Writing About Literature in the Media Age

Daniel Anderson
University of North Carolina at Chapel Hill

New York San Francisco Boston
London Toronto Sydney Tokyo Singapore Madrid
Mexico City Munich Paris Cape Town Hong Kong Montreal

Vice President and Editor-in-Chief: Joseph Terry
Managing Editor: Erika Berg
Development Manager: Janet Lanphier
Development Editor: Lai T. Moy
Executive Marketing Manager: Ann Stypuloski
Senior Supplements Editor: Donna Campion
Production Manager: Charles Annis
Project Coordination, Text Design, and Electronic Page Makeup: Electronic Publishing
    Services Inc., NYC
Cover Designer/Manager: John Callahan
Cover Image: "Dream Journal IV" by Jennifer Berringer, from *Collage Art* by Jennifer
    Atkinson, Rockport Publishers.
Photo Research: Photosearch, Inc.
Manufacturing Buyer: Roy Pickering
Printer and Binder: Quebecor World Taunton
Cover Printer: Phoenix Color Corp.

For permission to use copyrighted material, grateful acknowledgment is made to the copyright holders on pp. 958–964, which are hereby made part of this copyright page.

Library of Congress Cataloging-in-Publication Data

Anderson, Daniel.
Writing about literature in the media age / Daniel Anderson.
        p. cm.
Includes indexes.
ISBN 0-321-19835-2
1.   English language—Rhetoric—Problems, exercises, etc. 2. Criticism—Authorship—
        Problems, exercises, etc. 3. Mass media—Authorship—Problems, exercises, etc.
        4. Report writing—Problems, exercises, etc. 5. College readers. I Title.

PE1479.C7A53 2005
808′.066—dc22
        2004022816

Please visit our website at http://www.ablongman.com.

ISBN 0-321-19835-2

2 3 4 5 6 7 8 9 10—QWT—07 06 05

In loving memory of Lucille Lee Hubbell and
with love for Cindy, Peter, and Palmer.

Contents

Audio, video, and images   Video tutorials   Resources online and on the CD
Enhanced Reading   Extended Inquiry

CHAPTER 2

Analyzing and Writing About Literature   34

CHAPTER 3

Synthesizing Ideas and Considering Modes of Discourse   58

CHAPTER 4

Researching and Evaluating Sources   94

PART II
Argument and the Writing Process 131

C H A P T E R 5
Argument and the Rhetorical Situation 133

C H A P T E R 6
Prewriting to Develop Ideas 152

CHAPTER 11

Thinking and Writing About Drama and Film   283

CHAPTER 12

Thinking and Writing About Art and Advertising   316

CHAPTER 13

Critical Approaches to Literature 346

PART IV
Thematic Collection of Works   367

CHAPTER 14
Choice and Consequence   369

CHAPTER **16**
Innocence and Experience **637**

A P P E N D I X

Documenting and Using Sources   935

APPENDIX
Documenting and Using Sources 935

Contents by Genre

Essays

Poetry and Songs

DRAMA AND FILM

ART AND IMAGES

Preface to Instructors

Instructors know the frustrations felt by students who find themselves struggling to read and write, especially critically, about literature. *Writing About Literature in the Media Age* addresses these challenges by suggesting that students can start simply, employing thinking skills like evaluation, analysis, and synthesis, and then develop interpretations. To overcome writing barriers, the book emphasizes prewriting and open-ended drafting; moreover, it teaches students to provide helpful feedback and practice revising, editing, and polishing their work.

However, this book also celebrates what is best about teaching writing and literature. The positives start with engagement. The book meets students halfway, covering images, films, music, and aspects of culture familiar to students' lives, while offering a range of compelling poems, plays, dramas, and essays. The book also celebrates the power of bringing students together to read, write, and learn and of encouraging them to pursue questions and express ideas.

Ultimately, this book moves in two directions. It minimizes the challenges students can have with reading and writing about literature. At the same time, it strives to maximize engagement, promote collaboration, and encourage a healthy posture of inquiry. Students *can* move in both directions as they conduct intellectual work.

THE ORGANIZATION OF THE BOOK

The first half of the book discusses reading, thinking, writing, research, and literary studies. The second half provides thematic collections of works.

Chapters 1–4 emphasize critical thinking and research. They advocate a process of inquiry that starts simply, and then uses critical thinking and research to lead to interpretations.

Chapters 5–8 cover argument and the writing process. Chapter 5 focuses on arguable topics, evidence, objections, assumptions, and other specific elements of argument. Chapters 6–8 cover prewriting, drafting, revising, editing, and polishing papers.

Chapters 9–12 discuss reading and writing about genres. Chapter 9 covers fiction; Chapter 10 covers music and poetry; Chapter 11 covers drama and film; and Chapter 12 covers images and advertisements. Numerous concerns are treated in these chapters—for example, characters, narration, rhythm, melody, rhyme, diction, stage directions, and cinematography. Chapter 13 explores critical theories, casting theories as interpretive angles for thinking and writing about works.

Writing About Literature in the Media Age offers numerous critical thinking and writing activities. However, the general trajectory begins with *inquiry*, introducing reading and thinking, and then covering more complex treatments of writing and literature. The chapters in the second half of the book provide thematic groupings of works. Each addresses a large topic as well as a number of smaller themes. For instance, Chapter 14 addresses the topic of *Choice and Consequence* and includes sections on *crime and death, language and power, the consequences of war,* and *responding to injustice.* Chapters 15 treats topics and themes related to the *Self and Society.* Chapters 16 and 17 cover *Innocence and Experience,* and

Family and Relationships, and Chapter 18 explores *Art and Representations of the Natural World*.

Throughout the book you will find a number of pedagogical features:

- **Exercises**: promote thinking, writing, and the study of literature. Some ask students to reflect on works; some ask them to work in groups; others offer writing prompts. The exercises reinforce skills and concepts covered in the book.
- **Inquiring Further Sections**: follow all of the works in the book, providing thinking and writing opportunities and suggestions for exploring further.
- **Checklists**: distill important lessons, providing a reference for assignments and highlighting key concepts.
- **Extended Inquiries**: provide critical commentary, multimedia, and contextual materials related to an author, theme, or literary work; these inquiries are further extended on the CD.

THE CD CONNECTION

The integrated CD-ROM, a unique feature to this text, provides a variety of electronic assets that enable students to investigate clips from films, reproductions of works of art, recordings of poets reading their work, music, and additional texts and primary resources. The goal when developing these resources has been to directly enhance students' experiences with primary works and key concepts. Film versions of stories, for instance, allow students to see how others have interpreted fiction and illuminate discussions of narrative. Recordings of readings help us grasp the aural components of poetry. Paintings and photographs reveal aspects of culture related to the themes and works covered in the book.

Additionally, the CD contains numerous video tutorials. These tutorials provide immersive instruction that integrates technical skills with thinking, writing, and studying literature. For instance, a video detailing how to use Internet search engines is presented in terms of refining the focus of a research project—the technical instruction is delivered in terms of the lesson in thinking. Students can also study enhanced readings on the CD—these annotated texts demonstrate how works reveal thematic concerns and offer opportunities for writing.

Five types of icon indicate CD connections throughout the book. These icons point to assets on the CD and offer students a chance to extend the activities and materials available in the book. These connections include:

Media: audio recordings of poetry readings, music, video clips, and images that help meet the challenge of engaging students with the materials.

Video Tutorial: instructional videos covering skills and concepts from the book, modeling for students how they can conduct activities necessary for thinking and writing.

Enhanced-Reading (E-reading): works of literature annotated with commentary and prompts that guide students through the process of reading works critically.

Resources: additional information available online or on the CD that prepares students to embark on their own explorations of resources.

Extended Inquiry: materials on the CD that represent key components of the in-depth case studies in the book; also includes extended coverage of themes, authors, or works; readings of poems, reproductions of images, and music and video clips.

RESOURCES FOR INSTRUCTORS AND STUDENTS

The Instructor's Manual. The manual offers effective tips on how to discuss with students the concepts of inquiry and critical thinking, the writing process, and the social dimensions of writing and literature underpinning the book. Also discussed are literary genres and their critical relationship with media like photographs or films. Realizing that not all instructors will want to use the CD, the manual includes both information and topics for class discussions and writing assignments based on the readings in the book and as well as sections covering how to incorporate the materials and activities on the CD into teaching.

The Writing About Literature in the Media Age **Web site** extends the resources available on our CD, connecting the concepts and texts covered in the book with the wealth of materials on the Internet. The Web site (http://writingaboutliterature.com) ensures that sources of information for the book and CD remain current. It also provides a good starting place for students wishing to reach quality online information.

Other Longman supplements available for both the instructor and student include:

MyLiteratureLab. This online resource features the Longman Lectures. Richly illustrated and narrated by award-winning teachers and performance poets, these audiovisual lectures demonstrate various ways to read, interpret, and write about works of literature. Other features of this lab include diagnostic tests, a glossary of literary and critical terms, interactive readings, writing and research resources, and a tutor center. This password-protected Web site is available free with this text, or may be purchased separately.

Video Program. For qualified adopters, an impressive selection of videotapes is available to enrich students' experience of literature. Contact your sales representative to learn how to qualify.

Responding to Literature: A Writer's Journal. This journal provides students with their own personal space for writing. Helpful prompts for responding to fiction, poetry, and drama are also included. Available free when value-packed with *Writing About Literature in the Media Age.*

Researching Online, **Fifth Edition, by David Munger.** This companion includes detailed information on Internet resources such as e-mail, listservs, and Usenet newsgroups; advanced techniques for using search engines; tips on assessing the validity of electronic sources; and a section on creating Web pages. Available free when value-packed with *Writing About Literature in the Media Age.*

Take Note! For students working on projects that require the use of outside sources, this cross-platform CD-ROM facilitates note taking, outlining, and bibliography management. Available at a discount when value-packed with *Writing About Literature in the Media Age.*

Penguin Discount Program (http://www.ablongmen.com/penguinacademics/). Offers a variety of Penguin paperbacks at a significant discount to accompany *Writing About Literature in the Media Age.*

ACKNOWLEDGMENTS

Before another line hits the page, I thank my family. Whatever words I might compose will never express what Cindy, Peter, and Palmer mean to me, but they come first, here and always.

Next I thank those who have helped me shape this book. Everyone should know that Erika Berg gets the credit for the insight and initiative behind the project; the vision here is hers. Lai Moy is responsible for developing this book; it is the work of her hands. Lauren Puccio deserves great recognition for her contributions to this project, both as a student reviewer and as a future teacher. At Longman I also must thank Janet Lanphier, Valerie Zaborski, Charles Annis, and Ruth Curry; without their attention to detail and unflagging efforts there would be nothing here.

There would be nothing to put in the book without the work of Marcy Lunetta and Julie Tesser who tirelessly tracked down the permissions for everything here and on the CD. Any connections between the book and the CD would be lost without Denise Olson, who brought the CD into being. Janette Afsharian is responsible for the CD design and Beth Strauss and Felicia Halpert for its production. Thanks also to Bob Stein from TK3 for his good advice. Special thanks to Scott Hitchcock who met every challenge imaginable in getting this book into print.

I mean it when I say this project represents the efforts of many people. Much of this work has made its way into the book or the CD and I take great pleasure in recognizing those special colleagues here—first, Heather Ross, the co-author of the *Instructor's Manual* and a big contributor to the CD. Also Michael Bogucki, co-author of the Appendix, and Brooke Lentz, Benjamin Sammons, and Sarah Wood, contributors to the CD.

I have also had much support at the University of North Carolina at Chapel Hill. I thank the Institute for the Arts and the Humanities for providing the collaborative environment and resources to help get this project off the ground. I am also grateful to the Department of English for its continued support of my work. Special thanks to Tyler Curtain for his responses to Chapter 13, Erin Carlston for her helpful suggestions, Joseph Viscomi for his insights, Allan Dessen and Jessica Wolfe for their expertise, and to Erika Lindemann for her perennial good counsel. There are still far too people who have offered advice and suggestions to name. I can only say, as I always do, these colleagues are remarkable not only for their knowledge, but also for their friendship and good will.

Let me also give a hand to those artists who have agreed to share their work in this project. In particular, I want to thank Seven Mary Three and Skating Club who both stepped up to the plate in a big way, offering advice and providing songs for the book and CD-ROM.

Finally, I would like to thank the following reviewers for their insightful comments and suggestions: James Allen, College of DuPage; Thomas P. Barber, Diablo Valley College; Martin Behr, California State University, Northridge; Barbara Bretcko, Raritan Valley Community College; Becky Childs, University of Georgia; Marilyn D. Daniels, Broward Community College; Rosemary B. Day, Albuquerque TVI Community College; Virginia Derrick, Holmes Community College; Kevin J. H. Dettmar, Southern Illinois University, Carbondale; Robert Dial, University of Akron; Vanessa Holford Diana, Westfield State College; Monika Elbert, Montclair State University; William Glenn Feeler, Midland College; Daniel Ferguson, Amarillo College; Dene Grigar, Texas Women's University; Bryon Lee Grigsby, Centenary College; John F. Healy, Central Methodist College; Kurt Hemmer, William Rainer Harper College; Michael Hennessy, Southwest Texas State Texas University; Kathleen M. Herndon, Weber State University; Caroline C. Hunt, College of Charleston; David Johnson, Volunteer State Community College; Daniel T. Kline, University of Alaska, Anchorage; Joleen Malcom, University of West Florida; Barry Mauer, University of Central Florida; Christopher McDermott, University of Georgia; University of Central Florida; Sean Nighbert, St. Philip's College; Lisa M. Reeves, University of Georgia; Donna Reiss, Tidewater Community College; Thomas W. Reynolds, Jr., Northwestern State University; David Rollison, College of Marin; Pamela Stinson, Northern Oklahoma College; Jessica Lyn Van Slooten, State University of West Georgia; Mary E. Vandiver, Henderson State University; Worth Weller, Manchester College; and Karin E. Westman, Kansas State University.

Daniel Anderson
University of North Carolina at Chapel Hill

A Note to Students

My goal for this book is simple: to give you a sense that you can accomplish academic work if you approach it with a posture of inquiry. When writing this book, for instance, I learned as much from the process as I knew going into the project. I had to focus my ideas, conduct research, read and think about texts, and then explain my thoughts through writing. As I introduce the book now, I want to suggest that you, too, can tap into this process of critical inquiry, and that doing so will help you accomplish a great deal of intellectual work in your current courses and throughout the rest of your lives.

As you study this text, consider a few points that can guide you as you read and practice writing:

- **Critical thinking** helps you inquire into topics and works. We divide critical thinking into *evaluation* (drawing conclusions), *analysis* (looking at details), and *synthesis* (making connections). You might not immediately understand something like a sonnet, but you can look at its details such as rhyme scheme, themes, or figurative language, discover and locate connections, and eventually develop interpretations and arguments. These critical skills will enable you to engage a range of media and situations—fine art, film, music, advertising, and cultural events and issues.
- **The writing process** can help you create better compositions. While you will no doubt go about writing in your own way, a healthy awareness of the process will strengthen your compositions through prewriting, drafting, feedback, revision, editing, and polishing.
- **The social contexts** of literature and writing can inform your reading and strengthen your compositions. Through *research*, that is locating and evaluating sources and evidence, you can critically examine how literature reflects and impacts culture. Further, awareness of the social dimensions of writing allows you to better communicate with your readers.

You will find great flexibility in this book; you may explore chapters out of sequence, or you may explore just some of the readings. Regardless, you should recognize big strands of critical thinking in each section, as well as repeated emphasis on the writing process, and the social contexts of literature and writing. Keep in mind, too, that *Writing About Literature in the Media Age* encourages you to follow your impressions, refine your ideas, and explain your positions to others. It is this posture of inquiry that will allow you to be successful in your academic work, including your studies in the writing and literature class.

Daniel Anderson
University of North Carolina at Chapel Hill

Introduction

Critical Thinking and the Writing Process

Cloth makers have a way of describing the strands used in the weaving of a piece of fabric. They call them the warp and the weft. The warp fibers are strung parallel to one another on the beams of a loom, and then the weft fibers are passed over and under the warp threads to create the cloth. The photograph above shows a Navajo woman weaving a blanket. The blanket in the figure helps us understand two things about the nature of thinking and writing:

1. Thinking or writing can be viewed separately; like the strands in the unfinished blanket, we can examine thinking and writing apart from one another to better understand their components.

2. In practice, thinking and writing intertwine; like the cloth of the finished blanket, thinking and writing are stronger when woven together.

If viewing thinking and writing both separately and in terms of one another seems contradictory, remember that most of what we study requires us to entertain such complexities. We can break things apart to examine them, but we must also consider how they relate to and inform one another.

RELATING THINKING AND WRITING

When we think, we **analyze** (break things apart to study them), **synthesize** (combine elements to see a bigger picture), and **evaluate** (interpret and draw conclusions). In this book, we classify these thinking activities as part of a process of **critical inquiry** or **critical thinking.** We can also inform our critical thinking and gain new knowledge through the **research process.** We discuss critical inquiry in the first three chapters and research in Chapter 4.

Writing, or **the writing process,** can be broken down into components as well. **Prewriting** allows us to explore possibilities informally through writing. When **drafting** we compose text that generates and explains knowledge. **Revising** strengthens and refines our writing. **Polishing** ensures that our compositions are error free and ready to be viewed by others. We work through the writing process to create **arguments** that will convince others that we have developed a worthwhile approach to a topic or a work of literature. We discuss argument in Chapter 5 and we explain the writing process in Chapters 6 through 8.

The components of critical thinking and the stages of the writing process also overlap with one another. When we begin looking closely (analysis) at unique characters within a short story, for instance, we also make judgments and draw conclusions about those characters (evaluation). When we compose an initial version of an essay (drafting) we also explore ideas and brainstorm (prewriting) and edit our compositions (revision).

Furthermore, thinking and writing go hand-in-hand. In this book, when we discuss a thinking skill like analysis, we integrate writing activities into the instruction because writing helps us generate and develop ideas. Clearly, separating concepts like thinking and writing can be useful, but in reality, successful thinkers and writers combine and move fluidly between activities like analyzing, synthesizing, drafting, and revising.

Once we know something about critical thinking and the writing process, we can apply that understanding to the study of literature. For instance, knowing that we can use analysis to break things into their component parts allows us to approach a short story by examining elements like its setting, characters, and plot. This approach also helps us expand the range of materials we study. For instance, we can consider how a movie conveys its message by analyzing elements of film like lighting, camera angles, and editing. In this book, then, we apply thinking and writing skills to a variety of artistic works. We look at essays in Chapter 3 and we discuss fiction, music, poetry, film, drama, art, and images in Chapters 9 through 12.

CONSIDERING THE SOCIAL CONTEXTS OF THINKING AND WRITING

Before we start exploring literature, we need to discuss one more key concept: the **social context** of thinking and writing. Context generally refers to the historical or social situation in which a person or a work of literature exists. Thinking about social context serves three purposes:

1. To help us understand our own positions and perspectives.

2. To act as a lens for viewing historical periods and works of literature.

3. To allow us to see how our own writing can have an impact on an audience.

Our contemporary social context and our personal backgrounds inform our thinking and perceptions. Twenty-first century readers may find the portrayal of Shylock, a Jewish moneylender in Shakespeare's *Merchant of Venice,* offensive. Readers from the United States' rural South may more easily recognize dialect in Flannery O'Connor's "A Good Man Is Hard to Find" (000–00) than those in the North. To think critically we must understand how our perspectives can be shaped by our social situation.

Social context also helps us learn about the places and periods in which a work originated. When we read Alice Walker's "Everyday Use," (134–40) for instance, we gain an understanding of the issues facing African Americans during the 1960s. Similarly, understanding social context helps us make sense out of the works we read; knowing that Elizabeth Bishop's "Roosters" (510–13) was written in 1940 helps us recognize military imagery in the poem.

Finally, the social nature of communication influences our own writing. We write because we believe we have something to say. This does not mean that our compositions must affect some kind of grand change in the world, or even that they must persuade every reader. It does mean, however, that we must discover approaches to literature that are worth sharing, and we must explain our approaches to others. These readers comprise the **audience** for our compositions, and we must assess this audience and consider how they will react to our explanations. We also must provide **evidence** that will help them appreciate and understand our thinking. We talk more about these challenges in Chapter 5.

THINKING AND WRITING ABOUT LITERATURE

We have to think critically to understand and come to conclusions about what we read. We also have to write well to show others that our thinking matters. Since there is never one single way of understanding literature, we must specifically articulate our approach and support it with evidence. Studying literature teaches us fundamental skills for becoming a critical thinker and a good writer: we must develop a focused approach, advocate for that approach in an organized way, and use evidence to support what we say.

Asking Questions About a Short Story

Exploring a short story will help us get a sense of how literature can engage our thinking and writing processes.

KATE CHOPIN

Kate Chopin (1851–1904) married in 1870 and moved to New Orleans where she developed an affinity with Cajun culture. She had six children with her husband, Oscar. After his death, she moved back to St. Louis where she began writing about the Creole and Cajun culture with which she had grown familiar. Bayou Folk was published in 1894 and represented her first collection of stories. She also began to write about the traditions women were expected to uphold. Her novel, The Awakening, *sparked a firestorm of controversy with its evocative theme of female sexuality and provocative protagonist. "The Story of an Hour" (1893) embodies similar concerns and sheds light on women's issues of the nineteenth century.*

The Story of an Hour

Knowing that Mrs. Mallard was afflicted with a heart trouble, great care was taken to break to her as gently as possible the news of her husband's death.

It was her sister Josephine who told her, in broken sentences; veiled hints that revealed in half concealing. Her husband's friend Richards was there, too, near her. It was he who had been in the newspaper office when intelligence of the railroad disaster was received, with Brently Mallard's name leading the list of "killed." He had only taken the time to assure himself of its truth by a second telegram, and had hastened to forestall any less careful, less tender friend in bearing the sad message.

She did not hear the story as many women have heard the same, with a paralyzed inability to accept its significance. She wept at once, with sudden, wild abandonment, in her sister's arms. When the storm of grief had spent itself she went away to her room alone. She would have no one follow her.

There stood, facing the open window, a comfortable, roomy armchair. Into this she sank, pressed down by a physical exhaustion that haunted her body and seemed to reach into her soul.

5   She could see in the open square before her house the tops of trees that were all aquiver with the new spring life. The delicious breath of rain was in the air. In the street below a peddler was crying his wares. The notes of a distant song which some one was singing reached her faintly, and countless sparrows were twittering in the eaves.

There were patches of blue sky showing here and there through the clouds that had met and piled one above the other in the west facing her window.

She sat with her head thrown back upon the cushion of the chair, quite motionless, except when a sob came up into her throat and shook her, as a child who has cried itself to sleep continues to sob in its dreams.

She was young, with a fair, calm face, whose lines bespoke repression and even a certain strength. But now there was a dull stare in her eyes, whose gaze was fixed away off yonder on one of those patches of blue sky. It was not a glance of reflection, but rather indicated a suspension of intelligent thought.

There was something coming to her and she was waiting for it, fearfully. What was it? She did not know; it was too subtle and elusive to name. But she felt it, creeping out of the sky, reaching toward her through the sounds, the scents, the color that filled the air.

10   Now her bosom rose and fell tumultuously. She was beginning to recognize this thing that was approaching to possess her, and she was striving to beat it back with her will—as powerless as her two white slender hands would have been.

When she abandoned herself a little whispered word escaped her slightly parted lips. She said it over and over under her breath: "free, free, free!" The vacant stare and the look of terror that had followed it went from her eyes. They stayed keen and bright. Her pulses beat fast, and the coursing blood warmed and relaxed every inch of her body.

She did not stop to ask if it were or were not a monstrous joy that held her. A clear and exalted perception enabled her to dismiss the suggestion as trivial.

She knew that she would weep again when she saw the kind, tender hands folded in death; the face that had never looked save with love upon her, fixed and gray and dead. But she saw beyond that bitter moment a long procession of years to come that would belong to her absolutely. And she opened and spread her arms out to them in welcome.

There would be no one to live for her during those coming years; she would live for herself. There would be no powerful will bending hers in that blind persistence with which men and women believe they have a right to impose a private will upon a fellow-creature. A kind intention or a cruel intention made the act seem no less a crime as she looked upon it in that brief moment of illumination.

15   And yet she had loved him—sometimes. Often she had not. What did it matter! What could love, the unsolved mystery, count for in face of this possession of self-assertion which she suddenly recognized as the strongest impulse of her being!

"Free! Body and soul free!" she kept whispering.

Josephine was kneeling before the closed door with her lips to the keyhole, imploring for admission. "Louise, open the door! I beg; open the door—you will make yourself ill. What are you doing, Louise? For heaven's sake open the door."

"Go away. I am not making myself ill." No; she was drinking in a very elixir of life through that open window.

Her fancy was running riot along those days ahead of her. Spring days, and summer days, and all sorts of days that would be her own. She breathed a quick prayer that life might be long. It was only yesterday she had thought with a shudder that life might be long.

20   She arose at length and opened the door to her sister's importunities. There was a feverish triumph in her eyes, and she carried herself unwittingly like a goddess of Victory. She clasped her sister's waist, and together they descended the stairs. Richards stood waiting for them at the bottom.

Some one was opening the front door with a latchkey. It was Brently Mallard who entered, a little travel-stained, composedly carrying his grip-sack and umbrella. He had been far from the scene of accident, and did not even know there had been one. He stood amazed at Josephine's piercing cry; at Richards' quick motion to screen him from the view of his wife.

But Richards was too late.

When the doctors came they said she had died of heart disease—of joy that kills.

On the surface, the story is not overly complicated. Mrs. Mallard (who has "a heart trouble") learns of her husband's death. She experiences grief, but quickly becomes excited at the prospect of freedom. Upon seeing her husband (who has not been killed after all), she herself dies. However, looking at the story more carefully can launch us into a process of inquiry.

As we have already mentioned, critical inquiry involves analyzing, synthesizing, and evaluating. Additionally, critical inquiry is driven by asking questions. We can start with a simple comparison: the character of Mrs. Mallard at the beginning and at the end of the story. Our comparison involves at least two ways of thinking:

1. Analysis—we first look at individual examples (the before and after Mrs. Mallard), and

2. Synthesis—we examine those two items in terms of one another and formulate some ideas about their relationship.

analysis

What do we know about Mrs. Mallard at the beginning of the story? What can we learn from the observation that she has "a heart trouble"? What do the actions of Richards and Josephine tell us about the character of Mrs. Mallard?

Example 1

Based on these questions we might develop a picture of Mrs. Mallard that reveals *a frail woman who is protected by those around her.*

But Mrs. Mallard appears differently at the end of the story. How does Mrs. Mallard exert herself when her sister demands that she open her door? What can we say about her character as she emerges from her room with "a feverish triumph in her eyes"? As she descends the stairs "like a goddess of Victory" we see *a self-assured woman filled with optimism for the days ahead.*

Example 2

synthesis

We just analyzed Mrs. Mallard by separating out two examples of her character. Now we can synthesize those two examples through a comparison. The initial Mrs. Mallard (Example 1) appears weak and constrained, while the Mrs. Mallard that emerges from her bedroom (Example 2) is vibrant and free. Perhaps, then, it is the prospect of reverting to her previous situation, rather than the shock of seeing her husband alive, that makes life unbearable for the "new and alive" Mrs. Mallard. The "joy that kills," then, is really not joy at all. This kind of twist in literature is called **irony.** Irony presents a contradiction or unexpected twist that prompts us to associate two dissimilar things, in this case death and happiness. (For more on irony, see page 260.)

Freewriting About an Image

Still frames and video clips from "The Story of an Hour"

By looking at an image taken from a film version of "The Story of an Hour," we can more fully understand the relationship between Mrs. and Mr. Mallard. We can also begin to see how writing can further our critical inquiries. Figure 1 reproduces a still frame taken from the film.

In the early stages of our writing process, we can use **freewriting** to raise questions and spur our inquiries. Freewriting lets us brainstorm without worrying about meeting the requirements of a formal essay or even having an organized approach. When you freewrite, the stakes are low. Do not worry about spelling, mechanics, editing, or revision.

Student Bridget Allen produced the sample freewriting below. In her freewriting, Bridget explores the image of Mrs. and Mr. Mallard taken from the film version of the story:

Bridget comments on the placement of Brently above Mrs. Mallard; the observation leads to questions about their relationship

A photo freezes things. The scene maybe with the photo symbolizes how the institution of marriage is forever like the photo. And that the placement of the couple in the photo with Mr. Mallard standing and with Mrs. Mallard sitting below him. Shows the unbalanced nature of power in the relationship. The first thing that is told to us is that Mrs. Mallard has a heart condition, meaning that she is physically and emotionally hurt. Nothing normal in matters of the heart. Firstly, you see a stern look on Mr. Mallard's face like he is some type of parental figure. Always standing over her telling her what to do, how to look and what she should be as his wife. Also, the picture was placed into a

FIGURE 1   The Mallards

Her exploration of the picture frame as a symbol of marriage prompts her to consider how marriage can be constraining

circular frame instead of a square frame to symbolize the wedding ring. Unity? Along with the unity is the unbroken bond of marriage, the bonds that keep a marriage together. The wedding ring shows you bonded to someone else. The frame bonds both. They both are bonded? Or just Mrs. Mallard? A constraint on men and women?

Bridget has used writing to generate questions and record observations about the image. Her inquiry will eventually lead her to a more focused approach to understanding the story, but for now she merely sketches possible ways of explaining what she sees. She comments on the placement of Brently above Mrs. Mallard in the image and asks questions about their relationship. She explores the implications of the picture frame as a symbol for the constraints of marriage. But she also begins to question the implications of marriage as a frame. Since the frame binds both Mr. and Mrs. Mallard, she asks whether marriage might be constraining to men **and** women. (The exercise at the end of this chapter offers you a chance to explore more images from the film through freewriting.)

✔ CHECKLIST FOR FREEWRITING

- [ ] **Remember that the goal with freewriting is to generate ideas.** Your freewriting is meant primarily for yourself. Even if your instructor or others ask to see your freewriting, continue to view the activity as a low-stakes opportunity to investigate and brainstorm.

- [ ] **Use a notebook or a computer to store and produce your freewriting.** Pencil and paper will simplify the logistics. Keyboards will allow you to generate text more quickly. Whatever method you use, retain your freewriting to refer to as you refine your thinking later.

- [ ] **Do not edit or revise while freewriting.** If you write something that is unclear, move on and clarify it with your next thought. Keep moving quickly. Use abbreviations and other shortcuts if they help you remain focused on brainstorming.

- [ ] **Try timing your freewriting sessions to make them more productive.** Limiting your freewriting to blocks of five or ten minutes will prompt you to toss out ideas quickly. After generating a number of ideas, it is useful to stop and reflect on them.

☐ **As you reflect on your freewriting, look for key ideas or questions.** There is no need to pursue every thought you have scratched onto the page. Instead, select one or two of the ideas and see if you can extend them with either additional freewriting or more focused exploration.

As you become more comfortable with the writing process, you will no doubt develop your own approach to freewriting. You might consider integrating freewriting with some of the other prewriting techniques discussed in Chapter 6. Creating lists, holding conversations, outlining, and freewriting can be combined and modified to help you generate ideas. Consider, also, freewriting after completing a draft or when you come to an impasse as you compose. Find a method that is well suited for you, then make a conscious effort to employ freewriting as you work.

Explicating a Passage from a Story

You can see how writing about an image from the film promotes critical thinking. The visual image provides concrete details that can be easily interpreted. Studying those details leads to questions, which in turn lead to possible explanations. The same approach can be applied to looking at the short story. With images, we look at elements like the picture frame or the placement of the figures. With the story we would look at passages from the text.

In the story, we might examine a detail like the narrator's observation that "[t]here would be no powerful will bending her in that blind persistence with which men and women believe they have a right to impose a private will upon a fellow-creature." When we examine literature, we locate details that raise questions or help us understand the work, and then we integrate these details as quotations in our own writing to explain and support what we say. (For more on integrating quotations into your writing, see pages 179–83.)

Initially we might argue that, since the "powerful will" associated with marriage acts on Mrs. Mallard by "bending her," the passage suggests that marriage constrains and controls women. At the same time, however, we might ask why the passage characterizes this control as "blind persistence" and why it suggests that both "men and women" are likely to "impose their private will upon their fellow-creature." Blind persistence suggests that any bending of the will is unintentional, and lumping men and women together depicts this imposing of the will as not only something practiced by Mr. Mallard, but also something inherently related to marriage and relationships.

This kind of discussion of the story differs from the freewriting above in two ways: it is exploring a passage from a story rather than the details of an image, and it is taking those details and drawing conclusions about their significance. We call this process **explication,** an exploration that carefully describes and also formulates explanations about a passage or aspect of a work. Both freewriting and formal explications involve us in the process of inquiry. In both cases we ask and pursue questions that help us recognize significant details in the work, and then we consider the implications of what we have discovered.

Explaining Ideas to Others

Freewriting works well at getting our thoughts flowing because we do not need to please or convince anyone but ourselves. We freewrite in the early stages of the writing process to explore our own ideas. We can refer to these early activities as **prewriting.** As we move along in the writing process, however, we are more likely to share what we have written with others. As we do so, we will focus our energies more on **drafting.** Later, we will devote more effort to **revision** and to **polishing** our work.

When we draft an explication or an essay, we begin with a reader in mind. We may write for our classmates or an instructor, or we may intend to share the work with a larger audience. Either way, we must anticipate how an audience might react to what we say. We also need to incorporate and discuss evidence. We cannot just say the story is about *the oppression of marriage* and not about *the oppression of women by men*. We must incorporate evidence in the form of quotations and explain how they demonstrate that possibility.

As we write for others, we are challenged also to find a concrete approach to understanding the work; we need an angle that will help us focus our explanations. This challenge should not overwhelm us; writer's block often comes from worrying about not having a revolutionary idea or a grasp on every complexity of what we are studying. However, the point is not that you have seen something unrecognized in Shakespeare during the last four centuries. The point is that, to communicate with others, you need a specific approach that will focus your ideas and organize your writing.

Sharing Ideas with Others

As you think and write you will also need to pay attention to what others have to say about a work. Learning from others can take place informally through in-class and electronic discussions. You can also learn a great deal by reading and responding to the papers of your peers. Finally, reading essays and articles allows you to consider the detailed interpretations that have been developed by others.

As you discuss works of literature, try not to feel as if you need to have all the answers before joining the conversation. Perhaps you have an observation from personal experience or an idea related to another work you have read. If you are really stuck, rely on your classmates to generate ideas, and be careful not to monopolize the conversation. Otherwise, view discussions as an opportunity to offer what you do know and participate as productively as you can.

You may also be asked to participate in online conversations using discussion forums or chat tools. In electronic conversations, try to post messages that generate debate rather than composing essay-like statements that offer the final word. Additionally, be careful to avoid personalizing the debates that take place in electronic forums and be sure to understand the social interactions that can arise in electronic discussions. Balance conversation with productive exploration of topics, and participate by posting messages that further the discussion. You can learn more about productively participating in online conversation on pages 160-61 or on our CD.

Participating in electronic discussions

You may also be asked to respond to the writing of classmates and accept feedback about your own papers. Offering constructive feedback requires that you take an interest in the work of your peers and respond as an inquisitive reader. You will need to spot the most significant problems in the papers that you read and recognize strengths in the writing of your partners that you can develop in your own work. Use feedback to guide the revisions you make to your writing, rethinking your approach to respond to the concerns of your readers. You can learn more about reading and responding to the work of your peers and revising your papers in Chapter 8.

You can also find out what others have said about a work by consulting articles and essays. Even a simple search on the Web reveals that hundreds of people have written about Chopin's "The Story of an Hour." You may want to explore some of these essays to refine your own understanding, but you will have to be careful to avoid **plagiarism** (representing someone else's work as your own, or failing to appropriately acknowledge sources you refer to). Eventually, you will refine your own essays by preparing them for others through the process of revising and polishing. In Chapter 4, we look in detail at how you can conduct literary research and avoid plagiarism, in Chapter 8 we cover editing and polishing strategies for your own writing, and in the Appendix we cover how to use proper methods of citation.

Considering the Social Contexts of a Work

As we mentioned in the opening of this introduction, to think critically, you must recognize how your own perspectives and background can influence your interpretations. Further, you must think about how social contexts may have influenced the composition of the works you read. From our contemporary perspective, we might wonder why Mrs. Mallard did not simply pursue her own interests within her marriage or perhaps divorce her husband. We are prone to expect in our relationships some of the independence that Mrs. Mallard believes she can achieve only through the death of her husband. Knowing something about marriage during the late nineteenth century (the period in which the story takes place) would temper this perspective and refine our understanding of the story.

We can also consider more specific contexts or biographical information that might illuminate the work. Kate Chopin, for instance, had already written a short story when she was married at age nineteen. In her marriage she had six children and worked with her husband in business. It was not until almost twenty years later (after the death of her husband) that she embarked on her literary career in earnest. We might argue that the story reflects Chopin's ambivalence toward a marriage that has rewarded her with children and companionship, but limited her opportunities to pursue her writing.

Exploring the women's suffrage movement

We might also gain insights into the story by exploring the status of women during Chopin's time, or by looking at Chopin's interest in the suffrage movement (the movement to give women the right to vote). We could conduct research into the movement. We would learn that while former slaves achieved the right to vote shortly after the Civil War, women were still lobbying for the privilege during the last two decades of the nineteenth century. (Women achieved the right to vote in 1920.) With this knowledge we could develop an approach arguing that the story works as a commentary on the position of women in the late nineteenth century.

Learning about nineteenth-century attitudes or the author's life opens possible approaches to the story. There are two concerns with these kinds of contextual approaches:

1. There must be ample evidence in the work itself to justify and support looking at it in terms of its context. Because "The Story of an Hour" explicitly refers to the relationship between Mr. and Mrs. Mallard, we can discuss its examples in terms of what we can discover about nineteenth-century marriage.

2. Great care must be taken when drawing conclusions about the relationship of the context with the story. It is one thing to say the story reflects or rep-

resents women's issues and quite another to say that Chopin explicitly meant to educate readers about women's voting rights. Sometimes we can more or less discover what an author had in mind, but generally we are better served by looking at the context for its influence without concluding that the story is "about" that context.

REVIEWING AND PRACTICING

We will soon look at an exercise that will let you practice thinking and freewriting. But first we should review what we have learned so far:

- *Thinking and writing* are complex and intertwining processes. We can separate activities like thinking and writing to examine and experiment with them, but in practice the processes are closely related and overlapping.

- *Thinking itself* is made up of a number of related activities. Analysis breaks things into their component parts, allowing us to look at the pieces to gain an understanding of them. Synthesis combines elements, helping us see relationships and formulate a sense of a bigger picture. Evaluation reveals key characteristics of elements and invites us to draw conclusions about their significance.

- *Writing can be broken down* into separate but related components. Prewriting generates ideas. Drafting translates ideas into more formal compositions. Revising tests and refines those ideas. Polishing prepares our writing for final presentation to others. All of these activities overlap during the writing process.

- *Critical inquiry combines* the component activities of thinking and writing. Questions drive the process of inquiry. Composition translates our thinking into writing and generates further thought. Through critical inquiry, we freely explore ideas, refine our thinking, and eventually arrive at a coherent approach to understanding what we study.

- *Our own social positions* and perspectives influence our interpretations of literature. We can participate in conversations and conduct research to learn what others think. At the same time, we write to explain our own thinking to an audience.

- *Literature reflects and reveals* the culture that produces it. We can better understand historical periods by evaluating works of literature. Moreover, we can bring our knowledge of historical periods and authors to our deliberations about literature.

We will continue exploring all of these lessons throughout this book. For now, we can experiment with some freewriting to explore how thinking, writing, and literature intertwine.

Exercise 1   *Freewriting About Film Shots*

Freewriting from prompts focuses our attention while allowing us to explore questions fluidly. In this exercise, we will look at some more still frames from the film *The Story of an Hour* and explore some freewriting prompts.

The still frames in Figure 2 are taken from a film version of "The Story of an Hour." The filmmakers have added this scene in which Mrs. Mallard is

Video clip of
Mrs.
Mallard
singing

FIGURE 2   Mrs. Mallard Singing

giving a singing performance at a party. In the middle of the song, she looks to Brently Mallard who instructs her to smile as she sings. The three frames show Mrs. Mallard as she looks toward her husband, his gesture, and her response to his instructions. (You can learn more about evaluating film in Chapter 11.)

Working with a group of classmates or on your own, examine the sequence of still frames above or the video clip on our CD that depicts this scene. As you consider this scene, respond to the prompts below. Begin by selecting a person to keep track of the group's work or by preparing to take notes on your own.

1. First, consider the ways the film portrays the characters of Mrs. and Mr. Mallard. How well does the film capture the traits of the characters in the short story? How might you portray the characters differently? How does seeing the actors in the roles of Mrs. and Mr. Mallard compare with the mental vision you might have gotten of them from reading the story? Write three or more sentences discussing your impressions of the characters in the still frames or in the excerpt from the film.

2. Second, consider the image of Mrs. Mallard in the first and third frame. Filmmakers never just capture a scene using a camera. Instead they make deliberate decisions about where to place the camera and what techniques to use when filming. These aspects of camera use are often referred to as **cinematography.** Camera distance (how near or far the camera is placed from the subject of a shot) represents a key cinematography technique. How does the placement of the camera affect the impression we get as we examine the three frames? What might be the significance of the close up of Mrs. Mallard in the third frame? Write three or more sentences discussing the ways that the distance of the camera from the subjects in the frames creates significance (again, see Chapter 11 for more on film).

3. Finally, consider the significance of the singing scene as an addition to the short story. Does the scene add to or detract from the story? How fairly do you think the filmmakers have represented the themes and issues in the story? How does the addition of the scene represent an interpretation of the story on the part of the filmmakers? What alternative scenes might be added to tell the story in a film? Write three or more sentences discussing your impressions of the added scene.

FIGURE 3   Election Day

FIGURE 4   Wanted!

FIGURE 5   Save Freedom of Speech

Figure 6   Reverse Sexism

Exercise 2   *Writing About Historical Contexts*

Images provide visual messages that can represent the concerns and attitudes of the cultures from which they originate. This exercise asks you to analyze images from different historical periods and to make comparisons and draw conclusions about the ideas they represent.

Color reproductions of WWII propaganda posters

Examine the images on this page and the preceding page, then write a one- to two-page comparison of two of the images. You might consider how the characterization of men differs from one image to another. You might compare the representation of women. You could contrast the ways that men and women are represented in the two World War II propaganda posters. You can also select another aspect to compare. (You can learn more about comparisons on pages 71–72.)

1. Begin by asking questions and determining an approach to two of the images that strike your interest, an angle you can use to develop your comparison.

2. Analyze each image in turn, looking at the details of the image and offering explanations about what the details might represent.

3. Reflect on the relationship between the two images, pointing out similarities and differences between the images and drawing conclusions about the significance of the comparison.

1

Evaluation and
Critical Reading

Reading without reflecting is like eating without digesting.
                                        —*Edmund Burke*

For most of us, reading is a familiar part of life. We often scan through magazines
at the doctor's office, check horoscopes on the Web, or just unwind with an exciting book. Sometimes, however, we need to stop and invest a good deal more energy into our reading. On these occasions, we reread passages to answer questions.
We look up unfamiliar words. We often take notes to clarify our thinking. We call
this process of carefully analyzing a work **critical reading.**

In addition to these deliberate examinations, critical reading asks us to draw
conclusions about what we read. On one level, we draw conclusions throughout
the process of critical reading. We might assess a single passage before moving
on to the rest of a work, or decide whether to ignore or emphasize a particular
theme in our reading. On another level, we make decisions about the possible
meanings of the work as a whole and about how our interpretation relates to
other possibilities. We call this process of making judgments **evaluation.**

As we study literature, we can take steps to promote critical reading and evaluation. We can read simply to gather **impressions** and we can **read actively,** asking questions and making notes about what we study. **Reading analytically** helps
us hone in on the details of a passage. We sometimes **read to synthesize** information, drawing connections and making comparisons. We bring all of these ways
of reading together as we evaluate a work.

This process eventually helps us draw conclusions that lead to **interpretations,** specific ways of understanding a work. We can articulate an interpretation in a **thesis.** We also learn to consider how our approach relates to
alternative perspectives and how to locate and discuss **evidence** that supports
our thinking. The goal is to develop a closer relationship with a work so that
we can not only appreciate how it appeals to us, but also understand that appeal
and explain it to others.

READING CRITICALLY

Evaluations begin with an initial assessment of what we read. Our initial perspective will likely develop through an overlapping process of **reading for impressions** and **reading actively.** We will look at a short poem by Gwendolyn Brooks
as we begin thinking about this process.

GWENDOLYN BROOKS

Brooks
reading "We
Real Cool"

Gwendolyn Brooks (1917-2000) was the first African American woman poet to be awarded the Pulitzer Prize. She received the award in 1950 for her collection of poetry titled Annie Allen. *She is also well known for her collection* The Bean Eaters *(1960), from which the poem "We Real Cool" was taken. Brooks was raised in Chicago and her writing often reflects the situations and issues of this urban background.*

We Real Cool

THE POOL PLAYERS.
SEVEN AT THE GOLDEN SHOVEL.

1   We real cool. We
       Left school. We

       Lurk late. We
       Strike straight. We

5   Sing sin. We
       Thin gin. We

       Jazz June. We
       Die soon.

Reading for Impressions

Before we analyze the details and consider the possible significance of what we read, we should try to get a general sense of the material. A good place to start is by asking some **brainstorming questions:**

Does the work appeal to you (do you like it)? Why or why not?

What aspects of the work seem most significant?

What aspects of the work are unclear or raise questions?

Questions like these help you get a handle on the work and consider where you might examine it more closely. A good strategy is to conduct a brief freewriting session to explore your impressions. Here is one student's response to these brainstorming questions:

> I like the jazzy feeling of the poem. It is short and I like that too. Easy to get a feel for the poem. It seems like the rhymes are the most significant thing to me. Each pair of lines has a rhyme. I guess I wonder about the opening description of the pool players. Who are they and why are they there?

Writing helps us develop and keep track of our impressions. You might keep a **reading journal** where you record your thoughts about works. You can also explore impressions as you discuss works with others. Here is an excerpt from a chat discussion about "We Real Cool":

> Deborah Reynolds > What does everyone think of the poem and the pool players?
>
> Catherine Hernandez > they are cool with everything
>
> Adam Marshal > sounds like an anthem or motto
>
> Rene Bishop > lazy, laid back, real cool
>
> Kamala Vira > but they die soon
>
> Ronald Gains > Slacker song
>
> Maria Abadi > i think so too
>
> Greg Casperson > it's a gang
>
> Adam Marshal > like a drinking song
>
> Bridget Allen > they're just trying to have a good time, they don't care about much
>
> Catherine Hernandez > well they are going to die soon
>
> Tamara Wilson > they are way cool if they listen to Jazz
>
> Bridget Allen > Kamala, what are they dying from?
>
> Kamala Vira > no clue
>
> Bill French > the gin?
>
> Rene Bishop > yeah but i think that they accept that they are going to die, they understand the way they live their life
>
> Bridget Allen > maybe they're dying from Jazz
>
> Greg Casperson > yeah, they're care free
>
> Catherine Hernandez > it depresses me
>
> Brian Simmons > I think it's some people who went to play pool after school and stayed late, and they will "die" once they go home and get in trouble with the 'rents . . . I can imagine my grandpa telling me this little story you know
>
> Ronald Gains > they just die from gun shot wounds, liver failure, crack, you know . . . the normal things. . . .
>
> Daniel Barrantes > yes
>
> Ronald Gains > shot
>
> Greg Casperson > and it's catching up on this speaker
>
> Bridget Allen > they don't have much motivation for much of anything
>
> Maria Abadi > it's kind of sad

Participating in chat conversations

You are probably already familiar with the informal nature of chat sessions. The sample above demonstrates how chats can promote exploration of a topic through free-flowing conversation. Not all of the participants share the same view, but together they have considered the carefree attitude of the pool players, questioned the significance of the fact that the players will "die soon," and noted a sense that the poem strikes some of them as sad. If you participate in online conversations with classmates, you, too, can use the opportunity to share your reactions and brainstorm.

Whether freewriting, exchanging electronic messages, or just thinking over your impressions, feel free to let your initial engagement with literature develop informally. Keep an open mind, look for questions, and try to figure out why a work does or does not appeal to you.

Reading Actively

Any impressions and questions you develop initially will guide you as you take a more active role in understanding what you read. Your impressions should help you identify specific questions about the work—you might write out a list of questions, or experiment with some of the prewriting questions on pages 158–60 to spark your active reading. You might also begin to identify specific passages that deserve closer attention. Eventually, you will return to the work, rereading it with a more purposeful sense of some of the issues you are interested in.

As you interact with the work through active reading, you should also practice writing. You can use a separate document to take notes and write down your observations. You can also refine ideas in a reading journal. Additionally, you can use discussion forums or chats to probe the concerns you discover as you develop a closer relationship with the text.

In many ways, however, the best strategy is annotating the text you are reading. Mark up texts with highlighting, check marks, underlining, and other notations that will help you evaluate the work. You can get a sense of how you might mark up passages initially from the sample annotations made by Catherine Hernandez shown below.

Tutorial for annotating a text

Notice how Catherine has not underlined or marked up every line—instead she has used arrows and brackets to emphasize key aspects of the passages. Notice also how she is writing as she evaluates the poem. A highlighter can flag passages, but a pen or pencil will let you explore ideas by writing out questions and observations.

Gwendolyn Brooks
We Real Cool

THE POOL PLAYERS.   — *Is this*
SEVEN AT THE GOLDEN SHOVEL.   *a real place?*

We real cool./We
Left school./We   → *Seven o'clock?*
                         Seven players?

Choppy Lurk late./We
sounds Strike straight./We

Sing sin. We   → *Structure of poem*
Thin gin. We   *makes we stand out*

Jazz June. We
Die soon. ──→ *Last line also stands*
              out because of structure . . . Final statement?

FIGURE 1.1   Student Annotations of "We Real Cool"

Reading Analytically

We can use analysis in two ways as we develop a closer relationship with a work. First, we can focus in on some of the components of a work to better understand what we read. For instance, we might look at the setting of a story or the use of rhyme in a poem. Second, we can use analysis to read for details, approaching a work at the level of the paragraph, sentence, or word.

Different forms of literature invite us to look in detail at a number of components. As we think more about Gwendolyn Brooks's "We Real Cool" we can perform an analytical reading using a proven strategy for studying poetry: considering the **speaker** of the poem. Poems generally offer a viewpoint or tell a story that represents the perspective or experiences of a person. This **voice** or perspective in the poem is known as the speaker. When thinking about a poem's speaker you can gain insights by asking some questions:

- *How would you characterize the speaker?* Imagine the speaker as a character in a story. What key traits does he or she have?

- *What might motivate the speaker?* Can you recognize a purpose behind the words or actions of the speaker? Does any agenda that the speaker might have add to or detract from the poem?

- *How might the speaker of the poem relate to the author?* This is a tricky and important question. You should not confuse the speaker of the poem with its author. The speaker is a fiction composed by the author. At the same time, the fictional speaker may carry and reflect the ideas of the author. You can consider the ideas and background of the author, but be sure that you understand and account for the speaker as a creation of the poet and not the poet herself.

We can now return to Brooks's poem to analyze the speaker. We might start by considering the **tone** used by the speaker. Tone indicates the attitude conveyed by the word choices and writing style of the speaker. To evaluate the tone of the speaker in "We Real Cool," we can analyze the poem's language. What do phrases like "Sing sin" or "Jazz June" tell us about the speaker's attitude? Does the last sentence, "We / Die soon," challenge us to revise our sense of the speaker's tone?

We can also use analysis to zoom in on the details of a work. We might examine carefully the pronoun "We" in "We Real Cool." The pronoun aligns the speaker with the group of pool players. As readers, we might consider the repetition of the pronoun. What can we make of the fact that each sentence in the poem begins with "We" as its subject? What might we say about the line breaks in the poem emphasizing the "We" subject of each sentence? Is there anything to be made of the fact that a total of seven lines end with the "We" pronoun?

We are still raising and exploring questions, but analysis has focused our attention on two components of the poem: the tone of the speaker and the significance of the pronoun, "We." We could analyze any number of components. We might look at the sounds in the poem, the arrangement of rhymed words, or the rhythm of each line. The point is that by selecting an element, we can get started with our evaluation.

Reading to Synthesize

If reading analytically focuses on the components and details of a work, reading to synthesize considers how the components and details relate to one another and to the work as a whole. We can begin to develop a sense of this bigger picture by considering the details in terms of the rest of the work. We can also make connections with information and ideas outside the work.

To continue our inquiry into Brooks's poem, we might look at the speaker's tone in the final line of the poem and ask how the line influences our understanding of the rest of the poem. Catherine Hernandez composed the paragraph below exploring this connection.

> As we read through each line of Gwendolyn Brooks's poem "We Real Cool," our sense of the attitude of the speaker toward the seven pool players described in the poem builds. The language used portrays the pool players in an easy-going way. They "Lurk late" and "Strike straight." The repeated sounds in these descriptions match the easy going attitude the pool players have toward life. The tone seems playful, almost appreciative. But when we arrive at the final line of the poem this tone changes. The line does not have the repetition of sounds. The word "die" also stands alone because it does not rhyme with any other word in the poem. The last line emphasizes death. The tone is much sadder. This more negative tone makes us see that the rest of the poem is less playful and appreciative than it first seemed. The use of the word, "lurk," for instance, now seems somewhat darker. Knowing the attitude of the speaker toward the pool players at the end of the poem, we are able to recognize that there is something not quite right with the phrase, "we real cool" and we see that the tone of the speaker is not only playful but also somewhat critical.

In the chat session earlier, Catherine noted that she felt the poem to be depressing. In her paragraph, she evaluated the tone of the speaker to help make sense of the feeling. Her exploration of the details of the sounds and structure of the poem represents analytical reading. Once she has drawn a conclusion about the tone of the speaker at the end of the work, she synthesizes that information by discussing the poem as a whole in terms of what she has learned about the last line. (For more on how to read and write about poetry, see Chapter 10.)

Synthesis also helps us consider the context or author of the work. If we play the audio recording of Brooks reading "We Real Cool" on our CD, we learn that the poem was written in response to witnessing some pool players in a pool hall. Brooks asked herself, "Why aren't they in school?" Here we must be careful not to apply the author's statement indiscriminately; it would not be fair to say the poem is about school attendance. However, we can relate this information to the poem. We might read the work again, exploring how the poem relates to urban conditions or the missed opportunities of youth. Exploring these connections moves us closer toward developing an interpretation of the work.

Exercise 1.1   *Evaluating a Reading of a Poem*

Working with a group of peers or on your own, develop an evaluation of Brooks's reading of "We Real Cool." Begin by selecting a person to keep track of the group's work or preparing to take notes on your own.

1. Read the poem out loud several times to get a sense of how you believe the lines should be spoken.

2. Play the recording of Brooks's reading on our CD. Play the recording as many times as you need to develop a clear sense of the reading.

3. Read over the poem again and identify any qualities that appear in a new light as a result of your hearing Brooks's reading.

4. Write a paragraph evaluating Brooks's reading. Consider how Brooks's reading differs from your own sense of the poem. Discuss how tone, style, and any other aspects of Brooks's reading add to your understanding of the poem.

Exercise 1.2   *Reading a Poem on Your Own*

Working on your own, read "The Women Who Clean Fish" by Erica Funkhouser (printed on the next page) and practice reading strategies.

1. Begin by reading the poem to gather impressions and responding to the following prompts:

   • Does the work appeal to you (do you like it)? Why or why not?

   • What aspects of the work seem most significant?

   • What passages or specific aspects of the work are unclear or raise questions?

2. Select one passage or a theme that you find interesting. You might, for instance, look at one of the **stanzas** (the major sections that divide the poem) or examine themes relating to smell or religious imagery in the poem. Analyze the passage or theme you have selected by annotating the poem. Raise questions and mark observations in the margins of the poem. (You can also take notes in a journal or on paper.)

Enhanced
reading of
"The
Women Who
Clean Fish"

3. Consider the theme or passage you just analyzed in light of the rest of the poem. Contrast your analysis with other themes or passages. Look for relationships. Use your analysis and your considerations of the poem as a whole to decide how you might explain the poem to a classmate. Write a paragraph demonstrating your explanation. (If you are having trouble with this exercise, you might explore the enhanced reading of this poem on our CD.)

Funkhouser
reading
"The
Women Who
Clean Fish"

Erica Funkhouser

Erica Funkhouser teaches poetry at the Massachusetts Institute of Technology in Cambridge. She has published four collections of poetry and also works as a playwright. "The Women Who Clean Fish" was published in 1983 in Funkhouser's first collection of poetry, Natural Affinities.

The Women Who Clean Fish

The women who clean fish are all named Rose
or Grace. They wake up close to the water,
damp and dreamy beneath white sheets,
thinking of white beaches.

5   It is always humid where they work.
Under plastic aprons, their breasts
foam and bubble. They wear old clothes
because the smell will never go.

On the floor, chlorine.
10   On the window, dry streams left by gulls.
When tourists come to watch them
working over belts of cod and hake,
they don't look up.

They stand above the gutter. When the belt starts
15   they pack the bodies in, ten per box,
their tails crisscrossed as if in sacrament.
The dead fish fall compliantly.

It is the iridescent scales that stick,
clinging to cheek and wrist,
20   lighting up hours later in a dark room.

The packers say they feel orange spawn
between their fingers, the smell of themselves
more like salt than peach.

DEVELOPING AN INTERPRETATION

Interpretations represent another stage in the process of understanding what we read. An **interpretation** requires us to make a solid claim about an effective way of approaching a work. Articulating an approach in a **tentative thesis** can help us begin developing an interpretation. We also must begin to weigh **alternative possibilities,** and recognize **evidence** that supports our approach.

We can use Sherwood Anderson's short story "Hands" to continue thinking about evaluation and to explore interpretations.

SHERWOOD ANDERSON

Sherwood Anderson (1876–1941) brought a diverse background to his writing. He served in the Spanish American war in 1898 and then worked in advertising and as a factory manager. In 1913, Anderson experienced a psychological crisis, walked out on his wife and children, and gave up his career in business to pursue writing. "Hands" is taken from Anderson's collection of short stories, Winesburg, Ohio, *published in 1919. In the collection, Anderson weaves a number of stories together to explore life in a small town community.*

Hands

Upon the half decayed veranda of a small frame house that stood near the edge of a ravine near the town of Winesburg, Ohio, a fat little old man walked nervously up and down. Across a long field that had been seeded for clover but that had produced only a dense crop of yellow mustard weeds, he could see the public highway along which went a wagon filled with berry pickers returning from the fields. The berry pickers, youths and maidens, laughed and shouted boisterously. A boy clad in a blue shirt leaped from the wagon and attempted to drag after him one of the maidens who screamed and protested shrilly. The feet of the boy in the road kicked up a cloud of dust that floated across the face of the departing sun. Over the long field came a thin girlish voice. "Oh, you Wing Biddlebaum, comb your hair, it's falling into your eyes," commanded the voice to the man, who was bald and whose nervous little hands fiddled about the bare white forehead as though arranging a mass of tangled locks.

Wing Biddlebaum, forever frightened and beset by a ghostly band of doubts, did not think of himself as in any way a part of the life of the town where he had lived for twenty years. Among all the people of Winesburg but one had come close to him. With George Willard, son of Tom Willard, the proprietor of the new Willard House, he had formed something like a friendship. George Willard was the reporter on the *Winesburg Eagle* and sometimes in the evenings he walked out along the highway to Wing Biddlebaum's house. Now as the old man walked up and down on the veranda, his hands moving nervously about, he was hoping that George Willard would come and spend the evening with him. After the wagon containing the berry pickers had passed, he went across the field through the tall mustard weeds and climbing a rail fence peered anxiously along the road to the town. For a moment he stood thus, rubbing his hands together and looking up and down the road, and then, fear overcoming him, ran back to walk again upon the porch on his own house.

In the presence of George Willard, Wing Biddlebaum, who for twenty years had been the town mystery, lost something of his timidity, and his shadowy personality, submerged in a sea of doubts, came forth to look at the world. With the young reporter at his side, he ventured in the light of day into Main Street or strode up and down on the rickety front porch of his own house, talking excitedly. The voice that had been low and trembling became shrill and loud. The bent figure straightened. With a kind of wriggle, like a fish returned to the brook by the fisherman, Biddlebaum the silent began to talk, striving to put into words the ideas that had been accumulated by his mind during long years of silence.

Wing Biddlebaum talked much with his hands. The slender expressive fingers, forever active, forever striving to conceal themselves in his pockets or behind his back, came forth and became the piston rods of his machinery of expression.

5   The story of Wing Biddlebaum is a story of hands. Their restless activity, like unto the beating of the wings of an imprisoned bird, had given him his name. Some obscure poet of the town had thought of it. The hands alarmed their owner. He wanted to keep them hidden away and looked with amazement at the quiet inexpressive hands of other men who worked beside him in the fields, or passed, driving sleepy teams on country roads.

When he talked to George Willard, Wing Biddlebaum closed his fists and beat with them upon a table or on the walls of his house. The action made him more comfortable. If the desire to talk came to him when the two were walking in the fields, he sought out a stump or the top board of a fence and with his hands pounding busily talked with renewed ease.

The story of Wing Biddlebaum's hands is worth a book in itself. Sympathetically set forth it would tap many strange, beautiful qualities in obscure men. It is a job for a poet. In Winesburg the hands had attracted attention merely because of their activity. With them Wing Biddlebaum had picked as high as a hundred and forty quarts of strawberries in a day. They became his distinguishing feature, the source of his fame. Also they made more grotesque an already grotesque and elusive individuality. Winesburg was proud of the hands of Wing Biddlebaum in the same spirit in which it was proud of Banker White's new stone house and Wesley Moyer's bay stallion, Tony Tip, that had won the two-fifteen trot at the fall races in Cleveland.

As for George Willard, he had many times wanted to ask about the hands. At times an almost overwhelming curiosity had taken hold of him. He felt that there must be a reason for their strange activity and their inclination to keep hidden away and only a growing respect for Wing Biddlebaum kept him from blurting out the questions that were often in his mind.

Once he had been on the point of asking. The two were walking in the fields on a summer afternoon and had stopped to sit upon a grassy bank. All afternoon Wing Biddlebaum had talked as one inspired. By a fence he had stopped and beating like a giant woodpecker upon the top board had shouted at George Willard, condemning his tendency to be too much influenced by the people about him. "You are destroying yourself," he cried. "You have the inclination to be alone and to dream and you are afraid of dreams. You want to be like others in town here. You hear them talk and you try to imitate them."

10   On the grassy bank Wing Biddlebaum had tried again to drive his point home. His voice became soft and reminiscent, and with a sigh of contentment he launched into a long rambling talk, speaking as one lost in a dream.

Out of the dream Wing Biddlebaum made a picture for George Willard. In the picture men lived again in a kind of pastoral golden age. Across a green open country came clean-limbed young men, some afoot, some mounted upon horses. In crowds the young men came to gather about the feet of an old man who sat beneath a tree in a tiny garden and who talked to them.

Wing Biddlebaum became wholly inspired. For once he forgot the hands. Slowly they stole forth and lay upon George Willard's shoulders. Something new and bold came into the voice that talked. "You must try to forget all you have learned," said the old man. "You must begin to dream. From this time on you must shut your ears to the roaring of the voices."

Pausing in his speech, Wing Biddlebaum looked long and earnestly at George Willard. His eyes glowed. Again he raised the hands to caress the boy and then a look of horror swept over his face.

With a convulsive movement of his body, Wing Biddlebaum sprang to his feet and thrust his hands deep into his trousers pockets. Tears came to his eyes. "I must be getting along home. I can talk no more with you," he said nervously.

15   Without looking back, the old man had hurried down the hillside and across a meadow, leaving George Willard perplexed and frightened upon the grassy slope. With a shiver of dread the boy arose and went along the road toward town. "I'll not ask him about his hands," he thought, touched by the memory of the terror he had seen in the man's eyes. "There's something wrong, but I don't want to know what it is. His hands have something to do with his fear of me and of everyone."

And George Willard was right. Let us look briefly into the story of the hands. Perhaps our talking of them will arouse the poet who will tell the hidden wonder story of the influence for which the hands were but fluttering pennants of promise.

In his youth Wing Biddlebaum had been a school teacher in a town in Pennsylvania. He was not then known as Wing Biddlebaum, but went by the less euphonic name of Adolph Myers. As Adolph Myers he was much loved by the boys of his school.

Adolph Myers was meant by nature to be a teacher of youth. He was one of those rare, little-understood men who rule by a power so gentle that it passes as a lovable weakness. In their feeling for the boys under their charge such men are not unlike the finer sort of women in their love of men.

And yet that is but crudely stated. It needs the poet there. With the boys of his school, Adolph Myers had walked in the evening or had sat talking until dusk upon the schoolhouse steps lost in a kind of dream. Here and there went his hands, caressing the shoulders of the boys, playing about the tousled heads. As he talked his voice became soft and musical. There was a caress in that also. In a way the voice and the hands, the stroking of the shoulders and the touching of the hair were a part of the schoolmaster's effort to carry a dream into the young minds. By the caress that was in his fingers he expressed himself. He was one of those men in whom the force that creates life is diffused, not centralized. Under the caress of his hands doubt and disbelief went out of the minds of the boys and they began also to dream.

20   And then the tragedy. A half-witted boy of the school became enamored of the young master. In his bed at night he imagined unspeakable things and in the morning went forth to tell his dreams as facts. Strange, hideous accusations fell from his loose-hung lips. Through the Pennsylvania town went a shiver. Hidden, shadowy doubts that had been in men's minds concerning Adolph Myers were galvanized into beliefs.

The tragedy did not linger. Trembling lads were jerked out of bed and questioned. "He put his arms about me," said one. "His fingers were always playing in my hair," said another.

One afternoon a man of the town, Henry Bradford, who kept a saloon, came to the schoolhouse door. Calling Adolph Myers into the school yard he began to beat him with his fists. As his hard knuckles beat down into the frightened face of the schoolmaster, his wrath became more and more terrible. Screaming with dismay, the children ran here and there like disturbed insects. "I'll teach you to put your hands on my boy, you beast," roared the saloon keeper, who, tired of beating the master, had begun to kick him about the yard.

Adolph Myers was driven from the Pennsylvania town in the night. With lanterns in their hands a dozen men came to the door of the house where he lived alone and commanded that he dress and come forth. It was raining and one of the men had a rope in his hands. They had intended to hang the schoolmaster, but something in his figure, so small, white, and pitiful, touched their hearts and they let him escape. As he ran away into the darkness they repented of their weakness and ran after him, swearing and throwing sticks and great balls of soft mud at the figure that screamed and ran faster and faster into the darkness.

For twenty years Adolph Myers had lived alone in Winesburg. He was but forty but looked sixty-five. The name of Biddlebaum he got from a box of goods seen at a freight station as he hurried through an eastern Ohio town. He had an aunt in Winesburg, a black-toothed old woman who raised chickens, and with her he lived until she died. He had been ill for a year after the experience in Pennsylvania, and after his recovery worked as a day laborer in the fields, going timidly about and striving to conceal his hands. Although he did not understand what had happened he felt that the hands must be to blame. Again and again the fathers of the boys had talked of the hands. "Keep your hands to yourself," the saloon keeper had roared, dancing with fury in the schoolhouse yard.

25   Upon the veranda of his house by the ravine, Wing Biddlebaum continued to walk up and down until the sun had disappeared and the road beyond the field was lost in the grey shadows. Going into his house he cut slices of bread and spread honey upon them. When the rumble of the evening train that took away the express cars loaded with the day's harvest of berries had passed and restored the silence of the summer night, he went again to walk upon the veranda. In the darkness he could not see the hands and they became quiet. Although he still hungered for the presence of the boy, who was the medium through which he expressed his love of man, the hunger became again a part of his loneliness and his waiting. Lighting a lamp, Wing Biddlebaum washed the few dishes soiled by his simple meal and, setting up a folding cot by the screen door that led to the porch, prepared to undress for the night. A few stray white bread crumbs lay on the cleanly washed floor by the table; putting the lamp upon a low stool he began to pick up the crumbs, carrying them to his mouth one by one with unbelievable rapidity. In the dense blotch of light beneath the table, the kneeling figure looked like a priest engaged in some service of his church. The nervous expressive fingers, flashing in and out of the light, might well have been mistaken for the fingers of the devotee going swiftly through decade after decade of his rosary.

We can begin to understand "Hands" by employing the strategies discussed earlier in this chapter. We might start with our impressions of the story. Do we feel any sympathy for Wing Biddlebaum? What can we say about his state of mind? What are our thoughts about the episode twenty years earlier when he was accused of molesting one of his pupils? We might take notes or freewrite about these questions to further develop our impressions.

We might analyze passages more closely. As we do so, we can rely on specific knowledge about literature. For instance, we might consider the importance of the role of the **narrator** in a short story. The narrator, like the speaker of a poem, helps us understand many of the perspectives put forth in the story. In "Hands" an **omniscient narrator** (a narrator with insights into the thoughts and actions of the characters) tells the story. We can focus on details such as the narrator's description of the boy in the episode as "half-witted." As we connect these details to other parts of the story, we will have opportunities to draw conclusions and develop interpretations. (For more on narrators, see pages 230–31.)

Developing a Thesis Statement

Our critical reading should involve a progression from exploring our impressions to developing an interpretation. As we move closer toward offering an interpretation, we can articulate an approach in the form of a **thesis.** A thesis makes a clearly stated **claim** about the work. Remember that thinking and writing evolve fluidly. As you continue to assess a work, your thesis may shift. We use the term **tentative thesis** to describe our initial attempt at spelling out an approach to a work. In your formal papers you will need to develop a specific **thesis statement** that articulates your understanding clearly. For now, think of a thesis as an initial claim that expresses an angle you can take to make sense of the work.

In some ways you must go out on a limb to develop a thesis. The claim you make (especially while you are early in the process of exploring) may be simple. You might begin with something as straightforward as a tentative thesis that states *the narrator's portrayal of the boy who accuses Biddlebaum and the townspeople in Pennsylvania makes us sympathetic toward Biddlebaum.* The key thing is making some kind of judgment and spelling out your approach.

Exercise 1.3   *Developing a Tentative Thesis*

Working with a group of classmates or on your own, explore a number of angles that might be used to evaluate "Hands" and express one of those angles in a tentative thesis. Begin by selecting a person to keep track of the group's work or by preparing to take notes, and then respond to the following prompts.

1. Develop a list of questions about the work. Consider your reactions when reading the story. Think about the most confusing aspects of "Hands." Raise concerns as they occur to you until you have a list of at least five questions.

2. Select a question that you wish to explore in more detail. Return to the story and locate a passage that speaks to the question and analyze the passage. Write at least three sentences explaining how the passage addresses or complicates your question.

3. Look for other passages in the story that relate to the explanation you have just written. Analyze at least one of these passages and write at

least three sentences discussing how the story as a whole addresses, relates to, or complicates your question.

4. Write a one-sentence claim that expresses a tentative thesis that can be used to understand the story.

Weighing Alternative Perspectives

The rich nature of literature and the diversity of readers' perspectives result in any number of possibilities for understanding a work. Sometimes a thesis can address these complexities. For instance, while our tentative thesis claimed that *the narrator's portrayal of the boy who accuses Biddlebaum and the townspeople in Pennsylvania makes us sympathetic toward Biddlebaum,* we might adjust our sense of the story after considering Biddlebaum's state of mind. We might revise our thesis to state that *while the narrator's portrayal of the townspeople in Pennsylvania evokes the reader's sympathy for Wing Biddlebaum, questions about Biddlebaum's state of mind raise doubts that prevent us from fully supporting the main character.*

As you consider alternative possibilities, remember that evaluations are clear but not fixed. Do not abandon the fluid approach to reading and thinking just because you are beginning to arrive at a more specific interpretation of a work. Consider what does not fit your interpretation, explore alternative possibilities, and subject your tentative thesis to revision, allowing yourself to modify, extend, even abandon the approach you are considering when called for.

Looking for Evidence

Because you make a specific claim in an interpretation, you will need to locate evidence that will convince others of the merits of your interpretation. We will talk more about evidence in Chapter 5, but generally you will refer to parts of the work, things others have said about the work, or information outside the work to support your interpretation.

Once you have a tentative thesis, you can revisit a work in search of evidence. If, say, you wanted to claim that *subtle characteristics of the narrator's description implicate Biddlebaum as responsible for inappropriate sexual behavior,* you would look over the story to find passages that support that contention. You might analyze the passage that describes Biddlebaum's interactions with his students:

> Here and there went his hands, caressing the shoulders of the boys, playing about the tousled heads. As he talked his voice became soft and musical. There was a caress in that also. In a way the voice and the hands, the stroking of the shoulders and the touching of the hair were a part of the schoolmaster's effort to carry a dream into the young minds. By the caress that was in his fingers he expressed himself. He was one of those men in whom the force that creates life is diffused, not centralized. Under the caress of his hands doubt and disbelief went out of the minds of the boys and they began also to dream. (27)

For evidence, you might discuss the description of Biddlebaum's voice as soft and musical. You could discuss the implications of words like "caress." You could explore the influence Biddlebaum's actions appear to have on the boys' thinking and discuss the possible meanings of their "doubt and disbelief." All of these details can support an interpretation that Biddlebaum may be guilty of sexual misconduct. (For more on incorporating evidence into your own writing, see pages 146–48.)

Reading for evidence will be more productive if you combine the process with note taking or annotating. Keep pencil in hand and mark passages that support your approach to both continue the process of inquiry, and help you pinpoint evidence.

REVIEWING AND PRACTICING

Here is a review of what we have covered so far.

- *Evaluation is a process.* It begins with simply trying to gather impressions and ends with drawing conclusions and developing interpretations. Remember that evaluation is fluid and that you will move back and forth between the many aspects that make up the process of evaluation.

- *An initial impression* begins the process. Reading for impressions with an open mind allows you to spot possible ways of understanding a work.

- *Readers play an active role* in studying literature. A process of inquiry that allows you to understand and converse with others must be driven by your own questions and insights.

- *Zooming in by reading analytically and zooming out to synthesize* information allows you to further develop your impression of a work.

- *Writing assists the process* of evaluation. Annotating the works you read, taking notes, freewriting, and responding to questions facilitates the process at every stage.

- *An interpretation concretizes* your evaluation by prompting you to make specific claims. Interpretations need not answer every question, but they should suggest a way of understanding a work that takes a specific angle and can be expressed in a thesis.

- *Interpretations require evidence.* Evidence can come in the form of passages or aspects of the work that you quote and discuss. Later we will see how you can use the interpretations of others or information gathered through research as evidence.

Here are two exercises that will allow you to practice evaluating some works of literature.

Exercise 1.4   *Drawing Conclusions*

Working in a small group, consider whether "Hands" portrays Wing Biddlebaum as guilty or innocent of sexual misconduct. (You may have trouble making an ultimate determination, but for this exercise, select a position one way or the other.) Begin by selecting a person to keep track of the group's deliberations.

1. Consider the story thoroughly, and then make a decision about which position you support. (Your instructor may also assign you a position to argue.) Write a tentative thesis articulating your position.

2. Locate key passages that can provide evidence for your position. Analyze the passages to pick out the details that best support your thesis. Make a list of at least three pieces of evidence you can discuss to support your claim.

3. Consider the alternative position. What are the strongest points to be made for the other side? How might you respond to these points in a debate? List at least two points that support the alternative position and write out a response for each point.

4. Develop a report that explains to your classmates why you believe your position is worth considering. Write up your report in two or three paragraphs that discuss your position, your reasons for believing your position has merit, and your responses to the alternative position. (You may be asked to report to the class in a brief speech rather than writing up your deliberations.)

Exercise 1.5   *Starting from Scratch*

On the next page is a short poem written by Ron Wallace. Respond in writing to the prompts below as a way of evaluating the work.

1. Read through the entire poem quickly. Does it appeal to you? Why or why not? What is most striking about the piece? What questions do you have? Write down in a sentence or two your initial impression of the work.

2. Go back and reread the poem. Focus on a passage of the poem more closely, detailing how the language and ideas work. Write at least two sentences about your close reading. (You can also annotate the passage in the margins.)

3. Write a sentence relating the passage you just analyzed to the poem as a whole.

4. Develop an interpretation of the poem. After weighing as many possibilities as you can, articulate in a tentative thesis your approach to understanding the poem.

5. Locate and list two passages you could use as evidence for your interpretation.

6. Write a sentence or two explaining why your interpretation is important for readers of the poem to understand.

RON WALLACE

Ron Wallace (born in 1945) directs the creative writing program at the University of Wisconsin. His poems have been called accessible and immediate. They emphasize humor and the importance of everyday human situations. He has written more than nine books of poetry, publishing his first collection, Plums, Stones, Kisses, and Hooks, *in 1981. "Hardware" is taken from* Long for this World, *published in 2003.*

Wallace reading "Hardware"

Hardware

What secret?

My father always knew the secret
name of everything—
stove bolt and wing nut,
set screw and rasp, ratchet
5   wrench, band saw, and ball
peen hammer. He was my
tour guide and translator
through that foreign country
with its short-tempered natives
10   in their crew cuts and tattoos,
who suffered my incompetence
with gruffness and disgust.
Pay attention, he would say,
and you'll learn a thing or two.

15   Now it's forty years later,
and I'm packing up his tools
(*If you know the proper
names of things you're never
at a loss*) tongue-tied, incompetent,
20   my hands and heart full
of doohickeys and widgets,
watchamacallits, thingamabobs.

This father seems to know a lot and wants to teach his son.

2

Analyzing and Writing About Literature

> If a writer of prose knows enough about what he is writing about he may omit things that he knows and the reader, if the writer is writing truly enough, will have a feeling of those things as strongly as though the writer had stated them. The dignity of movement of an iceberg is due to only one-eighth of it being above water.
>
> —*Ernest Hemingway*

The *iceberg principle* expressed in the Hemingway quotation above can be a serious source of frustration as we grapple with a work of literature. If much of the meaning of a work is hidden beneath the surface, how are we supposed to find it? How can we know if our interpretations make sense? How can we evaluate the interpretations of others?

We can use a process of **analysis** to take up these questions as we begin to explore literature in depth. Analysis helps us address complex problems and find possible solutions by breaking things apart so that we may examine them more carefully. In one sense, analysis is like working on a puzzle; it takes a problem and spreads its pieces out so we can make sense of them.

In this chapter, we will consider how breaking literature into components helps us identify issues and raise questions. We will also consider how components of literature like **settings,** or **characters** can help us delve deeper and explore the implications of what we read. Ultimately, analysis not only helps us get a handle on literature, but also moves us closer toward developing interpretations and arguments.

ANALYZING COMPONENTS OF LITERATURE

We can analyze many components as we think about literature. Dramas have stage directions, poetry has rhythm and rhyme, films use lighting and camera angles, and so forth. You can learn more about the aspects of fiction, poetry, music, drama, film, and art in Chapters 9 through 12. This chapter introduces some of the main elements of fiction (plot, setting, characters, and themes).

Plot refers to the sequence of events that unfold in a story; a plot usually has a conflict that generates much of the action. The **setting** describes the time and location in which a story takes place; settings often convey a sense of a work's mood. **Characters** can resemble people we meet in daily life; characters can be complex (round) or one-dimensional (flat). Finally, **themes** convey ideas or concerns related to the work; we can identify themes to develop interpretations.

To provide a sense of how to analyze these elements, we will explore a short story by Ernest Hemingway called "Hills Like White Elephants." As you read, keep in mind these four components of literature—plot, setting, characters, and themes—and make note of any observations you have about conflicts, moods, types of characters, or key concerns in the story.

ERNEST HEMINGWAY

Born in Oak Park, Illinois, Ernest Hemingway (1899–1961) grew up fishing and hunting and leading an active boyhood life. After high school, he worked as a reporter, and then volunteered as an ambulance driver in World War I. He was wounded, then sent to Italy to recover. He wrote prodigiously after the war, publishing his first novel, The Sun Also Rises, *in 1926. "Hills Like White Elephants" was included in his second collection of short stories published in 1927. He published his second novel,* A Farewell to Arms, *in 1928. He continued to travel the world as a correspondent, big game hunter, and a fisherman. In 1937, he covered the Spanish Civil War as a reporter. His 1953 novel,* The Old Man and The Sea, *won the Pulitzer Prize and in 1954 Hemingway was awarded the Nobel Prize for literature. He is well known for his sparse or direct style of writing and for an emphasis on men and male pursuits. After suffering through treatment for mental illness, he committed suicide in 1961.*

Hills Like White Elephants

The hills across the valley of the Ebro were long and white. On this side there was no shade and no trees and the station was between two lines of rails in the sun. Close against the side of the station there was the warm shadow of the building and a curtain, made of strings of bamboo beads, hung across the open door into the bar, to keep out flies. The American and the girl with him sat at a table in the shade, outside the building. It was very hot and the express from Barcelona would come in forty minutes. It stopped at this junction for two minutes and went on to Madrid.

Enhanced reading of "Hills Like White Elephants"

"What should we drink?" the girl asked. She had taken off her hat and put it on the table.

"It's pretty hot," the man said.

"Let's drink beer."

5   "Dos cervezas," the man said into the curtain.

"Big ones?" a woman asked from the doorway.

"Yes. Two big ones."

The woman brought two glasses of beer and two felt pads. She put the felt pads and the beer glasses on the table and looked at the man and the girl. The girl was looking off at the line of hills. They were white in the sun and the country was brown and dry.

"They look like white elephants," she said.

10   "I've never seen one," the man drank his beer.

"No, you wouldn't have."

"I might have," the man said. "Just because you say I wouldn't have doesn't prove anything."

The girl looked at the bead curtain. "They've painted something on it," she said. "What does it say?"

"Anis del Toro. It's a drink."

15   "Could we try it?"

The man called "Listen" through the curtain. The woman came out from the bar.

"Four reales."

"We want two Anis del Toro."

"With water?"

20   "Do you want it with water?"

"I don't know," the girl said. "Is it good with water?"

"It's all right."

"You want them with water?" asked the woman.

"Yes, with water."

25   "It tastes like licorice," the girl said and put the glass down.

"That's the way with everything."

"Yes," said the girl. "Everything tastes of licorice. Especially all the things you've waited so long for, like absinthe."

"Oh, cut it out."

"You started it," the girl said. "I was being amused. I was having a fine time."

30   "Well, let's try and have a fine time."

"All right. I was trying. I said the mountains looked like white elephants. Wasn't that bright?"

"That was bright."

"I wanted to try this new drink: That's all we do, isn't it—look at things and try new drinks?"

"I guess so."

35   The girl looked across at the hills.

"They're lovely hills," she said. "They don't really look like white elephants. I just meant the coloring of their skin through the trees."

"Should we have another drink?"

"All right."

The warm wind blew the bead curtain against the table.

40   "The beer's nice and cool," the man said.

"It's lovely," the girl said.

"It's really an awfully simple operation, Jig," the man said. "It's not really an operation at all."

The girl looked at the ground the table legs rested on.

"I know you wouldn't mind it, Jig. It's really not anything. It's just to let the air in."

45   The girl did not say anything.

"I'll go with you and I'll stay with you all the time. They just let the air in and then it's all perfectly natural."

"Then what will we do afterward?"

"We'll be fine afterward. Just like we were before."

"What makes you think so?"

50   "That's the only thing that bothers us. It's the only thing that's made us unhappy."

    The girl looked at the bead curtain, put her hand out and took hold of two of the strings of beads.

    "And you think then we'll be all right and be happy."

    "I know we will. You don't have to be afraid. I've known lots of people that have done it."

    "So have I," said the girl. "And afterward they were all so happy."

55   "Well," the man said, "If you don't want to you don't have to. I wouldn't have you do it if you didn't want to. But I know it's perfectly simple."

    "And you really want to?"

    "I think it's the best thing to do. But I don't want you to do it if you don't really want to."

    "And if I do it you'll be happy and things will be like they were and you'll love me?"

    "I love you now. You know I love you."

60   "I know. But if I do it, then it will be nice again if I say things are like white elephants, and you'll like it?"

    "I'll love it. I love it now but I just can't think about it. You know how I get when I worry."

    "If I do it you won't ever worry?"

    "I won't worry about that because it's perfectly simple."

    "Then I'll do it. Because I don't care about me."

65   "What do you mean?"

    "I don't care about me."

    "Well, I care about you."

    "Oh, yes. But I don't care about me. And I'll do it and then everything will be fine."

    "I don't want you to do it if you feel that way."

70   The girl stood up and walked to the end of the station. Across, on the other side, were fields of grain and trees along the banks of the Ebro. Far away, beyond the river, were mountains. The shadow of a cloud moved across the field of grain and she saw the river through the trees.

    "And we could have all this," she said. "And we could have everything and every day we make it more impossible."

    "What did you say?"

    "I said we could have everything."

    "We can have everything."

75   "No, we can't."

    "We can have the whole world."

    "No, we can't."

    "We can go everywhere."

    "No, we can't. It isn't ours any more."

80   "It's ours."

    "No, it isn't. And once they take it away, you never get it back."

    "But they haven't taken it away."

    "We'll wait and see."

    "Come on back in the shade," he said. "You mustn't feel that way."

85   "I don't feel any way," the girl said. "I just know things."

    "I don't want you to do anything that you don't want to do——"

"Nor that isn't good for me," she said. "I know. Could we have another beer?"

"All right. But you've got to realize——"

"I realize," the girl said. "Can't we maybe stop talking?"

90   They sat down at the table and the girl looked across at the hills on the dry side of the valley and the man looked at her and at the table.

"You've got to realize," he said, "that I don't want you to do it if you don't want to. I'm perfectly willing to go through with it if it means anything to you."

"Doesn't it mean anything to you? We could get along."

"Of course it does. But I don't want anybody but you. I don't want any one else. And I know it's perfectly simple."

"Yes, you know it's perfectly simple."

95   "It's all right for you to say that, but I do know it."

"Would you do something for me now?"

"I'd do anything for you."

"Would you please please please please please please please stop talking?"

He did not say anything but looked at the bags against the wall of the station. There were labels on them from all the hotels where they had spent nights.

100   "But I don't want you to," he said, "I don't care anything about it."

"I'll scream," the girl said.

The woman came out through the curtains with two glasses of beer and put them down on the damp felt pads. "The train comes in five minutes," she said.

"What did she say?" asked the girl.

"That the train is coming in five minutes."

105   The girl smiled brightly at the woman, to thank her.

"I'd better take the bags over to the other side of the station," the man said. She smiled at him.

"All right. Then come back and we'll finish the beer."

He picked up the two heavy bags and carried them around the station to the other tracks. He looked up the tracks but could not see the train. Coming back, he walked through the barroom, where people waiting for the train were drinking. He drank an Anis at the bar and looked at the people. They were all waiting reasonably for the train. He went out through the bead curtain. She was sitting at the table and smiled at him.

"Do you feel better?" he asked.

110   "I feel fine," she said. "There's nothing wrong with me. I feel fine."

Analyzing Plot

As we have noted, plot is the sequence of events that takes place in a work of literature. The plot is the unfolding of action, the story of what happens. Sometimes plot has a key role to play, as in Flannery O'Connor's short story "A Good Man is Hard to Find" (pages 370–80) where events conspire to place characters in difficult situations. Generally, however, plot becomes more meaningful in connection with the characters and themes that are influenced by it—this is why you should never include more than a minimal amount of plot summary in your writing.

You can analyze plot by considering its key components: exposition, conflict, and resolution. Sometimes plot can be explored with more complexity by considering five stages (see page 285). In general, however, plot provides a beginning, middle, and end for a story. **Exposition** sets the stage for the main action to take place. Think of the exposition as whatever events unfold at the beginning of a work to clue readers in to the **dramatic situation.** The dramatic situation describes places, people, or events that form the backdrop of a work. For instance, in "Hills Like White Elephants" the dramatic situation might be described as *A couple waiting at a train station order drinks and have a discussion.* By itself this information is of little interest, although it does help us begin to chart what takes place in the story.

    Conflict describes forces or characters in a work that create opposition or bring tension to the narrative. Sometimes conflict is quite directly related to an event in the plot, as in John Uplike's "A&P," (see pages 568–72) where an event creates a crisis for the narrator. Sometimes conflict comes in the form of an environmental force, as in Stephen Crane's "The Open Boat," where the conflict pits humans against the force of nature. "The Open Boat" also displays conflict that builds toward a **climax** (a moment of crisis and subsequent resolution). The story culminates with the men in the boat making a final attempt to reach safety. In other cases, the conflict will be more akin to what we find in Hemingway's short story— two characters with competing interests, personalities, and motivations.

Enhanced reading of "The Open Boat"

    Resolution consists of the events that take place after a crisis or conflict. It is often in the resolution that we are able to see prior events more clearly. Sometimes scholars of literature will use the French term **dénouement,** which means "an untying," to discuss the way events play out in the resolution. Edgar Allen Poe's "The Tell Tale Heart" uses **flashbacks** or retrospective storytelling to explain how the narrator arrived at his position. By the end of "The Tell Tale Heart," the last act of the narrator explains how he came to be relating the story and provides for his punishment, increasing our sense of resolution.

Enhanced reading of "The Tell Tale Heart"

    The resolution, however, need not always offer as tidy an ending as we would wish. In "Hills Like White Elephants" the lack of a dramatic conclusion to the story encourages us to consider exactly what has been resolved. It may be that the story simply offers a brief episode in the relationship between Jig and the American. It may end much as it began by portraying a couple in conflict. Or, the ending may prompt us to consider subtle changes in the characters' attitudes and to see either Jig or the American as having a new outlook on their relationship by the close of the story.

Exercise 2.1   *Analyzing Conflicts and Resolutions*

Working with a group of fellow students or on your own, analyze the conflict and the resolution in "Hills Like White Elephants." Begin by selecting someone to keep track of the group's work or preparing to take notes.

1. Consider the decision that Jig contemplates in the story. The nature of the medical operation is never explicitly spelled out in the story, but most readers believe she is debating whether or not to have an abortion. How does the narration of the story hide or reveal this information? Can you tell how Jig feels about the abortion? Write three or more sentences detailing Jig's feelings.

2. Consider how the American feels about the abortion. Is it possible to determine his feelings? How? Write three or more sentences discussing his views of the operation.

3. Next, think about how the views of Jig and the American create a conflict in the story. Would you describe the conflict as serious? Why or why not? How does the conflict relate to the plot in the story? Write three or more sentences explaining your views on conflict in the story.

4. Finally, consider the resolution of the story. Does the story have a resolution? If so, how would you characterize it? How does the resolution relate to the conflict? Write three or more sentences discussing the resolution.

Analyzing Setting

The **setting** provides the backdrop where the action takes place. If we look at the references to Barcelona and Madrid in the first paragraph, and the publication date of "Hills Like White Elephants," we might assume that the story takes place in Northern Spain during the 1920s. Examining the setting helps us situate the events and characters that we encounter. For instance, we can explore the fact that the American (and most likely Jig) are traveling far from home. We can consider that the station is described as a junction between Barcelona and Madrid. We might ask how this distance from home and this junction relate to the decision to have an abortion or to the motivations of the characters.

When we analyze settings, we can consider also how they establish a mood and influence characters in the story. You can think of the mood of a fictional piece as its emotional atmosphere. While there are other elements that go into creating this atmosphere, the setting helps convey this mood by providing a sense of the physical environment. Consider the opening of "Hills Like White Elephants":

> The hills across the valley of the Ebro were long and white. On this side there was no shade and no trees and the station was between two lines of rails in the sun. (35)

Even from this sparse description we can conduct an analysis of the setting. Looking more closely we can see that the passage actually describes two settings: 1.) the hills that provide the title of the story, and 2.) the station where the story takes place.

We can start asking questions about the setting: What can be made of the fact that the station side of the Ebro has "no shade and no trees"? What can be said about the contrast between the two sides of the valley? Would it be fair to say the station side reflects a mood of barrenness or desolation? What might the hills seen at a distance represent? Exploring the atmosphere created by the setting can contribute to our interpretations.

Settings can also relate to character development. While debating whether to go through with an abortion and just after announcing that she does not care about herself, Jig once again looks over the setting:

> The girl stood up and walked to the end of the station. Across, on the other side, were fields of grain and trees along the banks of the Ebro. Far away, beyond the river, were mountains. The shadow of a cloud moved across the field of grain and she saw the river through the trees. (37)

Compare the details in this description to those depicted at the opening of the story, where the focus was on the barrenness of the station side. What might this more detailed description of the setting say about Jig and her situation?

Analyzing Characters

We analyze characters every day. As we interact with our friends, neighbors, peers, or even strangers, we make judgments about their personalities—we say someone is pushy, mousy, caring, selfish, silly, sad. The same can be said for the characters you come across as you think and write about literature.

But literary characters have an added dimension because they are fictional—that is, an author has purposely depicted characters in a certain way. So, when a fictional character comes across as neurotic, we can question the significance of that character trait. We can also ask how a character relates to other figures in the story, or about how a trait relates to the plot or a theme.

In fiction, it is common to find one-dimensional or **flat characters.** Usually flat characters play a minor role in literature—the waitress in "Hills Like White Elephants," for example, serves mainly to move the story along. Sometimes a one-dimensional or minor character will shed light on the other characters or on themes within the work. For instance, by providing a Spanish-speaking character with whom Jig and the American interact, the waitress illuminates the status of the main characters as travelers and differences in their abilities to communicate comfortably in the setting. (The American speaks Spanish to the waitress, while Jig seems to rely on the American to translate.)

The most interesting characters in literature are usually more complex than the waitress in "Hills Like White Elephants." These characters are often said to be round or multi-dimensional. **Round characters** are more likely to struggle with conflicts and have weaknesses (think of Hamlet). The American might be characterized as *a calculating man who is opposed to the couple having a child.* At the same time, however, he has concerns for Jig and is frustrated with his inability to really control the situation. Perhaps the best way to think of the many dimensions of characters is to imagine a continuum with the flattest, one-dimensional character on one end and the roundest, multi-faceted character on the other. Most characters are likely to fall somewhere in between.

Here are some additional aspects you can consider when analyzing characters:

Protagonist: The main character. The protagonist is the character around which the action of the work is centered. The protagonist can be heroic (like Hamlet) or perhaps comic or awkward (like Wing Biddlebaum).

Antagonist: A character that opposes the protagonist. Whether directly challenging the actions of the main character or representing opposing characteristics and perspectives, the antagonist is a source of conflict for the main character.

Foil: A companion character that sheds light on a main character. The foil usually resembles a main character in some ways, with the exception of key differences that highlight the traits of the main character.

Stock character: Usually flat, the stock character fits a stereotype easily recognized by readers, such as the spoiled brat or the nagging spouse. Stock characters often help move the action forward.

Traits: The key qualities possessed by a character. Stock or one-dimensional characters are often associated entirely with their key trait. Multi-faceted characters are likely to possess a number of traits, but you should still be able to concentrate on one or more significant aspects of the character's personality.

Motivation: The reasons behind a character's actions. Motivations can include explicit goals, such as the American's attempts to convince Jig to have the abortion, or personality traits that influence the character's actions, such as Jig's desire to avoid conflict.

Character development: Changes that take place in the character. Characters may grow in response to events or the influences of other characters. In some cases the growth of a character can be the subject of a work. Whether and how Jig and the American develop in "Hills Like White Elephants" is a central question we might use to understand the characters in the story.

Writing a Character Analysis

A **character analysis** is a detailed evaluation of a character. Like other evaluations, it first tries to make sense of, and then offers some conclusions about, the significance of the character. Begin a character analysis by examining your impressions and asking questions about the character. Consider what type of character you are analyzing, what traits he or she possesses, what motivates the character, and any growth the character undergoes.

We can look at a sample to better understand how to write a character analysis:

Bridget Allen

Instructor Catherine Reynolds

English 102

25 April 2004

Happily Only After: The Two Jigs

The character, Jig, changes in the story "Hills Like White Elephants."

The transformation she experiences at first seems subtle, almost

unnoticeable. However, examining the role of travel in the story and events

from the past reveals that a change does take place. In the past, Jig has

experienced fulfillment through the travel and the relationship she has

shared with the American. As she contemplates the hills and her unborn

baby, however, she undergoes a change. By the end of the story she longs

for the fertility of the distant hills and is no longer content to go on as the

happy couple. Instead, she tells the American to "stop talking" because she

knows she can no longer experience fulfillment by traveling and drinking.

Even if she were traveling, it would only lead her backwards toward her

previous life.

The change Jig undergoes can be understood by examining the life the couple has shared together before arriving at the station. This life that comes before the story can be seen in the stickers that cover their luggage: "there were labels on them from all the hotels where they had spent nights" (38). The labels represent a life of traveling to exotic places and leisurely nights spent together as a couple. The Jig from the past was content to simply "look at things and try new drinks" (36). When she says, "And if I do it, you'll be happy and things will be like they were and you'll love me?" we see her contemplating her life in the past and considering what it would be like to return to it.

As Jig contemplates the fertile lands on the other side of the river, however, she undergoes a change in her views on her previous life. After looking at the "fields of grain and trees" across the river, she asks again if they could have everything. When the American responds that they "can go everywhere" (emphasis mine) it reveals the distance that has developed between them. She is concentrating on the fertility of a single place, while he is still stuck in the world of travel and their past life. Because she has changed and he has not, she has no choice but to contemplate a future on her own and to tell her partner to simply "stop talking." At the end of the story, it is significant that the American moves their luggage and has another drink. She has come to a new understanding of what it will take to find fulfillment in her life. In the end she knows that she will not go back to the past of carefree travel. Instead, she "feel[s] fine" because she remains seated, contemplating this new view of a fertile place, the hills that look like white elephants.

Notice how the analysis takes a specific approach (*the transformation of Jig must be understood in terms of her life in the past*) and uses evidence from the story to support the claims it makes about Jig's character. As you compose character analyses, use your own insights and interpretations to develop an approach, then detail the components of the character and discuss passages from the work to make your points.

☑ CHECKLIST FOR WRITING A CHARACTER ANALYSIS

☐ **Have a clear angle or approach.** Your approach may be relatively straightforward (Jig undergoes a change that makes her past life seem unfulfilling) or more complex (The concept of travel contrasts with sitting still and illuminates the change in Jig). The key is having an angle that will help you make sense of the character and organize your writing.

☐ **Consider what function the character serves** in the work. Is the character a protagonist, an antagonist, a foil, a stock character? The function of the character will determine the analysis you create—a stock character may not lend itself to fruitful analysis, a foil character might be discussed in terms of other characters, an antagonist might be discussed in terms of motivation.

☐ **Examine closely the character's traits.** If a character is one-dimensional, can you develop an approach to analyzing that trait with complexity? If a character is multi-faceted, are there traits that are most significant? Does the character display different traits at different times? If so, why?

☐ **Explain aspects of the character's motivation.** Can circumstances account for the character's traits? How is the character's personality related to his or her actions? How might relationships with other characters explain the actions and traits of a character?

☐ **Chart any development** that takes place in the character. Not every character evolves, but for those that do, growth provides a clear approach for discussing their traits and understanding their motivations. If a character undergoes growth, ask what might account for that development. Are other characters responsible? Do events force a change in the character? Does the character experience a personality change? Is it believable?

☐ **Provide evidence to support your analysis.** What in the work allows you to make the claims you want to make about the character? Consider evidence provided by the narrator, the way other characters interact with the character you are analyzing, and evidence revealed in the speech or thoughts of the character. You may also be able to support your approach by using evidence from outside sources, such as the interpretations of others or contextual information. Integrate your evidence into your analysis using quotations that clearly back up your points (for more on using quotations see pages 179–83).

Exercise 2.2   *Composing a Character Analysis*

Write a two- to three-page analysis of one of the main characters from "Hills Like White Elephants." Either character is suitable for analysis. (You may write an analysis of a character from another work if you wish or if your instructor prefers.)

Refer to the checklist on page 44 as you compose your analysis, making sure to have an approach in mind and using evidence to support your discussion.

ANALYZING TOPICS AND DETERMINING THEMES

Of all the components of literature, themes may be the most difficult to pin down. A **theme** is a central idea present in a work, an idea that generally relates to the concerns of humans and society. We might contrast thinking about themes with our understanding of plot. Plot is relatively easy to recognize and tells us what happened. Themes, on the other hand, are much harder to identify and shed light on why events happened and what they might mean.

In part, the difficulty in locating a theme results from the iceberg principle, alluded to by Hemingway at the beginning of this chapter. Authors do not often spell out a handy encapsulation of a theme, because a work that overtly hammered out its moral would end up reading more like a lecture than literature. Most literature, instead, explores ideas by expressing them *through* the work; our task is to recognize these ideas, and then to investigate their implications.

Exploring a theme is also difficult because most themes relate to human emotions, actions, or relationships. All of us understand that there is no single way of describing an idea like freedom or motherhood. In fact, abstract ideas like love, marriage, mortality, and justice are made tangible through literature. The complexity of these concerns ensures that literature is open to many interpretations and that our personal insights can help us recognize themes in a work. To identify themes we can employ two strategies: 1) we can begin by looking for insights related to **broad topics** that will help us locate the major concerns of a work, and 2) we can then analyze the work in order to refine these ideas about a general topic into a **specific theme.**

Exploring Broad Topics

Locating general topics or concerns will help us explore a work in more depth. It is impossible to pin down all of the ideas found in literature, but we can discover topics by relating them to human concerns. Think of the topics we encounter as we relate to others and our society. We daily wonder about our relationships, our communities, our bodies, our history, and our friends, to name a few possibilities.

Here is a partial list of topics frequently addressed in literature:

Work	Play	Money
Technology	Nature	Urban Life
Pleasure	Pain	Rural Life
Community	Friendship	Rebellion
Change	Tradition	Imagination
Writing	Storytelling	Communication
Love	Sex	Hate

Violence	Bodies	Medicine
Death	Psychology	Health
Marriage	Parents	Family
Sexual Orientation	Children	Morality
Justice	Authority	Oppression
Freedom	Innocence	Good
Evil	Religion	Politics
Experience	Alienation	Nationality
Gender	Ethnicity	Class
Identity	Individuals	Society

Trust your insights and keep an open mind as you inquire into a work. Looking back at "Hills Like White Elephants," we might start by simply listing topics we can explore further: love, communication, abortion, decisions, and so forth.

Identifying a Specific Theme

Once we have developed some possible topics we can begin narrowing our focus to arrive at a specific theme. The theme should allow us to analyze how the work relates to a broad topic. Are there unique things the work has to say about the topic? Does the work reveal a particular facet of the topic? At this point in our deliberations, we might identify a theme by articulating a statement, or **tentative thesis.**

Of Hemingway's story, we might look more closely at a broad topic such as *communication.* To refine the topic of communication into a theme we should revisit the story. We might start with the impression that neither character seems willing to clearly state his or her desires; instead they talk around their decision over and over. We might analyze the American's claim that an abortion is "just let[ting] the air in." What does this description leave unsaid? What does talking around the reality of the operation signify?

Our analysis might lead us to look for themes in the way communication breaks down in the story. We might look at how the couple's desire to please one another undermines their ability to communicate. From a theme like missed communication, we can formulate a specific statement to help us further focus our thinking. We could compose a simple statement like *the couple seeks to avoid conflict with one another, resulting in missed communication.* Articulating a statement about a theme will create a tentative thesis that can guide us as we continue to explore.

Exercise 2.3   *Evaluating a Theme*

Working with a group of fellow students or on your own, consider alternative themes related to communication in "Hills Like White Elephants." Begin by choosing a person to keep track of the group's work or preparing to take notes on your own.

Above we discussed how the topic of communication could be developed into a theme exploring miscommunication. We suggested a tentative thesis: *the couple seeks to avoid conflict with one another, resulting in missed communication.*

Return to "Hills Like White Elephants" and look for instances of *successful communication.* Once you have spotted some, determine which examples are worth exploring in more detail and write a tentative thesis articulating a theme relating to successful communication. Now answer the following:

1. Discuss one example from the story, detailing ways that communication is effective. Ask how and why it is effective. Is it clear? Is it understood, but not clear? Write as many sentences as you need to explain how communication succeeds in the example.

2. Consider other passages that show successful communication. How strong is the evidence? Do there seem to be plenty of examples to support a discussion of successful communication?

3. Look over the story for examples of unsuccessful communication. Again, find specific passages, but this time explore how they reveal communication breaking down. Write as many sentences as you need to explain how communication fails in these examples.

4. Write a sentence declaring whether you think communication is successful or unsuccessful in the story. (Perhaps it could be both.)

5. Revise one of your tentative theses to make a statement related to successful or unsuccessful communication. Conclude by writing three sentences that explain how you arrived at your revised thesis.

Exercise 2.4   *Identifying Alternative Themes*

Working with a group of classmates or on your own, reread "Hills Like White Elephants" and refine a broad topic into a statement articulating your understanding of a theme in the story. Begin by selecting a person to keep track of the group's deliberations or by preparing to take notes, and then respond to the following prompts:

1. Consider some broad topics that relate to the story. Think of topics like change, love, decision-making, or some other large concern. (Do not use the topic of communication.) After considering a number of possibilities, select and write down a topic you will use to guide your search for specific themes in the story.

2. Develop a list of three statements regarding the topic in the story. Consider what the topic represents. Think about contradictions related to the topic. Focus on the most significant messages the story conveys regarding your topic. Write out three sentences that refine your topic into specific statements or tentative theses related to a theme.

3. Select one of the statements from the list above and return to the story looking for evidence. List at least two passages that you could use to support a discussion of the theme you have selected.

4. Write a one-paragraph explanation of the theme you have selected. Use your tentative thesis to introduce your paragraph. Refer to the passage you have analyzed to support your discussion. The audience for your statement should be readers familiar with the story. Emphasize for them how the theme you have selected helps explain the story.

REVIEWING AND PRACTICING

We have seen that analysis involves a process of breaking things into component parts so we can understand them. Examining plot, settings, and characters helps us gain insights into literature. As we look more closely at the components that make up literature, we can examine the topics and themes that lie beneath the surface of the work. Additionally, as we discover possible themes, we can develop a tentative thesis that will help us explain our understanding to others.

We can also review some of the main components of literature in more detail:

- *Plot tells what happens in a work, the events that take place.* Examining plot is often most helpful when considered in terms of other aspects of a work—for example, how it influences the motivations of a character. Plot can be further divided into exposition (events that set the stage for what happens), conflict (tensions, characters, or forces that challenge the main characters), and resolution (events taking place as the story winds down).

- *Setting is the location and time in which the work takes place,* the background where the actions play out. Setting is generally a key component in establishing an atmosphere or mood within the work. Setting can also provide valuable clues about the context of the work, raising questions about historical places and times. Longer works are likely to have more than one setting. Settings can influence actions and characters.

- *You can begin making sense of a work by examining the characters.* Fictional characters can be described as flat (one-dimensional) or round (multi-faceted), but they often fall somewhere in between. Characters can serve specific functions in a work, ranging from stock characters, to protagonists, to antagonists, to foils. We can understand characters by analyzing their traits, motivations, and development. In writing a character analysis, we should have a clear approach and provide evidence.

- *Recognizing themes requires locating the main concerns or broad topics* in a work. Looking more closely at these topics (beneath the surface of the iceberg) helps us identify **specific themes** we can use to understand the work. Since most literature touches on human issues, we can begin to explore works by examining familiar concerns like family, history, or health, to name just a few possibilities.

Printed on pages 50–57 is another short story, "The Chrysanthemums," by John Steinbeck. Refer to the story as you complete exercises 2.5 and 2.6.

Exercise 2.5   *Analyzing a Short Story*

Consider the plot, setting, characters, and themes in "The Chrysanthemums." Begin by simply reading the story and taking notes about your impressions. Then return to the story and read it more closely as you compose responses to the following prompts:

1. Summarize the plot of the story. Remember a plot summary merely provides basic information about what happens in the story (this is why instructors do not like to receive plot summaries when they ask you to write about a work). As you summarize the plot, make note of instances where you clearly see exposition, conflict, or resolution. Write no more than four sentences summarizing the plot.

2. Discuss the setting of the story. Consider how the setting conveys a sense of atmosphere or mood. Consider what the setting tells you about the context of the story. Consider how the setting influences the actions of the characters. For each of these considerations, locate evidence in the form of quotations from the story that could support a discussion. Write a paragraph analyzing the setting.

3. Describe one of the characters in the story. What function does the character serve? How would you describe the key traits of the character and how might those traits help us understand the story? What motivates the character and why does it matter? Does the character experience any development? If so, what might that development suggest? Again, look for evidence that would support a discussion, and then write a paragraph analyzing the character.

4. Articulate in a tentative thesis a key theme in the story. Locate at least two passages that relate to this theme, and then use them as evidence to explain in a paragraph the significance of the theme you have selected.

Exercise 2.6   *Writing a Character Analysis*

Referring to the checklist for writing a character analysis on page 44, write an analysis of one of the characters from "The Chrysanthemums." Take your time to develop a clear approach to understanding the character, and then examine the function, traits, motivation, and development of the character in one or two pages. Be sure to use evidence from the story to support your analysis.

Exercise 2.7   *Exploring Plot and Characters in a Film*

View the samples from the film version of "The Chrysanthemums" on our CD. Once you have explored the clips, respond to the prompts on the CD related to plot and characters.

Video clips of "The Chrysanthemums"

JOHN STEINBECK

Born in Salinas, California, John Steinbeck (1902-1968) grew up in a comfortable home, enjoying his schoolwork and reading voraciously as a child. After dropping out of college, he took on a number of jobs as a manual laborer, getting to know migrant workers, drifters, and social outcasts; many of these characters eventually became the subjects of his stories. In 1939, he wrote The Grapes of Wrath, *a gritty tale of family survival during the Depression. His writing is unadorned and often bleak, depicting common characters in straightforward but powerful ways. "The Chrysanthemums" is taken from his collection of short stories,* The Long Valley, *published in 1938.*

The Chrysanthemums

Still
frames
and video
clips from
"The
Chrysan-
themums"

The high gray-flannel fog of winter closed off the Salinas Valley from the sky and from all the rest of the world. On every side it sat like a lid on the mountains and made of the great valley a closed pot. On the broad, level land floor the gang plows bit deep and left the black earth shining like metal where the shares had cut. On the foothill ranches across the Salinas River, the yellow stubble fields seemed to be bathed in pale cold sunshine, but there was no sunshine in the valley now in December. The thick willow scrub along the river flamed with sharp and positive yellow leaves.

It was a time of quiet and of waiting. The air was cold and tender. A light wind blew up from the southwest so that the farmers were mildly hopeful of a good rain before long; but fog and rain did not go together.

Across the river, on Henry Allen's foothill ranch there was little work to be done, for the hay was cut and stored and the orchards were plowed up to receive the rain deeply when it should come. The cattle on the higher slopes were becoming shaggy and rough-coated.

Elisa Allen, working in her flower garden, looked down across the yard and saw Henry, her husband, talking to two men in business suits. The three of them stood by the tractor shed, each man with one foot on the side of the little Fordson. They smoked cigarettes and studied the machine as they talked.

5   Elisa watched them for a moment and then went back to her work. She was thirty-five. Her face was lean and strong and her eyes were as clear as water. Her figure looked blocked and heavy in her gardening costume, a man's black hat pulled low down over her eyes, clod-hopper shoes, a figured print dress almost completely covered by a big corduroy apron with four big pockets to hold the snips, the trowel and scratcher, the seeds and the knife she worked with. She wore heavy leather gloves to protect her hands while she worked.

She was cutting down the old year's chrysanthemum stalks with a pair of short and powerful scissors. She looked down toward the men by the tractor shed now and then. Her face was eager and mature and handsome; even her work with the scissors was over-eager, over-powerful. The chrysanthemum stems seemed too small and easy for her energy.

She brushed a cloud of hair out of her eyes with the back of her glove, and left a smudge of earth on her cheek in doing it. Behind her stood the neat white farm house with red geraniums close-banked around it as high as the windows. It was a hard-swept looking little house, with hard-polished windows, and a clean mud-mat on the front steps.

Elisa cast another glance toward the tractor shed. The strangers were getting into their Ford coupe. She took off a glove and put her strong fingers down into the forest of new green chrysanthemum sprouts that were growing around the old roots. She spread the leaves and looked down among the close-growing stems. No aphids were there, no sowbugs or snails or cutworms. Her terrier fingers destroyed such pests before they could get started.

Elisa started at the sound of her husband's voice. He had come near quietly, and he leaned over the wire fence that protected her flower garden from cattle and dogs and chickens.

10 "At it again," he said. "You've got a strong new crop coming."

Elisa straightened her back and pulled on the gardening glove again. "Yes. They'll be strong this coming year." In her tone and on her face there was a little smugness.

"You've got a gift with things," Henry observed. "Some of those yellow chrysanthemums you had this year were ten inches across. I wish you'd work out in the orchard and raise some apples that big."

Her eyes sharpened. "Maybe I could do it, too. I've a gift with things, all right. My mother had it. She could stick anything in the ground and make it grow. She said it was having planters' hands that knew how to do it."

"Well, it sure works with flowers," he said.

15 "Henry, who were those men you were talking to?"

"Why, sure, that's what I came to tell you. They were from the Western Meat Company. I sold those thirty head of three-year-old steers. Got nearly my own price, too."

"Good," she said. "Good for you."

"And I thought," he continued, "I thought how it's Saturday afternoon, and we might go into Salinas for dinner at a restaurant, and then to a picture show— to celebrate, you see."

"Good," she repeated. "Oh, yes. That will be good."

20 Henry put on his joking tone. "There's fights tonight. How'd you like to go to the fights?"

"Oh, no," she said breathlessly. "No, I wouldn't like fights."

"Just fooling, Elisa. We'll go to a movie. Let's see. It's two now. I'm going to take Scotty and bring down those steers from the hill. It'll take us maybe two hours. We'll go in town about five and have dinner at the Cominos Hotel. Like that?"

"Of course I'll like it. It's good to eat away from home."

"All right, then. I'll go get up a couple of horses."

25 She said, "I'll have plenty of time to transplant some of these sets, I guess."

She heard her husband calling Scotty down by the barn. And a little later she saw the two men ride up the pale yellow hillside in search of the steers.

There was a little square sandy bed kept for rooting the chrysanthemums. With her trowel she turned the soil over and over, and smoothed it and patted it firm. Then she dug ten parallel trenches to receive the sets. Back at the chrysanthemum bed she pulled out the little crisp shoots, trimmed off the leaves of each one with her scissors and laid it on a small orderly pile.

A squeak of wheels and plod of hoofs came from the road. Elisa looked up. The country road ran along the dense bank of willows and cottonwoods that bordered the river, and up this road came a curious vehicle, curiously drawn. It was an old spring-wagon, with a round canvas top on it like the cover of a prairie schooner. It was drawn by an old bay horse and a little grey-and-white burro. A big stubble-bearded man sat between the cover flaps and drove the crawling team. Underneath the wagon, between the hind wheels, a lean and rangy mongrel dog walked sedately. Words were painted on the canvas in clumsy, crooked letters. "Pots, pans, knives, sisors, lawn mores, Fixed." Two rows of articles, and the triumphantly definitive "Fixed" below. The black paint had run down in little sharp points beneath each letter.

Elisa, squatting on the ground, watched to see the crazy, loose-jointed wagon pass by. But it didn't pass. It turned into the farm road in front of her house, crooked old wheels skirling and squeaking. The rangy dog darted from between the wheels and ran ahead. Instantly the two ranch shepherds flew out at him. Then all three stopped, and with stiff and quivering tails, with taut straight legs, with ambassadorial dignity, they slowly circled, sniffing daintily. The caravan pulled up to Elisa's wire fence and stopped. Now the newcomer dog, feeling outnumbered, lowered his tail and retired under the wagon with raised hackles and bared teeth.

30   The man on the wagon seat called out, "That's a bad dog in a fight when he gets started."

Elisa laughed. "I see he is. How soon does he generally get started?"

The man caught up her laughter and echoed it heartily. "Sometimes not for weeks and weeks," he said. He climbed stiffly down, over the wheel. The horse and the donkey drooped like unwatered flowers.

Elisa saw that he was a very big man. Although his hair and beard were graying, he did not look old. His worn black suit was wrinkled and spotted with grease. The laughter had disappeared from his face and eyes the moment his laughing voice ceased. His eyes were dark, and they were full of the brooding that gets in the eyes of teamsters and of sailors. The calloused hands he rested on the wire fence were cracked, and every crack was a black line. He took off his battered hat.

"I'm off my general road, ma'am," he said. "Does this dirt road cut over across the river to the Los Angeles highway?"

35   Elisa stood up and shoved the thick scissors in her apron pocket. "Well, yes, it does, but it winds around and then fords the river. I don't think your team could pull through the sand."

He replied with some asperity, "It might surprise you what them beasts can pull through."

"When they get started?" she asked.

He smiled for a second. "Yes. When they get started."

"Well," said Elisa, "I think you'll save time if you go back to the Salinas road and pick up the highway there."

40   He drew a big finger down the chicken wire and made it sing. "I ain't in any hurry, ma'am. I go from Seattle to San Diego and back every year. Takes all my time. About six months each way. I aim to follow nice weather."

Elisa took off her gloves and stuffed them in the apron pocket with the scissors. She touched the under edge of her man's hat, searching for fugitive hairs. "That sounds like a nice kind of a way to live," she said.

He leaned confidentially over the fence. "Maybe you noticed the writing on my wagon. I mend pots and sharpen knives and scissors. You got any of them things to do?"

"Oh, no," she said quickly. "Nothing like that." Her eyes hardened with resistance.

"Scissors is the worst thing," he explained. "Most people just ruin scissors trying to sharpen 'em, but I know how. I got a special tool. It's a little bobbit kind of thing, and patented. But it sure does the trick."

45   "No. My scissors are all sharp."

"All right, then. Take a pot," he continued earnestly, "a bent pot, or a pot with a hole. I can make it like new so you don't have to buy no new ones. That's a saving for you."

"No," she said shortly. "I tell you I have nothing like that for you to do."

His face fell to an exaggerated sadness. His voice took on a whining undertone. "I ain't had a thing to do today. Maybe I won't have no supper tonight. You see I'm off my regular road. I know folks on the highway clear from Seattle to San Diego. They save their things for me to sharpen up because they know I do it so good and save them money."

"I'm sorry," Elisa said irritably. "I haven't anything for you to do."

50   His eyes left her face and fell to searching the ground. They roamed about until they came to the chrysanthemum bed where she had been working. "What's them plants, ma'am?"

The irritation and resistance melted from Elisa's face. "Oh, those are chrysanthemums, giant whites and yellows. I raise them every year, bigger than anybody around here."

"Kind of a long-stemmed flower? Looks like a quick puff of colored smoke?" he asked.

"That's it. What a nice way to describe them."

"They smell kind of nasty till you get used to them," he said.

55   "It's a good bitter smell," she retorted, "not nasty at all."

He changed his tone quickly. "I like the smell myself."

"I had ten-inch blooms this year," she said.

The man leaned farther over the fence. "Look. I know a lady down the road a piece, has got the nicest garden you ever seen. Got nearly every kind of flower but no chrysanthemums. Last time I was mending a copper-bottom washtub for her (that's a hard job but I do it good), she said to me, 'If you ever run acrost some nice chrysanthemums I wish you'd try to get me a few seeds.' That's what she told me."

Elisa's eyes grew alert and eager. "She couldn't have known much about chrysanthemums. You can raise them from seed, but it's much easier to root the little sprouts you see there."

60   "Oh," he said. "I s'pose I can't take none to her, then."

"Why yes you can," Elisa cried. "I can put some in damp sand, and you can carry them right along with you. They'll take root in the pot if you keep them damp. And then she can transplant them."

"She'd sure like to have some, ma'am. You say they're nice ones?"

"Beautiful," she said. "Oh, beautiful." Her eyes shone. She tore off the battered hat and shook out her dark pretty hair. "I'll put them in a flower pot, and you can take them right with you. Come into the yard."

While the man came through the picket fence Elisa ran excitedly along the geranium-bordered path to the back of the house. And she returned carrying a big red flower pot. The gloves were forgotten now. She kneeled on the ground by the starting bed and dug up the sandy soil with her fingers and scooped it into the bright new flower pot. Then she picked up the little pile of shoots she had prepared. With her strong fingers she pressed them into the sand and tamped around them with her knuckles. The man stood over her. "I'll tell you what to do," she said. "You remember so you can tell the lady."

65   "Yes, I'll try to remember."

"Well, look. These will take root in about a month. Then she must set them out, about a foot apart in good rich earth like this, see?" She lifted a handful of dark soil for him to look at. "They'll grow fast and tall. Now remember this. In July tell her to cut them down, about eight inches from the ground."

"Before they bloom?" he asked.

"Yes, before they bloom." Her face was tight with eagerness. "They'll grow right up again. About the last of September the buds will start."

She stopped and seemed perplexed. "It's the budding that takes the most care," she said hesitantly. "I don't know how to tell you." She looked deep into his eyes, searchingly. Her mouth opened a little, and she seemed to be listening. "I'll try to tell you," she said. "Did you ever hear of planting hands?"

70   "Can't say I have, ma am."

"Well, I can only tell you what it feels like. It's when you're picking off the buds you don't want. Everything goes right down into your fingertips. You watch your fingers work. They do it themselves. You can feel how it is. They pick and pick the buds. They never make a mistake. They're with the plant. Do you see? Your fingers and the plant. You can feel that, right up your arm. They know. They never make a mistake. You can feel it. When you're like that you can't do anything wrong. Do you see that? Can you understand that?"

She was kneeling on the ground looking up at him. Her breast swelled passionately.

The man's eyes narrowed. He looked away self-consciously. "Maybe I know," he said. "Sometimes in the night in the wagon there—"

Elisa's voice grew husky. She broke in on him. "I've never lived as you do, but I know what you mean. When the night is dark—why, the stars are sharp-pointed, and there's quiet. Why, you rise up and up! Every pointed star gets driven into your body. It's like that. Hot and sharp and—lovely."

75   Kneeling there, her hand went out toward his legs in the greasy black trousers. Her hesitant fingers almost touched the cloth. Then her hand dropped to the ground. She crouched low like a fawning dog.

He said, "It's nice, just like you say. Only when you don't have no dinner, it ain't."

She stood up then, very straight, and her face was ashamed. She held the flower pot out to him and placed it gently in his arms. "Here. Put it in your wagon, on the seat, where you can watch it. Maybe I can find something for you to do."

At the back of the house she dug in the can pile and found two old and battered aluminum saucepans. She carried them back and gave them to him. "Here, maybe you can fix these."

His manner changed. He became professional. "Good as new I can fix them." At the back of his wagon he set a little anvil, and out of an oily tool box dug a small machine hammer. Elisa came through the gate to watch him while he pounded out the dents in the kettles. His mouth grew sure and knowing. At a difficult part of the work he sucked his under-lip.

80   "You sleep right in the wagon?" Elisa asked.

"Right in the wagon, ma'am. Rain or shine I'm dry as a cow in there."

"It must be nice," she said. "It must be very nice. I wish women could do such things."

"It ain't the right kind of a life for a woman."

Her upper lip raised a little, showing her teeth. "How do you know? How can you tell?" she said.

85   "I don't know, ma'am," he protested. "Of course I don't know. Now here's your kettles, done. You don't have to buy no new ones."

"How much?"

"Oh, fifty cents'll do. I keep my prices down and my work good. That's why I have all them satisfied customers up and down the highway."

Elisa brought him a fifty-cent piece from the house and dropped it in his hand. "You might be surprised to have a rival some time. I can sharpen scissors, too. And I can beat the dents out of little pots. I could show you what a woman might do."

He put his hammer back in the oily box and shoved the little anvil out of sight. "It would be a lonely life for a woman, ma'am, and a scarey life, too, with animals creeping under the wagon all night." He climbed over the singletree, steadying himself with a hand on the burro's white rump. He settled himself in the seat, picked up the lines. "Thank you kindly, ma'am," he said. "I'll do like you told me; I'll go back and catch the Salinas road."

90   "Mind," she called, "if you're long in getting there, keep the sand damp."

"Sand, ma'am? . . . Sand? Oh, sure. You mean around the chrysanthemums. Sure I will." He clucked his tongue. The beasts leaned luxuriously into their collars. The mongrel dog took his place between the back wheels. The wagon turned and crawled out the entrance road and back the way it had come, along the river.

Elisa stood in front of her wire fence watching the slow progress of the caravan. Her shoulders were straight, her head thrown back, her eyes half-closed, so that the scene came vaguely into them. Her lips moved silently, forming the words "Good-bye—good-bye." Then she whispered, "That's a bright direction. There's a glowing there." The sound of her whisper startled her. She shook herself free and looked about to see whether anyone had been listening. Only the dogs had heard. They lifted their heads toward her from their sleeping in the dust, and then stretched out their chins and settled asleep again. Elisa turned and ran hurriedly into the house.

In the kitchen she reached behind the stove and felt the water tank. It was full of hot water from the noonday cooking. In the bathroom she tore off her soiled clothes and flung them into the corner. And then she scrubbed herself with a little block of pumice, legs and thighs, loins and chest and arms, until her skin was scratched and red. When she had dried herself she stood in front of a mirror in her bedroom and looked at her body. She tightened her stomach and threw out her chest. She turned and looked over her shoulder at her back.

After a while she began to dress, slowly. She put on her newest underclothing and her nicest stockings and the dress which was the symbol of her prettiness. She worked carefully on her hair, pencilled her eyebrows and rouged her lips.

95   Before she was finished she heard the little thunder of hoofs and the shouts of Henry and his helper as they drove the red steers into the corral. She heard the gate bang shut and set herself for Henry's arrival.

His step sounded on the porch. He entered the house calling, "Elisa, where are you?"

"In my room, dressing. I'm not ready. There's hot water for your bath. Hurry up. It's getting late."

When she heard him splashing in the tub, Elisa laid his dark suit on the bed, and shirt and socks and tie beside it. She stood his polished shoes on the floor beside the bed. Then she went to the porch and sat primly and stiffly down. She looked toward the river road where the willow-line was still yellow with frosted leaves so that under the high grey fog they seemed a thin band of sunshine. This was the only color in the grey afternoon. She sat unmoving for a long time. Her eyes blinked rarely.

Henry came banging out of the door, shoving his tie inside his vest as he came. Elisa stiffened and her face grew tight. Henry stopped short and looked at her. "Why—why, Elisa. You look so nice!"

100   "Nice? You think I look nice? What do you mean by 'nice'?"

Henry blundered on. "I don't know. I mean you look different, strong and happy."

"I am strong? Yes, strong. What do you mean 'strong'?"

He looked bewildered. "You're playing some kind of a game," he said helplessly. "It's a kind of a play. You look strong enough to break a calf over your knee, happy enough to eat it like a watermelon."

For a second she lost her rigidity. "Henry! Don't talk like that. You didn't know what you said." She grew complete again. "I'm strong," she boasted. "I never knew before how strong."

105   Henry looked down toward the tractor shed, and when he brought his eyes back to her, they were his own again. "I'll get out the car. You can put on your coat while I'm starting."

Elisa went into the house. She heard him drive to the gate and idle down his motor, and then she took a long time to put on her hat. She pulled it here and pressed it there. When Henry turned the motor off she slipped into her coat and went out.

The little roadster bounced along on the dirt road by the river, raising the birds and driving the rabbits into the brush. Two cranes flapped heavily over the willow-line and dropped into the river-bed.

Far ahead on the road Elisa saw a dark speck. She knew.

She tried not to look as they passed it, but her eyes would not obey. She whispered to herself sadly, "He might have thrown them off the road. That wouldn't have been much trouble, not very much. But he kept the pot," she explained. "He had to keep the pot. That's why he couldn't get them off the road."

110   The roadster turned a bend and she saw the caravan ahead. She swung full around toward her husband so she could not see the little covered wagon and the mismatched team as the car passed them.

In a moment it was over. The thing was done. She did not look back. She said loudly, to be heard above the motor, "It will be good, tonight, a good dinner."

"Now you're changed again," Henry complained. He took one hand from the wheel and patted her knee. "I ought to take you in to dinner oftener. It would be good for both of us. We get so heavy out on the ranch."

"Henry," she asked, "could we have wine at dinner?"

"Sure we could. Say! That will be fine."

115   She was silent for a while; then she said, "Henry, at those prize fights, do the men hurt each other very much?"

"Sometimes a little, not often. Why?"

"Well, I've read how they break noses, and blood runs down their chests. I've read how the fighting gloves get heavy and soggy with blood."

He looked around at her. "What's the matter, Elisa? I didn't know you read things like that." He brought the car to a stop, then turned to the right over the Salinas River bridge.

"Do any women ever go to the fights?" she asked.

120   "Oh, sure, some. What's the matter, Elisa? Do you want to go? I don't think you'd like it, but I'll take you if you really want to go."

She relaxed limply in the seat. "Oh, no. No. I don't want to go. I'm sure I don't." Her face was turned away from him. "It will be enough if we can have wine. It will be plenty." She turned up her coat collar so he could not see that she was crying weakly—like an old woman.

INQUIRING FURTHER

1. How would you describe Steinbeck's writing style? How would you relate it to the style you find in "Hills Like White Elephants?" How might thinking of the style help you develop an interpretation of the story?

2. What can you say about the character of Elisa? How do you explain her actions at the end of the story when she asks about the boxing matches? Do you believe she undergoes a change in the story? If so, what might motivate that change? If not, how would you explain her actions at the end of the story?

3. What themes are suggested by the symbols in the story? In addition to the flowerpot, what other symbols seem most significant? How do they relate to broad topics or specific themes you can discover in the story? Develop a tentative thesis exploring one of the symbols in the story in terms of a theme.

3

Synthesizing Ideas and Considering Modes of Discourse

The collage at the opening of this chapter brings together more than bits of paper and pieces of cloth. Items like an old newspaper clipping or a scrap of fabric each express unique ideas. News clippings might offer recommendations about women's fashion. Fabric cut-outs of sweaters and pants might suggest an imaginative dress-up game. Together, these assembled pieces convey messages through the relationships between the ideas that they express. The serious fashion recommendations in the clippings become playful or ironic when considered in light of the make-believe game suggested by doll's clothes.

We may not always realize it, but these relationships between ideas are also present in the various forms of language that we use. Consider the quotation from Gilda Radner in the collage above, "I base my fashion sense on what doesn't itch." In the same way that a piece of fabric can change our thinking about the newspaper clipping, a humorous quotation about fashion might prompt us to reconsider the newspaper recommendations about shoes or hats.

When we study writing and literature, we can compare different means of communication to better understand what we read. We call these ways of communicating, **modes of discourse.** Each of these modes has unique characteristics. A short story, for instance, differs from an essay by emphasizing plot, characters, symbols, and themes. Modes of discourse range from imaginative works of fiction, to casual conversations, to formal articles, to popular essays, to advertising slogans, and so on. Each mode has unique **conventions.** An academic essay, for instance, relies on citation standards to help readers track sources; a brochure uses bulleted lists to convey essential information; a poem employs rhythm and distilled language to affect the imagination.

The process of synthesis helps us explore relationships among modes of discourse. It also helps us examine facets of a work in terms of one another. We should remember, though, that synthesis cannot be separated from other activities of critical thinking. When we consider poetry as a specific mode of discourse, we employ analysis to focus our attention on the elements of language that make it unique. We also evaluate modes of discourse as we study them, offering conclusions about when and how they provide for successful communication. Synthesis, then, relies on a back and forth movement among thinking activities, building upon the details we discover through analysis and the judgments we arrive at through evaluation.

In this chapter, we will look more closely at modes of discourse and at synthesizing ideas. We will consider the relationships between works of literature and essays. We will also explore some specific modes of discourse—proven ways of thinking and writing that make use of strategies like **definition** and **comparison.** Finally, we will discuss the role of synthesis in critical inquiry.

COMPARING ASPECTS OF LITERATURE

As we discuss modes of discourse and synthesis, we will refer to a short story by Raymond Carver called "Cathedral."

RAYMOND CARVER

Raymond Carver (1938-1988) was born in Clatskanie, Oregon and grew up among the working class. He was employed at a sawmill and at numerous part-time jobs. By age twenty, Carver was married with two children and working hard to pay the bills. He took courses and taught at a number of colleges and universities. His first collection of short stories, Will You Please Be Quiet, Please, *was published in 1976. Carver continued to struggle to support his family and fought a difficult battle with alcoholism. He eventually quit drinking, but only after many stays in recovery centers and struggles resulting in the breakup of his first marriage. Carver had his career as a writer cut short after a battle with lung cancer in 1988. For the ten years or so before his death he lived with the poet Tess Gallagher, wrote stories, and taught at Syracuse University; Carver and Gallagher married just before his death. "Cathedral" was published in 1983. In an interview, Carver reported that the story is meant to affirm positive change. Tess Gallagher has also reported that the story in many ways reflects Carver's own eventual victory over alcoholism.*

Enhanced
reading of
"Cathedral"

Cathedral

This blind man, an old friend of my wife's, he was on his way to spend the night. His wife had died. So he was visiting the dead wife's relatives in Connecticut: He called my wife from his in-laws'. Arrangements were made. He would come by train, a five-hour trip, and my wife would meet him at the station. She hadn't seen him since she worked for him one summer in Seattle ten years ago. But she and the blind man had kept in touch. They made tapes and mailed them back and forth. I wasn't enthusiastic about his visit. He was no one I knew. And his being blind bothered me. My idea of blindness came from the movies. In the movies, the blind moved slowly and never laughed. Sometimes they were led by seeing-eye dogs. A blind man in my house was not something I looked forward to.

That summer in Seattle she had needed a job. She didn't have any money. The man she was going to marry at the end of the summer was in officers' training school. He didn't have any money, either. But she was in love with the guy, and he was in love with her, etc. She'd seen something in the paper: HELP WANTED - *Reading to Blind Man,* and a telephone number. She phoned and went over, was hired on the spot. She'd worked with this blind man all summer. She read stuff to him, case studies, reports, that sort of thing. She helped him organize his little office in the country social-service department. They'd become good friends, my wife and the blind man. How do I know these things? She told me. And she told me something else. On her last day in the office, the blind man asked if he could touch her face. She agreed to this. She told me he touched his fingers to every part of her face, her nose—even her neck! She never forgot it. She even tried to write a poem about it. She was always trying to write a poem. She wrote a poem or two every year, usually after something really important had happened to her.

When we first started going out together, she showed me the poem. In the poem, she recalled his fingers and the way they had moved around over her face. In the poem, she talked about what she had felt at the time, about what went through her mind when the blind man touched her nose and lips. I can remember I didn't think much of the poem. Of course, I didn't tell her that. Maybe I just don't understand poetry. I admit it's not the first thing I reach for when I pick up something to read.

Anyway, this man who'd first enjoyed her favors, the officer-to-be, he'd been her childhood sweetheart. So okay. I'm saying that at the end of the summer she let the blind man run his hands over her face, said goodbye to him, married her childhood etc., who was now a commissioned officer, and she moved away from Seattle. But they'd kept in touch, she and the blind man. She made the first contact after a year or so. She called him up one night from an Air Force base in Alabama. She wanted to talk. They talked. He asked her to send him a tape and tell him about her life. She did this. She sent the tape. On the tape, she told the blind man about her husband and about their life together in the military. She told the blind man she loved her husband but she didn't like it where they lived and she didn't like it that he was a part of the military-industrial thing. She told the blind man she'd written a poem and he was in it. She told him that she was writing a poem about what it was like to be an Air Force officer's wife. The poem wasn't finished yet. She was still writing it. The blind man made a tape. He sent her the tape. She made a tape. This went on for years. My wife's officer was posted to one base and then another. She sent tapes from Moody AFB, McGuire, McConnell, and finally Travis, near Sacramento, where one night she got to feeling lonely and cut off from people she kept losing in that moving-around life. She got to feeling she couldn't go it another step. She went in and swallowed all the pills and capsules in the medicine chest and washed them down with a bottle of gin. Then she got into a hot bath and passed out.

5   But instead of dying, she got sick. She threw up. Her officer—why should he have a name? he was the childhood sweetheart, and what more does he want?—came home from somewhere, found her, and called the ambulance. In time, she put it all on a tape and sent the tape to the blind man. Over the years, she put all kinds of stuff on tapes and sent the tapes off lickety-split. Next to writing a poem every year, I think it was her chief means of recreation. On one tape, she told the blind man she'd decided to live away from her officer for a time. On another tape, she told him about her divorce. She and I began going out, and of course she told her blind man about it. She told him everything, or so it seemed to me. Once she asked me if I'd like to hear the latest tape from the blind man. This was a year ago. I was on the tape, she said. So I said okay, I'd listen to it. I got us drinks and we settled down in the living room. We made ready to listen. First she inserted the tape into the player and adjusted a couple of dials. Then she pushed a lever. The tape squeaked and someone began to talk in this loud voice. She lowered the volume. After a few minutes of harmless chitchat, I heard my own name in the mouth of this stranger, this blind man I didn't even know! And then this: 'From all you've said about him, I can only conclude—' But we were interrupted, a knock at the door, something, and we didn't ever get back to the tape. Maybe it was just as well. I'd heard all I wanted to.

Now this same blind man was coming to sleep in my house.

'Maybe I could take him bowling,' I said to my wife. She was at the draining board doing scalloped potatoes. She put down the knife she was using and turned around.

'If you love me,' she said, 'you can do this for me. If you don't love me, okay. But if you had a friend, any friend, and the friend came to visit, I'd make him feel comfortable.' She wiped her hands with the dish towel.

'I don't have any blind friends,' I said.

10   'You don't have *any* friends,' she said. 'Period. Besides,' she said, 'goddamn it, his wife's just died! Don't you understand that? The man's lost his wife!'

I didn't answer. She'd told me a little about the blind man's wife. Her name was Beulah. Beulah! That's a name for a colored woman.

'Was his wife a Negro?' I asked.

'Are you crazy?' my wife said. 'Have you just flipped or something?' She picked up a potato. I saw it hit the floor, then roll under the stove. 'What's wrong with you?' she said. 'Are you drunk?'

'I'm just asking,' I said.

15   Right then my wife filled me in with more detail than I cared to know. I made a drink and sat at the kitchen table to listen. Pieces of the story began to fall into place.

Beulah had gone to work for the blind man the summer after my wife had stopped working for him. Pretty soon Beulah and the blind man had themselves a church wedding. It was a little wedding—who'd want to go to such a wedding in the first place?—just the two of them, plus the minister and the minister's wife. But it was a church wedding just the same. It was what Beulah had wanted, he'd said. But even then Beulah must have been carrying the cancer in her glands. After they had been inseparable for eight years—my wife's word, *inseparable*—Beulah's health went into a rapid decline. She died in a Seattle hospital room, the blind man sitting beside the bed and holding on to her hand. They'd married, lived and worked together, slept together—had sex, sure—and then the blind man had to bury her. All this without his having ever seen what the goddamned woman looked like. It was beyond my understanding. Hearing this, I felt sorry for the blind man for a little bit. And then I found myself thinking what a pitiful life this woman must have led. Imagine a woman who could never see herself as she was seen in the eyes of her loved one. A woman who could go on day after day and never receive the smallest compliment from her beloved. A woman whose husband could never read the expression on her face, be it misery or something better. Someone who could wear makeup or not—what difference to him? She could, if she wanted, wear green eye-shadow around one eye, a straight pin in her nostril, yellow slacks and purple shoes, no matter. And then to slip off into death, the blind man's hand on her hand, his blind eyes streaming tears—I'm imagining now—her last thought maybe this: that he never even knew what she looked like, and she on an express to the grave. Robert was left with a small insurance policy and half of a twenty-peso Mexican coin. The other half of the coin went into the box with her. Pathetic.

So when the time rolled around, my wife went to the depot to pick him up. With nothing to do but wait—sure, I blamed him for that—I was having a drink and watching the TV when I heard the car pull into the drive. I got up from the sofa with my drink and went to the window to have a look.

I saw my wife laughing as she parked the car. I saw her get out of the car and shut the door. She was still wearing a smile. Just amazing. She went around to the other side of the car to where the blind man was already starting to get out. This blind man, feature this, he was wearing a full beard! A beard on a blind man! Too much, I say. The blind man reached into the back seat and dragged out a suitcase. My wife took his arm, shut the car door, and, talking all the way, moved him down the drive and then up the steps to the front porch. I turned off the TV. I finished my drink, rinsed the glass, dried my hands. Then I went to the door.

My wife said, 'I want you to meet Robert. Robert, this is my husband. I've told you all about him.' She was beaming. She had this blind man by his coat sleeve.

20   The blind man let go of his suitcase and up came his hand.

I took it. He squeezed hard, held my hand, and then he let it go.

'I feel like we've already met,' he boomed.

'Likewise,' I said. I didn't know what else to say. Then I said, 'Welcome, I've heard a lot about you.' We began to move then, a little group, from the porch into the living room, my wife guiding him by the arm. The blind man was carrying his suitcase in his other hand. My wife said things like, 'To your left here, Robert. That's right. Now watch it, there's a chair. That's it. Sit down right here. This is the sofa. We just bought this sofa two weeks ago.'

I started to say something about the old sofa. I'd liked that old sofa. But I didn't say anything. Then I wanted to say something else, small-talk, about the scenic ride along the Hudson. How going *to* New York, you should sit on the right-hand side of the train, and coming *from* New York, the left-hand side.

25   'Did you have a good train ride?' I said. 'Which side of the train did you sit on, by the way?'

'What a question, which side!' my wife said. 'What's it matter which side?' she said.

'I just asked,' I said.

'Right side,' the blind man said. 'I hadn't been on a train in nearly forty years. Not since I was a kid. With my folks. That's been a long time. I'd nearly forgotten the sensation. I have winter in my beard now,' he said. 'So I've been told, anyway. Do I look distinguished, my dear?' the blind man said to my wife.

'You look distinguished, Robert,' she said. 'Robert,' she said. 'Robert, it's just so good to see you.'

30 My wife finally took her eyes off the blind man and looked at me. I had the feeling she didn't like what she saw. I shrugged.

I've never met, or personally known, anyone who was blind. This blind man was late forties, a heavy-set, balding man with stooped shoulders, as if he carried a great weight there. He wore brown slacks, brown shoes, a light-brown shirt, a tie, a sports coat. Spiffy. He also had this full beard. But he didn't use a cane and he didn't wear dark glasses. I'd always thought dark glasses were a must for the blind. Fact was, I wished he had a pair. At first glance, his eyes looked like anyone else's eyes. But if you looked close, there was something different about them. Too much white in the iris, for one thing, and the pupils seemed to move around in the sockets without his knowing it or being able to stop it. Creepy. As I stared at his face, I saw the left pupil turn in toward his nose while the other made an effort to keep in one place. But it was only an effort, for that eye was on the roam without his knowing it or wanting it to be.

I said, 'Let me get you a drink. What's your pleasure? We have a little of everything. It's one of our pastimes.'

'Bub, I'm a Scotch man myself,' he said fast enough in this big voice.

'Right,' I said. Bub! 'Sure you are. I knew it.'

35 He let his fingers touch his suitcase, which was sitting alongside the sofa. He was taking his bearings. I didn't blame him for that.

'I'll move that up to your room,' my wife said.

'No, that's fine,' the blind man said loudly. 'It can go up when I go up.'

'A little water with the Scotch?' I said.

'Very little,' he said.

40 'I knew it,' I said.

He said, 'Just a tad. The Irish actor, Barry Fitzgerald? I'm like that fellow. When I drink water, Fitzgerald said, I drink water. When I drink whiskey, I drink whiskey.' My wife laughed. The blind man brought his hand up under his beard. He lifted his beard slowly and let it drop.

I did the drinks, three big glasses of Scotch with a splash of water in each. Then we made ourselves comfortable and talked about Robert's travels. First the long flight from the West Coast to Connecticut, we covered that. Then from Connecticut up here by train. We had another drink concerning that leg of the trip.

I remembered having read somewhere that the blind didn't smoke because, as speculation had it, they couldn't see the smoke they exhaled. I thought I knew that much and that much only about blind people. But this blind man smoked his cigarette down to the nubbin and then lit another one. This blind man filled his ashtray and my wife emptied it.

When we sat down at the table for dinner, we had another drink. My wife heaped Robert's plate with cube steak, scalloped potatoes, green beans. I buttered him up two slices of bread. I said, 'Here's bread and butter for you.' I swallowed some of my drink. 'Now let us pray,' I said, and the blind man lowered his head. My wife looked at me, her mouth agape. 'Pray the phone won't ring and the food doesn't get cold,' I said.

45   We dug in. We ate everything there was to eat on the table. We ate like there was no tomorrow. We didn't talk. We ate. We scarfed. We grazed that table. We were into serious eating. The blind man had right away located his foods, he knew just where everything was on his plate. I watched with admiration as he used his knife and fork on the meat. He'd cut two pieces of meat, fork the meat into his mouth, and then go all out for the scalloped potatoes, the beans next, and then he'd tear off a hunk of buttered bread and eat that. He'd follow this up with a big drink of milk. It didn't seem to bother him to use his fingers once in a while, either.

We finished everything, including half a strawberry pie. For a few moments, we sat as if stunned. Sweat beaded on our faces. Finally, we got up from the table and left the dirty plates. We didn't look back. We took ourselves into the living room and sank into our places again. Robert and my wife sat on the sofa. I took the big chair. We had us two or three more drinks while they talked about the major things that had come to pass for them in the past ten years. For the most part, I just listened. Now and then I joined in. I didn't want him to think I'd left the room, and I didn't want her to think I was feeling left out. They talked of things that had happened to them—to them!—these past ten years. I waited in vain to hear my name on my wife's sweet lips: 'And then my dear husband came into my life'—something like that. But I heard nothing of the sort. More talk of Robert. Robert had done a little of everything, it seemed, a regular blind jack-of-all-trades. But most recently he and his wife had had an Amway distributorship, from which, I gathered, they'd earned their living, such as it was. The blind man was also a ham radio operator. He talked in his loud voice about conversations he'd had with fellow operators in Guam, in the Philippines, in Alaska, and even in Tahiti. He said he'd have a lot of friends there if he ever wanted to go visit those places. From time to time, he'd turn his blind face toward me, put his hand under his beard, ask me something. How long had I been in my present position? (Three years.) Did I like my work? (I didn't.) Was I going to stay with it? (What were the options?) Finally, when I thought he was beginning to run down, I got up and turned on the TV.

My wife looked at me with irritation. She was heading toward a boil. Then she looked at the blind man and said, 'Robert, do you have a TV?'

The blind man said, 'My dear, I have two TVs. I have a color set and a black-and-white thing, an old relic. It's funny, but if I turn the TV on, and I'm always turning it on, I turn on the color set. It's funny, don't you think?'

I didn't know what to say to that. I had absolutely nothing to say to that. No opinion. So I watched the news program and tried to listen to what the announcer was saying.

50   'This is a color TV,' the blind man said. 'Don't ask me how, but I can tell.'

'We traded up a while ago,' I said.

The blind man had another taste of his drink. He lifted his beard, sniffed it, and let it fall. He leaned forward on the sofa. He positioned his ashtray on the coffee table, then put the lighter to his cigarette. He leaned back on the sofa and crossed his legs at the ankles.

My wife covered her mouth, and then she yawned. She stretched. She said, 'I think I'll go upstairs and put on my robe. I think I'll change into something else. Robert, you make yourself comfortable,' she said.

'I'm comfortable,' the blind man said.

55   'I want you to feel comfortable in this house,' she said.

'I am comfortable,' the blind man said.

After she'd left the room, he and I listened to the weather report and then to the sports roundup. By that time, she'd been gone so long I didn't know if she was going to come back. I thought she might have gone to bed. I wished she'd come back downstairs. I didn't want to be left alone with a blind man. I asked him if he wanted another drink, and he said sure. Then I asked if he wanted to smoke some dope with me. I said I'd just rolled a number. I hadn't, but I planned to do so in about two shakes.

'I'll try some with you,' he said.

'Damn right,' I said. 'That's the stuff.'

60   I got our drinks and sat down on the sofa with him. Then I rolled us two fat numbers. I lit one and passed it. I brought it to his fingers. He took it and inhaled.

'Hold it as long as you can,' I said. I could tell he didn't know the first thing.

My wife came back downstairs wearing her pink robe and her pink slippers.

'What do I smell?' she said.

'We thought we'd have us some cannabis,' I said.

65   My wife gave me a savage look. Then she looked at the blind man and said, 'Robert, I didn't know you smoked.'

He said, 'I do now, my dear. There's a first time for everything. But I don't feel anything yet.'

'This stuff is pretty mellow,' I said. 'This stuff is mild. It's dope you can reason with,' I said. 'It doesn't mess you up.'

'Not much it doesn't, bub,' he said, and laughed.

My wife sat on the sofa between the blind man and me. I passed her the number. She took it and toked and then passed it back to me. 'Which way is this going?' she said. Then she said, 'I shouldn't be smoking this. I can hardly keep my eyes open as it is. That dinner did me in. I shouldn't have eaten so much.'

70   'It was the strawberry pie,' the blind man said. 'That's what did it,' he said, and he laughed his big laugh. Then he shook his head.

'There's more strawberry pie,' I said.

'Do you want some more, Robert?' my wife said.

'Maybe in a little while,' he said.

We gave our attention to the TV. My wife yawned again. She said, 'Your bed is made up when you feel like going to bed, Robert. I know you must have had a long day. When you're ready to go to bed, say so.' She pulled his arm. 'Robert?'

75   He came to and said, 'I've had a real nice time. This beats tapes, doesn't it?'

I said, 'Coming at you,' and I put the number between his fingers. He inhaled, held the smoke, and then let it go. It was like he'd been doing it since he was nine years old.

'Thanks, bub,' he said. 'But I think this is all for me. I think I'm beginning to feel it,' he said. He held the burning roach out for my wife.

'Same here,' she said. 'Ditto. Me, too.' She took the roach and passed it to me. 'I may just sit here for a while between you two guys with my eyes closed. But don't let me bother you, okay? Either one of you. If it bothers you, say so. Otherwise, I may just sit here with my eyes closed until you're ready to go to bed,' she said. 'Your bed's made up, Robert, when you're ready. It's right next to our room at the top of the stairs. We'll show you up when you're ready. You wake me up now, you guys, if I fall asleep.' She said that and then she closed her eyes and went to sleep.

The news program ended. I got up and changed the channel. I sat back down on the sofa. I wished my wife hadn't pooped out. Her head lay across the back of the sofa, her mouth open. She'd turned so that her robe had slipped away from her legs, exposing a juicy thigh. I reached to draw her robe back over her, and it was then that I glanced at the blind man. What the hell! I flipped the robe open again.

80   'You say when you want some strawberry pie,' I said.

'I will,' he said.

I said, 'Are you tired? Do you want me to take you up to your bed? Are you ready to hit the hay?'

'Not yet,' he said. 'No, I'll stay up with you, bub. If that's all right. I'll stay up until you're ready to turn in. We haven't had a chance to talk. Know what I mean? I feel like me and her monopolized the evening.' He lifted his beard and he let it fall. He picked up his cigarettes and his lighter.

'That's all right,' I said. Then I said, 'I'm glad for the company.'

85   And I guess I was. Every night I smoked dope and stayed up as long as I could before I fell asleep. My wife and I hardly ever went to bed at the same time. When I did go to sleep, I had these dreams. Sometimes I'd wake up from one of them, my heart going crazy.

Something about the church and the Middle Ages was on the TV. Not your run-of-the-mill TV fare. I wanted to watch something else. I turned to the other channels. But there was nothing on them, either. So I turned back to the first channel and apologized.

'Bub, it's all right,' the blind man said. 'It's fine with me. Whatever you want to watch is okay. I'm always learning something. Learning never ends. It won't hurt me to learn something tonight. I got ears,' he said.

We didn't say anything for a time. He was leaning forward with his head turned at me, his right ear aimed in the direction of the set. Very disconcerting. Now and then his eyelids drooped and then they snapped open again. Now and then he put his fingers into his beard and tugged, like he was thinking about something he was hearing on the television.

On the screen, a group of men wearing cowls was being set upon and tormented by men dressed in skeleton costumes and men dressed as devils. The men dressed as devils wore devil masks, horns, and long tails. This pageant was part of a procession. The Englishman who was narrating the thing said it took place in Spain once a year. I tried to explain to the blind man what was happening.

90   'Skeletons,' he said. 'I know about skeletons,' he said, and he nodded.

The TV showed this one cathedral. Then there was a long, slow look at another one. Finally, the picture switched to the famous one in Paris, with its flying buttresses and its spires reaching up to the clouds. The camera pulled away to show the whole of the cathedral rising above the skyline.

There were times when the Englishman who was telling the thing would shut up, would simply let the camera move around over the cathedrals. Or else the camera would tour the countryside, men in fields walking behind oxen. I waited as long as I could. Then I felt I had to say something. I said, 'They're showing the outside of this cathedral now. Gargoyles. Little statues carved to look like monsters. Now I guess they're in Italy. Yeah, they're in Italy. There's paintings on the walls of this one church.'

'Are those fresco paintings, bub?' he asked, and he sipped from his drink.

I reached for my glass. But it was empty. I tried to remember what I could remember. 'You're asking me are those frescoes?' I said. 'That's a good question. I don't know.'

95   The camera moved to a cathedral outside Lisbon. The differences in the Portuguese cathedral compared with the French and Italian were not that great. But they were there. Mostly the interior stuff. Then something occurred to me, and I said, 'Something has occurred to me. Do you have any idea what a cathedral is? What they look like, that is? Do you follow me? If somebody says cathedral to you, do you have any notion what they're talking about? Do you know the difference between that and a Baptist church, say?'

He let the smoke dribble from his mouth. 'I know they took hundreds of workers fifty or a hundred years to build,' he said. 'I just heard the man say that, of course. I know generations of the same families worked on a cathedral. I heard him say that, too. The men who began their life's work on them, they never lived to see the completion of their work. In that wise, bub, they're no different from the rest of us, right?' He laughed. Then his eyelids drooped again. His head nodded. He seemed to be snoozing. Maybe he was imagining himself in Portugal. The TV was showing another cathedral now. This one was in Germany. The Englishman's voice droned on. 'Cathedrals,' the blind man said. He sat up and rolled his head back and forth. 'If you want the truth, bub, that's about all I know. What I just said. What I heard him say. But maybe you could describe one to me? I wish you'd do it. I'd like that. If you want to know, I really don't have a good idea.'

I stared hard at the shot of the cathedral on the TV. How could I even begin to describe it? But say my life depended on it. Say my life was being threatened by an insane guy who said I had to do it or else.

I stared some more at the cathedral before the picture flipped off into the countryside. There was no use. I turned to the blind man and said, 'To begin with, they're very tall.' I was looking around the room for clues. 'They reach way up. Up and up. Toward the sky. They're so big, some of them, they have to have these supports. To help hold them up, so to speak. These supports are called buttresses. They remind me of viaducts, for some reason. But maybe you don't know viaducts, either? Sometimes the cathedrals have devils and such carved into the front. Sometimes lords and ladies. Don't ask me why this is,' I said.

He was nodding. The whole upper part of his body seemed to be moving back and forth.

100   'I'm not doing so good, am I?' I said.

He stopped nodding and leaned forward on the edge of the sofa. As he listened to me, he was running his fingers through his beard. I wasn't getting through to him, I could see that. But he waited for me to go on just the same. He nodded, like he was trying to encourage me. I tried to think what else to say. 'They're really big,' I said. 'They're massive. They're built of stone. Marble, too, sometimes. In those olden days, when they built cathedrals, men wanted to be close to God. In those olden days, God was an important part of everyone's life. You could tell this from their cathedral-building. I'm sorry,' I said, 'but it looks like that's the best I can do for you. I'm just no good at it.'

'That's all right, bub,' the blind man said. 'Hey, listen. I hope you don't mind my asking you. Can I ask you something? Let me ask you a simple question, yes or no. I'm just curious and there's no offense. You're my host. But let me ask if you are in any way religious? You don't mind my asking?'

I shook my head. He couldn't see that, though. A wink is the same as a nod to a blind man. 'I guess I don't believe in it. In anything. Sometimes it's hard. You know what I'm saying?'

'Sure, I do,' he said.

105   'Right,' I said.

The Englishman was still holding forth. My wife sighed in her sleep. She drew a long breath and went on with her sleeping.

'You'll have to forgive me,' I said. 'But I can't tell you what a cathedral looks like. It just isn't in me to do it. I can't do any more than I've done.'

The blind man sat very still, his head down, as he listened to me.

I said, 'The truth is, cathedrals don't mean anything special to me. Nothing. Cathedrals. They're something to look at on late-night TV. That's all they are.'

110   It was then that the blind man cleared his throat. He brought something up. He took a handkerchief from his back pocket. Then he said, 'I get it, bub. It's okay. It happens. Don't worry about it,' he said. 'Hey, listen to me. Will you do me a favor? I got an idea. Why don't you find us some heavy paper? And a pen. We'll do something. We'll draw one together. Get us a pen and some heavy paper. Go on, bub, get the stuff,' he said.

So I went upstairs. My legs felt like they didn't have any strength in them. They felt like they did after I'd done some running. In my wife's room, I looked around. I found some ballpoints in a little basket on her table. And then I tried to think where to look for the kind of paper he was talking about.

Downstairs, in the kitchen, I found a shopping bag with onion skins in the bottom of the bag. I emptied the bag and shook it. I brought it into the living room and sat down with it near his legs. I moved some things, smoothed the wrinkles from the bag, spread it out on the coffee table.

The blind man got down from the sofa and sat next to me on the carpet.

He ran his fingers over the paper. He went up and down the sides of the paper. The edges, even the edges. He fingered the corners.

115   'All right,' he said. 'All right, let's do her.'

He found my hand, the hand with the pen. He closed his hand over my hand. 'Go ahead, bub, draw,' he said. 'Draw. You'll see. I'll follow along with you. It'll be okay. Just begin now like I'm telling you. You'll see. Draw,' the blind man said.

So I began. First I drew a box that looked like a house. It could have been the house I lived in. Then I put a roof on it. At either end of the roof, I drew spires. Crazy.

'Swell,' he said. 'Terrific. You're doing fine,' he said. 'Never thought anything like this could happen in your lifetime, did you, bub? Well, it's a strange life, we all know that. Go on now. Keep it up.'

I put in windows with arches. I drew flying buttresses. I hung great doors. I couldn't stop. The TV station went off the air. I put down the pen and closed and opened my fingers. The blind man felt around over the paper. He moved the tips of his fingers over the paper, all over what I had drawn, and he nodded.

120   'Doing fine,' the blind man said.

I took up the pen again, and he found my hand. I kept at it. I'm no artist. But I kept drawing just the same.

My wife opened up her eyes and gazed at us. She sat up on the sofa, her robe hanging open. She said, 'What are you doing? Tell me, I want to know.'

I didn't answer her.

The blind man said, 'We're drawing a cathedral. Me and him are working on it. Press hard,' he said to me. 'That's right. That's good,' he said. 'Sure. You got it, bub. I can tell. You didn't think you could. But you can, can't you? You're cooking with gas now. You know what I'm saying? We're going to really have us something here in a minute. How's the old arm?' he said. 'Put some people in there now. What's a cathedral without people?'

125   My wife said, 'What's going on? Robert, what are you doing? What's going on?'

'It's all right,' he said to her. 'Close your eyes now,' the blind man said to me.

I did it. I closed them just like he said.

'Are they closed?' he said. 'Don't fudge.'

'They're closed,' I said.

130   'Keep them that way,' he said. He said, 'Don't stop now. Draw.'

So we kept on with it. His fingers rode my fingers as my hand went over the paper. It was like nothing else in my life up to now.

Then he said, 'I think that's it. I think you got it,' he said. 'Take a look. What do you think?'

But I had my eyes closed. I thought I'd keep them that way for a little longer. I thought it was something I ought to do.

'Well?' he said. 'Are you looking?'

135   My eyes were still closed. I was in my house. I knew that. But I didn't feel like I was inside anything.

'It's really something,' I said.

Understanding Modes of Discourse in "Cathedral"

We might not think that a short story contains many modes of discourse. The story itself is one form of communication, so it would be simple enough to call "Cathedral" a work of fiction and stop at that. However, investigating a short story like Carver's helps us complicate our understanding of how language works. "Cathedral" does not simply "tell a story." It uses language in specific ways to convey the many messages that make up "the story." For instance, the narrator employs methods of **comparison** as he tells the story. He uses contrast by establishing his initial "idea of blindness [that comes] from the movies" (60). This initial perspective forms the basis for the evolution of the narrator's views as the story develops.

The narrator also uses **examples** to tell the story. Rather than simply saying that his wife traveled a great deal when she was married to the Air Force officer, he lists the many bases where they were posted: "Moody AFB, McGuire, McConnell, and finally Travis, near Sacramento" (61). The examples convey a sense of the migratory life of an Air Force couple more clearly than a direct statement would.

Similarly, the story employs a conscious use of **narration** to convey its tale. Narration on one level lists the events that take place in the story. On another level, however, it establishes a relationship between the narrator and the reader. When the narrator describes the Air Force officer and asks, "why should he have a name?" (61), we can see narration as a technique used deliberately to share information with readers.

Making comparisons, providing examples, and employing techniques of narration all represent specific ways of using language. We might not automatically look for these somewhat essay-like strategies when we examine a work of fiction. Instead, we might examine the use of dialog or the role of symbols in a short story—modes of discourse more frequently emphasized when studying fiction. Still, if we train ourselves to recognize all of these modes of discourse, we can use them to evaluate many forms of writing and to strengthen our own compositions.

EXPLORING MODES OF DISCOURSE

Beginning over 2,000 years ago with thinkers like Aristotle, writers have employed models to help them organize their ideas. By using techniques like narration, exemplification, definition, causation, and comparison (to name a few possibilities), writers can develop ideas using easily recognizable frameworks. Readers familiar with the frameworks can follow a writer's thinking more readily.

We must use care, however, when we investigate modes of discourse. If, for instance, we methodically dissect a work of literature in search of modes of discourse, we may forget how works appeal to us emotionally. Instead, a process of critical inquiry should drive our investigation. Similarly, in our own compositions, we can make comparisons, provide examples, define, narrate, and use other strategies; we should employ these techniques as needed based on our goals and the evolving demands of our writing.

An Overview of Modes of Discourse

Below is an overview of some common modes of discourse. Later, we will look in detail at two significant modes of discourse, **definitions** and **comparisons.** As you think about these ways of using language, remember that modes of discourse generally overlap. Literary works employ essay-like techniques, and essays can contain literary elements. Further, modes of discourse may be related. We often integrate examples as a way of describing something. We might blend techniques like comparison, narration, or definition as we compose. We can separate modes of discourse to analyze them, but in practice writers employ them flexibly.

Narration relates a series of events. We find narration not only in works of literature, but also in essays. Narration establishes a relationship between the person providing the information and the reader, as in "Cathedral" where the narrator frequently confides in the reader.

Exemplification offers expansion or support for ideas by providing examples. Examples give readers concrete details that help them appreciate more general concepts and bolster arguments by providing evidence. We might, for example, show the narrator of "Cathedral" to be dissatisfied with life by discussing his drinking or his drug use.

Description offers details that help readers understand ideas, objects, people, or events. Descriptions can serve to inform or entertain readers. In "Cathedral," the narrator's efforts to explain the television images of cathedrals use descriptions. He also employs description to relate the events at the end of the story.

Process analysis describes an activity or series of events. A process analysis might be used to demonstrate how to perform an activity such as setting up a two-way radio. Usually a step-by-step description makes up the analysis.

Causation considers events or actions and their consequences. We can look backward or forward to either trace the causes of something, or to project an outcome. Causation helps us see the influences that a character or event can have in a story; some of the tension in "Cathedral" might be traced to the influence of Robert's visit on the narrator and his wife. We also might examine the influences of an event in an author's life; a visit paid to Carver and his wife by a friend who had lost his sight provided the impetus for this story.

Establishing Definitions

Definitions provide writers and readers with a shared basis for agreement. At the simplest level, definitions demonstrate meaning so that writers can communicate without misunderstanding. If we wish to consider Robert's activities as a ham radio operator, for example, we can examine the definition of ham radio and learn that this form of communication provides a two-way connection between radio enthusiasts who share information over long distances during disasters or for personal communication.

Dictionary definitions can help reduce misunderstandings, but they represent only the first step in explaining the meaning of something. Knowing that Robert's hobby, for instance, involves communication between radio operators does little to demonstrate the significance of that definition. An essay on "Cathedral" would need to explore the implications of the communication as two-way, the distance between communicators, the use of ham radio during times of disaster, and whatever else might help make sense of the hobby as it relates to themes in the story.

We can also employ definition more deliberately to develop interpretations and arguments. To make such arguments we can develop **criteria** for **classifying** or defining an item, and then use synthesis to consider how a specific item relates to those criteria. This **criteria/match** approach could serve to organize an essay on "Cathedral" around defining a concept like friendship. We could develop a number of paragraphs exploring what we believe to be the essential qualities of friendship: must a friend be willing to help in times of trouble, have a shared interest, tell the truth, accept failings, offer encouragement, avoid arguments? Once we discuss in detail what we believe to be the criteria for friendship, we can consider the relationships between Robert, the narrator, and the narrator's wife in terms of these criteria.

Of course, these criteria may not be universally agreed upon. Our essay would need to explain *why* the criteria we select are important. We also need to select what we believe to be the most **essential qualities** related to a category—is honesty more important than encouragement in a friendship? If so, why? If we have done the work of justifying the criteria we use to define something, discussing a specific item in terms of those criteria should come easily.

Making Comparisons

Comparisons examine and relate two or more similar items. When we study literature, the key to this process is considering passages, characters, themes, and other aspects of literature **in terms of** one another. As we make comparisons, we are bound to discover not only similarities but also differences, so we can include discovering **contrasts** as a key component of making comparisons.

As we locate examples for comparison, we must select items that have a logical connection with one another. While exploring "Cathedral," relating the narrator's drinking habits with Robert's description of his train ride to the city will likely prove difficult. Relating the narrator's wife's use of tapes to Robert's conversations using ham radio provides a more logical basis for comparison.

Remember, as well, that your activities will move back and forth between synthesis, analysis, and evaluation as you think and write about literature. You would want to analyze the details of exchanging messages using tapes to understand that example of communication before relating it to ham radio. You would also need to evaluate and draw conclusions about the relationships you discover.

Further, in all of the thinking that you do about a work, remember that you ultimately want to discover and draw connections that will provide you with something engaging to explore. Rather than comparing the eating habits of the characters, make deliberate efforts to explore challenging questions. You might take up a major theme in the story, such as touch. You will also want to channel your comparisons toward developing a thesis, a way of explaining the relationships you discover that will be of interest to you and to others.

When considering touch, you might start with something like the closing scene from "Cathedral." You could explore the way that Robert "closed his hand over [the narrator's] hand" (68). You might consider other examples where touch is used to convey information. You might recognize that Robert's request to touch the face of the narrator's wife earlier in the story is related to this episode in the final scene.

Once you have spotted related occurrences, you can begin synthesizing them. Initially, you may look for similarities. In both the closing scene and the opening episode, for instance, touch represents a way that Robert gathers information. You will also want to locate differences, and then examine those variations in more detail. In the earlier episode, the narrator's wife is passive while Robert touches her face. In the closing scene, however, both Robert and the narrator work together through touch to draw the cathedral.

Locating associated instances allows you to evaluate the nature of their relationship. You might discover that one instance causes another. You might see in several passages a pattern that suggests a theme in the work. Similarities or differences should invite comparisons and help you begin to develop a thesis statement (see below) that can guide the creation of an essay.

✔ CHECKLIST FOR COMPARING ASPECTS OF LITERATURE

☐ **Select items that lend themselves to comparison.** Often decisions about what to compare will arise from your reading as you discover relationships and questions. You can also prompt yourself by looking for potential comparisons in settings, characters, events, symbols, and themes.

☐ **Develop a sense of the items** you are comparing on their own terms. A brief character sketch of the narrator, for instance, will allow you to understand his key traits before relating them to other characters.

☐ **Relate key examples to one another.** Compare each to each and make note of areas of similarity. Recognize areas of difference. Consider whether the similarities or the differences (or perhaps both) are significant and why.

☐ **For similarities, ask questions** about elements the items have in common. What are the qualities of any common characteristics or themes? How do these common elements relate to the larger work?

☐ **For differences, consider how significant** any contrasts might be. Are the differences fundamental or just superficial? For significant differences, consider possible explanations for the contrasts.

Exercise 3.1 *Comparing Passages*

Working with a group of fellow students or on your own, explore "Cathedral" and locate passages that relate to a key theme in the story. Begin by selecting someone to keep track of the group's work or preparing to take notes on your own.

1. Consider the major themes that you find of interest in the story. Create a list of at least three themes.

2. Return to the work and look for examples that are related to your three themes. Evaluate how well the passages in the story could be used to support a discussion of each of your three themes. Based on your evaluation, select one theme you wish to consider further and write it down.

3. Look over the passages in the story and select two that you believe to be most significant in understanding your theme. Analyze each passage and develop a statement about their relationship. Consider whether they are more similar or different. Think about questions raised by the passages. Write three or more sentences describing the relationship between the passages.

4. Return to the work and locate two additional passages that could be used to expand your exploration. Write a paragraph explaining the relationships between all of the passages you have selected.

SYNTHESIZING TO DEVELOP A THESIS

As we explore relationships in a work, and especially as we prepare to write, a thesis can help us synthesize what we discover. This does not mean that we have found the "best" way of understanding the connections, or even that we have made sense of every facet we are looking at. When we select a thesis based on comparisons or relationships, what we are really saying is that we have an interesting way of explaining aspects of the work in terms of one another or in relation to a larger message.

Using synthesis to develop a thesis

We should articulate our approach in a **thesis statement.** To develop a thesis statement, we need to take an angle that spells out the key relationships we have discovered. Of "Cathedral," we might develop a thesis about the relationship between the narrator and the reader of the story. We could explore how readers gather information from the story or how the relationship between the reader and the narrator evolves. We might develop a thesis statement like *the relationship that evolves between the narrator and reader in "Cathedral" draws the reader into the narrator's uplifting realization at the end of the story.* The statement you develop may not address every connection that runs through the work. Our statement would allow us to look more closely at the details and formal elements of the narration of the story.

✔ CHECKLIST FOR SYNTHESIZING A THESIS STATEMENT

☐ **Develop a sense of the topics** addressed in the work. (See the table on pages 45–46 for suggestions.) Look for patterns and explore relationships that will help you focus your thinking about the topics and themes you discover.

☐ **Identify specific passages** that deserve attention. Compare passages and try to place them within a framework for understanding the work as a whole.

☐ **Consider additional information** about the context of the work or about other's interpretations. Consider how contextual information can help you understand the work as a whole.

☐ **Stop and ask questions** about the interpretations you are formulating. Are there aspects of the work that you have not addressed that really need to be accounted for? Will the approach you are developing be engaging to you and your readers? What insights should be explored further?

☐ **Formulate a statement** that demonstrates a way of understanding the relationships you have uncovered and that will enable you to pursue lingering questions. Check that the thesis you are proposing will allow you to discuss the work with detail. Articulate your thesis in a sentence that could be used to organize an essay.

☐ **Return to the work to look for evidence** that will support your thesis statement. If you cannot find a rich set of examples or if you find counter-examples that undermine your thesis, revise your statement. If you find numerous examples, begin selecting those that will most directly help you explain your approach.

Exercise 3.2   *Developing a Thesis Statement*

Working with a group of peers or on your own, develop a thesis statement that articulates your understanding of two or more related aspects of "Cathedral." Begin by choosing a person to keep track of the group's work or preparing to take notes, and then respond to the following prompts:

1. Select a theme from the story. Consider communication, relationships, stereotypes, addiction, spirituality, storytelling, or another theme that relates to "Cathedral."

2. Develop a list of everything you know that relates to the theme. Toss out observations, offer interpretations, and draw conclusions. Write out your list as a series of statements offering observations or questions related to your theme.

3. Examine your list of statements, looking for contradictions, comparisons, connections, or any other relationships that seem significant.

4. Write a thesis statement that will allow you to explore and explain one of these relationships. Brainstorm until you find a way of approaching "Cathedral" that relates two or more aspects of the story. Try out sentences until you can compose a statement that articulates your approach.

Exercise 3.3   *Writing a Comparison Paper*

Read Raymond Carver's "Cathedral" or one of the other works in our book and write a three-or-more page comparison that illuminates an important theme. Your comparison should help readers understand the theme you select by relating settings, characters, events, symbols, themes, or passages to one another.

1. Select a theme and determine passages that you can discuss to make your comparison.

2. Encapsulate the relationship between what you are comparing in a thesis statement, and then develop an outline you can use to organize your work.

3. Develop a series of body paragraphs that relate passages to one another and explain your thesis.

4. Provide evidence in the form of quotations from the story to support your points. Discuss and document your quotations (see pages 179–83 and the Appendix).

A Sample Comparison Paper

Maria Abadi

Instructor Catherine Reynolds

English 102

17 March 2004

Getting in Touch: Comparing Characters in "Cathedral"

The characters in Raymond Carver's "Cathedral" differ in the ways they communicate. The narrator appears to be the most challenged when it comes to communication, preferring to watch television and dismissing the concerns of his wife. The narrator's wife, on the other hand, communicates well with her blind friend, but seems unable to have a meaningful conversation with her husband. Robert acts as a bridge connecting the two characters. While it seems that the narrator and his wife are complete opposites when it comes to their ability to communicate, through the blind friend, we see that they have more similarities than differences. In the final analysis, their desire for human contact overrides differences in their

Abadi 2

Thesis statement encapsulating the comparison

abilities to communicate and brings the narrator to a moment of realization that connects him to Robert and reconnects him with his wife.

The narrator has the most difficult time communicating. We can see this difficulty in the way that he approaches the poetry that his wife writes.

Section discussing the narrator's difficulty communicating

His wife tries to capture her most significant experiences in her poems, "usually after something really important ha[s] happened to her" (60). Early in the story, the narrator relates his reaction to reading his wife's poem describing her encounter with Robert touching her face:

Block quotation providing an example for the discussion (see page 83)

> I can remember I didn't think much of the poem. Of course I didn't tell her that. Maybe I just don't understand poetry. I admit it's not the first thing I reach for when I pick up something to read. (60)

We might think the biggest problem with the narrator and his communication has to do with his not wanting to tell his wife about her poetry. Perhaps he does not want to hurt her feelings, or perhaps he just does not appreciate reading about his wife's encounter with another man. What really gives away his difficulty, however, may be his tone and the

Conclusion drawn about significance of the narrator's communication problem

attitude he takes toward the incident. By suggesting that he "just [doesn't] understand poetry," he dismisses the incident. He is really fooling himself. By placing his wife's most important communication on the same level as "the first thing [he] reach[es] for when [he] picks up something to read," he ignores the real problem: his detachment from his wife.

The narrator's difficulty seems to originate from both his jealousy and the tension in his relationship with his wife. Tensions in the relationship are revealed through the example of the sofa, something the wife has thrown out (perhaps when getting ready for her friend's visit). He seems

In-text quotation providing an example for the discussion (see pages 179–83)

angry at his wife and he tells us, "I wanted to say something about the old sofa. I liked the old sofa. But I didn't say anything" (62). Again, he seems unable to communicate. In fact, he expresses a desire to challenge his wife,

but bites his tongue either because he does not want to make trouble or he
is simply incapable of sharing his feelings.

Unlike the narrator, the wife communicates her feelings clearly in the
story. Her ability to share her feelings and communicate can be seen in the

Section describing the wife's communication abilities in terms of differences with the narrator

many methods of communication she uses throughout the story. She
shares tapes with Robert. She writes poetry where she talks about her
feelings. She converses with both her husband and her blind friend. She
keeps in touch for years after her move away from Robert. Her ability to
connect with others and the contrast between her perspective and the
narrator's can be seen in his observations of her as she picks up Robert: "I
saw my wife, laughing as she parked the car. I saw her get out of the car
and shut the door. She was still wearing a smile. Just amazing" (62).

However, the narrator's wife does share some of the narrator's
difficulties. Her ability to communicate seems limited to her interactions
with Robert. We learn not only that her first marriage ended in divorce, but

Section discussing the wife's communication in terms of similarities with the narrator

also that her difficulties in her first marriage and a sense of alienation may
have led to her suicide attempt. We can also attribute some of the
communication problems in her current marriage to her own difficulties.
When she is discussing Robert's visit, she tells her husband, "If you love me

In-text quotation providing an example for the discussion

. . . you can do this for me. If you don't love me, okay. But if you had a
friend, any friend, and the friend came to visit, I'd make him feel
comfortable" (61). Her concern seems to be more with the treatment of her

Conclusion relating the wife's and the narrator's communication

blind friend than with the status of her marriage. By tossing out the
possibility that there is no love in her marriage, and dismissing the
concern with "okay," the wife is not much different than the narrator in the
way she talks around the real conflict in their marriage.

The narrator and his wife share the greatest similarities, however, in
their relationship with Robert. The wife is clearly able to share her inner

feelings with Robert and has a strong relationship as a result. The

narrator is confused about the nature of blindness and unsure how to

approach the subject, but the end of the story is powerful because it closes

with a connection between the narrator and Robert that is equally as strong

as the connection between Robert and the narrator's wife. The real power of

the ending is not that the narrator is finally able to communicate the idea

of a cathedral. Instead, through communicating, the narrator is able to

establish a relationship and connection with Robert. This connection

mirrors the connection established years ago when Robert touched the

narrator's wife to examine her face.

We see the narrator's need for this human connection in his response to

Robert's question about religious beliefs. The narrator admits that he doesn't

"believe in anything," but continues this religious thought by apologizing for

not being able to describe the cathedral: "The truth is, cathedrals don't mean

anything special to me. Nothing. Cathedrals. They are something to look at

on late-night T.V. That's all they are" (68). The narrator expresses his lack of

a religious background or of even believing in "anything" in terms of his

inability to communicate the idea of the cathedral. We can feel his alienation

and the sense of resignation in the tone of his response. He tells us he "just

can't do it. It just isn't in [him]" (68).

Robert's response prepares us to see how the final scene of the story

demonstrates more about human relationships than cathedrals or

communication. He tells the narrator, "we'll draw one together" (68). When

Robert places his hand over the narrator's and they begin drawing, the

same human connection that the narrator's wife found in Robert's touch

can be felt in the description: "He found my hand, the hand with the pen.

He closed his hand over my hand" (68). As they continue drawing together,

however, the reactions of the narrator take on a spiritual tone. Robert's

---

Section extending the comparison by discussing the significance of the similarities between the narrator and his wife—the essay is moving closer to making conclusions about the human connection outlined in the thesis

Examples showing narrator's need for human connection

Examples showing human connection in the closing of the story

touch gives the sense of orientation to the narrator that he has been missing. He closes his eyes and a sense of comfort enters in the story: "I had my eyes closed. I thought I would keep them that way."

Conclusion that does not repeat entire structure of the essay, but restates thesis to make final point

The narrator now has established a connection with Robert and through that connection has found something in common with his wife. The sense of comfort and the human contact he shares is profound for the narrator because it contrasts so much with his earlier sense of detachment and alienation. He not only finds a friend, he finds a sense of grounding. Through the touch that establishes this human contact, the narrator awakens to the awareness of his human connections.

[New page]

Works Cited

Works Cited page in MLA format (see the Appendix)

Carver, Raymond. "Cathedral." <u>Writing about Literature in the Media</u> <u>Age</u>. Ed. Daniel Anderson. New York: Pearson Longman, 2005.

INQUIRING FURTHER

1. What do you think of Maria's choice to compare the characters in "Cathedral?" How successful do you think she has been in explaining the relationship between characters? What other elements of the story might lend themselves to comparison?

2. What modes of discourse can you recognize in Maria's essay? Do you feel as if she has made a deliberate attempt to employ specific techniques of communication? What strategies do you find to be most successful and why?

3. How successful do you find Maria's thesis to be? How would you sum up her thesis? Does she organize the essay so that it expands on and clarifies her thesis as it develops? What recommendations would you give for strengthening the organization of the essay?

COMPARING LITERATURE AND ESSAYS

Essays share many characteristics with literature. Like literature, essays possess creative elements. Georgina Kleege's essay "Blind Rage: An Open Letter to Helen Keller" (see page 83) uses humor and personal anecdotes to tell the story of the author's day. Like literature, essays may appeal to our emotions. They use imagery to demonstrate insights. They seek to get our attention and teach us something about themes that relate to human concerns.

However, essays differ from literature in that they generally relate real events and discuss non-fictional characters. They frequently employ modes of discourse deliberately to make their points. They tend to directly offer a message about the issues they discuss. They also invite us to consider the **rhetorical situation** in which they communicate their messages and the **argumentative strategies** that their authors employ.

Considering Modes of Discourse in Essays

Essays rely on modes of discourse to help make their points. This does not mean that they follow a model in lockstep fashion. Instead, they capitalize on models to demonstrate relationships and make convincing points. Kleege's essay, for instance, is organized around narration. The essay tells a story; however, it does so to bring us closer to understanding Kleege's position on issues related to people with disabilities.

Sometimes an essay will be organized deliberately around a model. Judy Syfers Brady's "Why I Want a Wife" (pages 818–20) employs exemplification as it explores women's roles in marriage. Generally, however, essays will use modes of discourse as needed. In addition to narration, for instance, Kleege makes comparisons, provides descriptions, and uses examples to help make her points.

Additionally, essays may employ a particular mode of discourse strategically to drive home a point. Linton Weeks' "Aliteracy: Read All About It, or Maybe Not" (89–93) closes by pointing out the relationship between aliteracy (the phenomenon of readers who choose not to read) and illiteracy (the inability to read). Weeks invokes **causality** as he cites a number of sources suggesting that, unless the aliterate change their ways, their lack of interest in reading will result in illiteracy for the next generation.

Considering Essays and Their Rhetorical Situations

The **rhetorical situation** describes the key components necessary for communication to take place. First, there must be a **message** that is exchanged. There must also be a **speaker** who creates or disseminates the message. This speaker writes with a **purpose** that influences the message. Finally, there must be an - **audience** that receives the message. Essay writers rely heavily on understanding this rhetorical situation.

Enhanced reading of "Letter from Birmingham Jail"

The writer must present himself or herself as a competent and fair-minded **speaker.** Martin Luther King Jr., in his "Letter from Birmingham Jail" (pages 515–26), begins by acknowledging the positions and good will of his opponents and listing some of his credentials to establish his authority. Essay writers also convey a sense of their attitude and **credibility** as speakers through their **tone.** Often essayists convey a serious but accessible tone. The tone of an essay is usually evenhanded as well. A lighthearted or ironic tone sometimes helps readers see a serious subject in a new light.

As readers, we develop a better understanding of essays by examining the **purpose** behind their composition. We can begin by considering whether an author means to **inform, entertain,** or **persuade** an audience. (In most cases, an author may intend to do some combination of the three.) Identifying an author's purpose can be challenging. Even if we recognize that an essayist is trying to persuade us of something, we must still ask *what* that something might be. Again, considering the speaker is a good starting place. Knowing Martin Luther King Jr.'s background, we can infer that his letter is meant to prompt us to act on civil rights concerns. We can also look at specific examples and rhetorical strategies to determine purpose; when Weeks suggests that the future literacy of children might be at stake, we see that his purpose is to alert people to the dangers of "aliteracy" and to try to change people's reading habits.

Finally, thinking about the intended audience for an essay can help us make sense of an author's purpose and the strategies he or she uses. Essayists adjust their writing based upon the audience for which they compose. Judy Syfers Brady's "Why I Want a Wife" (818–20) first appeared in *Ms.* magazine. Knowing *Ms.* generally has a liberal readership, we can expect the essay to appeal to the values of that type of audience.

You can consider these rhetorical concerns as you read the essays included in this book. In Chapter 5, you can also learn more about strategies of argument, and about how to apply what you know about rhetorical situations to your own writing.

REVIEWING AND PRACTICING

In this chapter we have talked about **synthesis,** a way of putting components together to examine their connections. As we explore characters, themes, passages, and other elements of literature, we recognize patterns and **relationships.** Many of these relationships can be demonstrated using **modes of discourse.** Narratives, descriptions, definitions, examples, and other modes of discourse help writers tell stories and communicate ideas.

- *Comparisons look at two elements in terms of one another.* We can investigate related items and evaluate any similarities we find. We can ask whether differences we discover are significant and what those contrasts might represent. Finally, we can use the patterns and relationships we discover to develop a thesis that provides an angle for approaching the work. Articulating this approach in a thesis statement helps us further inquire into the work and explain our thinking to others.

- *Essays can make deliberate use of modes of discourse,* though they often employ more than one mode. We can understand essays by examining their use of these strategies. We can also consider the rhetorical situation in which an essay exists. As we examine the speaker of the essay we can consider her or his tone and credibility. We can also consider an author's purpose and the intended audience of a work to better understand the rhetorical strategies employed in an essay.

Exercise 3.4   *Examining an Essay*

Working with a group of peers or on your own, examine "Aliteracy: Read All About It, or Maybe Not" (see pages 89–93) or one of the other essays in our book. Begin by selecting a person to keep track of the group's work or preparing to take notes on your own, and then respond to the following prompts:

1. Consider whether the essay as a whole can be classified using a mode of discourse. Does the essay center around narration, comparison, causation, or some other mode? Does it present a combination of

modes? List the mode or modes you believe best represent the essay and write two sentences explaining your decision.

2. Locate the passage that you believe best shows the use of a mode of discourse to make a specific point. Ask what point is being made. Consider how the mode of discourse helps make that point. Ask whether this is the most appropriate mode for convincing a reader of this point. Write three or more sentences describing the strategy employed in the passage.

3. Examine the speaker of the essay. What efforts does the speaker make to establish credibility? How would you describe the tone of the speaker? What do you know about the speaker's background? How does your sense of the speaker influence your response to the essay? Write at least four sentences discussing the speaker.

4. Consider the purpose behind the essay. Can you recognize a single purpose or does there seem to be more than one goal? How do the rhetorical strategies used in the essay help to achieve the author's purpose? Write three or more sentences discussing purpose.

5. Consider the intended audience for the essay. Can you determine from the original source of the essay anything about its audience? What strategies does the essay employ that help you recognize its audience? How would you characterize the audience for the essay? Write at least three sentences discussing the essay's appeal to its audience.

6. Consider the success of the essay. Given its purpose, audience, and rhetorical strategies, do you believe the essay is successful? Write at least four sentences explaining your assessment.

Exercise 3.5   *Comparing Literature and Essays*

Read Georgina Kleege's "Blind Rage: An Open Letter to Helen Keller" (next page) and write a three- to four-page essay comparing the work to Carver's "Cathedral."

1. Begin by evaluating Kleege's essay. Consider its modes of discourse and rhetorical situation and develop a thesis that explains the work.

2. Develop a reading of "Cathedral." Think about the elements of literature and the themes found in the story. Develop a thesis for understanding "Cathedral."

3. Compare the two works, looking at relationships between themes and modes of discourse. Is it possible to view "Cathedral" as you would the essay? What purpose and rhetorical strategies might you focus on? Can you approach "Blind Rage: An Open Letter to Helen Keller" from a literary perspective? What elements of literature might you discuss?

4. Considering the works' themes, rhetorical or literary strategies, purposes, or any other related elements you deem significant, develop your essay:

   • Determine a thesis that articulates a way of viewing the two works in terms of one another.

- Consider how you might use modes of discourse to make your points—can you integrate definitions, examples, narration, causation, or some other strategy into your comparison to make your points?

- Sketch an outline that can organize your essay—your outline will emphasize comparisons between the two works.

- Work from your outline to develop a series of body paragraphs that relate passages to one another and that explain your thesis.

- Provide evidence in the form of quotations from the story and essay to support your points. Discuss and document your quotations (see pages 179–83 and the Appendix).

EXAMINING ESSAYS

Printed below are the essays "Blind Rage: An Open Letter to Helen Keller" by Georgina Kleege and "Aliteracy: Read All About It, or Maybe Not" by Linton Weeks. You can also find essays integrated throughout the book. To learn more about rhetorical strategies and modes of discourse in essays, you may also want to look at the enhanced reading of Martin Luther King Jr.'s "Letter from Birmingham Jail" on our CD.

GEORGINA KLEEGE

Georgina Kleege is a novelist, essayist, and translator who has written extensively on her life as a legally blind author. Her 1999 book, Sight Unseen, *explores the ways she has come to grips with failing eyesight—at age eleven she was declared legally blind after being diagnosed with a degenerative eye disease. Kleege also takes on stereotypes and places blindness within a larger framework of how humans experience culture and communicate. "Blind Rage: An Open Letter to Helen Keller" was first published in 1998.*

Blind Rage: An Open Letter to Helen Keller

February 3, 1998
Dear Helen Keller:

I'm writing to you because I'm having a bad day. I could spare you the details. But the whole point of writing to a dead person is that you don't have to worry about boring your reader. And if this is to have the therapeutic effect I'm hoping for, I need to get it all out, exorcise everything. So indulge me. I'll make it worth your while.

It all began with snow. Slush to be exact, a heavy wet snow about ankle deep by the time I left for work. I have nothing against snow, in the abstract. All things being equal, I'm happy to live in a climate that has the occasional snowfall. Snow in the abstract is pretty. It makes the world fresh and silent. But snow in reality makes it harder to get around. Especially when you're blind. As far as I know, you didn't use a white cane. But I do, and let me tell you, a white cane in snow is something of an adventure. You can't feel the texture of the surface underfoot. You lose landmarks. You can begin to feel disoriented. On top of this, I discover my waterproof boots are not what you'd call water-tight. Every third step I feel water seeping through seams. When I get to the bus stop, my feet are soaked. Then the bus is extra crowded, because of the snow. Which is probably why the driver forgets to announce my stop. Once she remembers me, I have to backtrack four blocks to start my regular route to my office. So by the time I get here, I'm damp and nervy. But weather is weather. And it's not the first time a bus driver has forgotten to announce my stop.

5   Then I find a message on the machine from the student I was supposed to be meeting. He can't make it. His car won't start. Needless to say the thought of taking the bus never occurs to him. This is car culture. The only people who take the bus are people who can't afford a car or can't drive. Suggest the bus to anyone else, and they get insulted.

But I'm here—early, damp and nervy—but I'm here. And it's not as if there's nothing to do. So I turn on my computer to check my e-mail and discover its synthesized voice is on the fritz. I fiddle with it for a while. Then I make phone calls. I say, "There's something wrong with the voice output."

The guy says, "Your computer talks to you?"

I want to say, "I'm blind, buddy. Not schizophrenic," but I don't. He's entitled, I suppose. He says he has to "consult with a colleague." This means he covers the receiver with his hand and yells at another computer guy across the room. Then he tells me, "That's a hardware problem. That software is on your hard drive. That software is not on the network."

I knew this already. I'm blind, not stupid. And I'm usually not this cranky. It's just that my feet are wet. I sigh. Did I call the wrong office? No, this is the right office, just the wrong guy. I want the hardware guy and the hardware guy is out today. Because of the snow. Also, there's a backlog. He takes my name, but says it may be a while. I don't ask what "a while" means.

10   Then I get a call from one of my readers, and she tells me she's leaving, moving out of town to get married. I say, "That's wonderful," but inside I'm thinking, "Now what am I going to do?" Not that she's my only reader, of course. I have other readers and I can hire a new one. And it's not that I'm fussy either. I can listen to any reader, any kind of voice—I can tolerate the computer's voice after all. But I really like her voice. I like the way she phrases things. It somehow coincides with my own voice, or the voice in my head when I'm reading. Listening to her is effortless. I never have to blot out a vocal tick or a funny accent. I'll find another reader, but I'll never find a better fit.

Of course I don't say this. I say, "I'm so happy for you." In fact, I am happy for her, just sad for myself. I consider mailing her stuff, but it will take that much more time. And I doubt the Postal Service's "Free Matter for the Blind" is going to apply here.

While I'm debating the postal question, another one of my readers shows up. This is actually a good thing. He can read me my e-mail. This reader is hired by my department. He's an ADA accommodation. He's good enough, though. We get along. We gripe about the weather for a while. His feet are also wet. And he's a graduate student so he generally has lots to gripe about. He tells me he's having trouble with the book I gave him to tape. The style makes it hard to read, he says.

"Don't worry about it," I say. I want to say, "You don't have to like it. All you have to do is read it into the tape recorder," but I don't. I mean, he doesn't get paid much for this.

I get him to read me my e-mail. I stop him mid-sentence and tell him to delete. He does it, but I sense it annoys him. It's as if he thinks I should hear the whole message since he's reading it aloud. Or else he finds the whole thing beneath him. I get a lot of stupid e-mail. Reading it aloud makes it seem all the stupider. But what can I do? I need to go through it to be sure there's nothing important. His attitude gets to me. He acts like he's doing me a favor. He thinks I should be more grateful. But I let it go. I let him go home early. On account of the snow.

15   Then it's time for class. Half of them are not there. Did I mention it's snowing? And the ones who are there are lackluster and cranky. I suspect they have not done the reading. I sense they feel *Pride and Prejudice* is not as relevant to their everyday lives as *The X Files.* I could give them a pop quiz but it would only make them surly. And I just let my reader go home early, so I'd have to wait until tomorrow to read it.

One of them comes back to my office after class to complain about the grade on his last paper. I gave him a B and he thinks it should be an A. He always got A's in high school. I tell him this isn't high school but he doesn't buy it. I've ruined his perfect GPA, and he seems ready to argue with me all afternoon. Why go out in the snow when he can stay here and make my life miserable? I make him read the paper aloud to me. I stop him sentence by sentence, telling him everything that's wrong. I say, "Hear that? That sentence doesn't make any sense."

He says, "But you get what I mean."

"I get what you mean because I read it five times," I say. I'm beginning to think a B was a gift. But I don't say this. I tell him he has a chance to redeem himself on his next paper. Then I clam up. He is sulky and dissatisfied. He thinks I'm being arbitrary and capricious. As he leaves he grumbles something under his breath that I'm not supposed to understand, but I am supposed to hear. I'm supposed to hear his dissatisfaction. He leaves a bad taste in my mouth. Do I need this, on a day like today?

Which brings me to the present moment, and to you, Helen Keller. I know what you're thinking. What's all this to you? And you're right in a way. You don't know me. You don't owe me anything, certainly not a sympathetic ear (so to speak). You think I should consider myself lucky to have a job like this, and all these wonderful things—white canes, waterproof boots, public transit, free mail for the blind, readers paid by my employer, computer voice interface, e-mail, the Internet, braille printers. For you a typewriter was a big deal. I know. You don't have to tell me, again, how lucky I am. I'm lucky to be educated, lucky to have a job at all, lucky to live in these advanced times with all this technology, lucky that able-bodied people at least pay lip service to notions of equality, equal opportunity, accessibility, and the rest of it. I should be grateful, cheerful in the face of such minimal inconveniences. I should adjust my attitude, put on a smiley face and get over it.

20   This is precisely why I'm writing to you Helen. (Mind if I call you Helen?) You've been saying this to me all my life. Not you in person, of course, but you in effect. People have been saying it in your stead. "Things could be worse," they say. "Think about Helen Keller. Yes, you're blind, but she was deaf too. And no one ever heard her complain."

Save your breath. I know how good I have it. And it's not as if I feel I've been singled out for suffering. Everyone has bad days. When it snows it snows on everyone. People miss appointments. People make annoying demands. People and things you rely on fail. And there are worse things too—disappointment, betrayal, illness, death, despair. But I'm talking about something else here. I'm talking about the fact that most of what's wrong with this day has to do with being blind, and this is what leaves me raging. I rage at myself, my body, my eyes, tears welling up in them, reminding me how useless they are. I rage against the world for being inaccessible to me. I rage against technology for offering the promise of access and then breaking down, being cumbersome, leaving me stranded.

So what I'd like you to tell me is this. What did you do with the rage, Helen? Because you must have felt it. There must have been days when you woke up and all you wanted to do was pull the covers over your head and say, "Chuck it. Fuck it all. What am I trying to prove here? I surrender. Someone please take care of me." There must have been days when you wanted to shred the sheets with your teeth.

I can't believe there weren't such days. I mean for God's sake Helen, when you read page proofs of your books, it meant someone had to spell the text letter by letter into your hand. Tell me that didn't make you grind your teeth and tear your hair. But you never let it show, Helen. I scan your writing for even a sign of ire or irritation. The most you ever express is the occasional nervous unease. But then you follow up with flowery praise for all the wonderful, kind people who did so much to help you, utterly effacing both the difficulty and your effort. Because you did this, you left a legacy behind for the rest of us—the likes of me. "Why can't you be more like Helen Keller, especially since you're really nowhere near as bad off as she was?" You set an impossible standard. You with your cheerfulness, your stiff upper lip, your valiant smile in the face of adversity. So those who came after you feel a moral imperative to fight back the tears, to minimize the trouble, to avoid asking for help.

And for what, Helen? Sure, when we emulate your plucky, chirpy self-reliance, the able-bodied find us tolerable. They gush, "You're so patient, so persevering. How ever do you manage?" But what are they really thinking? I'm talking about the doubt, Helen. You know about the doubt. It's that nagging uncertainty at the back of your mind whenever anything good happens. You're in school and you wonder, "Is the A on this paper a gift? Would a normal student get an A for this?" You get a job, but you wonder, "Do they really think I'm qualified or is this just some sort of affirmative action quota?"

25   The doubt, Helen. I know you felt it. I know, for instance that you were discouraged by the reception your writing received. Your volumes of memoirs about your life and your disabilities got a lot of play. But on the rare occasions when you published something on other topics—women's suffrage, socialism, religion—the general assumption was that some member of your entourage, Anne Sullivan or her husband, John Macy, ghost-wrote it for you. "Write what you know," someone told you. They thought what you knew was nothing but deafness and blindness. They couldn't imagine that you knew anything else, that you could tell them anything else worth knowing.

A bad day, Helen. Cast your mind back. Surely you remember a few. For instance, there was that day when you were eleven and you were accused of plagiarism. You were not only accused, but essentially put on trial by the faculty of the Perkins Institution where you were in school. Eleven years old—plagiarism. The sheer lunacy of the charge should have been enough to trigger a tantrum. If it were me, I would have sat on my hands and refused to dignify their questions with answers. But you answered all their questions earnestly, eager to clear your name, anxious to get back into their good graces. You were exonerated, but doubt lingered, in you and others. Later, you wrote about how the incident shook your faith in your writing. Afterwards you always questioned the provenance of every idea. When words came to you too easily you feared you were remembering them from something you'd read, and started over. When words come too easily to other writers they call it inspiration and keep at it. "Forget dinner. I'm on a roll!"

And there were other bad days for you. Admit it. Remember that man who asked you to marry him, who signed the marriage licence with you, but then your own mother and Anne Sullivan made him go away. Because even they had doubts about you. They did not believe you had the wherewithal to make that kind of decision on your own, to live that kind of life. They worried about the children you might have, and your ability to care for them. They may have been right about the man. Perhaps his intentions were not honorable. Perhaps they even convinced you of that. But their intervention, the imposition of their judgment over yours, must have hurt, Helen, must have hit the rawest nerve of all.

There's more. I could go on, Helen. I guess you could say I've made something of a study of your life. But I don't want to badger you. I'm not here to make you squirm. All I want to know is what you did with the feelings of betrayal, injustice, the rage, Helen? How did you get over it—shrug your shoulders and swallow hard? How did you get it down without choking? I only wish you could have let it show, just once. If you could have let the mask slip for a minute, Helen—one lousy sneer of derision, one tear of rage. It would have made it better for the rest of us, a little easier. What's more, it just might have let them see you as human.

But they might just as well have scorned you for it. Or worse. "If you can't stand the heat, get out of the kitchen. If all you can do is make a fuss, well, there are places for people like you." Is that the message, Helen? Did you keep that smile glued to your lips because you knew it was the only thing that stood between you and the institution, the asylum, the freak show?

30   Say it then. Speak to me. I wish you could get word to me somehow. E-mail? How about it Helen? hkeller.627@afterlife.com. Not that I really think you would tell me anything I want to know.

"Hi," you'd probably write. "Sorry to hear about your bad day. Try to look at the bright side. At least you've got your health. Buck up. Turn that frown upside down, and smile! Smile!! Smile!!!"

I don't know why I bother. I don't know what I expect from you. And maybe—take this as a concession, Helen—you couldn't help yourself. Once you figured out that the only way your words would be read by anyone was if you took on the role of the first, original disability poster child. So you vowed to be the best damn poster child the world has ever known. I guess I can't blame you if the insipid, feel-good aphorisms got to be a habit. But level with me, Helen. Give me something I can use. "Get with the program," you could say. "Show them your weakness and they'll put you away in the blink of an eye. You're here by sufferance. They'll only tolerate you as long as you keep up the front. Nobody likes a grumpy cripple."

I know this already. That's the thing about doubt. There you are, talking to a student and all the while you're wondering whether or not he's thinking, "This woman is blind. How can she judge me, my work? How can she presume?" And if he goes to complain to another professor or to my chair, would that person look sympathetic and say, "Well you know, son, people like that feel they need to be tougher than normal people. It's over-compensation. You can put up with it. Noblesse oblige."

I know a graduate student here who is in a wheelchair. He's someone who doesn't seem to suffer doubts about his value. In other words, he really knows how to complain. At the rate my luck has been running today, he'll be in here any minute, to complain about the snow, about the Handi-van being late, about the elevator in the library not working, about the construction they're doing outside his dorm and how it blocks his usual route, and whatever else may be going on. He complains because before he was here he went to school in California, where it not only never snows, but where they have better services for people with disabilities. I admit, when this guy starts in on things, even I roll my eyes at times. In the back of my mind I'm thinking, "When I was in school there was none of this, no adaptive technologies, no services for disabled students, no legislative mandates." And yet, this guy is right. Do we have to put up with all this stuff and smile about it too? The squeaky wheel gets the oil. Rattle the bars of the cage loud enough and someone will unlock the door just to shut you up.

35   Progress, is this what you're telling me, Helen? It's the sort of thing you'd say. It's a part of that American can-do attitude everyone loved you for. "I blazed this path," you're telling me. "If there are still bumps in the road you've got to deal with them yourself." You couldn't complain because the risks were too great. What are the risks for me? True, for me, institutionalization has never been a real threat. And no one ever tried to mess with my love life. Though raise the issue of reproductive rights for disabled people and all the ugly eugenics arguments still rise to the surface. But change doesn't happen overnight, or even over a century or two. And for now, I should quit apologizing for being blind. If my blindness slows me down, or makes me do things differently, I still have something to contribute. If they don't believe me, let them say it to my face.

A bad day, Helen. It makes me lose perspective, so to speak. It puts me on the defensive. Tomorrow will be better. And that's not just Helen Keller-ish optimism talking. In fact, things could improve any minute. Another student could come in and tell me how though I gave him a B—no, a C—on his paper, my comments were so helpful, he's inspired to do better. The computer could hiccup and the voice could come back on all by itself. The sun could come out and melt all the snow. Miracles happen. Or even without miracles, ninety-nine percent of my days are just fine. I get up, I go to work, I teach, I read, I write. The fact that I use aids and assistants to do some of these things is not really central to my consciousness. When everything works, I consider myself "normal." My blindness is just a fact of life, not an insurmountable obstacle blocking my path. I work around it. I ignore it. On a lot of days, it matters less than the weather.

I don't know, Helen. I sense there's more you would tell me if you could. Feel free to elaborate. A word, a sign, a dream vision, a shudder of recognition—whatever means you have at your disposal. I'd really appreciate it. Hell, I'll even be grateful.

Excuse me if I close with the language of the oppressor, but you know how that goes. I look forward to hearing from you soon.

Sincerely,

40   GK

I N Q U I R I N G F U R T H E R

1. How would you describe Kleege's tone in "Blind Rage: An Open Letter to Helen Keller"? How would you relate it to the tone of the narrator in "Cathedral"? How does the tone help shape the message of the essay?

2. What modes of discourse can you recognize in Kleege's essay? Do you recognize ways of communicating that you would normally associate with works of literature? How would you discuss the essay in terms of literature?

3. What themes related to stereotypes and communication can you find in "Blind Rage: An Open Letter to Helen Keller"? What significant relationships can you discover between them? Write a thesis statement that might be used to explore one of the themes in the essay.

LINTON WEEKS

Linton Weeks is a staff writer for the Washington Post. *He has written numerous articles related to literature and publishing. "Aliteracy: Read All About It, or Maybe Not" appeared in May 2001.*

Aliteracy: Read All About It, or Maybe Not

Jeremy Spreitzer probably wouldn't read this story if it weren't about him.

He is an aliterate—someone who can read, but chooses not to.

A graduate student in public affairs at Park University in Kansas City, Mo., Spreitzer, 25, gleans most of his news from TV. He skims required texts, draws themes from dust jackets and, when he absolutely, positively has to read something, reaches for the audiobook.

"I am fairly lazy when it comes to certain tasks," says Spreitzer, a long-distance runner who hopes to compete in the 2004 Olympics. "Reading is one of them."

5   As he grows older, Spreitzer finds he has less time to read. And less inclination. In fact, he says, if he weren't in school, he probably wouldn't read at all.

He's not alone. According to the survey firm NDP Group—which tracked the everyday habits of thousands of people through the 1990s—this country is reading printed versions of books, magazines and newspapers less and less. In 1991, more than half of all Americans read a half-hour or more every day. By 1999, that had dropped to 45 percent.

A 1999 Gallup Poll found that only 7 percent of Americans were voracious readers, reading more than a book a week, while some 59 percent said they had read fewer than 10 books in the previous year. Though book clubs seem popular now, only 6 percent of those who read belong to one. The number of people who don't read at all, the poll concluded, has been rising for the past 20 years. The reports on changes in reading cut to the quick of American culture. We pride ourselves on being a largely literate First World country while at the same time we rush to build a visually powerful environment in which reading is not required.

The results are inevitable. Aliteracy is all around. Just ask:

- Internet developers. At the Terra Lycos portal design lab in Waltham, Mass., researcher William Albert has noticed that the human guinea pigs in his focus groups are too impatient to read much. When people look up information on the Internet today, Albert explains, they are "basically scanning. There's very little actual comprehension that's going on." People, Albert adds, prefer to get info in short bursts, with bullets, rather than in large blocks of text.

- Transportation gurus. Chandra Clayton, who oversees the design of road signs and signals for the Virginia Department of Transportation, says, "Symbols can quickly give you a message that might take too long to read in text." The department is using logos and symbols more and more. When it comes to highway safety and getting lifesaving information quickly, she adds, "a picture is worth a thousand words."

- Packaging designers. "People don't take the time to read anything," explains Jim Peters, editor of BrandPackaging magazine. "Marketers and packagers are giving them colors and shapes as ways of communicating." For effective marketing, Peters says, "researchers tell us that the hierarchy is colors, shapes, icons and, dead last, words."

Some of this shift away from words—and toward images—can be attributed to our ever-growing multilingual population. But for many people, reading is passe or impractical or, like, so totally unnecessary in this day and age.

10   To Jim Trelease, author of "The Read-Aloud Handbook," this trend away from the written word is more than worrisome. It's wicked. It's tearing apart our culture. People who have stopped reading, he says, "base their future decisions on what they used to know."

"If you don't read much, you really don't know much," he says. "You're dangerous."

"The man who does not read good books has no advantage over the man who cannot read them."

—*Mark Twain*

One thing you can say for illiteracy: It can be identified, nailed down. And combated. Scores of programs such as the Greater Washington Literacy Council and the International Reading Association are geared toward fighting readinglessness in the home, the school and the workplace.

Aliteracy, on the other hand, is like an invisible liquid, seeping through our culture, nigh impossible to pinpoint or defend against. It's the kid who spends hours and hours with video games instead of books, who knows Sim Cities better than "A Tale of Two Cities."

It's the thousands of business people who subscribe to executive book summaries—for example, Soundview's easy-to-swallow eight-page pamphlets that take simply written management books such as "Secrets of Question-Based Selling" by Thomas A. Freese and make them even simpler.

15   It's the parent who pops the crummy movie of "Stuart Little" into a machine for his kid instead of reading E.B. White's marvelous novel aloud. Or the teacher

who assigns the made-for-TV movie "Gettysburg" instead of the book it was based on, "The Killer Angels" by Michael Shaara.

There may be untold collateral damage in a society that can read but doesn't. "So much of our culture is embedded in literature," says Philip A. Thompsen, professor of communications at West Chester University in West Chester, Pa. Thompsen has been watching the rise of aliteracy in the classroom for 20 years, and "students today are less capable of getting full value from textbooks than they were 10 years ago."

He adds that these aliterate students are "missing out on our cultural heritage."

That literature-based past included a reverence for reading, a celebration of the works and a worshipful awe of those who wrote.

To draw you a picture: Where we once deified the lifestyles of writers such as Ernest Hemingway and F. Scott Fitzgerald, we now fantasize about rock-and-roll gods, movie starlets or NBA super-studs (e.g. MTV's "Cribs"). The notion of writer-as-culture-hero is dead and gone. Comedic monologuists such as Jay Leno or David Letterman have more sex appeal than serious fiction writers. The grail quest for the Great American Novel has ended; it was a myth after all.

20   Where we once drew our mass-cult references from books ("He's a veritable Simon Legree"), we now allude to visual works—a Seinfeld episode (not that there's anything wrong with that . . .) or "The Silence of the Lambs" (the movie, not the book). A recent story in Salon speaks of "learning to read a movie."

Where we once believed that a well-read populace leads to a healthy democracy, many people now rely on whole TV broadcast operations built around politics and elections. Quick, name a Wolf Blitzer book.

Non-readers abound. Ask "Politically Incorrect" talk show host Bill Maher, who once boasted in print that he hadn't read a book in years. Or Noel Gallagher of the rock band Oasis, who has been quoted as saying he'd never read a book. You can walk through whole neighborhoods of houses in the country that do not contain books or magazines—unless you count catalogues.

American historian Daniel Boorstin saw this coming. In 1984, while Boorstin was serving as librarian of Congress, the library issued a landmark report: "Books in Our Future." Citing recent statistics that only about half of all Americans read regularly every year, he referred to the "twin menaces" of illiteracy and aliteracy. "In the United States today," Boorstin wrote, "aliteracy is widespread."

25   Several of the articles in the report alluded to the growing number of non-readers. In one essay, "The Computer and the Book," Edmund D. Pellegrino, a former president of Catholic University who is now a bioethicist at Georgetown University, observed: "The computer is simply the most effective, efficient and attractive form for transmittal of processed information. Added to the other nonbook devices like films, tapes, television and the popular media, the computer accelerates the atrophy of the intellectual skills acquired for personally reading the books from which the information is extracted."

Kylene Beers has talked about the evils of aliteracy for so long and so loud, she's losing her voice. Today she's in the lecture hall of Oakton High School bending the ears of 100 or so middle school teachers.

If someone graduates from high school and is aliterate, Beers believes, that person will probably never become a habitual reader.

One of the few academics who have written about the phenomenon, Beers, a professor of reading at the University of Houston, says there are two types of reading: efferent and aesthetic.

Efferent, which comes from the Latin word efferre (meaning to carry away), is purposeful reading, the kind students are taught day after day in schools.

Efferent readers connect cognitively with the words and plan to take something useful from it—such as answers for a test.

30   Aesthetic is reading for the sheer bliss of it, as when you dive deep into Dostoevski or get lost in Louisa May Alcott. Aesthetic readers connect emotionally to the story. Beers believes that more students must be shown the marvels of reading for pleasure.

On this late afternoon, she is mapping out strategies for teachers who hope to engage reluctant middle school readers. Teaching grammar and parts of speech, such as dangling participles, is the kiss of death, she says. "You don't want to talk about dangling anythings with middle-schoolers," she says in her Texas drawl. And the room laughs.

Aliteracy, she continues, is no laughing matter. Using an overhead projector, she explains that aliterate people just don't get it. Unlike accomplished readers, aliterates don't understand that sometimes you have to read efferently and sometimes you have to read aesthetically; that even the best readers occasionally read the same paragraph over and over to understand it and that to be a good reader you have to visualize the text.

To engage non-reading students—and adults—she proposes reading strategies, such as turning a chapter of a hard book into a dramatic production or relating tough words to easier words.

She writes the word "tepid" on the acetate sheet. Then she asks the audience to supply other words that describe water temperature. "Hot," someone calls out. "Freezing," somebody else says. Others suggest: cold, warm and boiling. Beers arranges the words in a linear fashion, from the coldest word, "freezing," to the hottest, "boiling." "Tepid" falls in the middle of the list. This method, she says, will help reluctant readers to connect words they don't know to words they do know. "Aliterates," she tells the teachers, "don't see relationships."

35   Apparently, teachers don't always see the relationships either. Jim Trelease is concerned that teachers do not read. The aliteracy rate among teachers, he says, is about the same, 50 percent, as among the general public.

There is some good news on the reading front, according to Trelease and others. The Harry Potter series has turned on a lot of young readers and megabookstores, such as Barnes & Noble and Borders, are acrawl with people.

But there is plenty of bad news, too. Lots of aliterates, according to Trelease, say they just don't have time to read anymore. "The time argument is the biggest hoax of all," he says. According to time studies, we have more leisure time than ever. "If people didn't have time, the malls would be empty, cable companies would be broke, video stores would go out of business. It's not a time problem, it's a value problem. You have 50 percent in the country who don't value reading."

Like Beers, Trelease believes that youngsters should be encouraged to read aesthetically. Reading aloud to children, according to Trelease and other reading specialists, is the single best way to ensure that someone will become a lifelong reader.

"Even Daniel Boorstin wasn't born wanting to read," Trelease says. "Michael Jordan wasn't born wanting to play basketball. The desire has to be planted."

40   Trelease and Beers and others are scrambling for ways to engage aliterates. For all kinds of reasons. "What aliteracy does is breed illiteracy," Beers explains. "If you go through school having learned to read and then you leave school not wanting to read, chances are you won't put your own children into a reading environment."

"What you have to do is play hardball," says Trelease. He suggests running public awareness campaigns on TV. "That's where the aliterates are."

Trelease says we should try to eradicate aliteracy in the way we went after tobacco. We should let people know, Trelease says, "what the consequences are to your family and children if you don't read."

"Aliteracy may be a significant problem today," says Philip Thompsen. "But on the other hand, a narrow view of literacy—one that defines literacy as the ability to read verbal texts—may be a significant problem as well."

Many of the messages that we have to interpret in day-to-day life, Thompsen says, "use multiple communication media. I think it is important to realize that as our society becomes more accustomed to using multimedia messages, we must also expand our thinking about what it means to be 'literate.'"

45   Olympic hopeful Jeremy Spreitzer plans to become a teacher and maybe go into politics someday. For now, he's just trying to get through graduate school.

He watches a lot of television. "I'm a major surfer," he says. He watches the History Channel, A&E, Turner Classic Movies and all of the news stations.

"I'm required to do a lot of reading," he says. "But I do a minimum of what I need to do."

But how do you get through grad school without reading? Spreitzer is asked.

He gives an example. One of his required texts is the recently published "Bowling Alone: The Collapse and Revival of American Community" by Robert Putnam. In the book, Putnam argues, among other things, that television has fragmented our society.

50   Spreitzer thumbed through the book, dipped into a few chapters and spent a while "skipping around" here and there.

He feels, however, that he understands Putnam and Putnam's theories as well as if he had read the book.

How is that? he is asked.

Putnam, he explains, has been on TV a lot. "He's on the news all the time," Spreitzer says. "On MSNBC and other places. Those interviews with him are more invaluable than anything else."

Inquiring Further

1. What modes of discourse can you recognize in Weeks's article? Is there one mode that is used more regularly than another? How effective do you find the techniques to be?

2. How would you compare Weeks's tone with the tone used by Kleege? Are they more similar or different? Do you find one to be more effective? Why or why not? How does tone relate to credibility in the essays?

3. What do you think of the comparison Weeks makes between not being able to read, and choosing not to read? Do you think this is an important distinction? Freewrite for five minutes about this comparison.

4. Weeks compares reading with other forms of media such as television. How important do you think it is that our culture maintains an interest in reading? Discuss the future of reading with a group of peers.

4

Researching and Evaluating Sources

> Research is formalized curiosity. It is poking and prying
> with a purpose. . . .
>
> —*Zora Neale Hurston*

Research *is* closely related to curiosity. Initially we may conduct research to gather background information that will help us understand what we read; ideally, however, our discoveries will spark our interest and lead us further into a process of inquiry. Throughout this process we must formulate questions and focus our ideas. We must also analyze search results and draw connections between sources. Additionally, as we engage research materials, we will explore them through writing, refining our ideas and using what we discover as evidence to support any arguments we might make.

In this chapter, we will look at three general types of research: collecting contextual information, exploring ideas with others, and locating arguments about literature. Each of these research activities requires different approaches. Sometimes you will find success researching online. At other times, you will need to locate sources in the library. In most cases you must be very deliberate at using Web gateways, Web sites like library pages or Internet search engines that lead to information. You will also need to know some keyword search strategies and understand something about evaluating research sources. As we think about the research process, we will look at a story related to the Vietnam War, "The Things They Carried" by Tim O'Brien; we will begin by exploring some background information.

GROUNDING READINGS THROUGH BACKGROUND RESEARCH

Contextual information helps us understand and make judgments about works. Research helps us locate this background information. For instance, we all know that the Vietnam War represented a major conflict for the United States during the twentieth century. However, we may not know how that war relates to other major conflicts such as World War II, or the more recent war in Iraq. Before we read Tim O'Brien's "The Things They Carried," we might conduct research to better understand the historical context in which the story takes place.

The Vietnam War represents a conflicted moment in the history of the world. After World War II ended in 1945, the French, who had a colony in Vietnam prior to the war, sought to reclaim their authority. A communist resistance to French rule developed and fighting continued until 1954 when the French relinquished their control and the country was divided into North Vietnam and South Vietnam. Between 1957 and 1965, the United States increased its support for the South Vietnamese government as the South Vietnamese fought with the North Vietnamese. North Vietnam was supported by communist China and the USSR. In 1965, the United States entered the war formally and began sending a large number of troops into the region.

Studying the Vietnam War

The Vietnam War was the last major conflict in which the United States relied on a military draft. At age eighteen, all males were required to register for the draft and could be pressed into military service. Opposition to the war escalated in the United States as the deployment of troops increased and as television broadcasts brought home images of the conflict and its casualties. (The Vietnam War also represented the first war in the television era.) As you read "The Things They Carried," consider how this background information helps you make sense of the materials.

Tim O'Brien

Tim O'Brien was drafted into the army in 1968 and served until 1970, carrying out a tour of duty in Vietnam in 1969 and 1970. In 1973 he published If I Die in a Combat Zone, Box Me Up and Ship Me Home, *a novel/memoir based on his tour in Vietnam. He published* The Things They Carried *in 1990 as a novel consisting of a number of anecdotes. The excerpt printed below is the first chapter from that book.*

The Things They Carried

First Lieutenant Jimmy Cross carried letters from a girl named Martha, a junior at Mount Sebastian College in New Jersey. They were not love letters, but Lieutenant Cross was hoping, so he kept them folded in plastic at the bottom of his rucksack. In the late afternoon, after a day's march, he would dig his foxhole, wash his hands under a canteen, unwrap the letters, hold them with the tips of his fingers, and spend the last hour of light pretending. He would imagine romantic camping trips into the White Mountains in New Hampshire. He would sometimes taste the envelope flaps, knowing her tongue had been there. More than anything, he wanted Martha to love him as he loved her, but the letters were mostly chatty, elusive on the matter of love. She was a virgin, he was almost sure. She was an English major at Mount Sebastian, and she wrote beautifully about her professors and roommates and midterm exams, about her respect for Chaucer and her great affection for Virginia Woolf. She often quoted lines of poetry; she never mentioned the war, except to say, Jimmy, take care of yourself. The letters weighed 10 ounces. They were signed Love, Martha, but Lieutenant Cross understood that Love was only a way of signing and did not mean what he sometimes pretended it meant. At dusk, he would carefully return the letters to his rucksack. Slowly, a bit distracted, he would get up and move among his men, checking the perimeter, then at full dark he would return to his hole and watch the night and wonder if Martha was a virgin.

The things they carried were largely determined by necessity. Among the necessities or near-necessities were P-38 can openers, pocket knives, heat tabs, wristwatches, dog tags, mosquito repellent, chewing gum, candy, cigarettes, salt tablets, packets of Kool-Aid, lighters, matches, sewing kits, Military Payment Certificates, C rations, and two or three canteens of water. Together, these items weighed between 15 and 20 pounds, depending upon a man's habits or rate of metabolism. Henry Dobbins, who was a big man, carried extra rations; he was especially fond of canned peaches in heavy syrup over pound cake. Dave Jensen, who practiced field hygiene, carried a toothbrush, dental floss, and several hotel-sized bars of soap he'd stolen on R&R[1] in Sydney, Australia. Ted Lavender, who was scared, carried tranquilizers until he was shot in the head outside the village of Than Khe in mid-April. By necessity, and because it was SOP,[2] they all carried steel helmets that weighed 5 pounds including the liner and camouflage cover. They carried the standard fatigue jackets and trousers. Very few carried underwear. On their feet they carried jungle boots—2.1 pounds—and Dave Jensen carried three pairs of socks and a can of Dr. Scholl's foot powder as a precaution against trench foot. Until he was shot, Ted Lavender carried 6 or 7 ounces of premium dope, which for him was a necessity. Mitchell Sanders, the RTO,[3] carried condoms. Norman Bowker carried a diary. Rat Kiley carried comic books. Kiowa, a devout Baptist, carried an illustrated New Testament that had been presented to him by his father, who taught Sunday school in Oklahoma City, Oklahoma. As a hedge against bad times, however, Kiowa also carried his grandmother's distrust of the white man, his grandfather's old hunting hatchet. Necessity dictated. Because the land was mined and booby-trapped, it was SOP for each man to carry a steel-centered, nylon-covered flak jacket, which weighed 6.7 pounds, but which on hot days seemed much heavier. Because you could die so quickly, each man carried at least one large compress bandage, usually in the helmet band for easy access. Because the nights were cold, and because the monsoons were wet, each carried a green plastic poncho that could be used as a raincoat or groundsheet or makeshift tent. With its quilted liner, the poncho weighed almost 2 pounds, but it was worth every ounce. In April, for instance, when Ted Lavender was shot, they used his poncho to wrap him up, then to carry him across the paddy, then to lift him into the chopper that took him away.

They were called legs or grunts.

To carry something was to hump it, as when Lieutenant Jimmy Cross humped his love for Martha up the hills and through the swamps. In its intransitive form, to hump meant to walk, or to march, but it implied burdens far beyond the intransitive.

5   Almost everyone humped photographs. In his wallet, Lieutenant Cross carried two photographs of Martha. The first was a Kodacolor snapshot signed Love, though he knew better. She stood against a brick wall. Her eyes were gray

---

[1]**R&R:** Rest and recuperation.
[2]**SOP:** Standard operating procedure.
[3]**RTO:** Radio transmitter operator.

and neutral, her lips slightly open as she stared straight-on at the camera. At night, sometimes, Lieutenant Cross wondered who had taken the picture, because he knew she had boyfriends, because he loved her so much, and because he could see the shadow of the picture-taker spreading out against the brick wall. The second photograph had been clipped from the 1968 Mount Sebastian yearbook. It was an action shot—women's volleyball—and Martha was bent horizontal to the floor, reaching, the palms of her hands in sharp focus, the tongue taut, the expression frank and competitive. There was no visible sweat. She wore white gym shorts. Her legs, he thought, were almost certainly the legs of a virgin, dry and without hair, the left knee cocked and carrying her entire weight, which was just over 100 pounds. Lieutenant Cross remembered touching that left knee. A dark theater, he remembered, and the movie was *Bonnie and Clyde,* and Martha wore a tweed skirt, and during the final scene, when he touched her knee, she turned and looked at him in a sad, sober way that made him pull his hand back, but he would always remember the feel of the tweed skirt and the knee beneath it and the sound of the gunfire that killed Bonnie and Clyde, how embarrassing it was, how slow and oppressive. He remembered kissing her good night at the dorm door. Right then, he thought, he should've done something brave. He should've carried her up the stairs to her room and tied her to the bed and touched that left knee all night long. He should've risked it. Whenever he looked at the photographs, he thought of new things he should've done.

What they carried was partly a function of rank, partly of field specialty.

As a first lieutenant and platoon leader, Jimmy Cross carried a compass, maps, code books, binoculars, and a .45-caliber pistol that weighed 2.9 pounds fully loaded. He carried a strobe light and the responsibility for the lives of his men.

As an RTO, Mitchell Sanders carried the PRC-25 radio, a killer, 26 pounds with its battery.

As a medic, Rat Kiley carried a canvas satchel filled with morphine and plasma and malaria tablets and surgical tape and comic books and all the things a medic must carry, including M&M's for especially bad wounds, for a total weight of nearly 20 pounds.

10   As a big man, therefore a machine gunner, Henry Dobbins carried the M-60, which weighed 23 pounds unloaded, but which was almost always loaded. In addition, Dobbins carried between 10 and 15 pounds of ammunition draped in belts across his chest and shoulders.

As PFCs or Spec 4s, most of them were common grunts and carried the standard M-16 gas-operated assault rifle. The weapon weighed 7.5 pounds unloaded, 8.2 pounds with its full 20-round magazine. Depending on numerous factors, such as topography and psychology, the riflemen carried anywhere from 12 to 20 magazines, usually in cloth bandoliers, adding on another 8.4 pounds at minimum, 14 pounds at maximum. When it was available, they also carried M-16 maintenance gear—rods and steel brushes and swabs and tubes of LSA oil—all of which weighed about a pound. Among the grunts, some carried the M-79 grenade launcher, 5.9 pounds unloaded, a reasonably light weapon except for the ammunition, which was heavy. A single round weighed 10 ounces. The typical load was 25 rounds. But Ted Lavender, who was scared, carried 34 rounds when he was shot and killed outside Than Khe, and he went down under an exceptional burden, more than 20 pounds of ammunition, plus the flak jacket and helmet and rations and water and toilet paper and tranquilizers and all the rest, plus the unweighed fear. He was dead weight. There was no twitching or flopping. Kiowa, who saw it happen, said it was like watching a rock fall, or a big sandbag or something—just boom, then down— not like the movies where the dead guy rolls around and does fancy spins and goes ass over teakettle—not like that, Kiowa said, the poor bastard just flat-fuck fell. Boom. Down. Nothing else. It was a bright morning in mid-April. Lieutenant Cross felt the pain. He blamed himself. They stripped off Lavender's canteens and ammo, all the heavy things, and Rat Kiley said the obvious, the guy's dead, and Mitchell Sanders used his radio to report one U.S. KIA[4] and to request a chopper. Then they wrapped Lavender in his poncho. They carried him out to a dry paddy, established security, and sat smoking the dead man's dope until the chopper came. Lieutenant Cross kept to himself. He pictured Martha's smooth young face, thinking he loved her more than anything, more than his men, and now Ted Lavender was dead because he loved her so much and could not stop thinking about her. When the dustoff arrived, they carried Lavender aboard. Afterward they burned Than Khe. They marched until dusk, then dug their holes, and that night Kiowa kept explaining how you had to be there, how fast it was, how the poor guy just dropped like so much concrete. Boom-down, he said. Like cement.

In addition to the three standard weapons—the M-60, M-16, and M-79—they carried whatever presented itself, or whatever seemed appropriate as a means of killing or staying alive. They carried catch-as-catch-can. At various times, in various situations, they carried M-14s and CAR-15s and Swedish Ks and grease guns and captured AK-47s and Chi-Coms and RPGs and Simonov carbines and black market Uzis and .38-caliber Smith & Wesson handguns and 66 mm LAWs and shotguns and silencers and blackjacks and bayonets and C-4 plastic explosives. Lee Strunk carried a slingshot; a weapon of last resort, he called it. Mitchell Sanders carried brass knuckles. Kiowa carried his grandfather's feathered hatchet. Every third or fourth man carried a Claymore antipersonnel mine—3.5 pounds with its firing device. They all carried fragmentation grenades—14 ounces each. They all carried at least one M-18 colored smoke grenade—24 ounces. Some carried CS or tear gas grenades. Some carried white phosphorus grenades. They carried all they could bear, and then some, including a silent awe for the terrible power of the things they carried.

In the first week of April, before Lavender died, Lieutenant Jimmy Cross received a good-luck charm from Martha. It was a simple pebble, an ounce at most. Smooth to the touch, it was a milky white color with flecks of orange and violet, oval-shaped, like a miniature egg. In the accompanying letter, Martha wrote that she had found the pebble on the Jersey shoreline, precisely where the land touched water at high tide, where things came together but also separated. It was this separate-but-together quality, she wrote, that had inspired her to pick up the pebble and to carry it in her breast pocket for several days, where it seemed weightless, and then to send it through the mail, by air, as a token of her truest feelings for him. Lieutenant Cross found this romantic. But he wondered what her truest feelings were, exactly, and what she meant by separate-but-together. He wondered how the tides and waves had come into play on that afternoon along the Jersey shoreline when Martha saw the peb-

---

[4]**KIA:** Killed in action.

ble and bent down to rescue it from geology. He imagined bare feet. Martha was a poet, with the poet's sensibilities, and her feet would be brown and bare, the toenails unpainted, the eyes chilly and somber like the ocean in March, and though it was painful, he wondered who had been with her that afternoon. He imagined a pair of shadows moving along the strip of sand where things came together but also separated. It was phantom jealousy, he knew, but he couldn't help himself. He loved her so much. On the march, through the hot days of early April, he carried the pebble in his mouth, turning it with his tongue, tasting sea salt and moisture. His mind wandered. He had difficulty keeping his attention on the war. On occasion he would yell at his men to spread out the column, to keep their eyes open, but then he would slip away into daydreams, just pretending, walking barefoot along the Jersey shore, with Martha, carrying nothing. He would feel himself rising. Sun and waves and gentle winds, all love and lightness.

What they carried varied by mission.

15   When a mission took them to the mountains, they carried mosquito netting, machetes, canvas tarps, and extra bug juice.

If a mission seemed especially hazardous, or if it involved a place they knew to be bad, they carried everything they could. In certain heavily mined AOs,[5] where the land was dense with Toe Poppers and Bouncing Betties, they took turns humping a 28-pound mine detector. With its headphones and big sensing plate, the equipment was a stress on the lower back and shoulders, awkward to handle, often useless because of the shrapnel in the earth, but they carried it anyway, partly for safety, partly for the illusion of safety.

On ambush, or other night missions, they carried peculiar little odds and ends. Kiowa always took along his New Testament and a pair of moccasins for silence. Dave Jensen carried night-sight vitamins high in carotene. Lee Strunk carried his slingshot; ammo, he claimed, would never be a problem. Rat Kiley carried brandy and M&M's candy. Until he was shot, Ted Lavender carried the starlight scope, which weighed 6.3 pounds with its aluminum carrying case. Henry Dobbins carried his girlfriend's pantyhose wrapped around his neck as a comforter. They all carried ghosts. When dark came, they would move out single file across the meadows and paddies to their ambush coordinates, where they would quietly set up the Claymores and lie down and spend the night waiting.

Other missions were more complicated and required special equipment. In mid-April, it was their mission to search out and destroy the elaborate tunnel complexes in the Than Khe area south of Chu Lai. To blow the tunnels, they carried one-pound blocks of pentrite high explosives, four blocks to a man, 68 pounds in all. They carried wiring, detonators, and battery-powered clackers. Dave Jensen carried earplugs. Most often, before blowing the tunnels, they were ordered by higher command to search them, which was considered bad news, but by and large they just shrugged and carried out orders. Because he was a big man, Henry Dobbins was excused from tunnel duty. The others would draw numbers. Before Lavender died there were 17 men in the platoon, and whoever drew the number 17 would strip off his gear and crawl in headfirst with a flash-light and Lieutenant Cross's .45-caliber pistol. The rest of them would fan out as security. They would sit down or kneel, not facing the hole, listening to the ground beneath them, imagining cobwebs and

[5]**AOs:** Areas of operation.

ghosts, whatever was down there—the tunnel walls squeezing in—how the flashlight seemed impossibly heavy in the hand and how it was tunnel vision in the very strictest sense, compression in all ways, even time, and how you had to wiggle in—ass and elbows—a swallowed-up feeling—and how you found yourself worrying about odd things: Will your flashlight go dead? Do rats carry rabies? If you screamed, how far would the sound carry? Would your buddies hear it? Would they have the courage to drag you out? In some respects, though not many, the waiting was worse than the tunnel itself. Imagination was a killer.

On April 16, when Lee Strunk drew the number 17, he laughed and muttered something and went down quickly. The morning was hot and very still. Not good, Kiowa said. He looked at the tunnel opening, then out across a dry paddy toward the village of Than Khe. Nothing moved. No clouds or birds or people. As they waited, the men smoked and drank Kool-Aid, not talking much, feeling sympathy for Lee Strunk but also feeling the luck of the draw. You win some, you lose some, said Mitchell Sanders, and sometimes you settle for a rain check. It was a tired line and no one laughed.

20   Henry Dobbins ate a tropical chocolate bar. Ted Lavender popped a tranquilizer and went off to pee.

After five minutes, Lieutenant Jimmy Cross moved to the tunnel, leaned down, and examined the darkness. Trouble, he thought—a cave-in maybe. And then suddenly, without willing it, he was thinking about Martha. The stresses and fractures, the quick collapse, the two of them buried alive under all that weight. Dense, crushing love. Kneeling, watching the hole, he tried to concentrate on Lee Strunk and the war, all the dangers, but his love was too much for him, he felt paralyzed, he wanted to sleep inside her lungs and breathe her blood and be smothered. He wanted her to be a virgin and not a virgin, all at once. He wanted to know her. Intimate secrets: Why poetry? Why so sad? Why that grayness in her eyes? Why so alone? Not lonely, just alone—riding her bike across campus or sitting off by herself in the cafeteria—even dancing, she danced alone—and it was the aloneness that filled him with love. He remembered telling her that one evening. How she nodded and looked away. And how, later, when he kissed her, she received the kiss without returning it, her eyes wide open, not afraid, not a virgin's eyes, just flat and uninvolved.

Lieutenant Cross gazed at the tunnel. But he was not there. He was buried with Martha under the white sand at the Jersey shore. They were pressed together, and the pebble in his mouth was her tongue. He was smiling. Vaguely, he was aware of how quiet the day was, the sullen paddies, yet he could not bring himself to worry about matters of security. He was beyond that. He was just a kid at war, in love. He was twenty-four years old. He couldn't help it.

A few moments later Lee Strunk crawled out of the tunnel. He came up grinning, filthy but alive. Lieutenant Cross nodded and closed his eyes while the others clapped Strunk on the back and made jokes about rising from the dead.

Worms, Rat Kiley said. Right out of the grave. Fuckin' zombie.

25   The men laughed. They all felt great relief.

Spook city, said Mitchell Sanders.

Lee Strunk made a funny ghost sound, a kind of moaning, yet very happy, and right then, when Strunk made that high happy moaning sound, when he went *Ahhooooo,* right then Ted Lavender was shot in the head on his way back from peeing. He lay with his mouth open. The teeth were broken. There was a swollen black bruise under his left eye. The cheekbone was gone. Oh shit, Rat Kiley said, the guy's dead. The guy's dead, he kept saying, which seemed profound—the guy's dead. I mean really.

The things they carried were determined to some extent by superstition. Lieutenant Cross carried his goodluck pebble. Dave Jensen carried a rabbit's foot. Norman Bowker, otherwise a very gentle person, carried a thumb that had been presented to him as a gift by Mitchell Sanders. The thumb was dark brown, rubbery to the touch, and weighed 4 ounces at most. It had been cut from a VC[6] corpse, a boy of fifteen or sixteen. They'd found him at the bottom of an irrigation ditch, badly burned, flies in his mouth and eyes. The boy wore black shorts and sandals. At the time of his death he had been carrying a pouch of rice, a rifle, and three magazines of ammunition.

You want my opinion, Mitchell Sanders said, there's a definite moral here.

30   He put his hand on the dead boy's wrist. He was quiet for a time, as if counting a pulse, then he patted the stomach, almost affectionately, and used Kiowa's hunting hatchet to remove the thumb.

Henry Dobbins asked what the moral was.

Moral?

You know. *Moral.*

Sanders wrapped the thumb in toilet paper and handed it across to Norman Bowker. There was no blood. Smiling, he kicked the boy's head, watched the flies scatter, and said, It's like with that old TV show—Paladin. Have gun, will travel.

35   Henry Dobbins thought about it.

Yeah, well he finally said. I don't see no moral.

There it *is,* man.

Fuck off.

They carried USO stationery and pencils and pens. They carried Sterno, safety pins, trip flares, signal flares, spools of wire, razor blades, chewing tobacco, liberated joss sticks and statuettes of the smiling Buddha, candles, grease pencils, *The Stars and Stripes,* fingernail clippers, Psy Ops[7] leaflets, bush hats, bolos, and much more. Twice a week, when the resupply choppers came in, they carried hot chow in green mermite cans and large canvas bags filled with iced beer and soda pop. They carried plastic water containers, each with a 2-gallon capacity. Mitchell Sanders carried a set of starched tiger fatigues for special occasions. Henry Dobbins carried Black Flag insecticide. Dave Jensen carried empty sandbags that could be filled at night for added protection. Lee Strunk carried tanning lotion. Some things they carried in common. Taking turns, they carried the big PRC-77 scrambler radio, which weighed 30 pounds with its battery. They shared the weight of memory. They took up what others could no longer bear. Often, they carried each other, the wounded or weak. They carried infections. They carried chess sets, basketballs, Vietnamese-English dictionaries, insignia of rank, Bronze Stars and Purple Hearts, plastic cards imprinted with the Code of Conduct. They carried diseases, among them malaria and dysentery. They carried lice and ringworm and leeches and paddy algae and various rots and molds. They carried the land itself—Vietnam, the place, the soil—a powdery orange-red dust that covered

---

[6]**VC:** Viet Cong, soldiers from the North Vietnamese army.
[7]**Psy Ops:** Psychological operations.

their boots and fatigues and faces. They carried the sky. The whole atmosphere, they carried it, the humidity, the monsoons, the stink of fungus and decay, all of it, they carried gravity. They moved like mules. By daylight they took sniper fire, at night they were mortared, but it was not battle, it was just the endless march, village to village, without purpose, nothing won or lost. They marched for the sake of the march. They plodded along slowly, dumbly, leaning forward against the heat, unthinking, all blood and bone, simple grunts, soldiering with their legs, toiling up the hills and down into the paddies and across the rivers and up again and down, just humping, one step and then the next and then another, but no volition, no will, because it was automatic, it was anatomy, and the war was entirely a matter of posture and carriage, the hump was everything, a kind of inertia, a kind of emptiness, a dullness of desire and intellect and conscience and hope and human sensibility. Their principles were in their feet. Their calculations were biological. They had no sense of strategy or mission. They searched the villages without knowing what to look for, not caring, kicking over jars of rice, frisking children and old men, blowing tunnels, sometimes setting fires and sometimes not, then forming up and moving on to the next village, then other villages, where it would always be the same. They carried their own lives. The pressures were enormous. In the heat of early afternoon, they would remove their helmets and flak jackets, walking bare, which was dangerous but which helped ease the strain. They would often discard things along the route of march. Purely for comfort, they would throw away rations, blow their Claymores and grenades, no matter, because by nightfall the resupply choppers would arrive with more of the same, then a day or two later still more, fresh watermelons and crates of ammunition and sunglasses and woolen sweaters—the resources were stunning—sparklers for the Fourth of July, colored eggs for Easter—it was the great American war chest—the fruits of science, the smokestacks, the canneries, the arsenals at Hartford, the Minnesota forests, the machine shops, the vast fields of corn and wheat—they carried like freight trains; they carried it on their backs and shoulders—and for all the ambiguities of Vietnam, all the mysteries and unknowns, there was at least the single abiding certainty that they would never be at a loss for things to carry.

40   After the chopper took Lavender away, Lieutenant Jimmy Cross led his men into the village of Than Khe. They burned everything. They shot chickens and dogs, they trashed the village well, they called in artillery and watched the wreckage, then they marched for several hours through the hot afternoon, and then at dusk, while Kiowa explained how Lavender died, Lieutenant Cross found himself trembling.

He tried not to cry. With his entrenching tool, which weighed 5 pounds, he began digging a hole in the earth.

He felt shame. He hated himself. He had loved Martha more than his men, and as a consequence Lavender was now dead, and this was something he would have to carry like a stone in his stomach for the rest of the war.

All he could do was dig. He used his entrenching tool like an ax, slashing, feeling both love and hate, and then later, when it was full dark, he sat at the bottom of his foxhole and wept. It went on for a long while. In part, he was grieving for Ted Lavender, but mostly it was for Martha, and for himself, because she belonged to another world, which was not quite real, and because she was a junior at Mount Sebastian College in New Jersey, a poet and a virgin and uninvolved, and because he realized she did not love him and never would.

Like cement, Kiowa whispered in the dark. I swear to God—boom, down. Not a word.

45   I've heard this, said Norman Bowker.

A pisser, you know? Still zipping himself up. Zapped while zipping.

All right, fine. That's enough.

Yeah, but you had to see it, the guy just—

I *heard,* man. Cement. So why not shut the fuck *up?*

50   Kiowa shook his head sadly and glanced over at the hole where Lieutenant Jimmy Cross sat watching the night. The air was thick and wet. A warm dense fog had settled over the paddies and there was the stillness that precedes rain.

After a time Kiowa sighed.

One thing for sure, he said. The lieutenant's in some deep hurt. I mean that crying jag—the way he was carrying on—it wasn't fake or anything, it was real heavy-duty hurt. The man cares.

Sure, Norman Bowker said.

Say what you want, the man does care.

55   We all got problems.

Not Lavender.

No, I guess not, Bowker said. Do me a favor, though.

Shut up?

That's a smart Indian. Shut up.

60   Shrugging, Kiowa pulled off his boots. He wanted to say more, just to lighten up his sleep, but instead he opened his New Testament and arranged it beneath his head as a pillow. The fog made things seem hollow and unattached. He tried not to think about Ted Lavender, but then he was thinking how fast it was, no drama, down and dead, and how it was hard to feel anything except surprise. It seemed unchristian. He wished he could find some great sadness, or even anger, but the emotion wasn't there and he couldn't make it happen. Mostly he felt pleased to be alive. He liked the smell of the New Testament under his cheek, the leather and ink and paper and glue, whatever the chemicals were. He liked hearing the sounds of night. Even his fatigue, it felt fine, the stiff muscles and the prickly awareness of his own body, a floating feeling. He enjoyed not being dead. Lying there, Kiowa admired Lieutenant Jimmy Cross's capacity for grief. He wanted to share the man's pain, he wanted to care as Jimmy Cross cared. And yet when he closed his eyes, all he could think was Boom-down, and all he could feel was the pleasure of having his boots off and the fog curling in around him and the damp soil and the Bible smells and the plush comfort of night.

After a moment Norman Bowker sat up in the dark.

What the hell, he said. You want to talk, *talk.* Tell it to me.

Forget it.

No, man, go on. One thing I hate, it's a silent Indian.

65   For the most part they carried themselves with poise, a kind of dignity. Now and then, however, there were times of panic, when they squealed or wanted to squeal but couldn't, when they twitched and made moaning sounds and covered their heads and said Dear Jesus and flopped around on the earth and fired their weapons blindly and cringed and sobbed and begged for the noise to stop and went wild and made stupid promises to themselves and to God and to their mothers and fathers, hoping not to die. In different ways, it happened to all of them. Afterward, when the firing ended, they would blink and peek up. They would touch their bodies, feeling shame, then quickly hiding it. They would force

themselves to stand. As if in slow motion, frame by frame, the world would take on the old logic—absolute silence, then the wind, then sunlight, then voices. It was the burden of being alive. Awkwardly, the men would reassemble themselves, first in private, then in groups, becoming soldiers again. They would repair the leaks in their eyes. They would check for casualties, call in dustoffs, light cigarettes, try to smile, clear their throats and spit and begin cleaning their weapons. After a time someone would shake his head and say, No lie, I almost shit my pants, and someone else would laugh, which meant it was bad, yes, but the guy had obviously not shit his pants, it wasn't that bad, and in any case nobody would ever do such a thing and then go ahead and talk about it. They would squint into the dense, oppressive sunlight. For a few moments, perhaps, they would fall silent, lighting a joint and tracking its passage from man to man, inhaling, holding in the humiliation. Scary stuff, one of them might say. But then someone else would grin or flick his eyebrows and say, Roger-dodger, almost cut me a new asshole, *almost.*

There were numerous such poses. Some carried themselves with a sort of wistful resignation, others with pride or stiff soldierly discipline or good humor or macho zeal. They were afraid of dying but they were even more afraid to show it.

They found jokes to tell.

They used a hard vocabulary to contain the terrible softness. *Greased* they'd say. *Offed, lit up, zapped while zipping.* It wasn't cruelty, just stage presence. They were actors. When someone died, it wasn't quite dying, because in a curious way it seemed scripted, and because they had their lines mostly memorized, irony mixed with tragedy, and because they called it by other names, as if to encyst and destroy the reality of death itself. They kicked corpses. They cut off thumbs. They talked grunt lingo. They told stories about Ted Lavender's supply of tranquilizers, how the poor guy didn't feel a thing, how incredibly tranquil he was.

There's a moral here, said Mitchell Sanders.

70   They were waiting for Lavender's chopper, smoking the dead man's dope.

The moral's pretty obvious, Sanders said, and winked. Stay away from drugs. No joke, they'll ruin your day every time.

Cute, said Henry Dobbins.

Mind blower, get it? Talk about wiggy. Nothing left, just blood and brains.

They made themselves laugh.

75   There it is, they'd say. Over and over—there it is, my friend, there it is—as if the repetition itself were an act of poise, a balance between crazy and almost crazy, knowing without going, there it is, which meant be cool, let it ride, because Oh yeah, man, you can't change what can't be changed, there it is there it absolutely and positively and fucking well *is.*

They were tough.

They carried all the emotional baggage of men who might die. Grief, terror, love, longing—these were intangibles, but the intangibles had their own mass and specific gravity, they had tangible weight. They carried shameful memories. They carried the common secret of cowardice barely restrained, the instinct to run or freeze or hide, and in many respects this was the heaviest burden of all, for it could never be put down, it required perfect balance and perfect posture. They carried their reputations. They carried the soldier's greatest fear, which was the fear of blushing. Men killed, and died, because they were embarrassed not to. It was what had brought them to the war in the first place, nothing positive, no dreams of glory or honor, just to avoid the blush of dishonor. They died so as not to die of embarrassment. They crawled into tunnels and walked point and advanced under fire. Each morning, despite the unknowns, they made their legs move. They endured. They kept humping. They did not submit to the obvious alternative, which was simply to close the eyes and fall. So easy, really. Go limp and tumble to the ground and let the muscles unwind and not speak and not budge until your buddies picked you up and lifted you into the chopper that would roar and dip its nose and carry you off to the world. A mere matter of falling, yet no one ever fell. It was not courage, exactly; the object was not valor. Rather, they were too frightened to be cowards.

By and large they carried these things inside, maintaining the masks of composure. They sneered at sick call. They spoke bitterly about guys who had found release by shooting off their own toes or fingers. Pussies, they'd say. Candy-asses. It was fierce, mocking talk, with only a trace of envy or awe, but even so the image played itself out behind their eyes.

They imagined the muzzle against flesh. So easy: squeeze the trigger and blow away a toe. They imagined it. They imagined the quick, sweet pain, then the evacuation to Japan, then a hospital with warm beds and cute geisha nurses.

80   And they dreamed of freedom birds.

At night, on guard, staring into the dark, they were carried away by jumbo jets. They felt the rush of takeoff. *Gone!* they yelled. And then velocity—wings and engines—a smiling stewardess—but it was more than a plane, it was a real bird, a big sleek silver bird with feathers and talons and high screeching. They were flying. The weights fell off; there was nothing to bear. They laughed and held on tight, feeling the cold slap of wind and altitude, soaring, thinking *It's over, I'm gone!*—they were naked, they were light and free—it was all lightness, bright and fast and buoyant, light as light, a helium buzz in the brain, a giddy bubbling in the lungs as they were taken up over the clouds and the war, beyond duty, beyond gravity and mortification and global entanglements—*Sin loi!*[8] they yelled. *I'm sorry, motherfuckers, but I'm out of it, I'm goofed, I'm on a space cruise, I'm gone!*—and it was a restful, unencumbered sensation, just riding the light waves, sailing that big silver freedom bird over the mountains and oceans, over America, over the farms and great sleeping cities and cemeteries and highways and the golden arches of McDonald's, it was flight, a kind of fleeing, a kind of falling, falling higher and higher, spinning off the edge of the earth and beyond the sun and through the vast, silent vacuum where there were no burdens and where everything weighed exactly nothing—*Gone!* they screamed. *I'm sorry but I'm gone!*—and so at night, not quite dreaming, they gave themselves over to lightness, they were carried, they were purely borne.

On the morning after Ted Lavender died, First Lieutenant Jimmy Cross crouched at the bottom of his foxhole and burned Martha's letters. Then he burned the two photographs. There was a steady rain falling, which made it difficult, but he used heat tabs and Sterno to build a small fire, screening it with his body, holding the photographs over the tight blue flame with the tips of his fingers.

---

[8]**Sin loi!**: Sorry.

He realized it was only a gesture. Stupid, he thought. Sentimental, too, but mostly just stupid.

Lavender was dead. You couldn't burn the blame.

85   Besides, the letters were in his head. And even now, without photographs, Lieutenant Cross could see Martha playing volleyball in her white gym shorts and yellow T-shirt. He could see her moving in the rain.

When the fire died out, Lieutenant Cross pulled his poncho over his shoulders and ate breakfast from a can.

There was no great mystery, he decided.

In those burned letters Martha had never mentioned the war, except to say, Jimmy, take care of yourself. She wasn't involved. She signed the letters Love, but it wasn't love, and all the fine lines and technicalities did not matter. Virginity was no longer an issue. He hated her. Yes, he did. He hated her. Love, too, but it was a hard, hating kind of love.

The morning came up wet and blurry. Everything seemed part of everything else, the fog and Martha and the deepening rain.

90   He was a soldier, after all.

Half smiling, Lieutenant Jimmy Cross took out his maps. He shook his head hard, as if to clear it, then bent forward and began planning the day's march. In ten minutes, or maybe twenty, he would rouse the men and they would pack up and head west, where the maps showed the country to be green and inviting. They would do what they had always done. The rain might add some weight, but otherwise it would be one more day layered upon all the other days.

He was realistic about it. There was that new hardness in his stomach. He loved her but he hated her.

No more fantasies, he told himself.

Henceforth, when he thought about Martha, it would be only to think that she belonged elsewhere. He would shut down the daydreams. This was not Mount Sebastian, it was another world, where there were no pretty poems or midterm exams, a place where men died because of carelessness and gross stupidity. Kiowa was right. Boom-down, and you were dead, never partly dead.

95   Briefly, in the rain, Lieutenant Cross saw Martha's gray eyes gazing back at him.

He understood.

It was very sad, he thought. The things men carried inside. The things men did or felt they had to do.

He almost nodded at her, but didn't.

Instead he went back to his maps. He was now determined to perform his duties firmly and without negligence. It wouldn't help Lavender, he knew that, but from this point on he would comport himself as an officer. He would dispose of his good-luck pebble. Swallow it, maybe, or use Lee Strunk's slingshot, or just drop it along the trail. On the march he would impose strict field discipline. He would be careful to send out flank security, to prevent straggling or bunching up, to keep his troops moving at the proper pace and at the proper interval. He would insist on clean weapons. He would confiscate the remainder of Lavender's dope. Later in the day, perhaps, he would call the men together and speak to them plainly. He would accept the blame for what had happened to Ted Lavender. He would be a man about it. He would look them in the eyes, keeping his chin level, and he would issue the new SOPs in a calm, impersonal tone of voice, a lieutenant's voice, leaving no room for argument or discussion. Commencing immediately, he'd tell them, they would no longer abandon equipment along the route of march. They would police up their acts. They would get their shit together, and keep it together, and maintain it neatly and in good working order.

100   He would not tolerate laxity. He would show strength, distancing himself.

Among the men there would be grumbling, of course, and maybe worse, because their days would seem longer and their loads heavier, but Lieutenant Jimmy Cross reminded himself that his obligation was not to be loved but to lead. He would dispense with love; it was not now a factor. And if anyone quarreled or complained, he would simply tighten his lips and arrange his shoulders in the correct command posture. He might give a curt little nod. Or he might not. He might just shrug and say, Carry on, then they would saddle up and form into a column and move out toward the villages west of Than Khe.

They train to kill.

INQUIRING FURTHER

1. What do you know either about the Vietnam War or about other aspects of the military? Do you know anyone currently in the military? Have you studied other conflicts?

2. How do you usually get your information about conflicts like the Vietnam War? How much of your information could be characterized as fictional? How much could be called factual? What other methods of gaining information can you think of?

3. What elements of "The Things They Carried" do you think transcend the focus on the war? Are there concerns that people who have not experienced combat can relate to?

4. What one or two questions can you come up with about the story?

FORMULATING RESEARCH QUESTIONS

Research begins with questions. After reading "The Things They Carried," we might want to know more about the drafting of soldiers during the Vietnam War. To guide our research, we can translate our concerns into **research questions.** A research question focuses our investigation by articulating our main area of inquiry in a formal question. We might formulate an approach to researching "The Things They Carried" with the question, *How is the phenomena of the draft represented in the story?* This research question resembles a thesis statement in the way it prompts us to narrow our approach to a work.

Our question can help us develop goals and **supporting questions** as we carry out the research process. For instance, we might decide we need to find out what percentage of soldiers volunteered, versus the number of soldiers who were drafted, during the Vietnam War. We might determine that we need to research the ethnic or economic backgrounds of the soldiers who were drafted. A good research question will help generate more focused supporting questions.

☑ CHECKLIST FOR FORMULATING A RESEARCH QUESTION

☐ **Rely on your impressions and reactions** to a work. Like an interpretation, a research question evolves from your own interests. Consider what you like, what bothers or puzzles you, and any other questions that strike your interest, and then refine these areas of concern into a concrete research focus.

☐ **Conduct initial background research.** Either before reading or as a first step in understanding a work, conduct general research. Look for background information that might help you recognize important themes or make connections between a work and its context.

☐ **Draw comparisons** to help you understand the historical nature of what you read. You might relate the experiences of volunteer soldiers in the recent war with Iraq with those of draftees in O'Brien's story. Or, you might compare the political climate of today with that of the late 1960s in the United States. Draw connections that allow you to identify and understand the research you discover.

☐ **Compose a formal question** that can guide your research. Phrase your question in a way that suggests an interesting and open avenue for exploration, but that allows you to focus your research on a specific concern.

☐ **Develop supporting questions** based upon your research question. List additional questions you need to explore. Ensure that your question generates a number of research possibilities. Once you have specific questions in mind, you can employ all of the search strategies discussed in this chapter.

Exercise 4.1   *Developing a Research Question*

Working on your own, after reading "The Things They Carried" or another short work of fiction, develop a research question that can guide your investigation of the work.

1. Begin by reading the work and noting your impressions and any questions that arise. Select an element of the story that concerns you or that you would like to know more about. If you have trouble latching on to a research area, conduct a few brief queries on an Internet search engine (see next page) to look for general information that might inform your thinking.

2. Articulate your area of inquiry in a formal research question. Write that question out and check that it conveys a focused angle that might be used to guide your research.

3. Develop a list of at least three supporting questions that might lead you to information that will help you explore your research question.

UNDERSTANDING WEB GATEWAYS TO RESEARCH

The Web is your gateway to not only Internet information, but also to the resources located in your library. Through the Web you will research using **Internet search engines,** access your **library catalog,** and search through **indexes, abstracts,** and **databases** that provide materials in journals, periodicals, news sources, and books. To become a successful researcher, you must understand how different Web gateways (for instance, a library Web site, versus the Google search engine) can lead to different kinds of information.

Consider the comparison of the two screen shots in Figures 4.1 and 4.2. The figures have been keyed with numbers to help explain the differences between these two Web gateways. The following explains the search results in Figure 4.1.

1. **Listing of databases that have been searched:** The screen shot shows the results of a search of the *MasterFile Premier* and *Academic Search Elite* databases conducted from the Web site of a college library. Libraries offer hundreds of such databases from their Web sites; each will contain listings of reviews and articles that have been published in journals, books, and news sources. You will need to select the most appropriate databases to be successful. (See the list on page 123 for some possibilities.)

2. **Types of sources found in databases:** Look at the entries from the search. One article is from the *Chronicle of Higher Education* news periodical and

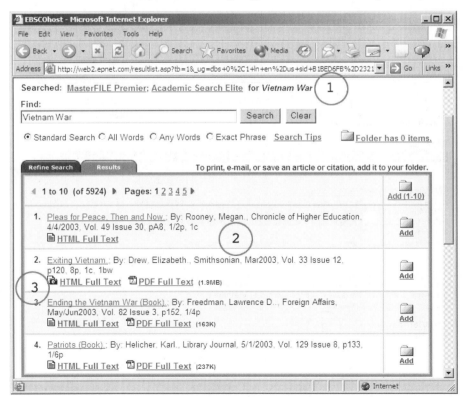

FIGURE 4.1 Library Database Search

another is from the academic journal *Smithsonian*. Other results from this search will contain similar sources—published articles by experts and professional news sources.

3. **Links to full text articles:** Notice how the entries in the library database search have links to HTML full text articles. Library searches conducted through the Web will often provide access to full text articles, so in terms of convenience there is little to lose and in terms of credibility there is much to be gained by searching through library resources.

As a contrast with the library database search shown in Figure 4.1, consider search results from the Google Internet search engine shown in Figure 4.2.

1. **Listing of search results:** Notice how the Google search returned over two million items. In general, Internet searches are going to bring back much more information, so you will need to sort through the results carefully and spend more time finding what is relevant.

2. **Interpreting search returns:** The first two returns appear to be Web sites sponsored by public broadcasting stations. The next entry appears to be sponsored by a commercial organization, vietnampix.com. (You can learn more about Internet domains on page 115.) The more you explore Internet sources, the more you will see how they can vary—you may find well-written articles by experts, images, business statements, or any range of other items.

FIGURE 4.2   Google Search Engine

You need a common-sense awareness of the differences between library resources and those found on the Internet at large. On the Internet, you can find materials offered by government-sponsored Web sites, commercial entities, non-profit organizations, educational institutions, and individuals, to name the most common possibilities. Through the library, you can find items like published articles, news stories, and historical documents. Since you will access both Internet and library resources through the Web, you must make a conscious effort to recognize how the Web gateway you use can influence the materials you will find.

CONDUCTING KEYWORD SEARCHES

Keywords are combinations of terms used to search for information in electronic databases. If we use the right keywords, our queries will find matches with the information in the database and our searches will be successful. Maintaining a **process of inquiry** as we research helps us develop the most appropriate keywords.

Tutorials
for
keyword
searches

The screen shots in Figure 4.3 have been annotated with numbers to help us discuss the keyword search process.

1. **Adding a search term:** Recall that our initial search of the Internet shown in Figure 4.2 used the keywords *Vietnam War* and returned over two million results. The first keyword query shown in Figure 4.3 has used the strategy of adding a term to the search, searching for *Vietnam War literature.* Adding or

FIGURE 4.3   Keyword Search Results

combining terms focuses search results. The number of search results has been reduced to about 300,000, and these items will be more directly related to the literature of the Vietnam War. However, 300,000 results is a big reduction from two million, but not nearly small enough to represent a focused search.

2. **Searching for an exact phrase:** The second search shown in the screen shot illustrates the strategy of searching for an exact phrase. By including a set of terms in quotation marks, the query returns items that contain that exact phrase. If we know we are interested in a person, work, event, or anything that can be identified uniquely, we can find related items by adding an exact phrase to our query. By searching for *Vietnam War "The Things They Carried,"* this query reduced the number of returns to just over 4,000.

3. **Evaluating search results:** This item listed in the search returns points to an online bookseller's catalog page for a companion book about "The Things They Carried." Evaluate search results to make adjustments to your strategies. At this point, the researcher is interested in finding information rather than buying a book, so she can remove some of these book selling results using advanced search strategies.

The screen shot in Figure 4.4 illustrates some advanced strategies.

1. **Combining terms and searching for exact phrases:** Keyword searches almost always offer a number of options beyond simply typing terms into a search field. The first two fields in this advanced search form represent our query for *Vietnam War "The Things They Carried,"* allowing us to combine terms and search for exact phrases.

2. **Broadening searches and excluding terms:** These two fields enable us to further refine our searches. Searching for at least one term or another is a way of broadening the results of a query. Rather than finding all of the items that contain both the terms *glossary* and *slang,* this query will bring back items with either of the terms. The next field allows us to exclude a search term from our query. If we discovered that a number of results were returning class assignments not related to our research question, we could compose a query that excluded any items containing the term *assignment.*

Tutorials
for
advanced
searching

3. **Filtering out unwanted results:** Most searches allow us to refine our queries even further. We can often filter results based on their format—looking for images instead of word processor documents, for instance. We might look for items in a particular language. With Web searches we can filter out results from a selected Web site or from a type of Web site—such as those with commercial, dot-com (.com), domains. (For more information on understanding Web sites, see page 115 and the tutorials on our CD-ROM.)

4. **Examining the query:** The results page demonstrates how the search engine has processed our query. The query can also be submitted from the main search field using shortcuts—for instance, we could type a minus sign (-) in front of the term *assignment* to quickly eliminate that item. Each search engine or database works differently, but all of them should support the strategies of combining, searching for exact phrases, searching for at least one term or another, and excluding a term. Learn the strategies, and then you can use shortcuts to make your searching more productive. You can bring these keyword search strategies with you as you investigate library resources.

5. **Narrowing down the results:** The number of search returns demonstrates how successful we have been in refining our query. Beginning with over two

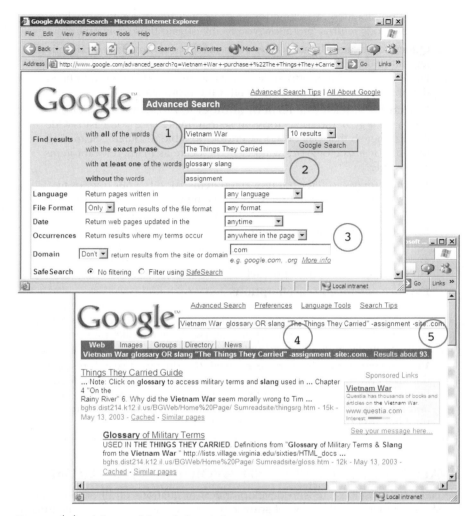

FIGURE 4.4   Advanced Search Strategies

million, we are now down to just 93 items. In the process, we have been thinking about our topic. Rather than the Vietnam War or its literature, we are now
researching "The Things We Carried" and the use of slang in the story.

✒CHECKLIST FOR CONDUCTING
KEYWORD SEARCHES

☐ **Be specific.** Searching for broad topics like the environment or war
literature will overwhelm you with the number of results and the range
of topics. Use the most precise terms you can to find specific sources.

☐ **Combine terms** to narrow your searches as you explore. A simple
combination of specific terms can limit results without excluding too

many possibilities. Searching for *Vietnam War literature music* will narrow your returns and allow you to investigate these concerns.

☐. **Query for exact phrases.** Quotation marks or advanced search options let you find a specific phrase, returning results directly related to the item you seek. Think of people, events, ideas, or other specific phrases that might help you locate highly relevant information.

☐ **Search for at least one term or another** to broaden returns. Once you have a goal and focus for your search, make sure you cast a wide enough net so that you do not overlook possible resources. Searching for *song* or *music* or *lyrics* will help you locate as many relevant items as possible.

☐ **Exclude terms** to filter out unwanted items. Modify your queries to remove items that are not relevant. Use a minus sign or the advanced search options to cut down on extraneous search returns.

☐ Learn to **interpret initial results** of searches. Look through the early results and evaluate the success of your queries. Consider the number and type of search returns and make adjustments to your queries and keywords to refine your approach.

☐ **Explore advanced search options** and search tool peculiarities. Do not be satisfied with simply typing terms in the basic search field. Use the advanced search form and learn the intricacies of search tools. Once you have learned the logistics, you can use shortcuts (like plus or minus signs) to implement advanced options.

☐ **View research and inquiry as related.** Conducting a search resembles thinking critically and writing about a topic. You need a narrow focus to be successful but you develop that focus through a process of inquiry and refinement. Experiment with search strategies and revise your thinking about your topic as your search evolves.

EVALUATING SOURCES AND AVOIDING PLAGIARISM

We can take conscious steps to develop critical evaluations of all of our sources. We should understand the **type of source** we are looking at, consider the **author** of the source, evaluate the **fairness of the source,** and determine the **correctness of the source.** We also must pay special attention to **Internet sources** and ensure that we avoid **plagiarism.**

Determining Types of Authors and Sources

By classifying the types of sources we find, we can make informed judgments about them. A message posted in an online discussion should be assessed using different criteria than something published in an academic journal. Additionally, knowing what kind of source we are using will help us make appropriate claims about the resource when we write—we might not use a discussion forum posting to verify statistics, but we could use it to show an alternative perspective. (See Chapter 7 for more on using sources in your writing.)

We can also inform our evaluation with information about an author. Authors carry with them a certain amount of credibility. An article written by a university professor is often seen as having authority because we assume that she has a high level of expertise with the subject matter. This authority is not automatic, however. A Vietnam veteran may have more authority when it comes to addressing the experience of the war.

Additionally, even authors with credentials have biases. Some writers make no efforts to hide their agendas, while others cloak them with care. Considering the author of a source requires us to probe these agendas and potential biases. We can look at the claims being made by the author and investigate the beliefs they may derive from. We can also find out if the author has said similar things elsewhere, or what others have said about the subject. Evaluate the source to determine potential biases and use these to help measure the author's credibility.

Assessing the Fairness and Correctness of Sources

We can also investigate the fairness of the source. We should know by now that rarely can a work or topic be addressed in a single way. Sources that suggest they have the answer, or that ignore alternative possibilities, should be viewed with skepticism. Instead, sources should acknowledge points of view that run directly counter to their own, and they should do so in a fair and reasonable way.

Finally, sources should demonstrate an attention to detail and correctness. Factual errors obviously undermine credibility, but so can mechanical errors and sloppiness. Do not discount a brilliant idea because of a misplaced comma, but do judge the care demonstrated in the writing and presentation of the source—sloppy compositions do not tend to inspire confidence in readers.

Understanding URLs

Every Web page has a unique address that indicates where it is located on the Internet. This address is provided by the Web page's **URL,** or **Uniform Resource Locator.**

The benefit of understanding URLs is that they can inform your judgments about Web materials. Consider the most common domains found on the Internet. Dot-edu (.edu) represents an educational institution; dot-com (.com) identifies a Web site sponsored by a commercial organization; dot-org (.org) represents a non-profit organization; and dot-gov (.gov) identifies a government agency. Because domains fall into different categories, we can compare the kinds of information that a given domain type is likely to provide.

Tutorials for understanding URLs and Internet domains

It is tempting to assume that sources from educational (.edu) and organizational (.org) domains are more credible than those from commercial domains. However, each source must be evaluated critically within the context of the Web domain that supports it. An individual's Web page put up on her college Web server is not necessarily a reliable source simply because it is hosted by an educational domain. Similarly, an academic journal might post scholarly articles at a commercial domain. Consider not only the domain, but also the organizations and individuals associated with it in terms of broader concerns of credibility.

Evaluating Internet Sources

The Web page shown in Figure 4.5 illustrates the value of many of the materials you can find on the Internet.

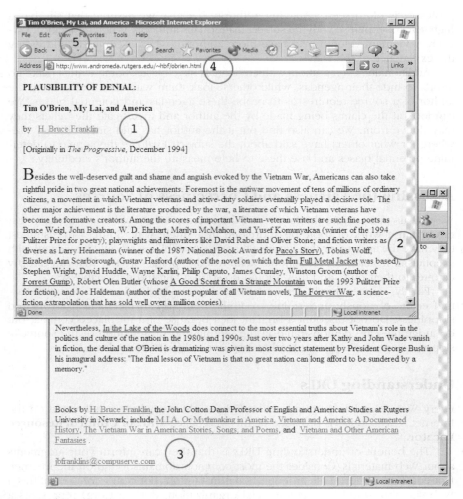

FIGURE 4.5 Credible Internet Sources

Tutorials
for
evaluating
Internet
sources

1. **Evaluating the type of source:** This page clearly lists the author of the work. Additionally, it provides information about the original publication of the piece. There are all types of materials available online; in this case we find an article much like we would see in a journal in our library. Knowing we are looking at a journal article, a personal Web page, an organization's information, or some other type of source is the first step in an evaluation.

2. **Determining the credibility of additional sources:** This source includes a number of references to other works that seem to bolster its credibility. If we look carefully, however, we will find no citation information given for these references. This information may have been lost when the original article was translated to the Web or it may just be missing, but in either case it diminishes the credibility of the source.

3. **Locating author contact information:** At the foot of this page we see information about the author, including his affiliation, a link to a Web site, and an e-mail address. We can use this information to find out more about the author, or we could try to contact the author to ask about the sources referenced in the piece. Sources with no information about their authors should be viewed skeptically.

4. **Examining the URL:** The URL for this page indicates that the file is hosted by Rutgers University. We must not automatically assume that materials located on educational or organizational servers are credible, but we can use the URL to inform our evaluations.

5. **Storing promising sites:** The Favorites menu (called the Bookmarks menu in some Web browsers) allows you to store the address of Web sites in a list managed by the Web browser. Add promising sites to your list of Favorites so that you can return to them later. For resources that seem especially valuable, you can save the resource to your own computer for retrieval. You will need to observe copyright concerns as you save these materials (see the Appendix).

Avoiding Plagiarism

We should look at one last Internet resource as a warning about what kinds of materials not to use when you conduct research online. The screen shot in Figure 4.6 depicts an online essay about "The Things They Carried." We can examine the essay to recognize the dangers of plagiarism.

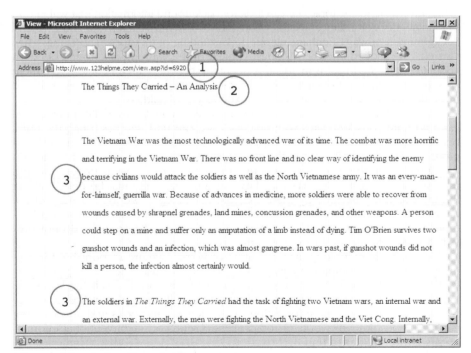

FIGURE 4.6 Online Essay Service

1. **Examining the URL:** The URL for this page reveals a problem immediately. The 123helpme.com domain tells us that the source resides on a commercial server. (This is not necessarily a problem, but it provides a clue we can use to make our judgment.) If we follow the URL back to the domain hosting the page, we will see that the source is an item provided by an online essay service.

2. **Examining the title:** Our next clue to problems with this source is the title. The title says nothing about the content of the paper. When you compose your papers, select a title that grabs the reader's interest and forecasts the thesis you wish to discuss. This paper likely has a vague title because it has little focus.

3. **Examining the content:** We can see also that the paper has put little care into the construction of its points or the style of its language. The phrase "because civilians would attack the soldiers as well as the North Vietnamese army" contains a misplaced modifier—it is unclear who is attacking whom. Further, the opening paragraph seems to discuss technology and medicine, but the paragraph at the bottom of the page drifts in an entirely new direction, again indicating that the paper has no controlling idea.

In addition to avoiding **paper mill** resources like the essay shown in Figure 4.6, you must be careful to cite and document properly all of the sources you use. We discuss strategies for keeping track of research information at the end of this chapter; we cover quoting sources, summarizing, and paraphrasing on pages 179–86. We provide more information on avoiding plagiarism in the Appendix.

EXPANDING OUR UNDERSTANDING OF CONTEXT

When investigating any topic, we can look for background information that will inform our judgments. For instance, we found out more about the Vietnam War and O'Brien's background as a way of enhancing our understanding of the story "The Things They Carried." We looked into the historical context of the war and also found out a bit about the draft. We might want to supplement this general sense of context with more specific information. Perhaps we could track down factual information or locate more documents detailing the personal experiences of soldiers.

Some of these reference sources seem relatively straightforward. For instance, we can find numerous Web sites with timelines. We can find statistics listing the number of casualties suffered during the war. We can also find information about the backgrounds of those who fought in the war or letters and memoirs written by soldiers.

While all of these sources provide a picture that can help us understand and interpret a story like "The Things They Carried," we still must be critical about the information presented by these external resources. If we look at most of the resources found on the Web, we will see that the statistics cover American soldiers and the letters present an American perspective. These items do not provide a complete picture of the Vietnam War.

As researchers looking at the context of works, we are responsible for seeing that context as completely as possible before we use it to develop an interpretation or argument. The nature of resources found on the Web (and to some extent in libraries) complicates this responsibility—the majority of Web sites are written in English and the information that makes it into books and articles often covers the best known works or topics. Less obvious or unconventional information is always harder to find.

The point is not that there is a problem with Tim O'Brien's story, or that this background information will not help us make sense of "The Things They Carried."

The point is that research represents an open-ended process of inquiry. As part of that process we are called to consider alternative possibilities—to question assumptions that often appear invisible. We will be better able to understand O'Brien's work if we understand the bigger picture. To learn more about the Vietnam conflict we might start by reading works by Vietnamese writers, or conducting research to investigate Vietnamese perspectives on the war.

Exercise 4.2   *Researching Alternative Perspectives*

Working on your own or with a group of fellow students, use an Internet search engine to find out as much as you can about the Vietnamese perspective on the war in Vietnam. (Consider as well the alternatives presented by both the North and the South Vietnamese perspectives.) Begin by selecting a person to keep track of the group's work (or preparing to take notes on your own).

Sample search for the North Vietnamese perspective

1. Go to an Internet search engine. (You can refer to our Web site for a list of search engines.) Conduct several keyword searches looking for information about the Vietnamese perspective.

2. Experiment with selecting keywords, combining terms, and searching for an exact phrase (use the advanced search options to refine your searches). Spend at least fifteen minutes looking for information and narrowing your searches.

3. Finally, based on the searching you have done, respond to the following prompts:

   • How would you characterize the search results? Was it difficult or easy to find information about the Vietnamese perspective? Did you discover other points of view as well? Write three or more sentences describing the process of searching for the Vietnamese perspective.

   • How would you characterize the Vietnamese perspectives that were represented in the research you discovered? Do you feel the materials provided a fair representation? What did you discover about any differences between North Vietnamese and South Vietnamese perspectives? How full a picture were you able to develop and how would you describe that picture? Write four or more sentences responding to these questions.

   • Finally, compare what you have discovered about the Vietnamese points of view to other perspectives on the Vietnam War. How does what you have learned relate to your own sense of the war? How does it relate to "The Things They Carried?" Write three or more sentences comparing perspectives.

Exercise 4.3   *Refining a Keyword Search*

Working on your own, conduct research looking for information on the Vietnam War (or some other historical event).

1. Begin by thinking through possible angles you might take as you research. Possibilities might include the North Vietnamese or South Vietnamese perspectives, the social dimensions of the war, representations of the war in film, the long-term effects of the war, or any other topic that appeals to you. If you cannot find an area of interest, conduct a broad search about the war and spend some time browsing through the results to get a feel for potential topics.

2. Develop a research question that helps you focus on a particular aspect of the topic you have chosen. Articulate a formal question that can guide your investigation.

3. Once you have a specific area that you would like to research, develop a list of potential keywords. Be as specific as you can in selecting keywords and think of possible people, places, events, or other terms you might use to search for exact phrases. Develop a list of at least five terms or phrases you could use as keywords.

4. Conduct several Internet searches using your list of terms. Combine terms and search for exact phrases. Keep track of the number of items returned. Adjust your queries based on what you discover. Work to reduce the search returns to a manageable number.

5. Once you have developed a well-focused query, explore four or more of the items that you have uncovered. Consider which of these might be useful for a continued investigation of the topic. Add the most useful items to your Favorites or Bookmarks list.

EXPLORING IDEAS WITH OTHERS

We might not think of talking with others as research, but holding conversations and exploring ideas is one of the best ways to get information and refine our thinking. Again, the key is maintaining an awareness of the nature of this kind of research, of its strengths and weaknesses. Exploring ideas with others helps us tap into a diverse pool of expertise and first-hand experiences. One strategy for conducting such research is to search through the archives of Internet conversations.

In **Internet conversations,** participants exchange messages about topics ranging from adoption to Zip cars. This means that you are going to find a wide range of experiences and agendas when you search through online conversations. Still, many Internet forums are frequented by people (often experts) with a genuine interest in the topics discussed by the group. You can find Internet conversations taking place on **Web message forums,** or in **Weblogs.** You will also find conversations taking place in **newsgroups.** Newsgroups are topic-based forums where users post messages. (For more on locating Internet conversations, see the resources on our CD.)

Locating
Internet
conversations

The simplest way to begin exploring these conversations is by looking through the archives of newsgroup discussions hosted by Google, as demonstrated in the screenshot in Figure 4.7. Examining the screen shot shows a number of characteristics shared by Internet conversations. (The screen shot has been keyed with numbers for discussion.)

1. **Considering the forum:** This conversation is taken from a newsgroup called soc.history.war.vietnam. Most online conversations are governed by the name

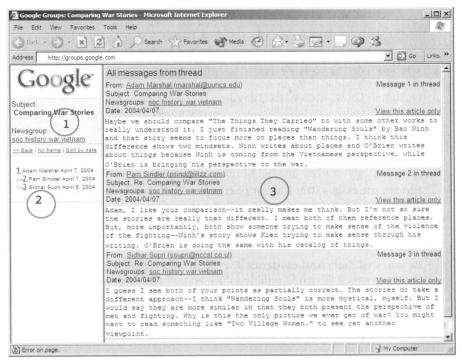

FIGURE 4.7   Google Groups Archive

or general topic of the forum in which they take place. If you can find a suitable newsgroup or message forum, you can rest assured that the members will likely be discussing topics that may be relevant to your research.

2. **Determining the conversation thread:** In the left-hand frame of the screen shot, we see that there are three messages posted in this conversation. In electronic conversations, an initial message is posted and subsequent messages respond to the points in the original posting. These postings and responses form what is called a **thread** of conversation. Threads illustrate the give and take nature of electronic discussions. In most cases, the follow up messages will offer alternative interpretations or ask for clarifications about the initial message. Sometimes these exchanges can become heated or drift from the original topic. Learn to recognize and ignore messages that personalize the debate or that fail to respond to the arguments of others.

3. **Evaluating the debate:** In this thread of discussion we can see how the first response challenges the original message. Pam accepts that comparing "The Things They Carried" with a work called "Wandering Souls" is helpful, but disagrees with Adam about the differences between the two stories. Sidri extends Pam's critique by offering an explanation that shows that both stories are similar in their focus on men and fighting. Sidri also suggests that reading a story called "Two Village Women" might inform Pam and Adam's thinking about the stories. While they question one another, these exchanges represent healthy debate—they are not personalizing the discussion, and they raise and follow up on objections in the spirit of moving the conversation forward.

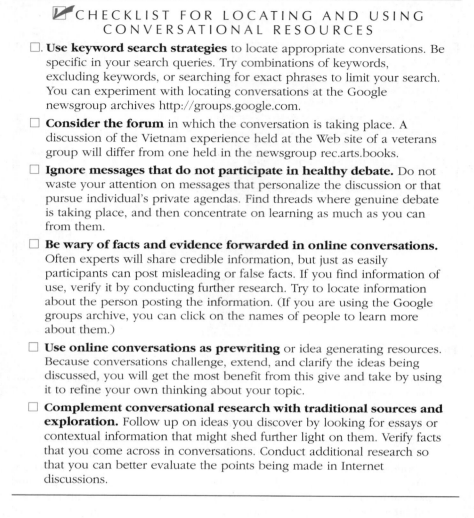

☑CHECKLIST FOR LOCATING AND USING
CONVERSATIONAL RESOURCES

☐. **Use keyword search strategies** to locate appropriate conversations. Be specific in your search queries. Try combinations of keywords, excluding keywords, or searching for exact phrases to limit your search. You can experiment with locating conversations at the Google newsgroup archives http://groups.google.com.

☐ **Consider the forum** in which the conversation is taking place. A discussion of the Vietnam experience held at the Web site of a veterans group will differ from one held in the newsgroup rec.arts.books.

☐ **Ignore messages that do not participate in healthy debate.** Do not waste your attention on messages that personalize the discussion or that pursue individual's private agendas. Find threads where genuine debate is taking place, and then concentrate on learning as much as you can from them.

☐ **Be wary of facts and evidence forwarded in online conversations.** Often experts will share credible information, but just as easily participants can post misleading or false facts. If you find information of use, verify it by conducting further research. Try to locate information about the person posting the information. (If you are using the Google groups archive, you can click on the names of people to learn more about them.)

☐ **Use online conversations as prewriting** or idea generating resources. Because conversations challenge, extend, and clarify the ideas being discussed, you will get the most benefit from this give and take by using it to refine your own thinking about your topic.

☐ **Complement conversational research with traditional sources and exploration.** Follow up on ideas you discover by looking for essays or contextual information that might shed further light on them. Verify facts that you come across in conversations. Conduct additional research so that you can better evaluate the points being made in Internet discussions.

FINDING ARGUMENTS ABOUT LITERATURE

As you narrow your focus on a topic, you may want to refer to specific and detailed arguments that others have put forth about a work or writer. Using an Internet search engine, you can no doubt find a number of essays on most works of literature. Be sure to read the section on pages 117–18 on plagiarism before spending any time with these kinds of arguments. Your instructor no doubt also knows how to find these paper mill essays and you need to learn to locate sources that have something of value to say (not every essay you find online does).

You can also locate essays that have been published in newspapers, books, and journals. These articles have the advantage of careful screening by publishers, and authorship by experts who have devoted a great deal of time and energy to their subject. Some of the essays have the disadvantage of being written for a specialized academic audience, meaning that you will need to invest some energy to get the most out of academic essays. (See Chapter 13 for advice on understanding specialized critical approaches to literature.)

To draw upon the arguments of others, you should learn to locate published articles and academic essays. For these searches, your library Web site will be your gateway. Once you access your library Web site, you will locate their list of **indexes, abstracts,** and **databases.** For every field of knowledge, and for many broad types of publications, databases collect listings of what has been published. (Many times these listings also provide full text versions of articles.)

Begin by locating the indexes, abstracts, and databases offered by your library. These resources are often listed on the library Web site as **Indexes and Abstracts,** or **Indexes and Databases.** Your library Web site should categorize many of these resources by subjects. You can begin with either a listing of broad subjects like *Arts and Humanities,* or with more specific subjects like *Literature.*

You can also go directly to one of the databases listed in the table below:

Searching indexes, abstracts, and databases

Useful General Research Databases	Useful Literature Research Databases
Academic Search Elite (provides popular and academic journal listings)	**ABELL** (lists literary works as well as articles, books, and periodicals about literature)
CQ Researcher (covers controversial public issues)	
LexisNexis Academic (provides legal, business, and medical listings)	**Chadwyck-Healey** (provides a number of databases covering poetry, drama, and fiction)
EBSCO (provides a gateway to many other databases)	**Literature in Context** (provides listings covering historical and reference materials)
Global Newsbank (offers news from international sources)	
Infotrac (several versions of Infotrac provide popular, news, and academic listings)	**Literature Online (LION)** (provides reference tools and online works of literature)
	MagillON (provides databases covering literary authors and texts)
Newsbank (provides listings from news sources)	**MLA International Bibliography** (lists articles on literature published in academic journals)
Popular Periodicals Index (covers hundreds of periodical listings)	
Proquest (provides news and periodical listings)	**Oxford English Dictionary** (offers detailed coverage of the meanings and histories of words)

Your library may not offer every one of these databases, but you should be able to locate at least several to use for general research or for research about specific works of literature.

Once you locate a database, you can conduct keyword searches to look for relevant information. The screen shot in Figure 4.8 (which has been keyed for discussion) shows a search of a specialized database, the *Literature Online (LION)* database. *LION* can help you locate original works, critical essays about works, and reference materials.

1. **Resource options:** The results of a database search provide information that will help you access and use the resources. These icons allow researchers to add this item to a saved list of records, link to bibliographic information,

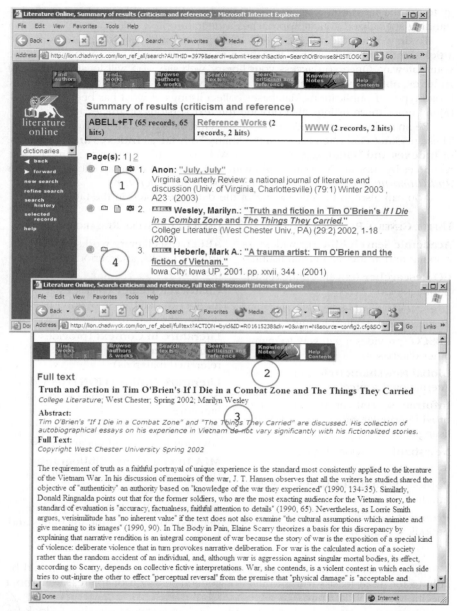

FIGURE 4.8   Literature Online

or to open a full text version of the listed article either as a Web page or an image. Each database will indicate options differently, but all will provide links and guidance to help you use the materials.

2. **Full text archives:** Following the link to the full text version of the source will provide a copy of the article. Publication information about the article should be listed at the top. You will need this information for your citations. Often arti-

cles will have an abstract that summarizes the major points of the piece. You can sometimes make a preliminary judgment about the article's usefulness from the abstract, but do not confuse the information in the abstract for the article itself.

3. **Relevant and credible resources:** The full text link offers a published article written by a scholar and directly related to "The Things They Carried." With a bit of effort locating the right database, we have discovered a resource that is relevant and credible. But we still must read critically and make sure that we integrate the resource into our own writing fairly.

4. **Tracking down items in your library:** Finally, it can be tempting to gravitate toward the full text listings returned from database searches. However, just as the best articles are often in the library database rather than on the Web, sometimes the best of the articles listed in the database are in the stacks of the library rather than linked as full text sources through the library Web page. Examine all of the items, make notes about resources that look relevant, and then track down any promising items in the library.

Each of the specialized databases for literature has its own strengths and weaknesses. You will want to learn the ins and outs of the resources available through your library's Web site, and then use them to your advantage as you work more extensively with literature.

✔ CHECKLIST FOR USING INDEXES, ABSTRACTS, AND DATABASES

☐ **Commit to using these resources.** The Web may seem more convenient, but when you factor in the ability to quickly find credible, published resources with the authority these sources will add to your writing, you cannot deny the benefits of learning to use these library databases.

☐ **Familiarize yourself with the offerings on your library Web page.** Each library provides these resources differently. Spend a few minutes learning which resources are available to you, and where they are located. If you do your research off-campus, find out how to access these materials through the Web. (Your library should have instructions for setting up remote access.)

☐ **Use keyword search strategies.** As with any electronic search, your results will improve with focused and relevant queries. Learn the options of the search tools you are using and be specific and thoughtful about your search terms.

☐ **Assess the range and type of resources.** Even among published sources in databases you will uncover a range of materials. Pieces from popular magazines may not offer as much insight or depth as you need. Articles from academic journals may provide too specialized a treatment. Understand the type of source you discover and adjust how you read and use the source accordingly.

☐ **Use full text articles critically.** The convenience of full text articles requires restraint in how you use them. Make sure they speak to your topic and ideas. Be sure not to confuse abstracts (brief summaries) of articles with the original article. Use care as you integrate sections of articles into your own work. Ensure that you write in your own words and use appropriate quotations, summaries, and paraphrases (see pages 179–86).

☐ **Track down relevant items on the shelves of the library.** Look through the list of items you discover and jot down publication information for those that seem most relevant. Find the location of the item (often you will look for the journal or source where it originates) and go to the library to evaluate it. Budget your time so that you can investigate these sources.

☐ **Ask for help.** The reference librarians have expertise in locating resources and in what is available at your school. Consult any tutorials or information they provide and ask for assistance if you need it.

TAKING NOTES AND CREATING A BIBLIOGRAPHY

Your research process should not be separated from the writing you do on a project. Initially, an emphasis on locating materials can help get you started on a project. Once you begin working, however, you may find that you slip comfortably between conducting research and composing. You will also have opportunities to write as you research by **taking notes** and creating a **bibliography** of your sources.

You can take notes using many methods. Note cards remain a handy option, as they allow you to sort and organize your information. You may also find it convenient to record information in a notebook or using pencil and paper. If you compose notes by hand, write legibly enough so that you can come back to them days later and still make out the information.

Composing notes electronically helps you eventually move information into a draft of your paper. You can also more easily integrate quotations and information into your notes if you are working with electronic sources. One convenient way of working with notes is to compose an e-mail message to yourself. This is especially useful if you are working in the library or away from the computer you normally use.

You can also compose your notes using a word processor. Again, this can make it easy to move fluidly between the research and note-taking phases of a project to the many activities of writing. The screen shot in Figure 4.9 shows one student's notes about an article on "The Things They Carried."

You can use note taking as a brainstorming opportunity, making sense of what you read as you translate ideas to your notes. Feel free to sketch out questions as you jot down observations and summaries. The notes in Figure 4.9 dovetail with the drafting process as they integrate analysis and evaluation with the information that is recorded. The author could easily turn these ideas into sections of a paper.

Be selective as you jot down quotations from your sources. Rather than copy wholesale passages into your notes, choose the selections that best represent the ideas you are reading. The notes in Figure 4.9 contain two quotations, each of which represents core ideas in the essay. Also, translate as much of the source as possible into your own words—this will help you make sense of the materials and make it easier to turn your notes into drafts later.

As you work with sources, you should also record documentation information. Notice how the notes shown in Figure 4.9 include the publication information for the article. Be sure to record this information as soon as you locate a source. It

Notes:

Calloway, Catherine. "'How to tell a true war story': Metafiction in The Things They Carried." Critique: Studies in Contemporary Fiction (Washington, *DC)* (36:4) [Summer 1995]

Begins with a review of TTTC—written in 95, TTTC published in 94? Looks at the way that individual stories are told. Talks about ambiguity and "epistemological ambivalence" of the story. Seems to be saying that determining the truth of the stories is impossible. The ambiguity is seen in the structure—the book has lots of different genres—essays, jokes, stories, anecdotes, etc. Calloway also points out "many parallels" between the protagonist and Tim O'Brien. Calls it a metafiction—a story about a story? Calloway quotes Patricia Waugh:

> Metafiction is a term given to fictional writing which self-consciously and systematically draws attention to its status as an artifact in order to pose questions about the relationship between fiction and reality.

Calloway discusses examples from the story where it is hard to tell reality from imagination. She shows how characters reappear in different chapters and how stories are told from different perspectives. She believes the story draws our attention to the way it is written, saying that the story "as much about the process of writing as it is the text of a literary work."

Sample research papers

FIGURE 4.9   Notes on an Article

is much easier to copy it into your notes or jot it down at the time, than to try to reproduce it later.

One method of collecting information about resources is to create a working **bibliography** as you research. Bibliographies help researchers by collecting in a single list a number of sources related to a topic. As you explore the topic in depth, you may not use every source listed in a working bibliography, but collecting the information will help ensure you have a breadth of coverage in the sources that you do use.

Sometimes researchers compose an **annotated bibliography.** For each entry, a brief annotation provides a summary of the source and may offer an evaluation of its relevance or value. To create an annotated bibliography, you will need to spend some time with the sources that you use so that you can summarize them accurately.

To compose a bibliography, list each item alphabetically, by the author's last name. Be sure to include the title, the publisher, and the date. Format the entries following the MLA documentation conventions covered on pages 935–46. If you are annotating your bibliography, compose a short gloss. The sample bibliography that follows contains entries that point toward sources for understanding "The Things They Carried." The first entry has been annotated.

Bibliography for "The Things They Carried"

Calloway, Catherine. "'How to Tell a True War Story': Metafiction in The

Things They Carried." <u>Critique: Studies in Contemporary Fiction</u>

36.4 (Summer 1995): 249–58.

[Calloway emphasizes the ambiguity found in the episodes told by the

narrator. She suggests that determining the truth of the stories is difficult.

She concludes that the work is a metafiction, "a story about stories."]

Naparsteck, Martin. "An Interview with Tim O'Brien." <u>Contemporary</u>

<u>Literature</u> 32 (Spring 1991): 1–11.

O'Brien, Tim. "The Things They Carried." <u>Writing about Literature in</u>

<u>the Media Age</u>. Ed. Daniel Anderson. New York: Longman, 2005.

95–107.

"Selective Service System: History and Records." 27 May, 2003. Selective

Service System. 03 February, 2004. <http://www.sss.gov/induct.htm>.

Sidhar, Supri. "Re: Comparing War Stories." Online Posting. 07 April,

2004. Soc.history.war.vietnam. 23 April, 2004.

<http://groups.google.com/groups?q=things+they+carried>.

You may not wish to keep a formal bibliography, but whatever you do, keep track of the sources you discover. If you do keep a bibliography, once you integrate any sources into your paper, you can quickly add the necessary entries into your **Works Cited** page (see pages 938–46).

Exercise 4.4   *Searching Indexes, Abstracts, and Databases*

Working with a group of fellow students (or on your own if your instructor prefers), search through several of the databases provided by your library.

1. Begin by locating the indexes, abstracts, and databases collection on your library's Web site. Spend a few minutes getting familiar with the organization of the resources.

2. Locate one of the general reference databases listed on page 123. Once you have accessed this database, develop a topic that you want to research and conduct several keyword queries looking for resources.

3. Find at least one item that contains a full text entry and follow the link to the full text article. Locate the bibliographic information for the article. Using the methods supported by your school (you can likely save or download articles, e-mail articles, or print articles) save a copy of the piece that you can access later.

4. Locate one of the specialized literature databases listed on page 123. Choose a text or author that you wish to investigate, and then conduct several keyword searches looking for resources.

5. Locate an item from your search of a literature-related database that contains a full text entry and follow the link to the article. Examine the language used in the article. If it seems too specialized, go back and look for others. If you find an article that seems useful, save it using the methods supported by your school.

6. Find one of the sources you have located in your searches that does not contain a full text link to the article. Using the publication information for the item, locate its source in your library. Visit the library and track down the item.

PART II

Argument and the Writing Process

5

Argument and the Rhetorical Situation

People generally quarrel because they cannot argue.
—*Gilbert K. Chesterton*

Argument might seem too strong a term for the writing that we do in most college classes. Arguments are verbal battles, drawn-out conflicts between people who will never see eye-to-eye. Right? Some disagreements do devolve into heated confrontations, but the arguments we engage in our academic writing are more like the debates that take place in a court of law than the quarrels we might encounter over dinner. In an academic argument, the parties must present a well-reasoned case that convinces others that their position has merit.

We argue our points intuitively all the time. In a class discussion we might claim that the setting of a story creates a desolate atmosphere. (We would probably provide **reasons** and discuss **examples** to support our position.) In the hallway we might debate the merits of a tough class. (We might weigh the pros and cons of the workload in terms of the learning benefits, accommodating **alternative possibilities**.) We might try to convince a friend to rent a film we want to see; we would consider the tastes of our friend (assessing our **audience**) and tailor our argument to appeal to those tastes. We can think of these examples as unique **rhetorical situations**. In these situations, we use elements of argument, though we might not realize it.

CONSIDERING OUR RHETORICAL SITUATION

Our **purpose** and **audience** determine the way we approach any writing task. These elements derive from our **rhetorical situation** (our task, our readers, and the context in which we write). We sometimes compose formal papers. We might write letters home, or letters to a newspaper editor or potential employer. We participate in all kinds of writing situations, and each demands a unique approach.

Writing for college presents a particular kind of rhetorical situation. Our **purpose** when we compose a formal academic argument will be to convince others that our thesis is worth considering, that it has merit. But we will also work from a number of smaller goals as we compose. We will have the goal of establishing our authority as we write. Our purpose in the body of our argument might be to use evidence as carefully and compellingly as possible. We might seek to defuse opposing points of view as our argument evolves. All of these purposes will determine how we approach the tasks we undertake when writing an argument.

An academic **audience** also shapes our use of language. If we are writing for our peers or instructor in a classroom setting, we will generally maintain an appropriate level of formality and adhere to the rules of standard American English. We should avoid slang or other non-standard language, write correct and complete sentences, and eliminate mechanical errors. We should also know that academic readers generally value organization, coherency, and fair-minded arguments. Understanding that we are writing in an academic rhetorical situation can help us assess our audience and refine our purpose as we compose.

Exploring Academic Arguments

To compose academic arguments, we must have an approach that lends itself to an argument. That is, our interpretations must entertain alternative possibilities and allow us to pursue open-ended questions about a work. This complexity will ensure that we have an **arguable topic**. We must then convince our readers that we can be trusted, by establishing our **authority** to speak on the subject. We should articulate our topic with a thesis, and then lay out a series of **convincing reasons** for accepting our approach. We must also entertain **opposing points of view** and either accommodate or refute them in our own argument. Finally, we must provide solid **evidence** that illustrates and supports the points that we make along the way.

Of course, when we read and write about literature, we cannot simply follow a formula in lockstep fashion. Because literature appeals to our emotions as well as our intellect, we must use argument to help us develop and express our interpretations. Argument is not simply about proving a point; it is about exploring an idea or issue that matters to us. Arguments will evolve organically as we draft them (see Chapter 6), but eventually they will help us explain what we discover as clearly as we can.

To get a sense for how academic arguments can promote this kind of process of inquiry we will examine a short story by Alice Walker called "Everyday Use."

Alice Walker

Alice Walker (born in 1944) grew up in a home with eight children in rural Eatonton, Georgia. Her parents were sharecroppers. In 1952 at age eight she was accidentally shot in the eye with a BB fired by one of her brothers. The injury resulted in a scar that discolored her eye. She was tormented by the scar and by the reactions of schoolmates until at age fourteen she underwent surgery and had the scar removed. By the time she graduated high school she was elected the most popular in her class. She went on to study at Sarah Lawrence college and published her first collection of poems, Once, *shortly after graduating. Walker's work includes poetry, short stories, novels, and essays. Her writing has been praised for its treatment of difficult subjects related to race, family, and poverty and for its honest, emotional, and lyrical qualities. She is perhaps best known for her Pulitzer Prize winning novel,* The Color Purple. *"Everyday Use" was first published in 1973.*

Everyday Use

For Your Grandmama

I will wait for her in the yard that Maggie and I made so clean and wavy yesterday afternoon. A yard like this is more comfortable than most people know. It is not just a yard. It is like an extended living room. When the hard clay is swept clean as a floor and the fine sand around the edges lined with tiny, irregular grooves, anyone can come and sit and look up into the elm tree and wait for the breezes that never come inside the house.

Background material for "Everyday Use"

Maggie will be nervous until after her sister goes: she will stand hopelessly in corners, homely and ashamed of the burn scars down her arms and legs, eyeing her sister with a mixture of envy and awe. She thinks her sister has held life always in the palm of one hand, that "no" is a word the world never learned to say to her.

You've no doubt seen those TV shows where the child who has "made it" is confronted, as a surprise, by her own mother and father, tottering in weakly from backstage. (A pleasant surprise, of course: What would they do if parent and child came on the show only to curse out and insult each other?) On TV mother and child embrace and smile into each other's faces. Sometimes the mother and father weep, the child wraps them in her arms and leans across the table to tell how she would not have made it without their help. I have seen these programs.

Sometimes I dream a dream in which Dee and I are suddenly brought together on a TV program of this sort. Out of a dark and soft-seated limousine I am ushered into a bright room filled with many people. There I meet a smiling, gray, sporty man like Johnny Carson who shakes my hand and tells me what a fine girl I have. Then we are on the stage and Dee is embracing me with tears in her eyes. She pins on my dress a large orchid, even though she has told me once that she thinks orchids are tacky flowers.

5   In real life I am a large, big-boned woman with rough, man-working hands. In the winter I wear flannel nightgowns to bed and overalls during the day. I can kill and clean a hog as mercilessly as a man. My fat keeps me hot in zero weather. I can work outside all day, breaking ice to get water for washing; I can eat pork liver cooked over the open fire minutes after it comes steaming from the hog. One winter I knocked a bull calf straight in the brain between the eyes with a sledge hammer and had the meat hung up to chill before nightfall. But of course all this does not show on television. I am the way my daughter would want me to be: a hundred pounds lighter, my skin like an uncooked barley pancake. My hair glistens in the hot bright lights. Johnny Carson has much to do to keep up with my quick and witty tongue.

But that is a mistake. I know even before I wake up. Who ever knew a Johnson with a quick tongue?

Who can even imagine me looking a strange white man in the eye? It seems to me I have talked to them always with one foot raised in flight, with my head turned in whichever way is farthest from them. Dee, though. She would always look anyone in the eye. Hesitation was no part of her nature.

"How do I look, Mama?" Maggie says, showing just enough of her thin body enveloped in pink skirt and red blouse for me to know she's there, almost hidden by the door.

"Come out into the yard," I say.

10   Have you ever seen a lame animal, perhaps a dog run over by some careless person rich enough to own a car, sidle up to someone who is ignorant enough to be kind to him? That is the way my Maggie walks. She has been like this, chin on chest, eyes on ground, feet in shuffle, ever since the fire that burned the other house to the ground.

Dee is lighter than Maggie, with nicer hair and a fuller figure. She's a woman now, though sometimes I forget. How long ago was it that the other house burned? Ten, twelve years? Sometimes I can still hear the flames and feel Maggie's arms sticking to me, her hair smoking and her dress falling off her in little black papery flakes. Her eyes seemed stretched open, blazed open by the flames reflected in them. And Dee. I see her standing off under the sweet gum tree she used to dig gum out of; a look of concentration on her face as she watched the last dingy gray board of the house fall in toward the red-hot brick chimney. Why don't you do a dance around the ashes? I'd wanted to ask her. She had hated the house that much.

I used to think she hated Maggie, too. But that was before we raised the money, the church and me, to send her to Augusta to school. She used to read to us without pity; forcing words, lies, other folks' habits, whole lives upon us two, sitting trapped and ignorant underneath her voice. She washed us in a river of make-believe, burned us with a lot of knowledge we didn't necessarily need to know. Pressed us to her with the serious way she read, to shove us away at just the moment, like dimwits, we seemed about to understand.

Dee wanted nice things. A yellow organdy dress to wear to her graduation from high school; black pumps to match a green suit she'd made from an old suit somebody gave me. She was determined to stare down any disaster in her efforts. Her eyelids would not flicker for minutes at a time. Often I fought off the temptation to shake her. At sixteen she had a style of her own: and knew what style was.

I never had an education myself. After second grade the school was closed down. Don't ask me why: in 1927 colored asked fewer questions than they do now. Sometimes Maggie reads to me. She stumbles along good-naturedly but can't see well. She knows she is not bright. Like good looks and money, quickness passed her by. She will marry John Thomas (who has mossy teeth in an earnest face) and then I'll be free to sit here and I guess just sing church songs to myself. Although I never was a good singer. Never could carry a tune. I was always better at a man's job. I used to love to milk till I was hooked in the side in '49. Cows are soothing and slow and don't bother you, unless you try to milk them the wrong way.

15   I have deliberately turned my back on the house. It is three rooms, just like the one that burned, except the roof is tin; they don't make shingle roofs any more. There are no real windows, just some holes cut in the sides, like the portholes in a ship, but not round and not square, with rawhide holding the shutters up on the outside. This house is in a pasture, too, like the other one. No doubt when Dee sees it she will want to tear it down. She wrote me once that no matter where we "choose" to live, she will manage to come see us. But she will never bring her friends. Mag gie and I thought about this and Maggie asked me, "Mama, when did Dee ever *have* any friends?"

She had a few. Furtive boys in pink shirts hanging about on washday after school. Nervous girls who never laughed. Impressed with her they worshiped the well-turned phrase, the cute shape, the scalding humor that erupted like bubbles in lye. She read to them.

When she was courting Jimmy T she didn't have much time to pay to us, but turned all her faultfinding power on him. He *flew* to marry a cheap city girl from a family of ignorant flashy people. She hardly had time to recompose herself.

When she comes I will meet—but there they are!

Maggie attempts to make a dash for the house, in her shuffling way, but I stay her with my hand. "Come back here," I say. And she stops and tries to dig a well in the sand with her toe.

20   It is hard to see them clearly through the strong sun. But even the first glimpse of leg out of the car tells me it is Dee. Her feet were always neat-looking, as if God himself had shaped them with a certain style. From the other side of the car comes a short, stocky man. Hair is all over his head a foot long and hanging from his chin like a kinky mule tail. I hear Maggie suck in her breath. "Uhnnnh," is what it sounds like. Like when you see the wriggling end of a snake just in front of your foot on the road. "Uhnnnh."

Dee next. A dress down to the ground, in this hot weather. A dress so loud it hurts my eyes. There are yellows and oranges enough to throw back the light of the sun. I feel my whole face warming from the heat waves it throws out. Earrings, too, gold, and hanging down to her shoulders. Bracelets dangling and making noises when she moves her arm up to shake the folds of the dress out of her armpits. The dress is loose and flows, and as she walks closer, I like it. I hear Maggie go "Uhnnnh" again. It is her sister's hair. It stands straight up like the wool on a sheep. It is black as night and around the edges are two long pig-tails that rope about like small lizards disappearing behind her ears.

"Wa-su-zo-Tean-o!" she says, coming on in that gliding way the dress makes her move. The short stocky fellow with the hair to his navel is all grinning and he follows up with "Asalamalakim,* my mother and sister!" He moves to hug Maggie but she falls back, right up against the back of my chair. I feel her trembling there and when I look up I see the perspiration falling off her chin.

"Don't get up," says Dee. Since I am stout it takes something of a push. You can see me trying to move a second or two before I make it. She turns, showing white heels through her sandals, and goes back to the car. Out she peeks next with a Polaroid. She stoops down quickly and lines up picture after picture of me sitting there in front of the house with Maggie cowering behind me. She never takes a shot without making sure the house is included. When a cow comes nibbling around the edge of the yard she snaps it and me and Maggie *and* the house. Then she puts the Polaroid in the back seat of the car, and comes up and kisses me on the forehead.

Meanwhile Asalamalakim is going through motions with Maggie's hand. Maggie's hand is as limp as a fish, and probably as cold, despite the sweat, and she keeps trying to pull it back. It looks like Asalamalakim wants to shake hands but wants to do it fancy. Or maybe he don't know how people shake hands. Anyhow, he soon gives up on Maggie.

25   "Well," I say. "Dee."

---

*Arabic greeting meaning "Peace be with you" used by members of the Islamic faith.

"No, Mama," she says. "Not 'Dee,' Wangero Leewanika Kemanjo!"

"What happened to 'Dee'?" I wanted to know.

"She's dead," Wangero said. "I couldn't bear it any longer, being named after the people who oppress me."

"You know as well as me you was named after your aunt Dicie," I said. Dicie is my sister. She named Dee. We called her "Big Dee" after Dee was born.

30   "But who was *she* named after?" asked Wangero.

"I guess after Grandma Dee," I said.

"And who was she named after?" asked Wangero.

"Her mother," I said, and saw Wangero was getting tired. "That's about as far back as I can trace it," I said. Though, in fact, I probably could have carried it back beyond the Civil War through the branches.

"Well," said Asalamalakim, "there you are."

35   "Uhnnnh," I heard Maggie say.

"There I was not," I said, "before 'Dicie' cropped up in our family, so why should I try to trace it that far back?"

He just stood there grinning, looking down on me like somebody inspecting a Model A car. Every once in a while he and Wangero sent eye signals over my head.

"How do you pronounce this name?" I asked.

"You don't have to call me by it if you don't want to," said Wangero.

40   "Why shouldn't I?" I asked. "If that's what you want us to call you, we'll call you."

"I know it might sound awkward at first," said Wangero.

"I'll get used to it," I said. "Ream it out again."

Well, soon we got the name out of the way. Asalamalakim had a name twice as long and three times as hard. After I tripped over it two or three times he told me to just call him Hakim-a-barber. I wanted to ask him was he a barber, but I didn't really think he was, so I didn't ask.

"You must belong to those beef-cattle peoples down the road," I said. They said "Asalamalakim" when they met you, too, but they didn't shake hands. Always too busy: feeding the cattle, fixing the fences, putting up salt-lick shelters, throwing down hay. When the white folks poisoned some of the herd the men stayed up all night with rifles in their hands. I walked a mile and a half just to see the sight.

45   Hakim-a-barber said, "I accept some of their doctrines, but farming and raising cattle is not my style." (They didn't tell me, and I didn't ask, whether Wangero (Dee) had really gone and married him.)

We sat down to eat and right away he said he didn't eat collards and pork was unclean. Wangero, though, went on through the chitlins and corn bread, the greens and everything else. She talked a blue streak over the sweet potatoes. Everything delighted her. Even the fact that we still used the benches her daddy made for the table when we couldn't afford to buy chairs.

"Oh, Mama!" she cried. Then turned to Hakim-a-barber. "I never knew how lovely these benches are. You can feel the rump prints," she said, running her hands underneath her and along the bench. Then she gave a sigh and her hand closed over Grandma Dee's butter dish. "That's it!" she said. "I knew there was something I wanted to ask you if I could have." She jumped up from the table and went over in the corner where the churn stood, the milk in it clabber by now. She looked at the churn and looked at it.

"This churn top is what I need," she said. "Didn't Uncle Buddy whittle it out of a tree you all used to have?"

"Yes," I said.

50   "Uh huh," she said happily. "And I want the dasher, too."

"Uncle Buddy whittle that, too?" asked the barber.

Dee (Wangero) looked up at me.

"Aunt Dee's first husband whittled the dash," said Maggie so low you almost couldn't hear her. "His name was Henry, but they called him Stash."

"Maggie's brain is like an elephant's," Wangero said, laughing. "I can use the churn top as a center-piece for the alcove table," she said, sliding a plate over the churn, "and I'll think of something artistic to do with the dasher."

55   When she finished wrapping the dasher the handle stuck out. I took it for a moment in my hands. You didn't even have to look close to see where hands pushing the dasher up and down to make butter had left a kind of sink in the wood. In fact, there were a lot of small sinks; you could see where thumbs and fingers had sunk into the wood. It was beautiful light yellow wood, from a tree that grew in the yard where Big Dee and Stash had lived.

After dinner Dee (Wangero) went to the trunk at the foot of my bed and started rifling through it. Maggie hung back in the kitchen over the dish-pan. Out came Wangero with two quilts. They had been pieced by Grandma Dee and then Big Dee and me had hung them on the quilt frames on the front porch and quilted them. One was in the Lone Star pattern. The other was Walk Around the Mountain. In both of them were scraps of dresses Grandma Dee had worn fifty and more years ago. Bits and pieces of Grandpa Jarrell's Paisley shirts. And one teeny faded blue piece, about the size of a penny matchbox, that was from Great Grandpa Ezra's uniform that he wore in the Civil War.

"Mama," Wangero said sweet as a bird. "Can I have these old quilts?"

I heard something fall in the kitchen, and a minute later the kitchen door slammed.

"Why don't you take one or two of the others?" I asked. "These old things was just done by me and Big Dee from some tops your grandma pieced before she died."

60   "No," said Wangero. "I don't want those. They are stitched around the borders by machine."

"That'll make them last better," I said.

"That's not the point," said Wangero. "These are all pieces of dresses Grandma used to wear. She did all this stitching by hand. Imagine!" She held the quilts securely in her arms, stroking them.

"Some of the pieces, like those lavender ones, come from old clothes her mother handed down to her," I said, moving up to touch the quilts. Dee (Wangero) moved back just enough so that I couldn't reach the quilts. They already belonged to her.

"Imagine!" she breathed again, clutching them closely to her bosom.

65   "The truth is," I said, "I promised to give them quilts to Maggie, for when she marries John Thomas."

She gasped like a bee had stung her.

"Maggie can't appreciate these quilts!" she said. "She'd probably be backward enough to put them to everyday use."

"I reckon she would," I said. "God knows I been saving 'em for long enough with nobody using 'em. I hope she will!" I didn't want to bring up how I had offered Dee (Wangero) a quilt when she went away to college. Then she had told me they were old-fashioned, out of style.

"But they're *priceless!*" she was saying now, furiously; for she has a temper. "Maggie would put them on the bed and in five years they'd be in rags. Less than that!"

70   "She can always make some more," I said. "Maggie knows how to quilt."

Dee (Wangero) looked at me with hatred. "You just will not understand. The point is these quilts, *these* quilts!"

"Well," I said, stumped. "What would *you* do with them?"

"Hang them," she said. As if that was the only thing you *could* do with quilts.

Maggie by now was standing in the door. I could almost hear the sound her feet made as they scraped over each other.

75   "She can have them, Mama," she said, like somebody used to never winning anything, or having anything reserved for her. "I can 'member Grandma Dee without the quilts."

I looked at her hard. She had filled her bottom lip with checkerberry snuff and it gave her face a kind of dopey, hangdog look. It was Grandma Dee and Big Dee who taught her how to quilt herself. She stood there with her scarred hands hidden in the folds of her skirt. She looked at her sister with something like fear but she wasn't mad at her. This was Maggie's portion. This was the way she knew God to work.

When I looked at her like that something hit me in the top of my head and ran down to the soles of my feet. Just like when I'm in church and the spirit of God touches me and I get happy and shout. I did something I never had done before: hugged Maggie to me, then dragged her on into the room, snatched the quilts out of Miss Wangero's hands and dumped them into Maggie's lap. Maggie just sat there on my bed with her mouth open.

"Take one or two of the others," I said to Dee.

But she turned without a word and went out to Hakim-a-barber.

80   "You just don't understand," she said, as Maggie and I came out to the car.

"What don't I understand?" I wanted to know.

"Your heritage," she said. And then she turned to Maggie, kissed her, and said, "You ought to try to make something of yourself, too, Maggie. It's really a new day for us. But from the way you and Mama still live you'd never know it."

She put on some sunglasses that hid everything above the tip of her nose and her chin.

Maggie smiled; maybe at the sunglasses. But a real smile, not scared. After we watched the car dust settle I asked Maggie to bring me a dip of snuff. And then the two of us sat there just enjoying, until it was time to go in the house and go to bed.

INQUIRING FURTHER

1. What is your position on Mrs. Johnson's decision to give the quilts to Maggie? Do you think Mrs. Johnson made the right decision at the end of the story? Why or why not?

2. For a minute, entertain the opposite position. Can you think of reasons why someone might disagree with your perspective on Mrs. Johnson's decision?

3. What assumptions might someone who disagreed with your position on Mrs. Johnson's decision have? What beliefs would prompt them to disagree with you?

4. What assumptions underlie your own position on Mrs. Johnson's decision? What beliefs prompt you to feel the way you do?

Finding an Arguable Topic

Arguments are based on disagreement, so your approach must have some complexity if it is to serve as a topic for an argument. Suggesting that *Maggie is the most likeable character in Alice Walker's "Everyday Use"* would constitute more of an opinion than an argument. Similarly, claiming that *Hakim-a-barber represents an outsider in "Everyday Use"* would not provide many avenues for discussion—what is there to argue about? However, a claim like *heritage limits opportunities in "Everyday Use"* might make a good topic for an argument, allowing a writer to explore the positive and negative aspects of tradition in the story with some complexity.

To write an argument, you must look past the obvious to find an angle that illuminates and acknowledges the many facets of a work. Instead of saying that *Maggie is the most likeable character*, you might argue that *the narrator's choice at the end to give the quilts to Maggie emphasizes family over African traditions*. To make this argument, you would need to address conflicts between family and African traditions. You would need to prepare for objections that might be raised to this perspective—are Mrs. Johnson and Maggie (and the personal traditions they represent) really presented entirely favorably? Are the traditions of the Johnson family different from those of Africa?

Topics that can be challenged lend themselves to arguments because they require writers to justify their way of thinking and to support that justification with credible evidence. Initially, these multi-faceted topics might seem to be more work than a simple "yes or no" discussion of the story. However, as you explore you will see how anticipating alternative possibilities and responding to them with your own explanations will give you more to write about and make your essay stronger in the long run.

☑ CHECKLIST FOR FINDING AN ARGUABLE TOPIC

- ☐ **Avoid topics that suggest something obvious** about the story or something that resembles a factual statement. Facts provide little room for argument.

- ☐ **Steer clear of topics that resemble opinions**. Refine your impressions and opinions into interpretations based on the evidence in the work.

- ☐ **Choose topics that can be challenged** or that challenge alternative approaches. Where there is mutual agreement, even about a theme, character, or message, there is little room for argument.

- ☐ **Anticipate objections when selecting a topic**. If you can find no objections to your approach, it probably lacks complexity. If you discover overwhelming objections, you may want to rethink your topic. An ideal topic will allow you to acknowledge and respond to legitimate objections as a way of building your own case.

- ☐ **Be sure that your topics can be discussed with evidence** from the text or with information you might gather through research. A complex and arguable topic will not be of much benefit if you cannot find ample evidence to support it.

Exercise 5.1   *Identifying Arguable Topics*

Working with a group of fellow students (or on your own if your instructor prefers), explore potential topics for arguing about "Everyday Use." Begin by selecting someone to keep track of the group's work (or preparing to take notes on your own).

1. Consider these topics:
   - "Everyday Use" demonstrates the importance of traditions to African Americans.
   - Names in "Everyday Use" represent tensions between family heritage and African heritage.
   - Quilts symbolize family history in "Everyday Use."
   - "Everyday Use" highlights the dangers of resisting change.
   - Family identity is maintained by women in "Everyday Use."
   - Dee is the central character in "Everyday Use."

2. For each topic, respond to the following prompts:
   - First, look at each topic and decide whether you believe it to be an arguable topic.
   - If you believe the topic to be arguable, write a sentence or two detailing an alternative position to the one listed in the topic.
   - If you do not believe the topic to be arguable, write a revision of the sentence that would make the topic arguable.

3. Develop two additional arguable topics on your own.

4. Look over all of the topics you have been considering. Select from these topics one that you believe would be the most useful for constructing an argument about "Everyday Use." Write two or three sentences explaining your decision.

Establishing Authority as a Writer

Others are more likely to accept your arguments if they believe you are knowledgeable, fair-minded, and careful. You can establish this credibility by presenting detailed research and discussion of a work to readers, composing with a reasonable tone that respects alternative perspectives, and maintaining a high standard of correctness in your writing.

When it comes to being knowledgeable about your topic, there are no shortcuts. You must invest the time and energy into reading and understanding the work before you can argue about it with authority. Of course, this requires a process of inquiry like the one we have been discussing throughout this book. You can begin thinking and writing about a work right away. However, as the process evolves, you should develop a closeness with the work that prepares you to discuss it in detail. You can also conduct research to help establish your authority (see Chapter 4).

Careful attention to detail will help establish your authority. Consider the passage below from an essay on "Everyday Use."

Through names, "Everyday Use" illustrates the conflicts between African

heritage and family heritage. Ultimately, names in the story privilege the

family heritage represented by Mrs. Johnson and Maggie. Initially, Mrs.

Johnson refers to her daughter by her given name, "Dee." When Dee

announces that she has changed her name to "Wangero Leewanika Kemanjo,"

Mrs. Johnson is willing to consider this African heritage. She refers to her

daughter as "Wangero" and tells her, "'If that's what you want us to call you,

we'll call you'" (139). As tensions emerge between the two heritages, the names

begin to blur. When referring to Muslim doctrines, Mrs. Johnson combines the

names using parentheses: "Wangero (Dee)." As Dee asks about family items

like the churn top, Mrs. Johnson again uses parentheses, but this time

emphasizes her daughter's given name: "Dee (Wangero)." As the story

concludes, Mrs. Johnson resumes calling her daughter "Dee," emphasizing

how family connections take precedence over African heritage in the story.

The writer here shows that she has spent some time thinking about how names relate to family tradition. She has tracked the evolution of names in the story. She also invests the effort in spelling out her points with details that will convince a reader that she is knowledgeable and willing to share her ideas with others.

You can also conduct research to help establish your authority. Consider this passage that incorporates ideas culled from two essays on "Everyday Use."

Essay on "Everyday Use"

Through names, "Everyday Use" illustrates the conflicts between

African heritage and family heritage. As Helga Hoel argues, "[the] names

Dee bases her new-found identity on resemble Kikuyu names, but they are all

[misspelled] . . . Dee has names representing the whole East African region.

Or more likely, she is confused and has only superficial knowledge of Africa

and all it stands for" (par. 12). This confusion illustrates the tensions

between recovering an African heritage and maintaining more recent family

connections. As Barbara Christian explains, "during the 1960s Walker

criticized the tendency among some African Americans to give up the names

their parents gave them—names which embodied the history of their recent past—for African names that did not relate to a single person they knew"

(13). Names demonstrate the power of both African and family heritage but

the confusion associated with the names Wangero and Hakim-a-barber

emphasizes the central role family heritage plays in the story.

This writer makes similar points, but uses evidence in the form of quotations from essays to back them up. Referring to these published sources also illustrates that the writer has taken the time to learn about the work. Equally important, these references suggest that the writer's perspective is informed by the ideas of others, that the writer is fair-minded and willing to entertain interpretations that run counter to her own. You can also establish this sense of fair-mindedness by responding to objections to your argument (discussed below).

Finally, both writers carefully present their ideas. They properly cite material they have introduced into their papers. They have revised and edited their writing to make it clear and correct. Taking the time to edit, proofread, and format your papers (see Chapter 8) helps to establish your credibility by showing that you care about your ideas.

EXPLORING CLAIMS, REASONS, AND ASSUMPTIONS

Argument has a close connection with logic, with thinking that moves from point A, to point B, to point C in an objective and predictable way. Logic can be used to try to "prove" something to be true—a formal argument might be *A: All dogs bark; B: Rover is a dog; therefore, C: Rover barks*. In this argument, a **claim** is made: *Rover barks*. Two **reasons** are provided to convince us of the claim: *All dogs bark*; and *Rover is a dog*.

But such proofs are less concrete than they would at first seem. Perhaps there are some dogs that do not bark, or perhaps Rover is a stuffed animal (not really a dog). We can also see the limits of such formal logic by constructing arguments that make no sense: *A: All dogs bark; B: Rover is barking; therefore C: Rover is a dog*. What if Rover is a seal or a teacher with a bad cough?

While this kind of formal logic is limited, it can help us understand something of the process of argument. First, it reveals that we cannot simply make a claim and assume that others will accept it. We must instead provide convincing reasons that will prompt others to believe the claim. Additionally, we must offer **evidence** that supports those reasons. We can show that Rover is indeed a kind of dog that barks; if we can provide that evidence, then the argument will be more convincing.

Further, logic prompts us to consider the **assumptions** that might be hidden beneath the reasons that ask us to believe something. For instance, the second example (*A: All dogs bark; B: Rover is barking; therefore C: Rover is a dog*) falls apart because there is an assumption that must be made to get from B to C (the assumption that *everything that barks must be a dog*). As readers and writers, learning to identify and explore these assumptions makes us critical consumers and producers of arguments.

When we write about literature, we can make similar use of formal elements of argument—as long as we understand their limitations and our purpose when composing. We are not out to "prove" the truth of a statement, but to make claims about our understanding and to convince others that our claims are worth believing. We do this by providing compelling reasons, considering assumptions under-lying our positions, and supporting what we say with evidence. We also must remember that literature has an emotional component. Our responses to litera-ture should still appeal to our interests and senses; our explanations of those responses will benefit from the reasoned structures that argument can provide.

Our claims should relate to the thesis we wish to explore in our argument. About "Everyday Use," we might start with a thesis like *when Mrs. Johnson gives the quilts to Maggie, she privileges family traditions and identity over African heritage.* We could then support that thesis with claims like *quilts uniquely represent family identity* (claim one), and *family identity is based on everyday activities* (claim two).

These claims, however, cannot stand on their own. Take the claim that *quilts uniquely represent family identity.* To convince others of the claim, we need to pro-vide **supporting reasons** that explain why the claim is believable. We might suggest that *the fabric used in the quilts symbolizes family history,* and *the stitch-ing symbolizes connections between generations.*

We might also explore the assumption beneath these two reasons and our claim. We can agree that fabric symbolizes family history and that stitching connects gen-erations, but what makes this a unique representation? Beneath our claim is an assumption that *quilts are unique in representing family identity.* We might explain this assumption by suggesting that *the arrangement of stitched fabric within the quilts tells a story,* giving them a unique way of presenting family identity.

We can represent the structure that our argument is taking by listing the the-sis, claim, supporting reasons, and assumptions:

Thesis: when Mrs. Johnson gives the quilts to Maggie, she privileges family traditions and identity over African heritage

Claim: quilts uniquely represent family identity

Reason: the fabric used in the quilts symbolizes family history

Reason: the stitching symbolizes connections between generations

Assumption: the arrangement of stitched fabric within the quilts tells a story in a unique way

Like an outline, the components of our argument can guide us as we draft the body of our paper. Additionally, by considering their relationships with our the-sis, we can be assured that the claims, reasons, and assumptions we discuss will help to convince our audience of the value of our overall approach.

Tutorial for understanding arguments

Exercise 5.2   *Supporting a Claim*

Working with a group of fellow students (or on your own if your instructor prefers), develop a list of reasons and explore assumptions to support a claim. Begin by selecting a person to keep track of the group's work (or preparing to take notes on your own).

1. First, consider the claim that *everyday activities represent shared traditions.* (You can also develop a claim of your own based on your understanding of "Everyday Use.")

2. Consider reasons that might support this claim. List the most significant reason as a sentence.

3. Think of another reason that follows from or supports the first reason that you have listed. Write a sentence that states your second reason.

4. Inquire into the assumptions that lie beneath the reasons you have stated above. An assumption might connect the reasons to one another or to the claim you are investigating. Once you have discovered an assumption that supports your reasons and claim, write a sentence that lists the assumption as a statement.

Providing Evidence

Evidence supports the claims and reasons we present in our argument. When writing about literature, evidence primarily comes in the form of **examples from works** we are discussing, quotations from **other readers**, or references to **contextual information** that illuminates the work.

Evidence from Works

Evidence from works should be directly related to the statements we seek to support. In supporting our statement that *the fabric used in the quilts symbolizes family history* we might cite the passage listing the pieces of fabric used in the quilt:

> In both of them were scraps of dresses Grandma Dee had worn fifty and more years ago. Bits and pieces of Grandpa Jarrell's Paisley shirts. And one teeny faded blue piece, about the size of a penny matchbox, that was from Great Grandpa Ezra's uniform that he wore in the Civil War. (139)

This citation provides compelling evidence to support our statement that the fabric pieces symbolize family history. If we wanted to bolster our point about stitching, however, we would need to find a more relevant example.

We also need to discuss carefully evidence that we use. If we cited the passage stating that "It was Grandma Dee and Big Dee who taught [Maggie] how to quilt herself" we would need to explain how the example relates to our point that the stitching represents connections between generations—we cannot assume that the example itself makes our point for us. We could also point out that Dee refuses the other quilts because they are "stitched around the borders by machine" and that Dee explains "these are all pieces of dresses Grandma used to wear. She did all this stitching by hand. Imagine!" In selecting quotations we need to be thorough and precise.

We must also be careful and fair. In the last example, for instance, the stitching Dee refers to is part of the dresses that are pieced into the quilt, rather than the stitches that hold the pieces of the quilt together. This is a subtle point, but to be fair we should explain that Dee identifies hand stitching in the scraps of dresses, not in the quilt. We can still claim that the threads that tie those pieces into the quilt connect generations, but this connection comes through a second act of stitching.

Evidence from Others

We can also support an argument by citing what others have said about a work. Again, we must ensure that our use of this evidence is both relevant and fair. For instance, an essay exploring the role of quilts in Alice Walker's *The Color Purple* might be relevant for our argument, but we would need to show our readers the relationship between the two works and not imply that a quotation about one could simply be applied to the other. We would also need to provide detailed discussion of the evidence that we integrate into our argument—consider using at least twice as much of your own words and explanations as those of others.

Additionally, when using others as sources of evidence, we must evaluate those sources, looking for potential credibility problems. An article in an online journal found through a library Web site carries a high level of authority based on its source. An essay found on a paper mill Web site carries little or no authority. In between these two extremes lies a range of sources that may provide strong evidence for our arguments. Avoid articles that do not consider the complexities of a topic or that fail to cite additional sources to support the claims that they make. Also, look for more than one source of information as you integrate the ideas of others into your arguments. You can spot biases and problems with credibility by conducting enough research to allow you to balance and compare the sources you use. (For more on finding and evaluating sources, see Chapter 4.)

Tutorial for evaluating sources

Contextual Evidence

Historical or biographical information about an author can also bolster an argument. Concerning "Everyday Use," for instance, we might discover that Alice Walker has traveled to Africa where she received an African name, or that Walker has written about quilts and about African-American identity. We could also investigate some of the cultural movements represented in "Everyday Use." We could discover historical parallels that shed light on the characters of Dee and Hakim-a-barber (and Mrs. Johnson and Maggie). We could learn about movements during the 1960s to recover African heritage or to collect and display artifacts that preserve cultural identity. All of this contextual information can be found through research.

Again, we must evaluate the credibility of this background information. Further, we must be careful not to let contextual evidence over-determine our interpretations of the story. Biographical information about Walker, for instance, can illuminate the characters, but it does not allow us to claim that the story depicts Walker's experience or that Walker thinks or feels a certain way. "Everyday Use" remains a story about the Johnsons and about themes of family and identity (among others). Locating compelling contextual information that illuminates those themes is not the same as saying the story is about that evidence. (For more on relating literature to its contexts, see Chapter 13.)

☑CHECKLIST FOR USING EVIDENCE

☐ **Draw carefully upon the work** you are discussing for evidence. Even if your argument relies on the interpretations of others or contextual information, you must connect your statements with the work itself and find support in the work for the points you make.

☐ **Learn to be a successful researcher** to discover the best evidence for your arguments. Understand the benefits and skills of library research and learn to locate resources available on the Internet. Make informed judgments about the sources you discover in the library and on the Internet.

☐ **Select the most relevant evidence** for your argument. Use passages from works that support your claims. Select research sources that speak directly to the works or topics you are arguing about. Spell out missing connections between the evidence you use and the statements you make.

- ☐ **Treat evidence fairly**. Be diligent in your reading of evidence and do not jump to conclusions about how evidence supports your points. Further, be sure not to ignore counter-evidence that can potentially undermine your argument.

- ☐ **Discuss the evidence you use**. Compose approximately twice as much text in your own words for every instance when you integrate evidence into your argument. Explain the significance of the evidence and discuss connections with your thesis, claims, and reasons.

- ☐ **Integrate the evidence you use smoothly** into the text of your argument. Compose introductory tags that demonstrate where the evidence comes from. Watch out for plagiarism. Use quotation and citation methods carefully to distinguish your evidence from your own writing. (See pages 946–47 for more on avoiding plagiarism and pages 179–83 for more on integrating quotations into your work.)

- ☐ **Evaluate the evidence that you use**. Consider the source and authority of your evidence. Look for biases within sources and consult a range of sources to fully understand the reliability of your evidence.

- ☐ **Do not allow contextual evidence (or the interpretations of others) to over-determine your argument**. Learn to consider critically the relationships between history, biography, and literature (see Chapter 13).

ADDRESSING OPPOSING POINTS OF VIEW

In an argument, we build a case point-by-point by stating a claim and then providing reasons and evidence to support that claim. Objections can be raised to our claims, the reasons that support our claims, and our evidence (as well as to any underlying assumptions beneath our claims and reasons). Additionally, people might disagree with our thesis as a whole. For our arguments to be convincing, we must address these possible objections head on by **anticipating, rebutting**, and **accommodating** opposing points of view.

Anticipating Opposing Points of View

As we compose arguments, we should determine where objections to our points are likely to arise. We can begin by considering our audience and the kinds of assumptions they hold. If we are making a statement about family, does it rely on a set of unique beliefs or is it something that most people are likely to agree about? How can we characterize our audience, and based on this characterization, which of our claims, reasons, and evidence is likely to be challenged by our audience?

We can also work through an outline of our argument as a way of anticipating potential objections. We could develop an argument around the claim that *family identity is based on everyday activities* and perhaps support the claim by showing how everyday activities bring family members together and create shared knowledge. We could sketch out a list of our reasons and assumptions as a way of anticipating objections to our argument:

Claim: family identity is based on everyday activities

   Possible objection: the disputed quilts are not really everyday items

Reason: everyday activities bring individuals together

   Evidence: quilting

      Possible objection: not all everyday activities bring connections—Dee's reading to the family is an exception

Reason: common experiences create shared knowledge

   Evidence: benches and other worn items

      Possible objection: familiar items go unnoticed by family

Assumption: shared knowledge creates family identity

   Evidence: outsider status of Hakim-a-barber

      Possible objection: outside forces also influence family identity

This outline does not represent a comprehensive list of ways we might argue that *family identity is based on everyday activities,* nor does it cover every objection. It does, however, help us anticipate possible objections so that we will be better able to rebut or accommodate them as we draft our argument.

Rebutting Opposing Points of View

Anticipating objections is only half the battle. To argue successfully, we must also address those objections directly in our writing. One strategy is to take issue with an objection or with the reasons or evidence that might support that objection. For instance, a possible objection to our claim that *everyday activities bring family members together* might be that *when Dee reads to Maggie and Mrs. Johnson it really pushes the family further apart.* We can refute this objection by pointing out that Dee's reading does not qualify as an everyday activity—it takes place apart from the daily work of the household and does not span generations like the other activities of the story.

Composing our rebuttal prompts us to think through these issues and refines our argument. In some cases we might directly challenge the opposing point of view—especially if we are working with the interpretations of others with whom we disagree. We might say that,

> arguments suggesting that shared activities do not create a connection between individuals fail to recognize the nature of the activities taking place. When activities involve a shared sense of work and span several generations, they do indeed inspire a sense of connection between family members.

We could also write a rebuttal that defuses the possible objection without challenging the opposing point of view directly. We could say

> Although not every activity brings the individuals of the family together, those that involve the daily maintenance of the household and that span several generations have a unique way of bonding individuals.

Such a refined statement shows that we are willing to entertain opposing points of view, but that we have focused our argument on the specific claims we want to make.

Accommodating Opposing Points of View

We need not refute every possible objection to our argument. In fact, were we to do so, our readers would likely find our approach one-sided and unconvincing. We can accommodate (acknowledge and concede to) smaller objections as we make our points. For instance, we might concede that *outside forces shape identity*, as is evidenced by Dee's relationship with the family—in fact, it would be hard to argue against the claim. But acknowledging the role of outside forces need not negate our claim about family identity. We argue that family identity is still shaped by shared knowledge, while we accept that individuals are also shaped by their external circumstances.

Accommodation also comes into play when we consider objections to our thesis as a whole. To our suggestion that *when Mrs. Johnson gives the quilts to Maggie, she privileges family traditions over African heritage*, one might respond that Mrs. Johnson is really acting to change the family traditions with this gesture—if Mrs. Johnson were to keep with the old identity and traditions, she would allow Dee to take the quilts, rather than choosing to give them to Maggie.

Because literature allows for more than one viable interpretation, we must advocate for our position while acknowledging those points of view that offer worthwhile alternatives. Here we might acknowledge the moment of change that takes place at the end of the story but suggest that the decision (while representing a change) results in keeping the quilts at the Johnson home and therefore carries more force in its emphasis on the family tradition.

However, objections and alternative interpretations can also demand that we change our approach (something we will learn more about as we study the writing process in the next chapters). It might be that we need to go back and rethink our interpretation in terms of this moment of growth. We might compose a new thesis that says, *when Mrs. Johnson gives the quilts to Maggie, she highlights the importance of growth and change in maintaining family traditions and identity*.

We would then find ourselves developing a new set of claims and reasons that could be used to argue the importance of change—we might look at Maggie's stature in the family, levels of change in Dee and Mrs. Johnson, or instances of positive or negative change. Fully accommodating this new perspective will take some work; however, if the objection is significant, our argument and our understanding of the story will both be made stronger by responding to the alternative possibility.

✔ CHECKLIST FOR RESPONDING TO OBJECTIONS

☐ **Anticipate opposing points of view** as you plan and draft your arguments. Consider any specific claims, reasons, or evidence that you provide, and then ask how each of these might be questioned. Also imagine objections to your thesis as a whole.

☐ **Assess the audience for your argument**. Consider the values they are likely to hold and how those values might influence their reception of your argument. Determine how claims, reasons, and evidence can be adjusted to appeal to the audience.

☐ **Create an outline that lists the major claims, reasons, and evidence** you will use in your argument. For each item, note possible objections. Sketch out possible responses you might offer to any objections you uncover.

☐ **Rebut objections that unreasonably undermine your argument**. Refute these objections concretely if you are placing your position in direct opposition to another. Defuse these objections if you can, to dismiss them and focus on the core of your own position.

☐ **Accommodate objections that do not undermine your own position**. Show relationships when opposing positions are able to coexist. Concede points that are solid when they do not completely undercut your own position.

☐ **Rethink your thesis when needed**. Maintain a posture of inquiry as you consider objections. When opposing perspectives demand a change in approach, adjust your argument to address these alternatives.

Exercise 5.3   *Responding to Objections*

Working with a group of fellow students (or on your own if your instructor prefers), respond to the following claims about "Everyday Use." Begin by selecting a person to keep track of the group's work (or preparing to take notes on your own).

1. Consider the following claims:

   ● The reference to Johnny Carson and other evidence reveals that Mrs. Johnson actually longs for the new identity that Wangero (Dee) represents.

   ● The quilts do not symbolize everyday use; instead, they are cherished, uncommon items.

   ● The sudden decision to give the blankets to Maggie is unrealistic.

   ● Mrs. Johnson, Maggie, and the family culture they represent are portrayed in a negative light.

2. For each claim, assume you are arguing that *the story emphasizes family over African traditions*, and then respond to the following prompts:

   ● First, how would you rebut each claim? Is there counter-evidence that can question the claim? Can you show the claim to be unrelated to your position that *the story emphasizes family over African traditions*? Are there assumptions or reasons needed to support the claim that you might question? Use these considerations, and then write a two or three sentence rebuttal that refutes the claim.

   ● Next, how would you accommodate the claim? Can the claim stand alongside your own position? If so, how are the two positions related? Does the claim completely undermine your position? If so, can you concede the point while maintaining the integrity of your argument? Use these considerations, then write a two or three sentence statement that accommodates the claim, or write one sentence that revises your position based on the opposing claim.

   ● Finally, would it be better to rebut or accommodate the claim? Why? Write two or three sentences explaining your answer.

Answer all three sets of these questions in writing as you refer to the claims above.

6

Prewriting to Develop Ideas

> Writing is an exploration. You start from nothing and
> learn as you go.
>
> — *E. L. Doctorow*

We often use words like exploration or investigation to describe the act of writing. Imagining writing as an organic process of discovery sounds somewhat corny, but there is no denying that often the best compositions evolve when we write to learn. In this book we apply that process of inquiry to literature, suggesting that we can use writing and thinking to develop not only a personal relationship with literature but also a critical understanding that evolves as we interpret and write about works.

Prewriting lends itself to both of these goals. Activities like **freewriting, listing,** and **answering questions** help us identify our personal responses to literature. **Researching, clustering ideas, outlining,** and **brainstorming with others** allow us to extend our personal responses with objective analysis and argument. Of course, activities like responding and interpreting are intertwined, sometimes taking place simultaneously. Prewriting generally helps us move from reaction toward reflection, but the processes will vary from writer to writer and task to task.

As we think more about prewriting, we will refer to two poems, "Embrace," by Billy Collins, and "A Blessing," by James Wright.

BILLY COLLINS

In 2002 Billy Collins (born in 1941) was appointed to his second term as the Poet Laureate (the official poet appointed to represent a nation) for the United States. As Poet Laureate, he has emphasized the fun and accessible nature of poetry. He created a project called Poetry 180 *that provides a poem a day for each day of the school year. Collins has published seven collections of poems. His work is witty, often playful, but ultimately addresses serious topics. "Embrace" is taken from the collection* The Apple that Astonished Paris, *published in 1988.*

Embrace

You know the parlor trick.
Wrap your arms around your own body
and from the back it looks like
someone is embracing you,
5   her hands grasping your shirt,
her fingernails teasing your neck.

From the front it is another story.
You never looked so alone,
your crossed elbows and screwy grin.
10   You could be waiting for a tailor
to fit you for a straitjacket,
one that would hold you really tight.

JAMES WRIGHT

James Wright (1927–1980) grew up as the son of working-class parents.
In high school, he suffered emotional distress and skipped a year of school.
He went on to college and graduate school, where he studied with the poet
Theodore Roethke. His first book of poetry was published in 1957, and his
subsequent collections influenced the state of poetry with their movement
away from formalism and toward free verse. He continued to teach and
write poetry until his death from cancer in 1980. "A Blessing" is taken from
the collection The Branch Will Not Break, *published in 1963.*

A Blessing

Just off the highway to Rochester, Minnesota,
Twilight bounds softly forth on the grass.
And the eyes of those two Indian ponies
Darken with kindness.
5   They have come gladly out of the willows
To welcome my friend and me.
We step over the barbed wire into the pasture
Where they have been grazing all day, alone.
They ripple tensely, they can hardly contain their
happiness
10   That we have come.
They bow shyly as wet swans. They love each other.
There is no loneliness like theirs.
At home once more,
They begin munching the young tufts of spring in the
darkness.
15   I would like to hold the slenderer one in my arms,

Garrison
Keillor
reading
"A
Blessing"

For she has walked over to me
And nuzzled my left hand.
She is black and white,
20   Her mane falls wild on her forehead,
And the light breeze moves me to caress her long ear
That is delicate as the skin over a girl's wrist.
Suddenly I realize
That if I stepped out of my body I would break
25   Into blossom.

FREEWRITING

We have looked at freewriting in our introduction and you can refer to the checklist on page 7 for more ideas. Remember that freewriting is personal. When freewriting, record and explore your own impressions, giving little thought to the mechanics of writing. Simply write ideas out as sentences or statements, letting them flow one after another. Freewriting is a simple, low stress, personal process that all of us can accomplish.

However, we can apply the process of freewriting in different ways as our engagement with literature evolves. For instance, we might explore a personal response to the two poems above by freewriting. To explore your personal response, ask questions like, *Do I like this work? How does it make me feel? What does it remind me of?* Be honest if something about it puzzles, dismays, worries, offends, or otherwise strikes you. The sample below represents one writer's freewriting about the two poems:

> That first poem is tricky. It mentions parlor trick. It seems so simple, just a kind of playful joke. But also about loneliness. It makes me feel like I don't quite get it all yet. There may be more to it. Also kind of weird with the self involvement. The trick is that you try to be two people at once. It makes me think of isolation. Sad to say, I've tried it—not at a party though. The second one feels more cerebral. If that is the right word. Horses. I'm not much for horses. The last line is pretty powerful but kind of hokie—hokie pokey? More of a peaceful feeling in the second one—definitely more positive. The main character seems a bit gushy. It also feels like it has some strangeness going on between the horses and man. I guess it's a man. Probably. Talks about caressing and a girl's wrist. The ending feels powerful. Maybe the build up. The first poem feels edgier. I like that.

When freewriting, you might explore your personal reaction to characters or events. You could consider your own background. If you know a little or a lot about horses or if you have ever tried the straightjacket parlor trick you can bring that experience into your exploration.

You might next direct your thoughts toward the works you are considering, as in this sample:

> I need to figure out what is going on in the second poem. The horses are
>
> a key. Might be a key. More about nature than horses maybe. They are kind.
>
> They are happy. But also lonely. Why lonely? What is the line—no loneliness
>
> like theirs. Weird. Happy and lonely. Why? Human contact. Do horses really
>
> need human contact? How would I know? It may be the man and the horses
>
> are key. The man also has a companion. Hmmn. Why does he want to join the
>
> horses then? The companion isn't mentioned much. Only called a friend. He
>
> wants to join the horses instead. Or also. The last line—about stepping out of
>
> his body—that's a key. He definitely wants to join the horses. Why?

Here the writer begins to train his thinking on Wright's "A Blessing." The process, though, is similar to that seen in the previous sample. He is asking questions and transcribing ideas directly into writing.

You can also apply freewriting to specific passages, as below:

> OK, I want to see what is happening in the last line. The man wants
>
> to step out of his body. Out of his skin? Isn't skin mentioned? The horse is
>
> like skin. The ear is like the skin of a girl's wrist. Hmmm. That seems
>
> kind of sexual. But it's a horse. The horse is like a girl. Weird. Or feeling
>
> the horse's ear is like feeling a girl's wrist. Really, that makes sense I
>
> guess. So the horse is compared to the human and we get this picture of
>
> human skin that stands for the horse. This line really sets up the next
>
> one. Stepping out of his body. If he does he will blossom. That seems to be
>
> more like saying he will step out of his skin. And the skin of the human
>
> is connected to the skin of the horse. Blossom may be more like transform
>
> instead of like a flower.

Here the writer is concerned with the last few lines of the poem. As he thinks about the passage, his personal response is refined by the intellectual measuring taking place as he moves closer to an interpretation. His freewriting, however, remains a device for exploration.

Exercise 6.1   *Computer Freewriting to Refine a Personal Response*

This exercise prompts you to ignore possible revisions and mechanical issues in your writing.

1. Begin by reading again Billy Collins's "Embrace." (You can choose another work from the book if you wish.) Do not stop and investigate the poem completely. Just read it through until you have a sense that you have taken it all in.

2. Open a word processing file on your computer. Place your cursor at the top of the page.

Prewriting resources

3. Prepare yourself to write by considering these three prompts:

- What is your personal response to the poem? How does it make you feel? (This question asks you to not focus on the poem, but instead to write freely about your own impressions.)

- What can you say about the poem as a whole? (This question asks you to write freely about the overall poem.)

- What do you think of specific passages or images in the poem? (This question asks you to write freely about the details of the work.)

4. Once you understand the progression your freewriting should take (moving from personal response, to response to the poem, to exploration of the details) you are ready to begin.

5. With your word processor file opened and your cursor at the top of the page, turn off the power or dim the brightness on your monitor so that you cannot see your computer screen. With your screen off, write freely for five minutes following the progression outlined above.

LISTING

Lists provide another form of prewriting. We can list ideas as they come to mind, not bothering to test or extend them. Or, we may develop more focused lists that respond to specific goals, listing all of the traits of a character, for instance. In both cases, the lists will be meant for our own purposes, to help generate and organize ideas.

A list may evolve initially in terms of what takes place in the work, as in this brainstorming list for "Embrace":

> You–poem addressed to reader
> Seen from the back
> Someone embracing
> A male?
> From the front
> Alone
> Tailor–outside person

Listing   157

Straightjacket-mental problems
Really tight-emotional loneliness

Or, lists can have a more specific purpose, as in this list on feelings in "Embrace":

Embrace-love
Grasping-passion
Teasing-playful or hurtful?
Alone-loneliness
Waiting-anxiety
Insanity-how severe is the problem?
Longing-shared with reader?

This list begins to focus on a particular aspect of the work, emotions, but still allows the author to explore freely. He includes items as they come to mind and even adds questions related to items in the list.

Lists can be as extensive and interrelated as you wish. The list below explores the relationship between the two poems and could easily serve as a framework for developing a more formal comparison of the works:

"Embrace"

Deals with emotions
Shows an ideal-love and passion
Deals with deceit or trickery
Shows a reality-loneliness
Related to gender?

"A Blessing"

Deals with emotions
Shows an ideal-but missing something
Horses have love but long for humans
Humans long for contact with horses
Ending brings humans and horses together

Comparisons

Humans vs. Humans and Horses
Loneliness and Longing
Last Lines-despair vs. transformation?

Questions

Does gender of speaker in poems matter?

Note how this writer has included unanswered questions in his list. Prewriting should remain a process of exploration, even as it helps you refine your thinking about a work. You can also develop your own strategies for using lists. You may find that lists help you open avenues for inquiry, or that lists easily lead to outlines (see below) that can help you get ready to write.

ASKING QUESTIONS

Sometimes responding to predefined questions can provide a better sense of a work and of how to begin writing.

Fill-in-the-Blank Questions

Here are some fill-in-the-blank questions you might find useful. (Note that many of these will be helpful for figuring out your own goals as a writer.)

Evaluation Questions

- What are the characteristics of _____?
- How would I define _____?
- How would others define _____?
- What are the most concrete examples of _____?
- How was _____ viewed in its original context?
- When do people get confused about _____?

Analysis Questions

- What group does _____ belong to?
- How can _____ be divided into parts?
- Which parts of _____ are the most significant and why?
- What will happen after _____?
- What must have happened before _____?

Synthesis Questions

- What is _____ similar to?
- What is _____ different from?
- What similarity or difference about _____ is most important?
- What patterns does _____ reveal?
- What is _____ superior to?
- What is _____ inferior to?

Social Context Questions

- What have others said about _____?
- When people discuss _____ what do they agree about?
- When people discuss _____ what do they disagree about?
- What facts do I know about _____?
- How is _____ portrayed by others?
- Who can I talk to about _____?

Asking any of these questions can help you gather ideas for writing. In fact, the best strategy is to use questions as prompts for freewriting, creating lists, or perhaps composing a paragraph that can become part of a larger essay. So, for instance, if you asked *What are the characteristics of Billy Collins's "Embrace?"* you might develop a list like this:

> It is somewhat humorous
> It directly addresses the reader–you
> It presents two views of the same person
> It uses free verse
> It saves its main metaphor for the end
> It does not reveal the gender of the speaker
> It closes with a concern for the speaker's sanity

This list could then form the basis of a freewrite or lead you to a specific topic or approach to the poem.

The Journalist's Questions

You can also use the questions frequently employed by journalists to help you begin a writing project. You can ask these questions about a work or about a writing task.

Who: Who are the main characters in a work? Who has something to say about the work? Who wrote the work? Who would be interested in the work? Who are you writing for?

What: What kind of work are you exploring? What happens in the work? What messages are emphasized in the work? What is your assignment? What must you do to fulfill your assignment?

Where: Where do the events in the work take place? Where was the work written or published? Where in the work can you locate key scenes? Where can you get more information?

When: When do the events in the work take place? When was the work written or published? Which events happen as a result of others in the work? When will you accomplish the tasks for your assignment?

Why: Why do events in the work take place? Why do characters in the work behave the way they do? Why might the author have written the work? Why have you selected this work to write about? Why might an approach to the work be of interest to others?

How: How does the work deliver its message? How are events, characters, and themes related in the work? How do you feel about the work? How can you refine that feeling into an interpretation? How will others view your approach? How will you complete your assignment?

Again, the key is to turn one or more of these questions into an activity that will allow you to begin writing to explore.

EXPLORING IDEAS WITH OTHERS

Investigating the ideas of others will help you formulate your own thinking. The key is maintaining an awareness of the nature of this kind of brainstorming, of its strengths and weaknesses. Two solid options for exploring ideas with others are investigating what others have said in **Internet conversations** and participating in **online class discussions.** (For more on investigating Internet conversations, see pages 120–21.)

You will most likely participate in online discussions by exchanging messages with classmates using forums that are part of a course Web site. The screen shot in Figure 6.1 demonstrates an online conversation conducted by the members of a class. Our discussion is keyed to the numbers in the screen shot.

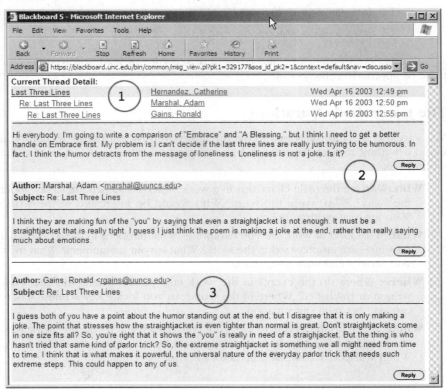

FIGURE 6.1 Brainstorming through Online Discussion

1. **Threads:** Discussions held with classmates will evolve as threads of conversation. The **thread** has a subject that provides a sense of the scope and topic under discussion and a series of replies that build on the initial message. Here we see an initial message posted by Catherine Hernandez. The nested responses indicate that Adam Marshal has responded to Catherine and that Ronald Gains has responded to Adam.

2. **An initial query:** In her message, Catherine asks about humor in the last three lines of "Embrace." When you initiate a thread of conversation with classmates, asking for opinions can open up the discussion. Catherine's message, however, is clear about the kinds of information she seeks. Postings that ask classmates to conduct research for you or that pose simple yes or no questions are liable to produce very little productive exploration. Instead, try to pose open-ended questions that will help others discuss real concerns about the work.

3. **Healthy debate:** Ronald's response follows Adam's message, but he refers to the earlier message posted by Catherine as well. If you are one of the later respondents, take time to read the other messages in the thread of discussion to understand the questions at play and to avoid repeating what has already been said. Notice also how Ronald does not personalize the debate about humor in the poem. Instead of questioning Adam, he addresses the issue of humor. Healthy debate requires good faith efforts to understand and respond to the ideas under discussion.

When conversing with classmates electronically you will write less formally than in an essay. You will also likely discuss larger points rather than offer an argument that accounts for every nuance of a topic. Still, you will display your thinking through the words you compose. Back up your claims by providing examples and respond to others by explaining alternative interpretations or spelling out your questions in writing. (For more on participating in online conversations, see the tutorials on our CD-ROM.)

Tutorial for brainstorming electronically

CLUSTERING AND OUTLINING

As you move closer toward a topic for a paper, you can focus on organizing your thoughts prior to drafting your essay. Two strategies are **clustering** (or mapping) and **outlining.** Clustering organizes ideas visually with maps that show connections between key concerns. The sample below demonstrates one such cluster map.

The map in Figure 6.2 demonstrates the writer's ideas about loneliness in "Embrace" and "A Blessing" and could serve to organize an essay comparing the two poems. You can also create cluster maps at earlier stages of the prewriting process and even during drafting and revision to help you keep ideas flowing.

Some writers prefer to organize ideas in outline form. An outline asks the writer to deliberately select which items to discuss and where they will fit in the overall scheme of the project. The outline below represents one way of organizing the items in the cluster map.

Common Theme: Loneliness

1. Loneliness identified with
    a. Speaker in "Embrace"
    b. Horses in "A Blessing"

2. Companions shown to be
    a. Others in "Embrace"
        1. Absent
        2. Watching
    b. Nature in "A Blessing"
        1. Human Companion is Unimportant
        2. Horses Lack but also Provide Companionship
3. Self depicted as
    a. Two-sided in "Embrace"
        1. Front
        2. Back
        3. Male/Female?
    b. Within body/skin in "A Blessing"
        1. Human/Nature
        2. Sets Stage for Transformation

There are software programs such as Inspiration that can help you create cluster maps, and your word processor has an outlining function that will automatically format outlines for you. However, do not feel like you need advanced technology to map your ideas or create outlines. Sketching ideas on paper lets you enjoy the messy nature of these prewriting activities.

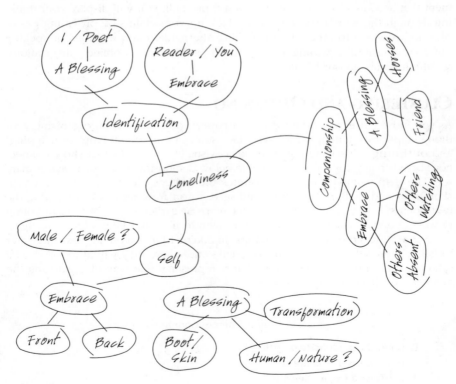

FIGURE 6.2   A Cluster Map

With both outlines and cluster maps, be mindful of the ways in which a writing project evolves as it progresses. Your outline or map can guide the organization of the project, but you may find that, as you draft, new ideas emerge and the project requires adjustment. Sometimes an entirely new direction evolves, and other times new issues must be incorporated into the overall scheme.

Exercise 6.2   *Creating a Cluster Map*

Start with a blank sheet of paper and prepare to sketch a cluster map with pencil, pens, or any other materials you might find useful.

1. Take a few moments and select one question that you have about either "Embrace" or "A Blessing." (You can choose another work if you prefer.)

2. Write this question in the center of your blank sheet of paper.

3. Develop a cluster map that represents your thinking about your question. You might develop offshoots that partially answer your question. You can explore additional questions. You could put down ideas and make note of relationships.

4. Look over the clusters that you have created. Consider whether this map or a new map based on one of the offshoots in the map might serve as the basis for organizing a paper.

Exercise 6.3   *Prewriting about a Poem*

Printed below is another poem by Billy Collins, "Thesaurus." Begin by reading the poem once or twice.

1. Choose from among listing, freewriting, or asking questions two methods of prewriting and apply them to the poem.

2. Develop a cluster map or an outline that could be used to organize an essay about "Thesaurus."

BILLY COLLINS

Thesaurus

Collins
reading
"Thesaurus"

It could be the name of a prehistoric beast
that roamed the Paleozoic earth, rising up
on its hind legs to show off its large vocabulary,
or some lover in a myth who is metamorphosed into a book.

5   It means treasury, but it is just a place
where words congregate with their relatives,
a big park where hundreds of family reunions
are always being held,
house, home, abode, dwelling, lodgings, and *digs,*

10   all sharing the same picnic basket and thermos;
hairy, hirsute, woolly, furry, fleecy, and *shaggy*
all running a sack race or throwing horseshoes,
inert, static, motionless, fixed and *immobile*
standing and kneeling in rows for a group photograph.

15   Here father is next to sire and brother close
to sibling, separated only by fine shades of meaning.
And every group has its odd cousin, the one
who traveled the farthest to be here:
astereognosis, polydipsia, or some eleven
20   syllable, unpronounceable substitute for the word *tool.*
Even their own relatives have to squint at their name tags.

I can see my own copy up on a high shelf.
I rarely open it, because I know there is no
such thing as a synonym and because I get nervous
25   around people who always assemble with their own kind,
forming clubs and nailing signs to closed front doors
while others huddle alone in the dark streets.

I would rather see words out on their own, away
from their families and the warehouse of Roget,
30   wandering the world where they sometimes fall
in love with a completely different word.
Surely, you have seen pairs of them standing forever
next to each other on the same line inside a poem,
a small chapel where weddings like these,
35   between perfect strangers, can take place.

INQUIRING FURTHER

1. It has been said of Collins's poetry that it is accessible. Do you find that to be true with "Thesaurus?" Why or why not?

2. How would you compare "Thesaurus" to "Embrace?"

3. Do you think humorous poems can be serious? Freewrite for five minutes on the relationship between humor and serious messages.

4. What do you think of the statement, "there is no / such thing as a synonym"? Do you think the statement is true? Write at least three sentences explaining your thinking.

5. What is the most pressing question that comes to your mind about the poem, or about the last stanza of the poem?

7

Drafting to Focus Ideas

The last thing one discovers in composing a work is what
to put first.

—Blaise Pascal

We can plan the details of many tasks. We select itineraries when we travel or make
lists before shopping. We organize events, inviting guests and choosing food or
music ahead of time. With writing, however, we often have to begin without knowing exactly how things will turn out. Writing is an organic process that can take any
number of turns as avenues of thought open up while we compose.

Still, there are some steps we can take to guide our thinking as we draft. First,
we should have an approach in mind before beginning. We need a thesis, not
so much to predefine our path, but to keep us moving from prewriting to drafting. Second, we need to understand the differences between drafting, revising,
and polishing; knowing the true nature of drafting as focused exploration can
help us overcome writer's block and promote a process of inquiry. We should
also know something about drafting introductions and conclusions and drafting
body paragraphs, including how to integrate and discuss summaries, paraphrases, and quotations.

We will use a short work of literature to illustrate the concepts discussed in this
and the next chapter. Here we will look at a story by Ambrose Bierce called "An
Occurrence at Owl Creek Bridge." We will also look at some still images taken from
a film version of the story.

AMBROSE BIERCE

*Ambrose Bierce (1842–1914?) enlisted in the Union Army during the Civil
War. He served in the army from 1861-1865 as a mapmaker and officer.
After the war, Bierce became a journalist, working in San Francisco. In
addition to his newspaper columns, Bierce wrote satires, ghost stories, and
tales based on his war experiences. "An Occurrence at Owl Creek Bridge"
was included in a collection of stories published in 1891. Bierce was born
in 1842, but his time of death is not known. In 1913, he disappeared,
supposedly riding to Mexico where he may have died participating in one
of the battles of the revolution in 1914.*

An Occurrence at Owl Creek Bridge

I

A man stood upon a railroad bridge in northern Alabama, looking down into the swift water twenty feet below. The man's hands were behind his back, the wrists bound with a cord. A rope closely encircled his neck. It was attached to a stout cross-timber above his head and the slack fell to the level of his knees. Some loose boards laid upon the sleepers supporting the metals of the railway supplied a footing for him and his executioners—two private soldiers of the Federal army, directed by a sergeant who in civil life may have been a deputy sheriff. At a short remove upon the same temporary platform was an officer in the uniform of his rank, armed. He was a captain. A sentinel at each end of the bridge stood with his rifle in the position known as "support," that is to say, vertical in front of the left shoulder, the hammer resting on the forearm thrown straight across the chest—a formal and unnatural position, enforcing an erect carriage of the body. It did not appear to be the duty of these two men to know what was occurring at the center of the bridge; they merely blockaded the two ends of the foot planking that traversed it.

Beyond one of the sentinels nobody was in sight; the railroad ran straight away into a forest for a hundred yards, then, curving, was lost to view. Doubtless there was an outpost farther along. The other bank of the stream was open ground—a gentle acclivity topped with a stockade of vertical tree trunks, loopholed for rifles, with a single embrasure through which protruded the muzzle of a brass cannon commanding the bridge. Midway of the slope between bridge and fort were the spectators—a single company of infantry in line, at "parade rest," the butts of the rifles on the ground, the barrels inclining slightly backward against the right shoulder, the hands crossed upon the stock. A lieutenant stood at the right of the line, the point of his sword upon the ground, his left hand resting upon his right. Excepting the group of four at the centre of the bridge, not a man moved. The company faced the bridge, staring stonily, motionless. The sentinels, facing the banks of the stream, might have been statues to adorn the bridge. The captain stood with folded arms, silent, observing the work of his subordinates, but making no sign. Death is a dignitary who when he comes announced is to be received with formal manifestations of respect, even by those most familiar with him. In the code of military etiquette silence and fixity are forms of deference.

The man who was engaged in being hanged was apparently about thirty-five years of age. He was a civilian, if one might judge from his habit, which was that of a planter. His features were good—a straight nose, firm mouth, broad forehead, from which his long, dark hair was combed straight back, falling behind his ears to the collar of his well-fitting frock-coat. He wore a mustache and pointed beard, but no whiskers; his eyes were large and dark gray, and had a kindly expression which one would hardly have expected in one whose neck was in the hemp. Evidently this was no vulgar assassin. The liberal military code makes provision for hanging many kinds of persons, and gentlemen are not excluded.

The preparations being complete, the two private soldiers stepped aside and each drew away the plank upon which he had been standing. The sergeant turned to the captain, saluted and placed himself immediately behind that officer, who in turn moved apart one pace. These movements left the condemned man and the sergeant standing on the two ends of the same plank, which spanned three of the cross-ties of the bridge. The end upon which the civilian stood almost, but not quite, reached a fourth. This plank had been held in place by the weight of the captain; it was now held by that of the sergeant. At a signal from the former the latter would step aside, the plank would tilt and the condemned man go down between two ties. The arrangement commended itself to his judgment as simple and effective. His face had not been covered nor his eyes bandaged. He looked a moment at his "unsteadfast footing," then let his gaze wander to the swirling water of the stream racing madly beneath his feet. A piece of dancing driftwood caught his attention and his eyes followed it down the current. How slowly it appeared to move! What a sluggish stream!

5   He closed his eyes in order to fix his last thoughts upon his wife and children. The water, touched to gold by the early sun, the brooding mists under the banks at some distance down the stream, the fort, the soldiers, the piece of drift—all had distracted him. And now he became conscious of a new disturbance. Striking through the thought of his dear ones was a sound which he could neither ignore nor understand, a sharp, distinct, metallic percussion like the stroke of a blacksmith's hammer upon the anvil; it had the same ringing quality. He wondered what it was, and whether immeasurably distant or near by—it seemed both. Its recurrence was regular, but as slow as the tolling of a death knell. He awaited each stroke with impatience and—he knew not why—apprehension. The intervals of silence grew progressively longer; the delays became maddening. With their greater infrequency the sounds increased in strength and sharpness. They hurt his ear like the thrust of a knife; he feared he would shriek. What he heard was the ticking of his watch.

He unclosed his eyes and saw again the water below him. "If I could free my hands," he thought, "I might throw off the noose and spring into the stream. By diving I could evade the bullets and, swimming vigorously, reach the bank, take to the woods and get away home. My home, thank God, is as yet outside their lines; my wife and little ones are still beyond the invader's farthest advance."

As these thoughts, which have here to be set down in words, were flashed into the doomed man's brain rather than evolved from it the captain nodded to the sergeant. The sergeant stepped aside.

II

Peyton Farquhar was a well-to-do planter, of an old and highly respected Alabama family. Being a slave owner and like other slave owners a politician he was naturally an original secessionist and ardently devoted to the Southern cause. Circumstances of an imperious nature, which it is unnecessary to relate here, had prevented him from taking service with the gallant army that had fought the disastrous campaigns ending with the fall of Corinth, and he chafed under the inglorious restraint, longing for the release of his energies, the larger life of the soldier, the opportunity for distinction. That opportunity, he felt, would come, as it comes to all in war time. Meanwhile he did what he could. No service was too humble for him to perform in aid of the South, no adventure too perilous for him to undertake if consistent with the character of a civilian who was at heart a soldier, and who in good faith and without too much qualification assented to at least a part of the frankly villainous dictum that all is fair in love and war.

One evening while Farquhar and his wife were sitting on a rustic bench near the entrance to his grounds, a gray-clad soldier rode up to the gate and asked for a drink of water. Mrs. Farquhar was only too happy to serve him with her own white hands. While she was fetching the water her husband approached the dusty horseman and inquired eagerly for news from the front.

10   "The Yanks are repairing the railroads," said the man, "and are getting ready for another advance. They have reached the Owl Creek bridge, put it in order and built a stockade on the north bank. The commandant has issued an order, which is posted everywhere, declaring that any civilian caught interfering with the railroad, its bridges, tunnels or trains will be summarily hanged. I saw the order."

"How far is it to the Owl Creek bridge?" Farquhar asked.

"About thirty miles."

"Is there no force on this side the creek?"

"Only a picket post half a mile out, on the railroad, and a single sentinel at this end of the bridge."

15   "Suppose a man—a civilian and student of hanging—should elude the picket post and perhaps get the better of the sentinel," said Farquhar, smiling, "what could he accomplish?"

The soldier reflected. "I was there a month ago," he replied. "I observed that the flood of last winter had lodged a great quantity of driftwood against the wooden pier at this end of the bridge. It is now dry and would burn like tow."

The lady had now brought the water, which the soldier drank. He thanked her ceremoniously, bowed to her husband and rode away. An hour later, after nightfall, he repassed the plantation, going northward in the direction from which he had come. He was a Federal scout.

III

As Peyton Farquhar fell straight downward through the bridge he lost consciousness and was as one already dead. From this state he was awakened—ages later, it seemed to him—by the pain of a sharp pressure upon his throat, followed by a sense of suffocation. Keen, poignant agonies seemed to shoot from his neck downward through every fiber of his body and limbs. These pains appeared to flash along well-defined lines of ramification and to beat with an inconceivably rapid periodicity. They seemed like streams of pulsating fire heating him to an intolerable temperature. As to his head, he was conscious of nothing but a feeling of fullness—of congestion. These sensations were unaccompanied by thought. The intellectual part of his nature was already effaced; he had power only to feel, and feeling was torment. He was conscious of motion. Encompassed in a luminous cloud, of which he was now merely the fiery heart, without material substance, he swung through unthinkable arcs of oscillation, like a vast pendulum. Then all at once, with terrible suddenness, the light about him shot upward with the noise of a loud splash; a frightful roaring was in his ears, and all was cold and dark. The power of thought was restored; he knew that the rope had broken and he had fallen into the stream. There was no additional strangulation; the noose about his neck was already suffocating him and kept the water from his lungs. To die of hanging at the bottom of a river!—the idea seemed to him ludicrous. He opened his eyes in the darkness and saw above him a gleam of light, but how distant, how inaccessible! He was still sinking, for the light became fainter and fainter until it was a mere glimmer. Then it began to grow and brighten, and he knew that he was rising toward the surface—knew it with reluctance, for he was now very comfortable. "To be hanged and drowned," he thought, "that is not so bad; but I do not wish to be shot. No; I will not be shot; that is not fair."

He was not conscious of an effort, but a sharp pain in his wrist apprised him that he was trying to free his hands. He gave the struggle his attention, as an idler might observe the feat of a juggler, without interest in the outcome. What splendid effort—what magnificent, what superhuman strength! Ah, that was a fine endeavor! Bravo! The cord fell away; his arms parted and floated upward, the hands dimly seen on each side in the growing light. He watched them with a new interest as first one and then the other pounced upon the noose at his neck. They tore it away and thrust it fiercely aside, its undulations resembling those of a water-snake. "Put it back, put it back!" He thought he shouted these words to his hands, for the undoing of the noose had been succeeded by the direst pang that he had yet experienced. His neck ached horribly; his brain was on fire; his heart, which had been fluttering faintly, gave a great leap, trying to force itself out at his mouth. His whole body was racked and wrenched with an insupportable anguish! But his disobedient hands gave no heed to the command. They beat the water vigorously with quick, downward strokes, forcing him to the surface. He felt his head emerge; his eyes were blinded by the sunlight; his chest expanded convulsively, and with a supreme and crowning agony his lungs engulfed a great draught of air, which instantly he expelled in a shriek!

20   He was now in full possession of his physical senses. They were, indeed, preternaturally keen and alert. Something in the awful disturbance of his organic system had so exalted and refined them that they made record of things never before perceived. He felt the ripples upon his face and heard their separate sounds as they struck. He looked at the forest on the bank of the stream, saw the individual trees, the leaves and the veining of each leaf—saw the very insects upon them: the locusts, the brilliant-bodied flies, the gray spiders stretching their webs from twig to twig. He noted the prismatic colors in all the dewdrops upon a million blades of grass. The humming of the gnats that danced above the eddies of the stream, the beating of the dragon-flies' wings, the strokes of the water-spiders' legs, like oars which had lifted their boat—all these made audible music. A fish slid along beneath his eyes and he heard the rush of its body parting the water.

He had come to the surface facing down the stream; in a moment the visible world seemed to wheel slowly round, himself the pivotal point, and he saw the bridge, the fort, the soldiers upon the bridge, the captain, the sergeant, the two privates, his executioners. They were in silhouette against the blue sky. They shouted and gesticulated, pointing at him. The captain had drawn his pistol, but did not fire; the others were unarmed. Their movements were grotesque and horrible, their forms gigantic.

Suddenly he heard a sharp report and something struck the water smartly within a few inches of his head, spattering his face with spray. He heard a second report, and saw one of the sentinels with his rifle at his shoulder, a light cloud of blue smoke rising from the muzzle. The man in the water saw the eye of the man on the bridge gazing into his own through the sights of the rifle. He observed that it was a gray eye and remembered having read that gray eyes were keenest, and that all famous marksmen had them. Nevertheless, this one had missed.

A counter-swirl had caught Farquhar and turned him half round; he was again looking into the forest on the bank opposite the fort. The sound of a clear, high voice in a monotonous singsong now rang out behind him and came across the water with a distinctness that pierced and subdued all other sounds, even the beating of the ripples in his ears. Although no soldier, he had frequented camps enough to know the dread significance of that deliberate, drawling, aspirated chant; the lieutenant on shore was taking a part in the morning's work. How coldly and pitilessly—with what an even, calm intonation,

presaging, and enforcing tranquillity in the men—with what accurately measured intervals fell those cruel words:

"Attention, company! . . . Shoulder arms! . . . Ready! . . . Aim! . . . Fire!"

25   Farquhar dived—dived as deeply as he could. The water roared in his ears
like the voice of Niagara, yet he heard the dulled thunder of the volley and,
rising again toward the surface, met shining bits of metal, singularly flattened,
oscillating slowly downward. Some of them touched him on the face and hands,
then fell away, continuing their descent. One lodged between his collar and
neck; it was uncomfortably warm and he snatched it out.

As he rose to the surface, gasping for breath, he saw that he had been a
long time under water; he was perceptibly farther down stream—nearer to
safety. The soldiers had almost finished reloading; the metal ramrods flashed
all at once in the sunshine as they were drawn from the barrels, turned in
the air, and thrust into their sockets. The two sentinels fired again, independently and ineffectually.

The hunted man saw all this over his shoulder; he was now swimming vigorously with the current. His brain was as energetic as his arms and legs; he
thought with the rapidity of lightning.

"The officer," he reasoned, "will not make that martinet's error a second time.
It is as easy to dodge a volley as a single shot. He has probably already given
the command to fire at will. God help me, I cannot dodge them all!"

An appalling plash within two yards of him was followed by a loud, rushing sound, *diminuendo*, which seemed to travel back through the air to the fort
and died in an explosion which stirred the very river to its deeps! A rising sheet
of water curved over him, fell down upon him, blinded him, strangled him! The
cannon had taken a hand in the game. As he shook his head free from the commotion of the smitten water he heard the deflected shot humming through
the air ahead, and in an instant it was cracking and smashing the branches in
the forest beyond.

30   "They will not do that again," he thought; "the next time they will use a
charge of grape.[1] I must keep my eye upon the gun; the smoke will apprise
me—the report arrives too late; it lags behind the missile. That is a good gun."

Suddenly he felt himself whirled round and round—spinning like a top. The
water, the banks, the forests, the now distant bridge, fort and men—all were
commingled and blurred. Objects were represented by their colors only; circular horizontal streaks of color—that was all he saw. He had been caught in
a vortex and was being whirled on with a velocity of advance and gyration that
made him giddy and sick. In a few moments he was flung upon the gravel at
the foot of the left bank of the stream—the southern bank—and behind a projecting point which concealed him from his enemies. The sudden arrest of his
motion, the abrasion of one of his hands on the gravel, restored him, and he
wept with delight. He dug his fingers into the sand, threw it over himself in
handfuls and audibly blessed it. It looked like diamonds, rubies, emeralds; he
could think of nothing beautiful which it did not resemble. The trees upon
the bank were giant garden plants; he noted a definite order in their arrangement, inhaled the fragrance of their blooms. A strange, roseate light shone
through the spaces among their trunks and the wind made in their branches
the music of æolian harps. He had no wish to perfect his escape—was content to remain in that enchanting spot until retaken.

---

[1]**grape:** small iron balls used as ammunition for a cannon, grape (or grapeshot) produces a hail of
projectiles.

A whiz and rattle of grapeshot among the branches high above his head roused him from his dream. The baffled cannoneer had fired him a random farewell. He sprang to his feet, rushed up the sloping bank, and plunged into the forest.

All that day he traveled, laying his course by the rounding sun. The forest seemed interminable; nowhere did he discover a break in it, not even a wood-man's road. He had not known that he lived in so wild a region. There was something uncanny in the revelation.

By nightfall he was fatigued, footsore, famishing. The thought of his wife and children urged him on. At last he found a road which led him in what he knew to be the right direction. It was as wide and straight as a city street, yet it seemed untraveled. No fields bordered it, no dwelling anywhere. Not so much as the barking of a dog suggested human habitation. The black bod-ies of the trees formed a straight wall on both sides, terminating on the hori-zon in a point, like a diagram in a lesson in perspective. Overhead, as he looked up through this rift in the wood, shone great golden stars looking unfamiliar and grouped in strange constellations. He was sure they were arranged in some order which had a secret and malign significance. The wood on either side was full of singular noises, among which—once, twice, and again—he distinctly heard whispers in an unknown tongue.

35   His neck was in pain and lifting his hand to it he found it horribly swollen. He knew that it had a circle of black where the rope had bruised it. His eyes felt congested; he could no longer close them. His tongue was swollen with thirst; he relieved its fever by thrusting it forward from between his teeth into the cold air. How softly the turf had carpeted the untraveled avenue—he could no longer feel the roadway beneath his feet!

Doubtless, despite his suffering, he had fallen asleep while walking, for now he sees another scene—perhaps he has merely recovered from a delirium. He stands at the gate of his own home. All is as he left it, and all bright and beau-tiful in the morning sunshine. He must have traveled the entire night. As he pushes open the gate and passes up the wide white walk, he sees a flutter of female garments; his wife, looking fresh and cool and sweet, steps down from the veranda to meet him. At the bottom of the steps she stands waiting, with a smile of ineffable joy, an attitude of matchless grace and dignity. Ah, how beautiful she is! He springs forward with extended arms. As he is about to clasp her he feels a stunning blow upon the back of the neck; a blinding white light blazes all about him with a sound like the shock of a cannon—then all is darkness and silence!

Peyton Farquhar was dead; his body, with a broken neck, swung gently from side to side beneath the timbers of the Owl Creek bridge.

Still frames and video clips from *An Occurrence at Owl Creek Bridge*

FIGURE 7.1   Still frames from *An Occurrence at Owl Creek Bridge*

MOVING FROM PREWRITING TO DRAFTING

As suggested earlier, the organic process of writing can still benefit from having an angle. If you begin drafting without any idea of the main questions you wish to explore, then you should think about brainstorming with some of the prewriting techniques covered in the last chapter. Through prewriting and by exploring your initial response to a work, you should be able to develop a reasonably specific approach to your topic, a thesis for the paper.

Narrowing your approach need not mean closing off exploration. Instead, a thesis helps you get started with the exploration that will take place through writing. Possible theses for the short story "An Occurrence at Owl Creek Bridge" might include:

Military customs limit personal responsibility.

The Civil War exposed hypocrisy within Southern plantation culture.

Narrative strategies in the story manipulate the reader in order to make a

    point about violence.

Perceptions of time change in extreme situations.

None of these angles explains the story completely, but they do provide a framework that can help us begin drafting.

As you develop a thesis, explore ways of adding interest to the essay you intend to compose. Of "An Occurrence at Owl Creek Bridge," for instance, we might begin with the thesis that military customs limit personal responsibility. We might inquire into ways of adding tension or complexity to this approach. Do we currently use strategies to limit responsibility in the military? Does the story shed light on personal responsibility or critique aspects of society other than the military? Look for ways of complicating your approach and consider how you might weave into your argument some of these surprises or unexpected insights. You do not want to make your paper a great mystery, but you do want to pursue an idea that has some complexity.

Exercise 7.1   *Drafting Thesis Statements*

The thesis statements above represent just a few of the ways we can approach "An Occurrence at Owl Creek Bridge." Consider the story on your own and develop a list of alternative theses that can be used to explain the work. Begin by preparing to take notes, and then respond to the following prompts:

1. Consider some large topics that might be used to understand the story. Think about ideas related to violence, imagination, politics, freedom, justice, authority, family, rebellion, nature, innocence, individuals, society, etc. (You can refer to a more comprehensive list of topics on pages 45–46.) Consider the story in light of these broad topics and select one that you might refine into a thesis.

2. Consider two passages from the story that relate to the broad topic you have selected. What messages do these passages present about the

topic? What themes do these two passages have in common? Sketch out at least three sentences relating the passages to your broad topic.

3. Finally, think about an interpretation of the story that relates to your deliberations so far. Refine your thinking into a statement that expresses your approach and that can act as a thesis for writing about the story.

Exercise 7.2 *Brainstorming about Film Images*

In many ways, a film version of a short story represents a filmmaker's interpretation of the work. By choosing to emphasize certain traits in a character or to portray a setting in a particular way, for instance, the filmmaker expresses her sense of what is significant about the story. This exercise asks you to analyze a filmmaker's portrayal of "An Occurrence at Owl Creek Bridge" in order to help you refine your own approach to the story.

Still frames and video clips from *An Occurrence at Owl Creek Bridge*

Working with a group of fellow students (or on your own if your instructor prefers), look over the materials and complete Exercise 7.2 on our CD.

In addition to selecting a thesis, as you move into the drafting stage of your project, consider developing an outline or cluster map that will help you plan your work. (See pages 1–63.) Your project can change or shift, but you should at least have a sense of the major areas you plan to cover before getting started.

You should also take the time to completely understand your assignment and audience. A character analysis differs from an argument or a comparison essay. If you are not completely comfortable with the assignment, ask your instructor for clarification. Further, think about your audience before putting pen to paper. Are you writing for your classmates, for your instructor, or for a larger audience? Have they read the work? What views are they likely to share with you? Where might they disagree? (You can review these audience issues in more detail on page 81.)

OVERCOMING WRITER'S BLOCK

Okay, so you have a thesis and you have a rough map or an outline. Now what? If you are still having trouble getting started, you can try the following strategies for overcoming writer's block.

- **Start early.** At times, writers procrastinate until putting off the draft is no longer an option. Do not do this. Deadlines are terrific motivators, but last-minute compositions are lousy examples of writing that should develop through a process of prewriting, drafting, revision, and polishing. Force yourself to begin your draft at least several days before the date it is due.

- **Start anywhere.** The introduction is often the most difficult part of an essay to write because you do not know exactly how you will treat every aspect of your paper. Sometimes it is easier to begin writing one of the body paragraphs and come back to the introduction later. If you have an insight, begin there and fit the writing you develop into the overall organization of your essay later.

- **Start simply.** Anxiety is one of the most common causes of writer's block. We all want to say something brilliant about our topics, but in practice most good writing succeeds because it explains concepts and ideas clearly. Rather than lower your expectations for your writing, take comfort in the fact that you do not need to compose something revolutionary to write something good.

- **Start talking.** If you are stuck, try talking out loud about your assignment or the work. (You might check that your roommates are not nearby with the tailor-made straightjacket.) Some writers use a tape recorder to keep track of ideas, but you can also simply speak aloud your thoughts until you have given voice to something that you can transcribe to your draft.

- **Start imagining.** You might try changing how you view your assignment. Pretend you are writing a letter to a friend. Suppose you are writing a screenplay for a film. Imagine you are composing a journal entry. Pretend you are composing a grocery list, if it helps loosen you up.

- **Start brainstorming.** Call on some prewriting techniques to get ideas flowing. Make lists, freewrite, pose questions to yourself, or create a cluster map or outline. Sketch ideas and otherwise brainstorm freely if you are having trouble fixing on an idea to write about.

- **Start writing.** Remember the stages of the writing process are not as distinct as they appear in discussions in books like this one. You will have a chance to revise later and you can prewrite now, so just go ahead and get something on paper.

DRAFTING INTRODUCTIONS

An **introduction** serves three important functions: 1.) it lays out for readers a thesis and a framework for understanding your work; 2.) it provides background information; and 3.) it engages the reader's interest. We can look at a sample introduction for a paper about "An Occurrence at Owl Creek Bridge" to explore these three elements. (We will refer to this draft in this and the next chapter.)

Peyton Farquhar was dead; his body, with a broken neck,

swung gently from side to side beneath the timbers of the Owl

Creek bridge.

"An Occurrence at Owl Creek Bridge," by Ambrose Bierce, opens with

the hanging of a well-to-do Southern planter, Peyton Farquhar. Set during

the Civil War, the story emphasizes the dangers of covering up the

atrocities of death and war. The story ends with the stark image of

Farquhar's body swinging "gently from side to side" from the hangman's

noose. But between the opening moments of the story and the gruesome

final scene, a journey takes place in Farquhar's imagination. This

intervening moment makes up the majority of Robert Enrico's 1962 film

version of the story and offers an escape through dreams. However, we learn at the end of the film that the dreams have been nothing more than a fiction that has allowed the viewer to ignore the reality of death. In the final analysis, the film's interpretation supports rather than undercuts the emphasis in the story on the atrocities of war and death.

Providing a Thesis

An introduction demonstrates the thesis of the essay and provides an overview of the major points of discussion. Often the thesis will be placed near the end of the introduction, as in the sample that concludes that *the film's interpretation supports rather than undercuts the emphasis in the story on the atrocities of war and death.* Ending with the thesis is not necessary, but it can bind together the introduction as a whole.

The introduction will also expand on the thesis by forecasting key points that will be covered in the essay. In the sample, the writer points out that an important *journey takes place in Farquhar's imagination.* The sample introduction also emphasizes the key role that *escape through dreams* plays in the film's interpretation of the story. The paragraph points to the central nature of the dream and explains the relationship between the story and the film. The thesis reinforces these key points.

Providing Background

An introduction also helps readers understand the work under discussion. Here, you will want to assess the potential audience for your paper. If your readers are not familiar with the work, you may need to provide a bit more detail. Be careful, however, not to fall into the trap of providing plot summary in the introduction. Instead of getting sidetracked explaining what happens, move on to discussing what it means.

Background might include historical information, biographical information about the author, research information about what others have said about the work, or information about the work itself. The introduction should also tell readers which authors and works you are writing about. In the sample introduction, the writer introduces both the short story and the film that will be discussed. The introduction gives some details about these items, but only enough to understand the main ideas that will be covered in the paper.

Engaging Your Readers

Finally, introductions often serve to hook readers, encouraging them to find out what you have to say. The sample uses a quotation to begin the essay, a common strategy. You might also use a definition or ask a question as a way of starting the essay and grabbing the attention of your readers. Be sure to remember, however, that a hook will not engage and maintain your readers' interests by itself. Nothing alienates readers more than confusion. Begin by spelling out a framework for understanding your essay. Once you clearly explain your points, any hook you add will have the desired effect.

Often introductions will move from a more general discussion to a specific statement like a thesis. But introductions that begin too generally usually represent false starts. If your introduction begins with a general statement like, "Litera-ture teaches many lessons," or "For centuries, society has struggled with issues of rebellion," then you probably have a false start and can edit the opening so that you begin with the heart of what you wish to say.

DRAFTING BODY PARAGRAPHS

In the body of an essay you present readers with a paragraph-by-paragraph expla-nation of your thinking. In general, each paragraph will serve to further your argument by making a key point. For this reason, you must make a clear claim about what you are trying to say in each paragraph and then provide detailed discussion that supports and illustrates that claim.

You can approach body paragraphs somewhat like you do your overall paper. In your paper you need a thesis or approach that will focus your ideas and organ-ize your writing. The same holds true with paragraphs. Most paragraphs will have a **topic sentence** or controlling idea that focuses the paragraph. In terms of argu-ment, the topic sentence spells out the central claim and the rest of the paragraph provides reasons and evidence to support that claim.

As you compose the rest of the paragraph, concentrate on illustrating and explaining the controlling idea in your topic sentence. Doing so will help you develop paragraphs that achieve unity, coherence, and depth. We will discuss these concepts by referring to a body paragraph taken from our sample paper about "An Occurrence at Owl Creek Bridge."

"An Occurrence at Owl Creek Bridge" suggests that military roles allow individuals to avoid responsibility for the atrocities of death and war. In the opening passages we're presented with a description of the scene of the hanging. This depiction, however, focuses primarily on the roles of the members of the military:

> Some loose boards laid upon the ties supporting the rails of the railway supplied a footing for him and his executioners—two private soldiers of the Federal army, directed by a sergeant who in civil life may have been a deputy sheriff. At a short remove upon the same temporary platform was an officer in the uniform of his rank, armed. He was a captain. A sentinel at each end of the bridge stood with his rifle in the position known as "support," that is to say, vertical in front of the left shoulder, the hammer resting on the forearm thrown straight across the chest—a formal and unnatural position, enforcing an erect carriage of the body. (166)

Two groups make up the scene. In the first group we find "two private soldiers . . . directed by a sergeant." This group is primarily responsible for carrying out the hanging, and the two privates most likely have bound Farquhar and placed the noose around his neck. However, the passage states that these privates were "directed by [the] sergeant," implying that they are not responsible for their actions. With each character depicted, the scene emphasizes the role but not the responsibility. The most we learn about the captain is that he wears "the uniform of his rank." Finally, at the ends of the bridge we find two sentinels. The sentinels bring home the point that military roles work against personal responsibility. A sentinel suggests one who watches, one on the alert for trouble, even injustice. Ironically, we are immediately told that "it did not appear to be the duty of these two men to know what was occurring at the center of the bridge; they merely blockaded the two ends of the foot planking that traversed it" (166).

Achieving Unity

Paragraph **unity** derives from having a clear sense of what the paragraph is about, that is a controlling idea (or topic sentence). A topic sentence is usually put forth near the beginning and then explored during the body of the paragraph. The sample paragraph states clearly that *military roles allow individuals to avoid responsibility for the atrocities of death and war.* This topic sentence relates to the thesis of the paper, which argues that the story and the film emphasize the dangers of overlooking the atrocities of death and war. The paragraph supports that claim by making specific points about how military roles figure into avoiding responsibility.

Achieving Coherence

Coherence refers to how the ideas and sentences within a paragraph fit together. On one level you can achieve coherence simply by staying focused on your topic sentence and maintaining the unity of your paragraph. Readers develop expectations based on what they have already understood about your writing. If they are told that military roles and responsibilities are the key themes of a paragraph, they expect the discussion that follows to refer to these themes. A sentence about Southern plantation culture in this paragraph would startle reader's expectations, diminishing the force of the paragraph.

On another more practical level, you can achieve coherence by tying together the ideas in each paragraph. In the sample paragraph, for instance, the writer frequently repeats the terms *roles* and *responsibilities.* The writer also provides clues to the reader about the relationships between the ideas and sentences—transitions like *however, ironically,* and *finally* connect the ideas to one another. By making a conscious effort to lead the reader from idea to idea and to spell out connections with the paragraph's controlling idea, the writer achieves coherence.

Achieving Depth

Depth simply requires taking the time to provide examples and evidence that explain your points. In the sample paragraph, the writer gives an extended quotation, then spends the majority of the paragraph detailing what he thinks it means. He highlights for the reader key phrases such as *rank, uniform,* and *duties* and shows how they can be understood in terms of roles and responsibilities. He brings his own ideas to bear on the discussion, pointing out the possible significance of the word *sentinel.* He does not assume that readers see the same things that he sees in the quotation. Instead he discusses the quotation, showing how it relates to his topic sentence and thesis.

Using
images in
your
writing

The full sample of the paper at the end of this chapter also discusses still images taken from the film version of the story. To achieve depth when discussing images, treat the images as you would quotations; do not assume that they convey meaning by themselves. Instead, discuss the image, referring explicitly to the visual details, drawing conclusions about what those details might represent, and finally explaining how those details and conclusions relate to your topic sentences and thesis.

Exercise 7.3   *Revising for Coherence*

Working with a group of fellow students (or on your own if your instructor prefers), look over the paragraph at the end of this exercise; the paragraph is taken from the sample draft in this chapter. This paragraph has some problems with coherency. Begin by choosing someone to keep track of the group's work or by preparing to take notes on your own, and then read through the paragraph and respond to the following prompts:

1. Write a sentence that restates the topic sentence or controlling idea of this paragraph.

2. List at least two places where the paragraph drifts from its controlling idea.

3. List at least two examples of poor use of repetitions, transitions or other devices that might add coherence to the paragraph.

4. Finally, revise the paragraph so that it achieves coherence.

Here is the sample paragraph:

In the film version of "An Occurrence at Owl Creek Bridge," we are

presented with a vivid depiction of the possibilities for escape through

dreams. The dream sequences are initiated in the film through the image of

water. Atop the railroad trestle, Farquhar witnesses a small piece of driftwood floating by on the stream. Shortly after, the scene shifts drastically to Farquhar's home and family. The rope is also a symbol of consciousness. When the sergeant steps off the board and Peyton Farquhar falls from the trestle, the rope snaps. The film provides several clues that the sequence that follows is part of a dream. First, Farquhar plunges into the water. Water can represent a symbol of the subconscious or the dream state. When Farquhar emerges from the water, the film adds to the sense of the dream through the use of slow motion photography and sound. Finally, the film techniques suggest that what is happening after the snapping of the rope is a dream. Next, when Farquhar escapes the scene of the hanging, he is carried off by a vortex of water. In the film, the vortex is represented as a series of rapids that hurry Farquhar away from the spot where his body will remain swinging back and forth from the Owl Creek bridge.

DRAFTING CONCLUSIONS

Conclusions can be tough to write because you are in some ways called to answer the question, "so what?" about your essay. You want to tell your audience what is really significant about what you have discussed. At the same time, however, conclusions do not really provide an opportunity for you to elaborate on ideas in depth. Because there is no chance to develop points you introduce, adding a twist or an important point at the end can often leave readers wondering why you did not address the issue in your essay in the first place.

Instead of introducing too much new information, you can use a conclusion to reiterate your main points. However, be careful not to simply repeat what you have already said. Repetition will only prolong the work your reader must do without providing a significant reward. Your task in the end is to convince readers that your approach is worth looking at, so any restating you do in the conclusion should emphasize *why* your argument matters.

In general, think of conclusions as reinforcing the central or final point of your argument. Make sure that you have addressed any major objections to your argument in the body of your paper. Then, see if you can offer an unexpected insight or forceful way of restating your main point. Or, see if you can reinforce connections or provide an evaluation of your own argument as a way of closing your essay.

WORKING WITH QUOTATIONS

The sample paragraph on pages 176–77 also shows how you can work with quotations to develop the body paragraphs of your essay. To work with quotations successfully you will need to do two things: 1.) realize that quotations cannot do any explaining for you—discuss quotations to demonstrate their significance (a good rule of thumb is to provide at least two parts discussion to one part quotation); and 2.) you must know how to **introduce, edit, discuss,** and **punctuate** quotations so that you can integrate them smoothly into your writing.

Introducing Quotations

You should compose your own sentences so that they prepare readers for quotations. For shorter quotations, you will insert the quoted material directly into your own text, as in

Integrating
quotations
into your
writing

> Ironically, we are immediately told that "it did not appear to be the duty
>
> of these two men to know what was occurring at the center of the bridge; they
>
> merely blockaded the two ends of the foot planking that traversed it" (166).

As you use quotations, learn to choose from a handy collection of **introductory tags,** words or phrases that prepare readers for quoted material. In many cases you can keep with simple and direct tags to introduce your quotations—tags like *says, tells, shows,* and *suggests* are mainstays. However, you may find that additional tags add variety and precision to your writing.

When writing about passages of literature, useful introductory tags include words like *reveals, depicts, affirms,* or *expresses,* as in

> The narrator <u>affirms</u> that "death . . . is to be received with formal
>
> manifestations of respect," but the description *reveals* only that "the
>
> company faced the bridge, staring stonily, motionless" (166).

When writing about what others have said or about the words of a character in a work, you might use introductory tags such as *acknowledges, argues, believes, asserts, insists, speculates,* or *asks,* as in

> Hargroves *acknowledges* that "the dream sequences provide a means of
>
> momentary escape," but *argues* that "the overall trajectory is toward despair."

Pay attention to subtle differences in meaning created by introductory tags. *Acknowledges* is not the same as *argues*—the latter suggests a more forceful point.

Longer quotations (quotations that take up more than four lines in prose or more than two lines in poetry) should be set off from the main text of your paper. These **block quotations** should be double spaced and indented ten spaces from your left-hand margin. Do not place quotation marks around a block quotation. You can use introductory tags to prepare readers for block quotations, but often you will introduce them with a colon, as in

> The story suggests that military roles limit personal responsibilities:
>
> > At a short remove upon the same temporary platform was an
> >
> > officer in the uniform of his rank, armed. He was a captain. A

sentinel at each end of the bridge stood with his rifle in the

position known as "support," that is to say, vertical in front of the

left shoulder, the hammer resting on the forearm thrown straight

across the chest—a formal and unnatural position, enforcing an

erect carriage of the body. (166)

Editing Quotations

When you edit quotations to make them fit more seamlessly into your own writing you must indicate the changes that you have made. Most commonly you will indicate deleted material, your own insertions, or minor editorial changes.

For deleted material you will use **ellipses,** the symbol formed by stringing periods together. For materials deleted from the middle of a quotation, use three ellipsis points with spaces on either side of them, as in

In the first group we find "two private soldiers . . . directed by a

sergeant."

For deleted material at the end of a quotation, use a period directly after the quoted material followed by three ellipsis points with spaces on either side of them, as in

"Some loose boards laid upon the ties supporting the rails of the

railway supplied a footing for him and his executioners—two private

soldiers of the Federal army, directed by a sergeant. . . ."

For edited material, use square brackets to indicate changes or to insert your own comments or clarifications, as in

However, the passage states that these privates were "directed by [the]

sergeant," implying that they are not responsible for their actions.

Hargroves acknowledges that "the dream sequences [described by

Villanova] provide a means of momentary escape," but argues that "the

overall trajectory [of the story] is toward despair."

To add emphasis to part of a quotation, italicize the material and indicate that you have added the emphasis in a parenthetical citation, as in

"It did not appear to be the <u>duty</u> of these two men to know what was

occurring at the center of the bridge" (166; emphasis added).

Punctuating Quotations

When integrating short quotations directly into your writing, follow the rules below.
For periods and commas, enclose the punctuation within the quotation marks, as in

The captain wears "the uniform of his rank."

Farquhar's dream offers only a "momentary escape," according to

Hargroves.

For semicolons and colons, place the punctuation outside of the quotation marks, as in

The sentinels take "a formal and unnatural position"; the suggestion is

that such decorum goes against human nature.

The captain wears "the uniform of his rank": a long frock or sack coat

and an officer's cap or hat.

For question marks, exclamation points, and dashes that are part of the original quotation, enclose the mark within the quotation marks, as in

Farquhar immediately asks the soldier, "How far is it to Owl Creek

Bridge?"

"Company! . . . Attention! . . . Shoulder arms! . . . Ready! . . . Aim! . . . Fire!"

"Midway of the slope between the bridge and the fort were the

spectators—"

The passage breaks its description after the "spectators."
For question marks, exclamation points, and dashes that are part of your own writing, place the punctuation outside of the quotation mark, as in

Why is it that "in the code of military etiquette silence and fixity are

forms of deference"?

There must be something wrong with a system in which those

witnessing a hanging stand by like statues "staring stonily"!

The sentinels "might have been statues"—they are without emotion.

For quotation marks within a short in-text quotation, change the double quotation mark to a single quotation mark, as in

> The dream sequence is cast as a waking dream: "He unclosed his eyes
>
> and saw again the water below him. 'If I could free my hands,' he thought,
>
> 'I might throw off the noose and spring into the stream. . . . ' "

For parenthetical documentation of in-text quotations, first place the quotation mark around the quoted material, followed by the source information in parentheses, followed by the punctuation mark, as in

> Hargroves claims that, "the overall trajectory [of the story] is toward
>
> despair" (32).

For parenthetical documentation of long block quotations, place the punctuation mark after the block quotation, followed by the source information in parentheses, as in

> He closed his eyes in order to fix his last thoughts upon his wife
>
> and children. The water, touched to gold by the early sun, the
>
> brooding mists under the banks at some distance down the stream,
>
> the fort, the soldiers, the piece of drift—all had distracted him. And
>
> now he became conscious of a new disturbance. (167)

SUMMARIZING AND PARAPHRASING

Summaries and paraphrases allow you to process what you read and to explain its significance in your own words. Summaries have the advantage of allowing you to distill and make sense of large amounts of information. Paraphrases allow you to integrate the ideas of others into your work, while maintaining your own voice.

Summarizing

Summaries distill large amounts of information into more manageable chunks. You are likely to use summaries to develop an overview of a work of literature or to understand the gist of an essay. Summaries relate directly to critical thinking. As you read a literary work or essay, you are called to recognize the key ideas put forward. You will need to analyze the work to get at the components that deserve attention. Summaries also ask you to evaluate and synthesize the ideas you encounter. You will need to make connections between key points and draw conclusions about their importance and relationships as you compose a summary.

To compose a summary, you can rely on some specific strategies. You might want to create a reverse outline (see page 193) that lists the key points of each section of the work. Once you have distilled the key points of each section or passage, try to develop a statement about the central idea of the piece as a whole. Using this central idea as a thesis statement and the reverse outline, compose a paragraph that encapsulates the work into a summary.

When composing summaries, be careful not to focus entirely on plot. A plot summary can be useful to help you understand what takes place in a work. However, an insightful summary will keep plot elements to a minimum and emphasize the significance of events that take place. You can see the difference between a plot summary and a summary emphasizing themes and interpretation by comparing the two examples below.

Plot Summary:

"An Occurrence at Owl Creek Bridge" tells the story of a Southern planter, Peyton Farquhar, who regrets not being able to participate in the Civil War. Farquhar is tricked by a Union soldier into sabotaging a railroad bridge, is captured, and then sentenced to hang from the Owl Creek bridge. The story details Farquhar's thoughts as he awaits the hanging. Thoughts of his family launch him into a dream state in which the execution fails as the hangman's rope breaks and Farquhar falls into the waters of Owl Creek below. The story details Farquhar's escape after falling into the water. He eludes gunfire and cannon shots and eventually is carried downstream. He emerges from Owl Creek and runs many miles to find his home. As he finally reaches his home and is about to join his family, he emerges from the dream state and the story ends with the moment of his hanging.

Summary Emphasizing Interpretation:

"An Occurrence at Owl Creek Bridge" tells the story of a Southern planter, Peyton Farquhar, who is caught and sentenced to hang, after trying to blow up a railroad bridge during the Civil War. While Farquhar awaits the hanging, he slips into a dream state. The dream state contrasts sharply with the opening of the story, which emphasizes the organized and unfeeling nature of military operations and of Farquhar. The dream state introduces emotions. Farquhar's imaginary escape is marked by pain and struggle. As his dream and escape progresses, his perceptions of the world around him sharpen. His pain and suffering increase along with his perceptions until, in a final moment of realization, Farquhar emerges from the dream state at the instant he is released from the bridge and hung by the neck.

Paraphrasing

In a paraphrase, you restate the writing of another in your own words. A paraphrase resembles a quotation in that it brings the ideas of another directly into your
writing. Paraphrases allow you to distill a source somewhat (not as much as you
would in a summary) to bring out the main ideas. They can also add variety to your
writing by allowing you to do more than simply insert and discuss quotations.
You are likely to paraphrase a passage from a work of fiction and you should learn
to paraphrase excerpts from essays.

To compose a paraphrase, deliberate until you have a sense of an excerpt's
main points. You should also examine the sentence structure and phrasing used
in the original passage. Restate the main idea in your own words and rewrite the
passage using a new sentence structure. Compare the two sample passages below
to get a sense of how to create a paraphrase. The first passage is an original excerpt
from an article on "An Occurrence at Owl Creek Bridge." The second passage is
a paraphrase of the original.

Original Passage:

Everything in Farquhar's dream originates in the split second point of his
death. Farquhar's perception when the dream begins is wide, encompass-
ing the Federal stockade and the bridge. In his hallucination, he falls into the
river, where his perception is sharper but narrower; he sees the banks along
the river and the guards on the bridge directly behind him. When he gains
the riverbank, he finally runs along a road, where "the black bodies of the
trees formed a straight wall on both sides, terminating on the horizon in a
point, like a diagram in a lesson in perspective" (193). When Farquhar reaches this "point" he dies. Bierce [maps] death as a topological terminus. The
dissipation of consciousness here is a culmination of space in perspective.
The story is an exercise in perspective with Farquhar's death as the controlling point, the point at which the reader realizes his own capacity for
error. (Conlogue Par. 2)

Paraphrase:

Conlogue believes that, while Farquhar's initial viewpoint takes in the

soldiers and bridge, his hallucination at the point of death represents a

more focused perception. The description of his escape culminates with

Farquhar running down a road that ends in a point in the distance. As he

reaches this physical point in his escape, his imaginative journey comes to

a corresponding closing point. The reader, who has been carried along with

Farquhar, reaches a similar point and realizes that her own perceptions

have been mistaken during the story (Conlogue Par. 2).

As you draft, think carefully about when to use a quotation, when to summarize, and when to paraphrase. You will sometimes want to summarize to
provide background information and make sense of what you read. In many

cases, as you analyze works of literature you will need to use quotations so that you can provide evidence from the text and explain the significance of passages.

If you are reading secondary articles about a work, you should lean toward summary and paraphrase equally as often as you use direct quotation. Summaries can guide readers by emphasizing the most important points in an essay. Paraphrases will help you weave the ideas of others into your own writing more seamlessly. Both will prompt you to make sense of what you read.

As with quotations, you must be careful to avoid plagiarism when you summarize and paraphrase materials. Even though you have put something into your own words, since the ideas you are using derive from someone else's writing, you must give that source credit. Cite in parentheses the original sources of materials that you paraphrase (see the Appendix).

EXAMINING A DRAFT OF A PAPER

Included below is a draft of the paper discussing the short story and the film version of "An Occurrence at Owl Creek Bridge." We will also use this paper in the next chapter on revision and polishing.

Ronald Gains

Instructor Reynolds

English 102

22 April 2004

The Dream Conceals a Nightmare

Peyton Farquhar was dead; his body, with a broken neck,

swung gently from side to side beneath the timbers of the Owl

Creek bridge.

Introduction provides background. Ronald highlights themes rather than providing plot summary.
"An Occurrence at Owl Creek Bridge," by Ambrose Bierce, opens with

the hanging of a well-to-do Southern planter, Peyton Farquhar. Set during

the Civil War, the story emphasizes the dangers of covering up the

atrocities of death and war. The story ends with the stark image of

Farquhar's body swinging "gently from side to side" from the hangman's

noose. But between the opening moments of the story and the gruesome

final scene, a journey takes place in Farquhar's imagination. This

intervening moment makes up the majority of the 1962 film version of the

story and at first glance provides an alternate interpretation of the theme

<table>
<tr>
<td>

Thesis statement. Introduction concludes by stating the main focus of the paper.

</td>
<td>

of death by offering an escape through dreams. However, we learn at the end of the film that the dreams have been nothing more than a fiction that has allowed the viewer to ignore the reality of death. In the final analysis, the film's interpretation supports rather than undercuts the emphasis in the story on the atrocities of war and death.

</td>
</tr>
<tr>
<td>

Body paragraph. Topic sentence introduces the central idea to be discussed in the paragraph, in this case military roles and responsibility.

</td>
<td>

"An Occurrence at Owl Creek Bridge" suggests that military roles allow individuals to avoid responsibility for the atrocities of death and war. In the opening passages we're presented with a description of the scene of the hanging. This depiction, however, focuses primarily on the roles of the members of the military:

</td>
</tr>
<tr>
<td>

Block quotation. Quotations of more than four lines are indented ten spaces and inserted without quotation marks. The parenthetical citation comes after the punctuation.

</td>
<td>

Some loose boards laid upon the ties supporting the rails of the railway supplied a footing for him and his executioners—two private soldiers of the Federal army, directed by a sergeant who in civil life may have been a deputy sheriff. At a short remove upon the same temporary platform was an officer in the uniform of his rank, armed. He was a captain. A sentinel at each end of the bridge stood with his rifle in the position known as "support," that is to say, vertical in front of the left shoulder, the hammer resting on the forearm thrown straight across the chest—a formal and unnatural position, enforcing an erect carriage of the body (166).

</td>
</tr>
<tr>
<td>

Discussion of quotation. Ronald analyzes the details and draws conclusions about the passage. Note the paragraph contains mechanical problems like the spelling of "Farquaar." At this point in the writing process Ronald is concentrating on ideas.

</td>
<td>

Two groups make up the scene. In the first group we find "two private soldiers . . . directed by a sergeant." This group is primarily responsible for carrying out the hanging, and the two privates most likely have bound Farquaar and placed the noose around his neck. However, the passage states that these privates were "directed by [the] sergeant," implying that they are not responsible for their actions. With each character depicted, the scene emphasizes the role but not the responsibility. The most we learn about the captain is that he wears "the uniform of his rank." Further from

</td>
</tr>
</table>

Gains 3

the hanging platform we find two sentinels. The sentinels bring home the

point that military roles work against personal responsibility. A sentinel

suggests one who watches, one on the alert for trouble, even injustice.

In-text quotation. Ronald restates a section of the quotation. What do you think of this strategy?

Ironically, however, we are immediately told that "it did not appear to be the

duty of these two men to know what was occurring at the center of the

bridge; they merely blockaded the two ends of the foot planking that

traversed it" (166).

We know that Bierce played an important role in the Civil War. This

Biographical information. This paragraph covers Bierce's background. How does this paragraph relate to what has already been said in the paper?

biographical information sheds light on much of the military description

provided in "An Occurrence at Owl Creek Bridge." The levels of detail Bierce

provides speaks to his first-hand experience as a soldier: "A sentinel at each

end of the bridge stood with his rifle in the position known as 'support,' that

is to say, vertical in front of the left shoulder, the hammer resting on the

forearm thrown straight across the chest—a formal and unnatural position,

enforcing an erect carriage of the body." If we can assume a certain truth to

these descriptions based on Bierce's experience, we should give the same

truth to the statements that reveal the impact that the military can have on

individual's emotions: "The company faced the bridge, staring stonily,

motionless." The description suggests that the members of the military are

without emotion. In a sense they are removed from the realities of their

duty—hanging a fellow human being—by their role in the military.

The film version of "An Occurrence at Owl Creek Bridge" seems to

Use of image. Ronald adds an image to the paper. What do you think of the discussion of the image? Check the second draft in the next chapter to see how Ronald revised the paragraph.

depict the same unemotional nature of the members of the military. In part

this is accomplished through images that

highlight the regimented nature of the

members of the company. This image shows

the way that military groups ignore

individuality.

Gains 4

In the film version of "An Occurrence at Owl Creek Bridge," we are

presented with a vivid depiction of the possibilities for escape through

dreams. The dream sequences are initiated in the film through the image of

water. Atop the railroad trestle, Farquhar witnesses a small piece of

driftwood floating by on the stream. Shortly after, the scene shifts

drastically to Farquhar's home and family. The rope is also a symbol of

consciousness. When the sergeant steps off the board and Peyton Farquhar

falls from the trestle, the rope snaps. The film provides several clues that

the sequence that follows is part of a dream. First, Farquhar plunges into

the water. Water can represent a symbol of the subconscious or the dream

like state. When Peyton emerges from the water, however, the film adds to

the sense of the dream through the use of slow motion photography and

sound. Finally, the film techniques suggest that what is happening after

the snapping of the rope is a dream. Next, when Farquhar escapes the

scene of the hanging, he is carried off by a

vortex of water. In the film, the vortex is

represented as a series of rapids that hurry

Farquhar away from the spot where his body

will remain swinging back and forth from the

Owl Creek bridge.

Unfortunately the dream is short lived. Even in the beginning we are

given clues that the idea of escape may not be a reality. We're told that

Farquhar "lost consciousness and was <u>as one already dead</u>" (168; emphasis

added). In dreams we lose consciousness and often drift off into an

imaginative state where our minds are freed from the concerns of waking

life. Here, however, the dream state is compared with death. It is not

something to be longed for. Unlike the members of the military, Farqahar is

able to see the realities of the situation he is in. When he looks up at the

---

Margin annotations:

Focus of paragraph. A topic sentence signals a focus for the paragraph, escape through dreams. The body of the paragraph, however, emphasizes the role of water imagery. The reference to the rope signals a drift in focus away from the water imagery. See the next chapter to find out how Ronald revised this paragraph.

Transition and tension. The topic sentence signals a transition. The shift also adds an interest factor or twist to the essay—things are not as simple as they seem.

soldiers who are firing at him, he sees them as evil: "Their movements were

Discussion of film techniques. The author analyzes film techniques using appropriate details and drawing conclusions. See Chapter 11 for more on writing about film.

grotesque and horrible, their forms gigantic" (169). The film techniques used

to represent this grotesque moment also comment on the painful realities of

war. In the seen, slow motion is used to show the actions of the soldiers on

the bridge. The technique makes the soldiers appear inhuman and

monsterous. Even more telling is the use of slowed speech by the soldiers in

the film. In one instance the speech is hard to recognize but eventually the

effect is lessened until the captain is heard to say "you're trapped like a rat in

a trap. . . ." This bit of dialog has been added by the filmmaker to suggest the

way that war can dehumanize individuals—the soldiers see Fraquhar not as

an individual but as an animal, in fact as a rodent.

Plot summary. The writer discusses the end of the story. Does the paragraph move too close to plot summary? What should Ronald emphasize instead of the plot in this paragraph?

As the dream state continues, the promise of escaping the atrocities of

war seems to increase. When Farquhar is carried downstream he lands on a

small bank in the creek that is presented as a kind of garden in the film.

The reality of his situation, however, intervenes as canon fire is heard and

he must get up and run for home. As he runs, he appears to be getting

closer and closer to an imaginative state of happiness, a good dream, in the

film, this sequence is demonstrated by the scenes where he enters the gate

of his plantation and runs steadily toward his wife. The film promises a

final escape through the dream. Only to have it yanked away in the final

scene. Just as Farquahar is about to rush into the arms of his wife, the

Conclusion. The closing sentences reiterate the main points and tie them into the thesis. What might be added to help show why the main points and thesis are of interest?

music builds to a peak and the scene shifts back to Owl Creek bridge. Just

as in the short story, the dream of escape

from the atrocities of death and war has been

a fantasy. In fact, the dream has been a

nightmare for in the end despite all of the

regimented codes of military conduct that

Gains 6

allow individuals to escape and despite Farquhar's personal escape through

dreams, "Peyton Farquhar was dead; his body, with a broken neck, swung

gently from side to side beneath the timbers of the Owl Creek bridge" (171).

INQUIRING FURTHER

1. What is your response to this paper? What are its biggest strengths? What are its major weaknesses?

2. This paper integrates images from the film into its discussion. How successful do you think the treatment is? How should writers incorporate images into their compositions?

3. The thesis at the opening of the paper suggests that both the story and the film emphasize the dangers of avoiding the realities of war and death. What objections do you have to this angle? What alternate argument might you make about the significance of the story?

4. What two recommendations for major revisions would you give to the writer of this paper?

8

Revising and Polishing

> Writing is not like painting where you add. It is not what
> you put on the canvas that the reader sees. Writing is
> more like a sculpture where you remove, you eliminate in
> order to make the work visible. Even those pages you
> remove somehow remain.
>
> —*Elie Wiesel*

We do not often think of writing as removing words. Still, we have all seen our papers improve as we trim away unnecessary information and rearrange ideas. Deleting and reorganizing sections of our compositions makes sense if we understand the roles of revising and polishing within the writing process. The revision stage lies smack in the middle of the writing process, while the polishing stage takes place toward the end.

Revision requires us to make wholesale changes that will help our explanations move from idea to idea more clearly. To facilitate revision, we must practice giving and receiving feedback. Additionally, revision asks us to return to prewriting and drafting as we delete, move, or add information to our papers. Polishing requires editing to tighten and clarify our language. It also requires careful proofreading to eliminate mechanical errors and proper formatting to make our writing easier to read and give it added authority.

As we cover these topics in this chapter we will refer to the writing sample and the short story "An Occurrence at Owl Creek Bridge" from the previous chapter.

EVALUATING YOUR OWN WRITING

Before evaluating any papers, understand the benefits of getting some distance on your work. As you move from brainstorming to drafting, to revising, to polishing you can develop a familiarity with your work that prevents you from recognizing potential problems. Allow some time between drafting and revising, so you can reflect and gain perspective on your writing.

Similarly, when possible, print out a copy of your work for reviewing. In one way, when you print a copy, it distances your writing from what you have been viewing on screen, allowing you to see things freshly as you look them over on paper. With a printout, you also can lay all of the pages out before you and gain a sense of the overall construction of the paper. You can easily mark sections and work in the margins as well. We will look at electronic options in a moment, but be sure to consider the benefits of printing copies of your papers in order to evaluate them.

Begin evaluating your paper by locating your thesis. If you cannot clearly spot your thesis, your approach should be clarified as part of any revisions. Next, look over your introduction. Is there too much plot summary? Are there false starts? Does it provide enough background information for your audience? Does your introduction engage the reader? Does it demonstrate a framework for understanding your paper?

For the body paragraphs, split your evaluation into two steps:

1. Assess each paragraph to see that it has a clear topic sentence. Check also that the paragraph achieves unity and coherence. Are there tangents or ideas that do not fit? Finally, examine the depth of discussion for each paragraph. Is there enough detail to explain and illustrate the main idea? How relevant is the evidence and how well is it discussed? Which sections are thin and how might they be fleshed out?

2. Once you have looked over each body paragraph to check its unity and coherence, consider the organization of the paragraphs within the essay as a whole. Can related sections be combined? Are there tangents that can be deleted or folded into other sections? Does the organization of the paper move the discussion from idea to idea logically?

To check the organization of your paper as a whole, you can develop a **reverse outline.** Begin by noting the central idea of each paragraph in the margin, as in the sample shown in Figure 8.1. In Figure 8.1 we can see that the writer has read over the draft and indicated the key ideas for each section. Here the writer has noted a shift in emphasis within the paragraph.

Once you have listed all of the main ideas in each paragraph, you can create an outline based on your observations. Here is a reverse outline for the sample paper that concluded our previous chapter:

Introduction: The film supports the message in the story—they both

emphasize the atrocities of death and war

Paragraph one: Military roles allow individuals to avoid responsibility

Paragraph two: Bierce's Civil War experience adds truth to descriptions—

this idea seems out of place

Paragraph three: The film echoes the story regarding military roles

Paragraph four: The film shows escape through dreams using water

imagery

Paragraph five: Drifts

Topic 1. Escape through dreams may not be a reality

Topic 2. Monstrous and inhuman nature of war

Conclusion: Death is the reality

Unfortunately the dream is short lived. Even in the beginning we are given clues that the idea of escape may not be a reality. We're told that Farquhar "lost consciousness and was <u>as one already dead</u>" (168; emphasis added). In dreams we lose consciousness and often drift off into an imaginative state where our minds are freed from the concerns of waking life. Here, however, the dream state is compared with death. It is not something to be longed for. Unlike the members of the military, Farquhar is able to see the realities of the situation he is in. When he looks up at the soldiers who are firing at him, he sees them as monsters: "Their movements were grotesque and horrible, their forms gigantic" (169). The film techniques used to represent this grotesque moment also comment on the painful realities of war. In the scene, slow motion is used to show the actions of the soldiers on the bridge. The technique makes the soldiers appear inhuman and monsterous. Even more telling is the use of slowed speech by the soldiers in the film. In one instance the speech is hard to recognize but eventually the effect is lessened until the captain is heard to say "you're trapped like a rat in a trap. . . . " this bit of dialog has been added by the flimmaker to suggest the way that war can dehumanize individuals—the soldiers see Farquhar not as an individual but as an animal, in fact as a rodent.

Dreams + Escape

?

Realities + Monsters

Unhuman

FIGURE 8.1   Observing the Main Ideas in a Paper

The reverse outline reflects the observation shown in Figure 8.1 indicating that paragraph five drifts from its initial focus on dreams and escape. If we look more closely at the outline, however, we can see another possible point of drift. Most of the paragraphs focus on messages in the story or the film. Paragraph two, however, centers on Bierce's Civil War experience. The writer should address this drift in the revision of the paper.

GIVING AND RECEIVING FEEDBACK

The reactions of others can reveal your writing's strengths and weaknesses. Additionally, reading the works of your peers can help you spot problem areas in your own papers. To be productive, however, you will need some strategies for providing feedback.

You might begin by composing a **front comment** about your paper. A front comment spells out your main points and any concerns you have about your writing. Often you will share such a comment with reviewers as you give them your paper, but you can also use it to begin the process of reflection before you evaluate your work. Here is a front comment written by the author of our sample paper.

> I'm trying to argue that the story is about the dangers of overlooking the atrocities of death and war. I guess I'm also saying that the film agrees with this interpretation. My biggest concern with the paper is the dream sequences. I need to address how the dream fits in with the theme of overlooking death and war–or really escape from the realities. I don't know how convincing I am in making this point.

Similarly, readers can compose an **end comment** after they have evaluated a paper. End comments list reactions and sum up advice for possible revisions. Here is an end comment written by a reviewer about our sample paper.

> I like the way you discuss military roles and responsibilities. I think that is the strongest part of your paper. My biggest question is about the relationship between the story and the film. In some paragraphs I'm not sure whether the focus is the film or the story or both–if that makes sense? You might consider reorganizing to make the film versus story relationship more clear. Two other things–one is a biggie. What about the idea of slavery and the Civil War? I don't know if you want to address this question, but you seem to discuss avoiding responsibility. What responsibility should Farquhar have for his actions? He is a plantation owner. He did try to blow up the bridge. The other question I had was with the images from the film. I wasn't convinced that they helped your argument. Some of them just seemed to be decoration. You might want to limit the images or try to work them more into the argument in your writing.

End comments are often more detailed than a front comment, but they should not get heavily into specifics about surface-level issues. Instead, they should point out the big concerns and sum up a reader's overall impression of the piece.

Giving Constructive Feedback

We can look at two possible ways of reviewing a section of our sample paper to better understand how to give constructive feedback. Figure 8.2 shows the responses of two reviewers. As a reader you should pinpoint organizational and argument-related concerns. The first set of comments in Figure 8.2 concentrates on mechanical and sentence-level issues in the paper. At this stage of the writing process, sentence-level feedback fails to offer advice that will lead to deep and meaningful revision. The second reader has spotted what appears to be a problem with the argument—the reader worries whether arguing that Farquhar sees things differently is too simplistic. The typos and language issues will still need to be addressed (later), but fixing this concern with the argument really will make the paper stronger.

A reviewer should also provide an interested reader's perspective. Feedback can present a fresh set of eyes and ideas. An interested reader will offer responses that show this point of view. You can bring your perspective as a reader out by detailing your impressions. The second reader says "I'm not sure why, but this

Here, however, the dream state is compared with death.

It is not something to be longed for. Unlike the

members of the military, (Farqahar) is able to see the   *You spelled this*
                          his   *differently the last time!*
realities of the situation ~~he is in.~~ When he looks up at

the soldiers who are firing at him, he sees them as evil: *You should use a*
                                                             different word
"Their movements were grotesque and horrible, their   *here.*

forms gigantic"

Here, however, the dream state is compared with death.   *I'm not sure why*
                                                          but this raises a
It is not something to be longed for. Unlike the   *question for me. Is*
                          SP.   *Farquhar this*
members of the military, Farqahar is able to see the   *aware earlier? Is*
                                                          he just trying to
realities of the situation he is in. When he looks up at *save his skin? If*
                                                          you can explain how
the soldiers who are firing at him, he sees them as evil: *he develops this*
                                                          awareness it would help me
"Their movements were grotesque and horrible, their   *make sense of his view.*

forms gigantic"

FIGURE 8.2   Responses from Two Reviewers

raises a question for me." React to the key points in the papers you read to show the impact the writing has on you.

Be selective in providing feedback. A litany of problem areas or suggestions for improvement will overwhelm any writer. Distill your thinking about major points for revision. The second reader in the sample, for instance, has flagged the misspelling of Farquhar since it must be corrected. Rather than overwhelm the author with stylistic advice, however, she has pinpointed the most significant problems—the spelling error and the potential problem with the argument.

A reviewer should also lead the writer back into a process of inquiry. An interested reader thinks through the key problems, but does not do the work of revision for the author. Instead, a good reader raises relevant questions ("Is Farquhar this aware earlier?") that will prompt the writer to explore and address possible revisions. For sentence-level issues, look for patterns rather than every example of a problem (like passive sentences) and suggest that the author concentrate on locating and learning to fix the examples as they occur throughout the paper.

Giving Feedback Electronically

Frequently writers share drafts and provide feedback using computers. You might send papers to a partner through e-mail or a class discussion forum. A reviewer could then reply to the original message and embed comments within the text of the response. The screenshot in Figure 8.3 has been keyed with numbers to show how you can give this kind of electronic feedback.

1. **Sharing files:** Catherine has attached a file to this message. She also has sent a carbon copy to her instructor. Exchanging files as attachments and sending messages to multiple people can help you share files and conduct reviews.

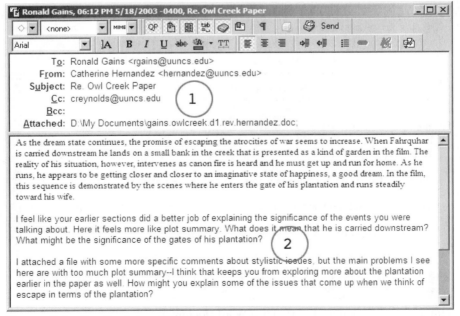

FIGURE 8.3   Feedback in an E-mail Message

2. **Cut-and-paste feedback:** In these most simple exchanges, the author can paste the text of his paper into the message. In the response, the reviewer will embed comments within the text of the original message. A reviewer can use a different font or capital letters to set off her comments. This method has the benefit of limiting the amount of surface-level attention one can give as a reader. Catherine focuses on the big questions, pointing out a problem with too much plot summary in this passage.

If you need to provide targeted feedback, you can exchange files and share comments using your word processor, as in the screen shot in Figure 8.4 which has been keyed with numbers.

1. **Inserting comments:** Using the Comment option found under the Insert menu, Adam has embedded a comment into the text of the paper he is reviewing. The comment then appears in colored brackets in the text of the paper.

2. **Viewing comments:** When a reader places the computer cursor over the bracketed comment, the response will appear in a floating pop-up window. You can make comments on small details in the text with this method. However, again, you will want to provide feedback that will do the writer the most good—here Adam points out the problem that the discussion of the rope brings to the coherency of the paragraph.

Tutorial for giving feedback electronically

If you are asked to provide feedback electronically, your instructor can give you more information about the logistics. (You should also explore the video tutorial on our CD-ROM; it provides detailed explanations about how best to use these tools.)

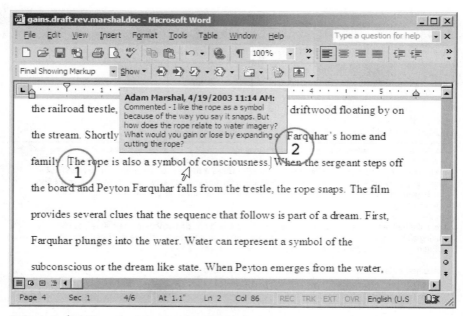

FIGURE 8.4   Comments Inserted in a Word Document

✔CHECKLIST FOR PROVIDING FEEDBACK

☐ **Check to see if the author of the paper has written a front comment** expressing major questions or concerns. If not, consider asking the writer to share impressions of the paper before you begin reviewing.

☐ **Read the paper once** without heavily marking or analyzing the details of the essay. Get a feel for the strengths and weaknesses of the paper.

☐ **See if you can locate the thesis** of the paper. If you cannot pinpoint a specific thesis, make note of your confusion and sketch out the approach being taken in the essay as best as you can.

☐ **Provide an interested reader** for the paper. Share with the author the impact that the writing is having on you. Avoid simply listing your feelings without connecting them to possible adjustments in the paper—rather than saying "I'm confused," say "I'm not convinced that there is a connection between the rope and water imagery here."

☐ **Focus on the big organizational concerns** in the essay. For each paragraph, look for unity and coherence and make note of paragraphs that drift from their central idea or that fail to present a clear topic sentence. Examine also the organization of the paper as a whole. Are there places where the ideas do not flow from one to another or where the paper drifts from its thesis?

☐ **Question the argument** put forth in the paper. Are there gaps in the logic? Are there alternative approaches that deserve attention? Is the argument and approach faithful to the work? (See Chapter 5 for more on arguments.)

☐ **Lead the writer back into a process of inquiry.** Carefully consider ways of resolving questions that you have, but phrase your deliberations to prompt the writer to investigate these possibilities on her own.

☐ **Leave most sentence-level proofreading for the author** to do at a later stage. When you spot larger patterns that indicate a stylistic or mechanical problem, alert the writer to the issue but do not nitpick at the expense of locating deep and meaningful opportunities for revision.

☐ **Compose an end comment** that distills your advice about revising the paper. Highlight the most significant questions you have and a few concrete steps the writer might take to strengthen the paper.

RETURNING TO PREWRITING AND DRAFTING

The good news and the bad news about revising is that you are far from finished with the drafting of your paper. You still have many opportunities to sharpen your focus and make explanations more clear and convincing. But you still have a lot of work to do after you hit save for the final time on the first draft of your composition.

The writer of our paper on "An Occurrence at Owl Creek Bridge," Ronald Gains, considered all of the feedback he received and decided to brainstorm about revisions to his paper. He began by listing three major concerns about his draft:

1. The biggie—what is Farquhar's role or guilt? Why not explore messages related to plantation culture as well as the military?

2. Images are not discussed. True. Should cut most out or connect with points about film.

3. Drifting focus—some paragraphs cover story, some cover film, some cover both. Also tangents in the paragraphs like "the rope." Need to reorganize to separate ideas more clearly.

You may find it useful to go all the way back to freewriting or listing (see pages 154–57) to help you refine your paper. Your revision also might benefit from a cluster map or an outline (pages 161–63). You will also, no doubt, return to the drafting stage of the writing process, having to produce new text or expand on ideas that are currently too thin.

The importance of drafting and reorganizing in the revision stage of the writing process can be seen if we track the changes we make to a document. To track the changes you make while revising, select the Track Changes option from the Tools menu of your word processor. Tracking the changes in a document allows you to revise more freely because nothing is deleted from the original. At a later point you can decide whether to accept or reject the changes you have made. Additionally, tracking changes helps you visualize your revision process. If the underline and strikethrough fonts reveal minor changes made on surface-level issues in the document, you should recheck your work to see if it needs deeper organizational revisions as well (most drafts do).

The numbers in the screen shot in Figure 8.5 shows some of the revising that has been tracked on Ronald Gains's paper.

Using word processors to revise papers

1. **New text is indicated with underlined font:** In this case, the writer has moved a sentence from the bottom of the paragraph closer to the top.

2. **Deleted text is indicated with a strikethrough font:** Here we see that the author has decided to eliminate the sentences discussing the rope as a symbol so that he can concentrate on the water imagery in the paragraph.

✔ CHECKLIST FOR REVISING A PAPER

☐ **Compose a front comment** encapsulating your major concerns for the paper and any questions you might like to ask reviewers. Share this comment with your peers before they review your paper.

☐ **Examine your introduction, body paragraphs, and conclusion.**
Does your introduction spell out a framework for reading the paper that includes a thesis? Does each body paragraph contain a clear topic sentence? Does each paragraph achieve unity, coherence, and depth? Does your conclusion tie things together or make a final point?

☐ **Create a reverse outline** listing the central ideas in each paragraph. Does the outline show sections where the paper drifts from the thesis? Is the organization of the paper logical? What rearrangements should you make?

☐ **Solicit feedback** from interested readers about your paper. Look for advice that will lead you toward meaningful organizational revisions.

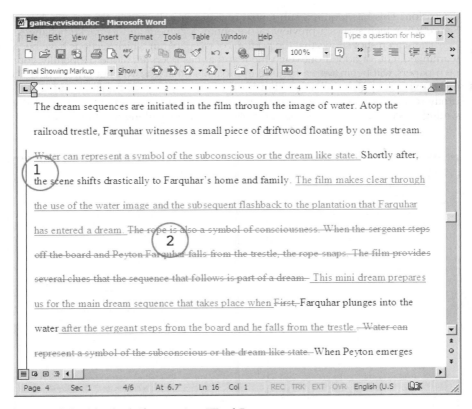

FIGURE 8.5   Tracked Changes in a Word Document

Take seriously any questions about your argument, considering revisions that will address gaps and inconsistencies spotted by your readers.

☐ **Return to prewriting and drafting** activities. Brainstorm to refine your approach and develop ideas for further writing. Draft new text, delete unnecessary material, and rearrange existing sections of your essay as you would when composing a draft.

☐ **Use your word processor skillfully** to make revisions. Save a duplicate copy of your draft with a new name to begin your revision. Experiment with Versioning or Track Changes functions to further your revision process. Use shortcuts and text moving strategies to work fluidly with the text of your essay.

EXAMINING A REVISION

The screen shot showing the tracked changes in Figure 8.5 illustrates the changes to one section of Ronald's paper. As he continued to revise, Ronald also shifted his focus to include plantation society and deleted the section on Bierce's Civil War experience. He also reorganized sections to separate the film from the story in his

Paper draft and revision samples

discussion. This has required substantial revision as indicated in the screen shot in Figure 8.6, which shows a preview of the entire document and its tracked changes.

The screen shot shows that the portions of the paper in which sections have been rearranged, cut, or added outweigh the text that has been left alone. Hopefully your own papers will begin with a focused approach so that you will not always have to make extensive, global changes, but be ready to adjust your thinking and significantly revise your work when necessary. Remember, there is an entire stage in the writing process left in which you can polish and tie everything together neatly.

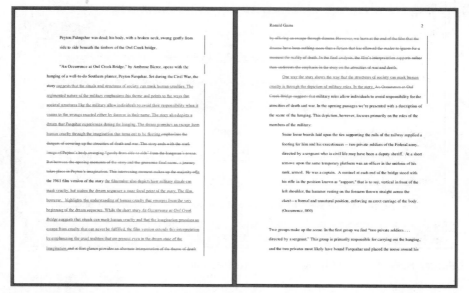

FIGURE 8.6   Tracked Changes Showing the Revisions to Ronald Gains's Paper

POLISHING A PAPER

The polishing process begins after the substantive changes you have made while revising. You then tighten and refine your writing through **editing.** Papers must then be combed through carefully for stylistic and mechanical problems that can be corrected through **proofreading.** Finally, the **formatting** of papers must be checked and adjusted before they are ready for viewing by others.

Editing

When drafting or revising, we write to explain and organize ideas. When editing, we examine how clearly and economically our writing expresses those ideas. Even after it has gone through a draft and revision, most writing can be improved by revising **flat** and **passive sentences** and **combining sentences** for concision and clarity.

Begin sharpening your writing by replacing flat and passive sentences with active language that demonstrates your points powerfully. Consider this paragraph from our sample paper:

One way the story shows the way that the structures of society can mask human cruelty is through the depiction of military roles. In the story, military roles allow individuals to avoid responsibility for the atrocities of death and war. In the opening passages we are presented with a description of the scene of the hanging. This depiction, however, focuses primarily on the roles of the members of the military.

We can edit the first sentence to make it more compelling and concise by replacing the "is through" verb construction with a stronger verb.

Original sentence: One way the story shows the way that the structures of society can mask human cruelty is through the depiction of military roles.

Revised sentence: Military roles illustrate how the structures of society can mask human cruelty.

Similarly, we can eliminate the passive language from the third sentence.

Original sentence: In the opening passages we are presented with a description of the scene of the hanging.

Revised sentence: The opening passages present a description of the hanging.

When editing, look for opportunities to eliminate the passive baggage attached to the core of your sentences. Look for phrases like "it is. . . . " or "there are. . . . " Where you find passive sentences, revise them to emphasize a concrete subject and a strong verb that demonstrate your meaning concisely.

Eliminating passive language and combining sentences

You can also combine sentences and delete unnecessary language to make your writing more powerful. In the sample, the first two sentences discuss military roles. Even without editing the passive language, the writing can benefit from consolidating the ideas.

Original sentences: One way the story shows the way that the structures of society can mask human cruelty is through the depiction of military roles. In the story, military roles allow individuals to avoid responsibility for the atrocities of death and war.

Revised sentence: Military roles illustrate how the structures of society can mask human cruelty and allow individuals to avoid responsibility for the atrocities of death and war.

We can also combine the last two sentences.

Original sentences: In the opening passages we are presented with a description of the hanging. This depiction, however, focuses primarily on the roles of the members of the military.

Revised sentence: The description of the hanging in the opening scene focuses primarily on the roles of the members of the military.

When combining sentences, first distill them into their core meanings, eliminating unnecessary language. Once you have distilled the ideas, look for opportunities to combine sentences to make your writing more powerful and concise.

Our revised passage expresses the same ideas with clarity and concision:

Military roles illustrate how the structures of society can mask human cruelty and allow individuals to avoid responsibility for the atrocities of death and war. The description of the hanging in the opening scene focuses primarily on the roles of the members of the military.

Exercise 8.1   *Eliminating Passive Language*

Working with a group of fellow students (or on your own if your instructor prefers), revise the sentences below to eliminate passive language. Begin by selecting someone to keep track of the group's work (or preparing to take notes on your own).

1. Identify the subject of the sentence, and then locate the passive verb that diminishes the force of the sentence.

2. Revise the sentence. First, emphasize its subject (usually beginning the sentence with its subject can focus the sentence). Second, select a strong verb to replace the passive construction in the sentence.

3. Eliminate any extraneous language to make the sentence as concise as possible.

Follow these steps to write revisions for the following sentences:

- Each time the promise of escape emerges, it is broken in upon by the reality of Peyton's impending fate.
- To understand plantation culture it is important to examine its roles and rituals.
- The imagination and its perceptions have a way of being refined by the stress of extreme situations.
- There are many depictions of the military in the film that resemble those in the story.
- Escape has been on Farquhar's mind throughout the story.
- It is necessary to view time as a flexible concept to understand the imaginative journey.
- In the film this sequence is demonstrated by the scenes where he runs steadily toward his wife.
- The key theme that emerges as the story unfolds is that water can be a means of changing consciousness.

Exercise 8.2   *Combining Sentences*

Working with a group of fellow students (or on your own if your instructor prefers), combine the sentences below to make the writing more concise. Begin by selecting a person to keep track of the group's work (or preparing to take notes on your own).

1. Identify the core meanings of each of the sentences.
2. Revise the sentences into one sentence that maintains the core meanings.
3. Eliminate any extraneous language to make the revised sentence as concise as possible.

Follow these steps to write revisions for the following grouped sentences:

- In the end, both the story and the film promote a similar message. They highlight the ways that structures like the military or the codes of conduct in plantation society mask human cruelty and responsibility.
- This image shows the way that military groups ignore individuality. In the image, the soldiers all assume the identical position.
- The lieutenant is distinguished by his hat and his raised bayonet. At the same time, the lieutenant is more similar in appearance than different from the rest of the men.
- Two groups make up the scene. In the first group we find "two private soldiers . . . directed by a sergeant." This group is primarily responsible for carrying out the hanging, and the two privates most likely have bound Farquhar and placed the noose around his neck.
- Further from the hanging platform we find two sentinels. The sentinels bring home the point that military roles work against personal responsibility.

Proofreading

At this stage in the writing process we may feel like we know every detail of our essay. That level of familiarity, unfortunately, can prevent us from seeing problems at all. The screen shot in Figure 8.7 shows some proofreading that has been performed on a few sentences from our sample essay. In the second line, the writer has deleted a repetition of the word *that*. These kinds of errors result directly from our familiarity with our work. We may have read the sentence fifteen times and we know what it says, so we overlook details like repeated words.

In the second line we see a common problem that results from relying on a word processor's spelling checker. The word *seen* is spelled correctly, but it is a **homonym** (a word that sounds exactly like another word) that is used incorrectly here. In line four, the spelling checker fails to recognize *an* as a problem because it is spelled correctly; however, the sentence requires the word *and*. To catch problems with homonyms or words spelled correctly but used incorrectly, you must rely on your own proofreading skills rather than your spelling checker.

The other corrections in the screen shot demonstrate the careful attention necessary for proofreading. Catching the comma splice at the end of line two demands that you see and hear your writing objectively. A good strategy is to work sentence by sentence through your essay. You can use a ruler or folded sheet of paper to "block out" each section as you read. When you stumble over a confusing phrase, consult your own knowledge and your grammar and style resources and revise to make things clear.

You should also try to print out a copy of your work as it nears the final stages. Take pencil in hand and mark the small mechanical problems like misused or missing words. Look out for any surface level details like missing or extra spaces. Use a system of proofreading marks so that you can note any changes to be made.

The techniques used by the filmmaker to represent this scene suggest

that ~~that~~ the realities of war are painful. In the *scene* seen, slow motion is

used, so that the actions of the soldiers on the bridge seem inhuman.

The technique makes the soldiers appear brutal an monstrous.

Their speech is hard to recognize but eventually the effect is lessened

until the captain is heard to say *you're* your trapped like a rat in a trap. . . ."

This bit of dialog has been added ~~by the filmmaker~~ to suggest that war

dehumanizes individuals.

Figure 8.7   Proofreading Marks

✔CHECKLIST FOR EDITING AND PROOFREADING

☐ **Eliminate passive language** to make your sentences more clear and compelling. Use "is" and "are" sentences sparingly. Instead emphasize the subject of the sentence and select a strong verb that demonstrates your meaning.

☐ **Evaluate the core meaning of your sentences** and see if you can eliminate unnecessary words. Look for opportunities to reduce repetition. Compare sentences with one another; when they make similar points, combine them to make your writing more coherent and concise.

☐ **Break away from the familiarity you have developed with your paper.** Read the paper aloud to develop an ear for catching potential problems with grammar and style. Experiment with strategies to disrupt your comfort level—read the paper backwards or evaluate your essay sentence by sentence to look for errors.

☐ **Use your word processor's spelling, grammar, and style checkers critically.** These tools can be of great assistance as you polish your paper. They can also trip you up if you fail to understand their strengths and weaknesses. Complement your word processor by reading carefully to spot errors unrecognized by the checker and to ensure your work is problem free.

☐ **Print out, when possible, a copy of your almost-completed paper** and read it several times with pencil in hand. Scan for surface-level problems and establish a proofreading system to note, and later fix, errors that you discover.

Formatting Documents

No matter how convincingly you have written your paper, it will find a poor reception if it is not properly prepared for viewing by others. This preparation requires checking and readying documentation about the sources that you have used. Documenting sources convinces others that you have done the work necessary to speak on the topic with authority. It also shows that you have made a good faith effort to help others follow up on your research. (You can find detailed information about documenting sources in the Appendix.)

Readying your documents for viewing also requires formatting the text of your paper and preparing margins, headers, and other conventional elements of a printed document. (The best information for how to format your documents can be found on our CD-ROM.) Some of the things to remember are illustrated in the screen shot in Figure 8.8, which has been keyed with numbers. Be sure to check with your instructor to see if there are any specific conventions required for your assignments.

Using word processors to format documents

1. **Name and course information:** Place your name, the name of your instructor, your class, and the date at the top of the first page of your paper. Use double spaces for these items.

2. **Name and page number:** Create a header, set one-half inch from the top of the page, with your name and page numbers. Do not add these page numbers or information by hand. Learn to use the features of your word processor to create a standardized header or footer and to vary that header from page to page. Note that the screen shot shows this information so that we can discuss where to place the header in a document. In most cases, however, you will begin the header on the second page—again, see our CD tutorials.

3. **Title:** Place your title at the top of the essay. Center the title and use a standard font. Invest some effort into finding a title that furthers the ideas in your essay.

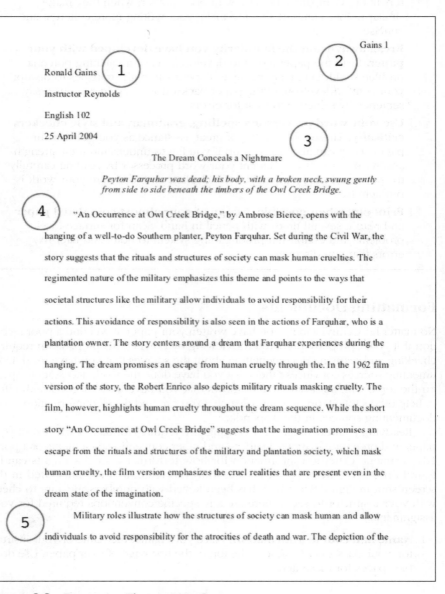

FIGURE 8.8   Formatting Elements in a Document

Never use a title like *Essay One* or *Hemingway Paper*. Instead, see if you can capture your thesis or set the tone for your essay as you select a title.

4. **Typeface:** Use a standard font (such as Times, Times New Roman, or Courier) for the text of your essay. Double space the text in the body paragraphs. Indent the first line of each paragraph five spaces.

5. **Margins:** Set margins of at least one inch (and not more than one and a quarter inches) at the top, bottom, left, and right sides of your document.

In some cases, you will make a cover page for your essay. The cover page will provide your name, the name of your instructor and class, the date, and the title of your paper. Use standard fonts and center the information on your cover page. If you use a cover page, you only need to add the title to the top of the first page of the paper. You will also need to make a **Works Cited** page (see the Appendix).

EXAMINING A POLISHED PAPER

Here is one last look at our sample paper. Ronald has made more revisions during the final stages of editing and has proofread and formatted the essay in preparation for submitting it. If you want to examine the development of the paper through the writing process, compare this final version to the first draft on pages 186–91.

Format and title. The paper has proper margins. It provides name and course information at the top. It uses double spacing and indents the first line of each paragraph five spaces. The title catches the reader's interest and alludes to the thesis of the paper.

Ronald Gains

Instructor Reynolds

English 102

25 April 2004

The Dream Conceals a Nightmare

Peyton Farquhar was dead; his body, with a broken neck,

swung gently from side to side beneath the timbers of the Owl

Creek bridge.

"An Occurrence at Owl Creek Bridge," by Ambrose Bierce, opens with

the hanging of a well-to-do Southern planter, Peyton Farquhar. Set during

the Civil War, the story suggests that the rituals and structures of society

can mask human cruelties. The regimented nature of the military

Revisions to main ideas. The paper now takes up the issue of Farquhar's role in the story, addressing the responsibility of plantation owners.

emphasizes this theme and points to the ways that societal structures like

the military allow individuals to avoid responsibility for their actions. This

avoidance of responsibility is also seen in the actions of Farquhar, who is a

plantation owner. The story centers around a dream that Farquhar

experiences during the hanging. The dream promises an escape from

Gains 2

human cruelty through the imagination. In the 1962 film version of the

story, Robert Enrico also depicts military rituals masking cruelty. The film,

however, highlights human cruelty throughout the dream sequence. While

Thesis statement. The introduction concludes with a revised thesis statement. the short story "An Occurrence at Owl Creek Bridge" suggests that the

imagination promises an escape from the cruelty hidden by military rituals

and plantation society, the film version emphasizes the cruel realities that

are present even in the dream state of the imagination.

Sentence-level polishing. Ronald has edited these sentences to make them clear. Military roles illustrate how the structures of society can mask human

cruelty and allow individuals to avoid responsibility for the atrocities of

death and war. The depiction of the hanging in the opening scene focuses

primarily on the roles of the members of the military:

> Some loose boards laid upon the ties supporting the rails of the
>
> railway supplied a footing for him and his executioners—two
>
> private soldiers of the Federal army, directed by a sergeant who in
>
> civil life may have been a deputy sheriff. At a short remove upon
>
> the same temporary platform was an officer in the uniform of his
>
> rank, armed. He was a captain. A sentinel at each end of the bridge
>
> stood with his rifle in the position known as "support," that is to
>
> say, vertical in front of the left shoulder, the hammer resting on the
>
> forearm thrown straight across the chest—a formal and unnatural
>
> position, enforcing an erect carriage of the body. (166)

Discussion of quotation. Ronald provides detailed explanations about how he interprets the passage he has quoted; he does not assume the reader will see the same thing he sees. In the scene we find "two private soldiers . . . directed by a sergeant."

This group is primarily responsible for carrying out the hanging, and the

two privates most likely have bound Farquhar and placed the noose around

his neck. However, the passage states that these privates were "directed by

[the] sergeant," implying that they are not accountable for their actions.

With each character depicted, the scene emphasizes the role but not the

responsibility. The most we learn about the captain is that he wears "the uniform of his rank." The uniform emphasizes the role not the individual.

Additionally, even these roles are brought into question through the

figures of the sentinel. A sentinel suggests one who watches, one on the

alert for trouble, even injustice. Ironically, however, we are told that "it did

not appear to be the duty of these two men to know what was occurring at

the center of the bridge; they merely blockaded the two ends of the foot

planking that traversed it" (167). The story suggests that the regimented

nature of the military enables individuals to overlook their responsibility

for the hanging.

> **Connections with thesis. Gains has added a sentence here tying the paragraph back in with the thesis.**

   As the story progresses, however, a number of clues reveal that this

criticism is not meant only for the military. In the behavior of Farquhar

and his wife at the plantation we also see regimented codes of conduct.

When the "gray-clad soldier" approaches, we're told that "Mrs. Farquhar

was only too happy to serve him with her own white hands" (167). This is

one of the few times in the story when race is highlighted. On one level, it

simply suggests that there are distinct roles within plantation society.

Mrs. Farquhar is willing to overlook them in this instance so that she can

serve the water to someone she thinks is a fellow member of Southern

society. Immediately after this simple gesture, however, Farquhar shows

> **New section. A paragraph has been added to discuss Farquhar's role and responsibility in the story. This was one of the major objections raised by Gains's classmates when reading his first draft.**

his own role in plantation society: "'Suppose a man—a civilian and

student of hanging—should elude the picket post and perhaps get the

better of the sentinel,' said Farquhar, smiling, 'what could he

accomplish?'" (168). Here we see that the realities of the roles and rituals

of Farquhar's society are more significant than simple rules about who

should serve a stranger a drink of water. The reality is death by hanging,

and yet, like the sentinels who act as statues, Farquhar is depicted as a

student of such atrocities, an observer who studies objectively rather than

shares in the responsibility for death.

Discussion of image. The paragraph has been expanded to discuss the details of the image and draw conclusions about their significance.

The film version of "An Occurrence at Owl Creek Bridge" depicts the same unemotional nature of the members of the military. In part this is accomplished through images that highlight the regimented nature of the company. The image of the soldiers on the ridge shows the way that military groups suppress individuality. In the image, the soldiers assume an identical position and wear similar uniforms. The lieutenant is distinguished by his hat and his raised sword. However, the lieutenant is more similar in appearance than different from the rest of the men. His individuality allows him to give the orders to fire at Farquhar, but his similarity and membership in the company diminishes his personal responsibility for giving those orders.

Relevant image. Gains has deleted images in the earlier draft and kept those that reflect directly the ideas in the paper.

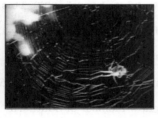

The film, <u>An Occurrence at Owl Creek Bridge</u>, differs the most from the story in its use of the dream sequence to make a point about the impossibility of fully masking the nature of human cruelty. The dream sequence that begins when Farquhar emerges from the water emphasizes the promise of escape by laying the sounds of nature and the song "A Living Man" over images of nature. On closer inspection, however, those images already suggest death and destruction. The scene ends with a close up of a spider's web and zooms in on the spider wrapping up its prey. The film is already sending forth the message that even in the dream we find death.

As the film cuts away from the scenes of nature, we see things from the dream perspective of Farquhar, a perspective revealing the realities beneath the dream. When he looks up at the soldiers who are firing at him,

Discussion of
film
techniques.
The writer
explores
details such as
slowed speech
and slow
motion
photography.
For more on
film
techniques, see
Chapter 11.
he sees them as monstrous. The film techniques representing this

grotesque moment comment on the painful realities of war. In the scene,

slow motion photography showing the actions of the soldiers on the bridge

makes the soldiers appear inhuman and monstrous. The use of slowed

speech by the soldiers in the film heightens this sense. When the slow

motion effects end, the captain is heard to say "you're trapped like a rat in a

trap. . . ." We see the grotesque nature of the soldier's actions. But we also

see that, like the spider in the web, Farquhar cannot escape his situation.

Again, the military and plantation society are connected as the soldiers and

the planter are bound by the web that makes up their roles in regimented

and ritualized societies.

As the dream state continues, each time the promise of escape emerges,

it is interrupted by the reality of Farquhar's impending fate. In the final

scene, as Farquhar runs, he appears to be getting closer and closer to the

safety of his plantation home. In the scene, Farquhar holds out his arms

longingly and a look of fulfillment enters his face. Ironically, however, as

his happiness grows and he reaches out, the scene snaps back to the

moment of his death. The message is that, even in the imaginative state of

the dream, escape is impossible.

Conclusion.
The final
paragraph
returns to the
comparison
between the
film and the
story and
reiterates the
thesis.
In the end, both the story and the film promote a similar message. They

highlight the ways that structures like the military or the codes of conduct in

plantation society mask human cruelty and responsibility. The film amplifies

this message through the use of slow motion camera techniques. Just as in

the short story, the dream of escape has been a fantasy. In fact, both the film

and the short story reveal that beneath the regimented codes of social conduct

and Farquhar's personal escape through the imagination, lie grotesque

scenes of destruction and death. The dream conceals a nightmare.

Gains 6

Works Cited

Bierce, Ambrose. "An Occurrence at Owl Creek Bridge." <u>Writing about</u>

<u>Literature in the Media Age</u>. Ed. Daniel Anderson. New York:

Pearson Longman, 2005.

<u>An Occurrence at Owl Creek Bridge</u>. Dir. Robert Enrico. 1962. Monterey

Media, 1996.

INQUIRING FURTHER

1. How would you characterize the revision that has taken place in Gains's paper? Do you find it significant? How well do you think Ronald has responded to the feedback of his peers?

2. How do Gains's revisions compare to your usual process of revision? Do you generally make the kind of large-scale revisions indicated on page 202?

3. How successfully do you think the paper discusses images from the film? Does the expanded discussion make you more convinced of the argument in the paper? What would you say to Ronald about his discussion of the film?

4. What further suggestions would you make to improve the paper? If you had to select one recommendation, what would it be?

PART III

Thinking and Writing About Literature and Art

9

Thinking and Writing About Fiction

> Good fiction reveals feeling, refines events, locates importance and, though its methods are as mysterious as they are varied, intensifies the experience of living our own lives.
>
> —*Vincent Canby*

Fiction *should* teach us something about "living our own lives." When we read fiction, we compare what we know (places, people, events) to the elements of fiction that make up stories: settings, characters, plot, tone, points of view, symbols and themes. Through fiction we relate imaginary situations and characters to our own experience, recognizing insights for daily living and deepening our appreciation of the works we read.

When we read stories and novels, we move from personal impressions of these fictional situations to critical awareness of their possible significance. The process allows us to react to what we read, refine impressions by considering the elements of fiction, test and revise our understanding by conducting research or constructing arguments, and write about our approach so we can share it with others.

REACTING TO SETTINGS, CHARACTERS, SYMBOLS, AND THEMES

In this chapter we will read two short stories to help us investigate fiction. We will start with "Where Are You Going, Where Have You Been?" by Joyce Carol Oates.

JOYCE CAROL OATES

Joyce Carol Oates (born in 1938) grew up on a farm near Millerstown, New York. Her childhood experiences were those of small-town life and economic hardship. She began writing in high school, completing several novels, none of which were published. In college she won the Mademoiselle *award for fiction and published in the* Best American Short Stories *collection, after which she turned her full attention to writing and teaching. Her fiction often reflects the rural settings and working class background of her youth. "Where Are You Going, Where Have You Been?" has several interesting sources that are discussed later in the chapter. The story was published in 1966.*

Where Are You Going, Where Have You Been?

For Bob Dylan

Her name was Connie. She was fifteen and she had a quick, nervous, giggling habit of craning her neck to glance into mirrors or checking other people's faces to make sure her own was all right. Her mother, who noticed everything and knew everything and who hadn't much reason any longer to look at her own face, always scolded Connie about it. "Stop gawking at yourself. Who are you? You think you're so pretty?" she would say. Connie would raise her eyebrows at these familiar old complaints and look right through her mother, into a shadowy vision of herself as she was right at that moment: she knew she was pretty and that was everything. Her mother had been pretty once too, if you could believe those old snapshots in the album, but now her looks were gone and that was why she was always after Connie.

"Why don't you keep your room clean like your sister? How've you got your hair fixed—what the hell stinks? Hair spray? You don't see your sister using that junk."

Her sister June was twenty-four and still lived at home. She was a secretary in the high school Connie attended, and if that wasn't bad enough—with her in the same building—she was so plain and chunky and steady that Connie had to hear her praised all the time by her mother and her mother's sisters. June did this, June did that, she saved money and helped clean the house and cooked and Connie couldn't do a thing, her mind was all filled with trashy daydreams. Their father was away at work most of the time and when he came home he wanted supper and he read the newspaper at supper and after supper he went to bed. He didn't bother talking much to them, but around his bent head Connie's mother kept picking at her until Connie wished her mother was dead and she herself was dead and it was all over. "She makes me want to throw up sometimes," she complained to her friends. She had a high, breathless, amused voice that made everything she said sound a little forced, whether it was sincere or not.

There was one good thing: June went places with girlfriends of hers, girls who were just as plain and steady as she, and so when Connie wanted to do that her mother had no objections. The father of Connie's best girlfriend drove the girls the three miles to town and left them at a shopping plaza so they could walk through the stores or go to a movie, and when he came to pick them up again at eleven he never bothered to ask what they had done.

5   They must have been familiar sights, walking around the shopping plaza in their shorts and flat ballerina slippers that always scuffed the sidewalk, with charm bracelets jingling on their thin wrists; they would lean together to whisper and laugh secretly if someone passed who amused or interested them. Connie had long dark blond hair that drew anyone's eye to it, and she wore part of it pulled up on her head and puffed out and the rest of it she let fall down her back. She wore a pull-over jersey blouse that looked one way when she was at home and another way when she was away from home. Everything about her had two sides to it, one for home and one for anywhere that was

not home: her walk, which could be childlike and bobbing, or languid enough to make anyone think she was hearing music in her head; her mouth, which was pale and smirking most of the time, but bright and pink on these evenings out; her laugh, which was cynical and drawling at home—"Ha, ha, very funny"—but highpitched and nervous anywhere else, like the jingling of the charms on her bracelet.

Sometimes they did go shopping or to a movie, but sometimes they went across the highway, ducking fast across the busy road, to a drive-in restaurant where older kids hung out. The restaurant was shaped like a big bottle, though squatter than a real bottle, and on its cap was a revolving figure of a grinning boy holding a hamburger aloft. One night in midsummer they ran across, breathless with daring, and right away someone leaned out a car window and invited them over, but it was just a boy from high school they didn't like. It made them feel good to be able to ignore him. They went up through the maze of parked and cruising cars to the bright-lit, fly-infested restaurant, their faces pleased and expectant as if they were entering a sacred building that loomed up out of the night to give them what haven and blessing they yearned for. They sat at the counter and crossed their legs at the ankles, their thin shoulders rigid with excitement, and listened to the music that made everything so good: the music was always in the background, like music at a church service; it was something to depend upon.

A boy named Eddie came in to talk with them. He sat backwards on his stool, turning himself jerkily around in semi-circles and then stopping and turning back again, and after a while he asked Connie if she would like something to eat. She said she would and so she tapped her friend's arm on her way out—her friend pulled her face up into a brave, droll look—and Connie said she would meet her at eleven, across the way. "I just hate to leave her like that," Connie said earnestly, but the boy said that she wouldn't be alone for long. So they went out to his car, and on the way Connie couldn't help but let her eyes wander over the windshields and faces all around her, her face gleaming with a joy that had nothing to do with Eddie or even this place; it might have been the music. She drew her shoulders up and sucked in her breath with the pure pleasure of being alive, and just at that moment she happened to glance at a face just a few feet from hers. It was a boy with shaggy black hair, in a convertible jalopy painted gold. He stared at her and then his lips widened into a grin. Connie slit her eyes at him and turned away, but she couldn't help glancing back and there he was, still watching her. He wagged a finger and laughed and said, "Gonna get you, baby," and Connie turned away again without Eddie noticing anything.

She spent three hours with him, at the restaurant where they ate hamburgers and drank Cokes in wax cups that were always sweating, and then down an alley a mile or so away, and when he left her off at five to eleven only the movie house was still open at the plaza. Her girlfriend was there, talking with a boy. When Connie came up, the two girls smiled at each other and Connie said, "How was the movie?" and the girl said, "*You* should know." They rode off with the girl's father, sleepy and pleased, and Connie couldn't help but look back at the darkened shopping plaza with its big empty parking lot and its signs that were faded and ghostly now, and over at the drive-in restaurant where cars were still circling tirelessly. She couldn't hear the music at this distance.

Next morning June asked her how the movie was and Connie said, "So-so."

10   She and that girl and occasionally another girl went out several times a week, and the rest of the time Connie spent around the house—it was summer vacation—getting in her mother's way and thinking, dreaming about the boys she met. But all the boys fell back and dissolved into a single face that was not even a face but an idea, a feeling, mixed up with the urgent insistent pounding of the music and the humid night air of July. Connie's mother kept dragging her back to the daylight by finding things for her to do or saying suddenly, "What's this about the Pettinger girl?"

And Connie would say nervously, "Oh, her. That dope." She always drew thick clear lines between herself and such girls, and her mother was simple and kind enough to believe it. Her mother was so simple, Connie thought, that it was maybe cruel to fool her so much. Her mother went scuffling around the house in old bedroom slippers and complained over the telephone to one sister about the other, then the other called up and the two of them complained about the third one. If June's name was mentioned her mother's tone was approving, and if Connie's name was mentioned it was disapproving. This did not really mean she disliked Connie, and actually Connie thought that her mother preferred her to June just because she was prettier, but the two of them kept up a pretense of exasperation, a sense that they were tugging and struggling over something of little value to either of them. Sometimes, over coffee, they were almost friends, but something would come up—some vexation that was like a fly buzzing suddenly around their heads—and their faces went hard with contempt.

One Sunday Connie got up at eleven—none of them bothered with church—and washed her hair so that it could dry all day long in the sun. Her parents and sister were going to a barbecue at an aunt's house and Connie said no, she wasn't interested, rolling her eyes to let her mother know just what she thought of it. "Stay home alone then," her mother said sharply. Connie sat out back in a lawn chair and watched them drive away, her father quiet and bald, hunched around so that he could back the car out, her mother with a look that was still angry and not at all softened through the windshield, and in the back seat poor old June, all dressed up as if she didn't know what a barbecue was, with all the running yelling kids and the flies. Connie sat with her eyes closed in the sun, dreaming and dazed with the warmth about her as if this were a kind of love, the caresses of love, and her mind slipped over onto thoughts of the boy she had been with the night before and how nice he had been, how sweet it always was, not the way someone like June would suppose but sweet, gentle, the way it was in movies and promised in songs; and when she opened her eyes she hardly knew where she was, the backyard ran off into weeds and a fence-like line of trees and behind it the sky was perfectly blue and still. The asbestos "ranch house" that was now three years old startled her—it looked small. She shook her head as if to get awake.

It was too hot. She went inside the house and turned on the radio to drown out the quiet. She sat on the edge of her bed, barefoot, and listened for an hour and a half to a program called XYZ Sunday Jamboree, record after record of hard, fast, shrieking songs she sang along with, interspersed by exclamations from "Bobby King": "An' look here, you girls at Napoleon's—Son and Charley want you to pay real close attention to this song coming up!"

And Connie paid close attention herself, bathed in a glow of slow-pulsed joy that seemed to rise mysteriously out of the music itself and lay languidly about the airless little room, breathed in and breathed out with each gentle rise and fall of her chest.

15   After a while she heard a car coming up the drive. She sat up at once, startled, because it couldn't be her father so soon. The gravel kept crunching all
the way in from the road—the driveway was long—and Connie ran to the
window. It was a car she didn't know. It was an open jalopy, painted a bright
gold that caught the sunlight opaquely. Her heart began to pound and her
fingers snatched at her hair, checking it, and she whispered, "Christ, Christ,"
wondering how bad she looked. The car came to a stop at the side door and
the horn sounded four short taps, as if this were a signal Connie knew.

She went into the kitchen and approached the door slowly, then hung out
the screen door, her bare toes curling down off the step. There were two boys
in the car and now she recognized the driver: he had shaggy, shabby black hair
that looked crazy as a wig and he was grinning at her.

"I ain't late, am I?" he said.

"Who the hell do you think you are?" Connie said.

"Toldja I'd be out, didn't I?"

20   "I don't even know who you are."

She spoke sullenly, careful to show no interest or pleasure, and he spoke
in a fast, bright monotone. Connie looked past him to the other boy, taking
her time. He had fair brown hair, with a lock that fell onto his forehead. His
sideburns gave him a fierce, embarrassed look, but so far he hadn't even bothered to glance at her. Both boys wore sunglasses. The driver's glasses were
metallic and mirrored everything in miniature.

"You wanta come for a ride?" he said.

Connie smirked and let her hair fall loose over one shoulder.

"Don'tcha like my car? New paint job," he said. "Hey."

25   "What?"

"You're cute."

She pretended to fidget, chasing flies away from the door.

"Don'tcha believe me, or what?" he said.

"Look, I don't even know who you are," Connie said in disgust.

30   "Hey, Ellie's got a radio, see. Mine broke down." He lifted his friend's arm
and showed her the little transistor radio the boy was holding, and now Connie began to hear the music. It was the same program that was playing inside
the house.

"Bobby King?" she said.

"I listen to him all the time. I think he's great."

"He's kind of great," Connie said reluctantly.

"Listen, that guy's *great*. He knows where the action is."

35   Connie blushed a little, because the glasses made it impossible for her to see
just what this boy was looking at. She couldn't decide if she liked him or if
he was just a jerk, and so she dawdled in the doorway and wouldn't come
down or go back inside. She said, "What's all that stuff painted on your car?"

"Can'tcha read it?" He opened the door very carefully, as if he were afraid
it might fall off. He slid out just as carefully, planting his feet firmly on the
ground, the tiny metallic world in his glasses slowing down like gelatin hardening, and in the midst of it Connie's bright green blouse. "This here is my
name, to begin with," he said. ARNOLD FRIEND was written in tarlike black letters on the side, with a drawing of a round, grinning face that reminded Connie of a pumpkin, except it wore sunglasses. "I wanta introduce myself, I'm
Arnold Friend and that's my real name and I'm gonna be your friend, honey,
and inside the car's Ellie Oscar, he's kinda shy." Ellie brought his transistor radio

up to his shoulder and balanced it there. "Now, these numbers are a secret code, honey," Arnold Friend explained. He read off the numbers 33, 19, 17 and raised his eyebrows at her to see what she thought of that, but she didn't think much of it. The left rear fender had been smashed and around it was written, on the gleaming gold background: DONE BY CRAZY WOMAN DRIVER. Connie had to laugh at that. Arnold Friend was pleased at her laughter and looked up at her. "Around the other side's a lot more—you wanta come and see them?"

"No."

"Why not?"

"Why should I?"

40   "Don'tcha wanta see what's on the car? Don'tcha wanta go for a ride?"

"I don't know."

"Why not?"

"I got things to do."

"Like what?"

45   "Things."

He laughed as if she had said something funny. He slapped his thighs. He was standing in a strange way, leaning back against the car as if he were balancing himself. He wasn't tall, only an inch or so taller than she would be if she came down to him. Connie liked the way he was dressed, which was the way all of them dressed: tight faded jeans stuffed into black, scuffed boots, a belt that pulled his waist in and showed how lean he was, and a white pull-over shirt that was a little soiled and showed the hard small muscles of his arms and shoulders. He looked as if he probably did hard work, lifting and carrying things. Even his neck looked muscular. And his face was a familiar face, somehow: the jaw and chin and cheeks slightly darkened because he hadn't shaved for a day or two, and the nose long and hawklike, sniffing as if she were a treat he was going to gobble up and it was all a joke.

"Connie, you ain't telling the truth. This is your day set aside for a ride with me and you know it," he said, still laughing. The way he straightened and recovered from his fit of laughing showed that it had been all fake.

"How do you know what my name is?" she said suspiciously.

"It's Connie."

50   "Maybe and maybe not."

"I know my Connie," he said, wagging his finger. Now she remembered him even better, back at the restaurant, and her cheeks warmed at the thought of how she had sucked in her breath just at the moment she passed him—how she must have looked to him. And he had remembered her. "Ellie and I come out here especially for you," he said. "Ellie can sit in back. How about it?"

"Where?"

"Where what?"

"Where're we going?"

55   He looked at her. He took off the sunglasses and she saw how pale the skin around his eyes was, like holes that were not in shadow but instead in light. His eyes were like chips of broken glass that catch the light in an amiable way. He smiled. It was as if the idea of going for a ride somewhere, to someplace, was a new idea to him.

"Just for a ride, Connie sweetheart."

"I never said my name was Connie," she said.

"But I know what it is. I know your name and all about you, lots of things," Arnold Friend said. He had not moved yet but stood still leaning back against the side of his jalopy. "I took a special interest in you, such a pretty girl, and found out all about you—like I know your parents and sister are gone some-wheres and I know where and how long they're going to be gone, and I know who you were with last night, and your best girl friend's name is Betty. Right?"

He spoke in a simple lilting voice, exactly as if he were reciting the words to a song. His smile assured her that everything was fine. In the car Ellie turned up the volume on his radio and did not bother to look around at them.

60 "Ellie can sit in the back seat," Arnold Friend said. He indicated his friend with a casual jerk of his chin, as if Ellie did not count and she should not bother with him.

"How'd you find out all that stuff?" Connie said.

"Listen: Betty Schultz and Tony Fitch and Jimmy Pettinger and Nancy Pet-tinger," he said in a chant. "Raymond Stanley and Bob Hutter—"

"Do you know all those kids?"

"I know everybody."

65 "Look, you're kidding. You're not from around here."

"Sure."

"But—how come we never saw you before?"

"Sure you saw me before," he said. He looked down at his boots, as if he were a little offended. "You just don't remember."

"I guess I'd remember you," Connie said.

70 "Yeah?" He looked up at this, beaming. He was pleased. He began to mark time with the music from Ellie's radio, tapping his fists lightly together. Con-nie looked away from his smile to the car, which was painted so bright it almost hurt her eyes to look at it. She looked at that name, ARNOLD FRIEND. And up at the front fender was an expression that was familiar—MAN THE FLYING SAUCERS. It was an expression kids had used the year before but didn't use this year. She looked at it for a while as if the words meant something to her that she did not yet know.

"What're you thinking about? Huh?" Arnold Friend demanded. "Not wor-ried about your hair blowing around in the car, are you?"

"No."

"Think I maybe can't drive good?"

"How do I know?"

75 "You're a hard girl to handle. How come?" he said. "Don't you know I'm your friend? Didn't you see me put my sign in the air when you walked by?"

"What sign?"

"My sign." And he drew an X in the air, leaning out toward her. They were maybe ten feet apart. After his hand fell back to his side the X was still in the air, almost visible. Connie let the screen door close and stood perfectly still inside it, listening to the music from her radio and the boy's blend together. She stared at Arnold Friend. He stood there so stiffly relaxed, pretending to be relaxed, with one hand idly on the door handle as if he were keeping himself up that way and had no intention of ever moving again. She recognized most things about him, the tight jeans that showed his thighs and buttocks and the greasy leather boots and the tight shirt, and even that slippery friendly smile of his, that sleepy dreamy smile that all the boys used to get across ideas they didn't want to put into words. She recognized all this and also the singsong way he talked, slight-ly mocking, kidding, but serious and a little melancholy, and she recognized the way he tapped one fist against the other in homage to the perpetual music behind him. But all these things did not come together.

She said suddenly, "Hey, how old are you?"

His smile faded. She could see then that he wasn't a kid, he was much older—thirty, maybe more. At this knowledge her heart began to pound faster.

80   "That's a crazy thing to ask. Can'tcha see I'm your own age?"

"Like hell you are."

"Or maybe a coupla years older. I'm eighteen."

"Eighteen?" she said doubtfully.

He grinned to reassure her and lines appeared at the corners of his mouth. His teeth were big and white. He grinned so broadly his eyes became slits and she saw how thick the lashes were, thick and black as if painted with a black tarlike material. Then, abruptly, he seemed to become embarrassed and looked over his shoulder at Ellie. "*Him,* he's crazy," he said. "Ain't he a riot? He's a nut, a real character." Ellie was still listening to the music. His sunglasses told nothing about what he was thinking. He wore a bright orange shirt unbuttoned halfway to show his chest, which was a pale, bluish chest and not muscular like Arnold Friend's. His shirt collar was turned up all around and the very tips of the collar pointed out past his chin as if they were protecting him. He was pressing the transistor radio up against his ear and sat there in a kind of daze, right in the sun.

85   "He's kinda strange," Connie said.

"Hey, she says you're kinda strange! Kinda strange!" Arnold Friend cried. He pounded on the car to get Ellie's attention. Ellie turned for the first time and Connie saw with shock that he wasn't a kid either—he had a fair, hairless face, cheeks reddened slightly as if the veins grew too close to the surface of his skin, the face of a forty-year-old baby. Connie felt a wave of dizziness rise in her at this sight and she stared at him as if waiting for something to change the shock of the moment, make it all right again. Ellie's lips kept shaping words, mumbling along with the words blasting in his ear.

"Maybe you two better go away," Connie said faintly.

"What? How come?" Arnold Friend cried. "We come out here to take you for a ride. It's Sunday." He had the voice of the man on the radio now. It was the same voice, Connie thought. "Don'tcha know it's Sunday all day? And honey, no matter who you were with last night, today you're with Arnold Friend and don't you forget it! Maybe you better step out here," he said, and this last was in a different voice. It was a little flatter, as if the heat was finally getting to him.

"No. I got things to do."

90   "Hey."

"You two better leave."

"We ain't leaving until you come with us."

"Like hell I am—"

"Connie, don't fool around with me. I mean—I mean, don't fool *around,*" he said, shaking his head. He laughed incredulously. He placed his sunglasses on top of his head, carefully, as if he were indeed wearing a wig, and brought the stems down behind his ears. Connie stared at him, another wave of dizziness and fear rising in her so that for a moment he wasn't even in focus but was just a blur standing there against his gold car, and she had the idea that he had driven up the driveway all right but had come from nowhere before that and belonged nowhere and that everything about him and even about the music that was so familiar to her was only half real.

95   "If my father comes and sees you—"

"He ain't coming. He's at a barbecue."

"How do you know that?"

"Aunt Tillie's. Right now they're—uh—they're drinking. Sitting around," he said vaguely, squinting as if he were staring all the way to town and over to Aunt Tillie's backyard. Then the vision seemed to get clear and he nodded energetically. "Yeah. Sitting around. There's your sister in a blue dress, huh? And high heels, the poor sad bitch—nothing like you, sweetheart! And your mother's helping some fat woman with the corn, they're cleaning the corn—husking the corn—"

"What fat woman?" Connie cried.

100   "How do I know what fat woman, I don't know every goddamn fat woman in the world!" Arnold Friend laughed.

"Oh, that's Mrs. Hornsby . . . Who invited her?" Connie said. She felt a little lightheaded. Her breath was coming quickly.

"She's too fat. I don't like them fat. I like them the way you are, honey," he said, smiling sleepily at her. They stared at each other for a while through the screen door. He said softly, "Now, what you're going to do is this: you're going to come out that door. You're going to sit up front with me and Ellie's going to sit in the back, the hell with Ellie, right? This isn't Ellie's date. You're my date. I'm your lover, honey."

"What? You're crazy—"

"Yes, I'm your lover. You don't know what that is but you will," he said. "I know that too. I know all about you. But look: it's real nice and you couldn't ask for nobody better than me, or more polite. I always keep my word. I'll tell you how it is, I'm always nice at first, the first time. I'll hold you so tight you won't think you have to try to get away or pretend anything because you'll know you can't. And I'll come inside you where it's all secret and you'll give in to me and you'll love me—"

105   "Shut up! You're crazy!" Connie said. She backed away from the door. She put her hands up against her ears as if she'd heard something terrible, something not meant for her. "People don't talk like that, you're crazy," she muttered. Her heart was almost too big now for her chest and its pumping made sweat break out all over her. She looked out to see Arnold Friend pause and then take a step toward the porch, lurching. He almost fell. But, like a clever drunken man, he managed to catch his balance. He wobbled in his high boots and grabbed hold of one of the porch posts.

"Honey?" he said. "You still listening?"

"Get the hell out of here!"

"Be nice, honey. Listen."

"I'm going to call the police—"

110   He wobbled again and out of the side of his mouth came a fast spat curse, an aside not meant for her to hear. But even this "Christ!" sounded forced. Then he began to smile again. She watched this smile come, awkward as if he were smiling from inside a mask. His whole face was a mask, she thought wildly, tanned down to his throat but then running out as if he had plastered makeup on his face but had forgotten about his throat.

"Honey—? Listen, here's how it is. I always tell the truth and I promise you this: I ain't coming in that house after you."

"You better not! I'm going to call the police if you—if you don't—"

"Honey," he said, talking right through her voice, "honey, I'm not coming in there but you are coming out here. You know why?"

She was panting. The kitchen looked like a place she had never seen before, some room she had run inside but that wasn't good enough, wasn't going to help her. The kitchen window had never had a curtain, after three years, and there were dishes in the sink for her to do—probably—and if you ran your hand across the table you'd probably feel something sticky there.

115   "You listening, honey? Hey?"

"—going to call the police—"

"Soon as you touch the phone I don't need to keep my promise and can come inside. You won't want that."

She rushed forward and tried to lock the door. Her fingers were shaking. "But why lock it," Arnold Friend said gently, talking right into her face. "It's just a screen door. It's just nothing." One of his boots was at a strange angle, as if his foot wasn't in it. It pointed out to the left, bent at the ankle. "I mean, anybody can break through a screen door and glass and wood and iron or anything else if he needs to, anybody at all, and specially Arnold Friend. If the place got lit up with a fire, honey, you'd come runnin' out into my arms, right into my arms an' safe at home—like you knew I was your lover and'd stopped fooling around. I don't mind a nice shy girl but I don't like no fooling around." Part of those words were spoken with a slight rhythmic lilt, and Connie somehow recognized them—the echo of a song from last year, about a girl rushing into her boyfriend's arms and coming home again—

Connie stood barefoot on the linoleum floor, staring at him. "What do you want?" she whispèred.

120   "I want you," he said.

"What?"

"Seen you that night and thought, that's the one, yes sir. I never needed to look anymore."

"But my father's coming back. He's coming to get me. I had to wash my hair first—" She spoke in a dry, rapid voice, hardly raising it for him to hear.

"No, your daddy is not coming and yes, you had to wash your hair and you washed it for me. It's nice and shining and all for me. I thank you sweetheart," he said with a mock bow, but again he almost lost his balance. He had to bend and adjust his boots. Evidently his feet did not go all the way down; the boots must have been stuffed with something so that he would seem taller. Connie stared out at him and behind him at Ellie in the car, who seemed to be looking off toward Connie's right, into nothing. This Ellie said, pulling the words out of the air one after another as if he were just discovering them, "You want me to pull out the phone?"

125   "Shut your mouth and keep it shut," Arnold Friend said, his face red from bending over or maybe from embarrassment because Connie had seen his boots. "This ain't none of your business."

"What—what are you doing? What do you want?" Connie said. "If I call the police they'll get you, they'll arrest you—"

"Promise was not to come in unless you touch that phone, and I'll keep that promise," he said. He resumed his erect position and tried to force his shoulders back. He sounded like a hero in a movie, declaring something important. But he spoke too loudly and it was as if he were speaking to someone behind Connie. "I ain't made plans for coming in that house where I don't belong but just for you to come out to me, the way you should. Don't you know who I am?"

"You're crazy," she whispered. She backed away from the door but did not want to go into another part of the house, as if this would give him permission to come through the door. "What do you . . . you're crazy, you . . ."

"Huh? What're you saying, honey?"

130   Her eyes darted everywhere in the kitchen. She could not remember what it was, this room.

"This is how it is, honey: you come out and we'll drive away, have a nice ride. But if you don't come out we're gonna wait till your people come home and then they're all going to get it."

"You want that telephone pulled out?" Ellie said. He held the radio away from his ear and grimaced, as if without the radio the air was too much for him.

"I toldja shut up, Ellie," Arnold Friend said, "you're deaf, get a hearing aid, right? Fix yourself up. This little girl's no trouble and's gonna be nice to me, so Ellie keep to yourself, this ain't your date—right? Don't hem in on me, don't hog, don't crush, don't bird dog, don't trail me," he said in a rapid, meaningless voice, as if he were running through all the expressions he'd learned but was no longer sure which of them was in style, then rushing on to new ones, making them up with his eyes closed. "Don't crawl under my fence, don't squeeze in my chipmunk hole, don't sniff my glue, suck my popsicle, keep your own greasy fingers on yourself!" He shaded his eyes and peered in at Connie, who was backed against the kitchen table. "Don't mind him, honey, he's just a creep. He's a dope. Right? I'm the boy for you and like I said, you come out here nice like a lady and give me your hand, and nobody else gets hurt, I mean, your nice old bald-headed daddy and your mummy and your sister in her high heels. Because listen: why bring them in this?"

"Leave me alone," Connie whispered.

135   "Hey, you know that old woman down the road, the one with the chickens and stuff—you know her?"

"She's dead!"

"Dead? What? You know her?" Arnold Friend said.

"She's dead—"

"Don't you like her?"

140   "She's dead—she's—she isn't here anymore—"

"But don't you like her, I mean, you got something against her? Some grudge or something?" Then his voice dipped as if he were conscious of a rudeness. He touched the sunglasses perched up on top of his head as if to make sure they were still there. "Now, you be a good girl."

"What are you going to do?"

"Just two things, or maybe three," Arnold Friend said. "But I promise it won't last long and you'll like me the way you get to like people you're close to. You will. It's all over for you here, so come on out. You don't want your people in any trouble, do you?"

She turned and bumped against a chair or something, hurting her leg, but she ran into the back room and picked up the telephone. Something roared in her ear, a tiny roaring, and she was so sick with fear that she could do nothing but listen to it—the telephone was clammy and very heavy and her fingers groped down to the dial but were too weak to touch it. She began to scream into the phone, into the roaring. She cried out, she cried for her mother, she felt her breath start jerking back and forth in her lungs as if it were something Arnold Friend was stabbing her with again and again with no tenderness. A noisy sorrowful wailing rose all about her and she was locked inside it the way she was locked inside this house.

145   After a while she could hear again. She was sitting on the floor with her wet back against the wall.

Arnold Friend was saying from the door, "That's a good girl. Put the phone back."

She kicked the phone away from her.

"No, honey. Pick it up. Put it back right."

She picked it up and put it back. The dial tone stopped.

150   "That's a good girl. Now, you come outside."

She was hollow with what had been fear but what was now just an emptiness. All that screaming had blasted it out of her. She sat, one leg cramped under her, and deep inside her brain was something like a pinpoint of light that kept going and would not let her relax. She thought, I'm not going to see my mother again. She thought, I'm not going to sleep in my bed again. Her bright green blouse was all wet.

Arnold Friend said, in a gentle-loud voice that was like a stage voice, "The place where you came from ain't there anymore, and where you had in mind to go is cancelled out. This place you are now—inside your daddy's house— is nothing but a cardboard box I can knock down any time. You know that and always did know it. You hear me?"

She thought, I have got to think. I have got to know what to do.

"We'll go out to a nice field, out in the country here where it smells so nice and it's sunny," Arnold Friend said. "I'll have my arms tight around you so you won't need to try to get away and I'll show you what love is like, what it does. The hell with this house! It looks solid all right," he said. He ran a fingernail down the screen and the noise did not make Connie shiver, as it would have the day before. "Now, put your hand on your heart, honey. Feel that? That feels solid too but we know better. Be nice to me, be sweet like you can because what else is there for a girl like you but to be sweet and pretty and give in?—and get away before her people come back?"

155   She felt her pounding heart. Her hand seemed to enclose it. She thought for the first time in her life that it was nothing that was hers, that belonged to her, but just a pounding, living thing inside this body that wasn't really hers either.

"You don't want them to get hurt," Arnold Friend went on. "Now, get up, honey. Get up all by yourself."

She stood.

"Now, turn this way. That's right. Come over here to me.—Ellie, put that away, didn't I tell you? You dope. You miserable creepy dope," Arnold Friend said. His words were not angry but only part of an incantation. The incantation was kindly. "Now, come out through the kitchen to me, honey, and let's see a smile, try it, you're a brave, sweet little girl and now they're eating corn and hot dogs cooked to bursting over an outdoor fire, and they don't know one thing about you and never did and honey, you're better than them because not a one of them would have done this for you."

Connie felt the linoleum under her feet; it was cool. She brushed her hair back out of her eyes. Arnold Friend let go of the post tentatively and opened his arms for her, his elbows pointing in toward each other and his wrists limp, to show that this was an embarrassed embrace and a little mocking, he didn't want to make her self-conscious.

160   She put out her hand against the screen. She watched herself push the door slowly open as if she were back safe somewhere in the other doorway, watch-

ing this body and this head of long hair moving out into the sunlight where Arnold Friend waited.

"My sweet little blue-eyed girl," he said in a half-sung sigh that had nothing to do with her brown eyes but was taken up just the same by the vast sunlit reaches of the land behind him and on all sides of him—so much land that Connie had never seen before and did not recognize except to know that she was going to it.

Some stories are closely related to historical events or experiences. Other stories are more clearly imaginative, but connect to our lives through their themes and characters. As we read and write about fiction, we investigate these relationships and messages. This investigation will eventually focus on an interpretation and argument, but it begins with our reactions.

We can start thinking about "Where Are You Going, Where Have You Been?" with some simple responses. We might begin with the setting. (For more on setting see page 40.) Do we get a concrete sense of time and place from reading the story? Can we relate the setting to places we are familiar with? Does it help us identify with the story?

Studying "Where Are You Going, Where Have You Been?"

We can also explore our reactions to the characters. Connie provides a good example because she is described as having "two sides." Connie represents a complex character. (For more on characters, see pages 41-42.) We may be able to identify with Connie in part because we recognize the confusion of adolescence or family tensions from our own experience.

We should also consider any important symbols in the work as well as the themes and ideas they represent. The screen door, for instance, in Oates's story acts as symbol for a passage between different states of mind (among other possibilities). This symbol presents us with topics for exploration, including rites of passage and movement from innocence to experience. We can decide which of these symbols and themes raises the most questions, or seems most significant.

As we react to elements of fiction like settings, characters, and themes, we can practice forms of prewriting to help us generate ideas. We might freewrite (page 154), create lists (156), or respond to questions (158). Catherine Hernandez used the first of the journalist's questions to develop these thoughts about the story:

> Who: Well the story is mainly about Connie. I can identify with her because she has the same kind of relationship with her parents—well her mother—that I had. I guess the father is just a stock character. Well, maybe? Maybe the fact that Arnold Friend is older can be related to the father. Absent father? A. Friend. What about that name? It is ironic, no doubt, but maybe there is more to it? Who is A. Friend and how does he relate to Connie?

Exercise 9.1   *Reacting to a Work of Fiction*

Following the example above, freewrite about your reactions to "Where Are You Going, Where Have You Been?" by responding to the journalist's questions. For each of the prompts below, spend at least two minutes exploring your ideas:

1. **Who:** Who wrote the work? Who do you identify with? Who raises questions for you in the story? Who in your own life comes to mind as you consider the work?

2. **Where:** Where does the story take place? What impresses you about the setting?

3. **What:** What happens in the work? What are some of the key messages? What questions do you have?

4. **When:** When do the events take place? When was the work written or published? What does this time frame mean to you?

5. **Why:** Why do characters do what they do? Why might the story be of interest to someone?

6. **How:** How do you feel about the work? How might you refine that feeling into an interpretation?

Write freely in response to these questions to see if you can feel an interpretation or a set of questions for further exploration taking shape.

UNDERSTANDING PLOT AND POINT OF VIEW

Some elements of fiction encourage an analytical approach to a work. When we consider the **plot** (see pages 38–39) of a story, for instance, we can more or less objectively look at the sequence of events that tells the story. In "Where Are You Going, Where Have You Been?," the basic plot depicts Connie sneaking to the drive-in restaurant and exchanging glances with Arnold Friend, who then shows up at her home on a subsequent Sunday and threatens her family if she does not agree to leave and, presumably, have sex with him.

We can also analyze the plot of individual scenes in the story. We might, for instance, consider the sequence of events at the end of the story. Connie "[hangs] out [of] the screen door." She later "let[s] the screen door close and [stands] perfectly still inside it," and then "back[s] away from the door." These actions, however, tell us not only about the specific sequence of events, but also about the development of Connie's character. As we assign significance to these details, we extend and refine our initial impressions and move closer to an interpretation we can argue about.

Similarly, exploring the **point of view** from which the story is told can provide a starting point for understanding the work on more critical terms. Point of view refers to the perspective of the **narrator** of the story. In "Where Are You Going, Where Have You Been?," for instance, the story is told by a narrator outside of the work. This storytelling by a narrator who relates the actions of others is called **third person narration.**

Third person perspective places the narrator in the position of an observer (sometimes third person narration is called **objective narration**). In some stories, this observer acts, for the most part, impartially. Shirley Jackson's "The Lottery" (pages 578–83) provides a well-known example of a narrator who essentially relates the details of the story without adding commentary or drawing conclusions about what characters may be thinking.

Often, however, third person narration is more connected to the characters than we might first suppose. In "Where Are You Going, Where Have You Been?" the narrator tells us what is going on in Connie's thoughts. Rather than simply observing the characters and events, this narrator relates the ideas and motivations of the characters; this all-knowing perspective is called **omniscient** narration.

Later in this chapter we will read Frank O'Connor's "First Confession," which is told in the **first person.** First person narration tells the story from the inside, usually using the pronoun "I" to represent the storyteller who is also a character in the work. First person narrators can be viewed as **reliable** or **unreliable.** We will see that, in "First Confession," our identification with the narrator is stronger if we take his reports at face value.

In other instances, we are invited to question the perspective of the narrator. "The Yellow Wallpaper," (pages 347–59) by Charlotte Perkins Gilman, for instance, details the changes in the narrator's state of mind as it tells the story. Our judgment of the work itself depends on understanding the narrator's reliability. (You can explore critical approaches to "The Yellow Wallpaper" in Chapter 13.)

"The Yellow Wallpaper"

Whether presenting a first person or third person perspective (or in some instances other variations), the narrator should be viewed as a construction of the author. Like a character in the story, the narrator serves a specific purpose. Joyce Carol Oates created a storyteller in "Where Are You Going, Where Have You Been?" who looks into the thoughts of the characters. We can discuss this narrator and the point of view as we refine our reactions to the work into interpretations.

Exercise 9.2   *Exploring a Narrator*

Working with a group of fellow students or on your own, respond to the following prompts as you consider the narrator of "Where Are You Going, Where Have You Been?" Begin by selecting someone to keep track of the group's work or preparing to take notes on your own.

1. Read the opening paragraph of the story. What can you learn about the narrator from this description? Does the narrator seem impartial? Why or why not? Based on the opening paragraph, write at least three sentences discussing the objectivity of the narrator.

2. Consider three of the characters in the story and the narrator's description of them. How would you describe the narrator's attitude toward each of the characters? Write at least three sentences discussing the narrator's approach to different characters.

3. Read the second-to-the-last paragraph of the story. What is the relationship between the narrator and Connie at this point? Write at least three sentences exploring how the relationship between the narrator and Connie here affects the story.

4. Consider the narrator throughout the story. Does your sense of the narrator change as the story evolves? How does the perspective of the narrator influence your understanding of the story? Write at least three sentences explaining how understanding the narrator can lead to an interpretation of the story.

UNDERSTANDING FICTION'S CONTEXT

Our personal reactions can help us begin to understand a work of fiction. We can complicate that understanding by considering connections outside the work. These connections may bring other works into conversation with the story. They may illuminate our thinking with historical or biographical information. Or, they may just deepen our sense of the setting and background in which the work is situated.

We know that "Where Are You Going, Where Have You Been?" was published in 1966. We can probably assume that the slang terms and references to music, drugs, and drive-in restaurants place the story sometime between the late 1950s and the mid 1960s. What conclusions might you draw based upon the time when the story takes place? Does the time frame shape the themes and characters in the story? How does the time frame make it easier or harder for you to relate to the story?

We can also explore more direct influences of context. We might start with the dedication to Bob Dylan that begins the story. Oates has reported that she was inspired by the Bob Dylan song "It's All Over Now Baby Blue" when she wrote the story. Oates also has reported thinking about a myth called "Death and the Maiden" and an article called "The Pied Piper of Tucson" that details the serial killer Charles Schmid.

All of this information tells us something about the social context of the work. The story reflects historical reports in magazines about real life depravity. It emerges from a culture in which music delivers important messages about issues such as change and authority. Additionally, the story carries forward recognizable themes from art and mythology.

However, knowing that a magazine article and a myth partially inspired the author does not alter the substance of the work itself. We cannot claim that the story is about a serial killer simply because Oates read an article about Charles Schmid. We might, however, see the story in an entirely new light based on this knowledge, perhaps arguing that the story depicts Connie as the victim of a predator.

Dylan singing "It's All Over Now Baby Blue" (margin note)

INTERPRETING FICTION

Exploring elements of fiction like settings, characters, plot, and point of view can help us refine impressions into a more measured understanding of the story. We can turn this understanding into a concrete interpretation by developing an argument. We will begin by selecting a thesis—one which can be considered arguable by allowing for disagreement. We can then build a case for our interpretation by supporting our thesis with claims and evidence. (See Chapter 5 for more on arguments.)

We can see how the process of developing an interpretation unfolds by considering a paper written by Catherine Hernandez. If you refer to the resources on our CD, you can see how Catherine developed a thesis and outline, and then composed the paper below.

Drafting and prewriting by Catherine Hernandez (margin note)

Catherine Hernandez

Instructor Reynolds

English 102

18 May 2004

Catherine gives a quick summary of the story—in her revision, she can also introduce information about Oates. (margin note)

A Friend in the Mirror

"Where Are You Going, Where Have You Been?" tells the story of Connie, a young girl who struggles to find her identity as she moves toward womanhood. Connie is initially divided between youthful innocence and sexual desire. As the story progresses, Connie begins a process of crossing over toward a mature sexual identity. Her understanding of sexuality initially is limited and naïve. In the allegorical figure of Arnold Friend, she discovers a darker sexuality that intensifies the distinctions between innocence and experience. As she crosses through the screen door at the end of the story, she makes a decision to discard her innocence and embrace her developing sexuality.

The story initially depicts Connie as divided between her status as both a girl and a woman: "Everything about her had two sides to it, one for home and one for anywhere that was not home" (Where Are You Going? 218–19). Connie is torn between being a young girl who moves with a "childlike and bobbing" walk at home and becoming a woman whose walk is "languid enough to make anyone think she was hearing music in her head" (219). These differences between her home and away-from-home identity illustrate the tension between Connie the girl and Connie the woman. Her home laugh is depicted as "cynical and drawling" but her away-from-home laugh is described as "high-pitched and nervous," suggesting that she is not entirely comfortable with her status as a mature woman.

Another way of understanding the two sides to Connie is by considering the symbol of the mirror in the story. The story begins with a description of Connie as having "a quick, nervous giggling habit of craning her neck to glance into mirrors or checking other people's faces to make sure her own was all right" (218). Again the suggestion is that Connie is not entirely comfortable with who she is. In fact, Connie is not only "nervous" about her status in the mirror, she is unable to see herself clearly. Instead, she sees "a shadowy vision of herself" (218). Additionally, this vision is associated with her physical status rather than her ideas, experiences, or relationships: "she was pretty and that was everything"

The introduction concludes with a thesis articulating Catherine's interpretation.

Catherine explores the two sides of Connie—a major claim for her interpretation. She discusses quotations to provide evidence for her claim.

Catherine discusses the symbol of the mirror. A transitional phrase opens the paragraph and indicates its topic.

She refers to a point made in the previous paragraph. Do you think this reference is repetitive? What other examples of repetition or reinforcement can you find in the paragraph?

(218). We usually think of mirrors as showing an accurate copy of what they reflect. In "Where Are You Going, Where Have You Been?," however, the mirror reveals that Connie is torn between her identity as a child and an alternate identity associated with physical beauty and womanhood.

Catherine introduces a new topic, crossing over from innocence to maturation. Again, she uses a transition and topic sentence.

Having established that Connie is divided between her status as a girl and her physical maturation into a woman, the story portrays the possibilities for crossing from one state to another. The setting for this crossing over is the drive-in restaurant. The drive-in is associated with maturity—it is a place where "older kids" hang out. It is also a place where kids meet and test their sexuality. Connie and her friend approach the drive-in with anticipation and desire:

> They went up through the maze of parked and cruising cars to the bright-lit, fly-infested restaurant, their faces pleased and expectant as if they were entering a sacred building that loomed up out of the night to give them what haven and blessing they yearned for. (219)

Catherine discusses the block quotation to explain its significance to her argument.

Connie's excitement at exploring her developing sexuality is clear in her "expectant face" and the significance of the transition she is considering is suggested in the religious associations given to the drive-in. Less clear, however, is the potential danger in making this transition; the unhealthy possibilities are only hinted at with the description of the drive-in as "fly-infested."

How well do you think this paragraph makes its point? What is the effect of ending the paragraph with a quotation?

The closer we examine the explorations Connie experiences at the drive-in, the more we see them as attempts to learn more about her developing other half. Connie sees her experiences as "sweet, gentle, the way it [is] in movies and promised in songs" (220). This sweet and innocent experience can be seen more clearly when contrasted to other possibilities in the story. When Connie's mother asks her "about the Pettinger girl," she

distinguishes herself from Pettinger: "'Oh, her. That dope.' She always drew
thick clear lines between herself and such girls. . . ." (220).

Catherine returns to the point about the two sides of Connie, connecting the paragraph with her thesis.

Connie is not like the Pettinger girl, but there is something in her
denial that suggests that she is still divided between her innocent and girl-
like status and the desire to embrace her sexuality and maturity completely.
Again, her response to her mother comes "nervously" and she wonders if it
may be "cruel to fool her [mother] so much" (218). As we consider Connie's
status, however, we see that she is also fooling herself. Her innocent
experimentation represented by the drive-in boys is contrasted with a more

What point do you think Catherine is trying to make with this quotation? How might her discussion be expanded?

significant longing for sexual maturity: "All the boys fell back and
dissolved into a single face that was not even a face but an idea, a feeling,
mixed up with the urgent insistent pounding of the music and the humid
night air of July" (220).

The idea represented by Arnold Friend's face suggests that Connie's
decision to leave her home at the end of the story acts as a final crossing
over from the innocent side of her identity to a mature version of Connie.

Catherine discusses the symbol of the screen door, using quotations and drawing conclusions.

The story makes this message clear through the symbol of the screen door.
Just as Connie earlier noticed a shadow version of herself in the mirror, she
now sees Arnold Friend on the other side of the door. Again, the scene is
associated with sexuality in that Connie "[feels] a little lightheaded" (225).
Now, however, the idea represented by Friend materializes in person and
"they [stare] at each other for a while through the screen door" (225). By
placing Connie on one side and Arnold Friend (representing the idea of
mature sexuality) on the other, the story suggests that passing through the
screen door is an act of finally moving from young girl to womanhood.

Connie's out of body experiences at the end of the story strengthen the
sense that she is crossing over from one state into another. This experience

builds as she succumbs to the seductions of Arnold Friend. When Friend

tells her to put her hand on her heart "she [thinks] for the first time in her

life that it [is] nothing that [is] hers, that belong[s] to her, but just a

pounding, living thing inside this body that [isn't] really hers either" (228).

The earlier experiments with sexuality seem limited in comparison with

Do you think a new paragraph should begin here? Why or why not?

this "first time" experience. The body Connie inhabits no longer seems her

own. Instead she begins a process of seeing herself anew, from outside of

her body. This process culminates with the conclusion of the story where

Connie observes her body as she might when looking at herself in a mirror:

"She watched herself push the door slowly open as if she were back safe

somewhere in the other doorway, watching this body and this head of long

hair moving out into the sunlight where Arnold Friend waited" (228–30).

The innocent Connie is left behind while mature Connie crosses through

the screen door to experience.

Again, Catherine restates and offers an explanation for why we might believe her thesis.

Interpreting "Where Are You Going, Where Have You Been?" as a

depiction of a young girl's crossing over into sexual maturity makes sense

when we consider the symbols and themes presented by the story. Connie is

shown as having two sides and the person of Arnold Friend is depicted as

representing the idea of mature sexuality. When Connie crosses the road to

the drive-in, her journey to maturity begins. When she crosses the doorway

Catherine accepts that there are alternative perspectives on the story. She spells out one interpretation that reveals a potential problem in her argument.

to Arnold Friend, it is completed. However, this may not be the most

obvious and it is certainly not the only interpretation of the story. In fact,

emphasizing the journey to sexual maturity overlooks the message about

the dangers of the situation Connie finds herself in and about the sinister

motives of Arnold Friend. Certainly the story is ironic in that Friend is no

friend at all. He is a crazed predator who uses Connie's allegiance to her

family to get what he wants.

Catherine suggests that viewing Connie as crossing over into sexual maturity is compatible with seeing Friend as a dangerous predator. Do you agree?

Interpreting Connie's decision at the end as a crossing over to maturity must be understood in conjunction with these more violent and disturbing possibilities. Seeing Connie as divided between innocence and sexual maturity offers us another way of understanding the work. This approach operates on a parallel track to the motives and actions of Arnold Friend. Perhaps it is this confusion within Connie that makes her susceptible to Friend's seductions. If so, then the two interpretations support one another.

Catherine addresses another possible objection to her interpretation. She gives a fair summary of this alternative perspective in this section.

Similar objections might be made about the way that interpreting the story as a crossing over into sexuality ignores the complexities of the family relationships depicted in the story. In many ways, "Where Are You Going, Where Have You Been?" is a story about relationships between Connie and her family. Connie and June serve as foils for one another. June represents the characteristics valued by Connie's mother. Connie's father is portrayed as detached. Connie's relationship with her mother is full of conflict. Given this family background, Connie's decision to go with Arnold Friend so that "her people" don't bear the brunt of his anger represents a choice to support and reaffirm the bonds she has with her family by trying to protect them.

As with the darker interpretations of Arnold Friend, however, seeing family relationships as central in the story can work with, rather than against, a reading that emphasizes crossing into sexual maturity. By the end of the story, the naïve picture Connie once had of sexual maturity is replaced by a cynical sense of the loss of innocence. With this knowledge comes an understanding of sexuality that represents a more complete crossing over into experience. Connie now understands the implications of sexual desire completely—both their sweet and gentle elements and their dark and violent components. Her decision to cross through the screen door represents both a

Hernandez 7

How would you describe Catherine's response to the interpretation about family relationships? Is her response successful?

desire to protect her family and a conscious decision to leave behind her divided self and embrace mature sexuality and all that it entails.

The story asks us to think allegorically. The significance of the name of the figure who represents sexuality—both its appealing and disturbing elements—cannot be overlooked. Arnold Friend is the seducer who comes to

The conclusion restates Catherine's thesis, makes connections with the title of the paper, and wraps up with a sentence that closes the essay.

destroy a young girl's innocence. However, he is also A. Friend who represents a part of Connie that struggles to find its place in her identity. Connie's decision to cross over from innocence to experience represents the maturation process teens go through as their identities change from child to adult. It is the process that helps all of us see where we are going and where we have been.

[New page]

Works Cited

Oates, Joyce Carol. "Where Are You Going, Where Have You Been?"

Writing about Literature in the Media Age. Ed. Daniel Anderson.

New York: Pearson Longman, 2005.

Catherine's paper is well polished, but it developed through a process of inquiry. She began by brainstorming about her impressions and developing an outline. Once she had an interpretation in mind, she composed a thesis arguing that Connie's crossing through the screen door represents "a decision to discard her innocence and embrace her developing sexuality." She then goes on to explain this approach in paragraphs that discuss Connie's divided sense of identity and the themes represented by the symbols of the mirror and the screen door. To make her argument stronger, she considers opposing points of view and shows how they relate to her own argument.

As you write about fiction, you can take a similar approach. You may emphasize the development of the characters or the importance of settings or other elements as you explain the themes that you discover. Whatever elements you focus on, begin with a thesis and then develop a series of paragraphs that use topic sentences to discuss the story and support your approach. Tie the paragraphs together by transitioning from one to another and making connections with your thesis. Support your points with evidence from the story and discuss your quotations. Finally, demonstrate how your approach relates to alternative possibilities.

☑CHECKLIST FOR WRITING ABOUT FICTION

☐ **Begin with your reactions to the work.** Give yourself permission to develop a personal response that explores your likes and dislikes. Experiment with freewriting, lists, or questions to generate ideas and explore your reactions.

☐ **Explore elements of fiction** to refine your thinking. Examine the setting and the mood it establishes. Consider the characters and whether you identify with them and why. Compare the places and people in fiction with what you know from life to help you develop your response.

☐ **Investigate plot and narrative point of view** to begin an objective analysis of the work. Develop a sketch of the events that take place in the story. Explore the narrator, determining what point of view is used to tell the story and what that perspective might mean.

☐ **Consider important themes** in the work. Note any symbols that recur and investigate those that seem most significant. Ask which themes these symbols speak to and how those themes relate to other elements of fiction.

☐ **Explore the context** of the story. Consider what you know about the time and place in which the story is set and also when and where it was written. Ask questions about the author that might illuminate the work. Conduct research to learn more about the work's context. Be careful, however, not to let context over-determine your reading.

☐ **Reread the work** to gain a deeper understanding of its elements and to develop an interpretation. Take notes and highlight passages that might be used in an argument.

☐ **Develop a thesis** that articulates your interpretation. Make a list sketching out ideas or questions related to the thesis. Refine your list into an outline or cluster map detailing a possible progression for an argument.

☐ **Consider opposing interpretations** and arguments. Probe the weaknesses in your own thinking. Select the most viable alternative approaches and consider them in detail. Revise your outline to refute or accommodate these opposing points of view. (See pages 148-51.) If necessary, revise your thesis and sketch out a new outline.

☐ **Draft an essay** that articulates your thesis and explains the points listed in your outline in terms of your thesis. Develop a topic sentence for each body paragraph and make connections with your topic sentence and your thesis as you compose. Quote from and discuss passages that provide evidence to support your points. Remain flexible as you draft, revising your outline or exploring new ideas that seem significant.

☐ **Revise your essay** using all of the strategies that make up the writing process. (See Chapter 8.) Gather feedback from peers and from your instructor. Assess your draft, concentrating on deep issues of argument and organization. Compose a revision that responds to deep issues. Polish this revision to address surface-level issues and ensure that formatting and documentation are correct.

FIGURE 9.1   *Death and the Maiden*

COMPARING WAYS OF TELLING STORIES

When we read a work of fiction, we learn through language about settings, characters, symbols, themes, perspectives, and events. But there are other ways of telling a story. Consider, for instance, the image in Figure 9.1 from a fifteenth-century woodcut depicting the myth of *Death and the Maiden.*

The image contains characters and a setting. It also reveals themes and tensions that we find in Oates's story. The image does not explain the motivations and concerns of the characters with the same detail that we find in the story, but it conveys a message that resonates in similar ways. Imagine how your reading of the woodcut might change if it were titled "Where Are You Going, Where Have You Been?"

Studying film

Now, consider how a filmmaker tells the same story in the adaptation of "Where Are You Going, Where Have You Been?" called *Smooth Talk.* The images in Figures 9.2 and 9.3 present two frames from the film.

The first still frame depicts Arnold Friend watching Connie from the driveway of her house. In the scene, Connie stands behind her screen door. The view, then, represents what Connie sees as she looks out from inside. The camera takes in both Friend and the country in the distance, suggesting something of the perspective of Connie's character as she talks with Friend.

In Figure 9.3, Connie has stepped outside. We now see both figures in the frame. The perspective shifts to that of a more omniscient narrator, one who, like the viewer of the film, watches the scene unfold. From this vantage, we can recognize elements of the film stills

FIGURE 9.2   Friend Watches Connie in *Smooth Talk*

FIGURE 9.3   Connie Joins Friend in *Smooth Talk*

that tell a story. The awkward stance of Friend, for instance, delivers the message that something is not quite natural with the character, a point made clear in the short story. The second frame also illustrates the importance of what is called **composition**—that is, the placement of the elements within the frame of the camera. By placing Connie and Friend at opposite ends of the frame, the shot creates a symmetry, but also suggests a distance between the two characters.

You can learn more about film in Chapter 11. To think about how the images in the still frames help demonstrate some of the themes from the story, you can complete Exercise 9.3.

Exercise 9.3   *Examining Still Frames*

Working with a group of fellow students or on your own, respond to the following prompts as you consider the still frames from *Smooth Talk*. Begin by selecting a person to keep track of the group's work or preparing to take notes on your own.

1. Relate the images from the film to your own impressions from the story. Do the actors capture your sense of the characters? What can you say about the setting in the images? What do you think of Connie stepping outside with Friend before the story ends? (In the film version of the story, Connie returns to the house, before deciding at last to leave with Friend.) Write three or more sentences discussing the film stills in terms of the story.

2. Examine the films stills as images, considering how elements like lighting, figures, and objects function in the images. Consider also how terms like emphasis, balance, contrast, or proportion can help you talk about the images. (You can learn more about exploring images in Chapter 12.) Write three or more sentences analyzing the composition of the still frames.

3. Write a paragraph exploring messages offered by the film stills. Connect themes from the "Where Are You Going, Where Have You Been?" to concrete discussion of the images as you explain how the film stills tell a story.

"Where Are You Going, Where Have You Been?" in its dedication to Bob Dylan and in the way Oates ascribes inspiration for the story to a particular song, encourages us to think about how music tells a story. Consider the lyrics printed below from Dylan's "It's All Over Now Baby Blue" (the song Oates credits with at least partially inspiring the story).

BOB DYLAN

Bob Dylan (born in 1941) began life as Robert Allen Zimmerman, growing up in Minnesota. In 1960 he dropped out of college, moved to New York to become a folk musician, and changed his name to Bob Dylan. He produced some of the most memorable folk music of the early 60s, including songs like "Blowin' in the Wind" and "Like a Rolling Stone." "It's All Over Now Baby Blue" was released in 1965 on his album Bringing it all Back Home.

It's All Over Now Baby Blue

You must leave now, take what you need, you think will last.
But whatever you wish to keep, you better grab it fast.
Yonder stands your orphan with his gun,
Crying like a fire in the sun.
5 Look out the saints are comin' through
And it's all over now, Baby Blue.

The highway is for gamblers, better use your sense.
Take what you have gathered from coincidence.
The empty-handed painter from your streets
10 Is drawing crazy patterns on your sheets.
This sky, too, is folding under you
And it's all over now, Baby Blue.

All your seasick sailors, they are rowing home.
All your reindeer armies, are all going home.
15 The lover who just walked out your door
Has taken all his blankets from the floor.
The carpet, too, is moving under you
And it's all over now, Baby Blue.

Leave your stepping stones behind, something calls for you.
20 Forget the dead you've left, they will not follow you.
The vagabond who's rapping at your door
Is standing in the clothes that you once wore.
Strike another match, go start anew
And it's all over now, Baby Blue.

"It's All
Over Now
Baby
Blue"

We can recognize elements from the song lyrics that resonate with Oates's fiction and we could construct an interpretation of the lyrics much as we would with a poem. To fully understand the story told by the song, however, we need to hear the intonations given to the lyrics and the musical accompaniment that also conveys meaning and tells a story. You can hear more songs and explore the ways music can tell a story in Chapter 10 and on our CD-ROM.

REVIEWING AND PRACTICING

We recognize aspects of our own lives in fiction. But we also realize that stories represent unique works of the imagination. We examine the settings, characters, symbols, themes, and other elements of fiction to understand how a work tells a story. As we explore these elements we deepen our personal responses by developing interpretations and arguments.

To practice this process of reacting to and writing about fiction, consider the short story by Frank O'Connor (242–47) or one of the other stories printed in our book, and respond to one of the following exercises.

Exercise 9.4   *Writing About a Work of Fiction*

Read Frank O'Connor's "First Confession" or one of the other works in our book and write an argument of four or more pages that explores an important theme in the story. Your argument should offer an interpretation that details an approach to understanding the theme you select.

1. Start by encapsulating that approach in a thesis statement, and then develop a series of body paragraphs with topic sentences that support and explain your thesis.

2. Consider and respond to alternative interpretations by acknowledging them in your argument and either refuting or accommodating them.

3. Provide evidence in the form of quotations from the story to support your points. Discuss and document your quotations. (See pages 180–83 and the Appendix.)

Exercise 9.5   *Comparing Ways of Storytelling*

Explore one of the film adaptations of a short story on our CD-ROM and the print version of the story in our book. Working from both versions, write a three-or-more-page comparison of the film and print versions. Consider the relationship between storytelling techniques, settings, characters, themes, or any other aspects you deem worth comparing. (For more on comparisons, see pages 71–72.)

Incorporating images into documents

1. Compose a thesis articulating your understanding of the relationship between the film and print version.

2. Develop a series of body paragraphs that contain topic sentences and that explain and expand on your thesis.

3. Consider and respond to objections by acknowledging them in your argument and either refuting or accommodating them.

4. Provide evidence in the form of quotations from the story or discussions of film still frames to support your points. (See the tutorials on our CD for instructions on incorporating still images into your papers.) Discuss and document the images and quotations that you use (See pages 180–83 and the Appendix.)

FRANK O'CONNOR

Frank O'Connor (1903-1966) grew up in poverty in the Southwest of Ireland in the city of Cork. He fought against the British in the Irish Republican Army during the early 1920s. O'Connor wrote plays, novels, and poems, but he is perhaps best known for his short stories that depict Irish life. "First Confession" reflects on O'Connor's boyhood experience. The edition here is taken from The Collected Stories of Frank O'Connor, *but the story was revised by O'Connor numerous times prior to this edition.*

First Confession

All the trouble began when my grandfather died and my grandmother—my father's mother—came to live with us. Relations in the one house are a strain at the best of times, but, to make matters worse, my grandmother was a real old country woman and quite unsuited to the life in town. She had a fat, wrinkled old face, and, to Mother's great indignation, went round the house in bare feet—the boots had her crippled, she said. For dinner she had a jug of porter and a pot of potatoes with—sometimes—a bit of salt fish, and she poured out the potatoes on the table and ate them slowly, with great relish, using her fingers by way of a fork.

Now, girls are supposed to be fastidious, but I was the one who suffered most from this. Nora, my sister, just sucked up to the old woman for the penny she got every Friday out of the old-age pension, a thing I could not do. I was too honest, that was my trouble; and when I was playing with Bill Connell, the sergeant-major's son, and saw my grandmother steering up the path with the jug of porter sticking out from beneath her shawl I was mortified. I made excuses not to let him come into the house, because I could never be sure what she would be up to when we went in.

When Mother was at work and my grandmother made the dinner I wouldn't touch it. Nora once tried to make me, but I hid under the table from her and took the bread-knife with me for protection. Nora let on to be very indignant (she wasn't, of course, but she knew Mother saw through her, so she sided with Gran) and came after me. I lashed out at her with the bread-knife, and after that she left me alone. I stayed there till Mother came in from work and made my dinner, but when Father came in later Nora said in a shocked voice: "Oh, Dadda, do you know what Jackie did at dinnertime?" Then, of course, it all came out; Father gave me a flaking; Mother interfered, and for days after that he didn't speak to me and Mother barely spoke to Nora. And all because of that old woman! God knows, I was heart-scalded.

Then, to crown my misfortunes, I had to make my first confession and Communion. It was an old woman called Ryan who prepared us for these. She was about the one age with Gran; she was well-to-do, lived in a big house on Montenotte, wore a black cloak and bonnet, and came every day to school at three o'clock when we should have been going home, and talked to us of Hell. She may have mentioned the other place as well, but that could only have been by accident, for Hell had the first place in her heart.

5   She lit a candle, took out a new half-crown, and offered it to the first boy who would hold one finger—only one finger!—in the flame for five minutes by the school clock. Being always very ambitious I was tempted to volun-

teer, but I thought it might look greedy. Then she asked were we afraid of holding one finger—only one finger!—in a little candle flame for five minutes and not afraid of burning all over in roasting hot furnaces for all eternity. "All eternity! Just think of that! A whole lifetime goes by and it's nothing, not even a drop in the ocean of your sufferings." The woman was really interesting about Hell, but my attention was all fixed on the half-crown. At the end of the lesson she put it back in her purse. It was a great disappointment; a religious woman like that, you wouldn't think she'd bother about a thing like a half-crown.

Another day she said she knew a priest who woke one night to find a fellow he didn't recognize leaning over the end of his bed. The priest was a bit frightened—naturally enough—but he asked the fellow what he wanted, and the fellow said in a deep, husky voice that he wanted to go to Confession. The priest said it was an awkward time and wouldn't it do in the morning, but the fellow said that last time he went to Confession, there was one sin he kept back, being ashamed to mention it, and now it was always on his mind. Then the priest knew it was a bad case, because the fellow was after making a bad confession and committing a mortal sin. He got up to dress, and just then the cock crew in the yard outside, and—lo and behold!—when the priest looked round there was no sign of the fellow, only a smell of burning timber, and when the priest looked at his bed didn't he see the print of two hands burned in it? That was because the fellow had made a bad confession. This story made a shocking impression on me.

But the worst of all was when she showed us how to examine our conscience. Did we take the name of the Lord, our God, in vain? Did we honor our father and our mother? (I asked her did this include grandmothers and she said it did.) Did we love our neighbor as ourselves? Did we covet our neighbor's goods? (I thought of the way I felt about the penny that Nora got every Friday.) I decided that, between one thing and another, I must have broken the whole ten commandments, all on account of that old woman, and so far as I could see, so long as she remained in the house I had no hope of ever doing anything else.

I was scared to death of Confession. The day the whole class went I let on to have a toothache, hoping my absence wouldn't be noticed; but at three o'clock, just as I was feeling safe, along comes a chap with a message from Mrs. Ryan that I was to go to Confession myself on Saturday and be at the chapel for Communion with the rest. To make it worse, Mother couldn't come with me and sent Nora instead.

Now, that girl had ways of tormenting me that Mother never knew of. She held my hand as we went down the hill, smiling sadly and saying how sorry she was for me, as if she were bringing me to the hospital for an operation.

10   "Oh, God help us! she moaned. "Isn't it a terrible pity you weren't a good boy? Oh, Jackie, my heart bleeds for you! How will you ever think of all your sins? Don't forget you have to tell him about the time you kicked Gran on the shin."

"Lemme go!" I said, trying to drag myself free of her. "I don't want to go to Confession at all."

"But sure, you'll have to go to Confession, Jackie," she replied in the same regretful tone. "Sure, if you didn't, the parish priest would be up to the house, looking for you. 'Tisn't, God knows, that I'm not sorry for you. Do you remember the time you tried to kill me with the bread-knife under the table? And

the language you used to me? I don't know what he'll do with you at all, Jackie. He might have to send you up to the Bishop."

I remember thinking bitterly that she didn't know the half of what I had to
tell—if I told it. I knew I couldn't tell it, and understood perfectly why the
fellow in Mrs. Ryan's story made a bad confession; it seemed to me a great
shame that people wouldn't stop criticizing him. I remember that steep hill
down to the church, and the sunlit hillsides beyond the valley of the river, which
I saw in the gaps between the houses like Adam's last glimpse of Paradise.

Then, when she had maneuvered me down the long flight of steps to the
chapel yard, Nora suddenly changed her tone. She became the raging malicious
devil she really was.

15   "There you are!" she said with a yelp of triumph, hurling me through the
church door. "And I hope he'll give you the penitential psalms, you dirty little caffler.[1]"

I knew then I was lost, given up to eternal justice. The door with the col-
ored-glass panels swung shut behind me, the sunlight went out and gave place
to deep shadow, and the wind whistled outside so that the silence within
seemed to crackle like ice under my feet. Nora sat in front of me by the confession box. There were a couple of old women ahead of her, and then a mis-
erable-looking poor devil came and wedged me in at the other side, so that I
couldn't escape even if I had the courage. He joined his hands and rolled his
eyes in the direction of the roof, muttering aspirations in an anguished tone,
and I wondered had he a grandmother too. Only a grandmother could account
for a fellow behaving in that heartbroken way, but he was better off than I,
for he at least could go and confess his sins; while I would make a bad confession and then die in the night and be continually coming back and burning people's furniture.

Nora's turn came, and I heard the sound of something slamming, and then
her voice as if butter wouldn't melt in her mouth, and then another slam, and
out she came. God, the hypocrisy of women! Her eyes were lowered, her head
was bowed, and her hands were joined very low down on her stomach, and she
walked up the aisle to the side altar looking like a saint. You never saw such
an exhibition of devotion; and I remembered the devilish malice with which she
had tormented me all the way from our door, and wondered were all religious
people like that, really. It was my turn now. With the fear of damnation in my
soul I went in, and the confessional door closed of itself behind me.

It was pitch-dark and I couldn't see priest or anything else. Then I really
began to be frightened. In the darkness it was a matter between God and me,
and He had all the odds. He knew what my intentions were before I even started; I had no chance. All I had ever been told about Confession got mixed up
in my mind, and I knelt to one wall and said: "Bless me, father, for I have
sinned; this is my first confession." I waited for a few minutes, but nothing happened, so I tried it on the other wall. Nothing happened there either. He had
me spotted all right.

It must have been then that I noticed the shelf at about one height with
my head. It was really a place for grown-up people to rest their elbows, but
in my distracted state I thought it was probably the place you were supposed
to kneel. Of course, it was on the high side and not very deep, but I was always
good at climbing and managed to get up all right. Staying up was the trouble. There was room only for my knees, and nothing you could get a grip on

----

[1]**Caffler:** an impertinent boy.

but a sort of wooden molding a bit above it. I held on to the molding and repeated the words a little louder, and this time something happened all right. A slide was slammed back; a little light entered the box, and a man's voice said: "Who's there?"

20   "'Tis me, father," I said for fear he mightn't see me and go away again. I couldn't see him at all. The place the voice came from was under the molding, about level with my knees, so I took a good grip of the molding and swung myself down till I saw the astonished face of a young priest looking up at me. He had to put his head on one side to see me, and I had to put mine on one side to see him, so we were more or less talking to one another upside-down. It struck me as a queer way of hearing confessions, but I didn't feel it my place to criticize.

"Bless me, father, for I have sinned; this is my first confession," I rattled off all in one breath, and swung myself down the least shade more to make it easier for him.

"What are you doing up there?" he shouted in an angry voice, and the strain the politeness was putting on my hold of the molding, and the shock of being addressed in such an uncivil tone, were too much for me. I lost my grip, tumbled, and hit the door before I found myself flat on my back in the middle of the aisle. The people who had been waiting stood up with their mouths open. The priest opened the door of the middle box and came our pushing his biretta back from his forehead; he looked something terrible. Then Nora came scampering down the aisle.

"Oh, you dirty little caffler!" she said. "I might have known you'd do it. I might have known you'd disgrace me. I can't leave you out of my sight for one minute."

Before I could even get to my feet to defend myself she bent down and gave me a clip across the ear. This reminded me that I was so stunned I had even forgotten to cry, so that people might think I wasn't hurt at all, when in fact I was probably maimed for life. I gave a roar out of me.

25   "What's all this about?" the priest hissed, getting angrier than ever and pushing Nora off me. "How dare you hit the child like that, you little vixen?"

"But I can't do my penance with him, father," Nora cried, cocking an outraged eye up at him.

"Well, go and do it, or I'll give you some more to do," he said, giving me a hand up. "Was it coming to Confession you were, my poor man?" he asked me.

"'Twas, father," said I with a sob.

"Oh," he said respectfully, "a big hefty fellow like you must have terrible sins. Is this your first?"

30   "'Tis, father," said I.

"Worse and worse," he said gloomily. "The crimes of a lifetime. I don't know will I get rid of you at all today. You'd better wait now till I'm finished with these old ones. You can see by the looks of them they haven't much to tell."

"I will, father," I said with something approaching joy.

The relief of it was really enormous. Nora stuck out her tongue at me from behind his back, but I couldn't even be bothered retorting. I knew from the very moment that man opened his mouth that he was intelligent above the ordinary. When I had time to think, I saw how right I was. It only stood to reason that a fellow confessing after seven years would have more to tell than people that went every week. The crimes of a lifetime, exactly as he said. It was only what he expected, and the rest was the cackle of old women and girls with their talk of Hell, the Bishop, and the penitential psalms. That was all they knew. I started to make my examination of conscience, and barring the one bad business of my grandmother it didn't seem so bad.

The next time, the priest steered me into the confession box himself and left the shutter back the way I could see him get in and sit down at the further side of the grille from me.

35 "Well, now," he said, "what do they call you?"

"Jackie, father," said I.

"And what's a-trouble to you, Jackie?"

"Father," I said, feeling I might as well get it over while I had him in good humor, "I had it all arranged to kill my grandmother."

He seemed a bit shaken by that, all right, because he said nothing for quite a while.

40 "My goodness," he said at last, "that'd be a shocking thing to do. What put that into your head?"

"Father," I said, feeling very sorry for myself, "she's an awful woman."

"Is she?" he asked. "What way is she awful?"

"She takes porter, father," I said, knowing well from the way Mother talked of it that this was a mortal sin, and hoping it would make the priest take a more favorable view of my case.

"Oh, my!" he said, and I could see he was impressed.

45 "And snuff, father," said I.

"That's a bad case, sure enough, Jackie," he said.

"And she goes round in her bare feet, father," I went on in a rush of self-pity, "and she knows I don't like her, and she gives pennies to Nora and none to me, and my da sides with her and flakes me, and one night I was so heart-scalded I made up my mind I'd have to kill her."

"And what would you do with the body?" he asked with great interest.

"I was thinking I could chop that up and carry it away in a barrow I have," I said.

50 "Begor, Jackie," he said, "do you know you're a terrible child?"

"I know, father," I said, for I was just thinking the same thing myself. "I tried to kill Nora too with a bread-knife under the table, only I missed her."

"Is that the little girl that was beating you just now?" he asked.

"'Tis, father."

"Someone will go for her with a bread-knife one day, and he won't miss her," he said rather cryptically. "You must have great courage. Between ourselves, there's a lot of people I'd like to do the same to but I'd never have the nerve. Hanging is an awful death."

55 "Is it, father?" I asked with the deepest interest—I was always very keen on hanging. "Did you ever see a fellow hanged?"

"Dozens of them," he said solemnly. "And they all died roaring."

"Jay!" I said.

"Oh, a horrible death!" he said with great satisfaction. "Lots of the fellows I saw killed their grandmothers too, but they all said 'twas never worth it."

He had me there for a full ten minutes talking, and then walked out the chapel yard with me. I was genuinely sorry to part with him, because he was the most entertaining character I'd ever met in the religious line. Outside, after the shadow of the church, the sunlight was like the roaring of waves on a beach; it dazzled me; and when the frozen silence melted and I heard the screech of trams on the road my heart soared. I knew now I wouldn't die in the night and come back, leaving marks on my mother's furniture. It would be a great worry to her, and the poor soul had enough.

60   Nora was sitting on the railing, waiting for me, and she put on a very sour puss when she saw the priest with me. She was mad jealous because a priest had never come out of the church with her.

"Well," she asked coldly, after he left me, "what did he give you?"

"Three Hail Marys," I said.

"Three Hail Marys," she repeated incredulously. "You mustn't have told him anything."

"I told him everything," I said confidently.

65   "About Gran and all?"

"About Gran and all."

(All she wanted was to be able to go home and say I'd made a bad confession.)

"Did you tell him you went for me with the bread-knife?" she asked with a frown.

"I did to be sure."

70   "And he only gave you three Hail Marys?"

"That's all."

She slowly got down from the railing with a baffled air. Clearly, this was beyond her. As we mounted the steps back to the main road she looked at me suspiciously.

"What are you sucking?" she asked.

"Bullseyes."

75   "Was it the priest gave them to you?"

" 'Twas."

"Lord God," she wailed bitterly, "some people have all the luck! 'Tis no advantage to anybody trying to be good. I might just as well be a sinner like you."

I N Q U I R I N G   F U R T H E R

1. Early in the story, the narrator, Jackie, states, "I was too honest, that was my trouble." Do you trust the narrator of the story? Why or why not? Freewrite for five minutes about the narrator.

2. How would you characterize the relationship between Jackie and Nora? Does the relationship say more about Jackie or Nora, or both? How does their relationship influence your understanding of the story?

3. What differences can you detect in the ways the story portrays men and women? Is it fair to say the story offers an unfriendly portrayal of women? Why or why not?

4. How does the age of the narrator influence your understanding of the story? Does the story have an adult message?

5. Think of some of the themes that can be found in the story—you might explore the treatment of women and men, issues of honesty, storytelling, childhood, religion, or any other theme you find significant. Write a thesis statement that could be used to develop an exploration of a theme from the work.

1 0

Thinking and Writing About Music and Poetry

> Poetry is, above all, an approach to the truth of feeling . . .
> A fine poem will seize your imagination intellectually—that
> is, when you reach it, you will reach it intellectually too—
> but the way is through emotion, through what we call
> feeling.
>
> —*Muriel Rukeyser*

> In a certain sense we all listen to music on three separate
> planes. For lack of a better terminology, one might name
> these: (1) the sensuous plane, (2) the expressive plane,
> (3) the sheerly musical plane. . . .
>
> —*Aaron Copland*

Muriel Rukeyser and Aaron Copland reveal some of the similarities between music and poetry: both forms appeal strongly to our senses, but both forms also demand that we apply our intellect if we are to develop a deeper understanding of the emotions they invoke. The process we go through as we learn to appreciate a song mirrors our progression as we analyze and write about poetry—we move from response, to refinement, to interpretation and argument.

However, music and poetry have even more in common. Like other forms of art, music is made up of distinct elements we can analyze to better understand what we hear. Songs, for instance, are characterized by **rhythm** (the beats that mark the time of the music) and **melody** (the rising and falling sounds played over the song's rhythm). If you are familiar with Outkast's "The Way You Move," you can hear the relationship between rhythm and melody in the steady *boom, boom, boom* bass notes established at the very opening of the song, and the melodious rapping and chorus layered over the rhythm.

Poetry contains literary elements like speakers, settings, diction, figures of speech, and imagery. However, poetry also contains elements that can help us investigate its musical qualities. Recognizing tone, aspects of sound, rhyme, rhythm, meter, and form helps us understand how poems appeal to our senses.

UNDERSTANDING THE ELEMENTS OF MUSIC

We encourage you to explore the resources on our CD-ROM for this chapter where you will find audio clips demonstrating the musical elements discussed here. As we explore music, we will draw connections with the elements of poetry discussed later in the chapter.

Relating Rhythm and Melody

The first audio clip for this chapter on our CD is a song by the group Seven Mary Three, called "Summer Is Over." The song opens with a cymbal crash that launches a steady drum rhythm. Accompanying this drumbeat is a bass line that layers a steady progression of notes over each **beat** of the drums. A repeated strumming of an electric guitar chord adds the final dimension to the opening beat. This combination of drum and guitars establishes the rhythm for the song, a foundation over which the other elements of the song can be layered.

The music of Seven Mary Three

In "Summer Is Over," the elements that make up the melody of the song are layered over its rhythm. The vocals enter, rising and falling in pitch and timing to weave their own sound pattern over the beat of the rhythm. More guitar notes and chords enter, matching the tempo of the beat but bringing a vertical and hard-driving sense to the overall sound. This overlapping pattern of sound and its variations represent the melody of the song.

Poetry, too, has a rhythm. The rhythm in poetry is established by the emphasis that is placed on the syllables of each word in the poem. Each syllable receives varying levels of emphasis or **stress** when spoken. The patterns created by the stresses form the poem's rhythm. Individual sounds of words also give a melodious sense to poems. We study poetry to understand how vowels, consonants, and other elements of sound shape our impressions and convey meaning. Consider the poem, "Résumé" by Dorothy Parker.

DOROTHY PARKER

Also a theater critic, writer of short stories, and playwright, Dorothy Parker (1893–1967) is best known for the wit and intensity of her work. "Résumé" was originally published in 1926 in the collection, Enough Rope.

Résumé

Razors pain you;
Rivers are damp;
Acids stain you;
And drugs cause cramp.
5 Guns aren't lawful;
Nooses give;
Gas smells awful;
You might as well live.

"Résumé" combines a strategy of emphasizing the first syllable of lines 1–3 and 5–7 with a regular use of rhyme to create a rhythm that can be felt when you read the poem. Try tapping out the beat of the poem as you read it and see if you can pick up on its rhythm.

Listening for Harmony and Tone

The music of Skating Club

The songs by the band Skating Club on our CD demonstrate **harmony.** "Come By or Call" blends together two different versions of the lead singer's voice to form a harmony that combines the pitches of both versions. Harmony also refers to the combination of specific notes to form **chords.** The song "Princess and the Pea" uses the harmony created by repeated strumming of guitar chords (a chord is formed by combining notes to make a harmony). Reverb effects are applied to the chord so that it resonates steadily. Harmony is not usually associated with poetry, but it might be found in instances when the meanings of the poem resonate with the poem's rhythm, structure, and sounds—see the discussion of the oily sounds in Elizabeth Bishop's "Filling Station" on page 265.

Tone describes the quality of a sound. Tone is often characterized in terms of color or temperature using adjectives like bright, dark, light, or warm. Another song on our CD, "Lucky," by Seven Mary Three, begins with two sung lines that have a warm, even, and open tone. The third sung line, however, shifts to a rougher, higher pitched, and more urgent tone. The contrast between the two tones foreshadows the themes of discontent and anxiety that make up the song. In poetry, tone generally refers to the attitude of the speaker of the poem, or to the mood that is conveyed by the poem as a whole.

Recognizing Form

Form refers to the organization that structures the musical piece. Bob Dylan's "It's All Over Now Baby Blue" uses a repeated refrain at the end of each verse to tie the song together. Classical music employs forms such as the **sonata** (a composition with three distinct sections) or the **rondo** (a composition that repeats passages in a specific pattern that can be mapped out with a scheme such as ABACAD).

Stanzas organize poems in similar ways. Forms like the sonnet resemble the models many musicians use to structure their lyrics. The sonnet requires poets to follow a fourteen-line structure that is familiar to readers. Poems also make use of rhyme schemes and recurring patterns of sound that establish relationships between lines and reinforce ideas and feelings.

Evaluating Lyrics

Song lyrics can be viewed sometimes as poems set to music. We can separate the text of the lyrics from the sounds of the song to analyze the message in the lyrics. Take these lyrics from Pink Floyd's song "Wish You Were Here."

SEVEN MARY THREE

Seven Mary Three scored their first hit on the college alternative music circuit with the independently produced "Cumbersome" in 1994. Led by Jason Ross, the band combines a hard driving, "post grunge" alternative

rock sound with lyrics that are both introspective and pop-focused. "Lucky"
is taken from their 1997 release, Rock Crown.

Man in Control

I count the cracks in the pavement.
Where the weeds and wishes grow.
Every car is a reminder.
That there's someplace else to go.

5   I'm a man who needs control.
A little space, just to soothe my soul.
And sometimes I'm too far away.

I steal a moment beside you.
Can you hear me whispering?
10   I don't know what divides you.
And I wonder if it's me.

I'm a man who needs control.
A little space, just to soothe my soul.
And sometimes I'm too far away.
15   I'm well enough to believe your lies.
And sick enough to believe you're mine.
If it's painful just because.
Don't be surprised if you're in love.

I'm a man who needs control.
20   A little space, just to soothe my soul.
And sometimes I'm too far away.
I'm well enough to believe your lies.
And sick enough to believe you're mine.
If it's painful just because.
25   Don't be surprised if you're in love.

We might begin interpreting the lyrics by looking at the narrative presented in the song. The opening verse acts somewhat like the first stanza of a poem, establishing a **setting** and introducing the voice or **speaker**. We can also look at figures of speech in the lyrics. In the first verse, the metaphor "Every car is a reminder," followed by the line "That there's someplace else to go" sheds light on the state of mind of the speaker, who appears discontented and is ready to move on. The lyrics also employ poetic language. For example, the repetition of the [w] consonant in the phrase "where the weeds and the wishes grow" represents alliteration, or consonance.

We can also examine the structure of the lyrics. After the first verse, the song introduces a pre-chorus, a verse that will be repeated and built upon as the song progresses. The pre-chorus complicates our understanding of the lyrics with contradictory suggestions; that is, although the speaker needs "a little space," he also sometimes feels "too far away." The sentiments raise questions about the motives and state of mind of the voice.

The second verse suggests that both the speaker and his companion may be suffering from conflicted emotions. The chorus builds upon the pre-chorus to finalize this message. The last line of the chorus offers a possible explanation for the tensions outlined in the previous verses and pre-chorus: "Don't be surprised if you're in love."

Seven Mary Three performing "Man in Control" with band member Jason Ross discussing songwriting

Ultimately, the song expresses concerns familiar to most relationships. Analyzing the lyrics gives us a sense of how the song conveys its message.

Examining Lyrics as Sound

We have analyzed the lyrics of "Man in Control," but to fully understand the meaning of the words of the song we may need to hear them as they are sung. Lyrics take on additional meaning as a singer gives them voice. Further, lyrics rely on melody to weave the words over the rhythm and into the texture of the song. The relationship between the melody represented by the lyrics and the rhythm and other musical elements of the song cannot be heard when lyrics are simply transcribed on paper.

Similarly, many songs are successful not because of the literary quality of their lyrics, but because of the vocal and musical elements that appeal to our senses. When we consider that one of the Beatles's first big hits developed around the repetition of the phrase, "She loves you, yeah, yeah, yeah," it is hard to conclude that all lyrics can be interpreted for their poetic elements.

As we consider lyrics, we can evaluate their performance and relationship with the other musical elements of the song. With poetry, we often look at the text on a page and forget that the poem also asks us to give voice to words that we read. As we turn our attention to the poetry later in this chapter, we will invite you to read poems aloud and to play clips of readings on our CD. By speaking and hearing poems, we can explore the ways that poems convey messages through both the sounds and the meanings of words.

Exercise 10.1   *Exploring an Argument about Lyrics*

We often hear claims that musical lyrics are like poetry in their language, imagery, and rhyme. The implications of this claim are that lyrics can stand on their own as a form of art. This exercise asks you to consider the relationship between song lyrics and music.

Working with a group of fellow students, respond to the argument that *song lyrics can be read as poetry*. Begin by selecting a recorder to keep track of the group's work.

1. Select a song that you would like to analyze.

2. Read the words of the song through once or twice to develop an initial impression of the significance of the lyrics.

3. Listen to the recording of the song on our CD. Play the song through as many times as needed, paying specific attention to the way the lyrics are integrated with the musical elements of the song.

4. Brainstorm a response to the claim that *song lyrics can be read as poetry*. Begin by deciding whether you agree or disagree with the claim. Write out a list of at least three reasons to support your position.

5. Develop a list of examples that can be discussed as evidence for your position. Whichever position you select, discuss examples from both the musical elements of the song and from the printed lyrics.

6. Once you have developed your list of reasons and possible evidence, report on your deliberations in a four- to six-minute speech to your classmates.

SEVEN MARY THREE

Lucky

Mean Mr. Mustard says he's bored
of life in The District.
Can't afford the French Quarter high,
says it gets old real quick
5   and he pales up next to me
scrawled on the pavement
It says: Son, time is all the Luck
you need.

And if I stay Lucky then my tongue
10   will stay tied, and I won't betray
the things that I hide.
There's not enough years underneath
this belt, for me to admit the way
that I felt.

15   Mean Mr. Mustard says don't be
the wave that crashes
From a sea of discontent, he says
he's wrestled with that blanket. . . .
It leaves you cold and wet
20   any way you stretch it
Divine apathy! Disease of my youth
watch that you don't catch it.

And if I stay Lucky then my tongue
will stay tied, and I won't betray
25   the things that I hide.
There's not enough years underneath
this belt, for me to admit the way
that I felt.

And I'm the wave that crashes
30   From a sea that turns itself
Inside out every chance I get to
See what it's like in hell.

And if I stay Lucky then my tongue
will stay tied, and I won't betray
35   the things that I hide.
There's not enough years underneath
this belt, for me to admit the way
that I felt.

And if I stay lucky then my tongue
40   will stay tied, and I won't betray
the things that I hide.
There's not enough years underneath
this belt, for me to admit the way
that I felt.

SKATING CLUB

Audio
recording
of
"Denver"

Skating Club produces their own CDs at their Boston recording studio. Their sound is mellow, even sad. Their lyrics are sparse, taking shape in the vocalization of lead singer, Aubrey Anderson. "Denver" is taken from their 2001 debut release, Skating Club.

Denver

i saw you there with your rock star intonations
i couldn't stop my eyes and their fixation
you shook my hand like a drunken Annie Oakley
the sight of you
5   was something true
and your group
was over laughing away

So later . . .

i sidled up to the bar and asked you questions
10   i made them up twenty reasons to keep talking
i even said that your shoes were kind of sexy
but it was true
the sight of you
makes me wonder
15   how far is Denver from here?

Writing About Music

Musical elements like rhythm, melody, and harmony appeal to our senses and convey messages. How we interpret those messages, however, is what aligns music most closely with literature: we react and bring our own perspectives to what we hear; we analyze, form connections, and draw conclusions about the elements of music; and we then develop interpretations and arguments about the significance of music.

Writers frequently evaluate music in reviews. To compose a review, keep an open mind and take an analytical approach to listening, considering not only which sounds impress you (positively or negatively) but also *how* those sounds work to appeal to your senses. Your review must describe for readers the sounds that you hear, so you will need to pick out specifics that will serve as evidence for the conclusions you put forward about the music.

Music
reviews

Writers also discuss music in arguments and research papers about issues, ideas, and events. Our Extended Inquiry on the Harlem Renaissance includes jazz and blues selections. An argument suggesting that the Harlem Renaissance embodies efforts to recognize and assert African-American identities in the early twentieth century could refer to these songs as evidence for its claims. The central role music plays in most cultures allows us to consider songs as key expressions of the tensions, themes, and time frames they represent.

☑ CHECKLIST FOR LISTENING TO AND WRITING ABOUT MUSIC

☐ **Appreciate music on multiple levels.** Enjoy the appeals of music to your senses, then move toward a more analytical view that considers how the elements of music create their appeals.

☐ **Learn to recognize the rhythm** of the music you hear. Contemporary music with drums and bass guitars presents a recognizable beat. Classical and other forms of music may require more effort to pick out the beat. Consider the meter and tempo of the beats you discover and how they appeal to your senses and create meaning.

☐ **Analyze the melodies** in music. Consider both vocal and instrumental melodies. Consider how the melodies interact with the underlying beat. Evaluate the rise and fall of the melodies and try to explain the significance of these vertical dimensions of the music.

☐ **Describe the tones** of the musical elements you hear. Consider how vocals and instruments set the mood of a piece through tone. Select adjectives that best describe the tone of vocals or of individual instruments and sounds. Consider how this tone influences your understanding of the piece.

☐ **Determine the structure** of the music you listen to. Distinguish verses, refrains, bridges, and choruses. Consider how the repetitions and other elements of the structure shape your impressions and understandings of the music.

☐ **Evaluate the lyrics** of songs to determine how they convey their messages. Explore how the performance of vocals translates the lyrics into sound. Consider the imagery and ideas in the lyrics as you would the elements of a poem. Explore how these poetic elements and lyrical messages interact with the instruments in the music.

☐ **Refer to specifics** as you write about music. Describe the elements of music with adjectives that will help your readers hear what you hear. Emphasize descriptions over opinions. Draw conclusions about the ways the sounds appeal to the senses and create meaning.

Exercise 10.2   *Writing a Music Review*

Listen to one of the music tracks on our CD and write a review detailing your evaluation of the song. (Your instructor may also allow you to choose a song on your own or to evaluate an entire CD.)

1. Look over the reviews and songs on our CD. Take note of how the reviews talk about the music they evaluate. Explore several of the songs,

comparing how the different types of music appeal to your senses and use elements of music.

2. Select a song you wish to write about. Listen to the song several times to evaluate your impressions of the music.

3. Prewrite by composing responses to the prompts below:
   - What about the song impresses you (pro or con)? How can you connect your impressions with specifics in the music? List three or more aspects of the song you might write about.
   - How would you evaluate the rhythm and melodies in the song? Describe the key instruments that create the song's rhythm. Make note of the tempo of the beat. Write two or more sentences describing the song's rhythm and melody.
   - What strikes you about the vocals in the song (if the song you have chosen has vocals)? What adjectives might describe the tone of the vocals? How do the vocals create melodies within the song? Write three or more sentences about the vocals.
   - What messages can you discover in the lyrics? How do the lyrics use imagery or other poetic techniques to create a message? Write three or more sentences describing the lyrics.

4. Open a word processor and compose a review of your own. Compose an opening paragraph giving background information to readers and demonstrating your views of the piece. Compose body paragraphs discussing the most significant elements of the song. As you discuss these elements, refer to specifics and use adjectives and comparisons to describe what you hear. Conclude by encapsulating the strengths and weaknesses of the piece and offering readers an insight that will help them make a decision about the song on their own.

UNDERSTANDING THE ELEMENTS OF POETRY

We placed music first in this chapter to prepare for our discussion of the musical elements in poetry. Elements like rhythm, rhyme, and sound all invite us to hear as well as read the poems we encounter. At the same time, poems contain many elements found in other works of literature. Symbols, themes, settings, characters, and so forth allow us to develop interpretations of the ideas and concerns addressed in poems. In this chapter we will consider both the literary elements and the musical aspects of poetry.

Evaluating Settings, Speakers, and Tone

As with fiction, we can begin a reading of a poem by considering the setting and the speaker of the work. To better understand how speakers and settings in poetry function, take a minute to read "Traveling Through the Dark," by William Stafford.

WILLIAM STAFFORD

William Stafford (1914-1993) was a conscientious objector to war, working on civilian projects rather than joining the army, during World War II. His lengthy teaching and writing career reflect his conviction to nonviolence. West of Your City, *his first book of poetry, appeared in 1960.* Traveling Through the Dark, *from which the title poem below is taken, won the National Book Award in 1963.*

Stafford
reading
"Traveling
through
the Dark"

Traveling through the Dark

Traveling through the dark I found a deer
dead on the edge of the Wilson River road.
It is usually best to roll them into the canyon:
that road is narrow; to swerve might make more dead.

5   By glow of the tail-light I stumbled back of the car
and stood by the heap, a doe, a recent killing;
she had stiffened already, almost cold.
I dragged her off; she was large in the belly.

My fingers touching her side brought me the reason—
10   her side was warm; her fawn lay there waiting,
alive, still, never to be born.
Beside that mountain road I hesitated.

The car aimed ahead its lowered parking lights;
under the hood purred the steady engine.
15   I stood in the glare of the warm exhaust turning red;
around our group I could hear the wilderness listen.

I thought hard for us all—my only swerving—,
then pushed her over the edge into the river.

In Stafford's poem, the setting is a narrow road at night. We can ask how this setting contributes to the mood of the poem and how the thoughts and actions of the speaker might be shaped by the setting. Some poems have a clear dramatic **setting,** while others are more abstract (as in Ron Wallace's "Hardware" on page 33).

The **speaker** is the persona or voice that narrates the work. Remember that the speaker is not the poet, but rather a construction of the poet, like the narrator of a work of fiction. In "Traveling through the Dark" the speaker is explicitly revealed in the opening line with the pronoun I. To begin analyzing the poem, we might ask how we would characterize this speaker and how any traits of the speaker influence our reading of the work.

In poetry, **tone** generally represents the emotional state of the speaker. We can recognize tone by considering the speaker's language. The choices of words and phrases can reflect the state of mind of the speaker. The tone of the speaker in "Traveling through the Dark" might be described as distanced, cool, and unemotional. The attitude of the speaker shapes the meaning of the poem as a whole. Consider this short poem by William Carlos Williams:

WILLIAM CARLOS WILLIAMS

Student essay on "This Is Just to Say"

William Carlos Williams (1883–1963) practiced medicine during his years as poet, believing that working both as a doctor and a poet would free him to write what he wanted. During the first two decades of the 1900s, he rejected the use of regular meter in his poetry, preferring instead to experiment with the rhythms of speech. "This Is Just to Say" was published in The Collected Poems *in 1934.*

This Is Just To Say

    I have eaten
    the plums
    that were in
    the icebox

5   and which
    you were probably
    saving
    for breakfast

    Forgive me
10   they were delicious
    so sweet
    and so cold

"This is Just to Say" has a matter-of-fact tone similar to Stafford's poem, but also complicates this unemotional tone with elements of playfulness and irony. Most people would not go into such detail about the plums, if they really felt remorseful about having eaten them.

When examining tone, pay special attention to instances of **irony.** Irony occurs when a work says one thing, but readers understand the meaning to be something almost entirely opposite of what is said. Williams's poem is ironic in that the speaker asks for forgiveness, but goes on to describe vividly the delicious nature of the plums, "so sweet / and so cold." The description suggests that the request for forgiveness is not genuine—in fact, the meaning of the poem partially hinges on this irony and its tone: is the speaker remorseful or teasing and ironic?

There are two basic types of irony. **Dramatic irony** (or situational irony) occurs when we as readers know something that the characters in a work are unaware of—as in Shakespeare's *The Taming of the Shrew* (page 841) or the film *10 Things I Hate About You.* In poetry we are more likely to encounter **verbal irony.** Verbal irony occurs when the literal meaning of words does not quite match up with their figurative or interpreted meanings. In Gwendolyn Brooks's poem "We Real Cool," (page 18) the final line, "We die soon," undercuts the title of the poem and the effect is an irony that changes the meaning of the poem as a whole.

Exercise 10.3   *Evaluating Settings, Speakers, and Tone*

Working with a group of fellow students or on your own, respond to the following prompts as you consider the poem "Mission Tire Factory, 1969" by Gary Soto. Select a classmate to keep track of the group's work or prepare to take notes on your own. Read the poem a couple of times. (You may want to listen to the recording of Soto reading the poem on our CD.)

1. First, consider the setting of the poem. How does the poem convey a sense of its setting? How does the setting influence your understanding of the poem? Write three or more sentences discussing the setting.

2. Explore the speaker of the poem. If you had to write a short description of the speaker, what evidence from the poem would you discuss? Write three or more sentences describing the speaker.

3. Evaluate the tone of the speaker. What adjectives would you use to describe the speaker's tone? Does the tone shift or stay consistent in the poem? How does the speaker's tone contribute to the mood of the poem? Write three or more sentences discussing the speaker's tone.

4. Consider the role of irony in the poem. Would you consider the irony to be verbal or dramatic irony? Why? How does the irony reshape your understanding of the poem as a whole? Write three or more sentences discussing irony in the poem.

GARY SOTO

Gary Soto (born in 1953) grew up in the agricultural San Joaquin Valley in California, where his family labored as farm workers. He graduated from college in 1974 and went on to receive an MFA in creative writing. He currently teaches at the University of California at Berkeley. "Mission Tire Factory, 1969" first appeared in the collection, Where Sparrows Work Hard, *published in 1981.*

Soto reading "Mission Tire Factory, 1969"

Mission Tire Factory, 1969

All through lunch Peter pinched at his crotch,
And Jesús talked about his tattoos,
And I let the flies crawl my arm, undisturbed,
Thinking it was wrong, a buck sixty-five,
5   The wash of rubber in our lungs,
The oven we would enter, squinting
—because earlier in the day Manny fell
From his machine, and when we carried him
To the workshed (blood from
10   Under his shirt, in his pants)
All he could manage, in an ignorance
Outdone only by pain, was to take three dollars
From his wallet, and say:
"Buy some sandwiches. You guys saved my life."

Evaluating Diction

Diction describes the decisions an author makes about words. The significance of these decisions is amplified in poetry, because poetry relies on precise and economical arrangements of words. Since poetry is distilled and musical, each word of the poem carries significance in both its meanings and its sounds.

Diction can also refer to the levels of formality in the words selected by an author. A high style uses elevated word choices and formal language. A low style uses informal language. To get a sense of how diction works in poetry, consider two poems that reflect different levels of formality.

WILLIAM WORDSWORTH

William Wordsworth (1770–1850) is perhaps the best known of the British Romantic poets. His poetry expresses the Romantic notion that people can have a close and meaningful relationship with nature, a notion repre- sented by Wordsworth's image of the "correspondent breeze" that links humans to the natural world. "My Heart Leaps Up" was published in 1802.

My Heart Leaps Up

My heart leaps up when I behold
  A Rainbow in the sky:
So was it when my life began;
So is it now I am a Man;
5   So be it when I shall grow old,
  Or let me die!
The Child is Father of the Man;
And I could wish my days to be
Bound each to each by natural piety.

RANDALL JARRELL

Randall Jarrell (1914–1965) taught at the University of Texas, before join- ing the Army during World War II. He later went on to a career as a col- lege instructor, poet, and writer of children's books. In the Army, he worked in a control tower where he developed relationships with the bomber crews. "The Death of the Ball Turret Gunner" is one of the many poems Jarrell wrote about the military. It first appeared in 1945.

The Death of the Ball Turret[1] Gunner

From my mother's sleep I fell into the State,
And I hunched in its belly till my wet fur froze.
Six miles from earth, loosed from its dream of life,
I woke to black flak[2] and the nightmare fighters.
5   When I died they washed me out of the turret with a hose.

---

[1]**Ball Turret:** The Plexiglas sphere beneath a bomber where a machine gunner would hang to fire at enemy fighters.

[2]**black flak:** The main antiaircraft weapon fired at Alllied bombers during World War II.

Compare the diction in Wordsworth's "My Heart Leaps Up" with the word choices found in "The Death of the Ball Turret Gunner." Wordsworth's poem uses a high style in both the arrangement and selection of its words. The way that words are arranged into sentences is called **syntax.** The first six lines of the poem present a complex syntax that uses a colon and a series of clauses to demonstrate the setting and state of mind of the speaker. Jarrell's poem uses a less formal style. If you listen to Jarrell's reading of the poem, you can hear how the informal nature of the diction is enhanced by the matter-of-fact tone Jarrell uses.

For both poems, understanding diction and syntax helps us develop interpretations. The series of clauses in "My Heart Leaps Up" refer to three times in the speaker's life—childhood, adulthood, and eventual old age. The syntax associates the speaker's state of mind when beholding the rainbow with each of these states, connecting the current sense of joy at seeing the rainbow to the past and the future and furthering the poem's message of timelessness.

In Jarrell's poem, we can notice subtle shifts in diction. The first line, "From my mother's sleep I fell into the State," suggests a formality similar to what we find in Wordsworth's poem. However, the poem takes on a less formal diction as it progresses. Some of the terms, such as "black flak," represent military jargon.

The shift in diction in "The Death of the Ball Turret Gunner" continues until the word choice is informal, almost commonplace. The everyday language of the final line contrasts with the more complex diction that opens the poem. It also contrasts with the serious emotional subject of the line that depicts the death of the gunner. The suggestion is that what initially appears formal, even stately or distinguished, is in the end, unfortunately, all too common.

Levels of diction can range between the high, formal style of Wordsworth's poem and a variety of styles that can include even **slang** and **dialect.** The diction in "The Death of the Ball Turret Gunner" might best be described as a medium, rather than a high formal or completely informal style. As another example, consider the lyrics from Linton Kwesi Johnson's "Di Great Insohreckshan." "Di Great Insohreckshan" not only incorporates slang and dialect into its diction, it relies on that diction to help deliver its message that challenges established authority.

LINTON KWESI JOHNSON

Linton Kwesi Johnson (born in 1952) moved from Jamaica to London when he was eleven years old. In 1974, his first collection of poems, Voices of the Living and the Dead, *appeared. In 1978 he released the adaptation of his second collection of poems as the album* Dread Beat an' Blood. *The album brought together Johnson's poetry with the sound of reggae, earning him recognition as the original "dub" poet. He continues to produce both poetry and music that addresses the social issues of urban England and the world. "Di Great Insohreckshan" is taken from* Making History, *released in 1984.*

The music and poetry of Linton Kwesi Johnson

Di Great Insohreckshan

it woz in april nineteen eighty wan
doun inna di ghetto af Brixtan
dat di babylan dem cauz such a frickshan

dat it bring about a great insohreckshan
5   an it spread all owevah di naeshan
it woz truly an historical occayshan

it woz event af di year
an I wish I ad been dere
wen wi run riat all owevah Brixtan
10   wen wi mash-up plenty police van
wen wi mash-up di wicked wan plan
wen wi mash-up di Swamp Eighty Wan[1]
fi wha?
fi mek di rulah dem andastan
15   dat wi naw tek noh more a dem oppreshan

an wen mi check out di ghetto grape vine
fi fine out all I couda fine
evry rebel jusa revel in dem story
dem a taak bout di powah an di glory
20   dem a taak bout di burnin an di lootin
dem a taak bout di smashin an di grabin
dem a tell mi bout di vanquish an di victri

dem seh di babylan dem went too far
soh wha
25   soh wi ad woz fi bun two cyar
an wan an two innocent get mar
but wha
noh soh it goh sometime inna war ein star
noh soh it goh sometime inna war?

30   dem seh wi bun dung di George[2]
wi couda bun di lanlaad
wi bun dung di George
wi nevah bun di lanlaad
wen wi run riat all owevah Brixtan
wen wi mash-up plenty police van
wen wi mash-up di wicked wan plan
wen wi mash-up di Swamp Eighty Wan

dem seh wi comandeer cyar
an wi ghadah ammunishan
40   wi bill wi baricade
an di wicked ketch afraid
wi sen out wi scout
fi goh fine dem whereabout
den wi faam-up wi passi
45   an wi mek wi raid

---

[1]**Swamp 81:** code name for Brixton police stop and search operation in 1981.

[2]**The George:** a public house on Railton Road, Brixton, with a reputation for racist attitudes.

well now dem run gaan goh plan countah-ackshan
but di plastic bullit an di waatah cannan
will bring a blam-blam
will bring a blam-blam
nevah mine Scarman[3]
will bring a blam-blam

Interpreting Sounds

Like music, poetry makes several sophisticated uses of sound. Individual words have unique **phonetic** characteristics associated with their vowels and consonants. These characteristics help determine the **stress** or emphasis given to their syllables. Relationships among and between words also create meaning—these relationships include alliteration, assonance, and rhyme. Additionally, poetry has a rhythm that (like the beat in music) provides a structure and pattern for the sounds that make up the work.

We can explore the poem "Filling Station" by Elizabeth Bishop to better understand some of these sound qualities.

ELIZABETH BISHOP

Elizabeth Bishop (1911-1979) spent a good deal of her life in Brazil, where she worked translating poems into English and deliberately composing and revising her own work. "Filling Station" was published in her collection, Questions of Travel, *in 1965. For more on Bishop, see "Roosters" (510), "The Fish" (871), and "Sestina" (274).*

Filling Station

Oh, but it is dirty!
—this little filling station,
oil-soaked, oil-permeated
to a disturbing, over-all
5   black translucency.
Be careful with that match!

Father wears a dirty,
oil-soaked monkey suit
that cuts him under the arms,
10   and several quick and saucy
and greasy sons assist him
(it's a family filling station),
all quite thoroughly dirty.

Do they live in the station?
15   It has a cement porch

[handwritten annotation: *oil everywhere]

---

[3]**Scarman:** Lord Scarman headed the public enquiry into the 1981 Brixton Riots.

behind the pumps, and on it
a set of crushed and grease-
impregnated wickerwork;
on the wicker sofa
20   a dirty dog, quite comfy.

Some comic books provide
the only note of color—
of certain color. They lie
upon a big dim doily
25   draping a taboret
(part of the set), beside
a big hirsute begonia.

Why the extraneous plant?
Why the taboret?
30   Why, oh why, the doily?
(Embroidered in daisy stitch
with marguerites, I think,
and heavy with gray crochet.)

Somebody embroidered the doily.
35   Somebody waters the plant,
or oils it, maybe. Somebody
arranges the rows of cans
so that they softly say:
ESSO—SO—SO—SO
40   to high-strung automobiles.
Somebody loves us all.

In the first stanza, we are introduced to the major theme of the poem and much of that introduction comes through sound.

Oh, but it is dirty!
—this little filling station,
oil-soaked, oil-permeated
to a disturbing, over-all
black translucency.
Be careful with that match!

The opening of the poem establishes the setting, a dirty filling station. The vowel sounds create the atmosphere that brings that setting to our senses. Say the third line out loud—oil-soaked, oil-permeated—and feel the way the vowels move. The blending of different vowel sounds and the shaping of the mouth required to articulate each syllable almost create a slippery sense of sliding on oil as the line moves from one sound to the next.

Another way that vowels convey meaning is in their relationships. Take the lines from the last stanza.

Somebody embroidered the doily.
Somebody waters the plant,
or oils it, maybe. Somebody

arranges the rows of cans
so that they softly say:
ESSO—SO—SO—SO
to high-strung automobiles.
Somebody loves us all.

The words "embroidered" and "doily" create a repetition of sound. The repetition of a vowel sound is called **assonance** and adds to the musical elements of the poem by creating a sense of echoing (and in this case a rhyme).

In the third from the last line of the poem, assonance is used to create an effect that mirrors the message of the poem. "ESSO—SO—SO—SO" combines four instances of a vowel sound. To articulate the vowel you must round your mouth and release your breath. Try it—say the line out loud. The assonance resembles the rush of air and sound suggested by a series of passing "high-strung" automobiles.

Consonants also contribute to the sense and meaning of poetry. Consonants like [t], [b], [p], [d], [k], and [g] are called **plosive** because they are made by releasing breath as we articulate the sounds. Words like buzz and explode are said to be **onomatopoeias**, because their sound coincides with their meaning.

Consider the consonant sounds that conclude the first stanza of "Filling Station." "Be careful with that match!" The line concludes with an exclamation point, but the repetition of [t] sounds in "that match" produces an effect that reinforces the sense of the punctuation—say the [t], [t], [tch] out loud and consider whether their sounds contribute to the sense of the striking of "that match." A repetition of consonants like the [t] and [tch] sounds in "that match" is called **alliteration** or **consonance**.

Exploring the assonance and consonance in "Filling Station" demonstrates how we might move from our impressions of a poem to an analysis of how the elements of sound create meaning. You need not read every work in this way, but you should learn to recognize the way that the sounds of words—even of individual vowels and consonants—give shape and meaning to poetry. (You can learn more about how to read poetry phonetically on our CD.)

Reading poetry for sound

Recognizing Rhyme and Rhythm

Rhyme and **rhythm** create meaning by establishing patterns in poetry. Again, as you learn to recognize rhyme and rhythm, realize that poetry conveys meaning in its sounds as well as its printed words. You can use your internal ear as you read, imagining the sounds of words as you scan them (or determine the patterns of stress). You can also read poems out loud, experimenting with different vocalizations of sounds. You may find it easier to sense the rhythm of a work if you tap out the beats as you scan from line to line. Use a pencil or your fingertips to practice picking up the rhythm of a piece by tapping at each stressed syllable (see below).

Rhyme consists of two or more words that have similar sounds. Recall how "Résumé" by Dorothy Parker used rhyme in conjunction with the rhythmic elements of the poem. Many longer poems have more complex ways of using rhyme to create meaning. Consider "The Tyger" by William Blake. (You can examine "The Tyger" in its original form as an etching and watercolor in the Extended Inquiry on Blake on our CD-ROM).

WILLIAM BLAKE

The prints
and
poetry of
William
Blake

*William Blake (1751–1827) was trained in an engraving shop where he
learned the art of etching. In the late 1780s, he invented a new method
of printing called relief etching. Using relief etching, Blake would print a
copy of a work, and then individually color the designs to create what
are known as illuminated books. "The Tyger" is taken from* The Songs of
Experience, *published in 1894.*

The Tyger

Tyger Tyger, burning bright, (A)
In the forest of the night, (A)
What immortal hand or eye (B)
Could frame thy fearful symmetry? (B)

5   In what distant deeps or skies (B)
Burnt the fire of thine eyes? (B)
On what wings dare he aspire? (C)
What the hand dare seize the fire? (C)

And what shoulder, and what art (D)
10   Could twist the sinews of thy heart? (D)
And when thy heart began to beat, (E)
What dread hand and what dread feet? (E)

What the hammer and what the chain? (F)
In what furnace was thy brain? (F)
15   What the anvil? What dread grasp (G)
Dare its deadly terrors clasp? (G)

When the stars threw down their spears, (H)
And watered heaven with their tears, (H)
Did he smile, his work to see? (E)
20   Did he who made the lamb make thee? (E)

Tyger Tyger, burning bright, (A)
In the forest of the night, (A)
What immortal hand or eye (B)
Dare frame thy fearful symmetry? (B)

[handwritten annotation: symmetry = balance]

The most easily recognized form of rhyme is **end rhyme**—rhymes that occur
at the end of the poem's lines. "The Tyger" is structured using pairs of end rhymes
like those at the end of the first two lines, "bright / night." These paired end rhymes
are called **couplets.** Couplets represent a longstanding form of rhyme common
to poetry and music. (Much of hip hop music relies on rhymed couplets.)

Sometimes rhymes are easy to recognize—bright and night are **exact rhymes**
in that they share the same sounds and spelling. Often, we must listen for the
sounds of the words rather than rely on spellings—in lines five and six, "skies" and
"eyes" rhyme based on their sounds, not on their spelling. In contrast to these more

common exact and **sound rhymes,** "The Tyger" also contains a **partial rhyme** between "eye" and "symmetry."

As we analyze poetry, we can create a **rhyme scheme** that demonstrates the rhyming structure of the poem. A rhyme scheme assigns the letter A to the first set of end rhymes, the letter B to the next set, and so on to chart the end rhymes in the poem. The rhyme scheme for "The Tyger" is AA, BB, BB, CC, DD, EE, FF, GG, HH, EE, AA, BB. Other poems will have more complex rhyme schemes and some poetic forms rely on precise structures that call for strict adherence to a particular rhyme scheme.

In addition to end rhyme, poems may also contain **internal rhymes**—rhymes that occur within or across lines. "Embroidered the doily" in "Filling Station" presents an internal rhyme within a single line. Gwendolyn Brooks's "We Real Cool" (page 18) capitalizes on internal rhyme to create a stuttering musical effect in the poem.

Similar to rhyme, rhythm creates patterns of sound that establish the musical sense of a poem. Rhythm refers to the rising and falling stresses that occur as words are read from line to line. **Stress** (sometimes called **accent**) is the emphasis given to words as they are spoken—in a word like opaque, the emphasis falls on the second syllable of the word; in a word like flower, the emphasis falls on the first syllable. Say "opaque flower" out loud and feel how the stresses fall.

When we read a line of poetry with attention to the patterns of stress, it is called **scanning.** There are many techniques you can use to scan the stresses in poetry, but the key is listening for the rising and falling rhythms. Some poems present a regular rhythm—think of the familiar de dum de dum de dum de dum de dum beat that we find in many lines from Shakespeare. In most instances, however, poems create meaning through the subtle variations that they enact once they have created a foundational meter and rhythm. (You can find out more about the rhythms of poetry and scanning poems on our CD.)

Scanning poetry and recognizing rhythms

🖋 CHECKLIST FOR EVALUATING SOUND, RHYME, AND RHYTHM IN POETRY

☐ **Read for sound** when exploring poetry. Recite poems out loud to hear their sounds and rhythms. When reading silently, imagine the sounds of the words on the page and consider how the sounds shape your impressions of the poem.

☐ **Analyze the sounds of vowels and consonants.** Consider how vowels in poems create a sense of movement. Explore how individual sounds create meaning and how assonance and alliteration (or consonance) influence the poem.

☐ **Track the rhymes within the poem.** Chart the progression of end rhymes in each line and look for patterns. Explore internal rhymes and consider how they shape your reading of the poem. Think about the way the rhymes appeal to your senses and create meaning.

☐ **Consider how stress and emphasis create sound and meaning.** Tap out the beats and stresses as you read to get a feel for the rhythm of the poem. Explore how the combinations of stresses increase or decrease the tempo of your reading. Think about the way these aspects of meter convey meaning.

☐ **Use a dictionary** to help you pronounce and determine the stress of words. Consider how the meter of poems works with or against the ways words are traditionally stressed.

Interpreting Words, Symbols, and Figures of Speech

As with other forms of literature, poetry asks us to interpret themes and explore ideas. The distilled nature of poetry requires us to concentrate on the ways that language conveys these themes and ideas. In poetry, we understand this process by exploring the meanings of words, the implications of symbols, and the significance of figures of speech.

The definitions and associations of individual words contribute to the meaning of each line and the poem as a whole. On one level, the meaning of words is relatively straightforward. **Denotation** describes the meaning of words on a simple definitional level. The word *flower,* for instance, refers to the colorful petals that grow at the end of a plant. *Flour* refers to a powder, usually made from wheat, used in cooking. We can look up these words in a dictionary and, for most purposes, understand their meanings.

Of course, denotations are not really as fixed or simple as we would like. Our definition of *flower* must consider whether the word is used as a verb (as in *to flower*) or a noun (as in *a flower*). Additionally, if we read a poem from the Middle Ages, we need to know that *flour* represents an Old English spelling of *flower* and denotes the petals of a plant. Further, if we read a passage from Geoffrey Chaucer's *Canterbury Tales, flour* might be used to refer to ground wheat, or to youth, or to a woman.

As words drift further from their dictionary meanings, we begin to evaluate their **connotations**—that is, the associations and symbolic meanings that they evoke. Some words on their own evoke connotations beyond their simple definitions. A word like *alone,* for instance, means more than just by oneself—it encompasses a set of feelings and associations that require more work to understand. Further, the connotation of words depends in part on our own experiences and sensibilities—alone might have different connotations to an only child than to someone who grew up in a family of eight.

Understanding the many possible meanings of words in poetry requires that we consider the way those words work within the poem and also how they relate to the poem's themes. Take a poem like James Applewhite's "The Story of a Drawer."

JAMES APPLEWHITE

James Applewhite (born in 1935) grew up in the tobacco farming town of Stantonsburg, North Carolina. He began writing poetry in college while studying William Wordsworth and earning his PhD. After college, he worked closely with the poet Randall Jarrell before returning to Duke where he teaches now. His work combines his critical training with his own rural background to create poems exploring memories. "The Story of a Drawer" was published in 1983.

The Story of a Drawer

Father amazed us waving his pistol
In his story of the station nearly robbed.
The thirty-eight special—blued steel glossy
As cobras—nested near the cash register handle
5   With foil-pack prophylactics, quarters.
We imagined his hand with that blue-black bolt
Of lightning upraised, the drunk punks slinking
For the door while he danced his explosive fist
At ceiling and window. We looked in awe at the thing
10   Exposed, then slid the drawer shut, were quiet.

Consider how the word "exposed" in the final line relates to the rest of the poem. What connotations does the word evoke? How are these connotations related to the speaker of the poem? How do the sounds, the rhymes, and the rhythms of the poem contribute to the different senses of the word?

"The Story of a Drawer" also illustrates how symbols and figures of speech convey meaning. A **symbol** is an image or word that stands for something else, that has a figurative meaning beyond its physical or literal sense. In Applewhite's poem, a drawer represents more than a place to store items inside a cabinet; it symbolizes the way humans compartmentalize and hide emotions and impulses.

Symbols can work at different levels in poetry. The symbol of the drawer appears in the title and last line of Applewhite's poem, and forms a kind of frame for the story told in the poem. Robert Frost's "Mending Wall" (page 584), on the other hand, weaves the symbol of the wall throughout the work, constructing the poem around this central image.

In "The Story of a Drawer," the image of the gun presented in the third and fourth lines, "blued steel glossy / As cobras—nested near the cash register handle," represents a similar kind of symbolic meaning—a cobra does have a glossy appearance, as a handgun might, but the power of the symbol comes from the sense of danger and death suggested by the poisonous snake. In this case, the poem uses a **simile** to invoke its symbol. A simile draws a comparison between two things using the words *like* or *as*—in this case the gun is as glossy *as* a cobra.

Metaphors work like similes, except they make their comparisons directly. When we read in Emily Dickinson's poem, "My life had stood a loaded gun," we know the poem is not suggesting that the speaker's life *is* a gun; rather like a loaded gun, the speaker's life may be full of unrealized potential. Poetry emphasizes meanings not normally found in other kinds of writing by employing similes and metaphors to create figurative language.

Figures of speech are combinations of words or phrases that represent ideas symbolically. Once figures of speech become familiar, they are said to be **clichés**. Fresh insights result from poems that subvert the expectations readers have about everyday language and figures of speech. Ron Wallace's "Blessings" plays with clichés to show the uses and limits of figures of speech.

RON WALLACE

Ron Wallace (born in 1945) has been praised for the wit and accessibility of his poems. "Blessings" is taken from Long for this World, *published in 2003. For more on Wallace, see "Hardware" (33).*

Blessings

    occur.
    Some days I find myself
    putting my foot in
    the same stream twice;
5   leading a horse to water
    and making him drink.
    I have a clue.
    I can see the forest
    for the trees.

10   All around me people
    are making silk purses
    out of sows' ears,
    getting blood from turnips,
    building Rome in a day.
15   There's a business
    like show business.
    There's something new
    under the sun.

    Some days misery
20   no longer loves company;
    it puts itself out of its.
    There's rest for the weary.
    There's turning back.
    There are guarantees.
25   I can be serious.
    I can mean that.
    You can quite
    put your finger on it.

    Some days I know
30   I am long for this world.
    I can go home again.
    And when I go
    I can
    take it with me.

By twisting the figures of speech in their opposite directions, "Blessings" builds a case for positive sentiments by portraying the figures in a fresh way.

Interpreting Form and Structure

We have already looked at some of the elements of form in this chapter. For instance, end rhymes create a structure for William Blake's "The Tyger." Some poems call for specific formal structures. For instance, the Elizabethan or **Shakespearian sonnet** is a poem with exactly fourteen lines of ten syllables each, as in Shakespeare's Sonnet 130.

WILLIAM SHAKESPEARE

William Shakespeare (1564–1616) is best known as a playwright. However, his sonnets represent some of his most sophisticated uses of rhyme and meter. Sonnets were a common form of poetry exchanged at court. They offered poets a chance to demonstrate their skills. Sonnet 130 seems to be satirizing many of the love poems that were likely exchanged at the time.

Sonnet 130

My mistress' eyes are nothing like the sun; (A)
Coral is far more red than her lips' red; (B)
If snow be white, why then her breasts are dun; (A)
If hairs be wires, black wires grow on her head. (B)
5   I have seen roses damask'd, red and white, (C)
But no such roses see I in her cheeks; (D)
And in some perfumes is there more delight (C)
Than in the breath that from my mistress reeks. (D)
I love to hear her speak, yet well I know (E)
10   That music hath a far more pleasing sound; (F)
I grant I never saw a goddess go: (E)
My mistress, when she walks, treads on the ground. (F)
   And yet, by heaven, I think my love as rare (G)
   As any she, belied with false compare. (G)

The Shakespearean sonnet is an example of a **closed form** of poetry, a form in which elements such as the structure, the line length, the rhyme scheme, and the rhythm of the poem are set by convention. Understanding these conventions allows us to analyze closed forms with more precision.

In addition to containing fourteen iambic pentameter lines, the Shakespearean sonnet has a conventional rhyme scheme. Notice how the end rhymes divide the poem into sets of four lines (called **quatrains**). The first quatrain is made up of the rhymes AB, AB; the second quatrain uses CD, CD; and the third EF, EF. The last two lines end in a couplet that usually offers a sense of closure or resolution for the sonnet.

A similar closed form of poetry is the Italian or **Petrarchan sonnet**—divided into a set of eight lines (the **octave**) and another set of six lines (the **sextet**). Another closed form is the **sestina,** a poem containing six stanzas that each have six lines with repeating but varied end words. The sestina ends with a three-line set (**tercet**) that provides closure. Now let's examine another poem written in closed form.

ELIZABETH BISHOP

Sestina (1965)

September rain falls on the house.
In the failing light, the old grandmother
sits in the kitchen with the child
beside the Little Marvel Stove,
5   reading the jokes from the almanac,
laughing and talking to hide her tears.

She thinks that her equinoctial tears
and the rain that beats on the roof of the house
were both foretold by the almanac,
10   but only known to a grandmother.
The iron kettle sings on the stove.
She cuts some bread and says to the child,

It's time for tea now; but the child
is watching the teakettle's small hard tears
15   dance like mad on the hot black stove,
the way the rain must dance on the house.
Tidying up, the old grandmother
hangs up the clever almanac

on its string. Birdlike, the almanac
20   hovers half open above the child,
hovers above the old grandmother
and her teacup full of dark brown tears.
She shivers and says she thinks the house
feels chilly, and puts more wood in the stove.

25   *It was to be,* says the Marvel Stove.
I know what I know, says the almanac.
With crayons the child draws a rigid house
and a winding pathway. Then the child
puts in a man with buttons like tears
30   and shows it proudly to the grandmother.

But secretly, while the grandmother
busies herself about the stove,
the little moons fall down like tears
from between the pages of the almanac
35   into the flower bed the child
has carefully placed in the front of the house.

Time to plant tears, says the almanac.
The grandmother sings to the marvellous stove
and the child draws another inscrutable house.

Elizabeth Bishop's "Sestina" demonstrates the ways that closed forms shape the construction of poetry. Conversely, in open forms, the poet creates a structure based on the thoughts, images, and sounds that make up the work. Open forms are some-times called **free verse.** This is not to say that open forms have no structure; rather the structure of the poem develops based on the evolving demands of the work. Consider how William Carlos Williams's "Poem" uses form.

WILLIAM CARLOS WILLIAMS

Poem (1934)

As the cat
climbed over
the top of

the jamcloset
5   first the right
forefoot

carefully
then the hind
stepped down

10   into the pit of
the empty
flowerpot

As Williams's poem unfolds, it moves from stanza to stanza, mirroring the care-ful stepping of the cat. Open forms let writers experiment with shape and struc-ture; free verse flows in concert with the ideas in the poem.

☑CHECKLIST FOR WRITING ABOUT POETRY

- ☐ **Move from impressions, to analysis, to interpretation, to argument.** Appreciate the way poems appeal to your senses and select poems that strike your interest. Refine this appreciation into an understanding of the elements of the poem.

- ☐ **Understand that sound plays a foundational role in poetry.** Learn to discuss the sounds and rhythms of the poems you write about and practice drawing connections between sound and meaning.

- ☐ **Evaluate imagery and themes** to understand their implications. Consider the associations of words and the significance of symbols, similes, and metaphors. Explore how figures of speech convey more than just their literal meanings.

- ☐ **Develop a thesis** that explains your approach. Consider elements of poetry as well as themes and topics, and then develop a specific statement that encapsulates your reading of the poem.

- ☐ **Entertain alternative interpretations.** Ask what objections others might have to your approach. Think about additional ways of reading the poem. Research to see what others have said about the work. Modify your approach to accommodate alternative possibilities.

☐ **Use evidence from poems** to support the points you make. Quote from the text of poems and explain your quotes in your own words. Use the reading techniques discussed in this chapter to demonstrate how the poem works. Document your sources using the models in the Appendix.

REVIEWING AND PRACTICING

As you read the poems printed on the next few pages, consider how you might develop interpretations based on some of the elements of poetry we have discussed in this chapter. Think about whether evaluating their sounds in detail might provide good evidence for an argument about their messages or techniques. Consider how their symbols and imagery work to convey ideas. Ask what role their structure plays in creating meaning.

As you write essays on poetry, you can develop arguments as you would when discussing any form of literature. First and foremost, you need to take an angle and develop a thesis to organize your work. You might argue that the poem makes an important statement about an issue or provides a unique message. You might suggest that the poem represents aspects of culture. You might argue about the significance of a specific poetic technique. In all of these cases, follow a process of inquiry to develop an arguable thesis, then use the strategies for thinking and writing about poetry discussed in this chapter to explain and support your thesis.

Exercise 10.4 *Arguing About a Poem*

Choose a poem from this chapter, and write a three- to five-page paper detailing what you believe to be the most significant message that the poem conveys. (If there is an audio recording of the poem on our CD, be sure to play the clip to hear the poet's vocalization of the piece.)

1. Freewrite, explore questions, create lists, develop maps or outlines, discuss the work with peers, conduct research, or use any other prewriting technique before beginning to draft the paper.

2. Develop a thesis statement that articulates the message in the poem you wish to focus on.

3. Compose body paragraphs that discuss in detail how the poem conveys its message—consider the poem's speaker, setting, tone, structure, sounds, rhythms, language, imagery, and any other significant elements.

4. Consider objections and alternative interpretations and respond to them in your paper.

5. Check that you have an introduction that maps out your key points and spells out your thesis. Check also that you make connections with your thesis as you compose, and that you have a conclusion that brings closure to the paper.

6. Make sure you integrate and discuss quotations correctly. Document your sources and format your paper.

7. When finished, gather feedback from peers or your instructor and revise the paper using the processes outlined in Chapter 8.

Exploring Poems

Here are additional poems. As you read through these works, consider how they relate to the elements of poetry we have been discussing in this chapter. Also, explore the messages conveyed by the works. Think about the themes that you discover and any potential topics you might use to write about the works. You can also find many poems among the thematic readings in Chapters 14–18.

SHARON OLDS

Sharon Olds (born in 1942) had not written any poetry growing up or in college, but after attending a poetry reading by Muriel Rukeyser, she decided on the spot that poetry was a love for her. After finishing her PhD, she took a chance and began composing poems. Her works often feature domestic situations and emotional issues while maintaining an accessible and uplifting tone. "The Race" was first published in Olds's collection, The Father, *in 1992.*

The Race

Student essay on "The Race"

When I got to the airport I rushed up to the desk,
bought a ticket, ten minutes later
they told me the flight was cancelled, the doctors
had said my father would not live through the night
5   and the flight was cancelled. A young man
with a dark blond moustache told me
another airline had a non-stop
leaving in seven minutes. See that
elevator over there, well go
10   down to the first floor, make a right, you'll
see a yellow bus, get off at the
second Pan Am terminal, I
ran, I who have no sense of direction
raced exactly where he'd told me, a fish
15   slipping upstream deftly against
the flow of the river. I jumped off that bus with those
bags I had thrown everything into
in five minutes, and ran, the bags
wagged me from side to side as if
20   to prove I was under the claims of the material,
I ran up to a man with a white flower on his breast,
I who always go to the end of the line, I said
Help me. He looked at my ticket, he said
Make a left and then a right, go up the moving stairs and then
25   run. I lumbered up the moving stairs,
at the top I saw the corridor,

and then I took a deep breath, I said
Goodbye to my body, goodbye to comfort,
I used my legs and heart as if I would
30   gladly use them up for this,
to touch him again in this life. I ran, and the
bags banged me, wheeled and coursed
in skewed orbits, I have seen pictures of
women running, their belongings tied
35   in scarves grasped in their fists, I blessed my
long legs he gave me, my strong
heart I abandoned to its own purpose,
I ran to Gate 17 and they were
just lifting the thick white
40   lozenge of the door to fit it into
the socket of the plane. Like the one who is not
too rich, I turned sideways and
slipped through the needle's eye, and then
I walked down the aisle toward my father. The jet
45   was full, and people's hair was shining, they were
smiling, the interior of the plane was filled with a
mist of gold endorphin light,
I wept as people weep when they enter heaven,
in massive relief. We lifted up
50   gently from one tip of the continent
and did not stop until we set down lightly on the
other edge, I walked into his room
and watched his chest rise slowly
and sink again, all night
55   I watched him breathe.

WILLIAM SHAKESPEARE

Sonnet 73

That time of year thou mayst in me behold
When yellow leaves, or none, or few do hang
Upon those boughs which shake against the cold
Bare ruined choirs where late the sweet birds sang.
5   In me thou see'st the twilight of such day
As after sunset fadeth in the west,
Which by-and-by black night doth steal away,
Death's second self, which seals up all in rest.
In me thou see'st the glowing of such fire
10   That on the ashes of his youth doth lie,
As the deathbed whereon it must expire,
Consumed with that which it was nourished by.
    This thou perceiv'st, which makes thy love more strong,
    To love that well which thou must leave ere long

DYLAN THOMAS

Recognized as an exemplary Welsh poet, Dylan Thomas (1914–1953) grew up with a love of poetry. His father was a school teacher who encouraged Thomas to read and study literature. Most of Thomas's success, however, cannot be attributed to formal education. He worked hard to establish himself in the London literary scene, publishing his first collection of poems in 1934 but not receiving much critical acclaim until later in life. "Do Not Go Gentle into that Good Night" was first published in 1937.

Do Not Go Gentle into that Good Night

Do not go gentle into that good night,
Old age should burn and rave at close of day;
Rage, rage against the dying of the light.

Though wise men at their end know dark is right,
5 Because their words had forked no lightning they
Do not go gentle into that good night.

Good men, the last wave by, crying how bright
Their frail deeds might have danced in a green bay,
Rage, rage against the dying of the light.

10 Wild men who caught and sang the sun in flight,
And learn, too late, they grieved it on its way,
Do not go gentle into that good night.

Grave men, near death, who see with blinding sight
Blind eyes could blaze like meteors and be gay,
15 Rage, rage against the dying of the light.

Grave—serious person

And you, my father, there on the sad height,
Curse, bless, me now with your fierce tears, I pray.
Do not go gentle into that good night.
Rage, rage against the dying of the light.

INQUIRING FURTHER

1. "The Race" does not appear to have a regular rhythm or make use of rhyme in a significant way. How does the poem use rhythm or other elements of sound to convey its message?

2. Sonnet 73 is written in Elizabethan English, the language used by the aristocracy in court some four hundred years ago. Treat the first four lines of the poem as a sentence and read it through until you understand the meaning of the sentence. How does the diction and syntax differ from forms of English you may be more familiar with? Read the rest of the poem as carefully as the first four lines, then write a short summary of what the speaker of the poem is saying.

3. Play the recording of one of the poems on our CD. Compare the poet's reading of the poem to your expectations of how the poem might sound. How does hearing the poem change your understanding of it?

4. "The Race," "Sonnet 73," and "Do Not Go Gentle into that Good Night" all touch on themes related to death. Which poem do you prefer and why? Write a paper comparing the way two or more of the works use elements of poetry (settings, speakers, rhythm, rhyme, sound, symbols, etc.) to treat their topics.

A Draft Essay on Poetry

Below you will find an essay on William Stafford's "Traveling through the Dark" (page 257). As you examine Greg's exploration of the poem, consider how the paper discusses elements of poetry to support its interpretation. Also, look over Stafford's poem again and see if you can raise any objections to the approach taken in the paper.

Greg Casperson

Instructor Reynolds

English 102

25 April 2004

Understanding through the Dark

William Stafford's poem, "Traveling through the Dark," tells the story of

a motorist driving at night who describes an encounter with a deer that has

been struck by a passing car. Stafford's tale may appear short and simple on

the surface, but like the character during his travels, a second look at things

reveals a picture deeply painted in meaning. Through contrasts between logic

and emotion, William Stafford explores a man's progressive understanding of

the conflicting relationship between his world and that of nature.

The first two stanzas present a very matter-of-fact analysis of the

situation. The narrator describes how he "stood by the heap, a doe, a recent

killing" ("Traveling" line 6). This cryptic description of the deer resembles a

mortician's surgical report, appropriately followed by the temperature and

texture of the animal. The first two stanzas are examples of typical human

logic. The speaker makes conclusions through sound reasoning that lead to

a decision to move the animal, preventing further harm to other motorists.

The narrator automatically responds in the most rational way, going
through the motions as a caring, good-natured driver would do (arguably
above and beyond most).

However, this routine task, similar to that of assisting a stranger with a
flat tire, becomes a tragic situation as he feels the unborn baby inside. This
change of events beautifully transitions into the last three stanzas, sharply
opposing the thought processes of the first two. The surprise discovery of
the fawn casts doubt on his previously well-rationalized decision to roll the
carcass into the canyon. The man is clearly troubled by this change in
events: "Beside that mountain road I hesitated," his first truly human action.

William Stafford has described a character found in the middle of two
worlds: one of soulless machinery and the other of the natural realm that
surrounds it. As a result of these contradictions, the poem's narrator is
challenged by the now tragically escalating situation and fearful of his own
general indifference toward nature. With his fears growing stronger, the
decision to dispose of the deer carcass and its living occupant becomes
impossible to reason through with simple logic.

As he ponders his next course of action, the "group" involved await his
decision: a car personified by the cat-like purring of the engine, the dead
mother and her unborn baby, and himself, the ambassador of our society. As
he mentally conducts his closing arguments against the listening
wilderness, the taillights shine through the exhaust smoke obstructing his
view. His inability to see what's happening in the world around him
comments on the priorities of the human race. The lesson is that not
everything is supposed to be categorized and sorted out for our own analysis.
Sometimes there are no answers; our sight blinds us from this conclusion.

Having come to such an understanding with the natural world, our
narrator must still make a decision regarding the unborn fawn. His "only

Casperson 3

swerving" ends up killing the fawn, but his decision to push her back into

the river was one based on his respect for nature and frustrations over the

conflict between the two worlds rather than the earlier precaution to

prevent further injury to other drivers. His understanding of the situation

and how the fawn could never really be saved was based on his awareness

of the two opposing forces of the earth and the machines that plague it.

Our narrator had no intent of contrasting these two conflicting worlds

as he pulled to the side of the road one evening. Yet as he comes face to face

with the responsibility of taking another life, he can't help but understand

the frustrating relationship in which we take so much with little moral

regard. From the beginning, each stanza brings the poem a little further

along and closer to our narrator's understanding of this relationship, as

well as his eventual realization that he had to close his eyes to better see

while traveling through the dark.

[New page]

Works Cited

Stafford, William. "Traveling through the Dark." <u>Writing about</u>

<u>Literature in the Media Age</u>. Ed. Daniel Anderson. New York:

Pearson Longman, 2005.

I N Q U I R I N G   F U R T H E R

1. Do you think the paper takes more of a thematic approach to explaining the story, or more of a formal approach that looks at elements of poetry like rhythm or diction? What recommendations would you make for revising the approach in the paper? Write an end comment that expresses your impressions of the strengths and weaknesses of the paper.

2. Look over "Traveling through the Dark" again. How does your reading of the poem differ from the one expressed in the paper? What alternative possibilities do you think the paper should address and why?

3. Stafford's poem can be difficult to write about because it narrates such a linear progression of events. The linear narration makes it easy to fall into the trap of providing plot summary instead of analyzing the poem from a particular angle. How well do you think Greg's paper handles this difficulty? What revisions might help with this issue?

11

Thinking and Writing About Drama and Film

Drama is life with the dull bits cut out.

—*Alfred Hitchcock*

Drama and film *are* like life. We can recognize in films or plays the conflicts that the actors undergo as events unfold. At the same time, as the term drama implies, plays and films operate with a higher emotional intensity than most of us could stand in our day-to-day existence. Drama centers on tensions and derives much of its power by building suspense, and then providing a sense of release as conflicts are resolved.

Like other forms of literature, drama employs a deliberate plot to tell its story. It emphasizes characters and presents information through dialog. Drama and film, however, differ from other forms of literature in that they rely on the performances of actors and the physical reproductions of settings to create a world. As readers (or viewers), we must keep this performative aspect in mind as we evaluate and write about drama and film.

Drama relies on elements of the stage such as sets, costumes, lighting, and sounds. Drama also has unique structures and conventions. Scenes, for instance, organize the structure of a play. Plays also may follow the conventions of tragedy or comedy. Film operates as a visual and auditory medium, demanding that we evaluate the way objects and figures appear in its scenes, its camera techniques (cinematography), its use of special effects, as well as its sounds and music. Further, film requires us to think about editing techniques that have been used to piece together the shots and scenes that tell the story.

UNDERSTANDING DRAMATIC CONVENTIONS

Above all else, we must realize that drama is intended to be performed. We often read the text of plays, but, as we do so, we should visualize how the settings might be constructed in a theater. We should also imagine how actors might bring the characters to life. When possible, we can attend or view recordings of performances to see how the text on the page is translated through performance on the stage.

Exploring Elements of the Stage

When reading a drama, we can explore elements within the text that help us imagine the play in performance. Foremost among these elements are **stage directions** (instructions about the appearance of the stage and the actions of the actors). Stage directions can be purely descriptive, or they can editorialize, offering a playwright's comments and setting the tone for the drama.

Other elements of the stage include **sets, costumes, lighting,** and **sounds.** Sometimes these aspects are spelled out clearly in the text of a play. In David Ives's *Sure Thing* (289–95), for instance, stage directions signal for a bell to ring at selected intervals in the play. The bell plays a key role in the action as it interrupts the dialog of the characters and creates separations between the episodes of conversation.

Sometimes these elements of drama are not always specified. **Costumes, lighting,** and **music** are often developed by directors, set builders, costume designers, and other collaborators putting on the play. Consider the way that a play like *Romeo and Juliet* has been reworked for contemporary audiences in the 1996 film version of the same title. The film is set in modern "Verona Beach" and the sets include handguns, fast cars, and helicopters. Part of your task as a viewer of drama (and film) is to evaluate the interpretations that go into the production of the piece.

Considering Characters

The actors provide perhaps the most significant interpretation of a play. As you study performances of actors and the characters they represent, you can use the strategies for understanding characters discussed on pages 41–42. Decide whether characters are **flat** (one-dimensional) or **round** (multifaceted). Determine which character you believe to be the **protagonist** (or main character) and which might act as **antagonists.** In drama, action often centers squarely around the protagonist, sometimes called the hero.

You can compose a character analysis (see page 42) that examines the traits of the characters. When evaluating an actor's performance, begin with your own sense of the key traits of the character. Draft a sketch of the traits emphasized by the performance. Compare the two versions and make note of aspects of the character you may have overlooked, or traits you believe the actor may have de-emphasized. Consider how the traits emphasized by the actor illuminate your thinking about the play as a whole.

Exercise 11.1   *Casting for Characters*

Working with a group of fellow students or on your own, consider *Sure Thing* or *Los Vendidos* included in this chapter, or one of the plays in Chapters 14–18 and respond to the following prompts. Begin by selecting a recorder to keep track of the group's work or preparing to take notes on your own.

1. Create a list of the main characters in the play. For two of the characters, develop a brief analysis of their traits. Consider the complexities of each character and how he or she relates to others in the play. Think about how events shed light on the character and about adjectives that might describe him or her. Sketch out your analysis of each character in three or more sentences.

2. For the first character on your list, select an actor or actress you think would be best suited to play the character. Think about actors that fit

your reading of the character. Think of actors who might add another dimension. Consider the benefits and drawbacks of different choices, then write down the name of the person you would cast into the role.

3. Justify your decision. Explain which traits the actor possesses that you considered in making your decision. Discuss ways you believe the actor might interpret the character. Think about how this choice sheds light on your understanding of the play. Repeat the process, selecting an actor and explaining your decision for the second character in your list. Report your choices and explain your decision in a brief speech to your classmates.

Recognizing Plot, Structure, and Genres

Fiction in general tends to follow a rising and falling structure that can be understood as moving from **exposition** (providing background), to **conflict** (whatever opposes the protagonist or complicates the narrative), to **resolution.** In drama, often this general movement is laid out in five stages:

Exposition → complication → crisis → falling action → resolution

Many dramas reflect this movement in their structure. Shakespeare's plays, for instance, have five acts. In fact, the resolution of many of Shakespeare's plays is often never really in doubt, as we know that in the fifth act most of the comedies will end in marriage and most of the tragedies will end in death.

Shakespeare's tragedies share characteristics with early **Greek dramas.** *Antigonê* by Sophocles (pages 788–814) demonstrates many of the key aspects of **Greek tragedy.** Creon, the king of Thebes, forbids the burial of Polyneicês, who was a traitor to the city. Polyneicês's sister, Antigonê, defies Creon's orders, and then Creon condemns her to death by starvation. Creon's son, Haimon, who was to marry Antigonê, challenges his father to release her. Creon eventually decides he has made a mistake and orders Antigonê released, but it is too late—Haimon has already committed suicide. Upon hearing of the death of her son, Creon's wife also kills herself.

The play illustrates the rising and falling pattern of the tragedy and the importance of a **plot** with a twist of fate. Creon's decision sets events in motion—the subsequent events unravel as the implications of his choice play out.

The play also demonstrates a central element of the protagonist, the **tragic flaw.** The **tragic hero** usually possesses positive qualities, but struggles with some key failing or personality trait. In Creon's case, his flaw may be his arrogance in thinking he can override the wishes of the community and his family, and his pride that prevents him from changing his mind sooner. (You can learn more about the elements of Greek drama on our CD.)

Resources for studying drama

Shakespeare's tragedies tend to have more subplots and emphasize the relationships between characters as well as the struggles of their protagonists. *Hamlet* (414–98), for instance, contains much subterfuge as Hamlet endeavors to learn the truth about his father's murder. Hamlet's relationships with his mother, his uncle, and his dead father drive the action as much or more so than the plot. Still, the story ends in tragedy and provides a resolution based on the development and eventual demise of the protagonist.

Shakespearean comedies, on the other hand, are marked by a happy resolution in their final acts. Shakespearean comedies emphasize the importance of subplots to the point of making them a key ingredient in the drama. *The Taming*

*The
Taming
of the
Shrew* on
stage and
on film

of the Shrew, for instance, weaves three romantic courtships into its plot. (See the extended inquiry on pages 837–43.) Subplots, disguises, mistaken identities, and magical manipulations mark the comedies. The resolution removes the impediments that have kept the lovers apart and restores order to the confusions of the plot.

Of course, these categories provide a general sense of the structure and nature of dramas. Many of Shakespeare's plays contain elements of comedy and tragedy. Tragedies provide comic relief, as in the gravedigger's scene from *Hamlet;* and comedies contain serious elements, as in the harsh treatment of Katharina in *The Taming of the Shrew.*

Modern dramas are even harder to compartmentalize. In many, a structure of rising and falling action can be distinguished. But in most, the conflicts and resolutions are messier and more realistic than what we would find in Greek or Shakespearean drama. Other plays experiment with the structure or staging techniques of drama. *Sure Thing* by David Ives structures the dialog using interruption and repetition to layer multiple versions of a single scene over one another. In evaluating varying forms of drama like these, keep in mind two key concerns:

1. Plays are structured to move toward a conclusion in a set amount of time, so their plots progress toward a moment of resolution.

2. Plays are meant to be performed, so imagine not only the words on the page, but also the enactment of the drama on stage and by actors. (When possible view live or filmed productions.)

Evaluating Imagery and Themes in Drama

As in other forms of literature, ideas are often conveyed through imagery. A symbolic meaning may run throughout an entire play. In Susan Glaspell's *Trifles* (pages 625–35), for instance, a bird cage provides a key symbol representing the role of women in the play. *Trifles* speaks to issues of gender and authority, so we might refer to the symbol of the bird cage as evidence for interpretations about the attitudes of men and women.

In *Los Vendidos,* by Luis Valdez (pages 296–303), the characters themselves take on symbolic roles. The figure of the Farmworker, the Revolucionario, and the Mexican American represent not characters, but caricatures that illuminate Hispanic stereotypes. The plot of the play provides a twist at the end that challenges our expectations for these stereotypes. Were we to write about themes of ethnic stereotyping in the play, we could refer to these figures and their characteristics to discuss how cultural expectations can influence views of identity.

✔ CHECKLIST FOR
UNDERSTANDING DRAMA

☐ **Remember that drama is meant to be acted out.** When reading drama, think about events as they might unfold in a production of the play. Consider how actors might bring the characters to life in a performance.

☐ **Pay attention to the elements of the stage.** Note any stage directions that demonstrate the atmosphere of the setting or the attitudes of the characters. Visualize descriptions of settings. Imagine how music, sounds, lighting, or costumes might influence the production of the drama.

☐ **Understand the characters** in drama. Consider how dialog works to demonstrate character traits. Explore relationships between characters, examining the protagonist and any antagonists. Evaluate the characters, considering whether they are flat or round and how they might be described.

☐ **Examine the plot and structure** of drama. Think about the general rising and falling organization of events in a drama and analyze how plays follow or vary from a model of exposition, complication, crisis, falling action, and resolution. Consider the final act of the drama and the significance of the resolution it provides.

☐ **Understand the conventions and context of plays.** Explore our CD or conduct research to learn more about Greek drama and Shakespearean theater. Consider the role drama plays in a culture, the audiences who might have viewed plays, and historical issues and events addressed by plays.

☐ **Recognize the genres of drama.** Consider the faults of the protagonists of tragedies. Think about how deceptions and confusion move the action and create meaning in comedies. Learn about figures and events addressed in historical plays. Explore how modern or experimental drama builds upon and modifies earlier forms.

☐ **Interpret the imagery and themes** in drama. Examine figurative language and key symbols. Explore themes relating to human, historical, and cultural concerns. Develop readings that explain your understanding of the significance of a play and how the elements of drama work to convey meaning.

Writing About Drama

As you write about plays, you can combine what you know about literature in general with an understanding of drama on its own terms. Drama tells a story. It provides a setting in which actions take place. It also features characters, imagery, and themes. You may write essays about the plays in this book as you would other works, developing arguments that interpret and explain their significance.

On the other hand, you may also concentrate on the aspects of a performance of a play. Attending or viewing a performance enables you to write about the interpretation of the work by the production company. You can specifically refer to elements of the stage, like lighting or sound, as you write. Similarly, you can think about how actors interpret their characters. Assessing the performance allows you to better understand your own reading of a play.

Exercise 11.2   *Reviewing a Performance*

Attend a production of a play and write a review evaluating the performance. You can also view a filmed version of a performance.

1. Begin by reading the text of the play. As you read, imagine how you would put on a performance of the play. How might the settings and

characters best be portrayed? Explore the play until you have a clear sense of the plot and its key themes.

2. Attend or view a performance of the play. Approach the play from the mindset of an attentive viewer—the play should be entertaining, but you will be watching to evaluate the elements of drama. (You can take notes and review scenes if you are watching a filmed version.)

3. Write a two-page review of the play. Begin your review with brief information about the production company, where the play was performed, the original author, and other background details. You can also encapsulate what you believe to be the strengths and weaknesses of the production.

4. Develop body paragraphs evaluating the quality of the production. Be careful not to merely list your impressions and opinions of the play. Instead, imagine yourself as the eyes and ears of your readers. Provide detailed descriptions of the play. Once you have described an aspect of the production in detail, you can draw conclusions about its strengths or weaknesses.

5. Address elements of the stage production in your evaluation—lighting, sound, music, costumes, and sets. Be sure to discuss the actors' performances on their own terms, and in terms of the ways they interpret the characters of the play. Finally, discuss the major themes of the play, describing and evaluating how the performance deals with the key concerns.

6. Close your review by encapsulating your evaluation of the performance. You may point out a specific aspect of the performance that illustrates the production as a whole. You may sum up your sense of the play with a comment that draws a final conclusion and makes a recommendation.

Exercise 11.3   *Arguing About Drama*

Choose one of the plays in our book and write a three- to five-page paper exploring a major theme that the play touches upon.

1. Begin by reading, and if possible viewing, a performance of the play. Mark key passages and note aspects of the performance that seem significant.

2. Freewrite, explore questions, create lists, maps, or outlines, discuss the work with peers, conduct research, or use any other prewriting technique before beginning to draft the paper.

3. Develop a thesis statement that articulates your understanding of the significance of a theme in the play.

4. Compose body paragraphs that discuss how the play provides a message concerning the theme you have selected—consider the elements of the stage, the characters, and the imagery. If you have viewed a performance of the play, discuss how the production supports or undercuts your interpretation.

5. Consider objections and alternative interpretations and respond to them in your paper.

6. Check that you have an introduction that maps out your key points and spells out your thesis. Check also that you have a conclusion that brings closure to the paper and that you make connections with your thesis as you compose.

7. Make sure you integrate and discuss quotations correctly. Document your sources and format your paper (see the Appendix).

8. When finished, gather feedback from peers or your instructor and revise the paper using the processes outlined in Chapter 8.

EXPLORING DRAMA

Printed below are two plays, *Sure Thing*, by David Ives, and *Los Vendidos*, by Luis Valdez. You can also find other plays on the pages listed below.

Hamlet, by William Shakespeare (414–98)

The Taming of the Shrew, by William Shakespeare (837–43)

A Doll's House, by Henrik Ibsen (667–715)

Antigone, by Sophocles (788–814)

Trifles, by Susan Glaspell (625–35)

DAVID IVES

David Ives began writing and staging drama after graduating from college. His early plays were put on in New York by the Circle Repertoire Company. His playwrighting convinced him to continue pursuing his interest in the theater so he enrolled at Yale and earned an MFA in drama. His writing emphasizes wit, short sketch-like pieces, and unorthodox methods of staging. He composed a series of short plays and published them in the collection All in the Timing *in 1994.* Sure Thing *is from that collection.*

Sure Thing

THE CHARACTERS
BILL and BETTY, both in their late twenties

The setting:
a cafe table, with a couple of chairs

Betty, reading at the table. An empty chair opposite her. Bill Enters.

BILL: Excuse me. Is this chair taken?
BETTY: Excuse me?
BILL: Is this taken?
BETTY: Yes it is.
BILL: Oh. Sorry.

BETTY: Sure thing. (*A bell rings softly.*)

BILL: Excuse me. Is this chair taken?

BETTY: Excuse me?

BILL: Is this taken?

BETTY: No, but I'm expecting somebody in a minute.

BILL: Oh. Thanks anyway.

BETTY: Sure thing. (*A bell rings softly.*)

BILL: Excuse me. Is this chair taken?

BETTY: No, but I'm expecting somebody very shortly.

BILL: Would you mind if I sit here till he or she or it comes?

BETTY: (*Glances at her watch.*) They seem to be pretty late . . .

BILL: You never know who you might be turning down.

BETTY: Sorry. Nice try, though.

BILL: Sure thing. (*Bell.*) Is this seat taken?

BETTY: No it's not.

BILL: Would you mind if I sit here?

BETTY: Yes I would.

BILL: Oh. (*Bell.*) Is this chair taken?

BETTY: No it's not.

BILL: Would you mind if I sit here?

BETTY: No. Go ahead.

BILL: Thanks. (*He sits. She continues reading.*) Everyplace else seems to be taken.

BETTY: Mm-hm.

BILL: Great place.

BETTY: Mm-hm.

BILL: What's the book?

BETTY: I just wanted to read in quiet, if you don't mind.

BILL: No. Sure thing. (*Bell.*)

BILL: Everyplace else seems to be taken.

BETTY: Mm-hm.

BILL: Great place for reading.

BETTY: Yes, I like it.

BILL: What's the book?

BETTY: "The Sound and the Fury."

BILL: Oh. Hemingway. (*Bell.*) What's the book?

BETTY: "The Sound and the Fury."

BILL: Oh. Faulkner.

BETTY: Have you read it?

BILL: Not . . . actually. I've sure read *about* . . . it, though. It's supposed to be great.

BETTY: It is great.

BILL: I hear it's great. (*Small pause.*) Waiter? (*Bell.*) What's the book?

BETTY: "The Sound and the Fury."

BILL: Oh. Faulkner.

BETTY: Have you read it?

BILL: I'm a Mets fan, myself. (*Bell.*)

BETTY: Have you read it?

BILL: Yeah, I read it in college.

BETTY: Where was college?

BILL: I went to Oral Roberts University. (*Bell.*)

BETTY: Where was college?

BILL: I was lying. I never really went to college. I just like to party. (*Bell.*)

BETTY: Where was college?

BILL: Harvard.

BETTY: Do you like Faulkner?

BILL: I love Faulkner. I spent a whole winter reading him once.

BETTY: I've just started.

BILL: I was so excited after ten pages that I went out and bought everything else he wrote. One of the greatest reading experiences of my life. I mean, all that incredible psychological understanding. Page after page of gorgeous prose. His profound grasp of the mystery of time and human existence. The smells of the earth . . . What do you think?

BETTY: I think it's pretty boring. (*Bell.*)

BILL: What's the book?

BETTY: "The Sound and the Fury."

BILL: Oh! Faulkner!

BETTY: Do you like Faulkner?

BILL: I love Faulkner.

BETTY: He's incredible.

BILL: I spent a whole winter reading him once.

BETTY: I was so excited after ten pages that I went out and bought everything else he wrote.

BILL: All that incredible psychological understanding.

BETTY: And the prose is so gorgeous.

BILL: And the way he's grasped the mystery of time—

BETTY: —and human existence. I can't believe I've waited this long to read him.

BILL: You never know. You might not have liked him before.

BETTY: That's true.

BILL: You might not have been ready for him. You have to hit these things at the right moment or it's no good.

BETTY: That's happened to me.

BILL: It's all in the timing. (*Small pause.*) My name's Bill, by the way.

BETTY: I'm Betty.

BILL: Hi.

BETTY: Hi. (*Small pause.*)

BILL: Yes I thought reading Faulkner was . . . a great experience.

BETTY: Yes. (*Small pause.*)

BILL: "The Sound and the Fury" . . . (*Another small pause.*)

BETTY: Well. Onwards and upwards. (*She goes back to her book.*)

BILL: Waiter—? (*Bell.*) You have to hit these things at the right moment or it's no good.

BETTY: That's happened to me.

BILL: It's all in the timing. My name's Bill, by the way.

BETTY: I'm Betty.

BILL: Hi.

BETTY: Hi.

BILL: Do you come in here a lot?

BETTY: Actually I'm just in town for two days from Pakistan.

BILL: Oh. Pakistan. (*Bell.*) My name's Bill, by the way.

BETTY: I'm Betty.

BILL: Hi.

BETTY: Hi.

BILL: Do you come in here a lot?

BETTY: Every once in a while. Do you?

BILL: Not much anymore. Not as much as I used to. Before my nervous breakdown. (*Bell.*) Do you come in here a lot?

BETTY: Why are you asking?

BILL: Just interested.

BETTY: Are you really interested, or do you just want to pick me up?

BILL: No, I'm really interested.

BETTY: Why would you be interested in whether I come in here a lot?

BILL: Just . . . getting acquainted.

BETTY: Maybe you're only interested for the sake of making small talk long enough to ask me back to your place to listen to some music, or because you've just rented some great tape for your VCR, or because you've got some terrific unknown Django Reinhardt record, only all you'll really want to do is fuck—which you won't do very well—after which you'll go into the bathroom and pee very loudly, then pad into the kitchen and get yourself a beer from the refrigerator without asking me whether I'd like anything, and then you'll proceed to lie back down beside me and confess that you've got a girlfriend named Stephanie who's away at medical school in Belgium for a year, and that you've been involved with her—*off and on*—in what you'll call a very "intricate" relationship, for about *seven YEARS*. None of which *interests* me, mister!

BILL: Okay. (*Bell.*) Do you come in here a lot?

BETTY: Every other day, I think.

BILL: I come in here quite a lot and I don't remember seeing you.

BETTY: I guess we must be on different schedules.

BILL: Missed connections.

BETTY: Yes. Different time zones.

BILL: Amazing how you can live right next door to somebody in this town and never even know it.

BETTY: I know.

BILL: City life.

BETTY: It's crazy.

BILL: We probably pass each other in the street every day. Right in front of this place, probably.

BETTY: Yep.

BILL: (*Looks around.*) Well the waiters here sure seem to be in some different time zone. I can't seem to locate one anywhere . . . Waiter! (*He looks back.*) So what do you—(*He sees that she's gone back to her book.*)

BETTY: I beg pardon?

BILL: Nothing. Sorry. (*Bell.*)

BETTY: I guess we must be on different schedules.

BILL: Missed connections.

BETTY: Yes. Different time zones.

BILL: Amazing how you can live right next door to somebody in this town and never even know it.

BETTY: I know.

BILL: City life.

BETTY: It's crazy.

BILL: You weren't waiting for somebody when I came in, were you?

BETTY: Actually I was.

BILL: Oh. Boyfriend?

BETTY: Sort of.

BILL: What's a sort-of boyfriend?

BETTY: My husband.

BILL: Ah-ha. (*Bell.*) You weren't waiting for somebody when I came in, were you?

BETTY: Actually I was.

BILL: Oh. Boyfriend?

BETTY: Sort of.

BILL: What's a sort-of boyfriend?

BETTY: We were meeting here to break up.

BILL: Mm-hm . . . (*Bell.*) What's a sort-of boyfriend?

BETTY: My lover. Here she comes right now! (*Bell.*)

BILL: You weren't waiting for somebody when I came in, were you?

BETTY: No, just reading.

BILL: Sort of a sad occupation for a Friday night, isn't it? Reading here, all by your-self?

BETTY: Do you think so?

BILL: Well sure. I mean, what's a good-looking woman like you doing out alone on a Friday night?

BETTY: Trying to keep away from lines like that.

BILL: No, listen—(*Bell.*) You weren't waiting for somebody when I came in, were you?

BETTY: No, just reading.

BILL: Sort of a sad occupation for a Friday night, isn't it? Reading here all by your-self?

BETTY: I guess it is, in a way.

BILL: What's a good-looking woman like you doing out alone on a Friday night anyway? No offense, but . . .

BETTY: I'm out alone on a Friday night for the first time in a very long time.

BILL: Oh.

BETTY: You see, I just recently ended a relationship.

BILL: Oh.

BETTY: Of rather long standing.

BILL: I'm sorry. (*Small pause.*) Well listen, since reading by yourself *is* such a sad occupation for a Friday night, would you like to go elsewhere?

BETTY: No . . .

BILL: Do something else?

BETTY: No thanks.

BILL: I was headed out to the movies in a while anyway.

BETTY: I don't think so.

BILL: Big chance to let Faulkner catch his breath. All those long sentences get him pretty tired.

BETTY: Thanks anyway.

BILL: Okay.

BETTY: I appreciate the invitation.

BILL: Sure thing. (*Bell.*) You weren't waiting for somebody when I came in, were you?

BETTY: No, just reading.

BILL: Sort of a sad occupation for a Friday night, isn't it? Reading here all by your-self?

BETTY: I guess I was trying to think of it as existentially romantic. You know—cappuccino, great literature, rainy night . . .

BILL: That only works in Paris. We *could* hop the late plane to Paris. Get on a Concorde. Find a cafe . . .

BETTY: I'm a little short on planefare tonight.

BILL: Darn it, so am I.

BETTY: To tell you the truth, I was headed to the movies after I finished this section. Would you like to come along? Since you can't locate a waiter?

BILL: That's a very nice offer, but . . .

BETTY: Uh-huh. Girlfriend?

BILL: Two, actually. One of them's pregnant, and Stephanie—(*Bell.*)

BETTY: Girlfriend?

BILL: No, I don't have a girlfriend. Not if you mean the castrating bitch I dumped last night. (*Bell.*)

BETTY: Girlfriend?

BILL: Sort of. Sort of.

BETTY: What's a sort-of girlfriend?

BILL: My mother. (*Bell.*) I just ended a relationship, actually.

BETTY: Oh.

BILL: Of rather long standing.

BETTY: I'm sorry to hear it.

BILL: This is my first night out alone in a long time. I feel a little bit at sea, to tell you the truth.

BETTY: So you didn't stop to talk because you're a Moonie, or you have some weird political affiliation—?

BILL: Nope. Straight-down-the-ticket Republican. (*Bell.*) Straight-down-the-ticket Democrat. (*Bell.*) Can I tell you something about politics? (*Bell.*) I like to think of myself as a citizen of the universe. (*Bell.*) I'm unaffiliated.

BETTY: That's a relief. So am I.

BILL: I vote my beliefs.

BETTY: Labels are not important.

BILL: Labels are not important, exactly. Like me, for example. I mean, what does it matter if I had a two-point at—(*Bell.*)—three-point at—(*Bell.*)—four-point at college, or if I did come from Pittsburgh—(*Bell.*)—Cleveland—(*Bell.*)—Westchester County?

BETTY: Sure.

BILL: I believe that a man is what he is. (*Bell.*) A person is what he is. (*Bell.*) A person is . . . what they are.

BETTY: I think so too.

BILL: So what if I admire Trotsky? (*Bell.*) So what if I once had a total-body liposuction? (*Bell.*) So what if I don't have a penis? (*Bell.*) So what if I once spent a year in the Peace Corps? I was acting on my convictions.

BETTY: Sure.

BILL: You can't just hang a sign on a person.

BETTY: Absolutely. I'll bet you're a Scorpio. (*Many bells ring.*) Listen, I was headed to the movies after I finished this section. Would you like to come along?

BILL: That sounds like fun. What's playing?

BETTY: A couple of the really early Woody Allen movies.

BILL: Oh.

BETTY: Don't you like Woody Allen?

BILL: Sure. I like Woody Allen.

BETTY: But you're not crazy about Woody Allen.

BILL: Those early ones kind of get on my nerves.

BETTY: Uh-huh. (*Bell.*)

BILL:	—(*simultaneously*)—	BETTY:
Y'know I was		I was
headed to the—		thinking about—

BILL: I'm sorry.

BETTY: No, go ahead.

BILL: I was going to say that I was headed to the movies in a little while, and . . .

BETTY: So was I.

BILL: The Woody Allen festival?

BETTY: Just up the street.

BILL: Do you like the early ones?

BETTY: I think anybody who doesn't ought to be run off the planet.

BILL: How many times have you seen "Bananas"?

BETTY: Eight times.

BILL: Twelve. So are you still interested? (*Long pause.*)

BETTY: Do you like Entenmann's crumb cake . . . ?

BILL: Last night I went out at two in the morning to get one. (*Small pause.*) Did you have an Etch-a-Sketch as a child?

BETTY: Yes! And do you like Brussels sprouts? (*Small pause.*)

BILL: I think they're gross.

BETTY: They *are* gross!

BILL: Do you still believe in marriage in spite of current sentiments against it?

BETTY: Yes.

BILL: And children?

BETTY: Three of them.

BILL: Two girls and a boy.

BETTY: Harvard, Vassar and Brown.

BILL: And will you love me?

BETTY: Yes.

BILL: And cherish me forever?

BETTY: Yes.

BILL: Do you still want to go to the movies?

BETTY: Sure thing.

BILL & BETTY: (*Together.*) *Waiter!*

   Blackout

INQUIRING FURTHER

1. How does *Sure Thing* compare to other plays you are familiar with? What is the effect of having just two actors and virtually no physical action in the play? Explain the story that the play tells and how it goes about telling its tale.

2. Do you feel as if the play allows you to develop a sense of Bill and Betty? How does the fragmented nature of the play impact your understanding of their characters? Write a paragraph discussing your sense of each of the characters and how the play's structure has impacted your assessment of them.

3. Think about how you might stage the play, *Sure Thing*. What actors would you envision playing Bill and Betty? What kind of setting would you select and why? Would you emphasize any actions or staging elements that are not spelled out in the text of the play?

LUIS VALDEZ

The son of migrant farm workers, Luis Valdez (born in 1940) has been instrumental in bringing Hispanic voices into contemporary theater. He worked in the fields growing up, then attended college at San Jose State, where he wrote and produced his first play, The Shrunken Head of Pancho Villa. *After college his work evolved in conjunction with the formation of El Teatro Campesino, a theater group founded by the United Farm Workers. The group produced many short plays, or* actos—*brief satirical skits concerning social issues.* Los Vendidos *is perhaps the best known of these actos and was first performed in 1967.*

Los Vendidos[1]

First Performance: *Brown Beret junta, Elysian Park, East Los Angeles.*

Characters

HONEST SANCHO
SECRETARY
FARMWORKER
PACHUCO
REVOLUCIONARIO
MEXICAN-AMERICAN

Scene: *HONEST SANCHO's* Used Mexican Lot and Mexican Curio Shop. Three models are on display in *HONEST SANCHO's* shop. To the right, there is a *REVOLUCIONARIO,* complete with sombrero, carrilleras and carabina 30–30.[2] At center, on the floor, there is the *FARMWORKER,* under a broad straw sombrero. At stage left is the *PACHUCO*[3], filero[4] in hand. *HONEST SANCHO* is moving among his models, dusting them off and preparing for another day of business.

SANCHO: *Bueno, bueno, mis monos, vamos a ver a quién vendemos ahora ¿no?*[5] *(To audience.) ¡Quihubo!* I'm Honest Sancho and this is my shop. Antes fui contratista, pero ahora logré tener mi negocito.[6] All I need now is a customer. *(A bell rings offstage.)* Ay, a customer!
SECRETARY: *(Entering.)* Good morning, I'm Miss Jimenez from . . .
SANCHO: *Ah, una chicana!* Welcome, welcome Señorita Jiménez.
SECRETARY: *(Anglo pronunciation.)* JIM-enez.

---

[1]**Los Vendidos:** The Sellouts.
[2]**carrileras . . . 30-30:** cartridge belt and a rifle.
[3]**Pachuco:** street tough living in the U.S.
[4]**filero:** knife.
[5]**Bueno . . . no?:** "Well, well, my cuties, let us see who we can sell now, Okay?"
[6]**Antes . . . negocito:** "I used to be a contractor, but now I have my own successful little business."

SANCHO: *¿Qué?*

SECRETARY: My name is Miss JIM-enez. Don't you speak English? What's wrong with you?

SANCHO: Oh, nothing, Señorita JIM-enez. I'm here to help you.

SECRETARY: That's better. As I was starting to say, I'm a secretary from Governor Reagan's office, and we're looking for a Mexican type for the administration.

SANCHO: Well, you come to the right place, lady. This is Honest Sancho's Used Mexican Lot, and we got all types here. Any particular type you want?

SECRETARY: Yes, we were looking for somebody suave . . .

SANCHO: Suave.

SECRETARY: Debonaire.

SANCHO: *De buen aire.*

SECRETARY: Dark.

SANCHO: *Prieto.*

SECRETARY: But of course, not too dark.

SANCHO: *No muy prieto.*

SECRETARY: Perhaps, beige.

SANCHO: Beige, just the tone. *Asi como cafecito con leche,*⁷ *¿no?*

SECRETARY: One more thing. He must be hard-working.

SANCHO: That could only be one model. Step right over here to the center of the shop, lady. (*They cross to the FARMWORKER.*) This is our standard farmworker model. As you can see, in the words of our beloved Senator George Murphy, he is "built close to the ground." Also, take special notice of his 4-ply Goodyear huaraches, made from the rain tire. This wide-brimmed sombrero is an extra added feature; keeps off the sun, rain and dust.

SECRETARY: Yes, it does look durable.

SANCHO: And our farmworker model is friendly. *Muy amable.*⁸ Watch. (*Snaps his fingers.*)

FARMWORKER: (*Lifts up head.*) *Buenos días, señorita.* (*His head drops.*)

SECRETARY: My, he is friendly.

SANCHO: Didn't I tell you? Loves his patrones! But his most attractive feature is that he's hard-working. Let me show you. (*Snaps fingers. FARMWORKER stands.*)

FARMWORKER: *¡El jale!*⁹ (*He begins to work.*)

SANCHO: As you can see he is cutting grapes.

SECRETARY: Oh, I wouldn't know.

SANCHO: He also picks cotton. (*Snaps. FARMWORKER begins to pick cotton.*)

SECRETARY: Versatile, isn't he?

SANCHO: He also picks melons. (*Snaps. FARMWORKER picks melons.*) That's his slow speed for late in the season. Here's his fast speed. (*Snap. FARMWORKER picks faster.*)

SECRETARY: *Chihuahua.* . . . I mean, goodness, he sure is a hardworker.

SANCHO: (*Pulls the FARMWORKER to his feet.*) And that isn't the half of it. Do you see these little holes on his arms that appear to be pores? During those hot sluggish days in the field when the vines or the branches get so entangled,

---

⁷**Asi . . . leche:** "Just like coffee with milk."

⁸**Muy amable:** very friendly.

⁹**¡el jale!:** the Job.

it's almost impossible to move, these holes emit a certain grease that allows
our model to slip and slide right through the crop with no trouble at all.

SECRETARY: Wonderful. But is he economical?

SANCHO: Economical? *Señorita,* you are looking at the Volkswagen of Mexicans.
Pennies a day is all it takes. One plate of beans and tortillas will keep him going
all day. That, and chile. Plenty of chile. *Chile jalapeños, chile verde, chile colorado.* But, of course, if you do give him chile, (*Snap. FARMWORKER turns
left face. Snap. FARMWORKER bends over.*) then you have to change his oil
filter once a week.

SECRETARY: What about storage?

SANCHO: No problem. You know these new farm labor camps our Honorable Governor Reagan has built out by Parlier or Raisin City? They were designed with
our model in mind. Five, six, seven, even ten in one of those shacks will give
you no trouble at all. You can also put him in old barns, old cars, riverbanks.
You can even leave him out in the field overnight with no worry!

SECRETARY: Remarkable.

SANCHO: And here's an added feature: every year at the end of the season, this
model goes back to Mexico and doesn't return, automatically, until next Spring.

SECRETARY: How about that. But tell me, does he speak English?

SANCHO: Another outstanding feature is that last year this model was programmed
to go out on STRIKE! (*Snap.*)

FARMWORKER: *¡Huelga! ¡Huelga! Hermanos, sálganse de esos files.*[10] (*Snap. He stops.*)

SECRETARY: No! Oh no, we can't strike in the State Capitol.

SANCHO: Well, he also scabs. (*Snap.*)

FARMWORKER: *Me vendo barato, ¿y qué?*[11] (*Snap.*)

SECRETARY: That's much better, but you didn't answer my question. Does he speak
English?

SANCHO: *Bueno . . . no, pero*[12] he has other. . . .

SECRETARY: No.

SANCHO: Other features.

SECRETARY: No! He just won't do!

SANCHO: Okay, okay, *pues.* We have other models.

SECRETARY: I hope so. What we need is something a little more sophisticated.

SANCHO: Sophisti-*qué?*

SECRETARY: An urban model.

SANCHO: Ah, from the city! Step right back. Over here in this corner of the shop
is exactly what you're looking for. Introducing our new 1969 JOHNNY PACHU-
CO model! This is our fast-back model. Streamlined. Built for speed, low-
riding, city life. Take a look at some of these features. Mag shoes, dual exhausts,
green chartruese paint-job, dark-tint windshield, a little poof on top. Let me just
turn him on. (*Snap. JOHNNY walks to stage center with a pachuco bounce.*)

SECRETARY: What was that?

SANCHO: That, *señorita,* was the Chicano shuffle.

SECRETARY: Okay, what does he do?

---

[10]**Huelga . . . files:** "Strike! Strike! Brothers, leave those rows."

[11]**Me . . . qué:** "I come cheap. So?"

[12]**Bueno . . . pero:** "Well, no, but."

SANCHO: Anything and everything necessary for city life. For instance, survival: he knife fights. (*Snaps. JOHNNY pulls out a switchblade and swings at SECRETARY. SECRETARY screams.*) He dances. (*Snap.*)

JOHNNY: (*Singing.*) "Angel Baby, my Angel Baby . . . " (*Snap.*)

SANCHO: And here's a feature no city model can be without. He gets arrested, but not without resisting, of course. (*Snap.*)

JOHNNY: *En la madre, la placa.*[13] I didn't do it! I didn't do it! (*JOHNNY turns and stands up against an imaginary wall, legs spread out, arms behind his back.*)

SECRETARY: Oh no, we can't have arrests! We must maintain law and order.

SANCHO: But he's bilingual.

SECRETARY: Bilingual?

SANCHO: *Simón que yes.* He speaks English! Johnny, give us some English. (*Snap.*)

JOHNNY: (*Comes downstage.*) Fuck-you!

SECRETARY: (*Gasps.*) Oh! I've never been so insulted in my whole life!

SANCHO: Well, he learned it in your school.

SECRETARY: I don't care where he learned it.

SANCHO: But he's economical.

SECRETARY: Economical?

SANCHO: Nickels and dimes. You can keep Johnny running on hamburgers, Taco Bell tacos, Lucky Lager beer, Thunderbird wine, yesca . . .

SECRETARY: Yesca?

SANCHO: Mota.

SECRETARY: Mota?

SANCHO: *Leños . . . marijuana.* (*Snap. JOHNNY inhales on an imaginary joint.*)

SECRETARY: That's against the law!

JOHNNY: (*Big smile, holding his breath.*) Yeah.

SANCHO: He also sniffs glue. (*Snap. JOHNNY inhales glue, big smile.*)

JOHNNY: Tha's too much man, ese.

SECRETARY: No, Mr. Sancho, I don't think this . . .

SANCHO: Wait a minute, he has other qualities I know you'll love. For example, an inferiority complex. (*Snap.*)

JOHNNY: (*To SANCHO.*) You think you're better than me, huh, ese? (*Swings switchblade.*)

SANCHO: He can also be beaten and he bruises. Cut him and he bleeds, kick him and he . . . (*He beats, bruises and kicks PACHUCO.*) Would you like to try it?

SECRETARY: Oh, I couldn't.

SANCHO: Be my guest. He's a great scapegoat.

SECRETARY: No really.

SANCHO: Please.

SECRETARY: Well, all right. Just once. (*She kicks PACHUCO.*) Oh, he's so soft.

SANCHO: Wasn't that good? Try again.

SECRETARY: (*Kicks PACHUCO.*) Oh, he's so wonderful! (*She kicks him again.*)

SANCHO: Okay, that's enough, lady. You'll ruin the merchandise. Yes, our Johnny Pachuco model can give you many hours of pleasure. Why, the LAPD just bought 20 of these to train their rookie cops on. And talk about maintenance. *Señorita,* you are looking at an entirely self-supporting machine. You're never going to find our Johnny Pachuco model on the relief rolls. No, sir, this model knows how to liberate.

---

[13]**En . . . placa:** "Wow, the cops."

SECRETARY: Liberate?

SANCHO: He steals. (*Snap. JOHNNY rushes to SECRETARY and steals her purse.*)

JOHNNY: *¡Dame esa bolsa, vieja!*[14] (*He grabs the purse and runs. Snap by* SANCHO, *he stops.* SECRETARY *runs after* JOHNNY *and grabs purse away from him, kicking him as she goes.*)

SECRETARY: No, no, no! We can't have any more thieves in the State Administration. Put him back.

SANCHO: Okay, we still got other models. Come on, Johnny, we'll sell you to some old lady. (*SANCHO takes JOHNNY back to his place.*)

SECRETARY: Mr. Sancho, I don't think you quite understand what we need. What we need is something that will attract the women voters. Something more traditional, more romantic.

SANCHO: Ah, a lover. (*He smiles meaningfully.*) Step right over here, señorita. Introducing our standard Revolucionario and/or Early California Bandit type. As you can see, he is well-built, sturdy, durable. This is the International Harvester of Mexicans.

SECRETARY: What does he do?

SANCHO: You name it, he does it. He rides horses, stays in the mountains, crosses deserts, plains, rivers, leads revolutions, follows revolutions, kills, can be killed, serves as a martyr, hero, movie star. Did I say movie star? Did you ever see *Viva Zapata? Viva Villa, Villa Rides, Pancho Villa Returns, Pancho Villa Goes Back, Pancho Villa Meets Abbott and Costello?*

SECRETARY: I've never seen any of those.

SANCHO: Well, he was in all of them. Listen to this. (*Snap.*)

REVOLUCIONARIO: (*Scream.*) *¡Viva Villaaaaa!*

SECRETARY: That's awfully loud.

SANCHO: He has a volume control. (*He adjusts volume. Snap.*)

REVOLUCIONARIO: (*Mousey voice.*) *Viva Villa.*

SECRETARY: That's better.

SANCHO: And even if you didn't see him in the movies, perhaps you saw him on TV. He makes commercials. (*Snap.*)

REVOLUCIONARIO: Is there a Frito Bandito in your house?

SECRETARY: Oh yes, I've seen that one!

SANCHO: Another feature about this one is that he is economical. He runs on raw horsemeat and tequila!

SECRETARY: Isn't that rather savage?

SANCHO: *Al contrario,* it makes him a lover. (*Snap.*)

REVOLUCIONARIO: (*To* SECRETARY.) *Ay, mamasota, cochota, ven pa 'ca!*[15] (*He grabs* SECRETARY *and folds her back, Latin-lover style.*)

SANCHO: (*Snap.* REVOLUCIONARIO *goes back upright.*) Now wasn't that nice?

SECRETARY: Well, it was rather nice.

SANCHO: And finally, there is one outstanding feature about this model I know the ladies are going to love: he's a genuine antique! He was made in Mexico in 1910!

SECRETARY: Made in Mexico?

SANCHO: That's right. Once in Tijuana, twice in Guadalajara, three times in Cuernavaca.

---

[14]**¡Dame . . . vieja!:** "Old lady, give me that bag!"

[15]**Ay . . . ca!:** "Hey sexy, get over here."

SECRETARY: Mr. Sancho, I thought he was an American product.

SANCHO: No, but . . .

SECRETARY: No, I'm sorry. We can't buy anything but American made products. He just won't do.

SANCHO: But he's an antique!

SECRETARY: I don't care. You still don't understand what we need. It's true we need Mexican models, such as these, but it's more important that he be American.

SANCHO: American?

SECRETARY: That's right, and judging from what you've shown me, I don't think you have what we want. Well, my lunch hour's almost over, I better . . .

SANCHO: Wait a minute! Mexican but American?

SECRETARY: That's correct.

SANCHO: Mexican but . . . (*A sudden flash.*) American! Yeah, I think we've got exactly what you want. He just came in today! Give me a minute. (*He exits. Talks from backstage.*) Here he is in the shop. Let me just get some papers off. There. Introducing our new 1970 Mexican-American! Tara-ra-raaaa! (SANCHO *brings out the* MEXICAN-AMERICAN *model, a clean-shaven middle class type in a business suit, with glasses.*)

SECRETARY: (*Impressed.*) Where have you been hiding this one?

SANCHO: He just came in this morning. Ain't he a beauty? Feast you eyes on him! Sturdy U.S. Steel frame, streamlined, modern. As a matter of fact, he is built exactly like our Anglo models, except that he comes in a variety of darker shades: naugahide, leather or leatherette.

SECRETARY: Naugahyde.

SANCHO: Well, we'll just write that down. Yes, señorita, this model represents the apex of American engineering! He is bilingual, college educated, ambitious! Say the word "acculturate" and he accelerates. He is intelligent, well-mannered, clean. Did I say clean? (*Snap.* MEXICAN-AMERICAN *raises his arm.*) Smell.

SECRETARY: (*Smells.*) Old Sobaco, my favorite.

SANCHO: (*Snap.* MEXICAN-AMERICAN *turns toward* SANCHO.) Eric? (*To SECRETARY.*) We call him Eric García. (*To ERIC.*) I want you to meet Miss JIM-enez, Eric.

MEXICAN-AMERICAN: Miss JIM-enez, I am delighted to make your acquaintance. (*He kisses her hand.*)

SECRETARY: Oh, my, how charming!

SANCHO: Did you feel the suction? He has seven especially engineered suction cups right behind his lips. He's a charmer all right!

SECRETARY: How about boards, does he function on boards?

SANCHO: You name them, he is on them. Parole boards, draft boards, school boards, taco quality control boards, surf boards, two by fours.

SECRETARY: Does he function in politics?

SANCHO: Señorita, you are looking at a political machine. Have you ever heard of the OEO, EOC, COD, WAR ON POVERTY? That's our model! Not only that, he makes political speeches.

SECRETARY: May I hear one?

SANCHO: With pleasure. (*Snap.*) Eric, give us a speech.

MEXICAN-AMERICAN: Mr. Congressman, Mr. Chairman, members of the board, honored guests, ladies and gentlemen. (SANCHO *and* SECRETARY *applaud.*) Please, please. I come before you as a Mexican-American to tell you about the problems of the Mexican. The problems of the Mexican stem from one thing and one thing only: he's stupid. He's uneducated. He needs to stay in school. He needs to be ambitious, foward-looking, harder-working. He needs to think American, American, American, American, American! God bless America! God bless America! God bless America! (*He goes out of control.* SANCHO *snaps frantically and the* MEXICAN-AMERICAN *finally slumps forward, bending at the waist.*)

SECRETARY: Oh my, he's patriotic too!

SANCHO: *Sí, señorita,* he loves his country. Let me just make a little adjustment here. (*Stands* MEXICAN-AMERICAN *up.*)

SECRETARY: What about upkeep? Is he economical?

SANCHO: Well, no, I won't lie to you. The Mexican-American costs a little bit more, but you get what you pay for. He's worth every extra cent. You can keep him running on dry Martinis, Langendorf bread . . .

SECRETARY: Apple pie?

SANCHO: Only Mom's. Of course, he's also programmed to eat Mexican food at ceremonial functions, but I must warn you, an overdose of beans will plug up his exhaust.

SECRETARY: Fine! There's just one more question. How much do you want for him?

SANCHO: Well, I tell you what I'm gonna do. Today and today only, because you've been so sweet, I'm gona let you steal this model from me! I'm gona let you drive him off the lot for the simple price of, let's see, taxes and license included, $15,000.

SECRETARY: Fifteen thousand dollars? For a Mexican!!!!

SANCHO: Mexican? What are you talking about? This is a Mexican-American! We had to melt down two pachucos, a farmworker and three gabachos[16] to make this model! You want quality, but you gotta pay for it! This is no cheap run-about. He's got class!

SECRETARY: Okay, I'll take him.

SANCHO: You will?

SECRETARY: Here's your money.

SANCHO: You mind if I count it?

SECRETARY: Go right ahead.

SANCHO: Well, you'll get your pink slip in the mail. Oh, do you want me to wrap him up for you? We have a box in the back.

SECRETARY: No, thank you. The Governor is having a luncheon this afternoon, and we need a brown face in the crowd. How do I drive him?

SANCHO: Just snap your fingers. He'll do anything you want. (SECRETARY *snaps.* MEXICAN-AMERICAN *steps forward.*)

MEXICAN-AMERICAN: *¡Raza querida, vamos levantando armas para liberarnos de estos desgraciados gabachos que nos explotan! Vamos. . . .*[17]

SECRETARY: What did he say?

SANCHO: Something about taking up arms, killing white people, etc.

SECRETARY: But he's not supposed to say that!

SANCHO: Look, lady, don't blame me for bugs from the factory. He's your Mexican-American, you bought him, now drive him off the lot!

---

[16]**gabachos:** whites.

[17]**¡Raza . . . Vamos:** "Beloved people, let's take up arms to liberate ourselves from those damned whites who exploit us!"

SECRETARY: But he's broken!

SANCHO: Try snapping another finger. (SECRETARY *snaps.* MEXICAN-AMERICAN *comes to life again.*)

MEXICAN-AMERICAN: *¡Esta gran humanidad ha dicho basta! ¡Y se ha puesto en marcha! ¡Basta! ¡Basta! ¡Viva la raza! ¡Viva la causa! ¡Viva la huelga! ¡Vivan los brown berets! ¡Vivan los estudiantes! ¡Chicano power!*[18] (*The* MEXICAN-AMERICAN *turns toward the* SECRETARY, *who gasps and backs up. He keeps turning toward the* PACHUCO, FARMWORKER *and* REVOLUCIONARIO, *snapping his fingers and turning each of them on, one by one.*)

PACHUCO: (*Snap. To* SECRETARY.) I'm going to get you, baby! *¡Viva la raza!*

FARMWORKER: (*Snap. to* SECRETARY.) *¡Viva la huelga! ¡Viva la huelga! ¡Viva la huelga!*

REVOLUCIONARIO: (*Snap. To* SECRETARY.) *¡Viva la revolución!* (*The three models join together and advance toward the* SECRETARY, *who backs up and runs out of the shop screaming.* SANCHO *is at the other end of the shop holding his money in his hand. All freeze. After a few seconds of silence, the* PACHUCO *moves and stretches, shaking his arms and loosening up. The* FARMWORKER *and* REVOLUCIONARIO *do the same.* SANCHO *stays where he is, frozen to his spot.*)

JOHNNY: Man, that was a long one, *ese.* (*Others agree with him.*)

FARMWORKER: How did we do?

JOHNNY: Pretty good, look at all that *lana,*[19] man! (*He goes over to* SANCHO *and removes the money from his hand.* SANCHO *stays where he is.*)

REVOLUCIONARIO: *En la madre,* look at all the money.

JOHNNY: We keep this up, we're going to be rich.

FARMWORKER: They think we're machines.

REVOLUCIONARIO: *Burros.*

JOHNNY: Puppets.

MEXICAN-AMERICAN: The only thing I don't like is how come I always get to play the goddamn Mexican-American?

JOHNNY: That's what you get for finishing high school.

FARMWORKER: How about our wages, *ese?*

JOHNNY: Here it comes right now. $3,000 for you, $3,000 for you, $3,000 for you and $3,000 for me. The rest we put back into the business.

MEXICAN-AMERICAN: Too much, man. Heh, where you vatos going tonight?

FARMWORKER: I'm going over to Concha's. There's a party.

JOHNNY: Wait a minute, *vatos.* What about our salesman? I think he needs an oil job.

REVOLUCIONARIO: Leave him to me. (*The* PACHUCO, FARMWORKER *and* MEXICAN-AMERICAN *exit, talking loudly about their plans for the night. The* REVOLUCIONARIO *goes over to* SANCHO, *removes his derby hat and cigar, lifts him up and throws him over his shoulder.* SANCHO *hangs loose, lifeless. To audience.*) He's the best model we got! *¡Ajúa!* (*Exit.*)

---

[18]**Esta . . . power!:** "The great mass of humanity has said enough! And it has begun to march! Enough! Enough! Long live the people! Long live the cause! Long live the strike! Long live the Brown Berets! Long live the students! Chicano power!"

[19]**lana:** Money.

INQUIRING FURTHER

1. How important is the social context of 1967 California to understanding *Los Vendidos*? What aspects of the play are most relevant today?

2. What is the effect of giving generic names to most of the characters? If you had to choose one character that stands out in the play, which would you select? Write a paragraph explaining your decision.

3. What would you say to someone who argued that the humor in *Los Vendidos* overshadows its social message? Would the play be more effective without the humor?

4. Would you say *Los Vendidos* is even handed in its portrayal of social groups or do the stereotypes favor one group over another? Freewrite for five minutes about stereotypes in *Los Vendidos*.

CONSIDERING CONVENTIONS OF FILM

Films share many similarities with plays. In the first place, films have a dramatic emphasis on conflict and resolution. Think of *Pretty Woman* (1990), *Meet the Parents* (2000), or most any other romantic comedy; the film develops as the couple falls in love, some force or deception intervenes to break them apart, then a final resolution brings the couple back together. The story sounds a lot like one of Shakespeare's plays.

At the same time, films have many unique characteristics that convey their messages. We can analyze the ways that films work as a visual medium, for instance. We can also look at the roles that sounds and music play in telling the story. We can also consider the cinematography, the aspects of film related to the use of the camera, and we need to understand the editing techniques used to create a narrative in a film.

Exploring Film as a Visual Medium

It is easy to overlook the amount of visual information we receive when watching a film. Each frame in a film depicts a setting that includes the objects in the background or foreground of the scene, the actors, the costumes, visual qualities such as lighting, and camera properties like shutter speed, that affect the appearance of what we see. Film studies uses the specialized term **mise-en-scène** to encapsulate all of this visual information. Mise-en-scène is French and means "putting in the scene."

A Rose for Emily

Mise-en-scène gives us a way of talking about the tone and composite feel created by all of the visual elements of a scene. Consider the still frames in Figure 11.1. The images are from the film version of William Faulkner's "A Rose for Emily" (586–92).

In these frames the objects, actors, and mood created by the visual composition result in a mise-en-scène that demonstrates the sad and eerie life of Emily Grangerford and her relationship with her community. These visual elements combine to create a sense of atmosphere.

We can analyze how individual elements such as lighting, effects, costumes, and the composition (the placement of objects, and the arrangement of **figures**)

FIGURE 11.1   Mise-en-scène in *A Rose for Emily*

contribute to the mise-en-scène. In the first frame, the dust floating in the air and the lighting emphasizing the antique wedding dress suggest an old sadness brought to light. The second frame arranges objects and adds cobwebs to the dust in the atmosphere to intensify the mood of the scene. The third frame emphasizes the figures and highlights Emily's status as an outsider and item of curiosity for the townspeople.

We can examine these visual aspects of film in even more detail. The unused mirror and hairbrush on the table suggest isolation and lost love; the costumes add historical accuracy and differentiate between the characters of the doctor and the women. The placement of figures also conveys meaning in the scene. The doctor in the foreground suggests an interested observer, while the women in the background might represent the judgment of the community.

To discuss arrangements of figures and objects in scenes we can analyze **framing techniques** and the relationship between the **figure** and the **ground.** The figure refers to objects or characters that make up the main subject for a frame. Consider the images from the film shown in Figure 11.2. In the first frame, the figure of Emily Grangerford occupies most of the visual field and captures our eye and interest. In the ground of the frame, however, we can barely make out the shape of an outsider looking in through the frosted glass at the end of the hallway. In this frame, the relationship between the figure and the ground mirrors the themes found in the story.

We can also consider how objects and figures are arranged within the space of the frame, what is called the **composition** of the frame. Arrangements may be **asymmetrical,** as in the first image where the right-hand half of the frame is filled with the figure. This asymmetrical framing reflects the earlier moment in the story where the emphasis is placed on Emily's psyche. The second scene presents a more

FIGURE 11.2   Composition and Framing in *A Rose for Emily*

symmetrical framing of the two women as they discover that Emily has kept and slept with the dead body of her lover. The framing emphasizes Emily's struggles and emotions in the first scene and the universal horror, fascination, and judgment of townspeople in the second frame.

As we look at something like the arrangement of figures in *A Rose For Emily,* we complement our emotional impressions with analysis that lets us examine filmmaking techniques like lighting or framing. But we also must explain what we find to be significant about those techniques, drawing upon what we know about critical thinking and argument. We can make connections between visual elements and the themes and storytelling of the film and draw conclusions about their significance, discussing the techniques in detail as evidence for the conclusions that we make.

Considering Elements of Sound

We often take elements of sound for granted when we watch films for pleasure; again we must make a deliberate effort to recognize and evaluate their significance. We can look specifically at how vocal elements such as actors' intonations and tones convey meaning. We can consider how the sound effects of a film create an atmosphere and help tell the story. We can also examine how music appeals to our senses and contributes to the themes and messages of the work.

In considering the vocal elements of film, we can rely on what we know about drama, music, and poetry. In the 1989 film *Do the Right Thing,* for instance, the diction of the characters reflects their status and roles in the film. Sal's speech conveys an ethnic Italian heritage and represents what is now a minority voice within the mostly black Brooklyn community of the film, a community represented in the speech of Mookie. As with visual elements our task is to analyze, then draw conclusions about these vocalizations.

Still images and video clips from *An Occurance at Owl Creek Bridge*

We can also consider the sound effects used to create a sense of realism and provide an atmosphere for the film. In the 1962 film version of the story "An Occurrence at Owl Creek Bridge," for instance, as Peyton Farquhar emerges from the water after escaping his death by hanging, we hear the sounds of birds in the background. The bird sounds complement a change in perception in Farquhar who begins to roll in the sand and smell the flowers as he enjoys his freedom.

The nature sounds, however, are interrupted by the whistling of a cannon ball followed by an explosion that shocks Farquhar out of his revelry. Farquhar runs. Immediately, a drum beat replaces the sounds of nature. The bird sounds and the freedom they represent were low pitched, rhythmic, and calming. The drum sounds are frenetic, replacing the earlier state of mind with a harried sense that Farquhar is being closely pursued. The drums in *An Occurrence at Owl Creek Bridge* also illustrate how background music supports the portrayal of the themes in the film.

Music is also used in films to make connections with themes and viewers. Songs reflect the cultures that produce them. They also have a history and cultural meaning that exists outside of their placement in a film. The music in the film *Apocalypse Now* (1979), for instance, reflects the culture and concerns of the Vietnam era. Viewers are asked to make those cultural connections as they watch the film and encounter the music of the 1960s. In *A Knight's Tale* (2001), this cultural association is turned on its head as modern rock music is used to create a comic irony and contemporary appeal for a medieval story.

Popular songs in films also appeal to us on a personal level. The song "Cruel to be Kind" played at the high school prom in the 1999 film *10 Things I Hate About You,* for instance, touches an emotional nerve for audience members who associate the song with a time in their life or with an emotional state. In contrast to background music, which tends to be instrumental and woven within or beneath the other elements of film, song tracks often stand out from the rest of the story—they may play over a **montage** (a sequence of images) or accompany a scene in which the characters and other sounds of the film drop out. (You can investigate some of the qualities of music in Chapter 10.)

In some films, music plays an even more central role in the story. In *O Brother, Where Art Thou?* (2000), music works on all the levels mentioned above. It provides a lens for looking at a cultural moment through the historical selections of music woven into the film. It also resonates with us emotionally as the characters perform songs that reflect their personalities and circumstances. Further, music plays a central role in the plot, as the musical career of the main characters takes off without their knowing it and eventually provides much of the resolution for the story.

Looking at Cinematography

Cinematography refers to the ways cameras are used to capture the scenes of a film. Some aspects of cinematography are related to the atmosphere in the mise-en-scène of a film—elements like lighting, or camera lenses and filters, that influence the look and feel of a scene. Other aspects have to do with the employment of the camera itself. The placement of the camera and the resulting camera angles and sense of distance create the perspectives in the film. Camera movements track the motions of characters and shape the way viewers see the actions and elements of a scene. These aspects of the camera and filming differentiate film from other forms of literature in the way it tells a story.

The frames from the film version of the short story "Young Goodman Brown," in Figures 11.3 and 11.4, illustrate some aspects of cinematography including lighting and filters, as well as camera angles, distance, and movement. Figure 11.3 reveals how aspects of camera distance can influence our impressions. Camera distance ranges from extreme **close ups,** to extreme **long shots** with many other possibilities in between. In the first frame, the camera is placed at an extreme distance, but the lens is **zoomed in** on the figure of Young Goodman Brown. As Brown approaches, the camera remains in position, but **zooms out,** so that the closer

FIGURE 11.3   Camera Distance in *Young Goodman Brown*

FIGURE 11.4   Camera Angle in *Young Goodman Brown*

Brown gets to the camera, the less significant his figure appears. This **pull-back** shot calls our attention to the setting (the forest where Brown will struggle with the devil) and the stature of the figure of Brown as this struggle is about to begin.

The frames in Figure 11.4 demonstrate how lighting, as well as camera angles, movement, and filters, appeal to our emotions and shape the scene. In the first frame in Figure 11.4 the camera is placed at a **high-angle** in the frame as Young Goodman Brown observes events in the forest. The angle adds a sense of vulnerability to the figure as the audience looks down upon Brown. The lighting in the frame intensifies the sense of vulnerability. The light source is placed above the figure; this **top-lighting** results in an emphasis on Brown's face and eyes. The rest of the scene, however, remains in shadow; this **low-key** lighting emphasizes both the thinking of Brown as he struggles to make sense of what he sees and the dark and ominous nature of the setting he finds himself in.

Still frames and video clips

The second frame in Figure 11.4 demonstrates aspects of cinematography that create atmosphere. It also shows the ways that camera movement captures motions and conveys a sense of action in a scene. As Brown's struggle with the devil reaches a crisis, he races through the forest. The scene is shot with a color filter that adds a red hue to all of the objects—the effect differs from the stark contrasts between dark and light in the rest of the film. The frame also demonstrates the effects of camera motion. Here the camera **pans** as it follows Brown's run through the forest—the position of the camera is fixed, but the lens is turned from side to side to follow the figure. The frantic sense of motion conveyed by the camera movement, and the hallucinogenic atmosphere created by the color filter, combine to reflect Young Goodman Brown's agitated state of mind.

Examining Editing Techniques

Editing techniques tie the sections of a film together to create a narrative structure. We can analyze components of a film to better understand the ways editors combine shots to create a narrative. Each **frame** represents a piece of a film broken down into its smallest component. When we explore editing, however, we generally discuss components on three larger levels. A **shot** represents a series of frames or a single uninterrupted take of the camera. A **scene** is a series of shots that have been combined to demonstrate an incident or episode in the story. A **sequence** combines a series of scenes to tell a larger part of the story.

Shots are self-contained in that they capture a single instance of filming—the shot begins when the camera is turned on and ends when the camera stops. The images in Figure 11.5 represent three shots taken underwater in the film *An Occurrence at*

Figure 11.5   Underwater Scene in *An Occurrence at Owl Creek Bridge*

Owl Creek Bridge. In the film, the protagonist, Peyton Farquhar, escapes a hanging when the noose breaks and he falls into the river beneath Owl Creek bridge.

The first frame in Figure 11.5 illustrates the opening shot showing Farquhar plunging into the water; the second frame depicts his struggle to free himself from the noose which has snapped; and the third frame depicts his rising toward the surface after untying himself. Together the shots combine to create the underwater scene. This series of shots serves to further the narrative by showing a small episode of the story—they represent a beginning, a middle, and an end to the scene.

But shots can also be used to emphasize imagery and themes within a scene. The bridge scene that takes place after Farquhar emerges from the water (Figure 11.6) uses different shots to create a juxtaposition between Fahrquhar and the soldiers who are trying to kill him.

The shots in the bridge scene shown in Figure 11.6 alternate camera positions and angles to create a back and forth sense of perspectives as the soldiers look down upon Farquhar from the bridge and he looks back from the water. As the scene progresses, close-up shots reinforce this mirroring of perspectives as both

Figure 11.6   Bridge Scene in *An Occurrence at Owl Creek Bridge*

the face of the soldier and of Farquhar fill the frame. Next, a **detail shot** (an extreme close-up) depicts a human eye. The alternating shots that precede the shot of the eye make it difficult to tell whether the eye belongs to Farquhar or the soldier—the confusion reinforces themes of perspective in the story.

The bridge scene ends when the soldier fires his gun and Farquhar begins swimming for his life. At this point, a swimming scene begins (see Figure 11.7). The swimming scene proceeds through a number of shots that eventually lead Farquhar through whitewater and to the shore and safety. The underwater scene, the bridge scene, and the swimming scene combine to tell the story of what happens immediately after the rope used to hang Farquhar breaks and he begins to make his escape. This combination of scenes creates a sequence. We might call this the *water escape sequence* of the film.

As the sequence ends, the final shot of the swimming scene uses a **transition** to demonstrate that this series of episodes is coming to a close and that a new sequence is about to begin. Figure 11.8 shows the transition at the end of the water escape sequence.

The first frame in Figure 11.8 shows the final shot of the swimming scene; the third frame shows a close-up shot of Farquhar that begins the next sequence. The second frame demonstrates the transition between the two sequences. This transition is a **dissolve**—the blending of one scene into another to create an overlapping image that connects the two scenes. A similar form of transition is the **fade,** in which the shot that begins or ends a scene fades in or out from a solid screen of (most frequently) black.

The most common transition in editing is the **cut.** Cuts instantly switch from one shot to another. Most cuts are used to transition from shot to shot (for instance, as camera angles change) or from scene to scene (for instance, as a series of

FIGURE 11.7   Swimming Scene in *An Occurrence at Owl Creek Bridge*

FIGURE 11.8   Transition in *An Occurrence at Owl Creek Bridge*

episodes play out to tell the story). A **cross-cut** transitions to a new setting or time frame within the film. Cross-cuts might be used to show two parallel but separate actions, to build suspense or weave scenes together.

Transitions take place as editors tie together shots, scenes, and sequences to create the story line for the film. The transitions editors use, and the choices they make about how to combine parts of the story, determine the narrative structure of the film. Most editing strives to achieve **continuity** in the film's narrative. Continuity provides a sense that the story is moving seamlessly from one scene to another. To create continuity, editors try to eliminate confusion and abrupt or illogical transitions.

Considering Genres, History, and Auteurs

Studying film genres

As with other forms of literature, films tend to rely on explicit conventions and traditions that shape the ways that we enjoy and interpret what we watch. These conventions are based on **genres** which create expectations about the story line, the characters, the themes, and even technical aspects of the filmmaking. The conventions of a genre can sometimes seem quite strict. Some Westerns take this expectation to the extreme, providing us with characters that can almost be reduced to the mere symbols of the white hat and the black hat. The film *Blazing Saddles* (1974) makes these stereotypical conventions the subject of ridicule to blend genres and create a satirical Western/comedy.

In general, films rely on, but also modify, established conventions. The film *Saving Private Ryan* (1998) fits neatly into the genre of the war film. It is constructed around fierce battle scenes, depicts the realities of combat, and explores the bonding of soldiers in extreme situations. But the film also challenges conventional elements of the war film. The film jars expectations with camera positions and lenses that create a war-footage feel. The film's characters and plot also raise questions about earlier depictions of war—the soldiers challenge typical conceptions of the war hero and the story does not hinge on capturing a key city or hill, but rather on finding a single soldier.

Considering genres also asks us to place a film in a **historical context.** When we view films historically, we often begin by comparing how a film relates to its predecessors or to similar works. We might compare *Saving Private Ryan* with the 1949 film *The Sands of Iwo Jima*. In the 1949 film, the director uses real war footage to add authenticity to the film. In *The Sands of Iwo Jima,* John Wayne plays Sergeant Stryker, a hard-as-nails commander who leads with toughness. We can see how *Saving Private Ryan* continues but also modifies this historical lineage.

In making such historical comparisons, however, we must also consider how genre and conventions relate to aspects of culture that exist outside of films. Both *The Sands of Iwo Jima* and *Saving Private Ryan* take the Second World War as their subject matter. However, each represents a different set of historical contexts. Consider the ending of the 1949 film that reenacts the historical flag raising that marked the conclusion of the battle. The images in Figure 11.9 reproduce the photo (left) and the film reenactment (right).

The reenactment of the famous photo illustrates the relationship between a film and its historical context—the image in 1949 represented (at least for many Americans) a shared sense of triumph and a specific historical moment fresh in the memory. From our contemporary perspective, the image carries a different cultural force. If we are unfamiliar with the cultural atmosphere of 1949 the image

FIGURE 11.9   Flag Raising over Iwo Jima

may not resonate as powerfully. On the other hand, if we have seen the very similar photo of firefighters raising the flag after the World Trade Center attacks, these images may take on new meaning.

When studying films, we also consider their authorship—that is, the vision or shaping of the film by the person most responsible for its creation. We can use the term **auteur** to describe this person. Conventionally the auteur of a film is its **director**—the person who makes decisions and oversees the creative aspects of the film. Sometimes we will apply an auteur approach to actors, looking at the characteristics of John Wayne films, for instance. We can discuss films in terms of a specific person to understand the themes and techniques we find to be significant about a filmmaker's work.

If we were writing about the *Kill Bill* films, we might try to place the film within a discussion of director Quentin Tarantino's other work. We might look at the film *Pulp Fiction* and note the ways that music or aspects of cinematography relate in the two films. We might consider how scenes from each movie could be discussed in an argument concerning the depiction of violence in Tarantino's films. Approaching a film from the perspective of an auteur provides a framework for talking about the filmmaking techniques and themes we discover.

Keep two things in mind as you think about and discuss the work of an individual director or auteur. First, understand that film is a collaborative art. Often directors have a great deal of control over a film. But, at the same time, market forces, editors, screenwriters, actors, and other collaborators influence every aspect of a movie. Second, recall from our critical thinking about literature that it is difficult to make the leap from evaluating the themes and messages we might find in a work, to drawing conclusions about the author's intentions. We discuss works in terms of their authors, but we must remember that what we see in a film is not necessarily an accurate representation of an auteur's thinking.

Writing About Film

When you write about film, you must focus on both the technical aspects of filmmaking and the interpretive issues related to a film's genre, history, auteur, and thematic concerns. The amount of energy you devote to each of these kinds of thinking will vary depending on your writing assignment. A film review may emphasize the formal elements, while an argument about a film's historical context will highlight concerns of culture.

✔CHECKLIST FOR WRITING ABOUT FILM

☐ **Relate film to other forms of literature.** Think of ways films differ from and resemble fiction or drama. Rely upon your skills in evaluating settings, characters, plot, imagery, and themes as you study film. Develop an understanding of film in terms of literature and also as a unique form of expression.

☐ **Explore sound and visual elements** in films. Analyze visual elements of films to better understand how images convey meaning. Evaluate the soundtracks and musical elements of films to learn how they appeal to your emotions and further the message of the movie.

☐ **Learn to read the mise-en-scène** of shots in a film. Consider how the composition of figures and objects conveys meaning. Look for the significance of aspects of framing. Consider how filters or other effects create atmosphere in films.

☐ **Recognize techniques of cinematography.** Examine how camera movements are used to capture the action of a shot. Consider the significance of distance and camera angles. Think about how lighting is used to convey a mood.

☐ **Understand how editing creates the story line** for a film. Learn to distinguish between shots, scenes, and sequences. Pay attention to transitions between shots. Decide if and how the editing conveys a sense of continuity and how the narrative sense of the film is accomplished.

☐ **Consider film genres.** Develop a sense of the conventions of the genres a film falls into. Think of ways the film reinforces or modifies those genres.

☐ **Examine the historical contexts** of films. Find out about similar works from the past and consider how films respond to their predecessors. Explore aspects of the culture in which a film exists. Think about how films both reflect and participate in their historical contexts.

☐ **Relate films to similar works by the same auteur.** Evaluate the style and recurring themes of an auteur. Understand that film is a collaborative medium and that pinpointing the vision of an auteur is not always possible.

☐ **Emphasize descriptions** rather than your opinions. Refer specifically to the elements of film, describing them for your readers. Use these descriptions as a basis for drawing conclusions that explain your understanding of their significance.

Exercise 11.4   *Writing a Film Review*

Write a film review that might be published in the entertainment section of a newspaper. Assume that the readers of the review have not seen the film.

Writing
film
reviews

1. Begin by studying the film. Watch the movie with an eye toward aspects of cinematography, uses of sound, and other elements of filmmaking. Evaluate the actors' performances. Consider how the editing moves the story along and how the film addresses its key concerns and themes. Also contextualize the film by relating it to others in the same genre and considering it in historical terms.

2. Next, compose your review. Introduce the film and provide just enough plot summary and background to help readers understand what the story is about.

3. In the body of your review, evaluate the formal elements of the film. Emphasize description over opinions—act as the eyes and ears of your readers and show them what is significant about the film.

4. Provide similar descriptions and explanations about the acting, editing, and themes covered in the film. Also cover the relevance of the film in terms of its genre and historical context.

5. Conclude by encapsulating your sense of the film with a few concrete evaluations and by offering a recommendation to readers who might be thinking about viewing the movie.

Exercise 11.5   *Writing About Genres*

Write a three- to five-page essay in which you compare two films from the same genre. (If you need help thinking through possible films to compare, look at the suggestions on our CD.)

1. Begin by developing a list of key characteristics for the genre you are working with. Be sure to not only think about elements of filmmaking, but also to consider how characters are typically portrayed and about important themes that are treated by the genre.

2. Compose an outline or a concept map to organize your work, and then develop the body of your essay by matching each film you wish to analyze with the set of characteristics you have developed. Additionally, relate the two films to one another based on your exploration of how they fit within the genre you are discussing.

3. Check that you have an introduction that maps out your key points and spells out your thesis. Check also that you have a conclusion that brings closure to the paper and that you tie ideas together with your thesis as you compose.

4. Make sure you integrate and discuss quotations correctly. When appropriate, integrate and discuss still images.

5. Finally, document your sources and format your paper (see the Appendix).

6. When finished, gather feedback from peers or your instructor and revise the paper using the processes outlined in Chapter 8.

Exercise 11.6   *Writing About Auteurs*

Write a three- to five-page essay in which you argue that a film represents the vision of a single auteur. Select an auteur responsible for at least two additional films, and then compare the films to develop your argument.

1. Freewrite, explore questions, create lists, maps, or outlines, discuss the work with peers, conduct research, or use any other prewriting technique before beginning to draft the paper.

2. Develop a thesis statement that articulates your argument that this film represents the work of the auteur. Develop an outline that will help you organize your essay.

3. Discuss the film in terms of the body of work by its auteur. Explain how the film you are discussing fits within this body of work. Finally, consider how seeing the film as the work of the auteur helps us understand its significance.

4. Check that you have an introduction that maps out your key points and spells out your thesis. Check also that you make connections with your thesis as you compose and that you have a conclusion that brings closure to the paper.

5. Make sure you integrate and discuss quotations correctly. When appropriate, integrate and discuss still images. Document your sources and format your paper (see the Appendix).

6. When finished, gather feedback from peers or your instructor and revise the paper using the processes outlined in Chapter 8.

12

Thinking and Writing About Art and Advertising

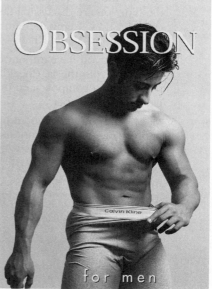

Scholars of art have a long tradition of analyzing paintings, photographs, and sculptures to discover the ways they create meaning and appeal to our emotions. More recently, scholars have begun applying similar analyses to images from advertising and other sources of popular media. Like literature, both art and media images represent artifacts that express ideas and reflect aspects of culture.

As with other forms of expression, we can begin exploring these images by analyzing some of their components. We can consider the **media** (or materials) that are used for a work. We can then explore how shape, texture, colors, patterns, and numerous other **elements of art** (and visual images) combine to create meaning. We can also look at how the subject matter of art and the content of visual compositions represent **themes and imagery** that appeal to both our sense and intellect. Additionally, we can ask questions about how these **cultural artifacts** relate to the contexts in which they are produced and received.

Further, we can bring our critical thinking and literary analysis skills to bear as we develop interpretations of images. We might ask about the settings or characters that we discover in an image. We can investigate the rhetorical situations in which art and images exist. We can consider the purpose behind art and images, the audience that views them, and the strategies they employ to communicate. All of these considerations relate art and images to our own thinking and writing.

EXPLORING THE ELEMENTS OF ART

Drawings, photographs, and paintings share a number of qualities that contribute to their messages and visual appeal. The materials that artists use influence their compositions. Lines and shapes combine to create the main subjects in an image. Color and light combine to create an atmosphere. We can analyze all of these elements to better understand the works we investigate.

Analyzing Materials, Lines, Shapes, and Textures

Materials such as oil paints, charcoal pencils, photochemicals, and stone represent some of the media used to create works of art. Materials determine some of the techniques artists will use—a photograph might manipulate lighting and color, while an etching might emphasize shapes and lines. In contemporary culture, we often also refer to media as the means used to transmit images—television or magazines represent media of transmission for images that might be photographic.

Rather than the straight marks between point A and point B, in visual images, **lines** represent any kind of significant mark. In practice, lines more accurately reproduce the edges and markings we might find in the natural world. Lines can be curved, or interrupted. They will take both horizontal and vertical directions, and they can be combined to create patterns and textures.

Lines also help create **shapes** within an image. Consider *The Frugal Repast* by Pablo Picasso in Figure 12.1. Picasso's piece is an etching made up of numerous lines. These lines create shape—look at the fingers of the man and woman or the lines that depict the man's neck. Additionally, lines are used in the etching to create a sense of **texture** and **shading.** Look at how lines create differences in texture on the wall in the background or in the tablecloth.

Color reproductions of images in this chapter

Texture need not only apply to painted or drawn works, however. Contrast the texture of Rodin's statue *The Thinker* that appears at the opening of this chapter with Michelangelo's *Pieta* in Figure 12.2. *The Thinker* presents a chiseled texture that emphasizes the status of the work as an artistic creation. *Pieta* displays a smooth texture that is every bit as artistic, but that draws attention away from the figures as chiseled artifacts.

Understanding Color and Light

Color and **light** contribute to the mood of a visual image and create focal points that attract our eyes. Colors are selected based on their relationships to one another. The combinations of choices form the **color palette** or **color scheme** for the image. When discussing color we can refer to this scheme or to the characteristics of a particular color. Colors are frequently described in terms of their intensity or warmth using adjectives like bright or dark, and warm or cool.

FIGURE 12.1   Picasso's *The Frugal Repast*

FIGURE 12.2   Michelangelo's *Pieta*

Similarly, light can draw our attention to elements of an image, create emphasis (see next page), and establish a mood. We can discuss the uses of lighting in terms of **value** (the relative amount of light or darkness present in a color) and

contrasts. The greatest contrast in values can be seen in black and white images. However, even a single color can have different values—think of the contrasts that are made when lightly pressing instead of firmly grinding a crayon into paper. We can discuss the light value of colors using adjectives that describe intensity or depth like deep, bright, dark, medium, or light.

Consider how color and light work in *The Nostalgia of the Infinite,* the oil on canvas painting by Giorgio de Chirico in Figure 12.3. The painting uses color to create a sharp contrast between the dark blue background of the sky and the bright beige swatch of dried grass in the middle of the frame. The portion of the painting in shadow in the foreground has a deep dark value. The dark foreground and the bright light side of the tower create an intense contrast that emphasizes the relationship between the two spaces.

In photography, light plays a similar role. By adjusting the amount of light exposed to the film in the camera and by manipulating sources of light, photographers create emphasis, patterns, and contrasts. László Moholy-Nagy's *Head* shown in Figure 12.4 demonstrates the use of light and the capturing of texture in a photographic image.

Figure 12.3   de Chirico's *The Nostalgia of the Infinite*

FIGURE 12.4   Moholy-Nagy's *Head*

Exercise 12.1   *Exploring Elements of Art*

Reproductions
of images in
this exercise

Working with a group of fellow students, consider Picasso's *The Frugal Repast* and *The Nostalgia of the Infinite* by Giorgio de Chirico. Select a classmate to keep track of the group's work.

1. Discuss the title of Picasso's etching. Without thinking about the etching (just concentrate on the theme in the title) write a one-sentence explanation of what you believe the title suggests.

2. Look at the lines and shapes in the etching. What impresses you about the lines and shapes? How do they convey meaning? Write three or more sentences explaining how the lines and shapes relate to the title.

3. Look at the textures and lighting in the etching. What aspects of the etching do textures and lighting emphasize? Write three or more sentences discussing texture and lighting in the work.

4. Move on to de Chirico's painting. Begin by analyzing the lines and shapes. What shapes stand out and what do you think they represent? What is significant about the lines? How do these shapes and lines relate to the subjects within the composition (the tower and the figures)? Write three or more sentences explaining what you believe is represented by the lines and shapes.

5. Consider the uses of light and color in the painting. How do they relate to the shapes and lines? How do they relate to the painting's subjects? Write three or more sentences discussing light and color in the work.

6. Based on your analysis of the painting, consider what you believe to be the painting's message. Now look at the title of the painting. How does this title relate to your sense of the message? Write at least three sentences explaining the title in terms of the painting.

Understanding Principles of Design

We can analyze elements of art like lines, shapes, colors, and light to illustrate some of the strategies artists use to convey meaning. These strategies can be discussed using principles of design that include emphasis, balance, and coherence.

We have already looked at how light and color can draw a viewer's eye toward particulars in an image to create emphasis. Similarly, the arrangement of items within the image can create emphasis. Consider how the placement of the figures in Gertrude Goodrich's *Scenes From American Life (The Beach)* in Figure 12.5 emphasizes the various characters in the painting. Emphasis focuses our attention; it helps us hone in on particulars as we develop an understanding of an image.

Balance refers to the relationships between elements in an image. Often balance applies to the shapes and proportions of an image. Compare Claude Monet's oil on canvas *On the Banks of the Sienne, Bennecourt* in Figure 12.6 with René Magritte's oil on canvas *The Human Condition* in Figure 12.7. *The Human Condition* displays a symmetrical structure to create a sense of balance. Monet's painting provides a more asymmetrical balance.

Viewers of Monet's painting may be initially drawn to the figure of the woman wearing stripes. The placement and proportion (the relative size of objects in the image) of the woman focus our attention on the near shore. Initially, the symmetrical balance in Magritte's painting might focus our gaze on the window that lies between the curtains. However, the painting that has been placed before the window pushes the balance of the image forward so that, while from left to right we see a great deal of symmetry, there is also a sense of depth from the front to the back of the painting.

FIGURE 12.5   Goodrich's *Scenes from American Life (The Beach)*

FIGURE 12.6   Monet's *On the Banks of the Seine, Bennecourt*
Claude Monet, French 1840–1926, On the Bank of the Seine, Bennecourt, *1868, oil on canvas, 81.5 x 100.7 cm, Potter Palmer Collection, 1922.427, Reproduction, The Art Institute of Chicago*

FIGURE 12.7   Magritte's *The Human Condition*

Coherence refers to the unity and logical arrangement of the elements in an image. A sense of coherence can be created through balance and proportion or through aspects of color or light. In Monet's *On the Banks of the Sienne, Bennecourt,* the woman in stripes is much larger than the figures on the far bank, but since the sizes reflect the relative distance of the figures their proportions are coherent. *The Human Condition* surprises expectations by providing a painting of a painting; the effect works because the two images resemble one another so closely in both subject and color.

Interpreting Images as Compositions

Elements like line, shape, light, and color give form to the settings, figures, and objects that make up an image. These components comprise the subject matter or **composition** of the image. The arrangement of the subject matter allows us to discuss the composition and its significance. Consider *People in the Sun,* by Edward Hopper in Figure 12.8.

The figures in *People in the Sun* demonstrate how arrangement can create **patterns** and **variety** in a composition. The figures in the front row all share similar postures. They also alternate between men and women. The man with the book fits, but also varies from this pattern. The relationships that are created by the pattern and the subtle variations create **motifs** (recurring elements) that allow us to discuss possible themes and messages in the image.

The compositions in photography also demonstrate patterns and thematic motifs. When considering photography, we must overcome the tendency to assume that the camera acts as an objective lens that reproduces reality. Instead, we should evaluate the choices a photographer makes in selecting or arranging subjects. Lewis Hine's photograph of an untethered construction worker on the Empire State Building (Figure 12.9) represents a shot that has been selected for not only its visual impact, but also for its emotional appeal.

The subject of a photograph is an essential component of its meaning. In addition, the placement of the camera, the arrangement of objects within the frame of the image, and the depth and focus given to objects within the photograph all represent ways in which photographs are composed.

FIGURE 12.8   Hopper's *People in the Sun*

☑CHECKLIST FOR EVALUATING ART AND IMAGES

☐ **Consider the medium.** Relate the piece to other works that use similar materials. Explore techniques in the work specific to its medium as well as those that cut across media.

☐ **Examine the lines** in a work, looking at their thickness and continuity and the ways they create shapes. Consider how combinations of lines and shapes create meaning.

☐ **Evaluate the uses of light.** Consider how light draws the viewer's eye to particulars in a work. Look at how light creates contrasts and patterns.

☐ **Examine the significance of color.** Consider the qualities of color and how cool, warm, dark, or bright colors affect the mood of a painting.

☐ **Consider the textures** in a work. Think about the impressions created by textures. Examine the significance of any shifts or variations of texture.

☐ **Explore the principles of art.** Notice areas of emphasis. Consider balance and proportion. Note the levels of coherence in a work. Explore the significance of all of these principles as they are revealed in the piece.

☐ **Interpret the composition** of a work. Examine the figures in a composition and imagine their characteristics and stories. Consider the significance of objects. Ask how the background or setting influences the composition.

☐ **Explore the imagery and motifs.** Search for recurring elements or themes that emerge in a work. Consider the possible symbolism of objects or figures. Determine what you believe to be the most significant messages conveyed by the work.

FIGURE 12.9   Hine's *Steel Worker, Empire State Building*

IMAGES FOR FURTHER EXPLORATION

To help you continue thinking about art and photography, we will provide a number of additional images. Be aware, as well, that the Web offers perhaps the best way of exploring images on your own. You can find links to a number of useful starting places on our CD and Web site.

Images and
resources
for further
exploration

GRANT WOOD

The paintings of Grant Wood (1891–1942) represent what has been called the school of American Landscape, or American Scene painting, which stressed realistic portrayals of diverse scenes from American life. American Gothic, *his best known work, was completed in 1930 using oil paint on a board surface.*

American Gothic

FIGURE 12.10   Wood's *American Gothic*
Grant Wood, American, 1891–1942, American Gothic, 1930, oil on beaver board, 30 11/16 x 25 11/16 in. (78 x 65.3 cm) unframed, Friends of American Art Collection, 1930.934, Reproduction, The Art Institute of Chicago

EDWARD CURTIS

Edward Curtis (1868–1952) is best known for his documentary photographs of Native Americans. Working for more than 35 years during the end of the 1800s and the early 1900s, Curtis took over 40,000 photographs, documenting every major Native American tribe. Maricopa Child *was taken around 1907.*

Maricopa Child

FIGURE 12.11   Curtis's *Maricopa Child*

GEORGE TOOKER

George Tooker (born in 1920) has been called a magical realist painter for the way his works add an element of fantasy or surrealism to common situations. Tooker grew up and studied art in New York. Many of his paintings reflect people in crowded, sometimes depersonalizing situations. The Waiting Room *uses a technique of mixing egg yolk with tempera pigment. It was painted on a board in 1959.*

The Waiting Room

FIGURE 12.12   Tooker's *The Waiting Room*

CINDY SHERMAN

The photography of Cindy Sherman (born in 1954) questions the distinctions between images that document reality and works of art that create a fictional world. She is best known for her Untitled Film Still *series, photographs intended to mimic frames that might be found in movies. In the images, Sherman dons costumes and stages scenes that call out for viewers to interpret the images as moments in a larger story. Notice the figure in the shadows in* Untitled Film Still 65, *taken in 1980.*

Untitled Film Still 65

FIGURE 12.13   Sherman's *Untitled Film Still 65*

WRITING ABOUT ART

As with other forms of expression, art enables writers to discuss both formal and thematic elements. In addition, art asks writers to think historically, considering the contexts in which works originate and the perspectives of the artists who created them. As you write about works of art, you can refer to the elements and principles discussed above to analyze and draw conclusions about what you see.

Sometimes you may be asked to simply describe in detail the formal elements of a work. In many **formal analyses,** however, you will argue that formal elements and principles of design create an impression and convey a message. You must read the details, looking at how the formal elements relate to themes and imagery. You might move from larger descriptions of the composition to more detailed discussion of specific elements of art. A thesis should guide your formal analysis so that, as you analyze the details of an image, you lead your reader toward an important point that you wish to make.

You may also write about the social or historical aspects of art. These connections can include key concerns that might have informed the creation of a piece or biographical information about an artist. You might also explore works from a specific era or school of art. This kind of exploration is sometimes called a **stylistic analysis** (meaning it looks at a work in terms of the shared techniques representing a style of art such as impressionism). Again, be sure to connect your discussion of the details you analyze to interpretations that explain the significance of those details.

You may wish to conduct research to better understand the history and context of a work. You might try the *Grove Dictionary of Art* or *Art Online* if your library provides them. You can find more art research resources on our CD. As with other kinds of writing about context, you must apply care in drawing conclusions based simply on historical information. Do not assume that art automatically reflects its history. Instead, begin with a thesis demonstrating a significant historical or biographical concern and discuss concrete evidence from the work that speaks to that concern.

Conducting
art
research

If your instructor asks you to use MLA format when writing about art, you should use underlining or italics to indicate the title of a work in the body of your paper. In your references provide the name and location of the institution (or collection) that houses the piece of art, as in the example below:

Tooker, George. <u>The Waiting Room.</u> 1959. Smithsonian American Art Museum, Washington, D.C.

Exercise 12.2   *Writing a Formal Analysis*

Select a work of art from this chapter, or an alternate piece of art, and compose a formal analysis that demonstrates how the work appeals to your senses and conveys a message.

1. Begin by exploring the work freely to find an approach that will guide your analysis. You might start with how the work appeals to your emotions. You might explore key imagery or themes. Spend as much time as it takes to develop a thesis statement about the meaning of the work.

2. Explore the formal elements of the work. Consider how principles of art such as patterns, emphasis, balance, and coherence work to further the message of the work. Examine elements of art such as color, contrast, light, value, texture, shape, and line. Sketch an outline detailing how you can discuss these formal elements in terms of your thesis.

3. Compose at least a two-page analysis that states your thesis and discusses in detail how the formal elements of the work convey meaning.

Exercise 12.3   *Writing an Art History Paper*

Examine a work of art in this chapter, or an alternate piece of art, in terms of its historical or social context.

1. Begin by exploring the themes and imagery in the work to develop an impression of its most significant messages. Explore key concerns representative of the work's context—you might think about important trends and events, or about issues of class, gender, politics, psychology, communication, and so forth. Select a historical concern that interests you and that can be discussed in terms of the piece of art.

2. Conduct library and Internet research to learn about the historical concern you are examining. Conduct research as well about the work you are examining.

3. Next, brainstorm an argument discussing how the work relates to the historical concern. Develop a thesis that articulates a way of understanding the work in terms of the concern.

4. Finally, compose a three- to five-page argument explaining how the work relates to the historical concern. Combine your knowledge of the historical issue with formal analysis of the work to make the claims that will support your argument. Use evidence from your research and from the work to support your points. Be sure to document your research using the style outlined above or specified by your instructor.

Exploring Literature and Art

Repro-
ductions
of paired
poems
and
paintings

Many authors have written creatively about works of art. In addition to providing a ready subject for expression, writing creatively about a work asks you to find an approach that strikes you on a personal level. You must then study the details of a work as you compose. Consider the paired poems and works of art on the following pages. (You can see full color versions of these paintings on our CD.)

JOHN STONE

John Stone represents many interests. A physician, musician, and linguist, Stone has written three volumes of poetry treating themes ranging from medicine, to art, to family. His poems display wit and accessibility and an ability to bridge the concerns of the sciences and the arts. "Three for the Mona Lisa" and "Early Sunday Morning" (see pages 332–33) are from his collection, Renaming the Streets, *published in 1985.*

Three for the Mona Lisa

1
It is not what she did
at 10 o' clock
last evening

accounts for the smile

5   It is
that she plans
to do it again

tonight.

2
Only the mouth
10   all those years
ever

letting on.

3
It's not the mouth
exactly

15   it's not the eyes
exactly either

it's not even
exactly a smile

But, whatever,
20   I second the motion.

LEONARDO DA VINCI

Leonardo da Vinci (1452–1519) is known for the breadth of his interests as much as his painting. He was an inventor, scientist, engineer, architect, and sculptor, as well as a successful painter. The Mona Lisa, *his (if not the world's) most famous painting, is best known for the subtle suggestions in the smile on the face of the woman in the portrait. The painting, however, is also unique for the way it employed techniques da Vinci introduced into the world of art. The shapes and lines of the painting are softened by creating a kind of smoky atmosphere that brings the subject and the landscape in the background into a complementary relationship. Da Vinci was said to have taken four years to paint the* Mona Lisa, *completing work sometime around 1507.*

Mona Lisa

FIGURE 12.14   da Vinci's *Mona Lisa*

EDWARD HOPPER

Edward Hopper (1882-1967) was a painter, illustrator, and printmaker who grew up in the Hudson River area of New York and trained in New York City. After traveling and studying in Europe, he eventually returned to New York where he felt unfulfilled, but found employment working as an illustrator. In 1923, he turned to watercolors and quickly found success. He continued to paint using oils and watercolors and began moving about the country looking for material. His paintings have a realistic, sometimes lonely and despondent quality. Early Sunday Morning *was painted in 1930 using oil on canvas.*

Early Sunday Morning

FIGURE 12.15   Hopper's *Early Sunday Morning*

Somewhere in the next block
someone may be practicing the flute
but not here

5   where the entrances
to four stores are dark
the awnings rolled in

nothing open for business
Across the second story
ten faceless windows

10   In the foreground
a barber pole, a fire hydrant
as if there could ever again

be hair to cut
fire to burn
15   And far off, still low

in the imagined East
the sun that is again
right on time

20 adding to the Chinese red
of the building
despite which color

I do not believe
the day
is going to be hot

25 It was I think
on just such a day
it is on just such a morning

that every Edward Hopper
finishes, puts down his brush
30 as if to say

As important
as what is
happening

is what is not.

Kitagawa Utamaro

Kitagawa Utamaro (1753–1806) collaborated with Japanese writers to produce a number of pairings of poetry and art. His paintings and woodblock engravings frequently depict women, often taking courtesans and other women recognized for their beauty as their subjects. The images he painted of women tended to emphasize sensual and generalized elements of female beauty, rather than depicting portraits of recognizable figures. Girl Powdering Her Neck *is a woodblock print produced around 1790.*

Figure 12.16   Utamaro's *Girl Powdering Her Neck*

CATHY SONG

Hawaiian poet Cathy Song (born in 1955) has written a number of poems dealing with Utamaro and his art, as well as poems associated with the artist Georgia O'Keeffe. Her poems have been called colorful, but quiet, emphasizing sensual elements or careful description. She published her first collection of poems, Picture Bride, *in 1983, in which "Girl Powdering Her Neck" appears.*

Girl Powdering Her Neck

The light is the inside
sheen of an oyster shell,
sponged with talc and vapor,
moisture from a bath.

5   A pair of slippers
are placed outside
the rice-paper doors.
She kneels at a low table
in the room,
10   her legs folded beneath her
as she sits on a buckwheat pillow.

Her hair is black
with hints of red,
the color of seaweed
15   spread over rocks.

Morning begins the ritual
wheel of the body,
the application of translucent skins.
She practices pleasure:
20   the pressure of three fingertips
applying powder.
Fingerprints of pollen
some other hand will trace.

The peach-dyed kimono
25   patterned with maple leaves
drifting across the silk,
falls from right to left
in a diagonal, revealing
the nape of her neck
30   and the curve of a shoulder
like the slope of a hill
set deep in snow in a country
of huge white solemn birds.
Her face appears in the mirror,

35   a reflection in a winter pond,
rising to meet itself.
She dips a corner of her sleeve
like a brush into water
to wipe the mirror;

40 she is about to paint herself.
The eyes narrow
in a moment of self-scrutiny.
The mouth parts
as if desiring to disturb
45 the placid plum face;
break the symmetry of silence.
But the berry-stained lips,
stenciled into the mask of beauty,
do not speak.

50 Two chrysanthemums
touch in the middle of the lake
and drift apart.

These poems about paintings represent several writers' interpretations of an image. In some instances, images and writing are more closely related, as in advertising images (see pages 337–43), or in the works of William Blake. In Blake's work, poems and art combine to create pictorial compositions of words and images, as in the poem "The Poison Tree" in Figure 12.17. (You can explore more of Blake's work on pages 726–34 and in the Extended Inquiry on our CD-ROM.)

The poetry and prints of William Blake

FIGURE 12.17 Blake's *A Poison Tree*

Exercise 12.4   *Writing Stories and Poetry About Art*

This exercise asks you to tell the story of one of the characters portrayed in the images in this chapter.

1. Begin by selecting a work that you think would lend itself to a story or perhaps a poem. Examine the image, looking at elements of the composition. Think about the setting that is displayed in the image. Look at any objects that might help tell the story.

2. Examine the characters and sketch out ideas about what traits they might have. Select a character that you believe to be the protagonist and consider how other characters might relate to him or her.

3. Imagine a plot that would explain how the protagonist got to be in the situation portrayed in the image. Alternatively, you might imagine forward and tell the story of what is about to happen to one of the characters. Create an outline for a story that introduces the character, builds tension and complication, and concludes with the moment depicted in the image or a resolution in the future.

4. Relying on your sense of the setting and characters, use your outline to draft one or more pages that tell the story of the protagonist.

(If you or your instructor prefers, you may compose a poem that describes the image you have chosen and that either tells the story of one or more of the characters or conveys a feeling present in the image.)

UNDERSTANDING IMAGES IN POPULAR CULTURE

Resources for studying popular media

In contemporary society, visual images surround us; from magazine covers, to television, to billboards, to the Web, images are there, vying for our attention. The most prevalent of these cultural images can be found in advertisements in the popular media. These media images sometimes inform, often entertain, and almost always seek to influence our beliefs and actions. As we investigate these images, we can apply what we know about **rhetorical situations** (that is, speakers and their purposes, audiences, and contexts).

Considering the Rhetorical Situation of Advertisements

Communication never takes place in a vacuum. Rather, individuals or entities act as speakers to produce communication with a specific purpose and target that communication to an audience. Both speakers and audiences are also shaped by the historical contexts they inhabit. All of these factors influence the way that messages are produced and received.

Consider the controversies regarding images used to advertise tobacco. How would you describe the target audience for the message conveyed by the "Joe Camel" image in Figure 12.18? Some have suggested that using a cartoon character to advertise cigarettes reveals that the target audience for the advertisement is children. (A report on logo recognition indicated that more than half of children ages 3–6 in a study associated the image of Joe Camel with cigarettes.)

FIGURE 12.18   Joe Camel Advertisement

In a 1998 settlement, tobacco companies agreed not to promote products to minors (the Joe Camel campaign ended in 1997). Still, public health officials and others have argued that, while U.S. laws prohibit selling (or even advertising) tobacco products to anyone under the age of eighteen, advertisements use images designed to appeal to teenage consumers.

We can also evaluate the speakers or entities producing images, and the rhetorical techniques used by these speakers. As we do so, we should remember the role of purpose as it relates to the rhetorical situation. Consider how the advertisement against fishing, in Figure 12.19, prompts us to think about the speaker and purposes behind the image. The ad is meant to raise our awareness of cruelty to fish by evoking our sympathies with the dog in the image. Knowing something about the entity that produced the advertisement helps us understand the purpose behind the image. People for the Ethical Treatment of Animals (PETA) takes an activist stance against animal cruelty, pushes people to consider the impact of human actions on animals, and encourages us to treat animals with standards much like those we apply to other humans.

We can see how the ad fulfills that purpose using rhetorical techniques expressed in the image. On the level of logic, we might question the tendency

FIGURE 12.19   PETA Advertisement

of PETA to equate humans and animals, or we might debate the merits of equating mammals with fish. The advertising image, however, achieves its purpose primarily through rhetorical techniques designed to appeal to our emotions. The image of the fishhook poking through the cheek of the fluffy dog evokes our sympathies and helps the ad deliver its message.

Most advertising images rely on appeals to our senses; many also include words that provoke thought, but the primary means of persuasion is usually based on emotion. Further, many advertising images try to tap into ideas that permeate the psyche of their audience. Because these images play upon emotions and ideas, they provide an illuminating lens for studying aspects of the culture in which they are produced and consumed.

Think about the image from a Body Shop advertising campaign reproduced in Figure 12.20. What does the Body Shop image say about the myth of the ideal woman? In many instances the primary purpose of such advertisements is to increase sales and make a profit. But in doing so, images may achieve a number of related goals such as associating a product with a feeling or idea like sexiness, power, or beauty. Consider the issues revealed in this excerpt from a chat conversation about the Body Shop image:

> Catherine Hernandez > I think it is a great ad for the body shop because the products they sell make everyone feel beautiful
>
> Julie Woods > most people know that the average person doesn't look like the women in magazines
>
> Samantha Billings > But women want to look like a supermodel, they want to be attractive, they don't want to look to obesity as a model
>
> Adam Marshal > companies are always looking for different angles to work in advertising. this is comedic and true

FIGURE 12.20   Body Shop "Ruby" Advertisement

Catherine Hernandez > but we are still made to feel like we should look like the women in magazines

Samantha Billings > I'm not saying that you have to look like a super-model to be attractive . . .

Rene Bishop > I just think it is trying to be realistic

Julie Woods > but supermodels are supermodels for a reason and people who only think that they are attractive if they look like a super-model have their own issues

Ronald Gains > perhaps they make more money b/c the viewer likes the thought that the body shop is a "good" corporation by thinking they care about these social values. when in reality all their products are made in china . . .

Bridget Allen > i don't like it

Greg Casperson > its just like the barbie idea

Bridget Allen > no it's not

Brenda Williams > I think the public desires the "role" models

Bridget Allen > barbies have perfect bodies

Greg Casperson > everyone wants a more realistic image

Kamala Vira > to sell products they're trying to relate to the most consumers, which is the 3 billion who don't look like supermodels; they're using a real woman's perspective to appeal to her, so she buys their product

Ronald Gains > i've been in one, MADE IN CHINA is stamped on every bot-tle of shampoo, lotion, etc . . .

Catherine Hernandez > society makes you feel this way, I don't think it is fair to say you have issues if you want to look this way

Bridget Allen > well according to whatever society tells us is perfect

Julie Woods > I don't think you can blame the media for people wanting to look like supermodels

Brenda Williams > yes you can

Brenda Williams > but you have to blame the people too

Samantha Billings > Probably a great deal, if we look back in history when Rubens was painting, the idea of a voluptuous woman was seen as the ideal because he painted them in a glorious light

Greg Casperson > is there something wrong with being healthy?

Bridget Allen > i don't want to look like a supermodel but i don't want to look like that either

Tamara Wilson > no you can't the media plays a role but people are far too impressionable

Adam Marshal > people need to think for themselves

Brenda Williams > I want to look like a supermodel

Traci Bridgeman > The media definitely plays a role, because when the images flash on tv in remote places, then anorexia suddenly shows up. Like it is now a factor in China.

Julie Woods > i don't feel pressured by magazines to look like a super-model

```
Adam Marshal > it plays a role but isn't to blame

Frank Conner > all companies are motivated by money, that's it

Samantha Billings > I feel the pressure

Kamala Vira > it's just to balance out all those pics of the skinny,
   flawless models with something real

Greg Casperson > i agree

Rene Bishop > I think that society does put a great deal of influence
   on our generation through ads, but i think that people are starting
   to realize this and this ad is an example of that.
```

Deliberations about images like these reveal how advertisements relate to concerns such as gender roles, the status of women and men, and health. Compare the Body Shop image with the image advertising Moschino jeans in Figure 12.21. To what extent do the images tap into similar ideas that permeate culture? What do the differences between the two images say about the speakers or entities that produce them or the audiences that receive them?

PRACTICING EVALUATING AND WRITING ABOUT IMAGES

Images
and video
clips on
advertising

You can explore and practice writing about advertising images below. We have provided a number of images, but you can also find many more by conducting Internet searches. You can also find more images on our CD and see video clips from scholars who study advertising and issues of culture.

FIGURE 12.21   Moschino Jeans Advertisement

Women and Sexuality

The images in Figures 12.22 and 12.23 represent two views on women's sexuality. The first image is a Russell & Bromley advertisement. The second image is from a 1932 advertisement for Listerine mouthwash.

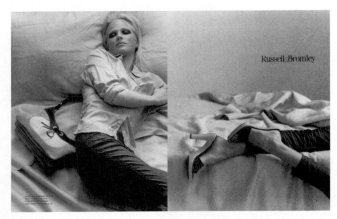

FIGURE 12.22   Russell & Bromley Advertisement for Shoes

FIGURE 12.23   Listerine Advertisement

Cities and Cars

Figures 12.24 and 12.25 present two differing images of cars and advertising. Figure 12.24 is taken from an exhibit by Alex Harris. Harris presents a series of photographs taken through the windshield of cars in Havana, Cuba. Advertising appears only subtly in the photograph. Figure 12.25 features a Hummer H2 SUV.

FIGURE 12.24   Alex Harris Havana Photograph

FIGURE 12.25   Hummer Advertisement

Selling Identity

The images in Figures 12.26 through 12.29 advertise identity. Figure 12.26 is a Tommy fragrance advertisement raising issues of group identification.

FIGURE 12.26   Tommy Fragrance Advertisement

FIGURE 12.27   Tommy Fragrance Advertisement Spoof

FIGURE 12.28   Calvin Klein Advertisement

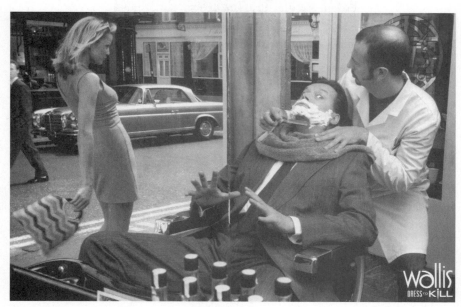

FIGURE 12.29   Wallis Advertisement

Exercise 12.5   *Brainstorming About an Advertising Image*

Working on your own, choose an ad from this chapter or an alternative image. Once you have selected an image, open a word processor document or take out some notepaper, and respond to the variations of the journalist's questions printed below.

1. **Who and Where:** Who is the speaker or entity that has created the image? What characteristics describe the speaker? Who is the image aimed at? How would you characterize this audience? Where does the image appear? How does this location influence the image? Write freely for two to three minutes about this prompt.

2. **What and Why:** In addition to advertising a product, what ideas does the image promote? What approach does the image take? Why might it be successful or unsuccessful? Write freely for two to three minutes.

3. **How:** How does the image deliver its message? What formal elements of art are used to create meaning? How does the image appeal to your senses? Does it use logic, emotions, or some other strategies to convey its message? How do you think viewers will respond? Write freely for two or three minutes.

Exercise 12.6   *Writing About Advertising Images*

Write a three- to five-page paper in which you analyze one or more advertising images in terms of the strategies they use to convey messages and their relationship to a trend or concern in society. You might, for instance, look at ads used to market designer clothing in terms of issues of body image and health. You might also look at issues such as violence, self esteem, social groups, consumers and labor practices, substance abuse, or some other issue related to the image you discuss.

1. You will need to start by conducting research on the social issue. You can refer to the Web sites and resources for this chapter on our CD for information about research, or conduct research using the strategies outlined in Chapter 4.

2. Next, write a thesis that will organize your work and narrow your focus—for instance, *problems with teen anorexia cannot be attributed solely to fashion advertising.* Construct an essay that explains your thesis by discussing the social issue and analyzing the advertising images.

3. As you analyze the images, be sure to look at aspects of their form, imagery, and themes. Just as you might when analyzing a work of art, explain how the formal elements of the image create a visual message for readers. You may want to analyze more than one image to make your point, but do not go overboard with more than three or so images—it is better to discuss fewer images in depth.

4. Document the images and sources that you use following the conventions outlined in the Appendix.

13

Critical Approaches to Literature

Theory is . . . a roadmap that shows new ways of doing old things, and new places to go. Theory is freedom from the apparently unchangeable way things are, which it unmasks as one possibility among hundreds. Theory breaks the ruts of coincidence and gives us the courage to undertake voyages of discovery.

—*Béla Balázs*

Some complain that approaching literature with too critical an eye can ruin our appreciation of it. The more we probe works intellectually, the less we enjoy their emotional appeal. However, investigating works critically can also open our reading experience to new pleasures. For instance, analyzing a work from a feminist perspective might help us realize how language reflects the relationships between men and women. Theories of literary criticism, then, intensify our intellectual engagements, but in doing so they help us discover new insights and enjoyments in literature.

READING A WORK THEORETICALLY

In this chapter we will discuss critical theories by showing how they can be used to interpret a short story called "The Yellow Wallpaper," written by Charlotte Perkins Gilman. As we explore "The Yellow Wallpaper," we will consider five theoretical approaches. Each of these theories can be used as a way to open avenues for interpreting the story.

1. **A formal/structural approach** examines a work's use of language and artistic techniques. As you read "The Yellow Wallpaper," keep in mind the narration of the story, its structure, and exceptional uses of language.

2. **Poststructural theories** consider formal elements of a work, but focus on how interpretations simultaneously lead to a number of alternative possibilities. Look for passages and language that reveal multiple interpretations and competing ideas.

3. **A feminist approach** considers how literature represents women and men. Feminism also looks at how writing by women has been received and perceived in society. Consider the significance of the narrator's status as a woman,

the relationships between men and women in the story, the ways language impacts men and women, and issues facing women in society as you read the story.

4. **A historical perspective** looks for concerns of the historical times and places in which literature is produced. They also sometimes touch on economic issues and themes. When reading "The Yellow Wallpaper," keep in mind historical conceptions of marriage, medicine, gender roles, and work. Consider, also, the biographical information on Gilman, below.

5. **A psychological perspective** looks at the human feelings and desires represented in a work, and at the ways individuals mature and develop identity. Consider the state of mind of the narrator, issues of maturation or development, and the concept of identity as you read the story.

It may be hard to keep all of these approaches in mind, but you should be able to recognize many of these perspectives as you read. The chart below can give further guidance.

Critical Approach	Formal/ Structural	Poststructural	Feminist	Historical	Psychological
Areas of Emphasis	Language/formal elements	Language/formal elements	Gender issues	Social contexts	Concerns of the mind
	Artistic techniques	Definitions of terms	Influence of language on identity	Political dimensions	Identity
	Structure	Competing messages	Access to communication/power	Economics	The unconscious
	Coherent messages	Multiple meanings	Resistance through writing	Influence of literature on culture	Relationships Maturation

As you read "The Yellow Wallpaper," be sure to annotate and take notes, as well as write down questions and ideas. (You can also use the Enhanced Reading on our CD to help you identify and explore these theoretical approaches.)

"The Yellow Wallpaper"

CHARLOTTE PERKINS GILMAN

With the publication of the book Women and Economics: A Study of the Economic Relation Between Men and Women as a Factor in Social Evolution *in 1898, Charlotte Perkins Gilman (1860–1935) offered an early critique of the social relationships of men and women, claiming that women existed in a state of exploitation. By essentially trading sex for the economic security offered by marriage, Gilman argued, the housewife becomes a prostitute. For Gilman, society dehumanizes women by offering them little means of support beyond the male-dominated institution of marriage.*

Fourteen years earlier, in 1884, Gilman married for the first time to an artist named Walter Stetson and shortly thereafter began to suffer depression. The next year, she gave birth to a daughter and her depression increased. Stetson encouraged her to undergo treatment from the well-known doctor S. Weir Mitchell. Mitchell had established an international reputation for his method of treating patients with nervous disorders. Mitchell developed a treatment known as the rest cure. *Patients were isolated and forbidden to read, write, or exert themselves mentally or physically. Gilman reported later that she wrote "The Yellow Wallpaper" as a response to her negative experiences under Mitchell's care. To critics who objected to the story, she explained that her intent was not "to drive people crazy, but to save people from being driven crazy."*

Gilman later divorced her first husband and remarried in 1900 to George Houghton Gilman. She increased her role as an advocate for women's issues, composing the feminist novel, Herland *in 1916.* Herland *depicts a utopian society where women work together to care for children and one another. In 1934, her second husband died. Gilman herself was stricken with breast cancer at the time and committed suicide shortly after her husband's death.*

The Yellow Wallpaper

It is very seldom that mere ordinary people like John and myself secure ancestral halls for the summer.

A colonial mansion, a hereditary estate, I would say a haunted house, and reach the height of romantic felicity—but that would be asking too much of fate!

Still I will proudly declare that there is something queer about it.

Else, why should it be let so cheaply? And why have stood so long untenanted?

5 John laughs at me, of course, but one expects that in marriage.

John is practical in the extreme. He has no patience with faith, an intense horror of superstition, and he scoffs openly at any talk of things not to be felt and seen and put down in figures.

John is a physician, and *perhaps*—(I would not say it to a living soul, of course, but this is dead paper and a great relief to my mind)—*perhaps* that is one reason I do not get well faster.

You see he does not believe I am sick!

And what can one do?

10 If a physician of high standing, and one's own husband, assures friends and relatives that there is really nothing the matter with one but temporary nervous depression—a slight hysterical tendency—what is one to do?

My brother is also a physician, and also of high standing, and he says the same thing.

So I take phosphates or phosphites—whichever it is, and tonics, and journeys, and air, and exercise, and am absolutely forbidden to "work" until I am well again.

Personally, I disagree with their ideas.

Personally, I believe that congenial work, with excitement and change, would do me good.

15   But what is one to do?

I did write for a while in spite of them; but it *does* exhaust me a good deal—having to be so sly about it, or else meet with heavy opposition.

I sometimes fancy that in my condition if I had less opposition and more society and stimulus—but John says the very worst thing I can do is to think about my condition, and I confess it always makes me feel bad.

So I will let it alone and talk about the house.

The most beautiful place! It is quite alone, standing well back from the road, quite three miles from the village. It makes me think of English places that you read about, for there are hedges and walls and gates that lock, and lots of separate little houses for the gardeners and people.

20   There is a *delicious* garden! I never saw such a garden—large and shady, full of box-bordered paths, and lined with long grape-covered arbors with seats under them.

There were greenhouses, too, but they are all broken now.

There was some legal trouble, I believe, something about the heirs and coheirs; anyhow, the place has been empty for years.

That spoils my ghostliness, I am afraid, but I don't care—there is something strange about the house—I can feel it.

I even said so to John one moonlight evening, but he said what I felt was a *draught,* and shut the window.

25   I get unreasonably angry with John sometimes. I'm sure I never used to be so sensitive. I think it is due to this nervous condition.

But John says if I feel so, I shall neglect proper self-control; so I take pains to control myself—before him, at least, and that makes me very tired.

I don't like our room a bit. I wanted one downstairs that opened on the piazza and had roses all over the window, and such pretty old-fashioned chintz hangings! but John would not hear of it.

He said there was only one window and not room for two beds, and no near room for him if he took another.

He is very careful and loving, and hardly lets me stir without special direction.

30   I have a schedule prescription for each hour in the day; he takes all care from me, and so I feel basely ungrateful not to value it more.

He said we came here solely on my account, that I was to have perfect rest and all the air I could get. "Your exercise depends on your strength, my dear," said he, "and your food somewhat on your appetite; but air you can absorb all the time." So we took the nursery at the top of the house.

It is a big, airy room, the whole floor nearly, with windows that look all ways, and air and sunshine galore. It was nursery first and then playroom and gymnasium, I should judge; for the windows are barred for little children, and there are rings and things in the walls.

The paint and paper look as if a boys' school had used it. It is stripped off—the paper—in great patches all around the head of my bed, about as far as I can reach, and in a great place on the other side of the room low down. I never saw a worse paper in my life.

One of those sprawling flamboyant patterns committing every artistic sin.

35   It is dull enough to confuse the eye in following, pronounced enough to constantly irritate and provoke study, and when you follow the lame uncertain curves for a little distance they suddenly commit suicide—plunge off at outrageous angles, destroy themselves in unheard of contradictions.

The color is repellent, almost revolting; a smouldering unclean yellow, strangely faded by the slow-turning sunlight.

It is a dull yet lurid orange in some places, a sickly sulphur tint in others.

No wonder the children hated it! I should hate it myself if I had to live in this room long.

There comes John, and I must put this away,—he hates to have me write a word.

40   We have been here two weeks, and I haven't felt like writing before, since that first day.

I am sitting by the window now, up in this atrocious nursery, and there is nothing to hinder my writing as much as I please, save lack of strength.

John is away all day, and even some nights when his cases are serious.

I am glad my case is not serious!

But these nervous troubles are dreadfully depressing.

45   John does not know how much I really suffer. He knows there is no *reason* to suffer, and that satisfies him.

Of course it is only nervousness. It does weigh on me so not to do my duty in any way!

I meant to be such a help to John, such a real rest and comfort, and here I am a comparative burden already!

Nobody would believe what an effort it is to do what little I am able,—to dress and entertain, and order things.

It is fortunate Mary is so good with the baby. Such a dear baby!

50   And yet I *cannot* be with him, it makes me so nervous.

I suppose John never was nervous in his life. He laughs at me so about this wallpaper!

At first he meant to repaper the room, but afterwards he said that I was letting it get the better of me, and that nothing was worse for a nervous patient than to give way to such fancies.

He said that after the wallpaper was changed it would be the heavy bed-stead, and then the barred windows, and then that gate at the head of the stairs, and so on.

"You know the place is doing you good," he said, "and really, dear, I don't care to renovate the house just for a three months' rental."

55   "Then do let us go downstairs," I said, "there are such pretty rooms there."

Then he took me in his arms and called me a blessed little goose, and said he would go down to the cellar, if I wished, and have it whitewashed into the bargain.

But he is right enough about the beds and windows and things.

It is as airy and comfortable a room as any one need wish, and, of course, I would not be so silly as to make him uncomfortable just for a whim.

I'm really getting quite fond of the big room, all but that horrid paper.

60   Out of one window I can see the garden, those mysterious deep-shaded arbors, the riotous old-fashioned flowers, and bushes and gnarly trees.

Out of another I get a lovely view of the bay and a little private wharf belonging to the estate. There is a beautiful shaded lane that runs down there from the house. I always fancy I see people walking in these numerous paths and arbors, but John has cautioned me not to give way to fancy in the least. He says that with my imaginative power and habit of story-making, a nervous weakness like mine is sure to lead to all manner of excited fancies, and that I ought to use my will and good sense to check the tendency. So I try.

I think sometimes that if I were only well enough to write a little it would relieve the press of ideas and rest me.

But I find I get pretty tired when I try.

It is so discouraging not to have any advice and companionship about my work. When I get really well, John says we will ask Cousin Henry and Julia down for a long visit; but he says he would as soon put fireworks in my pillow-case as to let me have those stimulating people about now.

65   I wish I could get well faster.

But I must not think about that. This paper looks to me as if it *knew* what a vicious influence it had!

There is a recurrent spot where the pattern lolls like a broken neck and two bulbous eyes stare at you upside down.

I get positively angry with the impertinence of it and the everlastingness. Up and down and sideways they crawl, and those absurd, unblinking eyes are everywhere. There is one place where two breadths didn't match, and the eyes go all up and down the line, one a little higher than the other.

I never saw so much expression in an inanimate thing before, and we all know how much expression they have! I used to lie awake as a child and get more entertainment and terror out of blank walls and plain furniture than most children could find in a toy-store.

70   I remember what a kindly wink the knobs of our big, old bureau used to have, and there was one chair that always seemed like a strong friend.

I used to feel that if any of the other things looked too fierce I could always hop into that chair and be safe.

The furniture in this room is no worse than inharmonious, however, for we had to bring it all from downstairs. I suppose when this was used as a playroom they had to take the nursery things out, and no wonder! I never saw such ravages as the children have made here.

The wallpaper, as I said before, is torn off in spots, and it sticketh closer than a brother—they must have had perseverance as well as hatred.

Then the floor is scratched and gouged and splintered, the plaster itself is dug out here and there, and this great heavy bed which is all we found in the room, looks as if it had been through the wars.

75   But I don't mind it a bit—only the paper.

There comes John's sister. Such a dear girl as she is, and so careful of me! I must not let her find me writing.

She is a perfect and enthusiastic housekeeper, and hopes for no better profession. I verily believe she thinks it is the writing which made me sick!

But I can write when she is out, and see her a long way off from these windows.

There is one that commands the road, a lovely shaded winding road, and one that just looks off over the country. A lovely country, too, full of great elms and velvet meadows.

80   This wallpaper has a kind of sub-pattern in a different shade, a particularly irritating one, for you can only see it in certain lights, and not clearly then.

But in the places where it isn't faded and where the sun is just so—I can see a strange, provoking, formless sort of figure, that seems to skulk about behind that silly and conspicuous front design.

There's sister on the stairs!

Well, the Fourth of July is over! The people are gone and I am tired out. John thought it might do me good to see a little company, so we just had mother and Nellie and the children down for a week.

Of course I didn't do a thing. Jennie sees to everything now.

85   But it tired me all the same.

John says if I don't pick up faster he shall send me to Weir Mitchell in the fall.

But I don't want to go there at all. I had a friend who was in his hands once, and she says he is just like John and my brother, only more so!

Besides, it is such an undertaking to go so far.

I don't feel as if it was worth while to turn my hand over for anything, and I'm getting dreadfully fretful and querulous.

90   I cry at nothing, and cry most of the time.

Of course I don't when John is here, or anybody else, but when I am alone.

And I am alone a good deal just now. John is kept in town very often by serious cases, and Jennie is good and lets me alone when I want her to.

So I walk a little in the garden or down that lovely lane, sit on the porch under the roses, and lie down up here a good deal.

I'm getting really fond of the room in spite of the wallpaper. Perhaps *because* of the wallpaper.

95   It dwells in my mind so!

I lie here on this great immovable bed—it is nailed down, I believe—and follow that pattern about by the hour. It is as good as gymnastics, I assure you. I start, we'll say, at the bottom, down in the corner over there where it has not been touched, and I determine for the thousandth time that I *will* follow that pointless pattern to some sort of a conclusion.

I know a little of the principle of design, and I know this thing was not arranged on any laws of radiation, or alternation, or repetition, or symmetry, or anything else that I ever heard of.

It is repeated, of course, by the breadths, but not otherwise.

Looked at in one way each breadth stands alone, the bloated curves and flourishes—a kind of "debased Romanesque" with delirium tremens—go waddling up and down in isolated columns of fatuity.

100   But, on the other hand, they connect diagonally, and the sprawling out-lines run off in great slanting waves of optic horror, like a lot of wallowing seaweeds in full chase.

The whole thing goes horizontally, too, at least it seems so, and I exhaust myself in trying to distinguish the order of its going in that direction.

They have used a horizontal breadth for a frieze, and that adds wonder-fully to the confusion.

There is one end of the room where it is almost intact, and there, when the crosslights fade and the low sun shines directly upon it, I can almost fancy radiation after all,—the interminable grotesques seem to form around a com-mon centre and rush off in headlong plunges of equal distraction.

It makes me tired to follow it. I will take a nap I guess.

105   I don't know why I should write this.

I don't want to.

I don't feel able.

And I know John would think it absurd. But I *must* say what I feel and think in some way—it is such a relief!

But the effort is getting to be greater than the relief.

110   Half the time now I am awfully lazy, and lie down ever so much.

John says I musn't lose my strength, and has me take cod liver oil and lots of tonics and things, to say nothing of ale and wine and rare meat.

Dear John! He loves me very dearly, and hates to have me sick. I tried to have a real earnest reasonable talk with him the other day, and tell him how I wish he would let me go and make a visit to Cousin Henry and Julia.

But he said I wasn't able to go, nor able to stand it after I got there; and I did not make out a very good case for myself, for I was crying before I had finished.

It is getting to be a great effort for me to think straight. Just this nervous weakness I suppose.

115   And dear John gathered me up in his arms, and just carried me upstairs and laid me on the bed, and sat by me and read to me till it tired my head.

He said I was his darling and his comfort and all he had, and that I must take care of myself for his sake, and keep well.

He says no one but myself can help me out of it, that I must use my will and self-control and not let any silly fancies run away with me.

There's one comfort, the baby is well and happy, and does not have to occupy this nursery with the horrid wallpaper.

If we had not used it, that blessed child would have! What a fortunate escape! Why, I wouldn't have a child of mine, an impressionable little thing, live in such a room for worlds.

120   I never thought of it before, but it is lucky that John kept me here after all, I can stand it so much easier than a baby, you see.

Of course I never mention it to them any more—I am too wise,—but I keep watch of it all the same.

There are things in that paper that nobody knows but me, or ever will.

Behind that outside pattern the dim shapes get clearer every day.

It is always the same shape, only very numerous.

125   And it is like a woman stooping down and creeping about behind that pattern. I don't like it a bit. I wonder—I begin to think—I wish John would take me away from here!

It is so hard to talk with John about my case, because he is so wise, and because he loves me so.

But I tried it last night.

It was moonlight. The moon shines in all around just as the sun does.

I hate to see it sometimes, it creeps so slowly, and always comes in by one window or another.

130   John was asleep and I hated to waken him, so I kept still and watched the moonlight on that undulating wallpaper till I felt creepy.

The faint figure behind seemed to shake the pattern, just as if she wanted to get out.

I got up softly and went to feel and see if the paper *did* move, and when I came back John was awake.

"What is it, little girl?" he said. "Don't go walking about like that—you'll get cold."

I thought it was a good time to talk, so I told him that I really was not gaining here, and that I wished he would take me away.

135   "Why darling!" said he, "our lease will be up in three weeks, and I can't see how to leave before."

"The repairs are not done at home, and I cannot possibly leave town just now. Of course if you were in any danger, I could and would, but you really are better, dear, whether you can see it or not. I am a doctor, dear, and I know. You are gaining flesh and color, your appetite is better, I feel really much easier about you."

"I don't weigh a bit more," said I, "nor as much; and my appetite may be better in the evening when you are here, but it is worse in the morning when you are away!"

"Bless her little heart!" said he with a big hug, "she shall be as sick as she pleases! But now let's improve the shining hours by going to sleep, and talk about it in the morning!"

"And you won't go away?" I asked gloomily.

140   "Why, how can I, dear? It is only three weeks more and then we will take a nice little trip of a few days while Jennie is getting the house ready. Really dear you are better!"

"Better in body perhaps—" I began, and stopped short, for he sat up straight and looked at me with such a stern, reproachful look that I could not say another word.

"My darling," said he, "I beg of you, for my sake and for our child's sake, as well as for your own, that you will never for one instant let that idea enter your mind! There is nothing so dangerous, so fascinating, to a temperament like yours. It is a false and foolish fancy. Can you not trust me as a physician when I tell you so?"

So of course I said no more on that score, and we went to sleep before long. He thought I was asleep first, but I wasn't, and lay there for hours trying to decide whether that front pattern and the back pattern really did move together or separately.

On a pattern like this, by daylight, there is a lack of sequence, a defiance of law, that is a constant irritant to a normal mind.

145   The color is hideous enough, and unreliable enough, and infuriating enough, but the pattern is torturing.

You think you have mastered it, but just as you get well underway in following, it turns a back-somersault and there you are. It slaps you in the face, knocks you down, and tramples upon you. It is like a bad dream.

The outside pattern is a florid arabesque, reminding one of a fungus. If you can imagine a toadstool in joints, an interminable string of toadstools, budding and sprouting in endless convolutions—why, that is something like it.

That is, sometimes!

There is one marked peculiarity about this paper, a thing nobody seems to notice but myself, and that is that it changes as the light changes.

150   When the sun shoots in through the east window—I always watch for that first long, straight ray—it changes so quickly that I never can quite believe it.

That is why I watch it always.

By moonlight—the moon shines in all night when there is a moon—I wouldn't know it was the same paper.

At night in any kind of light, in twilight, candle light, lamplight, and worst of all by moonlight, it becomes bars! The outside pattern I mean, and the woman behind it is as plain as can be.

I didn't realize for a long time what the thing was that showed behind, that dim sub-pattern, but now I am quite sure it is a woman.

155   By daylight she is subdued, quiet. I fancy it is the pattern that keeps her so still. It is so puzzling. It keeps me quiet by the hour.

I lie down ever so much now. John says it is good for me, and to sleep all I can.

Indeed he started the habit by making me lie down for an hour after each meal.

It is a very bad habit I am convinced, for you see I don't sleep.

And that cultivates deceit, for I don't tell them I'm awake—O no!

160   The fact is I am getting a little afraid of John.

He seems very queer sometimes, and even Jennie has an inexplicable look.

It strikes me occasionally, just as a scientific hypothesis,—that perhaps it is the paper!

I have watched John when he did not know I was looking, and come into the room suddenly on the most innocent excuses, and I've caught him several times *looking at the paper!* And Jennie too. I caught Jennie with her hand on it once.

She didn't know I was in the room, and when I asked her in a quiet, a very quiet voice, with the most restrained manner possible, what she was doing with the paper—she turned around as if she had been caught stealing, and looked quite angry—asked me why I should frighten her so!

165   Then she said that the paper stained everything it touched, that she had found yellow smooches on all my clothes and John's, and she wished we would be more careful!

Did not that sound innocent? But I know she was studying that pattern, and I am determined that nobody shall find it out but myself!

Life is very much more exciting now than it used to be. You see I have something more to expect, to look forward to, to watch. I really do eat better, and am more quiet than I was.

John is so pleased to see me improve! He laughed a little the other day, and said I seemed to be flourishing in spite of my wallpaper.

I turned it off with a laugh. I had no intention of telling him it was *because* of the wallpaper—he would make fun of me. He might even want to take me away.

170   I don't want to leave now until I have found it out. There is a week more, and I think that will be enough.

I'm feeling ever so much better! I don't sleep much at night, for it is so interesting to watch developments; but I sleep a good deal in the daytime.

In the daytime it is tiresome and perplexing.

There are always new shoots on the fungus, and new shades of yellow all over it. I cannot keep count of them, though I have tried conscientiously.

It is the strangest yellow, that wallpaper! It makes me think of all the yellow things I ever saw—not beautiful ones like buttercups, but old foul, bad yellow things.

175   But there is something else about that paper—the smell! I noticed it the moment we came into the room, but with so much air and sun it was not bad. Now we have had a week of fog and rain, and whether the windows are open or not, the smell is here.

It creeps all over the house.

I find it hovering in the dining-room, skulking in the parlor, hiding in the hall, lying in wait for me on the stairs.

It gets into my hair.

Even when I go to ride, if I turn my head suddenly and surprise it—there is that smell!

180   Such a peculiar odor, too! I have spent hours in trying to analyze it, to find what it smelled like.

It is not bad—at first, and very gentle, but quite the subtlest, most enduring odor I ever met.

In this damp weather it is awful, I wake up in the night and find it hanging over me.

It used to disturb me at first. I thought seriously of burning the house—to reach the smell.

But now I am used to it. The only thing I can think of that it is like is the *color* of the paper! A yellow smell.

185   There is a very funny mark on this wall, low down, near the mopboard. A streak that runs round the room. It goes behind every piece of furniture, except the bed, a long, straight, even *smooch,* as if it had been rubbed over and over.

I wonder how it was done and who did it, and what they did it for. Round and round and round—round and round and round—it makes me dizzy!

I really have discovered something at last.

Through watching so much at night, when it changes so, I have finally found out.

The front pattern *does* move—and no wonder! The woman behind shakes it!

190   Sometimes I think there are a great many women behind, and sometimes only one, and she crawls around fast, and her crawling shakes it all over.

Then in the very bright spots she keeps still, and in the very shady spots she just takes hold of the bars and shakes them hard.

And she is all the time trying to climb through. But nobody could climb through that pattern—it strangles so; I think that is why it has so many heads.

They get through, and then the pattern strangles them off and turns them upside down, and makes their eyes white!

If those heads were covered or taken off it would not be half so bad.

195   I think that woman gets out in the daytime!

And I'll tell you why—privately—I've seen her!

I can see her out of every one of my windows!

It is the same woman, I know, for she is always creeping, and most women do not creep by daylight.

I see her on that long road under the trees, creeping along, and when a carriage comes she hides under the blackberry vines.

200   I don't blame her a bit. It must be very humiliating to be caught creeping by daylight!

I always lock the door when I creep by daylight. I can't do it at night, for I know John would suspect something at once.

And John is so queer now, that I don't want to irritate him. I wish he would take another room! Besides, I don't want anybody to get that woman out at night but myself.

I often wonder if I could see her out of all the windows at once.

But, turn as fast as I can, I can only see out of one at a time.

205 And though I always see her, she *may* be able to creep faster than I can turn! I have watched her sometimes away off in the open country, creeping as fast as a cloud shadow in a high wind.

If only that top pattern could be gotten off from the under one! I mean to try it, little by little.

I have found out another funny thing, but I shan't tell it this time! It does not do to trust people too much.

There are only two more days to get this paper off, and I believe John is beginning to notice. I don't like the look in his eyes.

210 And I heard him ask Jennie a lot of professional questions about me. She had a very good report to give.

She said I slept a good deal in the daytime.

John knows I don't sleep very well at night, for all I'm so quiet!

He asked me all sorts of questions, too, and pretended to be very loving and kind.

As if I couldn't see through him!

215 Still, I don't wonder he acts so, sleeping under this paper for three months.

It only interests me, but I feel sure John and Jennie are secretly affected by it.

Hurrah! This is the last day, but it is enough. John is to stay in town over night, and won't be out until this evening.

Jennie wanted to sleep with me—the sly thing! but I told her I should undoubtedly rest better for a night all alone.

That was clever, for really I wasn't alone a bit! As soon as it was moonlight and that poor thing began to crawl and shake the pattern, I got up and ran to help her.

220 I pulled and she shook, I shook and she pulled, and before morning we had peeled off yards of that paper.

A strip about as high as my head and half around the room.

And then when the sun came and that awful pattern began to laugh at me, I declared I would finish it today!

We go away tomorrow, and they are moving all my furniture down again to leave things as they were before.

Jennie looked at the wall in amazement, but I told her merrily that I did it out of pure spite at the vicious thing.

225 She laughed and said she wouldn't mind doing it herself, but I must not get tired.

How she betrayed herself that time!

But I am here, and no person touches this paper but me—not *alive!*

She tried to get me out of the room—it was too patent! But I said it was so quiet and empty and clean now that I believed I would lie down again and sleep all I could; and not to wake me even for dinner—I would call when I woke.

So now she is gone, and the servants are gone, and the things are gone, and there is nothing left but that great bedstead nailed down, with the canvas mattress we found on it.

230   We shall sleep downstairs tonight, and take the boat home tomorrow.

I quite enjoy the room, now it is bare again.

How those children did tear about here!

This bedstead is fairly gnawed!

But I must get to work.

235   I have locked the door and thrown the key down into the front path.

I don't want to go out, and I don't want to have anybody come in, till John comes.

I want to astonish him.

I've got a rope up here that even Jennie did not find. If that woman does get out, and tries to get away, I can tie her!

But I forgot I could not reach far without anything to stand on!

240   This bed will *not* move!

I tried to lift and push it until I was lame, and then I got so angry I bit off a little piece at one corner—but it hurt my teeth.

Then I peeled off all the paper I could reach standing on the floor. It sticks horribly and the pattern just enjoys it! All those strangled heads and bulbous eyes and waddling fungus growths just shriek with derision!

I am getting angry enough to do something desperate. To jump out of the window would be admirable exercise, but the bars are too strong even to try.

Besides I wouldn't do it. Of course not. I know well enough that a step like that is improper and might be misconstrued.

245   I don't like to *look* out of the windows even—there are so many of those creeping women, and they creep so fast.

I wonder if they all come out of that wallpaper as I did?

But I am securely fastened now by my well-hidden rope—you don't get *me* out in the road there!

I suppose I shall have to get back behind the pattern when it comes night, and that is hard!

It is so pleasant to be out in this great room and creep around as I please!

250   I don't want to go outside. I won't, even if Jennie asks me to.

For outside you have to creep on the ground, and everything is green instead of yellow.

But here I can creep smoothly on the floor, and my shoulder just fits in that long smooch around the wall, so I cannot lose my way.

Why there's John at the door!

It is no use, young man, you can't open it!

255   How he does call and pound!

Now he's crying for an axe.

It would be a shame to break down that beautiful door!

"John dear!" said I in the gentlest voice, "the key is down by the front steps, under a plantain leaf!"

That silenced him for a few moments.

260   Then he said—very quietly indeed, "Open the door, my darling!"

"I can't", said I. "The key is down by the front door under a plantain leaf!"

And then I said it again, several times, very gently and slowly, and said it so often that he had to go and see, and he got it of course, and came in. He stopped short by the door.

"What is the matter?" he cried. "For God's sake, what are you doing!"

I kept on creeping just the same, but I looked at him over my shoulder.

265   "I've got out at last," said I, "in spite of you and Jane. And I've pulled off most of the paper, so you can't put me back!"

Now why should that man have fainted? But he did, and right across my path by the wall, so that I had to creep over him every time!

INQUIRING FURTHER

1. Which of the theories outlined on pages 346-47 did you find yourself focusing on as you read? Can you think of ways that these theoretical perspectives might help you develop an interpretation of the work?

2. Did you recognize moments when the narrator addressed the reader directly? Were there times when events in the story undercut the statements of the narrator?

3. What are your thoughts on the rest cure? What passages from the story would you interpret in terms of the cure? Can you recognize any other historical connections in the work?

4. Would issues of feminism help explain the relationship between the narrator and her husband? What role in the story does writing play for the female narrator?

5. What comes to mind when you think of the psychology of the narrator in the story? What factors are most significant in understanding the narrator's state of mind?

EXPLORING CRITICAL APPROACHES

To get a better sense of these critical theories, we will turn to a detailed discussion of formal/structural, poststructural, feminist, historical, and psychological approaches to literature. We will also continue our exploration of "The Yellow Wallpaper." Our discussion offers an overview aimed at helping you learn to use critical theories to develop interpretations. For more detailed information about critical theories, see the resources on our CD.

Formal and Structural Criticism

Formal or structural theories emphasize how works are structured and how language operates. Works can engage our senses through formal techniques like irony and through their organization and narrative structure. Further, works can be understood coherently; they present self-contained artifacts that can be examined on their own terms. Exploring literary techniques and structures requires an emphasis on close reading, analyzing and describing the formal details of a work.

Structuralism emphasizes the way that the formal elements of language combine to create understanding. Early structuralists like Ferdinand de Saussure, for instance, examined how words can be read as **signs;** we can determine the meaning of signs by relating them to other signs. Roland Barthes expanded on this notion by applying it to popular culture. Barthes contended that not only words, but also items like advertisements or photographs, even wrestling matches could be read as signs.

Studying
formalism

Formalist and structural approaches can help us analyze components of works (like characters, rhymes, or camera angles) and relate them to other components and patterns. We can explore words in terms of one another and analyze closely the elements of literature. At the same time, however, a number of alternative theories have pointed out that formalist approaches may overlook issues ranging from race, to gender, to history, to economics.

Reading "The Yellow Wallpaper" Formally

To explore formalist and structuralist approaches to "The Yellow Wallpaper," we might look at elements like the narration and structure of the work. Notice how the story is broken into episodes. Just before the first episode break in the story, for instance, the narrator begins to reveal her thinking about the wallpaper when she is interrupted by her husband's approach. Immediately, the narrator confides in the reader, "There comes John, and I must put this away—he hates to have me write a word" (350). The narrator breaks out of the typical first-person storytelling frame, shares a secret with the reader, and deliberately calls our attention to the fact that she is writing.

The structure and narrative techniques also reveal questions about the narrator's credibility. For instance, prior to one interruption, the narrator refers to a yellow smooch on her clothes. Later, we are told "there is a very funny mark on this wall, low down, near the mopboard . . . a long, straight, even *smooch,* as if it had been rubbed over and over" (356 emphasis added). Later still, the narrator observes that the bed had been gnawed, then admits that she has bitten "off a little piece" of the bed herself. By considering these patterns, we are able to see how the structure of the story undercuts the narrator's authority.

Exercise 13.1   *Investigating the Narrator's Credibility*

Working on your own, respond to the following prompts as you revisit "The Yellow Wallpaper." Begin by preparing to take notes.

1. Look through the story for moments when the narrator reveals information that sheds doubt on her credibility. Are there any patterns that emerge in these moments? Do they seem to be deliberate revelations or more like slips on the part of the narrator? Do they change during the course of the story? Write three or more sentences describing how these moments function.

2. Consider elements of the story that you accept at face value. What makes these passages seem believable? How do questions about the narrator's credibility elsewhere influence your understanding of these believable moments? Write three or more sentences describing the believable moments of the story.

3. Compose a two- or three-paragraph exploration of the credibility of the narrator. Develop an evaluation expressing your conclusions. Use examples to illustrate your points. Explore as well how your sense of

the narrator's credibility influences your interpretation of the story as a whole.

Poststructural Approaches to Literature

In some ways, poststructural theories of literature simply represent variations on the formal and structural approaches discussed above. **Deconstruction,** the best known example of poststructuralist theory, takes the kind of symbol system proposed by Saussure and examines it with a much less optimistic eye. Instead of signs taking on meaning based on their relationships with other signs, signs continually slip away from other signs as we try to establish their meaning. For the theorist who best represents deconstruction, Jacques Derrida, there is never an absolute reference for any sign, so language (and the meaning of literary works) is always open to interpretation.

Deconstruction in many ways enables other theories by demonstrating that language is not a transparent medium through which we communicate. Instead, distortions play out through language and influence our identities and beliefs in ways we are not fully aware of. Theorists like Michel Foucault and Louis Althusser have extended these kinds of criticisms by exploring how concepts like power and ideology exert influence on individuals and culture through the medium of language.

Studying poststructuralism

Poststructuralism in "The Yellow Wallpaper"

By questioning accepted interpretations, deconstruction opens avenues for exploring alternative perspectives. One deconstructive strategy is to place terms (like "men" and "women") under scrutiny until complexities and multiple meanings emerge. "The Yellow Wallpaper" provides a handy pair in its use of the sun and the moon to illustrate changes in the narrator's perception of the wallpaper. The narrator reports that,

> There is one marked peculiarity about this paper, a thing nobody seems to notice but myself, and that is that it changes as the light changes.
>
> When the sun shoots in through the east window—I always watch for that first long, straight ray—it changes so quickly that I never can quite believe it.
>
> That is why I watch it always.
>
> By moonlight—the moon shines in all night when there is a moon—I wouldn't know it was the same paper.
>
> At night in any kind of light, in twilight, candle light, lamplight, and worst of all by moonlight, it becomes bars! The outside pattern I mean, and the woman behind it is as plain as can be. (354–55)

We could develop a reading based on the relationships between the sun and the moon. We might trace the **etymology** (the history) of the terms sun and moon, and learn that the sun has been associated with religious gods and aligned with masculinity. Conversely, the moon has been associated with femininity. We might argue that the story sets up a distinction between masculinity and femininity through the contrasting figures of the sun and the moon.

However, we would be premature in supposing that this contrast privileges masculinity over femininity. The story ends in daylight, suggesting the feminine has once again been subjugated to the masculine. At the same time, the narrator clearly is in a superior position to her unconscious husband, so perhaps the feminine has also overturned the masculine. Were we to investigate these terms further, we would discover that even our original associations of the sun and moon with gender are suspect. Before the sun was associated with male gods, it was often seen instead as a feminine symbol. Ultimately, the suggestion is that neither the narrator or John, the feminine or the masculine, is able escape the confusion of language. From this investigation, we might proceed to consider further how issues of gender play out within the medium of language.

Feminism, and Theories of Race and Sexuality

Of particular interest to feminist critics is the way in which language exerts a male-dominated, or **patriarchic** influence on our identities and actions. The theorist Hélène Cixous, for instance, argues that the influence of language limits opportunities for women. For Cixous, language associates masculinity with action and speech while aligning femininity with passivity and silence. Cixous argues that language shapes our identities, so that we accept these associations as a normal part of our thinking. As Cixous puts it, "as soon as we exist, we are born into language and language speaks (to) us, dictates its law" (Cixous 482). For feminists, this law, this influence of language, privileges masculinity.

Some feminist theories suggest that women's writing is distorted by the male-centered medium of language. Others argue that by disrupting the established system of language, women can resist masculine influences and subvert the traditional associations that align men with power and women with passivity. Feminist theories also ask why some forms of writing have been privileged in both their reception in society and the attention given to them by scholarship. Comparing the responses to a work like *Moby Dick,* for instance, to the treatment of the poetry of Emily Dickinson can reveal potential biases toward masculine expression. Feminism seeks not only to rectify any disparities between the treatment of women and men, but also to educate us about the way language influences our understanding of the feminine and masculine.

Studying theories of gender, race, and sexuality

Like feminism, theoretical approaches concerned with race or sexuality suggest that language acts as a controlling or marginalizing force. For theories of race, the controlling forces of language and culture are primarily aligned with the values of Western or Anglo culture and expression. Theories of sexuality investigate the ways in which concepts such as homosexuality, heterosexuality, and even gender can be seen as constructs driven by the shaping forces of culture and language. (For more on theories of race and sexuality see the resources on our CD.)

Exercise 13.2   *Exploring Feminism in "The Yellow Wallpaper"*

Working on your own or with a group, explore the relationships between writing and gender in "The Yellow Wallpaper." Begin by selecting a person to keep track of the group's work or preparing to take notes on your own, and then respond to the following prompts.

1. What do you make of the importance of writing for the narrator? Make a list of at least three passages that could be used for an exploration of gender and writing.

2. Does the narrator conceal her writing from Jennie in the same way she conceals it from her husband? Write three or more sentences exploring the role of secrecy in the narrator's writing.

3. If you had to put a label on the wallpaper, would you associate it with the masculine or feminine? How does the label you apply relate to the narrator's descriptions of the wallpaper? Write three or more sentences exploring gender associations for the wallpaper.

4. Write a paragraph or two in which you explore the relationships between writing and gender in "The Yellow Wallpaper." Refer to passages from the text and consider acts of writing, secrecy, relationships, the wallpaper, the woman in the wallpaper, the state of mind of the narrator, or any other themes that help you discuss the narrator in terms of women's writing.

Historical Criticism

Historical approaches argue that a work is influenced by the society that produces it. This is quite a contrast from formalist conceptions of literature that see a work as an autonomous whole, something that can be understood coherently based on its own structure. Instead, in order to understand a work, historicists argue, we need to examine how artists respond to the cultural forces that surround them. Further, by examining works of literature, we can learn something about the historical eras in which they were produced.

Advocate of historical approaches, Stephen Greenblatt, argues that works of literature not only reveal aspects of history, but also act to influence the cultures in which they are produced. In some versions of historical criticism, because works are products of the history that shapes them, the autonomy of the author is diminished. In other versions, there is room for resistance of the dominant forces that shape culture. Ultimately, historical theories invite us to consider the relationships between culture and art at any given time.

Historical Approaches to "The Yellow Wallpaper"

We have already mentioned that Gilman composed "The Yellow Wallpaper" partially in response to treatments she received from S. Weir Mitchell for what was at the time diagnosed as a nervous condition. We might conduct research to locate medical treatises that shed light on thinking about neurosis in the nineteenth century, and then discuss the story in terms of that information. Initially, we might suppose that John represents a callous husband who is incapable of listening to the concerns of the narrator. However, historical knowledge reveals that John's behavior reflects what at the time was believed to be responsible medical practice. Perhaps, then, the story provides less of an indictment against John the husband and more of an illustration of John the nineteenth-century doctor.

Psychological Approaches

Psychological criticism focuses on feelings and desires, or on the relationships between the self, language, and others. Psychological approaches often refer to the work of Sigmund Freud, who established the field of **psychoanalysis.** Freud encouraged patients to recite stories of their childhood as a way of discovering hidden memories. A key concept for Freudian psychological criticism is the **unconscious,** an area of our thinking that we normally have no access to. Feelings from the past, especially those related to childhood, remain hidden, surfacing in dreams or slips of the tongue.

Freud's theories center around the process of maturation from infancy to adulthood. Infants are entirely dependent on their mothers, Freud suggests, only to realize as they grow older that a painful separation has developed between their own sense of self and the mother who has nurtured them. Sexuality becomes a key component of emotional development, with boys developing what Freud termed the Oedipus complex: a longing to kill their fathers to fulfill a desire for their mothers. Girls develop a sense of inadequacy as they realize that, like their mother, they lack a penis. Eventually, boys and girls replace these desires by identifying with the parent of their sex and transitioning into mature sexuality.

Studying psychological criticism

Obviously, Freud's conception of mental and sexual development is open to critique. Feminist criticism is quick to point out that when Freud associates inadequacy with a girl's longing for a penis, he may be simply projecting his own desire to dominate women. Still, psychological theories help us think about the ways that unconscious impulses and desires can be expressed. In addition to dreams, literature can be seen as one of the primary lenses through which we may view the workings beneath the surface of consciousness, opening a number of avenues for developing interpretations.

Psychological Approaches to "The Yellow Wallpaper"

Exploring the story from a psychological perspective can lead to a number of interpretations. We have already mentioned that the narrator at times breaks off her story as traumatic events come closer to the surface. We could trace the patterns of the narrative in more detail by looking at the relationship between the conscious and unconscious thoughts of the narrator and these interruptions.

We might also explore the story in terms of psychoanalytical theories of childhood and maturation. We could analyze the significance of the children who previously occupied the home, or the narrator's own child. Or, we could consider instances in the story where John refuses to treat the narrator as an adult. We can look more closely at these moments of **infantilization** (the treating of an adult as if she were a child). The infantilization can be seen as a response by John to the narrator's efforts to assert herself and intervene in her own treatment.

Exercise 13.3   *Considering Issues of Childhood*

Working with a group of fellow students or on your own, explore the theme of childhood in "The Yellow Wallpaper." Begin by selecting a recorder to keep track of the group's work or preparing to take notes on your own, and then respond to the following prompts.

1. How important is the fact that the narrator has recently given birth? How is this information revealed and emphasized in the work and what can

you say about its level of prominence in the story? Write three sentences, exploring issues related to the narrator as a mother.

2. What influence do the children who once occupied the home have on the story? How do we learn about them? How would you relate them to the setting of the story? How would you relate them to the narrator? Write three or more sentences exploring the children who used to live in the house.

3. How do views of childhood influence your reading of the story as a whole? What do you make of the relationship between John and the narrator in terms of childhood? How does the narrator's status as a new mother influence your thinking? Write two or three paragraphs exploring the theme of childhood in the story.

✔CHECKLIST FOR STUDYING CRITICAL APPROACHES TO LITERATURE

☐ **Think of theories as extensions of critical inquiry.** Theories provide avenues for exploring a work. Use theories to ground the analysis, synthesis, and evaluation you undertake as you develop interpretations.

☐ **Recognize concerns with language and culture** addressed by theory. Criticism tends to investigate not only particular works, but also the intersections of literature, language, and culture. Considering these dimensions can make theories more approachable.

☐ **Learn from formal and structural approaches.** Develop your own close reading skills and look for similar levels of detail in the interpretations of others. Expect other forms of theory to also employ techniques of close reading.

☐ **Use poststructural techniques** to scrutinize the meanings of words and the workings of language. Keep a healthy suspicion about interpretations, considering alternative possibilities and freely exploring multiple perspectives.

☐ **Employ psychological approaches** to explore dimensions of the self revealed through literature. Look also at the ways psychology illuminates issues of childhood and development.

☐ **Use historical perspectives** to investigate the relationships between literature and culture. Consider not only how culture shapes literature, but also how literature influences culture.

☐ **Explore the controlling and marginalizing influences of language.** Consider how works of literature privilege some identities and exclude others. Investigate how language relates to concepts like self, race, gender, nation, or sexuality.

☐ **Remember that literary theory invites you to make your own judgments.** Be prepared to recognize areas of overlap among critical theories. Select the approaches that best allow you to build upon your personal responses to develop critical interpretations.

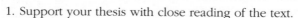

INQUIRING FURTHER

1. Why do you think critical theory expanded beyond the approaches of formalism and structuralism? Do you believe there is something inherently wrong with those approaches? If so, what and why? What role should purely formal approaches have in the study of literature?

2. What do you think of deconstruction's claims about the indeterminacy of language? Just how capable of communicating clearly do you believe language to be? What impact does confusion in communication have on our daily lives? What impact does it have on our engagements with literature?

3. Do you believe that our identities are shaped by language? Can you think of a way of expressing identity without language? Can you think of a way of not expressing, but simply conceptualizing identity without language? Freewrite for five minutes about the ways that language shapes our identities.

4. How powerfully do you think cultural forces are in shaping our beliefs and influencing our actions? Do you think that language and culture privilege certain groups? Write a paragraph explaining your position on the influences of language and culture.

Exercise 13.4 *Approaching "The Yellow Wallpaper" Critically*

Works to
consult for
further
study

Write an essay of four or more pages in which you take up one of the theoretical approaches discussed in this chapter and develop an interpretation of "The Yellow Wallpaper." You can use the discussion above as the basis for the approach you develop, refining and building upon the possible interpretations we have already sketched out. (If you feel as if you have already explored "The Yellow Wallpaper" extensively, you may wish to write about another work.) In your essay, articulate a thesis that draws upon a theoretical approach to offer a way of understanding the story.

1. Support your thesis with close reading of the text.

2. Extend this close reading by drawing conclusions that make connections with your thesis.

3. Revise your work using the strategies of the writing process discussed in Chapter 8. Be sure to document your sources (see the Appendix).

Thematic Collection
of Works

14

Choice and Consequence

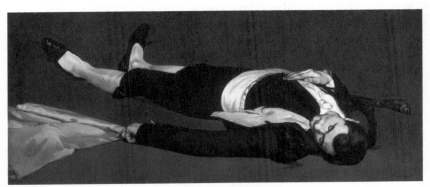

The Dead Toreador, *Widener Collection, Image © 2004 Board of Trustees, National Gallery of Art, Washington, D.C.*

Édourd Manet includes few objects in his nineteenth-century oil painting, *The Dead Toreador.* A cape is spread out in the lower left quadrant of the painting and the body of the toreador fills the rest of the frame. The techniques in the painting are equally direct. The strong use of darkness and light, a limited use of color, and striking shapes suggest simple distinctions, a scene where contrasts are as obvious as the fate of the fallen bullfighter.

Human choices and their results, however, are never that straightforward. Conflicts rarely offer us simple choices between black or white, and the impact of our decisions can be impossible to predict. Further, our backgrounds influence our choices and actions. These complexities ask us to make judgments about **ethics**, the consideration of human choices and the impact actions have on ourselves and others.

In this chapter, we will look at how the complexities of ethics reveal themselves in works of art and literature. Early selections explore crime and death. Later selections consider how we act collectively, and how we respond to one another. Selections at the end of the chapter consider dilemmas raised by war and economics. Obviously, the works represent a small percentage of what has been written about ethical questions. They also cannot be reduced to simple explanations of choosing between right and wrong.

As you explore the works below, look for overlap between the themes covered here. Consider, for instance, how death might relate to economics, or suicide to crime. Look also for ways of connecting the works to other topics found in literature—what other broad themes (such as self and society, or innocence and experience) might you use to evaluate a work? Be sure, also, to refer to related works on our CD as you explore these issues of choice and consequence.

CRIME AND DEATH

Criminal behavior and death are nothing new in human culture. The ethical questions surrounding crime and death, however, continue to call for our thinking and response. Among other things, we are asked to consider the causes of crime, the punishments that should be meted out for criminal actions, our beliefs about death, and the relationship between individuals and society (a key theme covered in Chapter 15 as well). As you explore the selections below, consider how these concerns are represented in the works, and how the works illuminate or complicate your own thinking about these issues.

FLANNERY O'CONNOR

Flannery O'Connor (1925–1964) stands as one of the American South's best-known writers. Her stories treat rural communities and characters in realistic detail; she grew up in Georgia, during the 1920s and 1930s. When she was 25, she became ill with Lupus disease (which had killed her father ten years earlier). O'Connor wrote much of her work while struggling with the disease. Our selection below is the title piece from her second collection of short stories which she published in 1955, A Good Man Is Hard to Find.

A Good Man Is Hard to Find

Studying
"A Good
Man Is
Hard to
Find"

The grandmother didn't want to go to Florida. She wanted to visit some of her connections in east Tennessee and she was seizing at every chance to change Bailey's mind. Bailey was the son she lived with, her only boy. He was sitting on the edge of his chair at the table, bent over the orange sports section of the *Journal*. "Now look here, Bailey," she said, "see here, read this," and she stood with one hand on her thin hip and the other rattling the newspaper at his bald head. "Here this fellow that calls himself The Misfit is aloose from the Federal Pen and headed toward Florida and you read here what it says he did to these people. Just you read it. I wouldn't take my children in any direction with a criminal like that aloose in it. I couldn't answer to my conscience if I did."

Bailey didn't look up from his reading so she wheeled around then and faced the children's mother, a young woman in slacks, whose face was as broad and innocent as a cabbage and was tied around with a green head-kerchief that had two points on the top like rabbit's ears. She was sitting on the sofa, feeding the baby his apricots out of a jar. "The children have been to Florida before," the old lady said. "You all ought to take them somewhere else for a change so they would see different parts of the world and be broad. They never have been to east Tennessee."

The children's mother didn't seem to hear her but the eight-year-old boy, John Wesley, a stocky child with glasses said, "If you don't want to go to Florida, why dontcha stay at home?" He and the little girl, June Star, were reading the funny papers on the floor.

"She wouldn't stay at home to be queen for a day," June Star said without raising her yellow head.

5   "Yes and what would you do if this fellow, The Misfit, caught you?" the grandmother asked.

"I'd smack his face," John Wesley said.

"She wouldn't stay at home for a million bucks," June Star said. "Afraid she'd miss something. She has to go everywhere we go."

"All right, Miss," the grandmother said. "Just remember that the next time you want me to curl your hair."

June Star said her hair was naturally curly.

10   The next morning the grandmother was the first one in the car, ready to go. She had her big black valise that looked like the head of a hippopotamus in one corner, and underneath it she was hiding a basket with Pitty Sing, the cat, in it. She didn't intend for the cat to be left alone in the house for three days because he would miss her too much and she was afraid he might brush against one of the gas burners and accidentally asphyxiate himself. Her son, Bailey, didn't like to arrive at a motel with a cat.

She sat in the middle of the back seat with John Wesley and June Star on either side of her. Bailey and the children's mother and the baby sat in front and they left Atlanta at eight forty-five with the mileage on the car at 55890. The grandmother wrote this down because she thought it would be interesting to say how many miles they had been when they got back. It took them twenty minutes to reach the outskirts of the city.

The old lady settled herself comfortably, removing her white cotton gloves and putting them up with her purse on the shelf in front of the back window. The children's mother still had on slacks and still had her head tied up in a green kerchief, but the grandmother had on a navy blue straw sailor hat with a bunch of white violets on the brim and a navy blue dress with a small white dot in the print. Her collars and cuffs were white organdy trimmed with lace and at her neckline she had pinned a purple spray of cloth violets containing a sachet. In case of an accident, anyone seeing her dead on the highway would know at once that she was a lady.

She said she thought it was going to be a good day for driving, neither too hot nor too cold, and she cautioned Bailey that the speed limit was fifty-five miles an hour and that the patrolmen hid themselves behind billboards and small clumps of trees and sped out after you before you had a chance to slow down. She pointed out interesting details of the scenery: Stone Mountain; the blue granite that in some places came up to both sides of the highway; the brilliant red clay banks slightly streaked with purple; and the various crops that made rows of green lace-work on the ground. The trees were full of silver-white sunlight and the meanest of them sparkled. The children were reading comic magazines and their mother had gone back to sleep.

"Let's go through Georgia fast so we won't have to look at it much," John Wesley said.

15   "If I were a little boy," said the grandmother, "I wouldn't talk about my native state that way. Tennessee has the mountains and Georgia has the hills."

"Tennessee is just a hillbilly dumping ground," John Wesley said, "and Georgia is a lousy state too."

"You said it," June Star said.

"In my time," said the grandmother, folding her thin veined fingers, "children were more respectful of their native states and their parents and everything else. People did right then. Oh look at the cute little pickaninny!" she said and pointed to a Negro child standing in the door of a shack. "Wouldn't that make a picture, now?" she asked and they all turned and looked at the little Negro out of the back window. He waved.

"He didn't have any britches on," June Star said.

20   "He probably didn't have any," the grandmother explained. "Little niggers in the country don't have things like we do. If I could paint, I'd paint that picture," she said.

The children exchanged comic books.

The grandmother offered to hold the baby and the children's mother passed him over the front seat to her. She set him on her knee and bounced him and told him about the things they were passing. She rolled her eyes and screwed up her mouth and stuck her leathery thin face into his smooth bland one. Occasionally he gave her a far away smile. They passed a large cotton field with five or six graves fenced in the middle of it, like a small island.

"Look at the graveyard!" the grandmother said, pointing it out. "That was the old family burying ground. That belonged to the plantation."

"Where's the plantation?" John Wesley asked.

25   "Gone With the Wind," said the grandmother. "Ha Ha."

When the children finished all the comic books they had brought, they opened the lunch and ate it. The grandmother ate a peanut butter sandwich and an olive and would not let the children throw the box and the paper napkins out the window. When there was nothing else to do they played a game by choosing a cloud and making the other two guess what shape it suggested. John Wesley took one the shape of a cow and June Star guessed a cow and John Wesley said, no, an automobile, and June Star said he didn't play fair, and they began to slap each other over the grandmother.

The grandmother said she would tell them a story if they would keep quiet. When she told a story, she rolled her eyes and waved her head and was very dramatic. She said once when she was a maiden lady she had been courted by a Mr. Edgar Atkins Teagarden from Jasper, Georgia. She said he was a very good-looking man and a gentleman and that he brought her a watermelon every Saturday afternoon with his initials cut in it, E. A. T. Well, one Saturday, she said, Mr. Teagarden brought the watermelon and there was nobody at home and he left it on the front porch and returned in his buggy to Jasper, but she never got the watermelon, she said, because a nigger boy ate it when he saw the initials, E. A. T.! This story tickled John Wesley's funny bone and he giggled and giggled but June Star didn't think it was any good. She said she wouldn't marry a man that just brought her a watermelon on Saturday. The grandmother said she would have done well to marry Mr. Teagarden because he was a gentleman and had bought Coca-Cola stock when it first came out and that he had died only a few years ago, a very wealthy man.

They stopped at The Tower for barbecued sandwiches. The Tower was a part stucco and part wood filling station and dance hall set in a clearing outside of Timothy. A fat man named Red Sammy Butts ran it and there were signs stuck here and there on the building and for miles up and down the highway saying, TRY RED SAMMY'S FAMOUS BARBECUE. NONE LIKE FAMOUS RED SAMMY'S! RED SAM! THE FAT BOY WITH THE HAPPY LAUGH. A VETERAN! RED SAMMY'S YOUR MAN!

Red Sammy was lying on the bare ground outside The Tower with his head under a truck while a gray monkey about a foot high, chained to a small chinaberry tree, chattered nearby. The monkey sprang back into the tree and got on the highest limb as soon as he saw the children jump out of the car and run toward him.

30 Inside, The Tower was a long dark room with a counter at one end and tables at the other and dancing space in the middle. They all sat down at a board table next to the nickelodeon and Red Sam's wife, a tall burnt-brown woman with hair and eyes lighter than her skin, came and took their order. The children's mother put a dime in the machine and played "The Tennessee Waltz," and the grandmother said that tune always made her want to dance. She asked Bailey if he would like to dance but he only glared at her. He didn't have a naturally sunny disposition like she did and trips made him nervous. The grandmother's brown eyes were very bright. She swayed her head from side to side and pretended she was dancing in her chair. June Star said play something she could tap to so the children's mother put in another dime and played a fast number and June Star stepped out onto the dance floor and did her tap routine.

"Ain't she cute?" Red Sam's wife said, leaning over the counter. "Would you like to come be my little girl?"

"No I certainly wouldn't," June Star said. "I wouldn't live in a broken-down place like this for a million bucks!" and she ran back to the table.

"Ain't she cute?" the woman repeated, stretching her mouth politely.

"Arn't you ashamed?" hissed the grandmother.

35 Red Sam came in and told his wife to quit lounging on the counter and hurry up with these people's order. His khaki trousers reached just to his hip bones and his stomach hung over them like a sack of meal swaying under his shirt. He came over and sat down at a table nearby and let out a combination sigh and yodel. "You can't win," he said. "You can't win," and he wiped his sweating red face off with a gray handkerchief. "These days you don't know who to trust," he said. "Ain't that the truth?"

"People are certainly not nice like they used to be," said the grandmother.

"Two fellers come in here last week," Red Sammy said, "driving a Chrysler. It was a old beat-up car but it was a good one and these boys looked all right to me. Said they worked at the mill and you know I let them fellers charge the gas they bought? Now why did I do that?"

"Because you're a good man!" the grandmother said at once.

"Yes'm, I suppose so," Red Sam said as if he were struck with this answer.

40 His wife brought the orders, carrying the five plates all at once without a tray, two in each hand and one balanced on her arm. "It isn't a soul in this green world of God's that you can trust," she said. "And I don't count nobody out of that, not nobody," she repeated, looking at Red Sammy.

"Did you read about that criminal, The Misfit, that's escaped?" asked the grandmother.

"I wouldn't be a bit surprised if he didn't attact this place right here," said the woman. "If he hears about it being here, I wouldn't be none surprised to see him. If he hears it's two cent in the cash register, I wouldn't be a tall surprised if he . . . "

"That'll do," Red Sam said. "Go bring these people their Co'-Colas," and the woman went off to get the rest of the order.

"A good man is hard to find," Red Sammy said. "Everything is getting terrible. I remember the day you could go off and leave your screen door unlatched. Not no more."

45 He and the grandmother discussed better times. The old lady said that in her opinion Europe was entirely to blame for the way things were now. She said

the way Europe acted you would think we were made of money and Red Sam said it was no use talking about it, she was exactly right. The children ran outside into the white sunlight and looked at the monkey in the lacy chinaberry tree. He was busy catching fleas on himself and biting each one carefully between his teeth as if it were a delicacy.

They drove off again into the hot afternoon. The grandmother took cat naps and woke up every few minutes with her own snoring. Outside of Toombsboro she woke up and recalled an old plantation that she had visited in this neighborhood once when she was a young lady. She said the house had six white columns across the front and that there was an avenue of oaks leading up to it and two little wooden trellis arbors on either side in front where you sat down with your suitor after a stroll in the garden. She recalled exactly which road to turn off to get to it. She knew that Bailey would not be willing to lose any time looking at an old house, but the more she talked about it, the more she wanted to see it once again and find out if the little twin arbors were still standing. "There was a secret panel in this house," she said craftily, not telling the truth but wishing that she were, "and the story went that all the family silver was hidden in it when Sherman came through but it was never found . . . "

"Hey!" John Wesley said. "Let's go see it! We'll find it! We'll poke all the woodwork and find it! Who lives there? Where do you turn off at? Hey Pop, can't we turn off there?"

"We never have seen a house with a secret panel!" June Star shrieked. "Let's go to the house with the secret panel! Hey Pop, can't we go see the house with the secret panel!"

"It's not far from here, I know," the grandmother said. "It wouldn't take over twenty minutes."

50   Bailey was looking straight ahead. His jaw was as rigid as a horseshoe. "No," he said.

The children began to yell and scream that they wanted to see the house with the secret panel. John Wesley kicked the back of the front seat and June Star hung over her mother's shoulder and whined desperately into her ear that they never had any fun even on their vacation, that they could never do what THEY wanted to do. The baby began to scream and John Wesley kicked the back of the seat so hard that his father could feel the blows in his kidney.

"All right!" he shouted and drew the car to a stop at the side of the road. "Will you all shut up? Will you all just shut up for one second? If you don't shut up, we won't go anywhere."

"It would be very educational for them," the grandmother murmured.

"All right," Bailey said, "but get this: this is the only time we're going to stop for anything like this. This is the one and only time."

55   "The dirt road that you have to turn down is about a mile back," the grandmother directed. "I marked it when we passed."

"A dirt road," Bailey groaned.

After they had turned around and were headed toward the dirt road, the grandmother recalled other points about the house, the beautiful glass over the front doorway and the candle-lamp in the hall. John Wesley said that the secret panel was probably in the fireplace.

"You can't go inside this house," Bailey said. "You don't know who lives there."

"While you all talk to the people in front, I'll run around behind and get in a window," John Wesley suggested.

60   "We'll all stay in the car," his mother said.

They turned onto the dirt road and the car raced roughly along in a swirl of pink dust. The grandmother recalled the times when there were no paved roads and thirty miles was a day's journey. The dirt road was hilly and there were sudden washes in it and sharp curves on dangerous embankments. All at once they would be on a hill, looking down over the blue tops of trees for miles around, then the next minute, they would be in a red depression with the dust-coated trees looking down on them.

"This place had better turn up in a minute," Bailey said, "or I'm going to turn around."

The road looked as if no one had traveled on it in months.

"It's not much farther," the grandmother said and just as she said it, a horrible thought came to her. The thought was so embarrassing that she turned red in the face and her eyes dilated and her feet jumped up, upsetting her valise in the corner. The instant the valise moved, the newspaper top she had over the basket under it rose with a snarl and Pitty Sing, the cat, sprang onto Bailey's shoulder.

65   The children were thrown to the floor and their mother, clutching the baby, was thrown out the door onto the ground; the old lady was thrown into the front seat. The car turned over once and landed right-side-up in a gulch off the side of the road. Bailey remained in the driver's seat with the cat—gray-striped with a broad white face and an orange nose—clinging to his neck like a caterpillar.

As soon as the children saw they could move their arms and legs, they scrambled out of the car, shouting, "We've had an ACCIDENT!" The grandmother was curled up under the dashboard, hoping she was injured so that Bailey's wrath would not come down on her all at once. The horrible thought she had had before the accident was that the house she had remembered so vividly was not in Georgia but in Tennessee.

Bailey removed the cat from his neck with both hands and flung it out the window against the side of a pine tree. Then he got out of the car and started looking for the children's mother. She was sitting against the side of the red gutted ditch, holding the screaming baby, but she only had a cut down her face and a broken shoulder. "We've had an ACCIDENT!" the children screamed in a frenzy of delight.

"But nobody's killed," June Star said with disappointment as the grandmother limped out of the car, her hat still pinned to her head but the broken front brim standing up at a jaunty angle and the violet spray hanging off the side. They all sat down in the ditch, except the children, to recover from the shock. They were all shaking.

"Maybe a car will come along," said the children's mother hoarsely.

70   "I believe I have injured an organ," said the grandmother, pressing her side, but no one answered her. Bailey's teeth were clattering. He had on a yellow sport shirt with bright blue parrots designed in it and his face was as yellow as the shirt. The grandmother decided that she would not mention that the house was in Tennessee.

The road was about ten feet above and they could see only the tops of the trees on the other side of it. Behind the ditch they were sitting in there were more woods, tall and dark and deep. In a few minutes they saw a car some distance away on top of a hill, coming slowly as if the occupants were watching them. The grandmother stood up and waved both arms dramatically to attract their attention. The car continued to come on slowly, disappeared around a bend and appeared again, moving even slower, on top of the hill they had gone over. It was a big black battered hearse-like automobile. There were three men in it.

It came to a stop just over them and for some minutes, the driver looked down with a steady expressionless gaze to where they were sitting, and didn't speak. Then he turned his head and muttered something to the other two and they got out. One was a fat boy in black trousers and a red sweat shirt with a silver stallion embossed on the front of it. He moved around on the right side of them and stood staring, his mouth partly open in a kind of loose grin. The other had on khaki pants and a blue striped coat and a gray hat pulled down very low, hiding most of his face. He came around slowly on the left side. Neither spoke.

The driver got out of the car and stood by the side of it, looking down at them. He was an older man than the other two. His hair was just beginning to gray and he wore silver-rimmed spectacles that gave him a scholarly look. He had a long creased face and didn't have on any shirt or undershirt. He had on blue jeans that were too tight for him and was holding a black hat and a gun. The two boys also had guns.

"We've had an ACCIDENT!" the children screamed.

75   The grandmother had the peculiar feeling that the bespectacled man was some-one she knew. His face was as familiar to her as if she had known him all her life but she could not recall who he was. He moved away from the car and began to come down the embankment, placing his feet carefully so that he wouldn't slip. He had on tan and white shoes and no socks, and his ankles were red and thin. "Good afternoon," he said. "I see you all had you a little spill."

"We turned over twice!" said the grandmother.

"Oncet," he corrected. "We seen it happen. Try their car and see will it run, Hiram," he said quietly to the boy with the gray hat.

"What you got that gun for?" John Wesley asked. "Whatcha gonna do with that gun?"

"Lady," the man said to the children's mother, "would you mind calling them children to sit down by you? Children make me nervous. I want all you all to sit down right together there where you're at."

80   "What are you telling US what to do for?" June Star asked.

Behind them the line of woods gaped like a dark open mouth. "Come here," said their mother.

"Look here now," Bailey began suddenly, "we're in a predicament! We're in . . ."

The grandmother shrieked. She scrambled to her feet and stood staring. "You're The Misfit!" she said. "I recognized you at once!"

"Yes'm," the man said, smiling slightly as if he were pleased in spite of himself to be known, "but it would have been better for all of you, lady, if you hadn't of reckernized me."

85   Bailey turned his head sharply and said something to his mother that shocked even the children. The old lady began to cry and The Misfit red-dened.

"Lady," he said, "don't you get upset. Sometimes a man says things he don't mean. I don't reckon he meant to talk to you thataway."

"You wouldn't shoot a lady, would you?" the grandmother said and removed a clean handkerchief from her cuff and began to slap at her eyes with it.

The Misfit pointed the toe of his shoe into the ground and made a little hole and then covered it up again. "I would hate to have to," he said.

"Listen," the grandmother almost screamed, "I know you're a good man. You don't look a bit like you have common blood. I know you must come from nice people!"

90   "Yes mam," he said, "finest people in the world." When he smiled he showed a row of strong white teeth. "God never made a finer woman than my mother and my daddy's heart was pure gold," he said. The boy with the red sweat shirt had come around behind them and was standing with his gun at his hip. The Misfit squatted down on the ground. "Watch them children, Bobby Lee," he said. "You know they make me nervous." He looked at the six of them huddled together in front of him and he seemed to be embarrassed as if he couldn't think of anything to say. "Ain't a cloud in the sky," he remarked, looking up at it. "Don't see no sun but don't see no cloud neither." "Yes, it's a beautiful day," said the grandmother. "Listen," she said, "you shouldn't call yourself The Misfit because I know you're a good man at heart. I can just look at you and tell."

"Hush!" Bailey yelled. "Hush! Everybody shut up and let me handle this!" He was squatting in the position of a runner about to sprint forward but he didn't move.

"I pre-chate that, lady," The Misfit said and drew a little circle in the ground with the butt of his gun.

"It'll take a half a hour to fix this here car," Hiram called, looking over the raised hood of it.

"Well, first you and Bobby Lee get him and that little boy to step over yonder with you," The Misfit said, pointing to Bailey and John Wesley. "The boys want to ast you something," he said to Bailey. "Would you mind stepping back in them woods there with them?"

95   "Listen," Bailey began, "we're in a terrible predicament! Nobody realizes what this is," and his voice cracked. His eyes were as blue and intense as the parrots in his shirt and he remained perfectly still.

The grandmother reached up to adjust her hat brim as if she were going to the woods with him but it came off in her hand. She stood staring at it and after a second she let it fall on the ground. Hiram pulled Bailey up by the arm as if he were assisting an old man. John Wesley caught hold of his father's hand and Bobby Lee followed. They went off toward the woods and just as they reached the dark edge, Bailey turned and supporting himself against a gray naked pine trunk, he shouted, "I'll be back in a minute, Mamma, wait on me!"

"Come back this instant!" his mother shrilled but they all disappeared into the woods.

"Bailey Boy!" the grandmother called in a tragic voice but she found she was looking at The Misfit squatting on the ground in front of her. "I just know you're a good man," she said desperately. "You're not a bit common!"

"Nome, I ain't a good man," The Misfit said after a second as if he had considered her statement carefully "but I ain't the worst in the world neither. My daddy said I was a different breed of dog from my brothers and sisters. 'You know,' Daddy said, 'it's some that can live their whole life out without asking about it and it's others has to know why it is, and this boy is one of the latters. He's going to be into everything!' " He put on his black hat and looked up suddenly and then away deep into the woods as if he were embarrassed again. "I'm sorry I don't have on a shirt before you ladies," he said, hunching his shoulders slightly. "We buried our clothes that we had on when we escaped and we're just making do until we can get better. We borrowed these from some folks we met," he explained.

100   "That's perfectly all right," the grandmother said. "Maybe Bailey has an extra shirt in his suitcase."

"I'll look and see terrectly," The Misfit said.

"Where are they taking him?" the children's mother screamed.

"Daddy was a card himself," The Misfit said. "You couldn't put anything over on him. He never got in trouble with the Authorities though. Just had the knack of handling them."

"You could be honest too if you'd only try," said the grandmother. "Think how wonderful it would be to settle down and live a comfortable life and not have to think about somebody chasing you all the time."

105   The Misfit kept scratching in the ground with the butt of his gun as if he were thinking about it. "Yes'm, somebody is always after you," he murmured.

The grandmother noticed how thin his shoulder blades were just behind his hat because she was standing up looking down on him. "Do you ever pray?" she asked.

He shook his head. All she saw was the black hat wiggle between his shoulder blades. "Nome," he said.

There was a pistol shot from the woods, followed closely by another. Then silence. The old lady's head jerked around. She could hear the wind move through the tree tops like a long satisfied insuck of breath. "Bailey Boy!" she called.

"I was a gospel singer for a while," The Misfit said. "I been most everything. Been in the arm service, both land and sea, at home and abroad, been twict married, been an undertaker, been with the railroads, plowed Mother Earth, been in a tornado, seen a man burnt alive oncet," and he looked up at the children's mother and the little girl who were sitting close together, their faces white and their eyes glassy; "I even seen a woman flogged," he said.

110   "Pray, pray," the grandmother began, "pray, pray . . . "

"I never was a bad boy that I remember of," The Misfit said in an almost dreamy voice, "but somewheres along the line I done something wrong and got sent to the penitentiary. I was buried alive," and he looked up and held her attention to him by a steady stare.

"That's when you should have started to pray," she said. "What did you do to get sent to the penitentiary that first time?"

"Turn to the right, it was a wall," The Misfit said, looking up again at the cloudless sky. "Turn to the left, it was a wall. Look up it was a ceiling, look down it was a floor. I forget what I done, lady. I set there and set there, trying to remember what it was I done and I ain't recalled it to this day. Oncet in a while, I would think it was coming to me, but it never come."

"Maybe they put you in by mistake," the old lady said vaguely.

115   "Nome," he said. "It wasn't no mistake. They had the papers on me."

"You must have stolen something," she said.

The Misfit sneered slightly. "Nobody had nothing I wanted," he said. "It was a head-doctor at the penitentiary said what I had done was kill my daddy but I known that for a lie. My daddy died in nineteen ought nineteen of the epidemic flu and I never had a thing to do with it. He was buried in the Mount Hopewell Baptist churchyard and you can go there and see for yourself."

"If you would pray," the old lady said, "Jesus would help you."

"That's right," The Misfit said.

120   "Well then, why don't you pray?" she asked trembling with delight suddenly.

"I don't want no hep," he said. "I'm doing all right by myself."

Bobby Lee and Hiram came ambling back from the woods. Bobby Lee was dragging a yellow shirt with bright blue parrots in it.

"Thow me that shirt, Bobby Lee," The Misfit said. The shirt came flying at him and landed on his shoulder and he put it on. The grandmother couldn't name what the shirt reminded her of. "No, lady," The Misfit said while he was buttoning it up, "I found out the crime don't matter. You can do one thing or you can do another, kill a man or take a tire off his car, because sooner or later you're going to forget what it was you done and just be punished for it."

The children's mother had begun to make heaving noises as if she couldn't get her breath. "Lady," he asked, would you and that little girl like to step off yonder with Bobby Lee and Hiram and join your husband?"

125   "Yes, thank you," the mother said faintly. Her left arm dangled helplessly and she was holding the baby, who had gone to sleep, in the other. "Hep that lady up, Hiram," The Misfit said as she struggled to climb out of the ditch, "and Bobby Lee, you hold onto that little girl's hand."

"I don't want to hold hands with him," June Star said. "He reminds me of a pig."

The fat boy blushed and laughed and caught her by the arm and pulled her off into the woods after Hiram and her mother.

Alone with The Misfit, the grandmother found that she had lost her voice. There was not a cloud in the sky nor any sun. There was nothing around her but woods. She wanted to tell him that he must pray. She opened and closed her mouth several times before anything came out. Finally she found herself saying, "Jesus. Jesus," meaning, Jesus will help you, but the way she was saying it, it sounded as if she might be cursing.

"Yes'm," The Misfit said as if he agreed. "Jesus thown everything off balance. It was the same case with Him as with me except, He hadn't committed any crime and they could prove I had committed one because they had the papers on me. Of course," he said "they never shown me my papers. That's why I sign myself now. I said long ago, you get you a signature and sign everything you do and keep a copy of it. Then you'll know what you done and you can hold up the crime to the punishment and see do they match and in the end you'll have something to prove you ain't been treated right. I call myself The Misfit," he said, "because I can't make what all I done wrong fit what all I gone through in punishment."

130   There was a piercing scream from the woods, followed closely by a pistol report. "Does it seem right to you, lady, that one is punished a heap and another ain't punished at all?"

"Jesus!" the old lady cried. "You've got good blood! I know you wouldn't shoot a lady! I know you come from nice people! Pray! Jesus, you ought not to shoot a lady. I'll give you all the money I've got!"

"Lady," The Misfit said, looking beyond her far into the woods, "there never was a body that give the undertaker a tip."

There were two more pistol reports and the grandmother raised her head like a parched old turkey hen crying for water and called, "Bailey Boy, Bailey Boy!" as if her heart would break.

"Jesus was the only One that ever raised the dead," The Misfit continued, "and He shouldn't have done it. He thown everything off balance. If He did what He said then it's nothing for you to do but thow away everything and follow Him, and if He didn't, then it's nothing for you to do but enjoy the few minutes you got left the best way you can—by killing somebody or burning down his house or doing some other meanness to him. No pleasure but meanness," he said and his voice had become almost a snarl.

135   "Maybe He didn't raise the dead," the old lady mumbled, not knowing what she was saying and feeling so dizzy that she sank down in the ditch with her legs twisted under her.

"I wasn't there so I can't say He didn't," The Misfit said. "I wisht I had of been there," he said, hitting the ground with his fist. "It ain't right I wasn't there because if I had of been there I would of known. Listen lady," he said in a high voice, "if I had of been there I would of known and I wouldn't be like I am now." His voice seemed about to crack and the grandmother's head cleared for an instant. She saw the man's face twisted close to her own as if he were going to cry and she murmured, "Why you're one of my babies. You're one of my own children!" She reached out and touched him on the shoulder. The Misfit sprang back as if a snake had bitten him and shot her three times through the chest. Then he put his gun down on the ground and took off his glasses and began to clean them.

Hiram and Bobby Lee returned from the woods and stood over the ditch, looking down at the grandmother who half sat and half lay in a puddle of blood with her legs crossed under her like a child's and her face smiling up at the cloudless sky.

Without his glasses, The Misfit's eyes were red-rimmed and pale and defense-less-looking. "Take her off and thow her where you thown the others," he said, picking up the cat that was rubbing itself against his leg.

"She was a talker, wasn't she?" Bobby Lee said, sliding down the ditch with a yodel.

140   "She would of been a good woman," The Misfit said, "if it had been some-body there to shoot her every minute of her life."

"Some fun!" Bobby Lee said.

"Shut up, Bobby Lee," The Misfit said. "It's no real pleasure in life."

INQUIRING FURTHER

1. What are your thoughts about The Misfit? What kind of character is he? What actions have shaped him? What decisions does he make? What ethical judgments might you make about him?

2. How do the forces that have shaped the Grandmother relate to The Misfit? What judgments can you make about her character?

3. Does the story convey a clear message about an ethical question? Does it treat multiple questions? What can you say about ethics in terms of the story?

DORIS LESSING

Doris Lessing (born in 1919) brings a background of many cultures to her writing. Although she moved from her birthplace in Persia (now Iran)

*to Rhodesia (now Zimbabwe), Africa as a child, both her parents were
British. In Rhodesia, the Lessings lived in an isolated settlement in the bush.
Lessing was sent from the settlement to school in Salisbury, but quickly
dropped out at the age of 14. Subsequently, she was married twice, had
a son, and explored communist and left-wing political movements. Her first
published novel,* The Grass Is Singing *(1949) reflects her experiences in
Rhodesia. "Homage for Issac Babel" was first published in 1961.*

Homage for Isaac Babel

The day I had promised to take Catherine down to visit my young friend Philip
at his school in the country, we were to leave at eleven, but she arrived at nine.
Her blue dress was new, and so were her fashionable shoes. Her hair had
just been done. She looked more than ever like a pink and gold Renoir girl who
expects everything from life.

Catherine lives in a white house overlooking the sweeping brown tides of
the river. She helped me clean up my flat with a devotion which said that she
felt small flats were altogether more romantic than large houses. We drank
tea, and talked mainly about Philip, who, being fifteen, has pure stern tastes
in everything from food to music. Catherine looked at the books lying around
his room, and asked if she might borrow the stories of Isaac Babel to read on
the train. Catherine is thirteen. I suggested she might find them difficult, but she
said: 'Philip reads them, doesn't he?'

During the journey I read newspapers and watched her pretty frowning face
as she turned the pages of Babel, for she was determined to let nothing get
between her and her ambition to be worthy of Philip.

At the school, which is charming, civilized, and expensive, the two children walked together across green fields, and I followed, seeing how the sun
gilded their bright friendly heads turned towards each other as they talked.
In Catherine's left hand she carried the stories of Isaac Babel.

5   After lunch we went to the pictures. Philip allowed it to be seen that he
thought going to the pictures just for the fun of it was not worthy of intelligent people, but he made the concession, for our sakes. For his sake we chose
the more serious of the two films that were showing in the little town. It was
about a good priest who helped criminals in New York. His goodness, however, was not enough to prevent one of them from being sent to the gas chamber; and Philip and I waited with Catherine in the dark until she had stopped
crying and could face the light of a golden evening.

At the entrance of the cinema the doorman was lying in wait for anyone who
had red eyes. Grasping Catherine by her suffering arm, he said bitterly: 'Yes,
why are you crying? He had to be punished for his crime, didn't he?' Catherine stared at him, incredulous. Philip rescued her by saying with disdain: 'Some
people don't know right from wrong even when it's *demonstrated* to them.' The
doorman turned his attention to the next red-eyed emerger from the dark;
and we went on together to the station, the children silent because of the cruelty of the world.

Finally Catherine said, her eyes wet again: 'I think it's all absolutely beast-
ly, and I can't bear to think about it.' And Philip said: 'But we've got to
think about it, don't you see, because if we don't it'll just go on and *on*, don't
you see?'

In the train going back to London I sat beside Catherine. She had the stories open in front of her, but she said: 'Philip's awfully lucky. I wish I went
to that school. Did you notice that girl who said hullo to him in the garden?
They must be great friends. I wish my mother would let me have a dress like
that, it's *not* fair.'

'I thought it was too old for her.'

10   'Oh *did* you?'

Soon she bent her head again over the book, but almost at once lifted it
to say: 'Is he a very famous writer?'

'He's a marvellous writer, brilliant, one of the very best.'

'Why?'

'Well, for one thing, he's so simple. Look how few words he uses, and how
strong his stories are.'

15   'I see. Do you know him? Does he live in London?'

'Oh no, he's dead.'

'Oh. Then why did you—I thought he was alive, the way you talked.'

'I'm sorry, I suppose I wasn't thinking of him as dead.'

'When did he die?'

20   'He was murdered. About twenty years ago, I suppose.'

'*Twenty years.*' Her hands began the movement of pushing the book over
to me, but then relaxed. 'I'll be fourteen in November,' she stated, sounding
threatened, while her eyes challenged me.

I found it hard to express my need to apologize, but before I could speak,
she said, patiently attentive again: 'You said he was murdered?'

'Yes.'

'I expect the person who murdered him felt sorry when he discovered he
had murdered a famous writer.'

25   'Yes, I expect so.'

'Was he old when he was murdered?'

'No, quite young really.'

'Well, that was bad luck, wasn't it?'

'Yes, I suppose it was bad luck.'

30   'Which do you think is the very best story here? I mean, in your honest opinion, the very very best one.'

I chose the story about killing the goose. She read it slowly, while I sat
waiting, wishing to take it from her, wishing to protect this charming little
person from Isaac Babel.

When she had finished she said: 'Well, some of it I don't understand.
He's got a funny way of looking at things. Why should a man's legs in boots
look like *girls?*' She finally pushed the book over at me, and said: 'I think
it's all morbid.'

'But you have to understand the kind of life he had. First, he was a Jew in
Russia. That was bad enough. Then his experience was all revolution and civil
war and . . .'

But I could see these words bouncing off the clear glass of her fiercely denying gaze; and I said: 'Look, Catherine, why don't you try again when you're
older? Perhaps you'll like him better then?'

35   She said gratefully: 'Yes, perhaps that would be best. After all, Philip is two
years older than me, isn't he?'

A week later I got a letter from Catherine.

Thank you very much for being kind enough to take me to visit Philip at his school. It was the most lovely day in my whole life. I am extremely grateful to you for taking me. I have been thinking about the Hoodlum Priest. That was a film which demonstrated to me beyond any shadow of doubt that Capital Punishment is a Wicked Thing, and I shall never forget what I learned that afternoon, and the lessons of it will be with me all my life. I have been meditating about what you said about Isaac Babel, the famed Russian short story writer, and I now see that the conscious simplicity of his style is what makes him, beyond the shadow of a doubt, the great writer that he is, and now in my school compositions I am endeavouring to emulate him so as to learn a conscious simplicity which is the only basis for a really brilliant writing style. Love, Catherine. P.S. Has Philip said anything about my party? I wrote but he hasn't answered. Please find out if he is coming or if he just forgot to answer my letter. I hope he comes, because sometimes I feel I shall die if he doesn't. P.P.S. Please don't tell him I said anything, because I should die if he knew. Love, Catherine.

INQUIRING FURTHER

1. During the 1930s, Babel was increasingly silenced for his views opposing the Stalinist government in the Soviet Union. He was arrested by Soviet authorities in 1939 and killed under orders by Joseph Stalin in a Siberian prison camp in 1940. How does this knowledge influence your understanding of the story?

2. The story references the murder of the Jewish author, Isaac Babel. It also refers to a film depicting a priest ministering to criminals. Is it fair to say the story is about murder and punishment? What other themes seem significant in the story?

3. In some ways the work comes across as an essay rather than a typical short story. Write a paragraph exploring how the essay-like elements of the piece influence your understanding of the work.

STEVE EARLE

Steve Earle (born in 1955) is best known as a rebel in the world of country music. He has been hailed for his tough lyrics and the heavy-hitting subject matter of his songs. He has also experienced a good deal of turmoil in his life, battling with drug addiction in the 1980s, and eventually spending time in prison for narcotics possession. In 1994, he emerged from detoxification and began corresponding with a number of death row inmates. "A Death in Texas" was published in 2001 and represents his reflections on being asked to serve as a witness for the execution of Jonathan Wayne Nobles. In addition to the essay below, Earle has written a short story and song about Nobles's execution.

A Death in Texas

"Hey, man." Jonathan Wayne Nobles grins at me through inch-thick wire-reinforced glass, hunching over to speak in a deep, resonant voice through

Earle and his music

the steel grate below. A feeble "What's up?" is the best I can manage. The visiting area in Ellis One Unit is crowded with other folks who have traveled, in some cases thousands of miles, to visit relatives and correspondents on Texas's Death Row. They sit at intervals in wooden chairs surrounding a cinder block and steel cage that dominates the center of the room. There are cages within the cage as well, reserved for inmates under disciplinary action and "death watch" status. Falling into the latter category, Jon must squeeze his considerable bulk into one of these phone-booth-sized enclosures.

It's an awkward moment for both of us. In the ten years we have corresponded we have never met face to face. The occasion is auspicious. Jon and I will spend eight hours a day together for the next three days and then another three days next week. Then, the state of Texas will transport Jon, chained hand and foot, eleven miles to the Walls unit in downtown Huntsville. There he will be pumped full of chemicals that will collapse his lungs and stop his heart forever. This is not a worst-case scenario. It is a certainty. The only action pending in the courts on Jon's behalf is an unprecedented petition to have Jon's vital organs harvested and donated for transplant before his execution. The supposedly "non-violent" lethal injection process literally destroys the lungs and renders all the other organs too toxic for transplantation. Neither Jon nor his attorneys have any faith that their motion will prevail. There is no doubt in my mind (or Jon's for that matter) that Jonathan Noble has precisely ten days to live. And I, at Jon's request, will attend the execution as one of his witnesses.

Over the next few days a routine develops. I arrive at Ellis at 8:30 in the morning. We usually spend the first two hours talking about music, politics, religion—subjects that we have covered thoroughly enough in letters over the years to know that we have widely divergent views and tastes. We fill the long awkward silences that seem inevitable in prison visiting areas with trips to the vending machines for soft drinks, candy, and potato chips. I pass Jon's goodies to the guard on duty through a small opening in the steel mesh.

Inevitably, we move on to life behind bars, drugs, and recovery—topics where we share considerably more common ground. We are both recovering addicts who got clean only when we were locked up. Jon began reading about recovery and attending "twelve step" meetings in prison years ago. I can remember a time, back when I was still using drugs, when the "recovery-speak" that filled his letters made me extremely uncomfortable. Now it is a language that we share—sort of a spiritual shorthand that cuts through the testosterone and affords us a convenient, if uncomfortable, segue to the business at hand.

5   There are arrangements to be made. If Jon's body goes unclaimed, as is the case with half of the men executed in Texas, he would be buried in the prison cemetery on the outskirts of Huntsville. Called "Peckerwood Hill" by the locals, it is lonely space filled with concrete crosses, adorned only with the interred inmates' prison numbers. Those executed by the state are easily identifiable by the "X" preceding their number. There are, however, no names on the stones. Jon doesn't want to wind up there.

Instead, he wants to be buried in Oxford, England—a place he's never seen. One of his pen pals, a British subject called Pam Thomas, has described it to him in her letters. He likes the picture Pam paints of the springtime there, when the bluebells are in bloom. Jon says that Pam is working on permission from the landowner. I, for my part, have a Plan B on the back burner. A Dominican community in Galway, Ireland has offered Jon a final resting place. At some

point in the proceedings it dawns on me that I have spent the last hour helping a living, breathing man plan his own burial.

One thing Jon and I don't talk about much is the movement to abolish the
death penalty. In fact, Jon is suspicious of abolitionists. We were "introduced"
by a pen pal of his and an acquaintance of mine. She had heard that I sometimes corresponded with inmates and asked if she could give Jon my address.
I said "sure." Within a month I received my first letter. It was a page and a
half long in a beautiful flowing script that made me more than a little jealous.
It contained a lot of the usual tough rhetoric and dark humor I had learned
to expect in letters from men and women in prison. After several readings I realized that all of the jailhouse small talk was merely a medium, a vehicle for
one pertinent piece of information—that Jonathan Wayne Nobles was guilty
of the crimes he was charged with.

Jon Nobles was found guilty (almost entirely on the strength of his own confession) of stabbing Kelley Farquar and Mitzi Nalley to death in 1986. He also
admitted struggling with and stabbing Ron Ross, Nalley's boyfriend. Ross lost
an eye in the attack. Jon never took the stand during his trial. He sat impassively as the guilty verdict was read and, according to newspaper accounts, only
flinched slightly when District Judge Bob Jones sentenced him to death.

When Jon arrived at Ellis he quickly alienated all of the guards and most
of the inmates. He once broke away from guards while being returned to his
cell from the exercise yard and climbed the exposed pipes and bars like an animal, kicking down television sets suspended outside on the bottom tier. Not
exactly the way to win friends and influence people in the penitentiary. On
another occasion he cut himself with a razor blade, knowing that the guards
would have to open his cell to prevent him from bleeding to death. He just
wanted to hit one officer before he passed out.

10   But somehow, somewhere along the line, in what is arguably the most inhumane environment in the "civilized" world, Jonathan Nobles began to change.
He became interested in Catholicism and began to attend Mass. He befriend-
ed the Catholic clergy who ministered in the prison system, including members of the Dominican Order of Preachers. He admired the Dominicans so much
that he set his sights on becoming one of them. He eventually achieved that
goal, becoming a lay member of the order and ministering to his fellow inmates,
even standing as godfather at inmate Cliff Boguss's baptism. He later helped
officiate at the Mass that was celebrated the night before Boguss' execution.
When I mentioned in a letter that I had found a bag of pot in my oldest son
Justin's laundry, Jon suggested that I bring him to Ellis. He believed his word
might carry a little more weight than mine, coming from the other side of the
razor wire. I was tempted, but in the final analysis I couldn't bring myself to
drag my firstborn through the gates of Hell.

I watched this transformation in the letters that I received. There is no doubt
in my mind or my heart that the Jonathan Nobles that sat on the other side
of the glass from me in September of 1998 is a different man than the one
that the State of Texas sentenced to die almost twelve years ago. The greatest
evidence of this fact is the way that Jon is treated by everyone he encounters, inmates and prison officials alike. A prison clerk, displaying obvious,
genuine regret, interrupts our visit. She needs Jon to sign some papers. Jon does
so and then informs me that the documents allow me to pick up his personal
property and distribute it to a list of people detailed in a note that the clerk

will hand me on my way out. He winks and says that he has left something special to me. Inmate Richard Bethard on his way down the line to visit with a family member stops to talk and Jon introduces us. Bethard beams, saying that he is one of my biggest fans. The guard patiently waits until the exchange is over before escorting him along to his assigned cubicle. Such socialization during inmate transfer is a clear violation of policy at Ellis, but a lot of the rules have relaxed for Jon. He says that it's like the last week of the school year. I believe that it's more likely that he has earned the genuine respect of everyone at Ellis.

The scene is repeated all afternoon. One visitor is a prison employee, who three years earlier went out and bought the *Dead Man Walking* soundtrack CD so that Jon could hear my contribution, a song called "Ellis Unit One," about a corrections officer suffering a crisis of conscience. There is an elderly woman who has moved to Huntsville from England to be near the twenty-six inmates she corresponds with. She is a recovering alcoholic, and when Jon tells her that I'm in the program she offers to take me to a meeting that night. At this point I could use a meeting so I make a date to meet her at a local church at 7:00. Richard Bethard's codefendant Gene Hathorn stops by. Hathorn, it so happens, is one of my other correspondents at Ellis. "Hey Jon, I hear you got a date. Is it serious?" Jon visibly stiffens. He and Hathorn were friends once but something happened years ago, something Jon is reluctant to talk about.

"Serious enough that they're going to kill me."

Hathorn moves on without another word. I excuse myself to go to the bathroom. The truth is I simply need a break.

15   On the way back I run into Father Stephen Walsh, a Franciscan friar from Boston who makes regular trips to Ellis to minister to its Catholic inmates. He will serve as Jonathan's spiritual advisor. In that capacity he will wait with Jon in the holding cell over at the Walls until he's escorted into the death chamber itself and will administer the last rights. Fr. Walsh introduces me to Bishop Carmody, of the East Texas Diocese in Tyler, who like me has been asked to witness on Jonathan's behalf. He is a native of County Kerry, Ireland, but has lived in the States for forty years, twenty of them in Texas. Being a sometime resident of County Galway, a little further up the island's west coast, I find his accent familiar and comforting. He has never witnessed an execution before and admits to being just as scared as I am. "With God's help," he says, "we'll get through this thing together, Stephen."

Every visit ends the same way. A guard gives us a five-minute warning, and Jon hurriedly dictates a list of "things to do" which I must commit to memory, as visitors are not allowed to bring writing instruments and paper into the unit. Then Jon presses his palm against the glass and I mirror his with mine. Jon says, "I love you. I'll see you tomorrow." That is until Wednesday, October 7 rolls around. It's hot and humid, even at 8:00 am as I thread my rented Lincoln through the drive-thru of a fast food restaurant near my motel. As I pull up to the window, a pretty Hispanic girl in her early twenties takes my money and hands me my breakfast: an egg and sausage taco and a medium Dr. Pepper. She smiles and says, "You don't recognize me, do you?" Before I can place her myself she volunteers, "I work at Ellis." Of course—behind the reception desk. I received Jon's property from her last night. "I just wanted to say I'm sorry. Jon's a good guy."

I glance at her nametag. "Thank you, Delores. I'll tell him you said that. It will mean a lot." I guess that she is probably around the same age as Mitzi Nalley was when she died.

Over the last few days the other witnesses have arrived in Huntsville. I had dinner the night before with Dona Hucka, Jon's aunt. She is the only blood relative to make the trip. She has driven all night to be here. Pam Thomas is in from England as well. Both are already on the unit when I arrive. Jon's fifth witness is the director of chaplain's services for the Texas Department of Corrections, Rev. Richard Garza. We take turns leaning close to the glass while a prison employee takes Polaroid snapshots of each of us with Jon. The prison provides this service for the nominal fee of eight dollars each.

10:00. There isn't much time left. At 12:30 we will be asked to leave the unit and Jon will be transported to the Walls. In the death chamber we will be able to hear Jon over a speaker in the witness room, but this is our last opportunity to speak to him. Jon divides the remaining time between us more or less equally. I go first. Jon looks tired; the stress is showing for the first time. He leans down and motions me closer. I realize he's assessing my condition as well. "You all right, man?" I tell him that I'm okay. Jon is not convinced.

20 "I'm worried about you. You don't have to be Superman or nothin'. This is insane shit that's goin' on here today. You don't have to be strong for the women if that's what you're thinkin'. They're big girls. You need to take care of yourself."

"I know, Jon. I'm all right. I went to a meeting last night and my manager's here now. I've also got a couple of friends up from Houston who have done this before."

"Witnessed?"

"Yeah." That seemed to make him feel better.

"OK, but if you need to cry, it's all right, go ahead and cry."

25 "When this is all over I'll cry."

"Promise?"

"I promise."

Jon shifts gears suddenly. Back to business. He looks both ways to make sure the guard isn't watching. "Take this." With much effort he pushes a tiny slip of tightly rolled paper, the diameter of a toothpick, through the impossibly tight mesh. Somehow he pulls it off. "That's my daughter's phone number in California. Dona read it to me over the phone last night. They're going to strip search me and I can't take anything to the Walls and I'm afraid I'll forget it. Give it to Father Walsh. Then I'll have it when I make my last phone calls."

I poke the paper in the watch pocket of my Levi's. There were a few other requests. He wants me to call his foster mother and his sister after the execution, and send flowers to two women who worked for the prison who had been kind to him over the years. I promise that I won't forget. "All right, bro. Take care of yourself and your kids. Tell Dona to come back." Hands against the glass one last time.

30 "I love you, Jonathan."

"I love you too, bro."

Noon. I head back into Huntsville. My manager, Dan Gillis, arrived last night and not a moment too soon. Suddenly, driving has become difficult. It's weird. I'm simply not as coordinated as usual and the world has taken on a kind of surrealistic patina. I need someone to drive for the rest of the day. Also waiting at the hotel are two friends from the abolition movement, Karen Sebung and Ward Larkin. Both have witnessed executions and they have made the trip to support me and assist in any way they can. We talk over arrangements for the transportation and cremation of Jon's body, which, as it turns out, Dan has already taken care of. I make a couple of phone calls and check my messages. Then I shower, shave, and put on a pair of black jeans, a blue short-sleeve shirt and a black linen sport coat.

4:00. We leave the hotel and Dan drives us to Hospitality House, a guest residence operated by the Baptist church for the families of inmates. Dona and Pam, as well as Pam's friend Caroline, are staying there. Bishop Carmody and Rev. Garza are already there when we arrive. We are assembled here for an orientation session to be conducted by Rev. Robert Brazile, the chaplain at the Walls unit. He and the warden will be the only two human beings inside the chamber with Jon when he dies. He goes through the execution process step by step so that "we will know what to expect" and, though it's obvious he speaks with authority, I'm not listening. I can't concentrate so I just nod a lot. It doesn't matter. No matter how well or poorly the witnesses are prepared, they are going to kill Jon anyway.

5:05. Rev. Brazile answers his cell phone and it's Fr. Walsh. He is over at the Walls with Jon and wants the phone number. The one that Jon passed me through the . . . oh my God. I can't find it. I was sure that I transferred the slip from my other jeans into my wallet when I changed clothes but it's simply not there. Dan runs to the hotel and checks my room, but it's hopeless; it was tiny. Rev. Brazil relays the bad news back to Fr. Walsh. I feel awful.

35   5:30. We arrive at the visitors' center across the street from the Walls unit. Karen Sebung accompanies me as far as the waiting area where we witnesses are searched, then Dona and Pam are escorted to another room by a female officer. When they return a large man enters the room and introduces himself as an officer of the prison's Internal Affairs Division. He informs us that if we should feel faint, medical attention is available. He also warns us that anyone who in any way attempts to disrupt the "process," as he calls it, will be removed from the witness area immediately. Bishop Carmody sits down next to me and asks when I was last in Ireland. I can't remember. Nothing about my body is working right. My feet and hands are cold and the side of my neck is numb. The bishop is telling me a story about his childhood in Kerry but I can't get the thread of it. I am suddenly fixated on the idea that somewhere nearby Ron Ross and Mitzy Nalley's mother are undergoing a similar process. They are waiting for the closure that the State of Texas promised them twelve years ago. I sincerely hope that they get it.

5:55. The corrections officer returns. "Follow me, please." I haul myself to my feet. We walk across the street and through the front door of the old gothic prison administration building. We turn left as soon as we enter and find ourselves in the waiting area of the governor's office, where we are asked to wait once again. There are two reporters already there. The other three members of the press pool, along with the victims' family members, have already been escorted to the witness area, which is divided by a cinder block wall. The procedure has been carefully planned and rehearsed, so that the two sets of witnesses will never come in contact with each other.

6:00. A corrections officer enters the room. I hear him tell the Internal Affairs officer that "they're ready." We walk through a visiting area similar to the one at Ellis, then out into the bright evening sun for a moment and turn left down a short sidewalk. Another left and we enter the first door of two set side by side in a small brick building built into the side of the perimeter wall. We enter the tiny room in single file. Father Walsh appears from somewhere inside the death chamber to join us. The reporters enter last and the door is locked behind us. I can hear the reporters scratching on their notepads with their pencils. There is only room for three of us on the front row, Dona, myself, and Pam. Dona grabs my left hand and squeezes it hard and then realizing she may be hurting me, she whispers an apology and relaxes her grip a little. She already has tears in her eyes.

Jon is strapped to a hospital gurney with heavy leather straps across his chest, hips, thighs, ankles, and wrists. His arms are extended at his sides on arm boards like you see in the blood bank and they are wrapped in ace bandages. At either wrist clear plastic tubes protrude from the wrappings, snaking back under the gurney and disappearing through a plastic tube set in a bright blue cinderblock wall. I think I see movement behind the one-way glass mirror on the opposite wall—the executioner getting into position. Jon is smiling at us, his great neck twisted uncomfortably sideways. A microphone suspended from the ceiling hangs a few inches above his head. The speaker above our heads crackles to life and Jon speaks, craning his head around to see the victims' witnesses in the room next door.

"I know some of you won't believe me, but I am truly sorry for what I have done. I wish that could undo what happened back then and bring back your loved ones but I can't." Jon begins to sob as he addresses Mitzi Nalley's mother. "I'm sorry. I'm so sorry. I wish I could bring her back to you. And Ron . . . I took so much from you. I'm sorry. I know you probably don't want my love, but you have it."

40   Turning to me he seems to regain his composure, somewhat. He even manages to smile again. "Steve, I can't believe that I had to go through all this to see you in a suit coat. Hey man, don't worry about the phone number, bro. You've done so much. I love you. Dona, thank you for being here. I know it was hard for you. I love you. Pam, thank you for coming from so far away. Thanks for all you have done. I love you. Bishop Carmody, thank you so much. Rev. Garza and you, Father Walsh, I love you all. I have something I want to say. It comes from I Corinthians. It goes . . . " and Jon recites the lengthy piece of scripture that he agonized over for weeks, afraid he would forget when the time came. He remembers every word.

When he finished reciting he took a deep breath and said, "Father into thy hands I commend my spirit." The warden, recognizing the prearranged signal he and John had agreed on, nodded towards the unseen executioner and Jon began to sing.

Silent night / Holy night . . .

He got as far as "mother and child" and suddenly the air exploded from his lungs, making a loud barking noise, deep and incongruous, like a child with whooping cough—"HUH!!!!" His head pitched forward with such force that his heavy, prison issue glasses flew off his face, bouncing from his chest and falling to the green tile floor below.

And then he didn't move at all—ever again. I actually watched his eyes fix and glaze over, my heart pounding in my chest and Dona squeezing my hand. We could all see that he was gone. Dead men look . . . well, dead. Vacant. No longer human. But there was a protocol to be satisfied. The warden checked his watch several times during the longest five minutes of my life. When time was up, he walked across the room and knocked on the door. The doctor entered, his stethoscope's earpieces already in place. He listened first at Jon's neck, then at his chest, then at his side. He shined a small flashlight into Jon's eyes for an instant and then, glancing up at the clock on his way out, intoned, "6:18."

45   We were ushered out the same way we came, but I don't think any of us are the same people that crossed the street to the prison that day. I know I'm not. I can't help but wonder what happens to the people that work at the Walls, who see this horrific thing happen as often as four times a week. What do they see when they turn out the lights? I can't imagine.

I do know that Jonathan Nobles changed profoundly while he was in prison. I know that the lives of other people who he came in contact with changed as well, including mine. Our criminal justice system isn't known for rehabilitation. I'm not sure that, as a society, we are even interested in that concept anymore. The problem is that most people who go to prison get out one day and walk among us. Given as many people as we lock up, we better learn to rehabilitate someone. I believe Jon might have been able to teach us how. Now we'll never know.

INQUIRING FURTHER

1. "A Death in Texas" takes the form of a personal narrative essay. Are there aspects of the essay that you find compelling? What key messages does the essay convey, and how does the narrative form relate to those messages?

2. Images appeal to our senses and emotions as well as to our intellect. What can you say about the messages conveyed by the image of the electric chair in Figure 14.1? How does the image in Figure 14.1 use emotions to convey its message? How does it use logic?

3. How does Andy Warhol's adaptation in Figure 14.2 alter the message conveyed by the image of the electric chair? Write a paragraph comparing the documentary elements and the artistic components of the two images.

FIGURE 14.1   Death Chamber and Electric Chair at Sing Sing

ͻURE 14.2   *Electric Chair* by Andy Warhol

MAY SWENSON

May Swenson (1913–1989) was raised along with nine brothers and sisters in the town of Logan, Utah. She received a strong religious upbringing, but did not follow in the Mormon church of her parents, calling herself "the only black sheep among [her] living four brothers and four sisters." She took an English degree in college, and worked in journalism and as an office typist before finding success as a poet. Her first collection of poems, Another Animal, *was published in 1954. "That the Soul May Wax Plump" appeared in the collection* New and Selected Things Taking Place, *published in 1978.*

That the Soul May Wax Plump

"He who has reached the highest degree of emptiness
will be secure in repose."
—A Taoist Saying

Recording
of Swenson
reading
"That the
Soul May
Wax
Plump"

My dumpy little mother on the undertaker's slab
had a mannequin's grace. From chin to foot
the sheet outlined her, thin and tall. Her face
uptilted, bloodless, smooth, had a long smile.
5   Her head rested on a block under her nape,
her neck was long, her hair waved, upswept. But later,
at "the viewing," sunk in the casket in pink tulle,
an expensive present that might spoil, dressed

in Eden's green apron, organdy bonnet on,
10   she shrank, grew short again, and yellow. Who
put the gold-rimmed glasses on her shut face, who
laid her left hand with the wedding ring on
her stomach that really didn't seem to be there
under the fake lace?

15   Mother's work before she died was self-purification,
a regimen of near starvation, to be worthy to go
to Our Father, Whom she confused (or, more aptly, fused)
with our father, in Heaven long since. She believed
in evacuation, an often and fierce purgation,
20   meant to teach the body to be hollow, that the soul
may wax plump. At the moment of her death, the wind
rushed out from all her pipes at once. Throat and rectum
sang together, a galvanic spasm, hiss of ecstasy.
Then, a flat collapse. Legs and arms flung wide,
25   like that female Spanish saint slung by the ankles
to a cross, her mouth stayed open in a dark O. So,
her vigorous soul whizzed free. On the undertaker's slab, she
lay youthful, cool, triumphant, with a long smile.

INQUIRING FURTHER

1. Swenson has been praised for the level of detail and observation in her poems. What can you say about the use of details in "That the Soul May Wax Plump"?

2. How would you characterize the tone of the speaker in Swenson's poem? How would you relate the tone to the speaker's attitude toward her mother? Could you also relate the tone and attitude toward death?

3. How do you think the subject matter of Swenson's poem influences the artistic expression in the work? Write a paragraph exploring the relationship between death and art in the poem.

BILLIE HOLIDAY

Billie Holiday (1915–1959) had a turbulent childhood. Her father abandoned the family, and, after her mother moved to New York, she was forced to live with relatives. When she moved to New York to be with her mother, she claims to have been arrested for prostitution. In the 1930s she found success, first by singing in bars, later by accompanying many of the era's top musicians, and eventually by signing her own recording contract. The song "Strange Fruit" was originally written as a poem by Abel Meeropol. Meeropol wrote the poem after viewing an anti-lynching exhibit. Holiday began singing the song in clubs where it met with both enthusiasm and controversy. The song has enjoyed an incredible longevity since Holiday first recorded it, evolving into a work deeply connected with race relations and issues of free speech.

Strange Fruit

Southern trees bear a strange fruit,
Blood on the leaves and blood at the root,
Black body swinging in the Southern breeze,
Strange fruit hanging from the poplar trees.

5   Pastoral scene of the gallant South,
The bulging eyes and the twisted mouth,
Scent of magnolia sweet and fresh,
And the sudden smell of burning flesh!

Here is a fruit for the crows to pluck,
10   For the rain to gather, for the wind to suck,
For the sun to rot, for a tree to drop,
Here is a strange and bitter crop.

MARTIN GANSBERG

Martin Gansberg wrote for the New York Times *between 1945 and 1985. The article below reports on the murder of Kitty Genovese. The murder took place on March 14, 1964. The failure of anyone to come to the aid of the victim shocked readers and eventually led social scientists to develop the term "Genovese Syndrome," the phenomenon of refusing to act when others are in need.*

Thirty Seven Who Saw Murder Didn't Call the Police

For more than half an hour 38 respectable, law-abiding citizens in Queens watched a killer stalk and stab a woman in three separate attacks in Kew Gardens.

Twice the sound of their voices and the sudden glow of their bedroom lights interrupted him and frightened him off. Each time he returned, sought her out and stabbed her again. Not one person telephoned the police during the assault; one witness called after the woman was dead.

That was two weeks ago today. But Assistant Chief Inspector Frederick M. Lussen, in charge of the borough's detectives and a veteran of 25 years of homicide investigations, is still shocked.

He can give a matter-of-fact recitation of many murders. But the Kew Gardens slaying baffles him—not because it is a murder, but because the "good people" failed to call the police.

5   "As we have reconstructed the crime," he said, "the assailant had three chances to kill this woman during a 35—minute period. He returned twice to complete the job. If we had been called when he first attacked, the woman might not be dead now."

This is what the police say happened beginning at 3:20 AM in the staid, middle-class, tree-lined Austin Street area:

Twenty-eight-year-old Catherine Genovese, who was called Kitty by almost everyone in the neighborhood, was returning home from her job as manager of a bar in Hollis. She parked her red Fiat in a lot adjacent to the Kew Gardens Long Island Rail Road Station, facing Mowbray Place. Like many residents of the neighborhood, she had parked there day after day since her arrival from Connecticut a year ago, although the railroad frowns on the practice.

She turned off the lights to her car, locked the door and started to walk the 100 feet to the entrance of her apartment at 82–70 Austin Street, which is in a Tudor building, with stores on the first floor and apartments on the second.

The entrance to the apartment is in the rear of the building because the front is rented to retail stores. At night the quiet neighborhood is shrouded in the slumbering darkness that marks most residential areas.

10   Miss Genovese noticed a man at the far end of the lot, near a seven-story apartment house at 82–40 Austin Street. She halted. Then, nervously, she headed up Austin Street toward Lefferts Boulevard, where there is a call box to the 102nd Police Precinct in nearby Richmond.

She got as far as a street light in front of a bookstore before the man grabbed her. She screamed. Lights went on in the 10-story apartment house at 82–67 Austin Street, which faces the bookstore. Windows slid open, and voices punctured the early-morning stillness.

Miss Genovese screamed: "Oh, my God, he stabbed me! Please help me! Please help me!"

From one of the upper windows in the apartment house, a man called down: "Let that girl alone!"

The assailant looked up at him, shrugged and walked down Austin Street toward a white sedan parked a short distance away. Miss Genovese struggled to her feet.

15   Lights went out. The killer returned to Miss Genovese, now trying to make her way around the side of the building by the parking lot to get to her apartment. The assailant stabbed her again.

"I'm dying!" she shrieked. "I'm dying!"

Windows were opened again, and lights went on in many apartments. The assailant got into his car and drove away. Miss Genovese staggered to her feet. A city bus, Q-10, the Lefferts Boulevard line to Kennedy International Airport, passed. It was 3:35 AM.

The assailant returned. By then, Miss Genovese had crawled to the back of the building, where the freshly painted brown doors to the apartment house held out hope of safety. The killer tried the first door; she wasn't there. At the second door, 82–62 Austin Street, he saw her slumped on the floor at the foot of the stairs. He stabbed her a third time—fatally.

It was 3:50 by the time the police received their first call, from a man who was a neighbor of Miss Genovese. In two minutes they were at the scene. The neighbor, a 70-year-old woman and another woman were the only persons on the street. Nobody else came forward.

20   The man explained that he had called the police after much deliberation. He had phoned a friend in Nassau County for advice and then he had crossed the roof of the building to the apartment of the elderly woman to get her to make the call.

"I didn't want to get involved," he sheepishly told the police.

Six days later, the police arrested Winston Moseley, a 29-year-old business-machine operator, and charged him with the homicide. Moseley had no previous record. He is married, has two children and owns a home at 133-19 Sutter Avenue, South Ozone Park, Queens. On Wednesday, a court committed him to Kings County Hospital for psychiatric observation.

When questioned by the police, Moseley also said that he had slain Mrs. Annie Mae Johnson, 24, of 146-12 133rd Avenue, Jamaica, on Feb. 29 and Barbara Kralik, 15, of 174-17 140th Avenue, Springfield Gardens, last July. In the Kralik case, the police are holding Alvin L. Mitchell, who is said to have confessed to that slaying.

The police stressed how simple it would have been to have gotten in touch with them. "A phone call," said one of the detectives, "would have done it." The police may be reached by dialing "O" for operator or SPring 7-3100.

25   The question of whether the witnesses can be held legally responsible in any way for the failure to report the crime was put to the Police Department's legal bureau. There, a spokesman said:

"There is no legal responsibility, with few exceptions, for any citizen to report a crime."

Under the statutes of the city, he said, a witness to a suspicious or violent death must report it to the medical examiner. Under the state law, a witness cannot withhold information in a kidnapping.

Today witnesses from the neighborhood, which is made up of one-family homes in the $35,000 to $60,000 range with the exception of the two apartment houses near the railroad station, find it difficult to explain why they didn't call the police.

Lieutenant Bernard Jacobs, who handled the investigation by the detectives, said: "It is one of the better neighborhoods. There are few reports of crimes. You only get the usual complaints about boys playing or garbage cans being turned over."

30   The police said most persons had told them they had been afraid to call but had given meaningless answers when asked what they had feared.

"We can understand the reticence of people to become involved in an area of violence," Lieutenant Jacobs said, "but when they are in their homes, near phones, why should they be afraid to call the police?"

He said his men were able to piece together what happened—and capture the suspect—because the residents furnished all the information when detectives rang doorbells during the days following the slaying.

"But why didn't someone call us that night?" he asked unbelievingly.

Witnesses—some of them unable to believe what they had allowed to happen—told a reporter why.

35   A housewife, knowingly if quite casual, said, "We thought it was a lover's quarrel." A husband and wife both said, "Frankly, we were afraid." They seemed aware of the fact that events might have been different. A distraught woman, wiping her hands in her apron, said, "I didn't want my husband to get involved."

One couple, now willing to talk about that night, said they heard the first screams. The husband looked thoughtfully at the bookstore where the killer first grabbed Miss Genovese.

"We went to the window to see what was happening," he said, "but the light from our bedroom made it difficult to see the street." The wife, still apprehensive, added: "I put out the light, and we were able to see better."

Asked why they hadn't called the police, she shrugged and replied: "I don't know."

A man peeked out from a slight opening in the doorway to his apartment and rattled off an account of the killer's second attack. Why hadn't he called the police at the time? "I was tired," he said without emotion. "I went back to bed."

40   It was 4:25 AM when the ambulance arrived for the body of Miss Genovese. It drove off. "Then," a solemn police detective said, "the people came out."

RAFAEL CAMPO

Rafael Campo (born in 1964) practices medicine at Harvard Medical School. He has brought together his experiences as a physician and talents as a poet in collections published throughout the 1990s. "The Distant Moon" is taken from The Other Man Was Me, *published in 1994.*

The Distant Moon

Campo
reading
"The
Distant
Moon"

I

Admitted to the hospital again.
The second bout of pneumocystis back
In January almost killed him; then,
He'd sworn to us he'd die at home. He baked
5   Us cookies, which the student wouldn't eat,
Before he left—the kitchen on 5A
Is small, but serviceable and neat.
He told me stories: Richard Gere was gay
And sleeping with a friend of his, and AIDS
10   Was an elaborate conspiracy
Effected by the government. He stayed
Four months. He lost his sight to CMV.[1]

II

One day, I drew his blood, and while I did
He laughed, and said I was his girlfriend now,
15   His blood-brother. "Vampire-slut," he cried,
"You'll make me live forever!" Wrinkled brows
Were all I managed in reply. I know
I'm drowning in his blood, his purple blood.
I filled my seven tubes; the warmth was slow
20   To leave them, pressed inside my palm. I'm sad
Because he doesn't see my face. Because
I can't identify with him. I hate
The fact that he's my age, and that across
My skin he's there, my blood-brother, my mate.

III

25   He said I was too nice, and after all
If Jodie Foster was a lesbian,
Then doctors could be queer. Residual

---

[1]**CMV:** Cytomegalovirus, a form of herpes.

Guilts tingled down my spine. "OK, I'm done,"
I said as I withdrew the needle from
30   His back, and pressed. The CSI² was clear;
I never answered him. That spot was framed
In sterile, paper drapes. He was so near
Death, telling him seemed pointless. Then, he died.
Unrecognizable to anyone
35   But me, he left my needles deep inside
His joking heart. An autopsy was done.

IV
I'd read to him at night. His horoscope,
The New York Times, The Advocate;
Some lines by Richard Howard gave us hope.
40   A quiet hospital is infinite,
The polished, ice-white floors, the darkened halls
That lead to almost anywhere, to death
Or ghostly, lighted Coke machines. I call
To him one night, at home asleep. His breath,
45   I dreamed, had filled my lungs—his lips, my lips
Had touched. I felt as though I'd touched a shrine.
Not disrespectfully, but in some lapse
Of concentration. In a mirror shines
The distant moon.

INQUIRING FURTHER

1. "Strange Fruit" was originally a poem, and then adapted into a song by Billie Holiday. Listen to a recording of the song and consider how hearing the song influences your understanding of it. Do you think the song is more powerful than the poem? Why or why not?

2. Compare the song "Strange Fruit" with the story of the murder of Kitty Genovese. Can you imagine a song based on the murder of Genovese? How would "Strange Fruit" differ if it were written as a newspaper article? Develop a list of what is similar and different about the two pieces.

3. How does the subject matter of Rafael Campo's "The Distant Moon" influence your reading of the piece as poetry? What ethical issues can you discover in the poem? How does the piece relate to Gansberg's newspaper article or to Holiday's song?

LANGUAGE AND POWER

We rarely pay much attention to the ways that language shapes us. However, the more we consider how language influences our thinking, the more we realize that words themselves can have a direct impact on human lives. The selections below explore this power of the word and its implications for the decisions we make.

---

²**CSI:** Caregiver Strain Index.

ROBERT BROWNING

*Although he took an early interest in poetry, composing a volume of poet-
ry at the age of twelve, it was not until Robert Browning (1812–1889) was
in his early 20s that his works began to see publication. In 1846, Browning married Elizabeth Barret, herself a well-known poet. "My Last Duchess"
first appeared in 1842. It is one of Browning's most often reproduced poems
and provides a clear example of a dramatic monologue (a poem shaped
around the speech of its speaker).*

My Last Duchess

Video
enactment
of "My
Last
Duchess"

Ferrara[1]

That's my last Duchess painted on the wall,
Looking as if she were alive. I call
That piece a wonder, now: Fra Pandolf's[2] hands
Worked busily a day, and there she stands.
5   Will't please you sit and look at her? I said
"Fra Pandolf" by design, for never read
Strangers like you that pictured countenance,
The depth and passion of its earnest glance,
But to myself they turned (since none puts by
10   the curtain I have drawn for you, but I)
And seemed as they would ask me, if they durst,
How such a glance came there; so, not the first
Are you to turn and ask thus. Sir, 'twas not
Her husband's presence only, called that spot
15   Of joy into the Duchess' cheek: perhaps
Fra Pandolf chanced to say "Her mantle laps
Over my lady's wrist too much," or "Paint
Must never hope to reproduce the faint
Half-flush that dies along her throat"; such stuff
20   Was courtesy, she thought, and cause enough
For calling up that spot of joy. She had
A heart—how shall I say—too soon made glad,
Too easily impressed; she liked whate'er
She looked on, and her looks went everywhere.
25   Sir, 'twas all one! My favour at her breast,
The dropping of the daylight in the West,
The bough of cherries some officious fool
Broke in the orchard for her, the white mule
She rode with round the terrace—all and each
30   Would draw from her alike the approving speech,
Or blush, at least. She thanked men—good! but thanked
Somehow—I know not how—as if she ranked
My gift of a nine-hundred-years-old name

---

[1]**Ferrara**: an Italian town known for its sixteenth-century duke who remarried after the death of his
first wife.
[2]**Fra Pandolf**: a fictional painter.

35
40
45
50
55

      With anybody's gift. Who'd stoop to blame
      This sort of trifling? Even had you skill
      In speech (which I have not) to make your will
      Quite clear to such an one, and say, "Just this
      Or that in you disgusts me; here you miss,
      Or there exceed the mark"—and if she let
      Herself be lessoned so, nor plainly set
      Her wits to yours, forsooth, and made excuse,
      E'en that would be some stooping; and I choose
      Never to stoop. Oh sir, she smiled, no doubt,
      Whene'er I passed her; but who passed without
      Much the same smile? This grew; I gave commands;
      Then all smiles stopped together. There she stands
      As if alive. Will't please you rise? We'll meet
      The company below, then. I repeat,
      The Count your master's known munificence
      Is ample warrant that no just pretence
      Of mine for dowry will be disallowed;
      Though his fair daughter's self, as I avowed
      At starting, is my object. Nay, we'll go
      Together down, sir. Notice Neptune, though,
      Taming a sea-horse, thought a rarity,
      Which Claus of Innsbruck[3] cast in bronze for me!

Inquiring Further

1. How would you characterize the speaker, the Duke, of the poem? How does he characterize himself? What can be said about the relationship between the Duke and the Duchess?

2. How does the Duke use language in the poem? What is the relationship between the Duke's use of language and the fate of the Duchess? Does the Duke's use of language work on the reader? Write an essay exploring the connections between language and power in the poem.

WILLIAM BUTLER YEATS

William Butler Yeats (1865–1939) was born in Dublin, Ireland but spent much of his first fifteen years in England. After returning to Ireland at the age of fifteen, Yeats began to compose poetry exploring Irish folklore. His early work emphasized his Irish background and mythological themes. After about 1910, he began to incorporate a more direct style into his poetry and address political turmoil in his native Ireland. One of his most political poems, "Easter 1916," was written in response to the killing of Irish leaders by the British in the failed Easter Rising in which a number of Irish tried to seize control of Dublin from the British. "Leda and the Swan" first appeared in 1918, though it was revised by Yeats over the next decade.

---

[3]**Claus of Innsbruck**: a fictional sculptor.

Leda and the Swan

A sudden blow: the great wings beating still
Above the staggering girl, her thighs caressed
By the dark webs, her nape caught in his bill,
He holds her helpless breast upon his breast.

5   How can those terrified vague fingers push
The feathered glory from her loosening thighs?
And how can body, laid in that white rush,
But feel the strange heart beating where it lies?

A shudder in the loins engenders there
10   The broken wall, the burning roof and tower
And Agamemnon dead.
                  Being so caught up,
So mastered by the brute blood of the air,
Did she put on his knowledge with his power
Before the indifferent beak could let her drop?

LUCILLE CLIFTON

Lucille Clifton (born in 1936) writes children's books as well as poetry. She attended Howard University and has taught at the University of California at Santa Cruz, American University in Washington, D.C., and St. Mary's College of Maryland. Her first collection of poems, Good Times, *appeared in 1969. The leda poems reproduced here appeared in* Blessing the Boats: New and Selected Poems, *published in 2000.*

leda 1

there is nothing luminous
about this.
they took my children.
I live alone in the backside
5   of the village.
my mother moved
to another town. my father
follows me around the well,
his thick lips slavering,
10   and at night my dreams are full
of the cursing of me
fucking god fucking me.

leda 2

a note on visitations
sometimes another star chooses.
the ones coming in from the east
are dagger-fingered men,
princes of no known kingdom.
5   the animals are raised up in their stalls

battering the stable door.
sometimes it all goes badly;
the inn is strewn with feathers,
the old husband suspicious,
10   and the fur between her thighs
is the only shining thing.

leda 3

a personal note (re: visitations)
always pyrotechnics;
stars spinning into phalluses
of light, serpents promising
sweetness, their forked tongues
5   thick and erect, patriarchs of bird
exposing themselves in the air.
this skin is sick with loneliness.
You want what a man wants,
next time come as a man
10   or don't come.

INQUIRING FURTHER

1. In the myth of Leda, the Greek god Zeus is overwhelmed by Leda's beauty and, disguising himself in the form of a swan, swoops down and takes Leda by force. As a result, Leda gives birth to Helen who eventually is responsible

Reproductions
of the Leda
paintings

FIGURE 14.3   *Leda and the Swan* by Leonardo Bottega

FIGURE 14.4   *Leda Col Cigno* by Michaelangelo Buonarroti

for the Trojan wars. What do you take to be the main message of this myth? Do you think Yeats's poem supports or undercuts that message? Why?

2. Clifton's three Leda poems can be seen as a response to the myth of Leda and to Yeats's "Leda and the Swan." What message do the poems by Clifton send? How does language work in Clifton's poems to deliver that message?

3. Contrast the two paintings of the Leda myth. Which painting would you associate with Yeats's poem? Why? Which painting would you associate with Clifton's poems? Write a paragraph comparing the messages conveyed by the paintings.

AUDRE LORDE

Audre Lorde (1934–1992) was born in New York City, but her parents had immigrated from the West Indies. In college, Lorde became editor of the school literary magazine and began developing her poetry and establishing her identity as a lesbian. Her first volume of poetry, The First Cities, *was published in 1968. She continued to publish poetry and undertook a lengthy college teaching career. In 1977, she delivered the essay, "The Transformation of Silence into Action" as a presentation for fellow college teachers.*

The Transformation of Silence into Action[1]

I have come to believe over and over again that what is most important to me must be spoken, made verbal and shared, even at the risk of having it bruised or misunderstood. That the speaking profits me, beyond any other effect. I am standing here as a Black lesbian poet, and the meaning of all that

---

[1]Paper delivered at the Modern Language Association's "Lesbian Literature Panel," Chicago, Illinois, December 28, 1977. First published in *Sinister Wisdom* 6 (1978) and *The Cancer Journals* (Spinster, Ink. San Francisco, 1980).

waits upon the fact that I am still alive, and might not have been. Less than two months ago I was told by two doctors, one female and one male, that I would have to have breast surgery, and that there was a 60 to 80 percent chance that the tumor was malignant. Between that telling and the actual surgery, there was a three-week period of the agony of an involuntary reorganization of my entire life. The surgery was completed, and the growth was benign.

But within those three weeks, I was forced to look upon myself and my living with a harsh and urgent clarity that has left me still shaken but much stronger. This is a situation faced by many women, by some of you here today. Some of what I experienced during that time has helped elucidate for me much of what I feel concerning the transformation of silence into language and action.

In becoming forcibly and essentially aware of my mortality, and of what I wished and wanted for my life, however short it might be, priorities and omissions became strongly etched in a merciless light and what I most regretted were my silences. Of what had I *ever* been afraid? To question or to speak as I believed could have meant pain, or death. But we all hurt in so many different ways, all the time, and pain will either change or end. Death, on the other hand, is the final silence. And that might be coming quickly, now, without regard for whether I had ever spoken what needed to be said, or had only betrayed myself into small silences, while I planned someday to speak, or waited for someone else's words. And I began to recognize a source of power within myself that comes from the knowledge that while it is most desirable not to be afraid, learning to put fear into a perspective gave me great strength.

I was going to die, if not sooner then later, whether or not I had ever spoken myself. My silences had not protected me. Your silence will not protect you. But for every real word spoken, for every attempt I had ever made to speak those truths for which I am still seeking, I had made contact with other women while we examined the words to fit a world in which we all believed, bridging our differences. And it was the concern and caring of all those women which gave me strength and enabled me to scrutinize the essentials of my living.

5   The women who sustained me through that period were Black and white, old and young, lesbian, bisexual, and heterosexual, and we all shared a war against the tyrannies of silence. They all gave me a strength and concern without which I could not have survived intact. Within those weeks of acute fear came the knowledge—within the war we are all waging with the forces of death, subtle and otherwise, conscious or not—I am not only a casualty, I am also a warrior.

What are the words you do not yet have? What do you need to say? What are the tyrannies you swallow day by day and attempt to make your own, until you will sicken and die of them, still in silence? Perhaps for some of you here today, I am the face of one of your fears. Because I am woman, because I am Black, because I am lesbian, because I am myself—a Black woman warrior poet doing my work—come to ask you, are you doing yours?

And of course I am afraid, because the transformation of silence into language and action is an act of self-revelation, and that always seems fraught with danger. But my daughter, when I told her of our topic and my difficulty with it, said, "Tell them about how you're never really a whole person if you remain silent, because there's always that one little piece inside you that wants to be spoken out, and if you keep ignoring it, it gets madder and madder and hotter and hotter, and if you don't speak it out one day it will just up and punch you in the mouth from the inside."

In the cause of silence, each of us draws the face of her own fear—fear of contempt, of censure, or some judgment, or recognition, of challenge, of annihilation. But most of all, I think, we fear the visibility without which we cannot truly live. Within this country where racial difference creates a constant, if unspoken, distortion of vision, Black women have on one hand always been highly visible, and so, on the other hand, have been rendered invisible through the depersonalization of racism. Even within the women's movement, we have had to fight, and still do, for that very visibility which also renders us most vulnerable, our Blackness. For to survive in the mouth of this dragon we call america, we have had to learn this first and most vital lesson—that we were never meant to survive. Not as human beings. And neither were most of you here today, Black or not. And that visibility which makes us most vulnerable is that which also is the source of our greatest strength. Because the machine will try to grind you into dust anyway, whether or not we speak. We can sit in our corners mute forever while our sisters and our selves are wasted, while our children are distorted and destroyed, while our earth is poisoned; we can sit in our safe corners mute as bottles, and we will still be no less afraid.

In my house this year we are celebrating the feast of Kwanza, the Africanamerican festival of harvest which begins the day after Christmas and lasts for seven days. There are seven principles of Kwanza, one for each day. The first principle is Umoja, which means unity, the decision to strive for and maintain unity in self and community. The principle for yesterday, the second day, was Kujichagulia—self-determination—the decision to define ourselves, name ourselves, and speak for ourselves, instead of being defined and spoken for by others. Today is the third day of Kwanza, and the principle for today is Ujima—collective work and responsibility—the decision to build and maintain ourselves and our communities together and to recognize and solve our problems together.

10   Each of us is here now because in one way or another we share a commitment to language and to the power of language, and to the reclaiming of that language which has been made to work against us. In the transformation of silence into language and action, it is vitally necessary for each one of us to establish or examine her function in that transformation and to recognize her role as vital within that transformation.

For those of us who write, it is necessary to scrutinize not only the truth of what we speak, but the truth of that language by which we speak it. For others, it is to share and spread also those words that are meaningful to us. But primarily for us all, it is necessary to teach by living and speaking those truths which we believe and know beyond understanding. Because in this way alone we can survive, by taking part in a process of life that is creative and continuing, that is growth.

And it is never without fear—of visibility, of the harsh light of scrutiny and perhaps judgment, of pain, of death. But we have lived through all of those already, in silence, except death. And I remind myself all the time now that if I were to have been born mute, or had maintained an oath of silence my whole life long for safety, I would still have suffered, and I would still die. It is very good for establishing perspective.

And where the words of women are crying to be heard, we must each of us recognize our responsibility to seek those words out, to read them and share them and examine them in their pertinence to our lives. That we not hide behind the mockeries of separations that have been imposed upon us and which so often we accept as our own. For instance, "I can't possibly teach Black women's writing—their experience is so different from mine." Yet how many years have you spent teaching Plato and Shakespeare and Proust? Or another, "She's a white woman and what could she possibly have to say to me?" Or, "She's a lesbian, what would my husband say, or my chairman?" Or again, "This woman writes of her sons and I have no children." And all the other endless ways in which we rob ourselves of ourselves and each other.

We can learn to work and speak when we are afraid in the same way we have learned to work and speak when we are tired. For we have been socialized to respect fear more than our own needs for language and definition, and while we wait in silence for that final luxury of fearlessness, the weight of that silence will choke us.

15   The fact that we are here and that I speak these words is an attempt to break that silence and bridge some of those differences between us, for it is not difference which immobilizes us, but silence. And there are so many silences to be broken.

ZORA NEAL HURSTON

Zora Neal Hurston's (1891–1960) literary career took off in conjunction with the Harlem Renaissance. Her early success led to an opportunity for further education in college and she embarked upon a two-year study of anthropology. She began investigating African-American traditions and culture. Her work led to her first novel, Jonah's Gourd, *which was published in 1934. She later incorporated more folk traditions into her novel,* Their Eyes Were Watching God. *"Sweat" is taken from the only published edition (1926) of a magazine that Hurston organized with the writer Langston Hughes,* Fire!!

Sweat

It was eleven o'clock of a Spring night in Florida. It was Sunday. Any other night, Delia Jones would have been in bed for two hours by this time. But she was a washwoman, and Monday morning meant a great deal to her. So she collected the soiled clothes on Saturday when she returned the clean things. Sunday night after church, she sorted them and put the white things to soak. It saved her almost a half day's start. A great hamper in the bedroom held the clothes that she brought home. It was so much neater than a number of bundles lying around.

She squatted in the kitchen floor beside the great pile of clothes, sorting them into small heaps according to color, and humming a song in a mournful key, but wondering through it all where Sykes, her husband, had gone with her horse and buckboard.

Just then something long, round, limp and black fell upon her shoulders and slithered to the floor beside her. A great terror took hold of her. It softened her knees and dried her mouth so that it was a full minute before she could cry out or move. Then she saw that it was the big bull whip her husband liked to carry when he drove.

She lifted her eyes to the door and saw him standing there bent over with laughter at her fright. She screamed at him.

5   "Sykes, what you throw dat whip on me like dat? You know it would skeer me—looks just like a snake, an' you knows how skeered Ah is of snakes."

"Course Ah knowed it! That's how come Ah done it." He slapped his leg with his hand and almost rolled on the ground in his mirth. "If you such a big fool dat you got to have a fit over a earth worm or a string, Ah don't keer how bad Ah skeer you."

"You aint got no business doing it. Gawd knows it's a sin. Some day Ah'm gointuh drop dead from some of yo' foolishness. 'Nother thing, where you been wid mah rig? Ah feeds dat pony. He aint fuh you to be drivin' wid no bull whip."

"You sho is one aggravatin' nigger woman!" he declared and stepped into the room. She resumed her work and did not answer him at once. "Ah done tole you time and again to keep them white folks' clothes outa dis house."

He picked up the whip and glared down at her. Delia went on with her work. She went out into the yard and returned with a galvanized tub and sit it on the washbench. She saw that Sykes had kicked all of the clothes together again, and now stood in her way truculently, his whole manner hoping, *praying*, for an argument. But she walked calmly around him and commenced to re-sort the things.

10   "Next time, Ah'm gointer kick 'em outdoors," he threatened as he struck a match along the leg of his corduroy breeches.

Delia never looked up from her work, and her thin, stooped shoulders sagged further.

"Ah aint for no fuss t'night Sykes. Ah just come from taking sacrament at the church house."

He snorted scornfully. "Yeah, you just come from de church house on a Sunday night, but heah you is gone to work on them clothes. You ain't nothing but a hypocrite. One of them amen-corner Christians—sing, whoop, and shout, then come home and wash white folks clothes on the Sabbath."

He stepped roughly upon the whitest pile of things, kicking them helter-skelter as he crossed the room. His wife gave a little scream of dismay, and quickly gathered them together again.

15   "Sykes, you quit grindin' dirt into these clothes! How can Ah git through by Sat'day if Ah don't start on Sunday?"

"Ah don't keer if you never git through. Anyhow, Ah done promised Gawd and a couple of other men, Ah aint gointer have it in mah house. Don't gimme no lip neither, else Ah'll throw 'em out and put mah fist up side yo' head to boot."

Delia's habitual meekness seemed to slip from her shoulders like a blown scarf. She was on her feet; her poor little body, her bare knuckly hands bravely defying the strapping hulk before her.

"Looka heah, Sykes, you done gone too fur. Ah been married to you fur fifteen years, and Ah been takin' in washin' fur fifteen years. Sweat, sweat, sweat! Work and sweat, cry and sweat, pray and sweat!"

"What's that got to do with me?" he asked brutally.

20   "What's it got to do with you, Sykes? Mah tub of suds is filled yo' belly with vittles more times than yo' hands is filled it. Mah sweat is done paid for this house and Ah reckon Ah kin keep on sweatin' in it."

She seized the iron skillet from the stove and struck a defensive pose, which act surprised him greatly, coming from her. It cowed him and he did not strike her as he usually did.

"Naw you won't," she panted, "that ole snaggle-toothed black woman you runnin' with aint comin' heah to pile up on *mah* sweat and blood. You aint paid for nothin' on this place, and Ah'm gointer stay right heah till Ah'm toted out foot foremost."

"Well, you better quit gittin' me riled up, else they'll be totin' you out sooner than you expect. Ah'm so tired of you Ah don't know whut to do. Gawd! how Ah hates skinny wimmen!"

A little awed by this new Delia, he sidled out of the door and slammed the back gate after him. He did not say where he had gone, but she knew too well. She knew very well that he would not return until nearly daybreak also. Her work over, she went on to bed but not to sleep at once. Things had come to a pretty pass!

25   She lay awake, gazing upon the debris that cluttered their matrimonial trail. Not an image left standing along the way. Anything like flowers had long ago been drowned in the salty stream that had been pressed from her heart. Her tears, her sweat, her blood. She had brought love to the union and he had brought a longing after the flesh. Two months after the wedding, he had given her the first brutal beating. She had the memory of his numerous trips to Orlando with all of his wages when he had returned to her penniless, even before the first year had passed. She was young and soft then, but now she thought of her knotty, muscled limbs, her harsh knuckly hands, and drew herself up into an unhappy little ball in the middle of the big feather bed. Too late now to hope for love, even if it were not Bertha it would be someone else. This case differed from the others only in that she was bolder than the others. Too late for everything except her little home. She had built it for her old days, and planted one by one the trees and flowers there. It was lovely to her, lovely.

Somehow, before sleep came, she found herself saying aloud: "Oh well, whatever goes over the Devil's back, is got to come under his belly. Sometime or ruther, Sykes, like everybody else, is gointer reap his sowing." After that she was able to build a spiritual earthworks against her husband. His shells could no longer reach her. *Amen.* She went to sleep and slept until he announced his presence in bed by kicking her feet and rudely snatching the cover away.

"Gimme some kivah heah, an' git yo' damn foots over on yo' own side! Ah oughter mash you in yo' mouf fuh drawing dat skillet on me."

Delia went clear to the rail without answering him. A triumphant indifference to all that he was or did.

The week was as full of work for Delia as all other weeks, and Saturday found her behind her little pony, collecting and delivering clothes.

30   It was a hot, hot day near the end of July. The village men on Joe Clarke's porch even chewed cane listlessly. They did not hurl the cane-knots as usual. They let them dribble over the edge of the porch. Even conversation had collapsed under the heat.

"Heah come Delia Jones," Jim Merchant said, as the shaggy pony came 'round the bend of the road toward them. The rusty buckboard was heaped with baskets of crisp, clean laundry.

"Yep," Joe Lindsay agreed. "Hot or col', rain or shine, jes ez reg'lar ez de weeks roll roun' Delia carries 'em an' fetches 'em on Sat'day."

"She better if she wanter eat," said Moss. "Syke Jones aint wuth de shot an' powder hit would tek tuh kill 'em. Not to *huh* he aint."

"He sho' aint," Walter Thomas chimed in. "It's too bad, too, cause she wuz a right pritty lil trick when he got huh. Ah'd uh mah'ied huh mahseff if he hadnter beat me to it."

35   Delia nodded briefly at the men as she drove past.

"Too much knockin' will ruin *any* 'oman. He done beat huh 'nough tuh kill three women, let 'lone change they looks," said Elijah Mosely. "How Syke kin stommuck dat big black greasy Mogul he's layin' roun' wid, gits me. Ah swear dat eight-rock couldn't kiss a sardine can Ah done thowed out de back do' 'way las' yeah."

"Aw, she's fat, thass how come. He's allus been crazy 'bout fat women," put in Merchant. "He'd a' been tied up wid one long time ago if he could a' found one tuh have him. Did Ah tell yuh 'bout him come sidlin' roun' *mah* wife—bringin' her a basket uh pee-cans outa his yard fuh a present? Yes-sir, mah wife! She tol' him tuh take 'em right straight back home, cause Delia works so hard ovah dat washtub she reckon everything on de place taste lak sweat an' soapsuds. Ah jus' wisht Ah'd a' caught 'im 'roun' dere! Ah'd a' made his hips ketch on fiah down dat shell road."

"Ah know he done it, too. Ah sees 'im grinnin' at every 'oman dat passes," Walter Thomas said. "But even so, he useter eat some mighty big hunks uh humble pie tuh git dat lil' 'oman he got. She wuz ez pritty ez a speckled pup! Dat wuz fifteen yeahs ago. He useter be so skeered uh losin' huh, she could make him do some parts of a husband's duty. Dey never wuz de same in de mind."

"There oughter be a law about him," said Lindsay. "He aint fit tuh carry guts tuh a bear."

40   Clarke spoke for the first time. "Taint no law on earth dat kin make a man be decent if it aint in 'im. There's plenty men dat takes a wife lak dey do a joint uh sugar-cane. It's round, juicy an' sweet when dey gits it. But dey squeeze an' grind, squeeze an' grind an' wring tell dey wring every drop uh pleasure dat's in 'em out. When dey's satisfied dat dey is wrung dry, dey treats 'em jes lak dey do a cane-chew. Dey thows 'em away. Dey knows whut dey is doin' while dey is at it, an' hates theirselves fuh it but they keeps on hangin' after huh tell she's empty. Den dey hates huh fuh bein' a cane-chew an' in de way."

"We oughter take Syke an' dat stray 'oman uh his'n down in Lake Howell swamp an' lay on de rawhide till they cain't say 'Lawd a' mussy.' He allus wuz uh ovahbearin' niggah, but since dat white 'oman from up north done teached 'im how to run a automobile, he done got to biggety to live—an' we oughter kill 'im." Old Man Anderson advised.

A grunt of approval went around the porch. But the heat was melting their civic virtue and Elijah Moseley began to bait Joe Clarke.

"Come on, Joe, git a melon outa dere an' slice it up for yo' customers. We'se all sufferin' wid de heat. De bear's done got *me!*"

"Thass right, Joe, a watermelon is jes' whut Ah needs tuh cure de eppizu-dicks," Walter Thomas joined forces with Moseley. "Come on dere, Joe. We all is steady customers an' you aint set us up in a long time. Ah chooses dat long, bowlegged Floridy favorite."

45   "A god, an' be dough You all gimme twenty cents and slice away," Clarke retorted. "Ah needs a col' slice m'self. Heah, everybody chip in. Ah'll lend y'll mah meat knife."

The money was quickly subscribed and the huge melon brought forth. At that moment, Sykes and Bertha arrived. A determined silence fell on the porch and the melon was put away again.

Merchant snapped down the blade of his jack-knife and moved toward the store door.

"Come on in, Joe, an' gimme a slab uh sow belly an' uh pound uh coffee—almost fuhgot 'twas Sat'day. Got to git on home." Most of the men left also.

Just then Delia drove past on her way home, as Sykes was ordering magnificently for Bertha. It pleased him for Delia to see.

50   "Git whutsoever yo' heart desires, Honey. Wait a minute, Joe. Give huh two botles uh strawberry soda-water, uh quart uh parched ground-peas, an' a block uh chewin' gum."

With all this they left the store, with Sykes reminding Bertha that this was his town and she could have it if she wanted it.

The men returned soon after they left, and held their watermelon feast.

"Where did Syke Jones git dat 'oman from no-how?" Lindsay asked.

"Ovah Apopka. Guess dey musta been cleanin' out de town when she lef'. She don't look lak a thing but a hunk uh liver wid hair on it."

55   "Well, she sho' kin squall," Dave Carter contributed. "When she gits ready tuh laff, she jes' opens huh mouf an' latches it back tuh de las' notch. No ole grandpa alligator down in Lake Bell ain't got nothin' on huh."

Bertha had been in town three months now. Sykes was still paying her room rent at Della Lewis'—the only house in town that would have taken her in. Sykes took her frequently to Winter Park to "stomps." He still assured her that he was the swellest man in the state.

"Sho' you kin have dat lil' ole house soon's Ah kin git dat 'oman outa dere. Everything b'longs tuh me an' you sho' kin have it. Ah sho' 'bominates uh skinny 'oman. Lawdy, you sho' is got one portly shape on you! You kin git *anything* you wants. Dis is *mah* town an' you sho' kin have it."

Delia's work-worn knees crawled over the earth in Gethsemane and up the rocks of Calvary many, many times during these months. She avoided the villagers and meeting places in her efforts to be blind and deaf. But Bertha nullified this to a degree, by coming to Delia's house to call Sykes out to her at the gate.

Delia and Sykes fought all the time now with no peaceful interludes. They slept and ate in silence. Two or three times Delia had attempted a timid friendliness, but she was repulsed each time. It was plain that the breaches must remain agape.

60   The sun had burned July to August. The heat streamed down like a million hot arrows, smiting all things living upon the earth. Grass withered, leaves browned, snakes went blind in shedding and men and dogs went mad. Dog days!

Delia came home one day and found Sykes there before her. She wondered, but started to go on into the house without speaking, even though he was standing in the kitchen door and she must either stoop under his arm or ask him to move. He made no room for her. She noticed a soap box beside the steps, but paid no particular attention to it, knowing that he must have brought it there. As she was stooping to pass under his outstretched arm, he suddenly pushed her backward, laughingly.

"Look in de box dere Delia, Ah done brung yuh somethin'!"

She nearly fell upon the box in her stumbling, and when she saw what it held, she all but fainted outright.

"Syke! Syke, mah Gawd! You take dat rattlesnake 'way from heah! You *gottuh*. Oh, Jesus, have mussy!"

65   "Ah aint gut tuh do nuthin' uh de kin'—fact is Ah aint got tuh do nothin'
but die. Taint no use uh you puttin' on airs makin' out lak you skeered uh
dat snake—he's gointer stay right heah tell he die. He wouldn't bite me cause
Ah knows how tuh handle 'im. Nohow he wouldn't risk breakin' out his fangs
'gin *yo'* skinny laigs."

"Naw, now Syke, don't keep dat thing 'roun' heah tuh skeer me tuh death.
You knows Ah'm even feared uh earth worms. Thass de biggest snake Ah
evah did see. Kill 'im Syke, please."

"Doan ast me tuh do nothin' fuh yuh. Goin' 'roun' tryin' tuh be so damn
asterperious. Naw, Ah aint gonna kill it. Ah think uh damn sight mo' uh him
dan you! Dat's a nice snake an' anybody doan lak 'im kin jes' hit de grit."

The village soon heard that Sykes had the snake, and came to see and ask
questions.

"How de hen-fire did you ketch dat six-foot rattler, Syke?" Thomas asked.

70   "He's full uh frogs so he caint hardly move, thass how Ah eased up on 'm.
But Ah'm a snake charmer an' knows how tuh handle 'em. Shux, dat aint
nothin'. Ah could ketch one eve'y day if Ah so wanted tuh."

"Whut he needs is a heavy hick'ry club leaned real heavy on his head.
Dat's de bes 'way tuh charm a rattlesnake."

"Naw, Walt, y'll jes' don't understand dese diamon' backs lak Ah do," said
Sykes in a superior tone of voice.

The village agreed with Walter, but the snake stayed on. His box remained
by the kitchen door with its screen wire covering. Two or three days later it had
digested its meal of frogs and literally came to life. It rattled at every movement in the kitchen or the yard. One day as Delia came down the kitchen steps
she saw his chalky-white fangs curved like scimitars hung in the wire meshes. This time she did not run away with averted eyes as usual. She stood for
a long time in the doorway in a red fury that grew bloodier for every second
that she regarded the creature that was her torment.

That night she broached the subject as soon as Sykes sat down to the table.

75   "Syke, Ah wants you tuh take dat snake 'way fum heah. You done starved
me an' Ah put up widcher, you done beat me an Ah took dat, but you done
kilt all mah insides bringin' dat varmint heah."

Sykes poured out a saucer full of coffee and drank it deliberately before
he answered her.

"A whole lot Ah keer 'bout how you feels inside uh out. Dat snake aint goin'
no damn wheah till Ah gits ready fuh 'im tuh go. So fur as beatin' is concerned, yuh aint took near all dat you gointer take ef yuh stay 'roun' *me*."

Delia pushed back her plate and got up from the table. "Ah hates you,
Sykes," she said calmly. "Ah hates you tuh de same degree dat Ah useter love
yuh. Ah done took an' took till mah belly is full up tuh mah neck. Dat's de
reason Ah got mah letter fum de church an' moved mah membership tuh Woodbridge—so Ah don't haftuh take no sacrament wid yuh. Ah don't wantuh see
yuh 'roun' me atall. Lay 'roun' wid dat 'oman all yuh wants tuh, but gwan
'way fum me an' mah house. At hates yuh lak uh suck-egg dog."

Sykes almost let the huge wad of corn bread and collard greens he was
chewing fall out of his mouth in amazement. He had a hard time whipping himself up to the proper fury to try to answer Delia.

80   "Well, Ah'm glad you does hate me. Ah'm sho' tiahed uh you hangin' ontuh
me. Ah don't want yuh. Look at yuh stringey ole neck! Yo' rawbony laigs an'

arms is enough tuh cut uh man tuh death. You looks jes' lak de devvul's doll-baby tuh *me*. You cain't hate me no worse dan Ah hates you. Ah been hatin' *you* fuh years.

"Yo' ole black hide don't look lak nothin' tuh me, but uh passle uh wrin-kled up rubber, wid yo' big ole yeahs flappin' on each side lak up paih uh buzzard wings. Don't think Ah'm gointuh be run 'way fum mah house nei-ther. Ah'm goin' tuh de white folks bout *you*, mah young man, de very nex' time you lay yo' han's on me. Mah cup is done run ovah." Delia said this with no signs of fear and Sykes departed from the house, threatening her, but made not the slightest move to carry out any of them.

That night he did not return at all, and the next day being Sunday, Delia was glad that she did not have to quarrel before she hitched up her pony and drove the four miles to Woodbridge.

She stayed to the night service—"love feast"—which was very warm and full of spirit. In the emotional winds her domestic trials were borne far and wide so that she sang as she drove homeward,

> *"Jurden water, black an' col'*
> *Chills de body, not de soul*
> *An' Ah wantah cross Jurden in uh calm time."*

She came from the barn to the kitchen door and stopped.

85   "Whut's de mattah, ol' satan, you aint kickin' up yo' racket?" She addressed the snake's box. Complete silence. She went on into the house with a new hope in its birth struggles. Perhaps her threat to go to the white folks had fright-ened Sykes! Perhaps he was sorry! Fifteen years of misery and suppression had brought Delia to the place where she would hope *anything* that looked towards a way over or through her wall of inhibitions.

She felt in the match safe behind the stove at once for a match. There was only one there.

"Dat niggah wouldn't fetch nothin' heah tuh save his rotten neck, but he kin run thew whut Ah brings quick enough. Now he done toted off nigh on tuh haff uh box uh matches. He done had dat 'oman heah in mah house, too."

Nobody but a woman could tell how she knew this even before she struck the match. But she did and it put her into a new fury.

Presently she brought in the tubs to put the white things to soak. This time she decided she need not bring the hamper out of the bedroom; she would go in there and do the sorting. She picked up the pot-bellied lamp and went in. The room was small and the hamper stood hard by the foot of the white iron bed. She could sit and reach through the bedposts—resting as she worked.

90   "Ah wantah cross Jurden in uh calm time." She was singing again. The mood of the "love feast" had returned. She threw back the lid of the basket almost gaily. Then, moved by both horror and terror, she spring back toward the door. *There lay the snake in the basket!* He moved sluggishly at first, but even as she turned round and round, jumped up and down in an insanity of fear, he began to stir vigorously. She saw him pouring his awful beauty from the bas-ket upon the bed, then she seized the lamp and ran as fast as she could to the kitchen. The wind from the open door blew out the light and the dark-ness added to her terror. She sped to the darkness of the yard, slamming the door after her before she thought to set down the lamp. She did not feel safe even on the ground, so she climbed up in the hay barn.

There for an hour or more she lay sprawled upon the hay a gibbering wreck.

Finally she grew quiet, and after that, coherent thought. With this, stalked through her a cold, bloody rage. Hours of this. A period of introspection, a space of retrospection, then a mixture of both. Out of this an awful calm.

"Well, Ah done de bes' Ah could. If things aint right, Gawd knows taint mah fault."

She went to sleep—a twitchy sleep—and woke up to a faint gray sky. There was a loud hollow sound below. She peered out. Sykes was at the wood-pile, demolishing a wire-covered box.

95   He hurried to the kitchen door, but hung outside there some minutes before he entered, and stood some minutes more inside before he closed it after him.

The gray in the sky was spreading. Delia descended without fear now, and crouched beneath the low bedroom window. The drawn shade shut out the dawn, shut in the night. But the thin walls held back no sound.

"Dat ol' scratch is woke up now!" She mused at the tremendous whirr inside, which every woods-man knows, is one of the sound illusions. The rattler is a ventriloquist. His whirr sounds to the right, to the left, straight ahead, behind, close under foot—everywhere but where it is. Woe to him who guesses wrong unless he is prepared to hold up his end of the argument! Sometimes he strikes without rattling at all.

Inside, Sykes heard nothing until he knocked a pot lid off the stove while trying to reach the match safe in the dark. He had emptied his pockets at Bertha's.

The snake seemed to wake up under the stove and Sykes made a quick leap into the bedroom. In spite of the gin he had had, his head was clearing now.

100   "Mah Gawd!" he chattered, "ef Ah could on'y strack uh light!"

The rattling ceased for a moment as he stood paralyzed. He waited. It seemed that the snake waited also.

"Oh, fuh de light! Ah thought he'd be too sick"—Sykes was muttering to himself when the whirr began again, closer, right underfoot this time. Long before this, Sykes' ability to think had been flattened down to primitive instinct and he leaped—onto the bed.

Outside Delia heard a cry that might have come from a maddened chimpanzee, a stricken gorilla. All the terror, all the horror, all the rage that man possibly could express, without a recognizable human sound.

A tremendous stir inside there, another series of animal screams, the intermittent whirr of the reptile. The shade torn violently down from the window, letting in the red dawn, a huge brown hand seizing the window stick, great dull blows upon the wooden floor punctuating the gibberish of sound long after the rattle of the snake had abruptly subsided. All this Delia could see and hear from her place beneath the window, and it made her ill. She crept over to the four-o'clocks and stretched herself on the cool earth to recover.

105   She lay there. "Delia, Delia!" She could hear Sykes calling in a most despairing tone as one who expected no answer. The sun crept on up, and he called. Delia could not move—her legs were gone flabby. She never moved, he called, and the sun kept rising.

"Mah Gawd!" She heard him moan, "Mah Gawd fum Heben!" She heard him stumbling about and got up from her flower-bed. The sun was growing warm. As she approached the door she heard him call out hopefully, "Delia, is dat you Ah heah?"

She saw him on his hands and knees as soon as she reached the door. He crept an inch or two toward her—all that he was able, and she saw his horribly swollen neck and his one open eye shining with hope. A surge of pity too strong to support bore her away from that eye that must, could not, fail to see the tubs. He would see the lamp. Orlando with its doctors was too far. She could scarcely reach the Chinaberry tree, where she waited in the growing heat while inside she knew the cold river was creeping up and up to extinguish that eye which must know by now that she knew.

INQUIRING FURTHER

1. Lorde writes in "The Transformation of Silence into Action" that speaking out is necessary to "[reclaim] that language which has been made to work against us." Who do you think she means by "us"? Do you believe that Lorde's advice applies to everyone? Why or why not?

2. In what ways can you see Hurston's archaeological background revealed in "Sweat?" Do you think the story is concerned more with the particulars of the community depicted in "Sweat" or with general themes and ideas? Why?

3. How would you interpret Hurston's story, "Sweat," in terms of Lorde's advice? Would you say that Delia's actions are justified? If so, what can you say about Lorde's advice? How far can one go with acts of resistance? Freewrite for five minutes about your judgments concerning Delia and the responsibility of women to speak out.

EXTENDED INQUIRY

The Political and the Personal in *Hamlet*

In many ways, *Hamlet* is about decisions. The central tension in the play involves Hamlet deliberating about suicide and revenge, encapsulated in his famous "to be or not to be" soliloquy. A number of other important choices are made, however. Many of these decisions have both personal and political implications. Claudius's decision to kill Hamlet's father and take over the kingdom, for instance, represents a political act, a grab for power on the part of Claudius.

Gertrude's decision to marry Claudius so shortly after the death of King Hamlet could also be seen in political terms; it represents a way of providing stability for the kingdom. However, the marriage between Gertrude and Claudius has personal elements as well, as both seem content, even happy, with their new relationship. In *Hamlet*, the tensions between the actions of individuals and the well-being of the kingdom ask us to consider the connections between the personal and the political. In this section we present the play of *Hamlet*, as well as some of the responses that have been developed by other authors in the 400 plus years since the play was written.

William Shakespeare

Hamlet, Prince of Denmark

Dramatis Personæ.

CLAUDIUS:	King of Denmark.
HAMLET:	Son to the late, and Nephew to the present King.
FORTINBRAS:	Prince of Norway.
HORATIO:	Friend to Hamlet.
POLONIUS:	Lord Chamberlain.
LAERTES:	his Son.
VOLTIMAND, CORNELIUS, ROSENCRANTZ, GUILDENSTERN, OSRIC:	Courtiers.
A Gentleman, A Priest.	
MARCELLUS, BERNARDO:	Officers.
FRANCISCO:	a Soldier.
REYNALDO:	Servant to Polonius.
A Captain. English Ambassadors.	
Players:	Two Clowns, Grave-diggers.
GERTRUDE:	Queen of Denmark and Mother to Hamlet.
OPHELIA:	Daughter to Polonius.

Lords, Ladies, Officers, Soldiers,
Sailors, Messengers, and Attendants.
Ghost of Hamlet's Father.

SCENE: *Elsinore.*

ACT I.

Scene I.—Elsinore. A Platform before the Castle.

FRANCISCO *at his post. Enter to him* BERNARDO.

BER: Who's there?
FRAN: Nay, answer me; stand, and unfold yourself.
BER: Long live the king!
FRAN: Bernardo?
BER: He.
FRAN: You come most carefully upon your hour.
BER: 'Tis now struck twelve; get thee to bed, Francisco.
FRAN: For this relief much thanks; 'tis bitter cold,
        And I am sick at heart.
BER: Have you had quiet guard?
FRAN: Not a mouse stirring.
BER: Well, good-night.

        If you do meet Horatio and Marcellus,
        The rivals of my watch, bid them make haste.
FRAN: I think I hear them. Stand, ho!, Who's there?

    Enter HORATIO *and* MARCELLUS.

HOR: Friends to this ground.
MAR: And liegemen to the Dane.
FRAN: Give you good-night.
MAR: O! farewell, honest soldier:
        Who hath reliev'd you?
FRAN: Bernardo has my place. Give you good-night.

    [*Exit*]

MAR: Holla! Bernardo!
BER: Say, What! is Horatio there?
HOR: A piece of him.
BER: Welcome, Horatio; welcome, good Marcellus.
MAR: What! has this thing appear'd again to-night?
BER: I have seen nothing.
MAR: Horatio says 'tis but our fantasy,
        And will not let belief take hold of him
        Touching this dreaded sight twice seen of us:
        Therefore I have entreated him along
        With us to watch the minutes of this night;
        That if again this apparition come,
        He may approve our eyes and speak to it.
HOR: Tush, tush! 'twill not appear.
BER: Sit down awhile,
        And let us once again assail your ears,
        That are so fortified against our story,
        What we two nights have seen.
HOR: Well, sit we down,
        And let us hear Bernardo speak of this.
BER: Last night of all,
        When yond same star that's westward from the pole
        Had made his course to illume that part of heaven
        Where now it burns, Marcellus and myself,
        The bell then beating one,—
MAR: Peace! break thee off; look, where it comes again!

    Enter GHOST.

BER: In the same figure, like the king that's dead.
MAR: Thou art a scholar; speak to it, Horatio.
BER: Looks it not like the king? mark it, Horatio.
HOR: Most like: it harrows me with fear and wonder.
BER: It would be spoke to.
MAR: Question it, Horatio.
HOR: What art thou that usurp'st this time of night,
        Together with that fair and war-like form
        In which the majesty of buried Denmark
        Did sometimes march? by heaven I charge thee, speak!

MAR: It is offended.

BER: See! it stalks away.

HOR: Stay! speak, speak! I charge thee, speak!

Exit GHOST.

MAR: 'Tis gone, and will not answer.

BER: How now, Horatio! you tremble and look pale:
    Is not this something more than fantasy?
    What think you on 't?

HOR: Before my God, I might not this believe
    Without the sensible and true avouch
    Of mine own eyes.

MAR: Is it not like the king?

HOR: As thou art to thyself:
    Such was the very armour he had on
    When he the ambitious Norway combated;
    So frown'd he once, when, in an angry parle,
    He smote the sledded Polacks on the ice.
    'Tis strange.

MAR: Thus twice before, and jump at this dead hour,
    With martial stalk hath he gone by our watch.

HOR: In what particular thought to work I know not;
    But in the gross and scope of my opinion,
    This bodes some strange eruption to our state.

MAR: Good now, sit down, and tell me, he that knows,
    Why this same strict and most observant watch
    So nightly toils the subject of the land;
    And why such daily cast of brazen cannon,
    And foreign mart for implements of war;
    Why such impress of shipwrights, whose sore task
    Does not divide the Sunday from the week;
    What might be toward, that this sweaty haste
    Doth make the night joint-labourer with the day:
    Who is 't that can inform me?

HOR: That can I;
    At least, the whisper goes so. Our last king,
    Whose image even but now appear'd to us,
    Was, as you know, by Fortinbras of Norway,
    Thereto prick'd on by a most emulate pride,
    Dar'd to the combat; in which our valiant Hamlet—
    For so this side of our known world esteem'd him—
    Did slay this Fortinbras; who, by a seal'd compact,
    Well ratified by law and heraldry,
    Did forfeit with his life all those his lands
    Which he stood seiz'd of, to the conqueror;
    Against the which, a moiety competent
    Was gaged by our king; which had return'd
    To the inheritance of Fortinbras,
    Had he been vanquisher; as, by the same covenant,
    And carriage of the article design'd,
    His fell to Hamlet. Now, sir, young Fortinbras,

Of unimproved mettle hot and full,
Hath in the skirts of Norway here and there
Shark'd up a list of lawless resolutes,
For food and diet, to some enterprise
That hath a stomach in 't; which is no other—
As it doth well appear unto our state—
But to recover of us, by strong hand
And terms compulsative, those foresaid lands
So by his father lost. And this, I take it,
Is the main motive of our preparations,
The source of this our watch and the chief head
Of this post-haste and romage in the land.

BER: I think it be no other but e'en so;
  Well may it sort that this portentous figure
  Comes armed through our watch, so like the king
  That was and is the question of these wars.

HOR: A mote it is to trouble the mind's eye.
  In the most high and palmy state of Rome,
  A little ere the mightiest Julius fell,
  The graves stood tenantless and the sheeted dead
  Did squeak and gibber in the Roman streets;
  As stars with trains of fire and dews of blood,
  Disasters in the sun; and the moist star
  Upon whose influence Neptune's empire stands
  Was sick almost to doomsday with eclipse;
  And even the like precurse of fierce events,
  As harbingers preceding still the fates
  And prologue to the omen coming on,
  Have heaven and earth together demonstrated
  Unto our climatures and countrymen.
  But, soft! behold! lo! where it comes again.

Re-enter GHOST.

  I'll cross it, though it blast me. Stay, illusion!
  If thou hast any sound, or use of voice,
  Speak to me:
  If there be any good thing to be done,
  That may to thee do ease and grace to me,
  Speak to me:
  If thou art privy to thy country's fate,
  Which happily foreknowing may avoid,
  O! speak;
  Or if thou hast uphoarded in thy life
  Extorted treasure in the womb of earth,
  For which, they say, you spirits oft walk in death,

[*Cock crows.*]

  Speak of it: stay, and speak! Stop it, Marcellus.

MAR: Shall I strike at it with my partisan?

HOR: Do, if it will not stand.

BER: 'Tis here!
HOR: 'Tis here!

[*Exit* Ghost.]

MAR: 'Tis gone!
    We do it wrong, being so majestical,
    To offer it the show of violence;
    For it is, as the air, invulnerable,
    And our vain blows malicious mockery.
BER: It was about to speak when the cock crew.
HOR: And then it started like a guilty thing
    Upon a fearful summons. I have heard,
    The cock, that is the trumpet to the morn,
    Doth with his lofty and shrill-sounding throat
    Awake the god of day; and at his warning,
    Whether in sea or fire, in earth or air,
    The extravagant and erring spirit hies
    To his confine; and of the truth herein
    This present object made probation.
MAR: It faded on the crowing of the cock.
    Some say that ever 'gainst that season comes
    Wherein our Saviour's birth is celebrated,
    The bird of dawning singeth all night long;
    And then, they say, no spirit can walk abroad;
    The nights are wholesome; then no planets strike,
    No fairy takes, nor witch hath power to charm,
    So hallow'd and so gracious is the time.
HOR: So have I heard and do in part believe it.
    But, look, the morn in russet mantle clad,
    Walks o'er the dew of yon high eastern hill;
    Break we our watch up; and by my advice
    Let us impart what we have seen to-night
    Unto young Hamlet; for, upon my life,
    This spirit, dumb to us, will speak to him.
    Do you consent we shall acquaint him with it,
    As needful in our loves, fitting our duty?
MAR: Let's do't, I pray; and I this morning know
    Where we shall find him most conveniently.

[*Exeunt.*]

Scene II.—A Room of State in the Castle.

Enter the KING, QUEEN, HAMLET, POLONIUS, LAERTES, VOLTIMAND, CORNELIUS, LORDS, *and* ATTENDANTS.

KING: Though yet of Hamlet our dear brother's death
    The memory be green, and that it us befitted
    To bear our hearts in grief and our whole kingdom
    To be contracted in one brow of woe,
    Yet so far hath discretion fought with nature

That we with wisest sorrow think on him,
Together with remembrance of ourselves.
Therefore our sometime sister, now our queen,
The imperial jointress of this war-like state,
Have we, as 'twere with a defeated joy,
With one auspicious and one dropping eye,
With mirth in funeral and with dirge in marriage,
In equal scale weighing delight and dole,
Taken to wife: nor have we herein barr'd
Your better wisdoms, which have freely gone
With this affair along: for all, our thanks.
Now follows, that you know, young Fortinbras,
Holding a weak supposal of our worth,
Or thinking by our late dear brother's death
Our state to be disjoint and out of frame,
Colleagued with the dream of his advantage,
He hath not fail'd to pester us with message,
Importing the surrender of those lands
Lost by his father, with all bands of law,
To our most valiant brother. So much for him.
Now for ourself and for this time of meeting.
Thus much the business is: we have here writ
To Norway, uncle of young Fortinbras,
Who, impotent and bed-rid, scarcely hears
Of this his nephew's purpose, to suppress
His further gait herein; in that the levies,
The lists and full proportions, are all made
Out of his subject; and we here dispatch
You, good Cornelius, and you, Voltimand,
For bearers of this greeting to old Norway,
Giving to you no further personal power
To business with the king more than the scope
Of these delated articles allow.
Farewell and let your haste commend your duty

COR:
VOL:} In that and all things will we show our duty.

KING: We doubt it nothing: heartily farewell.

[*Exeunt* VOLTIMAND *and* CORNELIUS.]

And now, Laertes, what's the news with you?
You told us of some suit; what is't, Laertes?
You cannot speak of reason to the Dane,
And lose your voice; what wouldst thou beg, Laertes,
That shall not be my offer, not thy asking?
The head is not more native to the heart,
The hand more instrumental to the mouth,
Than is the throne of Denmark to thy father.
What wouldst thou have, Laertes?

LAER: Dread my lord,
Your leave and favour to return to France;
From whence though willingly I came to Denmark,

To show my duty in your coronation,
Yet now, I must confess, that duty done,
My thoughts and wishes bend again toward France
And bow them to your gracious leave and pardon.

KING: Have you your father's leave? What says Polonius?

POL: He hath, my lord, wrung from me my slow leave
    By laboursome petition, and at last
    Upon his will I seal'd my hard consent:
    I do beseech you, give him leave to go.

KING: Take thy fair hour, Laertes; time be thine,
    And thy best graces spend it at thy will.
    But now, my cousin Hamlet, and my son,—

HAM: [*Aside.*] A little more than kin, and less than kind.

KING: How is it that the clouds still hang on you?

HAM: Not so, my lord; I am too much i' the sun.

QUEEN: Good Hamlet, cast thy nighted colour off,
    And let thine eye look like a friend on Denmark.
    Do not for ever with thy vailed lids
    Seek for thy noble father in the dust:
    Thou know'st 'tis common; all that live must die,
    Passing through nature to eternity.

HAM: Ay, madam, it is common.

QUEEN: If it be,
    Why seems it so particular with thee?

HAM: Seems, madam! Nay, it is; I know not 'seems.'
    'Tis not alone my inky cloak, good mother,
    Nor customary suits of solemn black,
    Nor windy suspiration of forc'd breath,
    No, nor the fruitful river in the eye,
    Nor the dejected haviour of the visage,
    Together with all forms, modes, shows of grief,
    That can denote me truly; these indeed seem,
    For they are actions that a man might play:
    But I have that within which passeth show;
    These but the trappings and the suits of woe.

KING: 'Tis sweet and commendable in your nature, Hamlet,
    To give these mourning duties to your father:
    But, you must know, your father lost a father;
    That father lost, lost his; and the survivor bound
    In filial obligation for some term
    To do obsequious sorrow; but to persever
    In obstinate condolement is a course
    Of impious stubbornness; 'tis unmanly grief:
    It shows a will most incorrect to heaven,
    A heart unfortified, a mind impatient,
    An understanding simple and unschool'd:
    For what we know must be and is as common
    As any the most vulgar thing to sense,
    Why should we in our peevish opposition
    Take it to heart? Fie! 'tis a fault to heaven,
    A fault against the dead, a fault to nature,
    To reason most absurd, whose common theme

Is death of fathers, and who still hath cried,
From the first corse till he that died to-day,
'This must be so.' We pray you, throw to earth
This unprevailing woe, and think of us
As of a father; for let the world take note,
You are the most immediate to our throne;
And with no less nobility of love
Than that which dearest father bears his son
Do I impart toward you. For your intent
In going back to school in Wittenberg,
It is most retrograde to our desire;
And we beseech you, bend you to remain
Here, in the cheer and comfort of our eye,
Our chiefest courtier, cousin, and our son.

QUEEN: Let not thy mother lose her prayers, Hamlet:
I pray thee, stay with us; go not to Wittenberg.

HAM: I shall in all my best obey you, madam.

KING: Why, 'tis a loving and a fair reply:
Be as ourself in Denmark. Madam, come;
This gentle and unforc'd accord of Hamlet
Sits smiling to my heart; in grace whereof,
No jocund health that Denmark drinks to-day,
But the great cannon to the clouds shall tell,
And the king's rouse the heavens shall bruit again,
Re-speaking earthly thunder. Come away.

[*Exeunt all except* HAMLET.]

HAM: O! that this too too solid flesh would melt,
Thaw and resolve itself into a dew;
Or that the Everlasting had not fix'd
His canon 'gainst self-slaughter! O God! O God!
How weary, stale, flat, and unprofitable
Seem to me all the uses of this world.
Fie on 't! O fie! 'tis an unweeded garden,
That grows to seed; things rank and gross in nature
Possess it merely. That it should come to this!
But two months dead: nay, not so much, not two:
So excellent a king; that was, to this,
Hyperion to a satyr; so loving to my mother
That he might not beteem the winds of heaven
Visit her face too roughly. Heaven and earth!
Must I remember? why, she would hang on him,
As if increase of appetite had grown
By what it fed on; and yet, within a month,
Let me not think on 't: Frailty, thy name is woman!
A little month; or ere those shoes were old
With which she follow'd my poor father's body,
Like Niobe, all tears; why she, even she,—
O God! a beast, that wants discourse of reason,
Would have mourn'd longer,—married with mine uncle,
My father's brother, but no more like my father
Than I to Hercules: within a month,

> Ere yet the salt of most unrighteous tears
> Had left the flushing in her galled eyes,
> She married. O! most wicked speed, to post
> With such dexterity to incestuous sheets.
> It is not nor it cannot come to good;
> But break, my heart, for I must hold my tongue!

Enter HORATIO, MARCELLUS, *and* BERNARDO.

HOR: Hail to your lordship!

HAM: I am glad to see you well: Horatio, or I do forget myself.

HOR: The same, my lord, and your poor servant ever.

HAM: Sir, my good friend; I'll change that name with you.
> And what make you from Wittenberg, Horatio?
> Marcellus?

MAR: My good lord,—

HAM: I am very glad to see you.
> [*To Bernardo.*] Good even, sir.
> But what, in faith, make you from Wittenberg?

HOR: A truant disposition, good my lord.

HAM: I would not hear your enemy say so,
> Nor shall you do mine ear that violence,
> To make it truster of your own report
> Against yourself; I know you are no truant.
> But what is your affair in Elsinore?
> We'll teach you to drink deep ere you depart.

HOR: My lord, I came to see your father's funeral.

HAM: I pray thee, do not mock me, fellow-student;
> I think it was to see my mother's wedding.

HOR: Indeed, my lord, it follow'd hard upon.

HAM: Thrift, thrift, Horatio! the funeral bak'd meats
> Did coldly furnish forth the marriage tables.
> Would I had met my dearest foe in heaven
> Ere I had ever seen that day, Horatio!
> My father, methinks I see my father.

HOR: O! where, my lord?

HAM: In my mind's eye, Horatio.

HOR: I saw him once; he was a goodly king.

HAM: He was a man, take him for all in all,
> I shall not look upon his like again.

HOR: My lord, I think I saw him yesternight.

HAM: Saw who?

HOR: My lord, the king your father.

HAM: The king, my father!

HOR: Season your admiration for a while
> With an attent ear, till I may deliver,
> Upon the witness of these gentlemen,
> This marvel to you.

HAM: For God's love, let me hear.

HOR: Two nights together had these gentlemen,
> Marcellus and Bernardo, on their watch,
> In the dead vast and middle of the night,
> Been thus encounter'd: a figure like your father,

    Armed at points exactly, cap-a-pe,
    Appears before them, and with solemn march
    Goes slow and stately by them: thrice he walk'd
    By their oppress'd and fear surprised eyes,
    Within his truncheon's length; whilst they, distill'd
    Almost to jelly with the act of fear,
    Stand dumb and speak not to him. This to me
    In dreadful secrecy impart they did,
    And I with them the third night kept the watch;
    Where, as they had deliver'd, both in time,
    Form of the thing, each word made true and good,
    The apparition comes. I knew your father;
    These hands are not more like.

HAM: But where was this?

MAR: My lord, upon the platform where we watch'd.

HAM: Did you not speak to it?

HOR: My lord, I did;
    But answer made it none; yet once methought
    It lifted up its head and did address
    Itself to motion, like as it would speak;
    But even then the morning cock crew loud,
    And at the sound it shrunk in haste away
    And vanish'd from our sight.

HAM: 'Tis very strange.

HOR: As I do live, my honour'd lord, 'tis true;
    And we did think it writ down in our duty
    To let you know of it.

HAM: Indeed, indeed, sirs, but this troubles me.
    Hold you the watch to-night?

MAR:
BER: }We do, my lord.

HAM: Arm'd, say you?

MAR:
BER: }Arm'd, my lord.

HAM: From top to toe?

MAR:
BER: }My lord, from head to foot.

HAM: Then saw you not his face?

HOR: O yes! my lord; he wore his beaver up.

HAM: What! look'd he frowningly?

HOR: A countenance more in sorrow than in anger.

HAM: Pale or red?

HOR: Nay, very pale.

HAM: And fix'd his eyes upon you?

HOR: Most constantly.

HAM: I would I had been there.

HOR: It would have much amaz'd you.

HAM: Very like, very like. Stay'd it long?

HOR: While one with moderate haste might tell a hundred.

MAR:
BER: }Longer, longer.

HOR: Not when I saw it.

HAM: His beard was grizzled, no?

HOR: It was, as I have seen it in his life,
　　　　A sable silver'd.

HAM: I will watch to-night;
　　　　Perchance 'twill walk again.

HOR: I warrant it will.

HAM: If it assume my noble father's person,
　　　　I'll speak to it, though hell itself should gape
　　　　And bid me hold my peace. I pray you all,
　　　　If you have hitherto conceal'd this sight,
　　　　Let it be tenable in your silence still;
　　　　And whatsoever else shall hap to-night,
　　　　Give it an understanding, but no tongue:
　　　　I will requite your loves. So, fare you well.
　　　　Upon the platform, 'twixt eleven and twelve,
　　　　I'll visit you.

ALL: Our duty to your honour.

HAM: Your loves, as mine to you. Farewell.

[*Exeunt* HORATIO, MARCELLUS, *and* BERNARDO.]

　　　　My father's spirit in arms! all is not well;
　　　　I doubt some foul play: would the night were come!
　　　　Till then sit still, my soul: foul deeds will rise,
　　　　Though all the earth o'erwhelm them, to men's eyes.

[*Exit.*]

Scene III.—A Room in Polonius' House.

Enter LAERTES *and* OPHELIA.

LAER: My necessaries are embark'd; farewell:
　　　　And, sister, as the winds give benefit
　　　　And convoy is assistant, do not sleep,
　　　　But let me hear from you.

OPH: Do you doubt that?

LAER: For Hamlet, and the trifling of his favour,
　　　　Hold it a fashion and a toy in blood,
　　　　A violet in the youth of primy nature,
　　　　Forward, not permanent, sweet, not lasting,
　　　　The perfume and suppliance of a minute;
　　　　No more.

OPH: No more but so?

LAER: Think it no more:
　　　　For nature, crescent, does not grow alone
　　　　In thews and bulk; but, as this temple waxes,
　　　　The inward service of the mind and soul
　　　　Grows wide withal. Perhaps he loves you now,
　　　　And now no soil nor cautel doth besmirch
　　　　The virtue of his will; but you must fear,
　　　　His greatness weigh'd, his will is not his own,

For he himself is subject to his birth;
He may not, as unvalu'd persons do,
Carve for himself, for on his choice depends
The safety and the health of the whole state;
And therefore must his choice be circumscrib'd
Unto the voice and yielding of that body
Whereof he is the head. Then if he says he loves you,
It fits your wisdom so far to believe it
As he in his particular act and place
May give his saying deed; which is no further
Than the main voice of Denmark goes withal.
Then weigh what loss your honour may sustain,
If with too credent ear you list his songs,
Or lose your heart, or your chaste treasure open
To his unmaster'd importunity.
Fear it, Ophelia, fear it, my dear sister;
And keep you in the rear of your affection,
Out of the shot and danger of desire.
The chariest maid is prodigal enough
If she unmask her beauty to the moon;
Virtue herself 'scapes not calumnious strokes;
The canker galls the infants of the spring
Too oft before their buttons be disclos'd,
And in the morn and liquid dew of youth
Contagious blastments are most imminent.
Be wary then; best safety lies in fear:
Youth to itself rebels, though none else near.

OPH: I shall th' effect of this good lesson keep,
As watchman to my heart. But, good my brother,
Do not, as some ungracious pastors do,
Show me the steep and thorny way to heaven,
Whiles, like a puff'd and reckless libertine,
Himself the primrose path of dalliance treads,
And recks not his own rede.

LAER: O! fear me not.
I stay too long; but here my father comes.

Enter POLONIUS.

A double blessing is a double grace;
Occasion smiles upon a second leave.

POL: Yet here, Laertes! aboard, aboard, for shame!
The wind sits in the shoulder of your sail,
And you are stay'd for. There, my blessing with thee!
And these few precepts in thy memory
Look thou character. Give thy thoughts no tongue,
Nor any unproportion'd thought his act.
Be thou familiar, but by no means vulgar;
The friends thou hast, and their adoption tried,
Grapple them to thy soul with hoops of steel;
But do not dull thy palm with entertainment
Of each new-hatch'd, unfledg'd comrade. Beware
Of entrance to a quarrel, but, being in,

Bear 't that th' opposed may beware of thee.
Give every man thine ear, but few thy voice;
Take each man's censure, but reserve thy judgment.
Costly thy habit as thy purse can buy,
But not express'd in fancy; rich, not gaudy;
For the apparel oft proclaims the man,
And they in France of the best rank and station
Are most select and generous, chief in that.
Neither a borrower, nor a lender be;
For loan oft loses both itself and friend,
And borrowing dulls the edge of husbandry.
This above all: to thine own self be true,
And it must follow, as the night the day,
Thou canst not then be false to any man.
Farewell; my blessing season this in thee!

LAER: Most humbly do I take my leave, my lord.
POL: The time invites you; go, your servants tend.
LAER: Farewell, Ophelia; and remember well
What I have said to you.
OPH: 'Tis in my memory lock'd,
And you yourself shall keep the key of it.
LAER: Farewell.

[*Exit.*]

POL: What is't, Ophelia, he hath said to you?
OPH: So please you, something touching the Lord Hamlet.
POL: Marry, well bethought:
'Tis told me, he hath very oft of late
Given private time to you; and you yourself
Have of your audience been most free and bounteous.
If it be so,—as so 'tis put on me,
And that in way of caution,—I must tell you,
You do not understand yourself so clearly
As it behoves my daughter and your honour.
What is between you? give me up the truth.
OPH: He hath, my lord, of late made many tenders
Of his affection to me.
POL: Affection! pooh! you speak like a green girl,
Unsifted in such perilous circumstance.
Do you believe his tenders, as you call them?
OPH: I do not know, my lord, what I should think.
POL: Marry, I'll teach you: think yourself a baby,
That you have ta'en these tenders for true pay,
Which are not sterling. Tender yourself more dearly;
Or,—not to crack the wind of the poor phrase,
Running it thus,—you'll tender me a fool.
OPH: My lord, he hath importun'd me with love
In honourable fashion.
POL: Ay, fashion you may call it: go to, go to.
OPH: And hath given countenance to his speech, my lord,
With almost all the holy vows of heaven.

POL: Ay, springes to catch woodcocks. I do know,
　　　　When the blood burns, how prodigal the soul
　　　　Lends the tongue vows: these blazes, daughter,
　　　　Giving more light than heat, extinct in both,
　　　　Even in their promise, as it is a-making,
　　　　You must not take for fire. From this time
　　　　Be somewhat scanter of your maiden presence;
　　　　Set your entreatments at a higher rate
　　　　Than a command to parley. For Lord Hamlet,
　　　　Believe so much in him, that he is young,
　　　　And with a larger lether may be walk
　　　　Than may be given you: in few, Ophelia,
　　　　Do not believe his vows, for they are brokers,
　　　　Not of that dye which their investments show,
　　　　But mere implorators of unholy suits,
　　　　Breathing like sanctified and pious bawds,
　　　　The better to beguile. This is for all:
　　　　I would not, in plain terms, from this time forth,
　　　　Have you so slander any moment's leisure,
　　　　As to give words or talk with the Lord Hamlet.
　　　　Look to 't, I charge you; come your ways.
OPH: I shall obey, my lord.
　　　　[*Exeunt.*]

Scene IV.—The Platform.

　　　　Enter HAMLET, HORATIO, and MARCELLUS.

HAM: The air bites shrewdly; it is very cold.
HOR: It is a nipping and an eager air.
HAM: What hour now?
HOR: I think it lacks of twelve.
MAR: No, it is struck.
HOR: Indeed? I heard it not: then it draws near the season
　　　　Wherein the spirit held his wont to walk.

　　　　[*A flourish of trumpets, and ordnance shot off, within.*]

　　　　What does this mean, my lord?
HAM: The king doth wake to-night and takes his rouse,
　　　　Keeps wassail, and the swaggering up-spring reels;
　　　　And, as he drains his draughts of Rhenish down,
　　　　The kettle-drum and trumpet thus bray out
　　　　The triumph of his pledge.
HOR: Is it a custom?
HAM: Ay, marry, is 't:
　　　　But to my mind,—though I am native here
　　　　And to the manner born,—it is a custom
　　　　More honour'd in the breach than the observance.
　　　　This heavy-headed revel east and west
　　　　Makes us traduc'd and tax'd of other nations;
　　　　They clepe us drunkards, and with swinish phrase
　　　　Soil our addition; and indeed it takes

> From our achievements, though perform'd at height,
> The pith and marrow of our attribute.
> So, oft it chances in particular men,
> That for some vicious mole of nature in them,
> As, in their birth,—wherein they are not guilty,
> Since nature cannot choose his origin,—
> By the o'ergrowth of some complexion,
> Oft breaking down the pales and forts of reason,
> Or by some habit that too much o'er-leavens
> The form of plausive manners; that these men,
> Carrying, I say, the stamp of one defect,
> Being nature's livery, or fortune's star,
> Their virtues else, be they as pure as grace,
> As infinite as man may undergo,
> Shall in the general censure take corruption
> From that particular fault: the dram of eale
> Doth all the noble substance of a doubt,
> To his own scandal.

Enter GHOST.

HOR: Look, my lord, it comes.
HAM: Angels and ministers of grace defend us!
> Be thou a spirit of health or goblin damn'd,
> Bring with thee airs from heaven or blasts from hell,
> Be thy intents wicked or charitable,
> Thou com'st in such a questionable shape
> That I will speak to thee: I'll call thee Hamlet,
> King, father; royal Dane, O! answer me:
> Let me not burst in ignorance; but tell
> Why thy canoniz'd bones, hearsed in death,
> Have burst their cerements; why the sepulchre,
> Wherein we saw thee quietly inurn'd,
> Hath op'd his ponderous and marble jaws,
> To cast thee up again. What may this mean,
> That thou, dead corse, again in complete steel
> Revisit'st thus the glimpses of the moon,
> Making night hideous; and we fools of nature
> So horridly to shake our disposition
> With thoughts beyond the reaches of our souls?
> Say, why is this? wherefore? what should we do?

[*The* GHOST *beckons* HAMLET.]

HOR: It beckons you to go away with it,
> As if it some impartment did desire
> To you alone.
MAR: Look, with what courteous action
> It waves you to a more removed ground:
> But do not go with it.
HOR: No, by no means.
HAM: It will not speak; then, will I follow it.

Hor: Do not, my lord.
Ham: Why, what should be the fear?
      I do not set my life at a pin's fee;
      And for my soul, what can it do to that,
      Being a thing immortal as itself?
      It waves me forth again; I'll follow it.
Hor: What if it tempt you toward the flood, my lord,
      Or to the dreadful summit of the cliff
      That beetles o'er his base into the sea,
      And there assume some other horrible form,
      Which might deprive your sovereignty of reason
      And draw you into madness? think of it;
      The very place puts toys of desperation,
      Without more motive, into every brain
      That looks so many fathoms to the sea
      And hears it roar beneath.
Ham: It waves me still. Go on, I'll follow thee.
Mar: You shall not go, my lord.
Ham: Hold off your hands!
Hor Be rul'd; you shall not go.
Ham: My fate cries out,
      And makes each petty artery in this body
      As hardy as the Nemean lion's nerve.

    [Ghost *beckons*.]

    Still am I call'd. Unhand me, gentlemen,

    [*Breaking from them*.]

    By heaven! I'll make a ghost of him that lets me:
    I say, away! Go on, I'll follow thee.

    [*Exeunt* Ghost *and* Hamlet.]

Hor: He waxes desperate with imagination.
Mar: Let's follow; 'tis not fit thus to obey him.
Hor: Have after. To what issue will this come?
Mar: Something is rotten in the state of Denmark.
Hor: Heaven will direct it.
Mar: Nay, let's follow him.

    [Exeunt.]

Scene V.—Another Part of the Platform.

    Enter Ghost *and* Hamlet.

Ham: Whither wilt thou lead me? speak; I'll go no further.
Ghost: Mark me.
Ham: I will.
Ghost: My hour is almost come,
      When I to sulphurous and tormenting flames

    Must render up myself.
HAM: Alas! poor ghost.
GHOST: Pity me not, but lend thy serious hearing
    To what I shall unfold.
HAM: Speak; I am bound to hear.
GHOST: So art thou to revenge, when thou shalt hear.
HAM: What?
GHOST: I am thy father's spirit;
    Doom'd for a certain term to walk the night,
    And for the day confin'd to fast in fires,
    Till the foul crimes done in my days of nature
    Are burnt and purg'd away. But that I am forbid
    To tell the secrets of my prison-house,
    I could a tale unfold whose lightest word
    Would harrow up thy soul, freeze thy young blood,
    Make thy two eyes, like stars, start from their spheres,
    Thy knotted and combined locks to part,
    And each particular hair to stand an end,
    Like quills upon the fretful porpentine:
    But this eternal blazon must not be
    To ears of flesh and blood. List, list, O list!
    If thou didst ever thy dear father love—
HAM: O God!
GHOST: Revenge his foul and most unnatural murder.
HAM: Murder!
GHOST: Murder most foul, as in the best it is;
    But this most foul, strange, and unnatural.
HAM: Haste me to know't, that I, with wings as swift,
    As meditation or the thoughts of love,
    May sweep to my revenge.
GHOST: I find thee apt;
    And duller shouldst thou be than the fat weed
    That rots itself in ease on Lethe wharf,
    Wouldst thou not stir in this. Now, Hamlet, hear:
    'Tis given out that, sleeping in mine orchard,
    A serpent stung me; so the whole ear of Denmark
    Is by a forged process of my death
    Rankly abus'd; but know, thou noble youth,
    The serpent that did sting thy father's life
    Now wears his crown.
HAM: O my prophetic soul! My uncle!
GHOST: Ay, that incestuous, that adulterate beast,
    With witchcraft of his wit, with traitorous gifts,—
    O wicked wit and gifts, that have the power
    So to seduce!—won to his shameful lust
    The will of my most seeming-virtuous queen.
    O Hamlet! what a falling-off was there;
    From me, whose love was of that dignity
    That it went hand in hand even with the vow
    I made to her in marriage; and to decline
    Upon a wretch whose natural gifts were poor

To those of mine!
But virtue, as it never will be mov'd,
Though lewdness court it in a shape of heaven,
So lust, though to a radiant angel link'd,
Will sate itself in a celestial bed,
And prey on garbage.
But, soft! methinks I scent the morning air;
Brief let me be. Sleeping within mine orchard,
My custom always in the afternoon,
Upon my secure hour thy uncle stole,
With juice of cursed hebona in a vial,
And in the porches of mine ears did pour
The leperous distilment; whose effect
Holds such an enmity with blood of man
That swift as quicksilver it courses through
The natural gates and alleys of the body,
And with a sudden vigour it doth posset
And curd, like eager droppings into milk,
The thin and wholesome blood: so did it mine;
And a most instant tetter bark'd about,
Most lazar-like, with vile and loathsome crust,
All my smooth body.
Thus was I, sleeping, by a brother's hand,
Of life, of crown, of queen, at once dispatch'd;
Cut off even in the blossoms of my sin,
Unhousel'd, disappointed, unanel'd,
No reckoning made, but sent to my account
With all my imperfections on my head:
O, horrible! O, horrible! most horrible!
If thou hast nature in thee, bear it not;
Let not the royal bed of Denmark be
A couch for luxury and damned incest.
But, howsoever thou pursu'st this act,
Taint not thy mind, nor let thy soul contrive
Against thy mother aught; leave her to heaven,
And to those thorns that in her bosom lodge,
To prick and sting her. Fare thee well at once!
The glow-worm shows the matin to be near,
And 'gins to pale his uneffectual fire;
Adieu, adieu! Hamlet, remember me.

    [*Exit.*]

HAM: O all you host of heaven! O earth! What else?
And shall I couple hell? O fie! Hold, hold, my heart!
And you, my sinews, grow not instant old,
But bear me stiffly up! Remember thee!
Ay, thou poor ghost, while memory holds a seat
In this distracted globe. Remember thee!
Yea, from the table of my memory
I'll wipe away all trivial fond records,
All saws of books, all forms, all pressures past,

That youth and observation copied there;
And thy commandment all alone shall live
Within the book and volume of my brain,
Unmix'd with baser matter: yes, by heaven!
O most pernicious woman!
O villain, villain, smiling, damned villain!
My tables,—meet it is I set it down,
That one may smile, and smile, and be a villain;
At least I'm sure it may be so in Denmark:

[*Writing.*]

So, uncle, there you are. Now to my word;
It is, 'Adieu, adieu! remember me.'
I have sworn 't.

HOR: [*Within.*] My lord! my lord!
MAR: [*Within.*] Lord Hamlet!
HOR: [*Within.*] Heaven secure him!
MAR: [*Within.*] So be it!
HOR: [*Within.*] Hillo, ho, ho, my lord!
HAM: Hillo, ho, ho, boy! come, bird, come.

Enter HORATIO *and* MARCELLUS.

MAR: How is't, my noble lord?
HOR: What news, my lord?
HAM: O! wonderful.
HOR: Good my lord, tell it.
HAM: No; you will reveal it.
HOR: Not I, my lord, by heaven!
MAR: Nor I, my lord.
HAM: How say you, then; would heart of man once think it?
    But you'll be secret?
HOR: }
MAR: } Ay, by heaven, my lord.
HAM: There's ne'er a villain dwelling in all Denmark,
    But he's an arrant knave.
HOR: There needs no ghost, my lord, come from the grave,
    To tell us this.
HAM: Why, right; you are i' the right;
    And so, without more circumstance at all,
    I hold it fit that we shake hands and part;
    You, as your business and desire shall point you,—
    For every man hath business and desire,
    Such as it is,—and, for mine own poor part,
    Look you, I'll go pray.
HOR: These are but wild and whirling words, my lord.
HAM: I am sorry they offend you, heartily;
    Yes, faith, heartily.
HOR: There's no offence, my lord.
HAM: Yes, by Saint Patrick, but there is, Horatio,
    And much offence, too. Touching this vision here,

It is an honest ghost, that let me tell you;
For your desire to know what is between us,
O'ermaster't as you may. And now, good friends,
As you are friends, scholars, and soldiers,
Give me one poor request.

HOR: What is 't, my lord? we will.

HAM: Never make known what you have seen to-night.

HOR:⎫
MAR:⎭My lord, we will not.

HAM: Nay, but swear't.

HOR: In faith,
   My lord, not I.

MAR: Nor I, my lord, in faith.

HAM: Upon my sword.

MAR: We have sworn, my lord, already.

HAM: Indeed, upon my sword, indeed.

GHOST: [*Beneath*.] Swear.

HAM: Ah, ha, boy! sayst thou so? art thou there, true-penny?
   Come on,—you hear this fellow in the cellar-age,—
   Consent to swear.

HOR: Propose the oath, my lord.

HAM: Never to speak of this that you have seen,
   Swear by my sword.

GHOST: [*Beneath*.] Swear.

HAM: *Hic et ubique?* then we'll shift our ground.
   Come hither, gentlemen,
   And lay your hands again upon my sword:
   Never to speak of this that you have heard,
   Swear by my sword.

GHOST: [*Beneath*.] Swear.

HAM: Well said, old mole! canst work i' the earth so fast?
   A worthy pioner! once more remove, good friends.

HOR: O day and night, but this is wondrous strange!

HAM: And therefore as a stranger give it welcome.
   There are more things in heaven and earth, Horatio,
   Than are dreamt of in your philosophy.
   But come;
   Here, as before, never, so help you mercy,
   How strange or odd soe'er I bear myself,
   As I perchance hereafter shall think meet
   To put an antic disposition on,
   That you, at such times seeing me, never shall,
   With arms encumber'd thus, or this head-shake,
   Or by pronouncing of some doubtful phrase,
   As, 'Well, well, we know,' or, 'We could, an if we would;'
   Or, 'If we list to speak,' or, 'There be, an if they might;'
   Or such ambiguous giving out, to note
   That you know aught of me: this not to do,
   So grace and mercy at your most need help you,
   Swear.

GHOST: [*Beneath*.] Swear.

[*They swear.*]

HAM: Rest, rest, perturbed spirit! So, gentlemen,
    With all my love I do commend me to you:
    And what so poor a man as Hamlet is
    May do, to express his love and friending to you,
    God willing, shall not lack. Let us go in together;
    And still your fingers on your lips, I pray.
    The time is out of joint; O cursed spite,
    That ever I was born to set it right!
    Nay, come, let's go together.

[*Exeunt.*]

ACT II.

Scene I.—A Room in Polonius' House.

    Enter POLONIUS *and* REYNALDO.

POL: Give him this money and these notes, Reynaldo.
REY: I will, my lord.
POL: You shall do marvellous wisely, good Reynaldo,
    Before you visit him, to make inquiry
    Of his behaviour.
REY: My lord, I did intend it.
POL: Marry, well said, very well said. Look you, sir,
    Inquire me first what Danskers are in Paris;
    And how, and who, what means, and where they keep,
    What company, at what expense; and finding
    By this encompassment and drift of question
    That they do know my son, come you more nearer
    Than your particular demands will touch it:
    Take you, as 'twere, some distant knowledge of him;
    As thus, 'I know his father, and his friends,
    And, in part, him;' do you mark this, Reynaldo?
REY: Ay, very well, my lord.
POL: 'And, in part, him; but,' you may say, 'not well:
    But if 't be he I mean, he's very wild,
    Addicted so and so;' and there put on him
    What forgeries you please; marry, none so rank
    As may dishonour him; take heed of that;
    But, sir, such wanton, wild, and usual slips
    As are companions noted and most known
    To youth and liberty.
REY: As gaming, my lord?
POL: Ay, or drinking, fencing, swearing, quarrelling,
    Drabbing; you may go so far.
REY: My lord, that would dishonour him.
POL: Faith, no; as you may season it in the charge.
    You must not put another scandal on him,

<pre>
                  That he is open to incontinency;
                  That's not my meaning; but breathe his faults so quaintly
                  That they may seem the taints of liberty,
                  The flash and outbreak of a fiery mind,
                  A savageness in unreclaimed blood,
                  Of general assault.
REY: But, my good lord,—
POL: Wherefore should you do this?
REY: Ay, my lord,
                  I would know that.
POL: Marry, sir, here's my drift;
                  And, I believe, it is a fetch of warrant:
                  You laying these slight sullies on my son,
                  As 'twere a thing a little soil'd i' the working,
                  Mark you,
                  Your party in converse, him you would sound,
                  Having ever seen in the prenominate crimes
                  The youth you breathe of guilty, be assur'd,
                  He closes with you in this consequence;
                  'Good sir,' or so; or 'friend,' or 'gentleman,'
                  According to the phrase or the addition
                  Of man and country.
REY: Very good, my lord.
POL: And then, sir, does he this,—he does,—what was
                  I about to say? By the mass I was about to say
                  something: where did I leave?
REY: At 'closes in the consequence.'
                  At 'friend or so,' and 'gentleman.'
POL: At 'closes in the consequence,' ay, marry;
                  He closes with you thus: 'I know the gentleman;
                  I saw him yesterday, or t' other day,
                  Or then, or then; with such, or such; and, as you say,
                  There was a' gaming; there o'ertook in 's rouse;
                  There falling out at tennis;' or perchance,
                  'I saw him enter such a house of sale,'
                  Videlicet, a brothel, or so forth.
                  See you now;
                  Your bait of falsehood takes this carp of truth;
                  And thus do we of wisdom and of reach,
                  With windlasses, and with assays of bias,
                  By indirections find directions out:
                  So by my former lecture and advice
                  Shall you my son. You have me, have you not?
REY: My lord, I have.
POL: God be wi' you; fare you well.
REY: Good my lord!
POL: Observe his inclination in yourself.
REY: I shall, my lord.
POL: And let him ply his music.
REY: Well, my lord.
POL: Farewell!
</pre>

[*Exit* REYNALDO.]

Enter OPHELIA.

How now, Ophelia! what's the matter?

OPH: Alas! my lord, I have been so affrighted.

POL: With what, in the name of God?

OPH: My lord, as I was sewing in my closet,
    Lord Hamlet, with his doublet all unbrac'd;
    No hat upon his head; his stockings foul'd,
    Ungarter'd, and down-gyved to his ancle;
    Pale as his shirt; his knees knocking each other;
    And with a look so piteous in purport
    As if he had been loosed out of hell
    To speak of horrors, he comes before me.

POL: Mad for thy love?

OPH: My lord, I do not know;
    But truly I do fear it.

POL: What said he?

OPH: He took me by the wrist and held me hard,
    Then goes he to the length of all his arm,
    And, with his other hand thus o'er his brow,
    He falls to such perusal of my face
    As he would draw it. Long stay'd he so;
    At last, a little shaking of mine arm,
    And thrice his head thus waving up and down,
    He rais'd a sigh so piteous and profound
    That it did seem to shatter all his bulk
    And end his being. That done, he lets me go,
    And, with his head over his shoulder turn'd,
    He seem'd to find his way without his eyes;
    For ont o' doors he went without their help,
    And to the last bended their light on me.

POL: Come, go with me; I will go seek the king.
    This is the very ecstasy of love,
    Whose violent property fordoes itself
    And leads the will to desperate undertakings
    As oft as any passion under heaven
    That does afflict our natures. I am sorry.
    What! have you given him any hard words of late?

OPH: No, my good lord; but, as you did command,
    I did repel his letters and denied
    His access to me.

POL: That hath made him mad.
    I am sorry that with better heed and judgment
    I had not quoted him; I fear'd he did but trifle,
    And meant to wrack thee; but, beshrew my jealousy!
    By heaven, it is as proper to our age
    To cast beyond ourselves in our opinions
    As it is common for the younger sort
    To lack discretion. Come, go we to the king;

This must be known; which, being kept close, might move
More grief to hide than hate to utter love.
Come.

[*Exeunt.*]

Scene II.—A Room in the Castle.

Enter KING, QUEEN, ROSENCRANTZ, GUILDENSTERN, *and* ATTENDANTS.

KING: Welcome, dear Rosencrantz and Guildenstern!
      Moreover that we much did long to see you,
      The need we have to use you did provoke
      Our hasty sending. Something have you heard
      Of Hamlet's transformation; so I call it,
      Since nor the exterior nor the inward man
      Resembles that it was. What it should be
      More than his father's death, that thus hath put him
      So much from the understanding of himself,
      I cannot dream of: I entreat you both,
      That, being of so young days brought up with him,
      And since so neighbour'd to his youth and humour,
      That you vouchsafe your rest here in our court
      Some little time; so by your companies
      To draw him on to pleasures, and to gather,
      So much as from occasion you may glean,
      Whe'r aught to us unknown afflicts him thus,
      That, open'd, lies within our remedy.
QUEEN: Good gentlemen, he hath much talk'd of you;
      And sure I am two men there are not living
      To whom he more adheres. If it will please you
      To show us so much gentry and good will
      As to expend your time with us awhile,
      For the supply and profit of our hope,
      Your visitation shall receive such thanks
      As fits a king's remembrance.
ROS: Both your majesties
      Might, by the sovereign power you have of us,
      Put your dread pleasures more into command
      Than to entreaty.
GUIL: But we both obey,
      And here give up ourselves, in the full bent,
      To lay our service freely at your feet,
      To be commanded.
KING: Thanks, Rosencrantz and gentle Guildenstern.
QUEEN: Thanks, Guildenstern and gentle Rosencrantz;
      And I beseech you instantly to visit
      My too much changed son. Go, some of you,
      And bring these gentlemen where Hamlet is.
GUIL: Heavens make our presence, and our practices
      Pleasant and helpful to him!

QUEEN: Ay, amen!

[*Exeunt* ROSENCRANTZ, GUILDENSTERN, *and some* ATTENDANTS.]

Enter POLONIUS.

POL: The ambassadors from Norway, my good lord,
    Are joyfully return'd.
KING: Thou still hast been the father of good news.
POL: Have I, my lord? Assure you, my good liege,
    I hold my duty, as I hold my soul,
    Both to my God and to my gracious king;
    And I do think—or else this brain of mine
    Hunts not the trail of policy so sure
    As it hath us'd to do—that I have found
    The very cause of Hamlet's lunacy.
KING: O! speak of that; that do I long to hear.
POL: Give first admittance to the ambassadors;
    My news shall be the fruit to that great feast.
KING: Thyself do grace to them, and bring them in.

    [*Exit* POLONIUS.]

    He tells me, my sweet queen, that he hath found
    The head and source of all your son's distemper.
QUEEN: I doubt it is no other but the main;
    His father's death, and our o'erhasty marriage.
KING: Well, we shall sift him.

    Re-enter POLONIUS, *with* VOLTIMAND *and* CORNELIUS.

    Welcome, my good friends!
    Say, Voltimand, what from our brother Norway?
VOLT: Most fair return of greetings, and desires.
    Upon our first, he sent out to suppress
    His nephew's levies, which to him appear'd
    To be a preparation 'gainst the Polack;
    But, better look'd into, he truly found
    It was against your highness: whereat griev'd,
    That so his sickness, age, and impotence
    Was falsely borne in hand, sends out arrests
    On Fortinbras; which he, in brief, obeys,
    Receives rebuke from Norway, and, in fine,
    Makes vow before his uncle never more
    To give the assay of arms against your majesty.
    Whereon old Norway, overcome with joy,
    Gives him three thousand crowns in annual fee,
    And his commission to employ those soldiers,
    So levied as before, against the Polack;
    With an entreaty, herein further shown,

    [*Giving a paper.*]

    That it might please you to give quiet pass
    Through your dominions for this enterprise,

On such regards of safety and allowance
As therein are set down.

KING: It likes us well;
And at our more consider'd time we'll read,
Answer, and think upon this business:
Meantime we thank you for your well-took labour.
Go to your rest; at night we'll feast together:
Most welcome home.

[*Exeunt* VOLTIMAND *and* CORNELIUS.]

POL: This business is well ended.
My liege, and madam, to expostulate
What majesty should be, what duty is,
Why day is day, night night, and time is time,
Were nothing but to waste night, day, and time.
Therefore, since brevity is the soul of wit,
And tediousness the limbs and outward flourishes,
I will be brief. Your noble son is mad:
Mad call I it; for, to define true madness,
What is 't but to be nothing else but mad?
But let that go.

QUEEN: More matter, with less art.

POL: Madam, I swear I use no art at all.
That he is mad, 'tis true; 'tis true 'tis pity;
And pity 'tis 'tis true: a foolish figure;
But farewell it, for I will use no art.
Mad let us grant him, then; and now remains
That we find out the cause of this effect,
Or rather say, the cause of this defect,
For this effect defective comes by cause;
Thus it remains, and the remainder thus.
Perpend.
I have a daughter, have while she is mine;
Who, in her duty and obedience, mark,
Hath given me this: now, gather, and surmise.
To the celestial, and my soul's idol, the most beautified Ophelia.—
That's an ill phrase, a vile phrase; 'beautified' is a vile phrase;
but you shall hear. Thus:
In her excellent white bosom, these, &c.—

QUEEN: Came this from Hamlet to her?

POL: Good madam, stay awhile; I will be faithful.

> *Doubt thou the stars are fire;*
> *Doubt that the sun doth move;*
> *Doubt truth to be a liar;*
> *But never doubt I love.*
> *O dear Ophelia! I am ill at these numbers: I have not art to reckon my*
>   *groans; but that I love thee best, O most best! believe it. Adieu.*
> *Thine evermore, most dear lady, whilst*
>   *this machine is to him,*
> *Hamlet.*

This in obedience hath my daughter shown me;
And more above hath his solicitings,

As they fell out by time, by means, and place,
All given to mine ear.
KING: But how hath she
    Receiv'd his love?
POL: What do you think of me?
KING: As of a man faithful and honourable.
POL: I would fain prove so. But what might you think,
    When I had seen this hot love on the wing,—
    As I perceiv'd it, I must tell you that,
    Before my daughter told me,—what might you,
    Or my dear majesty, your queen here, think,
    If I had play'd the desk or table-book,
    Or given my heart a winking, mute and dumb,
    Or look'd upon this love with idle sight;
    What might-you-think? No, I went round to work,
    And my young mistress thus I did bespeak:
    'Lord Hamlet is a prince, out of thy star;
    This must not be:' and then I precepts gave her,
    That she should lock herself from his resort,
    Admit no messengers, receive no tokens.
    Which done, she took the fruits of my advice;
    And he, repulsed,—a short tale to make,—
    Fell into a sadness, then into a fast,
    Thence to a watch, thence into a weakness,
    Thence to a lightness; and by this declension
    Into the madness wherein now he raves,
    And all we wail for.
KING: Do you think 'tis this?
QUEEN: It may be, very likely.
POL: Hath there been such a time,—I'd fain know that,—
    That I have positively said, ''Tis so,'
    When it prov'd otherwise?
KING: Not that I know.
POL: Take this from this, if this be otherwise:

    [*Pointing to his head and shoulder.*]

    If circumstances lead me, I will find
    Where truth is hid, though it were hid indeed
    Within the centre.
KING: How may we try it further?
POL: You know sometimes he walks four hours together
    Here in the lobby.
QUEEN: So he does indeed.
POL: At such a time I'll loose my daughter to him;
    Be you and I behind an arras then;
    Mark the encounter; if he love her not,
    And be not from his reason fallen thereon,
    Let me be no assistant for a state,
    But keep a farm, and carters.
KING: We will try it.
QUEEN: But look, where sadly the poor wretch comes reading.

POL: Away! I do beseech you, both away. I'll board him presently.

[*Exeunt* KING, QUEEN, *and* ATTENDANTS.]
Enter HAMLET, *reading*.

O! give me leave.
How does my good Lord Hamlet?

HAM: Well, God a mercy.

POL: Do you know me, my lord?

HAM: Excellent well; you are a fishmonger.

POL: Not I, my lord.

HAM: Then I would you were so honest a man.

POL: Honest, my lord!

HAM: Ay, sir; to be honest, as this world goes, is to be one man picked out of ten thousand.

POL: That's very true, my lord.

HAM: For if the sun breed maggots in a dead dog, being a good kissing carrion,—Have you a daughter?

POL: I have, my lord.

HAM: Let her not walk i' the sun: conception is a blessing; but not as your daughter may conceive. Friend, look to 't.

POL: [*Aside.*] How say you by that? Still harping on my daughter: yet he knew me not at first; he said I was a fishmonger: he is far gone, far gone: and truly in my youth I suffered much extremity for love; very near this. I'll speak to him again. What do you read, my lord?

HAM: Words, words, words.

POL: What is the matter, my lord?

HAM: Between who?

POL: I mean the matter that you read, my lord.

HAM: Slanders, sir: for the satirical rogue says here that old men have grey beards, that their faces are wrinkled, their eyes purging thick amber and plum-tree gum, and that they have a plentiful lack of wit, together with most weak hams: all which, sir, though I most powerfully and potently believe, yet I hold it not honesty to have it thus set down; for you yourself, sir, should be old as I am, if, like a crab, you could go backward.

POL: [*Aside.*] Though this be madness, yet there is method in 't. Will you walk out of the air, my lord?

HAM: Into my grave?

POL: Indeed, that is out o' the air.

[*Aside.*] How pregnant sometimes his replies are! a happiness that often madness hits on, which reason and sanity could not so prosperously be delivered of. I will leave him, and suddenly contrive the means of meeting between him and my daughter. My honourable lord, I will most humbly take my leave of you.

HAM: You cannot, sir, take from me any thing that I will more willingly part withal; except my life, except my life, except my life.

POL: Fare you well, my lord.

[*Going.*]

HAM: These tedious old fools!

Enter ROSENCRANTZ *and* GUILDENSTERN.

POL: You go to seek the Lord Hamlet; there he is.

Ros: [*To* Polonius.] God save you, sir!

[*Exit* Polonius.]

Guil: Mine honoured lord!

Ros: My most dear lord!

Ham: My excellent good friends! How dost thou, Guildenstern? Ah, Rosencrantz! Good lads, how do ye both?

Ros: As the indifferent children of the earth.

Guil: Happy in that we are not over happy; On Fortune's cap we are not the very button.

Ham: Nor the soles of her shoe?

Ros: Neither, my lord.

Ham: Then you live about her waist, or in the middle of her favours?

Guil: Faith, her privates we.

Ham: In the secret parts of Fortune? O! most true; she is a strumpet. What news?

Ros: None, my lord, but that the world's grown honest.

Ham: Then is doomsday near; but your news is not true. Let me question more in particular: what have you, my good friends, deserved at the hands of Fortune, that she sends you to prison hither?

Guil: Prison, my lord!

Ham: Denmark's a prison.

Ros: Then is the world one.

Ham: A goodly one; in which there are many confines, wards, and dungeons, Denmark being one o' the worst.

Ros: We think not so, my lord.

Ham: Why, then, 'tis none to you; for there is nothing either good or bad, but thinking makes it so: to me it is a prison.

Ros: Why, then your ambition makes it one; 'tis too narrow for your mind.

Ham: O God! I could be bounded in a nut shell, and count myself a king of infinite space, were it not that I have bad dreams.

Guil: Which dreams, indeed, are ambition, for the very substance of the ambitious is merely the shadow of a dream.

Ham: A dream itself is but a shadow.

Ros: Truly, and I hold ambition of so airy and light a quality that it is but a shadow's shadow.

Ham: Then are our beggars bodies, and our monarchs and outstretched heroes the beggars' shadows. Shall we to the court? for, by my fay, I cannot reason.

Ros: }
Guil: } We'll wait upon you.

Ham: No such matter; I will not sort you with the rest of my servants, for, to speak to you like an honest man, I am most dreadfully attended. But, in the beaten way of friendship, what make you at Elsinore?

Ros: To visit you, my lord; no other occasion.

Ham: Beggar that I am, I am even poor in thanks; but I thank you: and sure, dear friends, my thanks are too dear a halfpenny. Were you not sent for? Is it your own inclining? Is it a free visitation? Come, come, deal justly with me: come, come; nay, speak.

Guil: What should we say, my lord?

Ham: Why anything, but to the purpose. You were sent for; and there is a kind of confession in your looks which your modesties have not craft enough to colour: I know the good king and queen have sent for you.

Ros: To what end, my lord?

HAM: That you must teach me. But let me conjure you, by the rights of our fellowship, by the consonancy of our youth, by the obligation of our ever-preserved love, and by what more dear a better proposer could charge you withal, be even and direct with me, whether you were sent for or no!

ROS: [*Aside to* GUILDENSTERN.] What say you?

HAM: [*Aside.*] Nay, then, I have an eye of you. If you love me, hold not off.

GUIL: My lord, we were sent for.

HAM: I will tell you why; so shall my anticipation prevent your discovery, and your secrecy to the king and queen moult no feather. I have of late,—but wherefore I know not,—lost all my mirth, forgone all custom of exercises; and indeed it goes so heavily with my disposition that this goodly frame, the earth, seems to me a sterile promontory; this most excellent canopy, the air, look you, this brave o'erhanging firmament, this majestical roof fretted with golden fire, why, it appears no other thing to me but a foul and pestilent congregation of vapours. What a piece of work is a man! How noble in reason! how infinite in faculty! in form, in moving, how express and admirable! in action how like an angel! in apprehension how like a god! the beauty of the world! the paragon of animals! And yet, to me, what is this quintessence of dust? man delights not me; no, nor woman neither, though, by your smiling, you seem to say so.

ROS: My lord, there was no such stuff in my thoughts.

HAM: Why did you laugh then, when I said, man delights not me?'

ROS: To think, my lord, if you delight not in man, what lenten entertainment the players shall receive from you: we coted them on the way; and hither are they coming, to offer you service.

HAM: He that plays the king shall be welcome; his majesty shall have tribute of me; the adventurous knight shall use his foil and target; the lover shall not sigh gratis; the humorous man shall end his part in peace; the clown shall make those laugh whose lungs are tickle o' the sere; and the lady shall say her mind freely, or the blank verse shall halt for't. What players are they?

ROS: Even those you were wont to take delight in, the tragedians of the city.

HAM: How chances it they travel? their residence, both in reputation and profit, was better both ways.

ROS: I think their inhibition comes by the means of the late innovation.

HAM: Do they hold the same estimation they did when I was in the city? Are they so followed?

ROS: No, indeed they are not.

HAM: How comes it? Do they grow rusty?

ROS: Nay, their endeavour keeps in the wonted pace: but there is, sir, an aery of children, little eyases, that cry out on the top of question, and are most tyrannically clapped for't: these are now the fashion, and so berattle the common stages,—so they call them,—that many wearing rapiers are afraid of goose-quills, and dare scarce come thither.

HAM: What! are they children? who maintains 'em? how are they escoted? Will they pursue the quality no longer than they can sing? will they not say afterwards, if they should grow themselves to common players,—as it is most like, if their means are no better,—their writers do them wrong, to make them exclaim against their own succession?

ROS: Faith, there has been much to-do on both sides: and the nation holds it no sin to tarre them to controversy: there was, for a while, no money bid for argument, unless the poet and the player went to cuffs in the question.

HAM: Is it possible?

GUIL: O! there has been much throwing about of brains.

HAM: Do the boys carry it away?

ROS: Ay, that they do, my lord; Hercules and his load too.

HAM: It is not very strange; for my uncle is King of Denmark, and those that would make mows at him while my father lived, give twenty, forty, fifty, a hundred ducats a-piece for his picture in little. 'Sblood, there is something in this more than natural, if philosophy could find it out.

   [Flourish of trumpets within.]

GUIL: There are the players.

HAM: Gentlemen, you are welcome to Elsinore. Your hands, come then; the appurtenance of welcome is fashion and ceremony: let me comply with you in this garb, lest my extent to the players—which, I tell you, must show fairly outward—should more appear like entertainment than yours. You are welcome; but my uncle-father and aunt-mother are deceived.

GUIL: In what, my dear lord?

HAM: I am but mad north-north-west: when the wind is southerly I know a hawk from a handsaw.

   Enter POLONIUS.

POL: Well be with you, gentlemen!

HAM: Hark you, Guildenstern; and you too; at each ear a hearer: that great baby you see there is not yet out of his swaddling-clouts.

ROS: Happily he's the second time come to them; for they say an old man is twice a child.

HAM: I will prophesy he comes to tell me of the players; mark it. You say right, sir; o' Monday morning; 'twas so indeed.

POL: My lord, I have news to tell you.

HAM: My lord, I have news to tell you. When Roscius was an actor in Rome,—

POL: The actors are come hither, my lord.

HAM: Buzz, buzz!

POL: Upon my honour,—

HAM: Then came each actor on his ass,—

POL: The best actors in the world, either for tragedy, comedy, history, pastoral, pastoral-comical, historical-pastoral, tragical-historical, tragical-comical-historical-pastoral, scene individable, or poem unlimited: Seneca cannot be too heavy, nor Plautus too light. For the law of writ and the liberty, these are the only men.

HAM: O Jephthah, judge of Israel, what a treasure hadst thou!

POL: What a treasure had he, my lord?

HAM: Why

  One fair daughter and no more,
  The which he loved passing well.

POL: *[Aside.]* Still on my daughter.

HAM: Am I not i' the right, old Jephthah?

POL: If you call me Jephthah, my lord, I have a daughter that I love passing well.

HAM: Nay, that follows not.

POL: What follows, then, my lord?

HAM: Why,

  As by lot, God wot.
  And then, you know,
  It came to pass, as most like it was.—

The first row of the pious chanson will show you more; for look where my abridgment comes.

Enter four or five PLAYERS.

You are welcome, masters; welcome, all. I am glad to see thee well: welcome, good friends. O, my old friend! Thy face is valanced since I saw thee last: comest thou to beard me in Denmark? What! my young lady and mistress! By 'r lady, your ladyship is nearer heaven than when I saw you last, by the altitude of a chopine. Pray God, your voice, like a piece of uncurrent gold, be not cracked within the ring. Masters, you are all welcome. We'll e'en to 't like French falconers, fly at anything we see: we'll have a speech straight. Come, give us a taste of your quality; come, a passionate speech.

FIRST PLAY: What speech, my good lord?

HAM: I heard thee speak me a speech once, but it was never acted; or, if it was, not above once; for the play, I remember, pleased not the million; 'twas caviare to the general: but it was—as I received it, and others, whose judgments in such matters cried in the top of mine—an excellent play, well digested in the scenes, set down with as much modesty as cunning. I remember one said there were no sallets in the lines to make the matter savoury, nor no matter in the phrase that might indict the author of affectation; but called it an honest method, as wholesome as sweet, and by very much more handsome than fine. One speech in it I chiefly loved; 'twas Æneas' tale to Dido; and thereabout of it especially, where he speaks of Priam's slaughter. If it live in your memory, begin at this line: let me see, let me see:—

> *The rugged Pyrrhus, like the Hyrcanian beast,—*
> 'tis not so, it begins with Pyrrhus:—

> *The rugged Pyrrhus, he, whose sable arm,*
> *Black as his purpose, did the night resemble*
> *When he lay couched in the ominous horse,*
> *Hath now this dread and black complexion smear'd*
> *With heraldry more dismal; head to foot*
> *Now is he total gules; horridly trick'd*
> *With blood of fathers, mothers, daughters, sons,*
> *Bak'd and impasted with the parching streets,*
> *That tend a tyrannous and damned light*
> *To their vile murders: roasted in wrath and fire,*
> *And thus o'er-sized with coagulate gore,*
> *With eyes like carbuncles, the hellish Pyrrhus*
> *Old grandsire Priam seeks.*

So proceed you.

POL: 'Fore God, my lord, well spoken; with good accent and good discretion.

FIRST PLAY: *Anon, he finds him*
> *Striking too short at Greeks; his antique sword,*
> *Rebellious to his arm, lies where it falls,*
> *Repugnant to command. Unequal match'd,*
> *Pyrrhus at Priam drives; in rage strikes wide;*
> *But with the whiff and wind of his fell sword*
> *The unnerved father falls. Then senseless Ilium,*
> *Seeming to feel this blow, with flaming top*
> *Stoops to his base, and with a hideous crash*
> *Takes prisoner Pyrrhus' ear: for lo! his sword,*
> *Which was declining on the milky head*
> *Of reverend Priam, seem'd i' the air to stick:*

> *So, as a painted tyrant, Pyrrhus stood,*
> *And like a neutral to his will and matter,*
> *Did nothing.*
> *But, as we often see, against some storm,*
> *A silence in the heavens, the rack stand still,*
> *The bold winds speechless and the orb below*
> *As hush as death, anon the dreadful thunder*
> *Doth rend the region; so, after Pyrrhus' pause,*
> *Aroused vengeance sets him new a-work;*
> *And never did the Cyclops' hammers fall*
> *On Mars's armour, forg'd for proof elerne,*
> *With less remorse than Pyrrhus' bleeding sword*
> *Now falls on Priam.*
> *Out, out, thou strumpet Fortune! All you gods,*
> *In general synod, take away her power,*
> *Break all the spokes and fellies from her wheel,*
> *And bowl the round nave down the hill of heaven,*
> *As low as to the fiends!*

POL: This is too long.

HAM: It shall to the barber's, with your beard. Prithee, say on: he's for a jig or a tale of bawdry, or he sleeps. Say on; come to Hecuba.

FIRST PLAY: *But who, O! who had seen the mobled queen—*

HAM: 'The mobled queen?'—

POL: That's good; 'mobled queen' is good.

FIRST PLAY: *Run barefoot up and down, threat'ning the flames*
> *With bisson rheum; a clout upon that head*
> *Where late the diadem stood; and, for a robe,*
> *About her lank and all o'er-teemed loins,*
> *A blanket, in the alarm of fear caught up;*
> *Who this had seen, with tongue in venom steep'd,*
> *'Gainst Fortune's state would treason have pronounc'd:*
> *But if the gods themselves did see her then,*
> *When she saw Pyrrhus make malicious sport*
> *In mincing with his sword her husband's limbs,*
> *The instant burst of clamour that she made—*
> *Unless things mortal move them not at all—*
> *Would have made milch the burning eyes of heaven,*
> *And passion in the gods.*

POL: Look! wh'er he has not turned his colour and has tears in 's eyes. Prithee, no more.

HAM: 'Tis well; I'll have thee speak out the rest soon. Good my lord, will you see the players well bestowed? Do you hear, let them be well used; for they are the abstracts and brief chronicles of the time: after your death you were better have a bad epitaph than their ill report while you live.

POL: My lord, I will use them according to their desert.

HAM: God's bodikins, man, much better; use every man after his desert, and who should 'scape whipping? Use them after your own honour and dignity: the less they deserve, the more merit is in your bounty. Take them in.

POL: Come, sirs.

HAM: Follow him, friends: we'll hear a play to-morrow.

[*Exit* POLONIUS, *with all the* PLAYERS *but the* FIRST.]

Dost thou hear me, old friend; can you play the Murder of Gonzago?

FIRST PLAY: Ay, my lord.

HAM: We'll ha't to-morrow night. You could, for a need, study a speech of some dozen or sixteen lines, which I would set down and insert in't, could you not?

FIRST PLAY: Ay, my lord.

HAM: Very well. Follow that lord; and look you mock him not.

[*Exit* FIRST PLAYER.] [*To* ROSENCRANTZ *and* GUILDENSTERN.]

My good friends, I'll leave you till night; you are welcome to Elsinore.

ROS: Good my lord!

[*Exeunt* ROSENCRANTZ *and* GUILDENSTERN.]

HAM: Ay, so, God be wi' ye! Now I am alone.

    O! what a rogue and peasant slave am I:
    Is it not monstrous that this player here,
    But in a fiction, in a dream of passion,
    Could force his soul so to his own conceit
    That from her working all his visage wann'd,
    Tears in his eyes, distraction in 's aspect,
    A broken voice, and his whole function suiting
    With forms to his conceit? and all for nothing!
    For Hecuba!
    What's Hecuba to him or he to Hecuba
    That he should weep for her? What would he do
    Had he the motive and the cue for passion
    That I have? He would drown the stage with tears,
    And cleave the general ear with horrid speech,
    Make mad the guilty and appal the free,
    Confound the ignorant, and amaze indeed
    The very faculties of eyes and ears.
    Yet I,
    A dull and muddy-mettled rascal, peak,
    Like John-a-dreams, unpregnant of my cause,
    And can say nothing; no, not for a king,
    Upon whose property and most dear life
    A damn'd defeat was made. Am I a coward?
    Who calls me villain? breaks my pate across?
    Plucks off my beard and blows it in my face?
    Tweaks me by the nose? gives me the lie i' the throat,
    As deep as to the lungs? Who does me this?
    Ha!
    Swounds, I should take it, for it cannot be
    But I am pigeon-liver'd, and lack gall
    To make oppression bitter, or ere this
    I should have fatted all the region kites
    With this slave's offal. Bloody, bawdy villain!
    Remorseless, treacherous, lecherous, kindless villain!
    O! vengeance!
    Why, what an ass am I! This is most brave
    That I, the son of a dear father murder'd,

Prompted to my revenge by heaven and hell,
Must, like a whore, unpack my heart with words,
And fall a-cursing, like a very drab,
A scullion!
Fie upon't! foh! About, my brain! I have heard,
That guilty creatures sitting at a play
Have by the very cunning of the scene
Been struck so to the soul that presently
They have proclaim'd their malefactions;
For murder, though it have no tongue, will speak
With most miraculous organ. I'll have these players
Play something like the murder of my father
Before mine uncle; I'll observe his looks;
I'll tent him to the quick: if he but blench
I know my course. The spirit that I have seen
May be the devil: and the devil hath power
To assume a pleasing shape; yea, and perhaps
Out of my weakness and my melancholy—
As he is very potent with such spirits—
Abuses me to damn me. I'll have grounds
More relative than this: the play's the thing
Wherein I'll catch the conscience of the king.

[*Exit.*]

ACT III.

Scene I.—A Room in the Castle.

Enter KING, QUEEN, POLONIUS, OPHELIA, ROSENCRANTZ, *and* GUILDENSTERN.

KING: And can you, by no drift of circumstance,
    Get from him why he puts on this confusion,
    Grating so harshly all his days of quiet
    With turbulent and dangerous lunacy?
ROS: He does confess he feels himself distracted;
    But from what cause he will by no means speak.
GUIL: Nor do we find him forward to be sounded,
    But, with a crafty madness, keeps aloof,
    When we would bring him on to some confession
    Of his true state.
QUEEN: Did he receive you well?
ROS: Most like a gentleman.
GUIL: But with much forcing of his disposition.
ROS: Niggard of question, but of our demands
    Most free in his reply.
QUEEN: Did you assay him
    To any pastime?
ROS: Madam, it so fell out that certain players
    We o'er-taught on the way; of these we told him,
    And there did seem in him a kind of joy
    To hear of it: they are about the court,

And, as I think, they have already order
This night to play before him.

POL: 'Tis most true;
And he beseech'd me to entreat your majesties
To hear and see the matter.

KING: With all my heart; and it doth much content me
To hear him so inclin'd.
Good gentlemen, give him a further edge.
And drive his purpose on to these delights.

ROS: We shall, my lord.

[*Exeunt* ROSENCRANTZ *and* GUILDENSTERN.]

KING: Sweet Gertrude, leave us too;
For we have closely sent for Hamlet hither,
That he, as 'twere by accident, may here
Affront Ophelia.
Her father and myself, lawful espials,
Will so bestow ourselves, that, seeing, unseen,
We may of their encounter frankly judge,
And gather by him, as he is behav'd,
If 't be the affliction of his love or no
That thus he suffers for.

QUEEN: I shall obey you.
And for your part, Ophelia, I do wish
That your good beauties be the happy cause
Of Hamlet's wildness; so shall I hope your virtues
Will bring him to his wonted way again,
To both your honours.

OPH: Madam, I wish it may.

[*Exit* QUEEN.]

POL: Ophelia, walk you here. Gracious, so please you,
We will bestow ourselves.
[*To* OPHELIA.] Read on this book;
That show of such an exercise may colour
Your loneliness. We are oft to blame in this,
'Tis too much prov'd, that with devotion's visage
And pious action we do sugar o'er
The devil himself.

KING: [*Aside*.] O! 'tis too true;
How smart a lash that speech doth give my conscience!
The harlot's cheek, beautied with plastering art,
Is not more ugly to the thing that helps it
Than is my deed to my most painted word:
O heavy burden!

POL: I hear him coming; let's withdraw, my lord.

[*Exeunt* KING *and* POLONIUS.]

Enter HAMLET.

HAM: To be, or not to be: that is the question:
Whether 'tis nobler in the mind to suffer

The slings and arrows of outrageous fortune,
Or to take arms against a sea of troubles,
And by opposing end them? To die: to sleep;
No more; and, by a sleep to say we end
The heart-ache and the thousand natural shocks
That flesh is heir to, 'tis a consummation
Devoutly to be wish'd. To die, to sleep;
To sleep: perchance to dream: ay, there's the rub;
For in that sleep of death what dreams may come
When we have shuffled off this mortal coil,
Must give us pause. There's the respect
That makes calamity of so long life;
For who would bear the whips and scorns of time,
The oppressor's wrong, the proud man's contumely,
The pangs of dispriz'd love, the law's delay,
The insolence of office, and the spurns
That patient merit of the unworthy takes,
When he himself might his quietus make
With a bare bodkin? who would fardels bear,
To grunt and sweat under a weary life,
But that the dread of something after death,
The undiscover'd country from whose bourn
No traveller returns, puzzles the will,
And makes us rather bear those ills we have
Than fly to others that we know not of?
Thus conscience does make cowards of us all;
And thus the native hue of resolution
Is sicklied o'er with the pale cast of thought,
And enterprises of great pith and moment
With this regard their currents turn awry,
And lose the name of action. Soft you now!
The fair Ophelia! Nymph, in thy orisons
Be all my sins remember'd.

OPH: Good my lord,
  How does your honour for this many a day?
HAM: I humbly thank you; well, well, well.
OPH: My lord, I have remembrances of yours,
  That I have longed long to re-deliver;
  I pray you, now receive them.
HAM: No, not I;
  I never gave you aught.
OPH: My honour'd lord, you know right well you did;
  And, with them, words of so sweet breath compos'd
  As made the things more rich: their perfume lost,
  Take these again; for to the noble mind
  Rich gifts wax poor when givers prove unkind.
  There, my lord.
HAM: Ha, ha! are you honest?
OPH: My lord!
HAM: Are you fair?
OPH: What means your lordship?

HAM: That if you be honest and fair, your honesty should admit no discourse to your beauty.

OPH: Could beauty, my lord, have better commerce than with honesty?

HAM: Ay, truly; for the power of beauty will sooner transform honesty from what it is to a bawd than the force of honesty can translate beauty into his likeness: this was sometime a paradox, but now the time gives it proof. I did love thee once.

OPH: Indeed, my lord, you made me believe so.

HAM: You should not have believed me; for virtue cannot so inoculate our old stock but we shall relish of it: I loved you not.

OPH: I was the more deceived.

HAM: Get thee to a nunnery: why wouldst thou be a breeder of sinners? I am myself indifferent honest; but yet I could accuse me of such things that it were better my mother had not borne me. I am very proud, revengeful, ambitious; with more offences at my beck than I have thoughts to put them in, imagination to give them shape, or time to act them in. What should such fellows as I do crawling between heaven and earth? We are arrant knaves, all; believe none of us. Go thy ways to a nunnery. Where's your father?

OPH: At home, my lord.

HAM: Let the doors be shut upon him, that he may play the fool nowhere but in's own house. Farewell.

OPH: O! help him, you sweet heavens!

HAM: If thou dost marry, I'll give thee this plague for thy dowry: be thou as chaste as ice, as pure as snow, thou shalt not escape calumny. Get thee to a nunnery, go; farewell. Or, if thou wilt needs marry, marry a fool; for wise men know well enough what monsters you make of them. To a nunnery, go; and quickly too. Farewell.

OPH: O heavenly powers, restore him!

HAM: I have heard of your paintings too, well enough; God hath given you one face, and you make yourselves another: you jig, you amble, and you lisp, and nickname God's creatures, and make your wantonness your ignorance. Go to, I'll no more on't; it hath made me mad. I say, we will have no more marriages; those that are married already, all but one, shall live; the rest shall keep as they are. To a nunnery, go.

[*Exit.*]

OPH: O! what a noble mind is here o'er-thrown:
The courtier's, soldier's, scholar's, eye, tongue, sword;
The expectancy and rose of the fair state,
The glass of fashion and the mould of form,
The observ'd of all observers, quite, quite down!
And I, of ladies most deject and wretched,
That suck'd the honey of his music vows,
Now see that noble and most sovereign reason,
Like sweet bells jangled, out of tune and harsh;
That unmatch'd form and feature of blown youth
Blasted with ecstasy: O! woe is me,
To have seen what I have seen, see what I see!

Re-enter KING *and* POLONIUS.

KING: Love! his affections do not that way tend;

Nor what he spake, though it lack'd form a little,
Was not like madness. There's something in his soul
O'er which his melancholy sits on brood;
And, I do doubt, the hatch and the disclose
Will be some danger; which for to prevent,
I have in quick determination
Thus set it down: he shall with speed to England,
For the demand of our neglected tribute:
Haply the seas and countries different
With variable objects shall expel
This something-settled matter in his heart,
Whereon his brains still beating puts him thus
From fashion of himself. What think you on't?

POL: It shall do well: but yet do I believe
The origin and commencement of his grief
Sprung from neglected love. How now, Ophelia!
You need not tell us what Lord Hamlet said;
We heard it all. My lord, do as you please;
But, if you hold it fit, after the play,
Let his queen mother all alone entreat him
To show his griefs: let her be round with him;
And I'll be plac'd, so please you, in the ear
Of all their conference. If she find him not,
To England send him, or confine him where
Your wisdom best shall think.

KING: It shall be so:
Madness in great ones must not unwatch'd go.

[*Exeunt.*]

Scene II.—A Hall in the Castle.

Enter HAMLET *and certain* PLAYERS.

HAM: Speak the speech, I pray you, as I pronounced it to you, trippingly on the
tongue; but if you mouth it, as many of your players do, I had as lief the
town-crier spoke my lines. Nor do not saw the air too much with your hand,
thus; but use all gently: for in the very torrent, tempest, and—as I may say—
whirlwind of passion, you must acquire and beget a temperance, that may give
it smoothness. O! it offends me to the soul to hear a robustious periwig-pated
fellow tear a passion to tatters, to very rags, to split the ears of the groundlings,
who for the most part are capable of nothing but inexplicable dumb-shows
and noise: I would have such a fellow whipped for o'er-doing Termagant; it
out-herods Herod: pray you, avoid it.

FIRST PLAY: I warrant your honour.

HAM: Be not too tame neither, but let your own discretion be your tutor: suit the
action to the word, the word to the action; with this special observance, that
you o'erstep not the modesty of nature; for anything so overdone is from the
purpose of playing, whose end, both at the first and now, was and is, to
hold, as 'twere, the mirror up to nature; to show virtue her own feature, scorn
her own image, and the very age and body of the time his form and pressure. Now, this overdone, or come tardy off, though it make the unskilful

laugh, cannot but make the judicious grieve; the censure of which one must in your allowance o'erweigh a whole theatre of others. O! there be players that I have seen play, and heard others praise, and that highly, not to speak it profanely, that, neither having the accent of Christians nor the gait of Christian, pagan, nor man, have so strutted and bellowed that I have thought some of nature's journeymen had made men and not made them well, they imitated humanity so abominably.

FIRST PLAY I hope we have reformed that indifferently with us.

HAM: O! reform it altogether. And let those that play your clowns speak no more than is set down for them; for there be of them that will themselves laugh, to set on some quantity of barren spectators to laugh too, though in the mean time some necessary question of the play be then to be considered; that's villanous, and shows a most pitiful ambition in the fool that uses it. Go, make you ready.

[*Exeunt* PLAYERS.]

Enter POLONIUS, ROSENCRANTZ, *and* GUILDENSTERN.

How now, my lord! will the king hear this piece of work?

POL: And the queen too, and that presently.

HAM: Bid the players make haste.

[*Exit* POLONIUS.]

Will you two help to hasten them?

ROS: ⎫
GUIL: ⎭ We will, my lord.

[*Exeunt* ROSENCRANTZ *and* GUILDENSTERN.]

HAM: What, ho! Horatio!

Enter HORATIO.

HOR: Here, sweet lord, at your service.

HAM: Horatio, thou art e'en as just a man as e'er my conversation cop'd withal.

HOR: O! my dear lord,—

HAM: Nay, do not think I flatter;
　　　For what advancement may I hope from thee,
　　　That no revenue hast but thy good spirits
　　　To feed and clothe thee? Why should the poor be flatter'd?
　　　No; let the candied tongue lick absurd pomp,
　　　And crook the pregnant hinges of the knee
　　　Where thrift may follow fawning. Dost thou hear?
　　　Since my dear soul was mistress of her choice
　　　And could of men distinguish, her election
　　　Hath seal'd thee for herself; for thou hast been
　　　As one, in suffering all, that suffers nothing,
　　　A man that fortune's buffets and rewards
　　　Hast ta'en with equal thanks; and bless'd are those
　　　Whose blood and judgment are so well co-mingled
　　　That they are not a pipe for fortune's finger
　　　To sound what stop she please. Give me that man
　　　That is not passion's slave, and I will wear him

> In my heart's core, ay, in my heart of heart,
> As I do thee. Something too much of this.
> There is a play to-night before the king;
> One scene of it comes near the circumstance
> Which I have told thee of my father's death;
> I prithee, when thou seest that act afoot,
> Even with the very comment of thy soul
> Observe mine uncle; if his occulted guilt
> Do not itself unkennel in one speech,
> It is a damned ghost that we have seen,
> And my imaginations are as foul
> As Vulcan's stithy. Give him heedful note;
> For I mine eyes will rivet to his face,
> And after we will both our judgments join
> In censure of his seeming.

HOR: Well, my lord:

> If he steal aught the whilst this play is playing,
> And 'scape detecting, I will pay the theft.

HAM: They are coming to the play; I must be idle:

> Get you a place.

Danish march. A Flourish. Enter KING, QUEEN, POLONIUS, OPHELIA, ROSENCRANTZ, GUILDENSTERN, *and* OTHERS.

KING: How fares our cousin Hamlet?

HAM: Excellent, i' faith; of the chameleon's dish: I eat the air, promise-crammed; you cannot feed capons so.

KING: I have nothing with this answer, Hamlet; these words are not mine.

HAM: No, nor mine now.

> [*To* POLONIUS.] My lord, you played once i' the university, you say?

POL: That did I, my lord, and was accounted a good actor.

HAM: And what did you enact?

POL: I did enact Julius Cæsar: I was killed ' the Capitol; Brutus killed me.

HAM: It was a brute part of him to kill so capital a calf there. Be the players ready?

ROS: Ay, my lord; they stay upon your patience.

QUEEN: Come hither, my good Hamlet, sit by me.

HAM: No, good mother, here's metal more attractive.

POL: [*To the King.*] O ho! do you mark that?

HAM: Lady, shall I lie in your lap?

[*Lying down at* OPHELIA's *feet.*]

OPH: No, my lord.

HAM: I mean, my head upon your lap?

OPH: Ay, my lord.

HAM: Do you think I meant country matters?

OPH: I think nothing, my lord.

HAM: That's a fair thought to lie between maids' legs.

OPH: What is, my lord?

HAM: Nothing.

OPH: You are merry, my lord.

HAM: Who, I?

OPH: Ay, my lord.

HAM: O God, your only jig-maker. What should a man do but be merry? for, look you, how cheerfully my mother looks, and my father died within's two hours.

OPH: Nay, 'tis twice two months, my lord.

HAM: So long? Nay, then, let the devil wear black, for I'll have a suit of sables. O heavens! die two months ago, and not forgotten yet? Then there's hope a great man's memory may outlive his life half a year; but, by'r lady, he must build churches then, or else shall he suffer not thinking on, with the hobby-horse, whose epitaph is, 'For, O! for, O! the hobby-horse is forgot.'

Hautboys play. The dumb-show enters.

Enter a King *and a* Queen, *very lovingly; the* Queen *embracing him, and he her. She kneels, and makes show of protestation unto him. He takes her up, and declines his head upon her neck; lays him down upon a bank of flowers: she, seeing him asleep, leaves him. Anon comes in a fellow, takes off his crown, kisses it, and pours poison in the* King's *ears, and exit. The* Queen *returns, finds the* King *dead, and makes passionate action. The* Poisoner, *with some two or three* Mutes, *comes in again, seeming to lament with her. The dead body is carried away. The* Poisoner *wooes the* Queen *with gifts; she seems loath and unwilling awhile, but in the end accepts his love.*

[*Exeunt*]

OPH: What means this, my lord?

HAM: Marry, this is miching mallecho; it means mischief.

OPH: Belike this show imports the argument of the play.

Enter Prologue.

HAM: We shall know by this fellow: the players cannot keep counsel; they'll tell all.

OPH: Will he tell us what this show meant?

HAM: Ay, or any show that you'll show him; be not you ashamed to show, he'll not shame to tell you what it means.

OPH: You are naught, you are naught. I'll mark the play.

PRO: *For us and for our tragedy,*
  Here stooping to your clemency,
   We beg your hearing patiently.

HAM: Is this a prologue, or the posy of a ring?

OPH: 'Tis brief, my lord.

HAM: As woman's love.

Enter two PLAYERS, KING *and* QUEEN.

P. KING: *Full thirty times hath Phœbus' cart gone round*
  Neptune's salt wash and Tellus' orbed ground,
  And thirty dozen moons with borrow'd sheen
  About the world have times twelve thirties been,
  Since love our hearts and Hymen did our hands
  Unite commutual in most sacred bands.

P. QUEEN: *So many journeys may the sun and moon*
  Make us again count o'er ere love be done!
  But, woe is me! you are so sick of late,
  So far from cheer and from your former state,

> That I distrust you. Yet, though I distrust.
> Discomfort you, my lord, it nothing must;
> For women's fear and love holds quantity,
> In neither aught, or in extremity.
> Now, what my love is, proof hath made you know;
> And as my love is siz'd, my fear is so.
> Where love is great, the littlest doubts are fear;
> Where little fears grow great, great love grows there.

P. KING. *Faith, I must leave thee, love, and shortly too;*
> *My operant powers their functions leave to do;*
> *And thou shalt live in this fair world behind,*
> *Honour'd, belov'd; and haply one as kind*
> *For husband shalt thou—*

P. QUEEN: *O! confound the rest;*
> *Such love must needs be treason in my breast:*
> *In second husband let me be accurst;*
> *None wed the second but who kill'd the first.*

[Aside.]

HAM: Wormwood, wormwood.

P. QUEEN: *The instances that second marriage move,*
> *Are base respects of thrift, but none of love;*
> *A second time I kill my husband dead,*
> *When second husband kisses me in bed.*

P. KING: *I do believe you think what now you speak;*
> *But what we do determine off we break.*
> *Purpose is but the slave to memory,*
> *Of violent birth, but poor validity;*
> *Which now, like fruit unripe, sticks on the tree,*
> *But fall unshaken when they mellow be.*
> *Most necessary 'tis that we forget*
> *To pay ourselves what to ourselves is debt;*
> *What to ourselves in passion we propose.*
> *The passion ending, doth the purpose lose.*
> *The violence of either grief or joy*
> *Their own enactures with themselves destroy;*
> *Where joy most revels grief doth most lament,*
> *Grief joys, joy grieves, on slender accident.*
> *This world is not for aye, nor 'tis not strange,*
> *That even our love should with our fortunes change;*
> *For 'tis a question left us yet to prove*
> *Whe'r love lead fortune or else fortune love.*
> *The great man down, you mark his favourite flies;*
> *The poor advanc'd makes friends of enemies.*
> *And hitherto doth love on fortune tend,*
> *For who not needs shall never lack a friend;*
> *And who in want a hollow friend doth try*
> *Directly seasons him his enemy.*
> *But, orderly to end where I begun,*
> *Our wills and fates do so contrary run*

That our devices still are overthrown,
Our thoughts are ours, their ends none of our own;
So think thou wilt no second husband wed;
But die thy thoughts when thy first lord is dead.

P. QUEEN: *Nor earth to me give food, nor heaven light:*
Sport and repose lock from me day and night!
To desperation turn my trust and hope!
An anchor's cheer in prison be my scope!
Each opposite that blanks the face of joy
Meet what I would have well, and it destroy!
Both here and hence pursue me lasting strife,
If, once a widow, ever I be wife!

HAM: If she should break it now!

P. KING: *'Tis deeply sworn. Sweet, leave me here a while;*
My spirits grow dull, and fain I would beguile
The tedious day with sleep.

[*Sleeps*]

P. QUEEN: *Sleep rock thy brain;*
And never come mischance between us twain!

[*Exit.*]

HAM: Madam, how like you this play?

QUEEN: The lady doth protest too much, methinks.

HAM: O! but she'll keep her word.

KING: Have you heard the argument? Is there no offence in 't?

HAM: No, no, they do but jest, poison in jest; no offence i' the world.

KING: What do you call the play?

HAM: The Mouse-trap. Marry, how? Tropically. This play is the image of a murder done in Vienna: Gonzago is the duke's name; his wife, Baptista. You shall see anon; 'tis a knavish piece of work: but what of that? your majesty and we that have free souls, it touches us not: let the galled jade wince, our withers are unwrung.

Enter PLAYER *as* LUCIANUS.

This is one Lucianus, nephew to the king.

OPH: You are a good chorus, my lord.

HAM: I could interpret between you and your love, if I could see the puppets dallying.

OPH: You are keen, my lord, you are keen.

HAM: It would cost you a groaning to take off my edge.

OPH: Still better, and worse.

HAM: So you must take your husbands. Begin, murderer; pox, leave thy damnable faces, and begin. Come; the croaking raven doth bellow for revenge.

LUC. *Thoughts black, hands apt, drugs fit, and time agreeing;*
Confederate season, else no creature seeing;
Thou mixture rank, of midnight weeds collected,
With Hecate's ban thrice blasted, thrice infected,
Thy natural magic and dire property,
On wholesome life usurp immediately,

[Pours the poison into the Sleeper's ears.]

HAM: He poisons him i' the garden for 's estate. His name's Gonzago; the story is extant, and writ in very choice Italian. You shall see anon how the murderer gets the love of Gonzago's wife.

OPH: The king rises.

HAM: What! frighted with false fire?

QUEEN: How fares my lord?

POL: Give o'er the play.

KING: Give me some light: away!

ALL: Lights, lights, lights!

[*Exeunt all except* HAMLET *and* HORATIO.]

HAM: Why, let the stricken deer go weep,
    The hart ungalled play;
    For some must watch, while some must sleep:
    So runs the world away.
    Would not this, sir, and a forest of feathers, if the rest of my fortunes turn Turk with me, with two Provincial roses on my razed shoes, get me a fallowship in a cry of players, sir?

HOR: Half a share.

HAM: A whole one, I.
    For thou dost know, O Damon dear,
    This realm dismantled was
    Of Jove himself; and now reigns here
    A very, very—pajock.

HOR: You might have rimed.

HAM: O good Horatio! I'll take the ghost's word for a thousand pound. Didst perceive?

HOR: Very well, my lord.

HAM: Upon the talk of the poisoning?

HOR: I did very well note him.

HAM: Ah, ha! Come, some music! come, the recorders!
    For if the king like not the comedy,
    Why then, belike he likes it not, perdy.
    Come, some music!

Re-enter ROSENCRANTZ *and* GUILDENSTERN.

GUIL: Good my lord, vouchsafe me a word with you.

HAM: Sir, a whole history.

GUIL: The king, sir,—

HAM: Ay, sir, what of him?

GUIL: Is in his retirement marvellous distempered.

HAM: With drink, sir?

GUIL: No, my lord, rather with choler.

HAM: Your wisdom should show itself more richer to signify this to his doctor; for, for me to put him to his purgation would perhaps plunge him into far more choler.

GUIL: Good my lord, put your discourse into some frame, and start not so wildly from my affair.

HAM: I am tame, sir; pronounce.

GUIL: The queen, your mother, in most great affliction of spirit, hath sent me to you.

HAM: You are welcome.

GUIL: Nay, good my lord, this courtesy is not of the right breed. If it shall please you to make me a wholesome answer, I will do your mother's commandment; if not, your pardon and my return shall be the end of my business.

HAM: Sir, I cannot.

GUIL: What, my lord?

HAM: Make you a wholesome answer; my wit's diseased; but, sir, such answer as I can make, you shall command; or, rather, as you say, my mother: therefore no more, but to the matter: my mother, you say,—

ROS: Then, thus she says: your behaviour hath struck her into amazement and admiration.

HAM: O wonderful son, that can so astonish a mother! But is there no sequel at the heels of this mother's admiration? Impart.

ROS: She desires to speak with you in her closet ere you go to bed.

HAM: We shall obey, were she ten times our mother. Have you any further trade with us?

ROS: My lord, you once did love me.

HAM: So I do still, by these pickers and stealers.

ROS: Good my lord, what is your cause of distemper? you do surely bar the door upon your own liberty, if you deny your griefs to your friend.

HAM: Sir, I lack advancement.

ROS: How can that be when you have the voice of the king himself for your succession in Denmark?

HAM: Ay, sir, but 'While the grass grows,'—the proverb is something musty.

Enter PLAYERS, *with recorders.*

O! the recorders: let me see one. To withdraw with you: why do you go about to recover the wind of me, as if you would drive me into a toil?

GUIL O! my lord, if my duty be too bold, my love is too unmannerly.

HAM: I do not well understand that. Will you play upon this pipe?

GUIL: My lord, I cannot.

HAM: I pray you.

GUIL: Believe me, I cannot.

HAM: I do beseech you.

GUIL: I know no touch of it, my lord.

HAM: 'Tis as easy as lying; govern these ventages with your finger and thumb, give it breath with your mouth, and it will discourse most eloquent music. Look you, these are the stops.

GUIL: But these cannot I command to any utterance of harmony; I have not the skill.

HAM: Why, look you now, how unworthy a thing you make of me. You would play upon me; you would seem to know my stops; you would pluck out the heart of my mystery; you would sound me from my lowest note to the top of my compass; and there is much music, excellent voice, in this little organ, yet cannot you make it speak. 'Sblood, do you think I am easier to be played on than a pipe? Call me what instrument you will, though you can fret me, you cannot play upon me.

Enter POLONIUS.

God bless you, sir!

POL: My lord, the queen would speak with you, and presently.

HAM: Do you see yonder cloud that's almost in shape of a camel?

POL: By the mass, and 'tis like a camel, indeed.

HAM: Methinks it is like a weasel.

POL: It is backed like a weasel.

HAM: Or like a whale?

POL: Very like a whale.

HAM: Then I will come to my mother by and by.

[*Aside.*] They fool me to the top of my bent.

[*Aloud.*] I will come by and by.

POL: I will say so.

[*Exit.*]

HAM: By and by is easily said. Leave me, friends.

[*Exeunt all but* HAMLET.]

> 'Tis now the very witching time of night,
> When churchyards yawn and hell itself breathes out
> Contagion to this world: now could I drink hot blood,
> And do such bitter business as the day
> Would quake to look on. Soft! now to my mother.
> O heart! lose not thy nature; let not ever
> The soul of Nero enter this firm bosom;
> Let me be cruel, not unnatural;
> I will speak daggers to her, but use none;
> My tongue and soul in this be hypocrites;
> How in my words soever she be shent,
> To give them seals never, my soul, consent!

[*Exit.*]

Scene III.—A Room in the Castle.

Enter KING, ROSENCRANTZ, *and* GUILDENSTERN.

KING: I like him not, nor stands it safe with us
    To let his madness range. Therefore prepare you;
    I your commission will forthwith dispatch,
    And he to England shall along with you.
    The terms of our estate may not endure
    Hazard so dangerous as doth hourly grow
    Out of his lunacies.

GUIL: We will ourselves provide.
    Most holy and religious fear it is
    To keep those many many bodies safe
    That live and feed upon your majesty.

ROS: The single and peculiar life is bound
    With all the strength and armour of the mind
    To keep itself from noyance; but much more

    That spirit upon whose weal depend and rest
    The lives of many. The cease of majesty
    Dies not alone, but, like a gulf doth draw
    What's near it with it; it is a massy wheel,
    Fix'd on the summit of the highest mount,
    To whose huge spokes ten thousand lesser things
    Are mortis'd and adjoin'd; which, when it falls,
    Each small annexment, petty consequence,
    Attends the boisterous ruin. Never alone
    Did the king sigh, but with a general groan.

KING: Arm you, I pray you, to this speedy voyage;
    For we will fetters put upon this fear,
    Which now goes too free-footed.

ROS: }
GUIL: } We will haste us.

    [*Exeunt* ROSENCRANTZ *and* GUILDENSTERN.]

    Enter POLONIUS.

POL: My lord, he's going to his mother's closet:
    Behind the arras I'll convey myself
    To hear the process; I'll warrant she'll tax him home;
    And, as you said, and wisely was it said,
    'Tis meet that some more audience than a mother,
    Since nature makes them partial, should o'er-hear
    The speech, of vantage. Fare you well, my liege:
    I'll call upon you ere you go to bed
    And tell you what I know.

KING: Thanks, dear my lord.

    [*Exit* POLONIUS.]

    O! my offence is rank, it smells to heaven;
    It hath the primal eldest curse upon't;
    A brother's murder! Pray can I not,
    Though inclination be as sharp as will:
    My stronger guilt defeats my strong intent;
    And, like a man to double business bound,
    I stand in pause where I shall first begin,
    And both neglect. What if this cursed hand
    Were thicker than itself with brother's blood,
    Is there not rain enough in the sweet heavens
    To wash it white as snow? Whereto serves mercy
    But to confront the visage of offence?
    And what's in prayer but this two-fold force,
    To be forestalled, ere we come to fall,
    Or pardon'd, being down? Then, I'll look up;
    My fault is past. But, O! what form of prayer
    Can serve my turn? 'Forgive me my foul murder?'
    That cannot be; since I am still possess'd
    Of those effects for which I did the murder,
    My crown, mine own ambition, and my queen.

May one be pardon'd and retain the offence?
In the corrupted currents of this world
Offence's gilded hand may shove by justice,
And oft 'tis seen the wicked prize itself
Buys out the law; but 'tis not so above;
There is no shuffling, there the action lies
In his true nature, and we ourselves compell'd
Even to the teeth and forehead of our faults
To give in evidence. What then? what rests?
Try what repentance can: what can it not?
Yet what can it, when one can not repent?
O wretched state! O bosom black as death!
O limed soul, that struggling to be free
Art more engaged! Help, angels! make assay;
Bow, stubborn knees; and heart with strings of steel
Be soft as sinews of the new-born babe.
All may be well.

[*Retires and kneels.*]

Enter HAMLET.

HAM: Now might I do it pat, now he is praying;
        And now I'll do't: and so he goes to heaven;
        And so am I reveng'd. That would be scann'd:
        A villain kills my father; and for that,
        I, his sole son, do this same villain send
        To heaven.
        Why, this is hire and salary, not revenge.
        He took my father grossly, full of bread,
        With all his crimes broad blown, as flush as May;
        And how his audit stands who knows save heaven?
        But in our circumstance and course of thought
        'Tis heavy with him. And am I then reveng'd,
        To take him in the purging of his soul,
        When he is fit and season'd for his passage?
        No.
        Up, sword, and know thou a more horrid hent;
        When he is drunk asleep, or in his rage,
        Or in the incestuous pleasure of his bed,
        At gaming, swearing, or about some act
        That has no relish of salvation in't;
        Then trip him, that his heels may kick at heaven,
        And that his soul may be as damn'd and black
        As hell, where to it goes. My mother stays:
        This physic but prolongs thy sickly days.

    [*Exit.*]

The KING *rises and advances.*

KING: My words fly up, my thoughts remain below:

Words without thoughts never to heaven go.

[Exit.]

Scene IV.—The Queen's Apartment.

Enter QUEEN *and* POLONIUS.

POL: He will come straight. Look you lay home to him;
      Tell him his pranks have been too broad to bear with,
      And that your Grace hath screen'd and stood between
      Much heat and him. I'll silence me e'en here.
      Pray you, be round with him.
HAM: [*Within.*] Mother, mother, mother!
QUEEN: I'll warrant you;
      Fear me not. Withdraw, I hear him coming.

POLONIUS *hides behind the arras.*

Enter HAMLET.

HAM: Now, mother, what's the matter?
QUEEN: Hamlet, thou hast thy father much offended.
HAM: Mother, you have my father much offended.
QUEEN: Come, come, you answer with an idle tongue.
HAM: Go, go, you question with a wicked tongue.
QUEEN: Why, how now, Hamlet!
HAM: What's the matter now?
QUEEN: Have you forgot me?
HAM: No, by the rood, not so:
      You are the queen, your husband's brother's wife;
      And,—would it were not so!—you are my mother.
QUEEN: Nay then, I'll set those to you that can speak.
HAM: Come, come, and sit you down; you shall not budge;
      You go not, till I set you up a glass
      Where you may see the inmost part of you.
QUEEN: What will thou do? thou wilt not murder me?
      Help, help, ho!
POL: [*Behind.*] What, ho! help! help! help!
HAM: [*Draws.*] How now! a rat? Dead, for a ducat, dead!

    [*Makes a pass through the arras.*]

POL: [*Behind.*] O! I am slain.
QUEEN O me! what hast thou done?
HAM: Nay, I know not: is it the king?
QUEEN: O! what a rash and bloody deed is this!
HAM: A bloody deed! almost as bad, good mother,
      As kill a king, and marry with his brother.
QUEEN: As kill a king!
HAM: Ay, lady, 'twas my word.

    [*Lifts up the arras and discovers* POLONIUS.]

[*To* POLONIUS.]

    Thou wretched, rash, intruding fool, farewell!
    I took thee for thy better; take thy fortune;
    Thou find'st to be too busy is some danger.
    Leave wringing of your hands: peace! sit you down,
    And let me wring your heart; for so I shall
    If it be made of penetrable stuff,
    If damned custom have not brass'd it so
    That it is proof and bulwark against sense
QUEEN: What have I done that thou dar'st wag thy tongue
    In noise so rude against me?
HAM: Such an act
    That blurs the grace and blush of modesty,
    Calls virtue hypocrite, takes off the rose
    From the fair forehead of an innocent love
    And sets a blister there, makes marriage vows
    As false as dicers' oaths; O! such a deed
    As from the body of contraction plucks
    The very soul, and sweet religion makes
    A rhapsody of words; heaven's face doth glow,
    Yea, this solidity and compound mass,
    With tristful visage, as against the doom,
    Is thought-sick at the act.
QUEEN: Ay me! what act,
    That roars so loud and thunders in the index?
HAM: Look here, upon this picture, and on this;
    The counterfeit presentment of two brothers.
    See, what a grace was seated on this brow;
    Hyperion's curls, the front of Jove himself,
    An eye like Mars, to threaten and command,
    A station like the herald Mercury
    New-lighted on a heaven-kissing hill,
    A combination and a form indeed,
    Where every god did seem to set his seal,
    To give the world assurance of a man.
    This was your husband: look you now, what follows.
    Here is your husband; like a mildew'd ear,
    Blasting his wholesome brother. Have you eyes?
    Could you on this fair mountain leave to feed,
    And batten on this moor? Ha! have you eyes?
    You cannot call it love, for at your age
    The hey-day in the blood is tame, it's humble,
    And waits upon the judgment; and what judgment
    Would step from this to this? Sense, sure, you have,
    Else could you not have motion; but sure, that sense
    Is apoplex'd; for madness would not err,
    Nor sense to ecstasy was ne'er so thrall'd
    But it reserv'd some quantity of choice,
    To serve in such a difference. What devil was 't
    That thus hath cozen'd you at hoodman-blind?

Eyes without feeling, feeling without sight,
Ears without hands or eyes, smelling sans all,
Or but a sickly part of one true sense
Could not so mope.
O shame! where is thy blush? Rebellious hell,
If thou canst mutine in a matron's bones,
To flaming youth let virtue be as wax,
And melt in her own fire: proclaim no shame
When the compulsive ardour gives the charge,
Since frost itself as actively doth burn,
And reason panders will.

QUEEN: O Hamlet! speak no more;
Thou turn'st mine eyes into my very soul;
And there I see such black and grained spots
As will not leave their tinct.

HAM: Nay, but to live
In the rank sweat of an enseamed bed,
Stew'd in corruption, honeying and making love
Over the nasty sty,—

QUEEN: O! speak to me no more;
These words like daggers enter in mine ears;
No more, sweet Hamlet!

HAM: A murderer, and a villain;
A slave that is not twentieth part the tithe
Of your precedent lord; a vice of kings;
A cut-purse of the empire and the rule,
That from a shelf the precious diadem stole,
And put it in his pocket!

QUEEN: No more!

HAM: A king of shreds and patches,—

Enter GHOST.

Save me, and hover o'er me with your wings,
You heavenly guards! What would your gracious figure?

QUEEN: Alas! he's mad!

HAM: Do you not come your tardy son to chide,
That, laps'd in time and passion, lets go by
The important acting of your dread command?
O! say.

GHOST: Do not forget: this visitation
Is but to whet thy almost blunted purpose.
But, look! amazement on thy mother sits;
O! slep between her and her fighting soul;
Conceit in weakest bodies strongest works;
Speak to her, Hamlet.

HAM: How is it with you, lady?

QUEEN: Alas! how is't with you,
That you do bend your eye on vacancy
And with the incorporal air do hold discourse?
Forth at your eyes your spirits wildly peep;
And, as the sleeping soldiers in the alarm,

Your bedded hair, like life in excrements,
Starts up and stands an end. O gentle son!
Upon the heat and flame of thy distemper
Sprinkle cool patience. Whereon do you look?

HAM: On him, on him! Look you, how pale he glares!
His form and cause conjoin'd, preaching to stones,
Would make them capable. Do not look upon me;
Lest with this piteous action you convert
My stern effects; then what I have to do
Will want true colour; tears perchance for blood.

QUEEN: To whom do you speak this?

HAM: Do you see nothing there?

QUEEN: Nothing at all; yet all that is I see.

HAM: Nor did you nothing hear?

QUEEN: No, nothing but ourselves.

HAM: Why, look you there! look, how it steals away;
My father, in his habit as he liv'd;
Look! where he goes, even now, out at the portal.

[*Exit* GHOST.]

QUEEN: This is the very coinage of your brain:
This bodiless creation ecstasy
Is very cunning in.

HAM: Ecstasy!
My pulse, as yours, doth temperately keep time,
And makes as healthful music. It is not madness
That I have utter'd: bring me to the test,
And I the matter will re-word, which madness
Would gambol from, Mother, for love of grace,
Lay not that flattering unction to your soul,
That not your trespass but my madness speaks;
It will but skin and film the ulcerous place,
Whiles rank corruption, mining all within,
Infects unseen. Confess yourself to heaven;
Repent what's past; avoid what is to come;
And do not spread the compost on the weeds
To make them ranker. Forgive me this my virtue;
For in the fatness of these pursy times
Virtue itself of vice must pardon beg,
Yea, curb and woo for leave to do him good.

QUEEN: O Hamlet! thou hast cleft my heart in twain.

HAM: O! throw away the worser part of it,
And live the purer with the other half.
Good night; but go not to mine uncle's bed;
Assume a virtue, if you have it not.
That monster, custom, who all sense doth eat,
Of habits devil, is angel yet in this,
That to the use of actions fair and good
He likewise gives a frock or livery,
That aptly is put on. Refrain to-night;
And that shall lend a kind of easiness

To the next abstinence: the next more easy;
For use almost can change the stamp of nature,
And master ev'n the devil or throw him out
With wondrous potency. Once more, goodnight:
And when you are desirous to be bless'd,
I'll blessing beg of you. For this same lord,

[*Pointing to* POLONIUS.]

I do repent: but heaven hath pleas'd it so,
To punish me with this, and this with me,
That I must be their scourge and minister.
I will bestow him, and will answer well
The death I gave him. So, again, good-night.
I must be cruel only to be kind:
Thus bad begins and worse remains behind.
One word more, good lady.
QUEEN: What shall I do?
HAM: Not this, by no means, that I bid you do:
Let the bloat king tempt you again to bed;
Pinch wanton on your cheek; call you his mouse;
And let him, for a pair of reechy kisses,
Or paddling in your neck with his damn'd fingers,
Make you to ravel all this matter out,
That I essentially am not in madness,
But mad in craft. 'Twere good you let him know;
For who that's but a queen, fair, sober, wise,
Would from a paddock, from a bat, a gib,
Such dear concernings hide? who would do so?
No, in despite of sense and secrecy,
Unpeg the basket on the house's top,
Let the birds fly, and, like the famous ape,
To try conclusions, in the basket creep,
And break your own neck down.
QUEEN: Be thou assur'd, if words be made of breath,
And breath of life, I have no life to breathe
What thou hast said to me.
HAM: I must to England; you know that?
QUEEN: Alack!
I had forgot: 'tis so concluded on.
HAM: There's letters seal'd; and my two schoolfellows,
Whom I will trust as I will adders fang'd,
They bear the mandate; they must sweep my way,
And marshal me to knavery. Let it work;
For 'tis the sport to have the enginer
Hoist with his own petar: and it shall go hard
But I will delve one yard below their mines,
And blow them at the moon. O! 'tis most sweet,
When in one line two crafts directly meet.
This man shall set me packing;
I'll lug the guts into the neighbour room.
Mother, good-night. Indeed this counsellor

Is now most still, most secret, and most grave,
Who was in life a foolish prating knave.
Come, sir, to draw toward an end with you.
Good-night, mother.

[*Exeunt severally;* HAMLET *dragging in the body of* POLONIUS.]

ACT IV.

Scene I.—A Room in the Castle.

Enter KING, QUEEN, ROSENCRANTZ, *and* GUILDENSTERN.

KING: There's matter in these sighs, these profound heaves:
    You must translate; 'tis fit we understand them.
    Where is your son?

QUEEN:

    [*To* ROSENCRANTZ *and* GUILDENSTERN.]

    Bestow this place on us a little while.

    [*Exeunt* ROSENCRANTZ *and* GUILDENSTERN.]

    Ah! my good lord, what have I seen to-night.
KING: What, Gertrude? How does Hamlet?
QUEEN: Mad as the sea and wind, when both contend
    Which is the mightier. In his lawless fit,
    Behind the arras hearing something stir,
    Whips out his rapier, cries, 'A rat! a rat!'
    And, in his brainish apprehension, kills
    The unseen good old man.
KING: O heavy deed!
    It had been so with us had we been there.
    His liberty is full of threats to all;
    To you yourself, to us, to every one.
    Alas! how shall this bloody deed be answer'd?
    It will be laid to us, whose providence
    Should have kept short, restrain'd, and out of haunt,
    This mad young man: but so much was our love,
    We would not understand what was most fit,
    But, like the owner of a foul disease,
    To keep it from divulging, let it feed
    Even on the pith of life. Where is he gone?
QUEEN: To draw apart the body he hath kill'd;
    O'er whom his very madness, like some ore
    Among a mineral of metals base,
    Shows itself pure: he weeps for what is done.
KING: O Gertrude! come away.
    The sun no sooner shall the mountains touch
    But we will ship him hence; and this vile deed
    We must, with all our majesty and skill,
    Both countenance and excuse. Ho! Guildenstern!

Re-enter ROSENCRANTZ *and* GUILDENSTERN.

Friends both, go join you with some further aid:
Hamlet in madness hath Polonius slain,
And from his mother's closet hath he dragg'd him:
Go seek him out; speak fair, and bring the body
Into the chapel. I pray you, haste in this.

[*Exeunt* ROSENCRANTZ *and* GUILDENSTERN.]

Come, Gertrude, we'll call up our wisest friends,
And let them know both what we mean to do,
And what's untimely done: so, haply, slander,
Whose whisper o'er the world's diameter,
As level as the cannon to his blank
Transports his poison'd shot, may miss our name,
And hit the woundless air. O! come away;
My soul is full of discord and dismay.

[*Exeunt.*]

Scene II.—Another Room in the Same.

Enter *HAMLET.*

HAM: Safely stowed.

ROS:
GUIL: } [*Within.*] Hamlet! Lord Hamlet!

HAM: What noise? who calls on Hamlet?
    O! here they come.

Enter ROSENCRANTZ *and* GUILDENSTERN.

ROS: What have you done, my lord, with the dead body?

HAM: Compounded it with dust, whereto 'tis kin.

ROS: Tell us where 'tis, that we may take it thence
    And bear it to the chapel.

HAM: Do not believe it.

ROS: Believe what?

HAM: That I can keep your counsel and not mine own. Besides, to be demanded of a sponge! what replication should be made by the son of a king?

ROS: Take you me for a sponge, my lord?

HAM: Ay, sir, that soaks up the king's countenance, his rewards, his authorities. But such officers do the king best service in the end: he keeps them, like an ape, in the corner of his jaw; first mouthed, to be last swallowed: when he needs what you have gleaned, it is but squeezing you, and, sponge, you shall be dry again.

ROS: I understand you not, my lord.

HAM: I am glad of it: a knavish speech sleeps in a foolish ear.

ROS: My lord, you must tell us where the body is, and go with us to the king.

HAM: The body is with the king, but the king is not with the body. The king is a thing—

GUIL: A thing, my lord!

HAM: Of nothing: bring me to him. Hide fox, and all after.

[*Exeunt.*]

Scene III.—Another Room in the Same.

Enter KING, *attended.*

KING: I have sent to seek him, and to find the body.
　　　How dangerous is it that this man goes loose!
　　　Yet must not we put the strong law on him:
　　　He's lov'd of the distracted multitude,
　　　Who like not in their judgment, but their eyes;
　　　And where 'tis so, the offender's scourge is weigh'd,
　　　But never the offence. To bear all smooth and even,
　　　This sudden sending him away must seem
　　　Deliberate pause: diseases desperate grown
　　　By desperate appliance are reliev'd,
　　　Or not at all.

Enter ROSENCRANTZ.

　　　How now! what hath befall'n?
ROS: Where the dead body is bestow'd, my lord,
　　　We cannot get from him.
KING: But where is he?
ROS: Without, my lord; guarded, to know your pleasure.
KING: Bring him before us.
ROS: Ho, Guildenstern! bring in my lord.

Enter HAMLET *and* GUILDENSTERN.

KING: Now, Hamlet, where's Polonius?
HAM: At supper.
KING: At supper! Where?
HAM: Not where he eats, but where he is eaten: a certain convocation of politic
　　　worms are e'en at him. Your worm is your only emperor for diet: we fat all
　　　creatures else to fat us, and we fat ourselves for maggots: your fat king and
　　　your lean beggar is but variable service; two dishes, but to one table: that's
　　　the end.
KING: Alas, alas!
HAM: A man may fish with the worm that hath eat of a king, and eat of the fish that
　　　hath fed of that worm.
KING: What dost thou mean by this?
HAM: Nothing, but to show you how a king may go a progress through the guts
　　　of a beggar.
KING: Where is Polonius?
HAM: In heaven; send thither to see: if your messenger find him not there, seek
　　　him i' the other place yourself. But, indeed, if you find him not within this
　　　month, you shall nose him as you go up the stairs into the lobby.
KING: [*To some* Attendants.] Go seek him there.
HAM: He will stay till you come.

[*Exeunt* ATTENDANTS.]

KING: Hamlet, this deed, for thine especial safety,
     Which we do tender, as we dearly grieve
     For that which thou hast done, must send thee hence
     With fiery quickness: therefore prepare thyself;
     The bark is ready, and the wind at help,
     The associates tend, and every thing is bent
     For England.

HAM: For England!

KING: Ay, Hamlet.

HAM: Good.

KING: So is it, if thou knew'st our purposes.

HAM: I see a cherub that sees them. But, come; for England! Farewell, dear mother.

KING: Thy loving father, Hamlet.

HAM: My mother: father and mother is man and wife, man and wife is one flesh,
     and so, my mother. Come, for England!

> [*Exit.*]

KING: Follow him at foot; tempt him with speed aboard:
     Delay it not, I'll have him hence to-night,
     Away! for every thing is seal'd and done
     That else leans on the affair: pray you, make haste.

> [*Exeunt* ROSENCRANTZ *and* GUILDENSTERN.]

> And, England, if my love thou hold'st at aught,—
> As my great power thereof may give thee sense,
> Since yet thy cicatrice looks raw and red
> After the Danish sword, and thy free awe
> Pays homage to us,—thou mayst not coldly set
> Our sovereign process, which imports at full,
> By letters conjuring to that effect,
> The present death of Hamlet. Do it, England;
> For like the hectic in my blood he rages,
> And thou must cure me. Till I know 'tis done,
> Howe'er my haps, my joys were ne'er begun.

> [*Exit.*]

Scene IV.—A Plain in Denmark.

> *Enter* FORTINBRAS, *a* CAPTAIN, *and* SOLDIERS, *marching.*

FOR: Go, captain, from me greet the Danish king;
     Tell him that, by his licence, Fortinbras
     Claims the conveyance of a promis'd march
     Over his kingdom. You know the rendezvous.
     If that his majesty would aught with us,
     We shall express our duty in his eye,
     And let him know so.

CAP: I will do 't, my lord.

FOR: Go softly on.

[*Exeunt* FORTINBRAS *and* SOLDIERS.]

Enter HAMLET, ROSENCRANTZ, GUILDENSTERN, *&c.*

HAM: Good sir, whose powers are these?
CAP: They are of Norway, sir.
HAM: How purpos'd, sir, I pray you?
CAP: Against some part of Poland.
HAM: Who commands them, sir?
CAP: The nephew to old Norway, Fortinbras.
HAM: Goes it against the main of Poland, sir,
         Or for some frontier?
CAP: Truly to speak, and with no addition,
         We go to gain a little patch of ground
         That hath in it no profit but the name.
         To pay five ducats, five, I would not farm it;
         Nor will it yield to Norway or the Pole
         A ranker rate, should it be sold in fee.
HAM: Why, then the Polack never will defend it.
CAP: Yes, 'tis already garrison'd.
HAM: Two thousand souls and twenty thousand ducats
         Will not debate the question of this straw:
         This is the imposthume of much wealth and peace,
         That inward breaks, and shows no cause without
         Why the man dies. I humbly thank you, sir.
CAP: God be wi' you, sir.

     [*Exit.*]

ROS: Will 't please you go, my lord?
HAM: I'll be with you straight. Go a little before.

     [*Exeunt all except* HAMLET.]

         How all occasions do inform against me,
         And spur my dull revenge! What is a man,
         If his chief good and market of his time
         Be but to sleep and feed? a beast, no more.
         Sure he that made us with such large discourse,
         Looking before and after, gave us not
         That capability and god-like reason
         To fust in us unus'd. Now, whe'r it be
         Bestial oblivion, or some craven scruple
         Of thinking too precisely on the event,
         A thought, which, quarter'd, hath but one part wisdom,
         And ever three parts coward, I do not know
         Why yet I live to say 'This thing's to do;
         Sith I have cause and will and strength and means
         To do 't. Examples gross as earth exhort me:
         Witness this army of such mass and charge
         Led by a delicate and tender prince,
         Whose spirit with divine ambition puff'd
         Makes mouths at the invisible event,

Exposing what is mortal and unsure
To all that fortune, death and danger dare,
Even for an egg-shell. Rightly to be great
Is not to stir without great argument,
But greatly to find quarrel in a straw
When honour's at the stake. How stand I then,
That have a father kill'd, a mother stain'd,
Excitements of my reason and my blood,
And let all sleep, while, to my shame, I see
The imminent death of twenty thousand men,
That, for a fantasy and trick of fame,
Go to their graves like beds, fight for a plot
Whereon the numbers cannot try the cause,
Which is not tomb enough and continent
To hide the slain? O! from this time forth,
My thoughts be bloody, or be nothing worth!

[*Exit.*]

Scene V.—Elsinore. A Room in the Castle.

Enter QUEEN, HORATIO, *and a* GENTLEMAN.

QUEEN: I will not speak with her.
GENT: She is importunate, indeed distract: Her mood will needs be pitied.
QUEEN: What would she have?
GENT: She speaks much of her father; says she hears
There's tricks i' the world; and hems, and beats her heart;
Spurns enviously at straws; speaks things in doubt,
That carry but half sense: her speech is nothing,
Yet the unshaped use of it doth move
The hearers to collection; they aim at it,
And botch the words up fit to their own thoughts;
Which, as her winks, and nods, and gestures yield them,
Indeed would make one think there might be thought,
Though nothing sure, yet much unhappily.
HOR: 'Twere good she were spoken with, for she may strew
Dangerous conjectures in ill-breeding minds.
QUEEN: Let her come in.

[*Exit* GENTLEMAN.]

To my sick soul, as sin's true nature is,
Each toy seems prologue to some great amiss:
So full of artless jealousy is guilt,
It spills itself in fearing to be spilt.

Re-enter GENTLEMAN, *with* OPHELIA.

OPH: Where is the beauteous majesty of Denmark?
QUEEN: How now, Ophelia!
OPH: How should I your true love know
From another one?

> By his cockle hat and staff,
> And his sandal shoon.

QUEEN: Alas! sweet lady, what imports this song?

OPH: Say you? nay, pray you, mark.

> He is dead and gone, lady,
> He is dead and gone;
> At his head a grass-green turf.
> At his heels a stone.
>   O, ho!

QUEEN: Nay, but Ophelia,—

OPH: Pray you, mark.

> White his shroud as the mountain snow,—

Enter KING.

QUEEN: Alas! look here, my lord.

OPH: Larded with sweet flowers;
>   Which bewept to the grave did go
>   With true-love showers.

KING: How do you, pretty lady?

OPH: Well, God 'ild you! They say the owl was a baker's daughter. Lord! we know what we are, but know not what we may be. God be at your table!

KING: Conceit upon her father.

OPH: Pray you, let's have no words of this; but when they ask you what it means, say you this:

> To-morrow is Saint Valentine's day,
> All in the morning betime,
> And I a maid at your window,
> To be your Valentine:
> Then up he rose, and donn'd his clothes,
> And dupp'd the chamber door;
> Let in the maid, that out a maid
> Never departed more.

KING: Pretty Ophelia!

OPH: Indeed, la! without an oath, I'll make an end on 't:

> By Gis and by Saint Charity,
> Alack, and fie for shame!
> Young men will do't, if they come to't;
> By Cock they are to blame.
> Quoth she, before you tumbled me,
> You promis'd me to wed:
> So would I ha' done, by yonder sun,
> An thou hadst not come to my bed.

KING: How long hath she been thus?

OPH: I hope all will be well. We must be patient: but I cannot choose but weep, to think they should lay him i' the cold ground. My brother shall know of it: and so I thank you for your good counsel. Come, my coach! Good-night, ladies; good-night, sweet ladies; good-night, good-night.

> [*Exit.*]

KING: Follow her close; give her good watch, I pray you.

[*Exit* HORATIO.]

> O! this is the poison of deep grief; it springs
> All from her father's death. O Gertrude, Gertrude!
> When sorrows come, they come not single spies,
> But in battalions. First, her father slain;
> Next, your son gone; but he most violent author
> Of his own just remove: the people muddied,
> Thick and unwholesome in their thoughts and whispers,
> For good Polonius' death; and we have done but greenly,
> In hugger-mugger to inter him: poor Ophelia
> Divided from herself and her fair judgment,
> Without the which we are pictures, or mere beasts:
> Last, and as much containing as all these,
> Her brother is in secret come from France,
> Feeds on his wonder, keeps himself in clouds,
> And wants not buzzers to infect his ear
> With pestilent speeches of his father's death;
> Wherein necessity, of matter beggar'd,
> Will nothing stick our person to arraign
> In ear and ear. O my dear Gertrude! this,
> Like to a murdering-piece, in many places
> Gives me superfluous death.

[*A noise within.*]

QUEEN: Alack! what noise is this?

Enter a GENTLEMAN.

KING: Where are my Switzers? Let them guard the door.
What is the matter?
GEN: Save yourself, my lord;
The ocean, overpeering of his list,
Eats not the flats with more impetuous haste
Than young Laertes, in a riotous head,
O'erbears your officers. The rabble call him lord;
And, as the world were now but to begin,
Antiquity forgot, custom not known,
The ratifiers and props of every word,
They cry, 'Choose we; Laertes shall be king!'
Caps, hands, and tongues, applaud it to the clouds,
'Laertes shall be king, Laertes king!'
QUEEN: How cheerfully on the false trail they cry!
O! this is counter, you false Danish dogs!
KING: The doors are broke.

[*Noise within.*]

Enter LAERTES, *armed;* DANES *following.*

LAER: Where is the king? Sirs, stand you all without.
DANES: No, let's come in.

LAER: I pray you, give me leave.
DANES: We will, we will.

[*They retire without the door.*]

LAER: I thank you: keep the door. O thou vile king!
     Give me my father.
QUEEN: Calmly, good Laertes.
LAER: That drop of blood that's calm proclaims me bastard.
     Cries cuckold to my father, brands the harlot
     Even here, between the chaste unsmirched brow
     Of my true mother.
KING: What is the cause, Laertes,
     That thy rebellion looks so giant-like?
     Let him go, Gertrude; do not fear our person:
     There's such divinity doth hedge a king,
     That treason can but peep to what it would,
     Acts little of his will. Tell me, Laertes,
     Why thou art thus incens'd. Let him go, Gertrude.
     Speak, man.
LAER: Where is my father?
KING: Dead.
QUEEN: But not by him.
KING: Let him demand his fill.
LAER: How came he dead? I'll not be juggled with.
     To hell, allegiance! vows, to the blackest devil!
     Conscience and grace, to the profoundest pit!
     I dare damnation. To this point I stand,
     That both the worlds I give to negligence,
     Let come what comes; only I'll be reveng'd
     Most throughly for my father.
KING: Who shall stay you?
LAER: My will, not all the world:
     And, for my means, I'll husband them so well,
     They shall go far with little.
KING: Good Laertes,
     If you desire to know the certainty
     Of your dear father's death, is't writ in your revenge,
     That, swoopstake, you will draw both friend and foe,
     Winner and loser?
LAER: None but his enemies.
KING: Will you know them then?
LAER: To his good friends thus wide I'll ope my arms;
     And like the kind life-rendering pelican,
     Repast them with my blood.
KING: Why, now you speak
     Like a good child and a true gentleman,
     That I am guiltless of your father's death,
     And am most sensibly in grief for it,
     It shall as level to your judgment pierce
     As day does to your eye.
DANES:

[*Within.*]

      Let her come in.

LAER: How now! what noise is that?

Re-enter OPHELIA.

      O heat, dry up my brains! tears seven times salt,
      Burn out the sense and virtue of mine eye:
      By heaven, thy madness shall be paid by weight,
      Till our scale turn the beam. O rose of May!
      Dear maid, kind sister, sweet Ophelia!
      O heavens! is't possible a young maid's wits
      Should be as mortal as an old man's life?
      Nature is fine in love, and where 'tis fine
      It sends some precious instance of itself
      After the thing it loves.

OPH: They bore him barefac'd on the bier;
      Hey non nonny, nonny, hey nonny;
      And in his grave rain'd many a tear,—
      Fare you well, my dove!

LAER: Hadst thou thy wits, and didst persuade revenge,
      It could not move thus.

OPH: You must sing, a-down a-down,
      And you call him a-down-a.
      O how the wheel becomes it! It is the false steward that stole his mas-
ter's daughter.

LAER: This nothing's more than matter.

OPH: There's rosemary, that's for remembrance; pray, love, remember: and there's
pansies, that's for thoughts.

LAER: A document in madness, thoughts and remembrance fitted.

OPH: There's fennel for you, and columbines; there's rue for you; and here's some
for me; we may call it herb of grace o' Sundays. O! you must wear your rue
with a difference. There's a daisy; I would give you some violets, but they withered all when my father died. They say he made a good end,—
      For bonay sweet Robin is all my joy.

LAER: Thought and affliction, passion, hell itself,
      She turns to favour and to prettiness.

OPH: And will he not come again?
      And will he not come again?
      No, no, he is dead;
      Go to thy death-bed,
      He never will come again.
      His beard was as white as snow
      All flaxen was his poll,
      He is gone, he is gone,
      And we cast away moan:
      God ha' mercy on his soul!
      And of all Christian souls! I pray God. God be wi' ye!

[*Exit.*]

LAER: Do you see this, O God?

KING: Laertes, I must common with your grief,
   Or you deny me right. Go but apart,
   Make choice of whom your wisest friends you will,
   And they shall hear and judge 'twixt you and me.
   If by direct or by collateral hand
   They find us touch'd, we will our kingdom give,
   Our crown, our life, and all that we call ours,
   To you in satisfaction; but if not,
   Be you content to lend your patience to us,
   And we shall jointly labour with your soul
   To give it due content.

LAER: Let this be so:
   His means of death, his obscure burial,
   No trophy, sword, nor hatchment o'er his bones,
   No noble rite nor formal ostentation,
   Cry to be heard, as 'twere from heaven to earth,
   That I must call 't in question.

KING: So you shall;
   And where the offence is let the great axe fall.
   I pray you go with me.

  [*Exeunt.*]

Scene VI.—Another Room in the Same.

  Enter HORATIO *and a* SERVANT.

HOR: What are they that would speak with me?

SERV: Sailors, sir: they say, they have letters for you.

HOR: Let them come in.

  [*Exit* SERVANT.]

   I do not know from what part of the world
   I should be greeted, if not from Lord Hamlet.

  Enter SAILORS.

FIRST SAIL: God bless you, sir.

HOR: Let him bless thee too.

SEC. SAIL: He shall, sir, an't please him.
   There's a letter for you, sir;—it comes from the ambassador that was bound
  for England;—if your name be Horatio, as I am let to know it is.

HOR: *Horatio, when thou shalt have over-looked this, give these fellows some means
  to the* KING: *they have letters for him. Ere we were two days old at sea, a pirate
  of very war-like appointment gave us chase. Finding ourselves too slow of sail,
  we put on a compelled valour; in the grapple I boarded them: on the instant
  they got clear of our ship, so I alone became their prisoner. They have dealt with
  me like thieves of mercy, but they knew what they did; I am to do a good turn
  for them. Let the king have the letters I have sent; and repair thou to me with
  as much haste as thou wouldst fly death. I have words to speak in thine ear
  will make thee dumb; yet are they much too light for the bore of the matter. These*

*good fellows will bring thee where I am. Rosencrantz and Guildenstern hold
their course for England: of them I have much to tell thee. Farewell.*
    He that thou knowest thine,
    HAMLET.
    Come, I will give you way for these your letters;
    And do't the speedier, that you may direct me
    To him from whom you brought them.

[*Exeunt.*]

Scene VII.—Another Room in the Same.

    Enter KING *and* LAERTES.

KING: Now must your conscience my acquittance seal,
    And you must put me in your heart for friend,
    Sith you have heard, and with a knowing ear,
    That he which hath your noble father slain
    Pursu'd my life.
LAER: It well appears: but tell me
    Why you proceeded not against these feats,
    So crimeful and so capital in nature,
    As by your safety, wisdom, all things else,
    You mainly were stirr'd up.
KING: O! for two special reasons;
    Which may to you, perhaps, seem much unsinew'd,
    But yet to me they are strong. The queen his mother
    Lives almost by his looks, and for myself,—
    My virtue or my plague, be it either which,—
    She's so conjunctive to my life and soul,
    That, as the star moves not but in his sphere,
    I could not but by her. The other motive,
    Why to a public count I might not go,
    Is the great love the general gender bear him;
    Who, dipping all his faults in their affection,
    Would, like the spring that turneth wood to stone,
    Convert his gyves to graces; so that my arrows,
    Too slightly timber'd for so loud a wind,
    Would have reverted to my bow again,
    And not where I had aim'd them.
LAER: And so have I a noble father lost;
    A sister driven into desperate terms,
    Whose worth, if praises may go back again,
    Stood challenger on mount of all the age
    For her perfections. But my revenge will come.
KING: Break not your sleeps for that; you must not think
    That we are made of stuff so flat and dull
    That we can let our beard be shook with danger
    And think it pastime. You shortly shall hear more;
    I lov'd your father, and we love ourself,
    And that, I hope, will teach you to imagine,—

    Enter a MESSENGER.

      How now! what news?

MESS: Letters, my lord, from Hamlet:
    This to your majesty; this to the queen.

KING: From Hamlet! who brought them?

MESS: Sailors, my lord, they say; I saw them not:
    They were given me by Claudio, he receiv'd them
    Of him that brought them.

KING: Laertes, you shall hear them.
    Leave us.

    [*Exit* MESSENGER.]

    High and mighty, you shall know I am set naked on your kingdom. To-
morrow shall I beg leave to see your kingly eyes; when I shall, first asking your
pardon thereunto, recount the occasions of my sudden and more strange return
    HAMLET.

    What should this mean? Are all the rest come back?
    Or is it some abuse and no such thing?

LAER: Know you the hand?

KING: 'Tis Hamlet's character. 'Naked,'
    And in a postscript here, he says, 'alone.'
    Can you advise me?

LAER: I'm lost in it, my lord. But let him come:
    It warms the very sickness in my heart,
    That, I shall live and tell him to his teeth,
    'Thus diddest thou.'

KING: If it be so, Laertes,
    As how should it be so? how otherwise?
    Will you be rul'd by me?

LAER: Ay, my lord;
    So you will not o'er-rule me to a peace.

KING: To thine own peace. If he be now return'd,
    As checking at his voyage, and that he means
    No more to undertake it, I will work him
    To an exploit, now ripe in my device,
    Under the which he shall not choose but fall;
    And for his death no wind of blame shall breathe,
    But even his mother shall uncharge the practice
    And call it accident.

LAER: My lord, I will be rul'd;
    The rather, if you could devise it so
    That I might be the organ.

KING: It falls right.
    You have been talk'd of since your travel much,
    And that in Hamlet's hearing, for a quality
    Wherein, they say, you shine; your sum of parts
    Did not together pluck such envy from him
    As did that one, and that, in my regard,
    Of the unworthiest siege.

LAER: What part is that, my lord?

KING: A very riband in the cap of youth,
       Yet needful too; for youth no less becomes
       The light and careless livery that it wears
       Than settled age his sables and his weeds,
       Importing health and graveness. Two months since
       Here was a gentleman of Normandy:
       I've seen myself, and serv'd against, the French,
       And they can well on horseback; but this gallant
       Had witchcraft in't, he grew unto his seat,
       And to such wondrous doing brought his horse,
       As he had been incorps'd and demi-natur'd
       With the brave beast; so far he topp'd my thought,
       That I, in forgery of shapes and tricks,
       Come short of what he did.
LAER: A Norman was 't?
KING: A Norman.
LAER: Upon my life, Lamord.
KING: The very same.
LAER: I know him well; he is the brooch indeed
       And gem of all the nation.
KING: He made confession of you,
       And gave you such a masterly report
       For art and exercise in your defence,
       And for your rapier most especially,
       That he cried out, 'twould be a sight indeed
       If one could match you; the scrimers of their nation,
       He swore, had neither motion, guard, nor eye,
       If you oppos'd them. Sir, this report of his
       Did Hamlet so envenom with his envy
       That he could nothing do but wish and beg
       Your sudden coming o'er, to play with him.
       Now, out of this,—
LAER: What out of this, my lord?
KING: Laertes, was your father dear to you?
       Or are you like the painting of a sorrow,
       A face without a heart?
LAER: Why ask you this?
KING: Not that I think you did not love your father,
       But that I know love is begun by time,
       And that I see, in passages of proof,
       Time qualifies the spark and fire of it.
       There lives within the very flame of love
       A kind of wick or snuff that will abate it,
       And nothing is at a like goodness still,
       For goodness, growing to a plurisy,
       Dies in his own too-much. That we would do,
       We should do when we would, for this 'would' changes,
       And hath abatements and delays as many
       As there are tongues, are hands, are accidents;
       And then this 'should' is like a spendthrift sigh,
       That hurts by easing. But, to the quick o' the ulcer;

Hamlet comes back; what would you undertake
To show yourself your father's son in deed
More than in words?

LAER: To cut his throat i' the church.

KING: No place, indeed, should murder sanctuarize;
Revenge should have no bounds. But, good Laertes,
Will you do this, keep close within your chamber.
Hamlet return'd shall know you are come home;
We'll put on those shall praise your excellence,
And set a double varnish on the fame
The Frenchman gave you, bring you, in fine, together,
And wager on your heads: he, being remiss,
Most generous and free from all contriving,
Will not peruse the foils; so that, with ease
Or with a little shuffling, you may choose
A sword unbated, and, in a pass of practice
Requite him for your father.

LAER: I will do 't;
And, for that purpose, I'll anoint my sword,
I bought an unction of a mountebank,
So mortal that, but dip a knife in it,
Where it draws blood no cataplasm so rare,
Collected from all simples that have virtue
Under the moon, can save the thing from death
That is but scratch'd withal; I'll touch my point
With this contagion, that, if I gall him slightly,
It may be death.

KING: Let's further think of this;
Weigh what convenience both of time and means
May fit us to our shape. If this should fail,
And that our drift look through our bad performance
'Twere better not assay'd; therefore this project
Should have a back or second, that might hold,
If this should blast in proof. Soft! let me see;
We'll make a solemn wager on your cunnings:
I ha 't:
When in your motion you are hot and dry,—
As make your bouts more violent to that end,—
And that he calls for drink, I'll have prepar'd him
A chalice for the nonce, whereon but sipping,
If he by chance escape your venom'd stuck,
Our purpose may hold there. But stay! what noise?

Enter QUEEN.

How now, sweet queen!

QUEEN: One woe doth tread upon another's heel,
So fast they follow: your sister's drown'd, Laertes.

LAER: Drown'd! O, where?

QUEEN: There is a willow grows aslant a brook,
That shows his hoar leaves in the glassy stream;
There with fantastic garlands did she come,

Of crow-flowers, nettles, daisies, and long purples,
That liberal shepherds give a grosser name,
But our cold maids do dead men's fingers call them:
There, on the pendent boughs her coronet weeds
Clambering to hang, an envious sliver broke,
When down her weedy trophies and herself
Fall in the weeping brook. Her clothes spread wide,
And, mermaid-like, awhile they bore her up;
Which time she chanted snatches of old tunes,
As one incapable of her own distress,
Or like a creature native and indu'd
Unto that element; but long it could not be
Till that her garments, heavy with their drink,
Pull'd the poor wretch from her melodious lay
To muddy death.

LAER: Alas! then, she is drown'd?

QUEEN: Drown'd, drown'd.

LAER: Too much of water hast thou, poor Ophelia,
And therefore I forbid my tears; but yet
It is our trick, nature her custom holds,
Let shame say what it will; when these are gone
The woman will be out. Adieu, my lord!
I have a speech of fire, that fain would blaze,
But that this folly douts it.

[*Exit.*]

KING: Let's follow, Gertrude.
How much I had to do to calm his rage!
Now fear I this will give it start again;
Therefore let's follow.

[*Exeunt.*]

ACT V.

Scene I.—A Churchyard.

Enter two CLOWNS, *with spades and mattock.*

FIRST CLO: Is she to be buried in Christian burial that wilfully seeks her own salvation?

SEC. CLO: I tell thee she is; and therefore make her grave straight: the crowner hath sat on her, and finds it Christian burial.

FIRST CLO: How can that be, unless she drowned herself in her own defence?

SEC. CLO: Why, 'tis found so.

FIRST CLO: It must be *se offendendo*; it cannot be else. For here lies the point: if I drown myself wittingly it argues an act; and an act hath three branches; it is, to act, to do, and to perform: argal, she drowned herself wittingly.

SEC. CLO: Nay, but hear you, goodman delver,—

FIRST CLO: Give me leave. Here lies the water; good: here stands the man; good: if the man go to this water, and drown himself, it is, will he, nill he, he goes;

mark you that? but if the water come to him, and drown him, he drowns not himself: argal, he that is not guilty of his own death shortens not his own life.

SEC. CLO: But is this law?

FIRST CLO: Ay, marry, is 't; crowner's quest law.

SEC. CLO: Will you ha' the truth on 't? If this had not been a gentlewoman she should have been buried out o' Christian burial.

FIRST CLO: Why, there thou sayest; and the more pity that great folk should have countenance in this world to drown or hang themselves more than their even Christian. Come, my spade. There is no ancient gentlemen but gardeners, ditchers, and grave-makers; they hold up Adam's profession.

SEC. CLO: Was he a gentleman?

FIRST CLO: A' was the first that ever bore arms.

SEC. CLO: Why, he had none.

FIRST CLO: What! art a heathen? How dost thou understand the Scripture? The Scripture says, Adam digged; could he dig without arms? I'll put another question to thee; if thou answerest me not to the purpose, confess thyself—

SEC. CLO: Go to.

FIRST CLO: What is he that builds stronger than either the mason, the shipwright, or the carpenter?

SEC. CLO: The gallows-maker; for that frame outlives a thousand tenants.

FIRST CLO: I like thy wit well, in good faith; the gallows does well; but how does it well? it does well to those that do ill; now thou dost ill to say the gallows is built stronger than the church: argal, the gallows may do well to thee. To 't again; come.

SEC. CLO: Who builds stronger than a mason, a shipwright, or a carpenter?

FIRST CLO: Ay, tell me that, and unyoke.

SEC. CLO: Marry, now I can tell.

FIRST CLO: To 't.

SEC. CLO: Mass, I cannot tell.

Enter HAMLET *and* HORATIO *at a distance.*

FIRST CLO: Cudgel thy brains no more about it, for your dull ass will not mend his pace with beating; and, when you are asked this question next, say, 'a grave-maker,' the houses that he makes last till doomsday. Go, get thee to Yaughan; fetch me a stoup of liquor.

[*Exit Second* CLOWN.]

First Clown digs, and sings,

> In youth, when I did love, did love,
> Methought it was very sweet,
> To contract, O! the time, for-a my behove,
> O! methought there was nothing meet.

HAM: Has this fellow no feeling of his business, that he sings at grave-making?

HOR: Custom hath made it in him a property of easiness.

HAM: 'Tis e'en so; the hand of little employment hath the daintier sense.

FIRST CLO: But age, with his stealing steps,

> Hath claw'd me in his clutch.
> And hath shipped me intil the land,

As if I had never been such.

[*Throws up a skull.*]

HAM: That skull had a tongue in it, and could sing once; how the knave jowls it
to the ground, as if it were Cain's jaw-bone, that did the first murder! This might
be the pate of a politician, which this ass now o'er-offices, one that would
circumvent God, might it not?

HOR: It might, my lord.

HAM: Or of a courtier, which could say, 'Good morrow, sweet lord! How dost
thou good lord?' This might be my Lord Such-a-one, that praised my Lord Such-
a-one's horse when he meant to beg it, might it not?

HOR: Ay, my lord.

HAM: Why, e'en so, and now my Lady Worm's; chapless, and knocked about the
mazzard with a sexton's spade. Here's fine revolution an we had the trick to
see 't. Did these homes cost no more the breeding but to play at loggats with
'em? mine ache to think on 't.

FIRST CLO: A pick-axe, and a spade, a spade,
    For and a shrouding sheet;
    O! a pit of clay for to be made
    For such a guest is meet.

[*Throws up another skull.*]

HAM: There's another; why may not that be the skull of a lawyer? Where be his
quiddities now, his quillets, his cases, his tenures, and his tricks? why does
he suffer this rude knave now to knock him about the sconce with a dirty shovel, and will not tell him of his action of battery? Hum! This fellow might be
in 's time a great buyer of land, with his statutes, his recognizances, his fines,
his double vouchers, his recoveries; is this the fine of his fines, and the recovery of his recoveries, to have his fine pate full of fine dirt? will his vouchers
vouch him no more of his purchases, and double ones too, than the length
and breadth of a pair of indentures? The very conveyance of his lands will hardly lie in this box, and must the inheritor himself have no more, ha?

HOR: Not a jot more, my lord.

HAM: Is not parchment made of sheep-skins?

HOR: Ay, my lord, and of calf-skins too.

HAM: They are sheep and calves which seek out assurance in that. I will speak
to this fellow. Whose grave's this, sir?

FIRST CLO: Mine, sir,
    O! a pit of clay for to be made
    For such a guest is meet.

HAM: I think it be thine, indeed; for thou liest in 't.

FIRST CLO: You lie out on 't, sir, and therefore it is not yours; for my part, I do
not lie in 't, and yet it is mine.

HAM: Thou dost lie in 't, to be in 't and say it is thine: 'tis for the dead, not for
the quick; therefore thou liest.

FIRST CLO: 'Tis a quick lie, sir; 'twill away again, from me to you.

HAM: What man dost thou dig it for?

FIRST CLO: For no man, sir.

HAM: What woman, then?

FIRST CLO: For none, neither.

HAM: Who is to be buried in 't?

FIRST CLO: One that was a woman, sir; but, test her soul, she's dead.

HAM: How absolute the knave is! we must speak by the card, or equivocation will undo us. By the Lord, Horatio, these three years I have taken note of it; the age is grown so picked that the toe of the peasant comes so near the heel of the courtier, he galls his kibe. How long hast thou been a grave-maker?

FIRST CLO: Of all the days i' the year, I came to 't that day that our last King Hamlet overcame Fortinbras.

HAM: How long is that since?

FIRST CLO: Cannot you tell that? every fool can tell that; it was the very day that young Hamlet was born; he that is mad, and sent into England.

HAM: Ay, marry; why was he sent into England?

FIRST CLO: Why, because he was mad: he shall recover his wits there; or, if he do not, 'tis no great matter there.

HAM: Why?

FIRST CLO: 'Twill not be seen in him there; there the men are as mad as he.

HAM: How came he mad?

FIRST CLO: Very strangely, they say.

HAM: How strangely?

FIRST CLO: Faith, e'en with losing his wits.

HAM: Upon what ground?

FIRST CLO: Why, here in Denmark; I have been sexton here, man and boy, thirty years.

HAM: How long will a man lie i' the earth ere he rot?

FIRST CLO: Faith, if he be not rotten before he die,—as we have many pocky corses now-a-days, that will scarce hold the laying in,—he will last you some eight year or nine year; a tanner will last you nine year.

HAM: Why he more than another?

FIRST CLO: Why, sir, his hide is so tanned with his trade that he will keep out water a great while, and your water is a sore decayer of your whoreson dead body. Here's a skull now; this skull hath lain you i' the earth three-and-twenty years.

HAM: Whose was it?

FIRST CLO: A whoreson mad fellow's it was: whose do you think it was?

HAM: Nay, I know not.

FIRST CLO: A pestilence on him for a mad roguel a' poured a flagon of Rhenish on my head once. This same skull, sir, was Yorick's skull, the king's jester.

HAM: This!

FIRST CLO: E'en that.

HAM: Let me see.—

[*Takes the skull.*]

—Alas! poor Yorick. I knew him, Horatio; a fellow of infinite jest, of most excellent fancy; he hath borne me on his back a thousand times; and now, how abhorred in my imagination it is! my gorge rises at it. Here hung those lips that I have kissed I know not how oft. Where be your gibes now? your gambols? your songs? your flashes of merriment, that were wont to set the table on a roar? Not one now, to mock your own grinning? quite chapfallen? Now get you to my lady's chamber, and tell her, let her paint an inch thick, to this favour she must come; make her laugh at that. Prithee, Horatio, tell me one thing.

HOR: What's that, my lord?

HAM: Dost thou think Alexander looked o' this fashion i' the earth?

HOR: E'en so.

HAM: And smelt so? pah!

    [*Puts down the skull.*]

HOR: E'en so, my lord.

HAM: To what base uses we may return, Horatio! Why may not imagination trace the noble dust of Alexander, till he find it stopping a bung-hole?

HOR: 'Twere to consider too curiously, to consider so.

HAM: No, faith, not a jot; but to follow him thither with modesty enough, and likelihood to lead it; as thus: Alexander died, Alexander was buried, Alexander returneth into dust; the dust is earth; of earth we make loam, and why of that loam, whereto he was converted, might they not stop a beer-barrel?

    Imperious Cæsar, dead and turn'd to clay,
    Might stop a hole to keep the wind away:
    O! that that earth, which kept the world in awe,
    Should patch a wall to expel the winter's flaw.
    But soft! but soft! aside: here comes the king.

    Enter PRIESTS, *&c., in procession: the Corpse of* OPHELIA, LAERTES *and Mourners following;* KING, QUEEN, *their Trains, &c.*

    The queen, the courtiers: who is that they follow?
    And with such maimed rites? This doth betoken
    The corse they follow did with desperate hand
    Fordo its own life; 'twas of some estate.
    Couch we awhile, and mark.

    [*Retiring with* HORATIO.]

LAER: What ceremony else?

HAM: That is Laertes,
    A very noble youth: mark.

LAER: What ceremony else?

FIRST PRIEST: Her obsequies have been as far enlarg'd
    As we have warrantise: her death was doubtful.
    And, but that great command o'ersways the order,
    She should in ground unsanctified have lodg'd
    Till the last trumpet; for charitable prayers,
    Shards, flints, and pebbles should be thrown on her;
    Yet here she is allow'd her virgin crants,
    Her maiden strewments, and the bringing home
    Of bell and burial.

LAER: Must there no more be done?

FIRST PRIEST: No more be done:
    We should profane the service of the dead,
    To sing a requiem, and such rest to her
    As to peace-parted souls.

LAER: Lay her i' the earth;
    And from her fair and unpolluted flesh
    May violets spring! I tell thee, churlish priest,
    A ministering angel shall my sister be,

When thou liest howling.

HAM: What! the fair Ophelia?

QUEEN: Sweets to the sweet: farewell!

[*Scattering flowers.*]

I hop'd thou shouldst have been my Hamlet's wife;
I thought thy bride-bed to have deck'd, sweet maid,
And not have strew'd thy grave.

LAER: O! treble woe
Fall ten times treble on that cursed head
Whose wicked deed thy most ingenious sense
Depriv'd thee of. Hold off the earth awhile,
Till I have caught her once more in mine arms.

[*Leaps into the grave.*]

Now pile your dust upon the quick and dead,
Till of this flat a mountain you have made,
To o'er-top old Pelion or the skyish head
Of blue Olympus

HAM: [Advancing.] What is he whose grief
Bears such an emphasis? whose phrase of sorrow
Conjures the wandering stars, and makes them stand
Like wonder-wounded hearers? this is I,
Hamlet the Dane.

[*Leaps into the grave.*]

LAER The devil take thy soul!

[*Grapples with him.*]

HAM: Thou pray'st not well.
I prithee, take thy fingers from my throat;
For though I am not splenetive and rash
Yet have I in me something dangerous,
Which let thy wisdom fear. Away thy hand!

KING: Pluck them asunder.

QUEEN: Hamlet! Hamlet!

ALL: Gentlemen,—

HOR: Good my lord, be quiet.

[*The* ATTENDANTS *part them, and they come out of the grave.*]

HAM: Why, I will fight with him upon this theme
Until my eyelids will no longer wag.

QUEEN: O my son! what theme?

HAM: I lov'd Ophelia: forty thousand brothers
Could not, with all their quantity of love,
Make up my sum. What wilt thou do for her?

KING: O! he is mad, Laertes.

QUEEN: For love of God, forbear him.

HAM: 'Swounds, show me what thou 'it do:
Woo't weep? woo't fight? woo't fast? woo't tear thyself?

Woo't drink up eisel? eat a crocodile?
I'll do't. Dost thou come here to whine?
To outface me with leaping in her grave?
Be buried quick with her, and so will I:
And, if thou prate of mountains, let them throw
Millions of acres on us, till our ground,
Singeing his pate against the burning zone,
Make Ossa like a wart! Nay, an thou'lt mouth,
I'll rant as well as thou.

QUEEN: This is mere madness:
    And thus a while the fit will work on him;
    Anon, as patient as the female dove,
    When that her golden couplets are disclos'd,
    His silence will sit drooping.

HAM: Hear you, sir;
    What is the reason that you use me thus?
    I lov'd you ever: but it is no matter;
    Let Hercules himself do what he may,
    The cat will mew and dog will have his day.

    [*Exit.*]

KING: I pray you, good Horatio, wait upon him.

    [*Exit* HORATIO.]

    [To LAERTES.] Strengthen your patience in our last night's speech;
    We'll put the matter to the present push.
    Good Gertrude, set some watch over your son.
    This grave shall have a living monument:
    An hour of quiet shortly shall we see;
    Till then, in patience our proceeding be.

    [*Exeunt.*]

Scene II.—A Hall in the Castle.

Enter HAMLET *and* HORATIO.

HAM: So much for this, sir: now shall you see the other;
    You do remember all the circumstance?

HOR: Remember it, my lord?

HAM: Sir, in my heart there was a kind of fighting
    That would not let me sleep; methought I lay
    Worse than the mutines in the bilboes. Rashly,—
    And prais'd be rashness for it, let us know,
    Our indiscretion sometimes serves us well
    When our deep plots do pall; and that should teach us
    There's a divinity that shapes our ends,
    Rough-hew them how we will.

HOR: That is most certain.

HAM: Up from my cabin,
    My sea-gown scarf'd about me, in the dark

> Grop'd I to find out them, had my desire,
> Finger'd their packet, and in fine withdrew
> To mine own room again; making so bold—
> My fears forgetting manners—to unseal
> Their grand commission; where I found, Horatio,
> O royal knavery! an exact command,
> Larded with many several sorts of reasons
> Importing Denmark's health, and England's too,
> With, ho! such bugs and goblins in my life,
> That, on the supervise, no leisure bated,
> No, not to stay the grinding of the are,
> My head should be struck off.

HOR: Is 't possible?

HAM: Here's the commission: read it at more leisure.
> But wilt thou hear me how I did proceed?

HOR: I beseech you.

HAM: Being thus be-netted round with villanies,—
> Ere I could make a prologue to my brains
> They had begun the play,—I sat me down,
> Devis'd a new commission, wrote it fair;
> I once did hold it, as our statists do,
> A baseness to write fair, and labour'd much
> How to forget that learning; but, sir, now
> It did me yeoman's service. Wilt thou know
> The effect of what I wrote?

HOR: Ay, good my lord.

HAM: An earnest conjuration from the king,
> As England was his faithful tributary,
> As love between them like the palm should flourish,
> As peace should still her wheaten garland wear,
> And stand a comma 'tween their amities,
> And many such like 'As'es of great charge,
> That, on the view and knowing of these contents,
> Without debatement further, more or less,
> He should the bearers put to sudden death,
> Not shriving-time allow'd.

HOR: How was this seal'd?

HAM: Why, even in that was heaven ordinant.
> I had my father's signet in my purse,
> Which was the model of that Danish seal;
> Folded the writ up in form of the other,
> Subscrib'd it, gave 't th' impression, plac'd it safely.
> The changeling never known. Now, the next day
> Was our sea-fight, and what to this was sequent
> Thou know'st already.

HOR: So Guildenstern and Rosencrantz go to 't.

HAM: Why, man, they did make love to this employment;
> They are not near my conscience; their defeat
> Does by their own insinuation grow.
> 'Tis dangerous when the baser nature comes
> Between the pass and fell-incensed points

Of mighty opposites.

HOR: Why, what a king is this!

HAM: Does it not, thinks't thee, stand me now upon—
    He that hath kill'd my king and whor'd my mother,
    Popp'd in between the election and my hopes,
    Thrown out his angle for my proper life,
    And with such cozenage—is 't not perfect conscience
    To quit him with this arm? and is 't not to be damn'd
    To let this canker of our nature come
    In further evil?

HOR: It must be shortly known to him from England
    What is the issue of the business there.

HAM: It will be short: the interim is mine;
    And a man's life's no more than to say 'One.'
    But I am very sorry, good Horatio,
    That to Laertes I forgot myself;
    For, by the image of my cause, I see
    The portraiture of his: I'll count his favours:
    But, sure, the bravery of his grief did put me
    Into a towering passion.

HOR: Peace! who comes here?

Enter OSRIC.

OSR: Your lordship is right welcome back to Denmark.

HAM: I humbly thank you, sir. [*Aside to* HORATIO.] Dost know this water-fly?

HOR: [*Aside to* HAMLET.] No, my good lord.

HAM: [*Aside to* HORATIO.] Thy state is the more gracious; for 'tis a vice to know him. He hath much land, and fertile: let a beast be lord of beasts, and his crib shall stand at the king's mess: 'tis a chough; but, as I say, spacious in the possession of dirt.

OSR: Sweet lord, if your lordship were at leisure, I should impart a thing to you from his majesty.

HAM: I will receive it, sir, with all diligence of spirit. Your bonnet to his right use; 'tis for the head.

OSR: I thank your lordship, 'tis very hot.

HAM: No, believe me, 'tis very cold; the wind is northerly.

OSR: It is indifferent cold, my lord, indeed.

HAM: But yet methinks it is very sultry and hot for my complexion.

OSR: Exceedingly, my lord; it is very sultry, as 'twere, I cannot tell how. But, my lord, his majesty bade me signify to you that he has laid a great wager on your head. Sir, this is the matter,—

HAM: I beseech you, remember—

[HAMLET *moves him to put on his hat.*]

OSR: Nay, good my lord; for mine ease, in good faith. Sir, here is newly come to court Laertes; believe me, an absolute gentleman, full of most excellent differences, of very soft society and great showing; indeed, to speak feelingly of him, he is the card or calendar of gentry, for you shall find in him the continent of what part a gentleman would see.

HAM: Sir, his definement suffers no perdition in you; though, I know, to divide him inventorially would dizzy the arithmetic of memory, and yet but yaw neither, in respect of his quick sail. But, in the verity of extolment, I take him to be a soul of great article; and his infusion of such dearth and rareness, as, to make true diction of him, his semblable is his mirror; and who else would trace him, his umbrage, nothing more.

OSR: Your lordship speaks most infallibly of him.

HAM: The concernancy, sir? why do we wrap the gentleman in our more rawer breath?

OSR: Sir?

HOR: Is 't not possible to understand in another tongue? You will do 't, sir, really.

HAM: What imports the nomination of this gentleman?

OSR: Of Laertes?

HOR: His purse is empty already; all 's golden words are spent.

HAM: Of him, sir.

OSR: I know you are not ignorant—

HAM: I would you did, sir; in faith, if you did, it would not much approve me. Well, sir.

OSR: You are not ignorant of what excellence Laertes is—

HAM: I dare not confess that, lest I should compare with him in excellence; but, to know a man well, were to know himself.

OSR: I mean, sir, for his weapon; but in the imputation laid on him by them, in his meed he's unfellowed.

HAM: What's his weapon?

OSR: Rapier and dagger.

HAM: That's two of his weapons; but, well.

OSR: The king, sir, hath wagered with him six Barbary horses; against the which he has imponed, as I take it, six French rapiers and poniards, with their assigns, as girdle, hangers, and so: three of the carriages, in faith, are very dear to fancy, very responsive to the hilts, most delicate carriages, and of very liberal conceit.

HAM: What call you the carriages?

HOR: I knew you must be edified by the margent, ere you had done.

OSR: The carriages, sir, are the hangers.

HAM: The phrase would be more german to the matter, if we could carry cannon by our sides; I would it might be hangers till then. But, on; six Barbary horses against six French swords, their assigns, and three liberal-conceited carriages; that's the French bet against the Danish. Why is this 'imponed,' as you call it?

OSR: The king, sir, hath laid, that in a dozen passes between yourself and him, he shall not exceed you three hits; he hath laid on twelve for nine, and it would come to immediate trial, if your lordship would vouchsafe the answer.

HAM: How if I answer no?

OSR: I mean, my lord, the opposition of your person in trial.

HAM: Sir, I will walk here in the hall; if it please his majesty, 'tis the breathing time of day with me; let the foils be brought, the gentleman willing, and the king hold his purpose, I will win for him an I can; if not, I will gain nothing but my shame and the odd hits.

OSR: Shall I re-deliver you so?

HAM: To this effect, sir; after what flourish your nature will.

OSR: I commend my duty to your lordship.

HAM: Yours, yours.

   [*Exit* OSRIC.]

He does well to commend it himself; there are no tongues else for 's turn.

HOR: This lapwing runs away with the shell on his head.

HAM: He did comply with his dug before he sucked it. Thus has he—and many more of the same bevy, that I know the drossy age dotes on—only got the tune of the time and outward habit of encounter, a kind of yesty collection which carries them through and through the most fond and winnowed opinions; and do but blow them to their trial, the bubbles are out.

> *Enter a* LORD.

LORD: My lord, his majesty commended him to you by young Osric, who brings back to him, that you attend him in the hall; he sends to know if your pleasure hold to play with Laertes, or that you will take longer time.

HAM: I am constant to my purposes; they follow the king's pleasure: if his fitness speaks, mine is ready; now, or whensoever, provided I be so able as now.

LORD: The king, and queen, and all are coming down.

HAM: In happy time.

LORD: The queen desires you to use some gentle entertainment to Laertes before you fall to play.

HAM: She well instructs me.

> [*Exit* LORD.]

HOR: You will lose this wager, my lord.

HAM: I do not think so; since he went into France, I have been in continual practice; I shall win at the odds. But thou wouldst not think how ill all's here about my heart; but it is no matter.

HOR: Nay, good my lord,—

HAM: It is but foolery; but it is such a kind of gain-giving as would perhaps trouble a woman.

HOR: If your mind dislike any thing, obey it; I will forestal their repair hither, and say you are not fit.

HAM: Not a whit, we defy augury; there's a special providence in the fall of a sparrow. If it be now, 'tis not to come; if it be not to come, it will be now; if it be not now, yet it will come: the readiness is all. Since no man has aught of what he leaves, what is 't to leave betimes? Let be.

> [*Enter* KING, QUEEN, LAERTES, LORDS, OSRIC, *and* ATTENDANTS *with foils, &c.*]

KING: Come, Hamlet, come, and take this hand from me.

> [*The* KING *puts the hand of* LAERTES *into that of* HAMLET.]

HAM: Give me your pardon, sir; I've done you wrong;
But pardon 't, as you are a gentleman.
This presence knows,
And you must needs have heard, how I am punish'd
With sore distraction. What I have done,
That might your nature, honour and exception
Roughly awake, I here proclaim was madness.
Was 't Hamlet wrong'd Laertes? Never Hamlet:
If Hamlet from himself be ta'en away,
And when he's not himself does wrong Laertes,
Then Hamlet does it not; Hamlet denies it.
Who does it then? His madness. If 't be so,
Hamlet is of the faction that is wrong'd;

His madness is poor Hamlet's enemy.
Sir, in this audience,
Let my disclaiming from a purpos'd evil
Free me so far in your most generous thoughts,
That I have shot mine arrow o'er the house,
And hurt my brother.

LAER: I am satisfied in nature,
Whose motive, in this case, should stir me most
To my revenge; but in my terms of honour
I stand aloof, and will no reconcilement,
Till by some elder masters, of known honour,
I have a voice and precedent of peace,
To keep my name ungor'd. But till that time,
I do receive your offer'd love like love,
And will not wrong it.

HAM: I embrace it freely;
And will this brother's wager frankly play.
Give us the foils. Come on.

LAER: Come, one for me.

HAM: I'll be your foil, Laertes; in mine ignorance
Your skill shall, like a star i' the darkest night,
Stick fiery off indeed.

LAER: You mock me, sir.

HAM: No, by this hand.

KING: Give them the foils, young Osric. Cousin Hamlet,
You know the wager?

HAM: Very well, my lord;
Your Grace hath laid the odds o' the weaker side.

KING: I do not fear it; I have seen you both;
But since he is better'd, we have therefore odds.

LAER: This is too heavy; let me see another.

HAM: This likes me well. These foils have all a length?

OSR: Ay, my good lord.

[They prepare to play.]

KING: Set me the stoups of wine upon that table.
If Hamlet give the first or second hit,
Or quit in answer of the third exchange,
Let all the battlements their ordnance fire;
The king shall drink to Hamlet's better breath;
And in the cup an union shall he throw,
Richer than that which four successive kings
In Denmark's crown have worn. Give me the cups;
And let the kettle to the trumpet speak,
The trumpet to the cannoneer without,
The cannons to the heavens, the heavens to earth,
'Now the king drinks to Hamlet!' Come, begin;
And you, the judges, bear a wary eye.

HAM: Come on, sir.

LAER: Come, my lord.

[*They play.*]

HAM: One.
LAER: No.
HAM: Judgment.
OSR: A hit, a very palpable hit.
LAER: Well; again.
KING: Stay; give me drink. Hamlet, this pearl is thine;
    Here's to thy health. Give him the cup.

[*Trumpets sound; and cannon shot off within.*]

HAM: I'll play this bout first; set it by a while
    Come.—

[*They play.*]

    Another hit; what say you?
LAER: A touch, a touch, I do confess.
KING: Our son shall win.
QUEEN: He's fat, and scant of breath.
    Here, Hamlet, take my napkin, rub thy brows;
    The queen carouses to thy fortune, Hamlet.
HAM: Good madam!
KING: Gertrude, do not drink.
QUEEN: I will, my lord; I pray you, pardon me.
KING: [*Aside.*] It is the poison'd cup! it is too late.
HAM: I dare not drink yet, madam; by and by.
QUEEN: Come, let me wipe thy face.
LAER: My lord, I'll hit him now.
KING: I do not think 't
LAER: [*Aside.*] And yet 'tis almost 'gainst my conscience.
HAM: Come, for the third, Laertes. You but dally;
    I pray you, pass with your best violence.
    I am afeard you make a wanton of me.
LAER: Say you so? come on.

[*They play.*]

OSR: Nothing, neither way.
LAER: Have at you now.

[LAERTES *wounds* HAMLET; *then, in scuffling, they change rapiers, and* HAMLET *wounds* LAERTES.]

KING: Part them! they are incens'd.
HAM: Nay, come, again:

[*The* QUEEN *falls.*]

OSR: Look to the queen there, ho!
HOR: They bleed on both sides. How is it, my lord?
OSR: How is it, Laertes?
LAER: Why, as a woodcock to mine own springe, Osric;
    I am justly kill'd with mine own treachery.

HAM: How does the queen?
KING: She swounds to see them bleed.
QUEEN: No, no, the drink, the drink—O my dear Hamlet!
    The drink, the drink; I am poison'd.

    [*Dies.*]

HAM: O villany! Ho! let the door be lock'd:
    Treachery! seek it out.

    [LAERTES *falls.*]

LAER: It is here, Hamlet. Hamlet, thou art slain;
    No medicine in the world can do thee good;
    In thee there is not half an hour of life;
    The treacherous instrument is in thy hand,
    Unbated and envenom'd. The foul practice
    Hath turn'd itself on me; lo! here I lie,
    Never to rise again. Thy mother's poison'd.
    I can no more. The king, the king's to blame.
HAM: The point envenom'd too!—
    Then, venom, to thy work.

    [*Stabs the* KING.]

ALL: Treason! treason!
KING: O! yet defend me, friends; I am but hurt.
HAM: Here, thou incestuous, murderous, damned Dane,
    Drink off this potion;—is thy union here?
    Follow my mother.

    [KING *dies.*]

LAER: He is justly serv'd:
    It is a poison temper'd by himself.
    Exchange forgiveness with me, noble Hamlet:
    Mine and my father's death come not upon thee,
    Nor thine on me!

    [*Dies.*]

HAM: Heaven make thee free of it! I follow thee.
    I am dead, Horatio. Wretched queen, adieu!
    You that look pale and tremble at this chance,
    That are but mutes or audience to this act,
    Had I but time,—as this fell sergeant, death,
    Is strict in his arrest,—O! I could tell you—
    But let it be. Horatio, I am dead;
    Thou liv'st; report me and my cause aright
    To the unsatisfied.
HOR: Never believe it;
    I am more an antique Roman than a Dane:
    Here's yet some liquor left.
HAM: As thou'rt a man,
    Give me the cup: let go; by heaven, I'll have 't.

O God! Horatio, what a wounded name,
Things standing thus unknown, shall live behind me.
If thou didst ever hold me in thy heart,
Absent thee from felicity a while,
And in this harsh world draw thy breath in pain,
To tell my story.

[*March afar off, and shot within.*]

What war-like noise is this?

OSR: Young Fortinbras, with conquest come from Poland,
To the ambassadors of England gives
This war-like volley.
HAM: O! I die, Horatio;
The potent poison quite o'er-crows my spirit:
I cannot live to hear the news from England,
But I do prophesy the election lights
On Fortinbras: he has my dying voice;
So tell him, with the occurrents, more and less,
Which have solicited—The rest is silence.

[*Dies.*]

HOR: Now cracks a noble heart. Good-night, sweet prince,
And flights of angels sing thee to thy rest!
Why does the drum come hither?

[*March within.*]

Enter FORTINBRAS, *the English* AMBASSADORS, *and Others.*

FORT: Where is this sight?
HOR: What is it ye would see?
If aught of woe or wonder, cease your search.
FORT: This quarry cries on havoc. O proud death!
What feast is toward in thine eternal cell,
That thou so many princes at a shot
So bloodily hast struck?
FIRST AMB: The sight is dismal;
And our affairs from England come too late;
The ears are senseless that should give us hearing,
To tell him his commandment is fulfill'd,
That Rosencrantz and Guildenstern are dead.
Where should we have our thanks?
HOR: Not from his mouth,
Had it the ability of life to thank you:
He never gave commandment for their death.
But since, so jump upon this bloody question,
You from the Polack wars, and you from England,
Are here arriv'd, give order that these bodies
High on a stage be placed to the view;
And let me speak to the yet unknowing world
How these things came about: so shall you hear

Of carnal, bloody, and unnatural acts,
Of accidental judgments, casual slaughters;
Of deaths put on by cunning and forc'd cause,
And, in this upshot, purposes mistook
Fall'n on the inventors' heads; all this can I
Truly deliver.

FORT: Let us haste to hear it,
And call the noblest to the audience.
For me, with sorrow I embrace my fortune;
I have some rights of memory in this kingdom,
Which now to claim my vantage doth invite me.

HOR: Of that I shall have also cause to speak,
And from his mouth whose voice will draw on more:
But let this same be presently perform'd,
Even while men's minds are wild, lest more mischance
On plots and errors happen.

FORT: Let four captains
Bear Hamlet, like a soldier, to the stage;
For he was likely, had he been put on,
To have prov'd most royally: and, for his passage,
The soldiers' music and the rites of war
Speak loudly for him.
Take up the bodies: such a sight as this
Becomes the field, but here shows much amiss.
Go, bid the soldiers shoot.

[*A dead march. Exeunt, bearing off the bodies: after which a peal of ordnance is shot off.*]

INQUIRING FURTHER

1. One of the most famous lines from *Hamlet* is Marcellus's observation after seeing the ghost of King Hamlet that "Something is rotten in the State of Denmark" (Act 1, Scene 4). What do you take to be the meaning of Marcellus's observation? Spend five minutes freewriting about how you might interpret the rest of the play in terms of the statement.

2. *Hamlet* can also be viewed from the perspective of Hamlet's state of mind. What aspects of the play would you consider the most significant when you look at the work in terms of Hamlet's psychology? Develop a list of psychological themes and questions related to the play.

Responses to *Hamlet*

The works of Shakespeare have an incredible reach. Not only are quotations from his plays thrown around in our daily discourse, the larger messages of his works have become ingrained in the consciousness of contemporary society. Numerous artists have responded with paintings that represent scenes from Shakespeare's plays. Writers have composed adaptations and works that take up the key questions raised by the plays. Theater companies have produced versions of works like *Hamlet* continually for 400 years, and filmmakers regularly adapt Shakespeare's plays for the cinema. We offer some of these responses below.

MARGARET ATWOOD

Margaret Atwood (born in 1939) is one of Canada's most acclaimed contemporary authors. Her first book of poetry, The Circle Game, *appeared in 1966. She often takes up themes concerning relationships, human rights, and language and power. "Gertrude Talks Back" first appeared in the collection* Good Bones and Simple Murders *in 1994.*

Gertrude Talks Back

I always thought it was a mistake, calling you Hamlet. I mean, what kind of a name is that for a young boy? It was your father's idea. Nothing would do but that you had to be called after him. Selfish. The other kids at school used to tease the life out of you. The nicknames! And those terrible jokes about pork.

I wanted to call you George.

I am *not* wringing my hands. I'm drying my nails.

Darling, please stop fidgeting with my mirror. That'll be the third one you've broken.

5   Yes, I've seen those pictures, thank you very much.

I *know* your father was handsomer than Claudius. High brow, aquiline nose and so on, looked great in uniform. But handsome isn't everything, especially in a man, and far be it from me to speak ill of the dead, but I think it's about time I pointed out to you that your dad just wasn't a whole lot of fun. Noble, sure, I grant you. But Claudius, well, he likes a drink now and then. He appreciates a decent meal. He enjoys a laugh, know what I mean? You don't always have to be tiptoeing around because of some holier-than-thou principle or something.

By the way, darling, I wish you wouldn't call your stepdad *the bloat king*. He does have a slight weight problem, and it hurts his feelings.

The rank sweat of a *what?* My bed is certainly not *enseamed*, whatever that might be! A nasty sty, indeed! Not that it's any of your business, but I change those sheets twice a week, which is more than you do, judging from that student slum pigpen in Wittenberg. I'll certainly never visit you *there* again without prior warning! I see that laundry of yours when you bring it home, and not often enough either, by a long shot! Only when you run out of black socks.

And let me tell you, everyone sweats at a time like that, as you'd find out very soon if you ever gave it a try. A real girlfriend would do you a heap of good. Not like that pasty-faced what's-her-name, all trussed up like a prize turkey in those touch-me-not corsets of hers. If you ask me, there's something off about that girl. Borderline. Any little shock could push her right over the edge.

10   Go get yourself someone more down-to-earth. Have a nice roll in the hay. Then you can talk to me about nasty sties.

No, darling, I am not *mad* at you. But I must say you're an awful prig sometimes. Just like your Dad. *The Flesh* he'd say. You'd think it was dog dirt.

You can excuse that in a young person, they are always so intolerant, but in someone his age it was getting, well, very hard to live with, and that's the understatement of the year.

Some days I think it would have been better for both of us if you hadn't been an only child. But you realize who you have to thank for *that*. You have no idea what I used to put up with. And every time I felt like a little, you know, just to warm up my aging bones, it was like I'd suggested murder.

Oh! You think *what?* You think Claudius murdered your Dad? Well, no wonder you've been so rude to him at the dinner table!

If I'd known *that*, I could have put you straight in no time flat.

15   It wasn't Claudius, darling.

It was me.

JOHN EVERETT MILLAIS

The painting Ophelia *by John Everett Millais (1829–1896) is one of the best recognized works of art composed in response to a Shakespeare play. Millais was part of the movement in painting known as the Pre-Raphaelite Brotherhood, a group of young artists working in the 1850s who tried to break away from what they saw as formulaic methods of art taught by the Royal Academy of Art in London. Instead, the Pre-Raphaelites sought to return to a more realistic and everyday style. Millais was well known for the use of props and models and was said to have invested a large sum to purchase the dress depicted in* Ophelia. *The painting was composed in 1851 and 1852.*

Ophelia

Color reproduction and discussion of *Ophelia*

FIGURE 14.5   *Ophelia* by John Everett Millais

FREDERICK SEIDEL

The poems of Frederick Seidel have been called hard hitting with a some-times unapologetically male slant. His poem "Hamlet" appeared in the col-lection Life on Earth, *in 2001.*

Hamlet

The horsefly landing fatly on the page
And walking through words from left to right is rage.
It walks, stage right to left, across the stage.
The play is called *The Nest Becomes a Cage.*

5   I'm reading *Hamlet*, in which a bulging horsefly
Soliloquizes constantly, played by
Me. He's getting old, don't ask me why.
His lines are not familiar. Then I die.

I have been thinking, instead of weeping, tears,
10   And drinking everybody else's, for years.
They taste amazingly like urine. Cheers!
I tell you this—(But soft! My mother nears.)

You wonder how I know what urine tastes like?
I stuck my finger in a hole in a dike
15   And made the heart near-bursting burst. Strike
While it's hot. You have to seize the mike

And scream, "This is I! Hamlet the Dane!" True—
Too true—the lascivious iceberg you
Are cruising to, *Titanic*, is a Jew
20   Ophelia loved, a man she thought she knew.

One day I was bombing Belgrade, bombing Belgrade,
To halt the slaughter elsewhere, knowing aid
Arrives through the air in the form of a tirade
Hamlet stabs through the arras, like a man does a maid,

25   Only in this case it was the father of the girl,
Poor Polonius, her father. She is a pearl
At the bottom of a stream, and every curl
Of nothing but herself is drowned. I whirl

Around, and this is I! a fellow fanned
30   Into a flame. The horsefly that I land
On her has little legs—but on command
Struts back and forth on stage, princely, grand.

INQUIRING FURTHER

1. "Gertrude Talks Back" presents the perspective of Queen Gertrude. What is the message regarding sexuality presented by Gertrude? How does that message relate to the play? In what ways is the work also a commentary on the actions and the character of Hamlet?

2. Millais's painting of Ophelia has had a strong hold on the emotions of viewers and has been reproduced numerous times. In what ways is the influence of the painting rooted in the play? What aspects of the painting itself account for its appeal? Could it stand on its own? Freewrite for five minutes on the relationship between the painting and the play.

Shakespeare scholars discuss Hamlet

3. Frederick Seidel's poem "Hamlet" seems to emphasize issues of control and feelings of rage within the speaker of the poem. The speaker also seems to identify with Hamlet, Polonius, perhaps Ophelia, and with Shakespeare. Do you think the poem makes a significant comment on the play? Why or why not?

THE CONSEQUENCES OF WAR

Carl Von Clausewitz once said that "war is a continuation of diplomacy by other means," suggesting that wars represent an extension of the political conflicts that play out between nations. The truth is that wars do reflect the diplomatic agendas of countries. But they also have a decidedly human impact that refuses to be contained by the political ideologies of any of the nations involved. This human side is often taken up as the subject of literature.

Through photography, poetry, fiction, and every other form of expression, artists offer their interpretations about what war means to those it impacts directly. However, even these artistic expressions can have a political dimension. Rather than simply chronicling the realities of war, most works express a viewpoint about war. Whether these artistic expressions support or oppose a particular conflict, their impact on viewers gives works of art the potential to act as continuations of diplomacy in their own right.

STEPHEN CRANE

In his short-lived literary career, Stephen Crane (1871–1900) produced a number of stories concerning war. He is best known for The Red Badge of Courage, *a novel published in 1895 detailing the experiences of a young soldier in the Civil War. It was not until 1896, however, that Crane experienced war personally as a news correspondent covering the war between Greece and Turkey, and later the Spanish-American War in Cuba. "A Mystery of Heroism" takes as its subject the Civil War, and was originally published in 1895.*

A Mystery of Heroism

The dark uniforms of the men were so coated with dust from the incessant wrestling of the two armies that the regiment almost seemed a part of the clay bank which shielded them from the shells. On the top of the hill a battery was arguing in tremendous roars with some other guns, and to the eye of the infantry the artillerymen, the guns, the caissons, the horses, were distinctly outlined upon the blue sky. When a piece was fired, a red streak as round as a log flashed low in the heavens, like a monstrous bolt of lightning. The men of the battery wore white duck trousers, which somehow emphasized their legs; and when they ran and crowded in little groups at the bidding of the shouting officers, it was more impressive than usual to the infantry.

Fred Collins, of A Company, was saying: "Thunder! I wisht I had a drink. Ain't there any water round here?" Then somebody yelled: "There goes th' bugler!"

As the eyes of half the regiment swept in one machine-like movement, there was an instant's picture of a horse in a great convulsive leap of a death-wound and a rider leaning back with a crooked arm and spread fingers before his face. On the ground was the crimson terror of an exploding shell, with fibres of flame that seemed like lances. A glittering bugle swung clear of the rider's back as fell headlong the horse and the man. In the air was an odour as from a conflagration.

Sometimes they of the infantry looked down at a fair little meadow which spread at their feet. Its long green grass was rippling gently in a breeze. Beyond it was the grey form of a house half torn to pieces by shells and by the busy axes of soldiers who had pursued firewood. The line of an old fence was now dimly marked by long weeds and by an occasional post. A shell had blown the wellhouse to fragments. Little lines of grey smoke ribboning upward from some embers indicated the place where had stood the barn.

5   From beyond a curtain of green woods there came the sound of some stupendous scuffle, as if two animals of the size of islands were fighting. At a distance there were occasional appearances of swift-moving men, horses, batteries, flags, and with the crashing of infantry volleys were heard, often, wild and frenzied cheers. In the midst of it all Smith and Ferguson, two privates of A Company, were engaged in a heated discussion which involved the greatest questions of the national existence.

The battery on the hill presently engaged in a frightful duel. The white legs of the gunners scampered this way and that way, and the officers redoubled their shouts. The guns, with their demeanours of stolidity and courage, were typical of something infinitely self-possessed in this clamour of death that swirled around the hill.

One of a "swing" team was suddenly smitten quivering to the ground, and his maddened brethren dragged his torn body in their struggle to escape from this turmoil and danger. A young soldier astride one of the leaders swore and fumed in his saddle and furiously jerked at the bridle. An officer screamed out an order so violently that his voice broke and ended the sentence in a falsetto shriek.

The leading company of the infantry regiment was somewhat exposed, and the colonel ordered it moved more fully under the shelter of the hill. There was the clank of steel against steel.

A lieutenant of the battery rode down and passed them, holding his right arm carefully in his left hand. And it was as if this arm was not at all a part of him, but belonged to another man. His sober and reflective charger went slowly. The officer's face was grimy and perspiring, and his uniform was tousled as if he had been in direct grapple with an enemy. He smiled grimly when the men stared at him. He turned his horse toward the meadow.

10   Collins, of A Company, said: "I wish I had a drink. I bet there's water in that there ol' well yonder!"

"Yes; but how you goin' to git it?"

For the little meadow which intervened was now suffering a terrible onslaught of shells. Its green and beautiful calm had vanished utterly. Brown earth was being flung in monstrous handfuls. And there was a massacre of the young blades of grass. They were being torn, burned, obliterated. Some curious fortune of the battle had made this gentle little meadow the object of the red hate of the shells, and each one as it exploded seemed like an imprecation in the face of a maiden.

The wounded officer who was riding across this expanse said to himself: "Why, they couldn't shoot any harder if the whole army was massed here!"

A shell struck the grey ruins of the house, and as, after the roar, the shattered wall fell in fragments, there was a noise which resembled the flapping of shutters during a wild gale of winter. Indeed, the infantry paused in the shelter of the bank appeared as men standing upon a shore contemplating a madness of the sea. The angel of calamity had under its glance the battery upon the hill. Fewer white-legged men laboured about the guns. A shell had smitten one of the pieces, and after the flare, the smoke, the dust, the wrath of this blow were gone, it was possible to see white legs stretched horizontally upon the ground. And at the interval to the rear where it is the business of battery horses to stand with their noses to the fight, awaiting the command to drag their guns out of the destruction, or into it, or wheresoever these incomprehensible humans demanded with whip and spur—in this line of passive and dumb spectators, whose fluttering hearts yet would not let them forget the iron laws of man's control of them—in this rank of brute-soldiers there had been relentless and hideous carnage. From the ruck of bleeding and prostrate horses, the men of the infantry could see one animal raising its stricken body with its forelegs and turning its nose with mystic and profound eloquence toward the sky.

15   Some comrades joked Collins about his thirst. "Well, if yeh want a drink so bad, why don't yeh go git it?"

"Well, I will in a minnet, if yeh don't shut up!"

A lieutenant of artillery floundered his horse straight down the hill with as little concern as if it were level ground. As he galloped past the colonel of the infantry, he threw up his hand in swift salute. "We've got to get out of that," he roared angrily. He was a black-bearded officer, and his eyes, which resembled beads, sparkled like those of an insane man. His jumping horse sped along the column of infantry.

The fat major, standing carelessly with his sword held horizontally behind him and with his legs far apart, looked after the receding horseman and laughed. "He wants to get back with orders pretty quick, or there'll be no batt'ry left," he observed.

The wise young captain of the second company hazarded to the lieutenant-colonel that the enemy's infantry would probably soon attack the hill, and the lieutenant-colonel snubbed him.

20   A private in one of the rear companies looked out over the meadow, and then turned to a companion and said, "Look there, Jim!" It was the wounded officer from the battery, who some time before had started to ride across the meadow, supporting his right arm carefully with his left hand. This man had encountered a shell, apparently, at a time when no one perceived him, and

he could now be seen lying face downward with a stirruped foot stretched across the body of his dead horse. A leg of the charger extended slantingly upward, precisely as stiff as a stake. Around this motionless pair the shells still howled.

There was a quarrel in A Company. Collins was shaking his fist in the faces of some laughing comrades. "Dern yeh! I ain't afraid t' go: If yeh say much, I will go!"

"Of course, yeh will! You'll run through that there medder, won't yeh?"

Collins said, in a terrible voice: "You see now!"

At this ominous threat his comrades broke into renewed jeers.

25   Collins gave them a dark scowl, and went to find his captain. The latter was conversing with the colonel of the regiment.

"Captain," said Collins, saluting and standing at attention—in those days all trousers bagged at the knees—"Captain, I want t' get permission to go git some water from that there well over yonder!"

The colonel and the captain swung about simultaneously and stared across the meadow. The captain laughed. "You must be pretty thirsty, Collins?"

"Yes, sir, I am."

"Well—ah," said the captain. After a moment, he asked, "Can't you wait?"

30   "No, sir."

The colonel was watching Collins's face. "Look here, my lad," he said, in a pious sort of voice—"Look here, my lad"—Collins was not a lad—"don't you think that's taking pretty big risks for a little drink of water?"

"I dunno," said Collins uncomfortably. Some of the resentment toward his companions, which perhaps had forced him into this affair, was beginning to fade. "I dunno w'ether 'tis."

The colonel and the captain contemplated him for a time.

"Well," said the captain finally.

35   "Well," said the colonel, "if you want to go, why, go."

Collins saluted. "Much obliged t' yeh."

As he moved away the colonel called after him. "Take some of the other boys' canteens with you, an' hurry back, now."

"Yes, sir, I will."

The colonel and the captain looked at each other then, for it had suddenly occurred that they could not for the life of them tell whether Collins wanted to go or whether he did not.

40   They turned to regard Collins, and as they perceived him surrounded by gesticulating comrades, the colonel said: "Well, by thunder! I guess he's going."

Collins appeared as a man dreaming. In the midst of the questions, the advice, the warnings, all the excited talk of his company mates, he maintained a curious silence.

They were very busy in preparing him for his ordeal. When they inspected him carefully, it was somewhat like the examination that grooms give a horse before a race; and they were amazed, staggered, by the whole affair. Their astonishment found vent in strange repetitions.

"Are yeh sure a-goin'?" they demanded again and again.

"Certainly I am," cried Collins at last, furiously.

He strode sullenly away from them. He was swinging five or six canteens by their cords. It seemed that his cap would not remain firmly on his head, and often he reached and pulled it down over his brow.

There was a general movement in the compact column. The long animal-like thing moved slightly. Its four hundred eyes were turned upon the figure of Collins.

"Well, sir, if that ain't th' derndest thing! I never thought Fred Collins had the blood in him for that kind of business."

"What's he goin' to do, anyhow?"

"He's goin' to that well there after water."

50   "We ain't dyin' of thirst, are we? That's foolishness."

"Well, somebody put him up to it, an' he's doin' it."

"Say, he must be a desperate cuss."

When Collins faced the meadow and walked away from the regiment, he was vaguely conscious that a chasm, the deep valley of all prides, was suddenly between him and his comrades. It was provisional, but the provision was that he return as a victor. He had blindly been led by quaint emotions, and laid himself under an obligation to walk squarely up to the face of death.

But he was not sure that he wished to make a retraction, even if he could do so without shame. As a matter of truth, he was sure of very little. He was mainly surprised.

55   It seemed to him supernaturally strange that he had allowed his mind to manœuvre his body into such a situation. He understood that it might be called dramatically great.

However, he had no full appreciation of anything, excepting that he was actually conscious of being dazed. He could feel his dulled mind groping after the form and colour of this incident. He wondered why he did not feel some keen agony of fear cutting his sense like a knife. He wondered at this, because human expression had said loudly for centuries that men should feel afraid of certain things, and that all men who did not feel this fear were phenomena —heroes.

He was, then, a hero. He suffered that disappointment which we would all have if we discovered that we were ourselves capable of those deeds which we most admire in history and legend. This, then, was a hero. After all, heroes were not much.

No, it could not be true. He was not a hero. Heroes had no shames in their lives, and, as for him, he remembered borrowing fifteen dollars from a friend and promising to pay it back the next day, and then avoiding that friend for ten months. When, at home, his mother had aroused him for the early labour of his life on the farm, it had often been his fashion to be irritable, childish, diabolical; and his mother had died since he had come to the war.

He saw that, in this matter of the well, the canteens, the shells, he was an intruder in the land of fine deeds.

60   He was now about thirty paces from his comrades. The regiment had just turned its many faces toward him.

From the forest of terrific noises there suddenly emerged a little uneven line of men. They fired fiercely and rapidly at distant foliage on which appeared little puffs of white smoke. The spatter of skirmish firing was added to the thunder of the guns on the hill. The little line of men ran forward. A colour-sergeant fell flat with his flag as if he had slipped on ice. There was hoarse cheering from this distant field.

Collins suddenly felt that two demon fingers were pressed into his ears. He could see nothing but flying arrows, flaming red. He lurched from the shock of this explosion, but he made a mad rush for the house, which he viewed as a man submerged to the neck in a boiling surf might view the shore. In the air little pieces of shell howled, and the earthquake explosions drove him insane with the menace of their roar. As he ran the canteens knocked together with a rhythmical tinkling.

As he neared the house, each detail of the scene became vivid to him. He was aware of some bricks of the vanished chimney lying on the sod. There was a door which hung by one hinge.

Rifle bullets called forth by the insistent skirmishers came from the far-off bank of foliage. They mingled with the shells and the pieces of shells until the air was torn in all directions by hootings, yells, howls. The sky was full of fiends who directed all their wild rage at his head.

65   When he came to the well, he flung himself face downward and peered into its darkness. There were furtive silver glintings some feet from the surface. He grabbed one of the canteens and, unfastening its cap, swung it down by the cord. The water flowed slowly in with an indolent gurgle.

And now, as he lay with his face turned away, he was suddenly smitten with the terror. It came upon his heart like the grasp of claws. All the power faded from his muscles. For an instant he was no more than a dead man.

The canteen filled with a maddening slowness, in the manner of all bottles. Presently he recovered his strength and addressed a screaming oath to it. He leaned over until it seemed as if he intended to try to push water into it with his hands. His eyes as he gazed down into the well shone like two pieces of metal, and in their expression was a great appeal and a great curse. The stupid water derided him.

There was the blaring thunder of a shell. Crimson light shone through the swift-boiling smoke and made a pink reflection on part of the wall of the well. Collins jerked out his arm and canteen with the same motion that a man would use in withdrawing his head from a furnace.

He scrambled erect and glared and hesitated. On the ground near him lay the old well bucket, with a length of rusty chain. He lowered it swiftly into the well. The bucket struck the water and then, turning lazily over, sank. When, with hand reaching tremblingly over hand, he hauled it out, it knocked often against the walls of the well and spilled some of its contents.

70   In running with a filled bucket, a man can adopt but one kind of gait. So, through this terrible field over which screamed practical angels of death, Collins ran in the manner of a farmer chased out of a dairy by a bull.

His face went staring white with anticipation—anticipation of a blow that would whirl him around and down. He would fall as he had seen other men fall, the life knocked out of them so suddenly that their knees were no more quick to touch the ground than their heads. He saw the long blue line of the regiment, but his comrades were standing looking at him from the edge of an impossible star. He was aware of some deep wheel-ruts and hoof-prints in the sod beneath his feet.

The artillery officer who had fallen in this meadow had been making groans in the teeth of the tempest of sound. These futile cries, wrenched from him by his agony, were heard only by shells, bullets. When wild-eyed Collins came running, this officer raised himself. His face contorted and blanched from pain, he was about to utter some great beseeching cry. But suddenly his face straightened, and he called: "Say, young man, give me a drink of water, will you?"

Collins had no room amid his emotions for surprise. He was mad from the threats of destruction.

"I can't!" he screamed, and in his reply was a full description of his quaking apprehension. His cap was gone and his hair was riotous. His clothes made it appear that he had been dragged over the ground by the heels. He ran on.

75   The officer's head sank down, and one elbow crooked. His foot in its brassbound stirrup still stretched over the body of his horse, and the other leg was under the steed.

But Collins turned. He came dashing back. His face had now turned grey, and in his eyes was all terror. "Here it is! Here it is!"

The officer was as a man gone in drink. His arm bent like a twig. His head drooped as if his neck were of willow. He was sinking to the ground, to lie face downward.

Collins grabbed him by the shoulder. "Here it is. Here's your drink. Turn over. Turn over, man, for God's sake!"

With Collins hauling at his shoulder, the officer twisted his body and fell with his face turned toward that region where lived the unspeakable noises of the swirling missiles. There was the faintest shadow of a smile on his lips as he looked at Collins. He gave a sigh, a little primitive breath like that from a child.

80   Collins tried to hold the bucket steadily, but his shaking hands caused the water to splash all over the face of the dying man. Then he jerked it away and ran on.

The regiment gave him a welcoming roar. The grimed faces were wrinkled in laughter.

His captain waved the bucket away. "Give it to the men!"

The two genial, skylarking young lieutenants were the first to gain possession of it. They played over it in their fashion.

When one tried to drink, the other teasingly knocked his elbow. "Don't Billie! You'll make me spill it," said the one. The other laughed.

85   Suddenly there was an oath, the thud of wood on the ground, and a swift murmur of astonishment among the ranks. The two lieutenants glared at each other. The bucket lay on the ground, empty.

WILFRED OWEN

Studying
Owen's
war
poems

Wilfred Owen (1893–1918) enlisted in the British army in 1915 during the height of World War I. He was sent to battle on the front lines in 1916. In 1917, he was sent to a military hospital, diagnosed as shell-shocked. "Dulce et Decorum Est" was written in 1917 partially in response to authors who had never experienced combat but who were nonetheless composing poems promoting patriotism and war. "The Send Off" was composed in 1918.

Dulce et Decorum Est

Bent double, like old beggars under sacks,
Knock-kneed, coughing like hags, we cursed through sludge,
Till on the haunting flares we turned our backs
And towards our distant rest began to trudge.

5   Men marched asleep. Many had lost their boots
But limped on, blood-shod. All went lame; all blind;
Drunk with fatigue; deaf even to the hoots
Of tired, outstripped Five-Nines[1] that dropped behind.

Gas! Gas! Quick, boys!—An ecstasy of fumbling,
10   Fitting the clumsy helmets just in time;
But someone still was yelling out and stumbling,
And flound'ring like a man in fire or lime . . .
Dim, through the misty panes and thick green light,
As under a green sea, I saw him drowning.

15   In all my dreams, before my helpless sight,
He plunges at me, guttering, choking, drowning.

If in some smothering dreams you too could pace
Behind the wagon that we flung him in,
And watch the white eyes writhing in his face,
20   His hanging face, like a devil's sick of sin;
If you could hear, at every jolt, the blood
Come gargling from the froth-corrupted lungs,
Obscene as cancer, bitter as the cud
Of vile, incurable sores on innocent tongues,—
25   My friend, you would not tell with such high zest
To children ardent for some desperate glory,
The old Lie: Dulce et decorum est
Pro patria mori.[2]

Ironic = Sarcasum

The Send-Off

Down the close darkening lanes they sang their way
To the siding-shed,
And lined the train with faces grimly gay.

Their breasts were stuck all white with wreath and spray
5   As men's are, dead.

Dull porters watched them, and a casual tramp
Stood staring hard,
Sorry to miss them from the upland camp.

Then, unmoved, signals nodded, and a lamp
10   Winked to the guard.

So secretly, like wrongs hushed-up, they went.
They were not ours:
We never heard to which front these were sent;

Nor there if they yet mock what women meant
15   Who gave them flowers.

---

[1]**Five-Nines:** Artillery shells containing poison gas.
[2]**Dulce . . . mori:** From the poet Horace, Latin for, "It is sweet and fitting to die for one's country."

Shall they return to beating of great bells
In wild train-loads?
A few, a few, too few for drums and yells,

May creep back, silent, to village wells,
20   Up half-known roads.

ELIZABETH BISHOP

The poetry of Elizabeth Bishop (1911–1979) has been called meticulous and precise. Bishop was known to work on poems at great length, revising and polishing them for months, even years. Bishop was living in Key West, Florida at the time when "Roosters" was written in 1940. In a letter to friend and fellow poet Marian Moore, Bishop explains that she wanted the poem "to emphasize the essential baseness of militarism." You can read the letter to Moore below.

Roosters

At four o'clock
in the gun-metal blue dark
we hear the first crow of the first cock

just below
5   the gun-metal blue window
and immediately there is an echo

off in the distance,
then one from the backyard fence,
then one, with horrible insistence,

10   grates like a wet match
from the broccoli patch,
flares, and all over town begins to catch.

Cries galore
come from the water-closet door,
15   from the dropping-plastered henhouse floor,

where in the blue blur
their rustling wives admire,
the roosters brace their cruel feet and glare

with stupid eyes
20   while from their beaks there rise
the uncontrolled, traditional cries.

Deep from protruding chests
in green-gold medals dressed,
planned to command and terrorize the rest,

25   the many wives
who lead hens' lives
of being courted and despised;

deep from raw throats
a senseless order floats
30   all over town. A rooster gloats

over our beds
from rusty iron sheds
and fences made from old bedsteads,

over our churches
35   where the tin rooster perches,
over our little wooden northern houses,

making sallies
from all the muddy alleys,
marking out maps like Rand McNally's:

40   glass-headed pins,
oil-golds and copper greens,
anthracite blues, alizarins,

each one an active
displacement in perspective;
45   each screaming, "This is where I live!"

Each screaming
"Get up! Stop dreaming!"
Roosters, what are you projecting?

You, whom the Greeks elected
50   to shoot at on a post, who struggled
when sacrificed, you whom they labeled

"Very combative . . . "
what right have you to give
commands and tell us how to live,

55   cry "Here!" and "Here!"
and wake us here where are
unwanted love, conceit and war?

The crown of red
set on your little head
60   is charged with all your fighting blood.

Yes, that excrescence
makes a most virile presence,
plus all that vulgar beauty of iridescence.

Now in mid-air
65   by twos they fight each other.
Down comes a first flame-feather,

and one is flying,
with raging heroism defying
even the sensation of dying.

70   And one has fallen,
but still above the town
his torn-out, bloodied feathers drift down;

and what he sung
no matter. He is flung
75   on the gray ash-heap, lies in dung

with his dead wives
with open, bloody eyes,
while those metallic feathers oxidize.

St. Peter's sin
80   was worse than that of Magdalen
whose sin was of the flesh alone;

of spirit, Peter's,
falling, beneath the flares,
among the "servants and officers."

85   Old holy sculpture
could set it all together
in one small scene, past and future:

Christ stands amazed,
Peter, two fingers raised
90   to surprised lips, both as if dazed.

But in between
a little cock is seen
carved on a dim column in the travertine,

explained by *gallus canit;*
95   *flet Petrus* underneath it.
There is inescapable hope, the pivot;

yes, and there Peter's tears
run down our chanticleer's
sides and gem his spurs.

100   Tear-encrusted thick
as a medieval relic
he waits. Poor Peter, heart-sick,

still cannot guess
those cock-a-doodles yet might bless,
105   his dreadful rooster come to mean forgiveness,

a new weathervane
on basilica and barn,
and that outside the Lateran

there would always be
110   a bronze cock on a porphyry
pillar so the people and the Pope might see

that even the Prince
of the Apostles long since
had been forgiven, and to convince

115   all the assembly
that "Deny deny deny"
is not all the roosters cry.

In the morning
a low light is floating
120   in the backyard, and gilding

from underneath
the broccoli, leaf by leaf;
how could the night have come to grief?

gilding the tiny
125   floating swallow's belly   125
and lines of pink cloud in the sky,

the day's preamble
like wandering lines in marble.
The cocks are now almost inaudible.

130   The sun climbs in,
following "to see the end,"
faithful as enemy, or friend.

Letter to Marianne Moore

Murray Hill Hotel
New York
October 17, 1940

What I'm about to say, I'm afraid, will sound like ELIZABETH KNOWS BEST. However, I *have* changed [the first words of each line of "Roosters"] to small initial letters! and I have made several other of your corrections and suggestions, and left out one of the stanzas. But I can't seem to bring myself to give up the set form, which I'm afraid you think fills the poem with redundancies, etc. I feel that the rather rattletrap rhythm is appropriate—maybe I can explain it.

I cherish my "water-closet" and the other sordidities because I want to emphasize the essential baseness of militarism. In the first part I was thinking of Key West, and also of those aerial views of dismal little towns in Finland and Norway, when the Germans took over, and their atmosphere of poverty. That's why, although I see what *you* mean, I want to keep "tin rooster" instead of "gold," and not use "fastidious beds." And for the same reason I want to keep as the title the rather contemptuous word ROOSTERS rather than the more classical THE COCK; and I want to repeat the "gun-metal." (I also had in mind the violent roosters Picasso did in connection with his *Guernica* picture.)

About the "glass-headed pins": I felt the roosters to be placed here and there (by their various crowings) like the pins that point out war projects on a map—maybe I haven't made it clear enough. And I wanted to keep "to see the end" in quotes because, although it may not be generally recognized, I have always felt that expression used of Peter in the Bible to be extremely poignant.

4   It has been so hard to decide what to do, and I know that esthetically you are quite right, but I can't bring myself to sacrifice what (I think) is a very important "violence" of tone—which I feel to be helped by what *you* must feel to be just a bad case of the *Threes*. It makes me feel like a wonderful Klee picture I saw at his show the other day, *The Man of Confusion*. I wonder if you could be mesmerized across the bridge to see it again with me?

PABLO PICASSO

In 1937, Pablo Picasso (1881–1973) was commissioned to paint a mural to stand in the Spanish Pavilion at the World's Fair that was to be held in Paris in 1937. At that time, the Spanish Civil War was raging in Picasso's native country as rebels fought against the Fascist leader General Franco. In April of 1937, in alliance with Franco, German bombers attacked the village of Guernica as part of bombing practice exercises. The town was devastated and over 1500 civilians were killed or wounded. As public outrage over the attack boiled over, Picasso took the event as the subject matter for his mural. The result is Guernica, *a clear example of an artist's response to the atrocities of war.*

Guernica

FIGURE 14.6   *Guernica* by Pablo Piccaso

INQUIRING FURTHER

1. What can you say about the message conveyed by "A Mystery of Heroism"? Do you think the story has a moral? How do the elements of fiction (setting, characters, symbols, narration, and themes) work in the story to help convey its message?

2. Compare the settings in the two poems by Owen. How do the settings help to convey messages? How are the settings indicative of the way the poems dramatize the effects of war? Which do you find to be more powerful and why?

3. Read the letter to Marian Moore by Bishop. Based on your sense of the letter, what can you say about Bishop's goals for the poem? Return to "Roosters" and look for elements that work to achieve those goals. Make a list of the poetic techniques you find that help the poem convey its message.

4. Look over the image of Picasso's *Guernica*. You may also want to look at *Guernica* on our CD. How does the painting use line, shape, lighting, and other elements of art (see Chapter 12) to convey its message? Consider *Guernica* alongside the poem "Roosters" and write a paper where you develop a comparison of the artistic techniques used, and the messages conveyed, by the two works.

RESPONDING TO INJUSTICE

Unlike the death and violence associated with war, many of the conflicts we face in society are more pervasive and subtle. This is not to say that they do not erupt at times into violence or cause deep suffering and pain. It is just that some conflicts (for instance, those associated with race or class) are harder to untangle from the social and economic structures that make up our culture. These selections represent responses in writing and art to deep-seated social conflicts.

MARTIN LUTHER KING JR.

Martin Luther King Jr. (1929–1968) became an ordained minister at the age of nineteen and at age twenty-five was appointed minister of the Baptist Dexter Avenue Church in Montgomery, Alabama. King quickly established himself as a leader in the Civil Rights Movement, organizing and participating along with Rosa Parks in the successful Montgomery bus boycott. He continued to lobby for civil rights issues, employing the tactic of nonviolent protest. "Letter from Birmingham Jail" was composed while King was under arrest in 1963 for a protest held in Birmingham, Alabama. Following King's arrest, eight clergymen issued a statement questioning King's tactics. King wrote his response from his cell using whatever paper he could find. King was assassinated in Memphis, Tennessee on April 4, 1968. At the time, King was preparing to lead a protest in favor of better working conditions for sanitation workers.

"Letter from Birmingham Jail"

Letter from Birmingham Jail

April 16, 1963

MY DEAR FELLOW CLERGYMEN:

While confined here in the Birmingham city jail, I came across your recent statement calling my present activities "unwise and untimely." Seldom do I pause to answer criticism of my work and ideas. If I sought to answer all the criticisms that cross my desk, my secretaries would have little time for anything other than such correspondence in the course of the day, and I would have no time for constructive work. But since I feel that you are men of genuine good will and that your criticisms are sincerely set forth, I want to try to answer your statement in what I hope will be patient and reasonable terms.

I think I should indicate why I am here in Birmingham, since you have been influenced by the view which argues against "outsiders coming in." I have the honor of serving as president of the Southern Christian Leadership Conference, an organization operating in every southern state, with headquarters in Atlanta, Georgia. We have some eighty-five affiliated organizations across the South, and one of them is the Alabama Christian Movement for Human Rights. Frequently we share staff, educational and financial resources with our affiliates. Several months ago the affiliate here in Birmingham asked us to be on call to engage in a nonviolent direct-action program if such were deemed necessary. We readily consented, and when the hour came we lived up to our promise. So I, along with several members of my staff, am here because I was invited here. I am here because I have organizational ties here.

But more basically, I am in Birmingham because injustice is here. Just as the prophets of the eighth century B.C. left their villages and carried their "thus saith the Lord" far beyond the boundaries of their home towns, and just as the Apostle Paul left his village of Tarsus and carried the gospel of Jesus Christ to the far corners of the Greco-Roman world, so am I compelled to carry the gospel of freedom beyond my own home town. Like Paul, I must constantly respond to the Macedonian call for aid.

Moreover, I am cognizant of the interrelatedness of all communities and states. I cannot sit idly by in Atlanta and not be concerned about what happens in Birmingham. Injustice anywhere is a threat to justice everywhere. We are caught in an inescapable network of mutuality, tied in a single garment of destiny. Whatever affects one directly, affects all indirectly. Never again can we afford to live with the narrow, provincial "outside agitator" idea. Anyone who lives inside the United States can never be considered an outsider anywhere within its bounds.

5   You deplore the demonstrations taking place in Birmingham. But your statement, I am sorry to say, fails to express a similar concern for the conditions that brought about the demonstrations. I am sure that none of you would want to rest content with the superficial kind of social analysis that deals merely with effects and does not grapple with underlying causes. It is unfortunate that demonstrations are taking place in Birmingham, but it is even more unfortunate that the city's white power structure left the Negro community with no alternative.

In any nonviolent campaign there are four basic steps: collection of the facts to determine whether injustices exist; negotiation; self-purification; and direct action. We have gone through all these steps in Birmingham. There can be no gainsaying the fact that racial injustice engulfs this community. Birmingham is probably the most thoroughly segregated city in the United States. (Its ugly record of brutality is widely known.) Negroes have experienced grossly unjust treatment in the courts. There have been more unsolved bombings of Negro homes and churches in Birmingham than in any other city in the nation. (These are the hard, brutal facts of the case.) On the basis of these conditions, Negro leaders sought to negotiate with the city fathers. But the latter consistently refused to engage in good-faith negotiation.

Then, last September, came the opportunity to talk with leaders of Birmingham's economic community. In the course of the negotiations, certain promises were made by the merchants—for example, to remove the stores' humiliating racial signs. On the basis of these promises, the Reverend Fred Shuttlesworth and the leaders of the Alabama Christian Movement for Human Rights agreed to a moratorium on all demonstrations. As the weeks and months went by, we realized that we were the victims of a broken promise. A few signs, briefly removed, returned; the others remained.

As in so many past experiences, our hopes had been blasted, and the shadow of deep disappointment settled upon us. We had no alternative except to prepare for direct action, whereby we would present our very bodies as a means of laying our case before the conscience of the local and the national community. Mindful of the difficulties involved, we decided to undertake a process of self-purification. We began a series of workshops on nonviolence, and we repeatedly asked ourselves: "Are you able to accept blows without retaliating?" "Are you able to endure the ordeal of jail?" We decided to schedule our direct-action program for the Easter season, realizing that except for Christmas, this is the main shopping period of the year. Knowing that a strong economic-withdrawal program would be the by-product of direct action, we felt that this would be the best time to bring pressure to bear on the merchants for the needed change.

Then it occurred to us that Birmingham's mayoral election was coming up in March, and we speedily decided to postpone action until after election day. When we discovered that the Commissioner of Public Safety, Eugene "Bull" Connor, had piled up enough votes to be in the run-off, we decided again to postpone action until the day after the run-off so that the demonstrations could not be used to cloud the issues. Like many others, we waited to see Mr. Connor defeated, and to this end we endured postponement after postponement. Having aided in this community need, we felt that our direct-action program could be delayed no longer.

10   You may well ask: "Why direct action? Why sit-ins, marches and so forth? Isn't negotiation a better path?" You are quite right in calling for negotiation. Indeed, this is the very purpose of direct action. Nonviolent direct action seeks to create such a crisis and foster such a tension that a community which has constantly refused to negotiate is forced to confront the issue. It seeks so to dramatize the issue that it can no longer be ignored. My citing the creation of tension as part of the work of the nonviolent-resister may sound rather shocking. But I must confess that I am not afraid of the word "tension." I have earnestly opposed violent tension, but there is a type of constructive, non-violent tension which is necessary for growth. Just as Socrates felt that it was necessary to create a tension in the mind so that individuals could rise from the bondage of myths and half-truths to the unfettered realm of creative analysis and objective appraisal, so must we see the need for nonviolent gadflies to create the kind of tension in society that will help men rise from the dark depths of prejudice and racism to the majestic heights of understanding and brotherhood.

The purpose of our direct-action program is to create a situation so crisis-packed that it will inevitably open the door to negotiation. I therefore concur with you in your call for negotiation. Too long has our beloved Southland been bogged down in a tragic effort to live in monologue rather than dialogue.

One of the basic points in your statement is that the action that I and my associates have taken in Birmingham is untimely. Some have asked: "Why didn't you give the new city administration time to act?" The only answer that I can give to this query is that the new Birmingham administration must be prodded about as much as the outgoing one, before it will act. We are sadly mistaken if we feel that the election of Albert Boutwell as mayor will bring the millennium to Birmingham. While Mr. Boutwell is a much more gentle person than

Mr. Connor, they are both segregationists, dedicated to maintenance of the status quo. I have hope that Mr. Boutwell will be reasonable enough to see the futility of massive resistance to desegregation. But he will not see this without pressure from devotees of civil rights. My friends, I must say to you that we have not made a single gain in civil rights without determined legal and nonviolent pressure. Lamentably, it is an historical fact that privileged groups seldom give up their privileges voluntarily. Individuals may see the moral light and voluntarily give up their unjust posture; but, as Reinhold Niebuhr has reminded us, groups tend to be more immoral than individuals.[1]

We know through painful experience that freedom is never voluntarily given by the oppressor; it must be demanded by the oppressed. Frankly, I have yet to engage in a direct-action campaign that was "well timed" in the view of those who have not suffered unduly from the disease of segregation. For years now I have heard the word "Wait!" It rings in the ear of every Negro with piercing familiarity. This "Wait" has almost always meant "Never." We must come to see, with one of our distinguished jurists, that "justice too long delayed is justice denied."

We have waited for more than 340 years for our constitutional and God-given rights. The nations of Asia and Africa are moving with jetlike speed toward gaining political independence, but we still creep at horse-and-buggy pace toward gaining a cup of coffee at a lunch counter. Perhaps it is easy for those who have never felt the stinging darts of segregation to say, "Wait." But when you have seen vicious mobs lynch your mothers and fathers at will and drown your sisters and brothers at whim; when you have seen hate-filled policemen curse, kick and even kill your black brothers and sisters; when you see the vast majority of your twenty million Negro brothers smothering in an airtight cage of poverty in the midst of an affluent society; when you suddenly find your tongue twisted and your speech stammering as you seek to explain to your six-year-old daughter why she can't go to the public amusement park that has just been advertised on television and see tears welling up in her eyes when she is told that Funtown is closed to colored children and see ominous clouds of inferiority beginning to form in her little mental sky, and see her beginning to distort her personality by developing an unconscious bitterness toward white people; when you have to concoct an answer for a five-year-old son who is asking: "Daddy, why do white people treat colored people so mean?"; when you take a cross-country drive and find it necessary to sleep night after night in the uncomfortable corners of your automobile because no motel will accept you; when you are humiliated day in and day out by nagging signs reading "white" and "colored"; when your first name becomes "nigger," your middle name becomes "boy" (however old you are) and your last name becomes "John," and your wife and mother are never given the respected title "Mrs."; when you are harried by day and haunted by night by the fact that you are a Negro, living constantly at tiptoe stance, never quite knowing what to expect next, and are plagued with inner fears and outer resentments; when you are forever fighting a degenerating sense of "nobodiness"—then you will understand why we find it difficult to wait. There comes a time when the cup of endurance runs over, and men are no longer willing to be plunged into the abyss of despair. I hope, sirs, you can understand our legitimate and unavoidable impatience.

---

[1] **Reinhold Niebuhr:** American theologian concerned with ill effects of industrialization.

15   You express a great deal of anxiety over our willingness to break laws. This is certainly a legitimate concern. Since we so diligently urge people to obey the Supreme Court's decision of 1954 outlawing segregation in the public schools, at first glance it may seem rather paradoxical for us consciously to break laws. One may well ask: "How can you advocate breaking some laws and obeying others?" The answer lies in the fact that there are two types of laws: just and unjust. I would be the first to advocate obeying just laws. One has not only a legal but a moral responsibility to obey just laws. Conversely, one has a moral responsibility to disobey unjust laws. I would agree with St. Augustine that "an unjust law is no law at all."

Now, what is the difference between the two? How does one determine whether a law is just or unjust? A just law is a man-made code that squares with the moral law or the law of God. An unjust law is a code that is out of harmony with the moral law. To put it in the terms of St. Thomas Aquinas: An unjust law is a human law that is not rooted in eternal law and natural law. Any law that uplifts human personality is just. Any law that degrades human personality is unjust. All segregation statutes are unjust because segregation distorts the soul and damages the personality. It gives the segregator a false sense of superiority and the segregated a false sense of inferiority. Segregation, to use the terminology of the Jewish philosopher Martin Buber, substitutes an "I–it" relationship for an "I–thou" relationship and ends up relegating persons to the status of things. Hence segregation is not only politically, economically and sociologically unsound, it is morally wrong and sinful. Paul Tillich has said that sin is separation. Is not segregation an existential expression of man's tragic separation, his awful estrangement, his terrible sinfulness? Thus it is that I can urge men to obey the 1954 decision of the Supreme Court, for it is morally right; and I can urge them to disobey segregation ordinances, for they are morally wrong.

Let us consider a more concrete example of just and unjust laws. An unjust law is a code that a numerical or power majority group compels a minority group to obey but does not make binding on itself. This is *difference* made legal. By the same token, a just law is a code that a majority compels a minority to follow and that it is willing to follow itself. This is *sameness* made legal.

Let me give another explanation. A law is unjust if it is inflicted on a minority that, as a result of being denied the right to vote, had no part in enacting or devising the law. Who can say that the legislature of Alabama which set up that state's segregation laws was democratically elected? Throughout Alabama all sorts of devious methods are used to prevent Negroes from becoming registered voters, and there are some counties in which, even though Negroes constitute a majority of the population, not a single Negro is registered. Can any law enacted under such circumstances be considered democratically structured?

Sometimes a law is just on its face and unjust in its application. For instance, I have been arrested on a charge of parading without a permit. Now, there is nothing wrong in having an ordinance which requires a permit for a parade. But such an ordinance becomes unjust when it is used to maintain segregation and to deny citizens the First-Amendment privilege of peaceful assembly and protest.

20   I hope you are able to see the distinction I am trying to point out. In no sense do I advocate evading or defying the law, as would the rabid segregationist. That would lead to anarchy. One who breaks an unjust law must do so openly, lovingly, and with a willingness to accept the penalty. I submit that

an individual who breaks a law that conscience tells him is unjust, and who willingly accepts the penalty of imprisonment in order to arouse the conscience of the community over its injustice, is in reality expressing the highest respect for law.

Of course, there is nothing new about this kind of civil disobedience. It was evidenced sublimely in the refusal of Shadrach, Meshach and Abednego to obey the laws of Nebuchadnezzar, on the ground that a higher moral law was at stake.[2] It was practiced superbly by the early Christians, who were willing to face hungry lions and the excruciating pain of chopping blocks rather than submit to certain unjust laws of the Roman Empire. To a degree, academic freedom is a reality today because Socrates practiced civil disobedience. In our own nation, the Boston Tea Party represented a massive act of civil disobedience.

We should never forget that everything Adolf Hitler did in Germany was "legal" and everything the Hungarian freedom fighters did in Hungary was "illegal." It was "illegal" to aid and comfort a Jew in Hitler's Germany. Even so, I am sure that, had I lived in Germany at the time, I would have aided and comforted my Jewish brothers. If today I lived in a Communist country where certain principles dear to the Christian faith are suppressed, I would openly advocate disobeying that country's antireligious laws.

I must make two honest confessions to you, my Christian and Jewish brothers. First, I must confess that over the past few years I have been gravely disappointed with the white moderate. I have almost reached the regrettable conclusion that the Negro's great stumbling block in his stride toward freedom is not the White Citizen's Counciler or the Ku Klux Klanner, but the white moderate, who is more devoted to "order" than to justice; who prefers a negative peace which is the absence of tension to a positive peace which is the presence of justice; who constantly says: "I agree with you in the goal you seek, but I cannot agree with your methods of direct action"; who paternalistically believes he can set the timetable for another man's freedom; who lives by a mythical concept of time and who constantly advises the Negro to wait for a "more convenient season." Shallow understanding from people of good will is more frustrating than absolute misunderstanding from people of ill will. Lukewarm acceptance is much more bewildering than outright rejection.

I had hoped that the white moderate would understand that law and order exist for the purpose of establishing justice and that when they fail in this purpose they become the dangerously structured dams that block the flow of social progress. I had hoped that the white moderate would understand that the present tension in the South is a necessary phase of the transition from an obnoxious negative peace, in which the Negro passively accepted his unjust plight, to a substantive and positive peace, in which all men will respect the dignity and worth of human personality. Actually, we who engage in nonviolent direct action are not the creators of tension. We merely bring to the surface the hidden tension that is already alive. We bring it out in the open, where it can be seen and dealt with. Like a boil that can never be cured so long as it is covered up but must be opened with all its ugliness to the natural medicines of air and light, injustice must be exposed, with all the tension its exposure creates, to the light of human conscience and the air of national opinion before it can be cured.

---

[2]**Shadrach . . . stake:** From the book of Daniel, Shadrach, Meshach, and Abednego refused to worship a golden statue and were thrown into a fire.

25   In your statement you assert that our actions, even though peaceful, must be condemned because they precipitate violence. But is this a logical assertion? Isn't this like condemning a robbed man because his possession of money precipitated the evil act of robbery? Isn't this like condemning Socrates because his unswerving commitment to truth and his philosophical inquiries precipitated the act by the misguided populace in which they made him drink hemlock? Isn't this like condemning Jesus because his unique God-consciousness and never-ceasing devotion to God's will precipitated the evil act of crucifixion? We must come to see that, as the federal courts have consistently affirmed, it is wrong to urge an individual to cease his efforts to gain his basic constitutional rights because the quest may precipitate violence. Society must protect the robbed and punish the robber.

I had also hoped that the white moderate would reject the myth concerning time in relation to the struggle for freedom. I have just received a letter from a white brother in Texas. He writes: "All Christians know that the colored people will receive equal rights eventually, but it is possible that you are in too great a religious hurry. It has taken Christianity almost two thousand years to accomplish what it has. The teachings of Christ take time to come to earth." Such an attitude stems from a tragic misconception of time, from the strangely irrational notion that there is something in the very flow of time that will inevitably cure all ills. Actually, time itself is neutral; it can be used either destructively or constructively. More and more I feel that the people of ill will have used time much more effectively than have the people of good will. We will have to repent in this generation not merely for the hateful words and actions of the bad people but for the appalling silence of the good people. Human progress never rolls in on wheels of inevitability; it comes through the tireless efforts of men willing to be co-workers with God, and without this hard work, time itself becomes an ally of the forces of social stagnation. We must use time creatively, in the knowledge that the time is always ripe to do right. Now is the time to make real the promise of democracy and transform our pending national elegy into a creative psalm of brotherhood. Now is the time to lift our national policy from the quicksand of racial injustice to the solid rock of human dignity.

You speak of our activity in Birmingham as extreme. At first I was rather disappointed that fellow clergymen would see my nonviolent efforts as those of an extremist. I began thinking about the fact that I stand in the middle of two opposing forces in the Negro community. One is a force of complacency, made up in part of Negroes who, as a result of long years of oppression, are so drained of self-respect and a sense of "somebodiness" that they have adjusted to segregation; and in part of a few middle-class Negroes who, because of a degree of academic and economic security and because in some ways they profit by segregation, have become insensitive to the problems of the masses. The other force is one of bitterness and hatred, and it comes perilously close to advocating violence. It is expressed in the various black nationalist groups that are springing up across the nation, the largest and best-known being Elijah Muhammad's Muslim movement. Nourished by the Negro's frustration over the continued existence of racial discrimination, this movement is made up of people who have lost faith in America, who have absolutely repudiated Christianity, and who have concluded that the white man is an incorrigible "devil."

I have tried to stand between these two forces, saying that we need emulate neither the "do-nothingism" of the complacent nor the hatred and despair of the black nationalist. For there is the more excellent way of love and nonviolent protest. I am grateful to God that, through the influence of the Negro church, the way of nonviolence became an integral part of our struggle.

If this philosophy had not emerged, by now many streets of the South would, I am convinced, be flowing with blood. And I am further convinced that if our white brothers dismiss as "rabble-rousers" and "outside agitators" those of us who employ nonviolent direct action, and if they refuse to support our nonviolent efforts, millions of Negroes will, out of frustration and despair, seek solace and security in black-nationalist ideologies—a development that would inevitably lead to a frightening racial nightmare.

30   Oppressed people cannot remain oppressed forever. The yearning for freedom eventually manifests itself, and that is what has happened to the American Negro. Something within has reminded him of his birthright of freedom, and something without has reminded him that it can be gained. Consciously or unconsciously, he has been caught up by the *Zeitgeist*, and with his black brothers of Africa and his brown and yellow brothers of Asia, South America and the Caribbean, the United States Negro is moving with a sense of great urgency toward the promised land of racial justice. If one recognizes this vital urge that has engulfed the Negro community, one should readily understand why public demonstrations are taking place. The Negro has many pent-up resentments and latent frustrations, and he must release them. So let him march; let him make prayer pilgrimages to the city hall; let him go on freedom rides— and try to understand why he must do so. If his repressed emotions are not released in nonviolent ways, they will seek expression through violence; this is not a threat but a fact of history. So I have not said to my people: "Get rid of your discontent." Rather, I have tried to say that this normal and healthy discontent can be channeled into the creative outlet of nonviolent direct action. And now this approach is being termed extremist.

But though I was initially disappointed at being categorized as an extremist, as I continued to think about the matter I gradually gained a measure of satisfaction from the label. Was not Jesus an extremist for love: "Love your enemies, bless them that curse you, do good to them that hate you, and pray for them which despitefully use you, and persecute you." Was not Amos an extremist for justice: "Let justice roll down like waters and righteousness like an ever-flowing stream." Was not Paul an extremist for the Christian gospel: "I bear in my body the marks of the Lord Jesus." Was not Martin Luther an extremist: "Here I stand; I cannot do otherwise, so help me God." And John Bunyan: "I will stay in jail to the end of my days before I make a butchery of my conscience." And Abraham Lincoln: "This nation cannot survive half slave and half free." And Thomas Jefferson: "We hold these truths to be self-evident, that all men are created equal . . . " So the question is not whether we will be extremists, but what kind of extremists we will be. Will we be extremists for hate or for love? Will we be extremists for the preservation of injustice or for the extension of justice? In that dramatic scene on Calvary's hill three men were crucified. We must never forget that all three were crucified for the same crime—the crime of extremism. Two were extremists for immorality, and thus fell below their environment. The other, Jesus Christ, was an extremist for love, truth and goodness, and thereby rose above his environment. Perhaps the South, the nation and the world are in dire need of creative extremists.

I had hoped that the white moderate would see this need. Perhaps I was too optimistic; perhaps I expected too much. I suppose I should have realized that few members of the oppressor race can understand the deep groans and passionate yearnings of the oppressed race, and still fewer have the vision to see that injustice must be rooted out by strong, persistent and determined action. I am thankful, however, that some of our white brothers in the South have grasped the meaning of this social revolution and committed themselves to it. They are still all too few in quantity, but they are big in quality. Some—such as Ralph McGill, Lillian Smith, Harry Golden, James McBride Dabbs, Ann Braden and Sarah Patton Boyle—have written about our struggle in eloquent and prophetic terms. Others have marched with us down nameless streets of the South. They have languished in filthy, roach-infested jails, suffering the abuse and brutality of policemen who view them as "dirty nigger-lovers." Unlike so many of their moderate brothers and sisters, they have recognized the urgency of the moment and sensed the need for powerful "action" antidotes to combat the disease of segregation.

Let me take note of my other major disappointment. I have been so greatly disappointed with the white church and its leadership. Of course, there are some notable exceptions. I am not unmindful of the fact that each of you has taken some significant stands on this issue. I commend you, Reverend Stallings, for your Christian stand on this past Sunday, in welcoming Negroes to your worship service on a nonsegregated basis. I commend the Catholic leaders of this state for integrating Spring Hill College several years ago.

But despite these notable exceptions, I must honestly reiterate that I have been disappointed with the church. I do not say this as one of those negative critics who can always find something wrong with the church. I say this as a minister of the gospel, who loves the church; who was nurtured in its bosom; who has been sustained by its spiritual blessings and who will remain true to it as long as the cord of life shall lengthen.

35   When I was suddenly catapulted into the leadership of the bus protest in Montgomery, Alabama, a few years ago, I felt we would be supported by the white church. I felt that the white ministers, priests and rabbis of the South would be among our strongest allies. Instead, some have been outright opponents, refusing to understand the freedom movement and misrepresenting its leaders; all too many others have been more cautious than courageous and have remained silent behind the anesthetizing security of stained-glass windows.

In spite of my shattered dreams, I came to Birmingham with the hope that the white religious leadership of this community would see the justice of our cause and, with deep moral concern, would serve as the channel through which our just grievances could reach the power structure. I had hoped that each of you would understand. But again I have been disappointed.

I have heard numerous southern religious leaders admonish their worshipers to comply with a desegregation decision because it is the law, but I have longed to hear white ministers declare: "Follow this decree because integration is morally right and because the Negro is your brother." In the midst of blatant injustices inflicted upon the Negro, I have watched white churchmen stand on the sideline and mouth pious irrelevancies and sanctimonious trivialities. In the midst of a mighty struggle to rid our nation of racial and economic injustice, I have heard many ministers say: "Those are social issues, with which the gospel has no real concern." And I have watched many churches commit themselves to a completely otherworldly religion which makes a strange, un-Biblical distinction between body and soul, between the sacred and the secular.

I have traveled the length and breadth of Alabama, Mississippi and all the other southern states. On sweltering summer days and crisp autumn mornings I have

looked at the South's beautiful churches with their lofty spires pointing heavenward. I have beheld the impressive outlines of her massive religious-education
buildings. Over and over I have found myself asking: "What kind of people
worship here? Who is their God? Where were their voices when the lips of Governor Barnett dripped with words of interposition and nullification? Where were
they when Governor Wallace gave a clarion call for defiance and hatred? Where
were their voices of support when bruised and weary Negro men and women
decided to rise from the dark dungeons of complacency to the bright hills of
creative protest?"

Yes, these questions are still in my mind. In deep disappointment I have
wept over the laxity of the church. But be assured that my tears have been tears
of love. There can be no deep disappointment where there is not deep love.
Yes, I love the church. How could I do otherwise? I am in the rather unique
position of being the son, the grandson and the great-grandson of preachers.
Yes, I see the church as the body of Christ. But, oh! How we have blemished
and scarred that body through social neglect and through fear of being non-
conformists.

40   There was a time when the church was very powerful—in the time when
the early Christians rejoiced at being deemed worthy to suffer for what they
believed. In those days the church was not merely a thermometer that recorded the ideas and principles of popular opinion; it was a thermostat that transformed the mores of society. Whenever the early Christians entered a town, the
people in power became disturbed and immediately sought to convict the Christians for being "disturbers of the peace" and "outside agitators." But the Christians pressed on, in the conviction that they were "a colony of heaven," called
to obey God rather than man. Small in number, they were big in commitment.
They were too God-intoxicated to be "astronomically intimidated." By their
effort and example they brought an end to such ancient evils as infanticide
and gladiatorial contests.

Things are different now. So often the contemporary church is a weak,
ineffectual voice with an uncertain sound. So often it is an archdefender of
the status quo. Far from being disturbed by the presence of the church, the
power structure of the average community is consoled by the church's silent—
and often even vocal—sanction of things as they are.

But the judgment of God is upon the church as never before. If today's
church does not recapture the sacrificial spirit of the early church, it will lose
its authenticity, forfeit the loyalty of millions, and be dismissed as an irrele-
vant social club with no meaning for the twentieth century. Every day I meet
young people whose disappointment with the church has turned into outright
disgust.

Perhaps I have once again been too optimistic. Is organized religion too inex-
tricably bound to the status quo to save our nation and the world? Perhaps I
must turn my faith to the inner spiritual church, the church within the church,
as the true *ekklesia*[3] and the hope of the world. But again I am thankful to God
that some noble souls from the ranks of organized religion have broken loose from
the paralyzing chains of conformity and joined us as active partners in the struggle for freedom. They have left their secure congregations and walked the streets
of Albany, Georgia, with us. They have gone down the highways of the South
on tortuous rides for freedom. Yes, they have gone to jail with us. Some have been
dismissed from their churches, have lost the support of their bishops and fellow

[3]**ekklesia:** Greek word used to indicate a group of believers or the early Christian church.

ministers. But they have acted in the faith that right defeated is stronger than evil triumphant. Their witness has been the spiritual salt that has preserved the true meaning of the gospel in these troubled times. They have carved a tunnel of hope through the dark mountain of disappointment.

I hope the church as a whole will meet the challenge of this decisive hour. But even if the church does not come to the aid of justice, I have no despair about the future. I have no fear about the outcome of our struggle in Birmingham, even if our motives are at present misunderstood. We will reach the goal of freedom in Birmingham and all over the nation, because the goal of America is freedom. Abused and scorned though we may be, our destiny is tied up with America's destiny. Before the pilgrims landed at Plymouth, we were here. Before the pen of Jefferson etched the majestic words of the Declaration of Independence across the pages of history, we were here. For more than two centuries our forebears labored in this country without wages; they made cotton king; they built the homes of their masters while suffering gross injustice and shameful humiliation—and yet out of a bottomless vitality they continued to thrive and develop. If the inexpressible cruelties of slavery could not stop us, the opposition we now face will surely fail. We will win our freedom because the sacred heritage of our nation and the eternal will of God are embodied in our echoing demands.

45   Before closing I feel impelled to mention one other point in your statement that has troubled me profoundly. You warmly commended the Birmingham police force for keeping "order" and "preventing violence." I doubt that you would have so warmly commended the police force if you had seen its dogs sinking their teeth into unarmed, nonviolent Negroes. I doubt that you would so quickly commend the policemen if you were to observe their ugly and inhumane treatment of Negroes here in the city jail; if you were to watch them push and curse old Negro women and young Negro girls; if you were to see them slap and kick old Negro men and young boys; if you were to observe them, as they did on two occasions, refuse to give us food because we wanted to sing our grace together. I cannot join you in your praise of the Birmingham police department.

It is true that the police have exercised a degree of discipline in handling the demonstrators. In this sense they have conducted themselves rather "nonviolently" in public. But for what purpose? To preserve the evil system of segregation. Over the past few years I have consistently preached that nonviolence demands that the means we use must be as pure as the ends we seek. I have tried to make clear that it is wrong to use immoral means to attain moral ends. But now I must affirm that it is just as wrong, or perhaps even more so, to use moral means to preserve immoral ends. Perhaps Mr. Connor and his policemen have been rather nonviolent in public, as was Chief Pritchett in Albany, Georgia, but they have used the moral means of nonviolence to maintain the immoral end of racial injustice. As T. S. Eliot has said: "The last temptation is the greatest treason: To do the right deed for the wrong reason."

I wish you had commended the Negro sit-inners and demonstrators of Birmingham for their sublime courage, their willingness to suffer and their amazing discipline in the midst of great provocation. One day the South will recognize its real heroes. They will be the James Merediths,[4] with the noble sense of purpose that enables them to face jeering and hostile mobs, and with the

---

[4]**James Meredith:** Civil rights activist and the first African American to attend the University of Mississippi

agonizing loneliness that characterizes the life of the pioneer. They will be old, oppressed, battered Negro women, symbolized in a seventy-two-year-old woman in Montgomery, Alabama, who rose up with a sense of dignity and with her people decided not to ride segregated buses, and who responded with ungrammatical profundity to one who inquired about her weariness: "My feets is tired, but my soul is at rest." They will be the young high school and college students, the young ministers of the gospel and a host of their elders, courageously and nonviolently sitting in at lunch counters and willingly going to jail for conscience' sake. One day the South will know that when these disinherited children of God sat down at lunch counters, they were in reality standing up for what is best in the American dream and for the most sacred values in our Judaeo-Christian heritage, thereby bringing our nation back to those great wells of democracy which were dug deep by the founding fathers in their formulation of the Constitution and the Declaration of Independence.

Never before have I written so long a letter. I'm afraid it is much too long to take your precious time. I can assure you that it would have been much shorter if I had been writing from a comfortable desk, but what else can one do when he is alone in a narrow jail cell, other than write long letters, think long thoughts and pray long prayers?

If I have said anything in this letter that overstates the truth and indicates an unreasonable impatience, I beg you to forgive me. If I have said anything that understates the truth and indicates my having a patience that allows me to settle for anything less than brotherhood, I beg God to forgive me.

50   I hope this letter finds you strong in the faith. I also hope that circumstances will soon make it possible for me to meet each of you, not as an integrationist or a civil-rights leader but as a fellow clergyman and a Christian brother. Let us all hope that the dark clouds of racial prejudice will soon pass away and the deep fog of misunderstanding will be lifted from our fear-drenched communities, and in some not too distant tomorrow the radiant stars of love and brotherhood will shine over our great nation with all their scintillating beauty.

Yours for the cause of Peace and Brotherhood,

MARTIN LUTHER KING, JR.

INQUIRING FURTHER

1. "Letter from Birmingham Jail" has been praised for King's adept use of rhetorical strategies that create a convincing argument. How compelling did you find the essay to be? Find and list at least three rhetorical strategies you feel to be particularly effective.

2. In his letter, King highlights the distinction between just and unjust laws. What responsibility do you think individuals have regarding unjust laws? How can we determine when a law is unjust? Are there any unjust laws you are aware of today?

3. King advocates nonviolent forms of protest in his letter. Do you think these forms of protest are as effective today as they were in the 1960s? Are there ever times when you feel violent forms of protest are necessary? Is it possible to oppose injustice without protesting? Write a list of the possible ways one can protest injustice.

CATHERINE ANDERSON

Catherine Anderson (born in 1954) published her first book of poems, In the Mother Tongue, *in 1984. She has since published poems in a number of journals and a second collection of poems,* The Work of Hands *in 2000. "Womanhood" was first published in 1983.*

Womanhood

She slides over
the hot upholstery
of her mother's car,
this schoolgirl of fifteen
5   who loves humming & swaying
with the radio.
Her entry into womanhood
will be like all the other girls'—
a cigarette and a joke,
10   as she strides up with the rest
to a brick factory
where she'll sew rag rugs
from textile strips of kelly green,
bright red, aqua.

15   When she enters,
and the millgate closes,
final as a slap,
there'll be silence.
She'll see fifteen high windows
20   cemented over to cut out light.
Inside, a constant, deafening noise
and warm air smelling of oil,
the shifts continuing on . . .
All day she'll guide cloth along a line
25   of whirring needles, her arms & shoulders
rocking back & forth
with the machines—
200 porch size rugs behind her
before she can stop
30   to reach up, like her mother,
and pick the lint
out of her hair.

JIM DANIELS

Jim Daniels (born in 1956) worked at a Ford automotive plant during his college years. His first book of poetry, Places / Everyone *was published in 1985, and included "4ᵗʰ of July in the Factory." Since then, Daniels*

has published over a dozen books. He currently heads the creative writ-
ing program at Carnegie Mellon University.

4th of July in the Factory

Today there is no trouble
finding a parking spot.
There is no line
at the time clocks.

5   I walk down toward my department
past the deserted, motionless
assembly line in department 65,
past the dark cafeteria.

There is a doubleheader
10   at Tiger Stadium today.
Someone shouts the score of the first game
and I can hear him.

The foreman smiles
at the thought of all the money he will make today.
15   I smile with him.

The big press breaks down
after 20 minutes.
We all sit down and tell jokes,
waiting for the foreman to come by and notice.

20   Bobbie Joe brought in a bottle
and we pass it around.
Even K.Y. the hi-lo driver
gets off his seat
for the first time in recent history
25   and takes a hit.

When the foreman shows up
we tell him we need an electrician.
A half hour later
some guy with a flashlight
30   and a belt of tools
strolls toward us rubbing his eyes.
Another half hour goes by
before he gets the press fixed
with the foreman standing over him.
35   Then, we work until first break.

When we get back
someone wedges in a steel blank the wrong way.
Old Green, press repairman,
motions thumbs down
40   and walks away.

The foreman threatens to send us home
but instead
sends us on an early lunch.

We go outside to eat,
45   sitting on huge rolls of steel
and watching the sun set.
We talk about how wonderful it is
to make 20 dollars an hour
for sitting on our asses,
50   how wonderful it is
to hear voices
when the press is down.

Suddenly Old Green, who cannot speak,
lights up a joint
55   and takes a hit,
his wrinkled stone face
breaking into a smile
that today
could stop any machine.

INQUIRING FURTHER

1. How does the title of the poem, "Womanhood," influence your reading? Do you think the poem makes as much of a statement about the mother as about the fifteen-year-old girl? Can you find anything positive about the poem?

2. What kind of a message would you say "4th of July in the Factory" presents? What alternative messages are also present in the work? Make a list of all of the themes you find in the poem.

3. Compare "Womanhood" with "4th of July in the Factory." Do you find the poems to be more similar or different? Write an essay in which you relate the subject matter, poetic techniques, and messages of the poems.

EVELYN IRITANI AND TYLER MARSHAL

Iritani and Marshal wrote this report as part of a series of articles in the Los Angeles Times *investigating the economic and social impacts of Wal-Mart. The article appeared in the November 24, 2003 edition.*

The Wal-Mart Effect: Scouring the Globe to Give Shoppers an $8.63 Polo Shirt

San Pedro Sula, Honduras

When Wal-Mart Stores Inc. demands a lower price for the shirts and shorts it sells by the millions, the consequences are felt in a remote Chinese industrial town, at a port in Bangladesh and here in Honduras, under the corrugated metal roof of the Cosmos clothing factory.

Isabel Reyes, who has worked at the plant for 11 years, pushes fabric through her sewing machine 10 hours a day, struggling to meet the latest quota scrawled on a blackboard.

She now sews sleeves onto shirts at the rate of 1,200 garments a day. That's two shirts a minute, one sleeve every 15 seconds.

"There is always an acceleration," said Reyes, 37, who can't lift a cooking pot or hold her infant daughter without the anti-inflammatory pills she gulps down every few hours. "The goals are always increasing, but the pay stays the same."

5   Reyes, who earns the equivalent of $35 a week, says her bosses blame the long hours and low wages on big U.S. companies and their demands for ever-cheaper merchandise. Wal-Mart, the biggest company of them all, is the Cosmos factory's main customer.

Reyes is skeptical. Why, she asked, would a company in the richest country in the world care about a few pennies on a pair of shorts?

The answer: Wal-Mart built its empire on bargains.

The company's size and obsession with shaving costs have made it a global economic force. Its decisions affect wages, working conditions and manufacturing practices—even the price of a yard of denim—around the world.

From its headquarters in Bentonville, Ark., the company has established a network of 10,000 suppliers and constantly pressures them to lower their prices. At the same time, Wal-Mart buyers continually search the globe for still-cheaper sources of supply. The competition pits vendor against vendor, country against country.

10   "They control so much of retail that they can put someone into business or take someone out of business if they choose to," said Pat Danahy, a former chief executive at Cone Mills Corp. in Greensboro, N.C., one of the few surviving U.S. textile producers.

In Honduras, the pressure keeps factory managers on edge, always looking for ways to cut expenses without running afoul of labor laws or Wal-Mart's own contractor rules, which call for "reasonable employee work hours."

"I think we have reached the limit," said Shin Woo Kang, manager of the enormous Han Soll Textile Ltd. sewing plant on the outskirts of San Pedro Sula. The plant employs 1,600 workers, mostly young women. Wal-Mart is its biggest customer.

The brightly lighted factory is filled with humming machines, mounds of clothing parts and fast-moving hands. Down one production line, pieces of navy blue fabric take shape as Bobbie Brooks polo shirts, each bearing a Wal-Mart price tag of $8.63.

Kang said Wal-Mart was paying Han Soll about $3 a shirt — a few cents less than last year.

15   Asked what he would do if the retailer pressed for an even lower price, Kang grew quiet. "We would have to find something," he said finally. "Honestly speaking, I don't know what it is."

To cut costs, Honduran factories have reduced payrolls and become more efficient. The country produces the same amount of clothing as it did three years ago, but with 20% fewer workers, said Henry Fransen, director of the Honduran Apparel Manufacturers Assn., which represents nearly 200 export factories.

"We're earning less and producing more," he said with a laugh, "following the Wal-Mart philosophy."

That's harsh medicine for a developing country. The clothing industry is one of the few sources of decent jobs for unskilled workers in this nation of 6 million. Many of those jobs depend on Wal-Mart.

"You could be looking at a government meltdown if something were to happen to this industry," said Raja Rajan, a factory manager active in the apparel association.

20   In Rajan's view, Wal-Mart is so important to the stability of Honduras that leaders should cultivate stronger ties with the company, almost as they would a foreign country. He has lobbied the government to send high-level envoys to Wal-Mart's Arkansas headquarters, something Bangladesh and other countries already do.

Even with such efforts, Rajan fears that the migration of sewing jobs to China and other lower-cost countries can't be stopped, only slowed.

Chuck Wilburn figures that his 1,300 employees will be among the casualties. He manages a factory on the outskirts of San Pedro Sula that cranks out clothing for Wal-Mart, Target Corp. and other retailers.

Wilburn's employer, Oxford Industries of Atlanta, once owned 44 factories in the American South. It shuttered them all in the last 15 years and moved the work to cheaper locales. That's how Wilburn found himself in Honduras.

He is proud of his clean, modern factory. "It's nicer than the one I ran in South Carolina," Wilburn said.

25   Still, he has had trouble turning a profit. He laid off 500 employees two years ago. Even here, it's hard to meet Wal-Mart's prices. Wilburn expects that Oxford will close his factory in the next few years and move on to another country where basic cotton clothes, such as Wal-Mart's Old Glory khaki pants, can be produced for less.

"Our business is a lot of twill stuff," he said. "That will be gone."

Waving the Flag

It wasn't long ago that Wal-Mart was fighting to keep manufacturing jobs on U.S. soil.

In 1985, founder Sam Walton launched his "Bring It Home to the USA" program. "Wal-Mart believes American workers can make a difference," he told his suppliers, offering to pay as much as 5% more for U.S.-made products.

In his 1992 memoir, "Made in America," Walton claimed that the program had saved or created nearly 100,000 jobs by using "the power of this enormous enterprise as a force for change."

30   But the late Walton's much-trumpeted effort soon was overtaken by the rise of the global economy. The spread of the Internet and other technology, along with U.S.-led efforts to tear down trade barriers, made it easier to move goods and capital across borders.

To maintain its edge on pricing, Wal-Mart quietly joined other retailers in a worldwide search for the cheapest sources of production.

In apparel, the process begins with Celia Clancy. From a renovated warehouse near the company's headquarters, the Wal-Mart executive vice president oversees the world's largest clothing budget, estimated at $35 billion in 2000.

Clancy gives her buyers a "Plus One" mandate every year: For each item they handle, they must either lower the cost or raise the quality.

To demonstrate, she pulled a pair of girls' shorts off the wall of her cramped office and gave them a tug.

35   "This was a dumb little knit pull-on short," Clancy said. "We improved the fabric, put some more fashion in it and are selling it for the same price as last year — $5.19."

Keeping prices low like this means squeezing costs at every step. Clancy and her buyers have trimmed back the number of brands, styles and color schemes. That allows Wal-Mart to consolidate its purchases of fabric, accessories and thread and to wrangle steep discounts from suppliers.

Clancy's buyers used to rely on a Hong Kong company and other interme- diaries to find bargains overseas. This year, Wal-Mart established its own glob- al procurement division to hunt for the cheapest raw materials, manufactur- ers and shipping routes. Last year, for instance, the company rerouted cargo from a port in Hong Kong to the southern Chinese province of Guangdong, where shipping rates were lower. The savings: $650,000.

In purchasing fabrics such as denim and khaki, Wal-Mart plans to approach three to five mills around the world and pit them against each other. "We'll be putting our global muscle on them," said Ken Eaton, head of the global procurement division, which has 21 offices in 18 countries.

Eaton believes he can reduce costs at least 20% by cutting out the middle- man and buying directly from foreign factories. He feels a sense of urgency about his mission, in part because he believes the company's "Buy American" focus left it playing catch up.

40   "Honestly, we're kind of late to the party," he said. "There are a lot of com- panies out there that have been direct-importing and understanding the glob- al aspect of sourcing for a long, long time."

As late as 1995, Wal-Mart said imports accounted for no more than 6% of its products. Today, consulting firm Retail Forward estimates that 50% to 60% of the merchandise in the company's U.S. stores is imported.

Wal-Mart Chief Executive H. Lee Scott Jr. said in an interview that the trend reflected an inescapable reality: U.S. consumers aren't willing to pay even a little extra for a "Made in America" label.

"The customer ultimately drives that," he said.

Big in Bangladesh

Wal-Mart is the most powerful corporate citizen in Bangladesh, even though it doesn't operate a single store in the country.

45   When the company complained to Bangladesh's Export Promotion Bureau this spring about delays in moving cargo, the response was swift.

Officials in the southern port of Chittagong are speeding up efforts to reduce paperwork and modernize facilities. Over the objections of labor leaders, port officials also are building a five-berth container terminal that will be privately managed. Already, giant cranes have helped shorten a ship's turnaround time from six days to fewer than four.

It's no wonder Wal-Mart wields such clout in this country, where nearly half the population lives in poverty. The company bought 14% of the $1.9 bil- lion in apparel that Bangladesh shipped to the U.S. last year.

"Wal-Mart is our biggest customer and it's important to me," said Commerce Minister Amir Khasru Mahmud Chowdhury. But, he added, Wal-Mart's prices "are coming down all the time — that's the biggest threat to us."

Bangladeshi factory owners say Wal-Mart and other retailers have asked them to cut their prices by as much as 50% in recent years.

50   One apparel manufacturer described a visit from a Wal-Mart buyer who showed him a European-made garment that retailed for $100 to $130. The buyer asked the Bangladeshi to produce a knockoff for $10 a dozen. He declined.

"They say to come down in price, but we have to make a profit," complained another clothing maker. Hoping to land a Wal-Mart order for 600,000 fleece jackets this year, he bargained down his suppliers of fabric, thread and fastenings, and managed to cut his price by 20%.

It wasn't good enough for Wal-Mart. "They said they will place the order in Vietnam or China," he recalled.

Syed Naved Husain had hoped to avoid this sort of nickel-and-diming by going upscale.

As head of the apparel division for Beximco, Bangladesh's largest private company, Husain spent $300 million in 1995 to build a computerized textile and apparel manufacturing center in a rice paddy outside Dhaka. He hired hot designers from Asia and Europe.

55   Within a few years, he was manufacturing clothes for European retailers Diesel and Zara, and his lushly landscaped "manufacturing oasis" had become an industry showpiece.

But the market has started to change. Wal-Mart is selling more-fashionable clothes, and Husain's high-end customers are nervous. They are pushing him like never before to cut costs.

"Unfortunately," Husain said of Wal-Mart, "they've created a model that has taken the world by storm."

U.S. retailers began making their way to Bangladesh in the 1980s. They found a large population of poor, young women willing to work from dawn to dusk for a few pennies an hour.

Many factories lacked ventilation and fire escapes. Labor activists estimated in the mid-1990s that as many as 50,000 Bangladeshi children were sewing apparel for companies such as Wal- Mart and Kmart Corp.

60   The resulting outcry prompted a government crackdown on the use of child labor and led companies such as Wal-Mart to require suppliers to adhere to labor laws and safety standards.

Sheikh Nazma, a former child laborer, has seen the way Wal-Mart can help clean things up.

She worked at a Dhaka garment factory that had no clean drinking water and only a few filthy toilets for hundreds of employees. After the owner refused to pay their wages for three months, the employees complained to Wal-Mart, the factory's main customer.

"Wal-Mart interfered, and . . . the owner paid our salaries and overtime and even paid bonuses to each worker," recalled Nazma, who later helped launch the Bangladesh Independent Garment Workers Union Federation.

But Nazma and others say Wal-Mart undermines its good efforts with its incessant push for lower prices. To fill orders on short schedules, factories often force their employees to work overtime or stay on the job for weeks without a day off, according to Sayeeda Roxana Khan, a former factory manager in Dhaka. To conceal such practices, auditors say, some factories keep two sets of books.

65   "It's the workers who suffer when entrepreneurs have to survive by cutting corners," said Khan, who now works for Verite, a firm that conducts factory audits for Tommy Hilfiger, Levi Strauss and other U.S. companies.

Khadija Akhter can attest to that. For about $21 a month, nearly three times what a maid or cook would make, the 22-year-old worked in a Dhaka factory, performing final checks on men's shirts and trousers.

Employees, she said, often worked from 8 a.m. to 3 a.m. for 10 to 15 days at a stretch to fill big orders from Wal-Mart. Exhausted, she quit after a year and took a lower-paying but less grueling job.

All the speeding up by Bangladeshi factories may not be enough to satisfy Wal-Mart.

A. Hasnat, Wal-Mart's general manager in Bangladesh, said the country's factories need to become more efficient still. From his vantage, many are poorly managed, have outdated equipment and run too slowly.

70   "I think they need to improve," he said. "When I entered a factory in China, it seemed they are very fast."

3,000 Factories in China

Eyes down, hunched forward, 20-year-old Ping Qiuxia steered a pair of green women's briefs through a sewing machine. Then her fingers whipped the briefs 180 degrees and moved them back toward her, this time with elastic bands stitched neatly around the edges. Within seconds, she was at work on the next pair.

The garment was part of a 6,000-piece order scheduled for shipment to Wal-Mart stores in Germany. For nine hours a day, sometimes six days a week, Ping and other employees of the Gladpeer Garment Factory in the southern Chinese city of Dongguan churn out undergarments, sleepwear and children's clothing.

In southern China, Wal-Mart has found all the ingredients it needs to keep its "every day low prices" among the lowest in the world.

Although labor costs more here than it does in Bangladesh, China offers other advantages: low-cost raw materials; modern factories, highways and ports; and helpful government officials.

75   Wal-Mart has been instrumental in making this corner of China the world's fastest-growing manufacturing zone. Last year, the company shipped $12 billion in products out of China, 20% more than in 2001.

The marriage between the world's largest and most efficient retailer and China's low-cost factories is setting a new global "cost standard" for manufactured products, according to consulting firm Deloitte Touche Tohmatsu.

The phenomenon is rattling competitors worldwide and worrying international labor activists. They cite the Chinese government's hostility toward organized labor and its lack of worker protections.

"Wal-Mart has really been at the forefront in driving down wages and working conditions," said Kent Wong, director of the UCLA Labor Center, who has made two trips to China in the last year. "They're not only exporting the Wal-Mart name and the corporation and the identity. They're also exporting that way of doing business."

Wal-Mart has more than 3,000 supplier factories in China, and the number is expected to rise. But that doesn't mean workers in China are secure.

80   Gladpeer used to make clothes in Hong Kong. It moved production to China in the 1980s because costs were much lower, said Simon Lee, a managing director of the family-owned firm.

Gladpeer's 1,200 workers—mostly young women—are paid about $55 a month and live in clean but cramped dormitories, eight to a room.

But Lee is likely to reduce his employment in Dongguan soon. He is planning to open a new factory in Guangxi province, a remote region of western China where labor, electricity, housing and taxes are cheaper. "Competition is intense, and our biggest single issue is cost," Lee said. "Many customers look at cost first, then they look at the workmanship. That's why we're going to Guangxi."

LEWIS HINE

Lewis Hine (1874–1940) began taking photographs while a teacher at the University of Chicago. His first serious project involved photographing immigrants at Ellis Island, a project that helped him develop his skills for capturing the power and dignity of human struggle in difficult situations. He brought this skill to his subsequent work documenting labor practices in America, emphasizing the prevalence of child labor and the perseverance of workers in demanding occupations. Italian Track-walker on Pennsylvania Railroad *was photographed in 1930.*

Italian Track-walker on Pennsylvania Railroad

FIGURE 14.7 Hine's *Italian Track-walker on Pennsylvania Railroad*

INQUIRING FURTHER

1. What responsibility do you think employers have to provide living wages to employees? What other benefits do you believe employers should provide? Who is responsible for ensuring that individuals who work have benefits and earn a living wage?

2. What are your thoughts on the relationship between first world economies and third world countries? What responsibilities do you think consumers have

for the conditions under which goods they purchase are produced? Hold a class discussion concerning "The Wal-Mart Effect."

3. Examine *Italian Track-walker* in terms of the themes raised by "The Wal-Mart Effect." Do you see the same issues raised in the photograph? What details do you find most striking in the image? Freewrite for five minutes about the relationship between the article and the image.

MARGE PIERCY

Poet, novelist, and essayist Marge Piercy (born in 1936) grew up in a working class neighborhood in Detroit. During the 1960s, she became deeply involved in the antiwar movement as well as in Marxist political movements, writing poetry as her engagement with social issues increased. Eventually, Piercy turned toward feminism as well, where she focused much of her energy. Piercy is currently the poetry editor of Tikkun, *a bimonthly magazine that critiques politics, culture, and society from the Jewish perspective. "The Market Place" and "To Be of Use" are from her 1982 collection,* Circles on the Water.

The Market Economy

Suppose some peddler offered
you can have a color TV
but your baby will be
born with a crooked spine;
5   you can have polyvinyl cups
and wash and wear
suits but it will cost
you your left lung
rotted with cancer; suppose
10   somebody offered you
a frozen precooked dinner
every night for ten years
but at the end
your colon dies
15   and then you do,
slowly and with much pain.
You get a house in the suburbs
but you work in a new plastics
factory and die at fifty-one
20   when your kidneys turn off.

But where else will you
Work? where else can
you rent but Smog City?
The only houses for sale
25   are under the yellow sky.
You've been out of work for

a year and they're hiring
at the plastics factory.
Don't read the fine
30   print, there isn't any.

To Be of Use

The people I love the best
jump into work head first
without dallying in the shallows
and swim off with sure strokes almost out of sight.
5   They seem to become natives of that element,
the black sleek heads of seals
bouncing like half-submerged balls.

I love people who harness themselves, an ox to a heavy cart,
who pull like water buffalo, with massive patience,
10   who strain in the mud and the muck to move things forward,
who do what has to be done, again and again.

I want to be with people who submerge
in the task, who go into the fields to harvest
and work in a row and pass the bags along,
15   who are not parlor generals and field deserters
but move in common rhythm
when the food must come in or the fire be put out.

The work of the world is common as mud,
Botched, it smears the hands, crumbles to dust.
20   But the thing worth doing well done
has a shape that satisfies, clean and evident.
Greek amphoras for wine or oil,
Hopi vases that held corn, are put in museums
but you know they were made to be used.
25   The pitcher cries for water to carry
and a person for work that is real.

INQUIRING FURTHER

1. How does the choice of words, the diction, of "The Market Economy" relate to its message? How would you describe the tone of the speaker and what comments can you make about the language and tone?

2. How would you compare the messages conveyed in the first and second stanzas of "The Market Economy"? Does the second stanza offer a way of interpreting the first?

3. Would you say "to Be of Use" says more about work or about people? Could you develop a reading that addresses both work and people? What passages would you cite to explain your position?

15

Self and Society

The Soul selects her own Society—
Then—shuts the door—
To her divine Majority—
Present no more—

Unmoved—she notes the Chariots—pausing
At her low Gate—
Unmoved—an Emperor be kneeling
Upon her Mat—

I've known her—from an ample nation—
Choose One—
Then—close the Valves of her attention—
Like stone—

—Emily Dickinson

We have all at one time or another looked over our acquaintances and then decided to "choose one," selecting an individual to relate with on a close, personal level. We have also felt the need at times to ignore the world around us, to shut out the concerns of others and shelter behind closed doors with our closest friends or by ourselves. Emily Dickinson expresses these desires clearly in her poem above.

In daily life, however, our relationships and our sense of self are more complicated than the picture we find in Dickinson's poem. Whether we like it or not, society gives meaning to our lives. We cannot always seek comfort behind closed doors. Similarly, our sense of self is always complex, shaped by our physical traits, by the perceptions of others, and even by societal forces like organized religion or the media. In practice, we regularly interact with others and sometimes struggle to maintain our relationships and define our identity.

In this chapter, we explore the relationship between our selves and society. We begin by looking at some of the psychological dimensions of identity, considering how we often struggle to maintain a healthy sense of self. The chapter also examines how activities like work and play help define who we are. Later sections take up how our identities are shaped by the people and culture that surrounds us. Sections near the end of the chapter explore how conceptions of ethnicity and gender shape our definitions of self.

BODIES AND MINDS

We may associate our identity with labels and connections outside our selves—we may say I am a brother, a son, a screen name, and so on. However, at some level, we view all of these connections from the position of our own psyche. Further, we must consider the ways that our mental makeup may be connected with the physical functions of our minds. The selections below explore the relationship between our bodies and minds. The selections also consider how these connections influence our emotions and actions. We begin with a short story and an article related to the use of antidepressants.

GARY KRIST

Gary Krist is the author of numerous short stories and three novels. He also reviews books and writes editorials for the New York Times. *Krist often includes drugs as a thematic element in his works, but also emphasizes realistic characters rendered with depth. "Medicated" is taken from the collection* Bone by Bone, *published in 1994.*

Medicated

1.

He told me that he wanted to visit Houdini's grave.

He told me that small animals seemed attracted to him, and that this was causing problems on the job.

He told me that he was the owner of a hairbrush that had once belonged to Walt Disney.

He told me that I was the only woman whose knee he had ever touched with his tongue.

5   It seemed he had been talking continuously since Day One. We met at the Inverness Public Garden, where Jon worked as a landscaper, rotating the annuals, snapping the dead buds off roses, raking long, elegant strands of algae from the decorative ponds.

6   This was spring. I was taking one of my famous days off, one of those days when the thought of spoon-feeding Manifest Destiny to a roomful of ninth-graders was enough to make me break into a cold sweat.

7   Iceland poppies were in bloom. Forget-me-nots. Those cloying, throat-catching white hyacinths.

8   He approached me from behind in the Blaise Memorial Gazebo. "What do you know about watches?" he asked.

9   I turned, surprised by the voice so close to my ear. The person attached to it was young, sharp-featured, deep-eyed. He wore teal overalls with the word JON stitched into the breast pocket in orange thread. A long reddish-black ponytail emerged from the back of his cap like—well, like the tail of a pony.

10   Jon the gardener. I recognized him. I'd seen him on previous visits, wandering distractedly among the phlox and lupines. There was something about his manner, the nervous preoccupation, that interested me.

"Watches?" I asked.

"Digital. Quartz movement. Liquid-crystal display. The world of watches."

He sat down on the bench beside me and held up a smooth-muscled arm. Strapped to his wrist was one of those cheap plastic digitals that come with magazine subscriptions. It was flashing the wrong time, on and off, on and off, on and off.

"My brother gave it to me."

15   I gave him my best defensive smile. "I'm sorry, but I don't know anything about watches."

"That's all right," he said. "I'll just read the directions."

He paused, sighed once deeply, and turned to gaze out at the duck pond. The mallards were parading in front of us, making flat little snickering sounds like old men telling racy stories to themselves.

Then: "Have you seen what the deer have done to the tulip display?"

Two things flashed through my mind. One of them: Don't go anywhere with this man. The other: Go anywhere with this man.

20   He asked again: "Have you seen what they've done?"

I hadn't. That was the truth. "Is it very bad?" I asked finally.

It was. I could see that it upset him. And so I went with the man. We walked over, Jon and I, to have a look at the carnage.

2.

There were gifts. Jon was always presenting things, little hopeful tokens. It began that first afternoon, at the tulip display. I watched as he hopped around the trampled beds, pointing out toothmarked leaves, decapitated stems. He wore thick rubber boots that probably did as much damage to the flowers as the deer had. "Here," he said, handing me the severed head of a purple tulip. It was compact and smooth, streaked with white, like an Easter egg.

After that, over the next weeks, Jon gave me:

a Chinese coin;

a chestnut, burnished to a warm shine;

a pewter paperweight in the shape of a Japanese beetle;

a children's calendar from the makers of Jell-O brand pudding;

a pair of slipper-socks, slightly used;

two snapdragons;

a homemade cassette tape featuring himself playing Christmas carols on the flu-tophone;

a tailfeather from a mallard duck;

a postcard depicting the Blaise Memorial Gazebo with the words "A Place Near to Both Our Hearts" printed on the back;

another Chinese coin;

a cough drop.

25   What I gave Jon:

an extra pair of shoelaces;

a copy of Howard Belkin's Essential Guide for Home Video Rentals;

my word that I would not throw out anything he had given me.

One can impersonate a citadel for only so long.

3.

I had a husband who died when I was twenty-four years old. We were in graduate school together at Penn, I in Early American History, he in Classics. We married on a midterm break—foolishly, of course, since we had no money and no reason, really, to make our union legal. A justice of the peace performed the ceremony in his hideous green ranch house in Vermont, where I and my husband-to-be had driven on a whim to see the leaves changing. We were too early—most of the leaves hadn't even begun to blush pink at their centers— so we got married instead.

My husband had a nest of fine blond hair and a spray of birthmarks over his shoulders and back. He had a boyish smile and a very bad temper. He wore wire-rimmed glasses, one arm of which he scotch-taped to the rest of the frame.

One night, four months into our marriage, he went out to the Wawa Market for a bag of pretzels and was shot in the head by a jumpy crack-addict whose robbery seemed not to be going as smoothly as he would have liked. My husband was dead before anyone could call 911.

In an earlier century, of course, I would have known what to do. I would have returned to my father's house, to salve my grief with hard work and the care of younger siblings, playing the part of the stoic aunt who has known tragedy too soon. But this was impossible. My father had disappeared soon after my seventh birthday. My mother had since devoted her life and what was left of her emotions to another man, the little knock-kneed bagpiper on the bottle of Beefeater Gin. I had no choice but to put myself in the hands of the doctors.

30   Some of them, I should mention in the interest of fairness, were very kind.

But I don't deceive myself; it was the little green-and-white capsules that brought me back. That, and several years of distance. Pills and time.

Which is all to say that I did not go into this blindly. I knew what it was like to owe my soul to Pfizer Chemical. I knew what it was like to check the time whenever I felt the heaviness descending (4:30 every afternoon, like clock-work). I knew, in other words, what I was getting myself into with Jon.

4.

He wouldn't open his eyes the first time we made love. He said that my bare shoulders reminded him of something, but he couldn't remember what. I decid-ed to take that as a compliment. I hadn't gotten too many of those over the years.

This was summer now. School was out, my only teaching obligation a sum-mer-school class in American history, meeting three mornings a week. "Amer-ica," I would tell my students, "is about the replacement of kings by money, of oppression by abandonment, of poverty by emptiness." They would actually write this in their notebooks. A few—God love them—would even adore me for it.

35   Summer. It was all right. I was all right. I was a resident of this little New York town complete with firehouse and aluminum-sided diner and old school building that smelled comfortingly of marijuana and library paste. I was an active member of three organizations: the teacher's union, the local library asso-ciation, and Women Against Illegal Dumping (WAID). And I had two friends: Amy, the calculus teacher at school, and Mr. Donnapolis, my pharmacist.

And Jon. A third friend, now in my bed. He had let his hair down, so that it fell around his shoulders in damp curls. He looked like a figure from one of those brightly colored Bible illustrations—an unnamed shepherd, perhaps, or one of those dreamy olive sellers whose faces shine with the knowledge of routine miracles.

(Except for the watch. The watch was still strapped to his wrist, still blinking on and off, on and off, on and off. He hadn't read the directions yet.)

My mother would not approve, I told myself silently.

Afterward, he opened his eyes. "You won't hurt me in any of this, I hope," he said.

40   "Hurt you?" I'm sorry, but imagine someone looking at St. Sebastian and pleading: Don't shoot, please don't shoot. "No," I told him. "I'll try not to hurt you."

This seemed to confirm something in his mind. He closed his eyes again. He licked his lips and used them to kiss my navel.

5.

We went swimming together at a pond near the private boys' school. Jon wore cutoff jeans the color of rusted metal. His thighs were long—long, hairless, and smooth.

"Jon," I asked him, rubbing sunscreen onto the curves of his shoulders, "let me see the pills you're taking."

I felt his muscles rumple under my fingers. He pulled away from me and lay down on the bedspread we had set out on the grass. "You can't take them, you know. They're not that kind of pill. They won't do anything interesting."

45   I flinched at the misunderstanding. "No," I said quickly. "I just want to see them, see what they look like."

He stared up at a scrap of cloud that was inching along the tops of the maples. He reached for his sunglasses and put them up on the top of his head.

"Don't even tell me what they are," I said. "I don't want to know. I just want to see them. Please."

He relented. Sighing, he pulled the bottle from his knap-sack. The tablets were pink, with an odd dumbell-shaped hole in the center. He held them out to me in his palm. I worried them back and forth with an index finger. I had no idea what they were.

"And now," he said, watching me with a sly little smile, "you have to show me yours."

50   I looked at him sidelong, but of course I should have known that he knew. The brotherhood of the scarlet letter. M, this time, for medicated.

I hemmed a bit. But what's fair is fair. "Sure," I said finally. I opened my canvas bag and fished out my little Sucrets tin.

"Prozac," he announced, identifying the pills immediately.

"You've taken them?"

He chuckled. Then he frowned. "I've taken everything," he said.

6.

55   Jon's scent was of garlic and bell peppers whenever he worked out in my garden apartment. Sometimes I'd sit in the black armchair and watch him, his body soaked with the cold white light of my glowing Esso sign as he eked out a set of twenty push-ups. He was so slender, so sinewy. His body was like a mast, a floorbeam, something a person could cling to until the lifeboats reached her.

I introduced him to Amy (Mr. Donnapolis, the pharmacist, he already knew). The three of us got together at the diner in town for lunch one Saturday. Jon brought us gifts—three crocus bulbs each. He made us promise not to plant them until the recommended time in the fall.

Amy was cautious at first. I'd told her about Jon, and what I'd told her worried her. Amy knew all about what she called "unstable" men. She'd been married to a few.

"I've seen you before," Jon said to her after we ordered. "At the A&P. You asked me if I knew where the hell they kept the endive in that place."

Amy was surprised. "That was you?"

60   "You must have thought I worked there. I was wearing my garden overalls."

"That *was* you."

Jon turned to me. "I told her that the A&P didn't carry endive, that she should try the Shop-Rite."

"I was amazed," Amy said. "I thought it was just like Kriss Kringle in that old Christmas movie, where the Macy's Santa sends people over to Gimbel's."

"Miracle on 34th Street," he told her.

65   "Exactly."

I started breathing a little easier. Amy, I knew, would be well disposed to someone who knew where to buy endive.

I was right. "He's earnest," she said to me later that afternoon, after Jon returned to work. "Earnest and sexy and somehow innocent-seeming—not a combination you find very often. Just be careful, all right?"

I promised her I would be careful.

The summer turned hot. Jon cooked for me almost every weekend—at my place, which was air-conditioned. He had a heavy hand with ground cloves, and would throw a dash into the most unlikely dishes—tomato sauce, hamburgers, anything that struck him as too bland. Sometimes he'd bring me handfuls of gladiolas, irises, or even freesia from the Inverness greenhouses, and their smells would mingle with the cloves. I liked the effect. It made me think of us as refugees from an obscure spice island, reconstructing in this foreign town a tiny oasis of home.

70   Yes, there were episodes. Or whatever the medical term. There were days when Jon would mope, cry, eat doughnuts by the dozen. I learned to associate doughnuts with frustration—my own sense of helplessness when I found him that way, hunched over the white Entenmann's carton in the glow of my back porch light. One learned not to try to bring him out of such episodes. One learned to avoid the cloaked eyes, the whispered awfulnesses. The words he called one were like cornered animals—small, brutal things, capable of great hurt.

But it would pass. Balance would be restored.

I can *help* him, I told myself. And he can help me.

One evening, we lay naked on the floor in the dark, letting the warm breeze from the bedroom window sweep the smell of night over our bodies. Jon slid between my legs and rested his head on my belly, his hands raised to cup my breasts. He fell asleep that way. And I, after an hour, after two hours, watching the sheer curtains billow in and out like someone's indecisive ghost—I fell asleep too.

7.

A few weeks after starting on my first antidepressants, they began to work so well—lifting the gloom like a dentist's X-ray vest off my shoulders—that I almost felt depressed all over again. How could this be, I asked myself. Was my despair such a trivial thing that a few well-chosen chemicals could dispel it? Apparently my doctors thought so. I was cured, they said eventually, though not in so many words. And I suppose I believed them. I would occasionally miss one of my therapy sessions with Dr. Hagler, but I always made sure to keep the bottle of Prozac full to the brim.

75 One morning, about two years after my husband's death, I entered the Wawa Market—the very same one. I purchased a loaf of white bread and a quart of milk and a Kit-Kat bar. Then I left. I had breathed normally the whole time.

The next fall, I went back to school. I took up my old subject, everyday life in the Puritan era, with a special interest in the Salem witch trials. When I earned enough credits for my master's, I was done. My mother even managed to stumble her way to the commencement exercises—eyeliner smudged, silk dress askew, but there. She had found just the right dosage of Beefeater to get her through the event.

The miracles of modern science.

8.

We were fine until the evening of July 4th. Jon and I went to the fireworks at the high-school ballfield. We sat side by side on the blanket, drinking identical plastic glasses of lemonade. I kept scanning the crowds for Amy, who had promised to meet us there. Jon, I noticed, couldn't seem to keep still. His foot waggled continuously, like a fish on a hook.

"Jon," I said, "are you warm enough?"

80 "Fire works," he answered, not looking at me. He was twisting a hank of his long hair around an index finger. "It's a pun. Fire works. Kaleidoscope. This is really interesting."

A couple of eyes from other blankets strayed in our direction.

I moved closer to him and put a hand on his foot, stopping it. "Should we go home now, you think?"

One of my summer-school kids walked by then, one of my smarter, more conscientious kids. "Hey, Ms. Downey. Happy anniversary of the Declaration of Independence."

A clever line. I gave him an approving smile. "The same to you, Kevin."

85 Jon's head swiveled in my direction. His eyes seemed intense, but at the same time distant. "Happy anniversary of what?" he asked loudly.

"Just some history department humor," I told him. "One of my students."

"Is that what this is all about? Is that all? Shit!" He lay back and grasped his head. "Shit, shit, shit," he kept muttering, rocking back and forth.

The bombs bursting in air . . .

He was in the hospital two days later. The doctors had called his brother Larry in Connecticut, who then called me with the news. Jon had stopped taking his pills, Larry told me. Nobody knew why.

90 We met at the hospital. We had heard about each other, of course. Larry was the close brother. The far brother, Mike, lived in San Diego. The parents were dead.

Larry looked a lot like Jon, I thought as I shook his hand, except for the hair, which was short. And the eyes, which carried a weariness which told me that this was not the first time he was meeting his brother's new friend in the waiting room of a strange hospital.

"There's supposed to be a system for this," Larry said, leading me to the check-in desk. "There's supposed to be a system for making sure he takes his pills."

I knew that system. You have your regular appointments with the doctors. If you show up, they ask you if you're taking your pills. If you don't show up, they call you. If you don't answer the phone, they wait for the next appointment. That's the system.

Larry and I went upstairs. Jon seemed sedated, foggy. He managed a smile from the depths of the bed. "Sarah," he whispered.

95   "There," Larry said loudly, stepping toward him. "I brought her. Happy now?"

"Happy."

Larry began rearranging the pillows behind Jon's neck. Now that I saw them together, the resemblance was remarkable. Jon looked like an older, gaunter, more ravaged version of his brother, as if they were two formerly-identical lab mice, one of which had been injected with massive doses of caffeine over a long period of time.

"I won't be in here long, not long at all," Jon assured me while Larry fooled with his pillows.

"This is the second time in a year. Last time they found him running barefoot through the garage at the Milbrook DPW."

100   Jon looked at me. "Things—shitshitshit. OK. I mean, things don't always work the way they're supposed to."

"An obvious point," his brother added, punching pillows.

Afterward, Larry and I had coffee at the hospital canteen. I sat across from him in one of the red vinyl booths by the window. "OK, tell me everything," I said to him. "Tell me everything I need to know."

9.

There is a scholar at the University of Michigan who believes that the witches of Salem were actually mentally ill— schizophrenics, manic-depressives, sufferers of extreme psychological trauma. The witch trials of 1692, he argues, were the Puritans' way of neutralizing the threat presented by these people to an orderly religious community. Those accused often obliged by behaving in ways that supported the prosecution's contention of supernatural influence.

I tell my students about this theory every year, during my notorious lecture on Cotton Mather. I usually see one or two of them shaking their heads in disbelief. The idea is too farfetched for them. Such a lack of sympathy on the part of our forebears is unimaginable. Even three hundred years ago, they think, people couldn't have been *that* cruel.

105   Jon got out in time for my birthday. His doctor had given him a new prescription. He had lost eight pounds in the hospital.

"I'm looking for a new job," he told me as I drove him to the Red Lobster in Wappingers Falls, where we would celebrate with a king crab platter and clam stew.

I looked at him. "Why a new job?"

"They gave away my place at the garden. They said they needed somebody reliable."

I stopped the car. "You were sick," I said, the outrage seething in me. "They can't do that. It's illegal. Isn't it?"

110   "They gave it away before I got sick. I forgot to tell you."

My Nissan was clicking in the heat. The air wobbled over the hood in the late sunlight.

"I guess I missed some days," he went on, not looking at me, looking out the window. "The squirrels were really bothering me for a while there. So I didn't go in. I never really told you about that."

I didn't answer for a moment or two. How could I be angry with him? Who was I, after all, to scold someone who had stayed home from work for reasons that others would regard as nebulous? "So what will you do?" I asked.

"I've applied for other jobs. I've applied to be a health inspector in Poughkeepsie."

115   "But you're not qualified, are you?"

"People find it hard to lie to me," he said, bracing his hand against the dashboard. "What more qualification can you need?"

10.

Jon was unemployed for six weeks. He all but ran out of money by the end of July. There was some kind of stipend from his father's life insurance, but he could only get so much per month. Some arrangement the brothers had set up. Jon's tiny apartment (which I had seen only twice) was fortunately under Larry's name; somebody, probably Larry, paid the rent.

During the last weeks of July, Jon ate nothing but bagels and macaroni-and-cheese. And zucchini squash, which he stole from a garden on my street and cooked with butter and nutmeg and, of course, ground cloves.

"Let me lend you something," I told him in bed one night. I tried to spend as many nights as I could with him—to feed him, to make sure he was taking his pills. I was the new system, I guess.

120   "I don't need anything. I can live on almost nothing." Jon was running his thumb down the curved line of my jaw. It felt eerily satisfying, as if I were being sculpted.

"You can't live on nothing," I told him.

He pulled his thigh up over my belly. "I can," he whispered to me. "I can do anything in this world. Just wait."

We would watch cheerful movies on my VCR—*Miracle at Morgan's Creek, Splash, His Girl Friday.* Amy would come over sometimes and watch with us. She would tell us which of the characters behaved exactly like one of her ex-husbands. The night we watched Peter Pan, she had a field day.

One evening, Jon told Amy that she looked just like Julie Christie in the remake of *Heaven Can Wait.* I thought she might not like that, but she did. She knew it wasn't a line, I suppose—coming from Jon.

125   One night, I took his watch off the night table as he slept. I carried it into the kitchen, and there, under the amber light of the range hood, I fooled with its buttons until I had the time exactly right.

11.

He got a job at McDonald's in mid-August. He was a morning chef, specializing in fries. He would come to my door in his little paper hat, the long hair bound up in a net. "Is Sydney really not the capital of Australia?" he'd ask. Or else: "Is it true that there are no midgets anymore? Ella the cashier told me they've got this growth hormone now."

We would spend the long twilight in bed. His arms were covered with tiny splash burns from the hot oil. I'd kiss each one.

"The fries I make are feeding the world," he'd say, burying his face in my hair.

We swam nearly every day at the pond now, in the early afternoon. He continued to get thinner. The skin of his belly seemed concave over the waistband of his cutoffs. The wet hair squiggled down his shoulders like something in Arabic.

130   "Do you see that woman over there?" he asked me suddenly one afternoon. There were several other people swimming at the pond these days. The woman he was talking about was a mother with her twin toddler boys, a harried-looking blonde with a modest one-piece racing suit. "Do you see her?"

"Yes," I said.

"That woman is making me think about her. Do you know what that means? Do you know what that feels like?"

His foot was going again—the gasping fish.

No one answered at Larry's number. Jon said Larry had gone on vacation. To the Cayman Islands. Why did I ask?

135   "Jon," I asked him, "are you taking your pills?"

He had a wrinkle in his forehead that deepened whenever he felt affronted. "I'm taking my pills," he said flatly, his eyes revealing nothing.

I got the doctor's number. "What makes you think he's not taking his medication?" the man asked. His name was Dalton, Dr. Edward Dalton.

"He isn't acting right," I said. "I feel like he's . . . moving out there again, if you know what I mean." (My IQ has a tendency to fall fifty points whenever I talk to a member of an arrogant profession. It is something I regret but don't apologize for.)

I could hear Dr. Dalton sighing. "A man with Jon's illness cannot be expected to act right. That he can act in any way that is acceptable to you is something of a miracle."

140   I was silent, trying to think of a sentence of sufficient nastiness to answer back.

"He'll be in for his appointment on Friday," the man went on. "Let's see what he has to say for himself then, OK?"

That night, Jon threw a rock through my window.

I was awake when it happened. I saw the little shards of glass bouncing on the bedspread at my feet.

"Jon?" I whispered, pulling on sneakers. I went to the broken window. Glass crackled under my feet. He was out there, standing in the moonshadow of the rhododendrons. "Jon," I called to him. "Don't be afraid."

145   I could see his arms swinging back and forth. He was humming to himself.

I put on my bathrobe and went out to him.

As I crossed the lawn, he lay down on the damp grass—like someone resolutely going to sleep.

"Jon?" I asked as I stood over him. "Let's go to the hospital, OK, Jon?"

"Why? Are they having a party?" His face was as pale as the face of a clock. He was staring straight up at the sky.

150   "I think we should go to the hospital, Jon."

"I want to sleep. I want to sleep in the deep in my sleep. Don't ask me about the water times, cunt, I don't want to know!"

"Jon . . . "

I reached down to him, to turn his face toward me. He grabbed my wrist and pulled me down. We rolled on the grass until he was on top of me, his knees on my chest. "Don't ever touch me, goddamn it!" Something came into his eyes then that I had never seen before. My mistake was suddenly clear.

The police wanted me to press charges. It was advisable, they said, to press charges—assault and battery, at least—even if I dropped them later. Charges, they told me, would make picking him up a lot simpler.

155   I refused. Not that it made their job any more difficult. They caught Jon the next morning, at the DPW garage. There seemed to be something he liked about that place.

Larry came to see me at the hospital. Amy was there, but I didn't bother to introduce them. "Christ" was all Larry could say when he saw me. "Nothing like this ever happened before." Then: "I'm sorry."

"Where is he?" I asked.

Larry sat with his hands planted on his knees. "There's this place down in Westchester. He'll be in the locked ward, at least for a while."

"Am I allowed to visit him?"

160   He looked at me, eyebrows high. "You would want to?"

I didn't have an answer to that one. "Maybe not," I said finally, feeling Amy's eyes on me from across the room.

I went home the next day. Nuprin, the doctors had told me. Nuprin was what I needed right now.

Amy and I spent the afternoon cleaning up the glass in my bedroom. A warm breeze came in through the broken window, ruffling the edges of a paperback on my night table.

There, on my bureau, lay the chestnut, the paperweight in the shape of a Japanese beetle, the duck feather. They lay where I had left them, but they were strange objects to me now—mute, vaguely sinister. It was like the old optical illusion, the one that looks like a white goblet against a black background, until something shifts in your head and you see it as two faces, two blank silhouetted faces, staring nose to nose, and then it can't be seen as a goblet anymore. Those two awful faces are there; they've commandeered your perception; they won't go away no matter how hard you try to refocus your eyes.

165   "What are you thinking?" Amy asked, watching me. "I don't like what you're thinking. Don't you dare tell me that you plan to forget this."

12.

School started the next Monday, before the bruises had faded. I went into my first class, facing a new score of hopeful acned faces. I stood before them with my hands buried in my aching armpits. If I were one of those old Puritan sermonizers, I could speak to them as they needed to be spoken to. O children, I would say, beware this earthly world. It is not your home, for there is no shelter in it. Your time here is a time of pain and injustice and coldness. Expect nothing more.

But what I actually said to them was this: "Good morning, class. My name is Sarah Downey and our topic this year is the story of America."

1. How would you compare the narrator of "Medicated" with Jon? Do you believe Jon acts as a foil character for the narrator? What is the effect of depicting two people who are both undergoing psychological treatment in the story?

2. After relating the murder of her first husband, the narrator claims that if she had been born "in an earlier century" (542) she would not have needed the help of medication to respond to the tragedy. Write freely for five minutes about this statement.

3. The narrator closes by thinking about telling her students to expect nothing from life but "pain and injustice and coldness." She decides, instead, to tell them "the story of America" (549). What do you think she means? What may have motivated the narrator at the end? Write a paragraph explaining the narrator's decision.

DENISE GRADY AND GARDINER HARRIS

In early 2004, British health authorities warned doctors not to prescribe anti-depressant drugs to children, citing concerns that these medications are not effective for children (some research suggests that placebos or sugar pills offered as much benefit as the medications). Some studies have also suggested that these medications could increase the risk of suicide. In March, the U.S. Federal Drug Administration issued a similar warning, but did not go as far in recommending that specific medicines not be prescribed to children. In this article, Grady and Harris report on the FDA decision.

Overprescribing Prompted Warnings on Antidepressants

The government's warning on Monday that people newly taking antidepressants can become suicidal and must be closely monitored grew at least in part from a concern that the drugs were being handed out too freely and without enough follow-up, especially in children and teenagers.

Dr. Wayne K. Goodman, chairman of psychiatry at the University of Florida College of Medicine and a member of an expert panel that advised the Food and Drug Administration, said, "I think many physicians, and particularly nonpsychiatrists, have been lulled into the notion that these drugs are safe."

He emphasized that the drugs carried few serious physical side effects and a low risk of overdose. But, Dr. Goodman added, "I think what's been underestimated is this behavioral toxicity, which can indirectly lead to problems, including possibly suicidal behavior."

Yesterday many doctors acknowledged that the new warning was sound advice and yet said they worried it might discourage doctors and patients from treating depression.

5   Dr. Eva Ritvo, an associate professor of psychiatry at the University of Miami, said: "A depressed patient needs to be watched closely, particularly in the initial stages of treatment or when the dosage is raised. This is something we should be doing anyway as mental health professionals."

But, she added, "Untreated depression is dangerous and takes a huge toll on people's lives, and we can only hope this warning doesn't discourage people from seeking treatment."

Patients had mixed reactions.

Some people who suffered depression in the past but shunned medication said the new warnings reinforced their wariness.

Barry Owen, 51, a magazine consultant in San Francisco, refused antidepressants during an emotional crisis.

10 He said his doctor recommended the drugs a few years ago "because at that point I was pretty severely depressed and having panic attacks and couldn't eat and sleep." Mr. Owen added: "I decided then not to take her advice. And while I don't doubt the usefulness for a lot of people, this new information gives me one more question about them."

But patients who have done well on the drugs were not troubled by the new warnings. Paul Festa, 33, a San Francisco artist and writer, took Zoloft for about a year in 1999, and then Paxil for a year or so after the 2001 terrorist attacks. He said: "I would never hesitate to go back on these medications because I already know that I react extremely well to them. I feel like there should be a warning for people who are depressed that not taking these medications could lead to suicide. If you're depressed, you're putting yourself at risk for all sorts of self-destructive behaviors, up to and including suicide. When I was depressed, the thought of suicide was crossing my mind more than it ought to have, and the antidepressants got me out of that loop."

The advisory issued Monday by the drug agency asked manufacturers to put detailed warnings about a possible increased risk of suicidal behavior and the need for monitoring on the labels of 10 antidepressants: Prozac, Zoloft, Paxil, Wellbutrin, Luvox, Celexa, Lexapro, Effexor, Serzone and Remeron. The warning included both children and adults.

Studies in children taking the antidepressants have not found an increase in suicide. But studies of some drugs have suggested that they might increase the risk of suicidal thoughts and behaviors. Research has also failed to provide convincing evidence that the drugs are effective in children, making the potential risks even less acceptable. There is no solid data linking use of the drugs to suicide in adults.

Dr. Goodman of Florida said that panelists who met last month were troubled by reports that some doctors were giving patients samples of antidepressants and saying casually "Tell me how you do," rather than scheduling frequent follow-up appointments to make sure patients were tolerating the drugs.

15 "That is problematic," Dr. Goodman said, "and probably reflects people becoming a little lackadaisical about the downside of these medications in children."

Most antidepressants are now prescribed by primary care physicians, whose patients may never see a psychiatrist, because of concerns about cost or the perception of stigma attached to mental illness. Prozac, Paxil and other modern antidepressants became hugely popular in part because drug companies convinced family physicians that they were safe enough to use without a psychiatrist's intervention. Antidepressants are the third biggest selling category of drugs in the world behind cholesterol and heartburn pills.

Some psychiatrists speculated yesterday that their family-care colleagues might lose confidence in the drugs and become reluctant to prescribe them.

"We're hoping that doesn't happen, because primary care physicians have a major role to play in combating depression," said Dr. James H. Scully Jr., medical director of the American Psychiatric Association. "We hope they won't be scared off."

Dr. Robert Lee, a San Francisco physician of holistic medicine who sometimes prescribes antidepressants, said: "I don't think people already taking them will be concerned. But a lot of people who I think would benefit from these meds already won't take them because of various stigma reasons, so I'm a little concerned that this will raise that barrier even higher."

20   Dr. Lee said the new warning would not make him hesitate to prescribe the antidepressants.

He said, "People can get agitated from them, but I've never seen somebody get suicidal from them."

Dr. Joseph Gonzalez-Heydrich, chief of psychopharmacology at Children's Hospital Boston, said: "I've heard anecdotally that a lot of antidepressants were being prescribed by pediatricians without a lot of training or experience. I think the warning is appropriate. If it makes prescribers more vigilant or parents more vigilant, that's a good thing."

Dr. Gonzalez-Heydrich said that a sizable minority of children became more agitated and irritable on the antidepressants in question. "If we see it, we take them off it or reduce the dose," he said. "Doing it that way there are a lot of kids we feel do benefit from these medications, especially long term. But they're not for everybody."

Dr. Harold Koplewicz, director of New York University's Child Study Center, said, "The fear I have about this warning is that many teenagers will not get the medicine because it will build resistance among their parents, and that's really a tragic outcome." He noted that suicide rates in teenagers had gone down in the United States and Sweden as use of the drugs increased.

25   Several primary care doctors said that they had prescribed antidepressants with success for so many years that it was unlikely the FDA's new warnings would lead them to stop. Still, the warnings have given them pause, they said. They may think a bit harder before prescribing them to patients who are simply stressed, they said. And they will watch how the warnings play in the legal field, some said.

"We're going to continue to use these drugs pretty freely until we start seeing the ads in the newspapers from lawyers saying, 'Have you or your family member been prescribed these drugs? If so, you may have a case,'" said Dr. Phillip Kennedy, a family practice physician in Augusta, Ga. "When the big L word, liability, raises its ugly head, that's when things will really change."

Spokesmen for drug companies said that they would emphasize to physicians that the FDA's warning did not conclude that antidepressants cause suicide. "My hope is that people won't make a link with the drugs," said Jennifer Yoder, a spokeswoman for Eli Lilly & Company, maker of Prozac. "I think the message will be that suicide is an inherent part of the disease of depression, and physicians should carefully monitor their patients."

Critics of the medicines said the FDA's warning was long overdue.

"These warnings are not as strong as I would like, but they're an important first step," said Tom Woodward of North Wales, Pa. Mr. Woodward's teenage daughter, Julie, hanged herself six days after starting therapy with Zoloft.

INQUIRING FURTHER

1. Is it fair to say that antidepressants tell us as much about culture as about the state of medicine?

2. The advertisement in Figure 15.1 represents two states of mind using simple images. What message is conveyed by these images and by the advertisement?

FIGURE 15.1   Prozac Advertisement

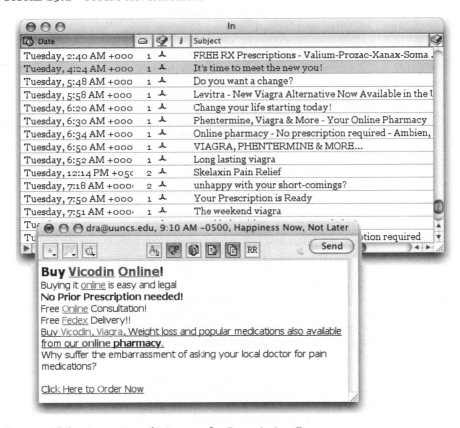

FIGURE 15.2   Spam E-mail Message for Prescription Drugs

3. Write an essay in which you explore the use of antidepressants to treat depression and mental illness. Consider relevant studies and the cultural dimensions of antidepressants. Conduct research, and then compose a four- or more-page paper exploring antidepressants in terms of identity and society. (For more on research, see Chapter 4.)

ETHERIDGE KNIGHT

Etheridge Knight (1931–1991) served eight years in Indiana State Prison where he began writing poetry. His first book of poems, Poems from Prison, *was published just prior to his release in 1968. Knight went on to publish four more books of poetry emphasizing concerns of race and poverty. "Hard Rock Returns to Prison from the Hospital for the Criminally Insane" is taken from* Poems from Prison.

Hard Rock Returns to Prison from the Hospital for the Criminally Insane

Hard Rock was "known not to take no shit
From nobody," and he had the scars to prove it:
Split purple lips, lumped ears, welts above
His yellow eyes, and one long scar that cut
5   Across his temple and plowed through a thick
Canopy of kinky hair.

The WORD was that Hard Rock wasn't a mean nigger
Anymore, that the doctors had bored a hole in his head,
Cut out part of his brain, and shot electricity
10   Through the rest. When they brought Hard Rock back,
Handcuffed and chained, he was turned loose,
Like a freshly gelded stallion, to try his new status.
And we all waited and watched, like indians at a corral,
To see if the WORD was true.

15   As we waited we wrapped ourselves in the cloak
Of his exploits: "Man, the last time, it took eight
Screws to put him in the Hole." "Yeah, remember when he
Smacked the captain with his dinner tray?" "He set
The record for time in the Hole—67 straight days!"
20   "Ol Hard Rock! man, that's one crazy nigger."
And then the jewel of a myth that Hard Rock had once bit
A screw on the thumb and poisoned him with syphilitic spit.
The testing came, to see if Hard Rock was really tame.
A hillbilly called him a black son of a bitch

25   And didn't lose his teeth, a screw who knew Hard Rock
From before shook him down and barked in his face.
And Hard Rock did *nothing*. Just grinned and looked silly,
His eyes empty like knot holes in a fence.
And even after we discovered that it took Hard Rock
30   Exactly 3 minutes to tell you his first name,

We told ourselves that he had just wised up,
Was being cool; but we could not fool ourselves for long,
And we turned away, our eyes on the ground. Crushed.
He had been our Destroyer, the doer of things
35   We dreamed of doing but could not bring ourselves to do,
The fears of years, like a biting whip,
Had cut grooves too deeply across our backs.

INQUIRING FURTHER

1. Would it be fair to say that Hard Rock is identified with his physical traits? Why or why not?

2. What is the relationship between Hard Rock and the speaker of the poem? How does the speaker define his identity in terms of Hard Rock's exploits?

3. Do you believe Knight's poem speaks more directly to issues of the justice system or issues of identity? Would you argue that it speaks to both? Write a paragraph explaining your position.

T. S. ELIOT

Thomas Stearns Eliot (1888–1965) represents one of the most intellectual literary figures of the twentieth century. He earned his Bachelor's degree in three years, and took a masters degree in his fourth year at Harvard. He studied at the Sorbonne in Paris, and then received a PhD in philosophy from Harvard in 1914. Eliot wrote influential literary criticism in which he stressed the importance of understanding art in terms of the traditions it refines. His poems are often associated with Modernism, a literary movement marked by disillusion with the mechanical and impersonal nature of modern society. "The Love Song of J. Alfred Prufrock" represents Eliot's first major poem; Eliot wrote the poem in 1911, while in Paris. Prufrock encapsulates many of the questions of identity and meaning associated with Modernism. The poem also demonstrates Eliot's tendency to refer to established literary works and themes.

The Love Song of J. Alfred Prufrock

S'io credesse che mia risposta fosse
A persona che mai tornasse al mondo,
Questa fiamma staria senza piu scosse.
Ma perciocche giammai di questo fondo
Non torno vivo alcun, s'i'odo il vero,
Senza tema d'infamia ti rispondo.[1]

Let us go then, you and I,
When the evening is spread out against the sky

---

[1]**Epigraph**: From Dante's *Inferno*, spoken by a poet suffering in hell: "If I thought my answer were to someone who would return to earth, this flame would cease. But since no spirit has ever returned—if what I have heard is true—I answer you without fear of infamy."

Like a patient etherized upon a table;
Let us go, through certain half-deserted streets,
5   The muttering retreats
Of restless nights in one-night cheap hotels
And sawdust restaurants with oyster-shells:
Streets that follow like a tedious argument
Of insidious intent
10   To lead you to an overwhelming question . . .
Oh, do not ask, "What is it?"
Let us go and make our visit.

In the room the women come and go
Talking of Michelangelo.

15   The yellow fog that rubs its back upon the window-panes,
The yellow smoke that rubs its muzzle on the window-panes,
Licked its tongue into the corners of the evening,
Lingered upon the pools that stand in drains,
Let fall upon its back the soot that falls from chimneys,
20   Slipped by the terrace, made a sudden leap,
And seeing that it was a soft October night,
Curled once about the house, and fell asleep.

And indeed there will be time
For the yellow smoke that slides along the street,
25   Rubbing its back upon the window-panes;
There will be time, there will be time
To prepare a face to meet the faces that you meet;
There will be time to murder and create,
And time for all the works and days of hands
30   That lift and drop a question on your plate;
Time for you and time for me,
And time yet for a hundred indecisions,
And for a hundred visions and revisions,
Before the taking of a toast and tea.

35   In the room the women come and go
Talking of Michelangelo.

And indeed there will be time
To wonder, "Do I dare?" and, "Do I dare?"
Time to turn back and descend the stair,
40   With a bald spot in the middle of my hair—
(They will say: "How his hair is growing thin!")
My morning coat, my collar mounting firmly to the chin,
My necktie rich and modest, but asserted by a simple pin—
(They will say: "But how his arms and legs are thin!")
45   Do I dare
Disturb the universe?
In a minute there is time
For decisions and revisions which a minute will reverse.

For I have known them all already, known them all:
50   Have known the evenings, mornings, afternoons,

I have measured out my life with coffee spoons;
I know the voices dying with a dying fall
Beneath the music from a farther room.
So how should I presume?

55   And I have known the eyes already, known them all—
The eyes that fix you in a formulated phrase,
And when I am formulated, sprawling on a pin,
When I am pinned and wriggling on the wall,
Then how should I begin

60   To spit out all the butt-ends of my days and ways?
And how should I presume?

And I have known the arms already, known them all—
Arms that are braceleted and white and bare
(But in the lamplight, downed with light brown hair!)

65   Is it perfume from a dress
That makes me so digress?
Arms that lie along a table, or wrap about a shawl.
And should I then presume?
And how should I begin?

70   Shall I say, I have gone at dusk through narrow streets
And watched the smoke that rises from the pipes
Of lonely men in shirt-sleeves, leaning out of windows? . . .

I should have been a pair of ragged claws
Scuttling across the floors of silent seas.

75   And the afternoon, the evening, sleeps so peacefully!
Smoothed by long fingers,
Asleep . . . tired . . . or it malingers,
Stretched on the floor, here beside you and me.
Should I, after tea and cakes and ices,

80   Have the strength to force the moment to its crisis?
But though I have wept and fasted, wept and prayed,
Though I have seen my head (grown slightly bald) brought in upon a
      platter,[2]
I am no prophet—and here's no great matter;
I have seen the moment of my greatness flicker,

85   And I have seen the eternal Footman hold my coat, and snicker,
And in short, I was afraid.

And would it have been worth it, after all,
After the cups, the marmalade, the tea,
Among the porcelain, among some talk of you and me,

90   Would it have been worth while,
To have bitten off the matter with a smile,
To have squeezed the universe into a ball[3]
To roll it toward some overwhelming question,
To say: "I am Lazarus, come from the dead,

---

[2]**head . . . platter**: A reference to John the Baptist, as described in the book of Matthew 14: 1–12.
[3]**squeezed . . . ball**: See Marvell's "To His Coy Mistress" on page 817.

95   Come back to tell you all, I shall tell you all"—
      If one, settling a pillow by her head,
            Should say: "That is not what I meant at all;
            That is not it, at all."

      And would it have been worth it, after all,
100   Would it have been worth while,
      After the sunsets and the dooryards and the sprinkled streets,
      After the novels, after the teacups, after the skirts that trail along the floor—
      And this, and so much more?—
      It is impossible to say just what I mean!
105   But as if a magic lantern threw the nerves in patterns on a screen:
      Would it have been worth while
      If one, settling a pillow or throwing off a shawl,
      And turning toward the window, should say:
      "That is not it at all,
110   That is not what I meant, at all."

      No! I am not Prince Hamlet, nor was meant to be;
      Am an attendant lord, one that will do
      To swell a progress, start a scene or two,
      Advise the prince; no doubt, an easy tool,
115   Deferential, glad to be of use,
      Politic, cautious, and meticulous;
      Full of high sentence, but a bit obtuse;
      At times, indeed, almost ridiculous—
      Almost, at times, the Fool.

120   I grow old . . . I grow old . . .
      I shall wear the bottoms of my trousers rolled.

      Shall I part my hair behind? Do I dare to eat a peach?
      I shall wear white flannel trousers, and walk upon the beach.
      I have heard the mermaids singing, each to each.

125   I do not think that they will sing to me.

      I have seen them riding seaward on the waves
      Combing the white hair of the waves blown back
      When the wind blows the water white and black.
      We have lingered in the chambers of the sea
130   By sea-girls wreathed with seaweed red and brown
      Till human voices wake us, and we drown.

INQUIRING FURTHER

1. What is the significance of the way the poem addresses another person in
   its opening line? Is it fair to suggest that the poem is addressing the reader?
   What conclusions can you draw about the opening?

2. How would you characterize the speaker of the poem? Does the speaker seem
   sure of himself? What seem to be his main concerns? If the poem explores
   the speaker's identity, what does it say about his sense of self?

VINCENT VAN GOGH

Vincent van Gogh (1853–1890) is as well known for his life story as for his painting. Van Gogh suffered heavily from mental illness. He is said to have cut off his ear in an episode of self-mutilation. He later spent time in an asylum and eventually committed suicide.

Self Portrait

Vincent van Gogh, Dutch, 1853–1890, Self-Portrait, 1886/87, oil on artist's board mounted on cradled panel, 41 x 32.5 cm, Joseph Winterbotham Collection, 1954.326, Photograph by Greg Williams. Reproduction, The Art Institute of Chicago

---

INQUIRING FURTHER

Vincent van Gogh

1. How does van Gogh's biography influence the way we look at the painting? Should it?

2. What do you think van Gogh's portrait says about the self? Consider elements of art in the painting like texture, line, shape, lighting, value, and color. What statements might these elements make about van Gogh? Do proportion, balance, arrangement, or emphasis suggest anything about the artist? Write a one- or more-page explication of the painting in terms of identity.

TILLIE OLSEN

Tillie Olsen (born in 1912) is recognized for her feminist beliefs and her contributions to studying issues of work and labor. She left school at age fifteen during the Depression and began a period where she worked in factories and as a secretary to help support her family. She turned to writing extensively only after raising her four children. "I Stand Here Ironing" is taken from her first collection of short stories, Tell Me a Riddle, *published in 1961.*

I Stand Here Ironing

"I Stand Here Ironing"

I stand here ironing, and what you asked me moves tormented back and forth with the iron.

"I wish you would manage the time to come in and talk with me about your daughter. I'm sure you can help me understand her. She's a youngster who needs help and whom I'm deeply interested in helping."

"Who needs help." Even if I came, what good would it do? You think because I am her mother I have a key, or that in some way you could use me as a key? She has lived for nineteen years. There is all that life that has happened outside of me, beyond me.

And when is there time to remember, to sift, to weigh, to estimate, to total? I will start and there will be an interruption and I will have to gather it all together again. Or I will become engulfed with all I did or did not do, with what should have been and what cannot be helped.

5   She was a beautiful baby. The first and only one of our five that was beautiful at birth. You do not guess how new and uneasy her tenancy in her now-loveliness. You did not know her all those years she was thought homely, or see her poring over her baby pictures, making me tell her over and over how beautiful she had been—and would be, I would tell her—and was now, to the seeing eye. But the seeing eyes were few or nonexistent. Including mine.

I nursed her. They feel that's important nowadays. I nursed all the children, but with her, with all the fierce rigidity of first motherhood, I did like the books then said. Though her cries battered me to trembling and my breasts ached with swollenness, I waited till the clock decreed.

Why do I put that first? I do not even know if it matters, or if it explains anything.

She was a beautiful baby. She blew shining bubbles of sound. She loved motion, loved light, loved color and music and textures. She would lie on the floor in her blue overalls patting the surface so hard in ecstasy her hands and feet would blur. She was a miracle to me, but when she was eight months old I had to leave her daytimes with the woman downstairs to whom she was no miracle at all, for I worked or looked for work and for Emily's father, who "could no longer endure" (he wrote in his good-bye note) "sharing want with us."

I was nineteen. It was the pre-relief, pre-WPA world of the depression. I would start running as soon as I got off the streetcar, running up the stairs, the place smelling sour, and awake or asleep to startle awake, when she saw me she would break into a clogged weeping that could not be comforted, a weeping I can hear yet.

10 After a while I found a job hashing at night so I could be with her days, and it was better. But it came to where I had to bring her to his family and leave her.

It took a long time to raise the money for her fare back. Then she got chicken pox and I had to wait longer. When she finally came, I hardly knew her, walking quick and nervous like her father, looking like her father, thin, and dressed in a shoddy red that yellowed her skin and glared at the pockmarks. All the baby loveliness gone.

She was two. Old enough for nursery school they said, and I did not know then what I know now—the fatigue of the long day, and the lacerations of group life in nurseries that are only parking places for children.

Except that it would have made no difference if I had known. It was the only place there was. It was the only way we could be together, the only way I could hold a job.

And even without knowing, I knew. I knew the teacher that was evil because all these years it has curdled into my memory, the little boy hunched in the corner, her rasp, "why aren't you outside, because Alvin hits you? that's no reason, go out, scaredy." I knew Emily hated it even if she did not clutch and implore "don't go Mommy" like the other children, mornings.

15 She always had a reason why we should stay home. Momma, you look sick, Momma. I feel sick. Momma, the teachers aren't there today, they're sick. Momma, we can't go, there was a fire there last night. Momma, it's a holiday today, no school, they told me.

But never a direct protest, never rebellion. I think of our others in their three-, four-year-oldness—the explosions, the tempers, the denunciations, the demands —and I feel suddenly ill. I put the iron down. What in me demanded that goodness in her? And what was the cost, the cost to her of such goodness?

The old man living in the back once said in his gentle way: "You should smile at Emily more when you look at her." What *was* in my face when I looked at her? I loved her. There were all the acts of love.

It was only with the others I remembered what he said, and it was the face of joy, and not of care or tightness or worry I turned to them—too late for Emily. She does not smile easily, let alone almost always as her brothers and sisters do. Her face is closed and sombre, but when she wants, how fluid. You must have seen it in her pantomimes, you spoke of her rare gift for comedy on the stage that rouses a laughter out of the audience so dear they applaud and applaud and do not want to let her go.

Where does it come from, that comedy? There was none of it in her when she came back to me that second time, after I had had to send her away again. She had a new daddy now to learn to love, and I think perhaps it was a better time.

20 Except when we left her alone nights, telling ourselves she was old enough.

"Can't you go some other time, Mommy, like tomorrow?" she would ask. "Will it be just a little while you'll be gone? Do you promise?"

The time we came back, the front door open, the clock on the floor in the hall. She rigid awake. "It wasn't just a little while. I didn't cry. Three times I called you, just three times, and then I ran downstairs to open the door so you could come faster. The clock talked loud. I threw it away, it scared me what it talked."

She said the clock talked loud again that night I went to the hospital to have Susan. She was delirious with the fever that comes before red measles, but she was fully conscious all the week I was gone and the week after we were home when she could not come near the new baby or me.

She did not get well. She stayed skeleton thin, not wanting to eat, and night after night she had nightmares. She would call for me, and I would rouse from exhaustion to sleepily call back: "You're all right, darling, go to sleep, it's just a dream," and if she still called, in a sterner voice, "now go to sleep, Emily, there's nothing to hurt you." Twice, only twice, when I had to get up for Susan anyhow, I went in to sit with her.

25   Now when it is too late (as if she would let me hold and comfort her like I do the others) I get up and go to her at once at her moan or restless stirring. "Are you awake, Emily? Can I get you something?" And the answer is always the same: "No, I'm all right, go back to sleep, Mother."

They persuaded me at the clinic to send her away to a convalescent home in the country where "she can have the kind of food and care you can't manage for her, and you'll be free to concentrate on the new baby." They still send children to that place. I see pictures on the society page of sleek young women planning affairs to raise money for it, or dancing at the affairs, or decorating Easter eggs or filling Christmas stockings for the children.

They never have a picture of the children so I do not know if the girls still wear those gigantic red bows and the ravaged looks on the every other Sunday when parents can come to visit "unless otherwise notified"—as we were notified the first six weeks.

Oh it is a handsome place, green lawns and tall trees and fluted flower beds. High up on the balconies of each cottage the children stand, the girls in their red bows and white dresses, the boys in white suits and giant red ties. The parents stand below shrieking up to be heard and the children shriek down to be heard, and between them the invisible wall "Not To Be Contaminated by Parental Germs or Physical Affection."

There was a tiny girl who always stood hand in hand with Emily. Her parents never came. One visit she was gone. "They moved her to Rose Cottage" Emily shouted in explanation. "They don't like you to love anybody here."

30   She wrote once a week, the labored writing of a seven-year-old. "I am fine. How is the baby. If I write my leter nicly I will have a star. Love." There never was a star. We wrote every other day, letters she could never hold or keep but only hear read—once. "We simply do not have room for children to keep any personal possessions," they patiently explained when we pieced one Sunday's shrieking together to plead how much it would mean to Emily, who loved so to keep things, to be allowed to keep her letters and cards.

Each visit she looked frailer. "She isn't eating," they told us.

(They had runny eggs for breakfast or mush with lumps, Emily said later, I'd hold it in my mouth and not swallow. Nothing ever tasted good, just when they had chicken.)

It took us eight months to get her released home, and only the fact that she gained back so little of her seven lost pounds convinced the social worker.

I used to try to hold and love her after she came back, but her body would stay stiff, and after a while she'd push away. She ate little. Food sickened her, and I think much of life too. Oh she had physical lightness and brightness, twinkling by on skates, bouncing like a ball up and down up and down over the jump rope, skimming over the hill; but these were momentary.

35   She fretted about her appearance, thin and dark and foreign-looking at a time when every little girl was supposed to look or thought she should look

a chubby blonde replica of Shirley Temple. The doorbell sometimes rang for her, but no one seemed to come and play in the house or be a best friend. Maybe because we moved so much.

There was a boy she loved painfully through two school semesters. Months later she told me how she had taken pennies from my purse to buy him candy. "Licorice was his favorite and I brought him some every day, but he still liked Jennifer better'n me. Why, Mommy?" The kind of question for which there is no answer.

School was a worry to her. She was not glib or quick in a world where glibness and quickness were easily confused with ability to learn. To her over-worked and exasperated teachers she was an overconscientious "slow learner" who kept trying to catch up and was absent entirely too often.

I let her be absent, though sometimes the illness was imaginary. How different from my now-strictness about attendance with the others. I wasn't work-ing. We had a new baby, I was home anyhow. Sometimes, after Susan grew old enough, I would keep her home from school, too, to have them all together.

Mostly Emily had asthma, and her breathing, harsh and labored, would fill the house with a curiously tranquil sound. I would bring the two old dresser mirrors and her boxes of collections to her bed. She would select beads and single earrings, bottle tops and shells, dried flowers and pebbles, old post-cards and scraps, all sorts of oddments; then she and Susan would play King-dom, setting up landscapes and furniture, peopling them with action.

40   Those were the only times of peaceful companionship between her and Susan. I have edged away from it, that poisonous feeling between them, that terrible balancing of hurts and needs I had to do between the two, and did so badly, those earlier years.

Oh there are conflicts between the others too, each one human, needing, demanding, hurting, taking—but only between Emily and Susan, no, Emily toward Susan that corroding resentment. It seems so obvious on the surface, yet it is not obvious. Susan, the second child, Susan, golden- and curly-haired and chubby, quick and articulate and assured, everything in appearance and manner Emily was not; Susan, not able to resist Emily's precious things, los-ing or sometimes clumsily breaking them; Susan telling jokes and riddles to company for applause while Emily sat silent (to say to me later: that was *my* riddle, Mother, I told it to Susan); Susan, who for all the five years' difference in age was just a year behind Emily in developing physically.

I am glad for that slow physical development that widened the difference between her and her contemporaries, though she suffered over it. She was too vulnerable for that terrible world of youthful competition, of preening and parad-ing, of constant measuring of yourself against every other, of envy, "If I had that copper hair," "If I had that skin. . . ." She tormented herself enough about not looking like the others, there was enough of the unsureness, the having to be conscious of words before you speak, the constant caring—what are they thinking of me? without having it all magnified by the merciless physical drives.

Ronnie is calling. He is wet and I change him. It is rare there is such a cry now. That time of motherhood is almost behind me when the ear is not one's own but must always be racked and listening for the child cry, the child call. We sit for a while and I hold him, looking out over the city spread in char-coal with its soft aisles of light. "*Shoogily*," he breathes and curls closer. I carry him back to bed, asleep. *Shoogily*. A funny word, a family word, inherited from Emily, invented by her to say: *comfort*.

In this and other ways she leaves her seal, I say aloud. And startle at my saying it. What do I mean? What did I start to gather together, to try and make coherent? I was at the terrible, growing years. War years. I do not remember them well. I was working, there were four smaller ones now, there was not time for her. She had to help be a mother, and housekeeper, and shopper. She had to set her seal. Mornings of crisis and near hysteria trying to get lunches packed, hair combed, coats and shoes found, everyone to school or Child Care on time, the baby ready for transportation. And always the paper scribbled on by a smaller one, the book looked at by Susan then mislaid, the homework not done. Running out to that huge school where she was one, she was lost, she was a drop; suffering over the unpreparedness, stammering and unsure in her classes.

45   There was so little time left at night after the kids were bedded down. She would struggle over books, always eating (it was in those years she developed her enormous appetite that is legendary in our family) and I would be ironing, or preparing food for the next day, or writing V-mail to Bill, or tending the baby. Sometimes, to make me laugh, or out of her despair, she would imitate happenings or types at school.

I think I said once: "Why don't you do something like this in the school amateur show?" One morning she phoned me at work, hardly understandable through the weeping: "Mother, I did it. I won, I won; they gave me first prize; they clapped and clapped and wouldn't let me go."

Now suddenly she was Somebody, and as imprisoned in her difference as she had been in anonymity.

She began to be asked to perform at other high schools, even in colleges, then at city and statewide affairs. The first one we went to, I only recognized her that first moment when thin, shy, she almost drowned herself into the curtains. Then: Was this Emily? The control, the command, the convulsing and deadly clowning, the spell, then the roaring, stamping audience, unwilling to let this rare and precious laughter out of their lives.

Afterwards: You ought to do something about her with a gift like that— but without money or knowing how, what does one do? We have left it all to her, and the gift has as often eddied inside, clogged and clotted, as been used and growing.

50   She is coming. She runs up the stairs two at a time with her light graceful step, and I know she is happy tonight. Whatever it was that occasioned your call did not happen today.

"Aren't you ever going to finish the ironing, Mother? Whistler painted his mother in a rocker. I'd have to paint mine standing over an ironing board." This is one of her communicative nights and she tells me everything and nothing as she fixes herself a plate of food out of the icebox.

She is so lovely. Why did you want me to come in at all? Why were you concerned? She will find her way.

She starts up the stairs to bed. "Don't get me up with the rest in the morning." "But I thought you were having midterms." "Oh, those," she comes back in, kisses me, and says quite lightly, "in a couple of years when we'll all be atom-dead they won't matter a bit."

She has said it before. She *believes* it. But because I have been dredging the past, and all that compounds a human being is so heavy and meaningful in me, I cannot endure it tonight.

55   I will never total it all. I will never come in to say: She was a child seldom smiled at. Her father left me before she was a year old. I had to work her first

six years when there was work, or I sent her home and to his relatives. There were years she had care she hated. She was dark and thin and foreign-looking in a world where the prestige went to blondeness and curly hair and dimples, she was slow where glibness was prized. She was a child of anxious, not proud, love. We were poor and could not afford for her the soil of easy growth. I was a young mother, I was a distracted mother. There were the other children pushing up, demanding. Her younger sister seemed all that she was not. There were years she did not want me to touch her. She kept too much in herself, her life was such she had to keep too much in herself. My wisdom came too late. She has much to her and probably nothing will come of it. She is a child of her age, of depression, of war, of fear.

Let her be. So all that is in her will not bloom—but in how many does it? There is still enough left to live by. Only help her to know—help make it so there is cause for her to know—that she is more than this dress on the ironing board, helpless before the iron.

INQUIRING FURTHER

1. What role do you believe physical influences play in the development of Emily's identity? Would readings on anti-depressants be helpful in developing an interpretation of "I Stand Here Ironing"? Why or why not?

2. What does "I Stand Here Ironing" tell us about the identity of the mother who narrates the story? Is it fair to say the story is as much about the narrator as about Emily? Write a one-page analysis of the mother's character.

3. What role do social influences play in the development of Emily's identity? What can be said about her relationship with her siblings? What do you think of her situation in school? Write a paragraph exploring the influences of others on Emily.

WORK, PLAY, AND LIFE-CHANGING SITUATIONS

Extreme situations, and even our regular work and play, shape who we are. This section explores some short stories, poems, and images dealing with work and its influence on our identity. It also covers works that treat life-changing situations. All of these contexts can be considered in terms of how they influence our sense of self.

HERMAN MELVILLE

Enhanced reading of "Bartleby, the Scrivener"

Herman Melville (1819–1891) descended from a well-respected New England family. His father, however, over-invested, lost the family fortune, and then suffered an emotional breakdown. When Melville was twelve, his father died. At fifteen he began working, taking positions as a bank clerk and a laborer. When he was twenty he went to sea, discovering a love of sailing and adventure. His adventures at sea informed his most successful books, including the classic, Moby Dick. *"Bartleby, The Scrivener" was published in 1853. For more on this story, see the Enhanced Reading on our Web site.*

Bartleby, The Scrivener: A Story of Wall-Street

JEAN-FRANCOIS MILLET

*Jean-Francois Millet (1814–1875) spent much of his early career paint-
ing portraits as a way of supporting himself. In 1848, he left the city and
turned his art toward rural scenes and occupations.*

L'homme à la Houe (The Man with the Hoe)

The J. Paul Getty Museum, Los Angeles, Millet, Jean-Francois, The Man with the Hoe,
1860–1862, oil on canvas, Unframed: 80 x 99.1 cm (31 1/2 x 39 in.)

EDWIN MARKHAM

*Edwin Markham was a school teacher from San Francisco when he pub-
lished "The Man with the Hoe" in 1899. The poem quickly captured national attention, sparking controversy for its portrayal of the social realities
of 1890s America. Markham was vaulted to the front of a movement that
saw in the poem a depiction of the downtrodden state of the poor, and a
critique of economic and religious leaders.*

The Man with the Hoe

Written after seeing Millet's World-Famous Painting

God made man in His own image,
in the image of God made He him.

—Genesis.

Bowed by the weight of centuries he leans
Upon his hoe and gazes on the ground,
The emptiness of ages in his face,
And on his back the burden of the world.
5   Who made him dead to rapture and despair,
A thing that grieves not and that never hopes,
Stolid and stunned, a brother to the ox?
Who loosened and let down this brutal jaw?
Whose was the hand that slanted back this brow?
10   Whose breath blew out the light within this brain?

Is this the Thing the Lord God made and gave
To have dominion over sea and land;
To trace the stars and search the heavens for power;
To feel the passion of Eternity?
15   Is this the Dream He dreamed who shaped the suns
And pillared the blue firmament with light?
Down all the stretch of Hell to its last gulf
There is no shape more terrible than this—
More tongued with censure of the world's blind greed—
20   More filled with signs and portents for the soul—
More fraught with menace to the universe.

What gulfs between him and the seraphim!
Slave of the wheel of labor, what to him
Are Plato and the swing of Pleiades?
25   What the long reaches of the peaks of song,
The rift of dawn, the reddening of the rose?
Through this dread shape the suffering ages look;
Time's tragedy is in that aching stoop;
Through this dread shape humanity betrayed,
30   Plundered, profaned and disinherited,
Cries protest to the Judges of the World,
A protest that is also prophecy.

O masters, lords and rulers in all lands,
Is this the handiwork you give to God,
35   This monstrous thing distorted and soul-quenched?
How will you ever straighten up this shape;
Touch it again with immortality;
Give back the upward looking and the light;
Rebuild in it the music and the dream;
40   Make right the immemorial infamies,
Perfidious wrongs, immedicable woes?

O masters, lords and rulers in all lands,
How will the Future reckon with this Man?
How answer his brute question in that hour
45   When whirlwinds of rebellion shake the world?
How will it be with kingdoms and with kings—
With those who shaped him to the thing he is—
When this dumb Terror shall reply to God,
After the silence of the centuries?

INQUIRING FURTHER

1. Would you say that *The Man with the Hoe* is best read as a portrait? Why or why not?

Paintings
by Millet

2. Millet's paintings *The Sower* (1850) and *The Gleaners* (1857) created controversy as they brought to light concerns about the living conditions of the poor. Can you recognize aspects of *The Man with the Hoe* that speak to social concerns? Make a list of artistic or thematic elements in the painting that could be used discuss the painting in terms of society.

JOHN UPDIKE

John Updike (born in 1932) credits his writing to having to occupy his time with fantasy worlds as a child. Updike grew up as an only child in Pennsylvania. He began his publishing career by editing and submitting stories and poems for magazines such as the New Yorker. *He has continued to write prolifically, composing novels, short stories, essays, and poetry—he is best known for his novels depicting "Rabbit" Angstrom, an ex-basketball player and unlikely hero. "A&P" was published in the collection,* Pigeon Feathers and Other Stories, *in 1962.*

A&P

In walks these three girls in nothing but bathing suits. I'm in the third checkout slot, with my back to the door, so I don't see them until they're over by the bread. The one that caught my eye first was the one in the plaid green two-piece. She was a chunky kid, with a good tan and a sweet broad soft-looking can with those two crescents of white just under it, where the sun never seems to hit, at the top of the backs of her legs. I stood there with my hand on a box of HiHo crackers trying to remember if I rang it up or not. I ring it up again and the customer starts giving me hell. She's one of these cash-register-watchers, a witch about fifty with rouge on her cheekbones and no eyebrows, and I know it made her day to trip me up. She'd been watching cash registers for fifty years and probably never seen a mistake before.

By the time I got her feathers smoothed and her goodies into a bag—she gives me a little snort in passing, if she'd been born at the right time they would have burned her over in Salem—by the time I get her on her way the girls had circled around the bread and were coming back, without a pushcart, back my way along the counters, in the aisle between the checkouts and the Special bins. They didn't even have shoes on. There was this chunky one, with the two-piece—it was bright green and the seams on the bra were still sharp and her belly was still pretty pale so I guessed she just got it (the suit)—there was this one, with one of those chubby berry faces, the lips all bunched together under her nose, this one and a tall one, with black hair that hadn't quite frizzed right and one of these sunburns right across under the eyes, and a chin that was too long—you know, the kind of girl other girls think is very "striking" and "attractive" but never quite makes it, as they very well know, which is why they like her so much—and then the third one, that wasn't quite so tall. She was the queen. She kind of led them, the other two peeking around and making their shoulders round. She didn't look around, not this queen, she just walked straight on slowly, on these long white prima-donna legs. She came down a little hard on her heels, as if she didn't walk in her bare feet that much, putting down her heels and then letting the weight move along to her toes as if she was testing the floor with every step, putting a little deliberate extra action into it. You never know for sure how girls' minds work (do you really think it's a mind in there or just a little buzz like a bee in a glass jar?) but you got the idea she had talked the other two into coming in here with her, and now she was showing them how to do it, walk slow and hold yourself straight.

She had on a kind of dirty-pink—beige maybe, I don't know—bathing suit with a little nubble all over it, and what got me, the straps were down. They were off her shoulders looped loose around the cool tops of her arms, and I guess as a result the suit had slipped a little on her, so all around the top of the cloth there was this shining rim. If it hadn't been there you wouldn't have known there could have been anything whiter than those shoulders. With the straps pushed off, there was nothing between the top of the suit and the top of her head except just *her*, this clean bare plane of the top of her chest down from the shoulder bones like a dented sheet of metal tilted in the light. I mean, it was more than pretty.

She had sort of oaky hair that the sun and salt had bleached, done up in a bun that was unravelling, and a kind of prim face. Walking into the A & P with your straps down, I suppose it's the only kind of face you *can* have. She held her head so high her neck, coming up out of those white shoulders, looked kind of stretched, but I didn't mind. The longer her neck was, the more of her there was.

5   She must have felt in the corner of her eye me and over my shoulder Stokesie in the second slot watching, but she didn't tip. Not this queen. She kept her eyes moving across the racks, and stopped, and turned so slow it made my stomach rub the inside of my apron, and buzzed to the other two, who kind of huddled against her for relief, and then they all three of them went up the cat-and-dog-food-breakfast-cereal-macaroni-rice-raisins-seasonings-spreads-spaghetti-soft-drinks-crackers-and-cookies aisle. From the third slot I look straight up this aisle to the meat counter, and I watched them all the way. The fat one with the tan sort of fumbled with the cookies, but on second thought she put the package back. The sheep pushing their carts down the aisle—the girls were walking against the usual traffic (not that we have one-way signs or anything)—were pretty hilarious. You could see them, when Queenie's white shoulders dawned on them, kind of jerk, or hop, or hiccup, but their eyes snapped back to their own baskets and on they pushed. I bet you could set off dynamite in an A & P and the people would by and large keep reaching and checking oatmeal off their lists and muttering "Let me see, there was a third thing, began with A, asparagus, no, ah, yes, applesauce!" or whatever it is they do mutter. But there was no doubt, this jiggled them. A few house-slaves in pin curlers even looked around after pushing their carts past to make sure what they had seen was correct.

You know, it's one thing to have a girl in a bathing suit down on the beach, where what with the glare nobody can look at each other much anyway, and another thing in the cool of the A & P, under the fluorescent lights, against all those stacked packages, with her feet paddling along naked over our checkerboard green-and-cream rubber-tile floor.

"Oh Daddy," Stokesie said beside me. "I feel so faint."

"Darling," I said. "Hold me tight." Stokesie's married, with two babies chalked up on his fuselage already, but as far as I can tell that's the only difference. He's twenty-two, and I was nineteen this April.

"Is it done?" he asks, the responsible married man finding his voice. I forgot to say he thinks he's going to be manager some sunny day, maybe in 1990 when it's called the Great Alexandrov and Petrooshki Tea Company or something.

10   What he meant was, our town is five miles from a beach, with a big summer colony out on the Point, but we're right in the middle of town, and the women generally put on a shirt or shorts or something before they get out of the car into the street. And anyway these are usually women with six children and varicose veins mapping their legs and nobody, including them, could care less. As I say, we're right in the middle of town, and if you stand at our front doors you can see two banks and the Congregational church and the newspaper store and three real-estate offices and about twenty-seven old freeloaders tearing up Central Street because the sewer broke again. It's not as if we're on the Cape; we're north of Boston and there's people in this town haven't seen the ocean for twenty years.

The girls had reached the meat counter and were asking McMahon something. He pointed, they pointed, and they shuffled out of sight behind a pyramid of Diet Delight peaches. All that was left for us to see was old McMahon patting his mouth and looking after them sizing up their joints. Poor kids, I began to feel sorry for them, they couldn't help it.

Now here comes the sad part of the story, at least my family says it's sad, but I don't think it's so sad myself. The store's pretty empty, it being Thursday afternoon, so there was nothing much to do except lean on the register and wait for the girls to show up again. The whole store was like a pinball machine and I didn't know which tunnel they'd come out of. After a while they come around out of the far aisle, around the light bulbs, records at discount of the Caribbean Six or Tony Martin Sings or some such gunk you wonder they waste the wax on, sixpacks of candy bars, and plastic toys done up in cellophane that fall apart when a kid looks at them anyway. Around they come, Queenie still leading the way, and holding a little gray jar in her hand. Slots Three through Seven are unmanned and I could see her wondering between Stokes and me, but Stokesie with his usual luck draws an old party in baggy gray pants who stumbles up with four giant cans of pineapple juice (what do these burns *do* with all that pineapple juice? I've often asked myself) so the girls come to me. Queenie puts down the jar and I take it into my fingers icy cold. Kingfish Fancy Herring Snacks in Pure Sour Cream: 49¢. Now her hands are empty, not a ring or a bracelet, bare as God made them, and I wonder where the money's coming from. Still with that prim look she lifts a folded dollar bill out of the hollow at the center of her nubbled pink top. The jar went heavy in my hand. Really, I thought that was so cute.

Then everybody's luck begins to run out. Lengel comes in from haggling with a truck full of cabbages on the lot and is about to scuttle into that door marked MANAGER behind which he hides all day when the girls touch his eye. Lengel's pretty dreary, teaches Sunday school and the rest, but he doesn't miss that much. He comes over and says, "Girls, this isn't the beach."

Queenie blushes, though maybe it's just a brush of sunburn I was noticing for the first time, now that she was so close. "My mother asked me to pick up a jar of herring snacks." Her voice kind of startled me, the way voices do when you see the people first, coming out so flat and dumb yet kind of tony, too, the way it ticked over "pick up" and "snacks." All of a sudden I slid right down her voice into her living room. Her father and the other men were standing around in ice-cream coats and bow ties and the women were in sandals picking up herring snacks on toothpicks off a big glass plate and they were all holding drinks the color of water with olives and sprigs of mint in them. When my parents have somebody over they get lemonade and if it's a real racy affair Schlitz in tall glasses with "They'll Do It Every Time" cartoons stencilled on.

15   "That's all right," Lengel said. "But this isn't the beach." His repeating this struck me as funny, as if it had just occurred to him, and he had been thinking all these years the A & P was a great big sand dune and he was the head lifeguard. He didn't like my smiling—as I say he doesn't miss much—but he concentrates on giving the girls that sad Sunday-school-superintendent stare.

Queenie's blush is no sunburn now, and the plump one in plaid, that I liked better from the back—a really sweet can —pipes up, "We weren't doing any shopping. We just came in for the one thing."

"That makes no difference," Lengel tells her, and I could see from the way his eyes went that he hadn't noticed she was wearing a two-piece before. "We want you decently dressed when you come in here."

"We *are* decent," Queenie says suddenly, her lower lip pushing, getting sore now that she remembers her place, a place from which the crowd that runs the A & P must look pretty crummy. Fancy Herring Snacks flashed in her very blue eyes.

"Girls, I don't want to argue with you. After this come in here with your shoulders covered. It's our policy." He turns his back. That's policy for you. Policy is what the kingpins want. What the others want is juvenile delinquency.

20   All this while, the customers had been showing up with their carts but, you know, sheep, seeing a scene, they had all bunched up on Stokesie, who shook open a paper bag as gently as peeling a peach, not wanting to miss a word. I could feel in the silence everybody getting nervous, most of all Lengel, who asks me, "Sammy, have you rung up their purchase?"

I thought and said "No" but it wasn't about that I was thinking. I go through the punches, 4, 9, GROC, TOT—it's more complicated than you think, and after you do it often enough, it begins to make a little song, that you hear words to, in my case "Hello (*bing*) there, you (*gung*) hap-py *pee*-pul (*splat*)!" —the *splat* being the drawer flying out. I uncrease the bill, tenderly as you may imagine, it just having come from between the two smoothest scoops of vanilla I had ever known were there, and pass a half and a penny into her narrow pink palm, and nestle the herrings in a bag and twist its neck and hand it over, all the time thinking.

The girls, and who'd blame them, are in a hurry to get out, so I say "I quit" to Lengel quick enough for them to hear, hoping they'll stop and watch me, their unsuspected hero. They keep right on going, into the electric eye; the door flies open and they flicker across the lot to their car, Queenie and Plaid and Big Tall Goony-Goony (not that as raw material she was so bad), leaving me with Lengel and a kink in his eyebrow.

"Did you say something, Sammy?"

"I said I quit."

25   "I thought you did."

"You didn't have to embarrass them."

"It was they who were embarrassing us."

I started to say something that came out "Fiddle-de-doo." It's a saying of my grandmother's, and I know she would have been pleased.

"I don't think you know what you're saying," Lengel said.

30   "I know you don't," I said. "But I do." I pull the bow at the back of my apron and start shrugging it off my shoulders. A couple customers that had been heading for my slot begin to knock against each other, like scared pigs in a chute.

Lengel sighs and begins to look very patient and old and gray. He's been a friend of my parents for years. "Sammy, you don't want to do this to your Mom and Dad," he tells me. It's true, I don't. But it seems to me that once you begin a gesture it's fatal not to go through with it. I fold the apron, "Sammy" stitched in red on the pocket, and put it on the counter, and drop the bow tie on top of it. The bow tie is theirs, if you've ever wondered. "You'll feel this for the rest of your life," Lengel says, and I know that's true, too, but remembering how he made that pretty girl blush makes me so scrunchy inside I punch the No Sale tab and the machine whirs "pee-pul" and the drawer splats out. One advantage to this scene taking place in summer, I can follow this up with a clean exit, there's no fumbling around getting your coat and galoshes, I just saunter into the electric eye in my white shirt that my mother ironed the night before, and the door heaves itself open, and outside the sunshine is skating around on the asphalt.

I look around for my girls, but they're gone, of course. There wasn't anybody but some young married screaming with her children about some candy they didn't get by the door of a powder-blue Falcon station wagon. Looking back in the big windows, over the bags of peat moss and aluminum lawn furniture stacked on the pavement, I could see Lengel in my place in the slot, checking the sheep through. His face was dark gray and his back stiff, as if he'd just had an injection of iron, and my stomach kind of fell as I felt how hard the world was going to be to me hereafter.

Ex-Basketball Player (1958)

Pearl Avenue runs past the high-school lot,
Bends with the trolley tracks, and stops, cut off
Before it has a chance to go two blocks,
At Colonel McComsky Plaza, Berth's Garage
5   Is on the corner facing west, and there,
Most days, you'll find Flick Webb, who helps Berth out.

Flick stands tall among the idiot pumps—
Five on a side, the old bubble-head style,
Their rubber elbows hanging loose and low.
10   One's nostrils are two S's, and his eyes
An E and O. And one is squat, without
A head at all—more of a football type.

Once Flick played for the high-school team, the Wizards.
He was good: in fact, the best. In '46
15   He bucketed three hundred ninety points,
A county record still. The ball loved Flick.

I saw him rack up thirty-eight or forty
In one home game. His hands were like wild birds.

20 He never learned a trade, he just sells gas,
Checks oil, and changes flats. Once in a while,
As a gag, he dribbles an inner tube,
But most of us remember anyway.
His hands are fine and nervous on the lug wrench.
It makes no difference to the lug wrench, though.

25 Off work, he hangs around Mae's luncheonette.
Grease-gray and kind of coiled, he plays pinball,
Smokes those thin cigars, nurses lemon phosphates.
Flick seldom says a word to Mae, just nods
Beyond her face toward bright applauding tiers
30 Of Necco Wafers, Nibs, and Juju Beads.

INQUIRING FURTHER

1. What role does the setting of the A&P grocery store play in the narrator's decision to quit his job? What passages from the story would help you discuss the influence of the setting on the narrator?

2. What are your thoughts on the way the narrator describes the girls in the story? Do you think the narrator is sexist? What do his descriptions say about his character?

3. What is the significance of the last line of the story in which the narrator describes "how hard the world was going to be to [him] hereafter"? Write a one- to two-page character analysis in which you explore the evolution of the narrator's sense of self.

4. Compare the narrator in "A&P" with Flick in "Ex-Basketball Player." In the future do you think Sammy might end up in a similar position as Flick? Why or why not?

STEPHEN CRANE

Stephen Crane (1871–1900) is best known for his war stories, including The Red Badge of Courage. *In 1897, Crane traveled as a newspaper correspondent to Cuba to cover the Spanish-American War. His boat, the* Commodore, *sank off the coast of Florida and Crane and three others took to a small lifeboat. During a thirty-hour ordeal, the group struggled to reach safety. Crane developed the experience into a short story shortly after being rescued. "The Open Boat" represents a classic example of* **Naturalism**, *a literary movement emphasizing the insignificance of humans as compared to nature and extreme forces or situations. The story is presented as an Enhanced Reading on our Web site.*

Enhanced
reading of
"The
Open
Boat"

The Open Boat

COMMUNITIES AND SELVES

When we consider issues of identity, we must also address our relationships with others. These relationships, however, shape more than our sense of self. They also define our responsibility toward others and their obligations toward us. Our dependence upon one another creates many of the dilemmas that mark us as humans. Not surprisingly, we can recognize these concerns in many works of literature.

ANTON CHEKHOV

Growing up in Russia, Anton Chekhov (1860–1904) worked long hours in his father's hardware store, until the business went bankrupt in 1876. He was then separated from his family, but continued to support them through tutoring and writing while going to medical school. At the age of twenty, he began publishing stories in Russian magazines and quickly found success. Unfortunately, Chekhov and his family were struck with tuberculosis. The disease took his brother's life in 1889, and afflicted Chekhov shortly after he began his publishing career. He battled the disease for the rest of his life. The following version of "Misery" was translated by Constance Garnett.

Misery

"To whom shall I tell my grief?"

The twilight of evening. Big flakes of wet snow are whirling lazily about the street lamps, which have just been lighted, and lying in a thin soft layer on roofs, horses' backs, shoulders, caps. Iona Potapov, the sledge-driver, is all white like a ghost. He sits on the box without stirring, bent as double as the living body can be bent. If a regular snowdrift fell on him it seems as though even then he would not think it necessary to shake it off. . . . His little mare is white and motionless too. Her stillness, the angularity of her lines, and the stick-like straightness of her legs make her look like a halfpenny gingerbread horse. She is probably lost in thought. Anyone who has been torn away from the plough, from the familiar gray landscapes, and cast into this slough, full of monstrous lights, of unceasing uproar and hurrying people, is bound to think.

It is a long time since Iona and his nag have budged. They came out of the yard before dinner-time and not a single fare yet. But now the shades of evening are falling on the town. The pale light of the street lamps changes to a vivid color, and the bustle of the street grows noisier.

"Sledge to Vyborgskaya!" Iona hears. "Sledge!"

Iona starts, and through his snow-plastered eyelashes sees an officer in a military overcoat with a hood over his head.

5   "To Vyborgskaya," repeats the officer. "Are you asleep? To Vyborgskaya!"

In token of assent Iona gives a tug at the reins which sends cakes of snow flying from the horse's back and shoulders. The officer gets into the sledge. The sledge-driver clicks to the horse, cranes his neck like a swan, rises in his seat, and more from habit than necessity brandishes his whip. The mare cranes her neck, too, crooks her stick-like legs, and hesitatingly sets off. . . .

"Where are you shoving, you devil?" Iona immediately hears shouts from the dark mass shifting to and fro before him. "Where the devil are you going? Keep to the r-right!"

"You don't know how to drive! Keep to the right," says the officer angrily.

A coachman driving a carriage swears at him; a pedestrian crossing the road and brushing the horse's nose with his shoulder looks at him angrily and shakes the snow off his sleeve. Iona fidgets on the box as though he were sitting on thorns, jerks his elbows, and turns his eyes about like one possessed as though he did not know where he was or why he was there.

10 "What rascals they all are!" says the officer jocosely. "They are simply doing their best to run up against you or fall under the horse's feet. They must be doing it on purpose."

Iona looks as his fare and moves his lips. . . . Apparently he means to say something, but nothing comes but a sniff.

"What?" inquires the officer.

Iona gives a wry smile, and straining his throat, brings out huskily: "My son . . . , er . . . my son died this week, sir."

"H'm! What did he die of?"

15 Iona turns his whole body round to his fare, and says:

"Who can tell! It must have been from fever. . . . He lay three days in the hospital and then he died. . . . God's will."

"Turn round, you devil!" comes out of the darkness. "Have you gone cracked, you old dog? Look where you are going!"

"Drive on! drive on! . . . " says the officer. "We shan't get there till tomorrow going on like this. Hurry up!"

The sledge-driver cranes his neck again, rises his seat, and with heavy grace swings his whip. Several times he looks round at the officer, but the latter keeps his eyes shut and is apparently disinclined to listen. Putting his fare down at Vyborgskaya, Iona stops by a restaurant, and again sits huddled up on the box. . . . Again the wet snow paints him and his horse white. One hour passes, and then another. . . .

20 Three young men, two tall and thin, one short and hunchbacked, come up, railing at each other and loudly stamping on the pavement with their galoshes.

"Cabby, to the Police Bridge!" the hunchback cries in a cracked voice. "The three of us, . . . twenty kopecks!"

Iona tugs at the reins and clicks to his horse. Twenty kopecks is not a fair price, but he has no thoughts for that. Whether it is a rouble or whether it is five kopecks does not matter to him now so long as he has a fare. . . . The three young men, shoving each other and using bad language, go up to the sledge, and all three try to sit down at once. The question remains to be settled: Which are to sit down and which one is to stand? After a long altercation, ill-temper, and abuse, they come to the conclusion that the hunchback must stand because he is the shortest.

"Well, drive on," says the hunchback in his cracked voice, settling himself and breathing down Iona's neck. "Cut along! What a cap you've got, my friend! You wouldn't find a worse one in all Petersburg. . . . "

"He-he! . . . he-he! . . . " laughs Iona. "It's nothing to boast of!"

25 "Well, then, nothing to boast of, drive on! Are you going to drive like this all the way? Eh? Shall I give you one in the neck?"

"My head aches," says one of the tall ones. "At the Dukmasovs' yesterday Vaska and I drank four bottles of brandy between us."

"I can't make out why you talk such stuff," says the other tall one angrily. "You lie like a brute."

"Strike me dead, it's the truth! . . . "

"It's about as true as that a louse coughs."

30   "He-he!" grins Iona. "Me-er-ry gentlemen!"

"Tfoo! the devil take you!" cries the hunchback indignantly. "Will you get on, you old plague, or won't you? Is that the way to drive? Give her one with the whip. Hang it all, give it her well."

Iona feels behind his back the jolting person and quivering voice of the hunchback. He hears abuse addressed to him, he sees people, and the feeling of loneliness begins little by little to be less heavy on his heart. The hunchback swears at him, till he chokes over some elaborately whimsical string of epithets and is overpowered by his cough. His tall companions begin talking of a certain Nadyezhda Petrovna. Iona looks round at them. Waiting till there is a brief pause, he looks round once more and says:

"This week . . . er . . . my . . . er . . . son died!"

"We shall all die, . . . " says the hunchback with a sigh, wiping his lips after coughing. "Come, drive on! drive on! My friends, I simply cannot stand crawling like this! When will he get us there?"

35   "Well, you give him a little encouragement . . . one in the neck!"

"Do you hear, you old plague? I'll make you smart. If one stands on ceremony with fellows like you one may as well walk. Do you hear, you old dragon? Or don't you care a hang what we say?"

And Iona hears rather than feels a slap on the back of his neck.

"He-he! . . . " he laughs. "Merry gentlemen . . . God give you health!"

"Cabman, are you married?" asks one of the tall ones.

40   "I? He he! Me-er-ry gentlemen. The only wife for me now is the damp earth. . . . He-ho-ho! . . . The grave that is! . . . Here my son's dead and I am alive. . . . It's a strange thing, death has come in at the wrong door . . . . . Instead of coming for me it went for my son. . . . "

And Iona turns round to tell them how his son died, but at that point the hunchback gives a faint sigh and announces that, thank God! they have arrived at last. After taking his twenty kopecks, Iona gazes for a long while after the revelers, who disappear into a dark entry. Again he is alone and again there is silence for him. . . . The misery which has been for a brief space eased comes back again and tears his heart more cruelly than ever. With a look of anxiety and suffering Iona's eyes stray restlessly among the crowds moving to and fro on both sides of the street: can he not find among those thousands someone who will listen to him? But the crowds flit by heedless of him and his misery. . . . His misery is immense, beyond all bounds. If Iona's heart were to burst and his misery to flow out, it would flood the whole world, it seems, but yet it is not seen. It has found a hiding-place in such an insignificant shell that one would not have found it with a candle by daylight. . . .

Iona sees a house-porter with a parcel and makes up his mind to address him.

"What time will it be, friend?" he asks.

"Going on for ten. . . . Why have you stopped here? Drive on!"

45   Iona drives a few paces away, bends himself double, and gives himself up to his misery. He feels it is no good to appeal to people. But before five minutes have passed he draws himself up, shakes his head as though he feels a sharp pain, and tugs at the reins. . . . He can bear it no longer.

"Back to the yard!" he thinks. "To the yard!"

And his little mare, as though she knew his thoughts, falls to trotting. An hour and a half later Iona is sitting by a big dirty stove. On the stove, on the floor, and on the benches are people snoring. The air is full of smells and stuffiness. Iona looks at the sleeping figures, scratches himself, and regrets that he has come home so early. . . . "I have not earned enough to pay for the oats, even," he thinks. "That's why I am so miserable. A man who knows how to do his work, . . . who has had enough to eat, and whose horse has had enough to eat, is always at ease. . . . "

In one of the corners a young cabman gets up, clears his throat sleepily, and makes for the water-bucket.

"Want a drink?" Iona asks him.

50   "Seems so."

"May it do you good. . . . But my son is dead, mate. . . . Do you hear? This week in the hospital. . . . It's a queer business. . . . "

Iona looks to see the effect produced by his words, but he sees nothing. The young man has covered his head over and is already asleep. The old man sighs and scratches himself. . . . Just as the young man had been thirsty for water, he thirsts for speech. His son will soon have been dead a week, and he has not really talked to anybody yet. . . . He wants to talk of it properly, with deliberation. . . . He wants to tell how his son was taken ill, how he suffered, what he said before he died, how he died. . . . He wants to describe the funeral, and how he went to the hospital to get his son's clothes. He still has his daughter Anisya in the country. . . . And he wants to talk about her too. . . . Yes, he has plenty to talk about now. His listener ought to sigh and exclaim and lament. . . . It would be even better to talk to women. Though they are silly creatures, they blubber at the first word.

"Let's go out and have a look at the mare," Iona thinks. "There is always time for sleep. . . . You'll have sleep enough, no fear. . . . "

He puts on his coat and goes into the stables where his mare is standing. He thinks about oats, about hay, about the weather. . . . He cannot think about his son when he is alone. . . . To talk about him with someone is possible, but to think of him and picture him is insufferable anguish. . . .

55   "Are you munching?" Iona asks his mare, seeing her shining eyes. "There, munch away, munch away. . . . Since we have not earned enough for oats, we will eat hay. . . . Yes, . . . I have grown too old to drive. . . . My son ought to be driving, not I. . . . He was a real cabman. . . . He ought to have lived. . . . "

Iona is silent for a while, and then he goes on:

"That's how it is, old girl. . . . Kuzma Ionitch is gone. . . . He said good-by to me. . . . He went and died for no reason. . . . Now, suppose you had a little colt, and you were mother to that little colt. . . . And all at once that same little colt went and died. . . . You'd be sorry, wouldn't you? . . . "

The little mare munches, listens, and breathes on her master's hands. Iona is carried away and tells her all about it.

INQUIRING FURTHER

1. In "Misery" Iona interacts with others three times. Would you agree with a statement that said all of these secondary characters are really the same in the story? Why or why not?

2. How would you characterize the treatment of Iona by the three revelers? Given their interactions with Iona, how do you explain the fact that Iona's misery "has been for a brief space eased" (576) in their company?

3. Are you startled by Iona's confiding in his horse at the close of the story? Develop a list of passages in the story that prepare the reader for the final scene.

SHIRLEY JACKSON

Shirley Jackson (1919–1965) by most accounts enjoyed a mixture of suc-
cess and struggle in life. In college, she published many short stories and
quickly established herself as one of the hardest working, and most talented,
writers of the later 1940s and 1950s. She also raised four children and nur-
tured friendships with a number of fellow authors, including Ralph Ellison.
At the same time, she suffered from depression and agoraphobia (fear of
leaving the house) during the later years of her adult life. She also suf-
fered from asthma and obesity, both of which may have contributed to
her death at age forty-five. Her best known work, "The Lottery" was pub-
lished in 1948.

The Lottery

The morning of June 27th was clear and sunny, with the fresh warmth of a
full-summer day; the flowers were blossoming profusely and the grass was richly green. The people of the village began to gather in the square, between
the post office and the bank, around ten o'clock; in some towns there were
so many people that the lottery took two days and had to be started on June
26th, but in this village, where there were only about three hundred people,
the whole lottery took less than two hours, so it could begin at ten o'clock in
the morning and still be through in time to allow the villagers to get home
for noon dinner.

The children assembled first, of course. School was recently over for the
summer, and the feeling of liberty sat uneasily on most of them; they tended
to gather together quietly for a while before they broke into boisterous play,
and their talk was still of the classroom and the teacher, of books and repri-
mands. Bobby Martin had already stuffed his pockets full of stones, and the
other boys soon followed his example, selecting the smoothest and roundest
stones; Bobby and Harry Jones and Dickie Delacroix—the villagers pronounced
this name "Dellacroy"—eventually made a great pile of stones in one corner
of the square and guarded it against the raids of the other boys. The girls
stood aside, talking among themselves, looking over their shoulders at the boys,
and the very small children rolled in the dust or clung to the hands of their older
brothers or sisters.

Soon the men began to gather, surveying their own children, speaking of
planting and rain, tractors and taxes. They stood together, away from the pile
of stones in the corner, and their jokes were quiet and they smiled rather than
laughed. The women, wearing faded house dresses and sweaters, came shortly after their menfolk. They greeted one another and exchanged bits of gossip as they went to join their husbands. Soon the women, standing by their husbands, began to call to their children, and the children came reluctantly, having
to be called four or five times. Bobby Martin ducked under his mother's grasping hand and ran, laughing, back to the pile of stones. His father spoke up
sharply, and Bobby came quickly and took his place between his father and his
oldest brother.

The lottery was conducted—as were the square dances, the teen-age club,
the Halloween program—by Mr. Summers, who had time and energy to
devote to civic activities. He was a round-faced, jovial man and he ran the

coal business, and people were sorry for him, because he had no children and his wife was a scold. When he arrived in the square, carrying the black wooden box, there was a murmur of conversation among the villagers, and he waved and called, "Little late today, folks." The postmaster, Mr. Graves, followed him, carrying a three-legged stool, and the stool was put in the center of the square and Mr. Summers set the black box down on it. The villagers kept their distance, leaving a space between themselves and the stool, and when Mr. Summers said, "Some of you fellows want to give me a hand?" there was a hesitation before two men, Mr. Martin and his oldest son, Baxter, came forward to hold the box steady on the stool while Mr. Summers stirred up the papers inside it.

5   The original paraphernalia for the lottery had been lost long ago, and the black box now resting on the stool had been put into use even before Old Man Warner, the oldest man in town, was born. Mr. Summers spoke frequently to the villagers about making a new box, but no one liked to upset even as much tradition as was represented by the black box. There was a story that the present box had been made with some pieces of the box that had preceded it, the one that had been constructed when the first people settled down to make a village here. Every year, after the lottery, Mr. Summers began talking again about a new box, but every year the subject was allowed to fade off without anything's being done. The black box grew shabbier each year; by now it was no longer completely black but splintered badly along one side to show the original wood color, and in some places faded or stained.

Mr. Martin and his oldest son, Baxter, held the black box securely on the stool until Mr. Summers had stirred the papers thoroughly with his hand. Because so much of the ritual had been forgotten or discarded, Mr. Summers had been successful in having slips of paper substituted for the chips of wood that had been used for generations. Chips of wood, Mr. Summers had argued, had been all very well when the village was tiny, but now that the population was more than three hundred and likely to keep on growing, it was necessary to use something that would fit more easily into the black box. The night before the lottery, Mr. Summers and Mr. Graves made up the slips of paper and put them in the box, and it was then taken to the safe of Mr. Summers' coal company and locked up until Mr. Summers was ready to take it to the square next morning. The rest of the year, the box was put away, sometimes one place, sometimes another; it had spent one year in Mr. Graves's barn and another year underfoot in the post office, and sometimes it was set on a shelf in the Martin grocery and left there. There was a great deal of fussing to be done before Mr. Summers declared the lottery open. There were the lists to make up—of heads of families, heads of households in each family, members of each household in each family. There was the proper swearing-in of Mr. Summers by the postmaster, as the official of the lottery; at one time, some people remembered, there had been a recital of some sort, performed by the official of the lottery, a perfunctory, tuneless chant that had been rattled off duly each year; some people believed that the official of the lottery used to stand just so when he said or sang it, others believed that he was supposed to walk among the people, but years and years ago this part of the ritual had been allowed to lapse. There had been also, a ritual salute, which the official of the lottery had had to use in addressing each person who came up to draw from the box, but this also had changed with time, until now it was felt necessary only for the official to speak to each person approaching. Mr. Summers was very good at all this; in his clean white shirt and blue jeans, with one hand resting carelessly on the black box, he seemed very proper and important as he talked interminably to Mr. Graves and the Martins.

Just as Mr. Summers finally left off talking and turned to the assembled villagers, Mrs. Hutchinson came hurriedly along the path to the square, her sweater thrown over her shoulders, and slid into place in the back of the crowd. Clean forgot what day it was," she said to Mrs. Delacroix, who stood next to her, and they both laughed softly. "Thought my old man was out back stacking wood," Mrs. Hutchinson went on, "and then I looked out the window and the kids was gone, and then I remembered it was the twenty-seventh and came a-running." She dried her hands on her apron, and Mrs. Delacroix said, "You're in time, though. They're still talking away up there."

Mrs. Hutchinson craned her neck to see through the crowd and found her husband and children standing near the front. She tapped Mrs. Delacroix on the arm as a farewell and began to make her way through the crowd. The people separated good-humoredly to let her through; two or three people said in voices just loud enough to be heard across the crowd. "Here comes your Missus, Hutchinson," and "Bill, she made it after all." Mrs. Hutchinson reached her husband, and Mr. Summers, who had been waiting, said cheerfully, "Though we were going to have to get on without you, Tessie." Mrs. Hutchinson said, grinning, "Wouldn't have me leave m'dishes in the sink, now, would you, Joe?," and soft laughter ran through the crowd as the people stirred back into position after Mrs. Hutchinson's arrival.

"Well, now," Mr. Summers said soberly, "guess we better get started, get this over with, so's we can go back to work. Anybody ain't here?"

10   "Dunbar," several people said. "Dunbar, Dunbar."

Mr. Summers consulted his list. "Clyde Dunbar," he said. "That's right. He's broke his leg, hasn't he? Who's drawing for him?"

"Me, I guess," a woman said, and Mr. Summers turned to look at her. "Wife draws for her husband," Mr. Summers said. "Don't you have a grown boy to do it for you, Janey?" Although Mr. Summers and everyone else in the village knew the answer perfectly well, it was the business of the official of the lottery to ask such questions formally. Mr. Summers waited with an expression of polite interest while Mrs. Dunbar answered.

"Horace's not but sixteen yet," Mrs. Dunbar said regretfully. "Guess I gotta fill in for the old man this year."

"Right," Mr. Summers said. He made a note on the list he was holding. Then he asked, "Watson boy drawing this year?"

15   A tall boy in the crowd raised his hand. "Here," he said "I'm drawing for m'mother and me." He blinked his eyes nervously and ducked his head as several voices in the crowd said things like "Good fellow, Jack," and "Glad to see your mother's got a man to do it."

"Well," Mr. Summers said, "guess that's everyone. Old Man Warner make it?"

"Here," a voice said, and Mr. Summers nodded.

A sudden hush fell on the crowd as Mr. Summers cleared his throat and looked at the list. "All ready?" he called "Now, I'll read the names—heads of families first—and the men come up and take a paper out of the box. Keep the paper folded in your hand without looking at it until everyone has had a turn. Everything clear?"

The people had done it so many times that they only half listened to the directions; most of them were quiet, wetting their lips, not looking around. Then Mr. Summers raised one hand high and said, "Adams." A man disengaged himself from the crowd and came forward. "Hi, Steve," Mr. Summers said, and Mr. Adams said, "Hi, Joe." They grinned at one another humorlessly and nervously. Then Mr. Adams reached into the black box and took out a folded paper. He held it firmly by one corner as he turned and went hastily back to his place in the crowd, where he stood a little apart from his family, not looking down at his hand.

20   "Allen," Mr. Summers said. "Anderson. . . . Bentham."

"Seems like there's no time at all between lotteries any more," Mrs. Delacroix said to Mrs. Graves in the back row. "Seems like we got through with the last one only last week."

"Time sure goes fast," Mrs. Graves said.

"Clark. . . . Delacroix."

"There goes my old man," Mrs. Delacroix said. She held her breath while her husband went forward.

25   "Dunbar," Mr. Summers said, and Mrs. Dunbar went steadily to the box while one of the women said, "Go on, Janey," and another said, "There she goes."

"We're next," Mrs. Graves said. She watched while Mr. Graves came around from the side of the box, greeted Mr. Summers gravely, and selected a slip of paper from the box. By now, all through the crowd there were men holding the small folded papers in their large hands, turning them over and over nervously. Mrs. Dunbar and her two sons stood together, Mrs. Dunbar holding the slip of paper.

"Harburt. . . . Hutchinson."

"Get up there, Bill," Mrs. Hutchinson said, and the people near her laughed. "Jones."

30   "They do say," Mr. Adams said to Old Man Warner, who stood next to him, "that over in the north village they're talking of giving up the lottery."

Old Man Warner snorted. "Pack of crazy fools," he said. "Listening to the young folks, nothing's good enough for *them*. Next thing you know, they'll be wanting to go back to living in caves, nobody work any more, live *that* way for a while. Used to be a saying about 'Lottery in June, corn be heavy soon.' First thing you know, we'd all be eating stewed chickweed and acorns. There's *always* been a lottery," he added petulantly. "Bad enough to see young Joe Summers up there joking with everybody."

"Some places have already quit lotteries," Mrs. Adams said.

"Nothing but trouble in *that*." Old Man Warner said stoutly. "Pack of young fools."

"Martin." And Bobby Martin watched his father go forward. "Overdyke. . . . Percy."

35   "I wish they'd hurry," Mrs. Dunbar said to her older son. "I wish they'd hurry."

"They're almost through," her son said.

"You get ready to run tell Dad," Mrs. Dunbar said.

Mr. Summers called his own name and then stepped forward precisely and selected a slip from the box. Then he called, "Warner."

"Seventy-seventh year I been in the lottery," Old Man Warner said as he went through the crowd. "Seventy-seventh time."

40   "Watson." The tall boy came awkwardly through the crowd. Someone said,
"Don't be nervous, Jack," and Mr. Summers said, "Take your time, son."
"Zanini."

After that, there was a long pause, a breathless pause, until Mr. Summers,
holding his slip of paper in the air, said, "All right, fellows." For a minute, no
one moved, and then all the slips of paper were opened. Suddenly, all the
women began to speak at once, saying, "Who is it?," "Who's got it?," "Is it the
Dunbars?," "Is it the Watsons?" Then the voices began to say, "It's Hutchinson. It's Bill," "Bill Hutchinson got it."
       "Go tell your father," Mrs. Dunbar said to her older son.
       People began to look around to see the Hutchinsons. Bill Hutchinson was
standing quiet, staring down at the paper in his hand. Suddenly, Tessie Hutchinson shouted to Mr. Summers, "You didn't give him time enough to take any
paper he wanted. I saw you. It wasn't fair!"
45   "Be a good sport, Tessie," Mrs. Delacroix called, and Mrs. Graves said, "All
of us took the same chance."
       "Shut up, Tessie," Bill Hutchinson said.
       "Well, everyone," Mr. Summers said, "that was done pretty fast, and now
we've got to be hurrying a little more to get done in time." He consulted his
next list. "Bill," he said, "you draw for the Hutchinson family. You got any other
house holds in the Hutchinsons?"
       "There's Don and Eva," Mrs. Hutchinson yelled. "Make *them* take their
chance!"
       "Daughters draw with their husbands' families, Tessie, Mr. Summers said
gently. "You know that as well as anyone else."
50   "It wasn't *fair*," Tessie said.
       "I guess not, Joe," Bill Hutchinson said regretfully. "My daughter draws with
her husband's family, that's only fair. And I've got no other family except the kids."
       "Then, as far as drawing for families is concerned, it's you," Mr. Summers
said in explanation, "and as far as drawing for households is concerned, that's
you, too. Right?"
       "Right," Bill Hutchinson said.
       "How many kids, Bill?" Mr. Summers asked formally.
55   "Three," Bill Hutchinson said. "There's Bill, Jr., and Nancy, and little Dave.
And Tessie and me."
       "All right, then," Mr. Summers said. "Harry, you got their tickets back?"
       Mr. Graves nodded and held up the slips of paper. "Put them in the box,
then," Mr. Summers directed. "Take Bill's and put it in."
       "I think we ought to start over," Mrs. Hutchinson said, as quietly as she could.
"I tell you it wasn't *fair*. You didn't give him time enough to choose. *Every*body
saw that."
       Mr. Graves had selected the five slips and put them in the box, and he
dropped all the papers but those onto the ground, where the breeze caught
them and lifted them off.
60   "Listen, everybody," Mrs. Hutchinson was saying to the people around her.
       "Ready, Bill?" Mr. Summers asked, and Bill Hutchinson, with one quick
glance around at his wife and children, nodded.
       "Remember," Mr. Summers said, "take the slips and keep them folded until
each person has taken one. Harry, you help little Dave." Mr. Graves took
the hand of the little boy, who came willingly with him up to the box. "Take

a paper out of the box, Davy," Mr. Summers said. Davy put his hand into the box and laughed. "Take just *one* paper," Mr. Summers said. "Harry, you hold it for him." Mr. Graves took the child's hand and removed the folded paper from the tight fist and held it while little Dave stood next to him and looked up at him wonderingly.

"Nancy next," Mr. Summers said. Nancy was twelve, and her school friends breathed heavily as she went forward, switching her skirt, and took a slip daintily from the box. "Bill, Jr.," Mr. Summers said, and Billy, his face red and his feet over-large, nearly knocked the box over as he got a paper out. "Tessie," Mr. Summers said. She hesitated for a minute, looking around defiantly, and then set her lips and went up to the box. She snatched a paper out and held it behind her.

"Bill," Mr. Summers said, and Bill Hutchinson reached into the box and felt around, bringing his hand out at last with the slip of paper in it.

65   The crowd was quiet. A girl whispered, "I hope it's not Nancy," and the sound of the whisper reached the edges of the crowd.

"It's not the way it used to be," Old Man Warner said clearly. "People ain't the way they used to be."

"All right," Mr. Summers said. "Open the papers. Harry, you open little Dave's."

Mr. Graves opened the slip of paper and there was a general sigh through the crowd as he held it up and everyone could see that it was blank. Nancy and Bill, Jr., opened theirs at the same time, and both beamed and laughed, turning around to the crowd and holding their slips of paper above their heads.

"Tessie," Mr. Summers said. There was a pause, and then Mr. Summers looked at Bill Hutchinson, and Bill unfolded his paper and showed it. It was blank.

70   "It's Tessie," Mr. Summers said, and his voice was hushed. "Show us her paper, Bill."

Bill Hutchinson went over to his wife and forced the slip of paper out of her hand. It had a black spot on it, the black spot Mr. Summers had made the night before with the heavy pencil in the coal-company office. Bill Hutchinson held it up, and there was a stir in the crowd.

"All right, folks," Mr. Summers said. "Let's finish quickly."

Although the villagers had forgotten the ritual and lost the original black box, they still remembered to use stones. The pile of stones the boys had made earlier was ready; there were stones on the ground with the blowing scraps of paper that had come out of the box. Mrs. Delacroix selected a stone so large she had to pick it up with both hands and turned to Mrs. Dunbar. "Come on," she said. "Hurry up."

Mrs. Dunbar had small stones in both hands, and she said, gasping for breath, "I can't run at all. You'll have to go ahead and I'll catch up with you."

75   The children had stones already, and someone gave little Davy Hutchinson a few pebbles.

Tessie Hutchinson was in the center of a cleared space by now, and she held her hands out desperately as the villagers moved in on her. "It isn't fair," she said. A stone hit her on the side of the head.

Old Man Warner was saying, "Come on, come on, everyone." Steve Adams was in the front of the crowd of villagers, with Mrs. Graves beside him.

"It isn't fair, it isn't right," Mrs. Hutchinson screamed, and then they were upon her.

INQUIRING FURTHER

1. Jackson received many outraged letters after publishing "The Lottery." Some readers of the *New Yorker* (where the story first appeared) cancelled their subscriptions. What do you think about these reactions to the story?

2. If you knew nothing of the dramatic ending of the story, how would you characterize the community portrayed in "The Lottery"? Does the setting seem out of the ordinary? What can be said of the relationships between the townspeople? Freewrite for five minutes about the portrayal of the community in the story.

3. "The Lottery" was published in 1948. What conclusions can you draw about the story based on this publication date? How does the story relate to our contemporary society?

ROBERT FROST

Robert Frost (1874–1963) was born in San Francisco, but moved to New Hampshire at age eleven after the death of his father. Frost was accepted to Dartmouth College, but dropped out during his first semester and began working and writing poetry. He spent almost the next twenty years working at odd jobs in New England, teaching at his mother's school, and running a poultry farm. In 1912, he traveled to England and soon after compiled many of his poems into his first two collections, A Boy's Will *and* North of Boston. *His work was received with much acclaim, and he returned to New York where he spent the rest of his life writing and giving poetry readings. "Mending Wall" was published in 1914, and "The Road Not Taken" was published in 1921.*

"Mending
Wall" and
"The
Road Not
Taken"

Mending Wall

Something there is that doesn't love a wall,
That sends the frozen-ground-swell under it,
And spills the upper boulders in the sun;
And makes gaps even two can pass abreast.
5   The work of hunters is another thing:
I have come after them and made repair
Where they have left not one stone on a stone,
But they would have the rabbit out of hiding,
To please the yelping dogs. The gaps I mean,
10   No one has seen them made or heard them made,
But at spring mending time we find them there.
I let my neighbour know beyond the hill;
And on a day we meet to walk the line
And set the wall between us once again.
15   We keep the wall between us as we go.
To each the boulders that have fallen to each.
And some are loaves and some so nearly balls

We have to use a spell to make them balance:
'Stay where you are until our backs are turned!'
20   We wear our fingers rough with handling them.
Oh, just another kind of out-door game,
One on a side. It comes to little more:
There where it is we do not need the wall:
He is all pine and I am apple orchard.
25   My apple trees will never get across
And eat the cones under his pines, I tell him.
He only says, 'Good fences make good neighbours.'
Spring is the mischief in me, and I wonder
If I could put a notion in his head:
30   'Why do they make good neighbours? Isn't it
Where there are cows? But here there are no cows.
Before I built a wall I'd ask to know
What I was walling in or walling out,
And to whom I was like to give offence.
35   Something there is that doesn't love a wall,
That wants it down.' I could say 'Elves' to him,
But it's not elves exactly, and I'd rather
He said it for himself. I see him there
Bringing a stone grasped firmly by the top
40   In each hand, like an old-stone savage armed.
He moves in darkness as it seems to me,
Not of woods only and the shade of trees.
He will not go behind his father's saying,
And he likes having thought of it so well
45   He says again, 'Good fences make good neighbours.'

The Road Not Taken

Two roads diverged in a yellow wood,
And sorry I could not travel both
And be one traveler long I stood
And looked down one as far as I could
5   To where it bent in the undergrowth;

Then took the other as just as fair,
And having perhaps the better claim,
Because it was grassy and wanted wear;
Though as for that the passing there
10   Had worn them really about the same,

And both that morning equally lay
In leaves no step had trodden black.
Oh, I kept the first for another day!
Yet knowing how way leads on to way,
15   I doubted if I should ever come back.

I shall be telling this with a sigh
Somewhere ages and ages hence:

Two roads diverged in a wood, and I—
I took the one less traveled by,
20   And that has made all the difference.

INQUIRING FURTHER

1. How would you characterize the speaker in "Mending Wall?" How would you describe the speaker's attitude toward his neighbor? What passages from the poem best illustrate this attitude?

2. Do you agree with the statement that "The Road Not Taken" portrays the speaker of the poem as a unique individual? What is your reaction to this statement? Can you think of alternative interpretations of the poem?

3. Which poem, "Mending Wall" or "The Road Not Taken," do you think speaks most clearly to the theme of the self and society? Write a paragraph explaining your decision.

WILLIAM FAULKNER

William Faulkner (1897–1962) was born into an established Southern family and grew up in a small town in Mississippi. He served in the Canadian and British Air Force during World War I, and began his writing career in earnest after the war. He studied briefly at the University of Mississippi and under the guidance of fellow author Sherwood Anderson. Many of his novels won critical acclaim (he won the Pulitzer Prize and the Nobel Prize for literature) but brought little money, forcing him to work for stints in Hollywood as a screen writer. In 1929, he was wedded through an arranged marriage that ended unhappily with divorce. "A Rose for Emily" was published in 1930.

A Rose for Emily

A Rose for Emily

1

When Miss Emily Grierson died, our whole town went to her funeral: the men through a sort of respectful affection for a fallen monument, the women mostly out of curiosity to see the inside of her house, which no one save an old manservant—a combined gardener and cook—had seen in at least ten years.

It was a big, squarish frame house that had once been white, decorated with cupolas and spires and scrolled balconies in the heavily lightsome style of the seventies, set on what had once been our most select street. But garages and cotton gins had encroached and obliterated even the august names of that neighbourhood; only Miss Emily's house was left, lifting its stubborn and coquettish decay above the cotton wagons and the gasoline pumps—an eyesore among eyesores. And now Miss Emily had gone to join the representatives of those august names where they lay in the cedar-bemused cemetery among the ranked and anonymous graves of Union and Confederate soldiers who fell at the battle of Jefferson.

Alive, Miss Emily had been a tradition, a duty, and a care; a sort of hereditary obligation upon the town, dating from that day in 1894 when Colonel Sartoris, the mayor—he who fathered the edict that no Negro woman should appear on the streets without an apron—remitted her taxes, the dispensation dating from the death of her father on into perpetuity. Not that Miss Emily would have accepted charity. Colonel Sartoris invented an involved tale to the effect that Miss Emily's father had loaned money to the town, which the town, as a matter of business, preferred this way of repaying. Only a man of Colonel Sartoris' generation and thought could have invented it, and only a woman could have believed it.

When the next generation, with its more modern ideas, became mayors and aldermen, this arrangement created some little dissatisfaction. On the first of the year they mailed her a tax notice. February came, and there was no reply. They wrote her a formal letter, asking her to call at the sheriff's office at her convenience. A week later the mayor wrote her himself, offering to call or to send his car for her, and received in reply a note on paper of an archaic shape, in a thin, flowing calligraphy in faded ink, to the effect that she no longer went out at all. The tax notice was also enclosed without comment.

5   They called a special meeting of the Board of Aldermen. A deputation waited upon her, knocked at the door through which no visitor had passed since she ceased giving china-painting lessons eight or ten years earlier. They were admitted by the old Negro into a dim hall from which a stairway mounted into still more shadow. It smelled of dust and disuse—a close, dank smell. The Negro led them into the parlour. It was furnished in heavy, leather-covered furniture. When the Negro opened the blinds of one window, they could see that the leather was cracked; and when they sat down, a faint dust rose sluggishly about their thighs, spinning with slow motes in the single sun-ray. On a tarnished gilt easel before the fireplace stood a crayon portrait of Miss Emily's father.

They rose when she entered—a small, fat woman in black, with a thin gold chain descending to her waist and vanishing into her belt, leaning on an ebony cane with a tarnished gold head. Her skeleton was small and spare; perhaps that was why what would have been merely plumpness in another was obesity in her. She looked bloated, like a body long submerged in motionless water, and of that pallid hue. Her eyes, lost in the fatty ridges of her face, looked like two small pieces of coal pressed into a lump of dough as they moved from one face to another while the visitors stated their errand.

She did not ask them to sit. She just stood in the door and listened quietly until the spokesman came to a stumbling halt. Then they could hear the invisible watch ticking at the end of the gold chain.

Her voice was dry and cold. "I have no taxes in Jefferson. Colonel Sartoris explained it to me. Perhaps one of you can gain access to the city records and satisfy yourselves."

"But we have. We are the city authorities, Miss Emily. Didn't you get a notice from the sheriff, signed by him?"

10   "I received a paper, yes," Miss Emily said. "Perhaps he considers himself the sheriff . . . I have no taxes in Jefferson."

"But there is nothing on the books to show that, you see. We must go by the—"

"See Colonel Sartoris. I have no taxes in Jefferson."

"But, Miss Emily—"

"See Colonel Sartoris." (Colonel Sartoris had been dead almost ten years.) "I have no taxes in Jefferson. Tobe!" The Negro appeared. "Show these gentlemen out."

2

15   So she vanquished them, horse and foot, just as she had vanquished their fathers thirty years before about the smell. That was two years after her father's death and a short time after her sweetheart—the one we believed would marry her—had deserted her. After her father's death she went out very little; after her sweetheart went away, people hardly saw her at all. A few of the ladies had the temerity to call, but were not received, and the only sign of life about the place was the Negro man—a young man then—going in and out with a market basket.

"Just as if a man—any man—could keep a kitchen properly," the ladies said; so they were not surprised when the smell developed. It was another link between the gross, teeming world and the high and mighty Griersons.

A neighbour, a woman, complained to the mayor, Judge Stevens, eighty years old.

"But what will you have me do about it, madam?" he said.

"Why, send her word to stop it," the woman said. "Isn't there a law?"

20   "I'm sure that won't be necessary," Judge Stevens said. "It's probably just a snake or a rat that nigger of hers killed in the yard. I'll speak to him about it."

The next day he received two more complaints, one from a man who came in diffident deprecation. "We really must do something about it, Judge. I'd be the last one in the world to bother Miss Emily, but we've got to do something." That night the Board of Aldermen met—three greybeards and one younger man, a member of the rising generation.

"It's simple enough," he said. "Send her word to have her place cleaned up. Give her a certain time to do it in, and if she don't . . . "

"Dammit, sir," Judge Stevens said, "will you accuse a lady to her face of smelling bad?"

So the next night, after midnight, four men crossed Miss Emily's lawn and slunk about the house like burglars, sniffing along the base of the brickwork and at the cellar openings while one of them performed a regular sowing motion with his hand out of a sack slung from his shoulder. They broke open the cellar door and sprinkled lime there, and in all the outbuildings. As they recrossed the lawn, a window that had been dark was lighted and Miss Emily sat in it, the light behind her, and her upright torso motionless as that of an idol. They crept quietly across the lawn and into the shadow of the locusts that lined the street. After a week or two the smell went away.

25   That was when people had begun to feel really sorry for her. People in our town, remembering how old lady Wyatt, her great-aunt, had gone completely crazy at last, believed that the Griersons held themselves a little too high for what they really were. None of the young men were quite good enough for Miss Emily and such. We had long thought of them as a tableau, Miss Emily a slender figure in white in the background, her father a spraddled silhouette in the foreground, his back to her and clutching a horsewhip, the two of them framed by the back-flung front door. So when she got to be thirty and was still single, we were not pleased exactly, but vindicated; even with insanity in the family she wouldn't have turned down all of her chances if they had really materialized.

When her father died, it got about that the house was all that was left to her; and in a way, people were glad. At last they could pity Miss Emily. Being left alone, and a pauper, she had become humanized. Now she too would know the old thrill and the old despair of a penny more or less.

The day after his death all the ladies prepared to call at the house and offer condolence and aid, as is our custom. Miss Emily met them at the door, dressed as usual and with no trace of grief on her face. She told them that her father was not dead. She did that for three days, with the ministers calling on her, and the doctors, trying to persuade her to let them dispose of the body. Just as they were about to resort to law and force, she broke down, and they buried her father quickly.

We did not say she was crazy then. We believed she had to do that. We remembered all the young men her father had driven away, and we knew that with nothing left, she would have to cling to that which had robbed her, as people will.

3

She was sick for a long time. When we saw her again, her hair was cut short, making her look like a girl, with a vague resemblance to those angels in coloured church windows—sort of tragic and serene.

30   The town had just let the contracts for paving the sidewalks, and in the summer after her father's death they began the work. The construction company came with niggers and mules and machinery, and a foreman named Homer Barron, a Yankee—a big, dark, ready man, with a big voice and eyes lighter than his face. The little boys would follow in groups to hear him cuss the niggers, and the niggers singing in time to the rise and fall of picks. Pretty soon he knew everybody in town. Whenever you heard a lot of laughing anywhere about the square, Homer Barron would be in the centre of the group. Presently we began to see him and Miss Emily on Sunday afternoons driving in the yellow-wheeled buggy and the matched team of bays from the livery stable.

At first we were glad that Miss Emily would have an interest, because the ladies all said, "Of course a Grierson would not think seriously of a Northerner, a day labourer." But there were still others, older people, who said that even grief could not cause a real lady to forget *noblesse oblige*—without calling it *noblesse oblige*. They just said, "Poor Emily. Her kinsfolk should come to her." She had some kin in Alabama; but years ago her father had fallen out with them over the estate of old lady Wyatt, the crazy woman, and there was no communication between the two families. They had not even been represented at the funeral.

And as soon as the old people said, "Poor Emily," the whispering began. "Do you suppose it's really so?" they said to one another. "Of course it is. What else could . . . " This behind their hands; rustling of craned silk and satin behind jalousies closed upon the sun of Sunday afternoon as the thin, swift clop-clop-clop of the matched team passed: "Poor Emily."

She carried her head high enough—even when we believed that she was fallen. It was as if she demanded more than ever the recognition of her dignity as the last Grierson; as if it had wanted that touch of earthiness to reaffirm her imperviousness. Like when she bought the rat poison, the arsenic. That was over a year after they had begun to say "Poor Emily," and while the two female cousins were visiting her.

"I want some poison," she said to the druggist. She was over thirty then, still a slight woman, though thinner than usual, with cold, haughty black eyes in a face the flesh of which was strained across the temples and about the eye-sockets as you imagine a lighthouse-keeper's face ought to look. "I want some poison," she said.

35   "Yes, Miss Emily. What kind? For rats and such? I'd recom——"

"I want the best you have. I don't care what kind."

The druggist named several. "They'll kill anything up to an elephant. But what you want is——"

"Arsenic," Miss Emily said. "Is that a good one?"

"Is . . . arsenic? Yes, ma'am. But what you want——"

40   "I want arsenic."

The druggist looked down at her. She looked back at him, erect, her face like a strained flag. "Why, of course," the druggist said. "If that's what you want. But the law requires you to tell what you are going to use it for."

Miss Emily just stared at him, her head tilted back in order to look him eye for eye, until he looked away and went and got the arsenic and wrapped it up. The Negro delivery boy brought her the package; the druggist didn't come back. When she opened the package at home there was written on the box, under the skull and bones: "For rats."

4

So the next day we all said, "She will kill herself"; and we said it would be the best thing. When she had first begun to be seen with Homer Barron, we had said, "She will marry him." Then we said, "She will persuade him yet," because Homer himself had remarked—he liked men, and it was known that he drank with the younger men in the Elks' Club—that he was not a marrying man. Later we said "Poor Emily" behind the jalousies as they passed on Sunday afternoon in the glittering buggy, Miss Emily with her head high and Homer Barron with his hat cocked and a cigar in his teeth, reins and whip in a yellow glove.

Then some of the ladies began to say that it was a disgrace to the town and a bad example to the young people. The men did not want to interfere, but at last the ladies forced the Baptist minister—Miss Emily's people were Episcopal—to call upon her. He would never divulge what happened during that interview, but he refused to go back again. The next Sunday they again drove about the streets, and the following day the minister's wife wrote to Miss Emily's relations in Alabama.

45   So she had blood-kin under her roof again and we sat back to watch developments. At first nothing happened. Then we were sure that they were to be married. We learned that Miss Emily had been to the jeweller's and ordered a man's toilet set in silver, with the letters H. B. on each piece. Two days later we learned that she had bought a complete outfit of men's clothing, including a nightshirt, and we said, "They are married." We were really glad. We were glad because the two female cousins were even more Grierson than Miss Emily had ever been.

So we were not surprised when Homer Barron—the streets had been finished some time since—was gone. We were a little disappointed that there was not a public blowing-off, but we believed that he had gone on to prepare for Miss Emily's coming, or to give her a chance to get rid of the cousins. (By that time it was a cabal, and we were all Miss Emily's allies to help circumvent the cousins.) Sure enough, after another week they departed. And, as we had expected all along, within three days Homer Barron was back in town. A neighbour saw the Negro man admit him at the kitchen door at dusk one evening.

And that was the last we saw of Homer Barron. And of Miss Emily for some time. The Negro man went in and out with the market basket, but the front door remained closed. Now and then we would see her at a window for a moment, as the men did that night when they sprinkled the lime, but for almost six months she did not appear on the streets. Then we knew that this was to be expected too; as if that quality of her father which had thwarted her woman's life so many times had been too virulent and too furious to die.

When we next saw Miss Emily, she had grown fat and her hair was turning grey. During the next few years it grew greyer and greyer until it attained an even pepper-and-salt iron-grey, when it ceased turning. Up to the day of her death at seventy-four it was still that vigorous iron-grey, like the hair of an active man.

From that time on her front door remained closed, save for a period of six or seven years, when she was about forty, during which she gave lessons in china-painting. She fitted up a studio in one of the downstairs rooms, where the daughters and grand-daughters of Colonel Sartoris' contemporaries were sent to her with the same regularity and in the same spirit that they were sent to church on Sundays with a twenty-five-cent piece for the collection plate. Meanwhile her taxes had been remitted.

50   Then the newer generation became the backbone and the spirit of the town, and the painting pupils grew up and fell away and did not send their children to her with boxes of colour and tedious brushes and pictures cut from the ladies' magazines. The front door closed upon the last one and remained closed for good. When the town got free postal delivery, Miss Emily alone refused to let them fasten the metal numbers above her door and attach a mailbox to it. She would not listen to them.

Daily, monthly, yearly we watched the Negro grow greyer and more stooped, going in and out with the market basket. Each December we sent her a tax notice, which would be returned by the post office a week later, unclaimed. Now and then we would see her in one of the downstairs windows—she had evidently shut up the top floor of the house—like the carven torso of an idol in a niche, looking or not looking at us, we could never tell which. Thus she passed from generation to generation—dear, inescapable, impervious, tranquil, and perverse.

And so she died. Fell ill in the house filled with dust and shadows, with only a doddering Negro man to wait on her. We did not even know she was sick; we had long since given up trying to get any information from the Negro. He talked to no one, probably not even to her, for his voice had grown harsh and rusty, as if from disuse.

She died in one of the downstairs rooms, in a heavy walnut bed with a curtain, her grey head propped on a pillow yellow and mouldy with age and lack of sunlight.

5

The Negro met the first of the ladies at the front door and let them in, with their hushed, sibilant voices and their quick curious glances; and then he disappeared. He walked right through the house and out the back and was not seen again.

55   The two female cousins came at once. They held the funeral on the second day, with the town coming to look at Miss Emily beneath a mass of bought flowers, with the crayon face of her father musing profoundly above the bier and the ladies sibilant and macabre; and the very old men—some in their brushed Confederate uniforms—on the porch and the lawn, talking of Miss Emily as if she had been a contemporary of theirs, believing that they had danced with her and courted her perhaps, confusing time with its mathematical progression, as the old do, to whom all the past is not a diminishing road but, instead, a huge meadow which no winter ever quite touches, divided from them now by the narrow bottle-neck of the most recent decade of years.

Already we knew that there was one room in that region above stairs which no one had seen in forty years, and which would have to be forced. They waited until Miss Emily was decently in the ground before they opened it.

The violence of breaking down the door seemed to fill this room with pervading dust. A thin, acrid pall as of the tomb seemed to lie everywhere upon this room decked and furnished as for a bridal: upon the valance curtains of faded rose colour, upon the rose-shaded lights, upon the dressing table, upon the delicate array of crystal and the man's toilet things backed with tarnished silver, silver so tarnished that the monogram was obscured. Among them lay a collar and tie, as if they had just been removed, which, lifted, left upon the surface a pale crescent in the dust. Upon a chair hung the suit, carefully folded; beneath it the two mute shoes and the discarded socks.

The man himself lay in the bed.

For a long while we just stood there, looking down at the profound and fleshless grin. The body had apparently once lain in the attitude of an embrace, but now the long sleep that outlasts love, that conquers even the grimace of love, had cuckolded him. What was left of him, rotted beneath what was left of the night-shirt, had become inextricable from the bed in which he lay; and upon him and upon the pillow beside him lay that even coating of the patient and biding dust.

60   Then we noticed that in the second pillow was the indentation of a head. One of us lifted something from it, and leaning forward, that faint and invisible dust dry and acrid in the nostrils, we saw a long strand of iron-grey hair.

INQUIRING FURTHER

1. How does "A Rose for Emily" help us understand the role of tradition in establishing relationships between our selves and society? Are traditions more important to individuals or to society as a whole? Perhaps to both?

2. Is it fair to relate "A Rose for Emily" to "Medicated" on page 540? Sketch out a list of ideas for an interpretation of the story in terms of Emily's state of mind?

3. Analyze the narrative strategies in "A Rose for Emily." How would you characterize the narrator's relationship with the reader? Can you recognize moments of foreshadowing or instances in the text that highlight specific themes? Write a three or more page paper analyzing the narration of the story.

4. Is Emily Grierson a victim of the conventions of society? How does the community influence her behavior? What can be said about her father and his place in the community? Hold a discussion with classmates concerning the responsibility of the community for Emily's behavior.

5. Consider the still frames and video clips from the film version of "A Rose for Emily" on our CD. Examine the Enhanced Reading exploring issues of identity and community.

NATHANIEL HAWTHORNE

*Nathaniel Hawthorne (1804–1864) descended from a prominent Puritan family that included a judge at the Salem witchcraft trials. His writing frequently explored the historical events and settings of New England. His work often emphasized **allegory**, the use of strong symbolism often associated with a moral. His best known work,* The Scarlet Letter, *exposes the hypocrisy and moral dimensions of Puritan society. "Young Goodman Brown" provides an allegorical tale that considers the relationships between individuals, religion, and Puritan communities. It was published in 1846.*

Young Goodman Brown

Young Goodman Brown came forth at sunset into the street at Salem village; but put his head back, after crossing the threshold, to exchange a parting kiss with his young wife. And Faith, as the wife was aptly named, thrust her own pretty head into the street, letting the wind play with the pink ribbons of her cap while she called to Goodman Brown.

Still frames and video clips from *Young Goodman Brown*

"Dearest heart," whispered she, softly and rather sadly, when her lips were close to his ear, "prithee put off your journey until sunrise and sleep in your own bed to-night. A lone woman is troubled with such dreams and such thoughts that she's afeard of herself sometimes. Pray tarry with me this night, dear husband, of all nights in the year."

"My love and my Faith," replied young Goodman Brown, "of all nights in the year, this one night must I tarry away from thee. My journey, as thou callest it, forth and back again, must needs be done twixt now and sunrise. What, my sweet, pretty wife, dost thou doubt me already, and we but three months married?"

"Then God bless you!" said Faith, with the pink ribbons; "and may you find all well when you come back."

5 "Amen!" cried Goodman Brown. "Say thy prayers, dear Faith, and go to bed at dusk, and no harm will come to thee."

So they parted; and the young man pursued his way until, being about to turn the corner by the meeting-house, he looked back and saw the head of Faith still peeping after him with a melancholy air, in spite of her pink ribbons.

"Poor little Faith!" thought he, for his heart smote him. "What a wretch am I to leave her on such an errand! She talks of dreams, too. Methought as she spoke there was trouble in her face, as if a dream had warned her what work is to be done tonight. But no, no; 't would kill her to think it. Well, she's a blessed angel on earth; and after this one night I'll cling to her skirts and follow her to heaven."

With this excellent resolve for the future, Goodman Brown felt himself justified in making more haste on his present evil purpose. He had taken a dreary road, darkened by all the gloomiest trees of the forest, which barely stood aside to let the narrow path creep through, and closed immediately behind. It was all as lonely as could be; and there is this peculiarity in such a solitude, that the traveller knows not who may be concealed by the innumerable trunks and the thick boughs overhead; so that with lonely footsteps he may yet be passing through an unseen multitude.

"There may be a devilish Indian behind every tree," said Goodman Brown to himself; and he glanced fearfully behind him as he added, "What if the devil himself should be at my very elbow!"

10   His head being turned back, he passed a crook of the road, and, looking forward again, beheld the figure of a man, in grave and decent attire, seated at the foot of an old tree. He arose at Goodman Brown's approach and walked onward side by side with him.

"You are late, Goodman Brown," said he. "The clock of the Old South was striking as I came through Boston, and that is full fifteen minutes agone."

"Faith kept me back a while," replied the young man, with a tremor in his voice, caused by the sudden appearance of his companion, though not wholly unexpected.

It was now deep dusk in the forest, and deepest in that part of it where these two were journeying. As nearly as could be discerned, the second traveller was about fifty years old, apparently in the same rank of life as Goodman Brown, and bearing a considerable resemblance to him, though perhaps more in expression than features. Still they might have been taken for father and son. And yet, though the elder person was as simply clad as the younger, and as simple in manner too, he had an indescribable air of one who knew the world, and who would not have felt abashed at the governor's dinner table or in King William's court, were it possible that his affairs should call him thither. But the only thing about him that could be fixed upon as remarkable was his staff, which bore the likeness of a great black snake, so curiously wrought that it might almost be seen to twist and wriggle itself like a living serpent. This, of course, must have been an ocular deception, assisted by the uncertain light.

"Come, Goodman Brown," cried his fellow-traveller, "this is a dull pace for the beginning of a journey. Take my staff, if you are so soon weary."

15   "Friend," said the other, exchanging his slow pace for a full stop, "having kept covenant by meeting thee here, it is my purpose now to return whence I came. I have scruples touching the matter thou wot'st of."

"Sayest thou so?" replied he of the serpent, smiling apart. "Let us walk on, nevertheless, reasoning as we go; and if I convince thee not thou shalt turn back. We are but a little way in the forest yet."

"Too far! too far!" exclaimed the goodman, unconsciously resuming his walk. "My father never went into the woods on such an errand, nor his father before him. We have been a race of honest men and good Christians since the days of the martyrs; and shall I be the first of the name of Brown that ever took this path and kept"—

"Such company, thou wouldst say," observed the elder person, interpreting his pause. "Well said, Goodman Brown! I have been as well acquainted with your family as with ever a one among the Puritans; and that's no trifle to say. I helped your grandfather, the constable, when he lashed the Quaker woman so smartly through the streets of Salem; and it was I that brought your father a pitch-pine knot, kindled at my own hearth, to set fire to an Indian village, in King Philip's war. They were my good friends, both; and many a pleasant walk have we had along this path, and returned merrily after midnight. I would fain be friends with you for their sake."

"If it be as thou sayest," replied Goodman Brown, "I marvel they never spoke of these matters; or, verily, I marvel not, seeing that the least rumor of the sort would have driven them from New England. We are a people of prayer, and good works to boot, and abide no such wickedness."

20   "Wickedness or not," said the traveller with the twisted staff, "I have a very general acquaintance here in New England. The deacons of many a church have drunk the communion wine with me; the selectmen of divers towns make me their chairman; and a majority of the Great and General Court are firm supporters of my interest. The governor and I, too—But these are state secrets."

"Can this be so?" cried Goodman Brown, with a stare of amazement at his undisturbed companion. "Howbeit, I have nothing to do with the governor and council; they have their own ways, and are no rule for a simple husbandman like me. But, were I to go on with thee, how should I meet the eye of that good old man, our minister, at Salem village? Oh, his voice would make me tremble both Sabbath day and lecture day."

Thus far the elder traveller had listened with due gravity; but now burst into a fit of irrepressible mirth, shaking himself so violently that his snake-like staff actually seemed to wriggle in sympathy.

"Ha! ha! ha!" shouted he again and again; then composing himself, "Well, go on, Goodman Brown, go on; but, prithee, don't kill me with laughing."

"Well, then, to end the matter at once," said Goodman Brown, considerably nettled, "there is my wife, Faith. It would break her dear little heart; and I'd rather break my own."

25   "Nay, if that be the case," answered the other, "e'en go thy ways, Goodman Brown. I would not for twenty old women like the one hobbling before us that Faith should come to any harm."

As he spoke he pointed his staff at a female figure on the path, in whom Goodman Brown recognized a very pious and exemplary dame, who had taught him his catechism in youth, and was still his moral and spiritual adviser, jointly with the minister and Deacon Gookin.

"A marvel, truly, that Goody Cloyse should be so far in the wilderness at nightfall," said he. "But with your leave, friend, I shall take a cut through the woods until we have left this Christian woman behind. Being a stranger to you, she might ask whom I was consorting with and whither I was going."

"Be it so," said his fellow-traveller. "Betake you to the woods, and let me keep the path."

Accordingly the young man turned aside, but took care to watch his companion, who advanced softly along the road until he had come within a staff's length of the old dame. She, meanwhile, was making the best of her way, with singular speed for so aged a woman, and mumbling some indistinct words—a prayer, doubtless—as she went. The traveller put forth his staff and touched her withered neck with what seemed the serpent's tail.

30   "The devil!" screamed the pious old lady.

"Then Goody Cloyse knows her old friend?" observed the traveller, confronting her and leaning on his writhing stick.

"Ah, forsooth, and is it your worship indeed?" cried the good dame. "Yea, truly is it, and in the very image of my old gossip, Goodman Brown, the grandfather of the silly fellow that now is. But—would your worship believe it?—

my broomstick hath strangely disappeared, stolen, as I suspect, by that unhanged witch, Goody Cory, and that, too, when I was all anointed with the juice of smallage, and cinquefoil, and wolf's bane"—

"Mingled with fine wheat and the fat of a new-born babe," said the shape of old Goodman Brown.

"Ah, your worship knows the recipe," cried the old lady, cackling aloud. "So, as I was saying, being all ready for the meeting, and no horse to ride on, I made up my mind to foot it; for they tell me there is a nice young man to be taken into communion to-night. But now your good worship will lend me your arm, and we shall be there in a twinkling.

35   "That can hardly be," answered her friend. "I may not spare you my arm, Goody Cloyse; but here is my staff, if you will."

So saying, he threw it down at her feet, where, perhaps, it assumed life, being one of the rods which its owner had formerly lent to the Egyptian magi. Of this fact, however, Goodman Brown could not take cognizance. He had cast up his eyes in astonishment, and, looking down again, beheld neither Goody Cloyse nor the serpentine staff, but his fellow-traveller alone, who waited for him as calmly as if nothing had happened.

"That old woman taught me my catechism," said the young man; and there was a world of meaning in this simple comment.

They continued to walk onward, while the elder traveller exhorted his companion to make good speed and persevere in the path, discoursing so aptly that his arguments seemed rather to spring up in the bosom of his auditor than to be suggested by himself. As they went, he plucked a branch of maple to serve for a walking stick, and began to strip it of the twigs and little boughs, which were wet with evening dew. The moment his fingers touched them they became strangely withered and dried up as with a week's sunshine. Thus the pair proceeded, at a good free pace, until suddenly, in a gloomy hollow of the road, Goodman Brown sat himself down on the stump of a tree and refused to go any farther.

"Friend," said he, stubbornly, "my mind is made up. Not another step will I budge on this errand. What if a wretched old woman do choose to go to the devil when I thought she was going to heaven: is that any reason why I should quit my dear Faith and go after her?"

40   "You will think better of this by and by," said his acquaintance, composedly. "Sit here and rest yourself a while; and when you feel like moving again, there is my staff to help you along."

Without more words, he threw his companion the maple stick, and was as speedily out of sight as if he had vanished into the deepening gloom. The young man sat a few moments by the roadside, applauding himself greatly, and thinking with how clear a conscience he should meet the minister in his morning walk, nor shrink from the eye of good old Deacon Gookin. And what calm sleep would be his that very night, which was to have been spent so wickedly, but so purely and sweetly now, in the arms of Faith! Amidst these pleasant and praiseworthy meditations, Goodman Brown heard the tramp of horses along the road, and deemed it advisable to conceal himself within the verge of the forest, conscious of the guilty purpose that had brought him thither, though now so happily turned from it.

On came the hoof tramps and the voices of the riders, two grave old voices, conversing soberly as they drew near. These mingled sounds appeared to pass along the road, within a few yards of the young man's hiding-place; but, owing doubtless to the depth of the gloom at that particular spot, neither the travellers nor their steeds were visible. Though their figures brushed the small boughs by the wayside, it could not be seen that they intercepted, even for a moment, the faint gleam from the strip of bright sky athwart which they must have passed. Goodman Brown alternately crouched and stood on tiptoe, pulling aside the branches and thrusting forth his head as far as he durst without discerning so much as a shadow. It vexed him the more, because he could have sworn, were such a thing possible, that he recognized the voices of the minister and Deacon Gookin, jogging along quietly, as they were wont to do, when bound to some ordination or ecclesiastical council. While yet within hearing, one of the riders stopped to pluck a switch.

"Of the two, reverend sir," said the voice like the deacon's, "I had rather miss an ordination dinner than to-night's meeting. They tell me that some of our community are to be here from Falmouth and beyond, and others from Connecticut and Rhode Island, besides several of the Indian powwows, who, after their fashion, know almost as much deviltry as the best of us. Moreover, there is a goodly young woman to be taken into communion."

"Mighty well, Deacon Gookin!" replied the solemn old tones of the minister. "Spur up, or we shall be late. Nothing can be done, you know, until I get on the ground."

45   The hoofs clattered again; and the voices, talking so strangely in the empty air, passed on through the forest, where no church had ever been gathered or solitary Christian prayed. Whither, then, could these holy men be journeying so deep into the heathen wilderness? Young Goodman Brown caught hold of a tree for support, being ready to sink down on the ground, faint and overburdened with the heavy sickness of his heart. He looked up to the sky, doubting whether there really was a heaven above him. Yet there was the blue arch, and the stars brightening in it.

"With heaven above and Faith below, I will yet stand firm against the devil!" cried Goodman Brown.

While he still gazed upward into the deep arch of the firmament and had lifted his hands to pray, a cloud, though no wind was stirring, hurried across the zenith and hid the brightening stars. The blue sky was still visible, except directly overhead, where this black mass of cloud was sweeping swiftly northward. Aloft in the air, as if from the depths of the cloud, came a confused and doubtful sound of voices. Once the listener fancied that he could distinguish the accents of towns-people of his own, men and women, both pious and ungodly, many of whom he had met at the communion table, and had seen others rioting at the tavern. The next moment, so indistinct were the sounds, he doubted whether he had heard aught but the murmur of the old forest, whispering without a wind. Then came a stronger swell of those familiar tones, heard daily in the sunshine at Salem village, but never until now from a cloud of night There was one voice of a young woman, uttering lamentations, yet with an uncertain sorrow, and entreating for some favor, which, perhaps, it would grieve her to obtain; and all the unseen multitude, both saints and sinners, seemed to encourage her onward.

"Faith!" shouted Goodman Brown, in a voice of agony and desperation; and the echoes of the forest mocked him, crying, "Faith! Faith!" as if bewildered wretches were seeking her all through the wilderness.

The cry of grief, rage, and terror was yet piercing the night, when the unhappy husband held his breath for a response. There was a scream, drowned immediately in a louder murmur of voices, fading into far-off laughter, as the dark cloud swept away, leaving the clear and silent sky above Goodman Brown. But something fluttered lightly down through the air and caught on the branch of a tree. The young man seized it, and beheld a pink ribbon.

50   "My Faith is gone!" cried he, after one stupefied moment. "There is no good on earth; and sin is but a name. Come, devil; for to thee is this world given."

And, maddened with despair, so that he laughed loud and long, did Goodman Brown grasp his staff and set forth again, at such a rate that he seemed to fly along the forest path rather than to walk or run. The road grew wilder and drearier and more faintly traced, and vanished at length, leaving him in the heart of the dark wilderness, still rushing onward with the instinct that guides mortal man to evil. The whole forest was peopled with frightful sounds—the creaking of the trees, the howling of wild beasts, and the yell of Indians; while sometimes the wind tolled like a distant church bell, and sometimes gave a broad roar around the traveller, as if all Nature were laughing him to scorn. But he was himself the chief horror of the scene, and shrank not from its other horrors.

"Ha! ha! ha!" roared Goodman Brown when the wind laughed at him.

"Let us hear which will laugh loudest. Think not to frighten me with your deviltry. Come witch, come wizard, come Indian powwow, come devil himself, and here comes Goodman Brown. You may as well fear him as he fear you."

In truth, all through the haunted forest there could be nothing more frightful than the figure of Goodman Brown. On he flew among the black pines, brandishing his staff with frenzied gestures, now giving vent to an inspiration of horrid blasphemy, and now shouting forth such laughter as set all the echoes of the forest laughing like demons around him. The fiend in his own shape is less hideous than when he rages in the breast of man. Thus sped the demoniac on his course, until, quivering among the trees, he saw a red light before him, as when the felled trunks and branches of a clearing have been set on fire, and throw up their lurid blaze against the sky, at the hour of midnight. He paused, in a lull of the tempest that had driven him onward, and heard the swell of what seemed a hymn, rolling solemnly from a distance with the weight of many voices. He knew the tune; it was a familiar one in the choir of the village meeting-house. The verse died heavily away, and was lengthened by a chorus, not of human voices, but of all the sounds of the benighted wilderness pealing in awful harmony together. Goodman Brown cried out, and his cry was lost to his own ear by its unison with the cry of the desert.

55   In the interval of silence he stole forward until the light glared full upon his eyes. At one extremity of an open space, hemmed in by the dark wall of the forest, arose a rock, bearing some rude, natural resemblance either to an alter or a pulpit, and surrounded by four blazing pines, their tops aflame, their stems untouched, like candles at an evening meeting. The mass of foliage that had overgrown the summit of the rock was all on fire, blazing high into the night and fitfully illuminating the whole field. Each pendent twig and leafy festoon was in a blaze. As the red light arose and fell, a numerous congregation alternately shone forth, then disappeared in shadow, and again grew, as it were, out of the darkness, peopling the heart of the solitary woods at once.

"A grave and dark-clad company," quoth Goodman Brown.

In truth they were such. Among them, quivering to and fro between gloom and splendor, appeared faces that would be seen next day at the council board of the province, and others which, Sabbath after Sabbath, looked devoutly heavenward, and benignantly over the crowded pews, from the holiest pulpits in the land. Some affirm that the lady of the governor was there. At least there were high dames well known to her, and wives of honored husbands, and widows, a great multitude, and ancient maidens, all of excellent repute, and fair young girls, who trembled lest their mothers should espy them. Either the sudden gleams of light flashing over the obscure field bedazzled Goodman Brown, or he recognized a score of the church members of Salem village famous for their especial sanctity. Good old Deacon Gookin had arrived, and waited at the skirts of that venerable saint, his revered pastor. But, irreverently consorting with these grave, reputable, and pious people, these elders of the church, these chaste dames and dewy virgins, there were men of dissolute lives and women of spotted fame, wretches given over to all mean and filthy vice, and suspected even of horrid crimes. It was strange to see that the good shrank not from the wicked, nor were the sinners abashed by the saints. Scattered also among their pale-faced enemies were the Indian priests, or powwows, who had often scared their native forest with more hideous incantations than any known to English witchcraft.

"But where is Faith?" thought Goodman Brown; and, as hope came into his heart, he trembled.

Another verse of the hymn arose, a slow and mournful strain, such as the pious love, but joined to words which expressed all that our nature can conceive of sin, and darkly hinted at far more. Unfathomable to mere mortals is the lore of fiends. Verse after verse was sung; and still the chorus of the desert swelled between like the deepest tone of a mighty organ; and with the final peal of that dreadful anthem there came a sound, as if the roaring wind, the rushing streams, the howling beasts, and every other voice of the unconcerted wilderness were mingling and according with the voice of guilty man in homage to the prince of all. The four blazing pines threw up a loftier flame, and obscurely discovered shapes and visages of horror on the smoke wreaths above the impious assembly. At the same moment the fire on the rock shot redly forth and formed a glowing arch above its base, where now appeared a figure. With reverence be it spoken, the figure bore no slight similitude, both in garb and manner, to some grave divine of the New England churches.

60   "Bring forth the converts!" cried a voice that echoed through the field and rolled into the forest.

At the word, Goodman Brown stepped forth from the shadow of the trees and approached the congregation, with whom he felt a loathful brotherhood by the sympathy of all that was wicked in his heart. He could have well-nigh sworn that the shape of his own dead father beckoned him to advance, looking downward from a smoke wreath, while a woman, with dim features of despair, threw out her hand to warn him back. Was it his mother? But he had no power to retreat one step, nor to resist, even in thought, when the minister and good old Deacon Gookin seized his arms and led him to the blazing rock. Thither came also the slender form of a veiled female, led between Goody Cloyse, that pious teacher of the catechism, and Martha Carrier, who had received the devil's promise to be queen of hell. A rampant hag was she. And there stood the proselytes beneath the canopy of fire.

"Welcome, my children," said the dark figure, "to the communion of your race. Ye have found thus young your nature and your destiny. My children, look behind you!"

They turned; and flashing forth, as it were, in a sheet of flame, the fiend worshippers were seen; the smile of welcome gleamed darkly on every visage.

"There," resumed the sable form, "are all whom ye have reverenced from youth. Ye deemed them holier than yourselves, and shrank from your own sin, contrasting it with their lives of righteousness and prayerful aspirations heavenward. Yet here are they all in my worshipping assembly. This night it shall be granted you to know their secret deeds: how hoary-bearded elders of the church have whispered wanton words to the young maids of their households; how many a woman, eager for widows' weeds, has given her husband a drink at bedtime and let him sleep his last sleep in her bosom; how beardless youths have made haste to inherit their fathers' wealth; and how fair damsels—blush not, sweet ones—have dug little graves in the garden, and bidden me, the sole guest to an infant's funeral. By the sympathy of your human hearts for sin ye shall scent out all the places—whether in church, bedchamber, street, field, or forest—where crime has been committed, and shall exult to behold the whole earth one stain of guilt, one mighty blood spot. Far more than this. It shall be yours to penetrate, in every bosom, the deep mystery of sin, the fountain of all wicked arts, and which inexhaustibly supplies more evil impulses than human power—than my power at its utmost—can make manifest in deeds. And now, my children, look upon each other."

65   They did so; and, by the blaze of the hell-kindled torches, the wretched man beheld his Faith, and the wife her husband, trembling before that unhallowed altar.

"Lo, there ye stand, my children," said the figure, in a deep and solemn tone, almost sad with its despairing awfulness, as if his once angelic nature could yet mourn for our miserable race. "Depending upon one another's hearts, ye had still hoped that virtue were not all a dream. Now are ye undeceived. Evil is the nature of mankind. Evil must be your only happiness. Welcome again, my children, to the communion of your race."

"Welcome," repeated the fiend worshippers, in one cry of despair and triumph.

And there they stood, the only pair, as it seemed, who were yet hesitating on the verge of wickedness in this dark world. A basin was hollowed, naturally, in the rock. Did it contain water, reddened by the lurid light? or was it blood? or, perchance, a liquid flame? Herein did the shape of evil dip his hand and prepare to lay the mark of baptism upon their foreheads, that they might be partakers of the mystery of sin, more conscious of the secret guilt of others, both in deed and thought, than they could now be of their own. The husband cast one look at his pale wife, and Faith at him. What polluted wretches would the next glance show them to each other, shuddering alike at what they disclosed and what they saw!

"Faith! Faith!" cried the husband, "look up to heaven, and resist the wicked one."

70   Whether Faith obeyed he knew not. Hardly had he spoken when he found himself amid calm night and solitude, listening to a roar of the wind which died heavily away through the forest. He staggered against the rock, and felt it chill and damp; while a hanging twig, that had been all on fire, besprinkled his cheek with the coldest dew.

The next morning young Goodman Brown came slowly into the street of Salem village, staring around him like a bewildered man. The good old minister was taking a walk along the graveyard to get an appetite for breakfast and meditate his sermon, and bestowed a blessing, as he passed, on Goodman Brown. He shrank from the venerable saint as if to avoid an anathema. Old Deacon Gookin was at domestic worship, and the holy words of his prayer were heard through the open window. "What God doth the wizard pray to?" quoth Goodman Brown. Goody Cloyse, that excellent old Christian, stood in the early sunshine at her own lattice, catechizing a little girl who had brought her a pint of morning's milk. Goodman Brown snatched away the child as from the grasp of the fiend himself. Turning the corner by the meeting-house, he spied the head of Faith, with the pink ribbons, gazing anxiously forth, and bursting into such joy at sight of him that she skipped along the street and almost kissed her husband before the whole village. But Goodman Brown looked sternly and sadly into her face, and passed on without a greeting.

Had Goodman Brown fallen asleep in the forest and only dreamed a wild dream of a witch-meeting?

Be it so if you will; but, alas! it was a dream of evil omen for young Goodman Brown. A stern, a sad, a darkly meditative, a distrustful, if not a desperate man did he become from the night of that fearful dream. On the Sabbath day, when the congregation were singing a holy psalm, he could not listen because an anthem of sin rushed loudly upon his ear and drowned all the blessed strain. When the minister spoke from the pulpit with power and fervid eloquence, and, with his hand on the open Bible, of the sacred truths of our religion, and of saint-like lives and triumphant deaths, and of future bliss or misery unutterable, then did Goodman Brown turn pale, dreading lest the roof should thunder down upon the gray blasphemer and his hearers. Often, waking suddenly at midnight, he shrank from the bosom of Faith; and at morning or eventide, when the family knelt down at prayer, he scowled and muttered to himself, and gazed sternly at his wife, and turned away. And when he had lived long, and was borne to his grave a hoary corpse, followed by Faith, an aged woman, and children and grandchildren, a goodly procession, besides neighbors not a few, they carved no hopeful verse upon his tombstone, for his dying hour was gloom.

INQUIRING FURTHER

1. Explore the still frames and video clips from the film *Young Goodman Brown* on our CD. How do these clips help you to think about the psychological and social dimensions of the work?

2. "Young Goodman Brown" has been said to present an allegorical story that offers a moral. Would you say the story differs from other works in the way it uses symbolism to convey a message? What might make this story more allegorical than others? Freewrite for five minutes about reading "Young Goodman Brown" allegorically.

3. Can you develop an interpretation that treats Brown's journey into the forest in psychological terms? Sketch out a list of ideas that could be used to create such an interpretation.

EXTENDED INQUIRY

Identity and the Harlem Renaissance

The Harlem Renaissance is frequently viewed as a central moment in the emergence of twentieth-century African-American culture. Fueled by migration to the northern cities after World War I, New York's Harlem experienced a surge of literature, music, theater, and art during the 1920s and 1930s. A number of artists came to Harlem to give voice to what they saw as the unique aspects of African-American culture and identity.

However, viewing the Harlem Renaissance as a groundswell of achievement for African Americans overlooks some of the tensions present even in the days of optimism that marked the beginning of what Langston Hughes has called "the period when the negro was in vogue." While there was much enthusiasm for the artists emerging in Harlem, there were also many problems with society and with the position of African Americans.

Some of these problems relate to the daily lives of African Americans. The movement of African Americans to the large urban centers of the north reflected worsening economic and social conditions in the rural south. In many instances, African Americans did find opportunities in the urban north. But in many cases, they did not find a life that matched the upbeat message proclaiming social and artistic freedom associated with the Harlem Renaissance.

Additionally, the relationship between African-American artists of the Harlem Renaissance and mainstream publishers and benefactors is also complex. Many of the performing artists of Harlem played to mixed houses of African and Anglo Americans. Some performances were staged for exclusively white audiences. African Americans had to deal with the question of whether their work was becoming accepted for its artistic merit, or simply because it satisfied the curiosity of mainstream audiences.

All of these tensions can be seen in the works of Harlem Renaissance artists. In literature, painting, and music artists expressed hope in what was at the time known as the **New Negro Movement**. These artists explored their heritage as slaves and displaced Africans, while celebrating their identity as African Americans participating in a rebirth. They also considered the conditions of their day, and used their art to give voice to concerns of social and economic justice that called for attention.

Jazz Music and the Poetry of Langston Hughes

Langston Hughes (1902–1967) reports in *The Big Sea* that a central event in his young life took place in his early twenties, when he took work on ocean liners traveling to Africa. Upon seeing Africa, Hughes claims "something took hold of me inside. My Africa, Motherland of the Negro peoples! And me a Negro! The real thing!" Already Hughes had been writing poetry, but this experience confirmed for him his desire to communicate the heritage and contemporary issues of African Americans in his writing.

Hughes recognized some of the most dramatic expressions of African-American identity in blues and jazz music. Blues could trace its roots to the days of slavery, providing a connection with a heritage of suffering and oppression. Jazz offered a more contemporary alternative, a liberating expression of possibility. For Hughes, blues and jazz expressed the heritage, social concerns, and causes for celebration of African Americans. Hughes often took music as a subject for his work and incorporated musical elements into many of his poems.

The readings below should help you learn more about the connections between poetry and music in Hughes' work. Be sure, also, to explore audio clips on our CD, so that you can listen to Hughes read his work and hear some of the blues and jazz music that inspired the poems.

The Negro Speaks of Rivers (1921)

(To W. E. B. DuBois)

I've known rivers:
I've known rivers ancient as the world and older than the flow of
    human blood in human veins.

My soul has grown deep like the rivers.

I bathed in the Euphrates when dawns were young.
5   I built my hut near the Congo and it lulled me to sleep.
I looked upon the Nile and raised the pyramids above it.
I heard the singing of the Mississippi when Abe Lincoln
    went down to New Orleans, and I've seen its muddy
    bosom turn all golden in the sunset.

I've known rivers:
Ancient, dusky rivers.
10   My soul has grown deep like the rivers.

Trumpet Player: 52nd Street (1926)

The Negro
With the trumpet at his lips
Has dark moons of weariness
Beneath his eyes
5   Where the smoldering memory
Of slave ships
Blazed to the crack of whips
About his thighs.

The Negro
10   With the trumpet at his lips
Has a head of vibrant hair
Tamed down,
Patent-leathered now
Until it gleams
15   Like jet—
Were jet a crown.

The music
From the trumpet at his lips
Is honey
20   Mixed with liquid fire.
The rhythm
From the trumpet at his lips
Is ecstasy
Distilled from old desire—

25   Desire
     That is longing for the moon
     Where the moonlight's but a spotlight
     In his eyes,
     Desire
30   That is longing for the sea
     Where the sea's a bar-glass
     Sucker size.

     The Negro
     With the trumpet at his lips
35   Whose jacket
     Has a *fine* one-button roll,
     Does not know
     Upon what riff the music slips
     Its hypodermic needle
40   To his soul—

     But softly
     As the tune comes from his throat
     Trouble
     Mellows to a golden note.

Dream Boogie (1925)

     Good morning, daddy!
     Ain't you heard
     The boogie-woogie rumble
     Of a dream deferred?

5   Listen closely:
     You'll hear their feet
     Beating out and Beating out a—

     You think
     It's a happy beat?

10   Listen to it closely:
     Ain't you heard
     something underneath
     like a—

     What did I say?

15   Sure,
     I'm happy!
     Take it away!

     Hey, pop!
     Re-bop!
20   Mop!

     Y-e-a-h!

Weary Blues (1925)

Droning a drowsy syncopated tune,
Rocking back and forth to a mellow croon,
   I heard a Negro play.
Down on Lenox Avenue the other night
5   By the pale dull pallor of an old gas light
     He did a lazy sway . . .
     He did a lazy sway . . .
To the tune o' those Weary Blues.
With his ebony hands on each ivory key
10   He made that poor piano moan with melody.
     O Blues!
Swaying to and fro on his rickety stool
He played that sad raggy tune like a musical fool.
     Sweet Blues!
15   Coming from a black man's soul.
     O Blues!
In a deep song voice with a melancholy tone
I heard that Negro sing, that old piano moan—
     "Ain't got nobody in all this world,
20   Ain't got nobody but ma self.
     I's gwine to quit ma frownin'
     And put ma troubles on the shelf."

Thump, thump, thump, went his foot on the floor.
He played a few chords then he sang some more—
25   "I got the Weary Blues
     And I can't be satisfied.
     Got the Weary Blues
     And can't be satisfied—
     I ain't happy no mo'
30   And I wish that I had died."
And far into the night he crooned that tune.
The stars went out and so did the moon.
The singer stopped playing and went to bed
While the Weary Blues echoed through his head.
35   He slept like a rock or a man that's dead.

Hughes's
poetry,
jazz, and
blues
music

Harlem (1951)

What happens to a dream deferred?

Does it dry up
like a raisin in the sun?
Or fester like a sore—
5   And then run?
Does it stink like rotten meat?
Or crust and sugar over—
like a syrupy sweet?

Maybe it just sags
10   like a heavy load.

Or does it explode?

---

1. "The Negro Speaks of Rivers" aligns rivers with the speaker of the poem's soul. How does the metaphor of the river address issues of African-American identity? Are these issues unique to African Americans?

2. The Harlem Renaissance is often described as a time of rebirth, a movement marked by optimism and a flourishing of African-American expression. What do you make of Hughes's poem, "Harlem," in light of this characterization? Freewrite for five minutes about the relationship between "Harlem" and The Harlem Renaissance.

3. Listen to the audio recordings of jazz and blues on our CD. Do you feel as if Hughes's poems capture the musical elements of these songs? Can you recognize specific elements of the poems such as rhyme, structure, rhythm, or sound that can be described as musical? Consider the music and poetry on the CD to further explore these relationships.

The Stories of Rudolph Fisher

Rudolph Fisher (1897-1934) was both a successful doctor and a writer. He depicted many aspects of Harlem life in his fiction, portraying both poor blacks from working-class backgrounds, and upwardly mobile black artists and intellectuals. His work emphasizes the issues raised by the economic advancement of African Americans. It often explores the disparity between the success of a relative few artists and professionals, and the everyday lives of working-class blacks. He also explores the tensions between black and white culture illuminated by the Harlem Renaissance.

Miss Cynthie (1933)

For the first time in her life somebody had called her "madam."

She had been standing, bewildered but unafraid, while innumerable Red Caps appropriated piece after piece of the baggage arrayed on the platform. Neither her brief seventy years' journey through life nor her long two days' travel northward had dimmed the live brightness of her eyes, which, for all their bewilderment, had accurately selected her own treasures out of the row of luggage and guarded them vigilantly.

"These yours, madam?"

The biggest Red Cap of all was smiling at her. He looked for all the world like Doc Crinshaw's oldest son back home. Her little brown face relaxed; she smiled back at him.

5   "They got to be. You all done took all the others."

He laughed aloud. Then—"Carry 'em in for you?"

She contemplated his bulk. "Reckon you can manage it—puny little feller like you?"

Thereupon they were friends. Still grinning broadly, he surrounded himself with her impedimenta, the enormous brown extension-case on one shoulder, the big straw suitcase in the opposite hand, the carpet-bag under one arm. She herself held fast to the umbrella.

"Always like to have sump'm in my hand when I walk. Can't never tell when you'll run across a snake."

10   "There aren't any snakes in the city."

"There's snakes everywhere, chile."

They began the tedious hike up the interminable platform. She was small and quick. Her carriage was surprisingly erect, her gait astonishingly spry. She said:

"You liked to took my breath back yonder, boy, callin' me 'madam.' Back home everybody call me 'Miss Cynthie.' Even my own chillun. Even their chillun. Black folks, white folks too. 'Miss Cynthie.' Well, when you come up with that 'madam' o' yourn, I say to myself. 'Now, I wonder who that chile's a-grinnin' at? 'Madam' stand for mist'ess o' the house, and I sho' ain' mist'ess o' nothin' in this hyeh New York."

"Well, you see, we call everybody 'madam.'"

15   "Everybody?—Hm." The bright eyes twinkled. "Seem like that'd worry me some—if I was a man."

He acknowledged his slip and observed, "I see this isn't your first trip to New York."

"First trip any place, son. First time I been over fifty mile from Waxhaw. Only travelin' I've done is in my head. Ain' seen many places, but I's seen a passel o' people, Reckon places is pretty much alike after people been in 'em awhile."

"Yes, ma'am. I guess that's right."

"You ain' no reg'lar bag-toter, is you?"

20   "Ma'am?"

"You talk too good."

"Well, I only do this in vacation-time. I'm still in school."

"You is. What you aimin' to be?"

"I'm studying medicine."

25   "You is?" She beamed. "Aimin' to be a doctor, huh? Thank the Lord for that. That's what I always wanted my David to be. My grandchile hyeh in New York. He's to meet me hyeh now."

"I bet you'll have a great time."

"Mussn't bet, chile. That's sinful. I tole him 'fo' he left home, I say, 'Son, you the only one o' the chillun what's got a chance to amount to sump'm. Don' th'ow it away. Be a preacher or a doctor. Work yo' way up and don' stop short. If the Lord don' see fit for you to doctor the soul, then doctor the body. If you don' get to be a reg'lar doctor, be a tooth-doctor. If you jes' can't make that, be a foot-doctor. And if you don' get that fur, be a undertaker. That's the least you must be. That ain' so bad. Keep you acquainted with the house of the Lord. Always mind the house o' the Lord—whatever you do, di like a church-steeple: aim high and go straight.'"

"Did he get to be a doctor?"

"Don' b'lieve he did. Too late startin', I reckon. But he's done succeeded at sump'm. Mus' be at least a undertaker, 'cause he started sendin' the homefolks money, and he come home las' year dressed like Judge Pettiford's boy what went off to school in Virginia. Wouldn't tell none of us 'zackly what he was doin', but he said he wouldn't never be happy till I come and see for myself. So hyeh I is." Something softened her voice. "His mammy died befo' he knowed her. But he was always seeh a good chile—" The something was apprehension. "Hope he *is* a undertaker."

30   They were mounting a flight of steep stairs leading to an exit-gate, about which clustered a few people still hoping to catch sight of arriving friends. Among these a tall young brown-skinned man in a light grey suit suddenly waved his panama and yelled, "Hey, Miss Cynthie!"

Miss Cynthie stopped, looked up, and waved back with a delighted umbrella. The Red Cap's eyes lifted too. His lower jaw sagged.

"Is that your grandson?"

"It sho' is," she said and distanced him for the rest of the climb. The grandson, with an abandonment that superbly ignored onlookers, folded the little woman in an exultant, smothering embrace. As soon as she could, she pushed him off with breathless mock impatience.

"Go 'way, you fool, you. Aimin' to squeeze my soul out my body befo' I can get a look at this place?" She shook herself into the semblance of composure. "Well. You don't look hungry, anyhow."

35   "Ho-ho! Miss Cynthie in New York! Can y'imagine this? Come on. I'm parked on Eighth Avenue."

The Red Cap delivered the outlandish luggage into a robin's egg blue open Packard with scarlet wheels, accepted the grandson's dollar and smile, and stood watching the car roar away up Eighth Avenue.

Another Red Cap came up. "Got a break, hey, boy?"

"Dave Tappen himself—can you beat that?"

"The old lady hasn't seen the station yet—starin' at him."

40   "That's not the half of it, bozo. That's Dave Tappen's grandmother. And what do you s'pose she hopes?"

"What?"

"She hopes that Dave has turned out to be a successful undertaker!"

"Undertaker? Undertaker!"

They stared at each other a gaping moment, then doubled up with laughter.

45   "Look—through there—that's the Chrysler Building. Oh, hell-elujah! I meant to bring you up Broadway—"

"David—"

"Ma'am?"

"This hyeh wagon yourn?"

"Nobody else's. Sweet buggy, ain't it?"

50   "David—you ain't turned out to be one of them moonshiners, is you?"

"Moonshiners—? Moon—Ho! No indeed, Miss Cynthie. I got a better racket 'n that."

"Better which?"

"Game. Business. Pick-up."

"Tell me, David. What is yo' racket?"

55   "Can't spill it yet, Miss Cynthie. Rather show you. Tomorrow night you'll know the worst. Can't you make out till tomorrow night?"

"David, you know I always wanted you to be a doctor, even if 'twasn' nothin' but a foot-doctor. The very leas' I wanted you to be was a undertaker."

"Undertaker! Oh, Miss Cynthie!—with my sunny disposition?"

"Then you ain' even a undertaker?"

"Listen, Miss Cynthie. Just forget 'bout what I am for awhile. Just till tomorrow night. I want you to see for yourself. Tellin' you will spoil it. Now stop askin', you hear?—because I'm not answerin'—I'm surprisin' you. And don't expect anybody you meet to tell you. It'll mess up the whole works. Understand? Now give the big city a break. There's the elevated train going up Columbus Avenue. Ain't that hot stuff?"

60   Miss Cynthie looked. "Humph!" she said. "'Tain' half high as that trestle two mile from Waxhaw."

She thoroughly enjoyed the ride up Central Park West. The stagger lights, the extent of the park, the high, close, kingly dwellings, remarkable because their stoves cooled them in summer as well as heated them in winter, all drew nods of mild interest. But what gave her special delight was not these: it was that David's car so effortlessly sped past the headlong drove of vehicles racing northward.

They stopped for a red light; when they started again their machine leaped forward with a triumphant eagerness that drew from her an unsuppressed "Hot you, David! That's it!"

He grinned appreciatively. "Why, you're a regular New Yorker already."

"New Yorker nothin'! I done the same thing fifty years ago—befo' I knowed they was a New York."

65   "What!"

"'Deed so. Didn' I use to tell you 'bout my young mare, Betty? Chile, I'd hitch Betty up to yo' grandpa's buggy and pass anything on the road. Betty never knowed what another horse's dust smelt like. No 'ndeedy. Shuh, boy, this ain' nothin' new to me. Why that broke-down Fo'd you' uncle Jake's got ain' nothin'—nothin' but a sorry mess. Done got so slow I jes' won' ride in it—I declare I'd rather walk. But this hyeh thing, now, this is right nice." She settled back in complete, complacent comfort, and they sped on, swift and silent.

Suddenly she sat erect with abrupt discovery.

"David—well—bless my soul!"

"What's the matter, Miss Cynthie?"

70   Then he saw what had caught her attention. They were traveling up Seventh Avenue now, and something was miraculously different. Not the road; that was as broad as ever, wide, white gleaming in the sun. Not the houses; they were lofty still, lordly, disdainful, supercilious. Not the cars; they continued to race impatiently onward, innumerable, precipitate, tumultuous. Something else, something at once obvious and subtle, insistent, pervasive, compelling.

"David—this mus' be Harlem!"

"Good Lord, Miss Cynthie—!"

"Don' use the name of the Lord in vain, David."

"But I mean—gee!—you're no fun at all. You get everything before a guy can tell you."

75   "You got plenty to tell me, David. But don' nobody need to tell me this. Look a yonder."

Not just a change of complexion. A completely dissimilar atmosphere. Sidewalks teeming with leisurely strollers, at once strangely dark and bright. Boys in white trousers, berets, and green shirts, with slickened black heads and proud swagger. Bareheaded girls in crisp organdie dresses, purple, canary, gay scarlet. And laughter, abandoned strong Negro laughter, some falling full on the ear, some not heard at all, yet sensed—the warm life-breath of the tireless carnival to which Harlem's heart quickens in summer.

"This is it," admitted David. "Get a good eyeful. Here's One Hundred and Twenty-fifth Street—regular little Broadway. And here's the Alhambra, and up ahead we'll pass the Lafayette."

"What's them?"

"Theatres."

80   "Theatres? Theatres. Humph! Look, David—is that a colored folks church?" They were passing a fine gray-stone edifice.

"That? Oh. Sure it is. So's this one on this side."

"No! Well, ain' that fine? Splendid big church like that for colored folks."

Taking his cue from this, her first tribute to the city, he said, "You ain't seen nothing yet. Wait a minute."

They swung left through a side-street and turned right on a boulevard. "What do you think o' that?" And he pointed to the quarter-million-dollar St. Mark's.

85   "That a colored church, too?"

"'Tain' no white one. And they built it themselves, you know. Nobody's hand-me-down gift."

She heaved a great happy sigh. "Oh, yes, it was a gift, David. It was a gift from on high." Then, "Look a hyeh—which a one you belong to?"

"Me? Why, I don't belong to any—that is, none o' these. Mine's over in another section. Y'see, mine's Baptist. These are all Methodist. See?"

"M-m. Uh-huh. I see."

90   They circled a square and slipped into a quiet narrow street overlooking a park, stopping before the tallest of the apartment-houses in the single commanding row.

Alighting, Miss Cynthie gave this imposing structure one sidewise, upward glance, and said, "Y'all live like bees in a hive, don't y'?—I boun' the women does all the work, too." A moment later, "So this is a elevator? Feel like I'm glory-bound sho' nuff."

Along a tiled corridor and into David's apartment. Rooms leading into rooms. Luxurious couches, easy-chairs, a brown-walnut grand piano, gay-shaded floor lamps, panelled walls, deep rugs, treacherous glass-wood floors—and a smiling golden-skinned girl in a gingham house-dress, approaching with outstretched hands.

"This is Ruth, Miss Cynthie."

"Miss Cynthie!" said Ruth.

95   They clasped hands. "Been wantin' to see David's girl ever since he first wrote us 'bout her."

"Come—here's your room this way. Here's the bath. Get out of your things and get comfy. You must be worn out with the trip."

"Worn out? Worn out? Shuh. How you gon' get worn out on a train? Now if 'twas a horse, maybe, or Jake's no-'count Fo'd—but a train—didn' but one thing bother me on that train."

"What?"

"When the man made them beds down, I jes' couldn' manage to undress same as at home. Why, s'posin' sump'm bus' the train open—where'd you be? Naked as a jay-bird in dew-berry time."

100   David took in her things and left her to get comfortable. He returned, and Ruth, despite his reassuring embrace, whispered:

"Dave, you can't fool old folks—why don't you go ahead and tell her about yourself? Think of the shock she's going to get—at her age."

David shook his head. "She'll get over the shock if she's there looking on. If we just told her, she'd never understand. We've got to railroad her into it. Then she'll be happy."

"She's nice. But she's got the same ideas as all old folks—"

"Yea—but with her you can change 'em. Specially if everything is really all right. I know her. She's for church and all, but she believes in good times too, if they're right. Why, when I was a kid—" He broke off. "Listen!"

105 Miss Cynthie's voice came quite distinctly to them, singing a jaunty little rhyme:

"Oh I danced with the gal with the hole in her stockin',

And her toe kep' a-kickin' and her heel kep' a-knockin'—

Come up, Jesse, and get a drink o' gin,

'Cause you near to the heaven as you'll ever get ag'in."

"She taught me that when I wasn't knee-high to a cricket," David said.

Miss Cynthie still sang softly and merrily:

"Then I danced with the gal with the dimple in her cheek,

And if she'd 'a' kep' a-smilin', I'd a' danced for a week—"

"God forgive me," prayed Miss Cynthie as she discovered David's purpose the following night. She let him and Ruth lead her, like an early Christian martyr, into the Lafayette Theatre. The blinding glare of the lobby produced a merciful self-anaesthesia, and she entered the sudden dimness of the interior as involuntarily as in a dream—

Attendants outdid each other for Mr. Dave Tappen. She heard him tell them, "Fix us up till we go on," and found herself sitting between Ruth and David in the front row of a lower box. A miraculous device of the devil, a motion-picture that talked, was just ending. At her feet the orchestra was assembling. The motion-picture faded out amid a scattered round of applause. Lights blazed and the orchestra burst into an ungodly rumpus.

110 She looked out over the seated multitude, scanning row upon row of illumined faces, black faces, white faces, yellow, tan, brown; bald heads, bobbed heads, kinky and straight heads; and upon every countenance, expectancy,—scowling expectancy in this case, smiling in that, complacent here, amused there, commentative elsewhere, but everywhere suspense, abeyance, anticipation.

Half a dozen people were ushered down the nearer aisle to reserved seats in the second row. Some of them caught sight of David and Ruth and waved to them. The chairs immediately behind them in the box were being shifted. "Hello, Tap!" Miss Cynthie saw David turn, rise, and shake hands with two men. One of them was large, bald and pink, emanating good cheer, the other short, thin, sallow with thick black hair and a sour mien. Ruth also acknowledged their greeting. "This is my grandmother," David said proudly. "Miss Cynthie, meet my managers, Lou and Lee Goldman." "Pleased to meet you," managed Miss Cynthie. "Great lad, this boy of yours," said Lou Goldman. "Great little partner he's got, too," added Lee. They also settled back expectantly.

"Here we go!"

The curtain rose to reveal a cotton-field at dawn. Pickers in blue denim overalls, bandanas, and wide-brimmed straws, or in gingham aprons and sunbonnets, were singing as they worked. Their voices, from clearest soprano to richest bass, blended in low concordances, first simply humming a series of harmonies, until, gradually, came words, like figures forming in mist. As the sound grew, the mist cleared, the words came round and full, and the sun rose bringing light as if in answer to the song. The chorus swelled, the radiance grew, the two, as if emanating from a single source, fused their crescendos, till at last they achieved a joint transcendence of tonal and visual brightness.

"Swell opener," said Lee Goldman.

115   "Ripe," agreed Lou.

David and Ruth arose. "Stay here and enjoy the show, Miss Cynthie. You'll see us again in a minute."

"Go to it, kids," said Lou Goldman.

"Yea—burn 'em up," said Lee.

Miss Cynthie hardly noted that she had been left, so absorbed was she in the spectacle. To her, the theatre had always been the antithesis of the church. As the one was the refuge of righteousness, so the other was the stronghold of transgression. But this first scene awakened memories, captured and held her attention by offering a blend of truth and novelty. Having thus baited her interest, the show now proceeded to play it like the trout through swift-flowing waters of wickedness. Resist as it might, her mind was caught and drawn into the impious subsequences.

120   The very music that had just rounded out so majestically now distorted itself into ragtime. The singers came forward and turned to dancers; boys, a crazy, swaying background, threw up their arms and kicked out their legs in a rhythmic jamboree; girls, an agile, brazen foreground, caught their skirts up to their hips and displayed their copper calves, knees, thighs, in shameless, incredible steps. Miss Cynthie turned dismayed eyes upon the audience, to discover that mob of sinners devouring it all with fond satisfaction. Then the dancers separated and with final abandon flung themselves off the stage in both directions.

Lee Goldman commented through the applause, "They work easy, them babies."

"Yea," said Lou. "Savin' the hot stuff for later."

Two black-faced cotton-pickers appropriated the scene, indulging in dialogue that their hearers found uproarious.

"Ah'm tired."

125   "Ah'm hongry."

"Dis job jes' wears me out."

"Starves me to death."

"Ah'm so tired—you know what Ah'd like to do?"

"What?"

130   "Ah'd like to go to sleep and dream I was sleepin'."

"What good dat do?"

"Den I could wake up and still be 'sleep."

"Well y' know what Ah'd like to do?"

"No. What?"

135   "Ah'd like to swaller me a hog and a hen."

"What good dat do?"

"Den Ah'd always be full o' ham and eggs."

"Ham? Shuh. Don't you know a hog has to be smoked 'fo' he's a ham?"

"Well, if I swaller him, he'll have a smoke all around him, won' he?"

140   Presently Miss Cynthie was smiling like everyone else, but her smile soon fled. For the comics departed, and the dancing girls returned, this time in scant travesties on their earlier voluminous costumes—tiny sunbonnets perched jauntily on one side of their glistening bobs, bandanas reduced to scarlet neck-ribbons, waists mere brassieres, skirts mere gingham sashes.

And now Miss Cynthie's whole body stiffened with a new and surpassing shock; her bright eyes first widened with unbelief, then slowly grew dull with misery. In the midst of a sudden great volley of applause her grandson had broken through that bevy of agile wantons and begun to sing.

He too was dressed as a cotton-picker, but a Beau Brummel among cotton-pickers; his hat bore a pleated green band, his bandana was silk, his overalls blue satin, his shoes black patent leather. His eyes flashed, his teeth gleamed, his body swayed, his arms waved, his words came fast and clear. As he sang, his companions danced a concerted tap, uniformly wild, ecstatic. When he stopped singing, he himself began to dance, and without sacrificing crispness of execution, seemed to absorb into himself every measure of the energy which the girls, now merely standing off and swaying, had relinquished.

"Look at that boy go," said Lee Goldman.

"He ain't started yet," said Lou.

145   But surrounding comment, Dave's virtuosity, the eager enthusiasm of the audience were all alike lost on Miss Cynthie. She sat with stricken eyes watching this boy whom she'd raised from a babe, taught right from wrong, brought up in the church, and endowed with her prayers, this child whom she had dreamed of seeing a preacher, a regular doctor, a tooth-doctor, a foot-doctor, at the very least an undertaker—sat watching him disport himself for the benefit of a sinsick, flesh-hungry mob of lost souls, not one of whom knew or cared to know the loving kindness of God; sat watching a David she'd never foreseen, turned tool of the devil, disciple of lust, unholy prince among sinners.

For a long time she sat there watching with wretched eyes, saw portrayed on the stage David's arrival in Harlem, his escape from "old friends" who tried to dupe him; saw him working as a trap-drummer in a night-club, where he fell in love with Ruth, a dancer; not the gentle Ruth Miss Cynthie knew, but a wild and shameless young savage who danced like seven devils—in only a girdle and breast-plates; saw the two of them join in a song-and-dance act that eventually made them Broadway headliners, an act presented *in toto* as the pre-finale of this show. And not any of the melodies, not any of the sketches, not all the comic philosophy of the tired-and-hungry duo, gave her figure a moment's relaxation or brightened the dull defeat in her staring eyes. She sat apart, alone in the box, the symbol, the epitome of supreme failure. Let the rest of the theatre be riotous, clamoring for more and more of Dave Tappen, "Tap," the greatest tapster of all time, idol of uptown and downtown New York. For her, they were lauding simply an exhibition of sin which centered about her David.

"This'll run a year on Broadway," said Lee Goldman.

"Then we'll take it to Paris."

Encores and curtains with Ruth, and at last David came out on the stage alone. The clamor dwindled. And now he did something quite unfamiliar to even the most consistent of his followers. Softly, delicately, he began to tap a routine designed to fit a particular song. When he had established the rhythm, he began to sing the song:

"Oh I danced with the gal with the hole in her stockin',

And her toe kep' a-kickin' and her heel kep' a-knockin'

Come up, Jesse, and get a drink o' gin,

'Cause you near to the heaven as you'll ever get ag'in—"

150   As he danced and sang this song, frequently smiling across at Miss Cynthie, a visible change transformed her. She leaned forward incredulously, listened intently, then settled back in limp wonder. Her bewildered eyes turned on the crowd, on those serried rows of shriftless sinners. And she found in their

faces now an overwhelmingly curious thing: a grin, a universal grin, a gleeful and sinless grin such as not the nakedest chorus in the performance had produced. In a few seconds, with her own song, David had dwarfed into unimportance, wiped off their faces, swept out of their minds every trace of what had seemed to be sin; had reduced it all to mere trivial detail and revealed these revelers as a crowd of children, enjoying the guileless antics of another child. And Miss Cynthie whispered her discovery aloud:

"Bless my soul! They didn't mean nothin' . . . They jes' didn't see no harm in it—"

"Then I danced with the gal with the dimple in her cheek,

And if she'd 'a' kep' a-smilin' I'd 'a' danced for a week—

Come up, Jesse—"

The crowd laughed, clapped their hands, whistled. Someone threw David a bright yellow flower. "From Broadway!"

He caught the flower. A hush fell. He said:

"I'm really happy tonight, folks. Y'see this flower? Means success, don't it? Well, listen. The one who is really responsible for my success is here tonight with me. Now what do you think o' that?"

155   The hush deepened.

"Y'know folks, I'm sump'm like Adam—I never had no mother. But I've got a grandmother. Down home everybody calls her Miss Cynthie. And everybody loves her. Take that song I just did for you. Miss Cynthie taught me that when I wasn't knee-high to a cricket. But that wasn't all she taught me. For back as I can remember, she used to always say one thing: 'Son, do like a church steeple—aim high and go straight.' And for doin' it—" he grinned, contemplating the flower—"I get this."

He strode across to the edge of the stage that touched Miss Cynthie's box. He held up the flower.

"So y'see, folks, this isn't mine. It's really Miss Cynthie's." He leaned over to hand it to her. Miss Cynthie's last trace of doubt was swept away. She drew a deep breath of revelation; her bewilderment vanished, her redoubtable composure returned, her eyes lighted up; and no one but David, still holding the flower toward her, heard her sharply whispered reprimand:

"Keep it, you fool you. Where's yo' manners—givin' 'way what somebody give you?"

160   David grinned:

"Take it, tyro. What you tryin' to do—crab my act?"

Thereupon, Miss Cynthie, smiling at him with bright, meaningful eyes, leaned over without rising from her chair, jerked a tiny twig off the stem of the flower, then sat decisively back, resolutely folding her arms, with only a leaf in her hand.

"This'll do me," she said.

The finale didn't matter. People filed out of the theatre. Miss Cynthie sat awaiting her children, her foot absently patting time to the orchestra's jazz recessional. Perhaps she was thinking, "God moves in a mysterious way," but her lips were unquestionably forming the words:

"—danced with the gal—hole in her stockin'—

—toe kep' a-kickin'—heel kep' a-knockin'—"

More on
Fisher
and his
stories

INQUIRING FURTHER

1. How would you characterize Miss Cynthie? Make a list of all of the values you think she represents.

2. Toward the end of the story, Miss Cynthie changes her attitude toward the revelers in the club, saying, "Bless my soul! They didn't mean nothin' . . . They jes' didn' see no harm in it—". Do you believe she has also changed her assessment of the performances as well? Write a paragraph explaining your stance.

Identity in Harlem Renaissance Art

Art provides a particularly vivid example of the tensions between the optimism of the Harlem Renaissance and the concerns of everyday African Americans. Painters like Aaron Douglas (1899–1979), for instance, portrayed African origins to emphasize slavery as a key component of African-American identity. Artists like William H. Johnson (1901–1970) and Palmer Hayden (1890–1973) complemented this concern for heritage with colorful portrayals of Harlem life. Together, these works demonstrate African heritage, the realities of working class life, and the celebration of African-American identity.

Harlem
Renaissance
paintings

AARON DOUGLAS

Into Bondage (1936, oil on canvas)

1996.9, Aaron Douglas, Into Bondage, *1936, oil on canvas, 60 3/8 x 60 1/2 in., Corcoran Gallery of Art, Washington, D.C., Museum Purchase and partial gift from Thurlow Evans Tibbs, Jr., The Evans-Tibbs Collection*

INQUIRING FURTHER

1. In the painting *Into Bondage*, what is the significance of having the point of view in the painting originate on the shore where slaves are being captured? What might the natural world symbolize in terms of slave trade and the painting's perspective?

2. How does *Into Bondage* use color, lighting, and value to help convey its message? Make a list of all of the elements of art you can recognize in the painting.

PALMER HAYDEN

The Janitor Who Paints (1937, oil on canvas)

WILLIAM H. JOHNSON

Chain Gang (1942, oil on wood)

INQUIRING FURTHER

1. Examine the objects in *The Janitor Who Paints*. What objects do you think are the most significant in the painting and why?

2. Many consider *The Janitor Who Paints* to be a self-portrait by Hayden who, in addition to painting, worked as a janitor. Which occupation would you say is highlighted in the painting? Freewrite for five minutes about occupations in the painting and identity.

3. Comment on the figures in *Chain Gang*. How would you relate the image to concerns of identity?

PALMER HAYDEN

Midsummer Night in Harlem (1938, oil on canvas)

WILLIAM H. JOHNSON

Moon Over Harlem (1944, oil on wood)

INQUIRING FURTHER

1. Despite the difficulties brought on by the economic struggles of the Depression, African Americans continued to flock to Harlem in the 1930s. As the population increased, the lack of opportunities persisted. Make a list of things to say about *Midsummer Night in Harlem* in terms of this historical context.

2. Johnson's *Moon Over Harlem* depicts the Harlem Riots that broke out in 1943. Keeping this subject matter in mind, examine the details of the painting. Consider the significance of the objects in the painting. Examine the figures. Which characters stand out and why? Write a paragraph describing the relationship between the style and techniques seen in the painting and its subject matter.

GENDER AND IDENTITY

We all recognize the ways that gender can influence identity. Boy babies may be dressed in blue, and girls in pink, for example. Society may associate boys with competition or physical strength, while recognizing nurturing and social traits in girls. At the same time, definitions of what constitutes women or men can be arbitrary and constraining. When we see qualities of nurturing in men, or of competition in women, what do we think? Do we try to stamp those qualities out? Why? This section explores works that speak to these and related questions. (For more on feminist approaches to studying literature, see pages 362–63.)

JAMAICA KINCAID

Jamaica Kincaid (born in 1949) began life as Elaine Potter Richardson on the island of Antigua. She had an early love of learning, but was forced to attend school as a seamstress while the family devoted their resources to sending her three brothers to college. She moved to New York at age seventeen, and worked as a nanny and secretary. She changed her name to Jamaica Kincaid in 1973, and also began to work with members of the New York publishing industry, eventually taking a job at the New Yorker. *"Girl" was Kincaid's first published short story, appearing in the* New Yorker *in 1976.*

Girl

Wash the white clothes on Monday and put them on the stone heap; wash the color clothes on Tuesday and put them on the clothesline to dry; don't walk barehead in the hot sun; cook pumpkin fritters in very hot sweet oil; soak your little cloths right after you take them off; when buying cotton to make yourself a nice blouse, be sure that it doesn't have gum on it, because that way it won't hold up well after a wash; soak salt fish overnight before you cook it; is it true that you sing benna[1] in Sunday school?; always eat your food in such a way that it won't turn someone else's stomach; on Sundays try to walk like a lady and not like the slut you are so bent on becoming; don't sing benna in Sunday school;

---

[1]**benna:** Calypso.

you mustn't speak to wharf-rat boys, not even to give directions; don't eat fruits on the street—flies will follow you; *but I don't sing benna on Sundays at all and never in Sunday school*; this is how to sew on a button; this is how to make a button-hole for the button you have just sewed on; this is how to hem a dress when you see the hem coming down and so to prevent yourself from looking like the slut I know you are so bent on becoming; this is how you iron your father's khaki shirt so that it doesn't have a crease; this is how you iron your father's khaki pants so that they don't have a crease; this is how you grow okra— far from the house, because okra tree harbors red ants; when you are growing dasheen,[2] make sure it gets plenty of water or else it makes your throat itch when you are eating it; this is how you sweep a corner; this is how you sweep a whole house; this is how you sweep a yard; this is how you smile to someone you don't like too much; this is how you smile to someone you don't like at all; this is how you smile to someone you like completely; this is how you set a table for tea; this is how you set a table for dinner; this is how you set a table for dinner with an important guest; this is how you set a table for lunch; this is how you set a table for breakfast; this is how to behave in the presence of men who don't know you very well, and this way they won't recognize immediate- ly the slut I have warned you against becoming; be sure to wash every day, even if it is with your own spit; don't squat down to play marbles—you are not a boy, you know; don't pick people's flowers—you might catch something; don't throw stones at blackbirds, because it might not be a blackbird at all; this is how to make a bread pudding; this is how to make doukona; this is how to make pepper pot; this is how to make a good medicine for a cold; this is how to make a good medicine to throw away a child before it even becomes a child; this is how to catch a fish; this is how to throw back a fish you don't like, and that way something bad won't fall on you; this is how to bully a man; this is how a man bullies you; this is how to love a man, and if this doesn't work there are other ways, and if they don't work don't feel too bad about giving up; this is how to spit up in the air if you feel like it, and this is how to move quick so that it doesn't fall on you; this is how to make ends meet; always squeeze bread to make sure it's fresh; *but what if the baker won't let me feel the bread?*; you mean to say that after all you are really going to be the kind of woman who the baker won't let near the bread?

INQUIRING FURTHER

1. Imagine the dramatic situation in "Girl." Who is giving the advice? How old does the girl seem to be? What can you say about the attitude of the girl or of the advice giver?

2. How would you respond to the statement that "Girl" tells us more about the identity of men than women? Do you disagree with the statement? Make two lists, one noting all the messages the story provides about identity and men, and the other covering identity and women.

3. Do you find the recommendations given in the story to be consistent? Is there an overriding message in the work? Write a paragraph summarizing the advice provided by "Girl."

---

[2]**dasheen**: A Caribbean herb.

LAURA SESSIONS STEPP

Laura Sessions Stepp is a Pulitzer Prize-winning journalist who writes about issues of family and children. She is the author Our Last Best Shot: Guiding Our Children Through Early Adolescence. *"Nothing to Wear" was published in the* Washington Post *in June of 2002.*

Nothing to Wear: From the Classroom to the Mall, Girls' Fashions Are Long on Skin, Short on Modesty

The 12- and 13-year-olds swarm like bees through the Gap in Georgetown. They buzz past the khaki pants and polo shirts that used to define the Gap look, on their way to ultra-low-rise bluejeans that ride well below the navel and black knit camisoles only slightly wider than a knee sock. They land at a rack of short cotton dresses with empire waists and spaghetti straps. A conversation ensues:

Would a girl wear a bra of the same color with this?

Or would bra straps show off better in a contrasting hue?

How about wearing no bra at all?

This is the world of naked fashion for girls from high school on down — even to elementary school—the less-is-more look flaunting breasts, bellies and bottoms. Many, if not most, schools forbid or discourage it, parents and teachers complain about fighting the "whore wars," and yet the trend shows no signs of letting go after a decade of growth.

What many find truly astonishing is the tender age at which it's first aimed, a trend that older teenage girls themselves tag as disgusting.

You can find terry-cloth bikinis at GapKids, metallic-looking bras and bikini underpants labeled "Girl Identity" in the girls' department of Sears, and thongs for girls ages 7 to 14 at abercrombie, the kids' arm of the youth chain Abercrombie & Fitch.

5   "Do you actually sell any of these?" a visitor asked an abercrombie clerk in Virginia recently, holding up a pink-and- yellow-striped piece of stretch cotton only slightly larger than a Band-Aid.

"Unfortunately, yes," replied the clerk, no more than 21 or 22 herself. "Last week a mother came in here accompanied by two girls—they were maybe 10 or younger—and said she had to buy a thong for each of her daughters because they told her every other girl in their classes had one."

An abercrombie spokesman announced last week that the company would no longer supply youngsters' thongs because of a letter campaign by aggrieved parents. But they could still be found on the shelves of several local stores.

Elizabeth Ely, an elder stateswoman in Washington area private education, is a well-known champion of student expression at the Field School, a private school she started in the District that has never had a dress code. Yet even she has started pulling girls into her office because of bare midriffs and exposed cleavage.

Skimpy dress, she says, sighing, "has never been so widespread."

10   Comedian Janeane Garofalo has dubbed this trend "thong feminism," and certainly it gets you more attention than first prize in the science fair or a varsity

letter in soccer. Also, it's easier to plunk down a couple of hundred bucks at Wet Seal (if you have a lot of disposable income, which many girls do) than monitor root-cell division for nine months. It's also a rebellion against parents and other adults who seem to have forgotten their own fling with hot pants, miniskirts and the no-bra look.

Stop by the fashion marketing class taught by Melanie Coughlan and Cara Kirby, a Fairfax County multi-school program that meets at the Springfield Mall, and you will find a bunch of high-school-age thong feminists. The classroom is decorated with posters displaying the nearly nude bods of Britney Spears and Jennifer Lopez, and some of the students are clad, on many days, in outfits that rival their pop idols'.

Coughlan says her students make her feel prudish. "I still think of thongs as flip-flops," she says, laughing, of the floss-thin underwear. She and Kirby share the unenviable task of teaching the selling power of the very looks that Fairfax County says girls can't wear in school.

"They want to go with the tightest, the lowest, the I-don't-know- what," says Kirby, who is appalled by the bare look.

Coughlan, a former retail buyer in New York, doesn't get quite as upset: "But I do say, 'Someone let you out of the house in that?' They'll have a comeback, always."

15   Karen Gutierrez, a marketing student, pulls off a long-sleeve shirt, worn to comply with rules at her high school, to reveal the black tube top that is stretched across her ample chest.

"Clothing like this makes me feel confident," Gutierrez says. "People's eyes are on me, not another girl."

Classmate Simge Yildrim arrives dressed in snug lime-green pants and a white halter top, purchased the day before at Abercrombie & Fitch. A matching lime-green jacket over the halter makes her presentable to school authorities, but the point, she says, is this: When she put on her outfit that morning and stood in front of a mirror, "I said to myself, 'You look good.' If I'm comfortable with myself, I don't ask anyone else."

If a teacher objects to what she is wearing, say the fact that her back is bared, "I'll say, 'So what?' and walk on."

Across the Potomac at the Field School, Katie Phillips, a slender and poised senior, says she was a shy girl in middle school who dressed in T-shirts, jeans and, occasionally, long skirts. Now her preferences have expanded to include low-cut blouses and short, low- waisted skirts that show off her flat abdomen.

20   This has nothing to do with attracting guys, she says. "I've become more confident with my body, and I'm comfortable with what I like. If you can pull it off and not look gross, why not dress this way?"

Certainly not all girls share the enthusiasm for their bodies that Phillips has for hers; too many girls are struggling with eating disorders to say that. And yet, Michael Wood, vice president of Teenage Research Unlimited, which does market analysis, says adults "shouldn't underestimate the confidence teen girls have."

It's not just the stick-figure girls who are confident, he continues. "We find it in all sizes and shapes." Retailers such as Hot Topic have started carrying skimpy fashion for fuller-figure girls, he says.

Laura Webster, one of the eighth-graders shopping in Georgetown, clearly has just as much fun as her slimmer classmates trying on different outfits. "I think you should like what you wear," she says. "That's what's important."

Some things haven't changed. Among any group of girls shopping, or arriving at school in the morning, you'll see several strutting around to impress one another. Women have always dressed more for other women than for men, and girls are no different.

They'll also whisper to each other the name of the classmate who constantly pulls at a leather skirt that is several sizes too small. They think nothing of baring their own lingerie ("It's no big deal. We don't even think about it"), but they do have standards that are not always apparent to the outsider.

"There's a difference between provocative and trashy," says Noelle Goff, a fashion marketing student. And that would be? "If she's going all the way."

For an eighth-grader at Field: "If a girl is doing sexual things."

So reputation is based more on behavior than dress? For girls, apparently. But perhaps not for boys.

Somsack Vongvirath, one of a handful of male students in fashion marketing, says outright, "Hot girls send a message." Don't get him wrong, he welcomes the distraction: "They brighten up the class." But as far as a relationship goes? He'd pick a cute girl ("dressed more feminine") over a hot girl ("dressed like a girlie picture") every time. "There would be too many guys trying to get the hot girl."

Girls tend to shrug off such comments. "Guys are going to hit on us no matter what we wear," Gutierrez says. "If they're bothered, it's their problem."

Phillips, at Field, agrees. "Girls have as much right to express themselves as boys do," she says. "It's not a girl's job either to please or keep the boys on track."

That's straight feminist rhetoric that appeals to people like Sharon Lamb, psychologist and author of the new book "The Secret Lives of Girls: What Good Girls Really Do—Sex Play, Aggression and Their Guilt."

Lamb says: "Girls are saying, 'Why can't he learn to control himself? I want you to look at me and say I'm sexy but not have sex with me.' They're not buying into the age-old idea that women are temptresses and men aren't responsible for their own sexuality."

But don't girls share some of that responsibility? Ely thinks so. One of the girls she pulled into her office at Field told her she should "change the boys." To which she said something like, "You can't stop nature, and it would be foolish to try."

"Sex is so much more pervasive in society than it used to be," says Tina Johnson, executive editor of Teen People magazine. "Kids can't help but be influenced by that in their dress and every other way."

In terms of sexy dress and power, there was no bigger celebrity than pop singer Madonna. Girls who weren't even born in the 1980s know that's when Madonna started turning underwear into outerwear. Through her MTV videos, Madonna made sure we knew she was a self-possessed woman who would take from life exactly what she wanted, regardless of what any man might want from her. She was followed, of course, by vocalists Spears and Lopez, who reinforced the idea to millions of fans that titillation equals liberation.

During these same years, designers, manufacturers and retailers bought into a concept called "deconstructionism," meaning the near elimination of clothing. In 1989, the same year that Madonna sang "Express Yourself" as she grabbed her crotch, bare-breasted models were walking the runways followed by women in corsets and black stockings, hip-slung pants and slip dresses. (Fashion analysts at the time gave the slip dress less than a year. They were wrong, as any middle school dance will prove.)

Adult lines started ad campaigns featuring teenage girls, and it was only a matter of time before the juniors market stepped in, followed by children's wear. Stores like Wet Seal, Hot Topic and Gadzooks picked up the Playboy line, then Hotkiss, whose marketing director knew exactly what to say: "We appeal to an independent girl with enough self-confidence to wear our body-conscious and provocative clothing."

Teen fashion magazines popularized the attitude, according to Ruth Rubenstein, associate professor of sociology at Manhattan's Fashion Institute of Technology. "They liked to portray sexy dressing as power."

40   The result has paid off big for retailers, according to Teenage Research's Wood. Currently, girls ages 12 to 18 spend more than $37 billion on clothes, a stable figure that kept companies afloat in the latest economic slowdown. "Marketers now have their eyes aimed at even younger girls," Wood says. "They don't want to wait until kids become teens." Perhaps abercrombie has stopped selling its thongs for children, but you can bet that someone else will jump in to meet the perceived desire.

Where has this marketing push left girls? With lots of revealing clothes to choose from and little else. Katie Phillips went shopping over Memorial Day weekend for a graduation dress that, she says, "is what my mom would call 'grandmother-appropriate.'" She canvassed two large shopping malls and several individual stores before finally finding a skirt and blouse at Neiman Marcus.

When girls complain to school administrators that they can't find anything but short-shorts or tummy-exposing jeans, they're not far off. Teenage girls' dress has a sameness about it that is noticeable. The students of Coughlan and Kirby recently sponsored a fashion show at the mall. Once the show was over, "I got confused which clothing had to be returned to which store," Coughlan says.

Strangely enough, another generation gap seems to have been created. With thongs being marketed to 7-year-olds, the prudishness and authority of age can be seen in high school girls.

Coughlan's students criticize the fashion industry for selling skimpy dress to younger girls. One of them says, "If I saw my little sister wearing a thong, I would cut it off." Wood says his company has seen this protectiveness over and over in focus groups of older girls. So has Ely, who is using it in her campaign, urging junior and senior girls at Field to consider how they are role models to the seventh- and eighth-graders.

45   Ely knows her older students seek to be influential; she believes they can be persuaded to "take responsibility for their environment, to discriminate, to show younger girls that it's okay to dress that way in some circumstances but not in others."

Ah, but what circumstances, and for what girls? And what happens when girls stop imagining adulthood as the life of Britney Spears and begin imagining themselves as doctors or bank presidents? What is empowerment, anyway, without the wisdom to know when to use that power?

Can any of this be explained by a single theory, or book, or expert or girl? Wait. Watch.

INQUIRING FURTHER

1. What are your thoughts on trends in youth fashion? Do you believe that children should wear revealing clothing? Is there an age at which revealing clothes become inappropriate? Hold a discussion with your classmates regarding the concerns raised in the article.

2. Weigh in on the role model controversies surrounding celebrities like Britney Spears. What criteria would you use to define a role model? How would you apply these criteria to trend-setting men and women? Make a list of three people whom you believe to be role models for youth and explain why each one qualifies for that title.

3. Write a paper in which you explore fashion trends or celebrity role models in terms of the advice provided in Jamaica Kincaid's "Girl." Use details from "Girl" to discuss ideals for women's identity, or for being a role model. Examine contemporary examples of trends or role models to explore the relationships between "Girl" and contemporary culture.

SUSAN GLASPELL

Susan Glaspell (1876–1948) took work as a reporter just after college, and then devoted the early part of her career to writing sentimental fiction. She published The Glory of the Conquered, *a romantic best-seller in 1909. In 1915, after marrying the social critic George Cook, she formed a theater group called the Provincetown Players and began composing plays that often featured female protagonists, and explored the relationships between men and women, and individuals and society.* Trifles *was written and first performed in 1916.*

Trifles

Original Cast

GEORGE HENDERSON,	*Country Attorney*
HENRY PETERS,	*Sheriff*
LEWIS HALE,	*A Neighboring Farmer*
MRS. PETERS	
MRS. HALE	

Scene: The kitchen in the now abandoned farm-house of JOHN WRIGHT, *a gloomy kitchen, and left without having been put in order—unwashed pans under the sink, a loaf of bread outside the bread-box, a dish-towel on the table—other signs of incompleted work. At the rear the outer door opens and the* SHERIFF *comes in followed by the* COUNTY ATTORNEY *and* HALE. *The* SHERIFF *and* HALE *are men in mid-*

dle life, the COUNTY ATTORNEY *is a young man; all are much bundled up and go at once to the stove. They are followed by the two women— the* SHERIFF'*s wife first; she is a slight wiry woman, a thin nervous face.* MRS. HALE *is larger and would ordinarily be called more comfortable looking, but she is disturbed now and looks fearfully about as she enters. The women have come in slowly, and stand close together near the door.*

COUNTY ATTORNEY: [*Rubbing his hands.*] This feels good. Come up to the fire, ladies.

MRS. PETERS: [*After taking a step forward.*] I'm not—cold.

SHERIFF: [*Unbuttoning his overcoat and stepping away from the stove as if to mark the beginning of official business.*]

Now, Mr. Hale, before we move things about, you explain to Mr. Henderson just what you saw when you came here yesterday morning.

COUNTY ATTORNEY: By the way, has anything been moved? Are things just as you left them yesterday?

SHERIFF: [*Looking about.*] It's just the same. When it dropped below zero last night I thought I'd better send Frank out this morning to make a fire for us—no use getting pneumonia with a big case on, but I told him not to touch anything except the stove—and you know Frank.

COUNTY ATTORNEY: Somebody should have been left here yesterday.

SHERIFF: Oh—yesterday. When I had to send Frank to Morris Center for that man who went crazy—I want you to know I had my hands full yesterday. I knew you could get back from Omaha by today and as long as I went over everything here myself—

COUNTY ATTORNEY: Well, Mr. Hale, tell just what happened when you came here yesterday morning.

HALE: Harry and I had started to town with a load of potatoes. We came along the road from my place and as I got here I said, "I'm going to see if I can't get John Wright to go in with me on a party telephone." I spoke to Wright about it once before and he put me off, saying folks talked too much anyway, and all he asked was peace and quiet—I guess you know about how much he talked himself; but I thought maybe if I went to the house and talked about it before his wife, though I said to Harry that I didn't know as what his wife wanted made much difference to John—

COUNTY ATTORNEY: Let's talk about that later, Mr. Hale. I do want to talk about that, but tell now just what happened when you got to the house.

HALE: I didn't hear or see anything; I knocked at the door, and still it was all quiet inside. I knew they must be up, it was past eight o'clock. So I knocked again, and I thought I heard somebody say, "Come in." I wasn't sure, I'm not sure yet, but I opened the door—this door [*indicating the door by which the two women are still standing*] and there in that rocker—[*pointing to it*] sat Mrs. Wright.

[*They all look at the rocker.*]

COUNTY ATTORNEY: What—was she doing?

HALE: She was rockin' back and forth. She had her apron in her hand and was kind of—pleating it.

COUNTY ATTORNEY: And how did she—look?

HALE: Well, she looked queer.

COUNTY ATTORNEY: How do you mean—queer?

HALE: Well, as if she didn't know what she was going to do next. And kind of done up.

COUNTY ATTORNEY: How did she seem to feel about your coming?

HALE: Why, I don't think she minded—one way or other. She didn't pay much attention. I said, "How do, Mrs. Wright, it's cold, ain't it?" And she said, "Is it?"—and went on kind of pleating at her apron. Well, I was surprised; she didn't ask me to come up to the stove, or to set down, but just sat there, not even looking at me, so I said, "I want to see John." And then she— laughed. I guess you would call it a laugh. I thought of Harry and the team outside, so I said a little sharp: "Can't I see John?" "No," she says, kind o' dull like. "Ain't he home?" says I. "Yes," says she, "he's home." "Then why can't I see him?" I asked her, out of patience. "'Cause he's dead," says she. "*Dead?*" says I. She just nodded her head, not getting a bit excited, but rockin' back and forth. "Why—where is he?" says I, not knowing what to say. She just pointed upstairs—like that [*himself pointing to the room above*]. I got up, with the idea of going up there. I walked from there to here— then I says, "Why, what did he die of?" "He died of a rope round his neck," says she, and just went on pleatin' at her apron. Well, I went out and called Harry. I thought I might—need help. We went upstairs and there he was lyin'—

COUNTY ATTORNEY: I think I'd rather have you go into that upstairs, where you can point it all out. Just go on now with the rest of the story.

HALE: Well, my first thought was to get that rope off. It looked . . . [*Stops, his face twitches*] . . . but Harry, he went up to him, and he said, "No, he's dead all right, and we'd better not touch anything." So we went back down stairs. She was still sitting that same way. "Has anybody been notified?" I asked. "No," says she, unconcerned. "Who did this, Mrs. Wright?" said Harry. He said it business-like—and she stopped pleatin' of her apron. "I don't know," she says. "You don't *know?*" says Harry. "No," says she. "Weren't you sleepin' in the bed with him?" says Harry. "Yes," says she, "but I was on the inside." "Somebody slipped a rope round his neck and strangled him and you didn't wake up?" says Harry. "I didn't wake up," she said after him. We must 'a looked as if we didn't see how that could be, for after a minute she said, "I sleep sound." Harry was going to ask her more questions but I said maybe we ought to let her tell her story first to the oroner, or the sheriff, so Harry went fast as he could to Rivers' place, where there's a telephone.

COUNTY ATTORNEY: And what did Mrs. Wright do when she knew that you had gone for the coroner?

HALE: She moved from that chair to this one over here [*Pointing to a small chair in the corner*] and just sat there with her hands held together and looking down. I got a feeling that I ought to make come conversation, so I said I had come in to see if John wanted to put in a telephone, and at that she start-ed to laugh, and then she stopped and looked at me—scared. [*The* COUNTY ATTORNEY, *who has had his notebook out, makes a note.*] I dunno, maybe it wasn't scared. I wouldn't like to say it was. Soon Harry got back, and then Dr. Lloyd came, and you, Mr. Peters, and so I guess that's all I know that you don't.

COUNTY ATTORNEY: [*Looking around.*] I guess we'll go upstairs first—and then out to the barn and around there. [*To the* SHERIFF.] You're convinced that there was nothing important here—nothing that would point to any motive.

SHERIFF: Nothing here but kitchen things.

[*The* COUNTY ATTORNEY, *after again looking around the kitchen, opens the door of a cupboard closet. He gets up on a chair and looks on a shelf. Pulls his hand away, sticky.*]

COUNTY ATTORNEY: Here's a nice mess.

[*The women draw nearer.*]

MRS. PETERS: [*To the other woman.*] Oh, her fruit; it did freeze. [*To the Lawyer.*] She worried about that when it turned so cold. She said the fire'd go out and her jars would break.

SHERIFF: Well, can you beat the women! Held for murder and worryin' about her preserves.

COUNTY ATTORNEY: I guess before we're through she may have something more serious than preserves to worry about.

HALE: Well, women are used to worrying over trifles.

[*The two women move a little closer together.*]

COUNTY ATTORNEY: [*With the gallantry of a young politician.*] And yet, for all their worries, what would we do without the ladies? [*The women do not unbend. He goes to the sink, takes a dipperful of water from the pail and pouring it into a basin, washes his hands. Starts to wipe them on the roller-towel, turns it for a cleaner place.*] Dirty towels! [*Kicks his foot against the pans under the sink.*] Not much of a housekeeper, would you say, ladies?

MRS. HALE: [*Stiffly.*] There's a great deal of work to be done on a farm.

COUNTY ATTORNEY: To be sure. And yet [*With a little bow to her.*] I know there are some Dickson county farmhouses which do not have such roller towels.

[*He gives it a pull to expose its full length again.*]

MRS. HALE: Those towels get dirty awful quick. Men's hands aren't always as clean as they might be.

COUNTY ATTORNEY: Ah, loyal to your sex, I see. But you and Mrs. Wright were neighbors. I suppose you were friends, too.

MRS. HALE: [*Shaking her head.*] I've not seen much of her of late years. I've not been in this house—it's more than a year.

COUNTY ATTORNEY: And why was that? You didn't like her?

MRS. HALE: I liked her all well enough. Farmers' wives have their hands full, Mr. Henderson. And then—

COUNTY ATTORNEY: Yes—?

MRS. HALE: [*Looking about.*] It never seemed a very cheerful place.

COUNTY ATTORNEY: No—it's not cheerful. I shouldn't say she had the homemaking instinct.

MRS. HALE: Well, I don't know as Wright had, either.

COUNTY ATTORNEY: You mean that they didn't get on very well?

MRS. HALE: No, I don't mean anything. But I don't think a place'd be any cheer-fuller for John Wright's being in it.

COUNTY ATTORNEY: I'd like to talk more of that a little later. I want to get the lay of things upstairs now.

[*He goes to the left, where three steps lead to a stair door.*]

SHERIFF: I suppose anything Mrs. Peters does'll be all right. She was to take in some clothes for her, you know, and a few little things. We left in such a hurry yes-terday.

COUNTY ATTORNEY: Yes, but I would like to see what you take, Mrs. Peters, and keep an eye out for anything that might be of use to us.

MRS. PETERS: Yes, Mr. Henderson.

[*The women listen to the men's steps on the stairs, then look about the kitchen.*]

MRS. HALE: I'd hate to have men coming into my kitchen, snooping around and crit-icising.

[*She arranges the pans under sink which the Lawyer had shoved out of place.*]

MRS. PETERS: Of course it's no more than their duty.

MRS. HALE: Duty's all right, but I guess that deputy sheriff that came out to make the fire might have got a little of this on. [*Gives the roller towel a pull.*] Wish I'd thought of that sooner. Seems mean to talk about her for not having things slicked up when she had to come away in such a hurry.

MRS. PETERS: [*Who has gone to a small table in the left rear corner of the room, and lifted one end of a towel that covers a pan.*] She had bread set.

[*Stands still.*]

MRS. HALE: [*Eyes fixed on a loaf of bread beside the bread-box, which is on a low shelf at the other side of the room. Moves slowly toward it.*] She was going to put this in there. [*Picks up loaf, then abruptly drops it. In a manner of returning to familiar things.*] It's a shame about her fruit. I wonder if it's all gone. [*Gets up on the chair and looks.*] I think there's some here that's all right, Mrs. Peters. Yes—here; [*Holding it toward the window.*] this is cherries, too. [*Looking again.*] I declare I believe that's the only one. [*Gets down, bottle in her hand. Goes to the sink and wipes it off on the outside.*] She'll feel awful bad after all her hard work in the hot weather. I remember the afternoon I put up my cherries last summer.

[*She puts the bottle on the big kitchen table, center of the room. With a sigh, is about to sit down in the rocking-chair. Before she is seated realises what chair it is; with a slow look at it, steps back. The chair which she has touched rocks back and forth.*]

MRS. PETERS: Well, I must get those things from the front room closet. [*She goes to the door at the right, but after looking into the other room, steps back.*] You com-ing with me, Mrs. Hale? You could help me carry them.

[*They go in the other room; reappear,* MRS. PETERS *carrying a dress and skirt,* MRS. HALE *following with a pair of shoes.*]

MRS. PETERS: My, it's cold in there.

[*She puts the clothes on the big table, and hurries to the stove.*]

MRS. HALE: [*Examining the skirt.*] Wright was close. I think maybe that's why she kept so much to herself. She didn't even belong to the Ladies Aid. I suppose she felt she couldn't do her part, and then you don't enjoy things when you feel shabby. She used to wear pretty clothes and be lively, when she was Minnie Foster, one of the town girls singing in the choir. But that—oh, that was thirty years ago. This all you was to take in?

MRS. PETERS: She said she wanted an apron. Funny thing to want, for there isn't much to get you dirty in jail, goodness knows. But I suppose just to make her feel more natural. She said they was in the top drawer in this cupboard. Yes, here. And then her little shawl that always hung behind the door. [*Opens stair door and looks.*] Yes, here it is. [*Quickly shuts door leading upstairs.*]

MRS. HALE: [*Abruptly moving toward her.*] MRS. PETERS?

MRS. PETERS: Yes, Mrs. Hale?

MRS. HALE: Do you think she did it?

MRS. PETERS: [*In a frightened voice.*] Oh, I don't know.

MRS. HALE: Well, I don't think she did. Asking for an apron and her little shawl. Worrying about her fruit.

MRS. PETERS: [*Starts to speak, glances up, where footsteps are heard in the room above. In a low voice.*] Mr. Peters says it looks bad for her. Mr. Henderson is awful sarcastic in a speech and he'll make fun of her sayin' she didn't wake up.

MRS. HALE: Well, I guess John Wright didn't wake when they was slipping that rope under his neck.

MRS. PETERS: No, it's strange. It must have been done awful crafty and still. They say it was such a—funny way to kill a man, rigging it all up like that.

MRS. HALE: That's just what Mr. Hale said. There was a gun in the house. He says that's what he can't understand.

MRS. PETERS: Mr. Henderson said coming out that what was needed for the case was a motive; something to show anger, or—sudden feeling.

MRS. HALE: [*Who is standing by the table.*] Well, I don't see any signs of anger around here. [*She puts her hand on the dish towel which lies on the table, stands looking down at table, one half of which is clean, the other half messy.*] It's wiped to here. [*Makes a move as if to finish work, then turns and looks at loaf of bread outside the breadbox. Drops towel. In that voice of coming back to familiar things.*] Wonder how they are finding things upstairs. I hope she had it a little more red-up up there. You know, it seems kind of *sneaking.* Locking her up in town and then coming out here and trying to get her own house to turn against her!

MRS. PETERS: But Mrs. Hale, the law is the law.

MRS. HALE: I s'pose 'tis. [*Unbuttoning her coat.*] Better loosen up your things, Mrs. Peters. You won't feel them when you go out.

[*MRS. PETERS takes off her fur tippet, goes to hang it on hook at back of room, stands looking at the under part of the small corner table.*]

MRS. PETERS: She was piecing a quilt.

[*She brings the large sewing basket and they look at the bright pieces.*]

MRS. HALE: It's log cabin pattern. Pretty, isn't it? I wonder if she was goin' to quilt it or just knot it?

[*Footsteps have been heard coming down the stairs. The SHERIFF enters followed by HALE and the COUNTY ATTORNEY.*]

SHERIFF: They wonder if she was going to quilt it or just knot it!

[*The men laugh, the women look abashed.*]

COUNTY ATTORNEY: [*Rubbing his hands over the stove.*] Frank's fire didn't do much up there, did it? Well, let's go out to the barn and get that cleared up.

[*The men go outside.*]

MRS. HALE: [*Resentfully.*] I don't know as there's anything so strange, our takin' up our time with little things while we're waiting for them to get the evidence. [*She sits down at the big table smoothing out a block with decision.*] I don't see as it's anything to laugh about.

MRS. PETERS: [*Apologetically.*] Of course they've got awful important things on their minds. [*Pulls up a chair and joins MRS HALE at the table.*]

MRS. HALE: [*Examining another block.*] Mrs. Peters, look at this one. Here, this is the one she was working on, and look at the sewing! All the rest of it has been so nice and even. And look at this! It's all over the place! Why, it looks as if she didn't know what she was about!

[*After she has said this they look at each other, then start to glance back at the door. After on instant MRS. HALE has pulled at a knot and ripped the sewing.*]

MRS. PETERS: Oh, what are you doing, Mrs. Hale?

MRS. HALE: [*Mildly.*] Just pulling out a stitch or two that's not sewed very good. [*Threading a needle.*] Bad sewing always made me fidgety.

MRS. PETERS: [*Nervously.*] I don't think we ought to touch things.

MRS. HALE: I'll just finish up this end. [*Suddenly stopping and leaning forward.*] Mrs. Peters?

MRS. PETERS: Yes, Mrs. Hale?

MRS. HALE: What do you suppose she was so nervous about?

MRS. PETERS: Oh—I don't know. I don't know as she was nervous. I sometimes sew awful queer when I'm just tired. [*MRS. HALE starts to say something, looks at MRS. PETERS, then goes on sewing.*] Well I must get these things wrapped up. They may be through sooner than we think. [*Putting apron and other things together.*] I wonder where I can find a piece of paper, and string.

MRS. HALE: In that cupboard, maybe.

MRS. PETERS: [*Looking in cupboard.*] Why, here's a bird-cage. [*Holds it up.*] Did she have a bird, Mrs. Hale?

MRS. HALE: Why, I don't know whether she did or not—I've not been here for so long. There was a man around last year selling canaries cheap, but I don't know as she took one; maybe she did. She used to sing real pretty herself.

MRS. PETERS: [*Glancing around.*] Seems funny to think of a bird here. But she must have had one, or why would she have a cage? I wonder what happened to it.

MRS. HALE: I s'pose maybe the cat got it.

MRS. PETERS: No, she didn't have a cat. She's got that feeling some people have about cats—being afraid of them. My cat got in her room and she was real upset and asked me to take it out.

MRS. HALE: My sister Bessie was like that. Queer, ain't it?

MRS. PETERS: [*Examining the cage.*] Why, look at this door, It's broke. One hinge is pulled apart.

MRS. HALE: [*Looking too.*] Looks as if someone must have been rough with it.

MRS. PETERS: Why, yes.

[*She brings the cage forward and puts it on the table.*]

MRS. HALE: I wish if they're going to find any evidence they'd be about it. I don't like this place.

MRS. PETERS: But I'm awful glad you came with me, Mrs. Hale. It would be lonesome for me sitting here alone.

MRS. HALE: It would, wouldn't it? [*Dropping her sewing.*] But I tell you what I do wish, Mrs. Peters. I wish I had come over sometimes when *she* was here, I—[*Looking around the room.*]—wish I had.

MRS. PETERS: But of course you were awful busy, Mrs. Hale—your house and your children.

MRS. HALE: I could've come. I stayed away because it weren't cheerful—and that's why I ought to have come. I—I've never liked this place. Maybe because it's down in a hollow and you don't see the road. I dunno what it is, but it's a lonesome place and always was. I wish I had come over to see Minnie Foster sometimes. I can see now—[*Shakes her head.*]

MRS. PETERS: Well, you mustn't reproach yourself, Mrs. Hale. Somehow we just don't see how it is with other folks until—something comes up.

MRS. HALE: Not having children makes less work—but it makes a quiet house, and Wright out to work all day, and no company when he did come in. Did you know John Wright, Mrs. Peters?

MRS. PETERS: Not to know him; I've seen him in town. They say he was a good man.

MRS. HALE: Yes—good; he didn't drink, and kept his word as well as most, I guess, and paid his debts. But he was a hard man, Mrs. Peters. Just to pass the time of day with him—[*Shivers.*]Like a raw wind that gets to the bone. [*Pauses, her eye falling on the cage.*] I should think she would 'a wanted a bird. But what do you suppose went with it?

MRS. PETERS: I don't know, unless it got sick and died.

[*She reaches over and swings the broken door, swings it again, both women watch it.*]

MRS. HALE: You weren't raised round here, were you? [*MRS. PETERS shakes her head.*] You didn't know—her?

MRS. PETERS: Not till they brought her yesterday.

MRS. HALE: She—come to think of it, she was kind of like a bird herself—real sweet and pretty, but kind of timid and—fluttery. How—she—did—change. [*Silence; then as if struck by a happy thought and relieved to get back to every day things.*] Tell you what, Mrs. Peters, why don't you take the quilt in with you? It might take up her mind.

MRS. PETERS: Why, I think that's a real nice idea, Mrs. Hale. There couldn't possibly be any objection to it, could there? Now, just what would I take? I wonder if her patches are in here—and her things.

[*They look in the sewing basket.*]

MRS. HALE: Here's some red. I expect this has got sewing things in it. [*Brings out a fancy box.*] What a pretty box. Looks like something somebody would give you. Maybe her scissors are in here. [*Opens box. Suddenly puts her hand to her nose.*] Why—[*MRS. PETERS bends nearer, then turns her face away.*] There's something wrapped up in this piece of silk.

MRS. PETERS: Why, this isn't her scissors.

MRS. HALE: [*Lifting the silk.*] Oh, Mrs. Peters—its—[*MRS. PETERS bends closer.*]

MRS. PETERS: It's the bird.

MRS. HALE: [*Jumping up.*] But, Mrs. Peters—look at it! It's neck! Look at its neck! It's all—other side *to*.

MRS. PETERS: Somebody—wrung—its—neck.

[*Their eyes meet. A look of growing comprehension, of horror. Steps are heard outside. MRS. HALE slips box under quilt pieces, and sinks into her chair. Enter SHERIFF and COUNTY ATTORNEY. MRS. PETERS rises.*]

COUNTY ATTORNEY: [*As one turning from serious things to little pleasantries.*] Well, ladies, have you decided whether she was going to quilt it or knot it?

MRS. PETERS: We think she was going to—knot it.

COUNTY ATTORNEY: Well, that's interesting, I'm sure. [*Seeing the bird-cage.*] Has the bird flown?

MRS. HALE: [*Putting more quilt pieces over the box.*] We think the—cat got it.

COUNTY ATTORNEY: [*Preoccupied.*] Is there a cat?

[*MRS. HALE glances in a quick covert way at MRS. PETERS.*]

MRS. PETERS: Well, not *now*. They're superstitious, you know. They leave.

COUNTY ATTORNEY: [*To SHERIFF PETERS, continuing an interrupted conversation.*] No sign at all of anyone having come from the outside. Their own rope. Now let's go up again and go over it piece by piece. [*They start upstairs.*] It would have to have been someone who knew just the—

[*MRS. PETERS sits down. The two women sit there not looking at one another, but as if peering into something and at the same time holding back. When they talk now it is in the manner of feeling their way over strange ground, as if afraid of what they are saying, but as if they can not help saying it.*]

MRS. HALE: She liked the bird. She was going to bury it in that pretty box.

MRS. PETERS: [*In a whisper.*] When I was a girl—my kitten—there was a boy took a hatchet, and before my eyes—and before I could get there—[*Covers her face an instant.*] If they hadn't held me back I would have—[*Catches herself, looks upstairs where steps are heard, falters weakly*] —hurt him.

MRS. HALE: [*With a slow look around her.*] I wonder how it would seem never to have had any children around. [*Pause.*] No, Wright wouldn't like the bird— a thing that sang. She used to sing. He killed that, too.

MRS. PETERS: [*Moving uneasily.*] We don't know who killed the bird.

MRS. HALE: I knew John Wright.

MRS. PETERS: It was an awful thing was done in this house that night, Mrs. Hale. Killing a man while he slept, slipping a rope around his neck that choked the life out of him.

MRS. HALE: His neck. Choked the life out of him.

[*Her hand goes out and rests on the bird-cage.*]

MRS. PETERS: [*With rising voice.*] We don't know who killed him. We dont *know.*

MRS. HALE: [*Her own feeling not interrupted.*] If there'd been years and years of nothing, then a bird to sing to you, it would be awful—still, after the bird was still.

MRS. PETERS: [*Something within her speaking.*] I know what stillness is. When we homesteaded in Dakota, and my first baby died—after he was two years old, and me with no other then—

MRS. HALE: [*Moving.*] How soon do you suppose they'll be through, looking for the evidence?

MRS. PETERS: I know what stillness is. [*Pulling herself back.*] The law has got to punish crime, Mrs. Hale.

MRS. HALE: [*Not as if answering that.*] I wish you'd seen Minnie Foster when she wore a white dress with blue ribbons and stood up there in the choir and sang. [*A look around the room.*] Oh, I *wish* I'd come over here once in a while! That was a crime! That was a crime! Who's going to punish that?

MRS. PETERS: [*Looking upstairs.*] We mustn't—take on.

MRS. HALE: I might have known she needed help! I know how things can be— for women. I tell you, it's queer, Mrs. Peters. We live close together and we live far apart. We all go through the same things—it's all just a different kind of the same thing. [*Brushes her eyes, noticing the bottle of fruit, reaches out for it.*] If I was you I wouldn't tell her her fruit was gone. Tell her it *ain't.* Tell her it's all right. Take this in to prove it to her. She—she may never know whether it was broke or not.

MRS. PETERS: [*Takes the bottle, looks about for something to wrap it in; takes a petticoat from the clothes brought from the other room, very nervously begins winding this around the bottle. In a false voice.*] My, it's a good thing the men couldn't hear us. Wouldn't they just laugh! Getting all stirred up over a little thing like a—dead canary. As if that could have anything to do with—with —wouldn't they *laugh!*

[*The men are heard coming down stairs.*]

MRS. HALE: [*Under her breath.*] Maybe they would—maybe they wouldn't.

COUNTY ATTORNEY: No, Peters, it's all perfectly clear except a reason for doing it. But you know juries when it comes to women. If there was some definite thing.

Something to show—something to make a story about—a thing that would connect up with this strange way of doing it —

[*The women's eyes meet for an instant. Enter* HALE *from outer door.*]

HALE: Well, I've got the team around. Pretty cold out there.
COUNTY ATTORNEY: I'm going to stay here a while by myself. [*To the* SHERIFF.] You can send Frank out for me, can't you? I want to go over everything. I'm not satisfied that we can't do better.
SHERIFF: Do you want to see what Mrs. Peters is going to take in?

[*The* LAWYER *goes to the table, picks up the apron, laughs.*]

COUNTY ATTORNEY: Oh, I guess they're not very dangerous things the ladies have picked out. [*Moves a few things about, disturbing the quilt pieces which cover the box. Steps back.*] No, Mrs. Peters doesn't need supervising. For that matter, a sheriff's wife is married to the law. Ever think of it that way, Mrs. Peters?
MRS. PETERS: Not—just that way.
SHERIFF: [*Chuckling.*] Married to the law. [*Moves toward the other room.*] I just want you to come in here a minute, George. We ought to take a look at these windows.
COUNTY ATTORNEY: [*Scoffingly.*] Oh, windows!
SHERIFF: We'll be right out, Mr. Hale.

[HALE *goes outside. The* SHERIFF *follows the* COUNTY ATTORNEY *into the other room. Then* MRS. HALE *rises, hands tight together, looking intensely at* MRS. PETERS, *whose eyes make a slow turn, finally meeting* MRS. HALE's. *A moment* MRS. HALE *holds her, then her own eyes point the way to where the box is concealed. Suddenly* MRS. PETERS *throws back quilt pieces and tries to put the box in the bag she is wearing. It is too big. She opens box, starts to take bird out, cannot touch it, goes to pieces, stands there helpless. Sound of a knob turning in the other room.* MRS. HALE *snatches the box and puts it in the pocket of her big coat. Enter* COUNTY ATTORNEY *and* SHERIFF.]

COUNTY ATTORNEY: [*Facetiously.*] Well, Henry, at least we found out that she was not going to quilt it. She was going to—what is it you call it, ladies?
MRS. HALE: [*Her hand against her pocket.*] We call it—knot it, Mr. Henderson.

(*CURTAIN*)

INQUIRING FURTHER

1. How would you describe the portrayal of characters in *Trifles?* Is it fair to say any of them represent stock characters or stereotypes? What can be said about the portrayal of the characters in terms of gender and identity?

2. What do you think motivates Mrs. Hale and Mrs. Peters not to tell the men about the bird? Do you think they understand the significance of the bird for the investigation?

3. Do you think it is fair to say that Mrs. Hale is the protagonist of *Trifles?* Why or why not? Write a one-page character analysis of Mrs. Hale.

4. How does the staging of *Trifles* influence the messages in the play regarding gender? What do the descriptions of the characters tell us? How do stage directions add to our understanding? Sketch out a list of examples discussing the staging of the play in terms of gender issues.

16

Innocence and Experience

The photograph that opens this chapter was taken by Dorothea Lange, who gave up a successful career as a portrait photographer in San Francisco to document the effects of the Great Depression of 1930s America. Originally she titled the photo *Young Cotton Picker*. When Lange included the image as part of a book urging the public to provide more support for displaced farmers, she changed the caption of the photograph to read *Oklahoma Child with Cotton Sack Ready to go into Field with Parents at 7 A.M.* The new caption eliminates any hint of innocence that might be associated with the title *Young Cotton Picker*. Instead, the commentary fills in the details of the story behind the image. Cotton picking for this child is not a choice, but something that begins with each day, at 7 A.M. The plight of the child spreads to her entire family—she is not with friends or playmates, but sharing the fate of her displaced parents.

Lange's image and the revised caption document the states of innocence and experience as clearly as any government study, sociological essay, or symbolic short story could. The cotton sack resembling a child's blanket, and the girl's facial expression remind us of the state of sleep and dreams we normally associate with children. We see these markers of innocence even as we recognize the growing knowledge of hardship and resignation in the face of the child. Even the use of light in the image suggests a movement from the warmth of sunshine into the darker state of shadows. The image demonstrates how innocence gives way to experience; in this case the demonstration documents the effects of the Great Depression by highlighting a loss of innocence that is clearly tragic.

Of course, the twin states of innocence and experience are not only realized in times of tragedy. We all gain experience as we mature, often finding solace in the knowledge gained that compensates for innocence lost. Further, while there is a clear movement away from childlike understanding as we grow, we maintain within us elements of innocence throughout our lives. Innocence and experience, in fact, coexist in a complex relationship. An attitude of hope, and a joy in the simple pleasures of play and possibility need not be lost as we mature. At the same time, events and our changing understanding require us to take stock of our experiences, to make them a part of our maturing identity, even as we strive to hold on to some of the innocence of youth. This chapter considers how literature has addressed these complex relationships between innocence and experience.

FROM CHILD TO ADULT

Our growing sense of experience sometimes can be associated with the maturation we undergo as we move from childhood to adulthood. This transition, as we all know, is anything but smooth. Relationships with parents, our own assertions of personality and independence, and the physical process of maturation all play out as we leave behind our lives as children and move into adulthood. These selections treat the process of maturation in literature and in life.

SHARON OLDS

Sharon Olds (born in 1942) often writes poetry with a direct style that addresses themes of family and relationships. "Rites of Passage" is taken from the collection The Dead and the Living, *published in 1983. Consider reading "The Race," also by Olds, on page 277.*

Rites of Passage

As the guests arrive at my son's party
they gather in the living room—
short men, men in first grade
with smooth jaws and chins.
5   Hands in pockets, they stand around
jostling, jockeying for place, small fights
breaking out and calming. One says to another
How old are you? Six. I'm seven. So?
They eye each other, seeing themselves

10   tiny in the other's pupils. They clear their
throats a lot, a room of small bankers,
they fold their arms and frown. *I could beat you
up,* a seven says to a six,
the dark cake, round and heavy as a

15   turret, behind them on the table. My son,
freckles like specks of nutmeg on his cheeks,
chest narrow as the balsa keel of a
model boat, long hands
cool and thin as the day they guided him

20   out of me, speaks up as a host
for the sake of the group.
We could easily kill a two-year-old,
he says in his clear voice. The other
men agree, they clear their throats

25   like Generals, they relax and get down to
playing war, celebrating my son's life.

PETER MEINKE

*Peter Meinke (born in 1932) served two years in the military between 1955
and 1957, before working as a high school English teacher, and then as
a professor of English. He writes short stories and poems that often feature humor while taking on complex subjects. "Advice to My Son" was published in 1981 in the collection* Trying to Surprise God.

Advice to My Son

The trick is, to live your days
as if each one may be your last
(for they go fast, and young men lose their lives
in strange and unimaginable ways)

5   but at the same time, plan long range
(for they go slow: if you survive
the shattered windshield and the bursting shell
you will arrive
at our approximation here below

10   of heaven or hell).

To be specific, between the peony and the rose
plant squash and spinach, turnips and tomatoes;
beauty is nectar
and nectar, in a desert, saves—

15   but the stomach craves stronger sustenance
than the honied vine.
Therefore, marry a pretty girl
after seeing her mother;
speak truth to one man,

20   work with another;
and always serve bread with your wine.

But, son,
always serve wine.

Both "Rites of Passage" and "Advice to My Son" comment on what it means to grow from a boy to a man. Compare the picture painted by each of the poems. Are they more similar or different? Which do you think more accurately describes this transition from boy to man? Why?

LYNN SMITH

Lynn Smith writes for the Los Angeles Times *and the* Washington Post. *She frequently covers entertainment, media, politics, and culture. "Betwixt and Bewildered" first appeared in the* Washington Post *in September 2001.*

Betwixt and Bewildered: Scholars Are Intrigued by the Angst of "Emerging Adults"

When she was 18, the mother of a 21-year-old son recalled, she hardly could wait to go away to school and move out of her parents' house. Most of her friends felt the same way. Nobody knew who they went out with, where they went, what they did or when they got in.

But her son lives at home and likes it. A junior in the California State University system, he doesn't have to pay rent or buy groceries. "He has a TV, a computer and a double bed. What more could a guy want?"

"The one thing that's been weird has been having his girlfriend spend the night," said the single mother, who also has a boyfriend. "How can I say, 'I can, but you can't?'" she asked. "When do you say he's an adult?"

It's a common question, and one that a growing number of parents and researchers are trying to answer. Social and economic realities have suspended the traditional markers of adulthood—moving out, finishing school, starting a job, getting married and having children. Old expectations for independence have been joined by new ones for career success and happiness.

5   Indeed, scholars say the path to adulthood, never particularly smooth, is not only longer, but also more circuitous, complex, expensive and vaguely defined than ever before. Rather than settling down with a spouse and children as their grandparents did, most high school seniors go on to college or pursue advanced degrees. They move about and hop from job to job. They live with various friends or significant others. An ever-increasing number move back home with their parents at some point after they move out.

Some specialists in human development believe the years between 18 and 25 are more than an extended adolescence, that they compose a distinct life stage that is neither adolescent nor adult, a heretofore nameless world of angst and hope. Jeffrey Arnett, an independent scholar based at the University of Maryland, calls it "emerging adulthood." Terri Apter, a research psychologist in Cambridge, England, and author of "The Myth of Maturity," calls those young adults "thresholders."

The members of this group, Arnett said, are living in a state marked by more risk and exploration than adolescence itself. Emerging adults, he said, are "freer now than they have ever been in American history. It used to be just for the elite. Now it's for the majority."

Even as they document this new stage of life, scholars disagree about whether these changes should be a cause for celebration or concern. A boom-and-bust marketplace, overly involved parents and mixed expectations are creating new pressures for young adults who fear they might never make it on their own. Others say the longer transition offers an unparalleled opportunity. Especially for those from disadvantaged or dysfunctional families, they say, this make-or-break phase can be a chance to invent or reinvent a life.

"We're going through a real sea change in how we define what adulthood is, what maturity is, what dependence is, what a steady job is," said Stephanie Coontz, a family historian at Evergreen State College in Olympia, Wash. Although the young aren't the only ones trying to sort out their life paths, they are the most obvious, she said. "They have to make decisions right now—when to get married, when to move out."

10   Bill Fitzsimmons, Harvard University dean of admissions and financial aid, said he has seen a consistent growth in anxiety levels among college students over the last two decades. The cause, he believes, is too little freedom, rather than too much. Overscheduled and controlled throughout childhood by their parents, many students are burned out and unable to be introspective about their own futures, he said. Some college students are so frenzied, they have to schedule a 20-minute meeting at 7 a.m. just to catch up with a friend, he said. Others might fail classes, consciously or unconsciously, as a way to deal with parents who have imposed inappropriate majors on them.

University officials have found students mature remarkably in just a year if they can take time off from school, Fitzsimmons said. But Jeylan Mortimer, a life-course specialist at the University of Michigan, said most students don't have the resources to take time off, travel or spend time mulling over their possibilities. "They're struggling to find their way, moving in and out of school and work, running into financial problems. They struggle with the whole process."

Increasingly young people are unable to leave home permanently the first time they move out. "It's like stopping smoking. You have to keep trying a couple of times," said Frances Goldscheider, professor of sociology at Brown University. "In the 1930s, only 25 percent of those who left home returned. By the mid-'80s, it was up to 40 percent." Now, although she doesn't have current numbers, she estimates that the figures are higher.

Apter believes too many parents feel they shouldn't be helping their thresholder children. "We're used to thinking about the dangers of keeping our children connected to us. These are real concerns in some cases, but what's happened is our awareness of the dangers of being too close has made us devalue normal healthy closeness and connection," she said.

14   One problem with studying the transition to adulthood is that researchers usually have limited funds and turn most often to students as subjects. Another is

that there has been little information about how people experience that phase of life.

15   Among the first to describe how it feels to navigate this extended transition are Alexandra Robbins and Abby Wilner, authors of "Quarterlife Crisis." They say young adults like themselves face nearly unlimited options and are jolted by "overwhelming helplessness and cluelessness, indecision and apprehension."

The authors, in their twenties, have said many people mistakenly think the twenties are easy and carefree. In fact, they said, many young adults are emotionally paralyzed and turn to antidepressants to deal with the angst of growing up. One chapter of their book is titled, "What if I'm Scared to Stop Being a Kid?"

Arnett noted that many students do not finish college, or at least not in four consecutive years. Only one-third of the college population obtains a bachelor's degree in their twenties, he said. "They're talking about the most fortunate segment of the most affluent generation of the most affluent society in human history. And all they can talk about is how tough they have it? It's like a rich guy complaining about the problems he's having with his Mercedes."

Many emerging adults have legitimate problems stemming from educational loans and credit card debt, he said.

At the same time, a "lottery-based society" has created pressures unrelated to one's finances, background or parents, said family historian Coontz. "It doesn't matter how stable you grew up; the person next to you, just by luck, got out of the stock market at just the right time and is now wandering around a millionaire while someone else, just by luck, lost out. It creates a 'why me?' mindset interspersed with grandiose, narcissistic dreams of really making it."

20   Despite their problems, most of the 200 young people Arnett interviewed over the last seven years, he said, were much happier than they had been as adolescents.

They get along with parents and regret that they were rude, he said. Most are full of hope and ambition, even if their backgrounds were difficult.

Some scholars said emerging adulthood is a luxury of the educated middle and upper classes, experienced only by those who stay in school and remain childless.

Nevertheless, Arnett said, it is an especially important opportunity for people whose parents were poor or dysfunctional in some way. "Emerging adulthood represents a chance to remake your life," he said.

For the poor, it might be now or never. "Children and adolescents are really at the mercy of families, for better or worse. The chances to turn your life around are not in childhood and adolescence. And in a way, there won't be any once you take on new long-term commitments, especially children," he said.

25   Barbara Schneider, professor of sociology at the University of Chicago, said it is imperative to understand that young adults, although they might be grouped in a single generation, are not all alike, one way or another. In her studies of 1,221 adolescents whom she followed into adulthood, Schneider found they fell into three groups: those who had a clear idea about what they wanted to do in the future, a transitional group whose members are trying to find themselves, and a "diffuse" group of young adults who had no idea what they wanted to do.

The diffuse group tended most to founder, changing colleges and taking longer to get a degree. Transitional students also have a difficult time if they don't establish a path for themselves by their junior year, she said. "This is the group that at the end of college is more likely to feel they have not lived up to their expectations. Mom says, 'We spent all this money and you want to be a what?'"

INQUIRING FURTHER

1. How would you relate your own experiences to the points made in "Betwixt and Bewildered"? Do you feel the pressures of tight schedules and too little freedom? Would it be fair to say life is more difficult for young adults today than in the past? Why or why not?

2. What do you think of the label "thresholder" being applied to 18 to 25 year olds? How would you compare this stage in life with early adolescence? Is it fair to single out any stage in life as more difficult than others?

DORIS BETTS

Author of nine novels and short story collections, Doris Betts (born in 1932) has been a nationally recognized voice in contemporary Southern literature. She won the 1994 Southern Book Critics Circle Award. Her fiction often reflects biblical influences, and depicts ordinary people showing extraordinary perseverance and common sense in the face of life's troubles. Her most widely reprinted short story, "The Ugliest Pilgrim," (1969) was the basis for a musical, which won the New York Drama Critics Circle Award, and a film, which received an Academy Award.

The Ugliest Pilgrim

I sit in the bus station, nipping chocolate peel off a Mounds candy bar with my teeth, then pasting the coconut filling to the roof of my mouth. The lump will dissolve there slowly and seep into me the way dew seeps into flowers.

Enhanced reading of "The Ugliest Pilgrim"

I like to separate flavors that way. Always I lick the salt off cracker tops before taking my first bite.

Somebody sees me with my suitcase, paper sack, and a ticket in my lap. "You going someplace, Violet?"

Stupid. People in Spruce Pine are dumb and, since I look dumb, say dumb things to me. I turn up my face as if to count those dead flies piled under the light bulb. He walks away—a fat man, could be anybody. I stick out my tongue at his back; the candy oozes down. If I could stop swallowing, it would drip into my lung and I could breathe vanilla.

5   Whoever it was, he won't glance back. People in Spruce Pine don't like to look at me, full face.

A Greyhound bus pulls in, blows air; the driver stands by the door. He's black-headed, maybe part Cherokee, with heavy shoulders but a weak chest. He thinks well of himself—I can tell that. I open my notebook and copy his name off the metal plate so I can call him by it when he drives me home again. And next week, won't Mr. Wallace Weatherman be surprised to see how well I'm looking!

I choose the front seat behind Mr. Weatherman, settle my bag with the hat in it, then open the lined composition book again. Maybe it's half full of writing. Even the empty pages toward the back have one repeated entry, high, printed off Mama's torn catechism: GLORIFY GOD AND ENJOY HIM FOREVER.

I finish Mr. Weatherman off in my book while he's running his motor and getting us onto the highway. His nose is too broad, his dark eyes too skimpy—nothing in his face I want—but the hair is nice. I write that down, "Black hair?" I'd want it to curl, though, and be soft as a baby's.

Two others are on the bus, a nigger soldier and an old woman whose jaw sticks out like a shelf. There grow, on the backs of her hands, more veins than skin. One fat blue vessel, curling from wrist to knuckle, would be good; so on one page I draw a sample hand and let blood wind across it like a river. I write at the bottom: "Praise God, it is started. May 29, 1969," and turn to a new sheet. The paper's lumpy and I flip back to the thick envelope stuck there with adhesive tape. I can't lose that.

10   We're driving now at the best speed Mr. Weatherman can make on these winding roads. On my side there is nothing out the bus window but granite rock, jagged and wet in patches. The old lady and the nigger can see red rhododendron on the slope of Roan Mountain. I'd like to own a tight dress that flower color, and breasts to go under it. I write in my notebook, very small, the word "breasts," and turn quickly to another page. AND ENJOY HIM FOREVER.

The soldier bends as if to tie his shoes, but instead zips open a canvas bag and sticks both hands inside. When finally he sits back, one hand is clenched around something hard. He catches me watching. He yawns and scratches his ribs, but the right fist sets very lightly on his knee, and when I turn he drinks something out of its cup and throws his head quickly back like a bird or a chicken. You'd think I could smell it, big as my nose is.

Across the aisle the old lady says, "You going far?" She shows me a set of tan, artificial teeth.

"Oklahoma."

"I never been there. I hear the trees give out." She pauses so I can ask politely where she's headed. "I'm going to Nashville," she finally says. "The country-music capital of the world. My son lives there and works in the cellophane plant."

15   I draw in my notebook a box and two arrows. I crisscross the box.

"He's got three children not old enough to be in school yet."

I sit very still, adding new boxes, drawing baseballs in some, looking busy for fear she might bring out their pictures from her big straw pocketbook. The funny thing is she's looking past my head, though there's nothing out that window but rock wall sliding by. I mumble, "It's hot in here."

Angrily she says, "I had eight children myself."

My pencil flies to get the boxes stacked, eight-deep, in a pyramid. "Hope you have a nice visit."

20   "It's not a visit. I maybe will move." She is hypnotized by the stone and the furry moss in its cracks. Her eyes used to be green. Maybe, when young, she was red-haired and Irish. If she'll stop talking, I want to think about trying green eyes with that Cherokee hair. Her lids droop; she looks drowsy. "I am right tired of children," she says and lays her head back on the white rag they button on these seats.

Now that her eyes are covered, I can study that face—china white, and worn thin as tissue so light comes between her bones and shines through her whole head. I picture the light going around and around her skull, like water spinning in a jar. If I could wait to be eighty, even my face might grind down and look softer. But I'm ready, in case the Preacher mentions that. Did Elisha make Naaman bear into old age his leprosy? Didn't Jesus heal the withered hand, even on Sunday, without waiting for the work week to start? And put back the ear of Malchus with a touch? As soon as Job had learned enough, did his boils fall away?

Lord, I have learned enough.

The old lady sleeps while we roll downhill and up again; then we turn so my side of the bus looks over the valley and its thickety woods where, as a girl, I pulled armloads of galax, fern, laurel, and hemlock to have some spending money. I spent it for magazines full of women with permanent waves. Behind us, the nigger shuffles a deck of cards and deals to himself by fives. Draw poker—I could beat him. My papa showed me, long winter days and nights snowed in on the mountain. He said poker would teach me arithmetic. It taught me there are four ways to make a royal flush and, with two players, it's an even chance one of them holds a pair on the deal. And when you try to draw from a pair to four of a kind, discard the kicker; it helps your odds.

The soldier deals smoothly, using his left hand only with his thumb on top. Papa was good at that. He looks up and sees my whole face with its scar, but he keeps his eyes level as if he has seen worse things; and his left hand drops cards evenly and in rhythm. Like a turtle, laying eggs.

25   I close my eyes and the riffle of his deck rests me to the next main stop where I write in my notebook: "Praise God for Johnson City, Tennessee, and all the state to come. I am on my way."

At Kingsport, Mr. Weatherman calls rest stop and I go straight through the terminal to the ladies' toilet and look hard at my face in the mirror. I must remember to start the Preacher on the scar first of all—the only thing about me that's even on both sides.

Lord! I am so ugly!

Maybe the Preacher will claim he can't heal ugliness. And I'm going to spread my palms by my ears and show him—this is a crippled face! An infirmity! Would he do for a kidney or liver what he withholds from a face? The Preacher once stuttered, I read someplace, and God bothered with that. Why not me? When the Preacher labors to heal the sick in his Tulsa auditorium, he asks us at home to lay our fingers on the television screen and pray for God's healing. He puts forth his own ten fingers and we match them, pad to pad, on that glass. I have tried that, Lord, and the Power was too filtered and thinned down for me.

I touch my hand now to this cold mirror glass, and cover all but my pimpled chin, or wide nose, or a single red-brown eye. And nothing's too bad by itself. But when they're put together?

30   I've seen the Preacher wrap his hot, blessed hands on a club foot and cry out "HEAL!" in his funny way that sounds like the word "Hell" broken into two pieces. Will he not cry out, too, when he sees this poor, clubbed face? I will be to him as Goliath was to David, a need so giant it will drive God to action.

I comb out my pine-needle hair. I think I would like blond curls and Irish eyes, and I want my month so large it will never be done with kissing.

The old lady comes in the toilet and catches me pinching my bent face. She jerks back once, looks sad, then pets me with her twiggy hand. "Listen, honey," she says, "I had looks once. It don't amount to much."

I push right past. Good people have nearly turned me against you, Lord. They open their mouths for the milk of human kindness and boiling oil spews out.

So I'm half running through the terminal and into the café, and I take the first stool and call down the counter, "Tuna-fish sandwich," quick. Living in the mountains, I eat fish every chance I get and wonder what the sea is like. Then I see I've sat down by the nigger soldier. I do not want to meet his gaze, since he's a wonder to me, too. We don't have many black men in the mountains. Mostly they live east in Carolina, on the flatland, and pick cotton and tobacco instead of apples. They seem to me like foreigners. He's absently shuffling cards the way some men twiddle thumbs. On the stool beyond him is a paratrooper, white, and they're talking about what a bitch the army is. Being sent to the same camp has made them friends already.

35   I roll a dill-pickle slice through my mouth—a wheel, a bitter wheel. Then I start on the sandwich and it's chicken by mistake when I've got chickens all over my backyard.

"Don't bother with the beer," says the black one. "I've got better on the bus." They come to some agreement and deal out cards on the counter.

It's just too much for me. I lean over behind the nigger's back and say to the paratrooper, "I wouldn't play with him." Neither one moves. "He's a mechanic." They look at each other, not at me. "It's a way to cheat on the deal."

The paratrooper sways backward on his stool and stares around out of eyes so blue that I want them, right away, and maybe his pale blond hair. I swallow a crusty half-chewed bite. "One-handed grip; the mechanic's grip. It's the middle finger. He can second-deal and bottom-deal. He can buckle the top card with his thumb and peep."

"I be damn," says the paratrooper.

40   The nigger spins around and bares his teeth at me, but it's half a grin. "Lady, you want to play?"

I slide my dishes back. "I get mad if I'm cheated."

"And mean when you're mad." He laughs a laugh so deep it makes me retaste that bittersweet chocolate off the candy bar. He offers the deck to cut, so I pull out the center and restack it three ways. A little air blows through his upper teeth. "I'm Grady Fliggins and they call me Flick."

The paratrooper reaches a hand down the counter to shake mine. "Monty Harrill. From near to Raleigh."

"And I'm Violet Karl. Spruce Pine. I'd rather play five-card stud."

45   By the time the bus rolls on, we've moved to its wider backseat playing serious cards with a fifty-cent ante. My money's sparse, but I'm good and the deck is clean. The old lady settles into my front seat, stiffer than plaster. Sometimes she throws back a hurt look.

Monty, the paratrooper, plays soft. But Flick's so good he doesn't even need to cheat, though I watch him close. He drops out quick when his cards are bad; he makes me bid high to see what he's got; and the few times he bluffs, I'm fooled. He's no talker. Monty, on the other hand, says often, "Whose play is it?" till I know that's his clue phrase for a pair. He lifts his cards close to his nose and gets quiet when planning to bluff. And he'd rather use wild cards but we won't. Ah, but he's pretty, though!

After we've swapped a little money, mostly the paratrooper's, Flick pours us a drink in some cups he stole in Kingsport and asks, "Where'd you learn to play?"

I tell him about growing up on a mountain, high, with Mama dead, and shuffling cards by a kerosene lamp with my papa. When I passed fifteen, we'd drink together, too. Applejack or a beer he made from potato peel.

"And where you headed now?" Monty's windburned in a funny pattern, with pale goggle circles that start high on his cheeks. Maybe it's something paratroopers wear.

50   "It's a pilgrimage." They lean back with their drinks. "I'm going to see this preacher in Tulsa, the one that heals, and I'm coming home pretty. Isn't that healing?" Their still faces make me nervous. "I'll even trade if he says. . . . I'll take somebody else's weak eyes or deaf ears. I could stand limping a little."

The nigger shakes his black head, snickering.

"I tried to get to Charlotte when he was down there with his eight-pole canvas cathedral tent that seats nearly fifteen thousand people, but I didn't have money then. Now what's so funny?" I think for a minute I am going to have to take out my notebook, and unglue the envelope and read them all the Scripture I have looked up on why I should be healed. Monty looks sad for me, though, and that's worse. "Let the Lord twist loose my foot or give me a cough, so long as I'm healed of my looks while I'm still young enough—" I stop and tip up my plastic cup. Young enough for you, blue-eyed boy, and your brothers.

"Listen," says Flick in a high voice. "Let me go with you and be there for that swapping." He winks one speckled eye.

"I'll not take black skin, no offense." He's offended, though, and lurches across the moving bus and falls into a far seat. "Well, you as much as said you'd swap it off!" I call. "What's wrong if I don't want it any more than you?"

55   Monty slides closer. "You're not much to look at," he grants, sweeping me up and down till I nearly glow blue from his eyes. Shaking his head, "And what now? Thirty?"

"Twenty-eight. His drink and his cards, and I hurt Flick's feelings. I didn't mean that." I'm scared, too. Maybe, unlike Job, I haven't learned enough. Who ought to be expert in hurt feelings? Me, that's who.

"And you live by yourself?"

I start to say "No, there's men falling all over each other going in and out my door." He sees my face, don't he? It makes me call, "Flick? I'm sorry." Not one movement. "Yes. By myself." Five years now, since Papa had heart failure and fell off the high back porch and rolled downhill in the gravel till the hobble-bushes stopped him. I found him past sunset, cut from the rocks but not much blood showing. And what there was, dark, and already jellied.

Monty looks at me carefully before making up his mind to say, "That preacher's a fake. You ever see a doctor agree to what he's done?"

60   "Might be." I'm smiling. I tongue out the last liquor in my cup. I've thought of all that, but it may be what I believe is stronger than him faking. That he'll be electrified by my trust, the way a magnet can get charged against its will. He might be a lunatic or a dope fiend, and it still not matter.

Monty says, "Flick, you plan to give us another drink?"

"No." He acts like he's going to sleep.

"I just wouldn't count on that preacher too much." Monty cleans his nails with a matchbook corner and sometimes gives me an uneasy look. "Things are mean and ugly in this world—I mean *act* ugly, do ugly, be ugly."

He's wrong. When I leave my house, I can walk for miles and everything's beautiful. Even the rattlesnakes have grace. I don't mind his worried looks, since I'm writing in my notebook how we met and my winnings—a good sign, to earn money on a trip. I like the way army barbers trim his hair. I wish I could touch it.

65   "Took one furlough in your mountains. Pretty country. Maybe hard to live in? Makes you feel little." He looks toward Flick and says softer, "Makes you feel like the night sky does. So many stars."

"Some of them big as daisies." It's easy to live in, though. Some mornings a deer and I scare up each other in the brush, and his heart stops, and mine stops. Everything stops till he plunges away. The next pulsebeat nearly knocks you down. "Monty, doesn't your hair get lighter in the summers? That might be a good color hair to ask for in Tulsa. Then I could turn colors like the leaves. Spell your last name for me."

He does, and says I sure am funny. Then he spells Grady Fliggins and I write that, too. He's curious about my book, so I flip through and offer to read him parts. Even with his eyes shut, Flick is listening. I read them about my papa's face, a chunky block face, not much different from the Preacher's square one. After Papa died, I wrote that to slow down how fast I was forgetting him. I tell Monty parts of my lists: that you can get yellow dye out of gopherwood and Noah built his ark from that, and maybe it stained the water. That a cow eating snakeroot might give poison milk. I pass him a pressed maypop flower I'm carrying to Tulsa, because the crown of thorns and the crucifixion nails grow in its center, and each piece of the bloom stands for one of the apostles.

"It's a mollypop vine," says Flick out of one corner of his mouth. "And it makes a green ball that pops when you step on it." He stretches. "Deal you some blackjack?"

For no reason, Monty says, "We oughtn't to let her go."

70   We play blackjack till supper stop and I write in my book, "Praise God for Knoxville and two new friends." I've not had many friends. At school in the valley, I sat in the back rows, reading, a hand spread on my face. I was smart, too; but if you let that show, you had to stand for the class and present different things.

When the driver cuts out the lights, the soldiers give me a whole seat, and a duffelbag for a pillow. I hear them whispering, first about women, then about me; but after a while I don't hear that anymore.

By the time we hit Nashville, the old lady makes the bus wait while she begs me to stop with her. "Harvey won't mind. He's a good boy." She will not even look at Monty and Flick. "You can wash and change clothes and catch a new bus tomorrow."

"I'm in a hurry. Thank you." I have picked a lot of galax to pay for this trip.

"A girl alone. A girl that maybe feels she's got to prove something?" The skin on her neck shivers. "Some people might take advantage."

75   Maybe when I ride home under my new face, that will be some risk. I shake my head, and as she gets off she whispers something to Mr. Weatherman about looking after me. It's wasted, though, because a new driver takes his place and he looks nearly as bad as I do—oily-faced and toad-shaped, with eyeballs a dingy color and streaked with blood. He's the flat lands driver, I guess, because he leans back and drops one warty hand on the wheel and we go so fast and steady you can hardly tell it.

Since Flick is the tops in cards and we're tired of that, it's Monty's turn to brag on his motorcycle. He talks all across Tennessee till I think I could ride one by hearsay alone, that my wrist knows by itself how far to roll the throttle in. It's a Norton and he rides it in Scrambles and Enduro events, in his leathers, with spare parts and tools glued all over him with black electrician's tape.

"So this bastard tells me, 'Zip up your jacket because when I run over you I want some traction.'"

Flick is playing solitaire. "You couldn't get me on one of them killing things."

"One day I'm coming through Spruce Pine, flat out, throw Violet up behind me! We're going to lean all the way through them mountains. Sliding the right foot and then sliding the left." Monty lays his head back on the seat beside me, rolls it, watches. "How you like that? Take you through creeks and ditches like you was on a skateboard. You can just holler and hang on."

80   Lots of women have, I bet.

"The Norton's got the best front forks of anybody. It'll nearly roll up a tree trunk and ride down the other side." He demonstrates on the seat back. I keep writing. These are new things, two-stroke and four-stroke, picking your line on a curve, Milwaukee iron. It will all come back to me in the winters, when I reread these pages.

Flick says he rode on a Harley once. "Turned over and got drug. No more."

They argue about what he should have done instead of turning over. Finally Monty drifts off to sleep, his head leaning at me slowly, so I look down on his crisp, light hair. I pat it as easy as a cat would, and it tickles my palm. I'd almost ask them in Tulsa to make me a man if I could have hair like his, and a beard, and feel so different in so many places.

He slides closer in his sleep. One eyebrow wrinkles against my shoulder. Looking our way, Flick smokes a cigarette, then reads some magazine he keeps rolled in his belt. Monty makes a deep noise against my arm as if, while he slept, his throat had cleared itself. I shift and his whole head is on my shoulder now. Its weight makes me breathe shallow.

85   I rest my eyes. If I should turn, his hair would barely touch my cheek, the scarred one, like a shoebrush. I do turn and it does. For miles he sleeps that way and I almost sleep. Once, when we take a long curve, he rolls against me, and one of his hands drifts up and then drops in my lap. Just there, where the creases are.

I would not want God's Power to turn me, after all, into a man. His breath is so warm. Everywhere, my skin is singing. Praise God for that.

When I get my first look at the Mississippi River, the pencil goes straight into my pocketbook. How much praise would that take?

"Is the sea like this?"

"Not except they're both water," Flick says. He's not mad anymore. "Tell you what, Vi-oh-LETTE. When Monty picks you up on his cycle" ("sickle," he calls it), "you ride down to the beaches—Cherry Grove, O.D., around there. Where they work the big nets in the fall and drag them up on the sand with trucks at each end, and men to their necks in the surf."

90   "You do that?"

"I know people that do. And afterward they strip and dress by this big fire on the beach."

And they make chowder while this cold wind is blowing! I know that much, without asking. In a big black pot that sits on that whipping fire. I think they might let me sit with them and stir the pot. It's funny how much, right now, I feel like praising all the good things I've never seen, in places I haven't been.

Everybody has to get off the bus and change in Memphis, and most of them wait a long time. I've taken the long way, coming here; but some of Mama's cousins live in Memphis and might rest me overnight. Monty says they plan to stay the night, too, and break the long trip.

"They know you're coming, Violet?" It's Flick says my name that way, in pieces, carefully: Vi-oh-LETTE. Monty is lazier; Viii-lut. They make me feel like more than one.

95   "I've never even met these cousins. But soon as I call up and tell them who I am and that I'm here . . . "

"We'll stay some hotel tonight and then ride on. Why don't you come with us?" Monty is carrying my scuffed bag. Flick swings the paper sack. "You know us better than them."

"Kin people," grunts Flick, "can be a bad surprise."

Monty is nodding his head. "Only cousin I had got drunk and drove this tractor over his baby brother. Did it on purpose, too." I see by his face that Monty has made this up, for my sake.

"Your cousins might not even live here anymore. I bet it's been years since you heard from a one."

100   "We're picking a cheap hotel, in case that's a worry."

I never thought they might have moved. "How cheap?"

When Flick says "Under five," I nod; and my things go right up on their shoulders as I follow them into a Memphis cab. The driver takes for granted I'm Monty's afflicted sister and names a hotel right off. He treats me with pity and good manners.

And the hotel he chooses is cheap, all right, where ratty salesmen with bad territories spend half the night drinking in their rooms. Plastic palm bushes and a worn rug the color of wet cigars. I get Room 210 and they're down the hall in the teens. They stand in my doorway and watch me drop both shoes and walk the bed in bare feet. When Monty opens my window, we can hear some kitchen underneath—a fan, clattering noise, a man's crackly voice singing about the California earthquake.

It scares me, suddenly, to know I can't remember how home sounds. Not one bird call, nor the water over rocks. There's so much you can't save by writing down.

105   "Smell that grease," says Flick, and shakes his head till his lips flutter. "I'm finding an ice machine. You, Vi-oh-LETTE, come on down in a while."

Monty's got a grin I'll remember if I never write a word. He waves. "Flick and me going to get drunker than my old cousin and put wild things in your book. Going to draw dirty pictures. You come on down and get drunk enough to laugh."

But after a shower, damp in my clean slip, even this bed like a roll of fence wire feels good, and I fall asleep wondering if that rushing noise is a river wind, and how long I can keep it in my mind.

Monty and Flick edge into my dream. Just their voices first, from way downhill. Somewhere in a Shonny Haw thicket. "Just different," Monty is saying. "That's all. Different. Don't make some big thing out of it." He doesn't sound happy. "Nobody else," he says.

Is that Flick singing? No, because the song goes on while his voice says, "Just so . . . " and then some words I don't catch. "It don't hurt"? Or maybe, "You don't hurt"? I hear them climbing my tangled hill, breaking sticks and knocking the little stones loose. I'm trying to call to them which way the path is, but I can't make noise because the Preacher took my voice and put it in a black bag and carried it to a sick little boy in Iowa.

110   They find the path, anyway. And now they can see my house and me standing little by the steps. I know how it looks from where they are: the wood rained on till the siding's almost silver; and behind the house a wet-weather waterfall that's cut a stream bed downhill and grown pin cherry and bee balm on both sides. The high rock walls by the waterfall are mossy and slick, but I've scraped one place and hammered a mean-looking gray head that leans out of the hillside and stares down the path at whoever comes. I've been here so

long by myself that I talk to it sometimes. Right now I'd say, "Look yonder. We've got company at last!" if my voice wasn't gone.

"You can't go by looks," Flick is saying as they climb. He ought to know. Ahead of them, warblers separate and fly out on two sides. Everything moves out of their path if I could just see it—tree frogs and mosquitoes. Maybe the worms drop deeper just before a footstep falls.

"Without the clothes, it's not a hell of a lot improved," says Monty, and I know suddenly they are inside the house with me, inside my very room, and my room today's in Memphis. "There's one thing, though," Monty says, standing over my bed. "Good looks in a woman is almost like a wall. She can use it to shut you outside. You never know what she's like, that's all." He's wearing a T-shirt and his dog tags jingle. "Most of the time I don't even miss knowing that."

And Flick says, disgusted, "I knew that much in grammar school. You sure are slow. It's not the face you screw." If I opened my eyes, I could see him now, behind Monty. He says, "After a while, you don't even notice faces. I always thought, in a crowd, my mother might not pick Daddy out."

"*My* mother could," says Monty. "He was always the one *started* the fight."

115   I stretch and open my eyes. It's a plain slip, cotton, that I sewed myself and makes me look too white and skinny as a sapling.

"She's waking up."

When I point, Monty hands me the blouse off the doorknob. Flick says they've carried me a soda pop, plus something to spruce it up. They sit stiffly on two hard chairs till I've buttoned on my skirt. I sip the drink, cold but peppery, and prop on the bed with the pillows. "I dreamed you both came where my house is, on the mountain, and it had rained so the waterfall was working. I felt real proud of that."

After two drinks we go down to the noisy restaurant with that smelly grease. And after that, to a picture show. Monty grins widely when the star comes on the screen. The spit on his teeth shines, even in the dark. Seeing what kind of woman he really likes, black-haired as a gypsy and with a juicy mouth, I change all my plans. My eyes, too, must turn up on the ends and when I bend down my breasts must fall forward and push at each other. When the star does that in the picture, the cowboy rubs his mustache low in the front of her neck.

In the darkness, Monty takes my hand and holds it in his swelling lap. To me it seems funny that my hand, brown and crusty from hoeing and chopping, is harder than his. I guess you don't get calluses rolling a motorcycle throttle. He rubs his thumb up and down my middle finger. Oh, I would like to ride fast behind him, spraddle-legged, with my arms wrapped on his belt, and I would lay my face between his sharp shoulder blades.

120   That night, when I've slept awhile, I hear something brushing the rug in the hall. I slip to my door. It's very dark. I press myself, face first, to the wood. There's breathing on the other side. I feel I get fatter, standing there, that even my own small breasts might now be made to touch. I round both shoulders to see. The movement jars the door and it trembles slightly in its frame.

From the far side, by the hinges, somebody whispers, "Vi-oh-LETTE?"

Now I stand very still. The wood feels cooler on my skin, or else I have grown very warm. Oh, I could love anybody! There is so much of me now, they could line up strangers in the hall and let me hold each one better than he had ever been held before!

Slowly I turn the knob, but Flick's breathing is gone. The corridor's empty.
I leave the latch off.

Late in the night, when the noise from the kitchen is over, he comes into
my room. I wake when he bumps on a chair, swears, then scrabbles at the foot-
board.

125   "Viii-lut?"

I slide up in bed. I'm not ready, not now, but he's here. I spread both arms
wide. In the dark he can't tell.

He feels his way onto the bed and he touches my knee and it changes. Stops
being just my old knee, under his fingers. I feel the joint heat up and bubble.
I push the sheet down.

He comes onto me, whispering something. I reach up to claim him.

One time he stops. He's surprised, I guess, finding he isn't the first. How can
I tell him how bad that was? How long ago? The night when the twelfth grade
was over and one of them climbed with me all the way home? And he asked.
And I thought, *I'm entitled.* Won him a five-dollar bet. Didn't do nothing for me.

130   But this time I sing out and Monty says, "Shh," in my ear. And he starts
over, slow, and makes me whimper one other time. Then he turns sideways
to sleep and I try my face there, laid in the nest on his damp back. I reach
out my tongue. He is salty and good.

Now there are two things too big for my notebook but praise God! And
for the Mississippi, too!

There is no good reason for me to ride with them all the way to Fort Smith,
but since Tulsa is not expecting me, we change my ticket. Monty pays the extra.
We ride through the fertile plains. The last of May becomes June and the
Arkansas sun is blazing. I am stunned by this heat. At home, night means
blankets and even on hot afternoons it may rain and start the waterfall. I lie
against my seat for miles without a word.

"What's wrong?" Monty keeps asking; but, under the heat, I am happy.
Sleepy with happiness, a lizard on a rock. At every stop Monty's off the bus,
bringing me more than I can eat or drink, buying me magazines and gum. I
tell him and Flick to play two-handed cards, but mostly Flick lectures him in
a low voice about something.

I try to stop thinking of Memphis and think back to Tulsa. I went to the
Spruce Pine library to look up Tulsa in their encyclopedia. I thought sure it
would tell about the Preacher, and on what street he'd built his Hope and Glory
Building for his soul crusades. Tulsa was listed in the *Americana,* Volume 27,
Trance to Venial Sin. I got so tickled with that I forgot to write down the rest.

135   Now, in the hot sun, clogged up with trances and venial sins, I dream under
the drone of their voices. For some reason I remember that old lady back in
Nashville, moved in with Harvey and his wife and their three children. I hope
she's happy. I picture her on Harvey's back porch, baked in the sun like me,
in a rocker. Snapping beans.

I've left my pencil in the hotel and must borrow one from Flick to write in
my book. I put in, slowly, "This is the day which the Lord hath made." But,
before Monty, what kind of days was He sending me? I cross out the line. I have
this wish to praise, instead of Him, the littlest things. Honeybees, and the wet
slugs under their rocks. A gnat in some farmer's eye.

I give up and hand Flick his pencil. He slides toward the aisle and whispers, "You wish you'd stayed in your mountains?"

I shake my head and a piece of my no-color hair falls into the sunlight. Maybe it even shines.

He spits on the pencil point and prints something inside a gum wrapper. "Here's my address. You keep it. Never can tell."

So I tear the paper in half and give him back mine. He reads it a long time before tucking it away, but he won't send a letter till I do—I can tell that. Through all this, Monty stares out the window. Arkansas rolls out ahead of us like a rug.

Monty has not asked for my address, nor how far uphill I live from Spruce Pine, though he could ride his motorcycle up to me, strong as its engine is. For a long time he has been sitting quietly, lighting one cigarette off another. This winter, I've got to learn smoking. How to lift my hand up so every eye will follow it to my smooth cheek.

I put Flick's paper in my pocketbook and there, inside, on a round mirror, my face is waiting in ambush for me. I see the curved scar, neat as ever, swoop from the edge of one nostril in rainbow shape across my cheek, then down toward the ear. For the first time in years, pain boils across my face as it did that day. I close my eyes under that red drowning, and see again Papa's ax head rise off its locust handle and come floating through the air, sideways, like a gliding crow. And it drops down into my face almost daintily, the edge turned just enough to slash loose a flap of skin the way you might slice straight down on the curve of a melon. My papa is yelling, but I am under a red rain and it bears me down. I am lifted and run with through the woodyard and into the barn. Now I am slumped on his chest and the whipped horse is throwing us down the mountainside, and my head is wrapped in something big as a wet quilt. The doctor groans when he winds it off and I faint while he lifts up my flesh like the flap of a pulpy envelope, and sews the white bone out of sight.

Dizzy from the movement of the bus, I snap shut my pocketbook.

Whenever I cry, the first drop quivers there, in the curving scar, and then runs crooked on that track to the ear. I cry straight-down on the other side.

145   I am glad this bus has a toilet. I go there to cool my eyes with wet paper, and spit up Monty's chocolate and cola.

When I come out, he's standing at the door with his fist up. "You all right, Viii-lut? You worried or something?"

I see he pities me. In my seat again, I plan the speech I will make at Fort Smith and the laugh I will give. "Honey, you're good," I'll say, laughing, "but the others were better." That ought to do it. I am quieter now than Monty is, practicing it in my mind.

It's dark when we hit Fort Smith. Everybody's face looks shadowed and different. Mine better. Monty's strange. We're saying good-byes very fast. I start my speech twice and he misses it twice.

Then he bends over me and offers his own practiced line that I see he's worked up all across Arkansas, "I plan to be right here, Violet, in this bus station. On Monday. All day. You get off your bus when it comes through. Hear me, Viii-lut? I'll watch for you?"

150   No. He won't watch. Nor I come. "My schedule won't take me this road going back. Bye, Flick. Lots of good luck to you both."

"Promise me. Like I'm promising."

"Good luck to you, Vi-oh-LETTE." Flick lets his hand fall on my head and it feels as good as anybody's hand.

Monty shoves money at me and I shove it back. "Promise," he says, his voice furious. He tries to kiss me in the hair and I jerk so hard my nose cracks his chin. We stare, blurry-eyed and hurting. He follows Flick down the aisle, calls back, "I'm coming here Monday. See you then, hear? And you get off this bus!"

"No! I won't!"

155   He yells it twice more. People are staring. He's out of the bus pounding on the steel wall by my seat. I'm not going to look. The seats fill up with strangers and we ride away, nobody talking to anyone else. My nose where I hit it is going to swell—the Preacher will have to throw that in for free. I look back, but he's gone.

The lights in the bus go out again. Outside they bloom thick by the streets, then thinner, then mostly gone as we pass into the countryside. Even in the dark, I can see Oklahoma's mountains are uglier than mine. Knobs and hills, mostly. The bus drives into rain which covers up everything. At home I like that washing sound. We go deeper into the downpour. Perhaps we are under the Arkansas River, after all. It seems I can feel its great weight move over me.

Before daylight, the rain tapers off and here the ground looks dry, even barren. Cattle graze across long fields. In the wind, wheat fields shiver. I can't eat anything all the way to Tulsa. It makes me homesick to see the land grow brighter and flatter and balder. That old lady was right—the trees do give out—and oil towers grow in their place. The glare's in my eyes. I write in my notebook, "Praise God for Tulsa; I am nearly there," but it takes a long time to get the words down.

One day my papa told me how time got slow for him when Mama died. How one week he waded through the creek and it was water, and the next week cold molasses. How he'd lay awake a year between sundown and sunup, and in the morning I'd be a day older and he'd be three hundred and sixty-five.

It works the other way, too. In no time at all, we're into Tulsa without me knowing what we've passed. So many tall buildings. Everybody's running. They rush into taxis before I can get one to wait for me long enough to ask the driver questions. But still I'm speeded to a hotel, and the elevator yanks me to a room quicker than Elijah rode to Heaven. The room's not bad. A Gideon Bible. Inside are lots of dirty words somebody wrote. He must have been feeling bad.

160   I bathe and dress, trembling from my own speed, and pin on the hat which has traveled all the way from Spruce Pine for this. I feel tired. I go out into the loud streets full of fast cars. Hot metal everywhere. A taxi roars me across town to the Preacher's church.

It looks like a big insurance office, though I can tell where the chapel is by colored glass in the pointed windows. Carved in an arch over the door are the words "HOPE OF GLORY BUILDING." Right away, something in me sinks. All this time I've been hearing it on TV as the Hope *and* Glory Building. You wouldn't think one word could make that much difference.

Inside the door, there's a list of offices and room numbers. I don't see the Preacher's name. Clerks send me down long, tiled halls, past empty air-conditioned offices. One tells me to go up two flights and ask the fat woman, and the fat woman sends me down again. I'm carrying my notebook in a dry hand, feeling as brittle as the maypop flower.

At last I wait an hour to see some assistant—very close to the Preacher, I'm told. His waiting room is chilly, the leatherette chairs worn down to the mesh. I try to remember how much TB and cancer have passed through this very room and been jerked out of people the way Jesus tore out a demon and flung him into a herd of swine. I wonder what he felt like to the swine.

After a long time, the young man calls me into his plain office—wood desk, wood chairs. Shelves of booklets and colored folders. On one wall, a colored picture of Jesus with that fairy ring of light around His head. Across from that, one of His praying hands—rougher than Monty's, smoother than mine.

165   The young man wears glasses with no rims. In this glare, I am reflected on each lens, Vi-oh-LETTE and Viii-lut. On his desk is a box of postcards of the Hope and Glory Building. *Of* Glory. *Of* Glory.

I am afraid.

I feel behind me for the chair.

The man explains that he is presently in charge. The Preacher's speaking in Tallahassee, his show taped weeks ahead. I never thought of it as a show before. He waits.

I reach inside my notebook where, taped shut, is the thick envelope with everything written down. I knew I could never explain things right. When have I ever been able to tell what I really felt? But it's all in there—my name, my need. The words from the Bible which must argue for me. I did not sit there nights since Papa died, counting my money and studying God's Book, for nothing. Playing solitaire, then going back to search the next page and the next. Stepping outside to rest my eyes on His limitless sky, then back to the Book and the paper, building my case.

170   He starts to read, turns up his glitter-glass to me once to check how I look, then reads again. His chair must be hard, for he squirms in it, crosses his legs. When he has read every page, he lays the stack down, slowly takes off his glasses, folds them shining into a case. He leaves it open on his desk. Mica shines like that, in the rocks.

Then he looks at me, fully. Oh. He is plain. Almost homely. I nearly expected it. Maybe Samuel was born ugly, so who else would take him but God?

"My child," the man begins, though I'm older than he is, "I understand how you feel. And we will most certainly pray for your spirit. . . . "

I shut my eyes against those two flashing faces on his spectacles. "Never mind my spirit." I see he doesn't really understand. I see he will live a long life, and not marry.

"Our Heavenly Father has purpose in all things."

175   Stubbornly, "Ask Him to set it aside."

"We must all trust His will."

After all these years, isn't it God's turn to trust mine? Could He not risk a little beauty on me? Just when I'm ready to ask, the sober assistant recites, "'Favor is deceitful and beauty is vain.' That's in Proverbs."

And I cry, " 'The crooked shall be made straight!' Isaiah said that!" He draws back, as if I had brought the Gideon Bible and struck him with its most disfigured pages. "Jesus healed an impediment in speech. See my impediment! Mud on a blind man's eyes was all He needed! Don't you remember?" But he's read all that. Everything I know on my side lies, written out, under his sweaty hand. Lord, don't let me whine. But I whine, "He healed the ten lepers and only one thanked. Well, I'll thank. I promise. All my life."

He clears his long knotty throat and drones like a bee, " 'By the sadness of the countenance the heart is made better.' Ecclesiastes. Seven. Three."

180   Oh, that's not fair! I skipped those parts, looking for verses that suited me! And it's wrong, besides.

I get up to leave and he asks will I kneel with him? "Let us pray together for that inner beauty."

No, I will not. I go down that hollow hall and past the echoing rooms. Without his help I find the great auditorium, lit through colored glass, with its cross of white plastic and a pinker Jesus molded onto it. I go straight to the pulpit where the Preacher stands. There is nobody else to plead. I ask Jesus not to listen to everything He hears, but to me only.

Then I tell Him how it feels to be ugly, with nothing to look back at you but a deer or an owl. I read Him my paper, out loud, full of His own words.

"I have been praising you, Lord, but it gets harder every year." Maybe that sounds too strong. I try to ease up my tone before the Amens. Then the chapel is very quiet. For one minute I hear the whir of many wings, but it's only a fan inside an air vent.

185   I go into the streets of Tulsa, where even the shade from a building is hot. And as I walk to the hotel I'm repeating, over and over, "Praise God for Tulsa in spite of everything."

Maybe I say this aloud, since people are staring. But maybe that's only because they've never seen a girl cry crooked in their streets before.

Monday morning. I have not looked at my face since the pulpit prayer. Who can predict how He might act—with a lightning bolt? Or a melting so slow and tender it could not even be felt?

Now, on the bus, I can touch in my pocketbook the cold mirror glass. Though I cover its surface with prints, I never look down. We ride through the dust and I'm nervous. My pencil is flying: "Be ye therefore perfect as your Heavenly Father is perfect. Praise God for Oklahoma. For Wagoner and Sapulpa and Broken Arrow and every other name on these signs by the road."

Was that the wrong thing to tell Him? My threat that even praise can be withheld? Maybe He's angry. "Praise God for oil towers whether I like them or not." When we pass churches, I copy their names. Praise them all. I want to write, "Bless," but that's *His* job.

190   We cross the cool Arkansas River. As its damp rises into the bus and touches my face, something wavers there, in the very bottom of each pore; and I clap my rough hands to each cheek. Maybe He's started? How much can He do between here and Fort Smith? If He will?

For I know what will happen. Monty won't come. And I won't stop. That's an end to it.

No, Monty is there. Waiting right now. And I'll go into the bus station on tiptoe and stand behind him. He'll turn, with his blue eyes like lamps. *And he won't know me!* If I'm changed. So I will explain myself to him: how this gypsy hair and this juicy mouth is still Violet Karl. He'll say, "Won't old Flick be surprised?" He'll say, "Where is that place you live? Can I come there?"

But if, while I wait and he turns, he should know me by my old face . . . If he should say my name or show by recognition that my name's rising up now in his eyes like something through water . . . I'll be running by then. To the bus. Straight out that door to the Tennessee bus, saying, "Driver, don't let that man on!" It's a very short stop. We'll be pulling out quick. I don't think he'll follow, anyhow.

I don't even think he will come.

195   One hundred and thirty-one miles to Fort Smith. I wish I could eat.

I try to think up things to look forward to at home. Maybe the sourwoods are blooming early, and the bees have been laying-by my honey. If it's rained enough, my corn might be in tassel. Wouldn't it be something if God took His own sweet time, and I lived on that slope for years and years, getting prettier all the time? And nobody to know?

It takes nearly years and years to get to Fort Smith. My papa knew things about time. I comb out my hair, not looking once to see what color sheddings are caught in the teeth. There's no need feeling my cheek, since my finger expects that scar. I can feel it on me almost anywhere, by memory. I straighten my skirt and lick my lips till the spit runs out.

And they're waiting. Monty at one door of the terminal and Flick at another.

"Ten minutes," the driver says when the bus is parked, but I wait in my seat till Flick gets restless and walks to the cigarette machine. Then I slip through his entrance door and inside the station. Mirrors shine everywhere. On the vending machines and the weight machines and a full-length one by the phone booth. It's all I can do not to look. I pass the ticket window and there's Monty's back at the other door. My face remembers the shape of it. Seeing him there, how he's made, and the parts of him fitted, makes me forget how I look. And before I can stop, I call out his name.

200   Right away, turning, he yells to me "*Viii*-lut!"

So I know. I can look, then, in the wide mirror over a jukebox. Tired as I am and unfed, I look worse than I did when I started from home.

He's laughing and talking. "I been waiting here since daylight scared you wouldn't . . . " but by then I've run past the ugly girl in the glass and I race for the bus, for the road, for the mountain.

Behind me, he calls loudly, "Flick!"

I see that one step in my path like a floating dark blade, but I'm faster this time. I twist by him, into the flaming sun and the parking lot. How my breath hurts!

205   Monty's between me and my bus, but there's time. I circle the cabstand, running hard over the asphalt field, with a pain ticking in my side. He calls me. I plunge through the crowd like a deer through fetterbush. But he's running as hard as he can and he's faster than me. And, oh!

Praise God!

He's catching me!

INQUIRING FURTHER

1. Trace the influence of religion on Violet's character in the story. What can you say about the fact that Violet is on a pilgrimage? Do the depictions of religion change in the story? Freewrite for five minutes about religion in "The Ugliest Pilgrim."

2. How would you explain the flashbacks in the story in terms of Violet's identity? Would you emphasize her experiences from the past when explaining her character? Why or why not? How would you relate the past to the present?

3. Consider the theme of appearance in the story. What can be said about the significance of Violet's appearance? How does appearance relate to the other characters in the story? How does it relate to religion? Write a paper in which you discuss "The Ugliest Pilgrim" in terms of appearance.

LIFE LESSONS

Whether young or old, we may encounter an event or be forced into a situation that changes our views. Often these changes in perspective accompany life changes. Economic or social forces may prompt us to alter our behavior. We may change the way we relate to others, taking new initiatives or even replacing one set of acquaintances with another. All of these personal transformations are part of the movement from innocence to experience.

KATE CHOPIN

A champion of women's issues, Kate Chopin (1851–1904) also chronicled the culture and people from the Creole communities of Louisiana. She frequently depicted female characters that brought to light the conventions and social tensions associated with Southern culture. For more, read "The Story of an Hour" by Chopin on pages 4–5.

Désirée's Baby

As the day was pleasant, Madame Valmondé drove over to L'Abri to see Désirée and the baby.

It made her laugh to think of Désirée with a baby. Why, it seemed but yesterday that Désirée was little more than a baby herself; when Monsieur in riding through the gateway of Valmondé had found her lying asleep in the shadow of the big stone pillar.

The little one awoke in his arms and began to cry for "Dada." That was as much as she could do or say. Some people thought she might have strayed there of her own accord, for she was of the toddling age. The prevailing belief was that she had been purposely left by a party of Texans, whose canvas-covered wagon, late in the day, had crossed the ferry that Coton Maïs kept, just below the plantation. In time Madame Valmondé abandoned every speculation but the one that Désirée had been sent to her by a beneficent Providence to be the child of her affection, seeing that she was without child of the flesh. For the girl grew to be beautiful and gentle, affectionate and sincere,—the idol of Valmondé.

It was no wonder, when she stood one day against the stone pillar in whose shadow she had lain asleep, eighteen years before, that Armand Aubigny riding by and seeing her there, had fallen in love with her. That was the way all the Aubignys fell in love, as if struck by a pistol shot. The wonder was that he had not loved her before; for he had known her since his father brought him home from Paris, a boy of eight, after his mother died there. The passion that awoke in him that day, when he saw her at the gate, swept along like an avalanche, or like a prairie fire, or like anything that drives headlong over all obstacles.

5   Monsieur Valmondé grew practical and wanted things well considered: that is, the girl's obscure origin. Armand looked into her eyes and did not care. He was reminded that she was nameless. What did it matter about a name when he could give her one of the oldest and proudest in Louisiana? He ordered the *corbeille*[1] from Paris, and contained himself with what patience he could until it arrived; then they were married.

---

[1] **Corbeille:** Wedding gifts.

Madame Valmondé had not seen Désirée and the baby for four weeks. When she reached L'Abri she shuddered at the first sight of it, as she always did. It was a sad looking place, which for many years had not known the gentle presence of a mistress, old Monsieur Aubigny having married and buried his wife in France, and she having loved her own land too well ever to leave it. The roof came down steep and black like a cowl, reaching out beyond the wide galleries that encircled the yellow stuccoed house. Big, solemn oaks grew close to it, and their thick-leaved, far-reaching branches shadowed it like a pall. Young Aubigny's rule was a strict one, too, and under it his negroes had forgotten how to be gay, as they had been during the old master's easy-going and indulgent lifetime.

The young mother was recovering slowly, and lay full length, in her soft white muslins and laces, upon a couch. The baby was beside her, upon her arm, where he had fallen asleep, at her breast. The yellow nurse woman sat beside a window fanning herself.

Madame Valmondé bent her portly figure over Désirée and kissed her, holding her an instant tenderly in her arms. Then she turned to the child.

"This is not the baby!" she exclaimed, in startled tones. French was the language spoken at Valmondé in those days.

10   "I knew you would be astonished," laughed Désirée, "at the way he has grown. The little *cochon de lait!*[2] Look at his legs, mamma, and his hands and finger-nails,—real finger-nails. Zandrine had to cut them this morning. Isn't it true, Zandrine?"

The woman bowed her turbaned head majestically, "Mais si, Madame."

"And the way he cries," went on Désirée, "is deafening. Armand heard heard him the other day as far away as La Blanche's cabin."

Madame Valmondé had never removed her eyes from the child. She lifted it and walked with it over to the window that was lightest. She scanned the baby narrowly, then looked as searchingly at Zandrine, whose face was turned to gaze across the fields.

"Yes, the child has grown, has changed;" said Madame Valmondé, slowly, as she replaced it beside its mother. "What does Armand say?"

15   Désirée's face became suffused with a glow that was happiness itself.

"Oh, Armand is the proudest father in the parish, I believe, chiefly because it is a boy, to bear his name; though he says not,–that he would have loved a girl as well. But I know it isn't true. I know he says that to please me. And mamma," she added, drawing Madame Valmondé's head down to her, and speaking in a whisper, "he hasn't punished one of them—not one of them— since baby is born. Even Négrillon, who pretended to have burnt his leg that he might rest from work—he only laughed, and said Négrillon was a great scamp. Oh, mamma, I'm so happy; it frightens me."

What Désirée said was true. Marriage, and later the birth of his son, had softened Armand Aubigny's imperious and exacting nature greatly. This was what made the gentle Désirée so happy, for she loved him desperately. When he frowned she trembled, but loved him. When he smiled, she asked no greater blessing of God. But Armand's dark, handsome face had not often been disfigured by frowns since the day he fell in love with her.

When the baby was about three months old, Désirée awoke one day to the conviction that there was something in the air menacing her peace. It was at first too subtle to grasp. It had only been a disquieting suggestion; an air

---

[2]**Cochon de lait:** A piglet.

of mystery among the blacks; unexpected visits from far-off neighbors who could hardly account for their coming. Then a strange, an awful change in her husband's manner, which she dared not ask him to explain. When he spoke to her, it was with averted eyes, from which the old love-light seemed to have gone out. He absented himself from home; and when there, avoided her presence and that of her child, without excuse. And the very spirit of Satan seemed suddenly to take hold of him in his dealings with the slaves. Désirée was miserable enough to die.

She sat in her room, one hot afternoon, in her *peignoir,* listlessly drawing through her fingers the strands of her long, silky brown hair that hung about her shoulders. The baby, half naked, lay asleep upon her own great mahogany bed, that was like a sumptuous throne, with its satin-lined half-canopy. One of La Blanche's little quadroon boys—half naked too—stood fanning the child slowly with a fan of peacock feathers. Désirée's eyes had been fixed absently and sadly upon the baby, while she was striving to penetrate the threatening mist that she felt closing about her. She looked from her child to the boy who stood beside him, and back again; over and over. "Ah!" It was a cry that she could not help; which she was not conscious of having uttered. The blood turned like ice in her veins, and a clammy moisture gathered upon her face.

20   She tried to speak to the little quadroon boy; but no sound would come, at first. When he heard his name uttered, he looked up, and his mistress was pointing to the door. He laid aside the great, soft fan, and obediently stole away, over the polished floor, on his bare tiptoes.

She stayed motionless, with gaze riveted upon her child, and her face the picture of fright.

Presently her husband entered the room, and without noticing her, went to a table and began to search among some papers which covered it.

"Armand," she called to him, in a voice which must have stabbed him, if he was human. But he did not notice. "Armand," she said again. Then she rose and tottered towards him. "Armand," she panted once more, clutching his arm, "look at our child. What does it mean? tell me."

He coldly but gently loosened her fingers from about his arm and thrust the hand away from him. "Tell me what it means!" she cried despairingly.

25   "It means," he answered lightly, "that the child is not white; it means that you are not white."

A quick conception of all that this accusation meant for her nerved her with unwonted courage to deny it. "It is a lie; it is not true, I am white! Look at my hair, it is brown; and my eyes are gray, Armand, you know they are gray. And my skin is fair," seizing his wrist. "Look at my hand; whiter than yours, Armand," she laughed hysterically.

"As white as La Blanche's," he returned cruelly; and went away leaving her alone with their child.

When she could hold a pen in her hand, she sent a despairing letter to Madame Valmondé.

"My mother, they tell me I am not white. Armand has told me I am not white. For God's sake tell them it is not true. You must know it is not true. I shall die. I must die. I cannot be so unhappy, and live."

30   The answer that came was as brief:

"My own Désirée: Come home to Valmondé; back to your mother who loves you. Come with your child."

When the letter reached Désirée she went with it to her husband's study, and laid it open upon the desk before which he sat. She was like a stone image: silent, white, motionless after she placed it there.

In silence he ran his cold eyes over the written words. He said nothing. "Shall I go, Armand?" she asked in tones sharp with agonized suspense.

"Yes, go."

35   "Do you want me to go?"

"Yes, I want you to go."

He thought Almighty God had dealt cruelly and unjustly with him; and felt, somehow, that he was paying Him back in kind when he stabbed thus into his wife's soul. Moreover he no longer loved her, because of the unconscious injury she had brought upon his home and his name.

She turned away like one stunned by a blow, and walked slowly towards the door, hoping he would call her back.

"Good-by, Armand," she moaned.

40   He did not answer her. That was his last blow at fate.

Désirée went in search of her child. Zandrine was pacing the sombre gallery with it. She took the little one from the nurse's arms with no word of explanation, and descending the steps, walked away, under the live-oak branches.

It was an October afternoon; the sun was just sinking. Out in the still fields the negroes were picking cotton.

Désirée had not changed the thin white garment nor the slippers which she wore. Her hair was uncovered and the sun's rays brought a golden gleam from its brown meshes. She did not take the broad, beaten road which led to the far-off plantation of Valmondé. She walked across a deserted field, where the stubble bruised her tender feet, so delicately shod, and tore her thin gown to shreds.

She disappeared among the reeds and willows that grew thick along the banks of the deep, sluggish bayou; and she did not come back again.

45   Some weeks later there was a curious scene enacted at L'Abri. In the centre of the smoothly swept back yard was a great bonfire. Armand Aubigny sat in the wide hallway that commanded a view of the spectacle; and it was he who dealt out to a half dozen negroes the material which kept this fire ablaze.

A graceful cradle of willow, with all its dainty furbishings, was laid upon the pyre, which had already been fed with the richness of a priceless *layette*. Then there were silk gowns, and velvet and satin ones added to these; laces, too, and embroideries; bonnets and gloves; for the *corbeille* had been of rare quality.

The last thing to go was a tiny bundle of letters; innocent little scribblings that Désirée had sent to him during the days of their espousal. There was the remnant of one back in the drawer from which he took them. But it was not Désirée's; it was part of an old letter from his mother to his father. He read it. She was thanking God for the blessing of her husband's love:—

"But, above all," she wrote, "night and day, I thank the good God for having so arranged our lives that our dear Armand will never know that his mother, who adores him, belongs to the race that is cursed with the brand of slavery."

INQUIRING FURTHER

1. How would you characterize the relationship between Désirée and Armand when the baby is first born? Is it fair to say that Armand was never in love with Désirée? Why or why not?

2. What passages from the story represent aspects of Southern culture most significantly? What kind of picture do these representations portray? Write one or two paragraphs exploring these representations.

3. How does the narration of the story convey its message? Can you recognize instances of foreshadowing? Does the narrator offer insights into the thinking of the characters? How do these narrative elements relate to the ending of the story?

TONI CADE BAMBARA

Toni Cade Bambara (1939–1995) was educated in New York, Italy, and Paris. Early in her career she worked as an investigator for the New York State Department of Social Welfare but later devoted herself for many years to teaching and writing. She edited a groundbreaking collection of African American women's writing, The Black Woman: An Anthology *(1970). Much of her writing focuses on African American women, particularly as they confront experiences that force them to new awareness. "The Lesson" is taken from Bambara's collection,* Gorilla My Love, *published in 1972.*

The Lesson

Back in the days when everyone was old and stupid or young and foolish and me and Sugar were the only ones just right, this lady moved on our block with nappy hair and proper speech and no makeup. And quite naturally we laughed at her, laughed the way we did at the junk man who went about his business like he was some big-time president and his sorry-ass horse his secretary. And we kinda hated her too, hated the way we did the winos who cluttered up our parks and pissed on our handball walls and stank up our hallways and stairs so you couldn't halfway play hide-and-seek without a goddamn gas mask. Miss Moore was her name. The only woman on the block with no first name. And she was black as hell, cept for her feet, which were fish-white and spooky. And she was always planning these boring-ass things for us to do, us being my cousin, mostly, who lived on the block cause we all moved North the same time and to the same apartment then spread out gradual to breathe. And our parents would yank our heads into some kinda shape and crisp up our clothes so we'd be presentable for travel with Miss Moore, who always looked like she was going to church, though she never did. Which is just one of things the grown-ups talked about when they talked behind her back like a dog. But when she came calling with some sachet she'd sewed up or some gingerbread she'd made or some book, why then they'd all be too embarrassed to turn her down and we'd get handed over all spruced up. She'd been to college and said it was only right that she should take responsibility for the young ones' education, and she not even related by marriage or blood. So they'd go for it. Specially Aunt Gretchen. She was the main gofer in the family. You got some ole dumb shit foolishness you want somebody to go for, you send for Aunt Gretchen. She been screwed into the go-along for so long, it's a blood-deep natural thing with her. Which is how she got saddled with me and Sugar and Junior in the first place while our mothers were in a la-de-da apartment up the block having a good ole time.

So this one day Miss Moore rounds us all up at the mailbox and it's puredee hot and she's knockin herself out about arithmetic. And school suppose to let up in summer I heard, but she don't never let up. And the starch in my pinafore scratching the shit outta me and I'm really hating this nappy-head bitch and her goddamn college degree. I'd much rather go to the pool or to the show where it's cool. So me and Sugar leaning on the mailbox being surly, which is a Miss Moore word. And Flyboy checking out what everybody brought for lunch. And Fat Butt already wasting his peanut-butter-and-jelly sandwich like the pig he is. And Junebug punchin on Q.T.'s arm for potato chips. And Rosie Giraffe shifting from one hip to the other waiting for somebody to step on her foot or ask her if she from Georgia so she can kick ass, preferably Mercedes'. And Miss Moore asking us do we know what money is, like we a bunch of retards. I mean real money, she say, like it's only poker chips or monopoly papers we lay on the grocer. So right away I'm tired of this and say so. And would much rather snatch Sugar and go to the Sunset and terrorize the West Indian kids and take their hair ribbons and their money too. And Miss Moore files that remark away for next week's lesson on brotherhood, I can tell. And finally I say we oughta get to the subway cause it's cooler and besides we might meet some cute boys. Sugar done swiped her mama's lipstick, so we ready.

So we heading down the street and she's boring us silly about what things cost and what our parents make and how much goes for rent and how money ain't divided up right in this country. And then she gets to the part about we all poor and live in the slums, which I don't feature. And I'm ready to speak on that, but she steps out in the street and hails two cabs just like that. Then she hustles half the crew in with her and hands me a five-dollar bill and tells me to calculate 10 percent tip for the driver. And we're off. Me and Sugar and Junebug and Flyboy hangin out the window and hollering to everybody, putting lipstick on each other cause Flyboy a faggot anyway, and making farts with our sweaty armpits. But I'm mostly trying to figure how to spend this money. But they all fascinated with the meter ticking and Junebug starts laying bets as to how much it'll read when Flyboy can't hold his breath no more. Then Sugar lays bets as to how much it'll be when we get there. So I'm stuck. Don't nobody want to go for my plan, which is to jump out at the next light and run off to the first bar-b-que we can find. Then the driver tells us to get the hell out cause we there already. And the meter reads eighty-five cents. And I'm stalling to figure out the tip and Sugar say give him a dime. And I decide he don't need it bad as I do, so later for him. But then he tries to take off with Junebug foot still in the door so we talk about his mama something ferocious. Then we check out that we on Fifth Avenue and everybody dressed up in stockings. One lady in a fur coat, hot as it is. White folks crazy.

"This is the place," Miss Moore say, presenting it to us in the voice she uses at the museum. "Let's look in the windows before we go in."

5   "Can we steal?" Sugar asks very serious like she's getting the ground rules squared away before she plays. "I beg your pardon," say Miss Moore, and we fall out. So she leads us around the windows of the toy store and me and

Sugar screamin, "This is mine, that's mine, I gotta have that, that was made for me, I was born for that," till Big Butt drowns us out.

"Hey, I'm goin to buy that there."

"That there? You don't even know what it is, stupid."

"I do so," he say punchin on Rosie Giraffe. "It's a microscope."

"Whatcha gonna do with a microscope, fool?"

10   "Look at things."

"Like what, Ronald?" ask Miss Moore. And Big Butt ain't got the first notion. So here go Miss Moore gabbing about the thousands of bacteria in a drop of water and the somethinorother in a speck of blood and the million and one living things in the air around us is invisible to the naked eye. And what she say that for? Junebug go to town on that "naked" and we rolling. Then Miss Moore ask what it cost. So we all jam into the window smudgin it up and the price tag say $300. So then she ask how long'd take for Big Butt and Junebug to save up their allowances. "Too long," I say. "Yeh," adds Sugar, "outgrown it by that time." And Miss Moore say no, you never outgrow learning instruments. "Why, even medical students and interns and," blah, blah, blah. And we ready to choke Big Butt for bringing it up in the first damn place.

"This here costs four hundred eighty dollars," say Rosie Giraffe. So we pile up all over her to see what she pointin out. My eyes tell me it's a chunk of glass cracked with something heavy, and different-color inks dripped into the splits, then the whole thing put into a oven or something. But for $480 it don't make sense.

"That's a paperweight made of semi-precious stones fused together under tremendous pressure," she explains slowly, with her hands doing the mining and all the factory work.

"So what's a paperweight?" asks Rosie Giraffe.

15   "To weigh paper with, dumbbell," say Flyboy, the wise man from the East.

"Not exactly," say Miss Moore, which is what she say when you warm or way off too. "It's to weigh paper down so it won't scatter and make your desk untidy." So right away me and Sugar curtsy to each other and then to Mercedes who is more the tidy type.

"We don't keep paper on top of the desk in my class," say Junebug, figuring Miss Moore crazy or lyin one.

"At home, then," she say. "Don't you have a calendar and a pencil case and a blotter and a letter-opener on your desk at home where you do your homework?" And she know damn well what our homes look like cause she nosys around in them every chance she gets.

"I don't even have a desk," say Junebug. "Do we?"

20   "No. And I don't get no homework neither," say Big Butt.

"And I don't even have a home," say Flyboy like he do at school to keep the white folks off his back and sorry for him. Send this poor kid to camp posters, is his specialty.

"I do," says Mercedes. "I have a box of stationery on my desk and a picture of my cat. My godmother bought the stationery and the desk. There's a big rose on each sheet and the envelopes smell like roses."

"Who wants to know about your smelly-ass stationery," say Rosie Giraffe fore I can get my two cents in.

"It's important to have a work area all your own so that . . . "

25   "Will you look at this sailboat, please," say Flyboy, cuttin her off and pointin to the thing like it was his. So once again we tumble all over each other to gaze at this magnificent thing in the toy store which is just big enough to maybe

sail two kittens across the pond if you strap them to the posts tight. We all start reciting the price tag like we in assembly. "Handcrafted sailboat of fiberglass at one thousand one hundred ninety-five dollars."

"Unbelievable," I hear myself say and am really stunned. I read it again for myself just in case the group recitation put me in a trance. Same thing. For some reason this pisses me off. We look at Miss Moore and she lookin at us, waiting for I dunno what.

"Who'd pay all that when you can buy a sailboat set for a quarter at Pop's, a tube of glue for a dime, and a ball of string for eight cents? "It must have a motor and a whole lot else besides," I say. "My sailboat cost me about fifty cents."

"But will it take water?" say Mercedes with her smart ass.

"Took mine to Alley Pond Park once," say Flyboy. "String broke, Lost it. Pity."

30   "Sailed mine in Central Park and it keeled over and sank. Had to ask my father for another dollar."

"And you got the strap," laugh Big Butt. "The jerk didn't even have a string on it. My old man wailed on his behind."

Little Q.T. was staring hard at the sailboat and you could see he wanted it bad. But he too little and somebody'd just take it from him. So what the hell. "This boat for kids, Miss Moore?"

"Parents silly to buy something like that just to get all broke up," say Rosie Giraffe.

"That much money it should last forever," I figure.

35   "My father'd buy it for me if I wanted it."

"Your father, my ass," say Rosie Giraffe getting a chance to finally push Mercedes.

"Must be rich people shop here," say Q.T.

"You are a very bright boy," say Flyboy. "What was your first clue?" And he rap him on the head with the back of his knuckles, since Q.T. the only one he could get away with. Though Q.T. liable to come up behind you years later and get his licks in when you half expect it.

"What I want to know is," I says to Miss Moore though I never talk to her, I wouldn't give the bitch that satisfaction, "is how much a real boat costs? I figure a thousand'd get you a yacht any day."

40   "Why don't you check that out," she says, "and report back to the group?" Which really pains my ass. If you gonna mess up a perfectly good swim day least you could do is have some answers. "Let's go in," she say like she got something up her sleeve. Only she don't lead the way. So me and Sugar turn the corner to where the entrance is, but when we get there I kinda hang back. Not that I'm scared, what's there to be afraid of, just a toy store. But I feel funny, shame. But what I got to be shamed about? Got as much right to go in as anybody. But somehow I can't seem to get hold of the door, so I step away for Sugar to lead. But she hangs back too. And I look at her and she looks at me and this is ridiculous. I mean, damn, I have never ever been shy about doing nothing or going nowhere. But then Mercedes steps up and then Rosie Giraffe and Big Butt crowd in behind and shove, and next thing we all stuffed into the doorway with only Mercedes squeezing past us, smoothing out her jumper and walking right down the aisle. Then the rest of us tumble in like a glued-together jigsaw done all wrong. And people lookin at us. And it's like the time me and Sugar crashed into the Catholic church on a dare. But once we got in there and everything so hushed and holy and the candles and the bow-in and the handkerchiefs on all the drooping heads, I just

couldn't go through with the plan. Which was for me to run up to the altar and do a tap dance while Sugar played the nose flute and messed around in the holy water. And Sugar kept givin me the elbow. Then later teased me so bad I tied her up in the shower and turned it on and locked her in. And she'd be there till this day if Aunt Gretchen hadn't finally figured I was lyin about the boarder takin a shower.

Same thing in the store. We all walkin on tiptoe and hardly touchin the games and puzzles and things. And I watched Miss Moore who is steady watchin us like she waitin for a sign. Like Mama Drewery watches the sky and sniffs the air and takes note of just how much slant is in the bird formation. Then me and Sugar bump smack into each other, so busy gazing at the toys, 'specially the sailboat. But we don't laugh and go into our fat-lady bump-stomach routine. We just stare at that price tag. Then Sugar run a finger over the whole boat. And I'm jealous and want to hit her. Maybe not her, but I sure want to punch somebody in the mouth.

"Watcha bring us here for, Miss Moore?"

"You sound angry, Sylvia. Are you mad about something?" Givin me one of them grins like she tellin a grown-up joke that never turns out to be funny. And she's lookin very closely at me like maybe she plannin to do my portrait from memory. I'm mad, but I won't give her that satisfaction. So I slouch around the store bein very bored and say, "Let's go."

Me and Sugar at the back of the train watchin the tracks whizzin by large then small then gettin gobbled up in the dark. I'm thinkin about this tricky toy I saw in the store. A clown that somersaults on a bar then does chin-ups just cause you yank lightly at his leg. Cost $35. I could see me askin my mother for a $35 birthday clown. "You wanna who that costs what?" she'd say, cocking her head to the side to get a better view of the hole in my head. Thirty-five dollars could buy new bunk beds for Junior and Gretchen's boy. Thirty-five dollars and the whole household could go visit Granddaddy Nelson in the country. Thirty-five dollars would pay for the rent and the piano bill too. Who are these people that spend that much for performing clowns and $1,000 for toy sailboats? What kinda work they do and how they live and how come we ain't in on it? Where we are is who we are, Miss Moore always pointin out. But it don't necessarily have to be that way, she always adds then waits for somebody to say that poor people have to wake up and demand their share of the pie and don't none of us know what kind of pie she talkin about in the first damn place. But she ain't so smart cause I still got her four dollars from the taxi and she sure ain't gettin it. Messin up my day with this shit. Sugar nudges me in my pocket and winks.

45   Miss Moore lines us up in front of the mailbox where we started from, seem like years ago, and I got a headache for thinkin so hard. And we lean all over each other so we can hold up under the draggy-ass lecture she always finishes us off with at the end before we thank her for borin us to tears. But she just looks at us like she readin tea leaves. Finally she say, "Well, what did you think of F.A.O. Schwartz?"

Rosie Giraffe mumbles, "White folks crazy."

"I'd like to go there again when I get my birthday money," says Mercedes, and we shove her out the pack so she has to lean on the mailbox by herself.

"I'd like a shower. Tiring day," say Flyboy.

Then Sugar surprises me by sayin, "You know, Miss Moore, I don't think all of us here put together eat in a year what that sailboat costs." And Miss

Moore lights up like somebody goosed her. "And?" she say, urging Sugar on. Only I'm standin on her foot so she don't continue.

50   "Imagine for a minute what kind of society it is in which some people can spend on a toy what it would cost to feed a family of six or seven. What do you think?"

"I think," say Sugar pushing me off her feet like she never done before, cause I whip her ass in a minute, "that this is not much of a democracy if you ask me. Equal chance to pursue happiness means an equal crack at the dough, don't it?" Miss Moore is besides herself and I am disgusted with Sugar's treachery. So I stand on her foot one more time to see if she'll shove me. She shuts up, and Miss More looks at me, sorrowfully I'm thinkin. And somethin weird is goin on, I can feel it in my chest.

"Anybody else learn anything today?" lookin dead at me.

I walk away and Sugar has to run to catch up and don't even seem to notice when I shrug her arm off my shoulder.

"Well, we got four dollars anyway," she says.

55   "Uh hunh."

"We could go to Hascombs and get half a chocolate layer and then go to the Sunset and still have plenty money for potato chips and ice-cream sodas."

"Uh hunh."

"Race you to Hascombs," she say.

We start down the block and she gets ahead which is O.K. by me cause I'm goin to the West End and then over to the Drive to think this day through. She can run if she want to and even run faster. But ain't nobody gonna beat me at nuthin.

Inquiring Further

1. How would you characterize Sylvia at the beginning of "The Lesson"? Can you trace changes in her attitude as the story develops?

2. What do you think Sylvia refers to when she says, "ain't nobody gonna beat me at nothing"? Write three or more sentences paraphrasing the lesson she has learned.

Henrik Ibsen

Henrik Johan Ibsen (1828–1906) became the eldest of five children after the early death of an older brother. Described as an unsociable child, his sense of isolation increased at the age of sixteen when his father's business had to be sold to pay debts. Rumors also began to circulate that Henrik was the illegitimate son of another man. Ibsen himself fathered an illegitimate son while he was an apprentice hoping to study medicine. Though his plays suggest otherwise, Ibsen revered the state of marriage, believing that it was possible for two people to travel through life as perfect, happy equals. In 1864, his friends generously offered him money, allowing him to spend the next twenty-seven years living in Italy and Germany where he authored a number of successful works, including A Doll's House, *which was published in 1879.*

A Doll's House

Dramatis Personae

TORVALD HELMER.
NORA, his wife
DOCTOR RANK.
MRS. LINDE.
NILS KROGSTAD.
HELMER'S THREE YOUNG CHILDREN.
ANNE, their nurse
A HOUSEMAID.
A PORTER.

(The action takes place in Helmer's house.)

ACT I

(SCENE.—A room furnished comfortably and tastefully, but not extravagantly. At the back, a door to the right leads to the entrance-hall, another to the left leads to Helmer's study. Between the doors stands a piano. In the middle of the left-hand wall is a door, and beyond it a window. Near the window are a round table, arm-chairs and a small sofa. In the right-hand wall, at the farther end, another door; and on the same side, nearer the footlights, a stove, two easy chairs and a rocking-chair; between the stove and the door, a small table. Engravings on the walls; a cabinet with china and other small objects; a small book-case with well-bound books. The floors are carpeted, and a fire burns in the stove. It is winter.

A bell rings in the hall; shortly afterwards the door is heard to open. Enter NORA, humming a tune and in high spirits. She is in outdoor dress and carries a number of parcels; these she lays on the table to the right. She leaves the outer door open after her, and through it is seen a PORTER who is carrying a Christmas Tree and a basket, which he gives to the MAID who has opened the door.)

NORA: Hide the Christmas Tree carefully, Helen. Be sure the children do not see it until this evening, when it is dressed. (To the PORTER, taking out her purse.) How much?

PORTER: Sixpence.

NORA: There is a shilling. No, keep the change. (The PORTER thanks her, and goes out. NORA shuts the door. She is laughing to herself, as she takes off her hat and coat. She takes a packet of macaroons from her pocket and eats one or two; then goes cautiously to her husband's door and listens.) Yes, he is in. (Still humming, she goes to the table on the right.)

HELMER (calls out from his room): Is that my little lark twittering out there?

NORA (busy opening some of the parcels): Yes, it is!

HELMER: Is it my little squirrel bustling about?

NORA: Yes!

HELMER: When did my squirrel come home?

NORA: Just now. (Puts the bag of macaroons into her pocket and wipes her mouth.) Come in here, Torvald, and see what I have bought.

HELMER: Don't disturb me. (A little later, he opens the door and looks into the room, pen in hand.) Bought, did you say? All these things? Has my little spendthrift been wasting money again?

NORA: Yes but, Torvald, this year we really can let ourselves go a little. This is the first Christmas that we have not needed to economise.

HELMER: Still, you know, we can't spend money recklessly.

NORA: Yes, Torvald, we may be a wee bit more reckless now, mayn't we? Just a tiny wee bit! You are going to have a big salary and earn lots and lots of money.

HELMER: Yes, after the New Year; but then it will be a whole quarter before the salary is due.

NORA: Pooh! we can borrow until then.

HELMER: Nora! (Goes up to her and takes her playfully by the ear.) The same little featherhead! Suppose, now, that I borrowed fifty pounds today, and you spent it all in the Christmas week, and then on New Year's Eve a slate fell on my head and killed me, and. . . .

NORA (putting her hands over his mouth): Oh! don't say such horrid things.

HELMER: Still, suppose that happened,—what then?

NORA: If that were to happen, I don't suppose I should care whether I owed money or not.

HELMER: Yes, but what about the people who had lent it?

NORA: They? Who would bother about them? I should not know who they were.

HELMER: That is like a woman! But seriously, Nora, you know what I think about that. No debt, no borrowing. There can be no freedom or beauty about a home life that depends on borrowing and debt. We two have kept bravely on the straight road so far, and we will go on the same way for the short time longer that there need be any struggle.

NORA (moving towards the stove): As you please, Torvald.

HELMER (following her): Come, come, my little skylark must not droop her wings. What is this! Is my little squirrel out of temper? (Taking out his purse.) Nora, what do you think I have got here?

NORA (turning round quickly): Money!

HELMER: There you are. (Gives her some money.) Do you think I don't know what a lot is wanted for housekeeping at Christmas-time?

NORA (counting): Ten shillings—a pound—two pounds! Thank you, thank you, Torvald; that will keep me going for a long time.

HELMER: Indeed it must.

NORA: Yes, yes, it will. But come here and let me show you what I have bought. And all so cheap! Look, here is a new suit for Ivar, and a sword; and a horse and a trumpet for Bob; and a doll and dolly's bedstead for Emmy,—they are very plain, but anyway she will soon break them in pieces. And here are dress-lengths and handkerchiefs for the maids; old Anne ought really to have something better.

HELMER: And what is in this parcel?

NORA (crying out): No, no! you mustn't see that until this evening.

HELMER: Very well. But now tell me, you extravagant little person, what would you like for yourself?

NORA: For myself? Oh, I am sure I don't want anything.

HELMER: Yes, but you must. Tell me something reasonable that you would particularly like to have.

NORA: No, I really can't think of anything—unless, Torvald. . . .

HELMER: Well?

NORA (playing with his coat buttons, and without raising her eyes to his): If you really want to give me something, you might—you might. . . .

HELMER: Well, out with it!

NORA (speaking quickly): You might give me money, Torvald. Only just as much as you can afford; and then one of these days I will buy something with it.

HELMER: But, Nora—

NORA: Oh, do! dear Torvald; please, please do! Then I will wrap it up in beautiful gilt paper and hang it on the Christmas Tree. Wouldn't that be fun?

HELMER: What are little people called that are always wasting money?

NORA: Spendthrifts—I know. Let us do as you suggest, Torvald, and then I shall have time to think what I am most in want of. That is a very sensible plan, isn't it?

HELMER (smiling): Indeed it is—that is to say, if you were really to save out of the money I give you, and then really buy something for yourself. But if you spend it all on the housekeeping and any number of unnecessary things, then I merely have to pay up again.

NORA: Oh but, Torvald.

HELMER: You can't deny it, my dear little Nora. (Puts his arm round her waist.) It's a sweet little spendthrift, but she uses up a deal of money. One would hardly believe how expensive such little persons are!

NORA: It's a shame to say that. I do really save all I can.

HELMER (laughing): That's very true—all you can. But you can't save anything!

NORA (smiling quietly and happily): You haven't any idea how many expenses we skylarks and squirrels have, Torvald.

HELMER: You are an odd little soul. Very like your father. You always find some new way of wheedling money out of me, and, as soon as you have got it, it seems to melt in your hands. You never know where it has gone. Still, one must take you as you are. It is in the blood; for indeed it is true that you can inherit these things, Nora.

NORA: Ah, I wish I had inherited many of papa's qualities.

HELMER: And I would not wish you to be anything but just what you are, my sweet little skylark. But, do you know, it strikes me that you are looking rather—what shall I say—rather uneasy today?

NORA: Do I?

HELMER: You do, really. Look straight at me.

NORA (looks at him): Well?

HELMER (wagging his finger at her): Hasn't Miss Sweet Tooth been breaking rules in town today?

NORA: No; what makes you think that?

HELMER: Hasn't she paid a visit to the confectioner's?

NORA: No, I assure you, Torvald.

HELMER: Not been nibbling sweets?

NORA: No, certainly not.

HELMER: Not even taken a bite at a macaroon or two?

NORA: No, Torvald, I assure you really.

HELMER: There, there, of course I was only joking.

NORA (going to the table on the right): I should not think of going against your wishes.

HELMER: No, I am sure of that; besides, you gave me your word— (Going up to her.) Keep your little Christmas secrets to yourself, my darling. They will all be revealed tonight when the Christmas Tree is lit, no doubt.

NORA: Did you remember to invite Doctor Rank?

HELMER: No. But there is no need; as a matter of course he will come to dinner with us. However, I will ask him when he comes in this morning. I have ordered some good wine. Nora, you can't think how I am looking forward to this evening.

NORA: So am I! And how the children will enjoy themselves, Torvald!

HELMER: It is splendid to feel that one has a perfectly safe appointment, and a big enough income. It's delightful to think of, isn't it?

NORA: It's wonderful!

HELMER: Do you remember last Christmas? For a full three weeks beforehand you shut yourself up every evening until long after midnight, making ornaments for the Christmas Tree, and all the other fine things that were to be a surprise to us. It was the dullest three weeks I ever spent!

NORA: I didn't find it dull.

HELMER (smiling): But there was precious little result, Nora.

NORA: Oh, you shouldn't tease me about that again. How could I help the cat's going in and tearing everything to pieces?

HELMER: Of course you couldn't, poor little girl. You had the best of intentions to please us all, and that's the main thing. But it is a good thing that our hard times are over.

NORA: Yes, it is really wonderful.

HELMER: This time I needn't sit here and be dull all alone, and you needn't ruin your dear eyes and your pretty little hands.

NORA (clapping her hands): No, Torvald, I needn't any longer, need I! It's wonderfully lovely to hear you say so! (Taking his arm.) Now I will tell you how I have been thinking we ought to arrange things, Torvald. As soon as Christmas is over—(A bell rings in the hall.) There's the bell. (She tidies the room a little.) There's some one at the door. What a nuisance!

HELMER: If it is a caller, remember I am not at home.

MAID (in the doorway): A lady to see you, ma'am—a stranger.

NORA: Ask her to come in.

MAID (TO HELMER): The doctor came at the same time, sir.

HELMER: Did he go straight into my room?

MAID: Yes, sir.

(HELMER goes into his room. The MAID ushers in MRS. LINDE, who is in travelling dress, and shuts the door.)

MRS. LINDE (in a dejected and timid voice): How do you do, Nora?

NORA (doubtfully): How do you do—

MRS. LINDE: You don't recognise me, I suppose.

NORA: No, I don't know—yes, to be sure, I seem to—(Suddenly.) Yes! Christine! Is it really you?

MRS. LINDE: Yes, it is I.

NORA: Christine! To think of my not recognising you! And yet how could I—(In a gentle voice.) How you have altered, Christine!

MRS. LINDE: Yes, I have indeed. In nine, ten long years.

NORA: Is it so long since we met? I suppose it is. The last eight years have been a happy time for me, I can tell you. And so now you have come into the town, and have taken this long journey in winter—that was brave of you.

MRS. LINDE: I arrived by steamer this morning.

NORA: To have some fun at Christmas-time, of course. How delightful! We will have such fun together! But take off your things. You are not cold, I hope. (Helps her.) Now we will sit down by the stove, and be cosy. No, take this armchair; I will sit here in the rocking-chair. (Takes her hands.) Now you look like your old self again; it was only the first moment—You are a little paler, Christine, and perhaps a little thinner.

MRS. LINDE: And much, much older, Nora.

NORA: Perhaps a little older; very, very little; certainly not much. (Stops suddenly and speaks seriously.) What a thoughtless creature I am, chattering away like this. My poor, dear Christine, do forgive me.

MRS. LINDE: What do you mean, Nora?

NORA (gently): Poor Christine, you are a widow.

MRS. LINDE: Yes; it is three years ago now.

NORA: Yes, I knew; I saw it in the papers. I assure you, Christine, I meant ever so often to write to you at the time, but I always put it off and something always prevented me.

MRS. LINDE: I quite understand, dear.

NORA: It was very bad of me, Christine. Poor thing, how you must have suffered. And he left you nothing?

MRS. LINDE: No.

NORA: And no children?

MRS. LINDE: No.

NORA: Nothing at all, then.

MRS. LINDE: Not even any sorrow or grief to live upon.

NORA (looking incredulously at her): But, Christine, is that possible?

MRS. LINDE (smiles sadly and strokes her hair): It sometimes happens, Nora.

NORA: So you are quite alone. How dreadfully sad that must be. I have three lovely children. You can't see them just now, for they are out with their nurse. But now you must tell me all about it.

MRS. LINDE: No, no; I want to hear about you.

NORA: No, you must begin. I mustn't be selfish today; today I must only think of your affairs. But there is one thing I must tell you. Do you know we have just had a great piece of good luck?

MRS. LINDE: No, what is it?

NORA: Just fancy, my husband has been made manager of the Bank!

MRS. LINDE: Your husband? What good luck!

NORA: Yes, tremendous! A barrister's profession is such an uncertain thing, especially if he won't undertake unsavoury cases; and naturally Torvald has never been willing to do that, and I quite agree with him. You may imagine how pleased we are! He is to take up his work in the Bank at the New Year, and then he will have a big salary and lots of commissions. For the future we can live quite differently—we can do just as we like. I feel so relieved and so happy, Christine! It will be splendid to have heaps of money and not need to have any anxiety, won't it?

MRS. LINDE: Yes, anyhow I think it would be delightful to have what one needs.

NORA: No, not only what one needs, but heaps and heaps of money.

MRS. LINDE (smiling): Nora, Nora, haven't you learned sense yet? In our schooldays you were a great spendthrift.

NORA (laughing): Yes, that is what Torvald says now. (Wags her finger at her.) But "Nora, Nora" is not so silly as you think. We have not been in a position for me to waste money. We have both had to work.

MRS. LINDE: You too?

NORA: Yes; odds and ends, needlework, crotchet-work, embroidery, and that kind of thing. (Dropping her voice.) And other things as well. You know Torvald left his office when we were married? There was no prospect of promotion there, and he had to try and earn more than before. But during the first year he over-worked himself dreadfully. You see, he had to make money every way he could, and he worked early and late; but he couldn't stand it, and fell dreadfully ill, and the doctors said it was necessary for him to go south.

MRS. LINDE: You spent a whole year in Italy, didn't you?

NORA: Yes. It was no easy matter to get away, I can tell you. It was just after Ivar was born; but naturally we had to go. It was a wonderfully beautiful journey, and it saved Torvald's life. But it cost a tremendous lot of money, Christine.

MRS. LINDE: So I should think.

NORA: It cost about two hundred and fifty pounds. That's a lot, isn't it?

MRS. LINDE: Yes, and in emergencies like that it is lucky to have the money.

NORA: I ought to tell you that we had it from papa.

MRS. LINDE: Oh, I see. It was just about that time that he died, wasn't it?

NORA: Yes; and, just think of it, I couldn't go and nurse him. I was expecting little Ivar's birth every day and I had my poor sick Torvald to look after. My dear, kind father—I never saw him again, Christine. That was the saddest time I have known since our marriage.

MRS. LINDE: I know how fond you were of him. And then you went off to Italy?

NORA: Yes; you see we had money then, and the doctors insisted on our going, so we started a month later.

MRS. LINDE: And your husband came back quite well?

NORA: As sound as a bell!

MRS. LINDE: But—the doctor?

NORA: What doctor?

MRS. LINDE: I thought your maid said the gentleman who arrived here just as I did, was the doctor?

NORA: Yes, that was Doctor Rank, but he doesn't come here professionally. He is our greatest friend, and comes in at least once everyday. No, Torvald has not had an hour's illness since then, and our children are strong and healthy and so am I. (Jumps up and claps her hands.) Christine! Christine! it's good to be alive and happy!—But how horrid of me; I am talking of nothing but my own affairs. (Sits on a stool near her, and rests her arms on her knees.) You mustn't be angry with me. Tell me, is it really true that you did not love your husband? Why did you marry him?

MRS. LINDE: My mother was alive then, and was bedridden and helpless, and I had to provide for my two younger brothers; so I did not think I was justified in refusing his offer.

NORA: No, perhaps you were quite right. He was rich at that time, then?

MRS. LINDE: I believe he was quite well off. But his business was a precarious one; and, when he died, it all went to pieces and there was nothing left.

NORA: And then?

MRS. LINDE: Well, I had to turn my hand to anything I could find—first a small shop, then a small school, and so on. The last three years have seemed like one long working-day, with no rest. Now it is at an end, Nora. My poor mother needs me no more, for she is gone; and the boys do not need me either; they have got situations and can shift for themselves.

NORA: What a relief you must feel if. . . .

MRS. LINDE: No, indeed; I only feel my life unspeakably empty. No one to live for anymore. (Gets up restlessly.) That was why I could not stand the life in my little backwater any longer. I hope it may be easier here to find something which will busy me and occupy my thoughts. If only I could have the good luck to get some regular work—office work of some kind.

NORA: But, Christine, that is so frightfully tiring, and you look tired out now. You had far better go away to some watering-place.

MRS. LINDE (walking to the window): I have no father to give me money for a journey, Nora.

NORA (rising): Oh, don't be angry with me!

MRS. LINDE (going up to her): It is you that must not be angry with me, dear. The worst of a position like mine is that it makes one so bitter. No one to work for, and yet obliged to be always on the lookout for chances. One must live, and so one becomes selfish. When you told me of the happy turn your fortunes have taken—you will hardly believe it—I was delighted not so much on your account as on my own.

NORA: How do you mean?—Oh, I understand. You mean that perhaps Torvald could get you something to do.

MRS. LINDE: Yes, that was what I was thinking of.

NORA: He must, Christine. Just leave it to me; I will broach the subject very cleverly—I will think of something that will please him very much. It will make me so happy to be of some use to you.

MRS. LINDE: How kind you are, Nora, to be so anxious to help me! It is doubly kind in you, for you know so little of the burdens and troubles of life.

NORA: I? I know so little of them?

MRS. LINDE (smiling): My dear! Small household cares and that sort of thing!—You are a child, Nora.

NORA (tosses her head and crosses the stage): You ought not to be so superior.

MRS. LINDE: No?

NORA: You are just like the others. They all think that I am incapable of anything really serious.

MRS. LINDE: Come, come—

NORA: —that I have gone through nothing in this world of cares.

MRS. LINDE: But, my dear Nora, you have just told me all your troubles.

NORA: Pooh!—those were trifles. (Lowering her voice.) I have not told you the important thing.

MRS. LINDE: The important thing? What do you mean?

NORA: You look down upon me altogether, Christine—but you ought not to. You are proud, aren't you, of having worked so hard and so long for your mother?

MRS. LINDE: Indeed, I don't look down on anyone. But it is true that I am both proud and glad to think that I was privileged to make the end of my mother's life almost free from care.

NORA: And you are proud to think of what you have done for your brothers?

MRS. LINDE: I think I have the right to be.

NORA: I think so, too. But now, listen to this; I too have something to be proud and glad of.

MRS. LINDE: I have no doubt you have. But what do you refer to?

NORA: Speak low. Suppose Torvald were to hear! He mustn't on any account—no one in the world must know, Christine, except you.

MRS. LINDE: But what is it?

NORA: Come here. (Pulls her down on the sofa beside her.) Now I will show you that I too have something to be proud and glad of. It was I who saved Torvald's life.

Mrs. Linde: "Saved"? How?

Nora: I told you about our trip to Italy. Torvald would never have recovered if he had not gone there.

Mrs. Linde: Yes, but your father gave you the necessary funds.

Nora (smiling): Yes, that is what Torvald and all the others think, but. . . .

Mrs. Linde: But?

Nora: Papa didn't give us a shilling. It was I who procured the money.

Mrs. Linde: You? All that large sum?

Nora: Two hundred and fifty pounds. What do you think of that?

Mrs. Linde: But, Nora, how could you possibly do it? Did you win a prize in the Lottery?

Nora (contemptuously): In the Lottery? There would have been no credit in that.

Mrs. Linde: But where did you get it from, then?

Nora (humming and smiling with an air of mystery): Hm, hm! Aha!

Mrs. Linde: Because you couldn't have borrowed it.

Nora: Couldn't I? Why not?

Mrs. Linde: No, a wife cannot borrow without her husband's consent.

Nora (tossing her head): Oh, if it is a wife who has any head for business—a wife who has the wit to be a little bit clever.

Mrs. Linde: I don't understand it at all, Nora.

Nora: There is no need you should. I never said I had borrowed the money. I may have got it some other way. (Lies back on the sofa.) Perhaps I got it from some other admirer. When anyone is as attractive as I am. . . .

Mrs. Linde: You are a mad creature.

Nora: Now, you know you're full of curiosity, Christine.

Mrs. Linde: Listen to me, Nora dear. Haven't you been a little bit imprudent?

Nora (sits up straight): Is it imprudent to save your husband's life?

Mrs. Linde: It seems to me imprudent, without his knowledge, to. . . .

Nora: But it was absolutely necessary that he should not know! My goodness, can't you understand that? It was necessary he should have no idea what a dangerous condition he was in. It was to me that the doctors came and said that his life was in danger, and that the only thing to save him was to live in the south. Do you suppose I didn't try, first of all, to get what I wanted as if it were for myself? I told him how much I should love to travel abroad like other young wives; I tried tears and entreaties with him; I told him that he ought to remember the condition I was in, and that he ought to be kind and indulgent to me; I even hinted that he might raise a loan. That nearly made him angry, Christine. He said I was thoughtless, and that it was his duty as my husband not to indulge me in my whims and caprices—as I believe he called them. Very well, I thought, you must be saved—and that was how I came to devise a way out of the difficulty.

Mrs. Linde: And did your husband never get to know from your father that the money had not come from him?

Nora: No, never. Papa died just at that time. I had meant to let him into the secret and beg him never to reveal it. But he was so ill then—alas, there never was any need to tell him.

Mrs. Linde: And since then have you never told your secret to your husband?

Nora: Good Heavens, no! How could you think so? A man who has such strong opinions about these things! And besides, how painful and humiliating it would be for Torvald, with his manly independence, to know that he owed me anything! It would upset our mutual relations altogether; our beautiful happy home would no longer be what it is now.

MRS. LINDE: Do you mean never to tell him about it?

NORA (meditatively, and with a half smile): Yes—someday, perhaps, after many years, when I am no longer as nice-looking as I am now. Don't laugh at me! I mean, of course, when Torvald is no longer as devoted to me as he is now; when my dancing and dressing-up and reciting have palled on him; then it may be a good thing to have something in reserve—(Breaking off.) What nonsense! That time will never come. Now, what do you think of my great secret, Christine? Do you still think I am of no use? I can tell you, too, that this affair has caused me a lot of worry. It has been by no means easy for me to meet my engagements punctually. I may tell you that there is something that is called, in business, quarterly interest, and another thing called payment in installments, and it is always so dreadfully difficult to manage them. I have had to save a little here and there, where I could, you understand. I have not been able to put aside much from my housekeeping money, for Torvald must have a good table. I couldn't let my children be shabbily dressed; I have felt obliged to use up all he gave me for them, the sweet little darlings!

MRS. LINDE: So it has all had to come out of your own necessaries of life, poor Nora?

NORA: Of course. Besides, I was the one responsible for it. Whenever Torvald has given me money for new dresses and such things, I have never spent more than half of it; I have always bought the simplest and cheapest things. Thank Heaven, any clothes look well on me, and so Torvald has never noticed it. But it was often very hard on me, Christine—because it is delightful to be really well dressed, isn't it?

MRS. LINDE: Quite so.

NORA: Well, then I have found other ways of earning money. Last winter I was lucky enough to get a lot of copying to do; so I locked myself up and sat writing every evening until quite late at night. Many a time I was desperately tired; but all the same it was a tremendous pleasure to sit there working and earning money. It was like being a man.

MRS. LINDE: How much have you been able to pay off in that way?

NORA: I can't tell you exactly. You see, it is very difficult to keep an account of a business matter of that kind. I only know that I have paid every penny that I could scrape together. Many a time I was at my wits' end. (Smiles.) Then I used to sit here and imagine that a rich old gentleman had fallen in love with me—

MRS. LINDE: What! Who was it?

NORA: Be quiet!—that he had died; and that when his will was opened it contained, written in big letters, the instruction: "The lovely Mrs. Nora Helmer is to have all I possess paid over to her at once in cash."

MRS. LINDE: But, my dear Nora—who could the man be?

NORA: Good gracious, can't you understand? There was no old gentleman at all; it was only something that I used to sit here and imagine, when I couldn't think of any way of procuring money. But it's all the same now; the tiresome old person can stay where he is, as far as I am concerned; I don't care about him or his will either, for I am free from care now. (Jumps up.) My goodness, it's delightful to think of, Christine! Free from care! To be able to be free from care, quite free from care; to be able to play and romp with the children; to be able to keep the house beautifully and have everything just as Torvald likes it! And, think of it, soon the spring will come and the big blue sky! Perhaps we shall be able to take a little trip—perhaps I shall see the sea again! Oh, it's a wonderful thing to be alive and be happy. (A bell is heard in the hall.)

MRS. LINDE (rising): There is the bell; perhaps I had better go.

NORA: No, don't go; no one will come in here; it is sure to be for Torvald.

SERVANT (at the hall door): Excuse me, ma'am—there is a gentleman to see the master, and as the doctor is with him.

NORA: Who is it?

KROGSTAD (at the door): It is I, Mrs. Helmer. (Mrs. LINDE starts, trembles, and turns to the window.)

NORA (takes a step towards him, and speaks in a strained, low voice): You? What is it? What do you want to see my husband about?

KROGSTAD: Bank business—in a way. I have a small post in the Bank, and I hear your husband is to be our chief now.

NORA: Then it is. . . .

KROGSTAD: Nothing but dry business matters, Mrs. Helmer; absolutely nothing else.

NORA: Be so good as to go into the study, then. (She bows indifferently to him and shuts the door into the hall; then comes back and makes up the fire in the stove.)

MRS. LINDE: Nora—who was that man?

NORA: A lawyer, of the name of Krogstad.

MRS. LINDE: Then it really was he.

NORA: Do you know the man?

MRS. LINDE: I used to—many years ago. At one time he was a solicitor's clerk in our town.

NORA: Yes, he was.

MRS. LINDE: He is greatly altered.

NORA: He made a very unhappy marriage.

MRS. LINDE: He is a widower now, isn't he?

NORA: With several children. There now, it is burning up. Shuts the door of the stove and moves the rocking-chair aside.)

MRS. LINDE: They say he carries on various kinds of business.

NORA: Really! Perhaps he does; I don't know anything about it. But don't let us think of business; it is so tiresome.

DOCTOR RANK (comes out of HELMER'S study. Before he shuts the door he calls to him): No, my dear fellow, I won't disturb you; I would rather go in to your wife for a little while. (Shuts the door and sees Mrs. LINDE.) I beg your pardon; I am afraid I am disturbing you too.

NORA: No, not at all. (Introducing him) Doctor Rank, Mrs. Linde.

RANK: I have often heard Mrs. Linde's name mentioned here. I think I passed you on the stairs when I arrived, Mrs. Linde?

MRS. LINDE: Yes, I go up very slowly; I can't manage stairs well.

RANK: Ah! some slight internal weakness?

MRS. LINDE: No, the fact is I have been overworking myself.

RANK: Nothing more than that? Then I suppose you have come to town to amuse yourself with our entertainments?

MRS. LINDE: I have come to look for work.

RANK: Is that a good cure for overwork?

MRS. LINDE: One must live, Doctor Rank.

RANK: Yes, the general opinion seems to be that it is necessary.

NORA: Look here, Doctor Rank—you know you want to live.

RANK: Certainly. However wretched I may feel, I want to prolong the agony as long as possible. All my patients are like that. And so are those who are morally diseased; one of them, and a bad case too, is at this very moment with Helmer—

MRS. LINDE (sadly): Ah!

NORA: Whom do you mean?

RANK: A lawyer of the name of Krogstad, a fellow you don't know at all. He suffers from a diseased moral character, Mrs. Helmer; but even he began talking of its being highly important that he should live.

NORA: Did he? What did he want to speak to Torvald about?

RANK: I have no idea; I only heard that it was something about the Bank.

NORA: I didn't know this—what's his name—Krogstad had anything to do with the Bank.

RANK: Yes, he has some sort of appointment there. (To Mrs. LINDE.) I don't know whether you find also in your part of the world that there are certain people who go zealously snuffing about to smell out moral corruption, and, as soon as they have found some, put the person concerned into some lucrative position where they can keep their eye on him. Healthy natures are left out in the cold.

MRS. LINDE: Still I think the sick are those who most need taking care of.

RANK (shrugging his shoulders): Yes, there you are. That is the sentiment that is turning Society into a sick-house.
(NORA, who has been absorbed in her thoughts, breaks out into smothered laughter and claps her hands.)

RANK: Why do you laugh at that? Have you any notion what Society really is?

NORA: What do I care about tiresome Society? I am laughing at something quite different, something extremely amusing. Tell me, Doctor Rank, are all the people who are employed in the Bank dependent on Torvald now?

RANK: Is that what you find so extremely amusing?

NORA (smiling and humming): That's my affair! (Walking about the room.) It's perfectly glorious to think that we have—that Torvald has so much power over so many people. (Takes the packet from her pocket.) Doctor Rank, what do you say to a macaroon?

RANK: What, macaroons? I thought they were forbidden here.

NORA: Yes, but these are some Christine gave me.

MRS. LINDE: What! I?—

NORA: Oh, well, don't be alarmed! You couldn't know that Torvald had forbidden them. I must tell you that he is afraid they will spoil my teeth. But, bah!—once in a while—That's so, isn't it, Doctor Rank? By your leave! (Puts a macaroon into his mouth.) You must have one too, Christine. And I shall have one, just a little one—or at most two. (Walking about.) I am tremendously happy. There is just one thing in the world now that I should dearly love to do.

RANK: Well, what is that?

NORA: It's something I should dearly love to say, if Torvald could hear me.

RANK: Well, why can't you say it?

NORA: No, I daren't; it's so shocking.

MRS. LINDE: Shocking?

RANK: Well, I should not advise you to say it. Still, with us you might. What is it you would so much like to say if Torvald could hear you?

NORA: I should just love to say—Well, I'm damned!

RANK: Are you mad?

MRS. LINDE: Nora, dear!

RANK: Say it, here he is!

NORA (hiding the packet): Hush! Hush! Hush! (HELMER comes out of his room, with his coat over his arm and his hat in his hand.)

NORA: Well, Torvald dear, have you got rid of him?

HELMER: Yes, he has just gone.

NORA: Let me introduce you—this is Christine, who has come to town.

HELMER: Christine? Excuse me, but I don't know. . . .

NORA: Mrs. Linde, dear; Christine Linde.

HELMER: Of course. A school friend of my wife's, I presume?

MRS. LINDE: Yes, we have known each other since then.

NORA: And just think, she has taken a long journey in order to see you.

HELMER: What do you mean? Mrs. Linde. No, really, I.

NORA: Christine is tremendously clever at book-keeping, and she is frightfully anxious to work under some clever man, so as to perfect herself. . . .

HELMER: Very sensible, Mrs. Linde.

NORA: And when she heard you had been appointed manager of the Bank—the news was telegraphed, you know—she travelled here as quick as she could. Torvald, I am sure you will be able to do something for Christine, for my sake, won't you?

HELMER: Well, it is not altogether impossible. I presume you are a widow, Mrs. Linde?

MRS. LINDE: Yes.

HELMER: And have had some experience of book-keeping?

MRS. LINDE: Yes, a fair amount.

HELMER: Ah! well, it's very likely I may be able to find something for you.

NORA (clapping her hands): What did I tell you? What did I tell you?

HELMER: You have just come at a fortunate moment, Mrs. Linde.

MRS. LINDE: How am I to thank you?

HELMER: There is no need. (Puts on his coat.) But today you must excuse me.

RANK: Wait a minute; I will come with you. (Brings his fur coat from the hall and warms it at the fire.)

NORA: Don't be long away, Torvald dear.

HELMER: About an hour, not more.

NORA: Are you going too, Christine?

MRS. LINDE (putting on her cloak): Yes, I must go and look for a room.

HELMER: Oh, well then, we can walk down the street together.

NORA (helping her): What a pity it is we are so short of space here; I am afraid it is impossible for us. . . .

MRS. LINDE: Please don't think of it! Goodbye, Nora dear, and many thanks.

NORA: Goodbye for the present. Of course you will come back this evening. And you too, Dr. Rank. What do you say? If you are well enough? Oh, you must be! Wrap yourself up well. (They go to the door all talking together. Children's voices are heard on the staircase.)

NORA: There they are! There they are! (She runs to open the door. The NURSE comes in with the children.) Come in! Come in! (Stoops and kisses them.) Oh, you sweet blessings! Look at them, Christine! Aren't they darlings?

RANK: Don't let us stand here in the draught.

HELMER: Come along, Mrs. Linde; the place will only be bearable for a mother now!

(RANK, HELMER, and Mrs. LINDE go downstairs. The NURSE comes forward with the children; NORA shuts the hall door.)

NORA: How fresh and well you look! Such red cheeks like apples and roses. (The children all talk at once while she speaks to them.) Have you had great fun? That's splendid! What, you pulled both Emmy and Bob along on the sledge? —both at once?—that was good. You are a clever boy, Ivar. Let me take her for a little, Anne. My sweet little baby doll! (Takes the baby from the MAID and dances it up and down.) Yes, yes, mother will dance with Bob too. What! Have you been snowballing? I wish I had been there too! No, no, I will take their things off, Anne; please let me do it, it is such fun. Go in now, you look half frozen. There is some hot coffee for you on the stove.

(The NURSE goes into the room on the left. NORA takes off the children's things and throws them about, while they all talk to her at once.)

NORA: Really! Did a big dog run after you? But it didn't bite you? No, dogs don't bite nice little dolly children. You mustn't look at the parcels, Ivar. What are they? Ah, I daresay you would like to know. No, no—it's something nasty! Come, let us have a game! What shall we play at? Hide and Seek? Yes, we'll play Hide and Seek. Bob shall hide first. Must I hide? Very well, I'll hide first. (She and the children laugh and shout, and romp in and out of the room; at last NORA hides under the table, the children rush in and out for her, but do not see her; they hear her smothered laughter, run to the table, lift up the cloth and find her. Shouts of laughter. She crawls forward and pretends to frighten them. Fresh laughter. Meanwhile there has been a knock at the hall door, but none of them has noticed it. The door is half opened, and KROGSTAD appears, he waits a little; the game goes on.)

KROGSTAD: Excuse me, Mrs. Helmer.

NORA (with a stifled cry, turns round and gets up on to her knees): Ah! what do you want?

KROGSTAD: Excuse me, the outer door was ajar; I suppose someone forgot to shut it.

NORA (rising): My husband is out, Mr. Krogstad.

KROGSTAD: I know that.

NORA: What do you want here, then?

KROGSTAD: A word with you.

NORA: With me?—(To the children, gently.) Go in to nurse. What? No, the strange man won't do mother any harm. When he has gone we will have another game. (She takes the children into the room on the left, and shuts the door after them.) You want to speak to me?

KROGSTAD: Yes, I do.

NORA: Today? It is not the first of the month yet.

KROGSTAD: No, it is Christmas Eve, and it will depend on yourself what sort of a Christmas you will spend.

NORA: What do you mean? Today it is absolutely impossible for me—

KROGSTAD: We won't talk about that until later on. This is something different. I presume you can give me a moment?

NORA: Yes—yes, I can—although. . . .

KROGSTAD: Good. I was in Olsen's Restaurant and saw your husband going down the street.

NORA: Yes?

KROGSTAD: With a lady.

NORA: What then?

KROGSTAD: May I make so bold as to ask if it was a Mrs. Linde?

NORA: It was.

KROGSTAD: Just arrived in town?

NORA: Yes, today.

KROGSTAD: She is a great friend of yours, isn't she?

NORA: She is. But I don't see. . . .

KROGSTAD: I knew her too, once upon a time.

NORA: I am aware of that.

KROGSTAD: Are you? So you know all about it; I thought as much. Then I can ask you, without beating about the bush—is Mrs. Linde to have an appointment in the Bank?

NORA: What right have you to question me, Mr. Krogstad?—You, one of my husband's subordinates! But since you ask, you shall know. Yes, Mrs. Linde is to have an appointment. And it was I who pleaded her cause, Mr. Krogstad, let me tell you that.

KROGSTAD: I was right in what I thought, then.

NORA (walking up and down the stage): Sometimes one has a tiny little bit of influence, I should hope. Because one is a woman, it does not necessarily follow that—. When anyone is in a subordinate position, Mr. Krogstad, they should really be careful to avoid offending anyone who—who. . . .

KROGSTAD: Who has influence?

NORA: Exactly.

KROGSTAD (changing his tone): Mrs. Helmer, you will be so good as to use your influence on my behalf.

NORA: What? What do you mean?

KROGSTAD: You will be so kind as to see that I am allowed to keep my subordinate position in the Bank.

NORA: What do you mean by that? Who proposes to take your post away from you?

KROGSTAD: Oh, there is no necessity to keep up the pretence of ignorance. I can quite understand that your friend is not very anxious to expose herself to the chance of rubbing shoulders with me; and I quite understand, too, whom I have to thank for being turned off.

NORA: But I assure you. . . .

KROGSTAD: Very likely; but, to come to the point, the time has come when I should advise you to use your influence to prevent that.

NORA: But, Mr. Krogstad, I have no influence.

KROGSTAD: Haven't you? I thought you said yourself just now—

NORA: Naturally I did not mean you to put that construction on it. I! What should make you think I have any influence of that kind with my husband?

KROGSTAD: Oh, I have known your husband from our student days. I don't suppose he is any more unassailable than other husbands.

NORA: If you speak slightingly of my husband, I shall turn you out of the house.

KROGSTAD: You are bold, Mrs. Helmer.

NORA: I am not afraid of you any longer. As soon as the New Year comes, I shall in a very short time be free of the whole thing.

KROGSTAD (controlling himself): Listen to me, Mrs. Helmer. If necessary I am prepared to fight for my small post in the Bank as if I were fighting for my life.

NORA: So it seems.

KROGSTAD: It is not only for the sake of the money; indeed, that weighs least with me in the matter. There is another reason—well, I may as well tell you. My position is this. I daresay you know, like everybody else, that once, many years ago, I was guilty of an indiscretion.

NORA: I think I have heard something of the kind.

KROGSTAD: The matter never came into court; but every way seemed to be closed to me after that. So I took to the business that you know of. I had to do something; and, honestly, I don't think I've been one of the worst. But now

I must cut myself free from all that. My sons are growing up; for their sake I must try and win back as much respect as I can in the town. This post in the Bank was like the first step up for me—and now your husband is going to kick me downstairs again into the mud.

NORA: But you must believe me, Mr. Krogstad; it is not in my power to help you at all.

KROGSTAD: Then it is because you haven't the will; but I have means to compel you.

NORA: You don't mean that you will tell my husband that I owe you money?

KROGSTAD: Hm!—suppose I were to tell him?

NORA: It would be perfectly infamous of you. (Sobbing.) To think of his learning my secret, which has been my joy and pride, in such an ugly, clumsy way— that he should learn it from you! And it would put me in a horribly disagreeable position.

KROGSTAD: Only disagreeable?

NORA (impetuously): Well, do it, then!—and it will be the worse for you. My husband will see for himself what a blackguard you are, and you certainly won't keep your post then.

KROGSTAD: I asked you if it was only a disagreeable scene at home that you were afraid of?

NORA: If my husband does get to know of it, of course he will at once pay you what is still owing, and we shall have nothing more to do with you.

KROGSTAD (coming a step nearer): Listen to me, Mrs. Helmer. Either you have a very bad memory or you know very little of business. I shall be obliged to remind you of a few details.

NORA: What do you mean?

KROGSTAD: When your husband was ill, you came to me to borrow two hundred and fifty pounds.

NORA: I didn't know anyone else to go to.

KROGSTAD: I promised to get you that amount.

NORA: Yes, and you did so.

KROGSTAD: I promised to get you that amount, on certain conditions. Your mind was so taken up with your husband's illness, and you were so anxious to get the money for your journey, that you seem to have paid no attention to the conditions of our bargain. Therefore it will not be amiss if I remind you of them. Now, I promised to get the money on the security of a bond which I drew up.

NORA: Yes, and which I signed.

KROGSTAD: Good. But below your signature there were a few lines constituting your father a surety for the money; those lines your father should have signed.

NORA: Should? He did sign them.

KROGSTAD: I had left the date blank; that is to say, your father should himself have inserted the date on which he signed the paper. Do you remember that?

NORA: Yes, I think I remember.

KROGSTAD: Then I gave you the bond to send by post to your father. Is that not so?

NORA: Yes.

KROGSTAD: And you naturally did so at once, because five or six days afterwards you brought me the bond with your father's signature. And then I gave you the money.

NORA: Well, haven't I been paying it off regularly?

KROGSTAD: Fairly so, yes. But—to come back to the matter in hand—that must have been a very trying time for you, Mrs. Helmer?

NORA: It was, indeed.

KROGSTAD: Your father was very ill, wasn't he?

NORA: He was very near his end.

KROGSTAD: And died soon afterwards?

NORA: Yes.

KROGSTAD: Tell me, Mrs. Helmer, can you by any chance remember what day your father died?—on what day of the month, I mean.

NORA: Papa died on the 29th of September.

KROGSTAD: That is correct; I have ascertained it for myself. And, as that is so, there is a discrepancy (taking a paper from his pocket) which I cannot account for.

NORA: What discrepancy? I don't know. . . .

KROGSTAD: The discrepancy consists, Mrs. Helmer, in the fact that your father signed this bond three days after his death.

NORA: What do you mean? I don't understand.

KROGSTAD: Your father died on the 29th of September. But, look here; your father has dated his signature the 2nd of October. It is a discrepancy, isn't it? (NORA is silent.) Can you explain it to me? (NORA is still silent.) It is a remarkable thing, too, that the words "2nd of October," as well as the year, are not written in your father's handwriting but in one that I think I know. Well, of course it can be explained; your father may have forgotten to date his signature, and someone else may have dated it haphazard before they knew of his death. There is no harm in that. It all depends on the signature of the name; and that is genuine, I suppose, Mrs. Helmer? It was your father himself who signed his name here?

NORA (after a short pause, throws her head up and looks defiantly at him): No, it was not. It was I that wrote papa's name.

KROGSTAD: Are you aware that is a dangerous confession?

NORA: In what way? You shall have your money soon.

KROGSTAD: Let me ask you a question; why did you not send the paper to your father?

NORA: It was impossible; papa was so ill. If I had asked him for his signature, I should have had to tell him what the money was to be used for; and when he was so ill himself I couldn't tell him that my husband's life was in danger—it was impossible.

KROGSTAD: It would have been better for you if you had given up your trip abroad.

NORA: No, that was impossible. That trip was to save my husband's life; I couldn't give that up.

KROGSTAD: But did it never occur to you that you were committing a fraud on me?

NORA: I couldn't take that into account; I didn't trouble myself about you at all. I couldn't bear you, because you put so many heartless difficulties in my way, although you knew what a dangerous condition my husband was in.

KROGSTAD: Mrs. Helmer, you evidently do not realise clearly what it is that you have been guilty of. But I can assure you that my one false step, which lost me all my reputation, was nothing more or nothing worse than what you have done.

NORA: You? Do you ask me to believe that you were brave enough to run a risk to save your wife's life?

KROGSTAD: The law cares nothing about motives.

NORA: Then it must be a very foolish law.

KROGSTAD: Foolish or not, it is the law by which you will be judged, if I produce this paper in court.

NORA: I don't believe it. Is a daughter not to be allowed to spare her dying father anxiety and care? Is a wife not to be allowed to save her husband's life? I don't know much about law; but I am certain that there must be laws permitting such things as that. Have you no knowledge of such laws—you who are a lawyer? You must be a very poor lawyer, Mr. Krogstad.

KROGSTAD: Maybe. But matters of business—such business as you and I have had together—do you think I don't understand that? Very well. Do as you please. But let me tell you this—if I lose my position a second time, you shall lose yours with me. (He bows, and goes out through the hall.)

NORA (appears buried in thought for a short time, then tosses her head): Nonsense! Trying to frighten me like that!—I am not so silly as he thinks. (Begins to busy herself putting the children's things in order.) And yet? No, it's impossible! I did it for love's sake.

CHILDREN (in the doorway on the left): Mother, the stranger man has gone out through the gate.

NORA: Yes, dears, I know. But, don't tell anyone about the stranger man. Do you hear? Not even papa.

CHILDREN: No, mother; but will you come and play again?

NORA: No, no,—not now.

CHILDREN: But, mother, you promised us.

NORA: Yes, but I can't now. Run away in; I have such a lot to do. Run away in, my sweet little darlings. (She gets them into the room by degrees and shuts the door on them; then sits down on the sofa, takes up a piece of needlework and sews a few stitches, but soon stops.) No! (Throws down the work, gets up, goes to the hall door and calls out.) Helen! bring the Tree in. (Goes to the table on the left, opens a drawer, and stops again.) No, no! it is quite impossible!

MAID (coming in with the Tree): Where shall I put it, ma'am?

NORA: Here, in the middle of the floor.

MAID: Shall I get you anything else?

NORA: No, thank you. I have all I want. [Exit MAID.]

NORA (begins dressing the tree): A candle here-and flowers here—The horrible man! It's all nonsense—there's nothing wrong. The tree shall be splendid! I will do everything I can think of to please you, Torvald!—I will sing for you, dance for you—(HELMER comes in with some papers under his arm.) Oh! are you back already?

HELMER: Yes. Has anyone been here?

NORA: Here? No.

HELMER: That is strange. I saw Krogstad going out of the gate.

NORA: Did you? Oh yes, I forgot, Krogstad was here for a moment.

HELMER: Nora, I can see from your manner that he has been here begging you to say a good word for him.

NORA: Yes.

HELMER: And you were to appear to do it of your own accord; you were to conceal from me the fact of his having been here; didn't he beg that of you too?

NORA: Yes, Torvald, but—

HELMER: Nora, Nora, and you would be a party to that sort of thing? To have any talk with a man like that, and give him any sort of promise? And to tell me a lie into the bargain?

NORA: A lie?

HELMER: Didn't you tell me no one had been here? (Shakes his finger at her.) My little songbird must never do that again. A songbird must have a clean beak to chirp with—no false notes! (Puts his arm round her waist.) That is so, isn't it? Yes, I am sure it is. (Lets her go.) We will say no more about it. (Sits down by the stove.) How warm and snug it is here! (Turns over his papers.)

NORA (after a short pause, during which she busies herself with the Christmas Tree): Torvald!

HELMER: Yes.

NORA: I am looking forward tremendously to the fancy-dress ball at the Stenborgs' the day after tomorrow.

HELMER: And I am tremendously curious to see what you are going to surprise me with.

NORA: It was very silly of me to want to do that.

HELMER: What do you mean?

NORA: I can't hit upon anything that will do; everything I think of seems so silly and insignificant.

HELMER: Does my little Nora acknowledge that at last?

NORA (standing behind his chair with her arms on the back of it): Are you very busy, Torvald?

HELMER: Well?

NORA: What are all those papers?

HELMER: Bank business.

NORA: Already?

HELMER: I have got authority from the retiring manager to undertake the necessary changes in the staff and in the rearrangement of the work; and I must make use of the Christmas week for that, so as to have everything in order for the new year.

NORA: Then that was why this poor Krogstad. . . .

HELMER: Hm!

NORA (leans against the back of his chair and strokes his hair): If you hadn't been so busy I should have asked you a tremendously big favour, Torvald.

HELMER: What is that? Tell me.

NORA: There is no one has such good taste as you. And I do so want to look nice at the fancy-dress ball. Torvald, couldn't you take me in hand and decide what I shall go as, and what sort of a dress I shall wear?

HELMER: Aha! so my obstinate little woman is obliged to get someone to come to her rescue?

NORA: Yes, Torvald, I can't get along a bit without your help.

HELMER: Very well, I will think it over, we shall manage to hit upon something.

NORA: That is nice of you. (Goes to the Christmas Tree. A short pause.) How pretty the red flowers look. But, tell me, was it really something very bad that this Krogstad was guilty of?

HELMER: He forged someone's name. Have you any idea what that means?

NORA: Isn't it possible that he was driven to do it by necessity?

HELMER: Yes; or, as in so many cases, by imprudence. I am not so heartless as to condemn a man altogether because of a single false step of that kind.

NORA: No, you wouldn't, would you, Torvald?

HELMER: Many a man has been able to retrieve his character, if he has openly confessed his fault and taken his punishment.

NORA: Punishment—?

HELMER: But Krogstad did nothing of that sort; he got himself out of it by a cunning trick, and that is why he has gone under altogether.

NORA: But do you think it would—?

HELMER: Just think how a guilty man like that has to lie and play the hypocrite with every one, how he has to wear a mask in the presence of those near and dear to him, even before his own wife and children. And about the children—that is the most terrible part of it all, Nora.

NORA: How?

HELMER: Because such an atmosphere of lies infects and poisons the whole life of a home. Each breath the children take in such a house is full of the germs of evil.

NORA (coming nearer him): Are you sure of that?

HELMER: My dear, I have often seen it in the course of my life as a lawyer. Almost everyone who has gone to the bad early in life has had a deceitful mother.

NORA: Why do you only say—mother?

HELMER: It seems most commonly to be the mother's influence, though naturally a bad father's would have the same result. Every lawyer is familiar with the fact. This Krogstad, now, has been persistently poisoning his own children with lies and dissimulation; that is why I say he has lost all moral character. (Holds out his hands to her.) That is why my sweet little Nora must promise me not to plead his cause. Give me your hand on it. Come, come, what is this? Give me your hand. There now, that's settled. I assure you it would be quite impossible for me to work with him; I literally feel physically ill when I am in the company of such people.

NORA (takes her hand out of his and goes to the opposite side of the Christmas Tree): How hot it is in here; and I have such a lot to do.

HELMER (getting up and putting his papers in order): Yes, and I must try and read through some of these before dinner; and I must think about your costume, too. And it is just possible I may have something ready in gold paper to hang up on the tree. (Puts his hand on her head.) My precious little singing-bird! (He goes into his room and shuts the door after him.)

NORA (after a pause, whispers): No, no—it isn't true. It's impossible; it must be impossible.

(The NURSE opens the door on the left.)

NURSE: The little ones are begging so hard to be allowed to come in to mamma.

NORA: No, no, no! Don't let them come in to me! You stay with them, Anne.

NURSE: Very well, ma'am. (Shuts the door.)

NORA (pale with terror): Deprave my little children? Poison my home? (A short pause. Then she tosses her head.) It's not true. It can't possibly be true.

ACT II

(THE SAME SCENE.—THE Christmas Tree is in the corner by the piano, stripped of its ornaments and with burnt-down candle-ends on its dishevelled branches. NORA'S cloak and hat are lying on the sofa. She is alone in the room, walking about uneasily. She stops by the sofa and takes up her cloak.)

NORA (drops her cloak): Someone is coming now! (Goes to the door and listens.) No—it is no one. Of course, no one will come today, Christmas Day—nor tomorrow either. But, perhaps—(opens the door and looks out). No, nothing in the letterbox; it is quite empty. (Comes forward.) What rubbish! of course he can't be in earnest about it. Such a thing couldn't happen; it is impossible—I have three little children.

(Enter the NURSE from the room on the left, carrying a big cardboard box.)

NURSE: At last I have found the box with the fancy dress.

NORA: Thanks; put it on the table.

NURSE (doing so): But it is very much in want of mending.

NORA: I should like to tear it into a hundred thousand pieces.

NURSE: What an idea! It can easily be put in order—just a little patience.

NORA: Yes, I will go and get Mrs. Linde to come and help me with it.

NURSE: What, out again? In this horrible weather? You will catch cold, ma'am, and make yourself ill.

NORA: Well, worse than that might happen. How are the children?

NURSE: The poor little souls are playing with their Christmas presents, but. . . .

NORA: Do they ask much for me?

NURSE: You see, they are so accustomed to have their mamma with them.

NORA: Yes, but, nurse, I shall not be able to be so much with them now as I was before.

NURSE: Oh well, young children easily get accustomed to anything.

NORA: Do you think so? Do you think they would forget their mother if she went away altogether?

NURSE: Good heavens!—went away altogether?

NORA: Nurse, I want you to tell me something I have often wondered about— how could you have the heart to put your own child out among strangers?

NURSE: I was obliged to, if I wanted to be little Nora's nurse.

NORA: Yes, but how could you be willing to do it?

NURSE: What, when I was going to get such a good place by it? A poor girl who has got into trouble should be glad to. Besides, that wicked man didn't do a single thing for me.

NORA: But I suppose your daughter has quite forgotten you.

NURSE: No, indeed she hasn't. She wrote to me when she was confirmed, and when she was married.

NORA (putting her arms round her neck): Dear old Anne, you were a good mother to me when I was little.

NURSE: Little Nora, poor dear, had no other mother but me.

NORA: And if my little ones had no other mother, I am sure you would— What nonsense I am talking! (Opens the box.) Go in to them. Now I must. You will see tomorrow how charming I shall look.

NURSE: I am sure there will be no one at the ball so charming as you, ma'am. (Goes into the room on the left.)

NORA (begins to unpack the box, but soon pushes it away from her): If only I dared go out. If only no one would come. If only I could be sure nothing would happen here in the meantime. Stuff and nonsense! No one will come. Only I mustn't think about it. I will brush my muff. What lovely, lovely gloves! Out of my thoughts, out of my thoughts! One, two, three, four, five, six— (Screams.) Ah! there is someone coming—. (Makes a movement towards the door, but stands irresolute.)

(Enter MRS. LINDE from the hall, where she has taken off her cloak and hat.)

NORA: Oh, it's you, Christine. There is no one else out there, is there? How good of you to come!

MRS. LINDE: I heard you were up asking for me.

NORA: Yes, I was passing by. As a matter of fact, it is something you could help me with. Let us sit down here on the sofa. Look here. Tomorrow evening there is to be a fancy-dress ball at the Stenborgs', who live above us; and Torvald wants me to go as a Neapolitan fisher-girl, and dance the Tarantella that I learned at Capri.

MRS. LINDE: I see; you are going to keep up the character.

NORA: Yes, Torvald wants me to. Look, here is the dress; Torvald had it made for me there, but now it is all so torn, and I haven't any idea.

MRS. LINDE: We will easily put that right. It is only some of the trimming come unsewn here and there. Needle and thread? Now then, that's all we want.

NORA: It is nice of you.

MRS. LINDE (sewing): So you are going to be dressed up tomorrow Nora. I will tell you what—I shall come in for a moment and see you in your fine feathers. But I have completely forgotten to thank you for a delightful evening yesterday.

NORA (gets up, and crosses the stage): Well, I don't think yesterday was as pleasant as usual. You ought to have come to town a little earlier, Christine. Certainly Torvald does understand how to make a house dainty and attractive.

MRS. LINDE: And so do you, it seems to me; you are not your father's daughter for nothing. But tell me, is Doctor Rank always as depressed as he was yesterday?

NORA: No; yesterday it was very noticeable. I must tell you that he suffers from a very dangerous disease. He has consumption of the spine, poor creature. His father was a horrible man who committed all sorts of excesses; and that is why his son was sickly from childhood, do you understand?

MRS. LINDE (dropping her sewing): But, my dearest Nora, how do you know anything about such things?

NORA (walking about): Pooh! When you have three children, you get visits now and then from—from married women, who know something of medical matters, and they talk about one thing and another.

MRS. LINDE (goes on sewing. A short silence): Does Doctor Rank come here everyday?

NORA: Everyday regularly. He is Torvald's most intimate friend, and a great friend of mine too. He is just like one of the family.

MRS. LINDE: But tell me this—is he perfectly sincere? I mean, isn't he the kind of man that is very anxious to make himself agreeable?

NORA: Not in the least. What makes you think that?

MRS. LINDE: When you introduced him to me yesterday, he declared he had often heard my name mentioned in this house; but afterwards I noticed that your husband hadn't the slightest idea who I was. So how could Doctor Rank?

NORA: That is quite right, Christine. Torvald is so absurdly fond of me that he wants me absolutely to himself, as he says. At first he used to seem almost jealous if I mentioned any of the dear folk at home, so naturally I gave up doing so. But I often talk about such things with Doctor Rank, because he likes hearing about them.

MRS. LINDE: Listen to me, Nora. You are still very like a child in many things, and I am older than you in many ways and have a little more experience. Let me tell you this—you ought to make an end of it with Doctor Rank.

NORA: What ought I to make an end of?

MRS. LINDE: Of two things, I think. Yesterday you talked some nonsense about a rich admirer who was to leave you money.

NORA: An admirer who doesn't exist, unfortunately! But what then?

MRS. LINDE: Is Doctor Rank a man of means?

NORA: Yes, he is.

MRS. LINDE: And has no one to provide for?

NORA: No, no one; but. . . .

MRS. LINDE: And comes here everyday?

NORA: Yes, I told you so.

MRS. LINDE: But how can this well-bred man be so tactless?

NORA: I don't understand you at all.

MRS. LINDE: Don't prevaricate, Nora. Do you suppose I don't guess who lent you the two hundred and fifty pounds?

NORA: Are you out of your senses? How can you think of such a thing! A friend of ours, who comes here everyday! Do you realise what a horribly painful position that would be?

MRS. LINDE: Then it really isn't he?

NORA: No, certainly not. It would never have entered into my head for a moment. Besides, he had no money to lend then; he came into his money afterwards.

MRS. LINDE: Well, I think that was lucky for you, my dear Nora.

NORA: No, it would never have come into my head to ask Doctor Rank. Although I am quite sure that if I had asked him. . . .

MRS. LINDE: But of course you won't.

NORA: Of course not. I have no reason to think it could possibly be necessary. But I am quite sure that if I told Doctor Rank. . . .

MRS. LINDE: Behind your husband's back?

NORA: I must make an end of it with the other one, and that will be behind his back too. I must make an end of it with him.

MRS. LINDE: Yes, that is what I told you yesterday, but. . . .

NORA (walking up and down): A man can put a thing like that straight much easier than a woman.

MRS. LINDE: One's husband, yes.

NORA: Nonsense! (Standing still.) When you pay off a debt you get your bond back, don't you?

MRS. LINDE: Yes, as a matter of course.

NORA: And can tear it into a hundred thousand pieces, and burn it up—the nasty dirty paper!

MRS. LINDE (looks hard at her, lays down her sewing and gets up slowly): Nora, you are concealing something from me.

NORA: Do I look as if I were?

MRS. LINDE: Something has happened to you since yesterday morning. Nora, what is it?

NORA (going nearer to her): Christine! (Listens.) Hush! there's Torvald come home. Do you mind going in to the children for the present? Torvald can't bear to see dressmaking going on. Let Anne help you.

MRS. LINDE (gathering some of the things together): Certainly—but I am not going away from here until we have had it out with one another. (She goes into the room on the left, as HELMER comes in from the hall.)

NORA: (going up to HELMER) I have wanted you so much, Torvald dear.

HELMER: Was that the dressmaker?

NORA: No, it was Christine; she is helping me to put my dress in order. You will see I shall look quite smart.

HELMER: Wasn't that a happy thought of mine, now?

NORA: Splendid! But don't you think it is nice of me, too, to do as you wish?

HELMER: Nice?—because you do as your husband wishes? Well, well, you little rogue, I am sure you did not mean it in that way. But I am not going to disturb you; you will want to be trying on your dress, I expect.

NORA: I suppose you are going to work.

HELMER: Yes. (Shows her a bundle of papers.) Look at that. I have just been into the bank. (Turns to go into his room.)

NORA: Torvald.

HELMER: Yes.

NORA: If your little squirrel were to ask you for something very, very prettily?

HELMER: What then?

NORA: Would you do it?

HELMER: I should like to hear what it is, first.

NORA: Your squirrel would run about and do all her tricks if you would be nice, and do what she wants.

HELMER: Speak plainly.

NORA: Your skylark would chirp about in every room, with her song rising and falling.

HELMER: Well, my skylark does that anyhow.

NORA: I would play the fairy and dance for you in the moonlight, Torvald.

HELMER: Nora—you surely don't mean that request you made to me this morning?

NORA (going near him): Yes, Torvald, I beg you so earnestly.

HELMER: Have you really the courage to open up that question again?

NORA: Yes, dear, you must do as I ask; you must let Krogstad keep his post in the bank.

HELMER: My dear Nora, it is his post that I have arranged Mrs. Linde shall have.

NORA: Yes, you have been awfully kind about that; but you could just as well dismiss some other clerk instead of Krogstad.

HELMER: This is simply incredible obstinacy! Because you chose to give him a thoughtless promise that you would speak for him, I am expected to. . . .

NORA: That isn't the reason, Torvald. It is for your own sake. This fellow writes in the most scurrilous newspapers; you have told me so yourself. He can do you an unspeakable amount of harm. I am frightened to death of him.

HELMER: Ah, I understand; it is recollections of the past that scare you.

NORA: What do you mean?

HELMER: Naturally you are thinking of your father.

NORA: Yes—yes, of course. Just recall to your mind what these malicious creatures wrote in the papers about papa, and how horribly they slandered him. I believe they would have procured his dismissal if the Department had not sent you over to inquire into it, and if you had not been so kindly disposed and helpful to him.

HELMER: My little Nora, there is an important difference between your father and me. Your father's reputation as a public official was not above suspicion. Mine is, and I hope it will continue to be so, as long as I hold my office.

NORA: You never can tell what mischief these men may contrive. We ought to be so well off, so snug and happy here in our peaceful home, and have no cares— you and I and the children, Torvald! That is why I beg you so earnestly.

HELMER: And it is just by interceding for him that you make it impossible for me to keep him. It is already known at the Bank that I mean to dismiss Krogstad. Is it to get about now that the new manager has changed his mind at his wife's bidding?

NORA: And what if it did?

HELMER: Of course!—if only this obstinate little person can get her way! Do you suppose I am going to make myself ridiculous before my whole staff, to let people think that I am a man to be swayed by all sorts of outside influence? I should very soon feel the consequences of it, I can tell you! And besides, there is one thing that makes it quite impossible for me to have Krogstad in the Bank as long as I am manager.

NORA: Whatever is that?

HELMER: His moral failings I might perhaps have overlooked, if necessary.

NORA: Yes, you could—couldn't you?

HELMER: And I hear he is a good worker, too. But I knew him when we were boys. It was one of those rash friendships that so often prove an incubus in afterlife. I may as well tell you plainly, we were once on very intimate terms with one another. But this tactless fellow lays no restraint on himself when other people are present. On the contrary, he thinks it gives him the right to adopt a familiar tone with me, and every minute it is "I say, Helmer, old fellow!" and that sort of thing. I assure you it is extremely painful for me. He would make my position in the Bank intolerable.

NORA: Torvald, I don't believe you mean that.

HELMER: Don't you? Why not?

NORA: Because it is such a narrow-minded way of looking at things.

HELMER: What are you saying? Narrow-minded? Do you think I am narrow-minded?

NORA: No, just the opposite, dear—and it is exactly for that reason.

HELMER: It's the same thing. You say my point of view is narrow-minded, so I must be so too. Narrow-minded! Very well—I must put an end to this. (Goes to the hall door and calls.) Helen!

NORA: What are you going to do?

HELMER (looking among his papers): Settle it. (Enter MAID.) Look here; take this letter and go downstairs with it at once. Find a messenger and tell him to deliver it, and be quick. The address is on it, and here is the money.

MAID: Very well, sir. (Exit with the letter.)

HELMER (putting his papers together): Now then, little Miss Obstinate.

NORA (breathlessly): Torvald—what was that letter?

HELMER: Krogstad's dismissal.

NORA: Call her back, Torvald! There is still time. Oh Torvald, call her back! Do it for my sake—for your own sake—for the children's sake! Do you hear me, Torvald? Call her back! You don't know what that letter can bring upon us.

HELMER: It's too late.

NORA: Yes, it's too late.

HELMER: My dear Nora, I can forgive the anxiety you are in, although really it is an insult to me. It is, indeed. Isn't it an insult to think that I should be afraid of a starving quill-driver's vengeance? But I forgive you nevertheless, because it is such eloquent witness to your great love for me. (Takes her in his arms.) And that is as it should be, my own darling Nora. Come what will, you may be sure I shall have both courage and strength if they be needed. You will see I am man enough to take everything upon myself.

NORA (in a horror-stricken voice): What do you mean by that?

HELMER: Everything, I say.

NORA (recovering herself): You will never have to do that.

HELMER: That's right. Well, we will share it, Nora, as man and wife should. That is how it shall be. (Caressing her.) Are you content now? There! There!—not these frightened dove's eyes! The whole thing is only the wildest fancy!—Now, you must go and play through the Tarantella and practise with your tambourine. I shall go into the inner office and shut the door, and I shall hear nothing; you can make as much noise as you please. (Turns back at the door.) And when Rank comes, tell him where he will find me. (Nods to her, takes his papers and goes into his room, and shuts the door after him.)

NORA (bewildered with anxiety, stands as if rooted to the spot, and whispers): He was capable of doing it. He will do it. He will do it in spite of everything. No, not that! Never, never! Anything rather than that! Oh, for some help, some way out of it! (The door-bell rings.) Doctor Rank! Anything rather than that—anything, whatever it is! (She puts her hands over her face, pulls herself together, goes to the door and opens it. RANK is standing without, hanging up his coat. During the following dialogue it begins to grow dark.)

NORA: Good day, Doctor Rank. I knew your ring. But you mustn't go in to Torvald now; I think he is busy with something.

RANK: And you?

NORA (brings him in and shuts the door after him): Oh, you know very well I always have time for you.

RANK: Thank you. I shall make use of as much of it as I can.

NORA: What do you mean by that? As much of it as you can?

RANK: Well, does that alarm you?

NORA: It was such a strange way of putting it. Is anything likely to happen?

RANK: Nothing but what I have long been prepared for. But I certainly didn't expect it to happen so soon.

NORA (gripping him by the arm): What have you found out? Doctor Rank, you must tell me.

RANK (sitting down by the stove): It is all up with me. And it can't be helped.

NORA (with a sigh of relief): Is it about yourself?

RANK: Who else? It is no use lying to one's self. I am the most wretched of all my patients, Mrs. Helmer. Lately I have been taking stock of my internal economy. Bankrupt! Probably within a month I shall lie rotting in the churchyard.

NORA: What an ugly thing to say!

RANK: The thing itself is cursedly ugly, and the worst of it is that I shall have to face so much more that is ugly before that. I shall only make one more examination of myself; when I have done that, I shall know pretty certainly when it will be that the horrors of dissolution will begin. There is something I want to tell you. Helmer's refined nature gives him an unconquerable disgust at everything that is ugly; I won't have him in my sick-room.

NORA: Oh, but, Doctor Rank.

RANK: I won't have him there. Not on any account. I bar my door to him. As soon as I am quite certain that the worst has come, I shall send you my card with a black cross on it, and then you will know that the loathsome end has begun.

NORA: You are quite absurd today. And I wanted you so much to be in a really good humour.

RANK: With death stalking beside me?—To have to pay this penalty for another man's sin? Is there any justice in that? And in every single family, in one way or another, some such inexorable retribution is being exacted.

NORA (putting her hands over her ears): Rubbish! Do talk of something cheerful.

RANK: Oh, it's a mere laughing matter, the whole thing. My poor innocent spine has to suffer for my father's youthful amusements.

NORA (sitting at the table on the left): I suppose you mean that he was too partial to asparagus and pate de foie gras, don't you?

RANK: Yes, and to truffles.

NORA: Truffles, yes. And oysters too, I suppose?

RANK: Oysters, of course, that goes without saying.

NORA: And heaps of port and champagne. It is sad that all these nice things should take their revenge on our bones.

RANK: Especially that they should revenge themselves on the unlucky bones of those who have not had the satisfaction of enjoying them.

NORA: Yes, that's the saddest part of it all.

RANK (with a searching look at her): Hm!

NORA (after a short pause): Why did you smile?

RANK: No, it was you that laughed.

NORA: No, it was you that smiled, Doctor Rank!

RANK (rising): You are a greater rascal than I thought.

NORA: I am in a silly mood today.

RANK: So it seems.

NORA (putting her hands on his shoulders): Dear, dear Doctor Rank, death mustn't take you away from Torvald and me.

RANK: It is a loss you would easily recover from. Those who are gone are soon forgotten.

NORA (looking at him anxiously): Do you believe that?

RANK: People form new ties, and then. . . .

NORA: Who will form new ties?

RANK: Both you and Helmer, when I am gone. You yourself are already on the high road to it, I think. What did that Mrs. Linde want here last night?

NORA: Oho!—you don't mean to say you are jealous of poor Christine?

RANK: Yes, I am. She will be my successor in this house. When I am done for, this woman will.

NORA: Hush! don't speak so loud. She is in that room.

RANK: Today again. There, you see.

NORA: She has only come to sew my dress for me. Bless my soul, how unreasonable you are! (Sits down on the sofa.) Be nice now, Doctor Rank, and tomorrow you will see how beautifully I shall dance, and you can imagine I am doing it all for you—and for Torvald too, of course. (Takes various things out of the box.) Doctor Rank, come and sit down here, and I will show you something.

RANK (sitting down): What is it?

NORA: Just look at those!

RANK: Silk stockings.

NORA: Flesh-coloured. Aren't they lovely? It is so dark here now, but tomorrow. No, no, no! you must only look at the feet. Oh well, you may have leave to look at the legs too.

RANK: Him!

NORA: Why are you looking so critical? Don't you think they will fit me?

RANK: I have no means of forming an opinion about that.

NORA (looks at him for a moment): For shame! (Hits him lightly on the ear with the stockings.) That's to punish you. (Folds them up again.)

RANK: And what other nice things am I to be allowed to see?

NORA: Not a single thing more, for being so naughty. (She looks among the things, humming to herself.)

RANK (after a short silence): When I am sitting here, talking to you as intimately as this, I cannot imagine for a moment what would have become of me if I had never come into this house.

NORA (smiling): I believe you do feel thoroughly at home with us.

RANK (in a lower voice, looking straight in front of him:) And to be obliged to leave it all.

NORA: Nonsense, you are not going to leave it.

RANK (as before): And not be able to leave behind one the slightest token of one's gratitude, scarcely even a fleeting regret—nothing but an empty place which the first comer can fill as well as any other.

NORA: And if I asked you now for a? No!

RANK: For what?

NORA: For a big proof of your friendship.

RANK: Yes, yes!

NORA: I mean a tremendously big favour.

RANK: Would you really make me so happy for once?

NORA: Ah, but you don't know what it is yet.

RANK: No—but tell me.

NORA: I really can't, Doctor Rank. It is something out of all reason; it means advice, and help, and a favour.

RANK: The bigger a thing it is the better. I can't conceive what it is you mean. Do tell me. Haven't I your confidence?

NORA: More than anyone else. I know you are my truest and best friend, and so I will tell you what it is. Well, Doctor Rank, it is something you must help me to prevent. You know how devotedly, how inexpressibly deeply Torvald loves me; he would never for a moment hesitate to give his life for me.

RANK (leaning towards her): Nora—do you think he is the only one?

NORA (with a slight start): The only one?

RANK: The only one who would gladly give his life for your sake.

NORA (sadly): Is that it?

RANK: I was determined you should know it before I went away, and there will never be a better opportunity than this. Now you know it, Nora. And now you know, too, that you can trust me as you would trust no one else.

NORA (rises, deliberately and quietly): Let me pass.

RANK (makes room for her to pass him, but sits still): Nora!

NORA (at the hall door): Helen, bring in the lamp. (Goes over to the stove.) Dear Doctor Rank, that was really horrid of you.

RANK: To have loved you as much as anyone else does? Was that horrid?

NORA: No, but to go and tell me so. There was really no need.

RANK: What do you mean? Did you know—? (MAID enters with lamp, puts it down on the table, and goes out.) Nora—Mrs. Helmer—tell me, had you any idea of this?

NORA: Oh, how do I know whether I had or whether I hadn't? I really can't tell you—To think you could be so clumsy, Doctor Rank! We were getting on so nicely.

RANK: Well, at all events you know now that you can command me, body and soul. So won't you speak out?

NORA (looking at him): After what happened?

RANK: I beg you to let me know what it is.

NORA: I can't tell you anything now.

RANK: Yes, yes. You mustn't punish me in that way. Let me have permission to do for you whatever a man may do.

NORA: You can do nothing for me now. Besides, I really don't need any help at all. You will find that the whole thing is merely fancy on my part. It really is so—of course it is! (Sits down in the rocking-chair, and looks at him with a smile.) You are a nice sort of man, Doctor Rank!—don't you feel ashamed of yourself, now the lamp has come?

RANK: Not a bit. But perhaps I had better go—forever?

NORA: No, indeed, you shall not. Of course you must come here just as before. You know very well Torvald can't do without you.

RANK: Yes, but you?

NORA: Oh, I am always tremendously pleased when you come.

RANK: It is just that, that put me on the wrong track. You are a riddle to me. I have often thought that you would almost as soon be in my company as in Helmer's.

NORA: Yes—you see there are some people one loves best, and others whom one would almost always rather have as companions.

RANK: Yes, there is something in that.

NORA: When I was at home, of course I loved papa best. But I always thought it tremendous fun if I could steal down into the maids' room, because they never moralised at all, and talked to each other about such entertaining things.

RANK: I see—it is their place I have taken.

NORA (jumping up and going to him): Oh, dear, nice Doctor Rank, I never meant that at all. But surely you can understand that being with Torvald is a little like being with papa—(Enter MAID from the hall.)

MAID: If you please, ma'am. (Whispers and hands her a card.)

NORA (glancing at the card): Oh! (Puts it in her pocket.)

RANK: Is there anything wrong?

NORA: No, no, not in the least. It is only something—it is my new dress.

RANK: What? Your dress is lying there.

NORA: Oh, yes, that one; but this is another. I ordered it. Torvald mustn't know about it.

RANK: Oho! Then that was the great secret.

NORA: Of course. Just go in to him; he is sitting in the inner room. Keep him as long as. . . .

RANK: Make your mind easy; I won't let him escape.

(Goes into HELMER'S room.)

NORA (to the MAID): And he is standing waiting in the kitchen?

MAID: Yes; he came up the back stairs.

NORA: But didn't you tell him no one was in?

MAID: Yes, but it was no good.

NORA: He won't go away?

MAID: No; he says he won't until he has seen you, ma'am.

NORA: Well, let him come in—but quietly. Helen, you mustn't say anything about it to anyone. It is a surprise for my husband.

MAID: Yes, ma'am, I quite understand. (Exit.)

NORA: This dreadful thing is going to happen! It will happen in spite of me! No, no, no, it can't happen—it shan't happen! (She bolts the door of HELMER'S room. The MAID opens the hall door for KROGSTAD and shuts it after him. He is wearing a fur coat, high boots and a fur cap.)

NORA (advancing towards him): Speak low—my husband is at home.

KROGSTAD: No matter about that.

NORA: What do you want of me?

KROGSTAD: An explanation of something.

NORA: Make haste then. What is it?

KROGSTAD: You know, I suppose, that I have got my dismissal.

NORA: I couldn't prevent it, Mr. Krogstad. I fought as hard as I could on your side, but it was no good.

KROGSTAD: Does your husband love you so little, then? He knows what I can expose you to, and yet he ventures. . . .

NORA: How can you suppose that he has any knowledge of the sort?

KROGSTAD: I didn't suppose so at all. It would not be the least like our dear Torvald Helmer to show so much courage.

NORA: Mr. Krogstad, a little respect for my husband, please.

KROGSTAD: Certainly—all the respect he deserves. But since you have kept the matter so carefully to yourself, I make bold to suppose that you have a little clearer idea, than you had yesterday, of what it actually is that you have done?

NORA: More than you could ever teach me.

KROGSTAD: Yes, such a bad lawyer as I am.

NORA: What is it you want of me?

KROGSTAD: Only to see how you were, Mrs. Helmer. I have been thinking about you all day long. A mere cashier, a quill-driver, a—well, a man like me— even he has a little of what is called feeling, you know.

NORA: Show it, then; think of my little children.

KROGSTAD: Have you and your husband thought of mine? But never mind about that. I only wanted to tell you that you need not take this matter too seriously. In the first place there will be no accusation made on my part.

NORA: No, of course not; I was sure of that.

KROGSTAD: The whole thing can be arranged amicably; there is no reason why anyone should know anything about it. It will remain a secret between us three.

NORA: My husband must never get to know anything about it.

KROGSTAD: How will you be able to prevent it? Am I to understand that you can pay the balance that is owing?

NORA: No, not just at present.

KROGSTAD: Or perhaps that you have some expedient for raising the money soon?

NORA: No expedient that I mean to make use of.

KROGSTAD: Well, in any case, it would have been of no use to you now. If you stood there with ever so much money in your hand, I would never part with your bond.

NORA: Tell me what purpose you mean to put it to.

KROGSTAD: I shall only preserve it—keep it in my possession. No one who is not concerned in the matter shall have the slightest hint of it. So that if the thought of it has driven you to any desperate resolution. . . .

NORA: It has.

KROGSTAD: If you had it in your mind to run away from your home. . . .

NORA: I had.

KROGSTAD: Or even something worse.

NORA: How could you know that?

KROGSTAD: Give up the idea.

NORA: How did you know I had thought of that?

KROGSTAD: Most of us think of that at first. I did, too—but I hadn't the courage.

NORA (faintly): No more had I.

KROGSTAD (in a tone of relief): No, that's it, isn't it—you hadn't the courage either?

NORA: No, I haven't—I haven't.

KROGSTAD: Besides, it would have been a great piece of folly. Once the first storm at home is over. I have a letter for your husband in my pocket.

NORA: Telling him everything?

KROGSTAD: In as lenient a manner as I possibly could.

NORA (quickly): He mustn't get the letter. Tear it up. I will find some means of getting money.

KROGSTAD: Excuse me, Mrs. Helmer, but I think I told you just now.

NORA: I am not speaking of what I owe you. Tell me what sum you are asking my husband for, and I will get the money.

KROGSTAD: I am not asking your husband for a penny.

NORA: What do you want, then?

KROGSTAD: I will tell you. I want to rehabilitate myself, Mrs. Helmer; I want to get on; and in that your husband must help me. For the last year and a half I have not had a hand in anything dishonourable, amid all that time I have been struggling in most restricted circumstances. I was content to work my way up step by step. Now I am turned out, and I am not going to be satisfied with merely being taken into favour again. I want to get on, I tell you. I want to get into the Bank again, in a higher position. Your husband must make a place for me.

NORA: That he will never do!

KROGSTAD: He will; I know him; he dare not protest. And as soon as I am in there again with him, then you will see! Within a year I shall be the manager's right hand. It will be Nils Krogstad and not Torvald Helmer who manages the Bank.

NORA: That's a thing you will never see!

KROGSTAD: Do you mean that you will?

NORA: I have courage enough for it now.

KROGSTAD: Oh, you can't frighten me. A fine, spoilt lady like you.

NORA: You will see, you will see.

KROGSTAD: Under the ice, perhaps? Down into the cold, coal-black water? And then, in the spring, to float up to the surface, all horrible and unrecognisable, with your hair fallen out.

NORA: You can't frighten me.

KROGSTAD: Nor you me. People don't do such things, Mrs. Helmer. Besides, what use would it be? I should have him completely in my power all the same.

NORA: Afterwards? When I am no longer?

KROGSTAD: Have you forgotten that it is I who have the keeping of your reputation? (NORA stands speechlessly looking at him.) Well, now, I have warned you. Do not do anything foolish. When Helmer has had my letter, I shall expect a message from him. And be sure you remember that it is your husband himself who has forced me into such ways as this again. I will never forgive him for that. Goodbye, Mrs. Helmer. (Exit through the hall.)

NORA: (goes to the hall door, opens it slightly and listens) He is going. He is not putting the letter in the box. Oh no, no! that's impossible! (Opens the door by degrees.) What is that? He is standing outside. He is not going downstairs. Is he hesitating? Can he? (A letter drops into the box; then KROGSTAD'S footsteps are heard, until they die away as he goes downstairs. NORA utters a stifled cry, and runs across the room to the table by the sofa. A short pause.)

NORA: In the letter-box. (Steals across to the hall door.) There it lies—Torvald, Torvald, there is no hope for us now!

　　　(Mrs. LINDE comes in from the room on the left, carrying the dress.)

MRS. LINDE: There, I can't see anything more to mend now. Would you like to try it on?

NORA (in a hoarse whisper): Christine, come here.

MRS. LINDE (throwing the dress down on the sofa): What is the matter with you? You look so agitated!

NORA: Come here. Do you see that letter? There, look—you can see it through the glass in the letter-box.

MRS. LINDE: Yes, I see it.

NORA: That letter is from Krogstad.

MRS. LINDE: Nora—it was Krogstad who lent you the money!

NORA: Yes, and now Torvald will know all about it.

MRS. LINDE: Believe me, Nora, that's the best thing for both of you.

NORA: You don't know all. I forged a name.

MRS. LINDE: Good heavens!

NORA: I only want to say this to you, Christine—you must be my witness.

MRS. LINDE: Your witness? What do you mean? What am I to. . . .

NORA: If I should go out of my mind—and it might easily happen.

MRS. LINDE: Nora!

NORA: Or if anything else should happen to me—anything, for instance, that might prevent my being here—

MRS. LINDE: Nora! Nora! you are quite out of your mind.

NORA: And if it should happen that there were some one who wanted to take all the responsibility, all the blame, you understand.

MRS. LINDE: Yes, yes—but how can you suppose?

NORA: Then you must be my witness, that it is not true, Christine. I am not out of my mind at all; I am in my right senses now, and I tell you no one else has known anything about it; I, and I alone, did the whole thing. Remember that.

MRS. LINDE: I will, indeed. But I don't understand all this.

NORA: How should you understand it? A wonderful thing is going to happen!

MRS. LINDE: A wonderful thing?

NORA: Yes, a wonderful thing!—But it is so terrible, Christine; it mustn't happen, not for all the world.

MRS. LINDE: I will go at once and see Krogstad.

NORA: Don't go to him; he will do you some harm.

MRS. LINDE: There was a time when he would gladly do anything for my sake.

NORA: He?

MRS. LINDE: Where does he live?

NORA: How should I know? Yes (feeling in her pocket), here is his card. But the letter, the letter!

HELMER (calls from his room, knocking at the door): Nora!

NORA (cries out anxiously): Oh, what's that? What do you want?

HELMER: Don't be so frightened. We are not coming in; you have locked the door. Are you trying on your dress?

NORA: Yes, that's it. I look so nice, Torvald.

MRS. LINDE (who has read the card): I see he lives at the corner here.

NORA: Yes, but it's no use. It is hopeless. The letter is lying there in the box.

MRS. LINDE: And your husband keeps the key?

NORA: Yes, always.

MRS. LINDE: Krogstad must ask for his letter back unread, he must find some pretence.

NORA: But it is just at this time that Torvald generally. . . .

MRS. LINDE: You must delay him. Go in to him in the meantime. I will come back as soon as I can. (She goes out hurriedly through the hall door.)

NORA (goes to HELMER'S door, opens it and peeps in): Torvald!

HELMER (from the inner room): Well? May I venture at last to come into my own room again? Come along, Rank, now you will see—(Halting in the doorway.) But what is this?

NORA: What is what, dear?

HELMER: Rank led me to expect a splendid transformation.

RANK (in the doorway): I understood so, but evidently I was mistaken.

NORA: Yes, nobody is to have the chance of admiring me in my dress until tomorrow.

HELMER: But, my dear Nora, you look so worn out. Have you been practising too much?

NORA: No, I have not practised at all.

HELMER: But you will need to.

NORA: Yes, indeed I shall, Torvald. But I can't get on a bit without you to help me; I have absolutely forgotten the whole thing.

HELMER: Oh, we will soon work it up again.

NORA: Yes, help me, Torvald. Promise that you will! I am so nervous about it— all the people—. You must give yourself up to me entirely this evening. Not the tiniest bit of business—you mustn't even take a pen in your hand. Will you promise, Torvald dear?

HELMER: I promise. This evening I will be wholly and absolutely at your service, you helpless little mortal. Ah, by the way, first of all I will just—(Goes towards the hall door.)

NORA: What are you going to do there?

HELMER: Only see if any letters have come.

NORA: No, no! don't do that, Torvald!

HELMER: Why not?

NORA: Torvald, please don't. There is nothing there.

HELMER: Well, let me look. (Turns to go to the letter-box. NORA, at the piano, plays the first bars of the Tarantella. HELMER stops in the doorway.) Aha!

NORA: I can't dance tomorrow if I don't practise with you.

HELMER (going up to her): Are you really so afraid of it, dear?

NORA: Yes, so dreadfully afraid of it. Let me practise at once; there is time now, before we go to dinner. Sit down and play for me, Torvald dear; criticise me, and correct me as you play.

HELMER: With great pleasure, if you wish me to. (Sits down at the piano.)

NORA: (takes out of the box a tambourine and a long variegated shawl. She hastily drapes the shawl round her. Then she springs to the front of the stage and calls out.) Now play for me! I am going to dance!

(HELMER plays and NORA dances. RANK stands by the piano behind HELMER, and looks on.)

HELMER (as he plays): Slower, slower!

NORA: I can't do it any other way.

HELMER: Not so violently, Nora!

NORA: This is the way.

HELMER (stops playing): No, no—that is not a bit right.

NORA (laughing and swinging the tambourine): Didn't I tell you so?

RANK: Let me play for her.

HELMER (getting up): Yes, do. I can correct her better then.

(RANK sits down at the piano and plays. NORA dances more and more wildly. HELMER has taken up a position beside the stove, and during her dance gives her frequent instructions. She does not seem to hear him; her hair comes down and falls over her shoulders; she pays no attention to it, but goes on dancing. Enter Mrs. LINDE.)

MRS. LINDE (standing as if spell-bound in the doorway): Oh!

NORA: (as she dances) Such fun, Christine!

HELMER: My dear darling Nora, you are dancing as if your life depended on it.

NORA: So it does.

HELMER: Stop, Rank; this is sheer madness. Stop, I tell you! (RANK stops playing, and NORA suddenly stands still. HELMER goes up to her.) I could never have believed it. You have forgotten everything I taught you.

NORA (throwing away the tambourine): There, you see.

HELMER: You will want a lot of coaching.

NORA: Yes, you see how much I need it. You must coach me up to the last minute. Promise me that, Torvald!

HELMER: You can depend on me.

NORA: You must not think of anything but me, either today or tomorrow; you mustn't open a single letter—not even open the letter-box.

HELMER: Ah, you are still afraid of that fellow?

NORA: Yes, indeed I am.

HELMER: Nora, I can tell from your looks that there is a letter from him lying there.

NORA: I don't know; I think there is; but you must not read anything of that kind now. Nothing horrid must come between us until this is all over.

RANK (whispers to HELMER): You mustn't contradict her.

HELMER (taking her in his arms): The child shall have her way. But tomorrow night, after you have danced.

NORA: Then you will be free: (The MAID appears in the doorway to the right.)

MAID: Dinner is served, ma'am.

NORA: We will have champagne, Helen.

MAID: Very good, ma'am. [Exit.]

HELMER: Hullo!—are we going to have a banquet?

NORA: Yes, a champagne banquet until the small hours. (Calls out.) And a few macaroons, Helen—lots, just for once!

HELMER: Come, come, don't be so wild and nervous. Be my own little skylark, as you used to.

NORA: Yes, dear, I will. But go in now and you too, Doctor Rank. Christine, you must help me to do up my hair.

RANK (whispers to HELMER as they go out): I suppose there is nothing—she is not expecting anything?

HELMER: Far from it, my dear fellow; it is simply nothing more than this childish nervousness I was telling you of. (They go into the right-hand room.)

NORA: Well!

MRS. LINDE: Gone out of town.

NORA: I could tell from your face.

MRS. LINDE: He is coming home tomorrow evening. I wrote a note for him.

NORA: You should have let it alone; you must prevent nothing. After all, it is splendid to be waiting for a wonderful thing to happen.

MRS. LINDE: What is it that you are waiting for?

NORA: Oh, you wouldn't understand. Go in to them, I will come in a moment. (Mrs. LINDE goes into the dining-room. NORA stands still for a little while, as if to compose herself. Then she looks at her watch.) Five o'clock. Seven hours until midnight; and then four-and-twenty hours until the next midnight. Then the Tarantella will be over. Twenty-four and seven? Thirty-one hours to live.

HELMER (from the doorway on the right): Where's my little skylark?

NORA (going to him with her arms outstretched): Here she is!

ACT III

> (*THE SAME SCENE.—The table has been placed in the middle of the stage, with chairs around it. A lamp is burning on the table. The door into the hall stands open. Dance music is heard in the room above. Mrs. LINDE is sitting at the table idly turning over the leaves of a book; she tries to read, but does not seem able to collect her thoughts. Every now and then she listens intently for a sound at the outer door.*)

MRS. LINDE (looking at her watch): Not yet—and the time is nearly up. If only he does not. (Listens again.) Ah, there he is. (Goes into the hall and opens the outer door carefully. Light footsteps are heard on the stairs. She whispers.) Come in. There is no one here.

KROGSTAD (in the doorway): I found a note from you at home. What does this mean?

MRS. LINDE: It is absolutely necessary that I should have a talk with you.

KROGSTAD: Really? And is it absolutely necessary that it should be here?

MRS. LINDE: It is impossible where I live; there is no private entrance to my rooms. Come in; we are quite alone. The maid is asleep, and the Helmers are at the dance upstairs.

KROGSTAD (coming into the room): Are the Helmers really at a dance tonight?

MRS. LINDE: Yes, why not?

KROGSTAD: Certainly—why not?

MRS. LINDE: Now, Nils, let us have a talk.

KROGSTAD: Can we two have anything to talk about?

MRS. LINDE: We have a great deal to talk about.

KROGSTAD: I shouldn't have thought so.

MRS. LINDE: No, you have never properly understood me.

KROGSTAD: Was there anything else to understand except what was obvious to all the world—a heartless woman jilts a man when a more lucrative chance turns up?

MRS. LINDE: Do you believe I am as absolutely heartless as all that? And do you believe that I did it with a light heart?

KROGSTAD: Didn't you?

MRS. LINDE: Nils, did you really think that?

KROGSTAD: If it were as you say, why did you write to me as you did at the time?

MRS. LINDE: I could do nothing else. As I had to break with you, it was my duty also to put an end to all that you felt for me.

KROGSTAD (wringing his hands): So that was it. And all this—only for the sake of money!

MRS. LINDE: You must not forget that I had a helpless mother and two little brothers. We couldn't wait for you, Nils; your prospects seemed hopeless then.

KROGSTAD: That may be so, but you had no right to throw me over for anyone else's sake.

MRS. LINDE: Indeed I don't know. Many a time did I ask myself if I had the right to do it.

KROGSTAD (more gently): When I lost you, it was as if all the solid ground went from under my feet. Look at me now—I am a shipwrecked man clinging to a bit of wreckage.

MRS. LINDE: But help may be near.

KROGSTAD: It was near; but then you came and stood in my way.

MRS. LINDE: Unintentionally, Nils. It was only today that I learned it was your place I was going to take in the Bank.

KROGSTAD: I believe you, if you say so. But now that you know it, are you not going to give it up to me?

MRS. LINDE: No, because that would not benefit you in the least.

KROGSTAD: Oh, benefit, benefit—I would have done it whether or no.

MRS. LINDE: I have learned to act prudently. Life, and hard, bitter necessity have taught me that.

KROGSTAD: And life has taught me not to believe in fine speeches.

MRS. LINDE: Then life has taught you something very reasonable. But deeds you must believe in?

KROGSTAD: What do you mean by that?

MRS. LINDE: You said you were like a shipwrecked man clinging to some wreckage.

KROGSTAD: I had good reason to say so.

MRS. LINDE: Well, I am like a shipwrecked woman clinging to some wreckage—no one to mourn for, no one to care for.

KROGSTAD: It was your own choice.

MRS. LINDE: There was no other choice—then.

KROGSTAD: Well, what now?

MRS. LINDE: Nils, how would it be if we two shipwrecked people could join forces?

KROGSTAD: What are you saying?

MRS. LINDE: Two on the same piece of wreckage would stand a better chance than each on their own.

KROGSTAD: Christine I. . . .

MRS. LINDE: What do you suppose brought me to town?

KROGSTAD: Do you mean that you gave me a thought?

MRS. LINDE: I could not endure life without work. All my life, as long as I can remember, I have worked, and it has been my greatest and only pleasure. But now I am quite alone in the world—my life is so dreadfully empty and I feel so forsaken. There is not the least pleasure in working for one's self. Nils, give me someone and something to work for.

KROGSTAD: I don't trust that. It is nothing but a woman's overstrained sense of generosity that prompts you to make such an offer of yourself.

MRS. LINDE: Have you ever noticed anything of the sort in me?

KROGSTAD: Could you really do it? Tell me—do you know all about my past life?

MRS. LINDE: Yes.

KROGSTAD: And do you know what they think of me here?

MRS. LINDE: You seemed to me to imply that with me you might have been quite another man.

KROGSTAD: I am certain of it.

MRS. LINDE: Is it too late now?

KROGSTAD: Christine, are you saying this deliberately? Yes, I am sure you are. I see it in your face. Have you really the courage, then?

MRS. LINDE: I want to be a mother to someone, and your children need a mother. We two need each other. Nils, I have faith in your real character—I can dare anything together with you.

KROGSTAD (grasps her hands): Thanks, thanks, Christine! Now I shall find a way to clear myself in the eyes of the world. Ah, but I forgot—

MRS. LINDE (listening): Hush! The Tarantella! Go, go!

KROGSTAD: Why? What is it?

MRS. LINDE: Do you hear them up there? When that is over, we may expect them back.

KROGSTAD: Yes, yes—I will go. But it is all no use. Of course you are not aware what steps I have taken in the matter of the Helmers.

MRS. LINDE: Yes, I know all about that.

KROGSTAD: And in spite of that have you the courage to. . . .

MRS. LINDE: I understand very well to what lengths a man like you might be driven by despair.

KROGSTAD: If I could only undo what I have done!

MRS. LINDE: You cannot. Your letter is lying in the letter-box now.

KROGSTAD: Are you sure of that?

MRS. LINDE: Quite sure, but. . . .

KROGSTAD: (with a searching look at her) Is that what it all means?—that you want to save your friend at any cost? Tell me frankly. Is that it?

MRS. LINDE: Nils, a woman who has once sold herself for another's sake, doesn't do it a second time.

KROGSTAD: I will ask for my letter back.

MRS. LINDE: No, no.

KROGSTAD: Yes, of course I will. I will wait here until Helmer comes; I will tell him he must give me my letter back—that it only concerns my dismissal—that he is not to read it.

MRS. LINDE: No, Nils, you must not recall your letter.

KROGSTAD: But, tell me, wasn't it for that very purpose that you asked me to meet you here?

MRS. LINDE: In my first moment of fright, it was. But twenty-four hours have elapsed since then, and in that time I have witnessed incredible things in this house. Helmer must know all about it. This unhappy secret must be disclosed; they must have a complete understanding between them, which is impossible with all this concealment and falsehood going on.

KROGSTAD: Very well, if you will take the responsibility. But there is one thing I can do in any case, and I shall do it at once.

MRS. LINDE (listening): You must be quick and go! The dance is over; we are not safe a moment longer.

KROGSTAD: I will wait for you below.

MRS. LINDE: Yes, do. You must see me back to my door.

KROGSTAD: I have never had such an amazing piece of good fortune in my life! (Goes out through the outer door. The door between the room and the hall remains open.)

MRS. LINDE (tidying up the room and laying her hat and cloak ready): What a difference! what a difference! Someone to work for and live for—a home to bring comfort into. That I will do, indeed. I wish they would be quick and come. (Listens.) Ah, there they are now. I must put on my things. (Takes up her hat and cloak. HELMER'S and NORA'S voices are heard outside; a key is turned, and HELMER brings NORA almost by force into the hall. She is in an Italian costume with a large black shawl around her; he is in evening dress, and a black domino which is flying open.)

NORA (hanging back in the doorway, and struggling with him): No, no, no!—don't take me in. I want to go upstairs again; I don't want to leave so early.

HELMER: But, my dearest Nora.

NORA: Please, Torvald dear—please, please—only an hour more.

HELMER: Not a single minute, my sweet Nora. You know that was our agreement. Come along into the room; you are catching cold standing there. (He brings her gently into the room, in spite of her resistance.)

MRS. LINDE: Good evening.

NORA: Christine!

HELMER: You here, so late, Mrs. Linde?

MRS. LINDE: Yes, you must excuse me; I was so anxious to see Nora in her dress.

NORA: Have you been sitting here waiting for me?

MRS. LINDE: Yes, unfortunately I came too late, you had already gone upstairs; and I thought I couldn't go away again without having seen you.

HELMER (taking off NORA's shawl): Yes, take a good look at her. I think she is worth looking at. Isn't she charming, Mrs. Linde?

MRS. LINDE: Yes, indeed she is.

HELMER: Doesn't she look remarkably pretty? Everyone thought so at the dance. But she is terribly self-willed, this sweet little person. What are we to do with her? You will hardly believe that I had almost to bring her away by force.

NORA: Torvald, you will repent not having let me stay, even if it were only for half an hour.

HELMER: Listen to her, Mrs. Linde! She had danced her Tarantella, and it had been a tremendous success, as it deserved—although possibly the performance was a trifle too realistic—a little more so, I mean, than was strictly compatible with the limitations of art. But never mind about that! The chief thing is, she had made a success—she had made a tremendous success. Do you think I was going to let her remain there after that, and spoil the effect? No, indeed! I took my charming little Capri maiden—my capricious little Capri maiden, I should say—on my arm; took one quick turn round the room; a curtsey on either side, and, as they say in novels, the beautiful apparition disappeared. An exit ought always to be effective, Mrs. Linde; but that is what I cannot make Nora understand. Pooh! this room is hot. (Throws his domino on a chair, and opens the door of his room.) Hullo! it's all dark in here. Oh, of course—excuse me. (He goes in, and lights some candles.)

NORA (in a hurried and breathless whisper): Well?

MRS. LINDE (in a low voice): I have had a talk with him.

NORA: Yes, and?

MRS. LINDE: Nora, you must tell your husband all about it.

NORA (in an expressionless voice): I knew it.

MRS. LINDE: You have nothing to be afraid of as far as Krogstad is concerned; but you must tell him.

NORA: I won't tell him.

MRS. LINDE: Then the letter will.

NORA: Thank you, Christine. Now I know what I must do. Hush—!

HELMER (coming in again): Well, Mrs. Linde, have you admired her?

MRS. LINDE: Yes, and now I will say goodnight.

HELMER: What, already? Is this yours, this knitting?

MRS. LINDE (taking it): Yes, thank you, I had very nearly forgotten it.

HELMER: So you knit?

MRS. LINDE: Of course.

HELMER: Do you know, you ought to embroider.

MRS. LINDE: Really? Why?

HELMER: Yes, it's far more becoming. Let me show you. You hold the embroidery thus in your left hand, and use the needle with the right—like this—with a long, easy sweep. Do you see?

MRS. LINDE: Yes, perhaps.

HELMER: But in the case of knitting—that can never be anything but ungraceful; look here—the arms close together, the knitting-needles going up and down—it has a sort of Chinese effect. That was really excellent champagne they gave us.

MRS. LINDE: Well, goodnight, Nora, and don't be self-willed any more.

HELMER: That's right, Mrs. Linde.

MRS. LINDE: Goodnight, Mr. Helmer.

HELMER (accompanying her to the door): Goodnight, goodnight. I hope you will get home all right. I should be very happy to—but you haven't any great distance to go. Goodnight, goodnight. (She goes out; he shuts the door after her, and comes in again.) Ah!—at last we have got rid of her. She is a frightful bore, that woman.

NORA: Aren't you very tired, Torvald?

HELMER: No, not in the least.

NORA: Nor sleepy?

HELMER: Not a bit. On the contrary, I feel extraordinarily lively. And you?—you really look both tired and sleepy.

NORA: Yes, I am very tired. I want to go to sleep at once.

HELMER: There, you see it was quite right of me not to let you stay there any longer.

NORA: Everything you do is quite right, Torvald.

HELMER (kissing her on the forehead): Now my little skylark is speaking reasonably. Did you notice what good spirits Rank was in this evening?

NORA: Really? Was he? I didn't speak to him at all.

HELMER: And I very little, but I have not for a long time seen him in such good form. (Looks for a while at her and then goes nearer to her.) It is delightful to be at home by ourselves again, to be all alone with you—you fascinating, charming little darling!

NORA: Don't look at me like that, Torvald.

HELMER: Why shouldn't I look at my dearest treasure?—at all the beauty that is mine, all my very own?

NORA (going to the other side of the table): You mustn't say things like that to me tonight.

HELMER (following her): You have still got the Tarantella in your blood, I see. And it makes you more captivating than ever. Listen—the guests are beginning to go now. (In a lower voice.) Nora—soon the whole house will be quiet.

NORA: Yes, I hope so.

HELMER: Yes, my own darling Nora. Do you know, when I am out at a party with you like this, why I speak so little to you, keep away from you, and only send a stolen glance in your direction now and then?—do you know why I do that? It is because I make believe to myself that we are secretly in love, and you are my secretly promised bride, and that no one suspects there is anything between us.

NORA: Yes, yes—I know very well your thoughts are with me all the time.

HELMER: And when we are leaving, and I am putting the shawl over your beautiful young shoulders—on your lovely neck—then I imagine that you are my young bride and that we have just come from the wedding, and I am bringing you for the first time into our home—to be alone with you for the first time—quite alone with my shy little darling! All this evening I have longed for nothing but you. When I watched the seductive figures of the Tarantella, my blood was on fire; I could endure it no longer, and that was why I brought you down so early.

NORA: Go away, Torvald! You must let me go. I won't.

HELMER: What's that? You're joking, my little Nora! You won't—you won't? Am I not your husband? (A knock is heard at the outer door.)

NORA (starting): Did you hear?

HELMER (going into the hall): Who is it?

RANK (outside): It is I. May I come in for a moment?

HELMER (in a fretful whisper): Oh, what does he want now? (Aloud.) Wait a minute! (Unlocks the door.) Come, that's kind of you not to pass by our door.

RANK: I thought I heard your voice, and felt as if I should like to look in. (With a swift glance round.) Ah, yes!—these dear familiar rooms. You are very happy and cosy in here, you two.

HELMER: It seems to me that you looked after yourself pretty well upstairs too.

RANK: Excellently. Why shouldn't I? Why shouldn't one enjoy everything in this world?—at any rate as much as one can, and as long as one can. The wine was capital.

HELMER: Especially the champagne.

RANK: So you noticed that too? It is almost incredible how much I managed to put away!

NORA: Torvald drank a great deal of champagne tonight too.

RANK: Did he?

NORA: Yes, and he is always in such good spirits afterwards.

RANK: Well, why should one not enjoy a merry evening after a well-spent day?

HELMER: Well spent? I am afraid I can't take credit for that.

RANK (clapping him on the back): But I can, you know!

NORA: Doctor Rank, you must have been occupied with some scientific investigation today.

RANK: Exactly.

HELMER: Just listen!—little Nora talking about scientific investigations!

NORA: And may I congratulate you on the result?

RANK: Indeed you may.

NORA: Was it favourable, then?

RANK: The best possible, for both doctor and patient—certainty.

NORA (quickly and searchingly): Certainty?

RANK: Absolute certainty. So wasn't I entitled to make a merry evening of it after that?

NORA: Yes, you certainly were, Doctor Rank. Helmer. I think so too, so long as you don't have to pay for it in the morning.

RANK: Oh well, one can't have anything in this life without paying for it.

NORA: Doctor Rank—are you fond of fancy-dress balls?

RANK: Yes, if there is a fine lot of pretty costumes.

NORA: Tell me—what shall we two wear at the next?

HELMER: Little featherbrain!—are you thinking of the next already?

RANK: We two? Yes, I can tell you. You shall go as a good fairy.

HELMER: Yes, but what do you suggest as an appropriate costume for that?

RANK: Let your wife go dressed just as she is in everyday life.

HELMER: That was really very prettily turned. But can't you tell us what you will be?

RANK: Yes, my dear friend, I have quite made up my mind about that.

HELMER: Well?

RANK: At the next fancy-dress ball I shall be invisible.

HELMER: That's a good joke!

RANK: There is a big black hat—have you never heard of hats that make you invisible? If you put one on, no one can see you.

HELMER (suppressing a smile): Yes, you are quite right.

RANK: But I am clean forgetting what I came for. Helmer, give me a cigar—one of the dark Havanas.

HELMER: With the greatest pleasure. (Offers him his case.)

RANK (takes a cigar and cuts off the end): Thanks.

NORA (striking a match): Let me give you a light.

RANK: Thank you. (She holds the match for him to light his cigar.) And now goodbye!

HELMER: Goodbye, goodbye, dear old man!

NORA: Sleep well, Doctor Rank.

RANK: Thank you for that wish.

NORA: Wish me the same.

RANK: You? Well, if you want me to sleep well! And thanks for the light. (He nods to them both and goes out.)

HELMER (in a subdued voice): He has drunk more than he ought.

NORA (absently): Maybe. (HELMER takes a bunch of keys out of his pocket and goes into the hall.) Torvald! what are you going to do there?

HELMER: Emptying the letter-box; it is quite full; there will be no room to put the newspaper in tomorrow morning.

NORA: Are you going to work tonight?

HELMER: You know quite well I'm not. What is this? Someone has been at the lock.

NORA: At the lock?

HELMER: Yes, someone has. What can it mean? I should never have thought the maid—. Here is a broken hairpin. Nora, it is one of yours.

NORA (quickly): Then it must have been the children.

HELMER: Then you must get them out of those ways. There, at last I have got it open. (Takes out the contents of the letter-box, and calls to the kitchen.) Helen!— Helen, put out the light over the front door. (Goes back into the room and shuts the door into the hall. He holds out his hand full of letters.) Look at that— look what a heap of them there are. (Turning them over.) What on earth is that?

NORA: (at the window) The letter—No! Torvald, no!

HELMER: Two cards—of Rank's.

NORA: Of Doctor Rank's?

HELMER (looking at them): Doctor Rank. They were on the top. He must have put them in when he went out.

NORA: Is there anything written on them?

HELMER: There is a black cross over the name. Look there—what an uncomfortable idea! It looks as if he were announcing his own death.

NORA: It is just what he is doing.

HELMER: What? Do you know anything about it? Has he said anything to you?

NORA: Yes. He told me that when the cards came it would be his leave-taking from us. He means to shut himself up and die.

HELMER: My poor old friend! Certainly I knew we should not have him very long with us. But so soon! And so he hides himself away like a wounded animal.

NORA: If it has to happen, it is best it should be without a word—don't you think so, Torvald?

HELMER (walking up and down): He had so grown into our lives. I can't think of him as having gone out of them. He, with his sufferings and his loneliness, was like a cloudy background to our sunlit happiness. Well, perhaps it is best so. For him, anyway. (Standing still.) And perhaps for us too, Nora. We two are thrown quite upon each other now. (Puts his arms round her.) My darling wife, I don't feel as if I could hold you tight enough. Do you know, Nora, I have often wished that you might be threatened by some great danger, so that I might risk my life's blood, and everything, for your sake.

NORA (disengages herself, and says firmly and decidedly): Now you must read your letters, Torvald.

HELMER: No, no; not tonight. I want to be with you, my darling wife.

NORA: With the thought of your friend's death?

HELMER: You are right, it has affected us both. Something ugly has come between us—the thought of the horrors of death. We must try and rid our minds of that. Until then—we will each go to our own room.

NORA (hanging on his neck:) Goodnight, Torvald—Goodnight!

HELMER (kissing her on the forehead) Goodnight, my little singing-bird. Sleep sound, Nora. Now I will read my letters through. (He takes his letters and goes into his room, shutting the door after him.)

NORA (gropes distractedly about, seizes HELMER'S domino, throws it round her, while she says in quick, hoarse, spasmodic whispers): Never to see him again. Never! Never! (Puts her shawl over her head.) Never to see my children again either—never again. Never! Never!—Ah! the icy, black water—the unfathomable depths—If only it were over! He has got it now—now he is reading it. Goodbye, Torvald and my children! (She is about to rush out through the hall, when HELMER opens his door hurriedly and stands with an open letter in his hand.)

HELMER: Nora!

NORA: Ah!

HELMER: What is this? Do you know what is in this letter?

NORA: Yes, I know. Let me go! Let me get out!

HELMER (holding her back): Where are you going?

NORA (trying to get free): You shan't save me, Torvald!

HELMER (reeling): True? Is this true, that I read here? Horrible! No, no—it is impossible that it can be true.

NORA: It is true. I have loved you above everything else in the world.

HELMER: Oh, don't let us have any silly excuses.

NORA (taking a step towards him): Torvald!

HELMER: Miserable creature—what have you done?

NORA: Let me go. You shall not suffer for my sake. You shall not take it upon yourself.

HELMER: No tragic airs, please. (Locks the hall door.) Here you shall stay and give me an explanation. Do you understand what you have done? Answer me! Do you understand what you have done?

NORA (looks steadily at him and says with a growing look of coldness in her face): Yes, now I am beginning to understand thoroughly.

HELMER (walking about the room): What a horrible awakening! All these eight years—she who was my joy and pride—a hypocrite, a liar—worse, worse—a criminal! The unutterable ugliness of it all!—For shame! For shame! (NORA is silent and looks steadily at him. He stops in front of her.) I ought to have suspected that something of the sort would happen. I ought to have foreseen it. All your father's want of principle—be silent!—all your father's want of principle has come out in you. No religion, no morality, no sense of duty. How I am punished for having winked at what he did! I did it for your sake, and this is how you repay me.

NORA: Yes, that's just it.

HELMER: Now you have destroyed all my happiness. You have ruined all my future. It is horrible to think of! I am in the power of an unscrupulous man; he can do what he likes with me, ask anything he likes of me, give me any orders he pleases—I dare not refuse. And I must sink to such miserable depths because of a thoughtless woman!

NORA: When I am out of the way, you will be free.

HELMER: No fine speeches, please. Your father had always plenty of those ready, too. What good would it be to me if you were out of the way, as you say? Not the slightest. He can make the affair known everywhere; and if he does, I may be falsely suspected of having been a party to your criminal action. Very likely people will think I was behind it all—that it was I who prompted you! And I have to thank you for all this—you whom I have cherished during the whole of our married life. Do you understand now what it is you have done for me?

NORA (coldly and quietly): Yes.

HELMER: It is so incredible that I can't take it in. But we must come to some understanding. Take off that shawl. Take it off, I tell you. I must try and appease him some way or another. The matter must be hushed up at any cost. And as for you and me, it must appear as if everything between us were just as before—but naturally only in the eyes of the world. You will still remain in my house, that is a matter of course. But I shall not allow you to bring up the children; I dare not trust them to you. To think that I should be obliged to say so to one whom I have loved so dearly, and whom I still. No, that is all over. From this moment happiness is not the question; all that concerns us is to save the remains, the fragments, the appearance.

(A ring is heard at the front-door bell.)

HELMER: (with a start) What is that? So late! Can the worst? Can he? Hide yourself, Nora. Say you are ill.

(NORA stands motionless. HELMER goes and unlocks the hall door.)

MAID (half-dressed, comes to the door): A letter for the mistress.

HELMER: Give it to me. (Takes the letter, and shuts the door.) Yes, it is from him. You shall not have it; I will read it myself.

NORA: Yes, read it.

HELMER (standing by the lamp): I scarcely have the courage to do it. It may mean ruin for both of us. No, I must know. (Tears open the letter, runs his eye over a few lines, looks at a paper enclosed, and gives a shout of joy.) Nora! (She looks at him questioningly.) Nora!—No, I must read it once again—. Yes, it is true! I am saved! Nora, I am saved!

NORA: And I?

HELMER: You too, of course; we are both saved, both you and I. Look, he sends you your bond back. He says he regrets and repents—that a happy change in his life—never mind what he says! We are saved, Nora! No one can do anything to you. Oh, Nora, Nora!—no, first I must destroy these hateful things. Let me see—. (Takes a look at the bond.) No, no, I won't look at it. The whole thing shall be nothing but a bad dream to me. (Tears up the bond and both letters, throws them all into the stove, and watches them burn.) There—now it doesn't exist any longer. He says that since Christmas Eve you . . . These must have been three dreadful days for you, Nora.

NORA: I have fought a hard fight these three days.

HELMER: And suffered agonies, and seen no way out but. . . . No, we won't call any of the horrors to mind. We will only shout with joy, and keep saying, "It's all over! It's all over!" Listen to me, Nora. You don't seem to realise that it is all over. What is this?—such a cold, set face! My poor little Nora, I quite understand; you don't feel as if you could believe that I have forgiven you. But it is true, Nora, I swear it; I have forgiven you everything. I know that what you did, you did out of love for me.

NORA: That is true.

HELMER: You have loved me as a wife ought to love her husband. Only you had not sufficient knowledge to judge of the means you used. But do you suppose you are any the less dear to me, because you don't understand how to act on your own responsibility? No, no; only lean on me; I will advise you and direct you. I should not be a man if this womanly helplessness did not just give you a double attractiveness in my eyes. You must not think anymore about the hard things I said in my first moment of consternation, when I thought everything was going to overwhelm me. I have forgiven you, Nora; I swear to you I have forgiven you.

NORA: Thank you for your forgiveness. (She goes out through the door to the right.)

HELMER: No, don't go—. (Looks in.) What are you doing in there?

NORA (from within): Taking off my fancy dress.

HELMER (standing at the open door): Yes, do. Try and calm yourself, and make your mind easy again, my frightened little singing-bird. Be at rest, and feel secure; I have broad wings to shelter you under. (Walks up and down by the door.) How warm and cosy our home is, Nora. Here is shelter for you; here I will protect you like a hunted dove that I have saved from a hawk's claws; I will bring peace to your poor beating heart. It will come, little by little, Nora, believe me. Tomorrow morning you will look upon it all quite differently; soon everything will be just as it was before. Very soon you won't need me to assure you that I have forgiven you; you will yourself feel the certainty that I have done so. Can you suppose I should ever think of such a thing as repudiating you, or even reproaching you? You have no idea what a true man's heart is like, Nora. There is something so indescribably sweet and satisfying, to a man, in the knowledge that he has forgiven his wife—forgiven her freely, and with all his heart. It seems as if that had made her, as it were, doubly his own; he has given her a new life, so to speak; and she has in a way become both wife and child to him. So you shall be for me after this, my little scared, helpless darling. Have no anxiety about anything, Nora; only be frank and open with me, and I will serve as will and conscience both to you. What is this? Not gone to bed? Have you changed your things?

NORA (in everyday dress): Yes, Torvald, I have changed my things now.

HELMER: But what for?—so late as this.

NORA: I shall not sleep tonight.

HELMER: But, my dear Nora.

NORA (looking at her watch): It is not so very late. Sit down here, Torvald. You and I have much to say to one another. (She sits down at one side of the table.)

HELMER: Nora—what is this?—this cold, set face?

NORA: Sit down. It will take some time; I have a lot to talk over with you.

HELMER (sits down at the opposite side of the table): You alarm me, Nora!—and I don't understand you.

NORA: No, that is just it. You don't understand me, and I have never understood you either—before tonight. No, you mustn't interrupt me. You must simply listen to what I say. Torvald, this is a settling of accounts.

HELMER: What do you mean by that?

NORA (after a short silence): Isn't there one thing that strikes you as strange in our sitting here like this?

HELMER: What is that?

NORA: We have been married now eight years. Does it not occur to you that this is the first time we two, you and I, husband and wife, have had a serious conversation?

HELMER: What do you mean by serious?

NORA: In all these eight years—longer than that—from the very beginning of our acquaintance, we have never exchanged a word on any serious subject.

HELMER: Was it likely that I would be continually and forever telling you about worries that you could not help me to bear?

NORA: I am not speaking about business matters. I say that we have never sat down in earnest together to try and get at the bottom of anything.

HELMER: But, dearest Nora, would it have been any good to you?

NORA: That is just it; you have never understood me. I have been greatly wronged, Torvald—first by papa and then by you.

HELMER: What! By us two—by us two, who have loved you better than anyone else in the world?

NORA (shaking her head): You have never loved me. You have only thought it pleasant to be in love with me.

HELMER: Nora, what do I hear you saying?

NORA: It is perfectly true, Torvald. When I was at home with papa, he told me his opinion about everything, and so I had the same opinions; and if I differed from him I concealed the fact, because he would not have liked it. He called me his doll-child, and he played with me just as I used to play with my dolls. And when I came to live with you. . . .

HELMER: What sort of an expression is that to use about our marriage?

NORA (undisturbed): I mean that I was simply transferred from papa's hands into yours. You arranged everything according to your own taste, and so I got the same tastes as you or else I pretended to, I am really not quite sure which— I think sometimes the one and sometimes the other. When I look back on it, it seems to me as if I had been living here like a poor woman—just from hand to mouth. I have existed merely to perform tricks for you, Torvald. But you would have it so. You and papa have committed a great sin against me. It is your fault that I have made nothing of my life.

HELMER: How unreasonable and how ungrateful you are, Nora! Have you not been happy here?

NORA: No, I have never been happy. I thought I was, but it has never really been so.

HELMER: Not—not happy!

NORA: No, only merry. And you have always been so kind to me. But our home has been nothing but a playroom. I have been your doll-wife, just as at home I was papa's doll-child; and here the children have been my dolls. I thought it great fun when you played with me, just as they thought it great fun when I played with them. That is what our marriage has been, Torvald.

HELMER: There is some truth in what you say—exaggerated and strained as your view of it is. But for the future it shall be different. Playtime shall be over, and lesson-time shall begin.

NORA: Whose lessons? Mine, or the children's?

HELMER: Both yours and the children's, my darling Nora.

NORA: Alas, Torvald, you are not the man to educate me into being a proper wife for you.

HELMER: And you can say that!

NORA: And I—how am I fitted to bring up the children?

HELMER: Nora!

NORA: Didn't you say so yourself a little while ago—that you dare not trust me to bring them up?

HELMER: In a moment of anger! Why do you pay any heed to that?

NORA: Indeed, you were perfectly right. I am not fit for the task. There is another task I must undertake first. I must try and educate myself—you are not the man to help me in that. I must do that for myself. And that is why I am going to leave you now.

HELMER (springing up): What do you say?

NORA: I must stand quite alone, if I am to understand myself and everything about me. It is for that reason that I cannot remain with you any longer.

HELMER: Nora, Nora!

NORA: I am going away from here now, at once. I am sure Christine will take me in for the night.

HELMER: You are out of your mind! I won't allow it! I forbid you!

NORA: It is no use forbidding me anything any longer. I will take with me what belongs to myself. I will take nothing from you, either now or later.

HELMER: What sort of madness is this!

NORA: Tomorrow I shall go home—I mean, to my old home. It will be easiest for me to find something to do there.

HELMER: You blind, foolish woman!

NORA: I must try and get some sense, Torvald.

HELMER: To desert your home, your husband and your children! And you don't consider what people will say!

NORA: I cannot consider that at all. I only know that it is necessary for me.

HELMER: It's shocking. This is how you would neglect your most sacred duties.

NORA: What do you consider my most sacred duties?

HELMER: Do I need to tell you that? Are they not your duties to your husband and your children?

NORA: I have other duties just as sacred.

HELMER: That you have not. What duties could those be?

NORA: Duties to myself.

HELMER: Before all else, you are a wife and a mother.

NORA: I don't believe that any longer. I believe that before all else I am a reasonable human being, just as you are—or, at all events, that I must try and become one. I know quite well, Torvald, that most people would think you right, and that views of that kind are to be found in books; but I can no longer content myself with what most people say, or with what is found in books. I must think over things for myself and get to understand them.

HELMER: Can you not understand your place in your own home? Have you not a reliable guide in such matters as that?—have you no religion?

NORA: I am afraid, Torvald, I do not exactly know what religion is.

HELMER: What are you saying?

NORA: I know nothing but what the clergyman said, when I went to be confirmed. He told us that religion was this, and that, and the other. When I am away from all this, and am alone, I will look into that matter too. I will see if what the clergyman said is true, or at all events if it is true for me.

HELMER: This is unheard of in a girl of your age! But if religion cannot lead you aright, let me try and awaken your conscience. I suppose you have some moral sense? Or—answer me—am I to think you have none?

NORA: I assure you, Torvald, that is not an easy question to answer. I really don't know. The thing perplexes me altogether. I only know that you and I look at it in quite a different light. I am learning, too, that the law is quite another thing from what I supposed; but I find it impossible to convince myself that the law is right. According to it a woman has no right to spare her old dying father, or to save her husband's life. I can't believe that.

HELMER: You talk like a child. You don't understand the conditions of the world in which you live.

NORA: No, I don't. But now I am going to try. I am going to see if I can make out who is right, the world or I.

HELMER: You are ill, Nora; you are delirious; I almost think you are out of your mind.

NORA: I have never felt my mind so clear and certain as tonight.

HELMER: And is it with a clear and certain mind that you forsake your husband and your children?

NORA: Yes, it is.

HELMER: Then there is only one possible explanation.

NORA: What is that?

HELMER: You do not love me anymore.

NORA: No, that is just it.

HELMER: Nora!—and you can say that?

NORA: It gives me great pain, Torvald, for you have always been so kind to me, but I cannot help it. I do not love you any more.

HELMER (regaining his composure): Is that a clear and certain conviction too?

NORA: Yes, absolutely clear and certain. That is the reason why I will not stay here any longer.

HELMER: And can you tell me what I have done to forfeit your love?

NORA: Yes, indeed I can. It was tonight, when the wonderful thing did not happen; then I saw you were not the man I had thought you were.

HELMER: Explain yourself better. I don't understand you.

NORA: I have waited so patiently for eight years; for, goodness knows, I knew very well that wonderful things don't happen every day. Then this horrible misfortune came upon me; and then I felt quite certain that the wonderful thing was going to happen at last. When Krogstad's letter was lying out there, never for a moment did I imagine that you would consent to accept this man's conditions. I was so absolutely certain that you would say to him: Publish the thing to the whole world. And when that was done. . . .

HELMER: Yes, what then?—when I had exposed my wife to shame and disgrace?

NORA: When that was done, I was so absolutely certain, you would come forward and take everything upon yourself, and say: I am the guilty one.

HELMER: Nora!

NORA: You mean that I would never have accepted such a sacrifice on your part? No, of course not. But what would my assurances have been worth against yours? That was the wonderful thing which I hoped for and feared; and it was to prevent that, that I wanted to kill myself.

HELMER: I would gladly work night and day for you, Nora—bear sorrow and want for your sake. But no man would sacrifice his honour for the one he loves.

NORA: It is a thing hundreds of thousands of women have done.

HELMER: Oh, you think and talk like a heedless child.

NORA: Maybe. But you neither think nor talk like the man I could bind myself to. As soon as your fear was over—and it was not fear for what threatened me, but for what might happen to you—when the whole thing was past, as far as you were concerned it was exactly as if nothing at all had happened. Exactly as before, I was your little skylark, your doll, which you would in future treat with doubly gentle care, because it was so brittle and fragile. (Getting up.) Torvald—it was then it dawned upon me that for eight years I had been living here with a strange man, and had borne him three children. Oh, I can't bear to think of it! I could tear myself into little bits!

HELMER (sadly): I see, I see. An abyss has opened between us—there is no denying it. But, Nora, would it not be possible to fill it up?

NORA: As I am now, I am no wife for you.

HELMER: I have it in me to become a different man.

NORA: Perhaps—if your doll is taken away from you.

HELMER: But to part!—to part from you! No, no, Nora, I can't understand that idea.

NORA (going out to the right): That makes it all the more certain that it must be done. (She comes back with her cloak and hat and a small bag which she puts on a chair by the table.)

HELMER: Nora, Nora, not now! Wait until tomorrow.

NORA (putting on her cloak): I cannot spend the night in a strange man's room.

HELMER: But can't we live here like brother and sister?

NORA (putting on her hat): You know very well that would not last long. (Puts the shawl round her.) Goodbye, Torvald. I won't see the little ones. I know they are in better hands than mine. As I am now, I can be of no use to them.

HELMER: But some day, Nora—some day?

NORA: How can I tell? I have no idea what is going to become of me.

HELMER: But you are my wife, whatever becomes of you.

NORA: Listen, Torvald. I have heard that when a wife deserts her husband's house, as I am doing now, he is legally freed from all obligations towards her. In any case, I set you free from all your obligations. You are not to feel yourself bound in the slightest way, any more than I shall. There must be perfect freedom on both sides. See, here is your ring back. Give me mine.

HELMER: That too?

NORA: That too.

HELMER: Here it is.

NORA: That's right. Now it is all over. I have put the keys here. The maids know all about everything in the house—better than I do. Tomorrow, after I have left her, Christine will come here and pack up my own things that I brought with me from home. I will have them sent after me.

HELMER: All over! All over!—Nora, shall you never think of me again?

NORA: I know I shall often think of you, the children, and this house.

HELMER: May I write to you, Nora?

NORA: No—never. You must not do that.

HELMER: But at least let me send you. . . .

NORA: Nothing—nothing.

HELMER: Let me help you if you are in want.

NORA: No. I can receive nothing from a stranger.

HELMER: Nora—can I never be anything more than a stranger to you?

NORA (taking her bag): Ah, Torvald, the most wonderful thing of all would have to happen.

HELMER: Tell me what that would be!

NORA: Both you and I would have to be so changed that . . . Oh, Torvald, I don't believe any longer in wonderful things happening.

HELMER: But I will believe in it. Tell me! So changed that?

NORA: That our life together would be a real wedlock. Goodbye. (She goes out through the hall.)

HELMER (sinks down on a chair at the door and buries his face in his hands:) Nora! Nora! (Looks round, and rises.) Empty. She is gone. (A hope flashes across his mind.) The most wonderful thing of all?

(The sound of a door shutting is heard from below.)

INQUIRING FURTHER

1. What are your thoughts on Nora's honesty? Was it right for her to keep the loan from Krogstad a secret? What about her forging her father's signature? What role do her white lies play in the story? Freewrite for five minutes about honesty in the play.

2. How would you characterize the marriage between Nora and Torvald? What is the significance of the pet names he uses for her? What other aspects of their relationship deserve investigation?

3. How important is the relationship between Mrs. Linde and Krogstad to your understanding of the play? Do they operate more to move the plot along or do they speak to important themes in the work? How does their relationship compare with the relationship between Nora and Torvald?

RESPONSES TO TRAGEDY

Events like natural disasters, wars, or the terrorist attacks of September 11th, have a collective impact on our points of view and change the tenor of our culture, bringing a loss of innocence and a painful knowledge gained. In these instances, artists often bring out the personal dimensions of traumatic events. Responses may also offer hope or seek to promote positive change, even as they struggle to help us understand the significance of these tragedies. The following selections provide insight into just a few of the experiences that have shaken our faith in the innocence of the world.

DOROTHEA LANGE, ARTHUR ROTHSTEIN, AND LEE RUSSELL

Images of the Great Depression

Images and resources for studying The Great Depression

FIGURE 16.1   *Evicted sharecroppers along highway 60, New Madrid County, Missouri* by Arthur Rothstein

FIGURE 16.2   *Sign at the FSA (Farm Security Administration) mobile camp for farm workers at Wilder, Idaho* by Lee Russell

FIGURE 16.3   *Waiting for Work on Edge of the Pea Field, Holtville, Imperial Valley, California, February 1937* by Dorothea Lange

The J. Paul Getty Museum, Los Angeles, Lange, Dorothea, Waiting for Work on Edge of the Pea Field, Holtville, Imperial Valley, California, February 1937, Gelatin silver, Image: 20.5 x 19.2 cm (8 1/16 x 7 9/16 in.), Sheet: 25.7 x 20.3 cm (10 1/8 x 8 in.)

INQUIRING FURTHER

1. Dorothea Lange, Arthur Rothstein, and Lee Russell were just three of many photographers working for the government's Farm Securities Administration (FSA). Their task was to capture images that might convince the public to expand support for displaced farmers. Do you find their photographs well suited to this purpose? Why or why not?

2. Which of the images in Figures 16.1–16.3 do you find the most compelling? Which elements of photography do you find the most significant? Write a one-or-more-page analysis of an image explaining how the photograph conveys its message.

3. Consider the additional information and images about the FSA photographers and the Great Depression on our CD. Consider what the photographs say about the relationships between art and social change.

RICHARD PRICE AND ANN HUDSON-PRICE

Richard Price (born in 1949) is the author of seven novels and a number of screenplays for Hollywood films, including Sea of Love *and* The

Color of Money. *His latest novel,* Samaritan, *depicts a TV writer's attempts to help the underprivileged residents of public housing projects and to connect with his teenage daughter. Price cowrote "Word on the Street" with his own daughter, Ann (born in 1985). They compiled the essay from their recorded observations in the aftermath of the September 11th attacks on the World Trade Center.*

Word on the Street

Conversations from the New New York

Cabby No. 1, Sept. 13

The taxi pulls to the curb across the street from the Police Academy on 20th and 3rd. Two thickly built, sandy-haired young men emerge from the back seat.

As they exit, the driver, a Pakistani, pats his forehead with a paper towel and exhales so profoundly that it seems as if he had been holding his breath since they entered his cab five and a half dollars ago.

The new passenger, coming up on his blind side, slides into the back without warning, unthinkingly slamming the door behind him. The driver nearly levitates off his seat. "Broadway and 44th?"

"Please, sir," he says, his voice feathery with tension. "Just give me a moment."

Kids No. 1, Army-Navy Sept. 18

5   "Dad? Do you know where I can get a pair of camouflage pants? The whole team has to wear camo to school tomorrow."

"Why?"

"I don't know. It's game day. Everybody has to wear the same stuff on a game day."

"But why camo? With all that's going on right now, they have to pick camo?"

"*Dad,*" her voice edged with tears, edged with the last eight days of her life. "It's *not* my *choice.*"

10   "O.K., O.K.," he quickly retreats. "No problem. No problem. How about an Army-Navy store?" he backpedals. "Let me call the one on 23rd Street, see if . . . . ”

They answer on the first ring—"Sorry, no more gas masks"—then hang up.

Cabby No. 2, Sept. 19

The driver is a heavyset man with a cropped beard. "God Is Great" is inscribed in Arabic on a Lucite placard that dangles from his rearview mirror along with a photograph of his two kids. There are more American flags fixed to the outside of his car than on a presidential motorcade.

"Thirty-third and Lex?"

"Yes," punching the meter. "So, sir. Are you having a good day?"

15   "Not really," the passenger says to the eyes in the rearview. "Are those your kids?"

"Yes," he answers. "My son and his sister. The boy goes to Stuyvesant, which is a problem right now; he has to take his classes at Brooklyn Tech. But the girl goes to St. John's, so there's no problem there. You have children yourself?"

"Yeah, two girls." Then, encouraged by the driver's chattiness: "Let me ask you, are people giving you a hard time out here?"

The driver's face slams down like a riot gate.

"Sir?" the passenger persists, trying to seek him out via the rearview mirror, but the driver maintains his silence, eyes on the road, all the way to 33rd Street, looking away even as he reaches back to accept the fare and tip.

Kids No. 2, Sept. 20

20   It took more than an hour to make it uptown to pick up his older daughter from her evacuated school that afternoon, another half-hour to find her on the street and an hour and a half through the semi-locked-down streets of Midtown to bring her back home.

"It was insane," she said. "It's like we were sitting in the cafeteria and we heard the fire alarm but really faintly, and we're looking at each other like, What bad judgment to have a fire drill now. You know, with everybody already freaked out as is. But O.K., so, we leave the cafeteria, everybody's crammed into the hallways and you can't even move, I went maybe 10 feet in five minutes.

"Then they say it's a false alarm, so we go back to lunch and we're all looking at each other like, That was not cool. A minute later, someone comes in, says: 'Get out. It *is* a drill. Get out *now*.'

"We're back in the hallway, packed, and because of the World Trade Center, a few people, me included, start thinking, Bomb. We get outside the building, I go up to a teacher and ask, 'Is this a fire drill or something else?'

"She says: 'I don't know, I don't know. Pretend it's not a drill and just *walk*. Walk away *now*.'

25   "I say, 'Should we go to our assigned evacuation spots?' She says: 'No. Just go. *Go*.' Then we see the bomb squad pull up.

"The kids who have cell phones are calling their parents and then they do something so unusual. They go up to other kids they don't even know and ask if anyone would like to call their parents, you know, offering them their phones; other kids announce that they live only two, three blocks away, and if anybody wants, they can come stay at their houses if they don't want to be out in the street. Everybody became so generous. It was almost worth the scare to see it.

"But then something happened, Dad? I don't think I'll ever get it out of my mind. There was this girl, my age, someone who I never thought of as particularly mature, kind of the opposite in fact, and, this girl, she goes up to one of the teachers and says very calmly, 'I want to get my sister from her class.' Teacher says: 'No. No way I can let you go do that.' The girl says, 'My sister is 6 years old, she gets scared easily, I know she wants me, and I am going to get her.' The teacher says: 'Look, she's with her own group, her own teacher, I'm sure she's fine. They probably told her it was just a fire drill.' And then, Dad, this girl, she says, 'But *I* know what's going on, and I *want* my *sister* with *me*.' "

His daughter takes a breather, her eyes glistening with unspilled tears. "I don't know, this girl, it's like in one minute flat, she went from being this flighty kind of kid to this instant adult. It's like she turned into iron. She was so strong and clear about things. I don't even really know her, but I felt so proud for her. . . . But I also felt so sad."

Her tears finally ran the rims and spilled down her cheeks. "I wish I could really find the words to explain to you how I felt."

30   It took her three weeks, but the words finally came, showing up on her father's desk early one morning, deposited there on her way to school.

"Dad, it's like these days, there are adults, and there are children. Only two camps now, no intermediate zone for teenagers like myself. If you possess the information, if you understand what's going on in the world, you're an adult, no matter what your biological age; all others are children.

"There is nothing that traditional 'adults' know that this new breed of 'child-adult' doesn't, and the gut instinct of kids my age to go to their parents and demand comfort, answers or whatever doesn't work now, because we are *aware* that we know just as much about the world as you do.

"So many of us have been forced into this new group overnight, like that girl I was telling you about and to some extent, myself.

"And along with the scariness that comes with being a member of this new group of adults without any actual adult experience, is the sadness that we bear for the years we had to surrender in order to accept this mutual burden with you."

Royalty, Sept. 29

35   It's the night of the unification bout for the middleweight belt, Felix Trinidad versus Bernard Hopkins, and the garden is boiling over with both the near-insanity of a mass gathering so soon after the events of the 11th, and the anticipation of the state-of-the-art violence to come.

The crowd is mad for Felix Trinidad, and there are Puerto Rican flags everywhere, reproduced on T-shirts, head wraps, pennants, scarves and, of course, flags as flags, flags so big it takes two men to display them; dozens of these tag teams work the landings between the multitiered seating sections, racing their pride around the natural oval of the building, blocking the views of hundreds of fans at a clip, although the general consensus seems to be for people to restrain themselves from shouting out something rude and to the point, because the vibes are such that anything, it feels, can lead to anything.

After two interminable hours of prelims, the fanfare that precedes a title bout finally begins. First there's the spotlighting of the usually schizophrenic mix of New York royalty in the crowd; Sharpton, Trump, Spike, Latrell, etc., followed by the calling up into the ring of past middleweight champs: Jake LaMotta, Emile Griffith and other less memorable titleholders. The crowd doesn't really cut loose though until the spotlight falls on Roberto Duran. Looking more like a heavyweight these days, the ex-champ milks the cheers, grinning, dancing, bathing in the love. . . .

But then, in the middle of his moment, there seems to be a secondary roar overtaking the first like a succeeding wave, this one a little stronger, a little more from the gut and strangely enough, focused slightly to the side of the ring itself, people half-rising now, some to cheer more loudly, others to track down the source, and there they are, maybe a dozen New York firemen in F.D.N.Y. T-shirts and jeans, heading for their places of honor next to the cast of "Oz," walking a little stiffly, some displaying awkward smiles, others giving up half-waves of acknowledgment, and one can only imagine the great sense of disorientation they must feel; heroes, grievers, survivors; the garden really pouring it on now, the fervid cheers gradually becoming more articulate, breaking down into three distinct sounds: U.S.A. U.S.A. U.S.A.

Tentatively, as if lowering themselves into scalding water, the city's newest royalty take their seats. (P.S.: Hopkins won the fight.)

Cabby No. 3, Oct. 3

40   "Fifty-ninth and Madison?"

The cab heads uptown, flags fluttering, another Yankee Doodle express. "So how's it shaking out here?" the fare asks.

"Business is bad," the cabby says. "Very bad. Come 9, 10 o'clock? This city is dead."

"Are people giving you a hard time?"

"Not really." The driver turns to face his passenger at a red light. "They've been pretty good. Mostly it's kind of polite interrogations, like, 'Where are you from, what did you do back in your country before you came here, *why* did you come here?'" The light changes and he turns back to the traffic.

45   "Where do you come from?" the fare asks. "I'm just curious."

"Bangladesh," he says.

"So nothing ugly? Well, that's good to hear."

"I tell you," he says, making eye contact through the mirror. "Do you know what I miss the most? The small talk. I enjoyed that very much. Now they get in, say take me to such and such and then nothing. Except for, you know, like I said, the polite interrogations."

"No, I hear you," his passenger says.

50   "Like you," the driver says, briefly turning again. "Like now."

Kids No. 3, Oct. 9

"Dad? Can I tell you something, you promise not to get mad at me?"

"Not really."

"I dropped my cellphone in the toilet," his younger daughter says. "It's dead."

"Don't worry about it. Take mine."

55   "Seriously?" Then, with as much guilt as relief, "What are you going to use?"

"Not your problem. It's just, you know, with everything going on these days? It makes me breathe easier to know that I can reach you no matter what."

The kid's face went taut, not what he intended.

"Look," touching her arm. "Don't get me wrong. Right now, in this city, you need to keep your eyes open. You know, use common sense, or whatever. But it's also very important that you live your life as normally as you can." That one opened the flood gates.

"What if they bomb us?"

60   "Who bomb us? Nobody's going to bomb us. I don't even know who *they* are."

"What if they hijack another plane?"

"Look, here's the deal. You go to school. You work hard, no goofing off. You do your homework, you study for your tests. You go to your soccer practices. Game time rolls around? Not too many headers. Come the weekends? You hang with your friends. Saturday morning? Sunday morning? You have a contest with your sister, see who can sleep the latest, O.K.? You *live* your *life*, O.K.?"

"O.K.," her face lightening. A light peck and a dash for the door.

"Where you headed?"

65   "I'm going to hang out with Cole."

"Hey. Do me a favor?" stopping her with one foot in the street. "Don't go into any big stores tonight, O.K.?"

"What?" A little stutter in her step. "Why?"

"Just . . . humor me. It's nothing."

"O.K."

70   "And stay out of Washington Square."

"What's wrong with Washington Square?"

"Well, I never like you hanging out at Washington Square."

"What's *wrong* with Washington *Square?*"

"Absolutely probably nothing. I'm just not too crazy about crowds right now, O.K.?"

75   "O.K., O.K.," the tightness coming back into her face, but what could you do?

"And oh," he winced pre-emptively. "The subway? It doesn't exist for you, O.K.?" then, "Sorry."

By the time the kid hit the street, she looked as if someone had strapped a boulder onto her back; her father wondering if it was more dangerous for her inside the house than out.

Haven, Oct. 21

Rafiyq Abdellah, born Torrin Williams, enters the visitors' room wearing a gray Velcro-fastened jumpsuit and greets his guest with a standing hug. At first, the talk is of lawyers and postponements, but the conversation turns to the inescapable.

"Well, I'll tell you, this is not the greatest of times to have a name like mine, you know what I'm saying?"

80   "They breaking your back in here?"

"Yeah, well, I don't want to make too much of it, but like, O.K., what was it, 10 minutes ago I come in here? The, the guard who brought me up? He's like, 'Abdellah, Abdellah, were you tight with the hijackers?' And I'm like, 'Yo, look at my *face,* hear my *speech*—do you *think* I was tight with the hijackers?'

"Yeah, and then on the other end of the spectrum, the native-born Muslims in here? Sometimes they look at the African-American Muslims and they're all like, 'You ain't *pray*ing right, you don't understand the K*ora*n right, you this, you that. . . .' I mean, I'll tell you, when we all go to the *jumah* on Fridays? Man, there is like some spirited disputations in there these days, no lie. . . .

"I mean, most guys in here, they feel like everybody else about what happened, you know, the horror of it. . . . I mean, there's a few guys, political types, and for them, what happened, it's all about chickens coming home to roost. But I don't see how anybody could say that with an honest heart.

"And I saw it happen that morning, did I write you about that? You get a pretty good view of the skyline from in here, and when that first building went down? Man, I couldn't even close my mouth.

85   "I'd like to think the worst is over, but with the anthrax now and everything? Hey, you know how I feel about being incarcerated in here, right? But I have to say it, with what's going on out there on a day-to-day basis? Rikers might very well be the safest place in the city."

Not Norman Rockwell, Oct. 24

Under a cracklingly blue sky, New York is trying harder than ever to proceed with its spiritual comeback; the shops are more crowded, overheard conversation veers more often to the blissfully inane and erratic bursts of laughter punctuate the soundtrack of the streets, although let's not kid ourselves, the people of this city still carry themselves with a certain humped tension, as if waiting for the next unthinkable.

"Did you ever hear of Lord Buckley?" she asks her friend as they cruise the ground floor of a mammoth bookstore. "Kind of a hipster monologist from the 50s? He had this bit back then about Khrushchev and the H-bomb, and he says something like: 'In times of great uncertainty and terror, humor is the only thing that ensures us that we do not die before we're killed.'"

"Yeah, well, have you heard any good jokes lately?" her friend asks. "Because I sure haven't."

"How about this?" she responds, gesturing to a freestanding six-book display easel by the information desk. The three titles running across the top row are: "Rogue Regimes," "Bin Laden: The Man Who Declared War on America" and "Terrorism: Today's Biggest Threat to Freedom." At the far left on the lower row is "Living Terrors: What America Needs to Know to Survive the Coming Bioterrorist Catastrophe"; at the far right, "Jihad"; and dead center, surrounded by all the others, "New York Landmarks."

90 "Will that do?"

Back out on the street, they wander down Broadway and notice after a few blocks that the people in front of them have come to a standstill, their eyes on the approaching uptown traffic, where a fire truck is cruising back to its house.

Some of the people break out in applause. Others wave. The firemen wave back.

"Can you believe that?" she says. "It's like the 1950s. Like Norman Rockwell."

"No way," her friend says, joining in on the applause. "There's nothing sentimental about what those guys went through." She cut loose with a piercing two-fingered whistle. "And I'll tell you something else. Right about now? This is probably the least naive city in the world."

BILLY COLLINS

Billy Collins (born in 1941) was poet Laureate at the time he wrote "The Names." The poem was printed as an editorial in the New York Times and later read before Congress in a ceremonial joint session held to mark the anniversary of September 11th. For more on Collins, see "Embrace" (page 153) and "Thesaurus" (page 163).

The Names

Yesterday, I lay awake in the palm of the night.
A fine rain stole in, unhelped by any breeze,
And when I saw the silver glaze on the windows,
I started with A, with Ackerman, as it happened,
5 Then Baxter and Calabro,
Davis and Eberling, names falling into place
As droplets fell through the dark.

Names printed on the ceiling of the night.
Names slipping around a watery bend.
10   Twenty-six willows on the banks of a stream.
In the morning, I walked out barefoot
Among thousands of flowers
Heavy with dew like the eyes of tears,
And each had a name—
15   Fiori inscribed on a yellow petal
Then Gonzalez and Han, Ishikawa and Jenkins.

Names written in the air
And stitched into the cloth of the day.
A name under a photograph taped to a mailbox.
20   Monogram on a torn shirt,
I see you spelled out on storefront windows
And on the bright unfurled awnings of this city.
I say the syllables as I turn a corner—
Kelly and Lee,
25   Medina, Nardella, and O'Connor.

When I peer into the woods,
I see a thick tangle where letters are hidden
As in a puzzle concocted for children.
Parker and Quigley in the twigs of an ash,
30   Rizzo, Schubert, Torres, and Upton,
Secrets in the boughs of an ancient maple.

Names written in the pale sky.
Names rising in the updraft amid buildings.
Names silent in stone
35   Or cried out behind a door.
Names blown over the earth and out to sea.

In the evening—weakening light, the last swallows.
A boy on a lake lifts his oars.
A woman by a window puts a match to a candle,
40   And the names are outlined on the rose clouds—
Vanacore and Wallace,
(let X stand, if it can, for the ones unfound)
Then Young and Ziminsky, the final jolt of Z.

Names etched on the head of a pin.
45   One name spanning a bridge, another undergoing a tunnel.
A blue name needled into the skin.
Names of citizens, workers, mothers and fathers,
The bright-eyed daughter, the quick son.
Alphabet of names in green rows in a field.
50   Names in the small tracks of birds.
Names lifted from a hat
Or balanced on the tip of the tongue.
Names wheeled into the dim warehouse of memory.
So many names, there is barely room on the walls of the heart.

FIGURE 16.4   *Reflecting Absence,* Winning Design for WTC Memorial

---

INQUIRING FURTHER

1. How many voices can you identify in "Word on the Street"? Can you distinguish between the voices of the coauthors, Ann Hudson-Price and Richard Price? How would you describe the voices of other non-American cultures portrayed in the essay? Freewrite for five minutes about voices and perspectives in the essay.

2. How would you compare Collins's response to the September 11th attacks to the responses of others (politicians, citizens, victims, etc.)? What roles should art play in addressing national tragedies? How does "Names" use poetic techniques to craft a response? Do you find the poetic techniques up to the task? Why or why not?

3. Construct an interpretation of the winning design for the World Trade Center Memorial. What might be the significance of the trees and natural elements of the memorial? How does the design of the memorial relate to its title, *Reflecting Absence?* Analyzing details of the memorial, write a page explaining what you believe to be the messages conveyed by its design.

EXTENDED INQUIRY

Songs of Innocence and Experience by William Blake

In 1789, the printmaker and poet William Blake (1757–1827) produced one of his best known collections of works, titled *Songs of Innocence*. The collection took the form of an illuminated book, that is a book of poems accompanied by illustrations. The illustrations offered complementary images that functioned both as commentary on the text of Blake's poems and as unique works of art in their own right.

The collection made use of the technique of relief etching that Blake had recently invented. Blake had apprenticed as an engraver and knew well the amount of time required to create printing plates by etching their surface using hand tools. The etching method required an artist to carve lines into a copper plate representing the image to be produced. Acid was then applied to the plate—the acid would penetrate the etched surface, deepening the engraving and creating the image to be printed. (We are grateful to the Blake Archive, the source for the best information on Blake and his art. You can find out more about the archive and view color images of the works discussed here on our CD.)

Blake's relief etching, however, reversed this process. Blake would paint on the surface of the plate with an acid-resistant liquid, somewhat like ink. Using the resistant liquid, Blake composed a reverse image that would be protected when the plate was exposed to acid. The process simplified the preparation of the plate so that printing might be done more efficiently.

The real power of the relief etching Blake developed, however, lay in its ability to transform the composing process of the artist. Whereas, traditional etching might carefully reproduce the shapes and lines of an image while engraving the plate, Blake's process allowed him to compose directly on the plate, offering an organic medium for developing artistic images.

Further, in his illuminated books, Blake composed with both words and images. He would begin by drawing onto a plate the words of his poems. (The lines would be written backwards so that the reverse image would make sense in the final print.) Once the text of the work had been laid down, Blake would compose accompanying images by painting or drawing around his poems. In this way, words and images flowed together as each printing plate evolved under the hand of the artist.

Ultimately, Blake's illuminated books stand out less for the original efficiency he had envisioned made possible by relief etching, and more for their unique status as works of art that bring word and image, as well as creation and production, together. Blake acted as both poet and painter to create the relief etching plates. He also managed the complete process from composing text, to painting images, to preparing printing plates, to printing the works on paper, to final coloring and distribution. As such, he stands as an early example of a multimedia artist.

In 1794, Blake produced a collection called *Songs of Experience*. He used the same relief etching techniques, but complicated the concerns of the early *Songs* by emphasizing a contrary state of knowledge, a knowledge often more painful, despondent, and fully aware of the realities of suffering and death. In his later editions of these collections, Blake combined both versions into a single *Songs of Innocence and Experience*. The combined collections represent a more nuanced statement about the relationship between innocence and experience, suggesting a complementary relationship between these two contrary states. Even in innocence, there is room for concern, and even experience brings knowledge that can offer hope and growth.

The Shepherd

      How sweet is the Shepherds sweet lot,
      From the morn to the evening he strays;
      He shall follow his sheep all the day
      And his tongue shall be filled with praise.

5   For he hears the lambs innocent call,
      And he hears the ewes tender reply,
      He is watchful while they are in peace,
      For they know when their Shepherd is nigh.

The Divine Image

To Mercy Pity Peace and Love,
All pray in their distress:
And to these virtues of delight
Return their thankfulness.

5   For Mercy Pity Peace and Love,
Is God our father dear:
And Mercy Pity Peace and Love.
Is Man his child and care.

For Mercy has a human heart
10   Pity, a human face:
And Love, the human form divine.
And Peace. the human dress.

Then every man of every clime,
That prays in his distress,
15   Prays to the human form divine
Love Mercy Pity Peace,

And all must love the human form.
In heathen, turk or jew.
Where Mercy. Love & Pity dwell
20   There God is dwelling too.

INQUIRING FURTHER

1. How would you describe the tone of "The Shepherd"? Does this tone correspond with the atmosphere created by the image of the print? What elements of art in the print contribute to this atmosphere? Sketch out a list of ways in which elements of art create an image that corresponds to the message in the text of the poem

2. How do you interpret the visual elements of "The Divine Image"? What thoughts can you develop related to the figures in the image? What can you say about the lines and shapes created by the flowing vine? Write a paragraph or two exploring the relationship between the image and the message of the poem.

The Angel

> I Dreamt a Dream! what can it mean?
> And that I was a maiden Queen:
> Guarded by an Angel mild;
> Witless woe, was ne'er beguil'd!
>
> 5   And I wept both night and day
> And he wip'd my tears away

And I wept both day and night
And hid from him my hearts delight

So he took his wings and fled:
10   Then the morn blush'd rosy red;
I dried my tears & arm'd my fears,
With ten thousand shields and spears

Soon my Angel came again;
I was arm'd, he came in vain;
15   For the time of youth was fled
And grey hairs were on my head.

INQUIRING FURTHER

1. What story is told by the image in "The Angel"? What can you say about the touching of the figures? How would you explain the expression on the face of the woman? What is suggested by the look of the angel?

2. How would you relate "The Angel" to "The Shepherd"? Is it fair to say "The Angel" presents a less innocent picture? How would you relate both works to "The Divine Image"? Freewrite for five minutes about the relationship between the three works.

The Chimney Sweeper

Enhanced reading of "The Chimney Sweeper"

When my mother died I was very young,
And my father sold me while yet my tongue,
Could scarcely cry weep weep weep weep.
So your chimneys I sweep & in soot I sleep.

5   Theres little Tom Dacre, who cried when his head,
That curl'd like a lambs back, was shav'd, so I said,
Hush Tom never mind it, for when your head's bare,
You know that the soot cannot spoil your white hair.

And so he was quiet, & that very night,
10   As Tom was a sleeping he had such a sight,
That thousands of sweepers Dick, Joe, Ned & Jack
Were all of them lock'd up in coffins of black,

And by came an Angel who had a bright key
And he open'd the coffins & set them all free.
15   Then down a green plain leaping laughing they run
And wash in a river and shine in the Sun.

Then naked & white, all their bags left behind,
They rise upon clouds, and sport in the wind.
And the Angel told Tom if he'd be a good boy.
20   He'd have God for his father & never want joy.

And so Tom awoke and we rose in the dark
And got with our bags & our brushes to work.
Tho' the morning was cold, Tom was happy & warm,
So if all do their duty, they need not fear harm.

INQUIRING FURTHER

1. What is significant about the fact that the speaker of the poem is a child? Is it fair to say the voice in the poem is innocent? Why or why not?

2. How do you interpret Tom Dacre's dream? What is significant about the angel setting the children free? Is the message undercut by the fact that it occurs in a dream? Why or why not? Write a paragraph or two discussing the dream in terms of the last line of the poem.

The Human Abstract

Pity would be no more,
If we did not make somebody Poor:
And Mercy no more could be,
If all were as happy as we;

5   And mutual fear brings peace;
Till the selfish loves increase.
Then Cruelty knits a snare,
And spreads his baits with care.

He sits down with holy fears,
10   And waters the ground with tears:

Then Humility takes its root
Underneath his foot.

Soon spreads the dismal shade
Of Mystery over his head;
15   And the Catterpiller and Fly,
Feed on the Mystery.

And it bears the fruit of Deceit,
Ruddy and sweet to eat;
And the Raven his nest has made
20   In its thickest shade.

The Gods of the earth and sea,
Sought thro' Nature to find this Tree
But their search was all in vain;
There grows one in the Human Brain.

INQUIRING FURTHER

1. How do you interpret the first six lines of "The Human Abstract"? How does the personification of cruelty in the poem relate to the opening lines? Write two or three sentences paraphrasing the poem's message about human behavior.

2. Analyze the image in "The Human Abstract." Does the image provide any commentary on the text of the poem? How does the image use lighting, lines, shapes, or arrangement to convey its message? What thematic elements of the image are significant?

London

I wander thro' each charter'd street.
Near where the charter'd Thames does flow
And mark in every face I meet
Marks of weakness, marks of woe,

5   In every cry of every Man,
In every Infants cry of fear.
In every voice; in every ban,
The mind-forg'd manacles I hear

How the Chimney-sweepers cry
10   Every blackning Church appalls.
And the hapless Soldiers sigh
Runs in blood down Palace walls

But most thro' midnight streets I hear
How the youthful Harlots curse
15   Blasts the new-born Infants tear
And blights with plagues the Marriage hearse.

INQUIRING FURTHER

1. How do you interpret the phrase "mind-forg'd manacles"? How is the suffering depicted in the poem related to human choice and consciousness? How is it related to the political structures suggested by the "charter'd" streets, the church, and "Palace walls"?

2. The "Harlot's curse" is usually read as an allusion to syphilis, which causes the loss of sight in newborn children. What is the relationship between prostitution and the final line of the poem? What explanations might you develop for associating marriage with death?

3. What central concern does "London" highlight for readers? What does the work tell readers to do? How does the text of the poem instruct readers?

17

Family and Relationships

In those simple relationships of loving husband and wife,
affectionate sisters, children and grandmother, there are
innumerable shades of sweetness and anguish which
make up the pattern of our lives day by day. . . .

—Willa Cather

Willa Cather reveals the conflicted nature of the relationships we share with others. These connections with parents, friends, and lovers cannot help but bring feelings of peace, contentment, and joy. At the same time, these associations account for some of our most painful experiences. The close relationships in our lives bring both "sweetness and anguish," inspiring feelings of friendship, desire, and devotion as well as sorrow, jealousy, even rage.

Our earliest experiences and even our identity relates directly to those who serve as our primary nurturers, usually our parents. These relationships between children and parents (perhaps grandparents) are profound—we often hear of parents who would sacrifice their own lives for the lives of their children. Unfortunately, some children have an entirely different experience growing up, and even the most healthy parent-child connection sways back and forth between devotion and frustration as children develop and assert their own identities.

The same complexities emerge in relationships with close friends or siblings. We all recognize the desire to have and maintain connections with a select few individuals, our closest friends. We also have a built in closeness with brothers, sisters, and other members of extended families. Friendships usually try our patience as our own needs and the needs of our friends conflict over time. Similarly, sibling connections often blend the twin emotions of love and anguish, as children vie for their parents' attention and negotiate their own affinities and interests.

As we mature, our attention often shifts to a single significant other. We fall in love, and often marry. No doubt, we maintain our friendships and hopefully remain close to parents and family. At the same time, the personal bond that develops between two people fills our emotional lives and sometimes takes precedence over other connections. In this chapter we will examine how "sweetness and anguish" play out in the different relationships that evolve during our lives, from parents, to friends and family, to lovers, spouses, and significant others.

PARENTS AND CAREGIVERS

Parents and children share perhaps the most complex of relationships. Parents act as teachers, nurturers, wardens, judge, and jury in the lives of their young

children. Parents usually show devotion for children unparalleled in other relationships. Children often strive to imitate their parents as they grow older—they
may inherit many characteristics from their biological parents. Yet, eventually children assert their own identity, breaking away from parents, even challenging their
authority. Throughout all of these interactions, fathers, mothers, sons, and daughters negotiate issues of origins, identity, and responsibility. The selections below
explore these concerns of parents and children.

ISABEL ALLENDE

*Isabel Allende (born in 1942) is the daughter of a diplomat and the niece
of assassinated Chilean President Salvador Allende. She frequently emphasizes political issues in her fiction, but also features female characters and
concerns. Her work can be said to represent the feminine dimensions of
the school of **Magical Realism**, literature that blends a spiritual sense of
fantasy with gritty depictions of everyday life. "The Judge's Wife" was published in Spanish originally, in 1989.*

The Judge's Wife

Nicolás Vidal had always known that a woman would cost him his life. That
had been prophesied on the day he was born, and confirmed by the propri-
etress of the general store on the one occasion he had permitted her to read
his fortune in the coffee dregs; he could never have imagined, however, that
the woman would be Casilda, the wife of Judge Hidalgo. The first time he
had seen her was the day she arrived in town to be married. He did not find
her attractive; he preferred females who were brazen and brunette, and this
translucent young girl in her traveling suit, with bashful eyes and delicate fingers useless for pleasuring a man, seemed as insubstantial to him as a handful of ashes. Knowing his fate so well, he was cautious about women, and
throughout his life he fled from any sentimental attachments, hardening his
heart to love and limiting himself to hasty encounters aimed at outwitting
loneliness. Casilda seemed so insignificant and remote to him that he took no
precautions against her and, when the moment came, he lost sight of the pre-
diction that had always governed his decisions. From the roof of the building
where he was crouched with two of his men, he observed the young *señorita*
from the capital as she descended from her car on her wedding day. She had
arrived in the company of a half dozen of her family members, all as pale and
delicate as she, who had sat through the ceremony fanning themselves with
a frank air of consternation and then departed, never to return.

Like all the town's residents, Vidal was sure the bride would never survive
the climate and that soon the old women would be laying her out for her funeral. In the unlikely event she did endure the heat and dust that blew through the
skin and settled in the heart, she would without question succumb before the
foul humor and bachelor manias of her husband. Judge Hidalgo was several
times her age, and had slept alone for so many years that he did not know how
to begin to please a wife. His severity and stubbornness in carrying out the
law—even at the cost of justice—was feared in every corner of the province.
In the exercise of his duties he ignored any rationale for humaneness, punishing

with equal firmness the theft of a hen and premeditated murder. He dressed in rigorous black, so that everyone would be reminded of the dignity of his responsibilities, and despite the inescapable dust clouds of this town without dreams his high-topped shoes always gleamed with a beeswax shine. A man like that is not made to be wed, the gossips would say; their dire prophecies about the marriage, however, were not fulfilled. To the contrary, Casilda survived three pregnancies in a row, and seemed content. On Sundays, with her husband, she attended twelve o'clock mass, imperturbable beneath her Spanish mantilla, untouched by the inclemency of the never-ending summer, as colorless and silent as a shadow. No one ever heard anything more than a timid hello from her, nor witnessed gestures more bold than a nod of the head or a fleeting smile, she seemed weightless; on the verge of dematerializing in a moment of carelessness. She gave the impression of not being there, and that was why everyone was so surprised by the influence she exerted on the Judge, who underwent striking changes.

Although Hidalgo maintained the same appearance—funereal and sour-faced—his decisions in court took a strange turn. Before a stupefied public he let off a boy who had stolen from his employer, following the logic that for three years his *patrón* had underpaid him, and the money he had pilfered was a form of compensation. He similarly refused to punish an adulterous wife, arguing that the husband had no moral authority to demand rectitude from her when he himself kept a concubine. Gossiping tongues had it that Judge Hidalgo turned inside out like a glove when he crossed the threshold of his front door, that he removed his sepulchral clothing, played with the children, laughed, and dandled Casilda on his knees, but those rumors were never substantiated. Whatever the case, his wife was given credit for his new benevolence, and his reputation improved. Nicolás Vidal, however, was indifferent to all of this because he was outside the law, and he was sure that there would be no mercy for him the day he was led in shackles before the Judge. He ignored the gossip about *doña* Casilda; the few times he had seen her from a distance confirmed the first impression of a blurred ectoplasm.

Vidal had been born thirty years earlier in a windowless room of the only bordello in town, the son of Juana la Triste and an unknown father. He had no business in this world, and his sad mother knew it; that was why she had tried to tear him from her womb by means of herbs, candle stubs, lye douches, and other brutal methods, but the tiny creature had stubbornly hung on. Years later, Juana la Triste, pondering why her son was so different from others, realized that her drastic measures to eradicate him had, instead of dispatching him, tempered him, body and soul, to the hardness of iron. As soon as he was born, the midwife had held him up to the light of the kerosene lamp to examine him and had immediately noticed that he had four nipples.

5   "Poor mite, a woman will cost him his life," she had prophesied, guided by long experience in such matters.

Those words weighed on the boy like a deformity. With a woman's love, his life might have been less miserable. To compensate for the numerous attempts to eliminate him before he was born, his mother chose for him a noble-sounding first name and a solid surname selected at random. Even that princely appellation had not been enough to exorcise the fatal omens, and before he was ten the boy's face was scarred from knife fights, and very soon thereafter he had begun his life as a fugitive. At twenty, he was the leader of a gang of desperados. The habit of violence had developed the strength of his muscles, the street had made him merciless, and the solitude to which he had been condemned by fear of dying over love had determined the expression in his eyes. Anyone in the town could swear on seeing him that he was Juana la Triste's son because, just like hers, his eyes were always filled with unshed tears. Anytime a misdeed was committed anywhere in the region, the *guardia*, to silence the protests of the citizenry, went out with dogs to hunt down Nicolás Vidal, but after a few runs through the hills, they returned empty-handed. In fact they did not want to find him, because they did not want to chance a fight. His gang solidified his bad name to the point that small towns and large haciendas paid him to stay away. With those "donations" his men could have led a sedentary life, but Nicolás Vidal kept them riding, in a whirlwind of death and devastation, to prevent the men from losing their taste for a fight or their infamous reputation from dwindling. There was no one who dared stand up to them. On one or two occasions Judge Hidalgo had asked the government to send Army troops to reinforce his deputies, but after a few futile excursions the soldiers had returned to their barracks and the renegades to their old tricks.

Only once was Nicolás Vidal close to falling into the traps of justice; he was saved by his inability to feel emotion. Frustrated by seeing Vidal run roughshod over the law, Judge Hidalgo decided to put aside scruples and set a trap for the outlaw. He realized that in the name of justice he was going to commit a heinous act, but of two evils, he chose the lesser. The only bait he had been able to think of was Juana la Triste, because Vidal had no other family, nor known lovers. The Judge collected Juana from the whorehouse where she was scrubbing floors and cleaning latrines for want of clients willing to pay for her miserable services, and threw her into a made-to-measure cage he then placed in the very center of the Plaza de Armas, with a jug of water as her only comfort.

"When her water runs out, she'll begin to scream. Then her son will come, and I will be waiting with the soldiers," said the Judge.

Word of this torture, outdated since the time of runaway slaves, reached the ears of Nicolás Vidal shortly before his mother drank the last drop from her pitcher. His men watched as he received the news in silence: no flicker of emotion crossed the impassive, loner's mask of his face; he never lost a stroke in the calm rhythm of stropping his knife. He had not seen Juana la Triste for many years and had not a single happy memory of his childhood; this, however, was not a question of sentiment, it was a matter of honor. No man can tolerate such an offense, the outlaws thought, and they readied their weapons and mounts, willing to ride into the ambush and give up their lives if that was what it took. But their leader showed no signs of haste.

10   As the hours went by, tension heightened among the men. They exchanged glances, dripping with sweat, not daring to comment, impatient from waiting, hands on the butts of their revolvers, the manes of their horses, the coil of their lariats. Night came, and the only person in the whole camp who slept was Nicolás Vidal. At dawn the men's opinions were divided; some had decided that Vidal was much more heartless than they had ever imagined, others believed that their leader was planning a spectacular manner of rescuing his mother. The one thing no one thought was that he might lack courage, because he had too often demonstrated that—in spades. By noon they could bear the uncertainty no longer, and they went to ask him what he was going to do.

"Nothing," he said.

"But what about your mother?"

"We'll see who has more balls, the Judge or me," Nicolás Vidal replied, unperturbed.

By the third day Juana la Triste was no longer pleading or begging for water; her tongue was parched and her words died in her throat. She lay curled up like a fetus on the floor of her cage, her eyes expressionless, her lips swollen and cracked, moaning like an animal in moments of lucidity and dreaming of hell the remainder of the time. Four armed men guarded the prisoner to prevent townspeople from giving her water. Her wails spread through all the town; they filtered through closed shutters, the wind carried them through the chinks of doors, they clung to the corners of rooms, dogs caught them up and repeated them in their howling, they infected newborn babies, and grated on the nerves of any who heard them. The Judge could not prevent the parade of people through the plaza, commiserating with the old woman, nor stop the sympathy strike of the prostitutes, which coincided with the miners' payday. On Saturdays, the streets were taken over by these roughnecks from the mines, eager to spend their savings before returning to their caverns, but this week the town offered no diversion apart from the cage and the moan of pain carried from mouth to mouth, from the river to the coast highway. The priest headed a group of parishioners who presented themselves before Judge Hidalgo to remind him of Christian charity and to entreat him to release that poor innocent woman from her martyr's death; the magistrate shot the bolt to his office door and refused to hear them, wagering that Juana la Triste would last one more day and that her son would fall into his trap. That is when the town leaders decided to appeal to *doña* Casilda.

15   The Judge's wife received them in the darkened parlor of their home and listened to their arguments silently, eyes lowered, as was her custom. Her husband had been away from home for three days, locked in his office, waiting for Nicolás Vidal with senseless determination. Even without going to the window, she had known everything happening outside: the sound of that long torment had also invaded the vast rooms of their home. *Doña* Casilda waited until the visitors had retired, then dressed her children in their Sunday best and with them headed in the direction of the plaza. She carried a basket of food and a jug of fresh water for Juana la Triste. The guards saw her as she turned the corner, and guessed her intentions, but they had precise orders, and they crossed rifles before her, and when she tried to walk by them—watched by an expectant crowd—they took her arms to prevent her from passing. The children began to cry.

Judge Hidalgo was in his office on the plaza. He was the only person in town who had not put wax plugs in his ears, because all his attention was focused on the ambush: he was waiting for the sound of Nicolás Vidal's horses. For three days and nights he had withstood the sobs of the victim and the insults of the people crowded outside the building, but when he heard the voices of his children he realized he had reached the limits of his endurance. He left the Court of Justice wearing the beard that had been growing since Wednesday, totally exhausted, red-eyed from waiting, and with the weight of defeat on his shoulders. He crossed the street, stepped onto the square of the plaza, and walked toward his wife. They gazed at each other sorrowfully. It was the first time in seven years that she had confronted him, and she had chosen to do so before the whole town. Judge Hidalgo took the basket and water jug from *doña* Casilda's hands, and himself opened the cage to minister to his prisoner.

"I told you, he hasn't got the balls I have," laughed Nicolás Vidal when he heard what had happened.

But his guffaws turned sour the following day when he was told that Juana la Triste had hanged herself on the lamppost of the whorehouse where she had spent her life, because she could not bear the shame of having been abandoned by her son in that cage in the center of the Plaza de Armas.

"Now it's the Judge's turn!" swore Vidal.

20　　His plan was to ride into town at nightfall, take the Judge by surprise, kill him in some spectacular fashion, and stuff him in the damned cage; at dawn the next day his humiliated remains would be waiting for the whole world to see. He learned, however, that the Hidalgo family had left for a spa on the coast, hoping to wash away the bad taste of defeat.

The news that a revenge-bent Vidal and his men were on their trail overtook Judge Hidalgo in mid-route at an inn where they had stopped to rest. Without a detachment of the *guardia*, the place could not offer sufficient protection, but the Judge and his family had several hours' advantage and their car was faster than Vidal's horses. He calculated that he would be able to reach the next town and get help. He ordered his wife and children into the car, pressed the pedal to the floor, and sped off down the road. He should have reached the town with an ample margin of safety, but it was written that this was the day Nicolás Vidal would meet the woman from whom he had been fleeing all his life.

Weakened by sleepless nights, by the townspeople's hostility, by the embarrassment he had suffered, and by the tension of the race to save his family, Judge Hidalgo's heart gave a great leap and burst without a sound. The driverless car ran off the road, bumped along the shoulder, and finally rolled to a stop. It was a minute or two before *doña* Casilda realized what had happened. Since her husband was practically ancient she had often thought what it would be like to be widowed, but she had never imagined that he would leave her at the mercy of his enemies. She did not pause to mull that over, however, because she knew that she must act quickly if she was to save her children. Hurriedly she looked around for help; she nearly burst into hopeless tears: in all those sun-baked, barren reaches there was no trace of human life, only the wild hills and burning white sky. At second glance, however, she spied in the distance the shadow of a cave, and it was there she ran, carrying two babies in her arms with a third clinging to her skirttails.

Three times Casilda scaled the slope to the cave, carrying her children, one by one. It was a natural cave, like many others in those hills. She searched the interior, to be sure she had not happened into the den of some animal, settled the children in the rear, and kissed them without shedding a tear.

"In a few hours the *guardia* will come looking for you. Until then, don't come out for any reason, even if you hear me scream. Do you understand?" she instructed.

25　　The tots hugged each other in terror, and with a last farewell glance the mother ran down the hill. She reached the car, closed her husband's eyelids, brushed her clothes, straightened her hair, and sat down to wait. She did not know how many men were in Nicolás Vidal's band, but she prayed there were many; the more there were, the more time would be spent in taking their pleasure of her. She gathered her strength, wondering how long it would take to die if she concentrated on expiring inch by inch. She wished she were voluptuous and robust, that she could bear up longer and win more time for her children.

She did not have long to wait. She soon saw a dust cloud on the horizon and heard galloping hoofs; she gritted her teeth. Confused, she watched as with drawn pistol a single rider reined in his horse a few meters from her. By the knife scar on his face she recognized Nicolás Vidal, who had decided to pursue Judge Hidalgo alone: this was a private matter to be settled between the two of them. She understood then that she must do something much more difficult than die slowly.

With one glance the bandit realized that his enemy, sleeping his death in peace, was beyond any punishment, but there was his wife, floating in the reverberating light. He leapt from his horse and strode toward her. She did not look away, or flinch, and he stopped short; for the first time in his life someone was defying him without a hint of fear. For several seconds they took each other's measure in silence, calculating the other's strength, estimating their own tenacity, and accepting the fact they were facing a formidable adversary. Nicolás Vidal put away his revolver, and Casilda smiled.

The Judge's wife earned every instant of the next hours. She employed all the seductive tricks recorded since the dawn of human knowledge, and improvised others out of her need to gratify the man's every dream. She not only played on his body like a skilled performer, strumming every chord in the pursuit of pleasure, she also called upon the wiles of her own refinement. Both realized that the stakes of this game were their lives, and that awareness lent the ultimate intensity to their encounter. Nicolás Vidal had fled from love since the day of his birth; he had never known intimacy, tenderness, secret laughter, the celebration of the senses, a lover's joyful pleasure. With every minute the *guardia* were riding closer and closer, and, with them, the firing wall, but he was also closer, ever closer, to this stupendous woman, and he gladly traded *guardia* and wall for the gifts she was offering him. Casilda was a modest and shy woman; she had been married to an austere old man who had never seen her naked. She did not forget for one instant throughout that memorable afternoon that her objective was to gain time, but at some point she let herself go, marveling at her own sensuality, and somehow grateful to Vidal. That was why when she heard the distant sound of the troops, she begged him to flee and hide in the hills. Nicolás Vidal preferred to hold her in his arms and kiss her for the last time, thus fulfilling the prophecy that had shaped his destiny.

Inquiring Further

1. What do you think of the foreshadowing of the fate of Nicholas Vidal? How effective is this technique? How might it contribute to an interpretation of the story?

2. What are your thoughts on the description of Casilda's and Vidal's lovemaking? How do you interpret her feeling of gratitude toward Vidal? Is it fair to say she has forgotten her children when she gives in to her passion? Freewrite for five minutes about the encounter between Casilda and Vidal.

T. CORAGHESSAN BOYLE

Thomas John Boyle (born in 1948) changed his name at age seventeen to T. Coraghessan Boyle before attending college at the State University of New York. After college, he returned to his hometown to teach high school English for four years, before leaving to earn his PhD from the University of Iowa. He is now a professor of creative writing at University of Southern California. His fiction has been called surreal and satirical, often revealing a harsh reality beneath the sheen of contemporary culture. Boyle composed "The Love of My Life" (2000) in response to an article he read in a newspaper.

The Love of My Life

They wore each other like a pair of socks. He was at her house, she was at his. Everywhere they went—to the mall, to the game, to movies and shops and the classes that structured their days like a new kind of chronology—their fingers were entwined, their shoulders touching, their hips joined in the slow triumphant sashay of love. He drove her car, slept on the couch in the family room at her parents' house, played tennis and watched football with her father on the big thirty-six-inch TV in the kitchen. She went shopping with his mother and hers, a triumvirate of tastes, and she would have played tennis with his father, if it came to it, but his father was dead. "I love you," he told her, because he did, because there was no feeling like this, no triumph, no high— it was like being immortal and unconquerable, like floating. And a hundred times a day she said it too: "I love you. I love you."

They were together at his house one night when the rain froze on the streets and sheathed the trees in glass. It was her idea to take a walk and feel it in their hair and on the glistening shoulders of their parkas, an otherworldly drumming of pellets flung down out of the troposphere, alien and familiar at the same time, and they glided the length of the front walk and watched the way the power lines bellied and swayed. He built a fire when they got back, while she towelled her hair and made hot chocolate laced with Jack Daniel's. They'd rented a pair of slasher movies for the ritualized comfort of them— "Teens have sex," he said, "and then they pay for it in body parts"—and the maniac had just climbed out of the heating vent, with a meat hook dangling from the recesses of his empty sleeve, when the phone rang.

It was his mother, calling from the hotel room in Boston where she was curled up—shacked up?—for the weekend with the man she'd been dating. He tried to picture her, but he couldn't. He even closed his eyes a minute, to concentrate, but there was nothing there. Was everything all right? she wanted to know. With the storm and all? No, it hadn't hit Boston yet, but she saw on the Weather Channel that it was on its way. Two seconds after he hung up— before she could even hit the Start button on the VCR—the phone rang again, and this time it was her mother. Her mother had been drinking. She was calling from a restaurant, and China could hear a clamor of voices in the background. "Just stay put," her mother shouted into the phone. "The streets are like a skating rink. Don't you even think of getting in that car."

Well, she wasn't thinking of it. She was thinking of having Jeremy to herself, all night, in the big bed in his mother's room. They'd been having sex ever since they started going together at the end of their junior year, but it was always sex in the car or sex on a blanket or the lawn, hurried sex, nothing like she wanted it to be. She kept thinking of the way it was in the movies, where the stars ambushed each other on beds the size of small planets and then did it again and again until they lay nestled in a heap of pillows and blankets, her head on his chest, his arm flung over her shoulder, the music fading away to individual notes plucked softly on a guitar and everything in the frame glowing as if it had been sprayed with liquid gold. That was how it was supposed to be. That was how it was going to be. At least for tonight.

5   She'd been wandering around the kitchen as she talked, dancing with the phone in an idle slow saraband, watching the frost sketch a design on the window over the sink, no sound but the soft hiss of the ice pellets on the roof, and now she pulled open the freezer door and extracted a pint box of ice cream. She was in her socks, socks so thick they were like slippers, and a pair of black leggings under an oversized sweater. Beneath her feet, the polished floorboards were as slick as the sidewalk outside, and she liked the feel of that, skating indoors in her big socks. "Uh-huh," she said into the phone. "Uh-huh. Yeah, we're watching a movie." She dug a finger into the ice cream and stuck it in her mouth.

"Come on," Jeremy called from the living room, where the maniac rippled menacingly over the Pause button. "You're going to miss the best part."

"Okay, Mom, okay," she said into the phone, parting words, and then she hung up. "You want ice cream?" she called, licking her finger.

Jeremy's voice came back at her, a voice in the middle range, with a congenital scratch in it, the voice of a nice guy, a very nice guy who could be the star of a TV show about nice guys: "What kind?" He had a pair of shoulders and pumped-up biceps too, a smile that jumped from his lips to his eyes, and close-cropped hair that stood up straight off the crown of his head. And he was always singing—she loved that—his voice so true he could do any song, and there was no lyric he didn't know, even on the oldies station. She scooped ice cream and saw him in a scene from last summer, one hand draped casually over the wheel of his car, the radio throbbing, his voice raised in perfect synch with Billy Corgan's, and the night standing still at the end of a long dark street overhung with maples.

"Chocolate. Swiss chocolate almond."

10   "Okay," he said, and then he was wondering if there was any whipped cream, or maybe hot fudge—he was sure his mother had a jar stashed away somewhere, *Look behind the mayonnaise on the top row*—and when she turned around he was standing in the doorway.

She kissed him—they kissed whenever they met, no matter where or when, even if one of them had just stepped out of the room, because that was love, that was the way love was—and then they took two bowls of ice cream into the living room and, with a flick of the remote, set the maniac back in motion.

It was an early spring that year, the world gone green overnight, the thermometer twice hitting the low eighties in the first week of March. Teachers were holding sessions outside. The whole school, even the halls and the cafeteria, smelled of fresh-mowed grass and the unfolding blossoms of the fruit trees in the development across the street, and students—especially seniors—were cutting class to go out to the quarry or the reservoir or to just drive the back streets with the sunroof and the windows open wide. But not China. She was hitting the books, studying late, putting everything in its place like pegs in a board, even love, even that. Jeremy didn't get it. "Look, you've already been accepted at your first-choice school, you're going to wind up in the top ten G.P.A.-wise, and you've got four years of tests and term papers ahead of you, and grad school after that. You'll only be a high school senior once in your life. Relax. Enjoy it. Or at least *experience* it."

He'd been accepted at Brown, his father's alma mater, and his own G.P.A. would put him in the top ten percent of their graduating class, and he was content with that, skating through his final semester, no math, no science, taking art and music, the things he'd always wanted to take but never had time for— and Lit., of course, A.P. History, and Spanish 5. "*Tú eres el amor de mi vida,*" he would tell her when they met at her locker or at lunch or when he picked her up for a movie on Saturday nights.

"*Y tú también,*" she would say, "or is it '*yo también*'?"—French was her language. "But I keep telling you it really matters to me, because I know I'll never catch Margery Yu or Christian Davenport, I mean they're a lock for val and salut, but it'll kill me if people like Kerry Sharp or Jalapy Seegrand finish ahead of me—you should know that, you of all people—"

15   It amazed him that she actually brought her books along when they went backpacking over spring break. They'd planned the trip all winter and through the long wind tunnel that was February, packing away freeze-dried entrées, Power Bars, Gore-Tex windbreakers and matching sweatshirts, weighing each item on a handheld scale with a dangling hook at the bottom of it. They were going up into the Catskills, to a lake he'd found on a map, and they were going to be together, without interruption, without telephones, automobiles, parents, teachers, friends, relatives, and pets, for five full days. They were going to cook over an open fire, they were going to read to each other and burrow into the double sleeping bag with the connubial zipper up the seam he'd found in his mother's closet, a relic of her own time in the lap of nature. It smelled of her, of his mother, a vague scent of her perfume that had lingered there dormant all these years, and maybe there was the faintest whiff of his father too, though his father had been gone so long he didn't even remember what he looked like, let alone what he might have smelled like. Five days. And it wasn't going to rain, not a drop. He didn't even bring his fishing rod, and that was love.

When the last bell rang down the curtain on Honors Math, Jeremy was waiting at the curb in his mother's Volvo station wagon, grinning up at China through the windshield while the rest of the school swept past with no thought for anything but release. There were shouts and curses, T-shirts in motion, slashing legs, horns bleating from the seniors' lot, the school buses lined up like armored vehicles awaiting the invasion—chaos, sweet chaos—and she stood there a moment to savor it. "Your mother's car?" she said, slipping in beside him and laying both arms over his shoulders to pull him to her for a kiss. He'd brought her jeans and hiking boots along, and she was going to change as they drove, no need to go home, no more circumvention and delay, a stop at McDonald's, maybe, or Burger King, and then it was the sun and the wind and the moon and the stars. Five days. Five whole days.

"Yeah," he said, in answer to her question, "my mother said she didn't want to have to worry about us breaking down in the middle of nowhere—"

"So she's got your car? She's going to sell real estate in your car?"

He just shrugged and smiled. "Free at last," he said, pitching his voice down low till it was exactly like Martin Luther King's. "Thank God Almighty, we are free at last."

20   It was dark by the time they got to the trailhead, and they wound up camping just off the road in a rocky tumble of brush, no place on earth less likely or less comfortable, but they were together, and they held each other through the damp whispering hours of the night and hardly slept at all. They made the lake by noon the next day, the trees just coming into leaf, the air sweet with the smell of the sun in the pines. She insisted on setting up the tent, just in case—it could rain, you never knew—but all he wanted to do was stretch out on a gray neoprene pad and feel the sun on his face. Eventually, they both fell asleep in the sun, and when they woke they made love right there, beneath the trees, and with the wide blue expanse of the lake giving back the blue of the sky. For dinner, it was étouffée and rice, out of the foil pouch, washed down with hot chocolate and a few squirts of red wine from Jeremy's bota bag.

The next day, the whole day through, they didn't bother with clothes at all. They couldn't swim, of course—the lake was too cold for that—but they could bask and explore and feel the breeze out of the south on their bare legs and the places where no breeze had touched before. She would remember that always, the feel of that, the intensity of her emotions, the simple unrefined pleasure of living in the moment. Woodsmoke. Duelling flashlights in the night. The look on Jeremy's face when he presented her with the bag of finger-sized crayfish he'd spent all morning collecting.

What else? The rain, of course. It came midway through the third day, clouds the color of iron filings, the lake hammered to iron too, and the storm that crashed through the trees and beat at their tent with a thousand angry fists. They huddled in the sleeping bag, sharing the wine and a bag of trail mix, reading to each other from a book of Donne's love poems (she was writing a paper for Mrs. Masterson called "Ocular Imagery in the Poetry of John Donne") and the last third of a vampire novel that weighed eighteen-point-one ounces.

And the sex. They were careful, always careful—*I will never, never be like those breeders that bring their puffed-up squalling little red-faced babies to class,* she told him, and he agreed, got adamant about it, even, until it became a running theme in their relationship, the breeders overpopulating an overpopulated world and ruining their own lives in the process—but she had forgotten to pack her pills and he had only two condoms with him, and it wasn't as if there was a drugstore around the corner.

In the fall—or the end of August, actually—they packed their cars separately and left for college, he to Providence and she to Binghamton. They were separated by three hundred miles, but there was the telephone, there was E-mail, and for the first month or so there were Saturday nights in a motel in Danbury, but that was a haul, it really was, and they both agreed that they should focus on their course work and cut back to every second or maybe third week. On the day they'd left—and no, she didn't want her parents driving her up there, she was an adult and she could take care of herself—Jeremy followed her as far as the Bear Mountain Bridge and they pulled off the road and held each other till the sun fell down into the trees. She had a poem for him, a Donne poem, the saddest thing he'd ever heard. It was something about the moon.

More than moon, that was it, lovers parting and their tears swelling like an ocean till the girl—the woman, the female—had more power to raise the tides than the moon itself, or some such. More than moon. That's what he called her after that, because she was white and round and getting rounder, and it was no joke, and it was no term of endearment.

25   She was pregnant. Pregnant, they figured, since the camping trip, and it was their secret, a new constant in their lives, a fact, an inescapable fact that never varied no matter how many home pregnancy kits they went through. Baggy clothes, that was the key, all in black, cargo pants, flowing dresses, a jacket even in summer. They went to a store in the city where nobody knew them and she got a girdle, and then she went away to school in Binghamton and he went to Providence. "You've got to get rid of it," he told her in the motel room that had become a prison. "Go to a clinic," he told her for the hundredth time, and outside it was raining—or, no, it was clear and cold that night, a foretaste of winter. "I'll find the money—you know I will."

She wouldn't respond. Wouldn't even look at him. One of the *Star Wars* movies was on TV, great flat thundering planes of metal roaring across the screen, and she was just sitting there on the edge of the bed, her shoulders hunched and hair hanging limp. Someone slammed a car door—two doors in rapid succession—and a child's voice shouted, "Me! Me first!"

"China," he said. "Are you listening to me?"

"I can't," she murmured, and she was talking to her lap, to the bed, to the floor. "I'm scared. I'm so scared." There were footsteps in the room next door, ponderous and heavy, then the quick tattoo of the child's feet and a sudden thump against the wall. "I don't want anyone to know," she said.

He could have held her, could have squeezed in beside her and wrapped her in his arms, but something flared in him. He couldn't understand it. He just couldn't. "What are you thinking? Nobody'll know. He's a doctor, for Christ's sake, sworn to secrecy, the doctor-patient compact and all that. What are you going to do, keep it? Huh? Just show up for English 101 with a baby on your lap and say, 'Hi, I'm the Virgin Mary'?"

30   She was crying. He could see it in the way her shoulders suddenly crumpled and now he could hear it too, a soft nasal complaint that went right through him. She lifted her face to him and held out her arms and he was there beside her, rocking her back and forth in his arms. He could feel the heat of her face against the hard fiber of his chest, a wetness there, fluids, her fluids. "I don't want a doctor," she said.

And that colored everything, that simple negative: life in the dorms, roommates, bars, bullshit sessions, the smell of burning leaves and the way the light fell across campus in great wide smoking bands just before dinner, the unofficial skateboard club, films, lectures, pep rallies, football—none of it mattered. He couldn't have a life. Couldn't be a freshman. Couldn't wake up in the morning and tumble into the slow steady current of the world. All he could think of was her. Or not simply her—her and him, and what had come between them. Because they argued now, they wrangled and fought and debated, and it was no pleasure to see her in that motel room with the queen-size bed and the big color TV and the soaps and shampoos they made off with as if they were treasure. She was pigheaded, stubborn, irrational. She was spoiled, he could see that now, spoiled by her parents and their standard of living and the socioeconomic expectations of her class—of his class—and the promise of life as you like it, an unscrolling vista of pleasure and acquisition. He loved her. He didn't want to turn his back on her. He would be there for her no matter what, but why did she have to be so *stupid?*

* * * * *

Big sweats, huge sweats, sweats that drowned and engulfed her, that was her campus life, sweats and the dining hall. Her dormmates didn't know her, and so what if she was putting on weight? Everybody did. How could you shovel down all those carbohydrates, all that sugar and grease and the puddings and nachos and all the rest, without putting on ten or fifteen pounds the first semester alone? Half the girls in the dorm were waddling around like the Doughboy, their faces bloated and blotched with acne, with crusting pimples and whiteheads fed on fat. So she was putting on weight. Big deal. "There's more of me to love," she told her roommate, "and Jeremy likes it that way. And, really, he's the only one that matters." She was careful to shower alone, in the early morning, long before the light had begun to bump up against the windows.

On the night her water broke—it was mid-December, almost nine months, as best as she could figure—it was raining. Raining hard. All week she'd been having tense rasping sotto voce debates with Jeremy on the phone—arguments, fights—and she told him that she would die, creep out into the woods like some animal and bleed to death, before she'd go to a hospital. "And what am I supposed to do?" he demanded in a high childish whine, as if he were the one who'd been knocked up, and she didn't want to hear it, she didn't.

"Do you love me?" she whispered. There was a long hesitation, a pause you could have poured all the affirmation of the world into.

35   "Yes," he said finally, his voice so soft and reluctant it was like the last gasp of a dying old man.

"Then you're going to have to rent the motel."

"And then what?"

"Then—I don't know." The door was open, her roommate framed there in the hall, a burst of rock and roll coming at her like an assault. "I guess you'll have to get a book or something."

By eight, the rain had turned to ice and every branch of every tree was coated with it, the highway littered with glistening black sticks, no moon, no stars, the tires sliding out from under her, and she felt heavy, big as a sumo wrestler, heavy and loose at the same time. She'd taken a towel from the dorm and put it under her, on the seat, but it was a mess, everything was a mess. She was cramping. Fidgeting with her hair. She tried the radio, but it was no help, nothing but songs she hated, singers that were worse. Twenty-two miles to Danbury, and the first of the contractions came like a seizure, like a knife blade thrust into her spine. Her world narrowed to what the headlights would show her.

40   Jeremy was waiting for her at the door to the room, the light behind him a pale rinse of nothing, no smile on his face, no human expression at all. They didn't kiss—they didn't even touch—and then she was on the bed, on her back, her face clenched like a fist. She heard the rattle of the sleet at the window, the murmur of the TV: *I can't let you go like this*, a man protested, and she could picture him, angular and tall, a man in a hat and overcoat in a black-and-white world that might have been another planet, *I just can't.* "Are you—?" Jeremy's voice drifted into the mix, and then stalled. "Are you ready? I mean, is it time? Is it coming now?"

She said one thing then, one thing only, her voice as pinched and hollow as the sound of the wind in the gutters: "Get it out of me."

It took a moment, and then she could feel his hands fumbling with her sweats.

Later, hours later, when nothing had happened but pain, a parade of pain with drum majors and brass bands and penitents crawling on their hands and knees till the streets were stained with their blood, she cried out and cried out again. "It's like *Alien*," she gasped, "like that thing in *Alien* when it, it—"

"It's okay," he kept telling her, "it's okay," but his face betrayed him. He looked scared, looked as if he'd been drained of blood in some evil experiment in yet another movie, and a part of her wanted to be sorry for him, but another part, the part that was so commanding and fierce it overrode everything else, couldn't begin to be.

45   He was useless, and he knew it. He'd never been so purely sick at heart and terrified in all his life, but he tried to be there for her, tried to do his best, and when the baby came out, the baby girl all slick with blood and mucus and the lumped white stuff that was like something spilled at the bottom of a garbage can, he was thinking of the ninth grade and how close he'd come to fainting while the teacher went around the room to prick their fingers one by one so they each could smear a drop of blood across a slide. He didn't faint now. But he was close to it, so close he could feel the room dodging away under his feet. And then her voice, the first intelligible thing she'd said in an hour: "Get rid of it. Just get rid of it."

Of the drive back to Binghamton he remembered nothing. Or practically nothing. They took towels from the motel and spread them across the seat of her car, he could remember that much . . . and the blood, how could he forget the blood? It soaked through her sweats and the towels and even the thick cotton bathmat and into the worn fabric of the seat itself. And it all came from inside her, all of it, tissue and mucus and the shining bright fluid, no end to it, as if she'd been turned inside out. He wanted to ask her about that, if that was normal, but she was asleep the minute she slid out from under his arm and dropped into the seat. If he focused, if he really concentrated, he could remember the way her head lolled against the doorframe while the engine whined and the car rocked and the slush threw a dark blanket over the windshield every time a truck shot past in the opposite direction. That and the exhaustion. He'd never been so tired, his head on a string, shoulders slumped, his arms like two pillars of concrete. And what if he'd nodded off? What if he'd gone into a skid and hurtled over an embankment into the filthy gray accumulation of the worst day of his life? What then?

She made it into the dorm under her own power, nobody even looked at her, and no, she didn't need his help. "Call me," she whispered, and they kissed, her lips so cold it was like kissing a steak through the plastic wrapper, and then he parked her car in the student lot and walked to the bus station. He made Danbury late that night, caught a ride out to the motel, and walked right through the Do Not Disturb sign on the door. Fifteen minutes. That was all it took. He bundled up everything, every trace, left the key in the box at the desk, and stood scraping the ice off the windshield of his car while the night opened up above him to a black glitter of sky. He never gave a thought to what lay discarded in the Dumpster out back, itself wrapped in plastic, so much meat, so much cold meat.

He was at the very pinnacle of his dream, the river dressed in its currents, the deep hole under the cutbank, and the fish like silver bullets swarming to his bait, when they woke him—when Rob woke him, Rob Greiner, his roommate, Rob with a face of crumbling stone and two policemen there at the door behind him and the roar of the dorm falling away to a whisper. And that was strange, policemen, a real anomaly in that setting, and at first—for the first thirty seconds, at least—he had no idea what they were doing there. Parking tickets? Could that be it? But then they asked him his name, just to confirm it, joined his hands together behind his back, and fitted two loops of naked metal over his wrists, and he began to understand. He saw McCaffrey and Tuttle from across the hall staring at him as if he were Jeffrey Dahmer or something, and the rest of them, all the rest, every head poking out of every door up and down the corridor, as the police led him away.

"What's this all about?" he kept saying, the cruiser nosing through the dark streets to the station house, the man at the wheel and the man beside him as incapable of speech as the seats or the wire mesh or the gleaming black dashboard that dragged them forward into the night. And then it was up the steps and into an explosion of light, more men in uniform, stand here, give me your hand, now the other one, and then the cage and the questions. Only then did he think of that thing in the garbage sack and the sound it had made—its body had made—when he flung it into the Dumpster like a sack of flour and the lid slammed down on it. He stared at the walls, and this was a movie too. He'd never been in trouble before, never been inside a police station, but he knew his role well enough, because he'd seen it played out a thousand times on the tube: deny everything. Even as the two detectives settled in across from him at the bare wooden table in the little box of the overlit room he was telling himself just that: *Deny it, deny it all.*

50   The first detective leaned forward and set his hands on the table as if he'd come for a manicure. He was in his thirties, or maybe his forties, a tired-looking man with the scars of the turmoil he'd witnessed gouged into the flesh under his eyes. He didn't offer a cigarette ("I don't smoke," Jeremy was prepared to say, giving them that much at least), and he didn't smile or soften his eyes. And when he spoke his voice carried no freight at all, not outrage or threat or cajolery—it was just a voice, flat and tired. "Do you know a China Berkowitz?" he said.

And she. She was in the community hospital, where the ambulance had deposited her after her roommate had called 911 in a voice that was like a bone stuck in the back of her throat, and it was raining again. Her parents were there, her mother red-eyed and sniffling, her father looking like an actor who's forgotten his lines, and there was another woman there too, a policewoman. The policewoman sat in an orange plastic chair in the corner, dipping her head to the knitting in her lap. At first, China's mother had tried to be pleasant to the woman, but pleasant wasn't what the circumstances called for, and now she ignored her, because the very unpleasant fact was that China was being taken into custody as soon as she was released from the hospital.

For a long while no one said anything—everything had already been said, over and over, one long flood of hurt and recrimination—and the antiseptic silence of the hospital held them in its grip while the rain beat at the windows and the machines at the foot of the bed counted off numbers. From down the hall came a snatch of TV dialogue, and for a minute China opened her eyes and thought she was back in the dorm. "Honey," her mother said, raising a purgatorial face to her, "are you all right? Can I get you anything?"

"I need to—I think I need to pee."

"Why?" her father demanded, and it was the perfect non sequitur. He was up out of the chair, standing over her, his eyes like cracked porcelain. "Why didn't you tell us, or at least tell your mother—or Dr. Fredman? Dr. Fredman, at least. He's been—he's like a family member, you know that, and he could have, or he would have . . . What were you *thinking*, for Christ's sake?"

55   Thinking? She wasn't thinking anything, not then and not now. All she wanted—and she didn't care what they did to her, beat her, torture her, drag her weeping through the streets in a dirty white dress with "Baby Killer" stitched over her breast in scarlet letters—was to see Jeremy. Just that. Because what really mattered was what he was thinking.

The food at the Sarah Barnes Cooper Women's Correctional Institute was exactly what they served at the dining hall in college, heavy on the sugars, starches, and bad cholesterol, and that would have struck her as ironic if she'd been there under other circumstances—doing community outreach, say, or researching a paper for her sociology class. But given the fact that she'd been locked up for more than a month now, the object of the other girls' threats, scorn, and just plain *nastiness*, given the fact that her life was ruined beyond any hope of redemption, and every newspaper in the country had her shrunken white face plastered across its front page under a headline that screamed MOTEL MOM, she didn't have much use for irony. She was scared twenty-four hours a day. Scared of the present, scared of the future, scared of the reporters waiting for the judge to set bail so that they could swarm all over her the minute she stepped out the door. She couldn't concentrate on the books and magazines her mother brought her or even on the TV in the rec room. She sat in her room—it was a room, just like a dorm room, except that they locked you in at night—and stared at the walls, eating peanuts, M&M's, sunflower seeds by the handful, chewing for the pure animal gratification of it. She was putting on more weight, and what did it matter?

Jeremy was different. He'd lost everything—his walk, his smile, the muscles of his upper arms and shoulders. Even his hair lay flat now, as if he couldn't bother with a tube of gel and a comb. When she saw him at the arraignment, saw him for the first time since she'd climbed out of the car and limped into the dorm with the blood wet on her legs, he looked like a refugee, like a ghost. The room they were in—the courtroom—seemed to have grown up around them, walls, windows, benches, lights and radiators already in place, along with the judge, the American flag and the ready-made spectators. It was hot. People coughed into their fists and shuffled their feet, every sound magnified. The judge presided, his arms like bones twirled in a bag, his eyes searching and opaque as he peered over the top of his reading glasses.

China's lawyer didn't like Jeremy's lawyer, that much was evident, and the state prosecutor didn't like anybody. She watched him—Jeremy, only him—as the reporters held their collective breath and the judge read off the charges and her mother bowed her head and sobbed into the bucket of her hands. And Jeremy was watching her too, his eyes locked on hers as if he defied them all, as if nothing mattered in the world but her, and when the judge said "First-degree murder" and "Murder by abuse or neglect," he never flinched.

She sent him a note that day—"I love you, will always love you no matter what, More than Moon"—and in the hallway, afterward, while their lawyers fended off the reporters and the bailiffs tugged impatiently at them, they had a minute, just a minute, to themselves. "What did you tell them?" he whispered. His voice was a rasp, almost a growl; she looked at him, inches away, and hardly recognized him.

60   "I told them it was dead."

"My lawyer—Mrs. Teagues?—she says they're saying it was alive when we, when we put it in the bag." His face was composed, but his eyes were darting like insects trapped inside his head.

"It was dead."

"It looked dead," he said, and already he was pulling away from her and some callous shit with a camera kept annihilating them with flash after flash of light, "and we certainly didn't—I mean, we didn't slap it or anything to get it breathing. . . . "

And then the last thing he said to her, just as they were pulled apart, and it was nothing she wanted to hear, nothing that had any love in it, or even the hint of love: "You told me to get rid of it."

65   There was no elaborate name for the place where they were keeping him. It was known as Drum Hill Prison, period. No reform-minded notions here, no verbal gestures toward rehabilitation or behavior modification, no benefactors, mayors or role models to lend the place their family names, but then who in his right mind would want a prison named after him anyway? At least they kept him separated from the other prisoners, the gangbangers and dope dealers and sexual predators and the like. He was no longer a freshman at Brown, not officially, but he had his books and his course notes, and he tried to keep up as best he could. Still, when the screams echoed through the cell-block at night and the walls dripped with the accumulated breath of eight and a half thousand terminally angry sociopaths, he had to admit it wasn't the sort of college experience he'd bargained for.

And what had he done to deserve it? He still couldn't understand. That thing in the Dumpster—and he refused to call it human, let alone a baby— was nobody's business but his and China's. That's what he'd told his attorney, Mrs. Teagues, and his mother and her boyfriend, Howard, and he'd told them over and over again: "*I didn't do anything wrong.*" Even if it was alive, and it was, he knew in his heart that it was, even before the state prosecutor presented evidence of blunt-force trauma and death by asphyxiation and exposure, it didn't matter, or shouldn't have mattered. There was no baby. There was nothing but a mistake, a mistake clothed in blood and mucus. When he really thought about it, thought it through on its merits and dissected all his mother's pathetic arguments about where he'd be today if she'd felt as he did when she was pregnant herself, he hardened like a rock, like sand turning to stone under all the pressure the planet can bring to bear. Another unwanted child in an overpopulated world? They should have given him a medal.

It was the end of January before bail was set—three hundred and fifty thousand dollars his mother didn't have—and he was released to house arrest. He wore a plastic anklet that set off an alarm if he went out the door, and so did she, so did China, imprisoned like some fairy-tale princess at her parents' house. At first, she called him every day, but mostly what she did was cry—"I want to see it," she sobbed. "I want to see our daughter's *grave.*" That froze him inside. He tried to picture her—her now, China, the love of his life—and he couldn't. What did she look like? What was her face like, her nose, her hair, her eyes and breasts and the slit between her legs? He drew a blank. There was no way to summon her the way she used to be or even the way she was in court, because all he could remember was the thing that had come out of her, four limbs and the equipment of a female, shoulders rigid and eyes shut tight, as if she were a mummy in a tomb . . . and the breath, the shuddering long gasping rattle of a breath he could feel ringing inside her even as the black plastic bag closed over her face and the lid of the Dumpster opened like a mouth.

He was in the den, watching basketball, a drink in his hand (7Up mixed with Jack Daniel's in a ceramic mug, so no one would know he was getting shit-faced at two o'clock on a Sunday afternoon), when the phone rang. It was Sarah Teagues. "Listen, Jeremy," she said in her crisp, equitable tones, "I thought you ought to know—the Berkowitzes are filing a motion to have the case against China dropped."

His mother's voice on the portable, too loud, a blast of amplified breath and static: "On what grounds?"

70   "She never saw the baby, that's what they're saying. She thought she had a miscarriage."

"Yeah, right," his mother said.

Sarah Teagues was right there, her voice as clear and present as his mother's. "Jeremy's the one that threw it in the Dumpster, and they're saying he acted alone. She took a polygraph test day before yesterday."

He could feel his heart pounding the way it used to when he plodded up that last agonizing ridge behind the school with the cross-country team, his legs sapped, no more breath left in his body. He didn't say a word. Didn't even breathe.

"She's going to testify against him."

75   Outside was the world, puddles of ice clinging to the lawn under a weak afternoon sun, all the trees stripped bare, the grass dead, the azalea under the window reduced to an armload of dead brown twigs. She wouldn't have wanted to go out today anyway. This was the time of year she hated most, the long interval between the holidays and spring break, when nothing grew and nothing changed—it didn't even seem to snow much anymore. What was out there for her anyway? They wouldn't let her see Jeremy, wouldn't even let her talk to him on the phone or write him anymore, and she wouldn't be able to show her face at the mall or even the movie theater without somebody shouting out her name as if she was a freak, as if she was another Monica Lewinsky or Heidi Fleiss. She wasn't China Berkowitz, honor student, not anymore—she was the punch line to a joke, a footnote to history.

She wouldn't mind going for a drive, though—that was something she missed, just following the curves out to the reservoir to watch the way the ice cupped the shore, or up to the turnout on Route 9 to look out over the river where it oozed through the mountains in a shimmering coil of light. Or to take a walk in the woods, just that. She was in her room, on her bed, posters of bands she'd out-grown staring down from the walls, her high school books on two shelves in the corner, the closet door flung open on all the clothes she'd once wanted so desperately she could have died for each individual pair of boots or the cashmere sweaters that felt so good against her skin. At the bottom of her left leg, down there at the foot of the bed, was the anklet she wore now, the plastic anklet with the transmitter inside, no different, she supposed, than the collars they put on wolves to track them across all those miles of barren tundra or the bears sleeping in their dens. Except that hers had an alarm on it.

For a long while she just lay there gazing out the window, watching the rinsed-out sun slip down into the sky that had no more color in it than a TV tuned to an unsubscribed channel, and then she found herself picturing things the way they were an eon ago, when everything was green. She saw the azalea bush in bloom, the leaves knifing out of the trees, butterflies—or were they cabbage moths?—hovering over the flowers. Deep green. That was the color of the world. And she was remembering a night, summer before last, just after she and Jeremy started going together, the crickets thrumming, the air thick with humidity, and him singing along with the car radio, his voice so sweet and pure it was as if he'd written the song himself, just for her. And when they got to where they were going, at the end of that dark lane overhung with trees, to a place where it was private and hushed and the night fell in on itself as if it couldn't support the weight of the stars, he was as nervous as she was. She moved into his arms, and they kissed, his lips groping for hers in the dark, his fingers trembling over the thin yielding silk of her blouse. He was Jeremy. He was the love of her life. And she closed her eyes and clung to him as if that were all that mattered.

I N Q U I R I N G   F U R T H E R

1. What would you say to someone who argued that China and Jeremy were simply young and infatuated with one another? Do you think they were truly in love? What passages in the story might help you determine the nature of the relationship between China and Jeremy?

2. What are your thoughts on China's motivation not to have an abortion? How does this decision relate to her insisting on not seeing a doctor when she went into labor? Freewrite for five minutes about China's decisions.

EDGAR ALLEN POE

Edgar Allen Poe (1809–1849) had a rough life, living with a Richmond merchant after his parents died while he was yet a baby. He attended college and joined the army, but soon quit the university and was quickly discharged from the military for gambling. He is often associated with his belief that literature should be distilled, ideally enough to be appreciated in one sitting. His short stories enact this approach, compressing events and quickly establishing a sense of suspense. "The Tell-Tale Heart" (published in 1843) exemplifies the macabre themes associated with Poe, while exploring the dimensions of what it means to be a caregiver. We provide an enhanced reading of the story on our CD.

Enhanced reading of "The Tell-Tale Heart"

The Tell-Tale Heart

LI-YOUNG LEE

Indonesian poet Li-Young Lee (born in 1957) settled in the United States after fleeing persecution in Indonesia. Lee and his family traveled for several years after his father had been jailed, finally arriving in the United

States in 1964. Lee has studied and taught at many universities, while pub-
lishing several collections of poems. "The Gift" is taken from his 1986 col-
lection, Rose.

The Gift

To pull the metal splinter from my palm
my father recited a story in a low voice.
I watched his lovely face and not the blade.
Before the story ended, he'd removed
5   the iron sliver I thought I'd die from.

I can't remember the tale,
but hear his voice still, a well
of dark water, a prayer.
And I recall his hands,
10   two measures of tenderness
he laid against my face,
the flames of discipline
he raised above my head.

Had you entered that afternoon
15   you would have thought you saw a man
planting something in a boy's palm,
a silver tear, a tiny flame.
Had you followed that boy
you would have arrived here,
20   where I bend over my wife's right hand.

Look how I shave her thumbnail down
so carefully she feels no pain.
Watch as I lift the splinter out.
I was seven when my father
25   took my hand like this,
and I did not hold that shard
between my fingers and think,
Metal that will bury me,
christen it Little Assassin,
30   Ore Going Deep for My Heart.
And I did not lift up my wound and cry,

Death visited here!
I did what a child does
when he's given something to keep.
35   I kissed my father.

BARBARA DAFOE WHITEHEAD

Barbara Dafoe Whitehead (born in 1944) studies issues of parenting and
relationships. Her most recent books, The Divorce Culture, *and* Why There
are No Good Men Left *examine marriage and dating in light of the cul-*
tural changes of the last several decades. "Women and the Future of Father-
hood" first appeared as an essay in Wilson Quarterly *in 1996.*

Women and the Future of Fatherhood

Much of our contemporary debate over fatherhood is governed by the assumption that men can solve the fatherhood problem on their own. The organizers of last year's Million Man March asked women to stay home, and the leaders of Promise Keepers and other grass-roots fatherhood movements whose members gather with considerably less fanfare simply do not admit women.

There is a cultural rationale for the exclusion of women. The fatherhood movement sees the task of reinstating responsible fatherhood as an effort to alter today's norms of masculinity and correctly believes that such an effort cannot succeed unless it is voluntarily undertaken and supported by men. There is also a political rationale in defining fatherlessness as a men's issue. In the debate about marriage and parenthood, which women have dominated for at least 30 years, the fatherhood movement gives men a powerful collective voice and presence.

Yet however effective the grass-roots movement is at stirring men's consciences and raising their consciousness, the fatherhood problem will not be solved by men alone. To be sure, by signaling their commitment to accepting responsibility for the rearing of their children, men have taken the essential first step. But what has not yet been acknowledged is that the success of any effort to renew fatherhood as a social fact and a cultural norm also hinges on the attitudes and behavior of women. Men can't be fathers unless the mothers of their children allow it.

Merely to say this is to point to how thoroughly marital disruption has weakened the bond between fathers and children. More than half of all American children are likely to spend at least part of their lives in one-parent homes. Since the vast majority of children in disrupted families live with their mothers, fathers do not share a home or a daily life with their children. It is much more difficult for men to make the kinds of small, routine, instrumental investments in their children that help forge a good relationship. It is hard to fix a flat bike tire or run a bath when you live in another neighborhood or another town. Many a father's instrumental contribution is reduced to the postal or electronic transmission of money, or, all too commonly, to nothing at all. Without regular contact with their children, men often make reduced emotional contributions as well. Fathers must struggle to sustain close emotional ties across time and space, to "be there" emotionally without being there physically. Some may pick up the phone, send a birthday card, or buy a present, but for many fathers, physical absence also becomes emotional absence.

5   Without marriage, men also lose access to the social and emotional intelligence of women in building relationships. Wives teach men how to care for young children, and they also encourage children to love their fathers. Mothers who do not live with the father of their children are not as likely as married mothers to represent him in positive ways to the children; nor are the relatives who are most likely to have greatest contact with the children—the mother's parents, brothers, and sisters—likely to have a high opinion of the children's father. Many men are able to overcome such obstacles, but only with difficulty. In general, men need marriage in order to be good fathers.

If the future of fatherhood depends on marriage, however, its future is uncertain. Marriage depends on women as well as men, and women are less committed to marriage than ever before in the nation's history. In the past, women were economically dependent on marriage and assumed a disproportionately heavy responsibility for maintaining the bond, even if the underlying relationship was seriously or irretrievably damaged. In the last third of the 20th century, however, as women have gained more opportunities for paid work and the availability of child care has increased, they have become less dependent on marriage as an economic arrangement. Though it is not easy, it is possible for women to raise children on their own. This has made divorce far more attractive as a remedy for an unsatisfying marriage, and a growing number of women have availed themselves of the option.

Today, marriage and motherhood are coming apart. Remarriage and marriage rates are declining even as the rates of divorce remain stuck at historic highs and childbearing outside marriage becomes more common. Many women see single motherhood as a choice and a right to be exercised if a suitable husband does not come along in time.

The vision of the "first stage" feminism of the 1960s and '70s, which held out the model of the career woman unfettered by husband or children, has been accepted by women only in part. Women want to be fettered by children, even to the point of going through grueling infertility treatments or artificial insemination to achieve motherhood. But they are increasingly ambivalent about the ties that bind them to a husband and about the necessity of marriage as a condition of parenthood. In 1994, a National Opinion Research survey asked a group of Americans, "Do you agree or disagree: one parent can bring up a child as well as two parents together." Women split 50/50 on the question; men disagreed by more than two to one.

And indeed, women enjoy certain advantages over men in a society marked by high and sustained levels of family breakup. Women do not need marriage to maintain a close bond to their children, and thus to experience the larger sense of social and moral purpose that comes with raising children. As the bearers and nurturers of children and (increasingly) as the sole breadwinners for families, women continue to be engaged in personally rewarding and socially valuable pursuits. They are able to demonstrate their feminine virtues outside marriage.

10   Men, by contrast, have no positive identity as fathers outside marriage. Indeed, the emblematic absent father today is the infamous "deadbeat dad." In part, this is the result of efforts to stigmatize irresponsible fathers who fail to pay alimony and child support. But this image also reflects the fact that men are heavily dependent on the marriage partnership to fulfill their role as fathers. Even those who keep up their child support payments are deprived of the social importance and sense of larger purpose that comes from providing for children and raising a family. And it is the rare father who can develop the qualities needed to meet the new cultural ideal of the involved and "nurturing" father without the help of a spouse.

These differences are reflected in a growing virtue gap. American popular culture today routinely recognizes and praises the achievements of single motherhood, while the widespread failure of men as fathers has resulted in a growing sense of cynicism and despair about men's capacity for virtuous conduct in family life. The enormously popular movie *Waiting To Exhale* captures the essence of this virtue gap with its portrait of steadfast mothers and deadbeat fathers, morally sleazy men and morally unassailable women. And women feel free to vent their anger and frustration with men in ways that would seem outrageous to women if the shoe were on the other foot. In *Operating Instructions* (1993), her memoir of single motherhood, Anne Lamott mordantly observes, "On bad days, I think straight white men are so poorly wired, so emotionally unenlightened and unconscious that you must approach each one as if he were some weird cross between a white supremacist and an incredibly depressing T. S. Eliot poem."

Women's weakening attachment to marriage should not be taken as a lack of interest in marriage or in a husband-wife partnership in child rearing. Rather, it is a sign of women's more exacting emotional standards for husbands and their growing insistence that men play a bigger part in caring for children and the household. Given their double responsibilities as breadwinners and mothers, many working wives find men's need for ego reinforcement and other forms of emotional and physical upkeep irksome and their failure to share housework and child care absolutely infuriating. (Surveys show that husbands perform only one-third of all household tasks even if their wives are working full-time.) Why should men be treated like babies? women complain. If men fail to meet their standards, many women are willing to do without them. Poet and polemicist Katha Pollitt captures the prevailing sentiment: "If single women can have sex, their own homes, the respect of friends and interesting work, they don't need to tell themselves that any marriage is better than none. Why not have a child on one's own? Children are a joy. Many men are not."

For all these reasons, it is important to see the fatherhood problem as part of the larger cultural problem of the decline of marriage as a lasting relationship between men and women. The traditional bargain between men and women has broken down, and a new bargain has not yet been struck. It is impossible to predict what that bargain will look like—or whether there will even be one. However, it is possible to speculate about the talking points that might bring women to the bargaining table. First, a crucial proviso: there must be recognition of the changed social and economic status of women. Rightly or wrongly, many women fear that the fatherhood movement represents an effort to reinstate the status quo ante, to repeal the gains and achievements women have made over the past 30 years and return to the "separate spheres" domestic ideology that put men in the workplace and women in the home. Any effort to rethink marriage must accept the fact that women will continue to work outside the home.

Therefore, a new bargain must be struck over the division of paid work and family work. This does not necessarily mean a 50/50 split in the work load every single day, but it does mean that men must make a more determined and conscientious effort to do more than one-third of the household chores. How each couple arrives at a sense of what is fair will vary, of course, but the goal is to establish some mutual understanding and commitment to an equitable division of tasks.

15   Another talking point may focus on the differences in the expectations men and women have for marriage and intimacy. Americans have a "best friends" ideal for marriage that includes some desires that might in fact be more easily met by a best friend—someone who doesn't come with all the complicated entanglements of sharing a bed, a bank account, and a bathroom. Nonetheless, high expectations for emotional intimacy in marriage often are confounded by the very different understandings men and women have of intimacy. Much more than men, women seek intimacy and affection through talking and emotional disclosure. Men often prefer sex to talking, and physical disrobing to emotional disclosing. They tend to be less than fully committed to (their own) sexual fidelity, while women view fidelity as a crucial sign of commitment.

These are differences that the sexes need to engage with mutual recognition and tolerance.

In renegotiating the marital bargain, it may also be useful to acknowledge the biosocial differences between mothers and fathers rather than to assume an androgynous model for the parental partnership. There can be a high degree of flexibility in parental roles, but men and women are not interchangeable "parental units," particularly in their children's early years. Rather than struggle to establish identical tracks in career and family lives, it may be more realistic to consider how children's needs and well-being might require patterns of paid work and child rearing that are different for mothers and fathers but are nevertheless equitable over the course of a lifetime.

Finally, it may be important to think and talk about marriage in another kind of language than the one that suffuses our current discourse on relationships. The secular language of "intimate relationships" is the language of politics and psychotherapy, and it focuses on individual rights and individual needs. It can be heard most clearly in the personal-ad columns, a kind of masked ball where optimists go in search of partners who respect their rights and meet their emotional needs. These are not unimportant in the achievement of the contemporary ideal of marriage, which emphasizes egalitarianism and emotional fulfillment. But this notion of marriage as a union of two sovereign selves may be inadequate to define a relationship that carries with it the obligations, duties, and sacrifices of parenthood. There has always been a tension between marriage as an intimate relationship between a man and a woman and marriage as an institutional arrangement for raising children, and though the language of individual rights plays a part in defining the former, it cannot fully describe the latter. The parental partnership requires some language that acknowledges differences, mutuality, complementarity, and, more than anything else, altruism.

There is a potentially powerful incentive for women to respond to an effort to renegotiate the marriage bargain, and that has to do with their children. Women can be good mothers without being married. But especially with weakened communities that provide little support, children need levels of parental investment that cannot be supplied solely by a good mother, even if she has the best resources at her disposal. These needs are more likely to be met if the child has a father as well as a mother under the same roof. Simply put, even the best mothers cannot be good fathers.

INQUIRING FURTHER

1. What perspective on fathers is offered in "The Gift"? Is it fair to say that perspective is unique to Lee's Eastern culture? Why or why not?

2. Do you believe Whitehead promotes stereotypes? How does she characterize the emotional attitudes of men and women? Do you agree with her characterizations? If they seem to hold true, can these characterizations be called stereotypes?

3. How would you relate Whitehead's essay to Lee's poem, "The Gift"? Which do you think offers a more realistic picture of fatherhood? Why?

ANDREW WYETH

*Andrew Wyeth (born in 1917) was the youngest son of painter N. C. Wyeth.
Andrew suffered from poor health growing up; rather than attending
school, he stayed at home where he learned art from his father. In 1945
N. C. Wyeth was killed in a railway accident, launching Andrew into a
period of introspection that led to a number of melancholy paintings.*
Dodge's Ridge *was painted in 1947, two years after his father's death.*

Dodge's Ridge

INQUIRING FURTHER

1. How would you characterize the message portrayed in *Dodge's Ridge?* What
   might be the significance of the tire ruts on the hillside? How do elements
   of art such as lighting, lines, shapes, and arrangement work in the image? Write
   a paragraph or two analyzing how the image conveys a message.

2. What would you say to someone who argued that the painting did not speak
   to relationships because it lacks any human figures? Is it possible for any image
   to not touch on human concerns? Why or why not?

3. If you did not know the biographical information about the death of Wyeth's
   father, how might your interpretation of the painting change? How would you
   explain the relationship between the context and the meaning of the image?

BROTHERS AND SISTERS

Ever since Cain and Abel, stories of sibling rivalry have held our attention and confirmed what we may already be familiar with from our own relationships. Brothers and sisters do not always get along. In fact, since children sometimes see themselves as competing for the limited attention of parents, the conflicts between siblings can become intense, leading to frustration, anger, even violence. However, rivalry tells only half the story of what it means to live as brothers or sisters. Indeed, the bonds between siblings may be equally as strong as those between parents and children. The selections below reveal just how important these sibling connections can be.

LOUISE ERDRICH

Louise Erdrich (born in 1954) grew up in Wahpeton, North Dakota, a member of the Turtle Mountain Band of Chippewa. Her grandfather was for many years tribal chair of the reservation, where her parents taught in the Bureau of Indian Affairs School. She attended Dartmouth College, earning a degree in anthropology (1976) and Johns Hopkins University where she studied creative writing. She has published numerous novels, including Love Medicine *(1984), which won the National Book Critics Circle Award. "The Red Convertible" is taken from* Love Medicine.

The Red Convertible (1974)

Lyman Lamartine

I was the first one to drive a convertible on my reservation. And of course it was red, a red Olds. I owned that car along with my brother Henry Junior. We owned it together until his boots filled with water on a windy night and he bought out my share. Now Henry owns the whole car, and his younger brother Lyman (that's myself), Lyman walks everywhere he goes.

How did I earn enough money to buy my share in the first place? My one talent was I could always make money. I had a touch for it, unusual in a Chippewa. From the first I was different that way, and everyone recognized it. I was the only kid they let in the American Legion Hall to shine shoes, for example, and one Christmas I sold spiritual bouquets for the mission door to door. The nuns let me keep a percentage. Once I started, it seemed the more money I made the easier the money came. Everyone encouraged it. When I was fifteen I got a job washing dishes at the Joliet Café, and that was where my first big break happened.

It wasn't long before I was promoted to busing tables, and then the short-order cook quit and I was hired to take her place. No sooner than you know it I was managing the Joliet. The rest is history. I went on managing. I soon became part owner, and of course there was no stopping me then. It wasn't long before the whole thing was mine.

After I'd owned the Joliet for one year, it blew over in the worst tornado ever seen around here. The whole operation was smashed to bits. A total loss. The fryalator was up in a tree, the grill torn in half like it was paper. I was only sixteen. I had it all in my mother's name, and I lost it quick, but before I lost it I had every one of my relatives, and their relatives, to dinner, and I also bought that red Olds I mentioned, along with Henry.

5 The first time we saw it! I'll tell you when we first saw it. We had gotten a ride up to Winnipeg, and both of us had money. Don't ask me why, because we never mentioned a car or anything, we just had all our money. Mine was cash, a big bankroll from the Joliet's insurance. Henry had two checks—a week's extra pay for being laid off, and his regular check from the Jewel Bearing Plant.

We were walking down Portage anyway, seeing the sights, when we saw it. There it was, parked, large as life. Really as *if* it was alive. I thought of the word *repose*, because the car wasn't simply stopped, parked, or whatever. That car reposed, calm and gleaming, a FOR SALE sign in its left front window. Then, before we had thought it over at all, the car belonged to us and our pockets were empty. We had just enough money for gas back home.

We went places in that car, me and Henry. We took off driving all one whole summer. We started off toward the Little Knife River and Mandaree in Fort Berthold and then we found ourselves down in Wakpala somehow, and then suddenly we were over in Montana on the Rocky Boy, and yet the summer was not even half over. Some people hang on to details when they travel, but we didn't let them bother us and just lived our everyday lives here to there.

I do remember this one place with willows. I remember I laid under those trees and it was comfortable. So comfortable. The branches bent down all around me like a tent or a stable. And quiet, it was quiet, even though there was a powwow close enough so I could see it going on. The air was not too still, not too windy either. When the dust rises up and hangs in the air around the dancers like that, I feel good. Henry was asleep with his arms thrown wide. Later on, he woke up and we started driving again. We were somewhere in Montana, or maybe on the Blood Reserve—it could have been anywhere. Anyway it was where we met the girl.

All her hair was in buns around her ears, that's the first thing I noticed about her. She was posed alongside the road with her arm out, so we stopped. That girl was short, so short her lumber shirt looked comical on her, like a nightgown. She had jeans on and fancy moccasins and she carried a little suitcase.

10 "Hop on in," says Henry. So she climbs in between us.
"We'll take you home," I says. "Where do you live?"
"Chicken," she says.
"Where the hell's that?" I ask her.
"Alaska."
15 "Okay," says Henry, and we drive.
We got up there and never wanted to leave. The sun doesn't truly set there in summer, and the night is more a soft dusk. You might doze off, sometimes, but before you know it you're up again, like an animal in nature. You never feel like you have to sleep hard or put away the world. And things would grow up there. One day just dirt or moss, the next day flowers and long grass. The girl's name was Susy. Her family really took to us. They fed us and put us up. We had our own tent to live in by their house, and the kids would be in and out of there all day and night. They couldn't get over me and Henry being brothers, we looked so different. We told them we knew we had the same mother, anyway.

One night Susy came in to visit us. We sat around in the tent talking of this and that. The season was changing. It was getting darker by that time, and the cold was even getting just a little mean. I told her it was time for us to go. She stood up on a chair.

"You never seen my hair," Susy said.

That was true. She was standing on a chair, but still, when she unclipped her buns the hair reached all the way to the ground. Our eyes opened. You couldn't tell how much hair she had when it was rolled up so neatly. Then my brother Henry did something funny. He went up to the chair and said, "Jump on my shoulders." So she did that, and her hair reached down past his waist, and he started twirling, this way and that, so her hair was flung out from side to side.

20   "I always wondered what it was like to have long pretty hair," Henry says. Well we laughed. It was a funny sight, the way he did it. The next morning we got up and took leave of those people.

On to greener pastures, as they say. It was down through Spokane and across Idaho then Montana and very soon we were racing the weather right along under the Canadian border through Columbus, Des Lacs, and then we were in Bottineau County and soon home. We'd made most of the trip, that summer, without putting up the car hood at all. We got home just in time, it turned out, for the army to remember Henry had signed up to join it.

I don't wonder that the army was so glad to get my brother that they turned him into a Marine. He was built like a brick outhouse anyway. We liked to tease him that they really wanted him for his Indian nose. He had a nose big and sharp as a hatchet, like the nose on Red Tomahawk, the Indian who killed Sitting Bull, whose profile is on signs all along the North Dakota highways. Henry went off to training camp, came home once during Christmas, then the next thing you know we got an overseas letter from him. It was 1970, and he said he was stationed up in the northern hill country. Whereabouts I did not know. He wasn't such a hot letter writer, and only got off two before the enemy caught him. I could never keep it straight, which direction those good Vietnam soldiers were from.

I wrote him back several times, even though I didn't know if those letters would get through. I kept him informed all about the car. Most of the time I had it up on blocks in the yard or half taken apart, because that long trip did a hard job on it under the hood.

I always had good luck with numbers, and never worried about the draft myself. I never even had to think about what my number was. But Henry was never lucky in the same way as me. It was at least three years before Henry came home. By then I guess the whole war was solved in the government's mind, but for him it would keep on going. In those years I'd put his car into almost perfect shape. I always thought of it as his car while he was gone, even though when he left he said, "Now it's yours," and threw me his key.

25   "Thanks for the extra key," I'd said. "I'll put it up in your drawer just in case I need it." He laughed.

When he came home, though, Henry was very different, and I'll say this: the change was no good. You could hardly expect him to change for the better, I know. But he was quiet, so quiet, and never comfortable sitting still anywhere but always up and moving around. I thought back to times we'd sat still for whole afternoons, never moving a muscle, just shifting our weight along the ground, talking to whoever sat with us, watching things. He'd always had a joke, then, too, and now you couldn't get him to laugh, or when he did it was more the sound of a man choking, a sound that stopped up the throats of other people around him. They got to leaving him alone most of the time, and I didn't blame them. It was a fact: Henry was jumpy and mean.

I'd bought a color TV set for my mom and the rest of us while Henry was away. Money still came very easy. I was sorry I'd ever bought it though, because of Henry. I was also sorry I'd bought color, because with black-and-white the pictures seem older and farther away. But what are you going to do? He sat in front of it, watching it, and that was the only time he was completely still. But it was the kind of stillness that you see in a rabbit when it freezes and before it will bolt. He was not easy. He sat in his chair gripping the armrests with all his might, as if the chair itself was moving at a high speed and if he let go at all he would rocket forward and maybe crash right through the set.

Once I was in the room watching TV with Henry and I heard his teeth click at something. I looked over, and he'd bitten through his lip. Blood was going down his chin. I tell you right then I wanted to smash that tube to pieces. I went over to it but Henry must have known what I was up to. He rushed from his chair and shoved me out of the way, against the wall. I told myself he didn't know what he was doing.

My mom came in, turned the set off real quiet, and told us she had made something for supper. So we went and sat down. There was still blood going down Henry's chin, but he didn't notice it and no one said anything, even though every time he took a bite of his bread his blood fell onto it until he was eating his own blood mixed in with the food.

30   While Henry was not around we talked about what was going to happen to him. There were no Indian doctors on the reservation, and my mom couldn't come around to trusting the old man, Moses Pillager, because he courted her long ago and was jealous of her husbands. He might take revenge through her son. We were afraid that if we brought Henry to a regular hospital they would keep him.

"They don't fix them in those places," Mom said; "they just give them drugs."

"We wouldn't get him there in the first place," I agreed, "so let's just forget about it."

Then I thought about the car.

Henry had not even looked at the car since he'd gotten home, though like I said, it was in tip-top condition and ready to drive. I thought the car might bring the old Henry back somehow. So I bided my time and waited for my chance to interest him in the vehicle.

35   One night Henry was off somewhere. I took myself a hammer. I went out to that car and I did a number on its underside. Whacked it up. Bent the tail pipe double. Ripped the muffler loose. By the time I was done with the car it looked worse than any typical Indian car that has been driven all its life on reservation roads, which they always say are like government promises—full of holes. It just about hurt me. I'll tell you that! I threw dirt in the carburetor and I ripped all the electric tape off the seats. I made it look just as beat up as I could. Then I sat back and waited for Henry to find it.

Still, it took him over a month. That was all right, because it was just getting warm enough, not melting, but warm enough to work outside.

"Lyman," he says, walking in one day, "that red car looks like shit."

"Well it's old," I says. "You got to expect that."

"No way!" says Henry. "That car's a classic! But you went and ran the piss right out of it, Lyman, and you know it don't deserve that. I kept that car in A-one shape. You don't remember. You're too young. But when I left, that car was running like a watch. Now I don't even know if I can get it to start again, let alone get it anywhere near its old condition."

40   "Well you try," I said, like I was getting mad, "but I say it's a piece of junk."

Then I walked out before he could realize I knew he'd strung together more than six words at once.

After that I thought he'd freeze himself to death working on that car. He was out there all day, and at night he rigged up a little lamp, ran a cord out the window, and had himself some light to see by while he worked. He was better than he had been before, but that's still not saying much. It was easier for him to do the things the rest of us did. He ate more slowly and didn't jump up and down during the meal to get this or that or look out the window. I put my hand in the back of the TV set, I admit, and fiddled around with it good, so that it was almost impossible now to get a clear picture. He didn't look at it very often anyway. He was always out with that car or going off to get parts for it. By the time it was really melting outside, he had it fixed.

I had been feeling down in the dumps about Henry around this time. We had always been together before. Henry and Lyman. But he was such a loner now that I didn't know how to take it. So I jumped at the chance one day when Henry seemed friendly. It's not that he smiled or anything. He just said, "Let's take that old shitbox for a spin." Just the way he said it made me think he could be coming around.

We went out to the car. It was spring. The sun was shining very bright. My only sister, Bonita, who was just eleven years old, came out and made us stand together for a picture. Henry leaned his elbow on the red car's windshield, and he took his other arm and put it over my shoulder, very carefully, as though it was heavy for him to lift and he didn't want to bring the weight down all at once.

45   "Smile," Bonita said, and he did.

That picture. I never look at it anymore. A few months ago, I don't know why, I got his picture out and tacked it on the wall. I felt good about Henry at the time, close to him. I felt good having his picture on the wall, until one night when I was looking at television. I was a little drunk and stoned. I looked up at the wall and Henry was staring at me. I don't know what it was, but his smile had changed, or maybe it was gone. All I know is I couldn't stay in the same room with that picture. I was shaking. I got up, closed the door, and went into the kitchen. A little later my friend Ray came over and we both went back into that room. We put the picture in a brown bag, folded the bag over and over tightly, then put it way back in a closet.

I still see that picture now, as if it tugs at me, whenever I pass that closet door. The picture is very clear in my mind. It was so sunny that day Henry had to squint against the glare. Or maybe the camera Bonita held flashed like a mirror, blinding him, before she snapped the picture. My face is right out in the sun, big and round. But he might have drawn back, because the shadows on his face are deep as holes. There are two shadows curved like little hooks around the ends of his smile, as if to frame it and try to keep it there—that one, first smile that looked like it might have hurt his face. He has his field jacket on and the worn-in clothes he'd come back in and kept wearing ever since. After Bonita took the picture, she went into the house and we got into the car. There was a full cooler in the trunk. We started off, east, toward Pembina and the Red River because Henry said he wanted to see the high water.

The trip over there was beautiful. When everything starts changing, drying up, clearing off, you feel like your whole life is starting. Henry felt it, too. The top was down and the car hummed like a top. He'd really put it back in shape, even the tape on the seats was very carefully put down and glued back in layers. It's not that he smiled again or even joked, but his face looked to me as if it was clear, more peaceful. It looked as though he wasn't thinking of anything in particular except the bare fields and windbreaks and houses we were passing.

The river was high and full of winter trash when we got there. The sun was still out, but it was colder by the river. There were still little clumps of dirty snow here and there on the banks. The water hadn't gone over the banks yet, but it would, you could tell. It was just at its limit, hard swollen, glossy like an old gray scar. We made ourselves a fire, and we sat down and watched the current go. As I watched it I felt something squeezing inside me and tightening and trying to let go all at the same time. I knew I was not just feeling it myself; I knew I was feeling what Henry was going through at that moment. Except that I couldn't stand it, the closing and opening. I jumped to my feet. I took Henry by the shoulders and I started shaking him. "Wake up," I says, "wake up, wake up, wake up!" I didn't know what had come over me. I sat down beside him again.

50   His face was totally white and hard. Then it broke, like stones break all of a sudden when water boils up inside them.

"I know it," he says. "I know it. I can't help it. It's no use."

We start talking. He said he knew what I'd done with the car. It was obvious it had been whacked out of shape and not just neglected. He said he wanted to give the car to me for good now, it was no use. He said he'd fixed it just to give it back and I should take it.

"No way," I says. "I don't want it."

"That's okay," he says, "you take it."

55   "I don't want it, though," I says back to him, and then to emphasize, just to emphasize, you understand, I touch his shoulder. He slaps my hand off.

"Take that car," he says.

"No," I say. "Make me," I say, and then he grabs my jacket and rips the arm loose. That jacket is a class act, suede with tags and zippers. I push Henry backwards, off the log. He jumps up and bowls me over. We go down in a clinch and come up swinging hard, for all we're worth, with our fists. He socks my jaw so hard I feel like it swings loose. Then I'm at his rib cage and land a good one under his chin so his head snaps back. He's dazzled. He looks at me and I look at him and then his eyes are full of tears and blood and at first I think he's crying. But no, he's laughing. "Ha! Ha!" he says. "Ha! Ha! Take good care of it."

"Okay," I says. "Okay, no problem. Ha! Ha!"

I can't help it, and I start laughing, too. My face feels fat and strange, and after a while I get a beer from the cooler in the trunk, and when I hand it to Henry he takes his shirt and wipes my germs off. "Hoof-and-mouth disease," he says. For some reason this cracks me up, and so we're really laughing for a while, and then we drink all the rest of the beers one by one and throw them in the river and see how far, how fast, the current takes them before they fill up and sink.

60   "You want to go on back?" I ask after a while. "Maybe we could snag a couple nice Kashpaw girls."

He says nothing. But I can tell his mood is turning again.

"They're all crazy, the girls up here, every damn one of them."

"You're crazy too," I say, to jolly him up. "Crazy Lamartine boys!"

He looks as though he will take this wrong at first. His face twists, then clears, and he jumps up on his feet. "That's right!" he says. "Crazier 'n hell. Crazy Indians!"

65   I think it's the old Henry again. He throws off his jacket and starts springing his legs up from the knees like a fancy dancer. He's down doing something between a grass dance and a bunny hop, no kind of dance I ever saw before, but neither has anyone else on all this green growing earth. He's wild. He wants to pitch whoopee! He's up and at me and all over. All this time I'm laughing so hard, so hard my belly is getting tied up in a knot.

"Got to cool me off!" he shouts all of a sudden. Then he runs over to the river and jumps in.

There's boards and other things in the current. It's so high. No sound comes from the river after the splash he makes, so I run right over. I look around. It's getting dark. I see he's halfway across the water already, and I know he didn't swim there but the current took him. It's far. I hear his voice, though, very clearly across it.

"My boots are filling," he says.

He says this in a normal voice, like he just noticed and he doesn't know what to think of it. Then he's gone. A branch comes by. Another branch. And I go in.

70 By the time I get out of the river, off the snag I pulled myself onto, the sun is down. I walk back to the car, turn on the high beams, and drive it up the bank. I put it in first gear and then I take my foot off the clutch. I get out, close the door, and watch it plow softly into the water. The headlights reach in as they go down, searching, still lighted even after the water swirls over the back end. I wait. The wires short out. It is all finally dark. And then there is only the water, the sound of it going and running and going and running and running.

INQUIRING FURTHER

1. What role does the red convertible play in the brothers' relationship? Is it fair to say the car is more significant to Henry than to Lyman at the end? Freewrite for five minutes about the significance of the car.

2. What other concerns does the story emphasize? Could you also develop an interpretation of the work around topics like culture and identity, or innocence and experience? How might these themes be connected to the relationship of the two brothers? Write a paper in which you explain how the status of Henry and Lyman as brothers helps us understand another theme in the story.

JAMES BALDWIN

James Baldwin (1924–1987) grew up poor in Harlem. His mother worked cleaning offices and his father was, by all reports, a bitter tyrant who instilled in Baldwin a sense of inadequacy and disappointment. Baldwin worked a number of menial jobs before earning some recognition for essays on life in Harlem. It would be many years later that Baldwin would publish his first novel, Go Tell it on the Mountain *(1953), and establish his literary reputation. He frequently explores issues of race and the hardships of the poor in his essays and novels. "Sonny's Blues" was originally published in 1957.*

Sonny's Blues

I read about it in the paper, in the subway, on my way to work. I read it, and I couldn't believe it, and I read it again. Then perhaps I just stared at it, at the newsprint spelling out his name, spelling out the story. I stared at it in the swinging lights of the subway car, and in the faces and bodies of the people, and in my own face, trapped in the darkness which roared outside.

It was not to be believed and I kept telling myself that, as I walked from the subway station to the high school. And at the same time I couldn't doubt it. I was scared, scared for Sonny. He became real to me again. A great block of ice got settled in my belly and kept melting there slowly all day long, while I taught my classes algebra. It was a special kind of ice. It kept melting, sending trickles of ice water all up and down my veins, but it never got less. Sometimes it hardened and seemed to expand until I felt my guts were going to come spilling out or that I was going to choke or scream. This would always be at a moment when I was remembering some specific thing Sonny had once said or done.

When he was about as old as the boys in my classes his face had been bright and open, there was a lot of copper in it; and he'd had wonderfully direct brown eyes, and great gentleness and privacy. I wondered what he looked like now. He had been picked up, the evening before, in a raid on an apartment downtown, for peddling and using heroin.

I couldn't believe it: but what I mean by that is that I couldn't find any room for it anywhere inside me. I had kept it outside me for a long time. I hadn't wanted to know. I had had suspicions, but I didn't name them, I kept putting them away. I told myself that Sonny was wild, but he wasn't crazy. And he'd always been a good boy, he hadn't ever turned hard or evil or disrespectful, the way kids can, so quick, so quick, especially in Harlem. I didn't want to believe that I'd ever see my brother going down, coming to nothing, all that light in his face gone out, in the condition I'd already seen so many others. Yet it had happened and here I was, talking about algebra to a lot of boys who might, every one of them for all I knew, be popping off needles every time they went to the head. Maybe it did more for them than algebra could.

5   I was sure that the first time Sonny had ever had horse, he couldn't have been much older than these boys were now. These boys, now, were living as we'd been living then, they were growing up with a rush and their heads bumped abruptly

against the low ceiling of their actual possibilities. They were filled with rage. All they really knew were two darknesses, the darkness of their lives, which was now closing in on them, and the darkness of the movies, which had blinded them to that other darkness, and in which they now, vindictively, dreamed, at once more together than they were at any other time, and more alone.

When the last bell rang, the last class ended, I let out my breath. It seemed I'd been holding it for all that time. My clothes were wet—I may have looked as though I'd been sitting in a steam bath, all dressed up, all afternoon. I sat alone in the classroom a long time. I listened to the boys outside, downstairs, shouting and cursing and laughing. Their laughter struck me for perhaps the first time. It was not the joyous laughter which—God knows why—one associates with children. It was mocking and insular, its intent was to denigrate. It was disenchanted, and in this, also, lay the authority of their curses. Perhaps I was listening to them because I was thinking about my brother and in them I heard my brother. And myself.

One boy was whistling a tune, at once very complicated and very simple, it seemed to be pouring out of him as though he were a bird, and it sounded very cool and moving through all that harsh, bright air, only just holding its own through all those other sounds.

I stood up and walked over to the window and looked down into the courtyard. It was the beginning of the spring and the sap was rising in the boys. A teacher passed through them every now and again, quickly, as though he or she couldn't wait to get out of that courtyard, to get those boys out of their sight and off their minds. I started collecting my stuff. I thought I'd better get home and talk to Isabel.

The courtyard was almost deserted by the time I got downstairs. I saw this boy standing in the shadow of a doorway, looking just like Sonny. I almost called his name. Then I saw that it wasn't Sonny, but somebody we used to know, a boy from around our block. He'd been Sonny's friend. He'd never been mine, having been too young for me, and, anyway, I'd never liked him. And now, even though he was a grown-up man, he still hung around that block, still spent hours on the street corners, was always high and raggy. I used to run into him from time to time and he'd often work around to asking me for a quarter or fifty cents. He always had some real good excuse, too, and I always gave it to him, I don't know why.

10   But now, abruptly, I hated him. I couldn't stand the way he looked at me, partly like a dog, partly like a cunning child. I wanted to ask him what the hell he was doing in the school courtyard.

He sort of shuffled over to me, and he said, "I see you got the papers. So you already know about it."

"You mean about Sonny? Yes, I already know about it. How come they didn't get you?"

He grinned. It made him repulsive and it also brought to mind what he'd looked like as a kid. "I wasn't there. I stay away from them people."

"Good for you." I offered him a cigarette and I watched him through the smoke. "You come all the way down here just to tell me about Sonny?"

15   "That's right." He was sort of shaking his head and his eyes looked strange, as though they were about to cross. The bright sun deadened his damp dark brown skin and it made his eyes look yellow and showed up the dirt in his kinked hair. He smelled funky. I moved a little away from him and I said, "Well, thanks. But I already know about it and I got to get home."

"I'll walk you a little ways," he said. We started walking. There were a couple of kids still loitering in the courtyard and one of them said goodnight to me and looked strangely at the boy beside me.

"What're you going to do?" he asked me. "I mean, about Sonny?"

"Look. I haven't seen Sonny for over a year, I'm not sure I'm going to do anything. Anyway, what the hell *can* I do?"

"That's right," he said quickly, "ain't nothing you can do. Can't much help old Sonny no more, I guess."

20   It was what I was thinking and so it seemed to me he had no right to say it.

"I'm surprised at Sonny, though," he went on—he had a funny way of talking, he looked straight ahead as though he were talking to himself—"I thought Sonny was a smart boy, I thought he was too smart to get hung."

"I guess he thought so too," I said sharply, "and that's how he got hung. And how about you? You're pretty goddamn smart, I bet."

Then he looked directly at me, just for a minute. "I ain't smart," he said. "If I was smart, I'd have reached for a pistol a long time ago."

"Look. Don't tell *me* your sad story, if it was up to me, I'd give you one." Then I felt guilty—guilty, probably, for never having supposed that the poor bastard *had* a story of his own, much less a sad one, and I asked, quickly, "What's going to happen to him now?"

25   He didn't answer this. He was off by himself some place. "Funny thing," he said, and from his tone we might have been discussing the quickest way to get to Brooklyn, "when I saw the papers this morning, the first thing I asked myself was if I had anything to do with it. I felt sort of responsible."

I began to listen more carefully. The subway station was on the corner, just before us, and I stopped. He stopped, too. We were in front of a bar and he ducked slightly, peering in, but whoever he was looking for didn't seem to be there. The juke box was blasting away with something black and bouncy and I half watched the barmaid as she danced her way from the juke box to her place behind the bar. And I watched her face as she laughingly responded to something someone said to her still keeping time to the music. When she smiled one saw the little girl, one sensed the doomed, still-struggling woman beneath the battered face of the semi-whore.

"I never *give* Sonny nothing," the boy said finally, "but a long time ago I come to school high and Sonny asked me how it felt." He paused, I couldn't bear to watch him, I watched the barmaid, and I listened to the music which seemed to be causing the pavement to shake. "I told him it felt great." The music stopped, the barmaid paused and watched the juke box until the music began again. "It did."

All this was carrying me some place I didn't want to go. I certainly didn't want to know how it felt. It filled everything, the people, the houses, the music, the dark, quicksilver barmaid, with menace; and this menace was their reality.

"What's going to happen to him now?" I asked again.

30   "They'll send him away some place and they'll try to cure him." He shook his head. "Maybe he'll even think he's kicked the habit. Then they'll let him loose"—he gestured, throwing his cigarette into the gutter. "That's all."

"What do you mean, that's *all?*"

But I knew what he meant.

"I *mean*, that's *all*." He turned his head and looked at me, pulling down the corners of his mouth. "Don't you know what I mean?" he asked, softly.

"How the hell *would* I know what you mean?" I almost whispered it, I don't know why.

35   "That's right," he said to the air, "how would *he* know what I mean?" He turned toward me again, patient and calm, and yet I somehow felt him shaking, shaking as though he were going to fall apart. I felt that ice in my guts again, the dread I'd felt all afternoon; and again I watched the barmaid, moving about the bar, washing glasses, and singing. "Listen. They'll let him out and then it'll just start all over again. That's what I mean."

"You mean—they'll let him out. And then he'll just start working his way back in again. You mean he'll never kick the habit. Is that what you mean?"

"That's right," he said, cheerfully. "*You* see what I mean."

"Tell me," I said at last, "why does he want to die? He must want to die, he's killing himself, why does he want to die?"

He looked at me in surprise. He licked his lips. "He don't want to die. He wants to live. Don't nobody want to die, ever."

40   Then I wanted to ask him—too many things. He could not have answered, or if he had, I could not have borne the answers. I started walking. "Well, I guess it's none of my business."

"It's going to be rough on old Sonny," he said. We reached the subway station. "This is your station?" he asked. I nodded. I took one step down. "Damn!" he said, suddenly. I looked up at him. He grinned again. "Damn it if I didn't leave all my money home. You ain't got a dollar on you, have you? Just for a couple of days, is all."

All at once something inside gave and threatened to come pouring out of me. I didn't hate him any more. I felt that in another moment I'd start crying like a child.

"Sure," I said. "Don't sweat." I looked in my wallet and didn't have a dollar, I only had a five. "Here," I said. "That hold you?"

He didn't look at it—he didn't want to look at it. A terrible, closed look came over his face, as though he were keeping the number on the bill a secret from him and me. "Thanks," he said, and now he was dying to see me go. "Don't worry about Sonny. Maybe I'll write him or something."

45   "Sure," I said. "You do that. So long."

"Be seeing you," he said. I went on down the steps.

And I didn't write Sonny or send him anything for a long time. When I finally did, it was just after my little girl died, he wrote me back a letter which made me feel like a bastard.

Here's what he said:

> Dear brother,
> You don't know how much I needed to hear from you. I wanted to write you many a time but I dug how much I must have hurt you and so I didn't write. But now I feel like a man who's been trying to climb up out of some deep, real deep and funky hole and just saw the sun up there, outside. I got to get outside.
>   I can't tell you much about how I got here. I mean I don't know how to tell you. I guess I was afraid of something or I was trying to escape from something and you know I have never been very strong in the head (smile). I'm glad Mama and Daddy are dead and can't see what's happened to their son and I swear if I'd known what I was doing I would never have hurt you so, you and a lot of other fine people who were nice to me and who believed in me.

I don't want you to think it had anything to do with me being a musician. It's more than that. Or maybe less than that. I can't get anything straight in my head down here and I try not to think about what's going to happen to me when I get outside again. Sometime I think I'm going to flip and *never* get outside and sometime I think I'll come straight back. I tell you one thing, though, I'd rather blow my brains out than go through this again. But that's what they all say, so they tell me. If I tell you when I'm coming to New York and if you could meet me, I sure would appreciate it. Give my love to Isabel and the kids and I was sure sorry to hear about little Gracie. I wish I could be like Mama and say the Lord's will be done, but I don't know it seems to me that trouble is the one thing that never does get stopped and I don't know what good it does to blame it on the Lord. But maybe it does some good if you believe it.

> Your brother,
> Sonny

Then I kept in constant touch with him and I sent him whatever I could and I went to meet him when he came back to New York. When I saw him many things I thought I had forgotten came flooding back to me. This was because I had begun, finally, to wonder about Sonny, about the life that Sonny lived inside. This life, whatever it was, had made him older and thinner and it had deepened the distant stillness in which he had always moved. He looked very unlike my baby brother. Yet, when he smiled, when we shook hands, the baby brother I'd never known looked out from the depths of his private life, like an animal waiting to be coaxed into the light.

50   "How you been keeping?" he asked me.

"All right. And you?"

"Just fine." He was smiling all over his face. "It's good to see you again."

"It's good to see you."

The seven years' difference in our ages lay between us like a chasm: I wondered if these years would ever operate between us as a bridge. I was remembering, and it made it hard to catch my breath, that I had been there when he was born; and I had heard the first words he had ever spoken. When he started to walk, he walked from our mother straight to me. I caught him just before he fell when he took the first steps he ever took in this world.

55   "How's Isabel?"

"Just fine. She's dying to see you."

"And the boys?"

"They're fine, too. They're anxious to see their uncle."

"Oh, come on. You know they don't remember me."

60   "Are you kidding? Of course they remember you."

He grinned again. We got into a taxi. We had a lot to say to each other, far too much to know how to begin.

As the taxi began to move, I asked, "You still want to go to India?"

He laughed. "You still remember that. Hell, no. This place is Indian enough for me."

"It used to belong to them," I said.

65   And he laughed again. "They damn sure knew what they were doing when they got rid of it."

Years ago, when he was around fourteen, he'd been all hipped on the idea of going to India. He read books about people sitting on rocks, naked, in all kinds of weather, but mostly bad, naturally, and walking barefoot through hot coals and arriving at wisdom. I used to say that it sounded to me as though they were getting away from wisdom as fast as they could. I think he sort of looked down on me for that.

"Do you mind," he asked, "if we have the driver drive alongside the park? On the west side—I haven't seen the city in so long."

"Of course not," I said. I was afraid that I might sound as though I were humoring him, but I hoped he wouldn't take it that way.

So we drove along, between the green of the park and the stony, lifeless elegance of hotels and apartment buildings, toward the vivid, killing streets of our childhood. These streets hadn't changed, though housing projects jutted up out of them now like rocks in the middle of a boiling sea. Most of the houses in which we had grown up had vanished, as had the stores from which we had stolen, the basements in which we had first tried sex, the rooftops from which we had hurled tin cans and bricks. But houses exactly like the houses of our past yet dominated the landscape, boys exactly like the boys we once had been found themselves smothering in these houses, came down into the streets for light and air and found themselves encircled by disaster. Some escaped the trap, most didn't. Those who got out always left something of themselves behind, as some animals amputate a leg and leave it in the trap. It might be said, perhaps, that I had escaped, after all, I was a school teacher; or that Sonny had, he hadn't lived in Harlem for years. Yet, as the cab moved uptown through streets which seemed, with a rush, to darken with dark people, and as I covertly studied Sonny's face, it came to me that what we both were seeking through our separate cab windows was that part of ourselves which had been left behind. It's always at the hour of trouble and confrontation that the missing member aches.

70   We hit 110th Street and started rolling up Lenox Avenue. And I'd known this avenue all my life, but it seemed to me again, as it had seemed on the day I'd first heard about Sonny's trouble, filled with a hidden menace which was its very breath of life.

"We almost there," said Sonny.

"Almost." We were both too nervous to say anything more.

We live in a housing project. It hasn't been up long. A few days after it was up it seemed uninhabitably new, now, of course, it's already rundown. It looks like a parody of the good, clean, faceless life—God knows the people who live in it do their best to make it a parody. The beat-looking grass lying around isn't enough to make their lives green, the hedges will never hold out the streets, and they know it. The big windows fool no one, they aren't big enough to make space out of no space. They don't bother with the windows, they watch the TV screen instead. The playground is most popular with the children who don't play at jacks, or skip rope, or roller skate, or swing, and they can be found in it after dark. We moved in partly because it's not too far from where I teach, and partly for the kids; but it's really just like the houses in which Sonny and I grew up. The same things happen, they'll have the same things to remember. The moment Sonny and I started into the house I had the feeling that I was simply bringing him back into the danger he had almost died trying to escape.

Sonny has never been talkative. So I don't know why I was sure he'd be dying to talk to me when supper was over the first night. Everything went fine, the oldest boy remembered him, and the youngest boy liked him, and

Sonny had remembered to bring something for each of them; and Isabel, who is really much nicer than I am, more open and giving, had gone to a lot of trouble about dinner and was genuinely glad to see him. And she's always been able to tease Sonny in a way that I haven't. It was nice to see her face so vivid again and to hear her laugh and watch her make Sonny laugh. She wasn't, or, anyway, she didn't seem to be, at all uneasy or embarrassed. She chatted as though there were no subject which had to be avoided and she got Sonny past his first, faint stiffness. And thank God she was there, for I was filled with that icy dread again. Everything I did seemed awkward to me, and everything I said sounded freighted with hidden meaning. I was trying to remember everything I'd heard about dope addiction and I couldn't help watching Sonny for signs. I wasn't doing it out of malice. I was trying to find out something about my brother. I was dying to hear him tell me he was safe.

75   "Safe!" my father grunted, whenever Mama suggested trying to move to a neighborhood which might be safer for children. "Safe, hell! Ain't no place safe for kids, nor nobody."

He always went on like this, but he wasn't, ever, really as bad as he sounded, not even on weekends, when he got drunk. As a matter of fact, he was always on the lookout for "something a little better," but he died before he found it. He died suddenly, during a drunken weekend in the middle of the war when Sonny was fifteen. He and Sonny hadn't ever got on too well. And this was partly because Sonny was the apple of his father's eye. It was because he loved Sonny so much and was frightened for him, that he was always fighting with him. It doesn't do any good to fight with Sonny. Sonny just moves back, inside himself, where he can't be reached. But the principal reason that they never hit it off is that they were so much alike. Daddy was big and rough and loud-talking, just the opposite of Sonny, but they both had—that same privacy.

Mama tried to tell me something about this, just after Daddy died. I was home on leave from the army.

This was the last time I ever saw my mother alive. Just the same, this picture gets all mixed up in my mind with pictures I had of her when she was younger. The way I always see her is the way she used to be on a Sunday afternoon, say, when the old folks were talking after the big Sunday dinner. I always see her wearing pale blue. She'd be sitting on the sofa. And my father would be sitting in the easy chair, not far from her. And the living room would be full of church folks and relatives. There they sit, in chairs all around the living room, and the night is creeping up outside, but nobody knows it yet. You can see the darkness growing against the windowpanes and you hear the street noises every now and again, or maybe the jangling beat of a tambourine from one of the churches close by, but it's real quiet in the room. For a moment nobody's talking, but every face looks darkening, like the sky outside. And my mother rocks a little from the waist, and my father's eyes are closed. Everyone is looking at something a child can't see. For a minute they've forgotten the children. Maybe a kid is lying on the rug, half asleep. Maybe somebody's got a kid in his lap and is absent-mindedly stroking the kid's head. Maybe there's a kid, quiet and big-eyed, curled up in a big chair in the corner. The silence, the darkness coming, and the darkness in the faces frightens the child obscurely. He hopes that the hand which strokes his forehead will never stop—will never die. He hopes that there will never come a time when the old folks won't be sitting around the living room, talking about where they've come from, and what they've seen, and what's happened to them and their kinfolk.

But something deep and watchful in the child knows that this is bound to end, is already ending. In a moment someone will get up and turn on the light. Then the old folks will remember the children and they won't talk any more that day. And when light fills the room, the child is filled with darkness. He knows that every time this happens he's moved just a little closer to that darkness outside. The darkness outside is what the old folks have been talking about. It's what they've come from. It's what they endure. The child knows that they won't talk any more because if he knows too much about what's happened to *them*, he'll know too much too soon, about what's going to happen to *him*.

80   The last time I talked to my mother, I remember I was restless. I wanted to get out and see Isabel. We weren't married then and we had a lot to straighten out between us.

There Mama sat, in black, by the window. She was humming an old church song, *Lord, you brought me from a long ways off*. Sonny was out somewhere. Mama kept watching the streets.

"I don't know," she said, "if I'll ever see you again, after you go off from here. But I hope you'll remember the things I tried to teach you."

"Don't talk like that," I said, and smiled. "You'll be here a long time yet."

She smiled, too, but she said nothing. She was quiet for a long time. And I said, "Mama, don't you worry about nothing. I'll be writing all the time, and you be getting the checks. . . . "

85   "I want to talk to you about your brother," she said, suddenly. "If anything happens to me he ain't going to have nobody to look out for him."

"Mama," I said, "ain't nothing going to happen to you *or* Sonny. Sonny's all right. He's a good boy and he's got good sense."

"It ain't a question of his being a good boy," Mama said, "nor of his having good sense. It ain't only the bad ones, nor yet the dumb ones that gets sucked under." She stopped, looking at me. "Your Daddy once had a brother," she said, and she smiled in a way that made me feel she was in pain. "You didn't never know that, did you?"

"No," I said, "I never knew that," and I watched her face.

"Oh, yes," she said, "your Daddy had a brother." She looked out of the window again. "I know you never saw your Daddy cry. But *I* did—many a time, through all these years."

90   I asked her, "What happened to his brother? How come nobody's ever talked about him?"

This was the first time I ever saw my mother look old.

"His brother got killed," she said, "when he was just a little younger than you are now. I knew him. He was a fine boy. He was maybe a little full of the devil, but he didn't mean nobody no harm."

Then she stopped and the room was silent, exactly as it had sometimes been on those Sunday afternoons. Mama kept looking out into the streets.

"He used to have a job in the mill," she said, "and, like all young folks, he just liked to perform on Saturday nights. Saturday nights, him and your father would drift around to different place, go to dances and things like that, or just sit around with people they knew, and your father's brother would sing, he had a fine voice, and play along with himself on his guitar. Well, this particular Saturday night, him and your father was coming home from some place, and they were both a little drunk and there was a moon that night, it was bright like day. Your father's brother was feeling kind of good, and he was whistling to himself, and he had his guitar slung over his shoulder. They was coming down a hill and beneath them was a road that turned off from the highway. Well, your father's brother, being always kind of frisky, decided to run down this hill, and he did, with that guitar banging and clanging behind him, and he ran across the road, and he was making water behind a tree. And your father was sort of amused at him and he was still coming down the hill, kind of slow. Then he heard a car motor and that same minute his brother stepped from behind the tree, into the road, in the moonlight. And he started to cross the road. And your father started to run down the hill, he says he don't know why. This car was full of white men. They was all drunk, and when they seen your father's brother they let out a great whoop and holler and they aimed the car straight at him. They was having fun, they just wanted to scare him, the way they do sometimes, you know. But they was drunk. And I guess the boy, being drunk, too, and scared, kind of lost his head. By the time he jumped it was too late. Your father says he heard his brother scream when the car rolled over him, and he heard the wood of that guitar when it give, and he heard them strings go flying, and he heard them white men shouting, and the car kept on a-going and it ain't stopped till this day. And, time your father got down the hill, his brother weren't nothing but blood and pulp."

95   Tears were gleaming on my mother's face. There wasn't anything I could say.

"He never mentioned it," she said, "because I never let him mention it before you children. Your Daddy was like a crazy man that night and for many a night thereafter. He says he never in his life seen anything as dark as that road after the lights of that car had gone away. Weren't nothing, weren't nobody on that road, just your Daddy and his brother and that busted guitar. Oh, yes. Your Daddy never did really get right again. Till the day he died he weren't sure but that every white man he saw was the man that killed his brother."

She stopped and took out her handkerchief and dried her eyes and looked at me.

"I ain't telling you all this," she said, "to make you scared or bitter or to make you hate nobody. I'm telling you this because you got a brother. And the world ain't changed."

I guess I didn't want to believe this. I guess she saw this in my face. She turned away from me, toward the window again, searching those streets.

100   "But I praise my Redeemer," she said at last, "that He called your Daddy home before me. I ain't saying it to throw no flowers at myself, but, I declare, it keeps me from feeling too cast down to know I helped your father get safely through this world. Your father always acted like he was the roughest, strongest man on earth. And everybody took him to be like that. But if he hadn't had *me* there—to see his tears!"

She was crying again. Still, I couldn't move. I said, "Lord, Lord, Mama, I didn't know it was like that."

"Oh, honey," she said, "there's a lot that you don't know. But you are going to find it out." She stood up from the window and came over to me. "You got to hold on to your brother," she said, "and don't let him fall, no matter what it looks like is happening to him and no matter how evil you gets with him. You going to be evil with him many a time. But don't you forget what I told you, you hear?"

"I won't forget," I said. "Don't you worry, I won't forget. I won't let nothing happen to Sonny."

My mother smiled as though she were amused at something she saw in my face. Then, "You may not be able to stop nothing from happening. But you got to let him know you's *there*."

105   Two days later I was married, and then I was gone. And I had a lot of things on my mind and I pretty well forgot my promise to Mama until I got shipped home on a special furlough for her funeral.

And, after the funeral, with just Sonny and me alone in the empty kitchen, I tried to find out something about him.

"What do you want to do?" I asked him.

"I'm going to be a musician," he said.

For he had graduated, in the time I had been away, from dancing to the juke box to finding out who was playing what, and what they were doing with it, and he had bought himself a set of drums.

110   "You mean, you want to be a drummer?" I somehow had the feeling that being a drummer might be all right for other people but not for my brother Sonny.

"I don't think," he said, looking at me very gravely, "that I'll ever be a good drummer. But I think I can play a piano."

I frowned. I'd never played the role of the older brother quite so seriously before, had scarcely ever, in fact, *asked* Sonny a damn thing. I sensed myself in the presence of something I didn't really know how to handle, didn't understand. So I made my frown a little deeper as I asked: "What kind of musician do you want to be?"

He grinned. "How many kinds do you think there are?"

"Be *serious*," I said.

115   He laughed, throwing his head back, and then looked at me. "I *am* serious."

"Well, then, for Christ's sake, stop kidding around and answer a serious question. I mean, do you want to be a concert pianist, you want to play classical music and all that, or—or what?" Long before I finished he was laughing again. "For Christ's *sake*, Sonny!"

He sobered, but with difficulty. "I'm sorry. But you sound so—*scared!*" and he was off again.

"Well, you may think it's funny now, baby, but it's not going to be so funny when you have to make your living at it, let me tell you *that*." I was furious because I knew he was laughing at me and I didn't know why.

"No," he said, very sober now, and afraid, perhaps, that he'd hurt me, "I don't want to be a classical pianist. That isn't what interests me. I mean"—he paused, looking hard at me, as though his eyes would help me to understand, and then gestured helplessly, as though perhaps his hand would help—"I mean, I'll have a lot of studying to do, and I'll have to study *everything*, but, I mean, I want to play *with*—jazz musicians." He stopped. "I want to play jazz," he said.

120   Well, the word had never before sounded as heavy, as real, as it sounded that afternoon in Sonny's mouth. I just looked at him and I was probably frowning a real frown by this time. I simply couldn't see why on earth he'd want to spend his time hanging around nightclubs, clowning around on bandstands, while people pushed each other around a dance floor. It seemed—beneath him, somehow. I had never thought about it before, had never been forced to, but I suppose I had always put jazz musicians in a class with what Daddy called "good-time people."

"Are you *serious?*"

"Hell, *yes*, I'm serious."

He looked more helpless than ever, and annoyed, and deeply hurt.

I suggested, helpfully: "You mean—like Louis Armstrong?"

125   His face closed as though I'd struck him. "No. I'm not talking about none of that old-time, down home crap."

"Well, look, Sonny, I'm sorry, don't get mad. I just don't altogether get it, that's all. Name somebody—you know, a jazz musician you admire."

"Bird."

"Who?"

"Bird! Charlie Parker! Don't they teach you nothing in the goddamn army?"

130   I lit a cigarette. I was surprised and then a little amused to discover that I was trembling. "I've been out of touch," I said. "You'll have to be patient with me. Now. Who's this Parker character?"

"He's just one of the greatest jazz musicians alive," said Sonny, sullenly, his hands in his pockets, his back to me. "Maybe *the* greatest," he added, bitterly, "that's probably why *you* never heard of him."

"All right," I said, "I'm ignorant. I'm sorry. I'll go out and buy all the cat's records right away, all right?"

"It don't," said Sonny, with dignity, "make any difference to me. I don't care what you listen to. Don't do me no favors."

I was beginning to realize that I'd never seen him so upset before. With another part of my mind I was thinking that this would probably turn out to be one of those things kids go through and that I shouldn't make it seem important by pushing it too hard. Still, I didn't think it would do any harm to ask: "Doesn't all this take a lot of time? Can you make a living at it?"

135   He turned back to me and half leaned, half sat, on the kitchen table. "Everything takes time," he said, "and—well, yes, sure, I can make a living at it. But what I don't seem to be able to make you understand is that it's the only thing I want to do."

"Well, Sonny," I said, gently, "you know people can't always do exactly what they *want* to do—"

"*No*, I don't know that," said Sonny, surprising me. "I think people *ought* to do what they want to do, what else are they alive for?"

"You getting to be a big boy," I said desperately, "it's time you started thinking about your future."

"I'm thinking about my future," said Sonny, grimly. "I think about it all the time."

140   I gave up. I decided, if he didn't change his mind, that we could always talk about it later. "In the meantime," I said, "you got to finish school." We had already decided that he'd have to move in with Isabel and her folks. I knew this wasn't the ideal arrangement because Isabel's folks are inclined to be dicty and they hadn't especially wanted Isabel to marry me. But I didn't know what else to do. "And we have to get you fixed up at Isabel's."

There was a long silence. He moved from the kitchen table to the window. "That's a terrible idea. You know it yourself."

"Do you have a *better* idea?"

He just walked up and down the kitchen for a minute. He was as tall as I was. He had started to shave. I suddenly had the feeling that I didn't know him at all.

He stopped at the kitchen table and picked up my cigarettes. Looking at me with a kind of mocking, amused defiance, he put one between his lips. "You mind?"

145   "You smoking already?"

He lit the cigarette and nodded, watching me through the smoke. "I just wanted to see if I'd have the courage to smoke in front of you." He grinned and blew a great cloud of smoke to the ceiling. "It was easy." He looked at my face. "Come on, now. I bet you was smoking at my age, tell the truth."

I didn't say anything but the truth was on my face, and he laughed. But now there was something very strained in his laugh. "Sure. And I bet that ain't all you was doing."

He was frightening me a little. "Cut the crap," I said. "We already decided that you was going to go and live at Isabel's. Now what's got into you all of a sudden?"

"*You* decided it," he pointed out. "*I* didn't decide nothing." He stopped in front of me, leaning against the stove, arms loosely folded. "Look, brother. I don't want to stay in Harlem no more, I really don't." He was very earnest. He looked at me, then over toward the kitchen window. There was something in his eyes I'd never seen before, some thoughtfulness, some worry all his own. He rubbed the muscle of one arm. "It's time I was getting out of here."

150   "Where do you want to *go,* Sonny?"

"I want to join the army. Or the navy, I don't care. If I say I'm old enough, they'll believe me."

Then I got mad. It was because I was so scared. "You must be crazy. You goddamn fool, what the hell do you want to go and join the *army* for?"

"I just told you. To get out of Harlem."

"Sonny, you haven't even finished *school.* And if you really want to be a musician, how do you expect to study if you're in the *army?*"

155   He looked at me, trapped, and in anguish. "There's ways. I might be able to work out some kind of deal. Anyway, I'll have the G.I. Bill when I come out."

"*If* you come out." We stared at each other. "Sonny, please. Be reasonable. I know the setup is far from perfect. But we got to do the best we can."

"I ain't learning nothing in school," he said. "Even when I go." He turned away from me and opened the window and threw his cigarette out into the narrow alley. I watched his back. "At least, I ain't learning nothing you'd want me to learn." He slammed the window so hard I thought the glass would fly out, and turned back to me. "And I'm sick of the stink of these garbage cans!"

"Sonny," I said, "I know how you feel. But if you don't finish school now, you're going to be sorry later that you didn't." I grabbed him by the shoulders. "And you only got another year. It ain't so bad. And I'll come back and I swear I'll help you do *whatever* you want to do. Just try to put up with it till I come back. Will you please do that? For me?"

He didn't answer and he wouldn't look at me.

160   "Sonny. You hear me?"

He pulled away. "I hear you. But you never hear anything *I* say."

I didn't know what to say to that. He looked out of the window and then back at me. "OK," he said, and sighed. "I'll try."

Then I said, trying to cheer him up a little, "They got a piano at Isabel's. You can practice on it."

And as a matter of fact, it did cheer him up for a minute. "That's right," he said to himself. "I forgot that." His face relaxed a little. But the worry, the thoughtfulness, played on it still, the way shadows play on a face which is staring into the fire.

165   But I thought I'd never hear the end of that piano. At first, Isabel would write me, saying how nice it was that Sonny was so serious about his music and how, as soon as he came in from school, or wherever he had been when he was supposed to be at school, he went straight to that piano and stayed there until suppertime. And, after supper, he went back to that piano and stayed there until everybody went to bed. He was at the piano all day Saturday and all day Sunday. Then he bought a record player and started playing records. He'd play one record over and over again, all day long sometimes, and he'd improvise along with it on the piano. Or he'd play one section of the record, one chord, one change, one progression, then he'd do it on the piano. Then back to the record. Then back to the piano.

    Well, I really don't know how they stood it. Isabel finally confessed that it wasn't like living with a person at all, it was like living with sound. And the sound didn't make any sense to her, didn't make any sense to any of them—naturally. They began, in a way, to be afflicted by this presence that was living in their home. It was as though Sonny were some sort of god, or monster. He moved in an atmosphere which wasn't like theirs at all. They fed him and he ate, he washed himself, he walked in and out of their door; he certainly wasn't nasty or unpleasant or rude, Sonny isn't any of those things; but it was as though he were all wrapped up in some cloud, some fire, some vision all his own; and there wasn't any way to reach him.

    At the same time, he wasn't really a man yet, he was still a child, and they had to watch out for him in all kinds of ways. They certainly couldn't throw him out. Neither did they dare to make a great scene about that piano because even they dimly sensed, as I sensed, from so many thousands of miles away, that Sonny was at that piano playing for his life.

    But he hadn't been going to school. One day a letter came from the school board and Isabel's mother got it—there had, apparently, been other letters but Sonny had torn them up. This day, when Sonny came in, Isabel's mother showed him the letter and asked where he'd been spending his time. And she finally got it out of him that he'd been down in Greenwich Village, with musicians and other characters, in a white girl's apartment. And this scared her and she started to scream at him and what came up, once she began—though she denies it to this day—was what sacrifices they were making to give Sonny a decent home and how little he appreciated it.

    Sonny didn't play the piano that day. By evening, Isabel's mother had calmed down but then there was the old man to deal with, and Isabel herself. Isabel says she did her best to be calm but she broke down and started crying. She says she just watched Sonny's face. She could tell, by watching him, what was happening with him. And what was happening was that they penetrated his cloud, they had reached him. Even if their fingers had been a thousand times more gentle than human fingers ever are, he could hardly help feeling that they had stripped him naked and were spitting on that nakedness. For he also had to see that his presence, that music, which was life or death to him, had been torture for them and that they had endured it, not at all for his sake, but only for mine. And Sonny couldn't take that. He can take it a little better today than he could then but he's still not very good at it and, frankly, I don't know anybody who is.

170   The silence of the next few days must have been louder than the sound of all the music ever played since time began. One morning, before she went

to work, Isabel was in his room for something and she suddenly realized that all of his records were gone. And she knew for certain that he was gone. And he was. He went as far as the navy would carry him. He finally sent me a postcard from some place in Greece and that was the first I knew that Sonny was still alive. I didn't see him any more until we were both back in New York and the war had long been over.

He was a man by then, of course, but I wasn't willing to see it. He came by the house from time to time, but we fought almost every time we met. I didn't like the way he carried himself, loose and dreamlike all the time, and I didn't like his friends, and his music seemed to be merely an excuse for the life he led. It sounded just that weird and disordered.

Then we had a fight, a pretty awful fight, and I didn't see him for months. By and by I looked him up, where he was living, in a furnished room in the Village, and I tried to make it up. But there were lots of other people in the room and Sonny just lay on his bed, and he wouldn't come downstairs with me, and he treated these other people as though they were his family and I weren't. So I got mad and then he got mad, and then I told him that he might just as well be dead as live the way he was living. Then he stood up and he told me not to worry about him any more in life, that he *was* dead as far as I was concerned. Then he pushed me to the door and the other people looked on as though nothing were happening, and he slammed the door behind me. I stood in the hallway, staring at the door. I heard somebody laugh in the room and then the tears came to my eyes. I started down the steps, whistling to keep from crying, I kept whistling to myself, *You going to need me, baby, one of these cold, rainy days.*

I read about Sonny's trouble in the spring. Little Grace died in the fall. She was a beautiful little girl. But she only lived a little over two years. She died of polio and she suffered. She had a slight fever for a couple of days, but it didn't seem like anything and we just kept her in bed. And we would certainly have called the doctor, but the fever dropped, she seemed to be all right. So we thought it had just been a cold. Then, one day, she was up, playing, Isabel was in the kitchen fixing lunch for the two boys when they'd come in from school, and she heard Grace fall down in the living room. When you have a lot of children you don't always start running when one of them falls, unless they start screaming or something. And, this time, Grace was quiet. Yet, Isabel says that when she heard that *thump* and then that silence, something happened in her to make her afraid. And she ran to the living room and there was little Grace on the floor, all twisted up, and the reason she hadn't screamed was that she couldn't get her breath. And when she did scream, it was the worst sound, Isabel says, that she'd ever heard in all her life, and she still hears it sometimes in her dreams. Isabel will sometimes wake me up with a low, moaning, strangled sound and I have to be quick to awaken her and hold her to me and where Isabel is weeping against me seems a mortal wound.

I think I may have written Sonny the very day that little Grace was buried. I was sitting in the living room in the dark, by myself, and I suddenly thought of Sonny. My trouble made his real.

175   One Saturday afternoon, when Sonny had been living with us, or, anyway, been in our house, for nearly two weeks, I found myself wandering aimlessly about the living room, drinking from a can of beer, and trying to work up the courage to search Sonny's room. He was out, he was usually out whenever I

was home, and Isabel had taken the children to see their grandparents. Suddenly I was standing still in front of the living room window, watching Seventh Avenue. The idea of searching Sonny's room made me still. I scarcely dared to admit to myself what I'd be searching for. I didn't know what I'd do if I found it. Or if I didn't.

On the sidewalk across from me, near the entrance to a barbecue joint, some people were holding an old-fashioned revival meeting. The barbecue cook, wearing a dirty white apron, his conked hair reddish and metallic in the pale sun, and a cigarette between his lips, stood in the doorway, watching them. Kids and older people paused in their errands and stood there, along with some older men and a couple of very tough-looking women who watched everything that happened on the avenue, as though they owned it, or were maybe owned by it. Well, they were watching this, too. The revival was being carried on by three sisters in black, and a brother. All they had were their voices and their Bibles and a tambourine. The brother was testifying and while he testified two of the sisters stood together, seeming to say, amen, and the third sister walked around with the tambourine outstretched and a couple of people dropped coins into it. Then the brother's testimony ended and the sister who had been taking up the collection dumped the coins into her palm and transferred them to the pocket of her long black robe. Then she raised both hands, striking the tambourine against the air, and then against one hand, and she started to sing. And the two other sisters and the brother joined in.

It was strange, suddenly, to watch, though I had been seeing these street meetings all my life. So, of course, had everybody else down there. Yet, they paused and watched and listened and I stood still at the window. "*Tis the old ship of Zion,*" they sang, and the sister with the tambourine kept a steady, jangling beat, "*it has rescued many a thousand!*" Not a soul under the sound of their voices was hearing this song for the first time, not one of them had been rescued. Nor had they seen much in the way of rescue work being done around them. Neither did they especially believe in the holiness of the three sisters and the brother, they knew too much about them, knew where they lived, and how. The woman with the tambourine, whose voice dominated the air, whose face was bright with joy, was divided by very little from the woman who stood watching her, a cigarette between her heavy, chapped lips, her hair a cuckoo's nest, her face scarred and swollen from many beatings, and her black eyes glittering like coal. Perhaps they both knew this, which was why, when, as rarely, they addressed each other, they addressed each other as Sister. As the singing filled the air the watching, listening faces underwent a change, the eyes focusing on something within; the music seemed to soothe a poison out of them; and time seemed, nearly, to fall away from the sullen, belligerent, battered faces, as though they were fleeing back to their first condition, while dreaming of their last. The barbecue cook half shook his head and smiled, and dropped his cigarette and disappeared into his joint. A man fumbled in his pockets for change and stood holding it in his hand impatiently, as though he had just remembered a pressing appointment further up the avenue. He looked furious. Then I saw Sonny, standing on the edge of the crowd. He was carrying a wide, flat notebook with a green cover, and it made him look, from where I was standing, almost like a schoolboy. The coppery sun brought out the copper in his skin, he was very faintly smiling, standing very still. Then the singing stopped, the tambourine turned into a collection plate again. The furious man dropped in his coins and vanished, so did a couple of the women, and Sonny dropped some change in the plate, looking directly at the woman with a little smile. He started across the avenue, toward the house. He has a slow, loping walk, something like the way Harlem hipsters walk, only he's imposed on this his own half-beat. I had never really noticed it before.

I stayed at the window, both relieved and apprehensive. As Sonny disappeared from my sight, they began singing again. And they were still singing when his key turned in the lock.

"Hey," he said.

180   "Hey, yourself. You want some beer?"

"No. Well, maybe." But he came up to the window and stood beside me, looking out. "What a warm voice," he said.

They were singing *If I could only hear my mother pray again!*

"Yes," I said, "and she can sure beat that tambourine."

"But what a terrible song," he said, and laughed. He dropped his notebook on the sofa and disappeared into the kitchen. "Where's Isabel and the kids?"

185   "I think they went to see their grandparents. You hungry?"

"No." He came back into the living room with his can of beer. "You want to come some place with me tonight?"

I sensed, I don't know how, that I couldn't possibly say no. "Sure. Where?"

He sat down on the sofa and picked up his notebook and started leafing through it. "I'm going to sit in with some fellows in a joint in the Village."

"You mean, you're going to play, tonight?"

190   "That's right." He took a swallow of his beer and moved back to the window. He gave me a sidelong look. "If you can stand it."

"I'll try," I said.

He smiled to himself and we both watched as the meeting across the way broke up. The three sisters and the brother, heads bowed, were singing *God be with you till we meet again*. The faces around them were very quiet. Then the song ended. The small crowd dispersed. We watched the three women and the lone man walk slowly up the avenue.

"When she was singing before," said Sonny, abruptly, "her voice reminded me for a minute of what heroin feels like sometimes—when it's in your veins. It makes you feel sort of warm and cool at the same time. And distant. And—and sure." He sipped his beer, very deliberately not looking at me. I watched his face. "It makes you feel—in control. Sometimes you've got to have that feeling."

"Do you?" I sat down slowly in the easy chair.

195   "Sometimes." He went to the sofa and picked up his notebook again. "Some people do."

"In order," I asked, "to play?" And my voice was very ugly, full of contempt and anger.

"Well"—he looked at me with great, troubled eyes, as though, in fact, he hoped his eyes would tell me things he could never otherwise say—"they *think* so. And *if* they think so—!"

"And what do *you* think?" I asked.

He sat on the sofa and put his can of beer on the floor. "I don't know," he said, and I couldn't be sure if he were answering my question or pursuing his thoughts. His face didn't tell me. "It's not so much to *play*. It's to *stand* it, to be able to make it at all. On any level." He frowned and smiled: "In order to keep from shaking to pieces."

200   "But these friends of yours," I said, "they seem to shake themselves to pieces pretty goddamn fast."

"Maybe." He played with the notebook. And something told me that I should curb my tongue, that Sonny was doing his best to talk, that I should listen. "But of course you only know the ones that've gone to pieces. Some don't— or at least they haven't *yet* and that's just about all *any* of us can say." He paused. "And then there are some who just live, really, in hell, and they know it and they see what's happening and they go right on. I don't know." He sighed, dropped the notebook, folded his arms. "Some guys, you can tell from the way they play, they on something *all* the time. And you can see that, well, it makes something real for them. But of course," he picked up his beer from the floor and sipped it and put the can down again, "they *want* to, too, you've got to see that. Even some of them that say they don't—*some*, not all."

"And what about you?" I asked—I couldn't help it. "What about you? Do *you* want to?"

He stood up and walked to the window and remained silent for a long time. Then he sighed. "Me," he said. Then: "While I was downstairs before, on my way here, listening to that woman sing, it struck me all of a sudden how much suffering she must have had to go through—to sing like that. It's *repulsive* to think you have to suffer that much."

I said: "But there's no way not to suffer—is there, Sonny?"

205   "I believe not," he said and smiled, "but that's never stopped anyone from trying." He looked at me. "Has it?" I realized, with this mocking look, that there stood between us, forever, beyond the power of time or forgiveness, the fact that I had held silence—so long!—when he had needed human speech to help him. He turned back to the window. "No, there's no way not to suffer. But you try all kinds of ways to keep from drowning in it, to keep on top of it, and to make it seem—well, like *you*. Like you did something, all right, and now you're suffering for it. You know?" I said nothing. "Well you know," he said, impatiently, "why *do* people suffer? Maybe it's better to do something to give it a reason, *any* reason."

"But we just agreed," I said, "that there's no way not to suffer. Isn't it better, then, just to—take it?"

"But nobody just takes it," Sonny cried, "that's what I'm telling you! *Everybody* tries not to. You're just hung up on the *way* some people try—it's not *your* way!"

The hair on my face began to itch, my face felt wet. "That's not true," I said, "that's not true. I don't give a damn what other people do, I don't even care how they suffer. I just care how *you* suffer." And he looked at me. "Please believe me," I said, "I don't want to see you—die—trying not to suffer."

"I won't," he said, flatly, "die trying not to suffer. At least, not any faster than anybody else."

210   "But there's no need," I said, trying to laugh, "is there? in killing yourself."

I wanted to say more, but I couldn't. I wanted to talk about will power and how life could be—well, beautiful. I wanted to say that it was all within; but was it? or, rather, wasn't that exactly the trouble? And I wanted to promise that I would never fail him again. But it would all have sounded—empty words and lies.

So I made the promise to myself and prayed that I would keep it.

"It's terrible sometimes, inside," he said, "that's what's the trouble. You walk these streets, black and funky and cold, and there's not really a living ass to talk to, and there's nothing shaking, and there's no way of getting it out—that storm inside. You can't talk it and you can't make love with it, and when you finally try to get with it and play it, you realize *nobody's* listening. So *you've* got to listen. You got to find a way to listen."

And then he walked away from the window and sat on the sofa again, as though all the wind had suddenly been knocked out of him. "Sometimes you'll do *anything* to play, even cut your mother's throat." He laughed and looked at me. "Or your brother's." Then he sobered. "Or your own." Then: "Don't worry. I'm all right now and I think I'll *be* all right. But I can't forget—where I've been. I don't mean just the physical place I've been, I mean where I've *been*. And *what* I've been."

215   "What have you been, Sonny?" I asked.

He smiled—but sat sideways on the sofa, his elbow resting on the back, his fingers playing with his mouth and chin, not looking at me. "I've been something I didn't recognize, didn't know I could be. Didn't know anybody could be." He stopped, looking inward, looking helplessly young, looking old. "I'm not talking about it now because I feel *guilty* or anything like that— maybe it would be better if I did, I don't know. Anyway, I can't really talk about it. Not to you, not to anybody," and now he turned and faced me. "Sometimes, you know, and it was actually when I was most *out* of the world, I felt that I was in it, that I was *with* it, really, and I could play or I didn't really have to *play*, it just came out of me, it was there. And I don't know how I played, thinking about it now, but I know I did awful things, those times, sometimes, to people. Or it wasn't that I *did* anything to them—it was that they weren't real." He picked up the beer can; it was empty; he rolled it between his palms: "And other times—well, I needed a fix, I needed to find a place to lean, I needed to clear a space to *listen*—and I couldn't find it, and I—went crazy, I did terrible things to *me*, I was terrible *for* me." He began pressing the beer can between his hands, I watched the metal begin to give. It glittered, as he played with it, like a knife, and I was afraid he would cut himself, but I said nothing. "Oh well. I can never tell you. I was all by myself at the bottom of something, stinking and sweating and crying and shaking, and I smelled it, you know? *my* stink, and I thought I'd die if I couldn't get away from it and yet, all the same, I knew that everything I was doing was just locking me in with it. And I didn't know," he paused, still flattening the beer can, "I didn't know, I still *don't* know, something kept telling me that maybe it was good to smell your own stink, but I didn't think that *that* was what I'd been trying to do—and—who can stand it?" and he abruptly dropped the ruined beer can, looking at me with a small, still smile, and then rose, walking to the window as though it were the lodestone rock. I watched his face, he watched the avenue. "I couldn't tell you when Mama died—but the reason I wanted to leave Harlem so bad was to get away from drugs. And then, when I ran away, that's what I was running from—really. When I came back, nothing had changed, *I* hadn't changed, I was just—older." And he stopped, drumming with his fingers on the windowpane. The sun had vanished, soon darkness would fall. I watched his face. "It can come again," he said, almost as though speaking to himself. Then he turned to me. "It can come again," he repeated. "I just want you to know that."

"All right," I said, at last. "So it can come again. All right."

He smiled, but the smile was sorrowful. "I had to try to tell you," he said.

"Yes," I said. "I understand that."

220   "You're my brother," he said, looking straight at me, and not smiling at all.

"Yes," I repeated, "yes. I understand that."

He turned back to the window, looking out. "All that hatred down there," he said, "all that hatred and misery and love. It's a wonder it doesn't blow the avenue apart."

We went to the only nightclub on a short, dark street, downtown. We squeezed through the narrow, chattering, jam-packed bar to the entrance of the big room, where the bandstand was. And we stood there for a moment, for the lights were very dim in this room and we couldn't see. Then, "Hello, boy," said a voice and an enormous black man, much older than Sonny or myself, erupted out of all that atmospheric lighting and put an arm around Sonny's shoulder. "I been sitting right here," he said, "waiting for you."

He had a big voice, too, and heads in the darkness turned toward us.

225   Sonny grinned and pulled a little away, and said, "Creole, this is my brother. I told you about him."

Creole shook my hand. "I'm glad to meet you, son," he said, and it was clear that he was glad to meet me *there*, for Sonny's sake. And he smiled, "You got a real musician in *your* family," and he took his arm from Sonny's shoulder and slapped him, lightly, affectionately, with the back of his hand.

"Well. Now I've heard it all," said a voice behind us. This was another musician, and a friend of Sonny's, a coal-black, cheerful-looking man, built close to the ground. He immediately began confiding to me, at the top of his lungs, the most terrible things about Sonny, his teeth gleaming like a lighthouse and his laugh coming up out of him like the beginning of an earthquake. And it turned out that everyone at the bar knew Sonny, or almost everyone; some were musicians, working there, or nearby, or not working, some were simply hangers on, and some were there to hear Sonny play. I was introduced to all of them and they were all very polite to me. Yet, it was clear that, for them, I was only Sonny's brother. Here, I was in Sonny's world. Or, rather: his kingdom. Here, it was not even a question that his veins bore royal blood.

They were going to play soon and Creole installed me, by myself, at a table in a dark corner. Then I watched them, Creole, and the little black man, and Sonny, and the others, while they horsed around, standing just below the bandstand. The light from the bandstand spilled just a little short of them and, watching them laughing and gesturing and moving about, I had the feeling that they, nevertheless, were being most careful not to step into that circle of light too suddenly: that if they moved into the light too suddenly, without thinking, they would perish in flame. Then, while I watched, one of them, the small, black man, moved into the light and crossed the bandstand and started fooling around with his drums. Then—being funny and being, also, extremely ceremonious—Creole took Sonny by the arm and led him to the piano. A woman's voice called Sonny's name and a few hands started clapping. And Sonny, also being funny and being ceremonious, and so touched, I think, that he could have cried, but neither hiding it nor showing it, riding it like a man, grinned, and put both hands to his heart and bowed from the waist.

Creole then went to the bass fiddle and a lean, very bright-skinned brown man jumped up on the bandstand and picked up his horn. So there they were, and the atmosphere on the bandstand and in the room began to change and tighten. Someone stepped up to the microphone and announced them. Then there were all kinds of murmurs. Some people at the bar shushed others. The waitress ran around, frantically getting in the last orders, guys and chicks got closer to each other, and the lights on the bandstand, on the quartet, turned to a kind of indigo. Then they all looked different there. Creole looked about him for the last time, as though he were making certain that all his chickens were in the coop, and then he—jumped and struck the fiddle. And there they were.

230   All I know about music is that not many people ever really hear it. And even then, on the rare occasions when something opens within, and the music enters, what we mainly hear, or hear corroborated, are personal, private, vanishing evocations. But the man who creates the music is hearing something else, is dealing with the roar rising from the void and imposing order on it as it hits the air. What is evoked in him, then, is of another order, more terrible because it has no words, and triumphant, too, for that same reason. And his triumph, when he triumphs, is ours. I just watched Sonny's face. His face was troubled, he was working hard, but he wasn't with it. And I had the feeling that, in a way, everyone on the bandstand was waiting for him, both waiting for him and pushing him along. But as I began to watch Creole, I realized that it was Creole who held them all back. He had them on a short rein. Up there, keeping the beat with his whole body, wailing on the fiddle, with his eyes half closed, he was listening to everything, but he was listening to Sonny. He was having a dialogue with Sonny. He wanted Sonny to leave the shoreline and strike out for the deep water. He was Sonny's witness that deep water and drowning were not the same thing—he had been there, and he knew. And he wanted Sonny to know. He was waiting for Sonny to do the things on the keys which would let Creole know that Sonny was in the water.

And, while Creole listened, Sonny moved, deep within, exactly like someone in torment. I had never before thought of how awful the relationship must be between the musician and his instrument. He has to fill it, this instrument, with the breath of life, his own. He has to make it do what he wants it to do. And a piano is just a piano. It's made out of so much wood and wires and little hammers and big ones, and ivory. While there's only so much you can do with it, the only way to find this out is to try; to try and make it do everything.

And Sonny hadn't been near a piano for over a year. And he wasn't on much better terms with his life, not the life that stretched before him now. He and the piano stammered, started one way, got scared, stopped; started another way, panicked, marked time, started again; then seemed to have found a direction, panicked again, got stuck. And the face I saw on Sonny I'd never seen before. Everything had been burned out of it, and, at the same time, things usually hidden were being burned in, by the fire and fury of the battle which was occurring in him up there.

Yet, watching Creole's face as they neared the end of the first set, I had the feeling that something had happened, something I hadn't heard. Then they finished, there was scattered applause, and then, without an instant's warning, Creole started into something else, it was almost sardonic, it was *Am I Blue*. And, as though he commanded, Sonny began to play. Something began to happen. And Creole let out the reins. The dry, low, black man said something awful on the drums, Creole answered, and the drums talked back. Then the horn insisted, sweet and high, slightly detached perhaps, and Creole listened, commenting now and then, dry, and driving, beautiful and calm and old. Then they all came together again, and Sonny was part of the family again. I could tell this from his face. He seemed to have found, right there beneath his fingers, a damn brand-new piano. It seemed that he couldn't get over it. Then, for awhile, just being happy with Sonny, they seemed to be agreeing with him that brand-new pianos certainly were a gas.

Then Creole stepped forward to remind them that what they were playing was the blues. He hit something in all of them, he hit something in me, myself, and the music tightened and deepened, apprehension began to beat the air. Creole began to tell us what the blues were all about. They were not about anything very new. He and his boys up there were keeping it new, at the risk of ruin, destruction, madness, and death, in order to find new ways to make us listen. For, while the tale of how we suffer, and how we are delighted, and how we may triumph is never new, it always must be heard. There isn't any other tale to tell, it's the only light we've got in all this darkness.

235   And this tale, according to that face, that body, those strong hands on those strings, has another aspect in every country, and a new depth in every generation. Listen, Creole seemed to be saying, listen. Now these are Sonny's blues. He made the little black man on the drums know it, and the bright, brown man on the horn. Creole wasn't trying any longer to get Sonny in the water. He was wishing him Godspeed. Then he stepped back, very slowly, filling the air with the immense suggestion that Sonny speak for himself.

Then they all gathered around Sonny and Sonny played. Every now and again one of them seemed to say, amen. Sonny's fingers filled the air with life, his life. But that life contained so many others. And Sonny went all the way back, he really began with the spare, flat statement of the opening phrase of the song. Then he began to make it his. It was very beautiful because it wasn't hurried and it was no longer a lament. I seemed to hear with what burning he had made it his, with what burning we had yet to make it ours, how we could cease lamenting. Freedom lurked around us and I understood, at last, that he could help us to be free if we would listen, that he would never be free until we did. Yet, there was no battle in his face now. I heard what he had gone through, and would continue to go through until he came to rest in earth. He had made it his: that long line, of which we knew only Mama and Daddy. And he was giving it back, as everything must be given back, so that, passing through death, it can live forever. I saw my mother's face again, and felt, for the first time, how the stones of the road she had walked on must have bruised her feet. I saw the moonlit road where my father's brother died. And it brought something else back to me, and carried me past it, I saw my little girl again and felt Isabel's tears again, and I felt my own tears begin to rise. And I was yet aware that this was only a moment, that the world waited outside, as hungry as a tiger, and that trouble stretched above us, longer than the sky.

Then it was over. Creole and Sonny let out their breath, both soaking wet, and grinning. There was a lot of applause and some of it was real. In the dark, the girl came by and I asked her to take drinks to the bandstand. There was a long pause, while they talked up there in the indigo light and after awhile I saw the girl put a Scotch and milk on top of the piano for Sonny. He didn't seem to notice it, but just before they started playing again, he sipped from it and looked toward me, and nodded. Then he put it back on top of the piano. For me, then, as they began to play again, it glowed and shook above my brother's head like the very cup of trembling.

INQUIRING FURTHER

1. How does the night when the narrator's father witnesses the death of his younger brother relate to the rest of the story? Could we understand the motivations of the characters without this episode?

2. Is the suffering alluded to in the story something we can all relate to? Would you say the concerns in the story apply to most siblings, or are they rooted in issues of poverty and race?

CHRISTINA ROSSETTI

Christina Georgina Rossetti (1830–1894) suffered an emotional breakdown at age fourteen when financial problems forced her sister, Maria Francesca, to work outside the home. Christina recovered and worked with her mother to operate several schools before devoting much of her energy to social issues, working at the Highgate Penitentiary for Fallen Women and through the Anglican Church. At this time, her family, especially her brother, well-known painter Dante Gabriel Rossetti, helped her publish her poems and novels. Dante took a direct role in finding a publisher for the collection Goblin Market and other Poems *(1862), even editing and revising some of the works. "Goblin Market" has been interpreted as providing a painting in words that matches the colorful depictions of Pre-Raphaelite painting. We provide the poem as an enhanced reading on our Web site.*

Enhanced reading of "Goblin Market"

Goblin Market

SOPHOCLES

Sophocles (495–405 B.C.E.) lived and wrote at the height of the Greek empire. Theater was a staple of Greek culture—annual competitions for dramatists were a regular part of an artist's life. Audience members were highly aware of formalized conventions for telling stories through drama. Sophocles established his reputation in part by modifying these conventions. Earlier dramatists, for instance, often wrote trilogies, sets of plays that were produced together and told a story in three different works. Antigone *represents a play that refers to this tradition in the way it builds from Sophocles's* Oedipus the King, *but also changes the tradition in the way it tells a story that can stand on its own.* Oedipus the King *(the prequel to* Antigone*) was actually written some ten years later. Sophocles wrote over 120 plays in his lifetime, but only a handful survive.* Antigone *was first produced in 441 B.C.E.*

Antigonê

An English Version by Dudley Fitts and Robert Fitzgerald

List of Characters

ANTIGONÊ
ISMENÊ
EURYDICÊ
CREON
HAIMON
TEIRESIAS
A SENTRY
A MESSENGER
CHORUS

SCENE: *Before the palace of* CREON, *king of Thebes. A central double door, and two lateral doors. A platform extends the length of the façade, and from this platform three steps lead down into the "orchestra," or chorus-ground.*
TIME: *Dawn of the day after the repulse of the Argive army from the assault on Thebes.*

Prologue

ANTIGONÊ *and* ISMENÊ *enter from the central door of the palace.*

ANTIGONÊ: Ismenê, dear sister,
> You would think that we had already suffered enough
> For the curse on Oedipus.[1]
> I cannot imagine any grief
> That you and I have not gone through. And now—
> Have they told you of the new decree of our King Creon?
ISMENÊ: I have heard nothing: I know
> That two sisters lost two brothers, a double death
> In a single hour;[2] and I know that the Argive army
> Fled in the night; but beyond this, nothing.
ANTIGONÊ: I thought so. And this is why I wanted you
> To come out here with me. There is something we must do.
ISMENÊ: Why do you speak so strangely?
ANTIGONÊ: Listen, Ismenê:
> Creon buried our brother Eteoclês
> With military honors, gave him a soldier's funeral,

---

[1]**Oedipus:** Oedipus was the father of Antigonê, Ismenê, Polyneicês and Eteoclês. Through an accident of fate, Oedipus killed his father and married his mother, bringing down the wrath of the gods.
[2]**single hour:** Polyneicês and Eteoclês struggled to control Thebes after Oedipus fled the city; Polyneicês was exiled. The events in the play take place just after Polyneicês has returned to battle for control. In the fighting, the brothers kill one another, leaving the throne to Creon.

And it was right that he should; but Polyneicês,
Who fought as bravely and died as miserably,—
They say that Creon has sworn
No one shall bury him, no one mourn for him,
But his body must lie in the fields, a sweet treasure
For carrion birds to find as they search for food.[3]
That is what they say, and our good Creon is coming here
To announce it publicly; and the penalty—
Stoning to death in the public square!

                                    There it is,
And now you can prove what you are:
A true sister, or a traitor to your family.

ISMENÊ: Antigonê, you are mad! What could I possibly do?

ANTIGONÊ: You must decide whether you will help me or not.

ISMENÊ: I do not understand you. Help you in what?

ANTIGONÊ: Ismenê. I am going to bury him. Will you come?

ISMENÊ: Bury him! You have just said the new law forbids it.

ANTIGONÊ: He is my brother. And he is your brother, too.

ISMENÊ: But think of the danger! Think what Creon will do!

ANTIGONÊ: Creon is not strong enough to stand in my way.

ISMENÊ: Ah sister!
Oedipus died, everyone hating him
For what his own search brought to light, his eyes
Ripped out by his own hand; and Iocastê died,
His mother and wife at once: she twisted the cords
That strangled her life; and our two brothers died,
Each killed by the other's sword. And we are left:
But oh, Antigonê,
Think how much more terrible than these
Our own death would be if we should go against Creon
And do what he has forbidden! We are only women,
We cannot fight with men, Antigonê!
The law is strong, we must give in to the law
In this thing, and in worse. I beg the Dead
To forgive me, but I am helpless: I must yield
To those in authority. And I think it is dangerous business
To be always meddling.

ANTIGONÊ: If that is what you think,
I should not want you, even if you asked to come.
You have made your choice, you can be what you want to be.
But I will bury him; and if I must die,
I say that this crime is holy: I shall lie down
With him in death, and I shall be as dear
To him as he to me.
                    It is the dead,
Not the living, who make the longest demands:
We die for ever. . . .

---

[3]**food:** Creon has ordered that Eteoclês be honored, but that Polyneicês remain unburied as a mark of shame.

You may do as you like.
Since apparently the laws of the gods mean nothing to you.

ISMENÊ: They mean a great deal to me; but I have no strength
　　To break laws that were made for the public good.

ANTIGONÊ: That must be your excuse, I suppose. But as for me,
　　I will bury the brother I love.

ISMENÊ:　　　　　　　　　　　　Antigonê,
　　I am so afraid for you!

ANTIGONÊ: You need not be:
　　You have yourself to consider, after all.

ISMENÊ:　But no one must hear of this, you must tell no one!
　　I will keep it a secret, I promise!

ANTIGONÊ:　　　　　　　　　　O tell it! Tell everyone!
　　Think how they'll hate you when it all comes out
　　If they learn that you knew about it all the time!

ISMENÊ: So fiery! You should be cold with fear.

ANTIGONÊ: Perhaps. But I am doing only what I must.

ISMENÊ:　But can you do it? I say that you cannot.

ANTIGONÊ: Very well: when my strength gives out,
　　I shall do no more.

ISMENÊ: Impossible things should not be tried at all.

ANTIGONÊ:　Go away, Ismenê:
　　I shall be hating you soon, and the dead will too,
　　For your words are hateful. Leave me my foolish plan:
　　I am not afraid of the danger; if it means death,
　　It will not be the worst of deaths—death without honor.

ISMENÊ:　Go then, if you feel that you must.
　　You are unwise,
　　But a loyal friend indeed to those who love you.

Exit into the palace. ANTIGONÊ *goes off, left. Enter the* CHORUS.

Párodos

CHORUS: Now the long blade of the sun, lying　　　　　　*Strophe 1*[4]
　　Level east to west, touches with glory
　　Thebes of the Seven Gates. Open, unlidded
　　Eye of golden day! O marching light
　　Across the eddy and rush of Dircê's stream,
　　Striking the white shields of the enemy
　　Thrown headlong backward from the blaze of morning!

CHORAGOS: Polyneicês their commander
　　Roused them with windy phrases,
　　He the wild eagle screaming
　　Insults above our land,

---

[4]**(Strophe 1):** In classical Greek drama, speeches are often offered in two forms, the strophe, and the antistrophe. These passages are meant to complement or counter one another, offering commentary on the action through the varying perspectives they present. The Greek chorus is meant to present the viewpoints of the community and in these passages CHORAGOS often steps forward as the spokesperson for the chorus.

His wings their shields of snow,
His crest their marshalled helms.

CHORUS: Against our seven gates in a yawning ring   *Antistrophe 1*
The famished spears came onward in the night:
But before his jaws were sated with our blood,
Or pinefire took the garland of our towers,
He was thrown back; and as he turned, great Thebes—
No tender victim for his noisy power—
Rose like a dragon behind him, shouting war.

CHORAGOS: For God hates utterly
The bray of bragging tongues;
And when he beheld their smiling,
Their swagger of golden helms,
The frown of his thunder blasted
Their first man from our walls.

CHORUS: We heard his shout of triumph high in the air   *Strophe 2*
Turn to a scream; far out in a flaming arc
He fell with his windy torch, and the earth struck him.
And others storming in fury no less than his
Found shock of death in the dusty joy of battle.

CHORAGOS: Seven captains at seven gates
Yielded their clanging arms to the god
That bends the battle-line and breaks it.
These two only, brothers in blood,
Face to face in matchless rage.
Mirroring each the other's death,
Clashed in long combat.

CHORUS: But now in the beautiful morning of victory   *Antistrophe 2*
Let Thebes of the many chariots sing for joy!
With hearts for dancing we'll take leave of war:
Our temples shall be sweet with hymns of praise,
And the long nights shall echo with our chorus.

Scene I

CHORAGOS: But now at last our new King is coming:
Creon of Thebes, Menoikeus' son.
In this auspicious dawn of his reign
What are the new complexities
That shifting Fate has woven for him?
What is his counsel? Why has he summoned
The old men to hear him?

*Enter CREON from the palace, center. He addresses the CHORUS from the
top step.*

CREON: Gentlemen: I have the honor to inform you that our Ship of State, which
recent storms have threatened to destroy, has come safely to harbor at last,
guided by the merciful wisdom of Heaven. I have summoned you here this
morning because I know that I can depend upon you: your devotion to
King Laïos was absolute; you never hesitated in your duty to our late ruler
Oedipus; and when Oedipus died, your loyalty was transferred to his children. Unfortunately, as you know, his two sons, the princes Eteoclês and

Polyneicês, have killed each other in battle; and I, as the next in blood, have succeeded to the full power of the throne.

I am aware, of course, that no Ruler can expect complete loyalty from his subjects until he has been tested in office. Nevertheless, I say to you at the very outset that I have nothing but contempt for the kind of Governor who is afraid, for whatever reason, to follow the course that he knows is bestfor the State; and as for the man who sets private friendship above the public welfare,—I have no use for him, either. I call God to witness that if I saw my country headed for ruin, I should not be afraid to speak out plainly; and I need hardly remind you that I would never have any dealings with an enemy of the people. No one values friendship more highly than I: but we must remember that friends made at the risk of wrecking our Ship are not real friends at all.

These are my principles, at any rate, and that is why I have made the following decision concerning the sons of Oedipus: Eteoclês, who died as a man should die, fighting for his country, is to be buried with full military honors, with all the ceremony that is usual when the greatest heroes die; but his brother Polyneicês, who broke his exile to come back with fire and sword against his native city and the shrines of his fathers' gods, whose one idea was to spill the blood of his blood and sell his own people into slavery—Polyneicês, I say, is to have no burial: no man is to touch him or say the least prayer for him; he shall lie on the plain, unburied; and the birds and the scavenging dogs can do with him whatever they like.

This is my command, and you can see the wisdom behind it. As long as I am King, no traitor is going to be honored with the loyal man. But whoever shows by word and deed that he is on the side of the State—he shall have my respect while he is living and my reverence when he is dead.

CHORAGOS: If that is your will, Creon son of Menoikeus,
    You have the right to enforce it: we are yours.
CREON: That is my will. Take care that you do your part.
CHORAGOS: We are old men: let the younger ones carry it out.
CREON: I do not mean that: the sentries have been appointed.
CHORAGOS: Then what is it that you would have us do?
CREON: You will give no support to whoever breaks this law.
CHORAGOS: Only a crazy man is in love with death!
CREON: And death it is; yet money talks, and the wisest
    Have sometimes been known to count a few coins too many.

Enter SENTRY *from left.*

SENTRY: I'll not say that I'm out of breath from running, King, because every time I stopped to think about what I have to tell you, I felt like going back. And all the time a voice kept saying, "You fool, don't you know you're walking straight into trouble?"; and then another voice: "Yes, but if you let somebody else get the news to Creon first, it will be even worse than that for you!" But good sense won out, at least I hope it was good sense, and here I am with a story that makes no sense at all; but I'll tell it anyhow, because, as they say, what's going to happen's going to happen and—
CREON: Come to the point. What have you to say?
SENTRY: I did not do it. I did not see who did it. You must not punish me for what someone else has done.
CREON: A comprehensive defense! More effective, perhaps, if I knew its purpose. Come: what is it?

SENTRY: A dreadful thing . . . I don't know how to put it—
CREON: Out with it!
SENTRY: Well, then;
        The dead man—
                    Polyneicês—

Pause. The SENTRY *is overcome, fumbles for words.* CREON *waits impassively.*

                            out there—
                                someone,—
        New dust on the slimy flesh!

Pause. No sign from CREON.

        Someone has given it burial that way, and
        Gone. . . .

Long pause. CREON *finally speaks with deadly control.*

CREON: And the man who dared do this?
SENTRY: I swear I
        Do not know! You must believe me!
                                Listen:
        The ground was dry, not a sign of digging, no,
        Not a wheeltrack in the dust, no trace of anyone.
        It was when they relieved us this morning: and one of them,
        The corporal, pointed to it.
                            There it was,
        The strangest—
                    Look:
        The body, just mounded over with light dust: you see?
        Not buried really, but as if they'd covered it
        Just enough for the ghost's peace. And no sign
        Of dogs or any wild animal that had been there.

        And then what a scene there was! Every man of us
        Accusing the other: we all proved the other man did it,
        We all had proof that we could not have done it.
        We were ready to take hot iron in our hands,
        Walk through fire, swear by all the gods,
        It was not I!
        I do not know who it was, but it was not I!

CREON'*s rage has been mounting steadily, but the* SENTRY *is too intent upon his story to notice it.*

        And then, when this came to nothing, someone said
        A thing that silenced us and made us stare
        Down at the ground: you had to be told the news,
        And one of us had to do it! We threw the dice,
        And the bad luck fell to me. So here I am,
        No happier to be here than you are to have me:
        Nobody likes the man who brings bad news.

CHORAGOS: I have been wondering, King: can it be that the gods have done
   this?
CREON [*furiously*]: Stop!
        Must you doddering wrecks
        Go out of your heads entirely? "The gods"!
        Intolerable!
        The gods favor this corpse? Why? How had he served them?
        Tried to loot their temples, burn their images,
        Yes, and the whole State, and its laws with it!
        Is it your senile opinion that the gods love to honor bad men?
        A pious thought!—
                        No, from the very beginning
        There have been those who have whispered together,
        Stiff-necked anarchists, putting their heads together,
        Scheming against me in alleys. These are the men,
        And they have bribed my own guard to do this thing.
        [*Sententiously.*] Money!
        There's nothing in the world so demoralizing as money.
        Down go your cities,
        Homes gone, men gone, honest hearts corrupted.
        Crookedness of all kinds, and all for money!
        [*To* SENTRY.]   But you—!
        I swear by God and by the throne of God,
        The man who has done this thing shall pay for it!
        Find that man, bring him here to me, or your death
        Will be the least of your problems: I'll string you up
        Alive, and there will be certain ways to make you
        Discover your employer before you die;
        And the process may teach you a lesson you seem to have missed:
        The dearest profit is sometimes all too dear:
        That depends on the source. Do you understand me?
        A fortune won is often misfortune.
SENTRY: King, may I speak?
CREON: Your very voice distresses me.
SENTRY: Are you sure that it is my voice, and not your conscience?
CREON: By God, he wants to analyze me now!
SENTRY: It is not what I say, but what has been done, that hurts you.
CREON: You talk too much.
SENTRY: Maybe; but I've done nothing.
CREON: Sold your soul for some silver: that's all you've done.
SENTRY: How dreadful it is when the right judge judges wrong!
CREON: Your figures of speech
        May entertain you now; but unless you bring me the man,
        You will get little profit from them in the end.

        Exit CREON *into the palace.*

SENTRY: "Bring me the man"—!
        I'd like nothing better than bringing him the man!
        But bring him or not, you have seen the last of me here.
        At any rate, I am safe!   [*Exit* SENTRY.]

Ode I

CHORUS: Numberless are the world's wonders, but not   *Strophe 1*
    More wonderful than man; the stormgray sea
    Yields to his prows, the huge crests bear him high;
    Earth, holy and inexhaustible, is graven
    With shining furrows where his plows have gone
    Year after year, the timeless labor of stallions.

    The lightboned birds and beasts that cling to cover,   *Antistrophe 1*
    The lithe fish lighting their reaches of dim water,
    All are taken, tamed in the net of his mind;
    The lion on the hill, the wild horse windy-maned,
    Resign to him; and his blunt yoke has broken
    The sultry shoulders of the mountain bull.

    Words also, and thought as rapid as air,   *Strophe 2*
    He fashions to his good use; statecraft is his,
    And his the skill that deflects the arrows of snow,
    The spears of winter rain: from every wind
    He has made himself secure—from all but one:
    In the late wind of death he cannot stand.

    O clear intelligence, force beyond all measure!   *Antistrophe 2*
    O fate of man, working both good and evil!
    When the laws are kept, how proudly his city stands!
    When the laws are broken, what of his city then?
    Never may the anarchic man find rest at my hearth,
    Never be it said that my thoughts are his thoughts.

Scene II

    Reenter SENTRY *leading Antigonê.*

CHORAGOS: What does this mean? Surely this captive woman
    Is the Princess, Antigonê. Why should she be taken?
SENTRY: Here is the one who did it! We caught her
    In the very act of burying him.—Where is Creon?
CHORAGOS: Just coming from the house.

    Enter CREON, *center.*

CREON: What has happened?
    Why have you come back so soon?
SENTRY [*expansively*]:   O King,
    A man should never be too sure of anything:
    I would have sworn
    That you'd not see me here again: your anger
    Frightened me so, and the things you threatened me with;
    But how could I tell then
    That I'd be able to solve the case so soon?
    No dice-throwing this time: I was only too glad to come!
    Here is this woman. She is the guilty one:

We found her trying to bury him.
Take her, then; question her; judge her as you will.
I am through with the whole thing now, and glad of it.
CREON: But this is Antigonê! Why have you brought her here?
SENTRY: She was burying him, I tell you!
CREON [*severely*]:   Is this the truth?
SENTRY: I saw her with my own eyes. Can I say more?
CREON: The details: come, tell me quickly!
SENTRY: It was like this:
After those terrible threats of yours, King,
We went back and brushed the dust away from the body.
The flesh was soft by now, and stinking,
So we sat on a hill to windward and kept guard.
No napping this time! We kept each other awake.
But nothing happened until the white round sun
Whirled in the center of the round sky over us:
Then, suddenly,
A storm of dust roared up from the earth, and the sky
Went out, the plain vanished with all its trees
In the stinging dark. We closed our eyes and endured it.
The whirlwind lasted a long time, but it passed;
And then we looked, and there was Antigonê!
I have seen
A mother bird come back to a stripped nest, heard
Her crying bitterly a broken note or two
For the young ones stolen. Just so, when this girl
Found the bare corpse, and all her love's work wasted,
She wept, and cried on heaven to damn the hands
That had done this thing.
                              And then she brought more dust
And sprinkled wine three times for her brother's ghost.
We ran and took her at once. She was not afraid,
Not even when we charged her with what she had done.
She denied nothing.
                              And this was a comfort to me,
And some uneasiness: for it is a good thing
To escape from death, but it is no great pleasure
To bring death to a friend.
                              Yet I always say
There is nothing so comfortable as your own safe skin!
CREON [*slowly, dangerously*]: And you, Antigonê,
You with your head hanging,—do you confess this thing?
ANTIGONÊ: I do. I deny nothing.
CREON [*to Sentry*]:   You may go.   [*Exit* SENTRY.]
[*To* ANTIGONÊ.] Tell me, tell me briefly:
Had you heard my proclamation touching this matter?
ANTIGONÊ: It was public. Could I help hearing it?
CREON: And yet you dared defy the law.
ANTIGONÊ: I dared.
It was not God's proclamation. That final Justice
That rules the world below makes no such laws.

Your edict, King, was strong.
But all your strength is weakness itself against
The immortal unrecorded laws of God.
They are not merely now: they were, and shall be,
Operative for ever, beyond man utterly.
I knew I must die, even without your decree:
I am only mortal. And if I must die
Now, before it is my time to die,
Surely this is no hardship: can anyone
Living, as I live, with evil all about me,
Think Death less than a friend? This death of mine
Is of no importance; but if I had left my brother
Lying in death unburied, I should have suffered.
Now I do not.
        You smile at me. Ah Creon,
Think me a fool, if you like; but it may well be
That a fool convicts me of folly.

CHORAGOS: Like father, like daughter: both headstrong, deaf to reason!
    She has never learned to yield.

CREON: She has much to learn.
The inflexible heart breaks first, the toughest iron
Cracks first, and the wildest horses bend their necks
At the pull of the smallest curb.
                  Pride? In a slave?
This girl is guilty of a double insolence,
Breaking the given laws and boasting of it.
Who is the man here,
She or I, if this crime goes unpunished?
Sister's child, or more than sister's child,
Or closer yet in blood—she and her sister
Win bitter death for this!
    [*To* SERVANTS.]   Go, some of you,
Arrest Ismenê. I accuse her equally.
Bring her: you will find her sniffling in the house there.
Her mind's a traitor: crimes kept in the dark
Cry for light, and the guardian brain shudders;
But how much worse than this
Is brazen boasting of barefaced anarchy!

ANTIGONÊ: Creon, what more do you want than my death?

CREON: Nothing.
That gives me everything.

ANTIGONÊ: Then I beg you: kill me.
This talking is a great weariness: your words
Are distasteful to me, and I am sure that mine
Seem so to you. And yet they should not seem so:
I should have praise and honor for what I have done.
All these men here would praise me
Were their lips not frozen shut with fear of you.
[*Bitterly.*] Ah the good fortune of kings,
Licensed to say and do whatever they please!

CREON: You are alone here in that opinion.

ANTIGONÊ: No, they are with me. But they keep their tongues in leash.

CREON: Maybe. But you are guilty, and they are not.

ANTIGONÊ: There is no guilt in reverence for the dead.

CREON: But Eteoclês—was he not your brother too?

ANTIGONÊ: My brother too.

CREON: And you insult his memory?

ANTIGONÊ [*softly*]: The dead man would not say that I insult it.

CREON: He would: for you honor a traitor as much as him.

ANTIGONÊ: His own brother, traitor or not, and equal in blood.

CREON: He made war on his country. Eteoclês defended it.

ANTIGONÊ: Nevertheless, there are honors due all the dead.

CREON: But not the same for the wicked as for the just.

ANTIGONÊ: Ah Creon, Creon,
          Which of us can say what the gods hold wicked?

CREON: An enemy is an enemy, even dead.

ANTIGONÊ: It is my nature to join in love, not hate.

CREON [*finally losing patience*]: Go join them then; if you must have your love,
          Find it in hell!

CHORAGOS: But see, Ismenê comes:

> *Enter* ISMENÊ, *guarded.*

          Those tears are sisterly, the cloud
          That shadows her eyes rains down gentle sorrow.

CREON: You too, Ismenê,
          Snake in my ordered house, sucking my blood
          Stealthily—and all the time I never knew
          That these two sisters were aiming at my throne!
                                          Ismenê,
          Do you confess your share in this crime, or deny it?
          Answer me.

ISMENÊ: Yes, if she will let me say so. I am guilty.

ANTIGONÊ [*coldly*]: No, Ismenê. You have no right to say so.
          You would not help me, and I will not have you help me.

ISMENÊ: But now I know what you meant: and I am here
          To join you, to take my share of punishment.

ANTIGONÊ: The dead man and the gods who rule the dead
          Know whose act this was. Words are not friends.

ISMENÊ: Do you refuse me, Antigonê? I want to die with you:
          I too have a duty that I must discharge to the dead.

ANTIGONÊ: You shall not lessen my death by sharing it.

ISMENÊ: What do I care for life when you are dead?

ANTIGONÊ: Ask Creon. You're always hanging on his opinions.

ISMENÊ: You are laughing at me. Why, Antigonê?

ANTIGONÊ: It's a joyless laughter, Ismenê.

ISMENÊ: But can I do nothing?

ANTIGONÊ: Yes. Save yourself. I shall not envy you.
          There are those who will praise you; I shall have honor, too.

ISMENÊ: But we are equally guilty!

ANTIGONÊ: No more, Ismenê.
          You are alive, but I belong to Death.

CREON [*to the Chorus*]: Gentlemen, I beg you to observe these girls:
          One has just now lost her mind; the other,
          It seems, has never had a mind at all.

ISMENÊ: Grief teaches the steadiest minds to waver, King.

CREON: Yours certainly did, when you assumed guilt with the guilty!

ISMENÊ: But how could I go on living without her?

CREON: You are.
            She is already dead.

ISMENÊ: But your own son's bride!

CREON: There are places enough for him to push his plow.
            I want no wicked women for my sons!

ISMENÊ: O dearest Haimon, how your father wrongs you!

CREON: I've had enough of your childish talk of marriage!

CHORAGOS: Do you really intend to steal this girl from your son?

CREON: No; Death will do that for me.

CHORAGOS: Then she must die?

CREON [*ironically*]: You dazzle me.
                        —But enough of this talk!
            [*To* GUARDS.] You, there, take them away and guard them well:
            For they are but women, and even brave men run
            When they see Death coming.   *Exeunt* ISMENÊ, ANTIGONÊ, *and* GUARDS.

Ode II

CHORUS: Fortunate is the man who has never tasted   Strophe 1
            God's vengeance!
            Where once the anger of heaven has struck, that house is shaken
            For ever: damnation rises behind each child
            Like a wave cresting out of the black northeast,
            When the long darkness under sea roars up
            And bursts drumming death upon the windwhipped sand.

            I have seen this gathering sorrow from time long past   Antistrophe 1
            Loom upon Oedipus' children: generation from generation
            Takes the compulsive rage of the enemy god.
            So lately this last flower of Oedipus' line
            Drank the sunlight! but now a passionate word
            And a handful of dust have closed up all its beauty.

            What mortal arrogance   Strophe 2
            Transcends the wrath of Zeus?
            Sleep cannot lull him nor the effortless long months
            Of the timeless gods: but he is young for ever,
            And his house is the shining day of high Olympos.
            All that is and shall be,
            And all the past, is his.
            No pride on earth is free of the curse of heaven.

            The straying dreams of men   Antistrophe 2
            May bring them ghosts of joy:
            But as they drowse, the waking embers burn them;
            Or they walk with fixed eyes, as blind men walk.
            But the ancient wisdom speaks for our own time:

Fate works most for woe
With Folly's fairest show.

Man's little pleasure is the spring of sorrow.

Scene III

CHORAGOS: But here is Haimon, King, the last of all your sons.
Is it grief for Antigonê that brings him here,
And bitterness at being robbed of his bride?

Enter HAIMON.

CREON: We shall soon see, and no need of diviners.
—Son,
You have heard my final judgment on that girl:
Have you come here hating me, or have you come
With deference and with love, whatever I do?
HAIMON: I am your son, father. You are my guide.
You make things clear for me, and I obey you.
No marriage means more to me than your continuing wisdom.
CREON: Good. That is the way to behave: subordinate
Everything else, my son, to your father's will.
This is what a man prays for, that he may get
Sons attentive and dutiful in his house,
Each one hating his father's enemies,
Honoring his father's friends. But if his sons
Fail him, if they turn out unprofitably,
What has he fathered but trouble for himself
And amusement for the malicious?
So you are right
Not to lose your head over this woman.
Your pleasure with her would soon grow cold, Haimon,
And then you'd have a hellcat in bed and elsewhere.
Let her find her husband in Hell!
Of all the people in this city, only she
Has had contempt for my law and broken it.

Do you want me to show myself weak before the people?
Or to break my sworn word? No, and I will not.
The woman dies.
I suppose she'll plead "family ties." Well, let her.
If I permit my own family to rebel,
How shall I earn the world's obedience?
Show me the man who keeps his house in hand,
He's fit for public authority.
I'll have no dealings
With lawbreakers, critics of the government:
Whoever is chosen to govern should be obeyed—
Must be obeyed, in all things, great and small,
Just and unjust! O Haimon,

The man who knows how to obey, and that man only,
Knows how to give commands when the time comes.
You can depend on him, no matter how fast
The spears come: he's a good soldier, he'll stick it out.

Anarchy, anarchy! Show me a greater evil!
This is why cities tumble and the great houses rain down,
This is what scatters armies!
No, no: good lives are made so by discipline.
We keep the laws then, and the lawmakers,
And no woman shall seduce us. If we must lose,
Let's lose to a man, at least! Is a woman stronger than we?
CHORAGOS: Unless time has rusted my wits,
What you say, King, is said with point and dignity.
HAIMON [*boyishly earnest*]: Father:
Reason is God's crowning gift to man, and you are right
To warn me against losing mine. I cannot say—
I hope that I shall never want to say!—that you
Have reasoned badly. Yet there are other men
Who can reason, too; and their opinions might be helpful.
You are not in a position to know everything
That people say or do, or what they feel:
Your temper terrifies—everyone
Will tell you only what you like to hear.
But I, at any rate, can listen; and I have heard them
Muttering and whispering in the dark about this girl.
They say no woman has ever, so unreasonably,
Died so shameful a death for a generous act:
"She covered her brother's body. Is this indecent?
She kept him from dogs and vultures. Is this a crime?
Death?—She should have all the honor that we can give her!"

This is the way they talk out there in the city.

You must believe me:
Nothing is closer to me than your happiness.
What could be closer? Must not any son
Value his father's fortune as his father does his?
I beg you, do not be unchangeable:
Do not believe that you alone can be right.
The man who thinks that,
The man who maintains that only he has the power
To reason correctly, the gift to speak, the soul—
A man like that, when you know him, turns out empty.

It is not reason never to yield to reason!
In flood time you can see how some trees bend,
And because they bend, even their twigs are safe,
While stubborn trees are torn up, roots and all.
And the same thing happens in sailing:
Make your sheet fast, never slacken,—and over you go,
Head over heels and under: and there's your voyage.

Forget you are angry! Let yourself be moved!
I know I am young; but please let me say this:
The ideal condition
Would be, I admit, that men should be right by instinct;
But since we are all too likely to go astray,
The reasonable thing is to learn from those who can teach.

CHORAGOS: You will do well to listen to him, King,
If what he says is sensible. And you, Haimon,
Must listen to your father.—Both speak well.

CREON: You consider it right for a man of my years and experience
To go to school to a boy?

HAIMON: It is not right
If I am wrong. But if I am young, and right,
What does my age matter?

CREON: You think it right to stand up for an anarchist?

HAIMON: Not at all. I pay no respect to criminals.

CREON: Then she is not a criminal?

HAIMON: The City would deny it, to a man.

CREON: And the City proposes to teach me how to rule?

HAIMON: Ah. Who is it that's talking like a boy now?

CREON: My voice is the one voice giving orders in this City!

HAIMON: It is no City if it takes orders from one voice.

CREON: The State is the King!

HAIMON: Yes, if the State is a desert.

Pause.

CREON: This boy, it seems, has sold out to a woman.

HAIMON: If you are a woman: my concern is only for you.

CREON: So? Your "concern"! In a public brawl with your father!

HAIMON: How about you, in a public brawl with justice?

CREON: With justice, when all that I do is within my rights?

HAIMON: You have no right to trample on God's right.

CREON [*completely out of control*]: Fool, adolescent fool! Taken in by a woman!

HAIMON: You'll never see me taken in by anything vile.

CREON: Every word you say is for her!

HAIMON [*quietly, darkly*]:   And for you.
And for me. And for the gods under the earth.

CREON: You'll never marry her while she lives.

HAIMON: Then she must die.—But her death will cause another.

CREON: Another?
Have you lost your senses? Is this an open threat?

HAIMON: There is no threat in speaking to emptiness.

CREON: I swear you'll regret this superior tone of yours!
You are the empty one!

HAIMON: If you were not my father,
I'd say you were perverse.

CREON: You girlstruck fool, don't play at words with me!

HAIMON: I am sorry. You prefer silence.

CREON: Now, by God—
I swear, by all the gods in heaven above us,
You'll watch it, I swear you shall!
[*To the* SERVANTS.] Bring her out!

Bring the woman out! Let her die before his eyes!
Here, this instant, with her bridegroom beside her!
HAIMON: Not here, no; she will not die here, King.
And you will never see my face again.
Go on raving as long as you've a friend to endure you.   *Exit* HAIMON.
CHORAGOS: Gone, gone.
Creon, a young man in a rage is dangerous!
CREON: Let him do, or dream to do, more than a man can.
He shall not save these girls from death.
CHORAGOS: These girls?
You have sentenced them both?
CREON: No, you are right.
I will not kill the one whose hands are clean.
CHORAGOS: But Antigonê?
CREON. [*somberly*]:   I will carry her far away
Out there in the wilderness, and lock her
Living in a vault of stone. She shall have food,
As the custom is, to absolve the State of her death.
And there let her pray to the gods of hell:
They are her only gods:
Perhaps they will show her an escape from death,
Or she may learn,
                        though late,
That piety shown the dead is piety in vain.   [*Exit* CREON.]

Ode III

CHORUS: Love, unconquerable   *Strophe*
Waster of rich men, keeper
Of warm lights and all-night vigil
In the soft face of a girl:
Sea-wanderer, forest-visitor!
Even the pure Immortals cannot escape you,
And the mortal man, in his one day's dusk,
Trembles before your glory.

Surely you swerve upon ruin   *Antistrophe*
The just man's consenting heart,
As here you have made bright anger
Strike between father and son—
And none has conquered by Love!
A girl's glance working the will of heaven:
Pleasure to her alone who mocks us,
Merciless Aphroditê.

Scene IV

CHORAGOS [*as* ANTIGONÊ *enters guarded*] But I can no longer stand in awe of this,
Nor, seeing what I see, keep back my tears.
Here is Antigonê, passing to that chamber
Where all find sleep at last.
ANTIGONÊ: Look upon me, friends, and pity me   *Strophe 1*
Turning back at the night's edge to say

Good-by to the sun that shines for me no longer;
Now sleepy Death
Summons me down to Acheron,[5] that cold shore:
There is no bridesong there, nor any music.

CHORUS: Yet not unpraised, not without a kind of honor,
You walk at last into the underworld;
Untouched by sickness, broken by no sword.
What woman has ever found your way to death?

ANTIGONÊ: How often I have heard the story of Niobê,   *Antistrophe 1*
Tantalos' wretched daughter,[6] how the stone
Clung fast about her, ivy-close: and they say
The rain falls endlessly
And sifting soft snow; her tears are never done.
I feel the loneliness of her death in mine.

CHORUS: But she was born of heaven, and you
Are woman, woman-born. If her death is yours,
A mortal woman's, is this not for you
Glory in our world and in the world beyond?

ANTIGONÊ: You laugh at me. Ah, friends, friends   *Strophe 2*
Can you not wait until I am dead? O Thebes,
O men many-charioted, in love with Fortune,
Dear springs of Dircê, sacred Theban grove,
Be witnesses for me, denied all pity,
Unjustly judged! and think a word of love
For her whose path turns
Under dark earth, where there are no more tears.

CHORUS: You have passed beyond human daring and come at last
Into a place of stone where Justice sits.
I cannot tell
What shape of your father's guilt appears in this.

ANTIGONÊ: You have touched it at last: *Antistrophe 2*
That bridal bed
Unspeakable, horror of son and mother mingling:
Their crime, infection of all our family!
O Oedipus, father and brother!
Your marriage strikes from the grave to murder mine.
I have been a stranger here in my own land:
All my life
The blasphemy of my birth has followed me.

CHORUS: Reverence is a virtue, but strength
Lives in established law: that must prevail.
You have made your choice,
Your death is the doing of your conscious hand.

ANTIGONÊ: Then let me go, since all your words are bitter,   *Epode*
And the very light of the sun is cold to me.
Lead me to my vigil, where I must have
Neither love nor lamentation; no song, but silence.

---

[5]**Acheron:** a river in the underworld.
[6]**Tantalos' wretched daughter:** Niobê, daughter of Tantalos (who was tempted forever by the gods) angered the gods by bragging about her children; the gods killed her children and turned her into the stone of Mount Sipylus.

CREON *interrupts impatiently.*

CREON: If dirges and planned lamentations could put off death,
    Men would be singing for ever.
    [*To the* SERVANTS.]   Take her, go!
    You know your orders: take her to the vault
    And leave her alone there. And if she lives or dies,
    That's her affair, not ours: our hands are clean.
ANTIGONÊ: O tomb, vaulted bride-bed in eternal rock,
    Soon I shall be with my own again
    Where Persephonê welcomes the thin ghosts underground:[7]
    And I shall see my father again, and you, mother,
    And dearest Polyneicês—
                    dearest indeed
    To me, since it was my hand
    That washed him clean and poured the ritual wine:
    And my reward is death before my time!
    And yet, as men's hearts know, I have done no wrong,
    I have not sinned before God. Or if I have,
    I shall know the truth in death. But if the guilt
    Lies upon Creon who judged me, then, I pray,
    May his punishment equal my own.
CHORAGOS: O passionate heart,
    Unyielding, tormented still by the same winds!
CREON: Her guards shall have good cause to regret their delaying.
ANTIGONÊ: Ah! That voice is like the voice of death!
CREON: I can give you no reason to think you are mistaken.
ANTIGONÊ: Thebes, and you my fathers' gods,
    And rulers of Thebes, you see me now, the last
    Unhappy daughter of a line of kings,
    Your kings, led away to death. You will remember
    What things I suffer, and at what men's hands,
    Because I would not transgress the laws of heaven.
    [*To the* GUARDS, *simply.*] Come: let us wait no longer.

                      [*Exit* ANTIGONÊ, *left, guarded.*]

Ode IV

CHORUS: All Danaê's beauty was locked away   *Strophe 1*
    In a brazen cell where the sunlight could not come:
    A small room, still as any grave, enclosed her.
    Yet she was a princess too,
    And Zeus in a rain of gold poured love upon her.[8]
    O child, child,
    No power in wealth or war

---

[7] **Persephone:** daughter of Zeus and Demeter who was abducted by Hades and taken to live in the underworld.

[8] **love upon her:** Danaê was locked in a bronze room away from all men to prevent her from having children. Zeus, however, desired Danaê and poured through the roof in a shower of gold, giving her a son.

Or tough sea-blackened ships
Can prevail against untiring Destiny!

And Dryas' son[9] also, that furious king,   *Antistrophe 1*
Bore the god's prisoning anger for his pride:
Sealed up by Dionysos in deaf stone,
His madness died among echoes.
So at the last he learned what dreadful power
His tongue had mocked:
For he had profaned the revels,
And fired the wrath of the nine
Implacable Sisters that love the sound of the flute.

And old men tell a half-remembered tale   *Strophe 2*
Of horror where a dark ledge splits the sea
And a double surf beats on the gray shores:
How a king's new woman, sick
With hatred for the queen he had imprisoned,
Ripped out his two sons' eyes with her bloody hands[10]
While grinning Arês[11] watched the shuttle plunge
Four times: four blind wounds crying for revenge,

Crying, tears and blood mingled.—Piteously born,   *Antistrophe 2*
Those sons whose mother was of heavenly birth!
Her father was the god of the North Wind
And she was cradled by gales,
She raced with young colts on the glittering hills
And walked untrammeled in the open light:
But in her marriage deathless Fate found means
To build a tomb like yours for all her joy.

Scene V

Enter blind Teiresias, *led by a boy. The opening speeches of* Teiresias
should be in singsong contrast to the realistic lines of Creon.

Teiresias: This is the way the blind man comes, Princes, Princes,
           Lock-step, two heads lit by the eyes of one.
Creon: What new thing have you to tell us, old Teiresias?
Teiresias: I have much to tell you: listen to the prophet, Creon.
Creon: I am not aware that I have ever failed to listen.
Teiresias: Then you have done wisely, King, and ruled well.
Creon: I admit my debt to you. But what have you to say?
Teiresias: This, Creon: you stand once more on the edge of fate.

---

[9]**Dryas' son:** Lycurgis, son of Dryas tried to imprison Bacchus, also known as Dionysus, (the god of
wine and pleasure). Dionysus caused Lycurgis to go insane, eventually killing his own son.
[10]**bloody hands:** Eidothea was jealous of Cleopatra, her husband's first wife, and blinded both of her
stepsons; the boys and Cleopatra were descended from powerful Boreas, the North Wind, but fate
still caused Cleopatra to be imprisoned in a cave while her sons were attacked.
[11]**Arês:** the god of war.

CREON: What do you mean? Your words are a kind of dread.
TEIRESIAS: Listen, Creon:

> I was sitting in my chair of augury, at the place
> Where the birds gather about me. They were all a-chatter,
> As is their habit, when suddenly I heard
> A strange note in their jangling, a scream, a
> Whirring fury; I knew that they were fighting,
> Tearing each other, dying
> In a whirlwind of wings clashing. And I was afraid.
> I began the rites of burnt-offering at the altar,
> But Hephaistos[12] failed me: instead of bright flame,
> There was only the sputtering slime of the fat thigh-flesh
> Melting: the entrails dissolved in gray smoke,
> The bare bone burst from the welter. And no blaze!

> This was a sign from heaven. My boy described it,
> Seeing for me as I see for others.

> I tell you, Creon, you yourself have brought
> This new calamity upon us. Our hearths and altars
> Are stained with the corruption of dogs and carrion birds
> That glut themselves on the corpse of Oedipus' son.
> The gods are deaf when we pray to them, their fire
> Recoils from our offering, their birds of omen
> Have no cry of comfort, for they are gorged
> With the thick blood of the dead.
>   O my son,
> These are no trifles! Think: all men make mistakes,
> But a good man yields when he knows his course is wrong,
> And repairs the evil. The only crime is pride.

> Give in to the dead man, then: do not fight with a corpse—
> What glory is it to kill a man who is dead?
> Think, I beg you:
> It is for your own good that I speak as I do.
> You should be able to yield for your own good.

CREON: It seems that prophets have made me their especial province.

> All my life long
> I have been a kind of butt for the dull arrows
> Of doddering fortune-tellers!
>   No, Teiresias:
> If your birds—if the great eagles of God himself
> Should carry him stinking bit by bit to heaven,
> I would not yield. I am not afraid of pollution:
> No man can defile the gods.
>   Do what you will,
> Go into business, make money, speculate
> In India gold or that synthetic gold from Sardis,

---

[12] **Hephaistos:** the god of fire.

Get rich otherwise than by my consent to bury him.
Teiresias, it is a sorry thing when a wise man
Sells his wisdom, lets out his words for hire!
TEIRESIAS: Ah Creon! Is there no man left in the world—
CREON: To do what?—Come, let's have the aphorism!
TEIRESIAS: No man who knows that wisdom outweighs any wealth?
CREON: As surely as bribes are baser than any baseness.
TEIRESIAS: You are sick, Creon! You are deathly sick!
CREON: As you say: it is not my place to challenge a prophet.
TEIRESIAS: Yet you have said my prophecy is for sale.
CREON: The generation of prophets has always loved gold.
TEIRESIAS: The generation of kings has always loved brass.
CREON: You forget yourself! You are speaking to your King.
TEIRESIAS: I know it. You are a king because of me.
CREON: You have a certain skill; but you have sold out.
TEIRESIAS: King, you will drive me to words that—
CREON: Say them, say them!
Only remember: I will not pay you for them.
TEIRESIAS: No, you will find them too costly.
CREON: No doubt. Speak:
Whatever you say, you will not change my will.
TEIRESIAS: Then take this, and take it to heart!
The time is not far off when you shall pay back
Corpse for corpse, flesh of your own flesh.
You have thrust the child of this world into living night,
You have kept from the gods below the child that is theirs:
The one in a grave before her death, the other,
Dead, denied the grave. This is your crime:
And the Furies and the dark gods of Hell
Are swift with terrible punishment for you.

Do you want to buy me now, Creon?

                                    Not many days,
And your house will be full of men and women weeping,
And curses will be hurled at you from far
Cities grieving for sons unburied, left to rot
Before the walls of Thebes.

These are my arrows, Creon: they are all for you.
[*To* BOY.] But come, child: lead me home.
Let him waste his fine anger upon younger men.
Maybe he will learn at last
To control a wiser tongue in a better head.   [*Exit* TEIRESIAS.]
CHORAGOS: The old man has gone, King, but his words
Remain to plague us. I am old, too,
But I cannot remember that he was ever false.
CREON: That is true. . . . It troubles me.
Oh it is hard to give in! but it is worse
To risk everything for stubborn pride.
CHORAGOS: Creon: take my advice.

CREON: What shall I do?
CHORAGOS: Go quickly: free Antigonê from her vault
        And build a tomb for the body of Polyneicês.
CREON: You would have me do this!
CHORAGOS: Creon, yes!
        And it must be done at once: God moves
        Switftly to cancel the folly of stubborn men.
CREON: It is hard to deny the heart! But I
        Will do it: I will not fight with destiny.
CHORAGOS: You must go yourself, you cannot leave it to others.
CREON: I will go.
        —Bring axes, servants:
        Come with me to the tomb. I buried her, I
        Will set her free.
                        Oh quickly!
        My mind misgives—
        The laws of the gods are mighty, and a man must serve them
        To the last day of his life!   [*Exit* CREON.]

Paean[13]

CHORAGOS: God of many names   *Strophe 1*
CHORUS: O Iacchos
                                son
        of Kadmeian Sémelê
                                O born of the Thunder!
        Guardian of the West
                                Regent
        of Eleusis' plain
                                O Prince of Maenad Thebes
        and the Dragon Field by rippling Ismenós:
CHORAGOS: God of many names   *Antistrophe 1*
CHORUS: the flame of torches
        flares on our hills
                                the nymphs of Iacchos
        dance at the spring of Castalia:
        from the vine-close mountain
                                come ah come in ivy:
        Evohé evohé! sings through the streets of Thebes
CHORAGOS: God of many names   *Strophe 2*
CHORUS: Iacchos of Thebes
        heavenly Child
                                of Sémelê bride of the Thunderer!
        The shadow of plague is upon us:
                                come
        with clement feet
                                oh come from Parnassos
        down the long slopes
                                across the lamenting water

---

[13]**Paean:** a hymn or praise. Iacchos is a secret name for Dionysus. *Antigonê* was first performed at the festival for Dionysus; here the chorus offers its praise for the god of wine and pleasure.

CHORAGOS: Iô Fire! Chorister of the throbbing stars! *Antistrophe 2*
    O purest among the voices of the night!
    Thou son of God, blaze for us!
CHORUS: Come with choric rapture of circling Maenads
    Who cry *Iô Iacche!*
              God of many names!

Exodos

    Enter MESSENGER *from left.*

MESSENGER: Men of the line of Kadmos, you who live
    Near Amphion's citadel,[14]
              I cannot say
    Of any condition of human life "This is fixed,
    This is clearly good, or bad." Fate raises up,
    And Fate casts down the happy and unhappy alike:
    No man can foretell his Fate.
              Take the case of Creon:
    Creon was happy once, as I count happiness:
    Victorious in battle, sole governor of the land,
    Fortunate father of children nobly born.
    And now it has all gone from him! Who can say
    That a man is still alive when his life's joy fails?
    He is a walking dead man. Grant him rich,
    Let him live like a king in his great house:
    If his pleasure is gone, I would not give
    So much as the shadow of smoke for all he owns.
CHORAGOS: Your words hint at sorrow: what is your news for us?
MESSENGER: They are dead. The living are guilty of their death.
CHORAGOS: Who is guilty? Who is dead? Speak!
MESSENGER: Haimon.
    Haimon is dead; and the hand that killed him
    Is his own hand.
CHORAGOS: His father's? or his own?
MESSENGER: His own, driven mad by the murder his father had done.
CHORAGOS: Teiresias, Teiresias, how clearly you saw it all!
MESSENGER: This is my news: you must draw what conclusions you can from it.
CHORAGOS: But look: Eurydicê, our Queen:
    Has she overheard us?

    Enter EURYDICÊ *from the palace, center.*

EURYDICÊ: I have heard something, friends:
    As I was unlocking the gate of Pallas' shrine,[15]
    For I needed her help today, I heard a voice
    Telling of some new sorrow. And I fainted
    There at the temple with all my maidens about me.

---

[14]**Men . . . citadel:** here the messenger continues praising the history of Thebes; Kadmos was said to have founded Thebes by sowing the teeth of a dragon in the Ismenos river. Amphion was said to have created a wall around the city by playing on his lyre.
[15]**Pallas:** Eurydicê reports that he was praying to Pallas, or Athena the goddess of wisdom.

But speak again: whatever it is, I can bear it:
Grief and I are no strangers.

MESSENGER: Dearest Lady,
I will tell you plainly all that I have seen.
I shall not try to comfort you: what is the use,
Since comfort could lie only in what is not true?
The truth is always best.

I went with Creon
To the outer plain where Polyneicês was lying,
No friend to pity him, his body shredded by dogs.
We made our prayers in the place to Hecatê
And Pluto,[16] that they would be merciful. And we bathed
The corpse with holy water, and we brought
Fresh-broken branches to burn what was left of it,
And upon the urn we heaped up a towering barrow
Of the earth of his own land.

When we were done, we ran
To the vault where Antigonê lay on her couch of stone.
One of the servants had gone ahead,
And while he was yet far off he heard a voice
Grieving within the chamber, and he came back
And told Creon. And as the King went closer,
The air was full of wailing, the words lost,
And he begged us to make all haste. "Am I a prophet?"
He said, weeping, "And must I walk this road,
The saddest of all that I have gone before?
My son's voice calls me on. Oh quickly, quickly!
Look through the crevice there, and tell me
If it is Haimon, or some deception of the gods!"
We obeyed; and in the cavern's farthest corner
We saw her lying:
She had made a noose of her fine linen veil
And hanged herself. Haimon lay beside her,
His arms about her waist, lamenting her,
His love lost under ground, crying out
That his father had stolen her away from him.

When Creon saw him the tears rushed to his eyes
And he called to him: "What have you done, child?
Speak to me.
What are you thinking that makes your eyes so strange?
O my son, my son, I come to you on my knees!"
But Haimon spat in his face. He said not a word,
Staring—
And suddenly drew his sword
And lunged. Creon shrank back, the blade missed; and the boy,
Desperate against himself, drove it half its length
Into his own side, and fell. And as he died
He gathered Antigonê close in his arms again,

---

[16]**Hecatê and Pluto:** gods of the underworld.

Choking, his blood bright red on her white cheek.
And now he lies dead with the dead, and she is his
At last, his bride in the house of the dead.

Exit EURYDICÊ *into the palace.*

CHORAGOS: She has left us without a word. What can this mean?
MESSENGER: It troubles me, too; yet she knows what is best,
Her grief is too great for public lamentation,
And doubtless she has gone to her chamber to weep
For her dead son, leading her maidens in his dirge.

Pause.

CHORAGOS: It may be so: but I fear this deep silence.
MESSENGER: I will see what she is doing. I will go in.

Exit MESSENGER *into the palace.*

Enter CREON *with attendants, bearing* HAIMON's *body.*

CHORAGOS: But here is the king himself: oh look at him,
Bearing his own damnation in his arms.
CREON: Nothing you say can touch me any more.
My own blind heart has brought me
From darkness to final darkness. Here you see
The father murdering, the murdered son—
And all my civic wisdom!

Haimon my son, so young, so young to die,
I was the fool, not you; and you died for me.
CHORAGOS: That is the truth; but you were late in learning it.
CREON: This truth is hard to bear. Surely a god
Has crushed me beneath the hugest weight of heaven,
And driven me headlong a barbaric way
To trample out the thing I held most dear.

The pains that men will take to come to pain!

Enter MESSENGER *from the palace.*

MESSENGER: The burden you carry in your hands is heavy,
But it is not all: you will find more in your house.
CREON: What burden worse than this shall I find there?
MESSENGER: The Queen is dead.
CREON: O port of death, deaf world,
Is there no pity for me? And you, Angel of evil,
I was dead, and your words are death again.
Is it true, boy? Can it be true?
Is my wife dead? Has death bred death?
MESSENGER: You can see for yourself.

The doors are opened and the body of EURYDICÊ *is disclosed within.*

CREON: Oh pity!
All true, all true, and more than I can bear!
O my wife, my son!

MESSENGER: She stood before the altar, and her heart
    Welcomed the knife her own hand guided,
    And a great cry burst from her lips for Megareus[17] dead,
    And for Haimon dead, her sons; and her last breath
    Was a curse for their father, the murderer of her sons.
    And she fell, and the dark flowed in through her closing eyes.
CREON: O God, I am sick with fear.
    Are there no swords here? Has no one a blow for me?
MESSENGER: Her curse is upon you for the deaths of both.
CREON: It is right that it should be. I alone am guilty.
    I know it, and I say it. Lead me in,
    Quickly, friends.
    I have neither life nor substance. Lead me in.
CHORAGOS: You are right, if there can be right in so much wrong.
    The briefest way is best in a world of sorrow.
CREON: Let it come,
    Let death come quickly, and be kind to me.
    I would not ever see the sun again.
CHORAGOS: All that will come when it will; but we, meanwhile,
    Have much to do. Leave the future to itself.
CREON: All my heart was in that prayer!
CHORAGOS: Then do not pray any more: the sky is deaf.
CREON: Lead me away. I have been rash and foolish.
    I have killed my son and my wife.
    I look for comfort; my comfort lies here dead.
    Whatever my hands have touched has come to nothing.
    Fate has brought all my pride to a thought of dust.

As CREON *is being led into the house, the* CHORAGOS *advances and speaks directly to the audience.*

CHORAGOS: There is no happiness where there is no wisdom;
    No wisdom but in submission to the gods.
    Big words are always punished,
    And proud men in old age learn to be wise.

INQUIRING FURTHER

1. Do you think it was right of Ismenê to initially not support Antigonê? Why or why not?

2. What do you think of Creon's rationale for not burying Polyneicês? How important is the fact that Polyneicês was fighting against the city of Thebes? Would you say Polyneicês raises more political or family concerns in the play?

SPOUSES AND LOVERS

While every relationship combines joy and sorrow, the close relationships between spouses and lovers extend these complexities by introducing sex into the equation.

---

[17]**Megareus:** Creon and Eurydicê's son, Magereus, was killed in the attack on Thebes.

Sexual relations present numerous questions about desire, control, and the physical dimensions of relationships. Intimate partnerships ask us to consider gender roles and societal views about marriage or relationships. Eventually, many of the connections between lovers bring the complexities of relationships full circle as partners decide whether or not to have children and how to devote their energies to others in the world. The selections below look at these intimate connections between people.

MATTHEW ARNOLD

Matthew Arnold (1822–1888) was closely supervised in his studies by his father, Thomas Arnold, who was a well-known literary figure and educator. Matthew received a strict education in classical learning, eventually enrolling at Oxford where he studied poetry and launched his writing career. After Oxford he published several volumes of poetry, but chiefly established his reputation as a literary critic. He wrote many successful essays on literature and culture. "Dover Beach" was first published in 1867, though it was written in the late 1850s.

Dover Beach

The sea is calm tonight,
The tide is full, the moon lies fair
Upon the straits;—on the French coast the light
Gleams and is gone; the cliffs of England stand,
5   Glimmering and vast, out in the tranquil bay.
Come to the window, sweet is the night air!
Only, from the long line of spray
Where the sea meets the moon-blanch'd land,
Listen! you hear the grating roar
10   Of pebbles which the waves draw back, and fling,
At their return, up the high strand.
Begin, and cease, and then again begin,
With tremulous cadence slow, and bring
The eternal note of sadness in.

15   Sophocles long ago
Heard it on the Ægæan, and it brought
Into his mind the turbid ebb and flow[1]
Of human misery; we
Find also in the sound a thought,
20   Hearing it by this distant northern sea.

The Sea of Faith
Was once, too, at the full, and round earth's shore
Lay like the folds of a bright girdle furl'd.
But now I only hear
25   Its melancholy, long, withdrawing roar,
Retreating, to the breath
Of the night-wind, down the vast edges drear

---

[1]**ebb and flow**: in *Antigonê* (788), by Sophocles, the fates bring misery like the ebb and flow of the sea.

                And naked shingles of the world.

                Ah, love, let us be true
30   To one another! for the world, which seems
                To lie before us like a land of dreams,
                So various, so beautiful, so new,
                Hath really neither joy, nor love, nor light,
                Nor certitude, nor peace, nor help for pain;
35   And we are here as on a darkling plain
                Swept with confused alarms of struggle and flight,
                Where ignorant armies clash by night.

ANTHONY HECHT

*Having never taken an interest in literature before college, Anthony Hecht
(born in 1923) made up for lost time upon entering Bard College, deciding on the spot that he wished to become a poet. After serving in the Army
during World War II, Hecht returned to study under the poet John Crowe
Ransom, and soon began publishing in a number of magazines. Hecht's
work hearkens back to traditional forms while taking up political and
cultural themes that represent the concerns of the last half of the twentieth century. "The Dover Bitch" was published in 1968.*

The Dover Bitch

A Criticism of Life

For Andrew S. Wennng

                So there stood Matthew Arnold and this girl
                With the cliffs of England crumbling away behind them,
                And he said to her, "Try to be true to me,
                And I'll do the same for you, for things are bad
5   All over, etc., etc."
                Well now, I knew this girl. It's true she had read
                Sophocles in a fairly good translation
                And caught that bitter allusion to the sea,
                But all the time he was talking she had in mind
10   The notion of what his whiskers would feel like
                On the back of her neck. She told me later on
                That after a while she got to looking out
                At the lights across the channel, and really felt sad,
                Thinking of all the wine and enormous beds
15   And blandishments in French and the perfumes.
                And then she got really angry. To have been brought
                All the way down from London, and then be addressed
                As a sort of mournful cosmic last resort
20   Is really tough on a girl, and she was pretty.
                Anyway, she watched him pace the room
                And finger his watch-chain and seem to sweat a bit,
                And then she said one or two unprintable things.
                But you mustn't judge her by that. What I mean to say is,

She's really all right. I still see her once in a while
25   And she always treats me right. We have a drink
And I give her a good time, and perhaps it's a year
Before I see her again, but there she is,
Running to fat, but dependable as they come.
And sometimes I bring her a bottle of *Nuit d' Amour*.

INQUIRING FURTHER

1. How would you read "Dover Beach" as an argument? What purpose does the speaker of the poem have in mind? What reasons does he offer to the listener? Write two or three sentences paraphrasing the message of the speaker.

2. Arnold's poem is sometimes interpreted as commenting on nineteenth-century culture, expressing a loss of faith related to industrialization and the breakdown of social hierarchies. Do you agree that the poem is more concerned with culture than relationships?

3. Do you see "The Dover Bitch" as commenting on Arnold's poem? If so, what comment does the latter poem make? Write a paragraph or two discussing the poems in terms of one another.

ANDREW MARVELL

Andrew Marvell (1621–1678) enjoyed an academic life from an early age, enrolling at Cambridge when he was thirteen. After Cambridge, he traveled abroad for many years, then returned to England and began writing some of his best-known lyric poetry. Throughout his adult life, he negotiated the complex territory of being a well-known writer during the many political upheavals of seventeenth-century England, changing allegiances and taking on political appointments when necessary. "To His Coy Mistress" (1641) represents a lyrical work from Marvell's early career.

To His Coy Mistress

Had we but world enough, and time,
This coyness, Lady, were no crime
We would sit down and think which way
To walk and pass our long love's day.
5   Thou by the Indian Ganges' side
Shouldst rubies find; I by the tide
Of Humber would complain. I would
Love you ten years before the Flood,
And you should, if you please, refuse
10   Till the conversion of the Jews.
My vegetable love should grow
Vaster than empires, and more slow;
An hundred years should go to praise
Thine eyes and on thy forehead gaze,
15   Two hundred to adore each breast,

But thirty thousand to the rest;
An age at least to every part,
And the last age should show your heart.
For, Lady, you deserve this state,
20   Nor would I love at lower rate.

But at my back I always hear
Time's wingèd chariot hurrying near;
And yonder all before us lie
Deserts of vast eternity.
25   Thy beauty shall no more be found,
Nor, in thy marble vault, shall sound
My echoing song; then worms shall try
That long preserved virginity,
And your quaint honour turn to dust,
30   And into ashes all my lust.
The grave's a fine and private place,
But none, I think, do there embrace.

Now therefore, while the youthful hue
Sits on thy skin like morning dew,
35   And while thy willing soul transpires
At every pore with instant fires,
Now let us sport us while we may,
And now, like amorous birds of prey,
Rather at once our time devour
40   Than languish in his slow-chapt power.
Let us roll all our strength and all
Our sweetness up into one ball,
And tear our pleasures with rough strife
Thorough the iron gates of life:
45   Thus, though we cannot make our sun
Stand still, yet we will make him run.

INQUIRING FURTHER

1. How would you respond to someone who claimed that the poem is written mostly as a joke? What passages in the poem seem to be the least serious? How might any playfulness in the poem relate to the overall message?

2. How do you interpret the line, "Rather at once our time devour"? How do poetic techniques in the first and second section relate to the concept of time? How does the concept of time work in the speaker's argument to convince the lady to be his lover? Freewrite for five minutes about time in the work.

JUDY SYFERS-BRADY

Judy Syfers-Brady first presented "Why I Want a Wife" at a celebration of the fiftieth anniversary of the passage of women's suffrage (which gave

women the right to vote). Since that time it has been published twice by Ms.
magazine, the first time in the premier issue. In the essay, Syfers-Brady satir-
ically lists the numerous reasons for wanting a wife, in the process raising
questions about what it means to be a woman in a male-centered society.

Why I Want a Wife

I belong to that classification of people known as wives. I am A Wife. And, not altogether incidentally, I am a mother. Not too long ago a male friend of mine appeared on the scene fresh from a recent divorce. He had one child, who is, of course, with his ex-wife. He is obviously looking for another wife. As I thought about him while I was ironing one evening, it suddenly occurred to me that I, too, would like to have a wife. Why do I want a wife?

I would like to go back to school so that I can become economically inde-pendent, support myself, and, if need be, support those dependent upon me. I want a wife who will work and send me to school. And while I am going to school I want a wife to take care of my children. I want a wife to keep track of the children's doctor and dentist appointments. And to keep track of mine, too. I want a wife to make sure my children eat properly and are kept clean. I want a wife who will wash the children's clothes and keep them mend-ed. I want a wife who is a good nurturant attendant to my children, who arranges for their schooling, makes sure that they have an adequate social life with their peers, takes them to the park, the zoo, etc. I want a wife who takes care of the children when they are sick, a wife who arranges to be around when the children need special care, because, of course, I cannot miss classes at school. My wife must arrange to lose time at work and not lose the job. It may mean a small cut in my wife's income from time to time, but I guess I can tolerate that. Needless to say, my wife will arrange and pay for the care of the children while my wife is working.

I want a wife who will take care of *my* physical needs. I want a wife who will keep my house clean. A wife who will pick up after me. I want a wife who will keep my clothes clean, ironed, mended, replaced when need be, and who will see to it that my personal things are kept in their proper place so that I can find what I need the minute I need it. I want a wife who cooks the meals, a wife who is a *good* cook. I want a wife who will plan the menus, do the necessary grocery shopping, prepare the meals, serve them pleasant-ly, and then do the cleaning up while I do my studying. I want a wife who will care for me when I am sick and sympathize with my pain and loss of time from school. I want a wife to go along when our family takes a vacation so that someone can continue to care for me and my children when I need a rest and change of scene.

I want a wife who will not bother me with rambling complaints about a wife's duties. But I want a wife who will listen to me when I feel the need to explain a rather difficult point I have come across in my course of studies. And I want a wife who will type my papers for me when I have written them.

5   I want a wife who will take care of the details of my social life. When my wife and I are invited out by my friends, I want a wife who will take care of the babysitting arrangements. When I meet people at school that I like and want to entertain, I want a wife who will have the house clean, will prepare a spe-cial meal, serve it to me and my friends, and not interrupt when I talk about the things that interest me and my friends. I want a wife who will have arranged

that the children are fed and ready for bed before my guests arrive so that the children do not bother us.

And I want a wife who knows that sometimes I need a night out by myself.

I want a wife who is sensitive to my sexual needs, a wife who makes love passionately and eagerly when I feel like it, a wife who makes sure that I am satisfied. And, of course, I want a wife who will not demand sexual attention when I am not in the mood for it. I want a wife who assumes the complete responsibility for birth control, because I do not want more children. I want a wife who will remain sexually faithful to me so that I do not have to clutter up my intellectual life with jealousies. And I want a wife who understands that *my* sexual needs may entail more than strict adherence to monogamy. I must, after all, be able to relate to people as fully as possible.

If, by chance, I find another person more suitable as a wife than the wife I already have, I want the liberty to replace my present wife with another one. Naturally, I will expect a fresh, new life; my wife will take the children and be solely responsible for them so that I am left free.

When I am through with school and have a job, I want my wife to quit working and remain at home so that my wife can more fully and completely take care of a wife's duties.

10   My God, who *wouldn't* want a wife?

INQUIRING FURTHER

1. Syfers-Brady's essay is one of the most frequently anthologized essays of the last thirty years. Why do you think it is so popular? Do you believe the status of women has shifted dramatically since 1971? Hold a discussion with classmates regarding the relevance of the essay's message then and now.

2. What do you take to be the main point of Syfers-Brady's argument? Is she suggesting that women should not become wives? Is she arguing that women should look for wife-like qualities in men? What other possibilities can you think of?

3. What rhetorical strategies can you recognize in the essay? How effective is the humor of the piece? Does the essay present any alternative perspectives? Which strategies do you find to be the most effective and why?

4. If you had to write a "Why I Want a Husband" response to Syfers-Brady, what points would you make? Can you envision a similar essay written about friends, parents, or children? Write a one or two page essay either revising Syfer-Brady's approach or taking up your own theme about a relationship.

KATE CHOPIN

In her many stories and novels, Kate Chopin (1851–1904) frequently offers a view of life from a woman's perspective. In "The Storm" (1898) Chopin adds an element of nature to the mix, showing how an extreme situation can influence behavior. For more on Chopin, consider reading "The Story of an Hour" (4–5) or "Désirée's Baby" (658–61).

The Storm

A Sequel to the 'cadian Ball

The leaves were so still that even Bibi thought it was going to rain. Bobinôt, who was accustomed to converse on terms of perfect equality with his little son, called the child's attention to certain sombre clouds that were rolling with sinister intention from the west, accompanied by a sullen, threatening roar. They were at Friedheimer's store and decided to remain there till the storm had passed. They sat within the door on two empty kegs. Bibi was four years old and looked very wise.

"Mama'll be 'fraid, yes," he suggested with blinking eyes.

"She'll shut the house. Maybe she got Sylvie helpin' her this evenin'," Bobinôt responded reassuringly.

"No; she ent got Sylvie. Sylvie was helpin' her yistiday," piped Bibi.

5   Bobinôt arose and going across to the counter purchased a can of shrimps, of which Calixta was very fond. Then he returned to his perch on the keg and sat stolidly holding the can of shrimps while the storm burst. It shook the wooden store and seemed to be ripping great furrows in the distant field. Bibi laid his little hand on his father's knee and was not afraid.

II

Calixta, at home, felt no uneasiness for their safety. She sat at a side window sewing furiously on a sewing machine. She was greatly occupied and did not notice the approaching storm. But she felt very warm and often stopped to mop her face on which the perspiration gathered in beads. She unfastened her white sacque at the throat. It began to grow dark, and suddenly realizing the situation she got up hurriedly and went about closing windows and doors.

Out on the small front gallery she had hung Bobinôt's Sunday clothes to air and she hastened out to gather them before the rain fell. As she stepped outside, Alcée Laballière rode in at the gate. She had not seen him very often since her marriage, and never alone. She stood there with Bobinôt's coat in her hands, and the big rain drops began to fall. Alcée rode his horse under the shelter of a side projection where the chickens had huddled and there were plows and a harrow piled up in the corner.

"May I come and wait on your gallery till the storm is over, Calixta?" he asked.

"Come 'long in, M'sieur Alcée."

10   His voice and her own startled her as if from a trance, and she seized Bobinôt's vest. Alcée, mounting to the porch, grabbed the trousers and snatched Bibi's braided jacket that was about to be carried away by a sudden gust of wind. He expressed an intention to remain outside, but it was soon apparent that he might as well have been out in the open: the water beat in upon the boards in driving sheets, and he went inside, closing the door after him. It was even necessary to put something beneath the door to keep the water out.

"My! what a rain! It's good two years since it rain' like that," exclaimed Calixta as she rolled up a piece of bagging and Alcée helped her to thrust it beneath the crack.

She was a little fuller of figure than five years before when she married; but she had lost nothing of her vivacity. Her blue eyes still retained their melting quality; and her yellow hair, dishevelled by the wind and rain, kinked more stubbornly than ever about her ears and temples.

The rain beat upon the low, shingled roof with a force and clatter that threatened to break an entrance and deluge them there. They were in the dining room—the sitting room—the general utility room. Adjoining was her bedroom, with Bibi's couch along side her own. The door stood open, and the room with its white, monumental bed, its closed shutters, looked dim and mysterious.

Alcée flung himself into a rocker and Calixta nervously began to gather up from the floor the lengths of a cotton sheet which she had been sewing.

15   "If this keeps up, *Dieu sait*[1] if the levees goin' to stan' it!" she exclaimed.

"What have you got to do with the levees?"

"I got enough to do! An' there's Bobinôt with Bibi out in that storm—if he only didn' left Friedheimer's!"

"Let us hope, Calixta, that Bobinôt's got sense enough to come in out of a cyclone."

She went and stood at the window with a greatly disturbed look on her face. She wiped the frame that was clouded with moisture. It was stiflingly hot. Alcée got up and joined her at the window, looking over her shoulder. The rain was coming down in sheets obscuring the view of far-off cabins and enveloping the distant wood in a gray mist. The playing of the lightning was incessant. A bolt struck a tall chinaberry tree at the edge of the field. It filled all visible space with a blinding glare and the crash seemed to invade the very boards they stood upon.

20   Calixta put her hands to her eyes, and with a cry, staggered backward. Alcée's arm encircled her, and for an instant he drew her close and spasmodically to him.

"*Bonté!*" she cried, releasing herself from his encircling arm and retreating from the window, "the house'll go next! If I only knew w'ere Bibi was!" She would not compose herself; she would not be seated. Alcée clasped her shoulders and looked into her face. The contact of her warm, palpitating body when he had unthinkingly drawn her into his arms, had aroused all the old-time infatuation and desire for her flesh.

"Calixta," he said, "don't be frightened. Nothing can happen. The house is too low to be struck, with so many tall trees standing about. There! aren't you going to be quiet? say, aren't you?" He pushed her hair back from her face that was warm and steaming. Her lips were as red and moist as pomegranate seed. Her white neck and a glimpse of her full, firm bosom disturbed him powerfully. As she glanced up at him the fear in her liquid blue eyes had given place to a drowsy gleam that unconsciously betrayed a sensuous desire. He looked down into her eyes and there was nothing for him to do but to gather her lips in a kiss. It reminded him of Assumption.

"Do you remember—in Assumption, Calixta?" he asked in a low voice broken by passion. Oh! she remembered; for in Assumption he had kissed her and kissed and kissed her; until his senses would well nigh fail, and to save her he would resort to a desperate flight. If she was not an immaculate dove in those days, she was still inviolate; a passionate creature whose very defenselessness had made her defense, against which his honor forbade him to prevail. Now—well, now—her lips seemed in a manner free to be tasted, as well as her round, white throat and her whiter breasts.

---

[1]**Dieu sait**: God knows.

They did not heed the crashing torrents, and the roar of the elements made her laugh as she lay in his arms. She was a revelation in that dim, mysterious chamber; as white as the couch she lay upon. Her firm, elastic flesh that was knowing for the first time its birthright, was like a creamy lily that the sun invites to contribute its breath and perfume to the undying life of the world.

25 The generous abundance of her passion, without guile or trickery, was like a white flame which penetrated and found response in depths of his own sensuous nature that had never yet been reached.

When he touched her breasts they gave themselves up in quivering ecstasy, inviting his lips. Her mouth was a fountain of delight. And when he possessed her, they seemed to swoon together at the very borderland of life's mystery.

He stayed cushioned upon her, breathless, dazed, enervated, with his heart beating like a hammer upon her. With one hand she clasped his head, her lips lightly touching his forehead. The other hand stroked with a soothing rhythm his muscular shoulders.

The growl of the thunder was distant and passing away. The rain beat softly upon the shingles, inviting them to drowsiness and sleep. But they dared not yield.

The rain was over; and the sun was turning the glistening green world into a palace of gems. Calixta, on the gallery, watched Alcée ride away. He turned and smiled at her with a beaming face; and she lifted her pretty chin in the air and laughed aloud.

III

30 Bobinôt and Bibi, trudging home, stopped without at the cistern to make themselves presentable.

"My! Bibi, w'at will yo' mama say! You ought to be ashame'. You oughtn' put on those good pants. Look at 'em! An' that mud on yo' collar! How you got that mud on yo' collar, Bibi? I never saw such a boy!" Bibi was the picture of pathetic resignation. Bobinôt was the embodiment of serious solicitude as he strove to remove from his own person and his son's the signs of their tramp over heavy roads and through wet fields. He scraped the mud off Bibi's bare legs and feet with a stick and carefully removed all traces from his heavy brogans. Then, prepared for the worst—the meeting with an over-scrupulous housewife, they entered cautiously at the back door.

Calixta was preparing supper. She had set the table and was dripping coffee at the hearth. She sprang up as they came in.

"Oh, Bobinôt! You back! My! but I was uncasy. W'ere you been during the rain? An' Bibi? he ain't wet? he ain't hurt?" She had clasped Bibi and was kissing him effusively. Bobinôt's explanations and apologies which he had been composing all along the way, died on his lips as Calixta felt him to see if he were dry, and seemed to express nothing but satisfaction at their safe return.

"I brought you some shrimps, Calixta," offered Bobinôt, hauling the can from his ample side pocket and laying it on the table.

35 "Shrimps! Oh, Bobinôt! you too good fo' anything! and she gave him a smacking kiss on the cheek that resounded. "*J'vous réponds*,[2] we'll have a feas' to night! umph-umph!"

Bobinôt and Bibi began to relax and enjoy themselves, and when the three seated themselves at table they laughed much and so loud that anyone might have heard them as far away as Laballière's.

[2] **J'vous réponds:** "I tell you."

IV

Alcée Laballière wrote to his wife, Clarisse, that night. It was a loving letter, full of tender solicitude. He told her not to hurry back, but if she and the babies liked it at Biloxi, to stay a month longer. He was getting on nicely, and though he missed them, he was willing to bear the separation a while longer—realizing that their health and pleasure were the first things to be considered.

V

As for Clarisse, she was charmed upon receiving her husband's letter. She and the babies were doing well. The society was agreeable; many of her old friends and acquaintances were at the bay. And the first free breath since her marriage seemed to restore the pleasant liberty of her maiden days. Devoted as she was to her husband, their intimate conjugal life was something which she was more than willing to forego for a while.

So the storm passed and every one was happy.

INQUIRING FURTHER

1. Does the narrator seem dismissive of the adultery that has been committed in the story? Do you think it is fair to say that the storm is partially responsible for Calixta and Alcée's actions? Write a paragraph or two in which you explore the messages in the story about adultery.

2. Read "The Story of an Hour" and/or "Désirée's Baby." In what ways can "The Storm" be read as presenting a woman's point of view? How might the perspective in the story relate to the institution of marriage? Write a paper exploring women's perspectives and marriage, in two or more of Chopin's stories.

DOROTHY ALLISON

Dorothy Allison (born in 1949) is the author of the novels Bastard out of Carolina *and* Trash, *as well as numerous essays on women's issues. She often writes forcefully about feminism and sexuality while celebrating her status as a lesbian. "Little Enough" and "A Woman Like an Ocean" are taken from her collection of poetry,* The Women Who Hate Me.

A Woman Like an Ocean

All last spring I imagined
falling in love with the ocean
going down at midnight, dawn, sunset
to kneel and worship a female movement
5   slow jewel drops running forward and back.

In the city I have to take the D train
out to Coney Island, Brighton Beach
walk the rock slope, rotted boardwalk.
It is the same ocean, has to be
10   but not to be fallen in love with.

Greaseshine, weedlined, trash high
No one swims, no one my age,
Drunken boys throw each other forward
come up glistening, cursing.
15   It has to be the same ocean.
Has to be, can't be
can not be loved like the other.

On Brant Beach I knew her   a suburban ocean
a girl in a well-tailored suit.
20   Clean.   Watched over.   Protected.
Walking a line toward the horizon every day.
When after three weeks the storm came
we went down to watch her roll over and scream.
Foam gathered grease
25   layered yellow and cold.
Sunset brought in a dark wind
A chill went up my back
        like lust.

Little Enough

On President Street a lady standing in her yard
reminded me of every aunt I ever met, stiff-backed
and tired but laughing in a rough loud voice.
"You ever see such ugly furniture?" Everything for
5   sale; a chest, table, counter and chairs, bent lamps
and broken cabinets. *"But the way things are, if it
stands still, I'd sell it."* She laughed and I
could not leave, for hope she'd laugh again.
*"You girls out walking on such a pretty day,
10   why don't you just buy me out and let me go in?
You look at this stuff. This an't bad stuff.
Ugly but strong like they say, and clean, clean."*
Which it was—scrubbed up and polished, oiled shiny
in the sunlight, like that lady and her concrete yard.

15   *"You girls,"* she smiled at us, invited us in to
see her new kitchen, the furniture set aside,
the walls redone. *"I've lived here twenty years,
worked forty for the city. You got to work, you know
even when the body wants no part of it. You got to work."*
20   I know. I have always known. I smiled at her and
memorized her address, watched the light at her
temples, the tight hair lightening with age,
her hands swinging a spray bottle of polish and
a flat yellow cotton rag.   *I know.   I know.*
25   I praised her walls, her cabinets, hugged to myself
her forty years of stubborn work, survival.

The women I dream of loving take care of themselves,
their people, put up shelves in the evening,

boil off chicken stock before bed, sleep hard and
30   are up again before dawn for the quiet, the hope of
a few good lines, another little piece of a story.
Like her, that old woman on President Street, as sturdy
as her pine cabinets and hand-scraped doors.   *"You girls,"*
she said and I knew then why she'd stopped us, what
35   she'd seen in how Barbara touched my neck, knew that
none of us would say the word, say *lesbian* or even *lovers.*

We would talk instead of houses, kitchens and
furniture, and how it is, making your own way in a
world where nobody's handing out anything for free,
40   of soup recipes and bean dishes rescued from burning pots.
"God an't gonna reach down and smooth things," she laughed.
"God's got enough on his mind." She waved her hand as if
to say god's got little enough to do with us.
"But you can do it. Get yourself a piece of
45   *something important to you and work it, work it*
with time and effort and care." In the code
we were speaking, I could not tell if she meant
the house
or life
50   or love.

INQUIRING FURTHER

1. What do you think of associating the ocean with feminine characteristics in "A Woman Like an Ocean"? What might be the significance of the speaker's recognizing that the ocean is not the same as she had imagined? How do you interpret the storm described in the last stanza?

2. What is the significance of the many objects that are listed in "Little Enough"? What do these objects say about the relationship between the speaker of the poem and the lady with the yard sale?

LESLÉA NEWMAN

Lesléa Newman (born in 1955) writes for both children and adults. In most of her works, she deals with issues of lesbian identity, exploring topics like AIDS and same-sex parenthood. In "A Letter to Harvey Milk," published in 1988, Newman also explores Jewish identity, hearkening back to the Holocaust as she takes up issues of sexuality and relationships. Harvey Milk was an openly gay politician who was murdered in 1978 after helping to pass gay civil rights legislation.

A Letter to Harvey Milk

for Harvey Milk 1930-1978

I.

The teacher says we should write about our life, everything that happened today. So *nu*[1], what's there to tell? Why should today be different than any other day? May 5, 1986. I get up, I have myself a coffee, a little cottage cheese, half an English muffin. I get dressed. I straighten out the house a little, nobody should drop by and see I'm such a slob. I go down to the Senior Center and see what's doing. I play a little cards, I have some lunch, a bagel with cheese. I read a sign in the cafeteria: WRITING CLASS, 2:00. I think to myself, why not, something to pass the time. So at two o'clock I go in. The teacher says we should write about our life.

Listen, I want to say to this teacher, I.B. Singer I'm not. You think anybody cares what I did all day? Even my own children, may they live and be well, don't call. You think the whole world is waiting to hear what Harry Weinberg had for breakfast?

The teacher is young and nice. She says everybody has important things to say. Yeah, sure, when you're young, you believe things like that. She has short brown hair and big eyes, a nice figure, *zaftig*[2] like my poor Fannie, may she rest in peace. She's wearing a Star of David around her neck, hanging from a purple string, that's nice. She gave us all notebooks and told us we're gonna write something every day, and if we want, we can even write at home. Who'd a thunk it—me, Harry Weinberg, seventy-seven years old, scribbling in a notebook like a schoolgirl. Why not, it passes the time.

So after the class I go to the store, I pick myself up a little orange juice, a few bagels, a nice piece of chicken, I shouldn't starve to death. I go up, I put on my slippers, I eat the chicken, I watch a little TV, I write in this notebook, I get ready for bed. *Nu*, for this somebody should give me a Pulitzer Prize?

II.

5   Today the teacher tells us something about herself. She's a Jew, this we know from the *Mogen David*[3] she wears around her neck. She tells us she wants to collect stories from old Jewish people, to preserve our history. *Oy*, such stories that I could tell her shouldn't be preserved by nobody. She tells us she's learning Yiddish. For what, I wonder. I can't figure this teacher out. She's young, she's pretty, she shouldn't be with the old people so much. I wonder is she married. She don't wear a ring. Her grandparents won't tell her stories, she says, and she's worried that the Jews her age won't know nothing about the culture, about life in the *shtetls*.[4] Believe me, life in the *shtetl* is nothing worth knowing about. Hunger and more hunger. Better off we're here in America, the past is past.

---

[1] **nu:** so, well.
[2] **zaftig:** slightly chubby.
[3] **Mogen David:** six pointed Star of David.
[4] **shtetls:** small Jewish towns in Eastern Europe.

Then she gives us our homework, the homework we write in the class, it's a little *meshugeh*,[5] but all right. She wants us to write a letter to somebody from our past, somebody who's no longer with us. She reads us a letter a child wrote to Abraham Lincoln, like an example. Right away I see everybody's getting nervous. So I raise my hand. "Teacher," I say, "you can tell me maybe how to address such a letter? There's a few things I've wanted to ask my wife for a long time." Everybody laughs. Then they start to write.

I sit for a few minutes, thinking about Fannie, thinking about my sister Freida, my mother, my father, may they all rest in peace. But it's the strangest thing, the one I really want to write to is Harvey.

Dear Harvey,

You had to go get yourself killed for being a *faygeleh?*[6] You couldn't let somebody else have such a great honor? All right, all right, so you liked the boys, I wasn't wild about the idea. But I got used to it. I never said you wasn't welcome in my house, did I?

10   *Nu*, Harvey, you couldn't leave well enough alone? You had your own camera shop, your own business, what's bad? You couldn't keep still about the boys, you weren't satisfied until the whole world knew? Harvey Milk with the big ears and the big ideas, had to go make himself something, a big politician. I know, know, I said, "Harvey, make something of yourself. Don't be an old *shmegeggie*[7] like me, Harry the butcher." So now I'm eating my words, and they stick in my throat like an old chicken bone.

It's a rotten world, Harvey, and rottener still without you in it. You know what happened to that *momser*,[8] Dan White? They let him out of jail and he goes and kills himself so nobody else should have the pleasure. Now, you know me, Harvey, I'm not a violent man. In the old country, I saw things you shouldn't know from, things you couldn't imagine one person could do to another. But here in America, a man climbs through the window, kills the mayor of San Francisco, kills city supervisor Harvey Milk, and a couple years later he's out walking around on the street? This I never thought I'd see in my whole life. But from a country that kills the Rosenbergs, I should expect something different?

Harvey, you should be glad you wasn't around for the trial. I read about it in the papers. The lawyer, that son of a bitch, said Dan White ate too many Twinkies the night before he killed you, so his brain wasn't working right. Twinkies, *nu*, I ask you. My kids ate Twinkies when they was little, did they grow up to be murderers, God forbid? And now, since Twinkies are so dangerous, do they take them down from the shelves, somebody else shouldn't go a little crazy, climb through the windows and shoot somebody? No, they leave them there right next to the cupcakes and the doughnuts, to torture me every time I go to the store to pick up a few things, I shouldn't starve to death.

Harvey, I think I'm losing my mind. You know what I do every week? Every week I go to the store, I buy a bag of jellybeans for you, you should have something to *nosh*[9] on when you come over, I remember what a sweet tooth you have. I put them in a jar on the table, in case you should come in with another crazy

---

[5]**meshugeh:** crazy.
[6]**faygeleh:** homosexual.
[7]**shmegeggie:** a fool.
[8]**momser:** bastard.
[9]**nosh:** a snack or light meal.

petition for me to sign. Sometimes I think you're gonna walk through my door and tell me it was just another *meshugeh* publicity stunt.

Harvey, now I'm gonna tell you something. The night you died, the whole city of San Francisco cried for you. Thirty thousand people marched in the street, I saw it on TV. Me, I didn't go down. I'm an old man, I don't walk so good, they said there might be riots. But no, there was no riots. Just people walking in the street, quiet, each one with a candle, until the street looked like the sky all lit up with a million stars. Old people, young people, black people, white people, Chinese people, you name it, they was there. I remember thinking, Harvey must be so proud, and then I remembered you was dead, and such a lump rose in my throat, like a grapefruit it was, and then the tears ran down my face like rain. Can you imagine, Harvey, an old man like me, sitting alone in his apartment, crying and carrying on like a baby? But it's the God's truth. Never did I carry on so in all my life.

15   And then all of a sudden I got mad. I yelled at the people on TV: For getting shot you made him into such a hero? You couldn't march for him when he was alive, he couldn't *shep*[10] a little *naches?*[11] But *nu*, what good does getting mad do, it only makes my pressure go up. So I took myself a pill, calmed myself down.

Then they made speeches for you, Harvey. The same people who called you a *shmuck*[12] when you was alive, now you was dead, they was calling you a *mensch*.[13] You were a *mensch*, Harvey, a *mensch* with a heart of gold. You were too good for this rotten world. They just weren't ready for you.

Oy, Harveleh, alav ha-sholom,[14]

Harry

III.

Today the teacher asks me to stay for a minute after class. *Oy*, what did I do wrong now, I wonder. Maybe she didn't like my letter to Harvey?

20   After the class she comes and sits down next to me. She's wearing purple pants and a white T-shirt. "*Feh*,"[15] I can just hear Fannie say. "God forbid she should wear a skirt? Show off her figure a little? The girls today dressing like boys and the boys dressing like girls, this I don't understand."

"Mr. Weinberg," she says.

"Call me Harry," I says.

"Okay, Harry," she says. "I really liked the letter you wrote to Harvey Milk. It was terrific, really. It meant a lot to me. It even made me cry."

I can't even believe my own ears. My letter to Harvey Milk made the teacher cry?

25   "You see, Harry," she says, "I'm gay too. And I don't know many Jewish people your age that are so open-minded. So your letter gave me lots of hope. In fact, I'd like to publish it."

Publish my letter? Again I couldn't believe my own ears. Who would want to read a letter from Harry Weinberg to Harvey Milk? No, I tell her. I'm too old for fame and glory. I like the writing class, it passes the time. But what I write is my own business. The teacher looks sad for a minute, like a cloud passes over her eyes. Then she says, "Tell me about Harvey Milk. How did you meet

---

[10]**shep:** derive.
[11]**naches:** joy.
[12]**shmuck:** a fool.
[13]**mensch:** a person of character.
[14]**alav ha-sholom:** rest in peace.
[15]**Feh:** a word of disgust.

him? What was he like?" *Nu*, Harvey, you were a pain in the neck when you was alive, you're still a pain in the neck now that you're dead. Everybody only wants to hear about Harvey.

So I tell her. I tell her how I came into his camera shop one day with a roll of film from when I went to visit the grandchildren. How we started talking and I said, "Milk, that's not such a common name. Are you related to the Milks in Woodmere?" And so we found out we was practically neighbors forty years ago when the children was young, before we moved out here. Gracie was almost the same age as Harvey, a couple years older maybe, but they went to different schools. Still, Harvey leans across the counter and gives me such a hug, like I'm his own father.

I tell her more about Harvey, how he didn't believe there was a good *kosher* butcher in San Francisco, how he came to my shop just to see. But all the time I'm talking, I'm thinking to myself, no, it can't be true. Such a gorgeous girl like this goes with the girls, not with the boys? Such a *shanda*.[16] Didn't God in His wisdom make a girl a girl and a boy a boy—boom they meet, boom they marry, boom they make babies, and that's the way it is? Harvey I loved like my own son, but this I could never understand. And *nu*, why was the teacher telling me this, it's my business who she sleeps with? She has some sadness in her eyes, this teacher. Believe me, I've known such sadness in my life, I can recognize it a hundred miles away. Maybe she's lonely. Maybe after class one day, I'll take her out for a coffee, we'll talk a little bit, I'll find out.

IV.

It's three o'clock in the morning, I can't sleep. So *nu*, here I am with this crazy notebook. Who am I kidding, maybe I think I'm Yitzhak Peretz? What would the children think to see their old father sitting up in his bathrobe with a cup of tea, scribbling in his notebook? *Oy*, my *kinder*,[17] they should only live and be well and call their old father once in a while.

30   Fannie used to keep up with them. She could be such a nudge, my Fannie. "What's the matter, you're too good to call your old mother once in a while?" she'd yell into the phone. Then there'd be a pause. "Busy-shmizzie," she'd yell even louder. "Was I too busy to change your diapers? Was I too busy to put food into your mouth?" *Oy*, I haven't got the strength, but Fannie, could she yell and carry on.

You know, sometimes in the middle of the night I'll reach across the bed for Fannie's hand. Without even thinking, like my hand got a mind of its own, it creeps across the bed, looking for Fannie. After all this time, fourteen years she's been dead, but still, a man gets used to a few things. Forty-two years, the body don't forget. And my little *Faigl* had such hands, little *hentelehs*,[18] tiny like a child's. But strong. Strong from kneading *challah*,[19] from scrubbing clothes, from rubbing the children's backs to put them to sleep. My Fannie, she was so ashamed from those hands. After thirty-five years of marriage, when finally I could afford to buy her a diamond ring, she said no. She said it was too late already, she'd be ashamed. A girl needs nice hands to show off a diamond, her hands were already ruined, better yet buy a new stove.

---

[16]**shanda:** a disgrace, a shame.
[17]**kinder:** children.
[18]**hentelehs:** hands.
[19]**challah:** bread.

Ruined? *Feh*. To me her hands were beautiful. Small, with veins running through them like rivers and cracks in the skin like the desert. A hundred times I've kicked myself for not buying Fannie that ring.

V.

Today in the writing class the teacher read my notebook. Then she says I should make a poem about Fannie. "A poem," I says to her, "now Shakespeare you want I should be?" She says I have a good eye for detail. I says to her, "Excuse me, Teacher, you live with a woman for forty-two years, you start to notice a few things."

She helps me, we do it together, we write a poem called "Fannie's Hands."

> Fannie's hands are two little birds
> that fly into her lap.
> Her veins are like rivers.
> Her skin is cracked like the desert.
> Her strong little hands
> baked *challah*, scrubbed clothes
> rubbed the children's backs
> to put them to sleep.
> Her strong little hands
> and my big clumsy hands
> fit together in the night
> like pieces of a jigsaw puzzle
> made in Heaven, by God.

35   So *nu*, who says you can't teach an old dog new tricks? I read it to the class and such a fuss they made. "A regular Romeo," one of them says. "If only my husband, may he live and be well, would write such a poem for me," says another. I wish Fannie was still alive, I could read it to her. Even the teacher was happy, I could tell, but still, there was a ring of sadness around her eyes.

After the class I waited till everybody left, they shouldn't get the wrong idea, and I asked the teacher would she like to go get a coffee. "*Nu*, it's enough writing already," I says. "Come, let's have a little treat."

So we take a walk, it's a nice day. We find a diner, nothing fancy, but clean and quiet. I try to buy her a piece of cake, a sandwich maybe, but no, all she wants is coffee.

So we sit and talk a little. She wants to know about my childhood in the old country, she wants to know about the boat ride to America, she wants to know did my parents speak Yiddish when I was growing up. "Harry," she says to me, "when I hear old people talking Yiddish, it's like a love letter blowing in the wind. I run after it as fast as I can, but I just can't seem to catch it."

Oy, this teacher has some strange ideas. "Why do you want to talk Jewish?" I ask her. "Here in America, you don't need it. What's done is done, what's past is past. You shouldn't be with the old people so much. You should go out, make friends, have a good time. You got some problems you want to talk about? Maybe I shouldn't pry," I says, "but you shouldn't look so sad, a young girl like you. When you're old, you got plenty to be sad. You shouldn't think about the past so much. Let the dead rest in peace, what's done is done."

40   I took a swallow of my coffee to calm down my nerves. I was getting a little too excited.

"Harry, listen to me," the teacher says. "I'm thirty years old, and no one in my family will talk to me because I'm gay. It's all Harvey Milk's fault. You know what he said before he died, 'If a bullet enters my brain, let that bullet destroy every closet door.' So when he was killed, I came out to everyone: the people at work, my parents. I felt it was my duty, so the Dan Whites of the world couldn't get away with it. I mean, if every single gay person came out—just think of it!—everyone would see they had a gay friend or a gay brother or a gay cousin or a gay teacher. Then they couldn't say things like 'Those gays should be shot.' Because they'd be saying 'You should shoot my neighbor, or my sister, or my daughter's best friend.'"

I never saw the teacher get so excited before. Maybe a politician she should be. She reminded me a little bit of Harvey. "So *nu*," I asked, "what's the problem?"

"The problem is my parents," she says with a sigh, and such a sigh I never heard from a young person before. "My parents haven't spoken to me since I came out. 'How could you do this to us?' they said. I wasn't doing anything *to* them. I tried to explain I couldn't help being gay, like I couldn't help being Jewish, but that they didn't want to hear. So I haven't spoken to them in eight years."

"Eight years, *Gottinyu*."[20] This I never heard in all my life. A father and a mother cut off their own flesh and blood like that. Better they should cut off their own hand. I thought about Gracie, a perfect daughter she's not, but still, your child is your child. When she married the *goy*,[21] Fannie threatened to put her head in the oven, but she got over it. Not to see your own daughter for eight years, and such a smart, gorgeous girl she is, such a good teacher, what a *shanda*.

45   So what can I do, I ask. Does she want me to talk to them, a letter maybe I could write. Does she want I should adopt her, the hell with them, I make a little joke. She smiles. "Just talking to you makes me feel better," she says. So *nu*, now I'm Harry the social worker. She says that's why she wants the old people's stories so much, she doesn't know nothing about her own family history. She wants to know about her own people, maybe write a book, but it's hard to get the people to talk to her, she says, she don't understand.

"Listen, Teacher," I says to her. "These old people have stories you shouldn't know from. Hunger and more hunger. Suffering and more suffering. I buried my sister, over thirty years ago, my mother, my father, all dead. You think I could just start talking about them like I saw them yesterday? You think I don't think about them every day? Right here I keep them," I says, pointing to my heart. "I try to forget them, I should live in peace. The dead are gone. Talking about them won't bring them back. You want stories, go talk to somebody else. I ain't got no stories."

I sat down then. I didn't even know I was standing up, I got so excited. Everybody in the diner was looking at me, a crazy old man shouting at a young pretty girl. *Oy*, and now the teacher was crying. "I'm sorry," I says to her. "You want another coffee?"

"No, thanks, Harry," she says. "I'm sorry too."

"Forget it. We can just pretend it never happened," I say, and then we go.

---

[20]**Gottinyu:** dear God.
[21]**goy:** non-Jew

VI.

50   All this crazy writing has shaken me up inside a little bit. Yesterday I was walking home from the diner, I thought I saw Harvey walking in front of me. No, it can't be, I says to myself, and my heart started to pound so, I got afraid I shouldn't drop dead in the street from a heart attack. But then the man turned around and it wasn't Harvey. It didn't even look like him at all.

I got myself upstairs and took myself a pill. I could feel my pressure was going up. All this talk about the past: Fannie, Harvey, Freida, my mother, my father, what good does it do? This teacher and her crazy ideas. Did I ever ask my mother, my father what their childhood was like? What nonsense. Better I shouldn't know.

So today is Saturday, no writing class, but still I'm writing in this crazy notebook. I ask myself, Harry, what can I do to make you feel a little better? And I answer myself: Make me a nice chicken soup.

What, you think an old man like me can't make chicken soup? Let me tell you, on all the holidays it was Harry that made the soup. Every Passover it was Harry skimming the *shmaltz*[22] from the top of the pot, it was Harry making the *matzo* balls. *Nu*, I ask you, where is it written that a man shouldn't know from chicken soup?

So I take myself down to the store, I buy myself a nice chicken, some carrots, some celery, some parsley—onions I already got, parsnips I can do without. I'm afraid I shouldn't have a heart attack *shlepping*[23] all that food up the steps, but thank God, I make it all right.

55   I put up the pot with water, throw everything in one-two-three, and soon the whole house smells like a holiday.

I remember the time Harvey came to visit and there I was with my apron on, skimming the *shmaltz* from the soup. Did he kid me about that! The only way I could get him to keep still was to invite him to dinner. "Listen, Harvey," I says to him. "Whether you're a man or a woman, it don't matter. You gotta learn to cook. When you're old and alone, nobody will do for you. You gotta learn to do for yourself."

"I won't live past fifty, Harry," he says, smearing a piece of rye bread with *shmaltz.*

"Nobody wants to grow old, believe me, I know," I says to him. "But listen, it's not so terrible. What's the alternative? Nobody wants to die young either." I take off my apron and sit down with him.

"No, I mean it, Harry," he says to me with his mouth full. "I won't make it to fifty, I've always known it. I'm a politician. A gay politician. Somebody will take a potshot at me. It can't be helped."

60   The way he said it, I tell you, a chill ran down my back like I never felt before. He was forty-seven at the time, just a year before he died.

VII.

Today after the writing class, the teacher tells us she's going away for a few days. Everyone makes a big fuss, the class they like so much already. She tells us she's sorry, something came up she has to do. She says we can come have class without her, the room will be open, we can read to each other what we write in our notebooks. Someone asks her what we should write about.

---

[22]**shmaltz:** animal fat.
[23]**shlepping:** to move or carry with difficulty.

"Write me a letter," she says. "Write a story called, 'What I Never Told Anyone.'"

So after everybody leaves, I ask her does she want to go out, have a coffee, but she says no, she has to go home and pack. I tell her wherever she's going she should have a good time.

"Thanks, Harry," she says. "You'll be here when I get back?"

65   "Sure," I tell her. "I like this crazy writing. It passes the time."

She swings a big black book bag onto her shoulder, a regular Hercules this teacher is, and she smiles at me. "I have to run, Harry. Have a good week." She turns and walks away and something on her book bag catches my eye: a big shiny pin that spells out her name all fancy-shmancy in rhinestones: Barbara. And under that, right away I see sewn onto her book bag an upside-down pink triangle.

I stop in my tracks, stunned. No, it can't be, I says to myself. Maybe it's just a design? Maybe she don't know from this? My heart's beating fast now, I know I should go home, take myself a pill, my pressure, I can feel it going up.

But I just stand there. And then I get mad. What, she thinks I'm blind as well as old, I can't see what's right in front of my nose? Or maybe we don't remember such things? What right does she have to walk in here with that thing on her bag to remind us of what we've been through? Ain't we seen enough? Stories she wants. She wants we should cut our hearts open and give her stories so she can write a book. Well, all right, now I'll tell her a story.

This is what I never told anyone. One day, maybe seven, eight years ago, no, maybe longer, I think Harvey was still alive, one day Izzie comes knocking on my door. I open the door and there's Izzie standing there, his face white as a sheet. I bring him inside, I make him a coffee. "Izzie, what is it?" I says to him. "Something happened to the children, to the grandchildren, God forbid?"

70   He sits down, he don't drink his coffee. He looks through me like I'm not even there. Then he says, "Harry, I'm walking down the street, you know, I had a little lunch at the Center, and then I come outside, I see a young man, maybe twenty-five, a good-looking fella, walking toward me. He's wearing black pants, a white shirt, and on his shirt he's got a pink triangle."

"So," I says, "a pink triangle, a purple triangle, they wear all kinds of crazy things these days."

"Heschel," he says, "don't you understand? The gays are wearing pink triangles, just like the war, just like in the camps."

No, this I can't believe. Why would they do a thing like that? But if Izzie says it, it must be true. Who would make up such a thing?

"He looked a little bit like Yussl," Izzie says, and then he begins to cry, and such a cry like I never heard. Like a baby he was, with the tears streaming down his cheeks and his shoulders shaking with great big sobs. Such moaning and groaning I never heard from a grown man in all my life. I thought maybe he was gonna have a heart attack the way he was carrying on. I didn't know what to do. I was afraid the neighbors would hear, they shouldn't call the police, such sounds he was making. Fifty-eight years old he was, but he looked like a little boy sitting there sniffling. And who was Yussl? Thirty years we'd been friends, and I never heard about Yussl.

75   So finally I put my arms around him and I held him, I didn't know what else to do. His body was shaking so, I thought his bones would crack from

knocking against each other. Soon his body got quiet, but then all of a sudden his mouth got noisy.

"Listen, Heschel, I got to tell you something, something I never told nobody in my whole life. I was young in the camps, nineteen, maybe twenty when they took us away." The words poured from his mouth like a flood. "Yussl was my best friend in the camps. Already I saw my mother, my father, my Hannah marched off to the ovens. Yussl was the only one I had to hold on to.

"One morning during the selection, they pointed me to the right and Yussl to the left. I went a little crazy, I ran after him. 'No, he stays with me, they made a mistake,' I said, and I grabbed him by the hand and dragged him out of the death line. Why the guard didn't kill us right then, I couldn't tell you. Nothing made sense in that place.

"Yussl and I slept together on a wooden bench. That night I couldn't sleep. It happened pretty often in that place. I would close my eyes and see such things that would make me scream in the night, and for that I could get shot. I don't know what was worse, asleep or awake, all I saw was suffering.

"On this night, Yussl was awake too. He didn't move a muscle, but I could tell. Finally he said my name, just a whisper, but something broke in me, and I began to cry. He put his arms around me and we cried together, such a close call we had.

80   "And then he began to kiss me. 'You saved my life,' he whispered, and he kissed my eyes, my cheeks, my lips. And Harry, I kissed him back. I never told nobody this before, I . . . you know, that was such a hell, that place, I couldn't help it. The warmth of his body was just too much for me and Hannah was dead already and surely we would soon be dead too, so what did it matter?"

He looked up at me then, the tears streaming from his eyes. "It's okay, Izzie," I said. "Maybe I would have done the same."

"There's more, Harry," he says, and I got him a tissue, he should blow his nose. What more could there be?

"This went on for a couple of months maybe, just every once in a while when we couldn't sleep. He'd whisper my name and I'd answer with his, and then we'd, you know, we'd touch each other. We were very, very quiet, and who knows, maybe some other boys in the barracks were doing the same.

"To this day I don't know how it happened, but somehow, somebody found out. One day Yussl didn't come back to the barracks at night. I went almost crazy, you can imagine all the things that went through my mind, the things they might have done to him, those lousy Nazis. I looked everywhere, I asked everyone, three days he was gone. And then on the third day, they lined us up after supper, and there they had Yussl. I almost collapsed on the ground when I saw him. They had him on his knees with his hands tied behind his back. His face was swollen so, you couldn't even see his eyes. His clothes were stained with blood. And on his uniform they had sewn a pink triangle, big, twice the size of our yellow stars.

85   "*Oy*, did they beat him but good. 'Who's your friend?' they yelled. 'Tell us and we'll let you live.' But no, he wouldn't tell. He knew they were lying, he knew they'd kill us both. They asked him again and again, 'Who's your friend? Tell us.' And every time he said no, they'd crack him with a whip until the blood ran from him like a river. Such a sight he was, like I've never seen. How he remained conscious I'll never know.

"Everything inside me was broken after that. I wanted to run to his side, but I didn't dare, so afraid I was. At one point he looked at me, right in the eye, as though he was saying, *Izzie, save yourself. Me, I'm finished, but you, you got a chance to live through this and tell the world our story.*

"Right after he looked at me, he collapsed, and they shot him, Harry, right there in front of us. Even after he was dead they kicked him in the head a little bit. They left his body out there for two days as a warning to us. They whipped us all that night, and from then on we had to sleep with all the lights on and with our hands on top of the blankets. Anyone caught with their hands under the blankets would be shot.

"He died for me, Harry, they killed him for that, was it such a terrible thing? *Oy*, I haven't thought about Yussl for years, but when I saw that kid on the street today, it was too much." And then he started crying again, and he clung to me like a child.

So what could I do? I was afraid he shouldn't have a heart attack, maybe he was having a nervous breakdown, maybe I should get the doctor. *Oy*, I never saw anybody so upset in all my life. And such a story, *Gottinyu*.

90   "Izzie, come lie down," I says, and I took him by the hand to the bed. I laid him down, I took off his shoes, and still he was crying. So what could I do? I lay down with him, I held him tight, I told him he was safe, he was in America. I don't know what else I said, I don't think he heard me, still he kept crying.

I stroked his head, I held him tight. "Izzie, it's all right," I said. "Izzie, Izzie, Izzeleh." I said his name over and over, like a lullaby, until his crying got quiet. He said my name once softly, "Heschel," or maybe he said "Yussl," I don't know, but thank God he finally fell asleep. I tried to get up from the bed, but Izzie held on to me tight. So what could I do? Izzie was my friend for thirty years, for him I would do anything. So I held him all night long and he slept like a baby.

And this is what I never told nobody, not even Harvey. That there, in that bed where Fannie and I slept together for forty-two years, Izzie and I spent the night. Me, I didn't sleep a wink, such a lump in my throat I had, like the night Harvey died.

Izzie passed on a couple months after that. I saw him a few more times and he seemed different somehow. How, I couldn't say. We never talked about that night. But now that he had told someone his deepest secret, he was ready to go, he could die in peace. Maybe now that I told, I can die in peace too?

VIII.

Dear Teacher,

95   You said write what you never told nobody and write you a letter. I always did all my homework, such a student I was. So *nu*, I gotta tell you something. I can't write in this notebook no more, I can't come no more to the class. I don't want you should take offense, you're a good teacher and a nice girl. But me, I'm an old man, I don't sleep so good at night, these stories are like a knife in my heart. Harvey, Fannie, Izzie, Yussl, my mother, my father, let them all rest in peace. The dead are gone. Better to live for today. What good does remembering do, it don't bring back the dead. Let them rest in peace.

But Teacher, I want you should have my notebook. It don't have nice stories in it, no love letters, no happy endings for a nice girl like you. A bestseller it ain't, I guarantee. Maybe you'll put it in a book someday, the world shouldn't forget.

Meanwhile, good luck to you, Teacher. May you live and be well and not get shot in the head like poor Harvey, may he rest in peace. Maybe someday we'll go out, have a coffee again, who knows? But me, I'm too old for this crazy writing. I remember too much, the pen is like a knife twisting in my heart.

One more thing, Teacher. Between parents and children, it ain't so easy. Believe me, I know. Don't give up on them. One father, one mother, it's all you got. If you was my *tochter*,[24] I'd be proud of you.

Harry

INQUIRING FURTHER

1. How would you characterize the narrator's attitude toward Harvey Milk? What passages from the story might help you explore his attitude in a paper?

2. How do you find the writing style of the story? What are your thoughts on the Yiddish expressions woven into the narrative? Do you find the story compelling?

3. The story touches on the tragedy of the Holocaust, but does not make it the focus of the story. How central is the Holocaust to "A Letter to Harvey Milk"? How is the Holocaust related to the historical killing of Harvey Milk?

4. What are your thoughts on issues of sexuality revealed in the story? How does sexuality affect the relationships between the characters? Freewrite for five minutes about sexuality in the story.

EXTENDED INQUIRY

The Taming of the Shrew *on Stage and in Film*

The romantic films produced in Hollywood follow a familiar formula handed down for centuries. Occasionally, however, a romantic comedy may offer something more. The film *10 Things I Hate About You* (1999), for instance, depicts a boy who agrees to woo a girl as part of a challenge. The girl is sharp tongued and uninterested in romance. The story also depicts a second boy hopelessly in love with the first girl's younger sister. The younger sister has been forbidden to see boys until the mean-spirited sister agrees to date. We might view such a film and think we have discovered something original. In this case, however, we would be wrong. We have instead found an adaptation of Shakespeare's *The Taming of The Shrew*.

10 Things I Hate About You holds our interest because it presents a well-wrought tale that weaves together multiple relationships and interesting complications. A 1967 adaptation of Shakespeare's play sticks closer to the original script, but adds complexity through the actors Richard Burton and Elizabeth Taylor, whose real life marriage almost seems to inform their interactions on the screen. In 1948, the play was adapted into a Broadway musical called *Kiss Me Kate*. All of these revisions rely on an original play that blends intrigue with humor and romance. This section asks you to consider how such an engaging story is told both on stage and in the movies.

---

[24]**tochter:** daughter.

The Taming of The Shrew by William Shakespeare

First performed in 1594, Shakespeare's *The Taming of the Shrew* features one of the most intriguing devices of Elizabethan drama, the play within a play. The story opens with a deception played upon the drunken character, Sly, a lowly tinker. Sly is tricked into believing he is a lord and that a play is being put on for his entertainment. The story that follows centers around the conflict created by the wooing of two sisters, Katharina and Bianca. Baptista, the father, forbids his youngest daughter from receiving any suitors until after Katharina, the eldest, is married. The catch is that Katharina is strong-willed, sharp-tongued, and unlikely to be accepted by a husband.

As the play continues, Gremio, Hortensio, and Lucentio enlist Petruchio to marry Katharina, so that they may approach Bianca. Hortensio and Lucentio disguise themselves as teachers in order to woo Bianca in the meantime. Petruchio prevails upon Baptista and marries Katharina by overpowering her will. He then embarks on a mission to wear Katharina down by behaving as cruelly as he can toward her and toward others. Eventually, Katharina succumbs to his "taming," transforming into a subservient wife who willingly does her husband's bidding. In the meantime, Lucentio wins the love of Bianca and uses his servant to trick Baptista into granting him her hand in marriage.

As the drama unfolds, a concern found throughout Shakespeare's work appears: the confusion between appearances and reality. Related to this theme of appearances is the role of deceit in relationships. The initial **induction**, a prelude that frames the main action, is based on the deceit practiced on the drunken tinker, Sly. In most versions of the play, Sly drops out quickly after this induction; however, the point remains that appearances are not always what they seem. This concern continues to play out on a practical level, as Tranio and Lucentio change places and Hortensio and Lucentio disguise themselves to woo Bianca.

The theme of appearances and reality is also suggested in the behaviors of the main characters. Initially Katharina is portrayed as hard-hearted and stubborn, while Bianca appears to be sweet and conforming. These roles are eventually switched, however, as Katharina turns out to be the more accommodating of the two. Similarly, Petruchio initially comes across as wanting to marry Katharina for her money. Eventually, however, his motives shift to wanting to win over her heart, although there may be issues of power tied up with this desire (see below).

The theme of control and power is equally significant in the play. Petruchio overcomes Katharina's will, in part, by demonstrating the negative side of bad behavior. He mistreats his servants and sets his mind to wearing down the will of his new bride. His taming methods might be said to be misogynistic, even bordering on abuse. He withholds food and sleep from Katharina and eventually converts her into a subservient wife. *The Taming of the Shrew* raises questions about the limits of cruelty and control in its playful deception of Sly in the induction, the heavy-handed taming of Katharina, and the duping of various other characters throughout the play. The text of *The Taming of the Shrew* can be found on our Web site.

The Taming of the Shrew in Music

The 1948 Broadway adaptation of Shakespeare's play, *Kiss Me Kate*, is remarkable in large part for the songs crafted for the production by Cole Porter. Porter incorporated some of Shakespeare's language into the lyrics of the eighteen songs he wrote for the musical. The production won five Tony awards and ran for over three years. In 1999, *Kiss Me Kate* was revived on Broadway and ran for another four years.

Music also plays a central role in *10 Things I Hate About You*. In the film, Patrick breaks the ice with Kat by secretly learning her favorite bands and then attending a concert where he arranges to run into her. Music gives Kat and Patrick a bond, and the purchase of an electric guitar in the final scene serves as a peace offering after Kat has learned of Patrick's deception. Music also provides a background that establishes the tone for many scenes.

COLE PORTER

Cole Porter (1891–1964) published his first song at the age of 10. He attended law school, before deciding to transfer to the Yale Music School. His songwriting after graduating met with mixed success. He composed a number of musicals, but by the 1940s had produced two flops and was said to be washed up. However, in 1948 he wrote the songs for Kiss Me Kate, *resuscitating his career with what many consider to be his strongest work.*

So in Love

Strange dear, but true dear,
When I'm close to you, dear,
The stars fill the sky,
So in love with you am I.
5   Even without you,
My arms fold about you,
You know darling why,
So in love with you am I.
In love with the night mysterious,
10   The night when you first were there,
In love with my joy delirious,
When I knew that you could care,
So taunt me, and hurt me,
Deceive me, desert me,
15   I'm yours, till I die. . . .
So in love. . . . So in love. . . .
So in love with you, my love . . . am I. . . .

10 THINGS I HATE ABOUT YOU SOUNDTRACK

To fully understand a film, we must consider how sounds, especially music, contribute to the dramatic elements of a story. In many movies, this contribution is represented in a soundtrack collection that compiles some of the most significant songs from the film. The soundtrack for the film 10 Things I Hate About You *includes music by the bands Letters to Cleo, Madness, and Sister Hazel, as well as songs by artists like George Clinton and Joan Armatrading. For samples from songs from the movie, see our Web site.*

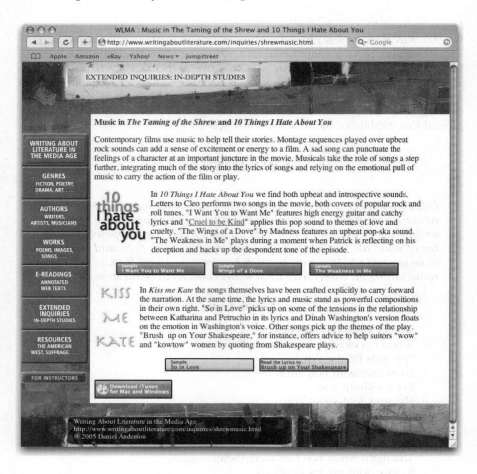

INQUIRING FURTHER

1. How well do you think Porter's "So in Love" captures the sentiments of Shakespeare's *The Taming of the Shrew*? Can you recognize any aspects of the lyrics that allude to specific passages in the play?

2. Read the lyrics to the songs "Brush up on Your Shakespeare" or "Cruel to be Kind" linked to our Web site. Is it fair to say these lyrics express attitudes no different from those in *The Taming of the Shrew*? What do these songs say about the relationships between men and women?

3. Sample some songs from adaptations of *The Taming of the Shrew* on our Web site. Consider how the musical elements complement the lyrics. Listen for vocal elements that express emotion. How do these musical pieces relate to the messages in Shakespeare's play?

The Taming of the Shrew on Film

Films tell stories differently than do drama productions. Elements of cinematography can convey a mood that is hard to put across on stage. Editing allows the filmmaker to present multiple perspectives and weave together scenes using continuity or cross-cuts that convey a unique sense of time. Music and sound contribute to the messages offered by the film. The 1967 version of *The Taming of the Shrew* coincides, for the most part, with Shakespeare's original, allowing us to consider how film modifies theater techniques to tell a story.

   10 Things I Hate About You (1999) presents a more radical adaptation of Shakespeare's play. The setting has been updated to a twentieth-century high school with all of its cliques and adolescent concerns. Contemporary music punctuates the scenes and enters the story as a plot element. The themes in the film, however, remain true to the core of the original. A film like *10 Things I Hate About You* allows us to see how authors build upon previous works in their creative endeavors (Shakespeare himself borrowed for some of his plays). The adaptation also reveals the long term appeal of the story and the continuing concerns of issues of appearances, deceit, control, and love.

The Taming of the Shrew

The 1967 film version of *The Taming of the Shrew* has been hailed for the dynamic interplay between Elizabeth Taylor (playing Katharina) and Richard Burton (in the role of Petruchio). The film represents an adaptation that remains true to much of the original play, deploying all of the cast and maintaining the Elizabethan speech. Director Franco Zeffirelli does expand on some scenes, omits others, and cuts back on some dialog. The film captures the bawdy humor of the comedy, while exploring the issues of relationships so prominent in Shakespeare's original.

The Taming of the Shrew

FIGURE 17.2   Elizabeth Taylor and Richard Burton in *The Taming of the Shrew*

I N Q U I R I N G   F U R T H E R

1. Figure 17.2 depicts a scene in which Katharina attacks Petruchio. What does this image say about the characters? What other aspects of the image seem significant?

2. Figure 17.2 also demonstrates some of the "taming" treatment Petruchio forces upon Katharina. Does the image evoke your sympathy for Katharina? Why or Why not?

3. View the resources for the film on our CD. Consider the elements of film in more detail and consider watching the movie after reading the play.

10 Things I Hate About You

10 Things I Hate About You

The 1999 adaptation, *10 Things I Hate About You*, updates Shakespeare's play by changing the setting to a contemporary high school, Padua High. Director Gil Junger keeps most of the story light and humorous, but the strength of the characters gives the movie depth that keeps us thinking even while we are entertained. Kat, in particular, displays many dimensions that move the film beyond simply another teen romance story to something that explores concerns related to women and relationships.

FIGURE 17.3   Heath Ledger and Julia Stiles in *10 Things I Hate About You*

INQUIRING FURTHER

1. As does Shakespeare's play, *10 Things I Hate About You* asks us to consider the relationship between Kat and Patrick. How do you interpret the arrangement and aspects of cinematography in the scene depicted in the first frame of Figure 17.3? What can you say about the relationship between the Kat and Patrick based on the image?

2. In the scene depicted in the middle frame, Kat and Patrick have overcome their distaste for one another and fallen in love. What aspects of the image convey information about their relationship? Compare the image to the first frame. Are there similarities between the two scenes?

3. The last frame depicts a scene at the senior prom when Kat finds out that Patrick has been paid to date her. View the film and think about the theme of deception. What would you say to someone who argued that manipulation in the film is merely a plot device? Freewrite for five minutes about the theme of manipulation in the film.

4. Explore the resources for *10 Things I Hate About You* on our CD. Compare the film with the 1967 film and with the original play. Write a paper in which you explore the adaptation in terms of its messages concerning women's issues, relationships, and manipulation, relating it with Shakespeare's play or the 1967 film.

18

Art and Representations of the Natural World

> A lot of people who . . . write poems that look sort of
> natural and wild, invoking this and that, have no
> experience whatsoever of what they write. They have
> never actually seen the glint in the eye of an eagle or the
> way a lizard's ribs quake when he does his pushups, or
> the way a trout turns and flicks, or how a bear backs up.
> If you haven't seen these things, you shouldn't write
> about them, whether you're an Indian or a white man.
>
> —*Gary Snyder*

Should we be able to write about things we have not seen? Gary Snyder seems to be suggesting that art should be based on actual experiences—that there should be some correspondence between witnessing the real world and writing about it. On one hand, Snyder's advice makes sense. Compositions are more likely to capture the essence of things if they are based on actual experiences. On the other hand, even what is artificial can sometimes present a picture of what is real. Further, some representations, while based on experience, do not always tell the whole story. In practice, art sometimes mimics and displays, but also manipulates and creates representations of the natural world.

Writers, painters, musicians, and storytellers have often studied the way that art represents reality. They have also explored in literature questions about art and creativity. Must an artist have first-hand knowledge of her subject? Can the viewing or reading of a work provide a real experience? How can literature represent the creative processes of artists? How central is art to understanding our identity and our culture?

Many artists also consider the role of art in representing the natural world. We can easily recognize the potential implications of representing nature as wild (in need of taming) or fertile (ready to provide resources). These metaphors can motivate our actions and shape the natural world. We may also recognize relationships between the world and our imaginations and psyche. We often find inspiration in nature. We sometimes fail to recognize our own role as components of the natural world. Relationships between ecology, human behavior, and imagination are revealed in their full complexity through art.

These interactions between art and the world have played out in representations of the American West. These representations often express competing world views. Explorers and adventurers might see the land as needing to be cataloged, mapped, brought under control. Others might view the natural world as a network in which humans exist as one member among many. Further, cultural histories play out in the American West, both the history of westward expansion during the last four and a half centuries, and the history of native peoples who came to the West during the last ice age. This chapter explores how art functions in our culture and its ability to represent the natural world.

THE ART OF REPRESENTATION

You may have heard the phrase "art for art's sake," which might be seen as the creative equivalent to the Nike slogan, "Just Do It." In practice, however, many artists reflect deeply on the nature of what it is that they do. Art has the power to offer viewers an argument about how to look at the world. At the same time, art does sometimes provide an individual with a canvas on which to experiment, to create something lasting and real, based on its aesthetic construction and status as an art object. These selections consider both how art can exemplify its techniques and materials, as well as construct representations of the world.

JOHN KEATS

English Romantic poet John Keats (1795–1821) lost both his parents at a young age and was sent to live with two London merchants. When Keats was fifteen, one of his guardians withdrew him from school to study medicine, and in 1818 he began caring for his brother, Tom, who suffered from tuberculosis. In late 1819 Keats contracted tuberculosis, and by the following February he felt that death was already upon him. Keats died in Rome in 1821 at the age of twenty-five. "Ode on a Grecian Urn" was published in 1820. In the poem the speaker describes a scene painted on an ancient urn and contemplates the nature of art and time.

Ode on a Grecian Urn

Thou still unravish'd bride of quietness,
   Thou foster-child of Silence and slow Time,
Sylvan[1] historian, who canst thus express
   A flowery tale more sweetly than our rhyme:
5   What leaf-fringed legend haunts about thy shape
   Of deities or mortals, or of both,
      In Tempe or the dales of Arcady?[2]
What men or gods are these? What maidens loth?
What mad pursuit? What struggle to escape?
10   What pipes and timbrels? What wild ecstasy?

Heard melodies are sweet, but those unheard
   Are sweeter; therefore, ye soft pipes, play on;
Not to the sensual ear, but, more endear'd,

---

[1]**Sylvan**: rural, forestlike; the scene on the urn depicts a rural setting.
[2]**Tempe . . . Arcady**: regions known for beautiful scenery.

Pipe to the spirit ditties of no tone:

15   Fair youth, beneath the trees, thou canst not leave
Thy song, nor ever can those trees be bare;
Bold Lover, never, never canst thou kiss,
Though winning near the goal—yet, do not grieve;
She cannot fade, though thou hast not thy bliss,
20   For ever wilt thou love, and she be fair!

Ah, happy, happy boughs! that cannot shed
Your leaves, nor ever bid the Spring adieu;
And, happy melodist, unwearièd,
For ever piping songs for ever new;
25   More happy love! more happy, happy love!
For ever warm and still to be enjoy'd,
For ever panting, and for ever young;
All breathing human passion far above,
That leaves a heart high-sorrowful and cloy'd,
30   A burning forehead, and a parching tongue.

Who are these coming to the sacrifice?
To what green altar, O mysterious priest,
Lead'st thou that heifer lowing at the skies,
And all her silken flanks with garlands drest?
35   What little town by river or sea-shore,
Or mountain-built with peaceful citadel,
Is emptied of its folk, this pious morn?
And, little town, thy streets for evermore
Will silent be; and not a soul, to tell
40   Why thou art desolate, can e'er return.

O Attic[3] shape! fair attitude! with brede[4]
Of marble men and maidens overwrought,
With forest branches and the trodden weed;
Thou, silent form! dost tease us out of thought
45   As doth eternity: Cold Pastoral!
When old age shall this generation waste,
Thou shalt remain, in midst of other woe
Than ours, a friend to man, to whom thou say'st,
'Beauty is truth, truth beauty,—that is all
50   Ye know on earth, and all ye need to know.'

INQUIRING FURTHER

1. What can you say about the relationship the poem sets up between the art object of the urn, and the imagination of the viewer of the urn? Make a list of passages from the poem that speak to this relationship.

2. What message do you believe the poem offers in the final stanza? How does the last stanza complicate your understanding of the relationship between art and time? How does the last stanza relate to the message of the poem as a whole?

---

[3]**Attic**: classic in shape, graceful.
[4]**brede**: design.

ELIZABETH BISHOP

Elizabeth Bishop (1911–1979) has been described as meticulous in the way she rewrote her poems to achieve a particular effect. "One Art" was written in response to the death of her long-time lover Lota de Macedo Soares, her subsequent return to America from Brazil (where she lived for almost twenty years with Soares), and the potential loss of her lover and caregiver, Alice Methfessel. The poem was published in the collection Geography III *in 1977.*

One Art

The art of losing isn't hard to master;
so many things seem filled with the intent
to be lost that their loss is no disaster.

Lose something every day. Accept the fluster
5   of lost door keys, the hour badly spent.
The art of losing isn't hard to master.

Then practice losing farther, losing faster:
places, and names, and where it was you meant
to travel. None of these will bring disaster.

10   I lost my mother's watch. And look! my last, or
next-to-last, of three loved houses went.
The art of losing isn't hard to master.

I lost two cities, lovely ones. And, vaster,
some realms I owned, two rivers, a continent.
15   I miss them, but it wasn't a disaster.

—Even losing you (the joking voice, a gesture
I love) I shan't have lied. It's evident
the art of losing's not too hard to master
though it may look like (*Write* it!) like disaster.

INQUIRING FURTHER

1. Bishop's poem is a villanelle, a fixed form consisting of five three-lined stanzas and a concluding quatrain. The villanelle also requires the repetition of the rhymes established in the first stanza in each subsequent stanza. What might be said about the relationship between this fixed form and the subject matter of the poem?

2. What do you think of the many items that are lost in the poem? Does it minimize the significance of some to lump them together with others? Freewrite for five minutes on the relationships between the items.

RICHARD WILBUR

Richard Wilbur (born in 1921) has published translations, books for children, and essays. He is best known, however, for his poetry. He has won numerous awards, including the Pulitzer Prize for his New and Collected Poems *in 1988. He has also served as Poet Laureate for the United States. His work is often grounded in tradition, but playful and accessible. "The Disappearing Alphabet" was published in 1977 in the* Atlantic Monthly.

The Disappearing Alphabet

If the alphabet began to disappear,
Some words would soon look raggedy and queer
(Like QUIRREL, HIMPANZEE, AND CHOOCHOO-TRAI),
While others would entirely fade away.
5   And since it is by words that we construe
The world, the world would start to vanish too. . . .

What if there were no letter **A**?
Cows would eat HY instead of HAY.
What's HY? It's an unheard-of diet,
10   And cows are happy not to try it.

In the word DUMB the letter **B** is mute,
But elsewhere its importance is acute.
If it were absent, say, from BAT and BALL,
There'd be no big or little leagues at all.

15   If there were no such thing as **C**,
Whole symphonies would be off-key,
And under every nut tree you'd
See HIPMUNKS gathering winter food.

If **D** did not exist, some creatures might
20   Wish, like the dodo bird, to fade from sight.
For instance, any self-respecting DUCK
Would rather be extinct than be an UCK.

The lordly ELEPHANT is one whom we
Would have no name for if there were no **E**,
25   And how it would offend him were we to
Greet him as "Bud," or "Big Boy," or "Hey, you!"
The ELEPHANT is thick-skinned, but I'll bet
That that's a thing he never would forget.

Hail, letter **F**! If it were not for you,
30   Our raincoats would be merely WATERPROO,
And that is such a stupid word, I doubt
That it would help to keep the water out.

If **G** did not exist, the color GREEN
Would have to vanish from the rural scene.
35   Would oak trees, then, be blue, and pastures pink?
We would turn green at such a sight, I think.

An **H** can be too scared to speak, almost.
In *gloomy* words like GHASTLY, GHOUL, and GHOST,
The sound of H can simply not be heard.
40   But how it loves to say a *cheerful* word

Like HEALTH, or HAPPINESS, or HOLIDAY!
Or HALLELUJAH! Or HIP, HIP, HURRAY!

Without the letter **I**, there'd be
No word for your IDENTITY,
45 And so you'd find it very tough
To tell yourself from other stuff.
Sometimes, perhaps, you'd think yourself
A jam jar on the pantry shelf.
Sometimes you'd make a ticking sound
50 And slowly move your hands around.
Sometimes you'd lie down like a rug,
Expecting to be vacuumed. Ugh!
Surely, my friends, you now see why
We need to keep the letter *I*.

55 If, all at once, there were no letter **J**.
A cloud of big blue birds might fly away,
And though they'd been an angry, raucous crew,
I think that I would miss them, wouldn't you?

Is **K** unnecessary? "Heavens, no!
60 It's in my name!" exclaims the ESKIMO.
"And if there were no *K*, my little craft,
The KAYAK, would be scuttled fore and aft."

It would be bitter, if there were no **L**,
To bid the LEMON or the LOON farewell,
65 And if the LLAMA, with its two-L name,
Should leave us, it would be a *double* shame,
But certainly it would be *triply* sad
If LOLLIPOPS no longer could be had.

M is a letter, but it alternates
70 As a Roman numeral often found in dates.
If *M* should vanish, we would lose, my dears,
MINCE PIE, MARSHMALLOWS, and a thousand years.

No **N**? In such a state of things,
Birds would have WIGS instead of WINGS,
75 And though a wig might suit the owl,
Who is a staid and judgelike fowl,
Most birds would rather fly than wear
A mat of artificial hair.
What would our proud bald eagle say
80 If he were offered a toupee?
I think it would be better, then,
For us to keep the letter *N*.

What if there were no letter **O**?
You couldn't COME, you couldn't GO,
85 You couldn't ROVE, you couldn't ROAM,
And yet you couldn't stay at HOME!
Where would you be had heaven not sent you
The letter *O* to orient you?

How strange that the banana's slippery PEEL,
90   Without its **P**, would be a slippery EEL!
It makes you think! However, it is not
Profound enough to think about a lot.

What if the letter **Q** should be destroyed?
Millions of *U*s would then be unemployed.
95   For *Q* and *U* belong like *tick* and *tock*,
Except, of course, in places like IRAQ.

What if there were no **R**? Your boat, I fear,
Would have no RUDDER, and so you couldn't steer.
How helplessly you'd drift then, and be borne
100   Through churning seas, and swept around the Horn!
But happily you couldn't come to grief
On ROCKS, or run aground upon a REEF.

What if the letter **S** were missing?
COBRAS would have no way of hissing,
105   And all their kin would have to take
The name of ERPENT or of NAKE.

At breakfast time the useful letter **T**
Preserves us all from eating SHREDDED WHEA.

Without the letter **U** you couldn't say,
110   "I think I'd like to visit URUGUAY,"
And so you'd stay forever in North Platte,
New Paltz, or Scranton, or some place like that.

Were there no **V**, would geese still fly
In V FORMATION in the sky,
115   Calling it something else instead,
Like "angle," "wedge," or "arrowhead"?
Perhaps. Or they might take the shape
Of smoke rings or of ticker tape.
Or spell out words like HERE WE GO
120   Or NUTS TO YOU. You never know.

What if there were no letter **W**?
The WEREWOLF would no longer trouble you,
And you'd be free of many evils
Like WARTS and WEARINESS and WEEVILS.
125   But then there'd be (alas!) no sweet
WATERMELONS for you to eat.

The letter **X** will never disappear:
The more you cross it out, the more it's here.
But if it vanished, treasure maps would not
130   Have anything with which to *mark the spot*,
And treasure isles would ring with the despair
Of puzzled pirates digging everywhere.

Lacking the letter **Y**, I guess
We'd have no way of saying YES,
135   Or even saying MAYBE, and so

There'd be no answer left but NO.
How horrible! Who wants to live
A life so very negative,
Refusing presents, RASPBERRY ice,
140   Fudge cake, and everything that's nice?

Because they're always BUZZING, honeybees
Could not be with us if there were no Zs,
And many Zs are needed, furthermore,
When people feel the need to SNOOZE and snore.
145   Long live the **Z**, then! Not for any money
Would I give up such things as sleep and honey.

Good heavens! It would be an awful mess
If everything dissolved to nothingness!
Be careful then, my friends, and do not let
150   *Anything happen to the alphabet.*

INQUIRING FURTHER

1. What does the speaker of the poem mean in saying that without the alphabet, "the world would start to vanish too"?
2. How does any playfulness in the poem relate to its message? Does the poem offer any serious messages about the relationship between language and the world?
3. How do the artistic techniques in the poem relate to the premise of the disappearing alphabet? Would you say art is an explicit or implicit concern in the poem? Freewrite for five minutes about the poem, art, and language.

KEN LIGHT

During the Democratic Primary for the 2004 presidential election, photographs of candidate John Kerry surfaced connecting him with actress and activist Jane Fonda. (Fonda's visit to Hanoi during the Vietnam War is frequently portrayed as unpatriotic.) One photograph depicts Fonda and Kerry together at the podium at a peace rally. The photograph turned out to be a fake. In this editorial for the Washington Post, *documentary photographer Ken Light reflects on the image and the events surrounding it.*

Fonda, Kerry and Photo Fakery

Anybody with Internet access and an interest in John Kerry has probably seen my photograph by now—or the part of it that I made, anyway. The other part is a fake, a visual lie. There's an AP credit down in the right corner. That's a lie, too. As far as I know, John Kerry never shared a demonstration podium with Jane Fonda, and the fact that a widely circulated photo showed him doing so—until it was exposed in recent weeks as a hoax—tells us more about the troublesome combination of Photoshop and the Internet than it does about the prospective Democratic candidate for president.

There have been two Kerry-Fonda pictures circulating around the Net, both promoted by conservative groups eager to link Kerry to Fonda's support for North Vietnam during the Vietnam War. One of these photos is real: the picture that shows the two of them in the same audience, some rows apart, at an anti-war rally. But the other, in which an angry-looking Fonda appears to be in mid-speech, with Kerry at her shoulder, is a paste-up job that started with a photo I made in 1971, when I was a 20-year-old student with big ideas about the power of photography.

I was trying to document the entire era with a camera. I believed photographs could bear witness, could help Americans understand each other, and I had spent the previous two years making images of a divided nation: anti-war rallies, veterans' parades, students facing off against national guardsmen. One afternoon in June, I attended a large rally in Mineola, N.Y., close to my parents' home. I recall the day vividly: the guy with a hardhat, the girl in a peasant blouse, the thousands of people sitting on the ground with American flags and peace signs. Speaker after speaker came to the stage to denounce the war in Vietnam. I kept shooting.

Finally, one speaker in particular caught my attention—a highly decorated Vietnam veteran named John Kerry. It was a powerful experience, hearing a war hero speak so forcefully against the war, and I made a few more photographs. I was still very young, but I'd learned enough to know that negatives are sacred, and that every roll of film must be carefully filed away for future use. So Roll 68 went into my file cabinet, where it remained until just a few weeks ago.

5   Watching Kerry emerge as the Democratic front-runner this year, I recalled that I had an image or two of him from way back when. The negatives were easy to find. Captioned and scanned, they flew off to the New York agency now representing some of my work. I have remained a photojournalist, and now teach students who are only a little older than I was in 1971, but who are working in a different world. Who could have predicted that my Ethical Problems in Photography presentation would be showing young journalists how National Geographic moved one of the Egyptian pyramids to make it fit on a cover better, or the way colleges seeking a more diverse image edit African American faces into sports crowds that look too white?

It's not that photographic imagery was ever unquestionable in its veracity; as long as pictures have been made from photographic film, people have known how to alter images by cropping. But what I've been trying to teach my students about how easy and professional-looking these distortions of truth have become in the age of Photoshop—and how harmful the results can be—had never hit me so personally as the day I found out somebody had pulled my Kerry picture off my agency's Web site, stuck Fonda at his side, and then used the massive, unedited reach of the Internet to distribute it all over the world.

I've spent a lot of time answering questions about this in the past couple of weeks, and this time, as far as I can tell, the Internet has come as close as it gets to a correction. If you use a search engine to look for my Kerry picture now, you'll find the hoax explanations before you see the photo itself. So what do I do now about the conspiratorial Web site that's trying to convince its readers that my original picture was the hoax—that Fonda really was at that podium with Kerry, and somebody edited "Hanoi Jane" out? All I can do is pull Roll 68 out of the file cabinet again. It's my visual record, my unretouched truth.

FIGURE 18.1   Forrest Gump with Richard Nixon

FIGURE 18.2   Forrest Gump with John F. Kennedy

INQUIRING FURTHER

1. What do you think of Ken Light's claim toward the end of his editorial that the negatives of his photographs present the "unretouched truth"? Would you agree or disagree? Why?

2. How would you relate the images in Figures 18.1 and 18.2 to Light's essay? Is it unfair to hold photography to a different standard of expression than film?

3. What are your thoughts on the more benign doctoring of photographs that takes place for magazine covers and advertisements? Would you say these are distortions of reality? What might you say to someone who argued that doctoring a photograph should never be acceptable?

4. Look for other manipulated images on the Internet. How easy is it for us to be deceived by art? When is distortion appropriate? Hold a discussion with classmates about the manipulation of images.

BILLY COLLINS

Billy Collins (born in 1941) has served two terms as the poet Laureate for the United States, and enjoys much popularity for the humor and accessibility of his works. He also frequently writes about paintings and the nature of poetry. For more on Collins, see "Embrace" (153), "Names" (723), and "Thesaurus" (163). "Marginalia" is taken from his collection, The Best Cigarette, *published in 1997.*

Marginalia

Collins
reading
"Marginalia"

Sometimes the notes are ferocious,
skirmishes against the author
raging along the borders of every page
in tiny black script.
5   If I could just get my hands on you,
Kierkegaard, or Conor Cruise O'Brien,
they seem to say,
I would bolt the door and beat some logic into your head.

Other comments are more offhand, dismissive—
10 "Nonsense." "Please!" "HA!!"—
that kind of thing.
I remember once looking up from my reading,
my thumb as a bookmark,
trying to imagine what the person must look like
15 why wrote "Don't be a ninny"
alongside a paragraph in The Life of Emily Dickinson.

Students are most modest
needing to leave only their splayed footprints
along the shore of the page.
20 One scrawls "Metaphor" next to a stanza of Eliot's.
Another notes the presence of "Irony"
fifty times outside the paragraphs of A Modest Proposal.

Or they are fans who cheer from the empty bleachers,
Hands cupped around their mouths.
25 "Absolutely," they shout
to Duns Scotus and James Baldwin.
"Yes." "Bull's-eye." "My man!"
Check marks, asterisks, and exclamation points
rain down along the sidelines.

30 And if you have managed to graduate from college
without ever having written "Man vs. Nature"
in a margin, perhaps now
is the time to take one step forward.

We have all seized the white perimeter as our own
35 and reached for a pen if only to show
we did not just laze in an armchair turning pages;

we pressed a thought into the wayside,
planted an impression along the verge.

Even Irish monks in their cold scriptoria
40   jotted along the borders of the Gospels
brief asides about the pains of copying,
a bird singing near their window,
or the sunlight that illuminated their page—
anonymous men catching a ride into the future
45   on a vessel more lasting than themselves.

And you have not read Joshua Reynolds,
they say, until you have read him
enwreathed with Blake's furious scribbling.

Yet the one I think of most often,
50   the one that dangles from me like a locket,
was written in the copy of Catcher in the Rye
I borrowed from the local library
one slow, hot summer.
I was just beginning high school then,
55   reading books on a davenport in my parents' living room,
and I cannot tell you
how vastly my loneliness was deepened,
how poignant and amplified the world before me seemed,
when I found on one page

60   A few greasy looking smears
and next to them, written in soft pencil—
by a beautiful girl, I could tell,
whom I would never meet—
"Pardon the egg salad stains, but I'm in love."

INQUIRING FURTHER

1. What is the significance of the last bit of marginalia next to the egg salad stain? Why do you think it affects the speaker of the poem so strongly?

2. How do readers of literary works complicate the concepts of art and representation? Do we often consider our own role in determining how well art captures reality? Freewrite for five minutes about the way we encounter works of art.

3. Mark up Collins' "Marginalia" with your own comments. What are your thoughts on marking up a text that is about marking up a text?

REPRESENTING NATURE

The works in this chapter have so far explored the relationship between art and reality. Art can represent the world more or less directly. It can also distort representations, or present pictures which may seem true without necessarily being real or complete. We can see these processes of representation in literature that explores the natural world. Art has a role to play in not only picturing the natural world, but also in helping us consider our role as members of the larger reality that makes up the world's ecosystem.

GARY SNYDER

Gary Snyder (born in 1930) spent much of his early childhood exploring the forests of Washington and Oregon. He also began writing poetry as a child, becoming more serious about both his outdoor experiences and his writing throughout high school. He studied literature and anthropology in college, worked for the Forest Service and at a number of outdoor jobs, and joined poets like Jack Kerouac and Allen Ginsberg in the San Francisco Beat scene, before moving to Japan in 1956 to study Zen Buddhism. His first published collection of poetry, Riprap *(1959), and his second volume,* Myths and Texts *(1960), emphasized the connections between outdoor experiences and Native American and Eastern philosophies that would characterize the rest of his work. His collections* Turtle Island *(1974) and* Axe Handles *(1983) stand as clear demonstrations of his ability to bring artistic mastery of poetry to a message that celebrates the value of the natural world both ecologically and philosophically.* Turtle Island *was awarded the Pulitzer Prize.*

Getting in the Wood

The sour smell,
  blue stain,
      water squirts out round the wedge,

Lifting quarters of rounds
5   covered with ants,
    "a living glove of ants upon my hand"
the poll of the sledge a bit peened over
so the wedge springs off and tumbles
  ringing like high-pitched bells
10   into the complex duff of twigs
      poison oak, bark, sawdust,
      shards of logs,

And the sweat drips down.
  Smell of crushed ants.
15 The lean and heave on the peavey
that breaks free the last of a bucked
    three-foot round,
      it lies flat on smashed oaklings—

Wedge and sledge, peavey and maul,
20   little axe, canteen, piggyback can
    of saw-mix gas and oil for the chain,
knapsack of files and goggles and rags,

All to gather the dead and the down.
    the young men throw splits on the piles
25   bodies hardening, learning the pace
and the smell of tools from this delve
  in the winter

The
poetry of
Gary
Snyder

death-topple of elderly oak.
30   Four cords.

Dillingham, Alaska, the Willow Tree Bar

Drills chatter full of mud and compressed air
all across the globe,
    low-ceilinged bars, we hear the same new songs

All the new songs.
5   In the working bars of the world.
After you done drive Cat. After the truck
    went home.
    Caribou slip,
    front legs folded first
10   under the warm oil pipeline
    set four feet off the ground—

On the wood floor, glass in hand,
    laugh and cuss with
    somebody else's wife.
15   Texans, Hawaiians, Eskimos,
Filipinos, Workers, always
on the edge of a brawl—
In the bars of the world.
Hearing those same new songs
20   in Abadan,
    Naples, Galveston, Darwin, Fairbanks,
    White or brown,
Drinking it down,

    the pain
25   of the work
of wrecking the world.

INQUIRING FURTHER

1. "Getting in the Wood" describes the use of tools to split wood and collect resources. What would you say to someone who argued that the poem presents a picture of humans exploiting the environment? What passages would help you construct a response to such a claim?

2. How would you characterize the tone of the speaker in "Dillingham, Alaska, the Willow Tree Bar"? How might you describe the speaker's attitude toward the occupants of the bar? Write a paragraph in which you explain how the speaker's attitude relates to the message of the poem.

One Should Not Talk to a Skilled Hunter About What Is Forbidden by the Buddha

Hsiang-yen

A gray fox, female, nine pounds three ounces.
39 5/8" long with tail.

Peeling skin back (Kai
reminded us to chant the *Shingyo* first)
5   cold pelt. crinkle; and musky smell
mixed with dead-body odor starting.

Stomach content: a whole ground squirrel well chewed
plus one lizard foot
and somewhere from inside the ground squirrel
10   a bit of aluminum foil.

The secret.
and the secret hidden deep in that.

Why Log Truck Drivers Rise Earlier Than Students of Zen

In the high seat, before-dawn dark,
Polished hubs gleam
And the shiny diesel stack
Warms and flutters
5   Up the Tyler Road grade
To the logging on Poorman creek.
Thirty miles of dust.

There is no other life.

INQUIRING FURTHER

1. How do you interpret the last line of "Why Log Truck Drivers Rise Earlier Than Students of Zen"? Would you say the picture painted of the drivers is positive or negative? Why?

2. The title of "One Should Not Talk to a Skilled Hunter about What is Forbidden by the Buddha" refers to a Buddhist proverb that suggests it may be wrong to judge people who, out of necessity, take on "forbidden" occupations. Do you believe that if an occupation is necessary, negative associations that go with it should be overlooked?

As for Poets

As for poets
The Earth Poets
Who write small poems,
Need help from no man.

5   The Air Poets
Play out the swiftest gales
And sometimes loll in the eddies.
Poem after poem,
Curling back on the same thrust.

10   At fifty below
Fuel oil won't flow
And propane stays in the tank.

Fire Poets
Burn at absolute zero
15   Fossil love pumped back up.

The first
Water Poet
Stayed down six years.
He was covered with seaweed.
20   The life in his poem
Left millions of tiny
Different tracks
Criss-crossing through the mud.

With the Sun and Moon
25   In his belly,
The Space Poet
Sleeps.
No end to the sky—
But his poems,
30   Like wild geese,
Fly off the edge.

A Mind Poet
Stays in the house.
The house is empty
35   And it has no walls.
The poem
Is seen from all sides,
Everywhere,
At once.

INQUIRING FURTHER

1. How do you interpret the last stanza of the poem? What might be the relationship between the house and the mind? Write a paraphrase of the last stanza.

2. What recommendations or statements about art can you discover in "As for Poets"? Is it fair to say "As for Poets" is a poem about art? Why or why not?

---

*Unnatural Writing**

"Nature writing" has become a matter of increased literary interest in the last few years. The subject matter "nature," and the concern for it (and us humans in it), have come—it is gratifying to note—to engage artists and writers. This interest may be another strand of postmodernism, since the modernist avant-garde was strikingly urban-centered. Many would-be writers approach this territory in a mode of curiosity, respect, and concern, without necessarily seeking personal gain or literary reputation. They are doing it for love—and the eco-warrior's passion, not money. (There is still a wide range of views and notions about what nature writing ought to be. There is an older sort of nature writing that might be seen as large-

*The original version of this essay was given as a talk the first year of the "Art of the Wild" nature-writing conference series, held at Squaw (Brodiaea Harvesters) Valley in June 1992.

ly essays and writing from a human perspective, middle-class, middlebrow Euro-American. It has a rhetoric of beauty, harmony, and sublimity. What makes us uncomfortable sometimes with John Muir's writing is an excess of this. He had contemporaries, now forgotten, who were far worse.)

Natural history writing is another branch. Semiscientific, objective, in the descriptive mode. Both these sorts are "naively realistic" in that they unquestioningly accept the front-mounted bifocal human eye, the poor human sense of smell, and other characteristics of our species, plus the assumption that the mind can, without much self-examination, directly and objectively "know" whatever it looks at. There has also always been a literature of heroic journals and adventure. And there is an old mix of science, nature appreciation, and conservation politics that has been a potent part of the evolution of the conservation movement in the United States. The best of this would be seen in the work of Rachel Carson and Aldo Leopold. All of these writings might be seen by some as mildly arthropocentric, but the work is worthy and good-hearted. We are in its debt.

Nature writing has been a class of literature held in less than full regard by the literary establishment, because it is focused on something other than the major subject matter of mainstream occidental writing, the moral quandaries, heroics, affairs of the heart, and soul searchings of highly gifted and often powerful people, usually male. Tales of the elites. In fact, up until a decade ago nature writing was relegated pretty much to a status like that of nineteenth-century women's writing—it was seen as a writing of sensibility and empathy and observation, but off to the side, not really serious, not important.

But if we look at the larger context of occidental history, educated elites, and literary culture, we see that the natural world is profoundly present in and an inescapable part of the great works of art. The human experience over the larger part of its history has been played out in intimate relationship to the natural world. This is too obvious even to say, yet it is often oddly forgotten. History, philosophy, and literature naturally foreground human affairs, social dynamics, dilemmas of faith, intellectual constructs. But a critical subtheme that runs through it all has to do with defining the human relationship to the rest of nature. In literature, nature not only provides the background, the scene, but also many of the characters. The "classical" world of myth is a world in which animal beings, supernatural figures, and humans are actors and interacters. Bears, bulls, and swans were not abstractions to the people of earlier times but real creatures in very real landscapes. The aurochs—the giant wild cow, *Bos primigenius*, who became Zeus to Europa—survived in pockets of the European forests until medieval times.

5   In *The Practice of the Wild*, I point out that through most of human history

populations were relatively small and travel took place on foot, by horse, or by sail. Whether Greece, Germania, or Han China, there were always nearby areas of forest, and wild animals, migratory waterfowl, seas full of fish and whales, and these were part of the experience of every active person. Animals as characters in literature and as universal presences in the imagination and in the archetypes of religion are there because they were *there*. Ideas and images of wastelands, tempests, wildernesses, and mountains are born not of abstraction but of experience: cisalpine, hyperboreal, circumpolar, transpacific, or beyond the pale. [This is the world people lived in up until the late nineteenth century. Plentiful wildlife, open space, small human population, trails instead of roads—and human lives of individual responsibility and existential intensity. It is not "frontier" that we're considering, but the Holocene era, our *present* era, in all its glory of salmon, bear, elk, deer, and moose.] Where do the sacred salmon of the Celts, the Bjorns and Brauns and Brun-(hilde)-s [bher = bear] of northern European literature, the dolphins of the Mediterranean, the Bear dances of Artemis, the Lion skin of Herakles come from but the wild systems the humans lived near?

Those images that yet

Fresh images beget

That dolphin-torn, that gong-tormented sea.

Many figures in the literary field, the critical establishment, and the academy are not enthralled with the natural world, and indeed some positively doubt its worth when compared to human achievement. Take this quote from Howard Nemerov, a good poet and a decent man:

Civilization, mirrored in language, is the garden where relations grow; outside the garden is the wild abyss.

The unexamined assumptions here are fascinating. They are, at worst, crystallizations of the erroneous views that enable the developed world to displace Third and Fourth World peoples and overexploit nature globally. Nemerov here proposes that language is somehow implicitly civilized or civilizing, that civilization is orderly, that intrahuman relations are the pinnacle of experience (as though all of us, and all life on the planet, were not interrelated), and that "wild" means "abyssal," disorderly, and chaotic.

First take language. Some theorists have latched onto "language" as that which somehow makes us different. They have the same enthusiasm for the "Logos" as the old Summer Institute of Linguistics had for Bible translation into unwritten languages. In fact, every recent writer who doesn't know what else to say about his or her work—when asked to give a sound bite—has declared, "Well, I'm just fascinated with language." The truth is language is part and parcel of consciousness, and we know virtually nothing about either one. Our study and respect should extend to them both.

On another tack, the European deconstructionists assume, because of their monotheistic background, that the Logos died along with God. Those who wish to decenter occidental metaphysics have begun to try to value both language and nature and declare them to be further tools of ruling-class mythology. In the past, the idea that the external world was our own invention came out of some variety of idealist thought. But *this* version leads to a weird philosophical position that, since the proponents are academic "meta-Marxists," might be called "materialist solipsism." But they are just talk.

10   There is some truly dangerous language in a term heard in some business and government circles: "sustainable development." Development is not compatible with sustainability and biodiversity. We must drop talking about development and concentrate on how to achieve a steady-state condition of real sustainability. Much of what passes for economic development is simply the further extension of the destabilizing, entropic, and disorderly functions of industrial civilization.

So I will argue that consciousness, mind, imagination, *and* language are fundamentally wild. "Wild" as in wild ecosystems—richly interconnected, interdependent, and incredibly complex. Diverse, ancient, and full of information. At root the real question is how we understand the concepts of order, freedom, and chaos. Is art an imposition of order on chaotic nature, or is art (also read "language") a matter of discovering the grain of things, of uncovering the measured chaos that structures the natural world? Observation, reflection, and practice show artistic process to be the latter.

Our school-in-the-mountains here at Squaw Valley is called "Art of the Wild." (I was wondering just what edible root might have been growing so profusely in this wet mountain bottomland to have caused it to be called "Squaw Valley." Any place with the word *squaw* in the name is usually where some early trappers saw numerous Native American women at work gathering wild food; here it might have been *Brodiaea* bulbs. This naming practice is as though some native women coming on a Euro-American farming community had called it White Boy Flats.)

The "art of the wild" is to see art in the context of the process of nature— nature *as* process rather than as product or commodity—because "wild" is a name for the way that phenomena continually actualize themselves. Seeing this also serves to acknowledge the autonomy and integrity of the nonhuman part of the world, an "Other" that we are barely beginning to be able to know. In disclosing, discovering, the wild world with our kind of writing, we may find ourselves breaking into unfamiliar territories that do not seem anything like what was called "nature writing" in the past. The work of the art of the wild can well be irreverent, inharmonious, ugly, frazzled, unpredictable, simple, and clear—or virtually inaccessible. Who will write of the odd barbed, hooked, bent, splayed, and crooked penises of nonhuman male creatures? Of sexism among spiders? Someone will yet come to write with the eye of an insect, write from the undersea world, and in other ways that step outside the human.

In *Practice* it says:

15   Life in the wild is not just eating berries in the sunlight. I like to imagine a "depth ecology" that would go to the dark side of nature—the ball of crunched bones in a scat, the feathers in the snow, the tales of insatiable appetite. Wild systems are in one elevated sense above criticism, but they can also be seen as irrational, moldy, cruel, parasitic. Jim Dodge told me how he had watched—with fascinated horror—orcas methodically batter a gray whale to death in the Chukchi Sea. Life is not just diurnal and a property of large interesting vertebrates, it is also nocturnal, anaerobic, canni-balistic, microscopic, digestive, fermentative: cooking away in the warm dark. Life is well maintained at a four mile ocean depth, is waiting and sustained on a frozen rock wall, and clinging and nourished in hundred-degree desert temperatures. And there is a world of nature on the decay side, a world of beings who do rot and decay in the shade. Human beings have made much of purity, and are repelled by blood, pollution, putre-faction. The other side of the "sacred" is the sight of your beloved in the underworld, dripping with maggots. Coyote, Orpheus, and Izanagi can-not help but look, and they lose her. Shame, grief, embarrassment, and fear are the anaerobic fuels of the dark imagination. The less familiar energies of the wild world, and their analogs in the imagination, have given us ecolo-gies of the imagination. . . .

Narratives are one sort of trace that we leave in the world. All our literatures are leavings, of the same order as the myths of wilderness peo-ples who leave behind only stories and a few stone tools. Other orders of beings have their own literatures. Narrative in the deer world is a track of scents that is passed on from deer to deer, with an art of inter-pretation which is instinctive. A literature of blood-stains, a bit of piss, a whiff of estrus, a hint of rut, a scrape on a sapling, and long gone. And there might be a "narrative theory" among these other beings—they might ruminate on "intersexuality," or "decomposition criticism."

I propose this to turn us loose to think about "wild writing" without preconception or inhibition, but at the same time with craft. The craft could be seen as the swoop of a hawk, the intricate galleries of burrowing and tunneling under the bark done by western pine bark beetles, the lurking at the bottom by a big old trout—or the kamikaze sting of a yellow jacket, the insouciant waddle of a porcupine, the constant steadiness of a flow of water over a boulder, the chatter of a squirrel, hyenas moaning and excavating the bowels of a dead giraffe under a serene moon. Images of our art. Nature's writing has the potential of becoming the most vital, radical, fluid, transgressive, pansexual, subductive, and morally challenging kind of writing on the scene. In becoming so, it may serve to help halt one of the most terrible things of our time—the destruction of species and their habitats, the elimination of some living beings forever.

Finally, let us not get drawn too far into dichotomous views and arguments about civilization versus nature, the domesticated versus the wild, the garden versus the wild abyss. Creativity draws on wildness, and wildness confers freedom; which is (at bottom) the ability to live in the real physical daily world at each moment, totally and completely.

Some Points for a "New Nature Poetics"

- That it be literate—that is, nature literate. Know who's who and what's what in the ecosystem, even if this aspect is barely visible in the writing.
- That it be grounded in a place—thus, place literate: informed about local specifics on both ecological-biotic and sociopolitical levels. And informed about history (social history and environmental history), even if this is not obvious in the poem.
- That it use Coyote as a totem—the trickster, always open, shape shifting, providing the eye of other beings going in and out of death, laughing with the dark side.
- That it use Bear as a totem—omnivorous, fearless, without anxiety, steady, generous, contemplative, and relentlessly protective of the wild.
- That it find further totems—this is the world of nature, myth, archetype, and ecosystem that we must each investigate. "Depth ecology."
- That it fear not science. Go *beyond* nature literacy into the emergent new territories in science: landscape ecology, conservation biology, charming chaos, complicated systems theory.
- That it go further with science—into awareness of the problematic and contingent aspects of so-called objectivity.
- That it study mind and language—language as wild system, mind as wild habitat, world as a "making" (poem), poem as a creature of the wild mind.
- That it be crafty and get the work *done*.

INQUIRING FURTHER

1. What do you make of the claim that "consciousness, mind, imagination, *and* language are fundamentally wild"? Can you paraphrase what Snyder intends the statement to mean? How does language relate to nature?

2. Do you think it is a fair representation to call animal communication a kind of literature or narrative? In what ways do animals tell stories? How is human thought and communication similar or different from that of animals?

3. How helpful do you find the points for a "New Nature Poetics" on page 867? Select one or two of these points and use them to develop a paper exploring one or more of the poems in this chapter.

SARAH ORNE JEWETT

Sarah Orne Jewett (1849–1909) has often been associated with the school of Regionalism in literature, because she wrote works describing in detail the characters and places of her native Maine. Her stories, however, touch on more than just local color, emphasizing the connections between individuals and places and raising important questions about relationships between men, women, and the environment. "A White Heron" is the title story to her collection published in 1886.

A White Heron

I.

The woods were already filled with shadows one June evening, just before eight o'clock, though a bright sunset still glimmered faintly among the trunks of the trees. A little girl was driving home her cow, a plodding, dilatory, provoking creature in her behavior, but a valued companion for all that. They were going away from whatever light there was, and striking deep into the woods, but their feet were familiar with the path, and it was no matter whether their eyes could see it or not.

There was hardly a night the summer through when the old cow could be found waiting at the pasture bars; on the contrary, it was her greatest pleasure to hide herself away among the huckleberry bushes, and though she wore a loud bell she had made the discovery that if one stood perfectly still it would not ring. So Sylvia had to hunt for her until she found her, and call Co'! Co'! with never an answering Moo, until her childish patience was quite spent. If the creature had not given good milk and plenty of it, the case would have seemed very different to her owners. Besides, Sylvia had all the time there was, and very little use to make of it. Sometimes in pleasant weather it was a consolation to look upon the cow's pranks as an intelligent attempt to play hide and seek, and as the child had no playmates she lent herself to this amusement with a good deal of zest. Though this chase had been so long that the wary animal herself had given an unusual signal of her whereabouts, Sylvia had only laughed when she came upon Mistress Moolly at the swampside, and urged her affectionately homeward with a twig of birch leaves. The old cow was not inclined to wander farther, she even turned in the right direction for once as they left the pasture, and stepped along the road at a good pace. She was quite ready to be milked now, and seldom stopped to browse. Sylvia wondered what her grandmother would say because they were so late. It was a great while since she had left home at half-past five o'clock, but everybody knew the difficulty of making this errand a short one. Mrs. Tilley had chased the hornéd torment too many summer evenings herself to blame any one else for lingering, and was only thankful as she waited that she had Sylvia, nowadays, to give such valuable assistance. The good woman suspected that Sylvia loitered occasionally on her own account; there never was such a child for straying about out-of-doors since the world was made! Everybody said that it was a good change for a little maid who had tried to grow for eight years in a crowded manufacturing town, but, as for Sylvia herself, it seemed as if she never had been alive at all before she came to live at the farm. She thought often with wistful compassion of a wretched geranium that belonged to a town neighbor.

"'Afraid of folks,'" old Mrs. Tilley said to herself, with a smile, after she had made the unlikely choice of Sylvia from her daughter's houseful of children, and was returning to the farm. "'Afraid of folks,' they said! I guess she won't be troubled no great with 'em up to the old place!" When they reached the door of the lonely house and stopped to unlock it, and the cat came to purr loudly, and rub against them, a deserted pussy, indeed, but fat with young robins, Sylvia whispered that this was a beautiful place to live in, and she never should wish to go home.

The companions followed the shady wood-road, the cow taking slow steps and the child very fast ones. The cow stopped long at the brook to drink, as if the pasture were not half a swamp, and Sylvia stood still and waited, letting her bare feet cool themselves in the shoal water, while the great twilight moths struck softly against her. She waded on through the brook as the cow moved away, and listened to the thrushes with a heart that beat fast with pleasure. There was a stirring in the great boughs overhead. They were full of little birds and beasts that seemed to be wide awake, and going about their world, or else saying good-night to each other in sleepy twitters. Sylvia herself felt sleepy as she walked along. However, it was not much farther to the house, and the air was soft and sweet. She was not often in the woods so late as this, and it made her feel as if she were a part of the gray shadows and the moving leaves. She was just thinking how long it seemed since she first came to the farm a year ago, and wondering if everything went on in the noisy town just the same as when she was there; the thought of the great red-faced boy who used to chase and frighten her made her hurry along the path to escape from the shadow of the trees.

5   Suddenly this little woods-girl is horror-stricken to hear a clear whistle not very far away. Not a bird's-whistle, which would have a sort of friendliness, but a boy's whistle, determined, and somewhat aggressive. Sylvia left the cow to whatever sad fate might await her, and stepped discreetly aside into the bushes, but she was just too late. The enemy had discovered her, and called out in a very cheerful and persuasive tone, "Halloa, little girl, how far is it to the road?" and trembling Sylvia answered almost inaudibly, "A good ways."

She did not dare to look boldly at the tall young man, who carried a gun over his shoulder, but she came out of her bush and again followed the cow, while he walked alongside.

"I have been hunting for some birds," the stranger said kindly, "and I have lost my way, and need a friend very much. Don't be afraid," he added gallantly. "Speak up and tell me what your name is, and whether you think I can spend the night at your house, and go out gunning early in the morning."

Sylvia was more alarmed than before. Would not her grandmother consider her much to blame? But who could have foreseen such an accident as this? It did not seem to be her fault, and she hung her head as if the stem of it were broken, but managed to answer "Sylvy," with much effort when her companion again asked her name.

Mrs. Tilley was standing in the doorway when the trio came into view. The cow gave a loud moo by way of explanation.

10   "Yes, you'd better speak up for yourself, you old trial! Where'd she tucked herself away this time, Sylvy?" But Sylvia kept an awed silence; she knew by instinct that her grandmother did not comprehend the gravity of the situation. She must be mistaking the stranger for one of the farmer-lads of the region.

The young man stood his gun beside the door, and dropped a lumpy game-bag beside it; then he bade Mrs. Tilley good-evening, and repeated his way-farer's story, and asked if he could have a night's lodging.

"Put me anywhere you like," he said. "I must be off early in the morning, before day; but I am very hungry, indeed. You can give me some milk at any rate, that's plain."

"Dear sakes, yes," responded the hostess, whose long slumbering hospital-ity seemed to be easily awakened. "You might fare better if you went out to the main road a mile or so, but you're welcome to what we've got. I'll milk right off, and you make yourself at home. You can sleep on husks or feathers," she proffered graciously. "I raised them all myself. There's good pasturing for geese just below here towards the ma'sh. Now step round and set a plate for the gentleman, Sylvy!" And Sylvia promptly stepped. She was glad to have some-thing to do, and she was hungry herself.

It was a surprise to find so clean and comfortable a little dwelling in this New England wilderness. The young man had known the horrors of its most prim-itive housekeeping, and the dreary squalor of that level of society which does not rebel at the companionship of hens. This was the best thrift of an old-fashioned farmstead, though on such a small scale that it seemed like a her-mitage. He listened eagerly to the old woman's quaint talk, he watched Sylvia's pale face and shining gray eyes with ever growing enthusiasm, and insisted that this was the best supper he had eaten for a month, and afterward the new-made friends sat down in the door-way together while the moon came up.

15   Soon it would be berry-time, and Sylvia was a great help at picking. The cow was a good milker, though a plaguy thing to keep track of, the hostess gossiped frankly, adding presently that she had buried four children, so Sylvia's moth-er, and a son (who might be dead) in California were all the children she had left. "Dan, my boy, was a great hand to go gunning," she explained sadly. "I never wanted for pa'tridges or gray squer'ls while he was to home. He's been a great wand'rer, I expect, and he's no hand to write letters. There, I don't blame him, I'd ha' seen the world myself if it had been so I could."

"Sylvy takes after him," the grandmother continued affectionately, after a minute's pause. "There ain't a foot o' ground she don't know her way over, and the wild creatures counts her one o' themselves. Squer'ls she 'll tame to come an' feed right out o' her hands, and all sorts o' birds. Last winter she got the jay-birds to bangeing here, and I believe she 'd 'a' scanted herself of her own meals to have plenty to throw out amongst 'em, if I had n't kep' watch. Anything but crows, I tell her, I 'm willin' to help support—though Dan he had a tamed one o' them that did seem to have reason same as folks. It was round here a good spell after he went away. Dan an' his father they did n't hitch,—but he never held up his head ag'in after Dan had dared him an' gone off."

The guest did not notice this hint of family sorrows in his eager interest in something else.

"So Sylvy knows all about birds, does she?" he exclaimed, as he looked round at the little girl who sat, very demure but increasingly sleepy, in the moonlight. "I am making a collection of birds myself. I have been at it ever since

I was a boy." (Mrs. Tilley smiled.) "There are two or three very rare ones I have been hunting for these five years. I mean to get them on my own ground if they can be found."

"Do you cage 'em up?" asked Mrs. Tilley doubtfully, in response to this enthusiastic announcement.

20   "Oh no, they're stuffed and preserved, dozens and dozens of them," said the ornithologist, "and I have shot or snared every one myself. I caught a glimpse of a white heron a few miles from here on Saturday, and I have followed it in this direction. They have never been found in this district at all. The little white heron, it is," and he turned again to look at Sylvia with the hope of discovering that the rare bird was one of her acquaintances.

But Sylvia was watching a hop-toad in the narrow footpath.

"You would know the heron if you saw it," the stranger continued eagerly. "A queer tall white bird with soft feathers and long thin legs. And it would have a nest perhaps in the top of a high tree, made of sticks, something like a hawk's nest."

Sylvia's heart gave a wild beat; she knew that strange white bird, and had once stolen softly near where it stood in some bright green swamp grass, away over at the other side of the woods. There was an open place where the sunshine always seemed strangely yellow and hot, where tall, nodding rushes grew, and her grandmother had warned her that she might sink in the soft black mud underneath and never be heard of more. Not far beyond were the salt marshes just this side the sea itself, which Sylvia wondered and dreamed much about, but never had seen, whose great voice could sometimes be heard above the noise of the woods on stormy nights.

"I can't think of anything I should like so much as to find that heron's nest," the handsome stranger was saying. "I would give ten dollars to anybody who could show it to me," he added desperately, "and I mean to spend my whole vacation hunting for it if need be. Perhaps it was only migrating, or had been chased out of its own region by some bird of prey."

25   Mrs. Tilley gave amazed attention to all this, but Sylvia still watched the toad, not divining, as she might have done at some calmer time, that the creature wished to get to its hole under the door-step, and was much hindered by the unusual spectators at that hour of the evening. No amount of thought, that night, could decide how many wished-for treasures the ten dollars, so lightly spoken of, would buy.

The next day the young sportsman hovered about the woods, and Sylvia kept him company, having lost her first fear of the friendly lad, who proved to be most kind and sympathetic. He told her many things about the birds and what they knew and where they lived and what they did with themselves. And he gave her a jack-knife, which she thought as great a treasure as if she were a desert-islander. All day long he did not once make her troubled or afraid except when he brought down some unsuspecting singing creature from its bough. Sylvia would have liked him vastly better without his gun; she could not understand why he killed the very birds he seemed to like so much. But as the day waned, Sylvia still watched the young man with loving admiration. She had never seen anybody so charming and delightful; the woman's heart, asleep in the child, was vaguely thrilled by a dream of love Some premonition of that great power stirred and swayed these young creatures who traversed the solemn woodlands with soft-footed silent care. They stopped to listen to a bird's song; they pressed forward again eagerly, parting the branches—speaking to each other rarely and in whispers; the young man going first and Sylvia following, fascinated, a few steps behind, with her gray eyes dark with excitement.

She grieved because the longed-for white heron was elusive, but she did not lead the guest, she only followed, and there was no such thing as speaking first. The sound of her own unquestioned voice would have terrified her—it was hard enough to answer yes or no when there was need of that. At last evening began to fall, and they drove the cow home together, and Sylvia smiled with pleasure when they came to the place where she heard the whistle and was afraid only the night before.

II.

Half a mile from home, at the farther edge of the woods, where the land was highest, a great pine-tree stood, the last of its generation. Whether it was left for a boundary mark, or for what reason, no one could say; the wood-choppers who had felled its mates were dead and gone long ago, and a whole forest of sturdy trees, pines and oaks and maples, had grown again. But the stately head of this old pine towered above them all and made a landmark for sea and shore miles and miles away. Sylvia knew it well. She had always believed that whoever climbed to the top of it could see the ocean; and the little girl had often laid her hand on the great rough trunk and looked up wistfully at those dark boughs that the wind always stirred, no matter how hot and still the air might be below. Now she thought of the tree with a new excitement, for why, if one climbed it at break of day could not one see all the world, and easily discover from whence the white heron flew, and mark the place, and find the hidden nest?

What a spirit of adventure, what wild ambition! What fancied triumph and delight and glory for the later morning when she could make known the secret! It was almost too real and too great for the childish heart to bear.

30   All night the door of the little house stood open and the whippoorwills came and sang upon the very step. The young sportsman and his old hostess were sound asleep, but Sylvia's great design kept her broad awake and watching. She forgot to think of sleep. The short summer night seemed as long as the winter darkness, and at last when the whippoorwills ceased, and she was afraid the morning would after all come too soon, she stole out of the house and followed the pasture path through the woods, hastening toward the open ground beyond, listening with a sense of comfort and companionship to the drowsy twitter of a half-awakened bird, whose perch she had jarred in passing. Alas, if the great wave of human interest which flooded for the first time this dull little life should sweep away the satisfactions of an existence heart to heart with nature and the dumb life of the forest!

There was the huge tree asleep yet in the paling moonlight, and small and silly Sylvia began with utmost bravery to mount to the top of it, with tingling, eager blood coursing the channels of her whole frame, with her bare feet and fingers, that pinched and held like bird's claws to the monstrous ladder reaching up, up, almost to the sky itself. First she must mount the white oak tree that grew alongside, where she was almost lost among the dark branches and the green leaves heavy and wet with dew; a bird fluttered off its nest, and a red squirrel ran to and fro and scolded pettishly at the harmless housebreaker. Sylvia felt her way easily. She had often climbed there, and knew that higher still one of the oak's upper branches chafed against the pine trunk, just where its lower boughs were set close together. There, when she made the dangerous pass from one tree to the other, the great enterprise would really begin.

She crept out along the swaying oak limb at last, and took the daring step across into the old pine-tree. The way was harder than she thought; she must reach far and hold fast, the sharp dry twigs caught and held her and scratched her like angry talons, the pitch made her thin little fingers clumsy and stiff as she went round and round the tree's great stem, higher and higher upward. The sparrows and robins in the woods below were beginning to wake and twitter to the dawn, yet it seemed much lighter there aloft in the pine-tree, and the child knew she must hurry if her project were to be of any use.

The tree seemed to lengthen itself out as she went up, and to reach farther and farther upward. It was like a great main-mast to the voyaging earth; it must truly have been amazed that morning through all its ponderous frame as it felt this determined spark of human spirit wending its way from higher branch to branch. Who knows how steadily the least twigs held themselves to advantage this light, weak creature on her way! The old pine must have loved his new dependent. More than all the hawks, and bats, and moths, and even the sweet voiced thrushes, was the brave, beating heart of the solitary gray-eyed child. And the tree stood still and frowned away the winds that June morning while the dawn grew bright in the east.

Sylvia's face was like a pale star, if one had seen it from the ground, when the last thorny bough was past, and she stood trembling and tired but wholly triumphant, high in the tree-top. Yes, there was the sea with the dawning sun making a golden dazzle over it, and toward that glorious east flew two hawks with slow-moving pinions. How low they looked in the air from that height when one had only seen them before far up, and dark against the blue sky. Their gray feathers were as soft as moths; they seemed only a little way from the tree, and Sylvia felt as if she too could go flying away among the clouds. Westward, the woodlands and farms reached miles and miles into the distance; here and there were church steeples, and white villages, truly it was a vast and awesome world!

35   The birds sang louder and louder. At last the sun came up bewilderingly bright. Sylvia could see the white sails of ships out at sea, and the clouds that were purple and rose-colored and yellow at first began to fade away. Where was the white heron's nest in the sea of green branches, and was this wonderful sight and pageant of the world the only reward for having climbed to such a giddy height? Now look down again, Sylvia, where the green marsh is set among the shining birches and dark hemlocks; there where you saw the white heron once you will see him again; look, look! a white spot of him like a single floating feather comes up from the dead hemlock and grows larger, and rises, and comes close at last, and goes by the landmark pine with steady sweep of wing and outstretched slender neck and crested head. And wait! wait! do not move a foot or a finger, little girl, do not send an arrow of light and consciousness from your two eager eyes, for the heron has perched on a pine bough not far beyond yours, and cries back to his mate on the nest and plumes his feathers for the new day!

The child gives a long sigh a minute later when a company of shouting cat-birds comes also to the tree, and vexed by their fluttering and lawlessness the solemn heron goes away. She knows his secret now, the wild, light, slender bird that floats and wavers, and goes back like an arrow presently to his home in the green world beneath. Then Sylvia, well satisfied, makes her perilous way down again, not daring to look far below the branch she stands on, ready to cry sometimes because her fingers ache and her lamed feet slip. Wondering over and over again what the stranger would say to her, and what he would think when she told him how to find his way straight to the heron's nest.

"Sylvy, Sylvy!" called the busy old grandmother again and again, but nobody answered, and the small husk bed was empty and Sylvia had disappeared.

The guest waked from a dream, and remembering his day's pleasure hurried to dress himself that might it sooner begin. He was sure from the way the shy little girl looked once or twice yesterday that she had at least seen the white heron, and now she must really be made to tell. Here she comes now, paler than ever, and her worn old frock is torn and tattered, and smeared with pine pitch. The grandmother and the sportsman stand in the door together and question her, and the splendid moment has come to speak of the dead hemlock-tree by the green marsh.

But Sylvia does not speak after all, though the old grandmother fretfully rebukes her, and the young man's kind, appealing eyes are looking straight in her own. He can make them rich with money; he has promised it, and they are poor now. He is so well worth making happy, and he waits to hear the story she can tell.

40   No, she must keep silence! What is it that suddenly forbids her and makes her dumb? Has she been nine years growing and now, when the great world for the first time puts out a hand to her, must she thrust it aside for a bird's sake? The murmur of the pine's green branches is in her ears, she remembers how the white heron came flying through the golden air and how they watched the sea and the morning together, and Sylvia cannot speak; she cannot tell the heron's secret and give its life away.

Dear loyalty, that suffered a sharp pang as the guest went away disappointed later in the day, that could have served and followed him and loved him as a dog loves! Many a night Sylvia heard the echo of his whistle haunting the pasture path as she came home with the loitering cow. She forgot even her sorrow at the sharp report of his gun and the sight of thrushes and sparrows dropping silent to the ground, their songs hushed and their pretty feathers stained and wet with blood. Were the birds better friends than their hunter might have been,—who can tell? Whatever treasures were lost to her, woodlands and summer-time, remember! Bring your gifts and graces and tell your secrets to this lonely country child!

INQUIRING FURTHER

1. What do you think of Sylvia's character at the beginning of the story? Does she seem to be a typical nine-year-old girl?

2. How would you analyze the description of Sylvia's climbing the tree to locate the nest of the heron? What do the passages say about Sylvia's relationship with nature? How might they relate to her attraction for the ornithologist? Write a paragraph or two interpreting the episode.

WILLIAM WORDSWORTH

A central figure in British Romanticism, William Wordsworth (1770–1850) represents in his poetry the Romantic conception of a close connection between humans and nature, what Wordsworth described with the image of the "correspondent breeze" that brings the poet and the surrounding world into a sympathetic relationship. Wordsworth collaborated often with his sister, Dorothy, during his life and with fellow poet Samuel Taylor Coleridge. "Lines Composed Above Tintern Abbey" established Wordsworth's status as a nature poet, with its complex treatment of the maturing relationship between nature and the speaker of the poem. We offer an enhanced reading of the poem on our CD.

Enhanced reading of "Tintern Abbey"

Lines Composed Above Tintern Abbey

ELIZABETH BISHOP

"The Fish" by Elizabeth Bishop (1911–1979) has been anthologized more than any of her other poems. Bishop wrote the piece in early 1940, while living in Key West, Florida where she frequently tried her hand at fishing. The poem has been praised for its close attention to detail that creates a vivid depiction of the fish, a sort of word picture. For another of Bishop's poems written in Key West, see "Roosters" on page 510.

The Fish

I caught a tremendous fish
and held him beside the boat
half out of water, with my hook
fast in a corner of his mouth.
5   He didn't fight.
He hadn't fought at all.
He hung a grunting weight,
battered and venerable
and homely. Here and there
10   his brown skin hung in strips
like ancient wallpaper,
and its pattern of darker brown
was like wallpaper:
shapes like full-blown roses
15   stained and lost through age.
He was speckled with barnacles,
fine rosettes of lime,
and infested
with tiny white sea-lice,
20   and underneath two or three
rags of green weed hung down.
While his gills were breathing in
the terrible oxygen
—the frightening gills,
25   fresh and crisp with blood,
that can cut so badly—
I thought of the coarse white flesh
packed in like feathers,
the big bones and the little bones,
30   the dramatic reds and blacks

of his shiny entrails,
and the pink swim-bladder
like a big peony.
I looked into his eyes
35   which were far larger than mine
but shallower, and yellowed,
the irises backed and packed
with tarnished tinfoil
seen through the lenses
40   of old scratched isinglass.
They shifted a little, but not
to return my stare.
—It was more like the tipping
of an object toward the light.
45   I admired his sullen face,
the mechanism of his jaw,
and then I saw
that from his lower lip
—if you could call it a lip—
50   grim, wet, and weaponlike,
hung five old pieces of fish-line,
or four and a wire leader
with the swivel still attached,
with all their five big hooks
55   grown firmly in his mouth.
A green line, frayed at the end
where he broke it, two heavier lines,
and a fine black thread
still crimped from the strain and snap
60   when it broke and he got away.
Like medals with their ribbons
frayed and wavering,
a five-haired beard of wisdom
trailing from his aching jaw.
65   I stared and stared
and victory filled up
the little rented boat,
from the pool of bilge
where oil had spread a rainbow
70   around the rusted engine
to the bailer rusted orange,
the sun-cracked thwarts,
the oarlocks on their strings,
the gunnels—until everything
75   was rainbow, rainbow, rainbow!
And I let the fish go.

INQUIRING FURTHER

1. How does the poem use description to convey a picture of the fish? List several examples of passages that you find to be exceptionally vivid.

2. How do you interpret the line, "and victory filled up / the little rented boat"? What might the victory refer to? How does the rest of the poem prepare us for the victory?

3. What do you think of the ending of the poem? How would the message of the poem change if the fish had not been let go?

Hudson River Artists

In the mid-nineteenth century, literary figures such as Ralph Waldo Emerson, William Cullen Bryant, and Walt Whitman called for a break from European allegiances in art, and the establishment of an American creative identity. One of the most significant responses to this call formed in the field of landscape painting, particularly in a movement known as the Hudson River School. Artists like Thomas Cole and Asher Durand painted majestic scenes of the American wilderness. Their images may be said to echo some of the sentiments of Romanticism, which ascribed a spiritual power to nature and a sympathetic relationship between people and the natural world. These lush landscapes expressed a pre-Civil War sense of a divine expanse of nature open with possibilities for exploration and an optimistic American identity.

Works by Hudson River artists

THOMAS BIRCH

Anticipating the Hudson River School painters, Thomas Birch (1779–1851) brought a European influence to his work, imitating the landscape and estate painting of English artists like John Constable. Birch's work expresses a sense of prosperity and promise for early nineteenth-century America, while capturing much of the natural beauty of the Eastern United States.

The Narrows, New York Bay

FIGURE 18.3   Thomas Birch, *The Narrows, New York Bay*
Thomas Birch, American, 1779–1851, The Narrows, New York Bay, 1812, oil on wood panel, 20 x 36 3/4 in., Fine Arts Museum of San Francisco, Gift of Mr. and Mrs. John D. Rockefeller, 1979.7.17

THOMAS COLE

Founder of the Hudson River School, Thomas Cole (1801–1848) empha-
sized the dramas present in natural scenes. His early work consisted of
majestic landscapes depicting the American wilderness. Upon returning
from Europe in 1832, he turned his attention toward paintings with
more explicit messages, composing a series of paintings called The Course of
Empire *(1832–1836) that depicted the rise and fall of an empire and*
reflected a growing ambivalence toward American expansionism. The
Arch of Nero *was painted in 1846.*

The Arch of Nero

FIGURE 18.4   Thomas Cole, *The Arch of Nero*

ASHER DURAND

Asher Durand (1796–1886) frequently painted works with an allegori-
cal message, or with literary associations. He also advocated painting as
a form of nature study, composing many of his landscapes based on obser-
vations and personal experience. Kindred Spirits *was painted just after the*
death of Thomas Cole, and depicts two figures believed to be Cole and
the poet William Cullen Bryant.

Kindred Spirits

FIGURE 18.5   Asher Durand, *Kindred Spirits*

INQUIRING FURTHER

1. How would you describe the atmosphere of Birch's *The Narrows, New York Bay*? What does the painting suggest about the relationship between humans and nature?

2. How would you interpret *The Arch of Nero* in terms of attitudes toward American expansion? Write a one-or-more-page analysis of the painting exploring its messages.

3. Although Durand advocated objective studies as a way of representing the natural world, the waterfalls in the background and the ledge on which the figures stand in *Kindred Spirits* are actually from two different settings. What do you think of this distortion of the natural world? What other strategies can you find in the painting that manipulate representation to convey a message?

4. In what ways can the paintings of Birch, Cole, and Durand be called literary? Where in the images can you find drama? Can you recognize ideas, history, or culture expressed in the images? Write a paper in which you explain how two or more of the paintings tell a story.

REPRESENTING THE AMERICAN WEST

Throughout the expansion of the American frontier, particularly in the last two hundred years, the West has held an allure of opportunity and adventure represented in the concept of Manifest Destiny (the belief that Americans had an obligation to open up and settle the West). At the same time, Native Americans have created and handed down their own stories about this region. These stories reflect longstanding relationships between native peoples and the natural world. We also find in representations of the West, elements of Hispanic cultures that have been a key part of the region for the last five hundred years. We see in the diverse images of Western life the tensions between expansion and preservation, the conflicting interests of people, and the shaping influence of the environment on life.

JANE TOMPKINS

Jane Tompkins stands as a key figure in efforts to open the literary canon to works by women writers. Her interests also include depictions of heroes in Western film and fiction. Her 1992 book West of Everything: The Inner Life of Westerns *explores how representations of the West have long-lasting influences on cultural attitudes and behavior. "At the Buffalo Bill Museum, June 1988" is taken from* West of Everything.

At the Buffalo Bill Museum, June 1988

Studying the American West

The video at the entrance to the Buffalo Bill Historical Center says that Buffalo Bill was the most famous American of his time, that by 1900 more than a billion words had been written about him, and that he had a progressive vision of the West. Buffalo Bill had worked as a cattle driver, a wagoneer, a Pony Express rider, a buffalo hunter for the railroad, a hunting guide, an army scout and sometime Indian fighter; he wrote dime novels about himself and an autobiography by the age of thirty-four, by which time he was already famous; and then he began another set of careers, first as an actor, performing on the urban stage in wintertime melodramatic representations of what he actually earned a living at in the summer (scouting and leading hunting expeditions), and finally becoming the impresario of his great Wild West show, a form of entertainment he invented and carried on as actor, director, and all-around idea man for thirty years. Toward the end of his life he founded the town of Cody, Wyoming, to which he gave, among other things, two hundred thousand dollars. Strangely enough, it was as a progressive civic leader that Bill Cody wanted to be remembered. "I don't want to die," the video at the entrance quotes him as saying, "and have people say—oh, there goes another old showman. . . . I would like people to say—this is man who opened Wyoming to the best of civilization."

"The best of civilization." This was the phrase that rang in my head as I moved through the museum, which is one of the most disturbing places I have ever visited. It is also a wonderful place. It is four museums in one: the Whitney Gallery of Western Art, which houses artworks on Western subjects; the Buffalo Bill Museum proper, which memorializes Cody's life; the Plains Indian Museum, which exhibits artifacts of American Indian civilization; and the Winchester Arms Museum, a collection of firearms historically considered.

The whole operation is extremely well designed and well run, from the video program at the entrance that gives an overview of all four museums, to the fresh-faced young attendants wearing badges that say "Ask Me," to the museum shop stacked with books on Western Americana, to the ladies room—a haven of satiny marble, shining mirrors, and flattering light. Among other things, the museum is admirable for its effort to combat prevailing stereotypes about the "winning of the West," a phrase it self-consciously places in quotation marks. There are placards declaring that all history is a matter of interpretation, and that the American West is a source of myth. Everywhere, except perhaps in the Winchester Arms Museum, where the rhetoric is different, you feel the effort of the museum staff to reach out to the public, to be clear, to be accurate, to be fair, not to condescend—in short, to educate in the best sense of the term.

On the day I went, the museum was featuring an exhibition of Frederic Remington's works. Two facts about Remington make his work different from that of artists usually encountered in museums. The first is that Remington's paintings and statues function as a historical record. Their chief attraction has always been that they transcribe scenes and events that have vanished from the earth. The second fact, related to this, is the brutality of their subject matter. Remington's work makes you pay attention to what is happening in the painting or the piece of statuary. When you look at his work you cannot escape from the subject.

5   Consequently, as I moved through the exhibit, the wild contortions of the bucking broncos, the sinister expression invariably worn by the Indians, and the killing of animals and men made the placards discussing Remington's use of the "lost wax" process seem strangely disconnected. In the face of unusual violence, or implied violence, their message was: what is important here is technique. Except in the case of paintings showing the battle of San Juan Hill, where white Americans were being killed, the material accompanying Remington's works did not refer to the subject matter of the paintings and statues themselves. Nevertheless, an undertone of disquiet ran beneath the explanations; at least I thought I detected one. Someone had taken the trouble to ferret out Remington's statement of horror at the slaughter on San Juan Hill; someone had also excerpted the judgment of art critics commending Remington for the lyricism, interiority, and mystery of his later canvasses—pointing obliquely to the fascination with bloodshed that preoccupied his earlier work.

The uneasiness of the commentary, and my uneasiness with it, were nothing compared to the blatant contradictions in the paintings themselves. A pastel palette, a sunlit stop-action haze, murderous movement arrested under a lazy sky, flattened onto canvas and fixed in azure and ochre—two opposed impulses nestle here momentarily. The tension that keeps them from splitting apart is what holds the viewer's gaze.

The most excruciating example of what I mean occurs in the first painting in the exhibit. Entitled *His First Lesson*, it shows a horse standing saddled but riderless, the white of the horse's eye signaling his fear. A man using an instrument to tighten the horse's girth, at arm's length, backs away from the reaction he clearly anticipates, while the man who holds the horse's halter is doing the same. But what can they be afraid of? For the horse's right rear leg is tied a foot off the ground by a rope that is also tied around his neck. He can't move. That is the whole point.

His First Lesson. Whose? And what lesson, exactly? How to stand still when terrified? How not to break away when they come at you with strange instruments? How to be obedient? How to behave? It is impossible not to imagine that Remington's obsession with physical cruelty had roots somewhere in his own experience. Why else, in statue after statue, is the horse rebelling? The bucking bronco, symbol of the state of Wyoming, on every licence plate, on every sign for every bar, on every belt buckle, mug, and decal—this image Remington cast in bronze over and over again. There is a wild diabolism in the bronzes; the horse and rider seem one thing, not so much rider and ridden as a single bolt of energy gone crazy and caught somehow, complicatedly, in a piece of metal.

In the paintings, it is different—more subtle and bizarre. The cavalry on its way to a massacre, sweetly limned, softly tinted, poetically seized in mid-career, and gently laid on the two-dimensional surface. There is about these paintings of military men in the course of performing their deadly duty an almost maternal tenderness. The idealization of the cavalrymen in their dusty uniforms on their gallant horses has nothing to do with patriotism; it is pure love.

10   Remington's paintings and statues, as shown in this exhibition, embody everything that was objectionable about his era in American history. They are imperialist and racist; they glorify war and the torture and killing of animals; there are no women in them anywhere. Never the West as garden, never as pastoral, never as home. But in their aestheticization of violent life, Remington's pictures speak (to me, at least) of some other desire. The maternal tenderness is not an accident, nor is the beauty of the afternoons or the warmth of the desert sun. In them Remington plays the part of the preserver, as if by catching the figures in color and line he could save their lives and absorb some of that life into himself.

In one painting that particularly repulsed and drew me, a moose is outlined against the evening sky at the brink of a lake. He looks expectantly into the distance. Behind him and to one side, hidden from his view and only just revealed to ours, for it is dark there, is a hunter poised in the back of a canoe, rifle perfectly aimed. We look closer; the title of the picture is *Coming to the Call*. Ah, now we see. This is a sadistic scene. The hunter has lured the moose to his death. But wait a moment. Isn't the sadism really directed at us? First we see the glory of the animal; Remington has made it as noble as he knows how. Then we see what is going to happen. The hunter is one up on the moose, but Remington is one up on us. He makes us feel the pain of the anticipated killing, and makes us want to hold it off, to preserve the moose, just as he has done. Which way does the painting cut? Does it go against the hunter—who represents us, after all—or does it go against the moose who came to the call? Who came, to what call? Did Remington come to the West in response to it—to whatever the moose represents or to whatever the desire to kill the moose represents? But he hasn't killed it; he has only preserved an image of a white man about to kill it. And what call do we answer when we look at this painting? Who is calling whom? What is being preserved here?

That last question is the one that for me hung over the whole museum.

The Whitney Gallery is an art museum proper. Its allegiance is to art as academic tradition has defined it. In this tradition, we come to understand a painting by having in our possession various bits of information. Something about the technical process used to produce it (pastels, watercolors, woodblock prints, etc.); something about the elements of composition (line and color and movement); something about the artist's life (where born, how educated, by whom influenced, which school belonged to or revolted against); something

about the artist's relation to this particular subject, such as how many times
the artist painted it or whether it contains a favorite model. Occasionally there
will be some philosophizing about the themes or ideas the paintings are said
to represent.

The problem is, when you're faced with a painter like Remington, these
bits of information, while nice to have, don't explain what is there in front of
you. They don't begin to give you an account of why a person should have
depicted such things. The experience of a lack of fit between the explanatory
material and what is there on the wall is one I've had before in museums, when,
standing in front of a painting or a piece of statuary, I've felt a huge gap
between the information on the little placard and what it is I'm seeing. I realize that works of art, so-called, all have a subject matter, are all engaged with
life, with some piece of life no less significant, no less compelling than Remington's subjects are, if we could only see its force. The idea that art is somehow separate from history, that it somehow occupies a space that is not the
same as the space of life, seems out of whack here.

15   I wandered through the gallery thinking these things because right next to
it, indeed all around it, in the Buffalo Bill Museum proper and in the Plains Indian Museum, are artifacts that stand not for someone's expertise or skill in manipulating the elements of an artistic medium, but for life itself; they are the residue
of life.

The Buffalo Bill Museum is a wonderful array of textures, colors, shapes, sizes,
forms. The fuzzy brown bulk of a buffalo's hump, the sparkling diamonds in
a stickpin, the brilliant colors of the posters—the mixture makes you want to
walk in and be surrounded by it, as if you were going into a child's adventure story. For a moment you can pretend you're a cowboy too; it's a museum where fantasy can take over. For a while.

As I moved through the exhibition, with the phrase "the best of civilization" ringing in my head, I came upon certain objects displayed in a section that
recreates rooms from Cody's house. Ostrich feather fans, peacock feather fans,
antler furniture—a chair and a table made entirely of antlers—a bearskin rug.
And then I saw the heads on the wall: Alaska Yukon Moose, Wapiti American Elk, Muskox (the "Whitney," the "DeRham"), Mountain Caribou (the
"Hyland"), Quebec Labrador Caribou (the "Elbow"), Rocky Mountain Goat
(the "Haase," the "Kilto"), Woodland Caribou (world's record, "DeRham"), the
"Rogers" freak Wapiti, the "Whitney" bison, the "Lord Rundlesham" bison. The
names that appear after the animals are the names of the men who killed them.
Each of the animals is scored according to measurements devised by the Boone
and Crockett Club, a big-game hunters' organization. The Lord Rundlesham
bison, for example, scores 124⅝, making it number 25 in the world for bison
trophies. The "Reed" Alaska Yukon Moose scores 247. The "Witherbee" Canada moose holds the world's record.

Next to the wall of trophies is a small enclosure where jewelry is displayed.
A buffalo head stickpin and two buffalo head rings, the heads made entirely
of diamonds, with ruby eyes, the gifts of the Russian crown prince. A gold
and diamond stickpin from Edward VII; a gold, diamond, and garnet locket
from Queen Victoria. The two kinds of trophies—animals and jewels—form
an incongruous set; the relationship between them compelling but obscure.

If the rest of the items in the museum—the dime novels with their outrageous covers, the marvelous posters, the furniture, his wife's dress, his daugh-

ter's oil painting—have faded from my mind it is because I cannot forget the heads of the animals as they stared down, each with an individual expression on its face. When I think about it I realize that I don't know why these animal heads are there. Buffalo Bill didn't kill them; perhaps they were gifts from the famous people he took on hunts. A different kind of jewelry.

20   After the heads, I began to notice something about the whole exhibition. In one display, doghide chaps, calfskin chaps, angora goathide chaps, and horsehide chaps. Next to these a rawhide lariat and a horsehair quirt. Behind me, boots and saddles, all of leather. Everywhere I looked there was tooth or bone, skin or fur, hide or hair, or the animal itself entire—two full-size buffalo (a main feature of the exhibition) and a magnificent stone sheep (a mountain sheep with beautiful curving horns). This one was another world's record. The best of civilization.

In the literature about Buffalo Bill you read that he was a conservationist, that if it were not for the buffalo in his Wild West shows the species would probably have become extinct. (In the seventeenth century 40 million buffalo roamed North America; by 1900 all the wild buffalo had been killed except for one herd in northern Alberta.) That the man who gained fame first as a buffalo hunter should have been an advocate for conservation of the buffalo is not an anomaly but typical of the period. The men who did the most to preserve America's natural wilderness and its wildlife were big-game hunters. The Boone and Crockett Club, founded by Theodore Roosevelt, George Bird Grinnell, and Owen Wister, turns out to have been one of the earliest organizations to devote itself to environmental protection in the United States. *The Reader's Encyclopedia of the American West* says that the club "supported the national park and forest reserve movement, helped create a system of national wildlife refuges, and lobbied for the protection of threatened species, such as the buffalo and antelope." At the same time, the prerequisites for membership in the club were "the highest caliber of sportsmanship and the achievement of killing 'in fair chase' trophy specimens [which had to be adult males] from several species of North American big game."

The combination big-game hunter and conservationist suggests that these men had no interest in preserving the animals for the animals' sake but simply wanted to ensure the chance to exercise their sporting pleasure. But I think this view is too simple; something further is involved here. The men who hunted game animals had a kind of love for them and a kind of love for nature that led them to want to preserve the animals they also desired to kill. That is, the desire to kill the animals was in some way related to a desire to see them live. It is not an accident, in this connection, that Roosevelt, Wister, and Remington all went west originally for their health. Their devotion to the West, their connection to it, their love for it are rooted in their need to reanimate their own lives. The preservation of nature, in other words, becomes for them symbolic of their own survival.

In a sense, then, there is a relationship between the Remington exhibition in the Whitney Gallery and the animal memorabilia in the Buffalo Bill Museum. The moose in *Coming to the Call* and the mooseheads on the wall are not so different as they might appear. The heads on the wall serve an aesthetic purpose; they are decorative objects, pleasing to the eye, which call forth certain associations. In this sense they are like visual works of art. The painting, on the other hand, has something of the trophy about it. The moose as Remington painted it is about to become a trophy, yet in another sense it already is one. Remington has simply captured the moose in another form. In both cases the subject matter, the life of a wild animal, symbolizes the life of the observer. It is the preservation of that life that both the painting and the taxidermy serve.

What are museums keeping safe for us, after all? What is it that we wish so much to preserve? The things we put in safekeeping, in our safe-deposit boxes under lock and key, are always in some way intended finally as safeguards of our own existence. The money and jewelry and stock certificates are meant for a time when we can no longer earn a living by the sweat of our brows. Similarly, the objects in museums preserve for us a source of life from which we need to nourish ourselves when the resources that would normally supply us have run dry.

25   The Buffalo Bill Historical Center, full as it is of dead bones, lets us see more clearly than we normally can what it is that museums are for. It is a kind of charnel house that houses images of living things that have passed away but whose life force still lingers around their remains and so passes itself on to us. We go and look at the objects in the glass cases and at the paintings on the wall, as if by standing there we could absorb into ourselves some of the energy that flowed once through the bodies of the live things represented. A museum, rather than being, as we normally think of it, the most civilized of places, a place most distant from our savage selves, actually caters to the urge to absorb the life of another into one's own life.

If we see the Buffalo Bill Museum in this way, it is no longer possible to separate ourselves from the hunters responsible for the trophies with their wondering eyes or from the curators who put them there. We are not, in essence, different from Roosevelt or Remington or Buffalo Bill, who killed animals when they were abundant in the Wild West of the 1880s. If in doing so those men were practicing the ancient art of absorbing the life of an animal into their own through the act of killing it, realizing themselves through the destruction of another life, then we are not so different from them, as visitors to the museum, we stand beside the bones and skins and nails of beings that were once alive, or stare fixedly at their painted images. Indeed our visit is only a safer form of the same enterprise as theirs.

So I did not get out of the Buffalo Bill Museum unscathed, unimplicated in the acts of rapine and carnage that these remains represent. And I did not get out without having had a good time, either, because however many dire thoughts I may have had, the exhibits were interesting and fun to see. I was even able to touch a piece of buffalo hide displayed especially for that purpose (it was coarse and springy). Everyone else had touched it too. The hair was worn down, where people's hands had been, to a fraction of its original length.

After this, the Plains Indian Museum was a terrible letdown. I went from one exhibit to another expecting to become absorbed, but nothing worked. What was the matter? I was interested in Indians, had read about them, taught some Indian literature, felt drawn by accounts of native religions. I had been prepared to enter this museum as if I were going into another children's story, only this time I would be an Indian instead of a cowboy or a cowgirl. But the objects on display, most of them behind glass, seemed paltry and insignificant. They lacked visual presence. The bits of leather and sticks of wood triggered no fantasies in me.

At the same time, I noticed with some discomfort that almost everything in those glass cases was made of feathers and claws and hide, just like the men's chaps and ladies' fans in the Buffalo Bill Museum, only there was no luxury here. Plains Indian culture, it seemed, was made entirely from animals. Their mode of life had been even more completely dedicated to carnage than Buffalo Bill's, dependent as it was on animals for food, clothing, shelter, equipment, everything. In the Buffalo Bill Museum I was able to say to myself, well, if these men had been more sensitive, if they had had a right relation to their environment and to life itself, the atrocities that produced these trophies would never have occurred. They never would have exterminated the Indians and killed off the buffalo. But the spectacle before me made it impossible to say that. I had expected that the Plains Indian Museum would show me how life in nature ought to be lived: not the mindless destruction of nineteenth-century America but an ideal form of communion with animals and the land. What the museum seemed to say instead was that cannibalism was universal. Both colonizer and colonized had had their hands imbrued with blood. The Indians had lived off animals and had made war against one another. Violence was simply a necessary and inevitable part of life. And a person who, like me, was horrified at the extent of the destruction was just the kind of romantic idealist my husband sometimes accused me of being. There was no such thing as the life lived in harmony with nature. It was all bloodshed and killing, an unending cycle, over and over again, and no one could escape.

30   But perhaps there was a way to understand the violence that made it less terrible. Perhaps if violence was necessary, a part of nature, intended by the universe, then it could be seen as sacramental. Perhaps it was true, what Calvin Martin had said in *Keepers of the Game*: that the Indians had a sacred contract with the animals they killed, that they respected them as equals and treated their remains with honor and punctilio. If so, the remains of animals in the Plains Indian Museum weren't the same as those left by Buffalo Bill and his friends. They certainly didn't look the same. Perhaps. All I knew for certain was that these artifacts, lifeless and shrunken, spoke to me of nothing I could understand. No more did the life-size models of Indians, with strange featureless faces, draped in costumes that didn't look like clothing. The figures, posed awkwardly in front of tepees too white to seem real, carried no sense of a life actually lived, any more than the objects in the glass cases had.

The more I read the placards on the wall, the more disaffected I became. Plains Indian life apparently had been not only bloody but exceedingly tedious. All those porcupine quills painstakingly softened, flattened, dyed, then appliqued through even more laborious methods of stitching or weaving. Four methods of attaching porcupine quills, six design groups, population statistics, patterns of migration. There wasn't any glamour here at all. No glamour in the lives the placards told about, no glamour in the objects themselves, no glamour in the experience of looking at them. Just a lot of shriveled things accompanied by some even drier information.

Could it be, then, that the problem with the exhibitions was that Plains Indian culture, if representable at all, was simply not readable by someone like me? Their stick figures and abstract designs could convey very little to an untrained Euro-American eye. One display in particular illustrated this. It was a piece of cloth, behind glass, depicting a buffalo skin with some marks on it. The placard read: "Winter Count, Sioux ca. 1910, after Lone Dog's, Fort Peck, Montana, 1877." The hide with its markings had been a calendar, each year represented by one image, which showed the most significant event in the life of the tribe. A thick pamphlet to one side of the glass case explained each image year by year: 1800–1801, the attack of the Uncapoo on a Crow Indian Fort; 1802–1803, a total eclipse of the sun. The images, once you knew what they represented, made sense, and seemed poetic interpretations of the experiences they stood for. But without explanation they were incomprehensible.

The Plains Indian Museum stopped me in my tracks. It was written in a language I had never learned. I didn't have the key. Maybe someone did, but I wasn't too sure. For it may not have been just cultural difference that made the text unreadable. I began to suspect that the text itself was corrupt, that the architects of this museum were going through motions whose purpose was, even to themselves, obscure. Knowing what event a figure stands for in the calendar doesn't mean you understand an Indian year. The deeper purpose of the museum began to puzzle me. Wasn't there an air of bad faith about preserving the vestiges of a culture one had effectively extinguished? Did the museum exist to assuage our guilt and not for any real educational reason? I do not have an answer to these questions. All I know is that I felt I was in the presence of something pious and a little insincere. It had the aura of a failed attempt at virtue, as though the curators were trying to present as interesting objects whose purpose and meaning even they could not fully imagine.

In a last-ditch attempt to salvage something, I went up to one of the guards and asked where the movie was showing which the video had advertised, the movie about Plains Indian life. "Oh, the slide show, you mean," he said. "It's been discontinued." When I asked why, he said he didn't know. It occurred to me then that that was the message the museum was sending, if I could read it, that that was the bottom line. Discontinued, no reason given.

35   The movie in the Winchester Arms Museum, *Lock, Stock, and Barrel*, was going strong. The film began with the introduction of cannon into European warfare in the Middle Ages, and was working its way slowly toward the nineteenth century when I left. I was in a hurry. Soon my husband would be waiting for me in the lobby. I went from room to room, trying to get a quick sense impression of the objects on display. They were all the same: guns. Some large drawings and photographs on the walls tried to give a sense of the context in which the arms had been used, but the effect was nil. It was case after case of rifles and pistols, repeating themselves over and over, and even when some slight variation caught my eye the differences meant nothing to me.

But the statistics did. In a large case of commemorative rifles, I saw the Antlered Game Commemorative Carbine. Date of manufacture: 1978. Number produced: 19,999. I wondered how many antlered animals each carbine had killed. I saw the Canadian Centennial (1962): 90,000; the Legendary Lawman (1978): 19,999; the John Wayne (1980–81): 51,600. Like the titles of the various sections of the museum, these names had a message. The message was: guns are patriotic. Associated with national celebrations, law enforcement, and cultural heroes. The idea that firearms were inseparable from the march of American history came through even more strongly in the titles given to the various exhibits: Firearms in Colonial America; Born in America: The Kentucky Rifle; The Era of Expansion and Invention; The Civil War: Firearms of the Conflict; The Golden Age of Hunting; Winning the West. The guns embodied phases of the history they had helped to make. There were no quotation marks here to indicate that expansion and conquest might not have been all they were cracked up to be. The fact that firearms had had a history seemed to consecrate them; the fact that they had existed at the time when certain

famous events had occurred seemed to make them not only worth preserving but worth studying and revering. In addition to the exhibition rooms, the
museum housed three "study galleries": one for hand arms, one for shoulder
arms, one for U.S. military firearms.

As I think back on the rows and rows of guns, I wonder if I should have
looked at them more closely, tried harder to appreciate the workmanship that
went into them, the ingenuity, the attention. Awe and admiration are the attitudes the museum invites. You hear the ghostly march of military music in
the background; you imagine flags waving and sense the implicit reference
to feats of courage in battle and glorious death. The place had the air of an
expensive and well-kept reliquary, or of the room off the transept of a cathedral where the vestments are stored. These guns were not there merely to be
seen or even studied; they were there to be venerated.

But I did not try to appreciate the guns. They were too technical, too foreign. I didn't have their language, and, besides, I didn't want to learn. I
rejoined my husband in the lobby. The Plains Indian Museum had been
incomprehensible, but in the Winchester Arms Museum I could hardly see the
objects at all, for I did not see the point. Or, rather, I did see it and rejected
it. Here in the basement the instruments that had turned live animals into
hides and horns, had massacred the Indians and the buffalo, were being
lovingly displayed. And we were still making them: 51,600 John Waynes in
1980–81. Arms were going strong.

As I bought my books and postcards in the gift shop, I noticed a sign that
read "Rodeo Tickets Sold Here," and something clicked into place. So that
was it. *Everything* was still going strong. The whole museum was just another rodeo, only with the riders and their props stuffed, painted, sculpted, immo-
bilized and put under glass. Like the rodeo, the entire museum witnessed a
desire to bring back the United States of the 1880s and 1890s. The American
people did not want to let go of the winning of the West. They wanted to win
it all over again, in imagination. It was the ecstasy of the kill, as much as the
life of the hunted, that we fed off here. The Buffalo Bill Historical Center did
not repudiate the carnage that had taken place in the nineteenth century. It celebrated it. With its gleaming rest rooms, cute snack bar, opulent museum shop,
wooden Indians, thousand rifles, and scores of animal trophies, it helped us
all reenact the dream of excitement, adventure, and conquest that was what the
Wild West meant to most people in this country.

40   This is where my visit ended, but it had a sequel. When I left the Buffalo Bill
Historical Center, I was full of moral outrage, an indignation so intense it made
me almost sick, though it was pleasurable too, as such emotions usually are.
But the outrage was undermined by the knowledge that I knew nothing about
Buffalo Bill, nothing of his life, nothing of the circumstances that led him to
be involved in such violent events. And I began to wonder if my reaction wasn't
in some way an image, however small, of the violence I had been objecting
to. So when I got home I began to read about Buffalo Bill, and a whole new
world opened up. I came to love Buffalo Bill.

"I have seen him the very personification of grace and beauty . . . dashing
over the free wild prairie and riding his horse as though he and the noble
animal were bounding with one life and one motion." That is the sort of thing
people wrote about Buffalo Bill. They said "he was the handsomest man I

ever saw." They said "there was never another man lived as popular as he was." They said "there wasn't a man woman or child that he knew or ever met that he didn't speak to." They said "he was handsome as a god, a good rider and a crack shot." They said "he gave lots of money away. Nobody ever went hungry around him." They said "he was way above the average, physically and every other way."

These are quotes from people who knew Cody, collected by one of his two most responsible biographers, Nellie Snyder Yost. She puts them in the last chapter, and by the time you get there they all ring true. Buffalo Bill was incredibly handsome. He was extremely brave and did things no other scout would do. He would carry messages over rugged territory swarming with hostile Indians, riding all night in bad weather and get through, and then take off again the next day to ride sixty miles through a blizzard. He was not a proud man. He didn't boast of his exploits. But he did do incredible things, not just once in a while but on a fairly regular basis. He had a great deal of courage; he believed in himself, in his abilities, in his strength and endurance and knowledge. He was very skilled at what he did—hunting and scouting—but he wasn't afraid to try other things. He wrote some dime novels, he wrote his autobiography by age thirty-four, without very much schooling; he wasn't afraid to try acting, even though the stage terrified him and he knew so little about it that, according to his wife, he didn't even know you had to memorize lines.

Maybe it was because he grew up on the frontier, maybe it was just the kind of person he was, but he was constantly finding himself in situations that required resourcefulness and courage, quick decisions and decisive action and rising to the occasion. He wasn't afraid to improvise.

He liked people, drank a lot, gave big parties, gave lots of presents, and is reputed to have been a womanizer (Cody, 16). When people came to see him in his office tent on the show grounds, to shake his hand or have their pictures taken with him, he never turned anyone away. "He kept a uniformed doorman at the tent opening to announce visitors," writes a biographer. "No matter who was outside, from a mayor to a shabby woman with a baby, the Colonel would smooth his mustache, stand tall and straight, and tell the doorman to 'show 'em in.' He greeted everyone the same" (Yost, 436).

45   As a showman, he was a genius. People don't say much about *why* he was so successful; mostly they describe the wonderful goings-on. But I get the feeling that Cody was one of those people who was connected to his time in an uncanny way. He knew what people wanted, he knew how to entertain them, because he *liked* them, was open to them, felt his kinship with them, or was so much in touch with himself at some level that he was thereby in touch with almost everybody else.

He liked to dress up and had a great sense of costume (of humor, too, they say). Once he came to a fancy dress ball, his first, in New York, wearing white tie and tails and a large Stetson. He knew what people wanted. He let his hair grow long and wore a mustache and beard, because, he said, he wouldn't be believable as a scout otherwise. Hence his Indian name, Pahaska, meaning "long hair," which people loved to use. Another kind of costume. He invented the ten-gallon hat, which the Stetson company made to his specifications. Afterward, they made a fortune from it. In the scores of pictures reproduced in the many books about him, he most often wears scout's clothes—usually generously fringed buckskin, sometimes a modified cavalryman's outfit—though often he's impeccably turned out in a natty-looking three-piece business suit (sometimes with overcoat, sometimes not). The photographs show him in a tuxedo, in something called a "Mexican suit" which looks like a cowboy outfit, and once he appears in Indian dress. In almost every case he is wearing some kind of hat, usually the Stetson, at exactly the right angle. He poses deliberately, and with dignity, for the picture. Cody didn't take himself so seriously that he had to pretend to be less than he was.

What made Buffalo Bill so irresistible? Why is he still so appealing, even now, when we've lost, supposedly, all the illusions that once supported his popularity? There's a poster for one of his shows when he was traveling in France that gives a clue to what it is that makes him so profoundly attractive a figure. The poster consists of a huge buffalo galloping across the plains, and against the buffalo's hump, in the center of his hump, is a cutout circle that shows the head of Buffalo Bill, white-mustachioed and bearded now, in his famous hat, and beneath, in large red letters, are the words "Je viens."

Je viens ("I am coming") are the words of a savior. The announcement is an annunciation. Buffalo Bill is a religious figure of a kind who makes sense within a specifically Christian tradition. That is, he comes in the guise of a redeemer, of someone who will save us, who will through his own actions do something for us that we ourselves cannot do. He will lift us above our lives, out of the daily grind, into something larger than we are.

His appeal on the surface is to childish desires, the desire for glamour, fame, bigness, adventure, romance. But these desires are also the sign of something more profound, and it is to something more profound in us that he also appeals. Buffalo Bill comes to the child in us, understood not as that part of ourselves that we have outgrown but as the part that got left behind, of necessity, a long time ago, having been starved, bound, punished, disciplined out of existence. He promises that that part of the self can live again. He has the power to promise these things because he represents the West, that geographical space of the globe that was still the realm of exploration and discovery, that was still open, that had not yet quite been tamed, when he began to play himself on the stage. He not only represented it, he *was* it. He brought the West itself with him when he came. The very Indians, the very buffalo, the very cowboys, the very cattle, the very stagecoach itself which had been memorialized in story. He performed in front of the audience the feats that had made him famous. He shot glass balls and clay pigeons out of the air with amazing rapidity. He rode his watersmooth silver stallion at full gallop. "Jesus he was a handsome man," wrote e. e. cummings in "Buffalo Bill's Defunct."

50   "I am coming." This appearance of Buffalo Bill, in the flesh, was akin to the apparition of a saint or of the Virgin Mary to believers. He was the incarnation of an ideal. He came to show people that what they had only imagined was really true. The West really did exist. There really were heroes who rode white horses and performed amazing feats. E. e. cummings was right to invoke the name of Jesus in his poem. Buffalo Bill was a secular messiah.

He was a messiah because people believed in him. When he died, he is reputed to have said, "Let my show go on." But he had no show at the time, so he probably didn't say that. Still, the words are prophetic because the desire for what Buffalo Bill had done had not only not died but would call forth the countless reenactments of the Wild West, from the rodeo—a direct descendant of his show—to the thousands of Western novels, movies, and television programs that comprise the Western genre in the twentieth century, a genre that came into existence as a separate category right about the time that Cody died. Don Russell maintains that the way the West exists in our minds today is largely the result of the way Cody presented it in his show. That was where people got their ideas of what the characters looked like. Though many Indian tribes wore no feathers and fought on foot, you will never see a featherless, horseless Indian warrior in the movies, because Bill employed only Sioux and other Plains tribes which had horses and traditionally wore feathered headdresses. "Similarly," he adds, "cowboys wear ten-gallon Stetsons, not because such a hat was worn in early range days, but because it was part of the costume adopted by Buffalo Bill for his show" (Russell, 470).

But the deeper legacy is elsewhere. Buffalo Bill was a person who inspired other people. What they saw in him was an aspect of themselves. It really doesn't matter whether Cody was as great as people thought him or not, because what they were responding to when he rode into the arena, erect and resplendent on his charger, was something intangible, not the man himself, but a possible way of being. William F. Cody and the Wild West triggered the emotions that had fueled the imaginative lives of people who flocked to see him, especially men and boys, who made up the larger portion of the audience. He and his cowboys played to an inward territory; a Wild West of the psyche that hungered for exercise sprang into activity when the show appeared. *Je viens* was a promise to redeem that territory, momentarily at least, from exile and oblivion. The lost parts of the self symbolized by buffalo and horses and wild men would live again for an hour while the show went on.

People adored it. Queen Victoria, who broke her custom by going to see it at all (she never went to the theater, and on the rare occasions when she wanted to see a play she had it brought to her), is supposed to have been lifted out of a twenty-five-year depression caused by the death of her husband after she saw Buffalo Bill. She liked the show so much that she saw it again, arranging for a command performance to be given at Windsor Castle the day before her Diamond Jubilee. This was the occasion when four kings rode in the Deadwood stagecoach with the Prince of Wales on top next to Buffalo Bill, who drove. No one was proof against the appeal. Ralph Blumenfeld, the London correspondent for the New York *Herald*, wrote in his diary while the show was in London that he'd had two boyhood heroes, Robin Hood and Buffalo Bill, and had delighted in Cody's stories of the Pony Express and Yellow Hand:

> Everything was done to make Cody conceited and unbearable, but he remained the simple, unassuming child of the plains who thought lords and ladies belonged in the picture books and that the story of Little Red Riding Hood was true. I rode in the Deadwood coach. It was a great evening in which I realized a good many of my boyhood dreams, for there was Buffalo Bill on his white rocking horse charger, and Annie Oakley behind him. (Weybright, 172)

55   Victor Weybright and Henry Blackman Sell, from whose book on the Wild West some of the foregoing information has come, dedicated their book to Buffalo Bill. It was published in 1955. Nellie Snyder Yost, whose 1979 biography is one of the two scholarly accounts of Cody's life, dedicates her book "to all those good people, living or dead, who knew and liked Buffalo Bill." Don Russell's *The Lives and Legends of Buffalo Bill* (1960), the most fact-filled scholarly biography, does not have a dedication, but in the final chapter, where he

steps back to assess Cody and his influence, Russell ends by exclaiming, "What more could possibly be asked of a hero? If he was not one, who was?" (Russell, 480).

Let me now pose a few questions of my own. Must we throw out all the wonderful qualities that Cody had, the spirit of hope and emulation that he aroused in millions of people, because of the terrible judgment history has passed on the epoch of which he was part? The kinds of things he stands for—courage, daring, strength, endurance, generosity, openness to other people, love of drama, love of life, the possibility of living a life that does not deny the body and the desires of the body—are these to be declared dangerous and delusional although he manifested some of them while fighting Indians and others while representing his victories to the world? And the feelings he aroused in his audiences, the idealism, the enthusiasm, the excitement, the belief that dreams could become real—must these be declared misguided or a sham because they are associated with the imperialistic conquest of a continent, with the wholesale extermination of animals and men?

It is not so much that we cannot learn from history as that we cannot teach history how things should have been. When I set out to discover how Cody had become involved in the killing of Indians and the slaughter of buffalo, I found myself unable to sustain the outrage I had felt on leaving the museum. From his first job as an eleven-year-old herder for an army supply outfit, sole wage earner for his ailing widowed mother who had a new baby and other children to support, to his death in Colorado at the age of seventy-one, there was never a time when it was possible to say, there, there you went wrong, Buffalo Bill, you should not have killed that Indian. You should have held your fire and made your living some other way and quit the army and gone to work in the nineteenth-century equivalent of the Peace Corps. You should have known how it would end. My reading made me see that you cannot prescribe for someone in Buffalo Bill's position what he should have done, and it made me reflect on how eager I had been to get off on being angry at the museum. The thirst for moral outrage, for self-vindication, lay pretty close to the surface.

I cannot resolve the contradiction between my experience at the Buffalo Bill Historical Center with its celebration of violent conquest and my response to the shining figure of Buffalo Bill as it emerged from the pages of books—on the one hand, a history of shame; on the other, an image of the heart's desire. But I have reached one conclusion that for a while will have to serve.

Major historical events like genocide and major acts of destruction are not simply produced by impersonal historical processes or economic imperatives or ecological blunders; human intentionality is involved and human knowledge of the self. Therefore, if you're really, truly interested in not having any more genocide or killing of animals, no matter what else you might do, if you don't first, or also, come to recognize the violence in yourself and your own anger and your own destructiveness, whatever else you do won't work. It isn't that genocide doesn't matter. Genocide matters, and it starts at home.

INQUIRING FURTHER

1. What do you think of Tompkins's claim that when we view trophies and mounted or stuffed animals in museums "we are not much different from [the hunters] who killed animals when they were abundant in the Wild West of

the 1880s"? Would you say Tompkins is exaggerating to make a point? What point is she trying to make?

2. Do you see Tompkins's experiences in the four museums as more similar or different? What do you think of her reactions to the exhibits? How do her reflections on the encounters relate to your own experiences with museums?

GEORGE CATLIN AND FREDERICK REMINGTON

George Catlin (1796–1882) practiced briefly as a lawyer before devoting himself to documenting the disappearing cultures of Native Americans. Beginning in 1830, he spent the next two decades traveling the American West and recording in his paintings the landscapes and people he encountered. Frederick Remington (1861–1909) studied fine art at Yale University before heading West in 1880 to document Native American and Western life. He spent the next decade moving between the West and New York, where he developed a successful career as an illustrator for magazines. He also began to publish short stories based on his encounters, and continued creating illustrations and oil paintings depicting the frontier.

Images of the American West

Paintings
by Catlin
and
Remington

FIGURE 18.6   *Catlin and His Indian Guide Approaching Buffalo under White Wolf Skins* by George Catlin

FIGURE 18.7   *The Wolf, a Chief* by George Catlin

FIGURE 18.8   *The Scout: Friends or Foes?* by Frederick Remington

FIGURE 18.9   *The Fall of the Cowboy* by Frederick Remington
1961.230—Frederic Remington, The Fall of the Cowboy, *oil on canvas, 1895, 25 x 35 1/8 inches, Amon Carter Museum, Forth Worth, Texas*

INQUIRING FURTHER

1. Of the paintings by Catlin and Remington in Figures 18.6–18.9, which do you prefer? Why?

2. From the title of Figure 18.6, *Catlin and His Indian Guide Approaching Buffalo under White Wolf Skins*, we can infer that Catlin is painting from memory of an experience he had hunting buffalo. Similarly, in his notes on *The Wolf, a Chief* Catlin reports details of the Wolf's dress and jewelry, suggesting that the paintings serve a documentary role. Do you find the paintings by Catlin more compelling as records of a culture or as works of art? How would you discuss the two functions in a paper?

MARY AUSTIN

Mary Austin (1868–1934) is often recognized as a naturalist for the detailed descriptions she wrote of the Owens Valley area of Northern California. She is further recognized for her activist stances on the environment and women's issues. Austin, however, also spent a good deal of time with Native Americans of the West. She wrote hundreds of short stories based on her experiences in California, Arizona, and New Mexico. "The Spirit of the Bear Walking" and "Stewed Beans" are taken from her collection, One Smoke Stories, *published in 1934.*

The Spirit of the Bear Walking

Hear now a Telling:

Whenever Hotándanai of the campody of Sagharawíte went hunting on the mountain, he took care to think as little as possible of Paháwitz-na'an, the Spirit of the Bear that Fathered Him. For it is well known that whoever can see Paháwitz-na'an without being seen by him will become the mightiest hunter of his generation, but he can never be seen by anybody who is thinking about him.

On the other hand, if a tribesman should himself be seen by the Spirit of the Bear Walking, there is no knowing what might happen. Hunters who have gone up on Toorape and never come back are supposed to have met with him. So between hope of seeing and fear of being seen, it is nearly impossible to hunt on the mountain without thinking of Paháwitz-na'an.

Hotándanai alone hoped to accomplish the impossible. He might have managed it at the time his thoughts were all taken up with wondering whether the daughter of Tinnemahá the Medicine Man could be persuaded to marry him, but at that time he did not hunt at all. He spent his time waiting at the spring where the maidens came with their mothers to fill their water-bottles, making a little flute of four notes and playing on it. After he was married, however, he tried again to dispossess his mind of the thought of Paháwitz-na'an. 'For,' he said, 'when my son is born he will have pride in me, and keep a soft place in the hut for the man who was the mightiest hunter of his generation.' Thus it was that he never went out to hunt on Toorape without thinking both of his son and the Bear Walking.

5   In due time the son was born, and though Hotándanai had not yet become the mightiest hunter, he was very happy. Always when he went on the mountain of Toorape he remembered his wish, and so missed it.

In the course of years the tribe fell into war with the people of the north and the son of Hotándanai went out to his first battle. But, as it turned out, the battle went against Sagharawíte, and the son of Hotándanai was brought home shot full of arrows. Then the heart of Hotándanai broke when he buried him. He said, 'Let me go, I will build a fire on the mountain to light the feet of my son's spirit, and there I will lament him.'

Clad in all his war gear he went up on Toorape, and all the way he thought only of his son and how he should miss him. So, when he had lighted the spirit fire, he said, 'Oh, my son, what profit shall I have of my life now you are departed!' And as he wept he saw something moving on the slope before him. He looked, for his eyes were by no means as keen as they had been, and behold, it was the Spirit of the Bear Walking.

Stewed Beans

Now I tellin' you thiss stewed beans story. Thass Apache story. Iss very fonny. You savvy stewed beans; how they make everybody go in his insides *r-r-r-ru, phutt-phutt!* Only if you not cook him right; if you pour the water off while they cooking two-three times, they not make. But if water is not poured off, then they make *phutt-phutt!* Well, I tellin' you.

There iss man in Apache Village in the Chirricahua Mountains, and his wife she not likin' him any more. She likin' 'nother man, only she don' tell him that, 'cause he don' live in her village. There iss three villages that make the same talk an' have one council, an' thiss man an' her husband they both bein' members of that council. So when thiss man from Lone Spring Village come over to Chirricahua Council, he visitin' that woman, an' some other times when he come on business. Thiss man is name Two-Comes-Over-the-Hill, an' thiss woman's husband is named Spotted Horse. Spotted Horse he think maybe Two-Comes-Over-the-Hill is comin' to see his wife, only he not sure. He never catch him; an' maybe he no like to catch him; only to make so that man don' think he not knowin'. He don' want to lose hees wife; only to make so that everybody been laughin' at thiss man an' not at Spotted Horse.

So then there is a Council, an' Spotted Horse think maybe so Two-Comes-Over-the-Hill will be visitin' hees wife. He watch an' he seein' hees wife makin' big supper, like when company comin', an' he stay 'roun' the house all after-noon. Hees wife she cookin' stewed beans; an' she want to go out an' pick some greens; so she say, 'I go pickin' greens, you watch those beans, an' make sure you pour the water off two-three times.'

So that man say, 'All right.' Well, he stayin' there while his wife pickin' greens, an' he don' pour that water off those beans, not one time. But when his wife come askin' him, he say, 'Yes, the water is pour off, two times.' So she fixin' the beans good; meat an' everything; an' when supper ready, he say he feel sorta sick an' he not carin' to eat any beans. Then he go to that Council, and when men sayin', 'How come you so early?' he sayin', 'Well, I didden' eat much sup-per tonight 'cause my wife left me to pour the water off the beans an' I for-got, so I not eatin' any beans,' an' everybody laugh an' make jokes with him 'bout those beans.

5   So it gettin' dark an' the Council wait until those mans from Lone Spring Vil-lage come, an' by an' by Two-Comes-Over-the-Hill come along an' sit in the Council. An' he sayin', 'You gotta excuse me 'cause I was eatin' supper with beans with meat an' greens,' so of course they excused him. Iss not polite for mans invit-ed to supper to eat too fast an' not eat a lot. So Spotted Horse say, 'I was goin' to ask you to supper at my house, but my wife left me to pour the water off the beans an' I forgot. You are a lot better off.' So they went on with the Coun-cil, an' by an' by the beans began to go *r-r-r-ru* in Two-Comes-Over-the-Hill's insides, an' pretty soon he begins to go *phutt-phutt!* An' Spotted Horse he kinda laughin' an' he say, 'Sounds like you been eatin' some of my wife's beans,' an' Two-Comes-Over-the-Hill he sayin', 'Oh, no, no, not at all.' An' the beans go *phutt-phutt!* An' pretty soon *phutt-phutt-phutt—phu—uttt!* An' everybody begin sort of laughin', so when the Governor of the Council calls for a vote, the beans goin' *r-r-r-ru, phutt!* An' somebody say, 'The beans don' got no vote.' Which make everybody laugh. An' Two-Comes-Over-the-Hill say, 'You gotta excuse me; I ain't feelin' so well.' An' Spotted Horse say, 'I gotta see my wife about this'; an' all the Council is laughin'. Every time Two-Comes-Over-the-Hill goes *phutt-phutt!* they laugh, an' Spotted Horse say, 'If you told me you were comin' to my house to supper, I would have poured the water off.' An' he act sorry like, so they all laugh an' laugh. So the Headman he say, 'You are excuse from this Council,' 'cause he don' like they all laughin' all the time.

So Two-Comes-Over-the-Hill he gathers up hees blanket an' he goes away from there. They watch an' see that he goes in the direction of Spotted Horse's house, an' go 'way from it in a few minutes. An' Spotted Horse when he get home see that his wife has been cryin'. 'Iss not your fault,' he say. 'I forgot to pour the water off. Next time old *Phutt-Phutt* is comin', I think you better tell me.' She say, 'There ain't goin' to be no next time. That Two-Comes-Over-the-Hill, he iss got no highness.' Sure 'nough, he is not comin' there again where he is call' *Phutt-Phutt*, an' somebody always ask him if he would like some stewed beans. That's very fonny story.

INQUIRING FURTHER

1. How does "The Spirit of the Bear Walking" represent the relationship between people and the environment? What message do you think is offered by the appearance of the Spirit of the Bear Walking at the end of that story?

2. How would you respond to someone who said "Stewed Beans" trivializes Native American culture? Can you see ways in which the story might be offensive?

VIRGINIA DRIVING HAWK SNEVE

A Rosebud Sioux, Virginia Driving Hawk Sneve (born in 1933) learned a great deal from her grandparents. Both of her grandmothers often told her traditional tales from the Lokata and other tribes. Sneve has written about these tales as well as about her family history and culture in a number of works for both children and adults. In addition to her writing, she teaches English and has raised three children. "Jimmy Yellow Hawk" is taken from her collection, Grandpa was a Cowboy and an Indian and Other Stories.

Jimmy Yellow Hawk

"Grandpa, I don't want to be called Little Jim anymore. How can I change my name?"

Grandpa cleared his throat and asked, "Why don't you want to be called Little Jim?"

The boy was a bit embarrassed as he answered, "The other kids tease me about being a little kid because of the 'Little' in my name."

"Your name is the same as your father's—James. Since he is older and had the name first, he is Big Jim and you are Little."

5   "I know," said the boy, kicking a rock on the ground. "But I still want to change my name."

"Your parents could have called you Junior—would that be better?"

Little Jim shook his head. "That still means a smaller Jim."

"Hmm," Grandpa thought. "So, you want a more grown-up name?"

Little Jim nodded. Grandpa cleared his throat and said, "In the old days, there was an Indian boy your age who got a new name because of a brave thing he did.

10   "It was in the time of the long cold winter when there was more snow than any of the old people had ever known. The men hunted but found no game. The only food the people had was the corn the women had dried in the summer. Soon that was almost gone. The people were starving, so one of the younger and stronger men made the long trip to see the government man at the agency. He hoped the man would give him some food for the people. He returned with a bag of corn and nothing more.

"Soon after the young man returned he got sick. It was a coughing sickness he had caught from the agency people. It wasn't long before others were sick and the men became too weak to hunt.

"There was a boy in the tribe who didn't get sick. His grandfather had taught him how to make snares to trap small animals. The boy had not been allowed to do any real trapping because the winter was so bad and his mother was afraid that he would get lost in a blizzard.

"When no one could go hunting, the boy decided that he would go down along the creek and set some snares. Maybe he could trap an animal they could eat. The boy did not tell anyone of his plan. He left the tipi in the morning while it was still dark and no one was awake.

"He went to the creek and then almost went home because it was so strange and different with the snow covering everything. He was scared, but he looked carefully along the bank and found tracks, so he knew that animals had been there. He set his snares and went home before anyone found out that he had been gone.

15   "The next morning he again left before anyone was awake. He checked his snares and found that he had caught two rabbits. He was happy and ran back to his tipi with the rabbits. His family was very proud of him and his mother made a stew with the rabbits and the corn from the agency. The stew gave needed strength to the hunters who were then able to go hunting again."

Grandpa paused to sip his coffee. He continued. "The whole band was very proud of the brave boy. In the spring when all were well and healthy again, a council was called and a feast was held to honor the boy.

"A deer was cooked for all the people and there was singing and dancing long into the night. At the end of the celebration the boy was given a new name. He was known as Goes Alone in the Morning and was not considered a little boy anymore but as one who was growing to be a man."

Little Jim liked the story and wished he had lived in the old times so that he could do a brave thing and not be called Little Jim anymore. Grandpa yawned and stretched so that Little Jim knew it was time to go to bed.

Little Jim dreamed about Goes Alone in the Morning, but in his dream he was the brave boy.

20   The summer was almost over, school would soon be starting, and still Little Jim hadn't thought of anything to do to change his name. One day he and his father were cleaning out the barn, and hanging way up in a corner, Little Jim spied what looked like odd-shaped metal tools.

"Hey, Dad," he called, "what are those?"

Big Jim smiled, "Why, I'd forgotten about them. They're my traps. I used to go trapping when I was a boy about your age. They sure are rusty."

Little Jim got all excited, "Do they still work, Dad?"

"Why, sure they will," answered Big Jim. "All they need is to be cleaned and oiled."

25   "Do you suppose I could use them," Little Jim asked eagerly.

"I don't know why you couldn't," answered his father. "In fact, I think trapping would be a good thing for you to learn."

Little Jim carefully took down the traps, found a rag, and started rubbing at the rust. "Whoa," said Big Jim. "You can't do any trapping till winter. Let's finish the barn first, then we'll work on the traps. There's a lot you'll have to learn about using them before you can trap this winter."

On the first day of school Little Jim rode his horse to his friend Shasha's house. His friend was often teased about his reddish hair and called "red red," which is what his nickname meant.

But Shasha didn't seem to mind being teased, like Little Jim did.

30   Little Jim told Shasha of his plan to do some trapping in the winter. "Maybe I'll catch a wolf or a bobcat and get an Indian name for doing a brave thing."

Shasha laughed. "Bobcats and wolves never get caught in traps, you dummy!"

Little Jim was hurt.

"Oh, all you'll probably get are rabbits," teased Shasha.

Little Jim felt bad that his friend didn't think much of his plan, but he was still going to do it. "Well, they might!" he said.

35   He'd show Shasha!

That evening after school Little Jim told Grandpa of his plan to be a trapper. Grandpa was pleased that Little Jim was going to learn how to trap but said it wouldn't be the same as Goes Alone in the Morning because Little Jim's family wasn't starving.

Now Little Jim was confused about the whole thing. He asked if it would be a brave thing if he trapped a bobcat or wolf.

"You will be using traps for small animals," answered Grandpa. "Bobcats or wolves are usually too smart to get caught in such traps."

"But could they?" insisted Little Jim.

40   "It's possible," answered Grandpa, "but if it did happen you would have to be very careful because they become vicious and very dangerous when trapped."

Grandpa went on to explain that there was bounty money for wolves and bobcats because they preyed on calves and sheep.

"What kind of a name would I get if I did catch one of them?" Little Jim asked.

"That," answered Grandpa. "would depend on how hard a job it was and how much the bounty was."

Grandpa smiled and went on, "You can trap rabbits. Some people buy their pelts, and they also make good stew."

45   Little Jim didn't think much of that idea. "I might be called Rabbit Boy if that's all I caught."

Big Jim went with him along the creek bottom and showed Little Jim the best places to set the traps.

"You have to pick a sheltered spot," he explained, "out of the wind where the snow won't drift in."

Little Jim listened carefully because he wanted to learn all he could so that he could trap by himself.

If Little Jim ever did trap a bobcat he was to leave it alone and get his father to help.

50   As soon as the first snows fell that winter, Little Jim took down his traps. After school, he rode his pony along the same places he'd checked for stray cattle in the summer, but now the snow made it all look different. He set his traps in the sheltered places along the creek that he and Big Jim had chosen.

All the next day in school he had trouble sitting still and paying attention to his lessons. He was so eager to get home he didn't even wait for Shasha, who yelled after him as he galloped out of the schoolyard.

"Hey, what's your hurry?"

"Gotta check my traps," Little Jim yelled back.

"Get your rabbits you mean," laughed Shasha.

55 But Little Jim didn't care and he hurried home. "Mama," he called as he rushed into the house, "I'm going to check my traps."

"Can't you say hello," Mama chided. "Don't you want a cookie or something to eat before you go? It will be a while before supper."

"Oh, yeah, hi!" said Little Jim. He stuffed cookies into the pocket of his parka and grabbed a burlap bag in which he would carry the animals home.

"Gotta hurry," he said, "see you later!"

That first day was disappointing, for he didn't trap a thing. But he carefully checked all of the traps and went home positive that the next day he would get something. Little Jim worked hard at trapping all winter. It never took him very long to check his lines because he rode his pony. Over his saddle was the bag to put the animals in. But, as Shasha had predicted, he caught only rabbits, and he was becoming discouraged. Grandpa liked rabbit stew and thought it was a good thing for Little Jim to trap rabbits. Although no one called him Rabbit Boy, he was still Little Jim, and it seemed to him that a trapper should have a better name.

60 One evening after school, when he'd been trapping for about two months, it was so bitterly cold and windy that Little Jim's mother didn't want him to go out to check his traps.

But Little Jim was sure that he must have caught something because there were unusual tracks, different from a rabbit's, around his traps.

He bundled up in his new parka and set out. The wind was blowing hard on his back as he rode and he was glad that he didn't have to ride into it. The first trap was empty, so he guided the pony through the deep snow to the next one. He had almost reached the brush where he had set it when he smelled the strong stink of skunk.

He reined in short. The pony danced around nervously and tried to turn toward home. Little Jim dismounted and walked cautiously to the trap. He didn't want to get any closer because of the awful stink, but he forced himself to move.

The skunk was lying still in the trap, and Little Jim let out the breath he had been holding. He knelt down to release the animal, but as he reached for the trap the skunk suddenly moved and Little Jim almost fell into the icy creek. The pony gave a loud whinny of fright and took off for home. Little Jim ran after it.

65 Little Jim's eyes hurt, his nose and lungs burned, and the awful stink was everywhere.

Coughing and gagging, with tears streaming from his eyes, Little Jim ran. He felt like throwing up.

Big Jim had finished chores in the barn and was in the yard when the pony ran through the gate. It had never come home alone before, and Big Jim knew something was wrong. He rushed into the house, grabbed his rifle and yelled, "I'm going out to look for Little Jim!"

He caught the pony and was about to mount it when he saw Little Jim floundering through the snow into the yard. Little Jim couldn't speak, but the skunkstink reached Big Jim before the boy did.

"Stop right there!" Big Jim ordered.

70 The boy was trying not to cry, especially since Grandpa had come outside and Mama peered out the door. She was holding her nose.

"Get a bath ready, Marie. Little Jim needs one!"

Big Jim made his son walk in front of him back to the place of the trapped skunk. From a safe distance, he shot the skunk. Little Jim released the animal, even as he gagged and retched at the terrible odor.

Big Jim handed him a length of twine he'd found in this pocket. "Hang it in a tree. In a few days we'll come back to get it—after the worst of the smell is gone."

At home, Big Jim told his son to go to the old shed behind the house where Mama and Grandpa had a tub of steaming hot water and soap waiting. Little Jim undressed and threw his clothes out the door. It was icy cold in the shed. Little Jim shivered, then gasped and jerked his foot back from the steaming hot water. But he lowered himself into the tub and Jim scrubbed himself all over. His mother wrapped him in a towel and a blanket, and Big Jim carried him into the house where Grandpa had warm pajamas and a chair waiting by the stove.

75   Big Jim had to pile all of the boy's clothes in the backyard, pour kerosene over the pile, and burn it because the skunk smell would never come out.

Little Jim, clean and not so smelly anymore, was terribly unhappy. Neither Grandpa nor his father had scolded him, but he knew his mother was upset about the expensive new parka that had to be burned.

Mama made hot chocolate for him and coffee for everybody else. They all sat around the stove not saying anything and then Grandpa cleared his throat as he usually did before starting to tell a story.

The story, this time, was about an Indian boy who didn't like his name and who wanted to change it because he thought he wasn't a little boy anymore. The boy had worked hard all winter learning to be a trapper and brought home many rabbits that made good stew. The boy had learned many things about trapping and his family was proud of him.

The boy had learned in a very hard way that it wasn't necessary to trap a big dangerous animal, like a bobcat, to have trouble. This boy hadn't earned a great name as Goes Alone in the Morning had, but neither did Lakota boys of today earn Indian names for deeds of valor in the old way.

80   Little Jim knew Grandpa was telling the story about him, but he said nothing.

Grandpa continued his story, "Now in the old way, this boy would have been given a name as a result of what had happened with the not-so-dangerous animal. Such a name might be Skunk Face, and he would have to go by that name whether he liked it or not. In the old way, when the people heard the name Skunk Face they would know right away how he had gotten his name."

Little Jim hung his head, but Grandpa went on.

"In the old way the boy would have to work very hard to show that he had learned from his experience. He would know that it is best to ride with the wind in his face when nearing a trap. He would know that he should never get close to the trap until he was sure the animal was dead."

Grandpa turned to Little Jim. "I think the name Little Jim is no longer right for you because you have learned many things as a trapper and provided your family with much good food this winter. But would you want to be named Skunk Face in the old way?"

85   Little Jim snuffled and wiped his nose. He shook his head. "No, I'd rather stay Little Jim."

His father put a hand on his son's shoulder. "When I was a boy I was called Jimmy. That is not a grand as Goes Alone in the Morning," then he smiled, "or as fancy as Skunk Face, but it would show that you are growing up."

"But the other kids will still call me Little Jim," he protested, wiping tears away.

"That," said his father," is not important because you know and we know that you are not a little kid anymore."

Mama rose and took the empty cups. "That's enough excitement for today," she said. "It's time for our boy, no matter what his name is, to go to bed." She gave him a hug before he went to his room.

90   "I think Jimmy is a fine name for a big boy," said Mama.

During the rest of the winter, Big Jim went out more often to help his son. He taught Little Jim where to look for rabbits and how to identify their tracks and tell them apart from the spoor of skunks and other wild creatures that sometimes foraged near the creek.

Little Jim came to know the special hunting grounds of all the animals that visited the creek. One day he pleased his father by recognizing the telltale signs left behind by a muskrat that had been digging for roots near the bank. Big Jim said, "If there were still mink around, that muskrat would be lucky to last through the winter."

"But minks are too tiny to hunt muskrats, aren't they?" Little Jim wanted to know.

"Don't you believe it," his father said. "Minks are lethal. They'll strike at anything that moves. Remember, they belong to the weasel family—the deadliest animals for their size that we know."

95   Mama was waiting supper for them one evening when Little Jim came bursting into the house, so excited that he didn't make much sense.

Mama and Grandpa grabbed their coats and went outside to see what all the commotion was about.

Big Jim, smiling very proudly, was holding up a mink for them to see. "See what our trapper got?"

"Oh, my," said Mama.

Grandpa said, "*waste!*" Both were very impressed. Mink had been scarce in the area for a long time and it was unusual for one to be trapped.

100   "Where did you get it, l'il . . . Jimmy?" asked Grandpa.

"In the same place I got the skunk," he answered, and they all laughed.

Big Jim helped skin and tan the pelt and then they took it to town. Big Jim was sure it would sell for enough money to buy a new parka.

The store was filled with people as they walked in. Shasha and his father were sitting on blocks of salt and greeted the Yellow Hawks warmly.

Big Jim placed the bag with the mink in it on the counter and took the pelt out when Mr. Haycock came over. "Hey, a mink!" the storekeeper said. He picked it up and carefully examined it. "They've been mighty scarce for a long time."

105   He held it up for all in the store to see, "Looks like a prime one, too. Where'd you trap it?" he asked.

Big Jim turned and spoke loud enough for everyone to hear, "My son, Jimmy, trapped it!" he said with pride in his voice.

"You don't say," said Mr. Haycock. He reached over to shake Jimmy's hand. "Boy, you're growing up! Congratulations."

To the others in the store he announced, "Hey, look here. Jimmy Yellow Hawk trapped this mink. Isn't that something?"

Jimmy couldn't stop grinning. He was happy about what he had done, but what pleased him more was that no one, not even Shasha, called him Little Jim. He had become Jimmy to everyone.

1. What role does the legend of Goes Alone in the Morning play in the story? In what ways is "Jimmy Yellow Hawk" a tale about storytelling?

2. What do you think of the way the relationship between people and the environment is represented in the story? How would you relate the trapping in the story to poems by Gary Snyder?

3. How would you compare "Jimmy Yellow Hawk" with other coming-of-age stories you have read? Would you say the story relates more to themes of innocence and experience than to Native American culture? Write a paper in which you explore the story from one of these perspectives, as you compare it with another work.

HONORÉ WILLSIE MORROW

"Breaking the Blue Roan" represents an example of the Western short story, a genre that has enjoyed considerable success in pulp magazines during the last century. The majority of these stories might fit stereotypically with our conceptions of Westerns; they feature rugged male heroes, bloody battles, and clear differences between the bad guys, good guys, and the women whom they either threaten or protect. At the same time, however, many Western stories were written by women, and the variety of pulp publications meant that countless stories that did not fit the mold made it into print. Honoré Willsie Morrow enjoyed great success publishing in the 1920s and 1930s. In her stories, she works with, but also modifies, the traditional themes of the Western. "Breaking the Blue Roan" was first published in 1921 in Everybody's Magazine.

Breaking the Blue Roan

John Hardy was born in Montana. But he did not grow up to be a sheepman, after all, because when John was a baby his father homesteaded in Wyoming. The homestead prospered and, when Bill Hardy died, he left John five thousand head of Herefords and a hundred or so of range horses. John was twenty-five when he inherited. At thirty-five he still was unmarried, a man of magnificent physique, best known for his taciturnity, his slowness, and his superb horsemanship.

In spite of his many acres and his herds John was not popular with the women of Lost Trail. Some of them said he was too lazy to make love. Some of them said that a man who was soft with horses, like John, never made a successful lover, others that John was too stupid to find a wife. All of which merely goes to prove that Lost Trail women were poor judges of men.

Quite unknown to the rest of the valley, John was in love, deeply, passionately in love, and had been ever since the new schoolma'am had come to the log schoolhouse on the mountainside. Not that Edith Archer, the schoolma'am, guessed this fact. She would probably have said that one of the Lost Trail girls bred to the saddle and to the bitter hard work of the ranch would be John's choice. At least she would have said this the first few months of her stay in Lost Trail. What she really said later is a part of this story.

Edith Archer was slender and gray eyed, with masses of chestnut hair wrapped around a finely shaped head. Her eyes and mouth were very beautiful, the eyes large, deeply set, and grave, the mouth richly curved and wistful. She was low voiced, an anomaly in Lost Trail where women spoke shrilly, and men spoke softly. She arrived at Lost Trail in September. By May the seven thousand feet of elevation at which the valley was set ceased to make her pant at the slightest exertion. She could stick on a well-broken horse, and she had tooled the Lost Trail school along at a pace unprecedented in the annals of that happy-go-lucky assemblage.

5   By May most of the eligible young riders of Lost Trail had offered themselves to Edith and had been refused. All but John Hardy and Dick Holton. Neither of these had proposed to the schoolma'am—John, because he did not want to add the pain of a refusal to his general sense of unfitness; Dick, because, for all that he was in love with Edith, he had plans afoot that did not harmonize with marriage. Edith herself looked on marriage as bondage which she had not the slightest desire to enter.

As John was loping past the schoolhouse late one May afternoon, Edith hailed him.

"Oh, Mister Hardy! Would you mind calling for my mail, too?"

John waved his hat and put his spurs to Nelly, who broke into a gallop and arrived at the post office in a sweating lather. A group of riders around the empty stove greeted him noisily. He grinned without losing the quiet dignity habitual to his blue eyes and said to the postmaster: "Give me Miss Archer's mail, too, Pete."

"How'd you get on that job, John?" demanded Pink Marshall. "I thought Dick here was on duty. Did you get yours, Dick? Say, I've done formed an ex-Archer club. Come on in, Dick, and Johnny, you'd better qualify!"

10   Dick, a good-looking man, dark and a little heavy around the jaw, laughed with the rest. "I ain't eligible yet, Pink. You go on with the mail, John. Maybe she likes elephants!"

"I don't know but what you'd better let me take her her letters, Pete," Pink went on. "A guy like John that's too lazy to court Edith Archer ain't got any love in him. And I still like to look at her, even if she don't want me."

"As for me," grunted Art Brown, "I like to listen to her. She's the only woman in the valley that don't bleat every time she opens her mouth."

One of the older men, Hank Lawson, spoke. "I'm going to make a try at breaking the blue roan mare tomorrow. Better come up, John."

"Handsomest horse in the valley. I wish you'd sell her to me, Hank," said John.

15   Hank shook his head.

"Anybody in Lost Trail that hasn't offered to buy the blue roan from you, Lawson?" asked Pete.

"Everybody's on record but Dick," replied the rancher.

Pete laughed. "Well, some folks has a prejudice against paying money for horseflesh."

There was an awkward pause. Dick had had some narrow escapes from the sheriff, but few people had the temerity to taunt him about it.

20   Pink came to the rescue. "You'd ought to form an ex-blue roan club, Hank!"

John laughed, lifted Pink by the collar and the slack of his breeches, and laid him across the empty stove, then went out.

Edith was sitting on the log door-step of the schoolhouse when John brought Nelly to her haunches before her.

She laughed. "Were you ever allowed to gallop alone on the enemy when you were in France, Mister Hardy?"

"I was put into the infantry," replied John with a smile.

25   "They didn't want you to scare the Germans to death, of course."

John's bigness was of bone and sinew. He jumped from the saddle without touching the stirrups, pulled off his hat, and handed Edith her mail. She looked up at him, still smiling.

"Little Charley Banes is watering my horse for me. Will you rest a bit, or must you go on?"

John pulled the reins over Nelly's head and sat down on the log beside the schoolma'am, who did not open her letters but sat waiting for the big rider to speak. Her eyes swept the powerful lines beneath the chaps and the soft silk shirt then paused on the stern modeling of the mouth and chin. Still John did not speak. His eyes lifted from the green-budding alfalfa in the valley to the menacing black saw edge of the Dead Fire range.

"Well," said Edith at last, "I hate to leave it all."

30   "When do you go?" asked the rider.

"I thought I'd wait for the Fourth of July rodeo," she said. "Shall you ride?" John nodded.

"Mister Lawson said he was going to ask you to come up to help him with the blue roan tomorrow." Edith looked at John inquiringly.

"Yes, I'll be up there, I guess."

35   "It must be a wonderful thing to have the skill with horses that you have," sighed the schoolma'am.

"You wouldn't think so if you'd been brought up in Lost Trail, and if you'd been brought up in Lost Trail, you'd have been spoiled."

"Spoiled! My word, man, what was there to spoil? If I'd been bred in this valley, I might have been wild and full of fight like the blue roan, but I'd have been really worth while. As it is, I'm just a soft Easterner."

"The blue roan wasn't bred in this valley. She's a wild horse Hank roped up in the Many Eagles a while back. And I can't see how anyone would want you to be bred in this rough, god-forsaken spot."

"Don't you like it?"

40   "Of course! But I'm rough and god-forsaken like the country. Nobody like you could put up with it very long."

The schoolma'am stared at the rancher curiously.

"Sometimes," John went on in his low-voiced drawl, "I get tired of it."

"What could you desire more than you have?" asked the school-ma'am.

"Well, even a rider likes something that's beautiful and fine in his life once in a while. The older I get the more I realize that the folks that marry just on cattle and . . . and like cattle . . . don't know anything at all about what there might be in love. There might be something that these Lost Trail folks don't realize exists, you know."

45   If Edith felt surprise, she did not show it. For long months she had tried to tempt John Hardy to share with her what thoughts lay behind the rugged dignity of his quiet face, and she was not going to stop the unexpected confidence by any show of amazement. She nodded her head. "There should be

the same beauty in love here that there is about those ranges yonder, just as subtle and just as enduring. But one would never expect to find it here . . . or anywhere else."

John drew a deep breath. But before he could speak, small Charley appeared with a little bay horse.

"Shall I help you?" asked John.

"If you don't mind," replied Edith.

But John did not offer his knee. Instead, he stepped up on the log, put his great hands around Edith's waist, and swung her to the saddle as if she were a child.

50   "Shucks!" cried Charley. "You don't have to do that. She can get on as well as anybody."

"That will do, Charles!" said Edith. "You may go now. We'll see you at the ranch tomorrow, then, Mister Hardy?"

"Yes, I'll be along."

John mounted and turned Nelly's head up the mountain. At the turn of the trail he looked back. Edith was still before the schoolhouse door. She waved her hand, and John waved back then rode on with an expression of profound depression on his sunburned face.

Edith boarded with the Lawsons at the north end of the valley. Their ranch of a thousand acres straddled Lost Trail Creek which tumbled like a liquid green opal past the corrals and down the alfalfa fields. The Lawsons' little log cabin was set in a grove of quivering aspens within easy access of the creek. There was no fence about the house, and cattle, horses, dogs, cats, and chickens inhabited the very door-step amid a litter of saddles, harness, spurs, lariat ropes, and nose-bags.

55   When John Hardy rode up the next morning about eleven o'clock, two or three riders were sitting on the fence. Mrs. Lawson was established on the hay wagon, and Edith was perched on the top bar of the corral gate, hugging the post. Hank Lawson was standing in the corral, holding a blue-roan mare by a lariat round her neck. John dismounted and tied Nelly to the hay rack.

"You're just in time, John!" cried Mame Lawson. "She's thrown the hull of 'em. She just dumped Dick, and they had to rope her to keep her from climbing the fence."

John lighted a cigarette and threw his long legs over the fence beside the other riders.

"She's sure a bird!" panted Lawson. "But ain't she a beauty? Got some Hambletonian in her, and some Morgan by her head."

"Gord, Hank, you'll be claiming Clydesdale for her yet, just because her mane's curly!" grunted Pink Lawson. "She's just the orneriest unbroke mare in Lost Trail, half Injun pony and the other half wildcat."

60   John, hunched on the topmost rail, looked from the panting horse to Edith and from Edith to the great white crest of Eagle's Peak which brooded with appalling intimacy over the Lawson ranch then back to the mare. She was about fifteen hands high, a spotless blue roan in color, with the magnificent mane and tail that the open winter range produces. She had the round strong back and barrel so desirable in the mountains, small feet and the lean, wiry neck that spelled ancestry, real if remote. She was panting, and her breast was foam flecked.

"Hard to mount?" asked John.

"Easy as a bolt of lightning," said Pink. "Look at the she hellion with her tail and neck as limp as a rag doll. Wouldn't you think she was stuffed with sawdust? Go to it, John! I hold the record to date. I stayed with her just six minutes. Hank's going to enter her down at Cheyenne Frontier Day as the Great Unbroke. I'd like to see one of those champeens tackle her."

John pulled off his coat and vest and dropped them across the fence. He drew his broad rider's belt tighter, adjusted his spurs, then put on his gloves again. "Who saddled her?" he asked.

"All of us," replied Hank promptly. "Everything's okay . . . new cinch and hackamore. But I warn you, she's got the makings of a killer in her."

65   Edith cleared her throat. "What's the idea of breaking her, poor thing? I've a queer sort of sympathy for her. You have a hundred horses, Mister Lawson."

Lawson looked from Edith's puzzled eyes to the row of grinning riders. "Well, she's got to be broke, ain't she?"

"I don't see why. You've lots of horses you never break."

"Yes, but she's a beauty, and she's got to be broke. Come on, John!"

John put his hand on the reins. The roan jerked her head high in the air. Lawson now shortened the lariat till he reached the animal's head then, with the mare backing and plunging violently, he loosened the noose and slipped the rope.

70   "You get on the fence, Hank," ordered John, "and don't make any more noise than you naturally feel you have to."

John had no quirt. With one hand gripping the reins firmly, he lighted another cigarette. As the match flared, the horse tried to rear, and the man jumped aside to avoid her forehoofs. Then he began to talk to her, now and again making a move as if to put his left hand, which held the reins, on the pommel. At each attempt the mare hinged violently backward.

"So, beauty, so! Why worry? Life is always like this. Better be broke by a man than by a mountain lion on the range. So. That's no way to act! So."

Edith, sitting on the gate, tried not to miss a word of the monologue.

"Wait, beauty, wait! You don't know what you've been missing. The best fun in life for horse or man is the saddle. Calmly now. Nobody is going to hit you over the head while I'm around."

75   Ten minutes of this and then Dick cried profanely: "Get onto the blankety-blank, John! What are you afraid of?"

Suddenly, and without touching the stirrups, John was in the saddle. The mare dropped her head. John established his feet quickly in the stirrups. She drew her legs together under belly; her tail flattened between her hind legs, and her ears lay back on her neck. She quivered, and the great muscles of her shoulders knotted. Then, with a wild squeal, she bucked, and the battle was on. She bucked all the way around the fence, coming down each time with a crack of her right side into the rails in the vain attempt to crush Hardy's leg. She split his boot, but if she hurt his leg, John gave no sign. When she had bucked so long that the spectators had lost track of the number of times she had circled the corral, she ceased her squealing and shot across the enclosure, straight for the gate.

"Get away, Miss Archer!" cried John.

The girl dropped without the gate just as the mare reared, jumped into the air, and came down on her side. John was standing beside her as she lay for a moment, kicking, and as she rose, he was in the saddle. With unmitigated enthusiasm the mare tore across the corral, again reared, and again came down on her side. Edith clambered up beside Pink Marshall.

"Will she kill him?" she asked.

80   "Shucks! Nobody hardly ever gets killed by horses out in this country," he answered. "You've got to hand it to old John! Sixteen minutes and she ain't budged him."

Edith drew a deep breath. Her eyes swept the glowing beauty of the range then dropped back to the blue roan and the rider whose soft silk shirt was wet with sweat. Again and again the mare, her eyes mad with fear and anger, jumped for the sun and fell back to her side.

"Twenty-five minutes!" cried Lawson.

As if she suddenly realized that she ought to be weary, the mare paused in the middle of the corral, head dropped, legs straddled. John warily lighted a fresh cigarette, but the tense muscles under his wet shirt did not relax nor did his spurs drop from the bloody flanks. His hat long since had rolled under the fence, and his damp yellow hair gleamed in the brilliant sunlight. No one spoke. For a full five minutes the roan stood quiescent; then, agile as a cat, she lay down and rolled. She enjoyed this pastime for several moments, evidently under the impression that she was crushing John into the muck of the corral. But when she regained her feet, he was in the saddle, and once more she resumed the bucking. John's face now was drawn and white under the dripping sweat. Again and again the blue roan threw herself against the fence.

"Fifty-two minutes, and he ain't pulled leather yet," grunted Lawson. "But he might as well quit. I'll send her down to Cheyenne."

85   "Don't engage space quite yet!" exclaimed Pink. "Watch this!"

The panting horse again was standing in the middle of the corral. John lifted the reins high above her neck and drove the rowels home. The blue roan broke into a gentle trot and slowly circled the corral until John brought her to pause and carefully and painfully dismounted.

"He sure grips 'em!" exclaimed Lawson.

"You'll note that she's spur and not quirt broke," added Pink.

"I ain't seen nothing better, not even on Frontier Day," cried Mame Lawson, "except when Annie Rice, the cowgirl, got killed!"

90   John walked over to the fence and looked up at Edith. She smiled a little unevenly.

"I'm glad you won," she said, "but I'm sorry for the blue roan."

John nodded. "I didn't hurt her. Not near as much as she hurt me. Maybe she'll live to thank me"—this with a smile that haunted Edith for many hours.

The other riders gathered about the haystack where Mrs. Lawson was dispensing coffee.

"I'd like to ride the blue roan," said Edith.

95   "You let her alone," John returned slowly, "till she's well broke. And I don't think Lawson can lady break her. Maybe he'll let me do it for him."

"Riding makes me sleep," said Edith. "For a year before I came to Lost Trail, I hadn't had a real night's sleep."

"What was the trouble?"

"Too much teaching and other things."

"A man?" asked John slowly.

100   Edith smiled. "I've liked many men, but I certainly never would admit that one of them had given me insomnia. And I don't think I'd walk in my sleep or dream queer dreams if I had the skill and courage to fight with the roan every day."

"You let her alone!" repeated John. "Even if you have liked many men, that doesn't teach you to control a wild horse."

Again Edith gave him a quick, inscrutable little smile. "Come and get some coffee."

John returned the smile and followed her to the hay rack.

"Well, Johnny," said Hank, "what are you going to charge me for breaking the beauty?"

105 "You mean you want me to take her home and get her in saddle-shape?"

"I sure don't! She's good enough for me to start with right now."

"You let me take her home, and I'll lady break her for you for nothing," said John.

"What's that for, Hank or the schoolma'am?" demanded Dick.

"Both," said John coolly.

110 "Don't you do it, Hank," said Dick. "It would be a shame to have a mare like that lady broke. And don't you think that John's taken the freedom out of her."

The others turned to follow Dick's gaze. The blue roan was standing on the far side of the corral, her head resting on the top bar of the gate. There was something dejected in the droop of the beautiful blue-brown body but something unquenchably spirited in the lift of the head toward the eternal hills. Edith looked from the blue roan to John and from John to Dick.

"I got a good horse that's lady broke that I'd admire to give you, Miss Archer," said Dick suddenly.

"No, thanks!" exclaimed Edith laughingly. "The blue roan or nothing!"

"Aw, she'll be running away the first chance she gets," retorted Dick. "Me, I hope she does." And he strode over to his dapple gray and trotted off.

115 There was a glorious moon that night. John could not sleep. All the long hours till midnight he lay tossing and thinking of Edith and wondering who the man might be who had given her insomnia for a year. After midnight he gave up the struggle, dressed, and went out to the corral where he talked to the horses and watched the dim outline of Eagle Mountain which guarded the Lawson ranch. He wondered if Edith were sleeping or awake with all the watchers of the moon that send weird calls into the whiteness of the night—coyote, dog, owl, and wildcat. They seemed indescribably melancholy to John, and he was glad when, with the coming of the dawn, the far calls ceased. He went to bed and to sleep.

At noon old Aunty Farmer, who kept house for John, woke him. "They want you to come and help hunt for the schoolma'am," she said.

John jerked on his trousers and strode into the dooryard. Pink Marshall and Art Brown were waiting for him.

"Hank sent word for us to come up," said Art. "Schoolma'am seems to have walked off somewhere last night."

Before he had finished speaking, John was throwing the saddle on Nelly.

120 "When did they miss her?" he asked, as they trotted out of the yard.

"Not an hour ago. Hank 'phoned to me then," replied Pink. "Said they always let her lie late on Sundays, she was such a poor sleeper. Mame tries to keep the house quiet. But when they went to call her for dinner, she wasn't there. At first they just thought she'd slipped out for a stroll without their noticing. Then Mame sees she hadn't dressed . . . just gone out in her nightgown and slippers."

"Her nerves must be in awful shape," volunteered Art. "How do you suppose Easterners get thata way? Whoever heard of a woman in Lost Trail having insomnia!"

"She'd better settle down here," said Pink. "She takes to this life fine."

"Shall we stop by for Dick?" asked John.

125 "He went to Cheyenne last night," replied Pink.

No one spoke again until they drew rein at the Lawsons' door. Mame greeted them.

"Hank's following the creek up. He said to tell you folks to scatter."

"Has he tried to put Shep on her scent?" asked John.

"Oh, yes, but you know Shep. He couldn't follow a skunk."

130 "Are you sure she went away in her sleep?" asked John.

"You just come in here, John," demanded Mame. "Art, you go get Shep. Maybe you'll have better luck. Hank's sort of harsh with dumb brutes."

"I'm better at it than Art," declared Pink, dismounting to collar the trembling collie.

John followed Mame to the door of Edith's room. It was tiny, with plain rough log walls but exquisitely clean. The bed was rumpled. The riding suit that Edith had worn the day before lay folded over the back of the chair. A little white pile of underwear was tossed across the chair seat. John stood with his sombrero in his hand, his quiet lips pressed in a thin line. Mame pulled aside the curtain which made a closet of one corner of the room.

"I know all her clothes, and there ain't a thing gone but her bathrobe and slippers. Besides, she told me that ever since she was a child, whenever anything disturbed her in the daytime, she was apt to walk in her sleep at night."

135 "What disturbed her yesterday?"

"How do I know? She never tells me what is really going on in her mind. But she's the nicest girl I ever saw, and I love her like she was my own kin."

John turned abruptly. "She must be right near. It's too rough a country for her to have gone far, dressed as she is."

"Why ain't she back then?" demanded Mame. "And there is another queer thing. The blue roan got away last night."

John made no comment. He already was mounting Nelly.

140 All day long they scoured the country in circles of ever-widening circumference. After sundown, before the moon rose, John returned to his house for a fresh horse and the equipment for living on the trail for a day or two. His arrangements made, he threw himself down to wait for the moonlight. And it seemed to him that he fell into a light doze and dreamed of Edith. He heard her low voice: *John! Help me, John! Help me!* He started from the couch with cold sweat on his forehead. "I'm going plumb crazy!" he muttered. "First time I've dreamed of her, though God knows she hasn't been out of my thoughts since she came here."

He pulled on his coat and went out to the corral. He mounted Pete and led Miss Lucky with a light pack on her saddle. The moon was just slipping over the far-flung silver line of the Indian range when Pete trotted out of the gate. John's first stop was at the Lawsons' for news.

"We ain't got a trace," reported Mame, "except one of the children found a little piece of her bathrobe on a nail in the corral. Looks like she must have dreamed of the blue roan."

"Let me see that piece of cloth," said John, following Mame into the kitchen.

The rancher's wife pointed to the bit of blue silk lying among the teacups on the table.

145 "What kind of a bathrobe was it?"

"One of those Chinese things you see in the store windows at Salt Lake. She said somebody brought it to her from China."

John stared at Mame with widening eyes. "You fix me a bundle of clothes for her, Mame," he said.

When she had done this, he rushed out of the room and put Pete to the lope. At the foot of Eagle Mountain he pulled up while he thought rapidly. He could recall a canyon weathered out of the pink sandstone which composed the chaos that lay between the Dead Fire range and Many Eagles, but it was so inaccessible that it seemed to him highly improbable that Edith could have come upon it. And yet, even as he sat debating with his common sense, he seemed to hear the low voice of his dream: *"John! Oh, John, help me!"*

With a groan he whistled to Miss Lucky and turned into the Many Eagles trail. He knew he was a fool. He knew that Edith must have wakened long before she had come this far, even if this had been her direction. Yet the potency of the dream overcame every protest advanced by his lifelong experience in the hills, and hour after hour he pushed toward the chaotic valley beyond Many Eagles.

150   It was after midnight when the trail around a mountainside opened into a canyon with sheer sides remotely edged by pines. The sides themselves were barren but in the moonlight of a brilliancy of color that was almost unbelievable. There were many rock heaps on the floor of the canyon. John threaded his way carefully among these, stopping to rest at frequent intervals. The elevation was over eight thousand feet, and the horses were making heavy work of it.

In one of these intervals he heard the dull, thudding tramp of an unshod horse. Before he could start his small cavalcade onward to meet the sound, a figure in a blue robe stumbled into view. It was Edith, and she was leading the blue roan.

When she saw John, she stopped and began to sob: "Oh, John! John Hardy!"

John dismounted and strode toward her. "Here I am, Miss Archer! What in heaven's name has happened?"

"I shot him!" sobbed Edith. "I had to!"

155   "Shot whom? Are you hurt?" John took the lead rope from her, and she clung to his arm, struggling to control her sobs.

"No, only bruised. Don't speak to me for a minute. I'm trying so hard not to make a fool of myself."

John stood patiently for a moment, then he said: "Suppose you don't try to talk at all until you get into the warm things I've got on Miss Lucky's saddle for you? You put 'em on while I go 'round the rocks here and make us a little camp."

Edith nodded, and John, after giving her the bundle of clothing, proceeded to make a great fire of sagebrush and scrub cedar. By the time the fire was going well, Edith appeared around the rocks in her riding suit, her face white and tense.

"Will you give me a drink of water?" she asked huskily.

160   John held his canteen to her lips. "Now, I'll put the coffee on to boil and get out the sandwiches Aunty Farmer fixed for me. Then you can tell me about it when you aren't so faint and cold."

"I must tell you now!" panted Edith.

John looked at her keenly. "Let me put the coffee pot on and then you can go ahead," he said. "Sit down here out of the smoke."

"I didn't get to sleep quickly Saturday night," began Edith, "and, when I did, I had troubled dreams. I kept dreaming of the blue roan and that both you and she were hurt. I thought I'd better go to your rescue, and in my dream I went out to the corral, roped the blue roan, and led her away. She was very hard to lead, and she kept pulling me down, and finally one specially hard fall wakened me. I was alone on a strange mountain trail, so cold and with my slippers all wet with dew. And I was so out of breath that I lay down under a cedar tree. While I was huddled there, I heard horses coming. I didn't know who it might be or whether it was just strays, so I didn't call. And then Dick Holton rode by with three horses, and one of them was the blue roan."

"The blue roan! Did you really let her out? I know you couldn't have roped her."

165   "I must have let her out. I always did dislike him, and he's the last man in Lost Trail I'd have wanted to rescue me. But I wasn't going to let him get away with that beautiful horse, especially as I felt guilty about her. So, after he had gone by, I followed him. I thought maybe he'd put her somewhere for safekeeping and then I could tell Mister Lawson."

"And you followed him? Far?"

"I don't know how far. It seemed a long time. And then I fell and, like a great baby, I cried out, and he heard me and came back. I was sitting against the rock I'd slipped off of, and he just stood and looked at me. I said: 'Where are you going with the blue roan?' and he said: 'I'm going to put her where your friend Hardy'll never glom his big hands on her. She was wandering loose, and she's mine now.'

"And then I saw that he'd been drinking heavily, and I told him I'd been walking in my sleep and that, if he'd tell me the way home, I'd be grateful. Then he laughed and said: 'God, lots of girls have been fond of me, but none of them ever followed me this way!' and he stooped over me, and I struck him as hard as I could, and he struck me back and tried to pick me up and kiss me. And he said: 'I'll fix it so you'll never want to tell anyone in Lost Trail you've seen me.'"

John walked up and down before the fire, his big hands opening and closing.

170   "Then I fought him and managed to get his six-shooter out of his belt, and I pressed it against him and pulled the trigger. And he dropped and rolled over . . . dead.

"Then I went and got the blue roan's lead rope and started for what I thought was home, and I got lost and I thought you'd never come."

John stood staring at her, cold sweat on his lips. "How do you know he is dead? Did you examine him? Where did the bullet go?"

"I don't know where it went. I couldn't have touched him, could I? I wasn't trying to run away. I am going to give myself up to the sheriff as soon as I get back."

"Give yourself up nothing!" cried John. "If you hadn't shot him, Lost Trail would have made a sieve of him. No one can get away with manhandling a woman or horse stealing on these ranges, even if he is a drunk. But maybe you didn't kill him."

175   He poured her a cup of coffee and held it to her lips with big hands that shook. She drank it and ate a couple of sandwiches.

"Could you sleep a little?" he asked when she had finished.

She looked at him with horror. "Sleep? No! How could I sleep with his awful voice in my ears?"

"Have you any idea where you were when it happened?"

"No," replied Edith.

180   "Was there any landmark you could describe? The moon was still high?"

Edith answered carefully: "The moon was just setting. There was a spring with a big tree growing above it."

"Blue Aspen Spring! Edith, you've swung clear around the mountain and aren't two miles from it now. We can get to it by a short cut up the wall yonder."

"Get to it? Do I have to see him again?"

"Edith, I want to see whether you really killed him or not before we report to Lost Trail. You can stay here. . . . "

185 Edith shook her head impatiently. "No. I told you I couldn't sleep with his voice in my ears."

"Will you do something for me?" asked John gently. "Won't you lie down on my blanket here by the fire and rest with your eyes closed until dawn?"

Edith looked up at him pitifully. "I know you despise me, but I don't dare close my eyes unless you promise to sit by me."

"I promise," said John simply.

He spread the blanket for her and, when she had laid down on it, he sat beside her. She slipped cold, trembling fingers into his and closed her eyes. John sat with his back against the rocks. The moon had set, and the firelight shone alone on the slender, rigid body of the girl, on her pale set face. A half hour slipped by, then John felt Edith's fingers relax, saw the lines between her eyes disappear, and knew that she slept. He tossed more wood on the fire with his free hand and waited. An owl hooted loudly. Edith started and jumped at once to her feet. Then she stared at John while recollection awoke.

190 "I'm ready to start," she said.

"The sun will be here in a few minutes." John nodded to the east.

Swiftly the dawn was pricking out the fronded tops of the pines far above them. Faintly above the farthest pines rose the gigantic white outline of the Indian range, moment by moment growing more vividly colorful until its splendor paled the prismatic tints of the canyon. They watched the mighty day arrive in silence. When the sun was free of the pines, John turned to the horses. They were pulling restlessly at their ropes.

"These poor brutes are thirsty," he said. "Did you water the blue roan yesterday?"

"Yes, in the afternoon at a little muddy spring. She grazed there, too."

195 "Did you have any trouble leading her?"

"No! Wasn't it queer!"

"Not so queer," mused John. "Sometimes you find a horse that's like a good dog and recognizes a friend. So, beauty!"—this to the restless blue roan as he approached her.

"Let me lead her," said Edith. "I do think a great deal of that horse."

"Yes?" John smiled a little. "One might not have suspected it. You mount Miss Lucky, and I'll give you the roan's lead."

200 And so they started. It was a short and not too arduous trip back to the Blue Aspen Spring. It came into view as they rounded the shoulder of the mountain. First they saw Dick's two cow ponies standing by the pool. Then they saw Dick lying by the water's edge. He raised his head at their approach. Edith gave a quick gasp. John dismounted and strode over to Dick's side.

"Where'd she get you?" he demanded.

"Left side and right hip," replied Dick weakly. "I was drunk."

"Bleeding much?"

"Not if I don't move." He lay staring at the sky, ghastly pale and worn.

205 "I'll leave you some grub," said John. "I'm going back and send the sheriff up here. I am not going to trust myself to touch you, you can bet on that. If

you aren't dead by the time he gets here, my advice is that you keep your mouth shut."

Dick's lips set in a grim line, but he said nothing. And so they watered the horses and rode away and left him. Edith did not speak for some moments. The relief was at first more than she could voice but, when after a mile of hard trail John called a halt for breakfast, she said: "It's like waking from a nightmare."

"I know," John nodded. "I'm about as relieved as you are but only for your sake. He deserved more than he got."

The breakfast was on the side of a mountain facing west. Remotely below lay the valley of Lost Trail. As they sat waiting for the coffee to boil, John said abruptly: "I wanted to kill him where he lay."

"After all"—Edith's eyes were on the red mists of Bear Mountain—"he didn't harm me, and I did save the blue roan."

210   John looked at Edith with something finer than admiration in his blue eyes. After a long pause he asked: "What are you going to tell the sheriff?"

"I am going to tell him the truth."

"You'd better let me say I shot him while I was taking the blue roan and that I picked you up elsewhere."

Edith looked at his grim face puzzled for a moment, then she exclaimed: "Oh, I see! But I'm not going to let you lie for me. Lies are very difficult. I never have met anyone I thought clever enough to lie. And what about the story Holton will tell?"

"I'll bet Dick tells nothing, and I'll bet he never stays in Lost Trail so long as I'm in it. And Lawson may shoot him up again for stealing the blue roan. He's good for a long stay in Rawlins if he gets well and, when he gets out of Rawlins, or before if I can get at him, I am going to beat him up so his own mother won't know him. But what I have got to do now is to keep the he and she gossips of Lost Trail from bandying your name about. Just leave the story to me, will you, Edith?"

215   He crossed over to her and sat down beside her, looking into her face with such a depth of earnestness that she said with a little uncertain color flaring in her cheeks: "Yes, if it won't get you into trouble."

"It won't!" He hesitated, then went on: "You haven't asked me how I came to be looking for you in such an unlikely spot." Edith watched his face without speaking, and John went on in his soft drawl: "We were all hunting for you from yesterday noon on. At dusk I went home for fresh horses, and I took a nap while I was waiting for the moon to rise. I dreamed that I saw you in the pink canyon in that blue Chinese thing and that you were calling to me like this: *'John! John! Help me, John!'* Did you really call to me?"

"Yes," admitted Edith reluctantly.

"Why?" Edith did not answer. "Did you call to the others, Hank and Pink and Art?" Still she did not reply, and John drew a sudden long breath. "Do you remember that talk we had at the schoolhouse, Friday afternoon, and I said that a man, even a rider, liked something beautiful and fine in his life once in a while. What did you think when I said that?"

"I thought how little the average woman really knows what goes on inside a man's mind. And I've been thinking that ever since. You see, any woman always thinks she's more refined, has more delicate perceptions than any man."

220   "Lots of 'em have," said John. "Me, I wouldn't know a delicate perception if I met one. Is that all you thought?"

Edith smiled whimsically. "No, I thought that most women were stupid egoists, me being among those present."

"I'm not sure what one of those critters is, but I know you aren't one. What did you really think about what I said, Edith?"

"Well, I thought how blind you were not to see the enchanting beauty of the Lost Trail country, and I thought, as I'd thought so many times before, how strange it was that all of Lost Trail's conversation was in sordid terms of cattle raising when some of it might quite normally be in terms of the most soul-stirring scenery that ever intrigued a poor, futile Easterner."

John stared at Bear Mountain and the glory of the brilliant clouds beyond it, as if he never before had seen them. "All my life," he said, "I have been look-ing for beauty till I found you."

225   "Me!" exclaimed Edith. "I'm just a tired Easterner with no nerve."

John grunted with a twisted smile at the blue roan then he said: "Do you remember that I said that maybe there might be something pretty fine about love that we Lost Trail folks didn't know existed? And you answered that there ought to be something as fine here in love as there was in the beauty of the ranges. Edith, will you tell me what love means to you?"

She answered a little hesitatingly: "I thought I knew when I was in my teens, but as I've grown older I've discovered that what I thought was love could never endure. Now I know that, no matter what anyone says to the contrary, the love that endures is a thing of the mind, intangible and permanent and based on the irresistible attraction of soul to soul and not of body to body."

John cleared his throat. "If your mind or soul or whatever it was called across the mountains to us yesterday and only I heard and answered, might it mean that I felt this . . . this . . . intangible . . . oh, Edith, help me! I never would have the courage to say this much if you had not called to me in my dream."

"I called only to you."

230   "Why?" urged John.

"When I saw you break the blue roan with gentleness, I knew that I could care for you, but I've always hated the thought of marriage so! But . . . but now after this experience . . . John, I guess you've broken me with gentle-ness, too."

"God!" breathed John. "Edith, could it mean that you would marry me?"

"It might." Her voice was a little uneven.

"Do you think you know how much and how little a man like me could bring you?"

235   Edith replied slowly: "I know that you are fine and simple and beautiful, like your great hills, and that your inner ear heard me call in my deep need."

John rose suddenly and lifted Edith to her feet. He took her tired face gently between his big palms and looked long into her eyes. Then he lifted her to his heart and kissed her. And she lay quietly, as if, after long wanderings, she had at last come home.

INQUIRING FURTHER

1. How does the setting of the story influence the characters? What elements of fiction seem significant in "Breaking the Blue Roan"?

2. What are your thoughts on the horse-breaking episode in the story? Does John come across positively? Is Edith's assessment that he broke the horse with gentleness accurate?

3. How would you analyze the story in terms of stereotypes? Are gender roles more complex than you would expect? How do thematic or plot elements relate to expectations for the genre? Write a one-or-more-page exploration of Western stereotypes in terms of the story.

4. How would you compare "Breaking the Blue Roan" with other stories that treat relationships between men and women?

EXTENDED INQUIRY

New Mexico in Word and Image

One particularly compelling environment for relating art, nature, and culture can be seen in the mountains, deserts, and mesas of New Mexico. Native American cultures have flourished for years in the Pueblos of New Mexico. Before Pueblo culture, the Native American history of the region reaches back well beyond the settlement of America by Europeans. There is also a strong Hispanic presence in New Mexico, dating to the settlement of the region by conquistadors beginning in the fifteenth century. During the last century and a half, the region has also attracted many artists, drawn by the diverse culture and dynamic natural landscapes.

Dating back over 25,000 years, Native people have lived and hunted in the regions of what are now New Mexico, Colorado, and Arizona. The highly evolved culture represented by the Anasazi peoples flourished from about the time of Christ up until the 1300s. Between the fourteenth and sixteenth centuries, this culture evolved into the nineteen pueblos that made up the networked society of New Mexico some 500 years ago. Navajo and Apache tribes have also established themselves in the region, living among the expansive environments of the northern mesas and the southern deserts. All of these Native American cultures continue to flourish in contemporary New Mexico.

European explorers have also found the region well suited to settlement. Early Spanish explorers, drawn by tales of the "Seven Cities of Gold," established missions and settlements. The history of this Spanish influence is complex. Attempts to convert Native Americans to Christianity and to control the region were met with resistance, culminating in the Pueblo Revolt of 1680. At the same time, Hispanic and Native American cultures have coexisted in New Mexico for the last five centuries and each plays a significant role in representing the people and places of the region.

Artists have found New Mexico to be well suited as a subject for their work. Many have also found in the region a spiritual environment in which they can develop their craft. Nineteenth-century artists frequently acted as recorders, using photography or painting to document the landscape and Native American people. In the early twentieth century, artists such as Georgia O'Keefe found in the region an atmosphere of spirituality and ready subjects for their art. Contemporary artists and writers continue to create images and stories representing the geography and people of New Mexico.

LESLIE MARMON SILKO

Although Leslie Marmon Silko (born in 1948) has a mixed heritage of white, Mexican, and Native American grandparents, she was raised in the culture of the Laguna Pueblo in New Mexico. She attended law school briefly, before devoting herself full time to writing. She is best known for her novel, Ceremony, *published in 1977. Her work often incorporates Native American stories and weaves mythic elements and rituals into the structure of her narratives. "Yellow Woman" is based upon a Laguna myth and was published as part of the collection* Storyteller *in 1981.*

Yellow Woman

My thigh clung to his with dampness, and I watched the sun rising up through the tamaracks and willows. The small brown water birds came to the river and hopped across the mud, leaving brown scratches in the alkali-white crust. They bathed in the river silently. I could hear the water, almost at our feet where the narrow fast channel bubbled and washed green ragged moss and fern leaves. I looked at him beside me, rolled in the red blanket on the white river sand. I cleaned the sand out of the cracks between my toes, squinting because the sun was above the willow trees. I looked at him for the last time, sleeping on the white river sand.

I felt hungry and followed the river south the way we had come the afternoon before, following our footprints that were already blurred by lizard tracks and bug trails. The horses were still lying down, and the black one whinnied when he saw me but he did not get up—maybe it was because the corral was made out of thick cedar branches and the horses had not yet felt the sun like I had. I tried to look beyond the pale red mesas to the pueblo. I knew it was there, even if I could not see it, on the sandrock hill above the river, the same river that moved past me now and had reflected the moon last night.

The horse felt warm underneath me. He shook his head and pawed the sand. The bay whinnied and leaned against the gate trying to follow, and I remembered him asleep in the red blanket beside the river. I slid off the horse and tied him close to the other horse, I walked north with the river again, and the white sand broke loose in footprints over footprints.

"Wake up."

5   He moved in the blanket and turned his face to me with his eyes still closed. I knelt down to touch him.

"I'm leaving."

He smiled now, eyes still closed. "You are coming with me, remember?" He sat up now with his bare dark chest and belly in the sun.

"Where?"

"To my place."

10   "And will I come back?"

He pulled his pants on. I walked away from him, feeling him behind me and smelling the willows.

"Yellow Woman," he said.

I turned to face him. "Who are you?" I asked.

He laughed and knelt on the low, sandy bank, washing his face in the river. "Last night you guessed my name, and you knew why I had come."

15   I stared past him at the shallow moving water and tried to remember the night, but I could only see the moon in the water and remember his warmth around me.

"But I only said that you were him and that I was Yellow Woman—I'm not really her—I have my own name and I come from the pueblo on the other side of the mesa. Your name is Silva and you are a stranger I met by the river yesterday afternoon."

He laughed softly. "What happened yesterday has nothing to do with what you will do today, Yellow Woman."

"I know—that's what I'm saying—the old stories about the ka'tsina spirit and Yellow Woman can't mean us."

My old grandpa liked to tell those stories best. There is one about Badger and Coyote who went hunting and were gone all day, and when the sun was going down they found a house. There was a girl living there alone, and she had light hair and eyes and she told them that they could sleep with her. Coyote wanted to be with her all night so he sent Badger into a prairie-dog hole, telling him he thought he saw something in it. As soon as Badger crawled in, Coyote blocked up the entrance with rocks and hurried back to Yellow Woman.

20   "Come here," he said gently.

He touched my neck and I moved close to him to feel his breathing and to hear his heart. I was wondering if Yellow Woman had known who she was—if she knew that she would become part of the stories. Maybe she'd had another name that her husband and relatives called her so that only the ka'tsina from the north and the storytellers would know her as Yellow Woman. But I didn't go on; I felt him all around me, pushing me down into the white river sand.

Yellow Woman went away with the spirit from the north and lived with him and his relatives. She was gone for a long time, but then one day she came back and she brought twin boys.

"Do you know the story?"

"What story?" He smiled and pulled me close to him as he said this. I was afraid lying there on the red blanket. All I could know was the way he felt, warm, damp, his body beside me. This is the way it happens in the stories, I was thinking, with no thought beyond the moment she meets the ka'tsina spirit and they go.

25   "I don't have to go. What they tell in stories was real only then, back in time immemorial, like they say."

He stood up and pointed at my clothes tangled in the blanket. "Let's go," he said.

I walked beside him, breathing hard because he walked fast, his hand around my wrist. I had stopped trying to pull away from him, because his hand felt cool and the sun was high, drying the river bed into alkali. I will see someone, eventually I will see someone, and then I will be certain that he is only a man—some man from nearby—and I will be sure that I am not Yellow Woman. Because she is from out of time past and I live now and I've been to school and there are highways and pickup trucks that Yellow Woman never saw.

It was an easy ride north on horseback. I watched the change from the cottonwood trees along the river to the junipers that brushed past us in the foothills, and finally there were only piñons, and when I looked up at the rim of the mountain plateau I could see pine trees growing on the edge. Once I stopped to look down, but the pale sandstone had disappeared and the river was gone and the dark lava hills were all around. He touched my hand, not speaking, but always singing softly a mountain song and looking into my eyes.

I felt hungry and wondered what they were doing at home now—my mother, my grandmother, my husband, and the baby. Cooking breakfast, saying, "Where did she go?—maybe kidnapped." And Al going to the tribal police with the details: "She went walking along the river."

30   The house was made with black lava rock and red mud. It was high above the spreading miles of arroyos and long mesas. I smelled a mountain smell of pitch and buck brush. I stood there beside the black horse, looking down on the small, dim country we had passed, and I shivered.

"Yellow Woman, come inside where it's warm."

He lit a fire in the stove. It was an old stove with a round belly and an enamel coffeepot on top. There was only the stove, some faded Navajo blankets, and a bedroll and cardboard box. The floor was made of smooth adobe plaster, and there was one small window facing east. He pointed at the box.

"There's some potatoes and the frying pan." He sat on the floor with his arms around his knees pulling them close to his chest and he watched me fry the potatoes. I didn't mind him watching me because he was always watching me— he had been watching me since I came upon him sitting on the river bank trimming leaves from a willow twig with his knife. We ate from the pan and he wiped the grease from his fingers on his Levi's.

"Have you brought women here before?" He smiled and kept chewing, so I said, "Do you always use the same tricks?"

35   "What tricks?" He looked at me like he didn't understand.

"The story about being a ka'tsina from the mountains. The story about Yellow Woman."

Silva was silent; his face was calm.

"I don't believe it. Those stories couldn't happen now," I said.

He shook his head and said softly, "But someday they will talk about us, and they will say, 'Those two lived long ago when things like that happened.'"

40   He stood up and went out. I ate the rest of the potatoes and thought about things—about the noise the stove was making and the sound of the mountain wind outside. I remembered yesterday and the day before, and then I went outside.

I walked past the corral to the edge where the narrow trail cut through the black rim rock. I was standing in the sky with nothing around me but the wind that came down from the blue mountain peak behind me. I could see faint mountain images in the distance miles across the vast spread of mesas and valleys and plains. I wondered who was over there to feel the mountain wind on those sheer blue edges— who walks on the pine needles in those blue mountains.

"Can you see the pueblo?" Silva was standing behind me.

I shook my head. "We're too far away."

"From here I can see the world." He stepped out on the edge. "The Navajo reservation begins over there." He pointed to the east. "The Pueblo boundaries are over here." He looked below us to the south, where the narrow trail seemed to come from. "The Texans have their ranches over there, starting with that valley, the Concho Valley. The Mexicans run some cattle over there too."

45   "Do you ever work for them?"

"I steal from them," Silva answered. The sun was dropping behind us and the shadows were filling the land below. I turned away from the edge that dropped forever into the valleys below.

"I'm cold," I said, "I'm going inside." I started wondering about this man who could speak the Pueblo language so well but who lived on a mountain and rustled cattle. I decided that this man Silva must be Navajo, because Pueblo men didn't do things like that.

"You must be a Navajo."

Silva shook his head gently. "Little Yellow Woman," he said, "you never give up, do you? I have told you who I am. The Navajo people know me, too." He knelt down and unrolled the bedroll and spread the extra blankets out on a piece of canvas. The sun was down, and the only light in the house came from outside—the dim orange light from sundown.

50   I stood there and waited for him to crawl under the blankets.

"What are you waiting for?" he said, and I lay down beside him. He undressed me slowly like the night before beside the river—kissing my face gently and running his hands up and down my belly and legs. He took off my pants and then he laughed.

"Why are you laughing?"

"You are breathing so hard."

I pulled away from him and turned my back to him.

55   He pulled me around and pinned me down with his arms and chest. "You don't understand, do you, little Yellow Woman? You will do what I want."

And again he was all around me with his skin slippery against mine, and I was afraid because I understood that his strength could hurt me. I lay underneath him and I knew that he could destroy me. But later, while he slept beside me, I touched his face and I had a feeling—the kind of feeling for him that overcame me that morning along the river. I kissed him on the forehead and he reached out for me.

When I woke up in the morning he was gone. It gave me a strange feeling because for a long time I sat there on the blankets and looked around the little house for some object of his—some proof that he had been there or maybe that he was coming back. Only the blankets and the cardboard box remained. The .30-30 that had been leaning in the corner was gone, and so was the knife I had used the night before. He was gone, and I had my chance to go now. But first I had to eat, because I knew it would be a long walk home.

I found some dried apricots in the cardboard box, and I sat down on a rock at the edge of the plateau rim. There was no wind and the sun warmed me. I was surrounded by silence. I drowsed with apricots in my mouth, and I didn't believe that there were highways or railroads or cattle to steal.

When I woke up, I stared down at my feet in the black mountain dirt. Little black ants were swarming over the pine needles around my foot. They must have smelled the apricots. I thought about my family far below me. They would be wondering about me, because this had never happened to me before. The tribal police would file a report. But if old Grandpa weren't dead he would tell them what happened—he would laugh and say, "Stolen by a ka'tsina, a mountain spirit. She'll come home—they usually do." There are enough of them to handle things. My mother and grandmother will raise the baby like they raised me. Al will find someone else, and they will go on like before, except that there will be a story about the day I disappeared while I was walking along the river. Silva had come for me; he said he had. I did not decide to go. I just went. Moon-flowers blossom in the sand hills before dawn, just as I followed him. That's what I was thinking as I wandered along the trail through the pine trees.

60   It was noon when I got back. When I saw the stone house I remembered that I had meant to go home. But that didn't seem important any more, maybe

because there were little blue flowers growing in the meadow behind the stone house and the gray squirrels were playing in the pines next to the house. The horses were standing in the corral, and there was a beef carcass hanging on the shady side of a big pine in front of the house. Flies buzzed around the clotted blood that hung from the carcass. Silva was washing his hands in a bucket full of water. He must have heard me coming because he spoke to me without turning to face me.

"I've been waiting for you."

"I went walking in the big pine trees."

I looked into the bucket full of bloody water with brown-and-white animal hairs floating in it. Silva stood there letting his hand drip, examining me intently.

"Are you coming with me?"

65 "Where?" I asked him.

"To sell the meat in Marquez."

"If you're sure it's O.K."

"I wouldn't ask you if it wasn't," he answered.

He sloshed the water around in the bucket before he dumped it out and set the bucket upside down near the door. I followed him to the corral and watched him saddle the horses. Even beside the horses he looked tall, and I asked him again if he wasn't Navajo. He didn't say anything; he just shook his head and kept cinching up the saddle.

70 "But Navajos are tall."

"Get on the horse," he said, "and let's go."

The last thing he did before we started down the steep trail was to grab the .30-30 from the corner. He slid the rifle into the scabbard that hung from his saddle.

"Do they ever try to catch you?" I asked.

"They don't know who I am."

75 "Then why did you bring the rifle?"

"Because we are going to Marquez where the Mexicans live."

The trail leveled out on a narrow ridge that was steep on both sides like an animal spine. On one side I could see where the trail went around the rocky gray hills and disappeared into the southeast where the pale sandrock mesas stood in the distance near my home. On the other side was a trail that went west, and as I looked far into the distance I thought I saw the little town. But Silva said no, that I was looking in the wrong place, that I just thought I saw houses. After that I quit looking off into the distance; it was hot and the wildflowers were closing up their deep-yellow petals. Only the waxy cactus flowers bloomed in the bright sun, and I saw every color that a cactus blossom can be; the white ones and the red ones were still buds, but the purple and the yellow were blossoms, open full and the most beautiful of all.

Silva saw him before I did. The white man was riding a big gray horse, coming up the trail towards us. He was traveling fast and the gray horse's feet sent rocks rolling off the trail into the dry tumbleweeds. Silva motioned for me to stop and we watched the white man. He didn't see us right away, but finally his horse whinnied at our horses and he stopped. He looked at us briefly before he lapped the gray horse across the three hundred yards that separated us. He stopped his horse in front of Silva, and his young fat face was shadowed by the brim of his hat. He didn't look mad, but his small, pale eyes moved from the blood-soaked gunny sacks hanging from my saddle to Silva's face and then back to my face.

"Where did you get the fresh meat?" the white man asked.

80 "I've been hunting," Silva said, and when he shifted his weight in the saddle the leather creaked.

"The hell you have, Indian. You've been rustling cattle. We've been looking for the thief for a long time."

The rancher was fat, and sweat began to soak through his white cowboy shirt and the wet cloth stuck to the thick rolls of belly fat. He almost seemed to be panting from the exertion of talking, and he smelled rancid, maybe because Silva scared him.

Silva turned to me and smiled. "Go back up the mountain, Yellow Woman."

The white man got angry when he heard Silva speak in a language he couldn't understand. "Don't try anything, Indian. Just keep riding to Marquez. We'll call the state police from there."

85 The rancher must have been unarmed because he was very frightened and if he had a gun he would have pulled it out then. I turned my horse around and the rancher yelled, "Stop!" I looked at Silva for an instant and there was something ancient and dark—something I could feel in my stomach—in his eyes, and when I glanced at his hand I saw his finger on the trigger of the .30-30 that was still in the saddle scabbard. I slapped my horse across the flank and the sacks of raw meat swung against my knees as the horse leaped up the trail. It was hard to keep my balance, and once I thought I felt the saddle slipping backward; it was because of this that I could not look back.

I didn't stop until I reached the ridge where the trail forked. The horse was breathing deep gasps and there was a dark film of sweat on its neck. I looked down in the direction I had come from, but I couldn't see the place. I waited. The wind came up and pushed warm air past me. I looked up at the sky, pale blue and full of thin clouds and fading vapor trails left by jets.

I think four shots were fired—I remember hearing four hollow explosions that reminded me of deer hunting. There could have been more shots after that, but I couldn't have heard them because my horse was running again and the loose rocks were making too much noise as they scattered around his feet.

Horses have a hard time running downhill, but I went that way instead of uphill to the mountain because I thought it was safer. I felt better with the horse running southeast past the round gray hills that were covered with cedar trees and black lava rock. When I got to the plain in the distance I could see the dark green patches of tamaracks that grew along the river; and beyond the river I could see the beginning of the pale sandrock mesas. I stopped the horse and looked back to see if anyone was coming; then I got off the horse and turned the horse around, wondering if it would go back to its corral under the pines on the mountain. It looked back at me for a moment and then plucked a mouthful of green tumbleweeds before it trotted back up the trail with its ears pointed forward, carrying its head daintily to one side to avoid stepping on the dragging reins. When the horse disappeared over the last hill, the gunny sacks full of meat were still swinging and bouncing.

I walked toward the river on a wood-hauler's road that I knew would eventually lead to the paved road. I was thinking about waiting beside the road for someone to drive by, but by the time I got to the pavement I had decided it wasn't very far to walk if I followed the river back the way Silva and I had come.

90   The river water tasted good, and I sat in the shade under a cluster of silvery willows. I thought about Silva, and I felt sad at leaving him; still, there was something strange about him, and I tried to figure it out all the way back home.

I came back to the place on the river bank where he had been sitting the first time I saw him. The green willow leaves that he had trimmed from the branch were still lying there, wilted in the sand. I saw the leaves and I wanted to go back to him—to kiss him and to touch him—but the mountains were too far away now. And I told myself, because I believe it, he will come back sometime and be waiting again by the river.

I followed the path up from the river into the village. The sun was getting low, and I could smell supper cooking when I got to the screen door of my house. I could hear their voices inside—my mother was telling my grandmother how to fix the Jell-O and my husband, Al, was playing with the baby. I decided to tell them that some Navajo had kidnaped me, but I was sorry that old Grandpa wasn't alive to hear my story because it was the Yellow Woman stories he liked to tell best.

INQUIRING FURTHER

1. How does the first person narration of the story influence your interpretation of "Yellow Woman"? Does the narrator seem reliable? What does the ending tell us about her sense of what has happened? What else would you say about her?

2. Consider the relationship between the past and the present in the story? What is the significance of the Yellow Woman stories from the past? What do you think of the story itself being told in the past? Write a page or two analyzing the relationships between the past and storytelling in "Yellow Woman."

3. Compare "Yellow Woman" with one of the stories about relationships in Chapter 17. In what ways might you say "Yellow Woman" is a typical love story? In what ways is it different? Write a paper relating "Yellow Woman" to one or more other stories.

E. A. MARES

E. A. Mares (born in 1938) studied and taught Spanish in college before devoting his attention to history and writing. His works include essays, plays, and poetry. "Once a Man Knew His Name" addresses the Pueblo Revolt of 1680. Spanish explorers began colonizing New Mexico beginning in the 1540s. Expeditions and mission colonies over the next 140 years experienced rising conflict with the Pueblo cultures, culminating in a revolt lead by a Tewa from the San Jaun Pueblo named Popé.

Once a Man Knew His Name

(dedicated to the memory of Popé, great leader of the Pueblo Revolt, 1680)

Enhanced
reading of
"Once a
Man Knew
His
Name"

My name was ripe with summer,
a cornucopia overflowing with food
for the Pueblos.
My name was the summer
5   and my name
gathered together the life giving maize,
the ripe squash, beans, and chile
that fed the people of Oke Oweenge
and all the Pueblos along the Rio Grande.

10   As a child
I ran along the banks of the river
and nibbled on the sweet grass that grew there.
I knew the blue grama, the little blue stem,
camomile, and the sunflowers,
15   the rainbow colors of the earth.

As a child
I learned the stories of the Tewa.
We came from beneath the Sandy Place Lake.
Our first mother was Blue Corn Woman,
20   the Summer Mother.
And our first mother was White Corn Maiden,
the Winter Mother.

All is sacred in our world:
Shimmering Mountain to the north.
25   Obsidian Covered Mountain to the west.
Turtle Mountain to the south.
Stone Man Mountain to the east.

All the hills are sacred.
All the shrines are sacred.
30   All the plazas are sacred.
All the dances in the plazas.
All the directions and their colors.
All, all are sacred for the Pueblo
the Spanish called San Juan.

35   The Spanish said our spirits were devils,
their faith the one true faith.
In the name of God, they destroyed our kivas.
In the name of God, they burned our katchinas.
In the name of God, they forbade our dances.
40   In the name of God, they flogged our caciques.
They took our Tewa names away.
Our mouths filled with the dust of our loss.

As a young man
I knew all the colors of life.
45   I followed blue to the north
and my authority returned to me.

I followed red to the south,
yellow to the west,
white to the east,
50   and my authority returned to me.

I visited the sacred hills and mountains.
I knew the Summer People.
I knew the Winter People.
And I knew we were one.
55   I knew my own name
and I was with the people.
I knew my own name.
My authority returned to me.

Then the Spanish took me.
60   They flogged me
but they could not take away my name.
My authority returned to me.

At Taos Pueblo, in the kiva,
I invoked the highest spirits to guide me.
65   I knew my name
and my authority returned to me.

In the kiva at Taos Pueblo,
I invoked P'ose Yemu,
he who scatters the mist before him,
70   and my authority returned to me.

Then the war leaders came to me.
I sent forth the runners
with the knotted cords
to the two dozen Pueblos,
75   to the six different languages,
to all the directions and their colors
from Taos to the Hopi villages.

When the time came
and the last knot unravelled,
80   we struck everywhere and all at once.
We raked a fire across the sun.
We let those Spaniards go
who had lived with us in peace.
We drove the rest away.
85   We let them all go.

When they came with an army
marching towards Santa Fe,
the Rio Grande rose
and their soldiers were scattered
90   with the mist.

We broke their arrogance
like bits of dry straw.
We drove them away.
We let them all go.

95   They came back
a better people
to become our compadres, our comadres,
as the people of all colors
come back together
100   and we are one.
We shine with the brilliance of stars.

I knew my own name.
Within and around the earth,
within and around the hills,
105   within and around the mountains,
my authority returned to me.

I knew my own name.
I knew my own name.
I knew my own name.

INQUIRING FURTHER

1. What can be said about the title of the poem? How do names relate to representation? How do names relate to the authority mentioned in the poem?

2. What is the significance of the many references to the past in the poem? Do the closing lines in the past tense raise any questions for you?

3. The Pueblo Revolt represents one of the most significant uprisings in the New World. By sending messengers from pueblo to pueblo with knotted cords, leaders communicated the date of the uprising and coordinated their attacks. The Spanish were driven out of New Mexico for almost fourteen years. Why do you suppose this event is frequently overlooked in discussions of American history?

LAURA GILPIN

Laura Gilpin (1891–1979) is often associated with landscape photographs, having broken much ground with her dramatic images of the Southwest. She also spent over two decades photographing Native Americans in New Mexico. Her work illustrates the lives and customs of Pueblo peoples and offers one of the strongest examples of documentary work by women photographers in the early twentieth century. Her 1941 book, The Pueblos, *is remarkable for its images as well as the commentary Gilpin provides. Her 1946 book on the Rio Grand River explores the dependence of people on the river as a water source, and emphasizes the extreme nature of the physical landscape of New Mexico.*

Images of New Mexico

FIGURE 18.10   *The Rio Grande Yields Its Surplus to the Sea*
P1979.95.35 Laura Gilpin, The Rio Grande Yields Its Surplus to the Sea, *gelatin silver print,*
1947, 8 11/16 x 13 3/4 inches, © 1979 Amon Carter Museum, Fort Worth, Texas, Gift of the artist.

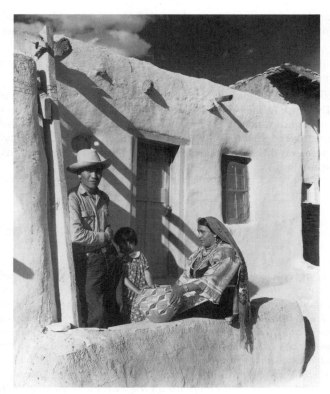

FIGURE 18.11   *Indian Family, Acoma Pueblo*

FIGURE 18.12   *The Hymn to the Sun*

INQUIRING FURTHER

1. How would you describe the tone created in *The Rio Grande Yields its Surplus to the Sea*? What aspects of the image do you find the most compelling?

2. What does *Indian Family, Acoma Pueblo* say about family relationships? Does it say anything specifically about Native American culture? What elements in the image seem most significant in discussing family?

3. Does the image in *The Hymn to the Sun* feel posed? Is it possible for a posed picture to still provide an accurate representation of a culture? Freewrite for five minutes about the image and representation.

4. How do Gilpin's photographs tell a story? Consider the photographic techniques, especially the composition of the images. Think about the people, cultures, and places represented in the images. Write a paper in which you explain how one or more of the images can be read as telling a story.

ED CHAVEZ

Ed Chavez was born in Albuquerque, New Mexico. He studies the history of the Southwest and writes poetry, stories and novels. "Death March" was published in a collection of literature from New Mexico called Voces *in 1987.*

Death March

It seemed a defiance of instinct, but a greater drive compelled the lizard to lie on the large, warm, flat rock. Daytime he spent in a cool place in the ground, and at night he came out to find warmth and food. The lizard lay in the open in the light of the full moon, protected by his chameleon-like coloring. And always his patience paid off.

An insect scampered onto the rock and carelessly meandered closer and closer to the lizard. Closer and closer until—spak!—the moth came too close and the lizard lifted him away with a hardly perceptible flick of the tongue.

Hardly, but perceptible enough for another patient night watcher. A shapeless tree branch immediately revealed its powerful wing span and swiftly it swooped down and clutched the lizard in its talons, then sailed back in a wide arc to a higher branch in another tree. It was all a simultaneous motion of a few seconds and the dead lizard was still wriggling involuntarily in the owl's claws when the owl perched on his new branch.

On the ground below the tree a frightened voice whispered, "Did you hear that, Loyd? The owl's sending us a warning."

5   "Don't be so superstitious, Tony. It's only calling because you're making so much noise."

But Eloyd didn't resist Tony huddling close to him. It was gloomy hiding there in the woods and very spooky for the ten year olds. They were hiding under a juniper, down on their bellies so they could look out and watch the path.

A loud whistle pierced the stillness and Tony hugged Eloyd and buried his face in his shoulder and whimpered, "I shouldn't have come, Loyd. I'll never see my mother again. We're going to die, Loyd! I know it!"

"Ssh!" Eloyd was just as frightened. But he had to know.

"Let's go back, Loyd. We can hear about it tomorrow when the big folks talk. They do every year after Las Tinieblas is over."

10   "Quiet!" Eloyd cupped his hand over Tony's mouth. Tony calmed down. Then he started wriggling again when the mournful tooting started.

"Be still! It's only the pitero, Tony."

They could see him now. A shuffling figure, all in white, swaying to the lament as he walked up the trail. Soon he would be close enough to touch, if they dared, but they would lay quietly on their bellies, holding their breath in the shadows.

Behind the pitero more figures emerged, some wearing peaked hats under their black shrouds. One of them began to sing, a wailing alabado with pitiful, quavering sounds.

From their place under the juniper the two boys could only see feet now, each stepping to a solemn deliberate pace. Three men walked apart, stripped to the waist. The sound of their whips lashing over their shoulders was a painful counterpoint to the alabado.

15   It was the scrape of a huge timber dragging on the hard packed trail that caused Eloyd to dare a bolder look. He lifted the lowest branch and saw a lone man pulling the enormous madero on his shoulder. The man slipped and others gathered quickly to help him. He wore a band of chamiso around his forehead. He was shirtless and Eloyd could see where the rough beam scraped the skin off his shoulder. His white calzones were damp with sweat and blood.

Eloyd gasped. He saw what he had come to see. One of the compañeros dabbed the man's face. His father's face!

So many wonderful things had happened in Eloyd's life the past few weeks. His father had returned after an absence of many years and he was greeted in Punta de Agua—in the whole county!—as a hero. As indeed he was. His father had fought in the war in the Phillipines, survived the Death March from Bataan, outlasted the atrocities of the Japanese internment, manfully regained his strength in a California hospital, and now the brotherhood had selected him to be the Cristo. The Cristo!

And why not? To Eloyd the logic was plain. Who else but his father was more deserving? It explained those looks Eloyd had noticed—the serene glow in his father's eyes, the adoring fussiness of his mother, the solicitude of the women and children, and the open respect of the men. It explained the murmurs that evaporated to a solemn hush when Eloyd chanced upon adult conversants in the village. They would gently smile at him, nod, and keep a respectful silence. Their manner indicated they knew something that would make Eloyd proud. And Eloyd knew better than to ask any direct questions. But he also knew they all shared a special knowledge. Even the most firmly kept secrets have a way of seeping among the people. And now Eloyd confirmed what he had guessed.

The brotherhood had conveyed the distinct honor on his father to be the Cristo in the annual reenactment of the Passion.

20   Three men helped his father lift the two hundred and fifty pound madero, constructed in the shape of a cross, and then he proceeded, genuine agony accompanying every step.

Eloyd strained for a better view as his father staggered up the loma. Mostly, he carried the load alone, but the Cyreños were there to assist when he weakened.

So overcome was Eloyd in watching his father that he failed to hear the creaking of the cart wheels. Tony stifled another whimper and Eloyd turned, ready to chide Tony, but instead he sucked his breath in horror. There, in a cart, sat a shawled figure with a bow and arrow poised right at him. And deep in the hood Eloyd saw the glowing green eyes of a skull.

"La Muerte," Eloyd whspered.

"Si!" Another voice whispered hoarsely. Eloyd felt long, nimble fingers cup his mouth with gentle firmness and he turned to see the stern face of Dedos. Tony started to scream, but Dedos shushed him and ordered, "Go home! To your mamá!"

25   Eloyd started to move but Dedos held him back with the same gentle firmness. "Not You! This baby here. Go! And don't look back!"

Tony obeyed and fled. Dedos dropped the venda over his face, took Eloyd's hand and admonished, "Stay with me and do only as I say."

Up the trail they went in the procesión de sangre, behind the Carreta del Muerto, across the camposanto, past the wooden gravemarkers, and up an ever steepening slope. El Calvario.

Dedos led Eloyd to the shaded side of the cart from where he could see without obstruction the continuing live enactment of the Passion. The flaring lights of the torches reflected off the walls of the barranca and lighted the scene.

Eloyd's breath quickened. He heard the sound of a steel hammer pounding on a spike, muffled at first until it pierced the flesh, then ringing more clearly as it was driven into the madero his father so recently carried. Were they actually going to *nail* him to the cross? Three times Eloyd heard the ringing clang of metal striking metal until the job was done.

30   Why didn't they bind him with ropes? Or had his father actually made this awful promise in Japan? Is this why they were doing it in the dark instead of in the afternoon as in prior years?

Eloyd watched as six men tugged at ropes while another five pushed from behind and lifted the cross to which his father was tied. There was a shuddering thud as it slipped into its hole in the ground. Eloyd observed how the five men quickly tumbled rocks and fitted supporting stumps into the slot to hold the madero upright.

He heard his father cry out, "Por el amor de Dios! Basta!"

He wanted to help. He wanted to scream or run away. He wanted to stop them, but all he could do was remember Dedo's warning to do as he was told. He averted his eyes and stared at La Muerte. She held her taut bow and arrow poised directly at him, as if she were deliberately threatening him.

"Dejame! No puedo mas!"

35   Something was wrong. Eloyd knew his father would be ashamed of him for getting anxious like a woman, but this was not expected. Real nails? He gulped a long, deep breath and slowly expelled it, the way the priest had taught him to control his emotions before receiving his First Communion, and he thought of Christ. Christ? *Not* Christ! Not now! Concentrate on something else.

Eloyd noticed La Muerte was a real skeleton and not a carved one as he had seen in other processions. Whose skeleton? He wondered. From the old Indian grave on the other side of the lagunita?

"Ten piedad!" His father cried.

Couldn't they hear his father? Don't get anxious. He is only saying the words of the Cristo. They will take him down soon, bathe him, and let him rest. And then, for a year at least, everyone will come to see his wounds, marvel at his courage and at his holiness, and ask him for a blessing. And he will bless them.

Eloyd had seen only one other with the scarred hands, an old man from Las Trampas, and now his own father would show the marks. Because he chose the nails, people would come to him for more than a year. They would come to him for the rest of his life.

40   It was too magnificent to think about. If only they would hurry and take him down. Eloyd chewed on his lower lip and tried to think of something else.

He stared at La Muerte square in the eyes. What causes that green glow? Yes. It was a real skull alright. Such long teeth. Large and yellow. Some of them missing.

"Hermanos! Ya no aguanto!"

Eloyd was numbed by a deafening clatter of the matracas and a thundering from corrugated tins. The noise boomed and raged louder in the deafening din, and all Eloyd could see were the glowing green eyes. He dared not move or even look away.

Dedos gently pulled Eloyd's arm.

45   "Is it finished?"

"Si. Let's go."

"Where's my father?"

"They're taking care of him. Come. We have to go back to the morada."

"Was I asleep?"

50   "You never closed your eyes." Dedos dismantled the bowstring from La Muerte's hand and dropped the black hood over her skull. "Hurry. They're waiting for us."

"Aren't we going to walk behind the cart?"

"No. We go behind the pitero now. Vamonos. It's almost time for the sun to rise."

The pitero piped a repetitious, melancholy dirge all the way back. People were already standing by the morada. When Eloyd saw his mother in the crowd, he wanted to go to her, but Dedos would not let his hand go. He wanted to comfort her. Why did she look so worried?

Eloyd entered the morada with all the men and was led to a spot in front of the altar. Above the piping of the pitero he could hear the squeak of the carreta as it entered the chapel, and above all these sounds he could hear his mother wail outside when she saw the hooded skull. Eloyd was ashamed she should carry on so. Didn't she know this was only a drama, a ceremony reenacting the death of Christ? Someone was leading her away and he could hear her fading wail, pleading, "¡Mi esposo! ¿Dónde 'sta Alberto? ¡Alberto! ¿Dónde 'sta?"

55   Dedos led Eloyd back through the chapel of the morada into a room he had never been permitted to enter before. He could still hear the pitero in the chapel while the rezador launched into a long prayer for the dead.

Only the Hermano Mayor, Dedos and Eloyd were in the secret room. Dario solemnly addressed Dedos. "Sangrador, prepare the novice."

Dedos nodded and removed Eloyd's shirt. He instructed Eloyd to shed the rest of his clothes and to put on the white cotton calzones he handed him.

In the chapel Eloyd could hear the sas! sas! sas! of wet lashes. It was the sound of yucca whips the flaggelants used to scourge themselves. Dedos dipped a similar whip in a mixture of romero herb tea and salt. "Toma!" He handed it to Eloyd. "To prepare yourself as a worthy hermano, you must scourge yourself."

Eloyd could not think of disobeying. He tentatively lashed the wet whip over his shoulder and felt the sting.

60   "Harder!"

Eloyd heard the rezador intone "Ven pecador y veras," and the voices of the entire brotherhood fearsomely continued the alabado.

Eloyd flailed himself again. In the chapel he could hear the sas! sas! sas! of the bloody wet whips.

"Harder!"

He closed his eyes and lashed himself over the other shoulder.

65   "Again!"

He whipped himself again.

"Faster!"

At first, the salted solution stung his welted back, but it had a perverse healing affect because of the romero juice. Eloyd kept whipping himself hypnotically without prompting until the Hermano Mayor intervened. "Basta!"

Exhausted, Eloyd let his whip drop.

70   The singing stopped in the chapel, but all the while the pitero piped away to a higher and more piercing crescendo.

The Hermano Mayor held out a cigar box and Dedos ceremoniously lifted the lid and selected a sharp flint. Then he stepped back and positioned himself behind Eloyd.

The Hermano Mayor intoned: "Is the Sangrador ready?"

"I am ready," Dedos replied.

"Then proceed," the Hermano Mayor ordered.

75   Immediately in the chapel the matracas began to clatter accompanied by booming tins. Eloyd did not resist nor did he even flinch because he knew there was no stopping the inevitable. Dedos deftly made six gashes on Eloyd's back, three on each side. It took considerable skill to be a sangrador, to know how to cut without severing a nerve or causing any permanent disability.

Eloyd cooperated without a whimper, fully conscious of the entire rite, until he felt the warm trickle down his back. Only then did he swoon.

"Que niño tan valiente," was Dario's only comment as he steadied Eloyd so that Dedos could finish his work. Dedos took a cloth soaked with romero brew and bathed Eloyd's wounds until they were clean and stopped bleeding.

"He is so young for the rite, Dario. Why so soon?"

"First, as the Hermano Mayor and the Maestro de Novicios, I decide who is ready. Also," Dario's tone became more soothing, "there has been an unbroken line, in his family, of membership in the hermandad ever since this morada was founded. I know Alberto—que en paz descanse—" Dario added, "would be pleased to know his son has not let the chain be interrupted. And finally, as an hermano, this young man is bound to secrecy. Or suffer the ultimate penalty."

80   Dedos nodded in agreement. "He should rest."

"Yes. Let him rest. The diggers should be finished. Only they, you, and I shall know Alberto's Gethsemani. He shall be buried upright to guarantee his salvation. The confradia will continue the sudario until we return."

Eloyd was very proud of his initiation at so young an age and he could not understand why his mother deplored it. That his father died as the Cristo was an extreme honor surely to guarantee his own, and their, salvation. But all she did was weep.

It was no wonder to Eloyd that women were not permitted to enter the brotherhood.

INQUIRING FURTHER

1. What significance do you give to the fact that Eloyd's father has just returned from World War II? How might this background help you develop an interpretation of the story?

2. Do you think the events described in the story are exceptional or just part of the yearly ritual? What passages from the text would you discuss to support your position?

3. How do you interpret the last sentence of the story? Would you say the statement is ironic? Freewrite for five minutes about men's and women's perspectives in "Death March," and how the ending can guide an interpretation of the story.

GEORGIA O'KEEFE AND E. MARTIN HENNINGS

E. Martin Hennings (1886–1956) once reported that New Mexico was likely to make a landscape painter out of him, although he preferred to include people as the subjects of his paintings. Hennings emphasized portrayals of Native Americans in contemporary settings and dress over posed subjects in costume. Hennings was a member of the Taos Society of Artists, a cooperative group of painters who lived in Taos and frequently emphasized striking Northern New Mexico landscapes and Native American and Hispanic subjects in their works. Georgia O'Keefe (1887–1986) studied art in Chicago and New York, before working briefly as a commercial artist. She soon became interested in abstract and symbolic art, creating a breakthrough series of charcoal sketches that caught the attention of photographer Alfred Stieglitz, whom she married in 1924. The couple divided their time between New York and Taos, with Georgia refining her abstract techniques with the influence of the photographic interests she developed from working with Stieglitz.

Art from Taos, New Mexico

Paintings by O'Keefe and Hennings

FIGURE 18.13   *Homeward Bound* by E. Martin Hennings

FIGURE 18.14   *Riders at Sunset* by E. Martin Hennings

FIGURE 18.15   *My Back Yard* by Georgia O'Keefe
Georgia O'Keeffe, My Backyard, oil on canvas, 1937, New Orleans Museum of Art: Museum purchase, City of New Orleans Capital Funds, 73.8

FIGURE 18.16   *Black Cross, New Mexico* by Georgia O'Keefe
Georgia O'Keeffe, American, 1887–1986, Black Cross, New Mexico, 1929, oil on canvas, 99.1 x 76.2 cm, Art Institute Purchase Fund, 1943.95, Reproduction, The Art Institute of Chicago

---

INQUIRING FURTHER

1. Which of the paintings in Figures 18.13–18.16 do you prefer and why?

2. How would you compare Hennings's paintings with the images created by George Catlin or Frederick Remington (pages 889–91)? Freewrite for five minutes about the way each artist represents the culture of the West.

3. What can you say about the messages conveyed by O'Keefe's abstract style? Can you recognize themes or symbols in the works? What do they tell you about art and representation?

4. In what way can O'Keefe's paintings be described as photographic? Can you find aspects of framing, lighting, or composition you might associate with photography in the paintings? Could you interpret Hennings's work similarly? Write a paper in which you explore the messages in one or more of the paintings in terms of photography.

FIGURE 26-16 ...

Appendix

Documenting and Using Sources

> When a thing has been said and said well, have no
> scruple. Take it and copy it.
>
> —*Anatole France*

What do you suppose Anatole France means when recommending that we "have no scruple" when copying what others have said? Do you believe France is suggesting that we can freely use the words of others in any way we please? More likely, France has in mind the responsible use of materials. A big part of participating in arguments about issues and works of literature is sharing knowledge. This allows us to draw upon the ideas of others, incorporating them into our compositions in the form of **paraphrases**, **summaries**, and **quotations**. At the same time, however, we must be very careful to attribute the ideas that we use to their authors, and to help our readers locate the original sources of the materials that we borrow. Indeed, the freedom to draw upon the work of others requires that we pay close attention to scruples, that we carefully attribute and accurately document the sources that we use.

This appendix provides guidance to help you use the works of others in your compositions. For the papers you write about literature, you will most likely adhere to the formats recommended by the Modern Language Association (MLA). These formats will help you develop **in-text citations** and create a list of **works cited** for your papers. Additionally, you will need to carefully avoid **plagiarism** as you integrate the words of others into your compositions. Finally, you will also need to observe issues of **copyright** to ensure that you are using materials fairly.

USING MLA STYLE

Different academic disciplines use their own documentation styles. For example, psychology students will follow APA style (American Psychological Association), political science students will follow CMS style (Chicago Manual of Style), and literature students will follow MLA style (Modern Language Association). The MLA style is fully described in the *MLA Handbook for Writers of Research Papers* (6th edition, 2003). More detailed information may be found in most writing handbooks. Here we provide some of the most common MLA formats for in-text citations and entries in the list of works cited.

Generally, MLA documentation has two main purposes: 1.) creating a citation in your paper whenever you summarize, paraphrase, or quote from a source, and 2.) creating a Works Cited page that provides your readers with full bibliographical details of the sources that you have used. In-text citations do not provide full, bibliographical details. Whenever in-text citations are used, the reader may expect to find a fuller bibliographic listing of the works at the end of the paper.

In-Text Citations

In the body of your paper, you should note each source as you use it. Generally, you should introduce material being cited with an **introductory tag**, or **signal phrase**. (You can find out more about introducing and punctuating quotations on pages 180–83.) As you note the use of a source in your paper, you should provide information about the author of a source and the page number, if available, from which you are citing.

1. **Author named in an introductory tag**. When you summarize, paraphrase, or quote a source in your paper, you can name the author directly in your introductory tag, and then give the page number(s) that the materials come from:

   Hans Bertens argues that, "racial discrimination is a recurrent theme

   in African-American writing" (104).

2. **Author named in parentheses**. If you do not name the author in your text, include his or her last name with the page number in parentheses:

   After World War One, literary studies began to emphasize diversity: "In

   the 1920s African-American writing, flowering in the so-called 'Harlem

   Renaissance,' becomes almost overnight a permanent force within the field

   of American literature" (Bertens 104).

3. **Two or three authors**. If your source has two or three authors, name them in the introductory tag or include them in the parenthetical reference.

   Culler and Lamb conclude that while some academic writing can be

   needlessly obscure, sometimes authors use strange styles as a way of

   making their point (9).

4. **Four or more authors**. If your source has four or more authors, you can include only the first author's name followed by "et al." (*Et alia* is Latin for "and others.") As with authors' names, this can be included in either the introductory tag or the parenthetical reference.

The publication of the resulting study demonstrated that much of the

environmental research had been on the wrong track for the past several

years (D'Angelo et al. 225).

5. **Unknown author**. If a source does not give an author, use the complete title in the introductory tag or a shortened version of the title in the parenthetical reference.

According to *The National Geographic Atlas of the World*, Australia's Great

Dividing Range ends only a few miles north of Melbourne ("Atlas" 54).

6. **Literary works**. Because some literary works are available in numerous editions, you will want to include enough information so that your reader will be able to find the passage you are citing in any edition.

Play. When citing a verse play, leave out the page number and give instead the act, scene, and line numbers, separated by periods:

On the Elizabethan stage, the actor playing Macbeth may very well

be addressing the three main sections of his audience when he says,

"Tomorrow, and tomorrow, and tomorrow / Creeps in this petty pace from

day to day / to the last syllable of recorded time. . . ." (5.5.19–21).

Poetry. For poetry, cite the stanza number (if the poem contains more than one stanza) and the line numbers. If the poem does not contain stanzas, include the word line(s) in your first citation:

Brooks emphasizes the importance of the speaker through the

structure of her poem: "We real cool. We / left school. We" (1.1–2).

Wright's "A Blessing" uses the imagery of skin to set up the out of

body experience of the speaker: "And the light breeze moves me to caress

her long ear / That is delicate as the skin over a girl's wrist" (lines 19–20).

7. **Work without page numbers**. If your source is not paginated, but is numbered in another way (such as by paragraphs or sections), include the name and number(s) of the part you are citing. ("par." or "pars." for paragraphs; "sec." for section; "pt." for part).

PBS's online forum points out that the Harlem Renaissance "was a profound literary and political movement" (par. 2).

8. **Electronic or nonprint source**. Give enough information in either the introductory tag or the parenthetical reference so that your reader can find your source in the list of works cited:

Langston Hughes avoided the high style of other poets in order to make "direct and unambiguous statements about the social plight of his fellow black Americans" (Literature Online).

Creating a List of Works Cited

Creating
a list
of Works
Cited

In your Works Cited list, you provide information that will help readers locate the sources that you use. This information demonstrates that you are using materials responsibly and helps readers who would like to follow up on your research by examining the materials you are citing. Your list, then, will offer **author**, **title**, and **publication information** about your sources. You will **double space** the **Works Cited** list, sort the entries **alphabetically**, and create what is called a hanging indent for items that take more than a single line.

Entries for Books

Generally, a book requires three pieces of information, followed by a period:

1. **Author's name, last name first**. For a book with multiple authors, only the first author's name is inverted.
2. **Title and subtitle, underlined**.
3. **Publication information, including the city, a shortened form of the publisher's name, and the date**.

Works published since 1900 include a publisher's name as well as a city, but publisher's names should be shortened whenever possible. Words such as "Company" and "Books" can be dropped, as well as abbreviations such as "Inc.," "Bro.," or "LTD." Abbreviate "University Press" to "UP." Whenever possible, shorten a publisher's name to one word. For example, "Charles Scribner's & Sons" becomes "Scribner's" and "Columbia University Press" becomes "Columbia UP." Publication information should be taken from the title page of the book and from the reverse side of the title page (the copyright page), not the outside cover. The date given in your Works Cited page should be the most recent copyright date.

1. **One author**. As noted above, the basic entry for a book provides the author, the title, and the publication information.

Hemingway, Ernest. <u>The Sun Also Rises</u>. New York: Scribner's, 1926.

2. **Two or more works by the same author**. Provide author, title, and publication information for the first work. For the second entry, use three hyphens to indicate the author.

McCarthy, Cormac. <u>All the Pretty Horses</u>. New York: Knopf, 1992.

- - -. <u>Blood Meridian: or the Evening Redness in the West</u>. New York:

Vintage, 1992.

3. **Two or more authors**. Name the authors in the order they appear on the title page, and reverse the name of only the first author.

Bolter, Jay David, and Richard Grusin. <u>Remediation: Understanding</u>

<u>New Media</u>. Cambridge: MIT, 2002.

4. **Unknown author**. Begin with the title and alphabetize the entry by its first word; remember not to count the articles "A," "An," or "The" as the first word of a title.

<u>Essential Atlas of the World</u>. New York: Barnes & Noble, 2001.

5. **Editor**. Follow the name of the editor with a comma and "ed." for editor or "eds." if there is more than one editor.

Hughes, Merrit Y., ed. <u>John Milton: Complete Poems and Prose</u>. New

York: Prentice, 1957.

6. **More than four authors or editors**. To save space, cite only the first author (name reversed), followed by "et al."

Anderson, Daniel, et al. <u>Connections: A Guide to Online Writing</u>. New

York: Allyn & Bacon, 1998.

7. **Selection in an anthology or chapter in an edited book**. List the author of the selection, the title of the selection, the title of the anthology, the editor of the anthology (preceded by "Ed."), the city, publisher, and date of publication, and the page numbers on which the selection appears.

Carver, Raymond. "Cathedral." <u>Writing About Literature in the Media</u>

<u>Age</u>. Ed. Daniel Anderson. New York: Pearson Longman, 2005.

60–69.

8. **Translation**. List the entry by the name of the original author of the work; after listing the title, distinguish the translator(s) by "Trans." followed by the translator's name.

> Dostoevsky, Fyodor. <u>Demons</u>. Trans. Richard Pevear and Larissa
>
> Volokhonsky. New York: Knopf, 1994.

9. **Article in a reference work**. List the author of the article (if any), the title of the article, the title of the reference work, the edition number (if any), and the date of the edition. Volume and page numbers are not necessary because entries are already alphabetized for quick reference. If the reference work is less well known, provide full publication information.

> "Iraq." <u>Encyclopedia Britannica</u>. 2004.

> "Iraq." <u>The Political Encyclopedia of the Middle East</u>. New York:
>
> Continuum, 1999.

Note that the most common types of citations from a book are listed here; for more detailed examples, go to our Web site.

Periodicals

The information for a periodical includes the three following elements, separated by periods:

1. **Author's name, last name first**. As for books, for periodicals with multiple authors, only the first author's name is inverted.
2. **Title of the article, in quotation marks**. Note that the period following the article title goes inside the closing quotation mark.
3. **Publication information**, including the periodical title (underlined), the volume and issue numbers (if any), the date of publication, and the page number(s).

1. **Article in a journal paginated by volume**. Provide the author, the title, the name of the journal (underlined), the volume number, the date (in parentheses), and the page number(s).

> Green, Richard Firth. "Chaucer's Victimized Women." <u>Studies in the Age</u>
>
> <u>of Chaucer</u> 10 (1988): 3–21.

2. **Article in a journal paginated by issue**. Provide the author, the title, the title of the journal (underlined), issue information, the date (in parentheses), and the page number(s).

> Sklar, Elizabeth S. "Guido, the Middle English Troy Books, and Chaucer:
>
> The English Connection." <u>Neophilologus</u> 76.4 (Oct. 1992): 616–28.

3. **Article in a monthly magazine**. Provide the author, the title, the title of the magazine (underlined), the month of publication, and the page number(s).

> Saul, John Ralston. "The Collapse of Globalism." <u>Harper's</u>. Mar. 2004: 33–43.

4. **Article in a weekly magazine**. Provide the author, the title, the title of the magazine (underlined), the date of publication, and the page number(s).

> Tyrangiel, Josh. "The Tao of Uma." <u>Time</u>. 29 Sept. 2003: 66–68.

5. **Article in a newspaper**. Provide the author, the title, the title of the newspaper (underlined), the date of publication, and the section and page number.

> McKinley, Jesse. "Library Given a Collection of the Makings of Hit
>
> Musicals." <u>New York Times</u> 16 June 2004, sec. E: 1.

6. **Editorial or letter to editor**. List the author (if known), the title, the phrase "Editorial" or "Letter" (if it is a letter from a reader), the title of the publication (underlined), the date, and the pages or section numbers.

> Mounger, Swyn. "The Poems of War." Editorial. <u>New York Times</u> 14 June
>
> 2004, sec. A: 20.

Entries for Electronic Sources

Especially in the case of electronic sources, you must make clear exactly where the source can be found. The documentation style for electronic sources discussed in this section is consistent with the MLA's most recent guidelines, which can be found in the *MLA Handbook for Writers of Research Papers* (6th edition, 2003). Beyond what is provided here, you can find more information about documenting electronic sources on our CD.

1. **CD-ROM**. Include the author's name, publication information for the print version of the text (if available), the title of the CD-ROM (underlined), the medium (CD-ROM), the city, the name of the publisher, and the date.

Documenting electronic sources

> Anderson, Daniel. <u>Writing About Literature in the Media Age</u>. CD-ROM.
>
> New York: Pearson Longman, 2005.

2. **Electronic database**. You will reach most electronic databases through your library Web site, but some are also published on CD, and most include sources originally published in print. Provide enough information to help readers locate the source in print (if applicable) or through the online (or CD) database. List the author's name (if available), the title, name of the publication, and publication information for any sources also available in print. For the database, if it is a CD-ROM database, provide the database name, the phrase "CD-ROM," the company producing the CD, and the date of publication.

For databases reached through a library Web site, provide the name of the database and any company providing the database service, the name of the library where the database was accessed, the city where the library is located, the date of access, and a URL that leads to the database.

Murphy, Mary. "Picture/Story: Representing Gender in Montana Farm

Security Administration Photographs." Frontiers 22.3 (2001):

93–117. Proquest. University of North Carolina Libraries, Chapel

Hill, NC. 15 July 2004 <http://proquest.umi.com/>.

3. **Document from a Web site**. When possible, include the author's name, the title of the document (work or posting), print publication information (if applicable), electronic publication information (if available), the date of access, and the URL within angle brackets.

Bresson, Robert. "Notes on Sound." 4 June 2004.

<http://filmsound.studienet.org/articles/bresson.htm>.

If a particular URL is extremely complicated, you can instead give the URL for the site's search page, if it exists, or for the site's home page. If a URL will not entirely fit on one line, it should be broken only after a slash.

4. **Entire Web site**. Include the name of the person or group who created the site (if relevant), the title of the site (underlined or italicized) or (if there is no title) a brief description such as "Home page," the electronic publication date or last update (if available), the name of any institution or organization associated with the site, the date of access, and the URL.

Spotlight on Technology. 21 April 2004. UNC, Chapel Hill Department of

English. 4 June 2004. <http://english.unc.edu/comp/technology/>.

5. **Online book**. Include the name of the author, editor, compiler, or translator. Then give the title and the name of anyone responsible for placing the materials online. If the online version of the text has not been published before, give the date of the electronic publication and the name of any sponsoring institution or organization. Then give any publication information (city, publisher, and/or year) for the original print version, the date of access, and the URL.

Thoreau, Henry David. "Civil Disobedience." The Thoreau Reader.

Richard Lenat, ed. EServer. 2004. Iowa State U. 4 Mar. 2004.

<http://eserver.org/thoreau/civil.html>.

6. **Article in an online periodical**. Follow the same format for documenting print periodicals, but use information necessary to the online medium. Include the page numbers of the article, or the total number of pages, paragraphs, parts, or other numbered sections (if any), the date of access, and the URL.

> Mieszkowski, Katharine. "The Gas Guzzlers Who Just Can't Quit." <u>Salon</u>
>
> 19 May 2004. 19 pars. 15 June 2003. <http://www.salon.com/tech/
>
> books/2004/05/19/end_of_oil/index_np.html>.

7. **Posting to a discussion group**. Give the author's name, the title of the posting, the phrase "Online posting," and the date of the posting. For a listserv posting, give the name of the listserv, the date of access, and either the URL of the listserv or (preferably) the URL of an archival version of the posting. If a URL is unavailable, give the email address of the list moderator. For a newsgroup posting, end with the date of access and the name of the newsgroup, in angle brackets.

> Marshal, Adam. "Comparing War Stories." Online posting. 7 April 2004.
>
> 16 June 2004. <news:soc.history.war.vietnam>.

> Gains, Ronald. "Re. Last Three Lines." Online posting. 16 April 2003.
>
> Blackboard Class Discussion. 12 June 2004.
>
> <https://blackboard.unc.edu/bin/common/course.pl?course_id=_14713_1>.

8. **E-mail message**. Include the writer's name, the subject line, the phrase "E-mail to the author" or "E-mail to [the recipient's name]," and the date of the message.

> Hernandez, Catherine. "Yellow Wallpaper Narrator." E-mail to Bridget
>
> Allen. 27 Feb. 2004.

9. **Synchronous communication (MOO, MUD, IM, or IRC)**. It can sometimes be difficult to cite synchronous exchanges in chat programs, Instant Messaging systems, and other collaborative environments, but you should try to include as much information as possible. Include the name of any specific speaker(s) you are citing, a description of the event, its date, the name of the forum, the date of access, and the URL of the posting or (preferably) the URL of an archival version.

> Vira, Kamala. Online chat. 12 Mar. 2004. Blackboard Virtual Classroom.
>
> 16 June 2004. <https://blackboard.unc.edu/bin/common/
>
> course.pl?course_id=_14713_1>.

Patuto, Jeremy, Simon Fennel, and James Goss. The Mytilene debate. 9

May 1996. MiamiMOO. 28 Mar. 1998 <http://moo.cas.muohio.edu>.

Other Sources

As with electronic media, the main goal when listing these sources is to convey efficiently as much relevant information as possible to your reader.

1. **Personal and published interview**. List the name of the person interviewed, the location of the interview (use the phrase "Personal Interview" for personal interviews), and the date.

   Kerrane, Kevin. Personal Interview. 2 Feb. 2004.

   Trippi, Joe. <u>The Connection</u>. Natl. Public Radio. WUNC, Chapel Hill.

   12 Dec. 2003.

2. **Personal letter**. List the name, the phrase "Letter to the author: [or to another known individual], and the date.

   Filipowicz, Norma. Letter to the author. 25 Jun. 2001.

3. **Film or videotape**. List the title, alphabetized by the first word (other than "a," "an," or "the"), and then list the relevant information in this order: writer (prefixed with "By"), director ("Dir."), narrator ("Narr."), producer ("Prod."), or main actors ("Perf."). These should be followed by the distributor and the year. For a videotape, add the word "Videocassette" before the distributor.

   <u>The Lord of the Rings: Return of the King</u>. Dir. Peter Jackson. Perf.

   Elijah Wood, Ian McKellen. New Line Cinema, 2003.

   <u>Sense and Sensibility</u>. Dir. Ang Lee. Perf. Emma Thompson, Hugh

   Grant, and Alan Rickman. Videocassette. TriStar Home Video, 1996.

4. **Television or radio program**. Begin with the same information as with a film (above), followed by the network, the local station (if any) that broadcast the program, the city, and the date of the broadcast.

   <u>Hardball</u>. Host Chris Matthews. MSNBC. 4 Mar. 2004.

5. **Television or radio interview**. Cite the person interviewed, followed by the word "interview," and then the information for the television or radio program.

Patterson, Orlando. Interview. <u>NewsHour with Jim Lehrer</u>. PBS.

>   30 Sept. 1998.

6. **Sound recording**. Start the citation with the composer (or author if the recording is spoken), then list the title of the work (underlined), pertinent artists (such as performers, readers, or musicians), the orchestra (if any), the conductor (if any), the manufacturer, and the date. If the recording is not a CD, indicate the medium (such as "audiocassette" or "LP") before the manufacturer's name.

Porter, Cole. <u>Night and Day</u>. Perf. Billie Holliday. The Billie Holliday

>   Orchestra. Columbia, 1940.

7. **Work of art (e.g., painting, sculpture, photograph)**. List the artist, the title of the piece, the date (if known), and the collection that houses the work.

Dalí, Salvador. <u>The Sacrament of the Last Supper</u>. 1955. Natl. Gallery of

>   Art, Washington, D.C.

If you have found the work in a book or online, also provide information about the publication where you found the item.

Lange, Dorothea. <u>Migrant Mother, Nipomo California</u>. 1936. Oakland

>   Museum of Art, Oakland CA. <u>The Masters of Photography Web Site</u>.

>   14 July 2004. <http://www.masters-of photography.com/L/lange/

>   lange_migrant_mother.html>.

8. **Live performance**. List the title and participant information as you would for a film, followed by the place of performance, and the date.

<u>King Lear</u>. By William Shakespeare. Dir. Mark Wing-Davey. Perf.

>   Michael Winters. Playmakers Repertory Company. Paul Green

>   Theatre, Chapel Hill. 14 Jan. 2004.

9. **Advertisement**. List the product, the phrase "Advertisement," the source, the date, and any relevant page numbers.

Nivea. Advertisement. <u>Vogue</u>. July 2004. 62.

Remember that the main purpose of your Works Cited page is to provide readers with a means of following up on your research by helping them track down the sources that you use. Strive to offer as complete a picture as possible of the authors, the titles, and the publication information for your sources. We have covered some of the most common forms, but you may also need to track down additional information on our CD. Finally, you will also need to format your papers according to MLA standards. You can get more information about formatting your papers on pages 207-09 and on our CD.

AVOIDING PLAGIARISM

Being scrupulous about using sources includes making the right decisions about which sources to use and how to incorporate them into your compositions. Carelessness and poor choices can easily result in **plagiarism**, passing off someone else's work as your own. On one level, attention to detail when quoting, summarizing, and paraphrasing will protect you against plagiarism. On another level, intellectual honesty must ultimately drive the decisions you make as a writer and prevent you from plagiarizing the work of others.

Fairly Quoting, Summarizing, and Paraphrasing

When you integrate quotations into your work, carelessness can easily result in plagiarism. For example, you might neglect to note that certain information came from a particular source; if your readers are aware that your work is not original, they can assume you are plagiarizing. Be careful, too, of haphazardly pasting online materials into your work, or of copying down large amounts of prose from a book in the midst of drafting. Not only are you more likely to forget to attribute the sources you have used, you will miss out on the process of inquiry that comes from distilling your sources, and then explaining their significance in your own words.

For summaries and paraphrases, *you must make sure that you give proper credit and that you thoroughly recast the materials in your own words.* (For more on integrating summaries and paraphrases into your writing, see pages 183–86.) When you reference a key idea or offer a summary of a source, *indicate the author in a parenthetical citation and include the source in your Works Cited page.* When paraphrasing, be sure to maintain the core ideas of the source, while developing statements that rely on your own thoughts and language. Consider the two sample paraphrases below.

Original Source:

The art of the Harlem Renaissance was optimistic because many artists and writers of the 1920s enjoyed greater opportunities to publish and disseminate their art than they had ever had before. For one thing, African American artists of the 1920s did not have to deny their racial identity by publishing works anonymously, as had James Weldon Johnson when he published *The Autobiography of an Ex-Colored Man* in 1912 or to write poems, short stories, novels, or create works of art that avoided the racial theme, as Henry O. Tanner, William Stanley Braithwaite, and others had done before the 1920s. For the first time in American culture, for better or worse, African American creative artists could claim that there was something distinctive about the Black experience, while at the same time arguing that it was an integral part of the American experience. That freedom was exhilarating for many. (PBS par. 4)

Acceptable Paraphrase:

New opportunities to produce and share their work gave Harlem Renaissance artists a sense of optimism. No longer did they have to avoid subjects of race or publish their work anonymously. Treating issues of race and claiming their own work helped artists create and celebrate unique expressions of African American experience. (PBS par. 4)

Unacceptable Paraphrase:

The Harlem Renaissance created optimistic art *because artists and writers* had more *opportunities to publish and disseminate their art* than they had in the past. Artists no longer had to publish works anonymously, as had James Weldon Johnson. Nor did they have to avoid racial themes, as *others had done before the 1920s.* Instead, African American artists could celebrate *the distinctive Black experience.* (PBS par. 4)

Compare the two paraphrases above. The first maintains the gist of the original passage, but reworks the material significantly, putting the passage into the writer's own words and restructuring the sentences and paragraph. The second paraphrase, however, contains many phrases that are lifted directly from the original passage—in these instances, the writer should use quotation marks to indicate any text taken from another source. Notice also how the second paraphrase has mimicked the structure of the original passage; the ideas flow in the same order and (while simplified) many of the sentences maintain the structure of the original. Finally, the second paraphrase is unscrupulous in its use of terms from the original passage; a phrase like "the distinctive Black experience" does not exactly match the wording of the original, but it is close enough to warrant quotation to indicate that the writer is borrowing material.

Using Materials Honestly

It is simple enough to find reference sources, articles, even paper mill essays on the Internet (see pages 117–18). Most instructors are familiar with spotting these kinds of writing and recognize when students have been passing off such sources as their own. Ultimately, using these materials scrupulously requires a conscious decision on your part to invest the energy necessary to incorporate them into your work fairly. Further, integrating materials that you discover into your own compositions can raise a number of copyright concerns. Especially with items like images and audio or video clips, you must be deliberate about following fair use guidelines and observing intellectual property concerns. You can get more information about copyright and fair use on our CD.

Guidelines for observing copyright and fair use

SAMPLE ESSAY IN MLA STYLE

Ultimately, working with research sources requires not only careful documentation of materials, but also thoughtful integration of the ideas of others into your own writing. You can see this how this process plays out in the sample research paper provided on our CD.

Student research paper

Glossary

Allegory   The use of strong symbolism often associated with a moral. Allegorical works often present one story that is meant to stand for another or to offer a political, religious, or moral message, as in "Young Goodman Brown," where the protagonist goes in search of Faith in the woods.

Alliteration   The repetition of consonant sounds, usually found in poetry (sometimes called *consonance*).

Allusion   A veiled reference to an idea or event or to a source in another work. Allusions rely on readers to have knowledge of other sources, as in "The Love Song of J. Alfred Prufrock," which opens with an epigraph from Dante's *Inferno.*

Alternative Perspectives   Positions that run counter to one another; most literature can be interpreted in multiple ways and most people differ over key human concerns. Acknowledging alternative perspectives improves our understanding and strengthens our arguments.

Analysis   The process of breaking concepts apart to examine their pieces in more detail. With concepts like fiction, we might look at characters, settings, plot, themes, and so on.

Antagonist   Opposed to the *protagonist*, the antagonist is a source of conflict for the main character.

Arguable topic   An approach to an essay that allows room for reasonable amounts of disagreement. Rather than making obvious points or discussing opinions, an arguable topic will find an angle that is open to discussion and considers the multi-faceted nature of works and human concerns.

Argument   Writing that stakes out a claim and then provides reasons and evidence to support that claim. Most academic arguments are not characterized by competition or verbal debate, but rather by deliberately organized essays addressing complex, or *arguable topics* and explaining the value of a given way of approaching the topic.

Assonance   The repetitions of vowels sounds, usually found in poetry.

Assumptions   Unstated positions necessary to support a claim or an argument. Some assumptions resemble values that may or may not be shared by an audience, others resemble hidden claims necessary to support the logic of an argument.

Audience   The recipient of a message or work of literature. Considering the audience helps us understand the aims of works that we read and how best to craft compositions to achieve our purposes when writing.

Authority   The amount of credibility readers are willing to grant a writer. As we examine essays we can consider the authority of their creators. As we compose we can strengthen our own authority by being fair-minded, providing evidence, and using care in our writing.

Bibliography   A listing of relevant sources for a topic or work. As part of the research process, investigators often develop a working bibliography to keep track of sources; an annotated bibliography contains a brief summary of the listed sources.

Block Quotations   Quotations of more than four lines of prose and more than two lines of poetry. Block quotations are double-spaced, indented ten spaces from the left-hand margin, and used without quotation marks.

948

Causation   Considering events or actions and their consequences. Causation helps us look forward to project an outcome or look backward to trace a cause.

Character Analysis   A short piece of writing evaluating a character in a work. Character analyses often describe the traits of a character, discuss motivations and growth, and offer conclusions about the character.

Character Development   Changes that take place in a character during a story. Often, character growth is a central theme in works of fiction.

Characters   The figures present in a work. Characters often resemble people we meet in daily life and may range from complex (multifaceted or round) to simple (flat or stock) characters.

Chat   A form of instantaneous communication over the Internet, useful for brainstorming. Common forms of chat include virtual classrooms and Instant Messaging.

Cinematography   The term used to discuss aspects of films related to the use of cameras. Cinematography includes aspects such as camera angles and distance, as well as elements like shutter speeds and filters, *lighting,* and film stocks.

Citation   A reference to information that has been incorporated into a composition. Examples include in-text citations, which alert readers to the use of the ideas or words of others in the body of an essay, and entries in a list of works cited, which instruct readers about locating the original source.

Claim   A statement articulating a position, a claim represents the basic building block of arguments. A thesis statement acts as a claim about the main focus of an essay or argument; additional claims function to explain and support the main claim.

Clustering   Brainstorming ideas for a project visually. Mapping ideas on paper or using software such as Inspiration allows writers to explore and organize materials using shapes, lines, and colors.

Coherence   The way ideas and sentences within paragraphs fit together. Writers can achieve coherence by developing paragraphs with unity and employing helpful transitions, repetitions, and references to key ideas.

Comedy   A form of drama characterized by happy endings, plot twists, and laughable characters. Shakespearean comedies are well known for plots in which a couple falls in love, encounters an obstacle to their romance, and then overcomes that obstacle in the resolution of the play—a formula still found in contemporary romantic comedies in film.

Comparison   The process of relating two or more items. Comparisons rely on *synthesis* to consider relationships and connections. Developing comparisons provides a handy strategy for exploring literature.

Composition   1) The creation of essays, images, works of literature, documents, and other messages meant to fulfill a purpose. 2) A term from visual studies (film, painting, and photography) used to discuss the arrangement of figures and objects within the frame of an image.

Conflict   An aspect of plot creating tension. Sometimes conflicts involve characters within a work, or events and forces that create the drama in the story.

Connotation   The symbolic or figurative meanings of words. In contrast to the *denotative* (or *definitional*) meaning, connotation opens avenues for interpretation as we consider the possible significance of words like "love," "freedom," or "mother."

Consonance   See *alliteration.*

Context   See Social Context.

Conventions   Characteristics associated with specific forms of writing. Dramas use conventions like stage directions and dialog, for instance, while poems might use rhythm and figures of speech, and essays might use quotations and documentation of sources.

Couplets   Paired sets of rhymes often found in poetry or music. Couplets are a staple in poetry, in some dramas, and in contemporary music.

Critical Inquiry   An approach to academic work characterized by an inquisitive posture. A fluid process, inquiry often begins with our reactions and personal responses, and then moves toward more measured, arguable positions. Critical inquiry goes hand-in-hand with *critical thinking*, the ability to *analyze*, *synthesize*, and *evaluate* concepts and consider alternative positions.

Critical Reading   The process of scrutinizing works with the aim of moving from response toward interpretation and argument. Critical reading asks us to look up unfamiliar words, reread difficult passages, take notes, and mark up texts.

Critical Theory   Sometimes known as *literary theory* or *literary criticism*, critical theory offers formalized approaches for interpreting literary texts. Theories provide angles for viewing a work—for instance, a feminist theory focuses attention on issues of gender, while a historical approach emphasizes the context of a work.

Critical Thinking   The process of *analyzing*, *synthesizing*, and *evaluating* concepts in order to understand them. Critical thinking supports a process of inquiry through which we investigate ideas, asking questions and developing arguable positions.

Definition   Providing a shared knowledge of something so that readers and writers can understand one another. Definitions can offer dictionary meanings to clarify terms, or they can consider key characteristics and classifications and show how an item relates to those criteria.

Denotation   The dictionary definitions of words. The denotative meaning of words represents their literal or non-symbolic meaning. See also Connotation.

Dénouement   A French term meaning "untying," dénouement is often used to discuss the way events are resolved after the conflict in a story.

Depth   The quality of paragraphs that provide a sufficient level of discussion about their key ideas. Writers can achieve depth by beginning with a narrow focus and providing detailed support and evidence for their points.

Description   Details that help readers understand ideas, objects, people, or events.

Diction   The word choices writers make as they compose. Diction might be high (resulting in lofty prose), low (leading to accessible everyday language), or somewhere in between.

Didactic Literature   Literature written to convey an overt message. Some claim that works with an explicit message suffer in their quality as literary texts.

Drafting   The activity of generating text. Drafting differs from revising in that it calls for open-ended composition that helps explore and explain ideas.

Editing   Examining papers to achieve writing that is clear and powerful. When editing, writers also check accuracy and make adjustments to eliminate flat language, unnecessary repetitions, and wordiness.

Elements of Art   Aspects of visual images that help convey meaning. Elements can include lines, shapes, textures, shading, lighting, and color.

Elements of the Stage   Aspects of drama related to the performance of the play. Elements can include costumes, lighting, sets, props, and sounds, as well as stage directions in the text of the play.

End Comment   A detailed comment written by a reviewer of a paper after reading a draft. Though longer than a comment written in the margins of a paper, an end comment should emphasize the most pressing needs for revision.

Etymology   The study of the development of the meaning of words over time. A word like "theory," for instance, can be traced to its Latin root theôria, which means "a viewing or spectacle"; from this root we can better understand how theory helps us develop an approach for looking at texts.

Evaluation   The process of drawing conclusions about things we study. Evaluations ask us to make judgments and eventually can lead to interpretations and arguments.

Evidence   Details and supporting claims that strengthen an argument. Evidence often comes in the form of quotations from works, the words of others, or research and contextual information.

Exemplification   Writing that expands or supports ideas by providing examples. Examples give readers concrete details that help them appreciate more general concepts and bolster arguments by providing evidence.

Explication   Writing that explains what is taking place in a work or a passage. Explications feature careful descriptions that help writers draw conclusions about passages.

Exposition   An aspect of plot representing the events that unfold to set the story in motion.

Feedback   Responses offered by reviewers of paper drafts. When giving feedback, concentrate generally on deep problems with the organization and argument of a paper draft.

Feminism   A critical theory that considers how literature represents women and men. Feminism also looks at how writing by women has been received and perceived in society, and at how language can operate as a medium of power.

Figures of Speech   Combinations of words or phrases that represent things or ideas symbolically; for instance, "the early bird gets the worm." Figures of speech (sometimes called figurative language) often become clichés from overuse.

First Person Narration   See *point of view.*

Flat Characters   One-dimensional characters in a story, flat characters often serve to help move the action forward.

Focused Freewriting   Freewriting in response to specific prompts. Often exercises will contain focused prompts that can spur freewriting activities, or we can refer to sets of questions (like the journalist's questions) to help us focus our freewriting.

Foil   A companion character that sheds light on a main character. The foil usually resembles a main character in some ways, with the exception of key differences that highlight the traits of the main character.

Formalism   Sometimes associated with structuralism, a critical theory that emphasizes a work's use of language and artistic techniques. Formalism and structuralism lend themselves to close readings of texts.

Formatting   Adjusting the way that information is displayed in a document. Most academic papers rely on a standard format, such as that recommended by the MLA, which provides guidelines about the appearance of the document.

Free Verse   An open form of poetry characterized by stream of consciousness structure, rather than strict formal patterns.

Freewriting   Open-ended writing meant to spur a process of inquiry. Freewriting asks us to compose quickly, allowing our thoughts to stream forth with little concern for correctness or audience.

Front Comment   A brief message written by an author before submitting a paper to reviewers for feedback.

Full-Text Archives   Databases containing links to reproductions of the text of articles. Reached through a library database, full-text articles quickly provide researchers with published information and represent one of the best sources for research.

Genre   Describes the categories that works fall into, such as poetry, drama, fiction, essays, and so on. Also applies to other kinds of works (e.g. action films or hip-hop) and to sub-categories (e.g. tragedies, comedies, or history plays).

Harmony   Blended sounds formed by combining two or more sounds of varying pitches to form a resonance. Often, popular music combines several vocal tracks to create harmonies, and musical chords represent harmonic combinations of individual notes.

Historicism   A critical theory that examines the historical times and places in which literature is produced. Historicism often considers economic issues and sometimes looks at biographical information related to an author.

Internet Conversations   Discussions facilitated through online tools and forums. Conversations range from entries in blogs, to postings in newsgroups or message boards, to chat sessions, to instant messaging. Exchanges in which messages are shared instantly are referred to as synchronous, or real-time conversations (generally useful for brainstorming); exchanges in which there is a lag between shared messages are termed asynchronous (generally useful for developing positions and sharing information).

Introductory Tags   Phrases used to integrate quotations into an essay. Sometimes called signal phrases, these tags alert readers to upcoming quotations and help writers blend the words of others smoothly into their own prose.

Irony   Instances when a work or phrase says one thing, but readers understand the meaning to be something almost entirely opposite of what is said. Irony can be dramatic, or situational (when readers understand something characters are unaware of), or verbal (when words say one thing, but mean another).

Keyword Searches   Searches using combinations of terms to locate information in electronic databases. Electronic searching benefits from using specific and relevant keywords.

Library Databases   Electronic collections of information containing listings of reviews and articles that have been published in journals, books, and news sources. Databases include those for popular or general research like *Proquest* or *EBSCO*, as well as specialized databases such as *Literature Online*.

Lighting   The techniques used to manipulate light sources in a scene from a film or a visual image.

Lines   Marks used to create meaning in a work of art. Rather than straight, uniform lines, most lines in works of art are disconnected and vary in value and form, combining to create textures, shading, and shapes.

Listing   A form of *prewriting* in which authors list ideas as they explore works or topics. Lists also can be developed into outlines.

Literary Criticism   See *critical theory*.

Literary Theory   See *critical theory*.

Mapping   See *clustering*.

Melody   The rising and falling sounds that add vertical dimensions to music. While *rhythm* establishes a foundation in the music, melody is woven over it to create an arrangement of sounds.

Metaphor   A comparison drawn between two things without the use of the words "like" or "as."

Mise-en-scène   A French term that literally means "putting in the scene," used to describe everything that appears within the frame of a film shot. Mise-en-scène includes the arrangement of figures and objects, aspects of the camera, and lighting, allowing us to discuss the overall atmosphere and composition of a scene.

Modern Language Association (MLA)   The professional organization for scholars of language. The MLA develops standards for the sharing of information about literature (e.g. MLA citation standards) and publishes bibliographies listing literary scholarship.

Modes of Discourse   Conventional ways of communicating designed to achieve specific aims. Modes of discourse include writing that seeks to narrate, explain with examples, define, show causation, or compare.

Mood   The emotional atmosphere of a work of literature. In poetry, mood is often associated with the *tone* of the speaker, while in fiction, *settings* often contribute to the mood of a piece. In other genres, like *film, lighting* or *cinematography* might convey mood.

Motivation   The reasons behind a character's actions. Motivations can include explicit goals or personality traits that influence the character's actions.

Narration   Telling a story by relating a series of events. We find narration not only in works of literature, but also in essays.

Narrator   The voice behind the telling of a story. The narrator should be viewed as a fictional construction (somewhat like a character) rather than equated directly to the author of a work.

Newsgroups   Internet forums devoted to specific topics, newsgroups facilitate conversations between participants who are interested in a particular topic. The archives of newsgroup conversations can be explored using Google's groups search.

Omniscient Narrator   A narrator capable of knowing and expressing the thoughts and motivations of the characters in the story, an "all knowing" narrator.

Onomatopoeias   Words whose sounds correspond with their meanings (e.g., bang).

Opposing Points of View   See *alternative perspectives*.

Outline   A plan for organizing an essay or writing project. Outlines pick out the key points to be covered and list them using a hierarchy to help writers prepare to compose.

Paper Mill Essays   Papers purchased or downloaded from an online essay service. A number of Web sites offer pre-written papers for a fee. Downloading and submitting these papers represents a severe form of *plagiarism*.

Paraphrases   Short sections of writing which restate the information found in a work. Paraphrases mirror what is said in a source, but ask writers to translate the ideas into their own words.

Passive Sentences   Sentences that employ forms of "to be" verbs such as "is" or "are," or in which the subject of the sentence is acted upon. Passive sentences can be revised to emphasize the subject of the sentence and an active verb.

Plagiarism   Claiming someone else's work as your own, or failing to acknowledge the sources you use in your own work. Plagiarism ranges from downloading *paper mill essays,* to pasting passages of others into your own papers, to failing to properly *cite* your sources.

Plot   The sequence of events that unfold in a story, usually characterized by *exposition, conflict,* and *resolution.* Plot is often helpful for initially understanding the action of a work, but does not help in developing complete interpretations.

Plot Summary   A summary which details the events that take place in a work. Plot summaries are of marginal use when it comes to developing interpretations of works and should be avoided or minimized in essays discussing literary works.

Point of View   The perspective presented by the narration of a story. Common forms of point of view include *first person*, in which the story is told through the eyes of the narrator using pronouns like "I," and *third person*, in which the story is told from the perspective of an outside narrator who relates the events.

Polishing   The final stage of the writing process, polishing addresses surface level errors and prepares a document for viewing by others.

Poststructuralism   A critical theory that focuses on how interpretations simultaneously lead to a number of alternative possibilities. The best known practice of poststructuralism, deconstruction, looks at formal elements of a work to reveal the ambiguity inherent in language.

Prewriting   Activities that help writers generate ideas and prepare to compose. Helpful prewriting activities include *freewriting, listing,* asking questions, *clustering, outlining,* and *research.*

Principles of Design   Tenets for creating and understanding visual images and other compositions. Principles can include emphasis, balance, coherence, and arrangement.

Proofreading   The process of editing papers to eliminate spelling and other mechanical errors. When proofreading, writers should strive to break away from familiarity with papers, and learn to recognize problems with spelling, grammar, and misused words with their own eyes rather than relying completely on their word processors.

Protagonist   The character around which the action of the work is centered, the main character.

Psychological Criticism   A *critical theory* that looks at the human feelings and desires represented in a work. Often associated with the thinking of Sigmund Freud and other psychologists, these approaches also emphasize the ways individuals mature and develop identity.

Purpose   The goal of a speaker in producing a message. Purposes range from personal exploration, to offering information, to entertaining, to persuading. We can examine works or messages to evaluate the purposes behind their creation, or we can use our own purpose as a guide while creating messages.

Quotations   Excerpts from literary works or from the words of others inserted into an essay to bolster a point or facilitate discussion. Writers should use quotations to draw upon their sources, but discuss quotations fully to show their own perspectives and evaluate the excerpts.

Reasons   See *supporting reasons.*

Research   The process of exploring a topic and locating resources. Research represents a key component of critical inquiry as it demands that we refine our approach and carefully assess what others have said about a topic.

Research Question   A question that focuses a research project by articulating a main area of inquiry in a formal question. Similar to a thesis statement, a research question requires investigators to narrow their approach as they formulate specific questions to explore.

Resolution   An aspect of plot representing what takes place after the crisis in a story. The French term, *dénouement,* is often used to discuss the way events are "unknotted" during the resolution of the story.

Reverse Outline   An outline created by reading the draft of a paper and listing the main ideas covered in each paragraph. A reverse outline is useful for evaluating the organization of a paper.

Revising   The process of rewriting something in order to make it stronger. Revising benefits from the feedback of readers and from deep changes that address issues of argument and organization.

Rhetorical Situation   The key components necessary for communication to take place. Crucial to the rhetorical situation are the components of *speaker,* audience, and message; additional components include the speaker's *purpose* and other elements of context.

Rhyme   The occurrence of two or more words containing similar sounds. Usually found in poetry or lyrics, rhyme contributes to the musical qualities of poems or songs.

Rhyme Scheme   A series of letters designating the rhyming structure of a poem. A rhyme scheme assigns the letter A to the first set of rhyming words and additional letters to subsequent rhymes to map the rhyme patterns in a poem.

Rhythm   1) The pattern of musical beats that forms the foundation of a song. 2) The rising and falling structure of a poem based on the patterns of stresses and sounds in its lines.

Round Characters   Sometimes called complex, round characters usually represent the major figures in a work and often struggle with a weakness or character trait. Round characters also tend to feature more character growth.

Scanning   The process of reading a poem while marking out the patterns of rising and falling stress assigned to each of its syllables.

Scene   1) An episode that represents a continuous sequence of action and which divides the acts in a work of drama. Most plays contain three or more acts with each containing a number of smaller scenes. 2) In film, an episode that takes place in one location or which represents a single incident.

Setting   The time and location in which a story takes place. Settings often help establish the mood for a work.

Simile   A comparison drawn between two things using the words "like" or "as."

Social Context   The historical or social situation in which a work of literature arises. Social context helps us understand how literature relates to historical circumstances, how our culture relates to others, and how writing can have social consequences.

Sonnet   A poem of fourteen lines usually written with an iambic pentameter meter. Petrarchan sonnets use a structure divided between an eight line question or statement (the octet) that is responded to in the final six lines (sextet); Shakespearean or Elizabethan sonnets consist of twelve lines that introduce and elaborate on a problem or idea, followed by a two-line couplet offering a response.

Speaker   1) The producer of a message in any exchange of communication; the speaker can be an individual, or a group or entity responsible for creating a work or message. 2) The *voice* present in a poem; similar to the narrator or a character in a work of fiction, the speaker is a fictional construct of the author.

Stage Directions   In dramas, instructions about the appearance of the stage and the actions of the actors. Stage directions can be purely descriptive, or they can editorialize, offering a playwright's comments on the scene or the characters.

Stanzas   The major sections of a poem. Somewhat like the paragraphs in an essay, stanzas provide organization and contribute to the meanings of some poems.

Stock Character   Usually flat, the stock character fits a stereotype easily recognized by readers, such as the spoiled brat or the nagging spouse.

Stress   The level of emphasis given to individual syllables in the words of a poem. As readers voice the syllables of words, they assign rising and falling levels of stress to each one depending on its pronunciation and placement in the poem; scanning the patterns of stress in a poem helps us explore its lyrical qualities and determine its meter.

Summaries   Short pieces of writing that distill a work into manageable chunks. Summaries emphasize the key points and ask readers to make connections and draw conclusions.

Supporting Reasons   Claims that are offered in support of larger points in an argument. Reasons can serve as evidence for larger claims, and they may require additional evidence or reasons to back them up.

Symbols   Objects or events in a work that represent themes and ideas beyond their literal meanings. Symbols can be traditional (e.g. a snake might represent evil, or sexuality) or they can be unique to a work (e.g. a screen door might represent rites of passage).

Synthesis   The process of bringing things together to examine their connections and relationships. With literature, we might look at a character's actions in terms of events in the plot or explore themes and works in terms of one another.

Tentative Thesis   An initial statement staking out a position on a work or issue. A tentative thesis makes a claim, but can be refined through further inquiry.

Theme   A central idea present in a work. Themes generally relate to human concerns and may not always be explicitly spelled out.

Theories of Race   Critical theories emphasizing the relations among ethnicities and the ways that concepts of race operate in language and literary works. Approaches like African American theory consider how language and literature contribute to constructions of race and identity.

Theories of Sexuality   Critical theories that emphasize issues of gender and sexuality in literary texts; approaches such as Queer theory consider how concepts like heterosexuality operate in language and literary works.

Thesis Statement   A specific statement that clearly articulates an understanding of a work or a position on a topic. A thesis statement helps writers and readers understand the main ideas to be covered in an essay; the angle the writer is taking.

Third Person Narration   See *point of view*.

Threads   An initial message and series of responses posted during an Internet conversation. Threads demonstrate the give and take of online discussions as they evolve.

Tone   1) The attitude conveyed by the word choices and writing style of a speaker. 2) The atmosphere or mood established by a work of art. 3) The quality of sound conveyed by a piece of music or a voice.

Topic   An idea to be discussed or an approach to understanding a work or an issue. Broad topics include concerns like communities, tradition, or relationships. Most essays require focusing a broad topic into a narrower thesis (for instance, thinking about relationships might lead to a topic on nineteenth-century marriage and literature).

Topic Sentence   A sentence articulating the main ideas to be covered in a paragraph. Often introduced near the opening of the paragraph, the topic sentence helps readers stay oriented and helps writers develop paragraphs with unity, coherence, and depth.

Tragedy   Drama characterized by a rising and falling plot as it relates to the protagonist, who generally represents a tragic hero. A character flaw leads to the hero's downfall and the destruction of those who are close to the hero.

Tragic Hero   A protagonist (generally in a drama) who suffers from a fatal flaw that brings about his or her downfall. Usually, tragic heroes are characterized by a mixture of good and bad qualities, but suffer from one tragic trait that cannot be overcome.

Traits   The key qualities possessed by a character. Stock or one-dimensional characters are often associated entirely with their key trait, while multifaceted characters are likely to possess a number of traits or to change traits during the story.

Uniform Resource Locator (URL)   The unique address that indicates the location of every page on the Web. URLs reveal information about the domain or entity hosting the resource and help us evaluate online information.

Unity   The quality of paragraphs that maintain focus on their topic sentences; paragraphs that drift require reorganizing to achieve unity.

Voice   See *tone.*

Web Gateways   Sites on the Web that lead to research sources. The Web serves as the gateway to both Internet and library research sources. Understanding the distinctions between Web gateways leads to more successful research.

Writer's Block   The inability to move forward with a writing project. Writer's block often stems from unreal expectations about writing goals and anxiety over the success of the project, as well as from poor planning.

Writing Process   The stages writers move through as they compose. We analyze the writing process by considering *prewriting, drafting, revising,* and *polishing,* but in practice writers move back and forth through these stages fluidly.

Literary Credits

Lewis Allan, "Strange Fruit" words and lyrics by Lewis Allan. Copyright © 1939 (renewed) by Music Sales Corporation (ASCAP). International copyright secured. All rights reserved. Reprinted by permission of Music Sales Corporation and Edward B. Marks Music Company; **Isabel Allende,** "The Judge's Wife" reprinted with the permission of Scribner, an imprint of Simon & Schuster Adult Publishing Group, from the *Stories of Eva Luna* by Isabel Allende, translated from the Spanish by Margaret Sayers Peden. Copyright © 1989 by Isabel Allende. English translation copyright © 1991 by Macmillan Publishing Company.; **Dorothy Allison,** "A Woman Like an Ocean" and "Little Enough" by Dorothy Allison from *The Women Who Hate Me*. Copyright © 1991 Dorothy Allison. Reprinted by permission of Frances Goldin Literary Agency; **Catherine Anderson,** "Womanhood" by Catherine Anderson from *The Work of Hands*. Copyright © Catherine Anderson. Used by permission of the author.; **Sherwood Anderson,** "Hands" from *Winesburg, Ohio* by Sherwood Anderson. Copyright © 1919 by B.W. Huebsch; copyright 1947 by Eleanor Copenhaver Anderson. Used by permission of Viking Penguin, a division of Penguin Group (USA) Inc.; **James Applewhite,** "The Story of a Drawer" by James Applewhite from *Ode to the Chinaberry Tree and Other Poems*. Copyright © 1986 by James Applewhite. Reprinted by permission of Louisiana State University Press; **Margaret Atwood,** "Gertrude Talks Back" from *Good Bones and Simple Murders* by Margaret Atwood; Copyright © 1983, 1992, 1994 by O. W. Toad Ltd., A Nan A. Talese Book. Used by permission of Doubleday, a division of Random House, Inc. and McClelland & Stewart Ltd., The Canadian Publishers, **Mary Austin,** "The Spirit of Bear Walking" and "Stewed Beans" from *One-Smoke Stories*. Copyright © 1934 by Mary Austin; copyright renewed © 1961 by Kenneth M. Chapman and Mary C. Wheelwright. Reprinted by permission of Houghton Mifflin Company. All rights reserved.; **Toni Cade Bambara,** "The Lesson" from *Gorilla, My Love* by Toni Cade Bambara. Copyright © 1972 by Toni Cade Bambara. Used by permission of Random House, Inc.; **James Baldwin,** "Sonny's Blues" copyright © 1965 by James Baldwin was originally published in Partisan Review. Copyright renewed. Collected in *Going to Meet the Man*, published by Vintage Books. Reprinted by arrangement with the James Baldwin Estate; **Doris Betts,** "The Ugliest Pilgrim." Reprinted with the permission of Scribner, an imprint of Simon & Schuster Adult Publishing Group and Russell & Volkening, as agents for the author, from *Beasts of the Southern Wild and Other Stories* by Doris Betts. Copyright © 1973 by Doris Betts.; **Elizabeth Bishop,** "One Art" "Filling Station" "The Fish" "Roosters" "Sestina" from *The Complete Poems: 1927–1979* by Elizabeth Bishop. Copyright © 1979, 1983 by Alice Helen Methfessel. Reprinted by permission of Farrar, Straus and Giroux, LLC. "Letter to Marianne Moore" from *One Art: Letters* by Elizabeth Bishop, selected and edited by Robert Giroux. Copyright © 1994 by Alice Methfessel. Reprinted by permission of Farrar, Straus and Giroux, LLC.; **T. Coraghessan Boyle,** "The Love of My Life" from *After the Plague*. Copyright © 2001 by T. Coraghessan Boyle. Used by permission of Viking Penguin, a division of Penguin Group (USA) Inc.; **Gwendolyn Brooks,** "We Real Cool" from *Blacks* (Third World Press) by Gwendolyn Brooks. Reprinted by consent of Brooks Permissions.; **Lucille Clifton,** "leda 1," "leda 2," and "leda 3," by Lucille Clifton from *The Book of Light*. Copyright © 1993 by Lucille Clifton. Reprinted with the permission of Copper Canyon Press, P.O. Box 271, Port Townsend, WA 98368-0271; **Billy Collins,** "Embrace" by Billy Collins from *The Apple That Astonished Paris*. Copyright © 1988 by Billy Collins. Reprinted by permission of the University of Arkansas Press. "Thesaurus" from *The Art of Drowning* by Billy Collins. Copyright © 1995. Reprinted by permission of the University of Pittsburgh Press. "Marginalia" from *Picnic, Lightning* by Billy Collins, © 1998. Reprinted by permission of the University of Pittsburgh Press. "The Names" by Billy Collins, *New York Times,* September 6, 2002. Copyright © 2002 The New York Times Co. Reprinted by permission.; **Raymond Carver,** "Cathedral" from *Cathedral* by Raymond Carver. Copyright © 1983 by Raymond Carver. Used by permission of Alfred A. Knopf, a

Image Credits

Page 1: Reproduced from the Collections of the Library of Congress; 7: Ishtar Films 11333 Moorpark St #460, Studio City, CA 91602 800-428-7136; 12: Ishtar Films 11333 Moorpark St #460, Studio City, CA 91602 800-428-7136; 13BL: King Visual Technology/National Archives and Records Administration; 13BR: Norman Rockwell Family Agency; 13T: Reproduced from the Collections of the Library of Congress; 14: The Advertising Archive, Ltd.; 58: Janice Brown; 109: © EBSCO Publishing 2004; 110: © Google, Inc. Used with permission.; 111: © Google, Inc. Used with permission.; 113: © Google, Inc. Used with permission; 116: Copyright © 2000 H. Bruce Franklin. All rights reserved.; 117: © 123helpme.com; 121: © Google, Inc. Used with permission.; 124: Literature online database; 171: Monterey Media, Inc.; 189: Monterey Media, Inc.; 191: Monterey Media, Inc.; 202: © 1999–2003 Microsoft, Inc. Used with permission.; 212: Monterey Media, Inc.; 240B: Goldcrest/The Kobal Collection/Ellison, Nancy; 240T: Bettmann/Corbis; 241T: Goldcrest/The Kobal Collection/Ellison, Nancy; 305: Pyramid Films Corporation; 307: Young Goodman Brown © 1972 American Film; 308: Young Goodman Brown © 1972 American Film; 309: Monterey Media, Inc.; 310: Monterey Media, Inc.; 312TR: National Archives and Records; 312TR: Everett Collection; 316L: Reunion des Musees Nationaux/Art Resource, NY; 316R: Courtesy www.adbusters.org; 318T: Art Resource, NY; 318B: Scala/Art Resource, NY; 319: Digital Image © The Museum of Modern Art/Licensed by SCALA/Art Resource, NY; 320: Digital Image © The Museum of Modern Art/ Licensed by SCALA/Art Resource, NY; 321: Smithsonian American Art Museum/Art Resource, NY; 322B: Phototheque R. Magritte-ADAGP/Art Resource, NY; 323: Smithsonian American Art Museum, Washington, DC/Art Resource, NY; 324: The New York Public Library/Art Resource, NY; 326B: Reproduced from the Collections of the Library of Congress; 327: Smithsonian American Art Museum, Washington, DC/Art Resource, NY; 328: Digital Image © The Museum of Modern Art/Licensed by SCALA/Art Resource, NY; 331: Reunion des Musees Nationaux/Art Resource, NY; 332: Whitney Museum of American Art; 333: Reunion des Musees Nationaux/Art Resource, NY; 335: Lessing J. Rosenwald Collection, Library of Congress. Copyright © 2004 the William Blake Archive. Used with permission.; 337T: The Advertising Archive, Ltd.; 337B: The Advertising Archive, Ltd.; 338: The Advertising Archive, Ltd.; 340: The Advertising Archive, Ltd.; 341B: The Advertising Archive, Ltd.; 341T: The Advertising Archive, Ltd.; 342T: From the Collection of the Manuscript, Rare Book, and Special Collections Library, Duke University. Copyright Alex Harris.; 342B: Photo Courtesy of GM/Newsmakers/Getty Images; 343B: Courtesy www.adbusters.org; 343T: The Advertising Archive, Ltd.; 344T: The Advertising Archive, Ltd.; 344B: The Advertising Archive, Ltd.; 390: Reproduced from the Collections of the Library of Congress; 391: The Andy Warhol Foundation, Inc./Art Resource, NY; 401: Scala/Art Resource, NY; 402: Alinari/Art Resource, NY; 500: Erich Lessing/Art Resource, NY; 514: Erich Lessing/Art Resource, NY; 535: The New York Public Library/Art Resource, NY; 553: The Advertising Archive, Ltd.; 614: Smithsonian American Art Museum, Washington, D.C./Art Resource, NY; 615: Smithsonian American Art Museum, Washington, D.C./Art Resource, NY; 616T: The Museum of African American Art, Los Angeles, California. Palmer C. Hayden Collection, gift of Miriam A.[Unknown font 2: Book Antiqua] [End Font: Book Antiqua]Hayden; 616B: Smithsonian American Art Museum, Washington, D.C./Art Resource, NY; 639: Reproduced from the Collections of the Library of Congress; 716T: Reproduced from the Collections of the Library of Congress; 716B: Reproduced from the Collections of the Library of Congress; 725: AP/Wide World Photos; 727: Lessing J. Rosenwald Collection, Library of Congress. Copyright © 2004 the William Blake Archive. Used with permission.; 728: Lessing J. Rosenwald Collection, Library of Congress. Copyright © 2004 the William Blake Archive. Used with permission.; 729: Lessing J. Rosenwald Collection, Library of Congress. Copyright © 2004 the WIlliam Blake Archive.

Index of Authors, Titles, and First Lines of Poems

Index of Terms